MW01202143

THE CAMBRIDGE HANDBOOK OF EUROPEAN MONETARY, ECONOMIC AND FINANCIAL INTEGRATION

This Handbook provides a comprehensive analysis of the past, present, and future of the European Economic and Monetary Union in its broader context. It incorporates economic, legal, and political science perspectives to provide an in-depth and forward-looking scrutiny of the rationales, the main features and the shortcomings of economic, monetary, and financial integration in the euro area. Studying its complex, highly interconnected governance structures, the authors suggest directions for necessary reforms. With contributions from a diverse group of leading experts in their fields, this volume is truly versatile in its scope and approach, whilst remaining accessible for readers of different academic backgrounds.

DARIUSZ ADAMSKI has published widely on economic governance in the euro area, as well as on legal aspects of the European Central Bank's (ECB) monetary policy and on regulation of financial institutions. He is the author of *Redefining European Economic Integration* (Cambridge University Press, 2018) and was awarded the 2018 ECB Legal Research Programme scholarship. He is a member of the Academic Board of the European Banking Institute.

FABIAN AMTENBRINK has published extensively on legal aspects of European economic and monetary (policy) integration and the European Banking Union. He is author of the widely cited *The Democratic Accountability of Central Banks: A Comparative Study* (1999). He is a member of the editorial board of the *European Law Review* and co-editor of *Nijhoff Studies in EU Law*. He is also a member of the Academic Board of the Erasmus Centre for Economic and Financial Governance.

JAKOB DE HAAN has published extensively on issues such as public debt, monetary policy, central bank independence, banking, and European integration. He is a member of the editorial boards of *Public Choice*, *European Union Politics*, the *Journal of International Money and Finance*, and the *Journal of Common Market Studies*. From 2009 to 2020 he was Head of Research at De Nederlandsche Bank.

The Cambridge Handbook of European Monetary, Economic and Financial Integration

Edited by

DARIUSZ ADAMSKI

University of Wrocław

FABIAN AMTENBRINK

Erasmus University Rotterdam

JAKOB DE HAAN

University of Groningen

CAMBRIDGE
UNIVERSITY PRESS

Shaftesbury Road, Cambridge CB2 8EA, United Kingdom

One Liberty Plaza, 20th Floor, New York, NY 10006, USA

477 Williamstown Road, Port Melbourne, VIC 3207, Australia

314–321, 3rd Floor, Plot 3, Splendor Forum, Jasola District Centre, New Delhi – 110025, India

103 Penang Road, #05-06/07, Visioncrest Commercial, Singapore 238467

Cambridge University Press is part of Cambridge University Press & Assessment, a department of the University of Cambridge.

We share the University's mission to contribute to society through the pursuit of education, learning and research at the highest international levels of excellence.

www.cambridge.org
Information on this title: www.cambridge.org/9781009364690

DOI: 10.1017/9781009364706

First published 2023

A catalogue record for this publication is available from the British Library

Library of Congress Cataloging-in-Publication Data
NAMES: Adamski, Dariusz, 1975- editor. | Amtenbrink, Fabian, editor. | Haan, Jakob de, editor.
TITLE: The Cambridge handbook of European monetary, economic and financial integration/ edited by Dariusz Adamski, University of Wroclaw; Fabian Amtenbrink, Erasmus Universiteit Rotterdam; Jakob de Haan, University of Groningen.
DESCRIPTION: Cambridge, United Kingdom ; New York : Cambridge University Press, 2022. | Series: Cambridge law handbooks | Includes bibliographical references and index.
IDENTIFIERS: LCCN 2023011483 (print) | LCCN 2023011484 (ebook) | ISBN 9781009364690 (hardback) | ISBN 9781009364706 (epub)
SUBJECTS: LCSH: Financial institutions–Law and legislation–European Union countries. | Money–Law and legislation–European Union countries. | Monetary policy–European Union countries. | Europe–Economic integration.
CLASSIFICATION: LCC KJE2188 .C36 2022 (print) | LCC KJE2188 (ebook) | DDC 346.4/082–dc23/eng/20230717
LC record available at https://lccn.loc.gov/2023011483
LC ebook record available at https://lccn.loc.gov/2023011484

ISBN 978-1-009-36469-0 Hardback

Contents

Contributors

Dariusz Adamski is Professor of Law and Head of the Centre for European Economic Law and Governance at the Faculty of Law, Administration and Economics of the University of Wrocław, Poland. Adamski has published widely on economic governance in the euro area, as well as on legal aspects of the ECB's monetary policy and regulation of financial institutions. He is the author of *Redefining European Economic Integration* (Cambridge University Press, 2018) and was awarded the 2018 ECB Legal Research Programme scholarship. He is a member of the Academic Board of the European Banking Institute.

Fabian Amtenbrink is Professor of European Union Law at the Erasmus University Rotterdam and Visiting Professor at the College of Europe (Bruges). He is also a member of the Academic Board of the Erasmus Centre for Economic and Financial Governance. Amtenbrink has published extensively on issues surrounding economic policy coordination in EMU, the ECB, and European financial market supervision, as well as on issues relating to institutional and substantive issues of European integration. He is a member of the editorial boards of the *European Law Review* and the *Netherlands Yearbook of International Law*, and an editor of *Nijhoff Studies in EU Law* (Brill).

Roel Beetsma is Professor of Macroeconomics and Dean of the Faculty of Economics and Business of the University of Amsterdam. He is fellow of the Centre for Economic Policy Research (CEPR) and CESifo. He has held visiting positions at DELTA (Paris), the University of British Columbia (Vancouver), the University of California in Berkeley, and the EUI Florence. Beetsma has been a consultant for various international policy institutions, and is a member of the European Fiscal Board, and the Supervisory Boards of the pension fund of the Dutch retail sector and a.s.r. Vermogensbeheer. He has published in journals such as the *American Economic Review*, the *Journal of Economic Literature*, and the *Economic Journal*.

Iain Begg is Professorial Research Fellow at the European Institute, London School of Economics and Political Science. His main research work is on the political economy of European integration and EU economic governance. He has directed and participated in a series of projects on different facets of EU policy, including work on EU and national fiscal frameworks and the EU budget. He has undertaken a number of advisory roles and acted as an expert witness or specialist adviser on EU issues for the House of Commons Treasury Committee, the House of Lords European Communities Committee, and the European Parliament.

Jens-Hinrich Binder is Professor in Private Law, Company Law, Banking and Securities Law at the University of Tübingen, Germany. His previous affiliations include the Universities of Wiesbaden, Mainz, Munich, and Freiburg. He is Fellow Academic Member of the European Banking Institute, Fellow of the Institute of Finance and Financial Regulation at the University of Piraeus, member of the Panel of Experts on Financial Regulation, German Ministry of Finance, and co-editor of the *Journal of Banking Law and Banking*. He holds a doctorate degree from the University of Freiburg and an LLM in Banking & Finance Law from the London School of Economics and Political Science.

Ana Bobić is référendaire to Advocate General Tamara Ćapeta at the Court of Justice of the European Union and Affiliate Research Fellow at the Hertie School in Berlin. Until 2021, she was a postdoctoral researcher for the Leviathan Project at the Hertie School, working on questions of legal accountability in EU economic governance. She obtained her DPhil at the University of Oxford as a Law Faculty Graduate Assistance Fund scholar in 2017. Recently she has published *The Jurisprudence of Constitutional Conflict in the EU* (Oxford University Press, 2022).

Elena Ríos Camacho is Research Associate and Lecturer at the Chair of European and Global Governance at the Technical University of Munich. Her research focuses on European economic governance, banking union, and financial reforms after the euro area crisis, EU institutions, European integration theory, and digital transformations in Europe. Ríos Camacho was a PhD researcher and lecturer at the University of Bamberg, and at the same time she was a Bluebook trainee at the Single Resolution Board in Brussels. She recently published *The Choice for Banking Union Power, Politics and the Trap of Credible Commitments* (Routledge, 2022).

Nauro F. Campos is Professor of Economics at University College London and Research Professor at ETH-Zürich. His main fields of interest are political economy and European integration. He has previously taught at CERGE-EI (Prague), California (Fullerton), Newcastle, Brunel, Bonn, Paris 1 Sorbonne, and Warwick. He is currently Research Fellow at IZA-Bonn, Professorial Fellow at UNU-MERIT (Maastricht University), a member of the Scientific Advisory Board of the (Central) Bank of Finland, and Senior Fellow of the ESRC Peer Review College. Campos is the editor-in-chief of *Comparative Economic Studies* and of Cambridge University Press' series Elements of Economics of European Integration.

Andrea Capati is a PhD researcher in the Department of Political Science at Luiss University, Rome. He holds a Double MA in International Relations from Luiss and the University of Brussels (ULB), both with first-class honours. In 2019, he was Academic Coordinator at the Luiss School of Government, where he also earned a Second-Level MA in International Public Affairs. His research interests are European governance, European integration, comparative politics, historical institutionalism, critical junctures analysis, fiscal policy, and financial policy.

Michele Chang is Director of the Transatlantic Affairs Programme and Professor at the European Political and Governance Studies Department of the College of Europe. She holds a PhD from the University of California San Diego. Her research interests include EMU, euro area economic governance, ECB, fiscal policy coordination, Banking Union, and financial crises. Previously she was affiliated to Boston University, the Centre for European Policy Studies, Cornell University, and Colgate University. She is a board member of the Trans-European Policy Studies Association and a member of the Scientific Committee of the Brexit Research and Policy Institute, Dublin City University.

Jacopo Cimadomo is Lead Economist in the Directorate General Economics of the European Central Bank. He has been working for the ECB since 2008. Before joining the ECB, he worked for the Italian Ministry of Finance in Rome, and at CEPII in Paris. He holds a master's degree and a PhD in economics and statistics from the Free University of Brussels (ULB) and a bachelor's degree in economics from Bocconi University, Milan. His research interests cover fiscal and monetary policies, financial economics, and forecasting. He has published in journals such as the *Journal of Monetary Economics*, the *Journal of Econometrics*, and the *European Economic Review*.

Mark Dawson is Professor of European Law and Governance at the Hertie School in Berlin. Dawson was previously Assistant Professor at Maastricht University. He has held visiting positions at LSE, the University of Wisconsin, and Harvard Kennedy School. Dawson holds degrees from the Universities of Edinburgh and Aberdeen as well as a PhD from the EUI in Florence, where he was in 2019 Fernand Braudel Fellow. He is a member of the Editorial Board of the *European Law Review* and the Advisory Board of the *Maastricht Journal of European and Comparative Law*. He is the Principal Investigator of LEVIATHAN, a research project exploring the legal and political accountability structure of EU economic governance.

Maria Demertzis is the interim Director at Bruegel. Previously, she served as Senior Economist at De Nederlandsche Bank from 2000 until 2012 and was Seconded National Expert at the European Commission from 2012 to 2016. She has also held academic positions at the Harvard Kennedy School of Government in the United States and the University of Strathclyde in the United Kingdom, from where she holds a PhD in economics, while she holds a master's in economics from the University of Glasgow, and a bachelor's degree in economics from the University of Athens. Demertzis was a visiting associate professor at the University of Amsterdam from 2012 to 2018.

Sebastian Diessner is Assistant Professor at the Faculty of Governance and Global Affairs at Leiden University. He was a Max Weber Fellow at the European University Institute and holds a PhD from the London School of Economics and Political Science. His thesis examined the political economy of central banking and central bank independence in Europe and Japan, and his research interests include the politics of macroeconomic policy and the interplay between technological and institutional change in the advanced capitalist democracies. He recently won a grant from the Leverhulme Trust for the research project 'The Political Economy of Knowledge-Based Growth'.

Marta Domínguez Jiménez is a PhD-track MPhil candidate at CEMFI in Madrid. Previously, she was a Research Analyst at Bruegel, where her research focused primarily on monetary policy, financial systems, and international trade and capital flows. She has published on these issues for Bruegel, in academic journals, and European Parliament and Commission reports. She holds a bachelor's degree from the University of Oxford and a master's from the College of Europe in Bruges. Previously, she was an analyst within the Markets division of Citigroup in London, where she worked on the structuring of fixed income products and developing systematic quantitative investment strategies.

Kenneth Dyson is Visiting Professor of European Political Studies at Cardiff University (United Kingdom), Fellow of the British Academy, and Fellow of the Royal Historical Society. Previous affiliations include the University of Liverpool and Bradford University. Visiting Professorships have included the Free University of Berlin (DAAD Distinguished Research Professor),

Konstanz University, McMaster University (Distinguished Hooker Professor), and Siena University. He is currently Honorary Visiting Professor at the universities of Leeds and Luxembourg. He was co-founder and chair of the Association for the Study of German Politics (ASGP). His research interests centre on the European state tradition, comparative and historical political economy, European integration, and German studies. His *The Road to Maastricht: Negotiating Economic and Monetary Union* (1999, with Featherstone) was *Choice* academic book of the year; his *States, Debt, and Power: 'Saints' and 'Sinners' in European History and Integration* (2015) was UACES Best Book.

Barry Eichengreen is George C. Pardee and Helen N. Pardee Chair and Distinguished Professor of Economics and Professor of Political Science at the University of California, Berkeley. He is a research associate of the NBER and Research Fellow at the CEPR. Eichengreen is a fellow of the American Academy of Arts and Sciences, a distinguished fellow of the AEA, a corresponding fellow of the British Academy, and a life fellow of the Cliometric Society. He has held Guggenheim and Fulbright Fellowships and been a fellow of the Center for Advanced Study in the Behavioral Sciences (Palo Alto) and the Institute for Advanced Study (Berlin). For fifteen years, he served as convener of the Bellagio Group of academics and officials. He is a regular columnist for *Project Syndicate*.

Edgars Eihmanis is a postdoctoral researcher in the project PANDEMO and an assistant professor at the University of Wrocław. He is also affiliated to the Johan Skytte Institute of Political Studies at the University of Tartu. He received master's degrees in sociology and political science from the University of Amsterdam and a PhD degree in political science from the EUI in Florence. As a doctoral student at the EUI, Eihmanis studied the politics of taxation in East and Central Europe. His second field of expertise is the EU's socio-economic governance. His research has been published in leading academic outlets.

Sergio Fabbrini is Professor of Politics and International Relations and Dean of the Political Science Department at the Luiss Guido Carli in Rome, where he holds the Intesa Sanpaolo Chair on European Governance. He was Pierre Keller Professor at the Harvard Kennedy School of Government, Jemolo Chair Professor at Nuffield College, Oxford University, Recurrent Visiting Professor at the University of California at Berkeley, Jean Monnet Chair Professor at the EUI in Florence. He has authored seventeen books, co-authored two books, edited or co-edited twenty books or journal special issues, and has published hundreds of scientific articles and essays in seven languages.

Bram Gootjes is a former PhD researcher in the Department of Economics, Econometrics, and Finance at the University of Groningen in the Netherlands. He has published several papers which deal with fiscal rules. He holds a Research Master's degree and a PhD degree from the University of Groningen.

Esther Gordo Mora is Director of the Economic Analysis Division Independent Authority for Fiscal Responsibility in Spain. She holds a Bachelor of Economics and Business from the Complutense University of Madrid. She has specialized in analysing the situation and economic policies of the Spanish economy and other EMU countries. For several years she represented the Bank of Spain and AIREF in several groups for the forecast and analysis of the economic situation and public finances of the ECB, the OECD, and the European Commission. She has published several papers which deal with globalization, the design of EMU governance, and fiscal policy.

Willem Pieter de Groen is a senior research fellow, and he heads the Financial Markets and Institutions Unit at CEPS. He is also a visiting professor at the College of Europe in Bruges. He has (co-)authored studies and coordinated projects on EU and Near East financial institutions regulation, diversity in bank ownership and business models, retail financial services, and financial instruments. Moreover, he works on obstacles to growth and access to finance of small and medium-sized enterprises as well as the collaborative economy and taxation. He holds a Masters in Finance from VU University, the Netherlands.

Jakob de Haan is Professor of Political Economy at the University of Groningen, the Netherlands. Currently, he is the President of SUERF and Fellow of CESifo. Previously, he was Head of Research of De Nederlandsche Bank and Director of the Graduate School and Research Institute of the Faculty of Economics and Business of the University of Groningen. He has published extensively on issues such as public debt, monetary policy, central bank independence, banking, and European integration. He is a member of the editorial board of *Public Choice, European Union Politics*, the *Journal of International Money and Finance*, and the *Journal of Common Market Studies*.

Markus Haverland holds the chair in Political Science at the Department of Public Administration and Sociology, Erasmus University Rotterdam. He is also a fellow of the Montesquieu Institute (The Hague) and the Netherlands Institute of Government, and a former fellow of the European University Institute (Florence). He is interested in EU policy-making amid politicization and the principal investigator of *The Politics of Reforming Europe's Economies* (Dutch Research Council). His research has been widely published in journals such as *European Union Politics*, the *Journal of Common Market Studies*, the *Journal of European Public Policy*, *Public Administration*, and *West European Politics*.

Harold James is Claude and Lore Kelly Professor in European Studies at Princeton University, Professor of History and International Affairs at the Woodrow Wilson School, and an associate at the Bendheim Center for Finance. His most recent books include *The Creation and Destruction of Value: The Globalization Cycle* (2009); *Making the European Monetary Union* (2012); *The Euro and the Battle of Economic Ideas* (with Markus K. Brunnermeier and Jean-Pierre Landau; 2016); *Making A Modern Central Bank: The Bank of England 1979–2003* (2020); and *The War of Words: A Glossary of Globalization* (2021). He was awarded the Helmut Schmidt Prize for Economic History, and the Ludwig Erhard Prize for writing about economics. He writes a monthly column for *Project Syndicate*.

George Kopits is a senior scholar at the Woodrow Wilson International Center for Scholars in Washington DC. He is also a member of Portugal's Public Finance Council and a member of the Commission on Reform of the Macro-Fiscal Framework in Peru. Kopits served as chairman of the Fiscal Council of Hungary (2009–11) and was a member of the Monetary Council of the National Bank of Hungary (2004–9). He previously also worked at the IMF's Fiscal Affairs Department, and the US Treasury Department. He has held visiting academic appointments at Bocconi, Budapest, Cape Town, Johns Hopkins, Siena, and Vienna universities. He holds a PhD in economics from Georgetown University and is a member of the Hungarian Academy of Sciences.

Marco Lamandini is Professor of Law at the Alma Mater Studiorum Università degli Studi di Bologna, a vice-chair of the Academic Board of the European Banking Institute and a member of the Academic Board of the European Capital Markets Institute, former President of the Board of Appeal of the European Financial Supervisory Authorities, a member of the Appeal Panel for the SRB, a member of the Italian Arbitro Bancario Finanziario, a member of the Informal Company Law Expert Group, and an external legal expert to the ECON Committee of the European Parliament on bank resolution matters.

Karel Lannoo has been Chief Executive of CEPS since 2000. He was an Independent Director of *Bolsas y Mercados Españolas*, which manages the Spanish securities markets. Lannoo has published several books on capital markets, MiFID, and the financial crisis. He is also the author of many op-eds and articles. Lannoo is a regular speaker in hearings for national and international institutions and at international conferences and executive learning courses. He holds a bachelor's degree in philosophy (1984) and an MA in modern history (1985) from the University of Leuven, Belgium, and obtained a postgraduate diploma in European studies from the University of Nancy, France (1986).

Menelaos Markakis is Assistant Professor of International and European Union Law at Erasmus University Rotterdam and co-coordinator of the Erasmus Center for Economic and Financial Governance. He also lectures in EU law at Worcester College, Oxford. He holds degrees from the Universities of Athens (LLB) and Oxford (MJur and DPhil). In 2020, he was awarded an EUR fellowship by Erasmus University Rotterdam for a project focusing on the accountability of the ECB. He is the author of *Accountability in the Economic and Monetary Union: Foundations, Policy, and Governance* (Oxford University Press 2020) and is co-editing a multidisciplinary *Handbook of Accountability Research: Politics, Law, Business, Work* (forthcoming with Edward Elgar).

Giuseppe Montalbano is a post-doctoral researcher at the Institute of Political Science of the University of Luxembourg. As a member of the research team of the PRO-Active Policymaking for Equal Lives project, he deals with qualitative methodologies to analyse and explain the making and impact of housing finance policies. Montalbano gained his PhD at LUISS University in Rome before working as a postdoctoral researcher and teaching assistant in different Italian institutions, such as LUISS, the Scuola Normale Superiore in Florence, and the University of Bologna. His research focuses on European financial governance, and interest groups' influence in policy-making.

David Ramos Muñoz is Associate Professor of Commercial Law at Universidad Carlos III de Madrid, and he also teaches at the University of Bologna. He has published extensively on financial law, corporate law, contract law, arbitration, and fundamental rights and the rule of law and has participated three times in the ECB Legal Research Programme. He is a fellow academic member of the European Banking Institute, an alternate member of the Appeal Panel of the SRB and the Board of Appeal of the European Supervisory Authorities, and an expert in bank resolution for the European Parliament.

Alessandra Anna Palazzo is a PhD researcher at the University of Maryland, USA. Previously, she was Research Analyst at the Fiscal Policies Division of the European Central Bank (between September 2018 and June 2019). She holds degrees from the Université Catholique de Louvain and Bocconi University (Research Master's in Economics 2016–17 and Master of Science – MS, Economics and Social Sciences 2015–17).

Katarzyna Parchimowicz is Assistant Professor at the Digital Justice Center of the University of Wrocław and Associated Researcher at the European Banking Institute. She received masters' degrees from the University of Wrocław and Goethe University, Frankfurt am Main. During her stay in Frankfurt, she completed an internship in banking supervision at the ECB. In 2019, she spent one term as Junior Academic Visitor at the University of Oxford. She received a three-year grant from National Science Centre for a project on regulation of global systemically important banks. Her research focuses on comparative European and international financial law, in particular on post-crisis regulation of global systemically important banks.

Waltraud Schelkle is Professor of European Public Policy at the European University Institute. She is also Adjunct Professor of Economics at the Free University of Berlin, (non-resident) Senior Fellow at Johns Hopkins University, Washington DC, and a member of the Advisory Board of the Research Centre for Inequality and Social Policy in Bremen. She has previously worked as a development economist at the German Institute of Development in Berlin. She published *The Political Economy of Monetary Solidarity: Understanding the Experiment of the Euro* (Oxford University Press, 2017). This work is continued in an ERC-funded research project on 'Policy Crisis and Crisis Politics: Sovereignty, Solidarity and Identity in Europe Post-2008'.

Dirk Schoenmaker is Professor of Banking and Finance at the Rotterdam School of Management (RSM), Erasmus University Rotterdam. His research and teaching focus on the areas of sustainable finance, central banking and financial stability, financial system architecture, and European financial integration. He is Research Fellow at CEPR and co-author of the textbooks *Principles of Sustainable Finance* (Oxford University Press), *Financial Markets and Institutions: A European Perspective* (Cambridge University Press), and author of *Governance of International Banking: The Financial Trilemma* (Oxford University Press). He earned his PhD in economics at LSE. Before joining RSM, he was Dean of the Duisenberg School of Finance. Previously, he served at the Netherlands Ministry of Finance and the Bank of England.

Hans Stegeman is an economist and chief strategist at Triodos Investment Management. He previously worked at the Netherlands Bureau for Economic Policy Analysis and was chief economist at Rabobank for a number of years. He studied at Maastricht University and is currently working on a PhD dissertation on the circular economy.

Diego Valiante is a senior officer and team leader at the European Commission and Adjunct Professor at Bologna University. Since joining the Commission, Valiante has been involved in both CMU and Banking Union files, including the Sustainable Finance Action Plan, the ESAs Review, the European Deposit Insurance Scheme, and Brexit. Between 2009 and 2016, he was Head of Financial Markets and Institutions at CEPS and Head of Research of the European Capital Markets Institute. He holds a PhD in Law and Economics from LUISS University (Rome), a Joint LLM in Law and Economics from Erasmus University Rotterdam and Bologna University, a MSc in Economic Analysis of Law, and a BSc in Business Economics from LUISS University (Rome).

Amy Verdun is Professor of Political Science at the University of Victoria, BC Canada, where she has been since 1997. Verdun holds a PhD from the European University Institute Florence Italy (1995). From 2018 to 2020 she served as Professor of European Politics and Political Economy at Leiden University. She is the (co-)author or (co-)editor of *European Union Governance and Policy Making: A Canadian Perspective* (University of Toronto Press, 2023), *Decision-Making in the EU before and after the Lisbon Treaty* (Routledge), and *Ruling Europe: The Politics of the Stability and Growth Pact* (Cambridge University Press), and was co-editor of *Journal of Common Market Studies* (2010–17).

Nicola Viegi has been the South African Reserve Bank Professor of Monetary Economics at the University of Pretoria, South Africa since 2010. Previous affiliations include the University of Strathclyde, the University of Kwazulu-Natal, and the University of Cape Town. He has had visiting positions at ESC Toulouse, the University of Malta, and De Nederlandsche Bank, Amsterdam. His research areas are monetary economics, economic policy theory, monetary fiscal policy interdependence, political economy of monetary institutions, economic policy under uncertainty, regional integration in Africa, political economy of government debt, the economics of colonization and decolonization, macro modelling for emerging countries, and economic growth and institutions.

Fabio Wasserfallen is Professor of European Politics and Managing Director of the Institute of Political Science at the University of Bern. He completed his PhD at the University of Zurich in 2014 and became Assistant Professor of Political Economy at the University of Salzburg, where he was promoted to Associate Professor in 2017. Previously, he was Professor of Comparative Politics at Zeppelin University in Friedrichshafen. His research interests include European integration, the institutions and politics of the European Union, public opinion, policy diffusion, federalism, and direct democracy. He has published in the *American Political Science Review*, *American Journal of Political Science*, *British Journal of Political Science*, and *European Journal of Political Research*.

Introduction

Dariusz Adamski, Fabian Amtenbrink, and Jakob de Haan

The aim of this volume is to provide a reference guide to the contemporary challenges faced by the European Economic and Monetary Union (EMU). With the goal of providing a holistic picture, the editors have brought together a multidisciplinary team of scholars specialized in economic history, economics, political sciences, and law. This combination of multidisciplinary approaches makes the book unique, as most publications on EMU take a monodisciplinary approach, while the challenges faced by EMU are arguably multifaceted and therefore require a multidisciplinary approach. The authors of the contributions in the volume have been invited to judge the state of integration in EMU, thereby in particular taking into account the decade of experiences following the Global Financial Crisis (GFC), the European sovereign debt crisis, and the responses to the economic impact of the COVID-19 pandemic.

The areas covered have undergone various alterations, redefinitions, and reforms in the past decade, aimed to rectify economic, political, and regulatory inconsistencies, loopholes, and failed paradigms, as well as to tackle unexpected challenges. The authors have been invited to ascertain the emerging picture, focusing on the following overarching questions: Where is the EMU heading? How much closer to an optimum currency area is it now compared to where it was in the wake of the GFC? Which reforms are required to ensure its survival? How urgent are they and how likely is it that they might actually be delivered? What are the broader implications of these findings for European integration more generally and beyond?

These questions are addressed and the consequences of the current setup of EMU are ascertained from the various perspectives represented by the individual contributors. Finally, conditions for further reforms in the most important fields covered by this volume are considered.

To provide for an easily recognizable structure and to enhance accessibility to the wealth of information included, the volume comprises four parts, covering all relevant policy areas pertaining to EMU.

PART I: THE ECONOMIC AND MONETARY UNION: POLITICAL, ECONOMIC, AND LEGAL RATIONALES

The EMU governance framework introduced by the 1992/1993 Treaty of European Union (Maastricht Treaty) encapsulates the economic, political, and legal thinking at the time of its drafting, bearing witness to 'contrasting philosophies' (Brunnermeier et al., 2016, p. 4) and national interests (see Chapters 2, 3, and 5, by Verdun, James, and Dyson).

Various theories have been offered to explain the coming into existence of EMU, inter alia including functionalist and constructivist approaches to the creation of EMU, and economic and monetary integration as the result of complex bargaining processes in interstate relations or 'multi-level games' (for details see Chapter 3 by James). Contributions to Part I pay tribute to the power of key Member States in pursuing their (economic) interests and policy preferences. Examples include Germany's geo-strategy and its foreign and security policies that shaped its approach to EMU and the interest of other Member States in addressing Germany's current account surpluses, but also France's reluctance to take austerity measures and Germany's antipathy to an expansionary economic policy (Chapters 3, 5, and 6 by James, Dyson, and Begg). The need to accommodate a plurality of domestic considerations is an important explanation for these diverse preferences. Still, in pursuing these interests, Member States also formed alliances, most notably France and Germany, building on a long tradition of bilateral collaboration on European integration issues (Chapters 3 and 5, by James and Dyson).

As regards the economic rationale for the establishment of EMU, a distinction can be drawn between adopting a single currency in the first place and specific choices of governance structures and institutional arrangements. Building on early integration theories (Chapter 2 by Verdun), the establishment of an economic and monetary union can be perceived as the final step of the process of economic integration and a logical extension of the common (internal) market project. Yet, as Eichengreen argues in Chapter 1, the view that a single currency substantially enhances the working of the internal market and in that regard constitutes a *conditio sine qua non* for the completion of the internal market can be challenged. If anything, critical voices about Member States' costs and benefits of participating in the single currency have increased, as the lessons of the GFC and the European sovereign debt crisis were drawn.

From the EU's internal market perspective, economic benefits associated with the single currency include the reduction of exchange rate risks and the associated costs (and uncertainties) of cross-border trade in goods and services, as well as the reduction of interest rate differentials (Chapter 8 by Campos; see also Eichengreen, 1990). Yet it is debatable whether such benefits necessitate the adoption of a common currency or could also be achieved through the completion of the internal market, the creation of a level playing field, and a system of managed exchange rates. This also applies to the question of how much transnational trade in the euro area since the introduction of the euro can be attributed to the establishment of the single currency (Chapter 1 by Eichengreen), and to what extent it can be attributed to other factors.

The cost of abandoning a national currency is the loss of an autonomous monetary policy and hence the ability to deal with asymmetric shocks through interest rate adjustments and devaluation/depreciation of the national currency to improve price competitiveness. Moreover, Member States have to 'issue debt in a currency they [have] no control over' (De Grauwe, 2013, p. 8). Implications of the loss of these instruments have come to the forefront during the European sovereign debt crisis and constitute the backdrop of debates on the need for a European fiscal capacity of some sort (e.g. Bénassy-Quéré et al., 2018).

As regards the rationale for the governance framework and institutional arrangements for EMU, two features touched upon by many authors in Parts I to III of this volume have been at the core of economic, political, and legal debates before, during, and ever after the establishment of the euro area: the (legal) design of the European Central Bank (ECB), and the lopsided integration of monetary and economic policy in EMU.

The creation of the independent ECB with its overriding price stability objective signified a clear makeover of ideas on the role of monetary policy and the broad recognition among economists of the benefits an independent and inflation-adverse monetary policy authority would produce (Chapter 2 by Verdun). In the same vein, Begg, in Chapter 6, refers to a paradigm shift away from Keynesianism. Together with the system of fiscal policy coordination following the 1997 Stability and Growth Pact (SGP), the Maastricht Treaty was a clear commitment to monetary dominance in the euro area (Schnabel, 2020). This was the outcome of complex political debates between the two biggest economies, France and Germany (Chapters 3 and 5, by James and Dyson), that also dominated the drafting of the SGP. In the endeavour to insulate the new supranational central bank from any political pressure from national governments or EU political institutions, the ECB has effectively been made one of the most independent central banks, as becomes clear from the fact that its legal basis has been elevated to a quasi-constitutional status, making any substantive amendments politically nearly impossible (Chapter 4 by Amtenbrink). The side effect of this emphasis on the depoliticization of monetary policy by law has been that the political accountability of the ECB vis-à-vis democratically elected institutions is limited. Concerns in this regard have increased as a result of the ECB's role in the financial assistance programmes for euro area Member States and its approach to monetary policy during the European sovereign debt crisis (Chapter 4 by Amtenbrink).

The second institutional feature of EMU that stands out is the asymmetry in the degree to which economic and monetary policy have been supra-nationalized in the euro area. Whereas monetary policy in the euro area is in the hands of an EU institution, a similar institutional arrangement cannot be found for fiscal policy. In fact, primary EU law in the EMU context refers to the economic policies of the Member States. Instead, the drafters of the Maastricht Treaty foresaw a rather complex system of fiscal policy coordination focused on ensuring budgetary discipline through a common fiscal rule (prohibition of excessive government deficits) and through the allegedly disciplining pressure of financial markets (namely the prohibition of monetary financing and the no-bailout clause), with the final aim to secure the abovementioned choice for monetary dominance. The complexity of these arrangements has only increased as a result of the reforms in response to the European sovereign debt crisis, which did not necessarily increase their efficiency (see Chapters 4, 6, and 17, by Amtenbrink, Begg, and Markakis).

From an economic point of view, the design choice to leave fiscal policy in a currency union at the level of the Member States is not self-evident. In Chapters 3 and 6, James and Begg provide evidence for this from the early days of the European Economic Community, as the need to consider monetary and fiscal policy in parallel and to provide for a system ensuring the close coordination of these two policy fields was recognized in key policy documents. Perhaps most informative in this regard, the 1970 Werner Report, which had been drafted mostly by central bankers, stressed that European decision-makers should 'exercise independently, in accordance with the Community interest, a decisive influence over the general economic policy of the Community' and 'to influence the national budgets, especially as regards the level and the direction of the balances and the methods for financing the deficits or utilizing the surplus' (Werner et al., 1970, pp. 11–12). By the time of drafting the 1989 Delors Report, and even more the Maastricht Treaty, these ambitions on the supra-nationalization of fiscal policy had been notably toned down (Chapter 3 by James). As these policies are core state powers, no political compromise in favour of transferring serious fiscal and economic powers to the supranational level has been possible, regardless of any negative consequences a mismatch between supranational monetary policy and essentially national economic and fiscal policies may entail.

A reoccurring theme in the majority of contributions in Part I is how the ideas of what constitutes a suitable governance framework for EMU have changed over time, in some instances softening political resistance against certain policy choices at the time of the establishment of EMU.[1] In Chapter 6, Begg describes this process fittingly as 'learning by doing', whereby EMU has developed organically as a result of many 'pragmatic choices' (see also Chapter 2 by Verdun).

One important driver of this change has been the experience with the application of the existing governance framework during normal times that has been diagnosed with various shortcomings which relate to broader systemic issues, such as the lack of a matching political integration (as highlighted in Chapters 2 and 4 by Verdun and Amtenbrink). Still, reforms that can be said to signify a shift in thinking have for a long time mainly focused on technical details, albeit important ones. Examples in this regard include the ECB's own approach to transparency and political accountability arrangements (see, for instance, Amtenbrink, 2019).

As is mainly stressed in Chapter 2 by Verdun, crises have been another important driver of change. Crises have not only pushed early ideas for the establishment of a single currency, such as the breakdown of the Bretton Woods system, but have also led to changes in the EMU policy agenda and to a revaluation of the role of the main actors during the crises of recent years. The ECB has gained an important role in securing the stability (and survival) of the single currency area and, more broadly, in ensuring financial stability (see Chapters 1–3 and 6, by Eichengreen, Verdun, James, and Begg). It has been granted microprudential supervisory tasks over significant banks. The ECB's forceful unconventional monetary policy interventions during and after the European sovereign debt crisis have certainly raised this EU institution from the obscurity often associated with autonomous and apolitical technocratic bodies, and led to reiterated debates on its mandate and the need for a greater European fiscal capacity, not least to preserve monetary dominance.

Regarding the impact of the crises on the approach to fiscal policy coordination in EMU, the uncompromising rhetoric of the early days on no bailout has given way to a more pragmatic approach that recognizes the room provided by the EU Treaties (albeit not always legally undisputed – see, for instance, Gordon, 2022) to provide temporary financial assistance to Member States if the financial stability of the euro area is at risk.[2] As Begg's chapter explains, reforms to fiscal coordination adopted during the sovereign debt crisis were to minimize moral hazard by linking financial assistance to economic reforms (conditionality).[3] Chapter 8 by Campos offers arguments how, paradoxically, this focus on fiscal consolidation (austerity) deepened the euro area crisis not only in economic but mainly in political terms.

The EU's approach to addressing the economic consequences of the COVID-19 pandemic highlights how a crisis may result not only in a shift of thinking but at times also in the lifting of taboos on topics that are politically sensitive. The Support to mitigate Unemployment Risks in an Emergency (SURE) and the Recovery and Resilience Facility (RRF) touch upon the controversial question of issuing common debt by the EU to support the economies of the Member States and of a supra-national stabilization function.[4] For Schelkle in Chapter 7, these

[1] The chapter by Verdun highlights how already prior to the establishment of EMU, ideational changes took place in the Member States that influenced the thinking about monetary integration.

[2] The temporary European Financial Stabilisation Mechanism was based on Article 122 TFEU, whereas the ECJ has confirmed that the Member States were competent to adopt the European Stability Mechanism by means of an intergovernmental treaty.

[3] See in this regard Article 136(3) TFEU.

[4] On these measures see in particular Chapters 2, 5, and 6 by Verdun, Dyson, and Begg.

institutional developments signify the emergence of a reinsurance system that potentially avoids some of the political and legal pitfalls of a full-blown centralization of fiscal and economic policies.

All in all, the Member States could be seen acting much faster collectively now, more in tune, more decisively, with less focus on the enforcement of EU budgetary rules, and overall, with a more accommodating attitude (see Chapter 3 by James) than during the European sovereign debt crisis, prompting Verdun to refer to 'a window of opportunity to expand the role and scope of fiscal federalism' (Chapter 2). To be sure, the new policy and institutional developments established in response to the COVID-19 pandemic have been limited in both scope and time. But their effects will last long not only because of the decades-long repayment schedules for the common debt issued by the EU (Chapter 6 by Begg) but also because these measures have shown political and legal avenues for a greater supranational fiscal capacity (Chapter 4 by Amtenbrink).

Another major area where crisis has resulted in a departure from previous national policy preferences concerns the EU's regulatory and supervisory powers relating to financial markets. Close links between banks and sovereigns (see Chapters 6 and 8 by Begg and Campos) in particular underscored the need for a European system of financial supervision and crisis management (see Chapters 1, 2, and 6 by Eichengreen, Verdun, and Begg), eventually resulting in the project of a European Banking Union, the main elements of which (the Single Rulebook, the Single Supervisory Mechanism, the Single Resolution Mechanism) are the focus of the contributions in Part IV of this volume.

PART II: THE MONETARY DIMENSION

The number of monetary policy programmes instituted by the ECB has grown significantly in the last several years. Their extended functions and implications have increased the economic and political significance of this institution, while raising legitimacy and accountability issues discussed in contributions to Part II.

Monetary policy always entails economic and political consequences. The most standard monetary policy instrument – official interest rates – influences lending conditions and stimulates or reduces economic activity in the real economy. However, such effects have been accepted as part and parcel of traditional central banking. Official interest rates aim at achieving price stability and operate through predictable, essentially market-neutral channels. The same cannot be said about non-standard monetary policy instruments.

Soon after the GFC broke out, the ECB was forced to enter new terrain, assuming the role of lender of last resort for a financial system undergoing severe stress. Even more than within the previous narrow inflation-control function, this new task brought the central bank and financial institutions closer to each other, increasing their interdependencies and undermining the market-neutrality paradigm discussed more broadly by Adamski, and Schoenmaker and Stegeman (Chapters 9 and 12). Still, the economic and fiscal effects of this new role were largely contained by the very characteristics of lender of last resort to financial institutions. While providing emergency liquidity to the financial sector influences the financial viability of financial institutions and their behaviour, liquidity support, guarantees on liabilities, or resolution of individual credit institutions are to be funded from other sources (primarily of national treasuries, regardless of the advancements of the banking union). In addition to this, when a central bank acts as lender of last resort to financial institutions this is always limited to periods of exceptional stress on international markets.

However, since the sovereign debt crisis, the ECB has gone further than this, as Chapters 9, 10, and 11, by Adamski, Chang, and de Haan, explain in more detail. It has embarked on two types of programmes based on large-scale purchases of government bonds: a selective type and an unselective type. The selective type has comprised three programmes so far: The Securities Markets Programme (SMP) implemented intermittently between May 2010 and summer 2012, the Outright Monetary Transactions (OMT) announced in September 2012, and the Transmission Protection Instrument (TPI) publicized in July 2022. The ECB has also instituted two unselective programmes: The Public Sector Purchase Programme[5] (PSPP) launched in early 2015 and the Pandemic Emergency Purchase Programme (PEPP) triggered in March 2020.

Both types of intervention programmes based on large-scale purchases of government bonds rely on so-called non-regular open market operations[6] and have been explained in monetary policy terms as maintaining monetary transmission. Both have also been contested from economic, political, and legal perspectives, as they have affected government debt markets (more directly in respect to country-selective interventions and less so regarding country-unselective interventions), with fiscal implications for the costs of servicing public debt.

Beyond the abovementioned common denominators, though, the two types of non-standard interventions differ. The country-unselective interventions were triggered when the euro area faced the risk of deflation (PSPP), or when the economy was decreasing fast due to COVID-19 pandemic-related lockdowns and other administrative barriers to economic activity (PEPP). Their monetary policy function was therefore very strong and interventions themselves followed the path charted by other major central banks. In contrast, all three programmes based on country-selective interventions (SMP, OMT, TPI) were launched either when inflation in the euro area was close to (SMP) or above the price stability target of the ECB (OMT and TPI). Therefore, their monetary policy justification – transmission of the monetary policy signals to the real economy – has been more problematic and their fiscal implications – providing respite to the most heavily indebted euro area sovereigns – more discernible compared to country-unselective interventions. On the other hand, while both country-unselective programmes have resulted in serious alterations in the balance sheet of the Eurosystem, among the country-selective interventions so far only SMP has led to actual (yet relatively limited and fading) asset purchases.

In two landmark decisions – *Gauweiler*[7] and *Weiss*[8] – the Court of Justice of the European Union (CJEU) has legally vindicated country-selective interventions and country-unselective interventions, respectively, as long as they can be justified in terms of the monetary transmission mechanism. Accordingly, when they meet this condition, the two types of large-scale purchases of government bonds are in line with the mandate of the Eurosystem and the Treaty prohibition

[5] The unselective nature of the PSPP is not complete, as Greek government paper has been excluded from it since the very beginning of the programme.

[6] Open market operations constitute the foundation of the Eurosystem monetary policy implementation framework (Guideline 2015/510 of the European Central Bank of 19 December 2014 on the implementation of the Eurosystem monetary policy framework (ECB/2014/60), OJ L 91, 2.4.2015, pp. 3–135, as subsequently amended). Regular open market operations comprise two types of liquidity-providing operations in euros: one-week main refinancing operations (MROs) or three-month longer-term refinancing operations (LTROs). Four non-regular open market operations have been undertaken by the ECB in recent times: PELTROs – pandemic emergency longer-term refinancing operations; TLTROs – targeted longer-term refinancing operations; APP – asset purchase programme (in which PSPP constitutes the biggest part); and PEPP – pandemic emergency purchase programme. For further details see ECB, Open market operations, www.ecb.europa.eu/mopo/implement/omo/html/index.en.html.

[7] Case C-62/14 *Gauweiler* [2015] EU:C:2015:400.

[8] Case C-493/17 *Weiss* [2018] EU:C:2018:1000.

of monetary financing.[9] However, as Chang argues in Chapter 10, the implications of these interventions for distribution of political power in the EU have been paramount, even if the political leadership and economic influences associated with these programmes have been given to the ECB largely because of the power vacuum created by inactivity of political leaders. Building on this finding, Adamski in Chapter 9 adds that the extensions of the monetary policy functions performed by the Eurosystem have seriously overburdened it. They have imposed on the ECB the role of mitigating consequences of actions taken by national economic and fiscal decision-makers, which a supranational monetary policy institution is not well placed to influence, with serious corresponding efficiency and legitimacy concerns down the road.

While fiscal implications of increased ECB interventions on government debt markets have been highly contestable, another new task assumed by the central bank is broadly applauded (although there is also critique).[10] This function – greening monetary policy – is comprehensively discussed in Part II by Schoenmaker and Stegeman. Political actors in charge of climate law-making and regulation have not fallen behind comparably to economic and fiscal policy-makers and – as the Green deal agenda demonstrates – the role of European institutions in shaping the regulatory agenda in this field is far greater. Efforts of the ECB to introduce climate mitigation aspects to its monetary policy can therefore be seen as an attempt to keep pace with the other decision-makers in delivering the crucial public good of a stable ecological system. Fiscal implications of this monetary policy reorientation are also incomparably smaller than those of large-scale purchases of government assets, regardless of the potential redistributive effects between classes of asset holders and the related sectors of the real economy entailed by greening monetary policy. Schoenmaker and Stegeman argue in Chapter 12 that such a policy shift not only remains within the mandate of the ECB, but also calls for corresponding adjustments in microprudential standards for banks.

The abovementioned extensions of ECB's monetary policy tasks pose serious problems for its legitimacy and accountability. As de Haan explains in Chapter 11, improving communication has been one of the most important methods used by the ECB to respond to these challenges. De Haan highlights three positive implications of better central bank communication. First, it increases the transparency of the ECB's actions and facilitates accountability. Second, it is key for managing expectations about interest rates and inflation. Third, better communication could help the ECB rebuild credibility and trust in its actions, tarnished since the onset of the GFC.[11]

As contributors to Part II emphasize, finding new ways of increasing the legitimacy of ECB actions is important because of its operational independence guaranteed by the Treaties, which in practice prohibits other actors from instructing the ECB how to conduct monetary policy. This legal environment curtails its legitimacy based on inputs from other actors (input legitimacy), as emphasized by Diessner in Chapter 13. In turn, output legitimacy – the ability of the ECB to meet its statutory objectives, stable prices in particular – has also proven difficult to achieve in practice: while inflation remained persistently below the ECB's stated target from early 2013 to mid-2018, since mid-2019 it has increased well above target. Foreclosed input legitimacy and hindered output legitimacy has attracted scholarly attention to throughput legitimacy – the quality of decision-making processes. This dimension of legitimacy – explored

[9] Article 123 TFEU.

[10] Issing (2019) argues, for instance, that 'A policy domain far outside of central banks' proper mandate cannot be brought within it, and attempts to do so will inevitably end more or less badly'.

[11] In early 2022, 44 per cent of respondents in EU27 trusted the ECB while 43 per cent expressed distrust (European Commission, 2022, Annex, T.46). Fifteen years earlier, in spring 2007, the results were 53 per cent and 25 per cent, respectively (European Commission, 2007, QA15.4). See also Roth and Jonung (2022).

in Part II especially by Diessner – relates to Chapter 11 by de Haan, as high standards of decision-making require good communication.

Better communication and throughput legitimacy are associated with central bank accountability. However, the ECB's political accountability has remained inherently shallow, limited to giving an account in the sense of informing broader audiences of the central bank's motives and intentions. However, deeper understandings of political accountability, in which the account-giving institution may face sanctions of some kind for not delivering according to its mandate, do not apply to the ECB due to the abovementioned statutory independence of the Eurosystem. More fundamentally still, as the euro area is not a sovereign state, different institutions can compete for the role of the accountability forum towards the ECB. While contributors to Part II agree that the European Parliament is the most natural candidate, the economic sovereignty still residing firmly at the national level could substantiate the argument that the Eurogroup or the European Council could also make a claim in this respect. Therefore, the fact that the creation of the monetary union has not gone hand in hand with establishing a political union has also produced serious implications for the political accountability of the ECB.

Another accountability mechanism of monetary policy – judicial review (judicial accountability) – is depicted by some as a promising method of remedying the problem of the tenuous political accountability of the ECB and therefore of its limited democratic (input and throughput) legitimacy. This argument is dealt with in Chapter 14 by Bobić and Dawson forcefully defended by the German Constitutional Court in its much-debated *Weiss* decision finding the PSPP programme *ultra vires* for its insufficient throughput legitimacy.[12] However, as Bobić and Dawson emphasize, judicial accountability of monetary policy interventions is seriously reduced by judicial deference of the CJEU in cases involving specialized EU authorities. One can hardly expect that the Luxembourg court may depart from this line in cases involving monetary policy – a particularly complex and intricate policy area.

The input legitimacy and deeper political accountability are therefore prevented by the Treaty requirement of the central bank's independence while judicial accountability of the ECB is curtailed by the judicial deference of the CJEU (see also Chapter 4 by Amtenbrink). This places responsibility for both successes and failures of its monetary policy squarely on the central bank, emphasizing the role of its output legitimacy. However, output legitimacy becomes particularly difficult to achieve when the ECB's functions go far beyond maintaining stable prices, as argued by Adamski in Chapter 9.

PART III: THE ECONOMIC AND FISCAL DIMENSIONS

Although national fiscal policy remains the primary responsibility of the Member States, the SGP and the Fiscal Compact impose specific rules that aim to impose budget discipline. There are three reasons for constraining national fiscal policy in a monetary union. Firstly, lack of budget discipline creates insufficient room for expansionary fiscal policies in times of crisis. In the euro area, this is particularly important because Member States may face country-specific shocks that cannot be absorbed by the common monetary policy. In addition, inadequate fiscal discipline in one EMU Member State may have an impact on other Member States, as the economies in the euro area are strongly interlinked. These effects are often not internalized, as pointed out in Chapter 15 by Demertzis, Jiménez, and Viegi. Finally, unsustainable fiscal

[12] German Constitutional Court, judgment of 5 May 2020, 2 BvR 859/15, 2 BvR 980/16, 2 BvR 2006/15, 2 BvR 1651/15 (*Weiss II*).

policies can undermine confidence in the ECB's monetary policy if financial markets come to expect that government debt will eventually be financed by money creation (Buti and Carnot, 2012).

The tools aimed to deliver economic policy coordination, including the fiscal policy framework, developed during the European sovereign debt crisis and brought together under the rubric of 'European Semester', as launched in 2011, are discussed in Chapter 16 by Eihmanis. He takes stock of the available evidence showing that the European Semester can significantly shape national debates and at times national policy outcomes.

The COVID-19 pandemic has further enhanced the significance of the European Semester, which will also serve to monitor and assess Member States' use of EU financial support under the RRF. Eihmanis points out that for most of the first decade of the Semester's operation, the Commission issued country-specific recommendations, while leaving implementation at the discretion of the individual Member States. However, it may be expected that since the Commission has become the chief administrator of RRF funds, its potential ability to shape national policies has significantly increased, even beyond the fiscal realm.

Not only coordination of national fiscal policies, but also coordination of fiscal and monetary policy is important for economic stabilization. Here a distinction can be made between normal and crisis times (Bartsch et al., 2020). Under normal circumstances, monetary policy aims at price stability and (to the extent that it is supportive to price stability) at stabilization of the business cycle. A policy stance that tends to stabilize the business cycle is said to be countercyclical; otherwise, it is either neutral (i.e. no systematic impact on the cyclicality of economic activity) or procyclical (i.e. it tends to amplify fluctuations). In principle, fiscal and monetary policy can be used for stabilization purposes. If the economy is in a recession, government may increase spending and/or lower taxes and finance its revenues shortfall by issuing government debt. This expansionary policy will stimulate the economy, just as a cut in interest rates would. Likewise, during an economic boom, the government may decide to increase taxes to reduce government debt (contractionary fiscal policy).

However, there are three key differences between fiscal and monetary policy (Bartsch et al., 2020). First, the transmission of fiscal policy operates more directly, impinging on households' incomes and firms' profitability, while monetary policy works indirectly by changing the price and availability of credit. Second, monetary policy decisions and their implementation take less time than fiscal policy decisions and their implementation. This reflects that the government needs parliamentary approval to change spending or taxes and this process takes time (the legislative lag). Moreover, once a fiscal policy bill is accepted by parliament, it takes time to implement it (the implementation lag). Finally, it takes time for fiscal policy to have an effect (the impact lag). These long lags make discretionary fiscal policy a less effective stabilization tool than monetary policy. Third, politicians tend to prefer expansionary fiscal policy over contractionary policy. Notably during economic good times, they prefer not to increase taxes and limit spending (Alesina et al., 2008). Consequently, fiscal policies are often procyclical, especially in good times. This holds true in EMU as well as shown in Chapter 15 by Demertzis, Jiménez, and Viegi, and Chapter 18 by de Haan and Gootjes. As central banks are (at least to some extent) insulated from the political process, they are typically more willing than fiscal policy authorities to use contractionary policy when the economy is booming, and inflation threatens to increase.

In crisis situations, like the COVID-19 pandemic, policymakers have no alternative but to massively deploy all instruments at their disposal. As pointed out by Demertzis, Jiménez, and Viegi, as the COVID-19 shock unravelled, monetary policy could only play an ancillary role to a fiscal response, aiming more at preventing financial fragmentation than actually counteracting the shock. It was fiscal policy that had to come to the rescue. To enable this, the European fiscal rules were suspended in the wake of the COVID-19-related economic decline. The ECB created fiscal policy space by (1) substantially lowering governments' borrowing costs and (2) by effectively providing what is called a monetary backstop to government debt. By the same token, the central bank commits to prevent self-fulfilling sovereign debt crises, as the ECB did when it introduced OMT after ECB President Mario Draghi's 'whatever it takes' speech. But there is a point beyond which stretching the ECB balance sheet could undermine its credibility. In fact, several observers have expressed concerns that the policy mix pursued to counter the impact of the COVID-19 pandemic may lead to what is called *fiscal dominance*, i.e. a situation where monetary policy is determined by the fiscal position of the government and is no longer directed at maintaining price stability (Bartsch et al., 2020).

The European fiscal rules have been severely criticized from different perspectives, as shown by de Haan and Gootjes in Chapter 18. Some observers have claimed that the rules would lead to pro-cyclical policies, while others argued that they would not be effective. Obviously, both arguments cannot be correct at the same time. Still, there is a broad consensus that the fiscal rules should be reformed, but there are different options on the table, as discussed by Markakis in Chapter 17. These proposals are very much influenced by the perceived effectiveness of the current set-up.

When a Member State gets into financial difficulties, it may receive support from the EU. The European Stability Mechanism (ESM) helped Member States in adjusting to the sovereign debt crisis and the RRF provided support for recovering from the pandemic crisis. However, as pointed out in Chapter 20 by Fabbrini and Capati, the ESM and the RRF have different aims. In fact, the authors argue that the EU moved from an approach of 'unconstrained intergovernmentalism' (ESM) to an approach of 'constrained supranationalism' (RRF).

The theory of optimum currency areas has emphasized the role of fiscal transfers in maintaining a single currency, also highlighting the inability of monetary policy alone to counter all shocks. Until recently, it seemed that a European stabilization mechanism was politically and legally not on the cards, but the COVID-19 pandemic has changed the debate, as shown by Wasserfallen in Chapter 19. The Franco-German compromise paving the way to the NextGenerationEU (NGEU) initiative, and the RRF in particular, have made the introduction of a European stabilization mechanism more likely. The NGEU extends the EU's fiscal capacity by adding €806 billion to the regular budget of €1,074 billion, while the Member States jointly finance the NGEU by issuing bonds. As Demertizis, Jiménez, and Viegi point out in Chapter 15, although not a fiscal stabilization tool in itself, the NGEU is an attempt to coordinate national fiscal policies at least at the level of investments needed to prepare next generations for the challenges that lie ahead. Although the NGEU programme is supposed to be exceptional and thus not anticipated to become a regular tool of fiscal policymaking, Wasserfallen argues that it remains to be seen whether that will really be the case. Indeed, the recent flurry of proposals for a European stabilization scheme suggests that at the very least, the experience with NGEU has changed the debate about such a scheme.

The proposals for a European stabilization mechanism can be split into four (Berger et al., 2019). First, some have proposed a counter-cyclical rainy-day fund that would collect contributions in times of economic growth to finance short-term transfers to countries experiencing asymmetric shocks. Others suggest issuing debt jointly guaranteed at the EU level (Eurobonds), which would decrease borrowing costs for countries in distress. A third option is a centralized budget with supranational taxation authority which extends common borrowing schemes.

Finally, EU-level support to national social security systems, such as a European unemployment insurance scheme, has been proposed.

The key challenge in designing any European fiscal risk-sharing mechanism is the moral hazard that such a scheme may create, notably if transfers to poorer regions are made unconditionally or if there are no mechanisms limiting permanent redistribution. A fiscal risk-sharing mechanism should thus strike a balance between adequate stabilization, while maintaining incentives for sufficient fiscal discipline. In Chapter 21, Beetsma and Kopits argue in favour of a mechanism to semi-automatically respond to region- and country-specific shocks via a central fiscal stabilization fund. To minimize moral hazard, only large exogenous shocks, above threshold values of some specified real-time indicators, should trigger support disbursement.

In comparison with the United States, private sector consumption is significantly lower in the euro area. In Chapter 22, Cimadomo, Gordo Mora, and Palazzo find that about 70 per cent of shocks is smoothed in the United States against 40 per cent in the euro area, although during the COVID-19 crisis risk sharing in the euro area has been more resilient than it was during the GFC. Risk sharing can be done via the public sector (e.g. through the scheme proposed by Beetsma and Kopits in Chapter 21), but also via the private sector (e.g. through financial markets). Further improvements to the private risk-sharing channels in the euro area are needed to ensure more effective cushioning against asymmetric shocks. This points to the need for more financial integration in the EMU.

PART IV: FINANCIAL INTEGRATION

The 1970 Werner Report – the first official action plan to establish a monetary union in what was then called the European Economic Community – considered 'the complete liberation of movements of capital' (Werner et al., 1970, pp. 10, 26) as an indispensable ingredient of monetary integration. EMU has thus conceptually been inseparably interwoven with financial integration. Another very influential report, published in 1990 under the telling title 'One Market, One Money', clarified that the 'liberation' of capital movements called for two decades earlier should entail nothing less than 'complete liberalization of capital transactions and full integration of banking and financial markets' (Emerson et al., 1990, p. 32). As its authors argued, thanks to coupling monetary integration with financial integration 'one can expect ... the supply of financial products to increase, presumably providing larger hedging opportunities, and also, some reduction in transaction and hedging costs because of economies of scale, technological change, and greater competition' (Emerson et al. 1990, p. 42).

Initial regulatory steps in this direction were very promising. One legislative instrument, adopted in 1988, removed restrictions on capital movements from 1 July 1990.[13] Another – the so-called Second Banking Directive,[14] passed one year later – aimed to pursue integration of the banking sector by centralizing supervision over individual institutions in one state and hence facilitating the free movement of establishment by means of bank branching. Due to these legal adjustments and others affecting the banking sector, discussed more broadly in Chapter 23 by Parchimowicz, interbank integration seriously progressed during the first years of the euro (even if retail markets remained mostly national). Foreign exposures of EU banks to other EU

[13] Council Directive 88/361/EEC of 24 June 1988 for the implementation of Article 67 of the Treaty, OJ L 178, 8.7.1988, pp. 5–18.

[14] Second Council Directive 89/646/EEC of 15 December 1989 on the coordination of laws, regulations and administrative provisions relating to the taking up and pursuit of the business of credit institutions and amending Directive 77/780/EEC, OJ L 386, 30.12.1989, pp. 1–13.

countries and cross-border credit provided by non-resident banks grew exponentially.[15] As capital was flowing mainly from the core to the periphery, it both increased profitability of the financial industry and boosted economic growth of the recipient countries.

The process, however, was advancing only until about 2005, while the GFC triggered its reversion (Hoffmann et al., 2020). Undermining market confidence, the crisis uncovered flaws in financial products, business models, and regulatory frameworks for the financial sector. As the seminal report of de Larosière Group (de Larosière et al., 2009) diagnosed, important segments of the financial system had been insufficiently regulated and supervised before the GFC, contributing to financial instability and volatility on wholesale funding markets. While the conclusions of the report spurred substantive reforms and institutional adjustments, soon different developments facilitated by the free movement of capital posed an even bigger challenge for the euro area. Capital outflows from the vulnerable periphery to the core countries precipitated the sovereign debt crisis (Merler and Pisani-Ferry, 2012). In addition, the market fragmentation which followed contributed to the destabilizing sovereign debt–domestic bank loop tightening between 2010 and 2012. Finally, the problem of the dominance of bank finance – a relatively small role in financing of the real economy played by financial markets (stock and bond markets) in the euro area – also surfaced during the sovereign debt crisis. It had serious implications going far beyond the financial sector, because integrated financial markets are an important shock-absorption mechanism, as Cimadomo, Gordo Mora, and Palazzo explain in Chapter 22, in Part III of this volume.

All in all, the financial integration progressing in the first few years of the single currency proved unsustainable and contributed to the sovereign debt crisis when financial flows subsequently reversed. Part IV deals with lessons drawn from these experiences for how the banking sector and financial markets are to be regulated and supervised to achieve more stable growth and further integration.

Banks are bound by prudential regulatory standards which have undergone a serious evolution in the last several years. While financial stability concerns drove the process shortly after the GFC, more recently new aspects – such as maintaining credit supply to the real economy during the COVID-19 pandemic, tackling climate change, or facilitating technological transition of the financial system – have emerged as important goals of banking regulation. In this context, Parchimowicz argues in Chapter 23 that for a long time, banking policymakers reacted to crises provoked by their earlier regulatory delays, inaction, and forbearance. Now they have become more proactive and future oriented. It is yet to be seen whether this shift suffices to avoid future systemic crises in the banking sector and whether it will be enough to produce genuine trans-border integration.

The intention to achieve precisely these goals has also been key for creating the European Banking Union (EBU). In its ultimate, mature version, the EBU should comprise three building blocks established on the foundation of common microprudential standards: common supervision, common bank resolution, and common deposit insurance. The decade since it was politically endorsed at the apex of the sovereign debt crisis in 2012 has brought the EBU half way, and further progress has virtually stalled since the wake of the COVID-19 pandemic. The accompanying economic crisis that hit the economies of the euro area's south harder than those of the euro area's north revived concerns about the vulnerabilities of the southern banking systems. The economic implications of the energy crisis caused by the Russian aggression in

[15] Even the central and eastern Member States of the EU, which at this stage all used their national currencies, experienced a similar process (Laeven and Tressel, 2014).

Ukraine have further diverted the attention of policymakers from completing this very important project.

Chapters by Ríos Camacho, Binder, and de Groen (Chapters 24–26) deal with political, legal, and economic enablers as well as barriers to the EBU since its inception a decade ago. Ríos Camacho pays particular attention to the fact that, while supranational layers of the EBU's governance have provided for common supervision and common bank resolution in the countries belonging to (and aspiring to become part of) the euro area, its institutional tissue has been crucially determined by complex bargaining between Member States striving to tailor legislative outcomes to their specific national interests and priorities. Because domestic interests and risk perceptions have been particularly hard to align in the field of deposit insurance, this important element of the banking union has remained very elusive. Little progress has been achieved since the Commission tabled its legislative proposal for a European deposit insurance scheme in 2015.

In Chapter 25, Binder focuses on the common banking resolution pillar of the EBU. On the one hand, since its establishment in 2014, the Single Resolution Mechanism (SRM) has improved resolvability of significant banks at the preventive stage, when individual credit institutions build specific buffers of capital and debt instruments, and when they design actions to be taken when the prospect of a failure becomes real. On the other hand, legal idiosyncrasies and political considerations have limited the role of the SRM at the subsequent – reactive – stage of resolution, when a credit institution is failing or likely to fail, with only two actual resolutions effectuated by the SRM so far. Binder emphasizes that it is still to be seen how the resolution toolbox now in place would fare in a systemic crisis. While bail-in rules, introduced to the banking resolution legislation to avoid future bailouts, have remained unused, the available funding for future resolutions has been seriously increased by financial backstops now offered for banking resolution purposes by both the ESM and the Single Resolution Fund (SRF). The key question is whether it will suffice to outweigh the potential consequences of the absence of a common deposit insurance scheme in the euro area and a persistently high level of non-performing loans in some of its Member States.

De Groen answers this very question in Chapter 26 by proposing two second-best solutions to the gridlocks so far preventing the first-best solutions to establishing a fully fledged EBU from making their way through the legislative process. The first of the two solutions – called Transitional Liquidity Assistance by de Groen – may increase liquidity in banking resolution by tapping additional resources of the Eurosystem. The other – a European Deposit Insurance Scheme (EDIS) restricted to a reinsurance scheme – could overcome the prevailing resistance to a full mutualization of the risks involved in a fully fledged EDIS. Such a reinsurance scheme would be a concrete manifestation of a more general concept presented by Schelkle (Chapter 7) in Part I of the volume.

In the face of a spectacular growth in assets managed by the financial system outside the banking sector, the regulatory framework for non-bank financial intermediation also witnessed multifaceted policy initiatives in recent years. As the ECB has highlighted in this context (ECB, 2022, p. 28):

> Total assets of the euro area non-bank financial sector[16] have almost doubled to around €50 trillion over the last decade and now represent almost 55% of total euro area financial sector assets ... The outstanding amount of debt securities issued by euro area NFCs [non-financial corporations] has roughly doubled over the past decade, growing from around €860 billion in January 2012 to around €1.6 trillion in December 2021.

[16] The non-bank financial sector comprises investment funds, money market funds, pension funds, insurance corporations, financial vehicle corporations, and the residual of other financial institutions.

Recognizing the role of financial integration outside the banking sector, the Juncker Commission in 2015 announced the Capital Market Union (CMU) programme. Construed as an internal market programme, and hence covering the territories of all the EU Member States, the CMU has been considered of paramount importance for the euro area, due to the role financial markets play in absorbing asymmetric economic shocks. However, the departure of the United Kingdom – the main European financial hub – from the EU deflated the original political salience of the 2015 CMU programme soon after it was launched, as Montalbano and Haverland point out in Chapter 27. Politics has determined the outcome of the CMU project in other respects as well. The programme has succeeded in producing tangible regulatory outcomes in more technical, less politically divisive areas – such as venture capital funds, securitization or covered bonds. Much less progress has been achieved in politically more salient (and more divisive) aspects, such as insolvency procedures or taxation of cross-border investments and business operations. Similar political dynamics may be expected to unfold in respect to the more recent legislative package (European Commission, 2021) associated with the 2020 Capital Markets Union Action Plan (European Commission, 2020).

Financial integration entails particularly salient regulatory challenges on markets for the technologically most advanced investments, services, and (intangible) goods. Chapters by Valiante, Lamandini, and Ramos Muñozu (Chapter 28) as well as Lannoo (Chapter 29) deal with this novel and fast-developing area, where less intrusive regulation (or lack of it) may be expected to support technological development more than stricter obligations, while the opposite is true if investor protection is prioritized.

Lannoo concentrates on regulatory and supervisory frameworks for crypto-assets and the market infrastructure based on the distributed ledger technology (DLT), emphasizing that a draft regulation on markets in crypto assets, tabled by the European Commission in 2020,[17] is based on a narrow, product-specific approach, rather than on an idea of extending the already existing regulatory framework to new market developments. Such a regulatory strategy adds to the complexity of financial markets regulation and enforcement, as well as facilitating regulatory arbitrage. Lannoo also highlights that those effects of the new regulatory framework for crypto assets, as well as of the related regulation on digital operational resilience for the financial sector[18] (once both of these pieces of legislation are adopted), will critically hinge on the operational efficiency of enforcement, for which developing appropriate practical cooperation mechanisms between national and European authorities will be crucial.

Although Chapter 28 by Valiante, Lamandini, and Ramos Muñozu deals with recent regulatory schemes for crypto assets and DLT market infrastructure, these authors extend their analysis to broader regulatory implications of digital finance. In particular, they discuss the Digital Single Market Strategy – adopted by the Commission in 2015 as a twin project to the CMU – and its subsequent evolution. They also ponder on broader company law and corporate governance questions and dilemmas produced by FinTech and digitalization of securities. These questions make it clear that further financial integration in the technologically most advanced segments may not justify entirely new regulatory frameworks for individual products, services, or infrastructures. Instead, it requires incremental changes and adjustments in highly technical rules dispersed across various pieces of legislation. The chapters by Montalbano and Haverland (Chapter 27), as well as by Lannoo (Chapter 29) point in the same direction.

[17] COM(2020)593.
[18] COM(2020)595.

REFERENCES

Alesina, A., Campante, F., and Tabellini, G. (2008). Why is fiscal policy often procyclical? *Journal of the European Economic Association* 6(5), 1006–1036.

Amtenbrink, F. (2019). The European Central Bank's intricate independence versus accountability conundrum in the post-crisis governance framework. *Maastricht Journal of European and Comparative Law* 26(1), 165–179.

Bartsch, E., Bénassy-Quéré, A., Corsetti, G., and Debrun, X. (2020). *It's All in the Mix. How Monetary and Fiscal Policies Can Work or Fail Together.* Geneva Reports on the World Economy 23, Geneva, ICMBS/London, CEPR.

Bénassy-Quéré, A., Brunnermeier, M., Enderlein, H., Farhi, E., Fratzscher, M., Fuest, C., Gourinchas, P.-O., Martin, P., Pisani-Ferry, J., Rey, H., Schnabel, I., Véron, N., Weder di Mauro, B., and Zettelmeyer, J. (2018). Reconciling risk sharing with market discipline: A constructive approach to euro area reform. CEPR Policy Insight No. 91, January 2018. https://cepr.org/publications/policy-insight-91-reconciling-risk-sharing-market-discipline-constructive-approach

Berger, H., Dell'Ariccia, G., and Obstfeld, M. (2019). Revisiting the economic case for fiscal union in the euro area. *IMF Economic Review* 67(3), 657–683.

Brunnermeier, M. K., James, H., and Landau, J.-P. (2016). *The Euro and the Battle of Ideas.* Princeton, NJ, Princeton University Press.

Buti, M., and Carnot, N. (2012). The EMU debt crisis: Early lessons and reforms. *Journal of Common Market Studies* 50(6), 899–911.

Emerson, M., Gros, D., and Italianer, A. (1990). One market, one money: An evaluation of the potential benefits and costs of forming an economic and monetary union. European Economy No. 44.

De Grauwe, P. (2013). Design failures in the Eurozone – Can they be fixed? European Economy, Economic Papers 491.

De Larosière, J., Balcerowicz, L., Issing, O., Masera, R., Mc Carthy, C., Nyberg, L., Pérez, J., and Ruding, O.(2009). Report of the High-Level Group on Financial Supervision in the EU. https://ec.europa.eu/economy_finance/publications/pages/publication14527_en.pdf

Eichengreen, B. (1990). Costs and benefits of European Monetary Unification. CEPR Discussion Paper No. 453.

European Central Bank (2022). Financial integration and structure in the euro area. April. www.ecb.europa.eu/pub/pdf/fie/ecb.fie202204~4c4f5f572f.en.pdf

European Commission (2007). Public opinion in the European Union. Standard Eurobarometer 67. https://europa.eu/eurobarometer/surveys/detail/664

European Commission. (2020). Capital Markets Union 2020 Action Plan: A capital markets union for people and businesses. https://finance.ec.europa.eu/capital-markets-union-and-financial-markets/capital-markets-union/capital-markets-union-2020-action-plan_en

European Commission. (2021). Capital Markets Union: Commission adopts package to ensure better data access and revamped investment rules. Communication. 25 November. https://finance.ec.europa.eu/publications/capital-markets-union-commission-adopts-package-ensure-better-data-access-and-revamped-investment_en

European Commission (2022). Public opinion in the European Union. Standard Eurobarometer 96. Winter 2021–2022. https://europa.eu/eurobarometer/surveys/detail/2553

Gordon, B. (2022). *The Constitutional Boundaries of European Fiscal Federalism.* Cambridge, Cambridge University Press.

Hoffmann, P., Kremer, M., and Zaharia, S. (2020). Financial integration in Europe through the lens of composite indicators. *Economics Letters* 194, 109344.

Issing, O. (2019). The problem with 'green' monetary policy. Project Syndicate. www.project-syndicate.org/commentary/central-banks-no-to-green-monetary-policy-by-otmar-issing-2019-11

Laeven, L., and Tressel, T. (2014). European Union financial integration before the crisis. In M. C. Enoch, M. L. Everaert, M. T. Tressel, and M. J. Zhou (eds.). *From Fragmentation to Financial Integration in Europe.* Washington, DC, International Monetary Fund, 49–68.

Merler, S., and Pisani-Ferry, J. (2012). Sudden stops in the euro area. Bruegel policy contribution No. 06.

Roth, F., and Jonung, L. (2022). Public support for the euro and trust in the ECB: The first two decades of the common currency. In F. Roth (ed.). *Public Support for the Euro: Essays on Labor Productivity, Monetary Economics, and Political Economy*, Vol. 2. Heidelberg, Springer.

Schnabel, I. (2020). The shadow of fiscal dominance: Misconceptions, perceptions and perspectives. Speech held at the Centre for European Reform and the Eurofi Financial Forum, Berlin, 11 September.

Werner, P., et al. (1970). Report to the Council and the Commission on the realization by stages of economic and monetary union the Community, 8 October. https://ec.europa.eu/economy_finance/publications/pages/publication6142_en.pdf

PART I

The Economic and Monetary Union

Political, Economic, and Legal Rationales

1

Conceptual Foundations of Economic and Monetary Union

The Economic Dimension

Barry Eichengreen

1.1 INTRODUCTION

The birth of the euro on 1 January 1999 marked the inauguration of Europe's economic and monetary union (EMU).[1] The event was the culmination of a half-century-long journey from the European Coal and Steel Community and the customs union to the European Monetary System and single market. In another sense, however, it was only a waystation along the path to forging a true economic and monetary union.

Search for information on EMU and one is directed, unsurprisingly, to the website of the European Commission. There one learns that EMU 'is not an end in itself' but is rather 'a means to provide stability and for stronger, more sustainable and inclusive growth across the euro area and the EU as a whole'. Advancing those objectives, one then learns, entails four core policies: ensuring that the single market runs smoothly; implementing an effective monetary policy; coordinating the fiscal policies of the Member States; and supervising and monitoring European financial institutions.

An interpretation of this list is that the single market is the European Union's signal economic achievement and that the other aspects – a price-stability-oriented central bank, fiscal coordination, and financial supervision and regulation – are flanking policies designed to support that creation. The single market entails the removal of barriers to the free movement of goods, services, capital, and labour (the so-called four freedoms). It commits the Member States to refrain from extending state aid and from pursuing other policies that might tilt the playing field. Firms are thereby fully exposed to the chill winds of competition from producers in other Member States, sharpening the incentive for them to boost productivity and efficiency in order to survive. No longer limited by the extent of the domestic market, Member States can further specialize along lines of comparative advantage. Producers are better able to exploit economies of scale and scope.

Economic studies, starting with some written well before the single market was a fact, are nearly unanimous in concluding that its economic benefits are substantial.[2] The disruptions to

[1] The physical euro was issued only three years later, but exchange rates between the members' so-called legacy currencies were irrevocably locked at the beginning of 1999, and the euro could already be used for non-cash transactions.

[2] These opinions were as near unanimous as economists are about anything. An early influential analysis was Baldwin (1989). Subsequent studies added precision and refined techniques without changing the overall conclusion. For a representative recent example, see Veld (2019).

British trade and production in early 2021, when the transitional period following Brexit ended and the United Kingdom lost its prior access to the single market, offered costly proof by counterexample. So too did the border closures that were imposed in the early stages of the COVID-19 pandemic.

The flanking policies are more controversial. Ever since the idea of the euro was first mooted, sceptics have questioned whether a single market needs a single currency. To put it another way, they have questioned how much adding a single currency to the single market enhances the four freedoms. There is disagreement about whether the role of the euro is to heighten price transparency, thereby strengthening the pro-competitive features of the single market, to facilitate cross-border trade within the euro area, to buttress currency and financial stability, or to fend off a political backlash against capricious exchange rate movements within the integrated economic zone. There are ongoing complaints about the costs to Member States of forgoing monetary policy autonomy and living with a one-size-fits-all monetary policy. More concretely, there is criticism of the European Central Bank (ECB) for interpreting its mandate too narrowly.

On the fiscal side, there are questions about exactly how closely fiscal policies must be coordinated in an economic and monetary union, and about how exactly such coordination should be achieved. The residents of different Member States have very different views of how large a budget deficit is acceptable and how much debt is too much (for evidence see, for example, European Commission, 2020). Even when there are benefits of fiscal centralization and coordination in a monetary union, club theory suggests going less far in that direction when preferences diverge (see e.g. Buchanan, 1965; Sandler and Tschirhart, 1997).

Moreover, the purported benefits of fiscal coordination achieved through the application of fiscal rules can be questioned. The counterargument is that the value of fiscal autonomy at the national level is greatest in a monetary union; eliminating distinct national monetary policies only strengthens the case for flexible national fiscal policies to address asymmetric shocks. A national government with its monetary hand tied behind its back has all the more reason to keep its fiscal hand free, as it is sometimes put. Insofar as the cross-border spillovers of national fiscal policies are small, the case for close coordination is weak, in which case giving Brussels oversight of national fiscal policies violates the principle of subsidiarity.[3]

The rebuttal starts with the observation that allowing Member States to accumulate excessive debt heightens the danger of 'fiscal dominance'. In the presence of heavy debts, the ECB will feel pressure to keep interest rates low in order to help Member States with their debt service costs, ultimately with inflationary consequences. In addition, when a government's debts become borderline unsustainable, confidence problems may spread contagiously to the bond markets of other countries, providing an additional rationale for preventing the development of those sustainability problems in the first place. Public debt crises can also become banking and financial crises, since banks, and not only in the debt-issuing jurisdiction, hold concentrations of government bonds.

Similarly, there is contestation over the need for and competences of a single financial supervisor at the EU or euro area level. The argument for a single supervisor is that banks do business with one another, and that Europe's big banks, in particular, do business with banks in other Member States. Even though what happens in one national banking system doesn't always

[3] The conclusion that cross-border spillovers are weak in a monetary union flows from standard versions of the Mundell–Fleming model: when a member runs larger budget deficits, for example, it sucks in more imports from other members, which is expansionary throughout the monetary union, but it also pushes up the common level of interest rates, which is contractionary throughout the monetary union. The two effects at least partially, if not completely, cancel each other out.

stay in that one national banking system, national supervisors may nonetheless have inadequate incentive to internalize the consequences for banks in other countries. Memoranda of understanding, in which separate national regulators agree on a division of labour and limited information sharing, have not been up to the task.

At the same time, banking systems in Europe are still mainly organized along national lines. Small banks still do most of their business at home. It can be argued on these grounds that they are best supervised by national authorities attuned to the nuances of local markets.

When the EU created its Single Supervisory Mechanism (SSM) in 2013, it opted to split the difference, giving supervisors within the ECB responsibility for oversight of Europe's biggest banks. Oversight of the others is reserved for national supervisors, operating in principle under the same rule book, of course. But the threshold above which banks are sufficiently large and systemically important to warrant supervision by the SSM is arbitrary. In addition, the Member States outside the monetary union can opt into the SSM, but only some (Croatia and Bulgaria) have chosen to do so.

1.2 EFFECTIVE MONETARY POLICY FOR THE EURO AREA

How important is the common currency for the operation of the single market? Intuition suggests that most of the benefits, in terms of competitive pressure or X-Efficiency (Leibenstein, 1966), economies of scale and scope, and national specialization, can be obtained by removing trade barriers at and behind the border and allowing the free movement of factors of production.[4] Obtaining them does not also require the addition of a common currency. This was the presumption of pre-euro studies such as Feldstein (1991), Obstfeld (1997), and Wyplosz (1997). Many examples support this conclusion. Danish exporters of dairy products, for example, do not appear to suffer from their country's retention of a separate national currency, the krone. It might be objected that this fact follows from Denmark's distinctive ability to hold its currency stable against the euro. But the United Kingdom has always had a more variable exchange rate and yet Scottish salmon processors did not obviously suffer major inconveniences from pre-Brexit Britain's retention of the pound sterling. Rather, the spanner in the works came later, at the beginning of 2021, when access to the single market was lost. Similarly, the United Kingdom's retention of a separate sovereign currency did not prevent London from becoming the leading centre for euro-related financial business. Rather, the City's ability to compete hinged not on the currency regime but on passporting rights conferred by the country's membership in the single market and its ability to attract financial talent (that is, it depended on labour mobility).

Some studies suggest, however, that the impact of monetary union on trade, and by implication on production and specialization, is large and significant. Rose (2000) famously found that two countries sharing a common currency trade three times as much with one another as their other characteristics would lead one to expect, even controlling for a long list of other country characteristics, including whether or not the partners are in a regional trade agreement. The objection, of course, is that the single market is more than a regional trade arrangement, so the large effect ascribed to monetary union is really picking up behind-the-border liberalization and other measures associated with the single market.

[4] In some models (Heckscher–Ohlin for example), factor mobility is redundant once trade barriers have been removed, at least as long as economies remain within the 'cone of diversification'. When factor endowments vary sharply and/or the strong assumptions of Heckscher–Ohlin are relaxed, however, this may no longer be the case.

Subsequent studies took advantage of the fact that additional members of the single market, starting with Greece, switched from their national currencies to the euro some years after entering the single market, strengthening the argument that the observed increase in trade following the switch was the effect of the common currency per se. Most such studies adopting this approach continued to find substantial effects of the single currency: Head and Mayer (2014) consider more than 100 such estimates and calculate that the mean effect is a doubling of trade. But Glick and Rose (2015) show that estimates of such effects are highly sensitive to methodological choices. They caution that it may be impossible to estimate the aggregate trade effect of currency unions such as Europe's with confidence. Not for the first time in the history of economic analysis, the jury remains out.

Another perspective is that the euro has been important not for trade but for financial flows. McKinnon (2000) was an early proponent of the view that the elimination of currency risk would foster the integration of national bond and equity markets and enhance the depth and liquidity of securities markets throughout the euro area. Capiello et al. (2006), among others, provided early evidence to this effect. On the side of financial stability, one can well imagine that, in the absence of the euro, there might have been sharp changes in the relative value of different EU currencies following the failure of Lehman Brothers in September 2008 and that this would have wreaked similar havoc. Banks and households with foreign-currency-denominated liabilities would have suffered additional balance-sheet distress had their central banks still been in the business of issuing national currencies and had some of those currencies depreciated sharply on the foreign exchange market.[5] Here Poland's experience with Swiss franc mortgage loans serves as a cautionary tale.

The retort in this case is that the euro has been as much the problem as the solution from a financial-stability perspective. The decade leading up to the Global Financial Crisis saw enormous financial flows between the northern and southern European members of the euro area and dramatic yield-spread compression (Lane, 2012). Some narrowing of spreads was justified, of course, by the narrowing of inflation differentials following the advent of the single currency. But there appears to have been a peculiar assumption on the part of investors that credit (default) risk also declined with adoption of the euro, justifying additional spread compression. There may have been false confidence that a member of a monetary union could not default on its debt (a misapprehension that would have been corrected by even a brief reconnaissance of the relevant history of public debt). There may have been false confidence in the efficacy of the euro area's fiscal rules. Or there may have been the belief that a Member State with debt difficulties would receive a bailout from its monetary union partners adequate for protecting its creditors from the application of a haircut.

The test case, Greece, received foreign financial assistance, as anticipated, but was nonetheless forced to restructure its domestic-law bonds, writing down their value. The creditors received a harsh reminder that the advent of the euro did not mean the elimination of credit risk. At the same time, the ECB insulated the bond markets of other euro area members from contagion by announcing a programme of Outright Monetary Transactions (OMT, potential purchases of government bonds on the secondary market). This was an impressive demonstration of the role of the central bank in ensuring the stability and smooth functioning of the euro

[5] Historically, banking crises have wreaked havoc with the stability of exchange rates and financial conditions. Recall for example the wider repercussions of the Finnish and Swedish banking crises of 1991–92. Finland and Sweden were not members of the European Community at that time, but their currencies were effectively pegged to the German Deutschmark, the anchor currency within the Exchange Rate Mechanism (Eichengreen and Naef, 2020).

area. The ECB responded with an even more extensive set of asset purchases in 2020, when Europe was battered by the COVID-19 pandemic and economic crisis.

In all, this history illustrates how conceptions of 'an effective monetary policy for the euro area' (to quote the Commission again) evolved over the first two decades of monetary union. At the outset, the ECB was conceived as responsible for implementing a monetary rule rather than acting as a regulator, lender, and liquidity provider of last resort (Folkerts-Landau and Garber, 1992). This reflected Germany's aversion to inflation and fidelity to policy rules; it reflected the practical calculation that no European monetary union could succeed without German participation. In its early years, the ECB saw itself as targeting inflation, pure and simple, rather than as influencing financial conditions.[6] As Jean-Claude Trichet, then ECB president, insisted in 2011, it was not the role of the ECB to backstop the bond market. Instead, governments were obliged to manage their affairs

> individually and collectively, to ensure financial stability. [This] is the way Europe has been constructed and it is the way, it seems to all of us, we must proceed. If it is not done by governments, it will not be credible ... On the concept of last-resort lending ... We don't intervene for financial stability reasons. We consider that is the responsibility of governments.[7]

This presumption changed, irrevocably it would seem, with Mario Draghi's 2012 pledge to 'do whatever it takes' to preserve the integrity of the euro area and, by implication, the single market. This, clearly, was not your mother's ECB. It was not even Jean-Claude Trichet's.

The focus and policies of the ECB continued to evolve over the subsequent decade. New objectives include fostering the EU's green transition: under Christine Lagarde, who succeeded Draghi in 2019, the ECB agreed to accept bonds with coupons linked to sustainability performance targets as collateral and invested in the euro-denominated green bonds of the Bank for International Settlements. In addition, Lagarde discussed the need for the ECB to prioritize issues of economic inequality, including gender inequality. These are controversial areas for a central bank by virtue of their non-traditional nature. They are not explicitly addressed in the central bank's statute and mandate, in contrast to the maintenance of price stability.[8]

Moreover, they pose special problems for the ECB, which is arguably the most independent central bank in the world. Central bank independence can only be sustained when it is accompanied by accountability – when the central bank's achievements can be gauged relative to its mandate and when its policy decisions are evaluated in those same terms.[9] In the absence of such accountability, an independent agency of government such as the ECB will lack democratic legitimacy, in which case a political backlash is apt to follow. Unfortunately, a central bank's success at mitigating climate change and inequality is harder to assess than its success at achieving price stability or even financial stability. The central bank's instruments are further removed from such targets, compared to its ability to influence and control inflation, and those unconventional targets are affected more powerfully by intervening variables controlled by other parties. This creates challenges for accountability. A central bank that strays too far in the

[6] Formally, the ECB had a two-pillar strategy, where it targeted inflation and monetary aggregates (this last target being an inheritance from the Bundesbank). For an early warning of the need for a central bank that does more than follow a monetary rule, see Folkerts-Landau and Garber (1992).

[7] Quoted from Trichet testimony before European Parliament (2011).

[8] Although one can argue that they are implicit secondary objectives of the ESCB under Article 127(1) TFEU (secondary in that they may be pursued insofar as they do not conflict with the primary objective of price stability). See also Adamski, Chapter 9 in this volume, Schoenmaker and Stegeman, Chapter 12 in this volume.

[9] In the words of Adrian and Khan (2019), central bank independence and accountability are 'two sides of the same coin'.

direction of pursuing these non-traditional objectives will have reason to worry about its independence. In addition, there is reason to worry about violating the Tinbergen rule, that the number of achievable policy goals cannot exceed the number of available policy instruments.

That said, the single market cannot function smoothly and provide for 'stronger, more sustainable and inclusive growth across the euro area and the EU as a whole' (European Commission, n.d.) if climate change and inequality remain unaddressed, since these are among the existential economic policy problems of our day. It would be more comfortable for all concerned were they addressed by other authorities possessing instruments more directly relevant to solving them. It would be more comfortable if the challenge of climate change was addressed by the fiscal authorities controlling the level of carbon taxation, and if inequality was addressed by tax and transfer policies more generally. But action by these other authorities can't be taken for granted. To the extent that climate change and inequality rise to the level of all-hands-on-deck emergencies, neither can they be ignored by Europe's monetary authorities. Doing too much will create risks for central bank independence. But so too would doing nothing at all.

1.3 COORDINATING THE FISCAL POLICIES OF EU COUNTRIES

Europe's best known, some would say most notorious, device for monitoring and coordinating national fiscal policies is the Stability and Growth Pact (SGP). The Pact was put in place in 1992, at Germany's behest, as a filter to determine which Member States might be eligible to participate in the monetary union.[10] It became notorious because the key provisions, that debt ratios could not exceed 60 per cent of GDP, or that they at least had to be converging to that level at an acceptable pace, while deficits could not exceed 3 per cent of GDP, were picked out of a hat, more or less. Sixty per cent just happened to be the Europe-wide debt-to-GDP ratio at the time, while 3 per cent was the deficit consistent with keeping it there, given then prevailing, equally arbitrary assumptions about growth rates and interest rates. From the start, there were doubts about the enforceability of these thresholds (Eichengreen and Wyplosz, 1998). Were arbitrary targets credible? Were European governments really prepared to sanction one another for violations, knowing that they themselves might next be called on the mat? Were they prepared to levy fines, given that the obligation to pay such penalties would be an additional budgetary burden on an already fiscally challenged government?

Nor is the justification for the Pact straightforward. The most compelling rationale for a procedure designed to safeguard against excessive deficits is to avoid fiscal dominance, prevent inflation, and avoid the need for emergency rescues of governments by the ECB. This rationale was widely advanced at the time (James, 2012). But the SGP is an obligation of all twenty-seven EU members, not just those that have adopted the euro. Its legal basis is Articles 121 and 126 of the Treaty on the Functioning of the European Union (the Treaty of Rome as updated and renamed in 2009), not any treaty relating specifically to the euro. Nothing that happens in Denmark, Sweden, or Poland in terms of fiscal policy obviously has first-order implications for ECB policy or for inflationary pressures in the euro area. So, applying the SGP to the EU as a whole seems like a non-sequitur.

[10] Strictly speaking, these provisions of the Maastricht Treaty were known as 'convergence criteria'. They were repurposed as provisions of the Stability Pact and extended into the period of monetary union itself at the behest of the German finance minister, Theo Waigel, in 1995.

It can be argued that the SGP is designed to encourage such Member States to ready themselves for membership in the euro area, by inter alia bringing their debt and deficit ratios down to prescribed levels. But it remains unclear why, in this case, the Pact should apply to members, such as Denmark and Sweden, that regard themselves as possessing opt-outs from euro adoption.

Alternatively, it could be argued that fiscal problems in a non-euro area Member State may disrupt the convergence process within the EU and risk putting unbearable strain on the Union. If what happened in Greece starting in 2010 happened in a non-euro area member such as Poland, the euro area would feel serious repercussions, given the spillover from recession, financial links, potential for significant migration, and political recrimination. There is of course the argument that what happened in Greece could not happen in Poland, since the latter, unlike the former, retains a national currency and a central bank capable of monetizing the public debt. But if the result is a sharp depreciation of the zloty, there still could be serious repercussions for the euro area. An obvious riposte is that Poland's problems, under these circumstances, are appropriately addressed by the International Monetary Fund (IMF), not by the European Commission, the ECB, or other EU Member States. Greece's experience starting in 2010 indicates that the EU is uncomfortable with this solution. At best, the question remains unresolved.

The original Stability Pact formulation having been rigid and unaccommodating of national circumstances, the EU has moved to make its fiscal rules and procedures more flexible. The procedures now start with multi-stage monitoring. The European Commission formulates forecasts for the Member States, assesses national budgets in their light, and publishes an 'Alert Mechanism Report' that points the finger at countries at risk of imbalances, including of a fiscal variety. At the prevention stage, EU Member States and the Commission negotiate Medium-Term Objectives designed to ensure the long-term sustainability of the public finances and national debt. These EU-wide recommendations are reinforced by a second set of preventative measures specific to euro area Member States, whose governments are obliged to draft and present budgetary plans annually to the Commission and their euro area partners.

If this were not enough, in addition there is the Fiscal Compact (formally the Treaty on Stability, Coordination and Governance). This is intended to limit the size of the structural (full employment) budget deficit that a government can run under normal circumstances to 0.5 per cent of GDP.[11] Signatories are obliged to transpose the Treaty's provisions into national law, in much the way that Germany's balanced-budget law, or debt brake, limiting structural deficits to 0.35 per cent of GDP, has now been embedded in that country's Basic Law, or constitution. The Fiscal Compact is an obligation of the nineteen members of the euro area; in addition, Denmark, Bulgaria, and Romania have opted in. It was designed, once again, to obtain German acquiescence to deepening economic and monetary union (notice the pattern). In effect, other countries adopted a Germany-style debt brake in return for Berlin agreeing to establish an emergency financial assistance mechanism – what became the European Stability Mechanism.

The rationale for focusing on the structural deficit rather than the headline deficit is to allow automatic fiscal stabilizers to respond to cyclical conditions. This makes sense insofar as rigid

[11] That limit can be increased to 1 per cent of GDP for governments with debt-to-GDP ratios significantly below 60 per cent. Where the structural deficit exceeds these limits, it must be adjusted by 0.5 per cent of GDP per annum (on average). The word 'intended' is meant to signal that there can be and have been gaps between aspiration and achievement.

application of the SGP may prevent automatic stabilizers from coming into play in countries close to or exceeding its thresholds. The problem is that the structural balance is not observable and is likely to be subject to significant measurement error; for example, estimating the structural balance requires knowing the full-employment level of GDP, about which there is no agreement.[12] And because the Fiscal Compact supplements rather than replaces the SGP, countries are simultaneously subject to conflicting ceilings on both their structural and headline deficits.

Again, arbitrary numerical thresholds, in this case 0.35 and 0.5 per cent of GDP, are difficult to defend. If their rationale is that structural deficits are permissible when used to finance productive public investment that pays for itself, then discussion should start by determining the cost of the productive public investment projects available to the government, and then solve for the permissible structural deficit, rather than starting with the latter. Historically, public investment in the euro area has run at 3 per cent of GDP (ECB, 2016). Not all of this is necessarily productive, of course, but much is. This means that enforcing a structural deficit limit of 0.5 per cent of GDP will require Member States to fund much of their productive public investment out of current revenues, which seems perverse, given that the returns on such investment accrue over time and can be used to pay off the resulting debt.

Finally, Member States whose overall budget deficits exceed 3 per cent of GDP or whose public debts exceed 60 per cent of GDP and are not declining at a satisfactory pace (the original Stability Pact limits) are required to submit to the EU's Excessive Deficit Procedure. This obliges them to eliminate each year a twentieth of the gap between the current debt ratio and the 60 per cent reference value. Thus, the Italian government, with a debt-to-GDP ratio of 160 per cent, is ostensibly obliged to lower that ratio by 5 percentage points of GDP each year for twenty years. In practice, of course, governments cannot commit their successors to a fiscal strategy, especially when it is defined for such a lengthy period. In addition, real interest rates have trended downward for several decades, which eases the process of debt management for a country in Italy's position and reduces the urgency of fiscal consolidation. While it is uncertain whether that trend will now reverse direction, for demographic or other reasons (as argued by Goodhart and Pradhan, 2020), the possibility cannot be ruled out. For a growth-challenged country like Italy, the assumption that the real growth rate will exceed the real interest rate for the next two decades is – how to put it? – optimistic. And as Eichengreen and Panizza (2016) have shown, instances in which countries succeed in running primary budget surpluses as large as 5 per cent of GDP for extended periods are rare.

The upshot is that the EU's fiscal rulebook has become extremely complicated, running to more than 200 pages (Wieser, 2018). This complexity reduces transparency, allowing politics to intrude into disputes among Member States, and creates tensions between governments and the Commission.

There is no consensus about the best direction for reform. One currently fashionable idea involves replacing all of the above with a country-specific public spending rule (see e.g. Claeys et al., 2016; Benassy-Quere et al., 2018). Governments would start with forecasts by independent experts of the growth of GDP and tax revenues, both in nominal terms. They would then solve for a path for the growth of public spending net of interest payments and perhaps also of unemployment spending that brings the debt ratio down at an acceptable pace. This procedure would have several advantages over the status quo. Since GDP and tax revenues are directly

[12] Orphanides and van Norden (2002) famously showed that ex post revisions of the output gap are of the same order of magnitude as estimates of the output gap themselves.

observed, unlike the output gap, they are easier to forecast than the structural balance. Nominal public expenditure can also be observed and, unlike the structural deficit, is directly controlled by the government. Automatic fiscal stabilizers are still allowed to operate on the revenue side, so the rule has reasonable cyclical properties.[13] The tendency to raise spending in the expansion phase of the business cycle, when revenues rise, a problem that is apparent in the historical record, would be directly restrained.

This proposed fiscal rule is not perfect (no rule is). Forecasting nominal GDP and revenues may be easier than forecasting the output gap, but easier is not the same as easy. The specific target for the debt-to-GDP ratio, whether 60 per cent as a holdover from the SGP or some other number, has no justification in economic logic. The length of time, perhaps twenty years, that countries are allowed to take in order to eliminate discrepancies from target is similarly arbitrary, boding problems of credibility and compliance and threatening continuing tensions between national governments and the Commission. Some (e.g. Eichengreen and Wyplosz, 2016) argue that European governments should focus on strengthening their national fiscal institutions by increasing the transparency of the budgeting process and delegating more powers to independent fiscal councils, and leave it at that. However, this does not seem to be Europe's way.[14]

A separate line of thought is that the problem is not the presence of complex and restrictive rules designed to avoid excessive deficits but rather the absence of a system for transferring fiscal resources among Member States, akin to the fiscal federalism that exists in the United States (or, for that matter, within Europe's own federal states, such as Germany). Its absence leaves Member States doubly constrained in the event of asymmetric shocks, given that this is when limits on the ability of heavily indebted Member States to borrow tend to kick in. In part, opposition to such a system flows from the fact that it would not be constructed behind a veil of ignorance: everyone knows (or knew) which way fiscal resources will flow within this 'transfer union'. (Or at least that's what people in the 'Frugal Five' countries will tell you.) In addition, opposition to such a system rested on moral hazard concerns, that additional resources would only encourage excessive spending by more profligate recipients.

In 2020, these reservations were finally overcome by the COVID-19 pandemic and its economic and financial effects. Member States agreed to the issuance of €750 billion of EU bonds to fund the Recovery Plan for Europe (also known as Next Generation EU). The plan was divided in roughly equal proportions between grants and loans. Loans can be requested in amounts up to 6.8 per cent of a member's 2019 Gross National Income. But since, in contrast to sovereign bonds, this additional debt will be backed by the full faith and credit of the entire group of members, and by transfers from the EU budget again funded by the entire group, the result will be fiscal federalism after a fashion.

Concerns about moral hazard and excessive spending took a back seat to European solidarity in response to a virus that was inadvertently imported into Europe, where additional public health spending and other measures to both staunch the economic losses from lockdowns and support recovery were of the essence. Concerns that the money would be used irresponsibly

[13] In addition, a negative (positive) demand shock that lowers (raises) inflation will translate into more rapidly (slowly) growing real public spending, providing another channel for automatic stabilization.

[14] The obvious explanation is that the problem of democratic accountability raised in Section 1.2 in the context of monetary policy is even more severe for independent fiscal institutions, given the prominent distributional dimension of fiscal policy. Blanchard, Leandro, and Zettelmeyer (2020) suggest a middle way, abandoning the EU's complex system of rules but replacing them with standards – e.g. qualitative prescriptions for what debt sustainability means in each individual country context – together with adjudication of whether those standards are being met by an independent body, such as the European Court of Justice.

were addressed by requiring governments to submit a detailed 'recovery and resilience plan' detailing how borrowed funds would be used to support recovery and transition to a green, digital post-pandemic Europe.

Still, this is no more than a baby step in the direction of fiscal federalism, much less fiscal union. Not only is €750 billion less than 5 per cent of the EU's €16 trillion economy, but the resulting resources will be transferred to the Member States over a period of six years. The only 'own resource' (dedicated source of EU revenues) associated with debt service was a tax on recycled plastic. So, it was unclear whether financial resources sufficient to service more than the initial €750 billion tranche would become available to the EU over time. Similarly unclear was whether EU Member States would be prepared to do in normal times what they did during a once-in-a-century pandemic. Much will depend, presumably, on how efficiently governments utilize the initial tranche of funds.

1.4 SUPERVISING AND MONITORING EUROPEAN FINANCIAL INSTITUTIONS

The idea that economic and monetary union should be accompanied by banking union was not part of EMU's original design. National banking systems differed in their particulars, favouring the delegation of financial supervision to national authorities, and the extent to which the different systems were interdependent was not fully appreciated. Interdependence was in fact relatively limited until the 1990s, reflecting strict financial regulation, extending to the maintenance of capital controls. Events like the failure of Herstatt Bank in 1974 should have been a wakeup call, but that episode focused attention on settlement risk in the foreign exchange market (Norman, 2015), not on the interdependence of internationally active banks more generally. Subsequent to Herstatt, capital standards for internationally active banks were negotiated in Basel, but they were then transposed into national and European law. In these respects, one can criticize European officials for their lack of foresight, but one can also criticize academics for their lack of insight. Early contributors to the literature on optimum currency areas, while focusing on asymmetric shocks, labour mobility, and fiscal federalism, said almost nothing about the need for banking union.[15]

This assignment of responsibilities was challenged and ultimately overturned by the Global Financial Crisis and the euro crisis. One factor contributing to the euro crisis was how freely northern European banks lent to southern European banks and governments. Once credit problems developed in Europe's south, the stability of those same northern European banks was called into question. The possibility of restructuring southern European debts, which might have taken some of the pressure off embattled governments and residents, was precluded by fear of the consequences for those same undercapitalized northern European financial institutions. Instead, it was necessary to throw large amounts of financial assistance, funded by EU Member States and the IMF, at teetering banks and governments across the euro area's periphery.

This experience made clear that national regulators had failed to adequately internalize the cross-border repercussions of their policies: French and German regulators failed to prevent domestic financial institutions from lending hand over fist to southern European banks and from accumulating large concentrations of southern European government bonds. In addition, national regulators failed to address the risks for the euro area as a whole created by the fragility of large, systemically important banks. Relatedly, those national authorities lacked adequate mechanisms for resolving, or winding up, insolvent financial institutions.

[15] I can point to having written one page on this subject in Eichengreen (1993).

Hence the sea change in 2013 that bequeathed the Single Supervisory Mechanism (SSM) situated in the ECB. The ECB directly supervises the euro area's largest banks while cooperating with national supervisors in supervising smaller institutions. Placing the SSM in the ECB was controversial, since it raised the possibility that the central bank might take its eye off inflation. But the ECB was the only EU entity with the necessary administrative capacity and technical expertise.[16] Assigning it this additional responsibility was yet another step in the evolution of the institution, as described in Section 1.2.

Accompanying the SSM was the Single Resolution Mechanism (SRM), intended to ensure that, in the event of failure of a systemically important bank, the institution in question would be recapitalized or wound up without resort to taxpayers' funds. The SRM takes the lead in resolving big banks, while the national authorities do so for other financial institutions (though early practice suggests that, in case of doubt, national authorities take the lead in such interventions). Resolution planning is by an independent Single Resolution Board. The decision of whether and how to implement the plan is then made in conjunction with the ECB (the relevant supervisor) and the European Commission (the relevant executive).[17] Injections of new capital from the SRM require, as a precondition, first writing down 8 per cent of the bank's balance sheet as the contribution of existing creditors.

In addition, the European Systemic Risk Board (ESRB) was established in 2010 to oversee macroprudential supervision and coordination at the national and EU levels. Three European supervisory authorities were then created to oversee specific markets. These were the European Banking Authority (EBA), the European Securities and Markets Authority (ESMA), and the European Insurance and Occupational Pensions Authority (EIOPA). The EBA was charged with coordinating banking supervision in the EU, since supervision of all but the largest banks remained the remit of national authorities, as noted, and with writing the single rulebook of banking activity in the EU. The other authorities did likewise for capital markets and the insurance industry, respectively.

The EU emerged from this round of reforms with a complex regulatory architecture. This was unavoidable, perhaps, since regulatory reform entailing negotiations among more than two dozen countries requires compromise over institutional design as well as substance.

How well have the resulting institutions done, in addressing banking sector risks in particular? The answer is: reasonably well, though they could have done better. Capital requirements for systemically important banks were raised starting in 2014. Non-performing loans as a share of total loans fell between 2014 and 2019. The fact that no systemically important bank failed in 2020 during the COVID-19 crisis testifies to the effectiveness of the regulatory measures to strengthen their balance sheets and internal processes taken in the preceding period.[18]

The glass-not-yet-full perspective would emphasize that the Single Resolution Fund, into which ECB-supervised banks pay in order to obviate the need for taxpayer bailouts, has yet to reach its full size of 1 per cent of the deposits in ECB-supervised banks. It is scheduled to do so in 2024, but even then – and even with the addition of the European Stability Mechanism (ESM) backstop – it can be questioned whether these resources are enough. Whether the 8 per cent bail-in rule can be applied is unclear, since in practice it is likely to be applied to wholesale (interbank) depositors, who will therefore have an incentive to exit at the first sign of trouble,

[16] In practice, physically housing the monetary policy and supervisory functions in different buildings and creating a separate Financial Stability Committee largely contained such conflicts.

[17] In some cases the European Council may also be involved.

[18] Of course, it also testifies to the response of the ECB as lender and liquidity provider of last resort, which was both more rapid and more powerful than during the Global Financial Crisis or the euro crisis.

resulting in funding instability, and worse. This points to the need to ensure that bank capital and subordinated long-term debt amount to at least 8 per cent of the balance sheet (which they presently, in general, do not, owing to their cost).

In addition, the banking union still lacks a common deposit insurance scheme, although the Commission continues to study proposals for moving in this direction. In the absence of common deposit insurance, there remains the possibility of deposit flight, in the event of stress, away from national schemes with relatively limited coverage and financial reserves. In terms of specific regulations and policies, the zero-capital charge on sovereign bonds continues to incentivize European banks to load up on the bonds of their own governments. In late 2020 and early 2021, lacking other attractive lending opportunities and enjoying an abundance of liquidity due to COVID-19, we again saw banks in the euro area periphery augment their holdings of such bonds. This raised the spectre of a 'diabolic loop', in which government debt problems created solvency problems for banks invested in government debt, together with banking sector problems that threatened further debt problems for governments on the hook for bailing out their banks.

1.5 CONCLUSION

It is customary to observe that Europe's economic and monetary union remains a work in progress. A more pertinent observation would be that Europe's economic and monetary union will *always* be a work in progress. European leaders, reflecting the input they received, not least from academics, started with a limited vision of what their union entailed. (No banking union, for instance.) They faced – and will continue to face – resistance to schemes for more fully building out the union. (No fiscal union, for instance.) The structure of the European economy will continue to evolve – it will become greener and more digital, and the economic and monetary union will have to adapt. Post-COVID-19, tourism-dependent economies will have problems. More heavily indebted governments will have problems. Growth-challenged economies and their banks will have problems. Which is to say that most of Europe, and its economic and monetary union, will have problems.

The question is whether a collection of countries bound up in an economic and monetary union has the capacity to address these challenges. Developing that capacity will require building out the economic and monetary union along dimensions where it remains incomplete, and reforming and renovating what exists. In some respects, what this implies is obvious. Build on the precedent of the Recovery Plan for Europe by further enlarging the EU's borrowing capacity. Develop revenue sources adequate for servicing and repaying EU debt. Reform and simplify the EU's maddeningly complex fiscal rules. Finish topping up the Single Resolution Fund. Create a fully funded EU-wide deposit insurance scheme.

Europe and the euro area have relied on rules – a numerical inflation target for the ECB, the numerical rules and reference values of the Stability and Growth Pact – to strengthen the democratic accountability and legitimacy of their macroeconomic policy-making institutions. But numerical rules are arbitrary, as we have seen, and arbitrary rules lack credibility and, as a result, legitimacy. They are not always faithfully respected. As social scientists have long emphasized, institutions can be erected on the basis of formal rules or informal norms and understandings. This would provide a superior basis for the operation of the euro area's policy-making institutions. But governance based on informal norms and understandings requires a high degree of trust between publics and policy makers, between the citizens of different EU Member States, and between Europe's north and south. All of which is to say that these challenges will not be met overnight.

REFERENCES

Adrian, T., and Khan, A. (2019). Central bank accountability, independence and transparency. IMF Blog (25 November). https://blogs.imf.org/2019/11/25/central-bank-accountability-independence-and-transparency/

Baldwin, R. (1989). The growth effects of 1992. *Economic Policy* 4, 247–281.

Bénassy-Quéré, A., Brunnermeier, M., Enderlein, H., Farhi, E., Fratzscher, M., Fuest, C., Gourinchas, P.-O., Martin, P., Pisani-Ferry, J., Rey, H., Schnabel, I., Véron, N., Weder di Mauro, B., and Zettelmeyer, J. (2018). Reconciling risk sharing with market discipline: A constructive approach to euro area reform. CEPR Policy Insight No. 91 (January). https://cepr.org/publications/policy-insight-91-reconciling-risk-sharing-market-discipline-constructive-approach

Blanchard, O., Leandro, A., and Zettelmeyer, J. (2020). Redesigning EU fiscal rules: From rules to standards. Unpublished manuscript, Peterson Institute of International Economics (August).

Buchanan, J. (1965). An economic theory of clubs. *Economica* 32, 1–14.

Capiello, L., Hordahl, P., Karareja, A., and Manganelli, S. (2006). The impact of the euro on financial markets. ECB Working Paper No. 598.

Claeys G., Darvas, Z. M., and Leandro, Á. (2016). A proposal to revive the European fiscal framework. Bruegel Policy Contribution 2016/07, Brussels: Bruegel.

Eichengreen, B. (1993). European monetary unification. *Journal of Economic Literature* 31, 1321–1357.

Eichengreen, B., and Naef, A. (2020). Imported or home grown? The 1992–3 EMS crisis. CEPR Discussion Paper No. 15340.

Eichengreen, B., and Panizza, U. (2016). A surplus of ambition: Can Europe rely on large primary surpluses to solve its debt problem? *Economic Policy* 31, 5–49.

Eichengreen, B., and Wyplosz, C. (1998). The Stability Pact: More than a minor nuisance? *Economic Policy* 13, 65–113.

Eichengreen, B., and Wyplosz, C. (2016). Minimal conditions for the survival of the euro. *Intereconomics* 1, 24–28.

European Central Bank (2016). Public investment in Europe. *ECB Economic Bulletin* 2, 1–14

European Commission (n.d.). How the Economic and Monetary Union works. Brussels: European Commission. https://ec.europa.eu/info/business-economy-euro/economic-and-fiscal-policy-coordination/economic-and-monetary-union/how-economic-and-monetary-union-works_en

European Commission (2020). *Standard Eurobarometer* 93 *(Summer 2020)*. Brussels: European Commission.

European Parliament, Committee on Economic and Monetary Affairs (2011). Trichet testimony (4 October). https://multimedia.europarl.europa.eu/en/committee-on-economic-and-monetary-affairs_20111004–1500-COMMITTEE-ECON_vd.

Feldstein, M. (1991). Does one market require one money? In Federal Reserve Bank of Kansas City, *Policy Implications of Trade and Currency Zones*. Kansas City, MO: Federal Reserve Bank of Kansas City, pp. 77–84.

Folkerts-Landau, D., and Garber, P. (1992). The ECB: A bank or a monetary policy rule? In M. Canzoneri, V. Grilli, and P. Masson (eds.), *Establishing a Central Bank: Issues in Europe and Lessons from the US*. Cambridge: Cambridge University Press, pp. 86–110.

Glick, R., and Rose, A. (2015). Currency unions and trade: A post-EMU mea culpa. NBER Working Paper No. 21535.

Goodhart, C., and Pradhan, M. (2020). *The Great Demographic Reversal: Ageing Societies, Waning Inequality, and an Inflation Revival*. London: Palgrave Macmillan.

Head, K., and Mayer, T. (2014). Gravity equations: Workhorse, toolkit and cookbook. In G. Gopinath, E. Helpman, and K. Rogoff (eds.), *Handbook of International Economics*, Vol. 4. Amsterdam: Elsevier, pp. 131–195.

James, H. (2012). *Making the European Monetary Union*. Cambridge, MA: Harvard University Press.

Lane, P. (2012). The European Sovereign Debt Crisis. *Journal of Economic Perspectives* 26, 49–68.

Leibenstein, H. (1966). Allocative efficiency vs. 'X-efficiency'. *American Economic Review* 56, 392–415.

McKinnon, R. (2000). Mundell, the euro, and optimum currency areas. Department of Economics, Stanford University Working Paper No. 00009.

Norman, B. (2015). BoE archives reveal little known lesson from the 1974 failure of Herstatt Bank. *Bank Underground* (24 June). https://bankunderground.co.uk/2015/06/24/boe-archives-reveal-little-known-lesson-from-the-1974-failure-of-herstatt-bank/

Obstfeld, M. (1997). Europe's gamble. *Brookings Papers on Economic Activity* 2, 241–317.

Orphanides, A., and van Norden, S. (2002). The unreliability of output-gap estimates in real time. *Review of Economics and Statistics* 84, 569–583.

Rose, A. (2000). One money, one market: The effect of common currencies on trade. *Economic Policy* 15, 7–45.

Sandler, T., and Tschirhart, J. (1997). Club theory: Thirty years later. *Public Choice* 93, 335–355.

Veld, J. in't (2019). The economic benefits of the EU single market in goods and services. *Journal of Policy Modeling* 41, 803–818.

Wieser, T. (2018). Fiscal rules and the role of the Commission. Bruegel Blog (22 May). www.bruegel.org/2018/05/fiscal-rules-and-the-role-of-the-commission/

Wyplosz, C. (1997). EMU: Why and how it might happen. *Journal of Economic Perspectives* 11, 3–22.

2

Theorizing Economic and Monetary Union

Between Concepts and Pragmatism

Amy Verdun

2.1 INTRODUCTION

This chapter offers an inquiry into how Economic and Monetary Union (EMU) has been conceptualized in the context of the European Union, in order to understand where EMU has ended up today. The chapter analyses the concepts and the directions of the past five decades, by focusing in particular on those that have shaped EMU as we know it today. The definition of what is on the agenda, and considered part of the scope of EMU, has had a major impact on what EMU actually covers. In the first decade (1999–2008), the focus was mostly on public debt and government deficits (although more the latter than the former), euro adoption in new Member States, and ensuring the credibility of the central bank. In the second decade (2009–18), the focus was on macroeconomic policy coordination and a continued question of the role of fiscal rules as well as conditions in the countries which needed support. In the third decade, plans aimed at completing EMU were (partially) implemented, with a focus on banking regulation, which includes branching out into the early steps of fiscal federalism. Each of these topics had been considered when conceptualizing early plans, but had often not been developed properly early on, as there was insufficient consensus or common ground to move forward.

The substance and scope of economic and monetary integration of the EU is the result of the conceptualization of what was possible in the immediate run-up to the creation of EMU in the 1960s, 1970s, and 1980s. The design of EMU once in place, in the late 1990s, reflected the thinking at the time. The EU encountered various crises in the twenty-first century, such as the financial crisis and sovereign debt crisis in the period 2008–15 (Caporaso, 2018), which shifted thinking further. Another major shock occurred with the COVID-19 crisis, due to which the EU was confronted with the largest recession since the Second World War, and a need to provide a forceful response. The EU embarked on providing EU-level support in the form of grants and loans but demanding that Member States had met the requirements for macroeconomic policy coordination in the context of the so-called European Semester (D'Erman and Verdun, 2022; Vanhercke and Verdun, 2022). To examine the path that has been taken towards deeper economic and monetary integration in the EU, this chapter examines the role of various theories of European economic and political integration that have impacted the creation and further development of EMU. A pragmatic understanding of what was feasible was at least as important for determining what became part of the institutional design of EMU. There had been an awareness of what EMU could entail. However, at each intersection in history, a pragmatic choice was made about the scope of possible agreement on what EMU would mean and where most of the attention would be placed. Crises were used to add issues onto the agenda. In this incremental way, the asymmetries, for example between 'economic' and 'monetary' union but also between monetary integration and banking supervision were addressed and more elements that had been considered in theory became part of the reality of EMU.

This argument is developed as follows: Section 2.2 offers an overview of the theoretical understanding of economic and monetary integration at the outset. Section 2.3 examines early plans for EMU in the three decades prior to the inclusion of EMU in the Maastricht Treaty. It argues that EMU was intended to incorporate a mix of established consensus on what the EU could do (cooperation on exchange rates and macroeconomic policy coordination) but left out the parts of EMU for which there was no consensus (banking regulation, fiscal federalism, automatic stabilizers). Section 2.4 examines how the early experience with EMU and the events of the day influenced thinking about what to change in the institutional design of EU economic and monetary governance. Section 2.5 examines how the financial crisis of 2007–8 and the sovereign debt crisis of 2009–12 and its aftermath affected what was needed to complete EMU. Most recently, leaders drew on the ideas that were floating around before the COVID-19 crisis in articulating a response to the pandemic as a way to address the economic crisis that was expected to follow. The chapter concludes by highlighting how most of the building blocks of a more complete EMU had been around in the realm of ideas since the outset.

2.2 TOWARDS EMU

2.2.1 *Stages of Integration*

Early scholarship on European economic integration emphasized that European integration would go through stages. Jan Tinbergen (1954), Bela Balassa (1961, 1975), Warner Max Corden (1972a, 1972b), Victoria Curzon Price (1974), and Fritz Machlup (1977) identified *stages of integration* that started with preferential trade agreements, a free trade area, a customs union through to a common market, a monetary union, a complete economic union, and possibly a more deeply integrated political union. Tinbergen (1954, p. 79) differentiated between positive and negative integration. Positive integration encompasses the creation of new or modified instruments and/or laws, whereas negative integration is defined as the removal of barriers to integration and an adherence to the principle of non-discrimination. As time went by, the idea that integration would necessarily have to pass through all of these stages in sequence became less obvious.

The study of European economic integration was informed by its practice. Hence, the focus of research was often on those areas in which there was observable integration. In the early years, some common policies generated revenue, such as trade policy, and the European Economic Community (EEC), as it was called by then, worked on gathering some revenue through indirect taxation (although the exact system varied in those early years and was only harmonized in the late 1960s). Much of the Community budget was spent on agricultural policy, and to a lesser extent on economic and social cohesion, infrastructure, and, from the 1970s onwards, also on regional policy. A system of own resources was set up in the first two decades. Levies on agriculture in the 1960s contributed to the budget but were insufficient. In the 1970s, the budgetary treaties, the 1970 Treaty of Luxembourg, and the Treaty of Brussels signed in 1975, facilitated an increase in the power of the European Parliament in the budgetary sphere. Member States' contributions were replaced with Communities' own resources which consisted of customs duties, the agricultural levies, but also a percentage of value added tax (*Journal officiel des Communautés européennes* L2 2 janvier 1971; *Official Journal of the European Communities* L359 31 December 1977; see also Laursen, 2019).

In the 1970s, Western Europe was confronted with various crises and difficulties, such as the oil crises, rising unemployment, stagflation, and diverging ideas about how to tackle these challenges. European integration picked up momentum in the late 1980s and 1990s. The theories that explained this process were not only these earlier theories, but increasingly those that focused on governance and changes in institutions and policy-making (Verdun, 2002, 2018).

2.2.1.1 The 1960s, 1970s, and the Werner Report

The aim to create EMU was not mentioned in the 1957 Rome Treaty; the initiative to establish it only came in the 1960s (Tsoukalis, 1977; Steinherr, 1994). Monetary integration had been tried in the period before the Second World War, but political willingness was often an obstacle to deeper integration (Vanthoor, 1996). The circumstances in the 1960s were quite particular: following the reconstruction after the Second World War, with support from the US Marshall Plan, there was high and stable economic growth in Western Europe and there existed an international system of fixed exchange rates (the Bretton Woods system), even though the continent was in the midst of the cold war. The six Member States of the EEC were making steady progress towards completing their customs union. These international circumstances started changing in the second half of the 1960s: revaluations and devaluations occurred among European currencies and between those currencies and the US dollar, leading to an exchange rate crisis. Various leaders felt strongly that exchange rate stability in Europe should be maintained, especially to secure the feasibility of the EEC flagship policy, the Common Agricultural Policy (CAP). By 1968, whilst there was a wave of protests and civil unrest – particularly in France – the EEC Member States had managed to create a customs union ahead of its schedule. Member States were discussing further steps in European integration. In December 1969, at the Summit of Heads of States and Governments in The Hague, political leaders agreed to explore the creation of an Economic and Monetary Union. In February 1970, the EEC finance ministers discussed a number of different plans but could not reach an agreement on a precise definition and a road to EMU. Nevertheless, similar views were held on two areas: the need to give the EEC some form of monetary organization and the wish to further deepen integration after the completion of the customs union (Magnifico, 1973; Kruse, 1980).

In March 1970, the Council of Ministers asked a group chaired by Pierre Werner, the prime minister and finance minister of Luxembourg, to draft an EMU proposal. A group of experts representing the Member States, who had experience with the European integration process, were tasked to write up the proposal (Werner Report 1970). These men were a closely knit community that trusted each other and had a vision of what was possible at this stage of European integration (Rosenthal, 1975; Verdun, 1998a). Throughout the spring, summer, and autumn of 1970 proposals were being discussed. There was a difference of opinion between what were called the 'economists' and the 'monetarists'. The former group was keen to have deeper integration first, with the single currency as the crowning feature ('coronation theory'; see Dyson and Featherstone, 1999); the monetarists preferred the opposite, namely to have a common currency first, assuming it would trigger deeper integration (Verdun, 2000; Quaglia and Maes, 2004; Maes and Verdun, 2005; Danescu, 2012).

The Commission drafted a memorandum based on the Werner Report (1970) but had omitted reference to institutional arrangements for the eventual transfer of sovereignty, whereas it strengthened provisions for action in the structural and regional fields (*Bulletin of the EC*, Supplement, 11, 1970, pp. 11–21). When the Council discussed the memorandum in November and mid-December, no agreement could be reached. The Dutch and West German delegations stressed that the supranational provisions needed to be installed, which was unacceptable to the French government officials (Kruse, 1980, pp. 75–76; Verdun, 2000, p. 60). In January 1971, at a Franco-German meeting, the West German officials proposed a clause which would ensure 'parallelism' between the economic and monetary provisions in the EMU arrangement (Rosenthal, 1975, p. 111; Verdun, 2000, p. 60). This compromise agreement was reached (Bulletin of the EC, Supplements 3 and 4, 1971; Verdun, 2000, p. 61). The process had begun, but the irreversible commitments were postponed for three years – a side effect of the fact that the governmental representatives stood by their national positions until the very last moment, thus making a far-reaching agreement very difficult.

During the rest of the 1970s it became clear that the compromise solution clause did not work. Already in the first semester after 22 March 1971, the date the Council formally launched EMU (*Journal Officiel des Communautés Européennes*, C28 and L73, 27 March 1971, and *Bulletin of the EC*, Supplement 4, 1971), it was apparent that the basis of common interests of the Member States was too narrow. The very same gap as the one that had existed a decade before re-emerged: the French were reluctant to accept any plans leading to the transfer of sovereignty to a European body. The powerful Gaullist groups in France strongly rejected the supranational element of the plans. Their opposition proved to be so strong that the French were obliged to change their policy on the subject of EMU (Howarth, 2001). Hence, the split between France, Belgium, and Luxembourg on the one hand, and Western Germany, the Netherlands, and to a lesser degree Italy on the other, was complete. Once again, a plan for further integration failed to materialize. Again, it was due to differences of opinion on which policies to coordinate or harmonize; that is, it was a disagreement about how to proceed towards a 'united Europe'.

In addition to the different interests among the EEC countries, international monetary events catalysed the breakdown of the EMU agreement. A major blow to the system came when on 15 August 1971 US President Richard Nixon announced suspension of the convertibility of the dollar into gold, together with import measures to protect the US domestic economy. It signalled the end of the Bretton Woods system. Unable to reach an agreement on joint action in response to the US policy change, the EEC countries and the Commission were left in a delicate situation. The result was that the EEC currencies were floating against each other, with the exception of the Benelux countries. As a result, a complicated system of border taxes and rebates, which was adjusted every week, was installed for the CAP (Ludlow, 2005; Burrell, 2009; Knudsen, 2011). The Member States used artificial rates of exchange of their currencies for the CAP in order to protect farm prices that would otherwise be subject to fluctuations in the exchange rate. This system was referred to as 'green currencies' (Law, 2009).

Given these changes, the EMU plan could not progress any further along the lines set on 22 March 1971. The EMU objective had quickly proven to be an unattainable ideal. To deal with the exchange rate fluctuations a new system of fixed but adjustable exchange rates among different European currencies was set up. This system was called the 'snake'. With the so-called Smithsonian Agreement, bands were set up ensuring that the European currencies would stay within 2.25 per cent of the US dollar (referred to as 'the tunnel'). But this system failed when the US dollar started to float in 1973. Not all EEC countries were able to keep the exchange rates fixed. With the rapidly changing external circumstances (e.g. stagflation and rising oil prices) and the lack of common priorities and policy objectives, EMU failed to be relaunched during the course of the 1970s (for a detailed discussion see Ungerer, 1997; Dyson and Featherstone, 1999; Verdun, 2000, pp. 61–75).

By the late 1970s, it was clear that the EMU plan had failed despite calls from various corners to advance the process (Basevi et al., 1978). In 1975, a group of experts, known as the study group 'Economic and Monetary Union 1980' chaired by Robert Marjolin, submitted its report spelling out the steps that needed to be taken to achieve EMU by 1980 (Marjolin, 1975). It includes calls for a monetary authority but also a significant Community budget. The plan did not materialize (Kruse, 1980; Schlosser, 2018). This expert report was not alone in calling for a larger Community budget; in the 1970s, various studies examined the need for fiscal federalism in the EU, in particular in combination with the aim for closer economic and monetary integration, such as the 1975 Tindemans Report and the MacDougall Report (Commission of the European Communities, 1977). Fiscal federalism is concerned with deciding at what level of government taxing and spending is best done. The question was whether there might be a larger role for the supranational ('European') level in this domain. But the reports did not lead to policy changes. A final attempt to move to European monetary integration came in 1978, with a proposal to launch a system of fixed but adjustable exchange rates (Exchange Rate Mechanism (ERM)), framed as part of the European Monetary System (EMS). It took off in 1979. Though not at all as ambitious as the EMU plan, it was still risky at this time to put forward a plan to create a community exchange rate system, especially in light of the lack of success of the European countries to keep their currencies in the snake arrangement (Ludlow, 1982). At the same time, the EMS was set up to pave the way for deeper monetary integration by keeping exchange rates stable and adopting the European Currency Unit (ECU) as a unit of account. It also reflected collaboration and willingness to move along on this path towards deeper integration (Mourlon-Druol, 2012).

2.2.1.2 The 1980s and the Delors Report

As the 1970s were ending, governments concluded that there was no long-term trade-off between inflation and unemployment. To the contrary, inflation meant that pensioners, wage earners, and savers lost money. If inflation was high and if wages and prices were indexed for inflation, then the net benefit of inflation was zero and, if anything, an interest rate premium had to be paid on the currency due to inflation risk.

Ideational changes occurred regarding monetary policy-making. West German monetary authorities pursued the most stringent policies (Verdun, 2000). Many of the others started to shadow their approach. The Netherlands, the United Kingdom, and Denmark decided that they should focus their monetary policy on safeguarding low inflation, a target the West German central bank (the Bundesbank) had already been focusing on (de Haan, 2000). Countries such as Belgium and Luxembourg, France, and Italy came around a few years later (Quaglia and Maes, 2004; Quaglia, 2004). As a result, the EMS, and in particular the ERM part of the EMS, turned out to be more of a success. To ensure that the exchange rates were in line with one another, central banks of European Member States would look closely at monetary policy changes in West Germany and then follow suit. This shadowing of Bundesbank policies stabilized exchange rates (Smeets, 1990; Herz and Roger, 1992; Loedel, 1999; Beyer et al., 2009).

Another important lesson was learnt by both France, in the early 1980s, and Italy, later in the mid-1980s (Marcussen, 1997, 2000; McNamara, 1998; Verdun, 2000; Howarth, 2001). An economy that is highly dependent on its neighbouring countries is unable to pursue an independent monetary policy. An isolationist policy easily leads to speculative attacks and undermines the objectives sought by the government of the day. 'Socialism in one country' (Hall, 1985) had become an outdated concept.

These three changes in ideas about monetary policy-making and the role of inflation are crucial to understanding the relaunch of EMU based on a depoliticized monetary policy. Instead, it became acceptable that a central bank should be independent, as that would mean it would be better equipped to safeguard price stability. The lesson learnt about inflation in the 1970s meant that there need not be political struggles over the redistributive effects of the monetary policy regime; all had agreed that inflation was undesirable.

The EMS was not very successful in the early period (1979–83), only moderately successful in the second period (1983–87), but quite successful in the last period, which witnessed the relaunch of EMU (1987–92).[1] Once it was decided that the EMS was a symbol of successful European integration, Member State governments started to consider the exchange rates as much more 'fixed' than was economically desirable. Germany acquired a hegemonic role in the EMS (Story, 1988; Barkin, 1996; Kaelberer, 1997; Heisenberg, 1999; Kaltenthaler, 2002).

The immediate impulse that led to the relaunch of EMU in the late 1980s was the signing of the Single European Act (SEA) in 1986 which amended the Treaties establishing the European Communities. Once it entered into force, in 1987, it provided the prospect of the completion of the single market (Padoa-Schioppa, 1987; Cecchini, 1988; Schure, 2013). The SEA enabled Member States to pass legislation pertaining to the single market by qualified majority vote in the Council. The Heads of State and Governments stated at the European Council meeting in Hanover on 27 and 28 June 1988 that 'in adopting the Single Act, the Member States of the Community confirmed the objective of progressive realization of economic and monetary union'.[2] It was decided to set up a committee of central bank presidents, with Jacques Delors (European Commission President) as Chair, to study and propose 'concrete stages leading towards this union' to be on the agenda at the June 1989 summit in Madrid.

The Delors Report was published in April 1989. It outlined in some detail three stages which would lead to the creation of an area with complete freedom of movement for persons, goods, services, and capital, as well as irrevocably fixed exchange rates between national currencies and, finally, a single currency (Delors Report, 1989, p. 17). The central bankers put forward a proposal to restructure monetary policy-making, and to transfer sovereignty over monetary policy to a new European institution, the European Central Bank (ECB). They left the political decision to the politicians, however. Much as the Werner Committee, the Delors Committee had worked as an epistemic community (Verdun, 1999), working within the boundaries of its expertise, guided by the ideas that drew on these past experiences.

By the late 1980s and early 1990s – although the creation of a European System of Central Banks and a European Central Bank, modelled after the German central bank, the Bundesbank, was envisaged – the plan to create EMU in three stages did not foresee a simultaneous creation of a federal economic authority; the design of EMU was 'asymmetrical' (Verdun, 1996, 2000). In the Maastricht Treaty, EMU was enshrined as a rather rigid legal construction geared towards specific objectives, on which societal preferences had largely converged (Dyson, 1994; Dyson

1 The ERM came under pressure in 1992 due to speculative attacks against the pound sterling, which had just joined the ERM. The United Kingdom was forced out of the ERM. The bands were widened for other currencies (except for the Dutch guilder). Most tried to stay within the original bands but the formal bands were stretched to 15 per cent.

2 Conclusions of the Hanover European Council, 27–28 June 1988, quoted in Delors Report (1989). It should be noted that no formal statement was made on the question of the possible establishment of a central bank.

and Featherstone, 1999), as well as an important step in deepening integration, one stage at a time (Padoa-Schioppa, 2000). Price stability and the soundness of fiscal policies had been at the basis of its constitutive framework and included in detail in the EU Treaty and primary law. In this way, the ECB enjoyed significant isolation from direct policy input (Gormley and de Haan, 1996). As stated above, the ECB's mandate had been solidly anchored in the policy preferences of EMU participants (Howarth and Loedel, 2005; Kalthenthaler, 2002).

2.3 EMU IN GOOD TIMES

EMU started in 1999 with the irrevocable fixing of exchange rates among eleven Member States. By 2002, banknotes and coins started circulating in now twelve Member States, as Greece had meanwhile also joined. The early period of EMU impacted the scope of what EMU was all about and how it would change as the Member States gained some experience of being in a monetary union together. Originally the rules of the Stability and Growth Pact (SGP) focused on the possible misuse of the financial space available to Member States (Heipertz and Verdun, 2004). The concerns were that once in EMU all Member States could borrow extensively and have budgetary deficits and public debt higher than the agreed limits. The rules were put in place to reduce the chance of that happening. However, during the first decade, a number of countries did not meet the rules of the SGP and exceeded the limits. Germany and France were notable violators, which led to an undermining of the rules and eventual reform (Heipertz and Verdun, 2010; see also de Haan and Gootjes, Chapter 18 in this volume).

Scholars in this early period focused on how EMU was working and what were the remaining challenges (Schelkle, 2006). After the first decade, various studies took stock of how EMU had done given the insights from the various academic bodies of literature (e.g. Amtenbrink et al., 1997; European Commission, 2008; Enderlein and Verdun, 2009; Verdun, 2010). This work considered whether theoretical challenges were materializing and, if not now, whether there would be a need to redesign EMU down the road in light of those considerations.

What were the considerations at this point in time? Verdun (2010) offered an assessment of how EMU fared by looking at five political science and five economic challenges (although a number of these issues were also discussed by legal scholars). The five challenges drawn from the Political Science literature at this point were: (1) that EMU would only go ahead and continue if it was in the interest of the large Member States; (2) the lack of economic government and political union; (3) the democratic deficit of EMU; (4) the lack of a common identity; and (5) EMU leading to welfare state retrenchment. The findings on these five points after its first decade were as follows. With reference to the first claim, one can argue that EMU has been in the interest of those large Member States that were part of it from the outset. Although only occurring later in the period, the United Kingdom's choice to depart the EU may have been influenced to some, albeit small, extent by the fact that the United Kingdom was not interested in deepening its relationship with the EU – for example, it was not committed to monetary union. Germany and France had been in the driver's seat. Collaboration between them typically was needed to keep the development of EMU on track (Heipertz and Verdun, 2010). Regarding the second point, an assessment after one decade of EMU, that is, by the end of 2008, did not support the theoretical claim that EMU would become unstable without further institutional change in the area of political union or more centralization of economic government. This insight would change after the second decade (see later). The same held for the third challenge, namely that EMU did not become unstable because of lack of sufficient transparency, accountability, or credibility in the first decades (again changes occurred in the second decade). Regarding the criterion of identity, a similar point was made about this matter based on the first decade. Furthermore, Eurobarometer studies after the first decade did not show a major change in identity formation in the EU over the previous ten years. However, these same studies do show support for the thesis of Kaelberer (2001), Risse et al. (1999) and others, namely that the euro is a part of the creation of a common identity. The final point, that EMU would force welfare state retrenchment, did not find support based on the experiences of the first decade; EMU did not undermine the capacity of Member States to determine their own level of support or the particular design of their welfare state, although Member States transgressed a fair bit from the SGP rules during this decade (Heipertz and Verdun, 2010; Bolukbasi 2021).

The five challenges identified by economists were as follows. The first in this group, voiced by Feldstein (1992, 1997), was that EMU will lead to war. Feldstein argued that there would be increased intra-European tensions over foreign policies and disagreements between the countries of the euro area on the one hand and partners (such as the United States) on the other. He also thought that there would be conflicts over the goals of monetary policy (price stability versus growth), with Germany advancing the first but others more interested in the latter (Feldstein, 1997, pp. 63–64). He foresaw a clash between the members and non-members (of EMU) within Europe, 'including the states of Eastern Europe and the former Soviet Union' (Feldstein, 1997, p. 61). He posits a prophetic warning when he writes: 'Although it is impossible to know for certain whether these conflicts would lead to war, it is too real a possibility to ignore in weighing the potential effects of EMU and the European political integration that would follow' (Feldstein, 1997, p. 62). The first decade did not support that notion. The civil war in Yugoslavia in the 1990s preceded EMU and was generally seen as separate from the issues around EMU. From today's vantage point, the notion of war has reappeared in the aftermath of 24 February 2022 when Russian forces started a full-scale invasion of Ukraine. Although Ukraine is outside the immediate EU borders, the EU responded quickly, providing Ukraine with humanitarian, political, financial, and military support. It has also adopted sanctions against Russia which have been aimed at weakening Russia's economy. It also accepted Ukraine as a candidate country (Council of the EU, 2022; Quaglia and Verdun 2023b).

The second challenge in this group, most often raised, is that countries participating in EMU do not form a so-called optimum currency area (OCA: Mundell, 1961; McKinnon, 1963; Eichengreen, 1993; Tavlas, 1993). Research done in the first decade, however, suggested that even though the Member States in EMU indeed do not form an OCA, to some extent EMU membership is part and parcel of the development of an OCA (i.e. it is endogenous; see Frankel and Rose, 1998; De Grauwe, 2006). The endogenous OCA literature suggested that countries may be more likely to have stronger trade connections and thus more synchronized business cycles once they have joined EMU. Furthermore, even existing federations are not all OCAs (especially large ones such as Canada or the United States), but they do have the extra ability to adjust to shocks through fiscal measures and automatic stabilizers. After the first decade, there was not a problem with EMU countries not forming an OCA (Kenen, 1995; Goodhart, 1998; Artis, 2003). Another challenge was the strength of the European Central Bank. Scholars had criticized the ECB for not having sufficient reputation and credibility yet (Artis and Winkler, 1997; de Haan et al., 2004). Observers wondered how well the ECB could execute its mandate without that reputation. The first decade did not provide evidence for these challenges as the inflation rate (the ECB's primary mandate) was managed well.

The final two claims were, first, that the SGP would stifle growth. Here the logic was that the SGP was pro-cyclical and did not allow Member States to pursue the policies necessary to meet the needs of the country at that time. The criticism was that during times of recession or very low growth, having to focus on keeping budgetary deficits low (or reducing the public debt) would further exacerbate that trend. The growth period of the first decade suggested that the countries in the south had performed well. In fact, these countries were overheating and wages were going up. Relatively speaking, the countries in the north were not growing as fast, in part because their monetary situation (cost of credit) had not dropped as much as in their counterparts in the south.

The final challenge was about the value of the euro. Depending on whose view was reflected, the literature was concerned about either overvaluation or undervaluation of the euro. In the first decade, the euro was relatively stable compared to major international currencies. Those who worried about the external value of the euro were moreover often forgetting that the euro area as a whole is (just as others, such as the United States) a relatively closed economy. The importance of over- or undervaluation of the currency of a small open economy is typically worse than that for the euro area as a whole vis-à-vis the rest of the world. The EU is relatively speaking not as open, but the economies of individual Member States are (Baldwin, 2006; Frankel and Rose, 2002). Research also suggests that joining EMU means that trade increases among those individual countries, but the effect on the euro area as a whole is very small. For example, Bun and Klaassen (2002, p. 1) find that the effect of a Member State joining the euro area is about 4 per cent in the first year and they estimate trade to increase to 40 per cent in the long run. Micco et al. (2003) noticed that trade among euro area members increased by 25 per cent. It seemed, however, that in the late 1990s and early 2000s, all countries across the globe were trading less with one another but that the trade among euro area Member States decreased less (Baldwin 2006, p. 37, see figure 10). Not all academics report the same results (e.g. Flam and Nordström, 2003; Chintrakarn, 2008). But the effects of EMU on trade are still considerable.

2.4 EMU IN BAD TIMES

Few expected that the world, and therefore the EU, would be confronted with a major financial crisis and the subsequent recession of the magnitude that started in 2007 and worsened in 2008. The financial crisis morphed into a sovereign debt crisis that from 2009 to 2012, and its aftermath, affected a number of EU Member States, such as Cyprus, Greece, Ireland, Italy, Portugal, and Spain; notably in Greece the situation was particularly perilous (Featherstone, 2011;Zagermann, 2024). These countries saw their economies contract, leading to an increase in public debt and rising unemployment. The EU responded to the situation by offering support to those Member States in need. In May 2010, the EU offered its first major coordinated response to the Greek crisis by providing it access to bailout funds. The so-called Troika of the European Commission, the ECB, and the International Monetary Fund (IMF), made €110 billion available to assist Greece (through an ad hoc arrangement referred to as the Greek Loan Facility, which used bilateral loans provided by Member States of the euro area, and some funds from the IMF). This ad hoc setup was outside the regular EU Treaty context and was modelled on how the IMF operates (Verdun, 2015, p. 226). A second programme for Greece was agreed in February 2012 and was provided by the European Financial Stability Facility (EFSF) – was created in June 2010 – and the IMF (Ardagna and Caselli, 2014; ESM, 2022). The EFSF was a temporary support system (three years). Financial support was also provided to Ireland and Portugal, by the EFSF, the European Financial Stabilisation Mechanism (EFSM) and the IMF. The EFSF was replaced by the European Stability Mechanism (ESM) (Gocaj and Meunier, 2013; Ioannou et al., 2015; Verdun, 2015), which was offered a larger lending ceiling. The ESM was created based on an intergovernmental treaty. The ESM, in operation from 2013 onwards, also supported Cyprus and Spain, and provided a third programme for Greece in 2015 (Henning, 2017). Even the US government played a significant role in seeking European solutions to these problems experienced by individual euro area Member States (Henning, 2019).[3] Demands for structural reforms were placed on the Member States receiving support, which often led to considerable social unrest (Verney and Bosco, 2013). Many observers believed that EMU, as a whole or in some part, would collapse if the EU Member States' leaders did not demonstrate the political will to support Member States facing problems (Chibber, 2011; Schoeller, 2018; Schulz and Verdun, 2022). However, the EU had included a so-called no-bailout clause which had originally been intended to be rather strict (Segers and Van Esch, 2007; Hinarejos, 2013). It took the Member States a long time to decide how to support those states facing problems. Various studies point to the fact that the lack of fast action (effectively a leadership deficiency of the German government) exacerbated the crisis situation (Schoeller, 2020). In particular, Chancellor Angela Merkel was not certain what path to take to solve the problems. The German ministry of finance as well as the level of the chancellor's office were concerned that supporting Member States in need could be in conflict with the EU no-bailout clause. In March 2010, Merkel remarked 'Greece is not insolvent and therefore we do not have to discuss the question of help now . . . It is the best solution for the euro if Greece solves its problems alone' (cited in Schoeller, 2020). The lack of clear German leadership early on led to a delay in making these decisions and arguably contributed to a worsening of the situation (Pagoulatos, 2020). Yet by 2011 it was clear that in Germany the importance of finding solutions had sunk in. Chancellor Merkel told the Bundestag on 26 October 2011 in the midst of the sovereign debt crisis: 'If the euro fails, Europe will fail' (Kornelius, 2013, p. 227). The ECB – ironically, as it is an institution that is set up to be not very 'political' – was among those that came to the rescue, when ECB President Mario Draghi pledged that the ECB would do 'whatever it takes to support the euro' (Draghi, 2012; Hodson, 2013; Baldassarri, 2017; Verdun, 2017; Wanke, 2017). He had received the back-up of Angela Merkel on this matter (Chang, 2016, p. 219). The EU had finally started to work on building EU-level institutions to support financial integration (Jones, 2015a).

During the tail-end of the crisis, the EU started to consider that the asymmetry between 'economic' and 'monetary' union (Verdun, 1996; Howarth and Verdun, 2020) meant a need to coordinate further fiscal policies as well as macroeconomic policies more widely defined (Drudi et al., 2012). One major decision to address this matter was to develop the European Semester – an attempt to coordinate macroeconomic policy-making. It drew on principles of benchmarking and best practices, developed in the area of social policy through the open method of coordination (Zeitlin and Vanhercke, 2018; D'Erman and Verdun, 2022).

In addition, EMU required deepening in the area of more supervision in banks through the formation of a Banking Union (Howarth and Quaglia, 2013; Jones, 2015b; De Rynck, 2016; Epstein and Rhodes, 2018). The Banking Union is based on three pillars: the Single Supervisory Mechanism (SSM); the Single Resolution Mechanism (SRM), and the European Deposit Insurance Scheme (EDIS). Having worked towards the creation of this Banking Union is generally considered one of the biggest achievements in deepening EMU since it started in 1998. The SSM provides supervision of the banking sector and improves cross-border cooperation. The ECB is responsible for the supervision of the most significant banks. However, not all elements (or 'pillars') are fully operational: the second pillar, i.e. the Single Resolution Mechanism, remains a challenge (Howarth and Quaglia, 2013). The SRM will deal with failing

[3] For details on the steps taken to create the ESM, see Gocaj and Meunier (2013), Verdun (2015), and Henning (2017).

banks. As to the third and final pillar, national deposit guarantee schemes exist that guarantee deposits up to €100,000 per person per bank, but there is no agreement yet on EDIS.

There were attempts to complete EMU spearheaded by Herman van Rompuy, the President of the Council, put forward the so-called Four Presidents' report. A few years later, Commission President Jean-Claude Juncker presided over the Five Presidents' report. It made the next steps towards deepening EMU, with stages towards fiscal federalism and political integration. The celebration of sixty years of the Treaty of Rome, in March 2017, was an opportunity to offer further plans to complete EMU. All in all, there was a plethora of ideas and proposals to advance EMU and deepen integration, many of them connecting back to those already existing during the early days (Verdun, 1998b). Although these plans provided clear blueprints about the next steps, they were thwarted somewhat when UK citizens voted in a referendum to leave the European Union (Cini and Verdun, 2018). But Brexit did not fundamentally alter the plans of the members of the euro area to deepen integration, as having the United Kingdom outside the EU removed a further veto-player in further deepening integration – potentially generating more space to complete EMU.

With the outbreak of the COVID-19 pandemic, Member States and supranational institutions drew on the ideas that were contained in the plans to complete EMU (Fabbrini, 2022). Member State governments, the ECB, and the European Commission indicated the need to support Member States that were most seriously affected (ECB, 2020; Lagarde, 2020). Early on the ECB played an important role. On 18 March, following a mishap in communication by the ECB president the week prior, the ECB provided a Pandemic Emergency Purchase Programme (PEPP), which aimed to reduce borrowing costs and increase lending (Jones, 2020). The amount was increased in steps to €1,850 billion. The ECB also lowered the standards for bank collateral for loans and increased the types of assets that could be used as collateral. In this way, the ECB was highly proactive in both the monetary domain but also in the domain of banking supervision (SSM) (see Quaglia and Verdun, 2023). Member States also developed plans to deal with COVID-19. Plans were put forward by the Spanish government, but the Franco-German leaders also planned to pool resources to support Member States in need (Fabbrini, 2022; Vanhercke and Verdun, 2022). The earlier plans to complete EMU had proposed various roadmaps for expanding the scope of EMU. Many Member States contributed to the debate on how to deepen EMU in response to the challenges posed by the COVID-19 pandemic. The latter offered a window of opportunity to expand the role and scope of fiscal federalism in the EU context. The choice was made for a short-term, temporary agreement to spend more money collectively and to explore possible steps towards taxation or refinancing. The European Council agreed in July 2020 to provide €750 billion to support member states. Building on ideas that had already been floating around in the decade prior, the new mechanism was called Next Generation EU, which is a temporary instrument intended to create capacity to support Member States in need (Jones, 2021; Vanhercke and Verdun, 2022). Although initially proposals circulated to use the ESM to provide support, these suggestions were shot down (Zagermann, 2024). Member States, especially those in the south, demanded that EU-level (not euro-area-level) support should be made available. The reasoning was that COVID-19 generated a health emergency unrelated to the macroeconomic or fiscal preconditions that the prior rules had sought to deal with. Thus, the support should reflect mutual solidarity; one should not consider this situation to be one of moral hazard (Buti and Fabbrini, 2023). The EU recovery programme includes options for temporary collective debt issuance, raising hopes that a more permanent new type of euro-denominated safe asset may emerge and that the European Commission will further develop a liquid and transparent market in EU bonds. Another initiative at this time is the European instrument for Temporary Support to mitigate Unemployment Risks in an Emergency (SURE) (European Commission, 2021). The EU issues social bonds to finance SURE (by March 2022 it had issued 92 billion social bonds in eight rounds – bonds of 5–30 years' duration, European Commission, 2022). This instrument provides loans to Member States to protect jobs and workers' income in the context of the COVID-19 pandemic. The notion of centralized, supranational unemployment support has often been discussed in the economics literature. The national unemployment schemes work as automatic stabilizers. Since the early days of conceptualizing EMU, these automatic stabilizers have been discussed as being necessary to offset imbalances. Although SURE is not the same as an EU-level unemployment benefit scheme, it is the first EU-level support system of this nature that helps Member States to secure workers' income and protect jobs (Vanhercke and Verdun, 2022). Funds have been used, for instance, for short-term work schemes. It was considered by scholars to be an important economic stabilizer (Claeys, 2020; Rhodes, 2021). The generous support for workers on furlough meant that unemployment was kept low because of the use of these funds for workers (Euronews, 2021). Making these funds available was also a response to earlier criticism when the EU focus on stability was seen to be procyclical and further deepening an economic downturn. Instead, SURE offered support to Member States to offset recession and unemployment.

2.5 CONCLUSION

Most of the building blocks of a more complete EMU had been around in the realm of ideas since the outset. There had been an awareness of what EMU could entail, with many being fully aware that economic and monetary integration was a step on a path towards deeper integration. Rather than building EMU following a concept or theory, at each intersection in history a pragmatic choice was made about the scope of possible agreement on what EMU would mean and where most of the attention would be placed. There were ambitious plans in the late 1960s that built on theories of economic integration. When international circumstances changed, and exchange rate volatility erupted, there was a lack of agreement on the exact path to take. The easiest option was to focus on exchange rate cooperation. Monetary authorities across the EU were willing de facto to follow the German model of monetary policy-making that focused on price stability. In this way, the exact content of economic and monetary integration of the EU followed the path that the Union chose more generally in the 1960s, 1970s, 1980s, and 1990s. The various crises, such as the financial crisis and the sovereign debt crisis in the late 2008–12 period, and its aftermath, but also the more recent COVID-19 crisis, have impacted the creation of EMU by deepening integration.

The insertion of EMU into the Maastricht Treaty came at a specific moment in time, namely following the end of the cold war. The immediate aftermath of that decision was difficult but in the end Member States chose to keep as many countries as possible on board. The motivation was political; the vision of exactly what economic and monetary policy rules were required was more a mediated settlement rather than following a careful understanding of theory. To ensure macroeconomic policy coordination, the focus was first and foremost on budgetary deficits and public debt. It made it possible for actors in the policy process to communicate the need to have rules. However, although Member States adjusted to EU rules, they were not always able to stay within the limits; they also did not fully solve various underlying structural problems. The financial crisis and sovereign debt crisis brought to the fore the fundamental imbalances among Member States as well as the need for members of the EU to provide mutual support. The incomplete design of EMU was dealt with somewhat at this time, but EMU was still not fully complete. Crises were used to add more to the agenda, such as banking union. In this incremental way, some of the asymmetries were addressed and more elements that had been considered in theory became part of the reality of EMU. Following the departure of the United Kingdom from the EU, and as the COVID-19 pandemic was raging, the EU responded by dabbling into more fiscal federalism. Many of these issues had been discussed in the early days when experts thought about what EMU would entail, but at the time there was insufficient support for this kind of deeper integration. There had not yet been the common ground, the lived experience, to have actionable points. Lacking those, some of the asymmetries were reinforced. It has been a mix of theoretical understanding of economic and monetary integration with practical understanding of what was in the realm of the possible that shaped economic and monetary integration. At the same time, Member States and citizens seem not prepared to dive into the deep end (political union). As the challenges that the EU is faced with persist, these realities keep changing.

REFERENCES

Amtenbrink, F., de Haan, J., and Sleijpen, O. (1997). Stability and Growth Pact: Placebo or panacea? (I). *European Business Law Review* 8(9), 202–210.

Ardagna, S., and Caselli, F. (2014) The political economy of the Greek debt crisis: A tale of two bailouts. *American Economic Journal: Macroeconomics* 6(4), 291–323.

Artis, M. J. (2003). Reflections on the optimal currency area (OCA) criteria in the light of EMU. *International Journal of Finance and Economics* 8(4), 297–307.

Artis, M. J. and Winkler, B. (1997). The Stability Pact: Safeguarding the credibility of the European Central Bank. CEPR Discussion Paper No. 1688.

Balassa, B. (1961). *The Theory of Economic Integration*, 1st ed. London: Allen and Unwin.

Balassa, B. (ed.) (1975). *European Economic Integration*. Amsterdam; Oxford: North-Holland; American Elsevier.

Baldassarri M. (2017). What would have happened in Europe if Mario Draghi had not been there? In M. Baldassarri (ed.), *The European Roots of the Eurozone Crisis*. Cham: Palgrave Macmillan, pp. 425–442.

Baldwin, R. (2006). The euro's trade effects. ECB Working Paper No. 594.

Barkin, J. S. (1996). Hegemony without motivation: Domestic policy priorities and German monetary policy. *German Politics and Society* 14(3), 54–72.

Basevi, G., et al. (1978). The All Saints' Day manifesto for European monetary union. In M. Fratianni, and T. Peeters (eds.), *One Money for Europe*. London: Palgrave Macmillan, pp. 37–43. https://doi.org/10.1007/978-1-349-04308-8_2.

Beyer, A., Gaspar, V., Gerberding, C., and Issing, O. (2009). Opting out of the great inflation: German monetary policy after the break down of Bretton Woods. ECB Working Paper No. 1010.

Bolukbasi, H. T. (2021). *Euro-Austerity and Welfare States: Comparative Political Economy Reforms during the Maastricht Decade*. Toronto: University of Toronto Press.

Bun, M., and Klaassen, F. (2002). Has the euro increased trade? University of Amsterdam, Tinbergen Institute Discussion 2002-108/2.

Burrell, A. (2009). The CAP: Looking back, looking ahead. *Journal of European Integration* 31(3), 271–289.

Buti, M., and Fabbrini, S. (2023) Next Generation EU and the future of economic governance: Towards a paradigm change or just a big one-off? *Journal of European Public Policy* 30(4), 676–695.

Caporaso, J. A. (2018). Europe's triple crisis and the uneven role of institutions: The euro, refugees and Brexit. *Journal of Common Market Studies* 56(60), 1345–1361.

Cecchini, P. (1988). *The European Challenge 1992: The Benefits of a Single Market*. Gower: Aldershot.

Chang, M. (2016) *Economic and Monetary Union*. Basingstoke: Palgrave.

Chibber, K. (2011). The domino effect in Europe's debt crisis. BBC News, 20 September. www.bbc.com/news/business-14985256

Chintrakarn, P. (2008). Estimating the euro effects on trade with propensity score matching. *Review of International Economics* 16(1), 186–198.

Cini, M., and Verdun, A. (2018). The implications of Brexit for the future of Europe. In B. Martill and U. Staiger (eds.), *Brexit and Beyond: Rethinking the Futures of Europe*. London: CL Press, pp. 63–71.

Claeys, G. (2020). The European Union's SURE plan to safeguard employment: A small step forward. Bruegel Blog Post, 20 May. At www.bruegel.org/2020/05/the-european-unions-sure-plan-to-safeguard-employment-a-small-step-forward/

Commission of the European Communities (1977). *Report of the Study Group on the Role of Public Finance in European Integration* (MacDougall Report), vols. 1–2. 1977-04.

Corden, W. M. (1972a). Economics of scale and customs union theory. *Journal of Political Economy* 80, 465–475.

Corden, W. M. (1972b). Monetary integration. Essays in International Finance No. 93, Princeton University.

Council of the EU (2022). EU response to Russia's invasion of Ukraine. www.consilium.europa.eu/en/policies/eu-response-ukraine-invasion

Curzon Price, V. (1974). *The Essentials of Economic Integration*. Basingstoke: Macmillan.

Danescu, E. R. (2012). Economists v. monetarists: Agreements and clashes in the drafting of the Werner Report. In *A Rereading of the Werner Report of* 8 *October* 1970 *in the Light of the Pierre Werner Family Archives*. Sanem: CVCE.

De Grauwe, P. (2006). What have we learnt about monetary integration since the Maastricht Treaty? *Journal of Common Market Studies* 44(4), 711–730.

De Haan, J. (ed.) (2000). *The History of the Bundesbank: Lessons for the European Central Bank*. London: Routledge.

De Haan, J., Ambtenbrink, F., and Waller, S. (2004). The transparency and credibility of the European Central Bank. *Journal of Common Market Studies* 42(4), 775–794.

Delors Report (1989). *Report on Economic and Monetary Union in the European Community* (Committee for the Study of Economic and Monetary Union). Luxembourg: Office for Official Publications of the EC 1989-04.

D'Erman, V., and Verdun, A. (2022). Introduction to the Special Issue: Macroeconomic policy coordination and domestic politics: Policy coordination in the EU from the European Semester to the Covid-19 crisis. *Journal of Common Market Studies* 60(1), 3–20.

De Rynck, S. (2016). Banking on a union: The politics of changing Eurozone banking supervision. *Journal of European Public Policy* 23(1), 119–135.

Draghi, Mario (2012). Verbatim of the remarks made by Mario Draghi. Speech at the Global Investment Conference, London, 26 July. www.ecb.europa.eu/press/key/date/2012/html/sp120726.en.html

Drudi, F., Durré, A., and Mongelli, F. P. (2012). The interplay of economic reforms and monetary policy: The case of the eurozone. *JCMS: Journal of Common Market Studies* 50(6), 881–898.

Dyson, K. (1994). *Elusive Union: The Process of Economic and Monetary Union in Europe*. London: Longman.

Dyson, K., and Featherstone, K. (1999). *The Road to Maastricht: Negotiating Economic and Monetary Union*. Oxford: Oxford University Press.

ECB (2020). ECB announces €750 billion Pandemic Emergency Purchase Programme (PEPP). 18 March. www.ecb.europa.eu/press/pr/date/2020/html/ecb.pr200318_1~3949d6f266.en.html

Eichengreen, B. (1993). Is Europe an optimum currency area. In S. Borner and H. Grubel (eds.), *The European Community after* 1992: *Perspectives from the Outside*. London: Macmillan, pp. 138–161.

Enderlein, H., and Verdun, A. (2009). EMU's teenage challenge: What have we learned and can we predict from political science? *Journal of European Public Policy* 16(4), 490–507.

Epstein, R., and Rhodes, M. (2018). From governance to government: Banking union, capital markets union and the new EU. *Competition & Change* 22(2), 205–224.

Euronews (2021). The EU scheme making 'SURE' unemployment stays low. 13 January. www.euronews.com/next/2021/01/13/the-eu-scheme-making-sure-unemployment-stays-low

European Commission (2008). EMU@10: Successes and challenges after ten years of Economic and Monetary Union. *European Economy*, No. 2, 2008. 2008-06.

European Commission (2021). Report from the Commission to the European Parliament, the Council, the Economic and Financial Committee and the Employment Committee. COM (2021) 596 final, Brussels. 2021-09-22.

European Commission (2022). *SURE. The European instrument for temporary Support to mitigate Unemployment Risks in an Emergency (SURE).* https://ec.europa.eu/info/business-economy-euro/economic-and-fiscal-policy-coordination/financial-assistance-eu/funding-mechanisms-and-facilities/sure_en

European Stability Mechanism (2022). Greece. Programme timeline for Greece. www.esm.europa.eu/assistance/greece

Fabbrini, F. (2022). The legal architecture of the economic responses to COVID-19: EMU beyond the pandemic. *Journal of Common Market Studies* 60(1), 186–203.

Featherstone, K. (2011). The Greek sovereign debt crisis and EMU: A failing state in a skewed regime. *Journal of Common Market Studies* 49(2), 193–217.

Feldstein, M. (1992). Europe's monetary union: The case against EMU. *The Economist*, 13 June, pp. 19–22.

Feldstein, M. (1997). EMU and international conflict. *Foreign Affairs* 76(6), 45–60.

Flam, H., and Nordstrom, H. (2003). *Trade Volume Effects of the Euro: Aggregate and Sector Estimates.* Stockholm: IIES.

Frankel, J. A., and Rose, A. K. (1998). The endogeneity of the optimum currency area criteria. *Economic Journal* 108(449), 1009–1025.

Frankel, J. A., and Rose, A. (2002). An estimate of the effect of currency unions on trade and income. *Quarterly Journal of Economics* 117(2), 437–466.

Gocaj, L., and Meunier, S. (2013). Time will tell: The EFSF, the ESM, and the euro crisis. *Journal of European Integration* 35(3), 239–253.

Goodhart, C. A. E. (1998). Two concepts of money: Implications for the analysis of optimal currency areas. *European Journal of Political Economy* 14(3), 402–432.

Gormley, L., and de Haan, J. (1996). The democratic deficit of the European Central Bank. *European Law Review* 21(2), 95–112.

Hall, P. A. (1985). Socialism in one country: Mitterrand and the struggle to define a new economic policy for France. In P. Cerny and M. Schain (eds.), *Socialism, the State and Public Policy in France.* London: Frances Pinter, pp. 81–107.

Heipertz, M., and Verdun, A. (2004). The dog that would never bite? On the origins of the Stability and Growth Pact. *Journal of European Public Policy* 11(5), 773–788.

Heipertz, M., and Verdun, A. (2010). *Ruling Europe: Theory and Politics of the Stability and Growth Pact.* Cambridge: Cambridge University Press.

Heisenberg, D. (1999). *The Mark of the Bundesbank: Germany's Role in European Monetary Cooperation.* Boulder, CO: Lynne Rienner.

Henning, C. R. (2017). *Tangled Governance: International Regime Complexity, the Troika, and the Euro Crisis.* Oxford: Oxford University Press.

Henning, C. R. (2019). US Policy in the euro crisis and the institutional deepening of the monetary union. *Journal of Economic Policy Reform* 23(3), 325–341.

Herz, B., and Roger, W. (1992). The EMS is a greater Deutschmark area. *European Economic Review* 36 (7), 1413–1425.

Hinarejos, A. (2013). Fiscal federalism in the European Union: Evolution and future choices for EMU. *Common Market Law Review* 50(6), 1621–1642.

Hodson, D. (2013). The eurozone in 2012: 'Whatever it takes to preserve the euro'? *JCMS: Journal of Common Market Studies* 51(S1), 183–200.

Howarth, D. J. (2001). *The French Road to European Monetary Union.* Basingstoke: Palgrave.

Howarth, D. J., and Loedel, P. H. (2005). *The European Central Bank: The New European Leviathan*, 2nd ed. Basingstoke: Palgrave.

Howarth, D., and Quaglia, L. (2013). Banking union as holy grail: Rebuilding the single market in financial services, stabilizing Europe's banks and 'completing' Economic and Monetary Union. *Journal of Common Market Studies* 51(S1), 103–123.

Howarth, D. and Verdun, A. (2020). Economic and Monetary Union at twenty: A stocktaking of a tumultuous second decade: introduction. *Journal of European Integration* 42(3), 287–293.

Ioannou, D., Leblond, D., and Niemann, A. (2015). European integration and the crisis: Practice and theory. *Journal of European Public Policy* 22(2), 155–176.
Jones, E. (2015a). The forgotten financial union. In M. Matthijs and M. Blyth (eds.), *The Future of the Euro*. Oxford: Oxford University Press, pp. 44–69.
Jones, E. (2015b). Getting the story right: How you should choose between different interpretations of the European crisis (and why you should care). *Journal of European Integration* 37(7), 817–832.
Jones, E. (2020) COVID-19 and the EU economy: Try again, fail better. *Survival* 62(4), 81–100.
Jones, E. (2021). Next Generation EU: Solidarity, *opportunity, and confidence*. European Policy Analysis, Sieps, 2021-06-11.
Kaelberer, M. (1997). Hegemony, dominance or leadership? Explaining Germany's role in European monetary cooperation. *European Journal of International Relations* 3(1), 35–60.
Kaelberer, M. (2001). *Money and Power in Europe: The Political Economy of European Monetary Cooperation*. Albany: State University of New York Press.
Kaltenthaler, K. (2002). German interests in European monetary integration. *Journal of Common Market Studies* 40(1), 69–87.
Kenen, P. B. (1995). *Economic and Monetary Union in Europe: Moving beyond Maastricht*. Cambridge: Cambridge University Press.
Kornelius, S. (2013). *Angela Merkel: The Chancellor and Her World*. Richmond: Alma Books.
Knudsen, A.-C. L. (2011). *Farmers on Welfare: The Making of Europe's Common Agricultural Policy*. Ithaca, NY: Cornell University Press.
Kruse, D. C. (1980). *Monetary Integration in Western Europe: EMU, EMS and Beyond*. London: Butterworth.
Lagarde, C. (2020). Our response to the coronavirus emergency. The ECB Blog. 19 March. www.ecb.europa.eu/press/blog/date/2020/html/ecb.blog200319~11f421e25e.en.html
Laursen, F. (2019). Budgetary treaties and European Union politics. *Oxford Research Encyclopedias*, 26 April, https://doi.org/10.1093/acrefore/9780190228637.013.1095
Law, J. (2009). Green currencies. In J. Law (ed.), *A Dictionary of Business and Management*, 5th ed. Oxford: Oxford University Press.
Loedel, P. H. (1999). *Deutsche Mark Politics: Germany in the European Monetary System*. London: Lynne Rienner.
Ludlow, P. (1982). *The Making of the European Monetary System: A Case Study of the Politics of the European Community*. London: Butterworth Scientific.
Ludlow, P. (2005). The making of the CAP: Towards a historical analysis of the EU's first major policy. *Contemporary European History* 14(3), 347–371.
Machlup, F. (1977). *A History of Thought on Economic Integration*. Basingstoke: Macmillan.
Maes, I., and Verdun, A. (2005). The role of medium-sized countries in the creation of EMU: The cases of Belgium and the Netherlands. *Journal of Common Market Studies* 43(2), 327–48.
Magnifico, G. (1973). *European Monetary Unification*. London: Macmillan.
Marcussen, M. (1997). The role of 'ideas' in Dutch, Danish and Swedish economic policy in the 1980s and the beginning of the 1990s. In P. Minkkinen and P. Heikki (eds.), *The Politics of Economic and Monetary Union*. Kluwer: Dordrecht, pp. 75–103.
Marcussen, M. (2000). *Ideas and Elites: The Social Construction of Economic and Monetary Union*. Vilborg: Aalborg University Press.
McKinnon, R. (1963). Optimum currency areas. *American Economic Review* 53(4), 717–725.
McNamara, K. R. (1998). *The Currency of Ideas: Monetary Politics in the European Union*. Ithaca, NY: Cornell University Press.
Marjolin, R., Bobba, F., Bosman, H. W. J., et al. (1975). Report of the Study Group Economic and Monetary Union 1980 (Marjolin Report), Commission of the European Communities, Brussels, Doc II/675/3/74, 1975-03-08.
Micco, A., Stein, E., Ordonez, G., Midelfart, K. H., and Viaene, J.-M. (2003). The currency union effect on trade: Early evidence from EMU. *Economic Policy* 18(37), 316–356.
Mourlon-Druol, E. (2012). *A Europe Made of Money: The Emergence of the European Monetary System*. Ithaca, NY: Cornell University Press.
Mundell, R. (1961). A theory of optimum currency areas. *American Economic Review* 51(4), 657–675.

Padoa-Schioppa, T. (1987). *Efficiency, Stability, and Equity: A Strategy for the Evolution of the Economic System of the European Community*. New York: Oxford University Press.

Padoa-Schioppa, T. (2000) *The Road to Monetary Union in Europe: The Emperor, the Kings, and the Genies*, 2nd ed. Oxford: Oxford University Press.

Pagoulatos, G. (2020). EMU and the Greek crisis: Testing the extreme limits of an asymmetric union. *Journal of European Integration* 42(3), 363–379.

Quaglia, L. (2004). Italy's policy towards European monetary integration: Bringing ideas back in? *Journal of European Public Policy* 11(6), 1096–1111.

Quaglia, L., and Maes, I. (2004). France and Italy's policies on European monetary integration: A comparison of 'strong' and 'weak' states. *Comparative European Politics* 2(1), 51–72.

Quaglia, L., and Verdun, A. (2023a). Explaining the response of the ECB to the Covid-19 related economic crisis: Inter-crisis and intra-crisis learning. *Journal of European Public Policy* 30(4), 635–654.

Quaglia, L., and Verdun, A. (2023b). Weaponisation of finance: The role of European central banks and financial sanctions against Russia. *West European Politics*. DOI: 10.1080/01402382.2022.2155906.

Risse, T., Engelmann-Martin, D., Knopf, H.-J., and Roscher, K. (1999). To euro or not to euro? The EMU and identity politics in the European Union. *European Journal of International Relations* 5(2), 147–187.

Rhodes, M. (2021). 'Failing forward': A critique in light of COVID-19. *Journal of European Public Policy* 28(10), 1537–1554.

Rosenthal, G. G. (1975). *The Men behind the Decisions: Cases in European Policy-Making*. Lexington, MA: Lexington Books, D. C Heath.

Schelkle, W. (2006). The theory and practice of economic governance in EMU revisited: What have we learnt about commitment and credibility? *Journal of Common Market Studies* 44(4), 669–686.

Schlosser, P. (2018). *Europe's New Fiscal Union*. Basingstoke: Palgrave Macmillan.

Schoeller, M. G. (2018). Leadership by default: The ECB and the announcement of outright monetary transactions. *Credit and Capital Markets* 51(1), 73–91.

Schoeller, M. G. (2020). Germany, the problem of leadership, and institution-building in EMU reform. *Journal of Economic Policy Reform* 23(3), 309–324.

Schulz, D. F., and Verdun, A. (2022). Differentiation and the European Central Bank: A bulwark against (differentiated) disintegration? In B. Leruth, S. Gänzle, and J. Trondal (eds.), *The Routledge Handbook of Differentiation in the European Union*. London: Routledge, pp. 200–214.

Schure, P. (2013). European financial market integration. In A. Verdun and A. Tovias (eds.), *Mapping Economic Integration*. Basingstoke: Palgrave Macmillan, pp. 105–124.

Segers, M. L. L., and Van Esch F. A. W. J. (2007). Behind the veil of budgetary discipline: The political logic of the budgetary rules in EMU and SGP. *Journal of Common Market Studies* 45(5), 1089–1109.

Smeets, H.-D. (1990). Does Germany dominate the EMS? *Journal of Common Market Studies* 29(1), 37–52.

Steinherr, A. (ed.) (1994). *Thirty Years of European Monetary Integration from the Werner Plan to EMU*. London: Longman.

Story, J. (1988). The launching of the EMS: An analysis of change in foreign economic policy. *Political Studies* 36(3), 397–412.

Tavlas, G. S. (1993). The 'new' theory of optimum currency areas. *The World Economy* 16(6), 663–685.

Tinbergen, J. (1954). *International Economic Integration*. Amsterdam: Elsevier.

Tsoukalis, L. (1977). *The Politics and Economics of European Monetary Integration*. London: Allen and Unwin.

Ungerer, H. (1997). *A Concise History of European Monetary Integration: From EPU to EMU*. London: Quorum Books.

Vanhercke, B., and Verdun, A. (2022). The European Semester as goldilocks: Macroeconomic policy coordination and the Recovery and Resilience Facility. *Journal of Common Market Studies* 60(1), 204–223.

Vanthoor, W. F. V. (1996). *European Monetary Union since 1848: A Political and Historical Analysis*. Cheltenham: Edward Elgar.

Verdun, A. (1996). An 'asymmetrical' Economic and Monetary Union in the EU: Perceptions of monetary authorities and social partners. *Journal of European Integration* 20(1), 59–81.

Verdun, A. (1998a). The increased influence of the EU Monetary Institutional Framework in determining monetary policies: A transnational monetary elite at work. In B. Reinalda and B. Verbeek (eds.), *Autonomous Policy Making by International Organizations*. London: Routledge, pp. 178–194.

Verdun, A. (1998b). Monetary integration in Europe: Ideas and evolution. In M. G. Cowles and M. Smith (eds.), *The State of the European Union Vol. 5: Risks, Reform, Resistance and Revival*. Oxford: Oxford University Press, pp. 91–109.

Verdun, A. (1999). The role of the Delors Committee in the creation of EMU: An epistemic community? *Journal of European Public Policy* 6(2), 308–328.

Verdun, A. (2000). *European Responses to Globalization and Financial Market Integration: Perceptions of Economic and Monetary Union in Britain, France and Germany*. Basingstoke: Palgrave.

Verdun, A. (2002). Why EMU happened: A survey of theoretical explanations. In P. M. Crowley (ed.), *Before and Beyond EMU: Historical Lessons and Future Prospects*. London: Routledge, pp. 71–98.

Verdun, A. (2010). Ten years EMU: An assessment of ten critical claims. *International Journal of Economics and Business Research* 2(1/2), 144–163.

Verdun, A. (2015). A historical institutionalist explanation of the EU's responses to the euro area financial crisis. *Journal of European Public Policy* 22(2), 219–237.

Verdun, A. (2017). Political leadership of the European Central Bank. *Journal of European Integration* 39 (2), 207–221.

Verdun, A. (2018). Theories of European integration and governance. In E. Brunet-Jailly, A. Hurrelmann, and A. Verdun (eds.), *European Union Governance and Policy Making: A Canadian Perspective*. Toronto: University of Toronto Press, pp. 105–124.

Verney, S., and Bosco, A. (2013). Living parallel lives: Italy and Greece in an age of austerity. *South European Society and Politics* 18(4), 397–426.

Wanke, S. (2017). Five years of 'whatever it takes': Three words that saved the euro. KfW Research, Economics in Brief, No. 139.

Werner Report (1970). Report to the Council and the Commission on the Realization by Stages of Economic and Monetary Union in the Community. Council and Commission of the EC, Bulletin of the EC, Supplement 11, Doc 16.956/11/70, 2011-10-08.

Zagermann, D. (2024). *Remaking European Political Economies: Financial Assistance in the Euro Crisis*. Toronto: University of Toronto Press.

Zeitlin, J., and Vanhercke, B. (2018). Socializing the European Semester: EU social and economic policy co-ordination in crisis and beyond. *Journal of European Public Policy* 25(2), 149–174.

3

Monetary Union and the Single Currency

Harold James

3.1 INTRODUCTION

This chapter examines the best way of conceptualizing the story of European monetary integration, but also reflects on the extent to which the peculiarities of that history may have been responsible for some major design flaws in the project. Europe's move to monetary integration with a common currency (the euro) was a quite unique process and is often held up as a model for monetary cooperation in other parts of the world: in the Gulf region, where there are periodic discussions of monetary unification, as well as in Asia and Latin America, where movements towards greater monetary integration also have some support but encounter a plethora of difficulties. Nevertheless, at the latest by the financial crisis of 2007–2008, it became clear that there were substantial design flaws in the concept of Economic and Monetary Union (EMU). As Patrick Honohan (2012) put it, 'release 1.0 of the euro was under-designed, and robust only to moderate shocks'.

What was the design flaw? It is often claimed – especially but not only by American economists – that the travails of the euro, as well as the history of past monetary unions (Bordo and Jonung, 2003), show that it is impossible to have a monetary union in the absence of a political union, which establishes a common political process for determining the distribution of fiscal costs. Paul de Grauwe (2013) stated the case quite simply: 'The Euro is a currency without a country. To make the Euro sustainable a country will have to be created.' Successive ECB Presidents rhetorically at least seemed to endorse this advice. Accepting the Charlemagne Prize in Aachen, Jean-Claude Trichet (2011) said: 'In a long-term historical perspective, Europe – which has invented the concept and the word of democracy – is called to complete the design of what it already calls a "Union".' Mario Draghi (2012) has been even more dramatic, demanding

> the collective commitment of all governments to reform the governance of the euro area. This means completing economic and monetary union along four key pillars: (i) a financial union with a single supervisor at its heart, to re-unify the banking system; (ii) a fiscal union with enforceable rules to restore fiscal capacity; (iii) an economic union that fosters sustained growth and employment; and (iv) a political union, where the exercise of shared sovereignty is rooted in political legitimacy.

This advice seems appallingly radical to many, since almost every politician denies that there is any real possibility of creating something resembling a European state, and almost every citizen recoils at the prospect. The fact that the discussion to which Draghi contributed had been going on for decades suggests that there were no very easy solutions. The simple version of the critique is that there was not enough politics in making the euro.

The monetary union that was accomplished in the 1990s in Europe is quite unprecedented in the story of interstate relations. It was long accepted that money was a creation of the state: even in the world of the gold standard, the state set the ratio of precious metal to a unit of currency through legislation. The new money was not only not a creation of a state; it was managed by a new institution, the European Central Bank (ECB), whose constitutional position within the European Union was left unspecified (until the Lisbon Treaty came into force). The ECB thus became the most independent central bank in the world.

3.2 CENTRAL BANKS AND CURRENT ACCOUNTS

The origins of a new phase of European monetary cooperation lie at the same moment as the creation of the European Economic Community (EEC) through the Treaty of Rome (1957).[1] In a 1957 speech at the Alpbach Economic Forum in Austria, Governor of the Netherlands Bank, Marius Holtrop, had gone further and asked whether a common central bank policy was necessary in a unified Europe, and then went on to answer the question in the affirmative (Holtrop, 1957; Vanthoor, 1991). On 10 November 1957, Holtrop circulated a note in which he suggested that the five central banks of the EEC countries (Luxembourg had none, as it was in a monetary union with Belgium) should send identical letters to the finance ministers proposing enhanced cooperation between central banks. The Belgian, French, and German governors responded sceptically, arguing that such a move would look like a concerted effort and only raise mutual national suspicions.

Germany in particular was persistently sceptical of all the cooperation talk and always found the compromise of monetary sovereignty difficult. Here is an example of the common pattern in international monetary relations: that cooperation is more attractive to smaller countries as it seems to provide more benefits for them, and it is the heavyweights that are likely to think that they can do it on their own. In the late 1950s, German current account surpluses started to increase, setting off a pattern of discussion that was echoed in the 1960s, the late 1970s, the late 1980s, but also after the establishment of a monetary union. From the perspective of Germany's central bank, the Deutsche Bundesbank, central bank cooperation might involve the demand for some German support operations, and thus involve pressure to follow policies that might be costly or inflationary. Bundesbank President Karl Blessing consequently spoke to German Chancellor Konrad Adenauer against any plan for funding of EEC countries.

The 1957 statement of a group of EEC central banks that everything was well and that no innovation was needed seems to have been accepted until an event occurred which showed that there was really not much central bank cooperation between Europeans. In March 1961, the Deutschmark and the Dutch guilder were revalued, following a long period of tensions in the markets, and a great deal of discussion within the IMF about the appropriate response to the build-up of German surpluses, but after no particular consultation with Germany's fellow EEC members. All the negotiation was done in Washington. In consequence, some European leaders thought they should bring European discussions back home.

[1] Treaty establishing the European Economic Community, 1957, https://eur-lex.europa.eu/legal-content/EN/TXT/?uri=CELEX:11957E/TXT.

The EEC Commission published its Action Programme for the Second Phase of EEC on 24 October 1962, referring to the desirability of a general liberalization of capital accounts, in accordance with the provisions of the Treaty of Rome. It concluded in a visionary way that made the logical link between monetary union and fiscal union explicit. That linkage, which also figured in the lead-up to the Maastricht Treaty, and became a recurrent centre of the debate during the eurozone crisis, was actually stated with greater clarity and force than it would be in the discussions of the 1990s. There would be parallel councils or committees to coordinate or determine ('fix') fiscal policy as well as monetary policy, because both were seen as part of the management of demand:

> The creation of a monetary union could become the objective of the third phase of the Common Market. The Finance or Economics Ministers of the Community, assembled in Council, would decide on conditions that should be fixed at an opportune time: the overall size of national budgets, and of the Community budget, and the general conditions of financing of these budgets. The Council of Central Bank Governors would become the central organ of the banking system of a federal type. (EEC, 1962)

It would begin to resemble what was later sometimes called a 'Eurofed'. This passage might be thought of as prophetic, in that the latter part of this suggestion was followed fairly precisely in the 1990s; but there was a major difference in that, by the end of the twentieth century, central banks placed a very substantial premium on devising legal guarantees of their institutional and operational independence.

What was the linkage between European initiatives and global debates? Were they complementary, or rather alternatives? UK Prime Minister James Callaghan, a veteran of many British struggles with the IMF, put the problem in this way when he thought that an overall solution was preferable: 'I think there comes a clear question – do we try to build a world monetary system or are we going to have a European one?' By contrast, the President of the European Commission, Roy Jenkins, replying to Callaghan, stated: 'I think we might move to a substantially more coordinated European monetary position which could help to create a better world monetary position.'

One more issue overshadowed the monetary debate. There was always an ambiguity in the story of monetary integration: was it designed primarily to deal with a technical issue – alternatively formulated as exchange rate volatility as a barrier to trade and thus to greater economic integration, or else as a quest for price stability – or was it part of a grand political plan, in which money was used to tie the European knot? Sometimes the monetary path just seemed politically and bureaucratically less fraught than, say, the task of coordinating European defence, with the hosts of national defence contractors and lobbyists obstructing progress. In 1950, Jacques Rueff, France's major mid-century thinker about money, coined a phrase that was subsequently often erroneously linked to the great architect of European integration Jean Monnet: 'L'Europe se fera par la monnaie ou ne se fera pas' (Rueff, 1978). (Europe will make itself by money, or it won't make it.) In the 1960s, a theory of optimum currency areas was developed by US-based economists (Mundell, 1961; McKinnon, 1963; Kenen, 1969): Although they continued to be influential figures in the European debate, their theories were irrelevant to the final push to monetary integration in the 1990s (Bayoumi and Eichengreen, 1993). The states that signed up to economic union had different expectations and hopes: some saw it as a way of building credibility and thus of reducing borrowing costs, while others focused on the constitutionalization of a stable monetary regime. How could the divergent visions of the potential gains from monetary integration and central bank cooperation be mutually reconciled?

There are five major conventional traditions of thinking about the history of monetary union:

1. In the logic of functionalism, increasing interaction creates a logic of yet more interaction. This was the mechanism laid out by Haas (1964); it has recently been reiterated by legal scholars who see a 1956 report by the Belgian foreign minister, Paul-Henri Spaak, laying a blueprint for the EEC but noting that the creation of a common market only represented a partial economic integration, as containing a normative and causal logic towards increased integration (Teixeira, 2020).
2. In a constructivist approach, the monetary union represents the victory of a new set of ideas – Kathleen McNamara's (1998) 'currency of ideas'.
3. Analysts who focus on interstate relations show how the monetary union was an outcome of a bargaining process between states (Moravcsik, 1998), in which a German view of central bank independence triumphed over a French philosophy of economic governance, and laid the basis for increased German ascendancy in the economics and politics of the EU (Marsh, 2011).
4. The negotiations might reflect the outcome of 'multi-level games', where institutions develop an autonomy in which they seek their preservation and strengthening through cross-national partnerships – in practice this argument is a sophisticated explanation of the logic that drives (1).
5. The project was conceived for strategic reasons, as an answer to the dominance/hegemony of the US dollar. The wish was to create a new international currency, that would rival or supplant the dollar.

How far can these theories be tested against a historical account of the evolution of monetary union?

1. The first appears as a worthy aspiration, but in practice prima facie implausible, as there are plenty of periods of stagnation and reversal, when there seems to be more disintegration than integration. Like most historical processes, the story of monetary union is not a one-way street.
2. The constructivist account faces the difficulty that there were plenty of ambitious plans for monetary unification (including the Werner Plan and the Fourcade Plan: see Mourlon-Druol, 2012) or monetary coordination and management (the Snake, the European Monetary Cooperation Fund, usually known by its French initials as FECOM, for Fonds européen de coopération monétaire) that were never or only imperfectly and partially realized; and conversely it is clear that a substantial number of the participants in the Delors Committee, which in retrospect seems to have laid down the fundamentally decisive mechanism for integration, at the time believed that their activities were fundamentally futile. In this sense, the policy community of central bankers, strong as it was, was incapable of exercising influence by itself
3. An intergovernmental approach raises the painful question (that has been constantly raised in French domestic politics) of whether France did not get a very bad bargain and, if so, what led France to accept the German view of central bank independence at the time of the Delors Report, and then to see the Delors Report as the only acceptable or realistic road to monetary union.
4. The fourth approach is enticing, but has so many actors and variables that it cannot really presented as creating a roadmap of the integration process. It sees the central banks as the major actors, in that the Bundesbank initially resisted Hans-Dietrich Genscher's

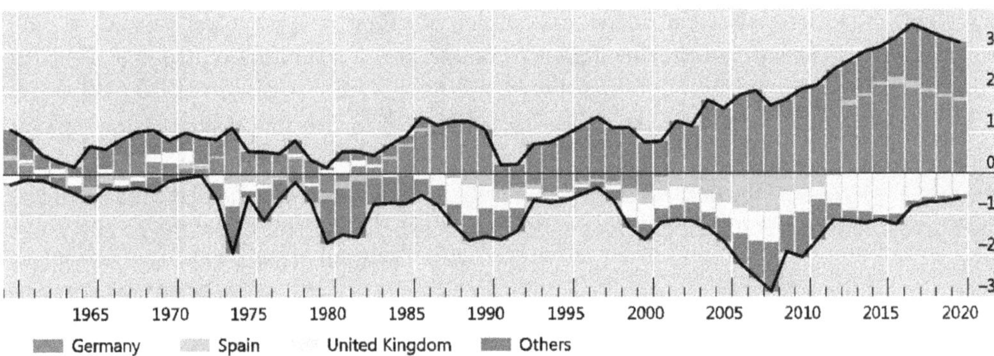

FIGURE 3.1. Current accounts in Europe, 1960–2020 (BIS data)

European plans and then used Europeanization to preserve its autonomy from the German government; while much more clearly Jacques de Larosière, Governor of the Banque de France at the time of the Delors Report, saw the mechanism as a way of providing for greater stability and reliability of French domestic policy. A few years later, however, the Bank of England obtained the same independence and autonomy (from the new Labour government in 1997) without needing the additional support of Europeanization. Did European central banks really need Europe to obtain operational independence?

5. The EU did surprisingly little after the 1990s to promote the euro as a rival to the dollar and seems to have been largely agnostic on the issue.

It is thus more helpful to focus on a sixth explanation, one which is surprisingly rare in the literature. The outbreak of the European debt crisis in 2010 called attention to what was actually a perennial issue: German current account surpluses (see Figure 3.1). In each phase of the negotiation about European monetary integration, Germany's partners tried to devise an institutional mechanism to control German surpluses. The debate went back a long way. For instance, the French economist Raymond Barre, then Vice-President of the European Commission, argued in 1968 that Germany should take 'energetic measures for speedier growth and the stimulation of imports' as well as 'special action to inhibit the flow of speculative capital into Germany' (Ungerer, 1997, p. 61).

In the Bretton Woods era of fixed exchange rates and controlled capital markets, even relatively small deficits could not be financed, and produced immediate pressure on the exchange markets. The deficit countries then had to apply fiscal brakes in a stop–go cycle. Germany's partners, notably France, were faced by the prospect of austerity and deflation in order to correct deficits. This alternative was unattractive to the French political elite, because it constrained growth and guaranteed electoral unpopularity. Their preferred policy alternative was thus German expansion, but this course was unpopular with a German public worried about the legacy of inflation and was opposed by the powerful and independent Bundesbank.

Solving the question of the German current account in the European setting at first appeared to require some sophisticated and ingenious political mechanism that would force French politicians to pursue more austerity than they would have liked, and Germans to pursue less price orthodoxy than they thought they needed. A political mechanism, however, requires continual negotiation and public deliberation, which would have been painful given the policy preferences in the two countries (and in those countries that lined up with either of the Big

Two). The increased attraction of monetary union was that it required no such drawn-out political process. The operation of an entirely automatic device would constrain political debate, initiative, and policy choice.

Monetary union was thus conceptualized as a way of simplifying or depoliticizing politics. This had been a feature of European arguments from the beginning: the German current account easily became the occasion of a blame game in which countries argued about who had the responsibility to adjust – the 'virtuous' creditor, where politicians presented the surplus as the outcome of good policy, or the 'spendthrift' debtor, which thought that it was the victim of a new mercantilism. Robert Triffin (1957, p. 289) had showed how a problem could be reduced to its most basic level: 'The significance of monetary unification, like that of exchange stability in a free market, is that both exclude any resort to any other corrective techniques except those of internal fiscal and credit policies.'

The problem of current accounts grew bigger, the surpluses and deficits ever larger. The monetary union occurred after a drive to capital market liberalization, and was intended to be the logical completion of that liberalization. Current account imbalances were apparently sustainable for much longer periods – though not forever. The effects of movements in capital in allowing current account imbalances to build up to a much greater extent, and ensuring that corrections, when they occurred, would be much more dramatic, was already noticeable in the late 1980s and early 1990s, before the move to monetary union. Indeed, those large build-ups in the imbalances were what convinced Europe's policymakers that a monetary union was the only way of avoiding the risk of periodic crises with currency realignments whose trade policy consequences threatened the survival of an integrated internal European market. The success of the early years of monetary union lies in the effective privatization of current account imbalances, as the imbalances could be easily financed by the private capital market until the outbreak of the European debt crisis of 2010; the issue thus disappeared for some time from the radar of policy debates. It would only reappear when the freezing up of the banking system after 2008 required the substitution of public sector claims for private claims: with that, the old problem of the politicization of current account imbalances immediately resurfaced.

The escalation of the German current account problem was also always linked to global debates about currency disorder. European monetary integration appeared urgent in the late 1960s, as the Bretton Woods regime disintegrated, again in the late 1970s, when US monetary policy was subject to big political pressures and the dollar collapsed, and finally – and with an apparently successful outcome – in the late 1980s, in the aftermath of a debate about global monetary stabilization at the Plaza and Louvre meetings of the major industrial countries.

3.3 THE DELORS INITIATIVE AND THE MAASTRICHT TREATY

When the dollar was soaring in the mid-1980s, when American manufacturing was threatened and when there appeared to be the possibility of a protectionist backlash, the finance ministers of the major industrial countries pushed for an exchange rate agreement. The G7 finance ministers' Louvre meeting in 1987 agreed to lock exchange rates into a system of target zones, i.e. a reference range (Funabashi, 1988).

In practice, nothing came of that global plan, but then Édouard Balladur, the French finance minister who had largely been responsible for the Louvre proposal, came up with a tighter European scheme. When the German foreign minister, Hans-Dietrich Genscher, appeared sympathetic, Europe's central bankers were asked by the President of the European Commission, Jacques Delors, to prepare a timetable and a plan for currency union. The

Delors Committee met between September 1988 and April 1989 at the Bank for International Settlements (BIS) in Basel, and produced its report at a moment when no one in Western Europe seriously thought that a profound geopolitical transformation such as the collapse of the Soviet bloc and of communist ideology could be at all likely (the fall of the Berlin Wall in November 1989 was a surprise to almost everyone, and certainly to the European governments). Gunter Baer, a BIS official, as rapporteur drew up the report; the second rapporteur, Tommaso Padoa-Schioppa, had been a past Director-General of Monetary Affairs in the Commission, was Vice-Director General of the Bank of Italy from 1984 to 1997 and a regular presence in Basel, and was a key intellectual influence on Delors's thinking about the consequences of capital liberalization and the need for a new institutional framework. These two men brought the world view of the BIS into the work of the Delors Committee.

A comparison of the integration discussions of the 1970s and 1980s is instructive. The negotiations to create the European Monetary System (EMS) and its associated Exchange Rate Mechanism (ERM) were largely governmental: though Roy Jenkins saw this as his initiative as Commission President, the actual success depended on the high-level cooperation of Helmut Schmidt and Valéry Giscard d'Estaing. This is the conventional picture and there is no reason to think it is wrong. By contrast, when Jenkins's successor Jacques Delors wanted to initiate a monetary discussion, he very deliberately started the process through an intense cultivation of the central bankers, largely through their regular meetings at the Committee of Central Bank Governors in Basel.

The positive outcome of the Delors Committee was a surprise in that the most powerful central banker in the Committee, Bundesbank President Karl Otto Pöhl, was generally believed to be opposed to any project for enhanced monetary cooperation, and the Eurosceptic UK government tried to keep the British member of the Committee working with Pöhl in order to frustrate such cooperation. Since the report required unanimity in order to be convincing or effective, it thus seemed more or less certain at the outset that the project would not lead to the visionary result intended by Jacques Delors. Some of the success of the Delors Report – or at least its ability to formulate any final report – arose out of the character of Pöhl.

The Delors Report clearly laid out the path to monetary union, defined as 'a currency area in which policies are managed jointly with a view to attaining common macroeconomic objectives'. But the Committee also added the rider:

> The adoption of a single currency, while not strictly necessary for the creation of a monetary union, might be seen for economic as well as psychological and political reasons as a natural and desirable further development of the monetary union. A single currency would clearly demonstrate the irreversibility of the move to monetary union, considerably facilitate the monetary management of the Community and avoid the transactions costs of converting currencies.

It provided for a three-stage process, in which the first stage simply expanded existing cooperative arrangements to which even the Eurosceptic government of Margaret Thatcher could have no objection.

In the second stage, a new European System of Central Banks (ESCB) would manage the transition from the combination of monetary policies of national central banks to a common monetary policy. In the third stage, exchange rates would be locked finally and irrevocably. The ESCB would pool reserves and manage interventions with regard to third currencies. 'With the establishment of the European System of Central Banks the Community would also have created an institution through which it could participate in all aspects of international monetary coordination' (Section 38 of the Delors Report). Delors emphasized that the monetary integration would need to be accompanied by a consolidation of the single market and competition policy, as well as by an evaluation and adaptation of regional policies (Section 56).

The central banks continued to play the dominant role in designing the new institutions. It is not surprising that they opted for a strong form of central bank independence, with a primary mandate for the new European central bank in the maintenance of price stability. The process reflected the outcome of a tussle between southern Europeans, who wanted to control German monetary policy, and Germans, who wanted to make European monetary policy in line with a German vision of *Ordnungspolitik* (Brunnermeier et al., 2016). The BIS commented in its 1992 Annual Report that 'to concede that the EMS has been an effective anti-inflationary instrument while seeking ways of softening its constraints may seem somewhat paradoxical' (BIS, 1992, p. 124).

The design of the Maastricht Treaty, which enshrined the conclusions of the Delors Report in the political decision to move towards EMU, eventually clearly reflected German preferences for limits on government fiscal activism. One of its provisions (now Article 123 TFEU) prohibited overdraft facilities from the central bank to governments (monetary financing). Another (now Article 124 TFEU) prohibited privileged access to financial institutions; and the 'no bailout' clause (Article 125 TFEU) stated that: 'The Community shall not be liable for or assume the commitments of central governments, regional, local or other public authorities, other bodies governed by public law, or public undertakings of any Member State, without prejudice to mutual financial guarantees for the joint execution of a specific project.' In practice, however, a consensus soon developed that government bonds would not be subject to a risk of default, and thus were not treated by financial markets as the equivalent of corporate bonds (Prati and Schinasi, 1997).

The German character of monetary union became clearer in the aftermath of Maastricht and of the major currency crises that shook the EMS in 1992–1993 and almost destroyed the integration project. The EMS was only rescued at the last moment in July 1993, with the suggestion by the UK Chancellor of the Exchequer Kenneth Clarke of moving to much wider exchange rate bands. The crises of 1992–1993 highlighted the centrality of the German position, as the Bundesbank suspended interventions in the French franc, and other currencies, on the argument that the extensive use of the Deutschmark for intervention would threaten German domestic monetary stability (at this moment the 1978 Emminger letter was used as the shield for Bundesbank actions).

The ERM experience was a game-changer in thinking about monetary policy and exchange rates. Before the speculative attacks on the lira, the pound, the peseta, and the escudo in September 1992, the way economists thought about currency crises was largely in terms of responses to bad and unsustainable fiscal policies. The responses of markets had been modelled by Paul Krugman in what was later termed the 'first-generation' currency crisis models (Krugman, 1979). The 'second generation' came when expectations about self-sustaining attacks were built in, most prominently in the model developed by Maurice Obstfeld. Such expectations could be applied very effectively to the European crisis. Willem Buiter, Giancarlo Corsetti, and Paolo Pesenti explained the origins in terms of a 'disinflation game', with a centre (Germany) committed to stable prices and a periphery where markets had diverging expectations about the extent and political tolerability of the output cost that would be involved in keeping inflation down and the exchange rate stable (Buiter et al., 1998; Obstfeld, 1994, 1996; Jeanne, 2000). To economic historians, that interpretation looked very like the traumatic 1931 crisis, when rumours of a naval mutiny at the Scottish base of Invergordon triggered a run on the pound, with the Bank of England being unable to stage a defence with higher interest rates, as that would make the pain of austerity worse. There existed multiple equilibria: markets would believe in the permanence of one exchange rate fix until a momentum developed to push to a different equilibrium. The crisis could thus be entirely explained in terms of the calculations of a George Soros. By the time of the 1997–1998 Asian crisis, where a similar pattern of radically revised exchange rate expectations drove a domino effect of one country after another collapsing, the 'second-generation' interpretation became canonical, and Asian leaders demonized Soros. Putting theory and history together led to the inescapable conclusion that the intermediate solution of a fixed and adjustable peg was unsustainable, and that, in consequence, there were only two realistic and stable options (corner solutions), namely either a publicly announced, credible, and time-consistent monetary policy, or monetary unification with only one central bank for a large currency area. By the late 1990s, it was easy to see that the United Kingdom was going on the first route and continental Europe on the second (Eichengreen, 2000). After 2016, that choice began to be referred to as an earlier version of Brexit (as was 1931, and perhaps also the 1533 legislation of the Henrician Reformation, when the Act in Restraint of Appeals rejected any jurisdiction outside England). The Asian crisis had seemed to demonstrate to both Europeans and UK policymakers that their decision was the correct or economically literate choice.

The implementation of EMU in fact occurred along German lines. Frankfurt was chosen as the location of the European Monetary Institute (EMI, the predecessor institution that would prepare the work of the ECB) in October 1993, and the name 'euro' was agreed in 1995 (as 'ECU' was thought to sound too French). Lamfalussy moved from his position at the BIS to become the first head of the EMI. At the same time, the German finance minister, Theo Waigel, pushed for a Stability Pact that would enforce the Maastricht deficit and debt levels. It became clear that convergence would not be complete by 1997, the first possible date under the Maastricht Treaty for the final stage of monetary union; but then attention focused on making the alternative date (1 January 1999) a reality, with the physical introduction of a new currency coming some years later (2002). In practice, although the old physical notes continued to circulate after 1999, the Deutschmark, francs, etc., were already then legally only units of a completely new currency.

3.4 PLANNING FOR MONETARY UNION: FISCAL FLAWS

The planning for monetary union was at the same time sober and meticulous, but also involved two potentially devastating flaws. In the debates of the central bankers' group that Delors chaired in 1988–1989, before the fall of the Berlin Wall, two really critical issues were highlighted – and they were the ones that really mattered. Neither was adequately resolved in the 1990s, and the monetary union was thus left incomplete.

The first concerned the fiscal discipline needed for currency union. An explicit discussion took place as to whether the capital market by itself was enough to discipline borrowers, and a consensus emerged that market discipline would not be adequate and that a system of rules was needed. The influential Belgian economist and BIS General Manager Lamfalussy, a member of the Delors Committee, brought up cases from the United States and Canada as well as from Europe, where cities and regions were insufficiently disciplined. Lamfalussy drew out the debate about whether market forces were to ensure fiscal convergence. The minutes of the December 1988 meeting of the Delors Committee record his suggestion that 'the idea, not shared by him, that market discipline was sufficient to bring about fiscal convergence should be considered in the report'.[2] Bundesbank President Karl Otto Pöhl said that 'the report should be clear in stating that [monetary union] required a substantial increase in the resources devoted to transfers'.

Lamfalussy went on to develop his proposal for an alternative to market discipline into a suggestion for the creation of a centre for fiscal policy coordination, which would allow Europe to make a significant contribution to global financial stability. In a memorandum written for the Delors Committee in response to a paper by Claudio Borio of the BIS on the fiscal arrangements of federal states, Lamfalussy noted:

> With widely divergent 'propensities to run deficits' prevailing in the various European countries, I doubt whether we could count in the foreseeable future on a convergence within a European EMU similar to that observed in most contemporary federal systems. Nor do I believe that it would be wise to rely principally on the free functioning of financial markets to iron out the differences in fiscal behaviour between member countries: (a) the interest premium to be paid by a high-deficit member country would be unlikely to be very large, since market participants would tend to act on the assumption that the EMU solidarity would prevent the 'bankruptcy' of the deficit country; and (b) to the extent that there was a premium, I doubt whether it would be large enough to reduce significantly the deficit country's propensity to borrow. There is therefore a serious risk that, in the absence of constraining policy coordination, major differences in fiscal behaviour would persist within a European EMU. This would be one contrast between most contemporary federal systems and a European EMU. ... Such a situation would appear even less tolerable once the EMU was regarded as part and parcel of the world economy, with a clear obligation to cooperate with the United States and Japan in an attempt to preserve (or restore) an acceptable pattern of external balances and to achieve exchange rate stabilization. To have the smallest chance of reaching these objectives, all cooperating partners need flexibility in the fiscal/monetary policy mix – as we have so often told the United States. In short, it would seem to me very strange if we did not insist on the need to make appropriate arrangements that would allow the gradual emergence, and the full operation once the EMU is completed, of a Community-wide macroeconomic fiscal policy that would be the natural complement to the common monetary policy of the Community.[3]

This clear statement that a monetary union also requires some measure of fiscal union seems apposite and intellectually compelling – and has indeed been borne out in the difficulties encountered in the eurozone in 2009 and since.

During the meetings of the Committee, Jacques Delors appropriately raised the prospect of a two- (or even multi-)speed Europe, in which one or two countries might need a 'different kind of marriage contract' (James, 2012, p. 243). There is a tendency for fiscal policy to be procyclical, particularly when the cycles are driven by property booms, in that enhanced fiscal revenue from real estate exuberance prompts politicians to think that the increase in their resources is permanent. But the procyclical fiscal element may be magnified in a currency union.

The need for fiscal discipline arising from spillover effects of large borrowing requirements is a European issue, but it is clearly not one confined to Europe alone. In emerging markets, this problem was identified after the 1997–1998 Asian crisis, and the problem of major fiscal strains became primarily one of the industrial world – and especially of the United States. An appropriate response would involve some democratically legitimated mechanism for limiting the debt build-up, as in the Swiss debt brake limiting expenditure to the level of structural, or cyclically adjusted, receipts (*Schuldenbremse*) which was supported by 85 per cent of voters in a referendum (2001).

[2] Committee of Governors archive at ECB, fourth meeting of Delors Committee, 13 December 1998 minutes.

[3] Committee of Governors archive at ECB, 31 January 1989, Alexander Lamfalussy note.

The debt and deficit criteria built into the Maastricht Treaty in fact proved to be at the centre of most of the debate in the 1990s. Germany insisted again and again on a strict interpretation of the Treaty: finance minister Theo Waigel repeated that 3.0 meant 3.0 with an insistence that led the French press to dub him 'Monsieur 3.0'. But in practice, some bending of the rules took place. First was the problem of Belgium, with a debt level that looked sustainable but exceeded 60 per cent of GDP (it was 130 per cent in 1997); but Belgium was in a currency union with Luxembourg, which qualified unambiguously, and Brussels was also the seat of the vital European institutions. Then, since Italy's debt level, at 120 per cent of GDP, was lower than that of Belgium, it was hard to exclude Italy. From the point of view of the high-debt countries, such as Italy, the great political attraction of membership in the currency union was the added credibility that would reduce interest rates, and thus bring an immediate fiscal saving. The downside was a loss of exchange rate flexibility, but many Italian policymakers and businessmen recognized that the cycles of inflation and devaluation that had characterized the 1970s and 1980s did nothing to increase productivity or output growth.

The original concept of a stability pact to perpetuate the eligibility criteria after the final stage of monetary union was cosmetically watered down to take account of French concerns about growth as a Stability and Growth Pact (SGP). A fatal blow came when France and Germany ignored the SGP and had it suspended in November 2003 as a counter to a – as it proved, spurious – threat of recession. In 2005 and 2011, the Pact was considerably reworked, and in the process became more complex and less transparent; in hindsight, it also did too little to push fiscal consolidation in a boom phase, and made the subsequent crisis years consequently harder and more painful.

3.5 FINANCIAL FLAWS

The second flaw in the European plans identified by the central bankers as they prepared monetary union was much more serious. In the original version of a plan for a central bank that would run a monetary union, the central bank would have overall supervisory and regulatory powers. That demand met strong resistance, above all from the Bundesbank, which worried that a role in maintaining financial stability might undermine the future central bank's ability to focus on price stability as the primary goal of monetary policy. There was also bureaucratic resistance to a European solution from the existing national regulators.

Just before the establishment of the Delors Committee, a subcommittee of the Committee of Governors of the Central Banks in the EEC (CoG) was established to deal with bank supervision. This new body was chaired by Brian Quinn, the chief banking supervisor for the Bank of England. The initiative had come from Huib Muller of the Netherlands Bank, who was also chair of the Basel Committee on Banking Supervision, and Tommaso Padio-Schioppa, the chair of the Banking Advisory Committee to the EC Commission (and who would later succeed Muller as chair of the Basel Committee). They argued that there was a satisfactory framework for drawing up legislative proposals on banking supervision in the Community, but no adequate way of drawing up policies on prudential supervision. Muller's memorandum specifically identified the novel policy problem posed by the development of transnational banking groups with ownership located in more than one EC member country.

In the CoG, Wim Duisenberg, the Dutch central banker who would eventually become the first President of the ECB, forcefully stated the view that banking supervision needed to occur at the European level. Such a move would deal with a very powerful objection to global attempts by the Basel Committee to develop what became the 'Core Principles of Banking Supervision':

Quinn, who was also a veteran member of the Basel Committee, repeatedly worried that global rules produced by a committee of central bankers might lack 'democratic legitimacy' (Goodhart, 2011, p. 551). Might Europe be a more viable umbrella for banking supervision? There was, however, considerable opposition to the CoG's developing a major competence for Europe in this field. The president of the German Credit Supervisory Office (Bundesaufsichtsamt für das Kreditwesen) wrote to Pöhl in early 1989 protesting at attempts to Europeanize banking supervision, which he saw as parallel to the initiatives of the G10 and the Basel Committee on Banking Supervision as potentially reducing the competitiveness of German banking. At the same time, Hans Tietmeyer (who was still at the finance ministry but would join the Bundesbank in 1990) argued that banking supervision was a responsibility of finance ministers, and not of central banks, and that the German ministry should be represented in CoG discussions of this issue. Pöhl tried to respond to these domestic German critiques by pointing out that any decision would need to be taken by governments and parliaments, and that such a moment of choice lay in the distant future. There was similar opposition from France's Banking Commission, which urged the Governor of the Bank of France to exercise 'vigilance' because Brian Quinn was believed to favour the transfer of supervisory and regulatory authority to the ECB.

In February 1990, at the EC Monetary Committee meeting in Brussels, there was complete agreement that the different national rules regarding bank regulation should be left in place. Delors was unwilling to force the pace on this issue and stated that the EC Commission approached the issue of banking supervision with an 'open mind': the ESCB should simply 'participate in the coordination of national policies but would not have a monopoly on those policies'.

On 29 June 1990, in the CoG alternates' meeting, Andrew Crockett of the Bank of England proposed that 'a further objective of the ESCB will be to preserve the integrity of the financial system'. Tietmeyer objected that this outcome should be considered a 'task' rather than an 'objective'. At the governors' meeting to discuss such a goal, the wording was softened, mostly in response to the German position. It was agreed that 'any suggestion that the system should undertake rescue operations in favour of individual banks should be avoided', though there might be a need to deal with (rather vaguely defined) 'sudden developments' in financial markets. The wording changed, so that 'preserve' became 'support', and 'integrity' became 'stability'. That phrasing seemed to preclude any responsibility to act as a classical central bank lender of last resort. In the end, the 'tasks' of Article 3 of the draft ECB Statute were watered down to the much less far-reaching and ambitious goal 'to promote the smooth operation of the payment system'.

In October 1990, when the alternates discussed the CoG's Banking Supervision Subcommittee proposals on draft articles for the central bank statute, Tietmeyer restated the sceptical position of the Bundesbank, which was consistently worried about the moral-hazard implications of central bank involvement in supervision. If the central bank took on the responsibility of regulating, it would also deliver an implicit commitment to rescue banks should there be bad developments that it had overlooked. Tietmeyer provided a neat encapsulation of the German philosophy of regulation: 'This did not mean from the view of the Board of the Deutsche Bundesbank that the ECB should not support the stability of the financial system, but that it should never be written down; this would be moral hazard.' The Luxembourg non-paper of 10 May 1991 spoke instead of the central bank participating in 'the coordination and execution of policies relating to the prudential control and stability of the financial system'.

In June 1991, the Intergovernmental Conference seemed to exclude any financial sector supervisory role of the ESCB and the ECB, contrary to the governors' draft statute. There was only a last-hope get-out clause, as a Spanish commentary on the ECB Statute now noted:

> The relevant provisions were introduced into the Statute with three considerations in mind: first, the System, even though operating strictly at the macroeconomic level, will have a broad oversight of developments in financial markets and institutions and therefore should possess a detailed working knowledge which would be of value to the exercise of supervisory functions. Secondly, there is a legitimate interest on the part of the system in the maintenance of sound and stable financial markets. Thirdly, legislative changes in regulatory provisions may have important technical consequences for the conduct of monetary policy. . . . However, the Statute recognizes the evolutionary character of financial markets and the concurrent need to adapt prudential supervision. For this reason Article 25.2 of the ECB Statute offers the possibility of designating the ECB as a competent supervisory authority, for example, if it were necessary and desirable to formulate and implement a Community-wide supervisory policy for pan-EC financial conglomerates. Such a task could be undertaken by the ECB only if it were designated as the competent supervisory authority through secondary Community legislation.

There was an opportunity to discuss a concrete example of the problem in September 1991, after the collapse of the Bank of Credit and Commerce International (BCCI) (Goodhart, 2011, pp. 392–95). Before that, bank failures and their consequences looked like such a remote possibility that the highly sensitive issues involved had not really been discussed since the 1974 Herstatt case, when the failure of a small German bank had raised the problem of international counterparty risk. Director of the Luxembourg Monetary Institute, Pierre Jaans, explained that the BCCI was legally based in Luxembourg and the Cayman Islands, but had extensive operations in London, the Middle East, the Far East, and Africa. As a result, the BCCI banking group could not be fitted into the philosophy of supervision on a consolidated basis that had been developed since the 1970s. The Bank of England Governor Robert ('Robin') Leigh-Pemberton asked whether a repetition of such a collapse was possible. It clearly was, although the systemic issues involved in large-scale banking crises only really became apparent in 2007–2008. For the moment, the BCCI looked idiosyncratically unique and banking in general reassuringly solid. Moreover, the BCCI affair also contributed to the erosion of any impetus to include a broader mandate for securing financial stability, because it brought considerable criticism of Brian Quinn, the Bank of England Director who had taken over Huib Muller's international role of pushing for more international coordination of banking supervision and regulation. Thus, far from strengthening the case for a sustained and coordinated European approach to the issues of a newly vigorous international banking system, the BCCI collapse actually weakened the demand for action.

Thus, the governors' draft referred to the possibility that the ECB would take over banking supervision and regulation functions, but, by the time this proposal was included in the Maastricht Treaty provisions on monetary policy, it was accompanied by so many provisos that it looked as if the hurdles to effective European banking supervision could not be set higher (Kenen, 1995, p. 33). The intrusion of politics had therefore resulted in a fundamental flaw in the new European monetary order.

The ECB was thus never given overall supervisory and regulatory powers, and until the outbreak of the financial crisis in 2007–2008 almost no one in positions of responsibility thought that was a problem. The critique remained largely academic; academic critics worried about the design of the European monetary order. The problems of European banking in the aftermath of the subprime crisis indicate that this was the major institutional flaw of Europe's monetary arrangements.

In the past, financial sector shocks have played a decisive role in the undermining of monetary regimes and the discrediting of the central banks responsible for their operation. The most dramatic of such episodes occurred in the interwar Great Depression, where banking panics in central Europe and the United States exacerbated the problems of the real economy. Unstable banks withdrew credits from borrowers, forcing firms that would otherwise have been solvent to liquidate stock at depressed prices. The major industrial countries that had significant banking problems fared significantly worse than those economies with no or only limited banking collapses. In particular the United States, with waves of banking panics after autumn 1930, and Germany, with a meltdown of the banking system in June and July 1931, were badly hit by the real consequences of the financial storm; these experiences have very obvious current echoes (that were not at all obvious even a few years ago).

The weakness of the American and German banks in the interwar era was at least in some measure the consequence of political federalism. Federalism:

1. encouraged the development of a banking system that was regional in character. In particular in the United States, state banks suffered because their risk was concentrated in particular sectors;
2. made for inefficiencies in regulating banks. In Germany, a major source of difficulty was the parallel system of Savings Banks (*Sparkassen*), which were controlled by local authorities, and which responded to local political pressures to lend;
3. produced a dispute about the appropriate monetary response of the central banking institutions. This may be an especially acute problem in the early life of the federation or the central bank. With regard to the United States, Eichengreen (1991) and Wheelock (1999) showed how the Federal Reserve found it difficult to resolve regional conflicts in the early 1920s. Friedman and Schwartz (1963) famously presented the major cause of the immobilization of the Federal Reserve System after 1930 as laying in tensions between the New York and Chicago banks.

Europe in the 1990s and 2000s was becoming a partly integrated capital market with national bank regulators that responded in different ways to incipient problems. There were still in some countries substantial and largely unwritten barriers to cross-national financial ownership. Nevertheless, financial institutions operated in this single capital market across national boundaries. Big mergers, such as those between Santander and Abbey National in 2004 and UniCredit and Hypovereinsbank (which had previously acquired a dominant share in the Austrian banking industry) in 2005, started to create Europe-wide superbanks.

The problem of a bank getting into difficulties because of engagements in a different country was widely recognized as a problem in theoretical or academic discussions (for instance, Prati and Schinasi, 1997). But a unification of banking regulation was unrealized until the financial crisis of 2008 and especially the debt crisis of 2010. Thus, at the same time as finance became internationalized and globalized from the 1990s, each country preserved its own idiosyncratic system of financial supervision and regulation. One obstacle is that regulation is inherently linked to implicit or explicit lender-of-last-resort functions, and thus to fiscal costs. When problems affected banks operating in several countries in the first stage of the Global Financial Crisis, they were simply handled bilaterally: by Belgium and the Netherlands in the case of Fortis, by Italy and Austria in the case of UniCredit.

Much of the earlier literature concentrated in consequence on the issue of how bailouts and rescues should be paid for after a financial crisis, as a consequence of the reluctance of national authorities (and their taxpayers) to bear the financial burden of bailing out depositors or creditors in other states (Goodhart and Schoenmaker, 2006). By 2010 and 2011, it had become clear that banks were a crucial part of the European story, since they were enmeshed in national doom loops: banks were unstable because of their holdings of government debt that might be subject to default; yet they would require recapitalization by governments, which would add to the fiscal strain. But the realization of the need for a banking union was slow in coming, as for some time at least in 2010 the problem was thought of as idiosyncratically Greek. It resulted from the prospect of large potential Spanish and Italian banking problems in 2012 that could not be dealt with through the type of rescue packages worked out with the IMF for smaller countries, Greece, Portugal, or Ireland.

The impulse came from Spain. In November 2011, a parliamentary election brought a staggering defeat for the socialist government of José Luis Rodríguez Zapatero. The centre-right People's Party under Mariano Rajoy formed the new government; during the first months of 2012, it seemed increasingly paralysed by the scale of the financial crisis. In particular, the winding up of insolvent banks was a politically intractable problem. It was also at the centre of a dispute between the new government and the Bank of Spain, which had been widely considered, both in Spain and internationally, a highly effective supervisor. Governor of the Bank of Spain, Miguel Ángel Fernández Ordóñez, hoped that economic recovery and higher growth might solve the problem, which was in any case restricted to a small number of institutions. In contrast, the new government saw an opportunity to clean up and avoid the long-term problem of bank zombification – which seemed to be the story of Japan since the 1990s and threatened to be the European story of the twenty-first century. At the beginning of December 2011, one incident highlighted Spain's vulnerability: all the potential bidders for the savings bank CAM dropped out, and the national deposit guarantee fund *Fondo de reestructuración ordenada bancaria* had to inject €5.25 billion in new capital and then sell the bank to the mid-sized Catalan bank Sabadell for €1, guaranteeing any losses up to 80 per cent for ten years. The incident was so significant because it coincided with a Europe-wide surge of spreads in the aftermath of the Cannes summit, the installation of technocratic governments in Greece and Italy, and the general belief of financial markets that Europe was on the brink of the precipice.

Spain's woes became instrumental in pushing Europe – and notably the key decision-makers in Berlin – to accept some broad-based reform scheme for banking, which became a key element in defusing the acute phase of the debt crisis in the summer of 2012. The European programme for Spain involved €100 billion in assistance from the EFSF. It focused on banking reform and recapitalization.

At the peak of the euro sovereign debt crisis, in a 25 June 2012 meeting in Brussels with Commission President José Manuel Barroso and European Council President Herman van Rompuy, ECB President Mario Draghi told the European leaders that they would be asked to guarantee emergency loans to commercial banks: without that support, the ECB would be unable to continue to provide liquidity. The ECB then started to contemplate a dramatic series of interventions that would reshape the eurozone, creating not only new institutions such as a banking union, which was implicit but not explicit in the 25 June agreement, but also new intervention procedures. On 30 June 2012, a Euro Summit announced the creation of what would become the first pillar of the Banking Union, the Single Supervisory Mechanism (SSM).

As a supervisory system, the Banking Union represented a unified system of law on the basis of a 'single rulebook', legislated and defined at the European level. But the application and enforcement of this rulebook, in the form of banking supervision and resolution, is a complex process: it is under the exclusive competence of European authorities, whose acts are subject to the judicial review of the European Court of Justice. But they are formally accountable to the European Parliament and the Council, and at the same time report to national parliaments (Teixeira, 2020). Is this a move to 'statiness' or the creation of a European sovereign, and to what extent is the accountability sufficient to establish democratic legitimacy and political credibility?

In 2014, and very cautiously and incrementally, the second pillar of the banking union, a common resolution mechanism, was established (Directive 2014/59/EU of 15 May 2014): resources for resolution would gradually built up by national authorities so that by the end of 2024 they would reach at least 1 per cent of the amount of covered deposits of all the institutions authorized in their territory. The Directive explained that: 'The inability of Member States to seize control of a failing institution and resolve it in a way that effectively prevents broader systemic damage can undermine Member States' mutual trust and the credibility of the internal market in the field of financial services.' But it contained an inherent vulnerability, in addition to the long transition phase to the end of 2024. In the case of resolution, 8 per cent of a bank's balance sheet would be 'bailed in', or subject to a 'haircut'. However, there were substantial protections for private customers and small and medium enterprises, so that it was in practice interbank deposits that would be subject to the bail-in; and the experience of 2007–8 showed that it was the interbank market that was more subject to runs than private depositors, who would likely keep their funds in longer (see Dewatripont et al., 2021).

A harmonized deposit guarantee scheme would logically form a third pillar of banking union, but in practice made little progress, because it raised most directly the issue of fiscal transfers from one country to another.

The reason that there were no serious Europe-wide banking problems after 2012 has more to do with the ECB's monetary policy, and the loose liquidity conditions created by successive waves of asset purchase programmes. The decisions on banking union were followed on 26 July 2012 by Mario Draghi's London speech in which he promised to 'do whatever it takes' to preserve the euro. That was monetary action, and a promise of (theoretically infinite) continuing monetary action. The difficulty of an effective Europe-wide response to financial sector problems began to be interpreted as an aspect of a more general problem with respect to the making of monetary policy: there may be a different political economy of money in regions of the eurozone and EU member countries, leading to contradictory pressures on policy. Monetary policy became a way of rescuing banks and defusing the problem of an inadequate financial regulatory and insurance framework.

The logic of European monetary integration did not provide an easy way of fixing flaws. An often-quoted aphorism from Jean Monnet suggested that crises would automatically produce new solutions. But crises, especially when they require fiscal commitments, produce blame games: it is tempting to try to identify villains whose behaviour must be curbed, and punished. The European debt crisis was thus replete with dangerous escalations, and games of chicken. Only, perhaps, when a crisis comes completely from the outside – as with the COVID-19 pandemic, or perhaps from climate change – is it possible to think of productive rather than retributive responses. From 2020, Europe's response to crisis was productive in ways that the reaction to the debt crisis after 2010 was not: both in terms of new coordinated fiscal action, and also in finding a path to a common debt asset which opens the way to a European safe asset that can be the stable foundation of an integrated European financial order. Major problems regarding the servicing of the common debt – which would require a new fiscal source of revenue – remained unsolved.

REFERENCES

Bayoumi, T., and Eichengreen, B. (1993). Shocking aspects of European monetary unification. In F. Torres and F. Giavazzi (eds.), *Adjustment and Growth in the European Monetary Union*. Cambridge: Cambridge University Press.

Bank for International Settlements (1992). *62nd Annual Report*.

Bordo, M. D., and Jonung, L. (2003). The future of EMU: What does the history of monetary unions tell us? In F. H. Capie and G. E. Wood (eds.), *Monetary Unions: Theory, History, Public Choice*. London: Routledge, pp. 42–69.

Brunnermeier, M., James, H., and Landau, J.-P. (2016). *The Euro and the Battle of Ideas*. Princeton, NJ: Princeton University Press.

Buiter, W., Corsetti, G., and Pesenti, P. (1998). *Interpreting the ERM crisis: Country-specific and systemic issues*. Princeton Studies in International Economics, International Economics Section, Department of Economics Princeton University.

De Grauwe, P. (2013). Design failures in the eurozone: Can they be fixed? LEQS Paper No. 57/2013. http://eprints.lse.ac.uk/53191/1/LEQSPaper57.pdf

Dewatripont, M., Reichlin, L., and Sapir, A. (2021). Urgent reform of the EU resolution framework is needed. VoxEU, 16 April, https://voxeu.org/article/urgent-reform-eu-resolution-framework-needed

Draghi, M. (2012). Remarks at 'A European Strategy for Growth and Integration with Solidarity', conference organized by the Directorate General of the Treasury, Ministry of Economy and Finance – Ministry for Foreign Trade, Paris, 30 November.

Eichengreen, B. (1991). Designing a central bank for Europe: A cautionary tale from the early years of the Federal Reserve System. NBER Working Papers 3840, National Bureau of Economic Research.

Eichengreen, B. (2000). The EMS crisis in retrospect. NBER Working Paper No. 8035.

European Economic Community (1962). Action programme for the second phase of EEC. 24 October.

Friedman, M., and Schwartz, A. J. (1963). *A Monetary History of the United States 1867–1960*. Princeton, NJ: Princeton University Press.

Funabashi, Y. (1988). *Managing the Dollar: From the Plaza to the Louvre*. Washington, DC: Institute for International Economics.

Goodhart, C. (2011). *The Basel Committee on Banking Supervision: A History of the Early Years, 1974–1997*. Cambridge: Cambridge University Press.

Goodhart, C., and Schoenmaker, D. (2006). Burden sharing in a banking crisis in Europe. *Sveriges Riksbank Economic Review* No. 2, 34–57.

Haas, E. B. (1964). *Beyond the Nation State*. Stanford, CA: Stanford University Press.

Holtrop, M. W. (1957). Is a common central bank policy necessary within a united Europe? *De Economist* 105, 642–661.

Honohan, P. (2012). A view from Ireland: The crisis and the euro. Address to the David Hume Institute and the Scottish Institute for Research in Economics, Edinburgh, 13 November.

James, H. (2012). *Making the European Monetary Union*. Cambridge, MA: Harvard University Press.

Jeanne, O. (2000). Currency crises: A perspective on recent theoretical developments. *Special Papers in International Economics* No. 20, International Finance Section, Princeton University.

Kenen, P. B. (1969). The theory of optimum currency areas: An eclectic view. In R. A. Mundell and A. K. Swoboda (eds.), *Monetary Problems in the International Economy*. Chicago, IL: University of Chicago Press, pp. 41–60.

Kenen, P. B. (1995). *Economic and Monetary Union in Europe: Moving beyond Maastricht*. Cambridge: Cambridge University Press.

Krugman, P. (1979). A model of balance of payments crises. *Journal of Money, Credit and Banking* 11, 311–325.

Marsh, D. (2011). *The Euro: The Battle for the New Global Currency*. New Haven, CT: Yale University Press.

McKinnon, R. I. (1963). Optimum currency areas. *American Economic Review* 53(4), 717–724.

McNamara, K. R. (1998). *The Currency of Ideas: Monetary Politics in the European Union*. Ithaca, NY: Cornell University Press.

Moravcsik, A. (1998). *The Choice for Europe: Social Purpose and State Power from Messina to Maastricht*. Ithaca, NY: Cornell University Press.

Mourlon-Druol, E. (2012). *A Europe Made of Money: The Emergence of the European Monetary System*. Ithaca, NY: Cornell University Press.

Mundell, R. A. (1961). A theory of optimum currency areas. *American Economic Review* 51(4), 657–665.

Obstfeld, M. (1994). The logic of currency crises. *Cahiers Economiques et Monétaires* 43, 189–213.

Obstfeld, M. (1996). Models of currency crises with self-fulfilling features. *European Economic Review* 40, 1037–1047.

Prati, A., and Schinasi, G. J. (1997). European Monetary Union and international capital markets: Structural implications and risks. IMF Working Paper No. 97/62.

Rueff, J. (1978). L'Europe se fera par la monnaie ou ne se fera pas. *Commentaire* 1978(3), 386–388.

Teixeira, P. G. (2020). *The Legal History of the European Banking Union: How European Law Led to the Supranational Integration of the Single Financial Market*. Oxford: Hart/Bloomsbury.

Trichet, J.-C. (2011). Building Europe, building institutions. Speech on receiving the Karlspreis 2011 in Aachen, 2 June.

Triffin, R. (1957). *Europe and the Money Muddle*. New Haven, CT: Yale University Press.

Ungerer, H. (1997). *A Concise History of European Monetary Integration: From EPU to EMU*. Westport, CT: Quorum.

Vanthoor, W. F. V. (1991). Een oog op Holtrop: Grondlegger van de Nederlanse monetaire analyse. PhD diss., Amsterdam University.

Wheelock, D. (1999). National monetary policy by regional design: The evolving role of the Federal Reserve banks in Federal Reserve System policy. No. 1998-010, Working Papers, Federal Reserve Bank of St. Louis.

4

On the Misalignment of Monetary, Economic, and Political Integration in European Economic and Monetary Union

Fabian Amtenbrink

4.1 INTRODUCTION

This contribution argues that Economic and Monetary Union (EMU) is characterized by a misalignment of the level of legal, economic, and political integration that is primarily rooted in the asymmetric integration of monetary and economic policy in EMU but can also to some extent be explained by the basic approach to European integration more generally. This is why some of the challenges monetary and economic policy (coordination) face in the euro area are unique to the European Union.

As is alluded to in various other contributions to this volume, economic integration lags behind monetary policy integration. In economic terms the rather weak supranational economic policy coordination framework has not delivered the envisaged budgetary stability in the euro area that could support monetary dominance. This put pressure on monetary policy during the Global Financial Crisis (GFC) and the sovereign debt crisis. The misalignment has also extended to the absence of adequate legal arrangements at the supranational level to ensure the democratic legitimacy of an EMU governance framework that has evolved substantially regarding both the scope of the supranational monetary policy and the claim made by EU law on the shaping of national economic policy decisions. The primary Union law-based separation of competences between the EU and its Member States has created an artificial rift between economic and monetary policy that has become the constitutional battleground between the EU and its Member States and especially between the German Federal Constitutional Court (Bundesverfassungsgericht) and the Court of Justice of the European Union (CJEU).

Substantially reforming the current EMU governance framework to align economic policy with monetary policy and to reinforce the democratic legitimacy of power exercised at the supranational level is anything but straightforward. The choice of the drafters of the Maastricht Treaty for an asymmetric integration in EMU has been locked in by primary Union law (namely the Treaty on the Functioning of the European Union) the amendment of which is legally complex and paved with political pitfalls. At the same time, the EU measures taken to deal with the economic consequences of the COVID-19 pandemic within the existing framework highlight the flexibility of primary Union law to accommodate change to some extent.

Hereafter, Section 4.2 first turns to the EU's approach to legal, economic, and political integration and its implications for political decision-making and the achievement of

I would like to thank Dariusz Adamski and Jakob de Haan for their feedback on a previous version of this chapter.

(economic) integration objectives pursued. Section 4.3 then turns to the EMU governance framework and explains how asymmetric policy integration in EMU is the root problem (Section 4.3.1) that has had a major impact on the working of the supranational monetary policy (Section 4.3.2) and economic policy coordination (Section 4.3.3) framework. Finally, Section 4.4 draws conclusions and discusses the thorny path towards the creation of a much-needed greater EU fiscal capacity at the EU level.

4.2 THE EU'S APPROACH TO LEGAL, ECONOMIC, AND POLITICAL INTEGRATION

EMU can be primarily perceived as a European integration project in economic (see Eichengreen, Chapter 1 in this volume) and political (see Verdun, Chapter 2 in this volume) terms. More intensive and effective economic and monetary policy coordination was considered necessary to facilitate the creation of a true internal market without competitive distortions and without thereby giving rise to structural or regional disequilibrium (Werner Report, 1970, p. 7; Committee for the Study of Economic and Monetary Union (Delors Report), 1989, p. 11), namely through the productive allocation of capital (Adamski, 2020, p. 218). The 1993 Treaty on European Union stated the objective of the EU as promoting economic and social progress which is balanced and sustainable, inter alia through the strengthening of economic and social cohesion and the establishment of economic and monetary union.[1] In this context, the benefits for the internal market of the adoption of a single currency were considered to outweigh its costs for the Member States, a position that has certainly not remained uncontested following the events triggered by the GFC and the sovereign debt crisis.

More broadly, economic convergence was considered necessary for the further development of the Community, as already stated in the 1986 Single European Act.[2] As such, EMU can also be considered a political integration project, albeit prior to the GFC and the sovereign debt crisis more in terms of being the outcome of complex negotiations against the background of partially attuned and partially competing political ideas (Calmfors et al., 1997; see also James, Chapter 3, and Dyson, Chapter 5 in this volume) than in terms of concrete political integration steps (Hodson, 2020). The latter statement is rather significant considering that the new EMU framework featured prominently in the 1993 Treaty on European Union (hereafter Maastricht Treaty), which was not only about creating a single currency but about addressing the much debated 'democratic deficit' of the then European Community.[3] The Maastricht Treaty was to signify the establishment of a European Union, which found its most prosaic expression in the reference to the creation of 'an ever closer union among the peoples of Europe'.[4] In more substantive legal terms, this entailed inter alia the expansion of the legislative role of the supranational European Parliament (EP), but also in the introduction of safeguards of remaining national prerogatives through the principles of subsidiarity and proportionality. Yet, as will become clear from the subsequent sections, this did not entail a level of political integration matching that of monetary integration and of the economic policy coordination framework.

[1] Title I, Article B, first indent, of the original Treaty on European Union.

[2] Title I, Article B, first indent, Single European Act, OJ 1987 L 169/1.

[3] To be sure, the notion of a democratic deficit of the EU has not remained uncontested. For an overview see Bellamy (2006).

[4] As stated in the Preamble to the Treaty on European Union.

During the sovereign debt crisis, with the legal disputes about financial rescue programmes and the ECB's unconventional monetary policy measures, it became clear to a broader audience that EMU is not only an economic and political phenomenon (as characterized early on by Eichengreen and Frieden, 1993), but – for better or for worse – also a legal one (Amtenbrink, 2018). This is hardly a controversial statement, as for European integration more generally the relationship between law, politics, and economics can be understood in terms of interlocking gear wheels. The somewhat stylized vision of the unification of Europe (at times used as a synonym for political integration) has been pursued – as already envisaged by Robert Schuman – through economic integration by means of *legalization*, that is through the creation of legally binding and precise obligations the implementation, interpretation, and application of which has been assigned to a third party (building in this context on a definition by Abbott et al., 2000, pp. 401–2). This has come in the shape of the creation and constant further development of a new supranational autonomous legal order with its own legislative and regulatory powers in specific policy fields and its own institutional framework to exercise and enforce these powers, as well as its own system of judicial review. In line with the abovementioned picture of interlocking wheels, this process of legalization in the EU has not only provided the necessary conditions for successful economic integration, but also functioned as a justification of further political integration.

Political integration in the EU has not necessarily been attuned to the degree of economic and legal integration. As a result, the transfer of powers from the national to the supranational level can result in a weakening of democratic politics at the national level, while the supranational governance framework may not necessarily provide for adequate substitutes (yet) ensuring the democratic legitimacy of powers exercised at the supranational level. This asynchrony or misalignment in integration can result in what has been described as 'juridification of the political' (Magnussen and Banasiak, 2013, p. 332), first and foremost because democratic decision-making is weakened to the extent that the transfer of powers to the EU to be exercised by supranational institutions is not matched by steps towards political integration.[5] The long-lasting debates on the existence of a *democratic deficit* of the EU can be attributed to this.[6]

What is more, resulting from legalization, political decisions may become virtually permanently removed from reconsideration or renegotiation (Magnussen and Banasiak, 2013, pp. 326 and 332). In the EU context, at the most fundamental level the locking in of political decisions takes place through the EU Treaties, and the attached Protocols and the vast amount of the procedural and substantive areas of EU law they cover, at least to the extent that they are beyond the type of judicial law-making by the CJEU referred to in the next paragraph. The reason for this is that while the EU Treaties and attached Protocols can be amended,[7] this comes with complex political bargaining, high costs of failure, and the realistic chance of practical unattainability due to the need for a consensus among all EU Member States and the requirement to have any such changes ratified by all national parliaments.

At the same time, European integration is also an example of how legalization can lead to the 'politicization of the law' (Magnussen and Banasiak, 2013, p. 335), in the sense that a judicial system may become 'more open to and influenced by general social and political discourses as they are formulated within politics' and courts are considered to intervene in policy-making

[5] On the concept of 'juridification', see e.g. Habermas (1987), Teubner (1987), and Blichner and Molander (2008).

[6] To be sure, the notion of a democratic deficit of the EU has not remained uncontested. For an overview see Bellamy (2006).

[7] Art. 48 TEU.

processes, namely by limiting powers of political decision-making bodies, and 'increasingly become places where substantive policy is made' (Ferejohn, 2002, p. 41). Such a proposition may seem controversial (at least from a legal point of view) given that in liberal-democratic systems the judiciary is commonly perceived as a non-political actor, tasked with the application and interpretation of the law as is. Yet, as Heywood (2019, p. 309) observes, 'judges, are clearly political, in the sense that their judgements have an undeniable political impact', in particular when considering the role of highest (constitutional) courts. In the EU context, the role of the CJEU in advancing European integration through its power as final arbiter on the interpretation and legality of EU law can hardly be overstated,[8] prompting many studies to conclude that the CJEU 'is an important political actor in its own right' (Schmidt, 2018, p. 27, with further references).

In keeping with the terminology used by Magnussen and Banasiak, European integration can also result in what may be referred to as the juridification of economics. To be sure, Europe's approach to economic integration certainly finds its roots in economic thinking. What this term is meant to describe in this contribution is the observation that the translation of this economic thinking into specific rules may lead to the creation of a governance framework that falls short of what is necessary to achieve the (economic) objectives pursued. Indeed, in the EU context a governance framework may not only reflect prevailing economic philosophies, but mainly also the Member States' interests and the complex political negotiations (see the introduction to this volume) resulting from this in the run-up to the adoption of concrete rules. In this context, it also needs to be recognized that (economic) integration in the EU has taken place in numerous waves, driven by partially shifting political agendas of Member States rather than by a master plan and economic considerations of which policy fields should be necessarily integrated (in parallel).

4.3 MISALIGNMENTS IN EMU AND THEIR CONSEQUENCES

What was argued in the previous section is that the EU's approach bears the inherent danger of a misalignment or partial mismatch between the level of economic integration (through law) and political integration, as well as between economic objectives and the legal framework that is adopted to achieve them. EMU is a clear case in point in this regard, and importantly also for the impact this has on the functioning of a governance framework.

4.3.1 *Asymmetric Policy Integration in EMU as the Root Problem*

At the core of the abovementioned misalignment lies the political choice at the time of the drafting of the Maastricht Treaty to vest the exclusive competence[9] for the exercise of monetary policy for the euro area Member States to a newly created supranational independent central bank (the European Central Bank, ECB),[10] while leaving the conduct of fiscal policies with the Member States. Primary Union law considers economic policy a national domain and consequently also part of the national democratic decision-making process. Member States are to consider *their* economic policies a matter of common concern and are supposed to coordinate

[8] See Art. 267 TFEU.
[9] Art. 3(1)(c) TFEU.
[10] A competence that arguably can only be retrieved by a Member State through a withdrawal from the EU (see Athanassiou, 2009).

them with the Council.[11] Correspondingly, the Maastricht Treaty provided for the coordination of decentralized economic policy decision-making through self-commitment and peer review under the preventive and corrective arm of the Stability and Growth Pact (Amtenbrink and de Haan, 2003, p. 1076), backed up by prohibition of monetary financing (Article 123 TFEU) and the so-called no-bail-out clause (Article 125 TFEU).

This decentralized rule-based supranational economic policy framework was the compromise between those that stressed the need for further economic integration (convergence) prior to the adoption of a single currency and those that considered the adoption of a single currency as a suitable driver for further economic integration; a debate that was already taking place during the debates for the establishment of an EMU in early 1970 (see Verdun, Chapter 2 in this volume). It reflected Germany's preference to restrict 'government fiscal activism' (see James, Chapter 3 in this volume) and to prevent moral hazard and free-rider behaviour (see Begg, Chapter 6 in this volume), but also the belief that market discipline alone would be insufficient as the guarantor of fiscal discipline in a currency union. Fiscal discipline, as expressed by Article 126(1) TFEU and the Protocol on the Excessive Deficit Procedure, was supposed to ensure that Member States would be able to deal with asymmetric shocks (see the contributions by Begg, Chapter 6, and de Haan and Gootjes, Chapter 18). The framework was thus aimed at ensuring monetary dominance (Praet, 2015), thereby ruling out a situation that 'could induce a central bank to deviate from its monetary policy objectives, endangering price stability' (Schnabel, 2020).

However, with this constitutional division of competences for monetary and economic policy, the drafters of the Maastricht Treaty created a legal fiction that is difficult to reconcile with economic realities and – as will be observed hereafter for monetary and economic policy separately –led to the juridification of politics and the politization of law referred to in the previous section. From a legal perspective, economic policy may be distinguished from monetary policy measures 'based on the overarching objectives pursued ... the instruments applied ... or the actors involved' (Amtenbrink and Repasi, 2020, pp. 760–61). Yet such a distinction becomes unworkable in practice 'when considering the economic interdependency, interactions, and mutual direct and indirect effects that measures taken by the different principles monetary policy and fiscal policy actors have' (Amtenbrink and Repasi, 2020, pp. 760–61). Monetary and economic policy have a symbiotic relationship (Wyplosz, 1999; Afonso et al., 2019), as has also been recognized by the ECB (2011) itself. Unsustainable fiscal policies in the shape of excessive government deficit and debt levels can lead to calls for the adjustment of monetary policy (Afonso et al., 2019). As will be further highlighted in the subsequent sections, the economic and political consequences of this lack of a European economic policy counterweight to monetary policy could be witnessed during the sovereign debt crisis (see also Begg, Chapter 6 in this volume).

This misalignment in integration has planted the seed for EMU over time becoming a 'constitutional battleground' (Amtenbrink, 2014) between the EU and its Member States regarding the legality and legitimacy of supranational interference with these policy fields. At the same time, the supranational economic policy coordination framework that was supposed to accommodate this vertical division of competences without endangering the functioning of the single currency has not worked properly. The transfer of monetary policy powers from the national to the supranational level has resulted in a weakening of democratic politics to the extent that this has not been matched by political integration steps. The extensive reform

[11] Arts. 120–121 TFEU.

measures taken in response to the sovereign debt crisis to reinforce the economic policy coordination framework have potentially only added to this misalignment, rather than closing the gap between monetary and fiscal integration in EMU.

4.3.2 *The Consequence of Asymmetric Integration for Monetary Policy*

In implementing the preferences of the main political actors at the time of the drafting of the Maastricht Treaty (see also Dyson, Chapter 5 in this volume) to separate monetary from economic policy and to assign the former to an independent supranational monetary policy authority that is insulated from political pressure from national and EU political institutions with an overriding single objective focused on maintaining price stability (Ioannidis, 2020, p. 375), the ECB has been given virtually unparalleled independence (de Haan, 1997; de Haan et al., 1999) that is guaranteed by primary Union law.[12] This also extends to the national central banks of the euro area Member States when carrying out European System of Central Banks (ESCB) related tasks. From the perspective of the Member States, the degree to which the transfer of monetary policy to the ECB has resulted in a depoliticization of monetary policy has varied and depended on the national legal arrangements existing at the time.[13]

The fragility of the EMU governance framework became evident during the sovereign debt crisis. In the absence of fiscal discipline in the euro area Member States and their political indecisiveness and lack of credible action in the face of the crisis, but also the lack of effective economic policy instruments at the disposal of the EU, the ECB could be seen taking unprecedented monetary policy measures (see Adamski, Chapter 9, and Chang, Chapter 10 in this volume; Tuori, 2020, pp. 641 ff.). Moreover, the latter became actively involved in the drafting and monitoring of the economic conditions attached to financial assistance granted to euro area Member States by the European Stability Mechanism (Karatzia and Markakis, 2017). The competence and democratic legitimacy of the ECB to take such actions was seriously questioned, drawing the attention of a whole new generation of mainly legal and political science scholars to this field of study. This heightened scholarly interest is hardly surprising in that during the euro crisis the ECB – like other non-euro area central banks – entered what Vujčić (2016) referred to as the 'redistribute realm of monetary policy, i.e., when monetary policy does somebody else's job'. Redistribution effects of the ECB's unconventional monetary policy measures have been discussed in terms of the potential allocation of risks (liabilities) between euro area Member States and their central banks, and also in terms of negative spillovers on economic developments that have been criticized for falling outside the powers assigned to the ECB and not being an EU competence in the first place. An unintended side effect of the actual (dis)functioning of the EMU governance framework has thus been the politicization of monetary policy in the sense that the latter is no longer necessarily perceived as a highly technical policy field that can be better left to independent experts (Amtenbrink, 2019). Rather, monetary policy in the shape of the ECB became the subject of legal and political contestation.

The lopsided integration of economic and monetary policy in EMU, the absence of an indisputable delineation in EU law of monetary from economic policy, and the actions of the ECB have also become a major source of judicial contestation in EMU. This has mainly played out in the German Federal Constitutional Court (Bundesverfassungsgericht) and the CJEU, ultimately leading to an unprecedented clash between these two – in their own right – powerful

[12] Arts. 130, 131, and 282(3) TFEU and Art. 7 of the Statute of the ESCB and ECB.

[13] For an overview of major EU central bank systems, see Amtenbrink (1999).

institutional actors that has briefly shaken the foundations of the European legal order.[14] Triggered by legal challenges to the validity of the ECB's action,[15] the CJEU has not only developed criteria for the delineation of monetary from economic policy, but also defined the scope of monetary financing (Article 123 TFEU) and determined the (in)significance of the so-called no-bail-out clause (Article 125 TFEU) for the legality of (un)conventional monetary policy measures. At the same time, the CJEU has effectively imposed on itself limitations to the scope of judicial review of monetary policy measures, referring in this context to the broad discretion required by the ECB when making choices of a technical nature and undertaking forecasts and complex assessments (see also Bobić and Dawson, Chapter 14 in this volume). The consequence has been a somewhat reduced judicial review of the proportionality of monetary policy measures by the Court of Justice that is focused on assessing whether the ECB has manifestly exceeded what is necessary to achieve its monetary policy objective (Amtenbrink and Repasi, 2020, pp. 764–65). This approach to the judicial review of monetary policy has fundamentally differed from that of the Bundesverfassungsgericht, which in its *Weiss* decision took the position that the ECB's statutory independence results in it operating 'on the basis of a diminished level of democratic legitimation' which calls for the possibility of a full judicial review of its measures in the light of its assigned powers.[16] These different viewpoints have resulted in an open conflict between the two courts in which the German judges have accused the European judges of an incomprehensible and objectively arbitrary interpretation of the EU Treaties that ultimately also lacks democratic legitimacy.[17] While this direct judicial confrontation has been settled for now, the underlying structural issues are here to stay: that is, 'the legitimate co-existence' of distinct legal orders in the EU and the lopsided integration of economic and monetary policy in EMU (Amtenbrink and Repasi, 2020, pp. 767–77).

Touching upon such politically charged topics as risk-sharing, redistribution, and solidarity in the euro area, the decisions by the CJEU in *Pringle*, *Gauweiler*, and *Weiss*[18] enter the sphere of policy- and law-making. They essentially deal with the limits of the powers of political decision-making at the national level (to the advantage of the supranational central bank), thereby not only having clear legal but also political implications. The same may also be observed for the national judiciary and especially the decision by the Bundesverfassungsgericht in the main proceedings in the *Weiss* case.[19] In fact, the significance of the judgment by the Bundesverfassungsgericht should not be reduced to its much-noted rejection of the CJEU's interpretation of primary Union law concerning the monetary policy competences of the ECB. Goldmann (2020) has observed that the German court's slating of the CJEU for its failure to give consideration to the economic and social policy effects of the Public Sector Purchase Programme (PSPP) in the context of the review of the proportionality of the ECB's measure actually signifies a major departure from its previous focus on the disciplinary character of the EMU legal framework, i.e. the delineation of monetary and economic policy competences between the EU and the euro area Member States, the focus of euro area monetary policy on

[14] See *German Law Journal*, Special Collection on 'European Constitutional Pluralism and the PSPP Judgment', 31 August 2020. https://germanlawjournal.com/german-law-journal-special-collection-on-european-constitutional-pluralism-and-the-pspp-judgment/.

[15] Which reached the CJEU through the preliminary reference procedure pursuant to Art. 267 TFEU.

[16] BVerfG, Judgment of the Second Senate of 5 May 2020 – 2 BvR 859/15, paras. 1–237, at para. 143.

[17] Ibid., at para. 118.

[18] Case C-370/12, *Pringle*, ECLI:EU:C:2012:756; case C-62/14, *Peter Gauweiler and Others*, ECLI:EU:C:2015:400; case C-493/17, *Heinrich Weiss and Others*, ECLI:EU:C:2018:1000.

[19] Weiss, Judgment of 5 May 2020, 2 BvR 859/15 (in English at www.bundesverfassungsgericht.de/SharedDocs/Entscheidungen/EN/2020/05/rs20200505_2bvr085915en.html

price stability, and the focus of economic policy coordination on budgetary discipline. In the opinion of Goldmann (2020, p. 1073): 'The [Bundesverfassungsgericht] replaces the disciplinary function of the [EMU] economic constitution with the flexibility and context-sensitivity of the proportionality test, representing a shift from discipline to welfare.' While only future judgments will tell whether the *Weiss* decision by the Bundesverfassungsgericht constitutes a shift in paradigm in Germany, it is a case in point for the role of the (national) judiciary in EMU.

Another main area of contestation concerns the democratic legitimacy of the position and action of the ECB. With the transfer of the exclusive competences for monetary policy for the euro area to the EU, any democratic legitimation of the exercise of this power beyond the initial act of its transfer to the supranational level by the Member States in accordance with the constitutional requirements (namely through ratification by national parliaments) must derive from the supranational (EU) level. Yet, in applying Vivien Schmidt's distinction of three basic normative criteria, i.e. input, throughput, and output legitimacy (Schmidt, 2012; see also Diessner, Chapter 13 in this volume), it can be observed that the throughput legitimacy of the ECB, and mainly its democratic accountability, is weak.[20] The reasons for this can be first, albeit certainly not only, found in the legal framework governing the ECB, which from its very inception has been criticized for its lack of legal mechanisms ensuring an adequate degree of democratic accountability for its exercise of monetary policy (e.g. already Gormley and de Haan, 1996). This relates to instruments in the hands of democratically legitimized institutions to assign consequences to an unfavourable assessment of the Bank's performance, such as a performance-based dismissal of central bank officials, the overriding of central bank decisions, and/or the realistic option to amend the legal basis of the central bank (Amtenbrink, 1999).[21] Indeed, instruments ensuring the democratic accountability of the ECB, thus contributing to its throughput legitimacy, have played a subsidiary role in the institutional design of the ECB (Amtenbrink, 1999, p. 359) and its *statutory* accountability arrangements are weak compared to those that can be found in other major central bank systems around the globe (de Haan et al., 1999).

The implications of this observation are particularly significant, given that the independence of the ECB naturally cannot be grounded in historical and political settings similar to those of some national central bank systems (Amtenbrink, 1999, p. 372). Thus, the ECB could not rely for its legitimacy on the same degree of public acceptance to be found, for example, for the Deutsche Bundesbank when it was still operating as an autonomous monetary policy authority. To be sure, even to the extent that the view has been entertained that the ECB's successful conduct of monetary policy, and thus 'policy effectiveness and outcomes' (Schmidt and Wood, 2019, p. 728, with further references to the notion of output legitimacy), would legitimize its independent exercise of monetary policy, this could not function as an adequate surrogate for mechanisms ensuring the continued back-coupling of the ECB's action to democratically elected institutions that ensure that the ECB acts in accordance with its statutory objective and, moreover, in accordance with (changing) policy preferences (as observed for EU policies in general by Kröger, 2019, pp. 770–71).

[20] According to Schmidt (2012), other aspects of throughput legitimacy may include efficacy, transparency, inclusiveness, and openness to interest intermediation.

[21] The law governing the ECB has been situated at the pinnacle of the EU legal order, i.e. the EU Treaties (primary Union law), rather than being cast in an ordinary legislative act that could be amended subject to the applicable European (ordinary) legislative procedure. This makes a reconsideration or renegotiation of the ECB's legal basis extremely difficult for the reasons stated in the previous section.

The monetary policy dialogue with the European Parliament, but also the ECB's enhanced communication and transparency strategy with the markets and the public more broadly (see de Haan, Chapter 11 in this volume), including the publication of accounts of the monetary policy decision-making meetings of the ECB's Governing Council since 2015, are geared towards explaining policy choices and gaining acceptance. Even if these arrangements contribute to the ECB's legitimacy in some regards (Amtenbrink and van Duin, 2009; Collignon and Diessner, 2016; Heidebrecht, 2019), they cannot provide a sufficient foundation for the democratic legitimacy of the ECB (Amtenbrink, 2019, p. 177), as any meaningful review of the Bank's action by the EU political institutions, and especially the EP, cannot be followed up by concrete action, which in the case of the possibility of an amendment of the legal basis would not only contribute to throughput legitimacy but ultimately also to input legitimacy. The focus in the creation of supranational monetary policy was on the insulation of the ECB from any political pressure and short-term political considerations to increase the money supply at the expense of price stability (Ioannidis, 2020, p. 414), rather than the embedding of the central bank in a supranational system of checks and balances with the only directly democratically legitimized EU institution – the EP – at the helm.

That judicial review of the ECB's measures can function as a surrogate for weak democratic accountability instruments for the exercise of the supranational monetary policy competence is doubtful. Even if it is argued that the judicial approval of monetary policy decisions through an interpretation of the legal framework by the CJEU legitimizes these decisions, as observed by Amtenbrink and Repasi (2020, p. 776): '[T]he issue of the fragile democratic legitimation of decisions with potentially far reaching implications is hardly solved by such a switching of actors', as 'one non-majoritarian body (a court) replaces the decision by another non-majoritarian body (a central bank)'. What is more, it is hard to imagine how the open clash of views between the Bundesverfassungsgericht and the CJEU could have enhanced the legitimacy of the ECB's action with the public at large.

4.3.3 *The Consequence of Asymmetric Integration for Economic Policy*

Overall, as far as the rules-based coordination of national economic policy is concerned, the Maastricht governance framework has proven incapable of providing economic stability mainly in the shape of sound budgetary policies in the currency union, even when considering the major reform measures. While economic policy coordination certainly cannot be said to have failed in its entirety (de Haan and Gootjes, Chapter 18 in this volume; De Jong and Gilbert, 2019), the system has been incapable of structurally preventing euro area Member States from pursuing pro-cyclical fiscal policies (European Commission, 2020, pp. 16–17), restricting the room for automatic stabilizers and discretionary economic policy in times of crisis. What is more, despite numerous long-lasting violations of the excessive deficit criteria by euro area Member States, the sanctioning regime foreseen in the excessive deficit procedure has never been executed. This has not even changed since the reinforcement of the legal framework as part of the Six Pack. The cancelling of the procedurally foreseen fines for Portugal and Spain in the context of the excessive deficit procedures against these two countries in August 2016 in favour of an extension of the deadlines for the correction of the respective excessive deficits are a case in point (Council of the European Union, 2016). This not only calls into question the effectiveness of the enforcement mechanisms of the system but, at a more fundamental level, to the extent that hard enforcement may politically or economically be considered undesirable or even counterproductive, the suitability of the current approach to achieving compliance with the supranational fiscal rules (Amtenbrink and Repasi, 2017).

The deliberate choice of the drafters of the Maastricht Treaty not to provide the EU with its own set of effective economic policy instruments, and a matching budgetary capacity[22] to allow for a macroeconomic stabilization function at the supranational level, has deprived EU institutions of the possibility to take resolute action – at least during the early stages of the sovereign debt crisis in 2010, when Greece received bilateral loans from euro area Member States (together with a loan from the IMF), pooled by the European Commission, as part of the so-called Greek Loan Facility. At the same time, in the face of high government deficits and debts and the absence of autonomous monetary policy instruments, Member States found themselves incapable of addressing the economic shocks themselves. This effectively made the ECB if not the only, then at least the crucial 'game in town'[23] during the sovereign debt crisis. It has created a situation in which monetary policy can (at times) no longer be considered in absolute isolation from the fiscal position of the euro area Member States. Asymmetric integration has in practice resulted in monetary policy in the euro area having to compensate for the lack of supranationalization of economic policy. As such, the economic policy coordination framework introduced by the Maastricht Treaty has failed to deliver on the rationale for its introduction. What is more, as was observed in the previous section, because of the role of the ECB as a crisis manager, its fragile democratic legitimacy has come under even more strain.

The sovereign debt crisis triggered a substantial amendment of the existing rules on economic policy coordination, partially through the adoption of new (Six Pack and Two Pack) and the amendment of existing secondary Union law acts (Stability and Growth Pact Council Regulations), and partially through the adoption of intergovernmental instruments outside the EU legal framework that pursue EMU objectives and that have recourse to EU institutions (Treaty on Stability, Coordination, and Governance (Fiscal Compact) and ESM Treaty). This has inter alia included tighter coordination rules in the European Semester for the national budgetary policies, including the requirement for euro area Member States to submit draft national budgets to the European Commission and to the Eurogroup, the monitoring of a much broader spectrum of national macroeconomic variables in the context of the new macroeconomic imbalances procedure, and the introduction of a sanctioning regime in the European Semester and at the outset of the excessive deficit procedure (see Markakis, Chapter 17 in this volume). Rather than closing the competence gap between monetary and economic policy in the euro area, these measures are geared towards an 'ever-closer coordination of economic policies [of the Member States] within the euro area'.[24] Holding on to the approach of the drafters of the Maastricht Treaty is not surprising, given that a relocation of economic policy powers from the national to the supranational level would have required an amendment of primary Union law (the EU Treaties). Still, the reform has aimed at increasing the supranational influence on national economic policy through a better alignment of the national budgetary and economic policies with the basic supranational fiscal rules.[25]

Whether these changes signify a development 'from coordination towards a quasi-common policy' (Keppenne, 2020, p. 792) can be questioned given the experience of compliance with and enforcement of the new framework in some euro area Member States. Still, the further

[22] In 2019, the EU budget was estimated at 'around 1% of combined EU income and only around 2% of public spending in the EU' (European Commission, 2019, p. 16).

[23] Referring here to Draghi's statement about monetary policy not being the only game in town (Draghi, 2015).

[24] See Preamble to the Fiscal Compact.

[25] See www.consilium.europa.eu/en/policies/european-semester/

legalization of economic policy at the supranational level should not be entirely dismissed as insignificant when it comes to the effects on national political decision-making and its significance for the legitimacy of EMU. Evidence suggests that while compliance with the EU fiscal framework, namely in the shape of the implementation of country-specific recommendations, certainly varies across Member States and over time, generally being 'affected by the macroeconomic environment, external and market pressure, and political factors' (Efstathiou and Wolff, 2019), it is difficult to argue that the framework has not had any impact on the direction of economic policy in the Member States.

The notable expansion of the legal framework governing the EU's engagement with national economic policy has raised concerns about a curtailing of the democratic decision-making processes on economic policy in the Member States and especially the diminishing role for national parliaments in the process (Amtenbrink, 2014; Crum and Merlo, 2020). This is particularly relevant considering that the legal reinforcement of the Maastricht framework has not been matched by steps towards political integration shifting powers from the intergovernmental (Council/Eurogroup) to the supranational democratically legitimized (EP) institutions, while national channels to ensure democratic legitimacy of the European actors in economic policy coordination are rather weak.

To be sure, with the introduction of the Six Pack and Two Pack reform measures, the importance of greater transparency and accountability has been explicitly recognized. Reference can be made in this context to the introduction of information requirements for the European Commission[26] and the economic dialogue with the EP (namely its Committees on Budgets and on Economic and Monetary Affairs (BUDG and ECON)). The latter can 'invite' the President of the Council, the Commission, and, where appropriate, the President of the European Council or the President of the Eurogroup to appear before the parliamentary committee to discuss the course of action, inter alia relating to EU surveillance of national budgetary plans and of national budgetary positions, the macroeconomic imbalances procedure, and the excessive deficit procedure.[27] Moreover, the EP can also enter into an exchange of view with Member States mainly concerning decisions and recommendations addressed to them. Regardless of the (unused) potential of these exchanges in creating more transparency and in reducing information asymmetries between the EP and the main institutional actors in economic policy coordination (see Fromage, 2018 for a critical assessment), their usefulness as a mechanism of throughput legitimacy depends on the ability of the EP, and – as far as the Council of the EU, the European Council, or the Eurogroup are concerned – also of national parliaments, to assign consequences to their assessment of the performance of these actors.

Compared to what has been observed for the democratic accountability of monetary policy, the EP has some more possibilities to assign consequences to its assessment of the execution of the European economic policy coordination framework. First, with the motion of censure the EP theoretically has a powerful tool at its disposal in relation to the European Commission. Yet in practice the hurdles are high, since such a motion requires a two-thirds majority of the votes cast. Moreover, the political threshold for application of this procedure is extremely high, as the Commission would be required to resign as a body, whereas removal of individual

[26] E.g. Art. 3 of Regulation 472/2013 on the strengthening of economic and budgetary surveillance of Member States in the euro area experiencing or threatened with serious difficulties with respect to their financial stability, (2013) OJ L 140/1.

[27] Exemplary for the rules on economic dialogue included in the different secondary Union law acts: Art. 2-ab of Council Regulation No. 1466/97 on the strengthening of the surveillance of budgetary positions and the surveillance and coordination of economic policies (as amended).

Commissioners, such as the President of the Commission or the Commissioner responsible for a specific policy area, is excluded (Amtenbrink and Vedder, 2021, p. 134). A similar power does not exist in relation to the Council of the EU, the European Council, and the Eurogroup, as they are composed of elected or appointed national government representatives. In the case of the Council and the European Council, the EP is authorized to initiate judicial review of actions or omissions of these institutions before the CJEU.[28] Yet, this is not the case for the Eurogroup, despite its practical importance (Craig, 2017), as the Court of Justice has declined to recognize it as a formal decision-making body that can take legally binding measures,[29] rightly raising concerns about its accountability (Staudinger, 2021) and more generally the liability of the EU for the behaviour of this body (Markakis and Karatzia, 2020).

Different to monetary policy, which is by and large based on primary Union law that can only be changed by a Treaty amendment, much of the operationalization of the current supranational economic policy coordination framework is based on secondary Union law in the shape of regulations and directives that can be redrafted or even repealed without the need for a Treaty amendment procedure. Key legislative acts of the post-crisis EMU legal framework, such as Regulation 1173/2011 on the effective enforcement of budgetary surveillance, Regulation 1176/2011 on the prevention and correction of macroeconomic imbalances, and Regulation 1174/2011 on enforcement measures to correct excessive macroeconomic imbalances in the euro area, include review clauses calling for a periodical evaluation of the effectiveness of these acts and proposal for amendments. The legal basis of these acts (Article 121(6) TFEU) calls for an application of the ordinary legislative procedure putting the EP in the position of co-legislator and allowing for qualified majority decisions in the Council. However, this is not in all instances the case, as becomes clear from a study of Council Regulation 1177/2011 on speeding up and clarifying the implementation of the excessive deficit procedure, which was based on Article 126 (14) TFEU, for which a special legislative procedure applies where the EP is only consulted alongside the ECB. Moreover, different to what can be found for national parliamentary systems, the EP does not have a formal right of initiative for legislative proposals, as this power is in the hands of the European Commission (Amtenbrink and Vedder, 2021, p. 127).

Next to the EP, the legitimacy of the European economic policy framework is primarily channelled through the governments of the Member States, which – subject to the specific constitutional arrangements in place – are accountable to national parliaments. National governments, both as a collective body but also in the shape of individual government ministers, are answerable to national parliaments for their actions whether in the national or EU context. Yet national governments or individual ministers, including heads of states or governments, can hardly be held accountable for their collective action at the supranational level by the Council of the EU, the European Council, or Eurogroup, in particular in the case of the application of qualified majority decision-making. At the same time, a collective responsibility of the Council in whatever composition at the supranational level is missing (Amtenbrink, 2007).

4.4 THE THORNY PATH AHEAD

Like the EU itself, EMU is as much a legal integration project as it is an economic and political one. And, like other EU policy fields, EMU is characterized by a misalignment of the level of

[28] Action for annulment (Art. 263 TFEU) or action for failure to act (Art. 265 TFEU).

[29] Joined cases C-105/15 P to C-109/15 P, *Mallis and Others*, ECLI:EU:C:2016:702; Joined cases C-597/18 P, C-598/18 P, C-603/18 P and C-604/18 P, *Council v. Chrysostomides & Co. and Others*, ECLI:EU:C:2020:1028.

legal, economic, and political integration. This is rooted in the political preference at the time of the drafting of the Maastricht Treaty for an asymmetric integration of monetary and economic policy and, linked to the absence of adequate legal arrangements at the supranational level to ensure the democratic legitimacy of an EMU governance framework that has evolved substantially both with regard to the scope of supranational monetary policy and the claim made by EU law on the shaping of national economic policy. At the same time, the rule-based fiscal coordination framework has not fully achieved the envisaged fiscal stability that could support monetary dominance in the euro area, triggering proposals for a further reform of EU economic governance.

The vertical division of competences between the EU and the euro area Member States for monetary and fiscal policies is at odds with the fact that monetary policy by its very definition 'affects the economy and market participants, including citizens ... in areas that fall in the general economic or fiscal policy domain for which ... the Member States remain in charge' (Amtenbrink and Repasi, 2020, p. 762); it affects the distribution of income and wealth (Bernanke, 2015). Direct decisions in this regard are usually assigned to economic policy decision-makers. In EMU, however, the decision-makers in the monetary and economic policy domains are situated at different levels of the EU constitutional system, i.e. the supranational and national levels respectively, with potentially incongruent policy preferences and distinct channels and degrees of democratic legitimation of economic policy-making. While the sovereign debt crisis reform measures reflect the supranational ambition to achieve the compliance of national economic policymakers with the European basic fiscal rules, they do not stand for the creation of an economic policy counterweight to monetary policy that would provide the EU with effective instruments to ensure fiscal stability, at least in times of crises, and that could moreover reinforce the democratic legitimacy of the EU in EMU.

Some of the shortcomings described above find their explanation not only in the legal design of EMU, but also in the constitutional characteristics of the supranational legal order in which the EMU governance framework has been implanted. The EU is not a body for intergovernmental cooperation between sovereign states only, nor does it take the place of the participating states; the EU is not a (federal) state. In this hybrid arrangement, national constitutional orders of the Member States continue to coexist alongside the EU legal order. They do not only continue to be a source of power, such as for economic policy in EMU, but also for the democratic legitimacy of the powers in respect to the fiscal coordination framework exercised at the supranational level. Much more so than in federal systems, the rules governing the distribution of powers between the two constitutional centres (national and EU) form the very fundament of this cooperation and a constant source of potential conflicts. As such, the asymmetric integration of the two very closely related policy fields in EMU laid the foundation for the constitutional conflict triggered by the ECB's unconventional monetary policy measures. The hybrid character of the EU legal order is also reflected in the inter-institutional balance between EU political institutions and the role they play in legitimation of the exercise of the EU's powers, as the Council of the EU and the European Council, which are dominated by the (euro area) Member States, in many regards are put on an equal footing with the directly elected EP that represents EU citizens.

As EMU thus forms an inseparable part of the EU legal order, the key to addressing the constraints identified in this chapter does not merely lie in a further development of the existing rules within the confinements of the current Treaty framework. This is in fact highlighted by the several attempts to address some of these limitations in the wake of the sovereign debt crisis that have not, and indeed could not have, resulted in a fundamental readjustment of the Maastricht Treaty EMU framework, thereby dealing with the root cause of the problem. This requires a substantive reorientation of the EMU governance framework in two ways: realignment of economic policy with monetary policy in the euro area and reinforcement of the democratic legitimacy of supranational policy-making in these policy fields.

Realigning fiscal with monetary policy in the euro area must be geared towards substantially decreasing asymmetric integration in EMU. This can in principle take different shapes but should entail an increase of the capacity of the supranational level to contribute to the aim to maintain sound and sustainable public finances and to prevent euro area Member States' deficits from becoming excessive.[30] The starting point must be a fundamental reconsideration of the basic assumptions on which the current rule-based framework is founded, such as the economic rationale of the numeric deficit and debt targets in Article 126(1) TFEU and the Protocol on the Excessive Deficit Procedure, which have been considered rather arbitrary (see Eichengreen, Chapter 1 in this volume; Afflatet, 2016), lacking a deeper economic logic (Buiter et al., 1992, pp. 62–63), and at times even outright unrealistic. A similar observation can be made for the key reference values that inform the economic policy coordination framework in EMU, such as the requirement for countries with an excessive deficit to reduce a government debt-to-GDP ratio that exceeds the 60 per cent reference value by 5 per cent points of GDP on an annual basis, and limitation by the Fiscal Compact of structural government budget deficits to 0.5 per cent of GDP.[31] Moreover, the viability of the no-bail-out clause of Article 125 TFEU and the underlying assumption that the framework must ensure that Member States remain subject to the logic of the markets when entering into debt deserve reconsideration given experience with the limited working of these rules during the sovereign debt crisis. Indeed, the question may be asked whether euro area Member States should remain in a position to refinance themselves on the markets without EU intervention.

While the complete supranationalization of economic policy in the euro area is neither politically achievable nor economically sensible, bringing the fiscal capacity of the EU in the euro area closer to its monetary policy capacity requires more than a reconsideration of the existing EU deficit and debt limits. Various proposals have been made in this regard in EU policy documents, such as the Four Presidents' Report 'Towards a genuine Economic and Monetary Union', the Five Presidents' Report on completing Economic and Monetary Union, and the European Commission's Reflection Paper on the deepening of the Economic and Monetary Union, but also in the academic literature. This includes the creation of a shared European safe asset (e.g. Delpla and Von Weizsäcker, 2010; Philippon, 2015; European Commission, 2017a, p. 22) and the introduction of a system of common debt issuing in the euro area with the aim not only of crisis mitigation but also 'to strengthen economic policy coordination and sound budgetary policies in the euro area in a more sustainable way' (Amtenbrink et al., 2016, p. 631). Moreover, the creation of a robust euro area-specific budget (European Commission, 2017a, p. 26; Claeys, 2020) that would allow for a countercyclical EU spending policy alongside a euro area-specific supranational shock absorption capacity (European Commission, 2020; European Fiscal Board, 2021, pp. 82 et seq.) has been suggested. Different proposals have been made regarding the latter, including the establishment of a cyclical shock insurance scheme financed by the Member States (Enderlein et al., 2013), and a European unemployment benefits or reinsurance scheme (Beblavý and Lenaerts, 2017; European Commission, 2017b). Introducing a substantial fiscal capacity at the supranational level would take pressure off the ECB, which

30 See, e.g., the Fiscal Compact, which considers this as an essential to safeguard the stability of the euro area.

31 Art. 3(1)(b) of the Fiscal Compact. To be sure, in exceptional circumstances countries can temporarily deviate from this objective, see Art. 3(3)(b).

during the sovereign debt crisis effectively had to fill the gap that was left wide open in this regard at the supranational level.

An increase of supranational fiscal capacity must go hand in hand with measures to increase democratic legitimacy not only of fiscal but also of monetary policy in EMU. The latter is justified because it has become clear since the sovereign debt crisis and during the COVID-19 pandemic that monetary policy is closely linked to economic policy and can have effects that are difficult to reconcile with the image of monetary policy as a highly technical and politically neutral field. The ECB's recent inclusion of climate objectives in its monetary policy (see Schoenmaker and Stegeman, Chapter 12 in this volume) is only reinforcing the case for an enhanced democratic accountability of the ECB. The focus should be on accountability instruments for the EP (Amtenbrink, 2019), including a stronger role in the appointment of the members of the ECB's Executive Board. As far as economic policy is concerned, new supranational mechanisms should foresee a decisive role for the EP in the decision-making process beyond the adoption of the EU's budget, for example regarding the actual application of an EU shock absorption instrument.

As far as the legal feasibility of a reform of the current EMU governance framework is concerned, it cannot be denied that any amendments that would change the current distribution of competences between the EU and the Member States laid down in Articles 3(1)(c) and 5 TFEU in favour of shifting economic policy onto the supranational level would require an amendment of the existing Treaty pursuant to Article 48 TEU, which would not only be legally complex but also paved with political pitfalls. This would, for example, apply to giving the EU the power of direct taxation as a source of its own resources, and a system of centralized debt-issuing that would require Member States to borrow from the EU rather than on the financial markets. It would entail a thorny path in the best of circumstances. What is more, the threat of a constitutional challenge in a national highest (constitutional) court on grounds of the protection of the national constitutional identity[32] hangs like a dark cloud over any attempts to expand the EU's competences.[33] Finally, addressing some of the more fundamental problems associated with the constitutional characteristics of the EU, such as the position of the EP vis-à-vis other EU institutions, that also affect EMU, will require an even more profound reconsideration of the EU constitutional order which far surpasses the working of EMU, as it would also affect the role of the EP in other policy fields.

A Treaty amendment may ultimately be inevitable to bring asymmetric integration of monetary and economic policy in EMU to an end, given that the scope of the existing EU legal framework to accommodate substantive changes towards an increased fiscal capacity of the EU is limited. Indeed, it can be observed that the EU's response to the COVID-19 pandemic highlights both the flexibility of the present framework to accommodate ad hoc and temporary measures, such as namely the European instrument for temporary support to mitigate unemployment risks in an emergency (SURE) and the recovery and resilience facility at the heart of NextGenerationEU.[34] At the same time, the measures point to the limitations of some of the legal bases utilized (namely Article 122 TFEU) to accommodate a permanent legally robust framework that recognizes the EU's own budgetary principles and procedures, while at the same time providing for a sufficient degree of democratic legitimacy of future arrangements that would potentially entail greater redistributional powers at the supranational level.

[32] Art. 4(2) TEU.

[33] An argument also advanced in the abovementioned *Weiss* judgment of the Bundesverfassungsgericht.

[34] Legal bases that have been utilized or discussed in this context include Arts. 122, 121(6), 126(14), 136(1), 175, 311 para. 3, 352(1) TFEU.

REFERENCES

Abbott, K. W., Keohane, R. O., Moravcsik, A., Slaughter, A. M., and Snidal, D. (2000). The concept of legalization. *International Organization* 54(3), 401–419.

Adamski, D. (2020). Objectives of the EMU. In F. Amtenbrink and C. Herrmann (eds.), *The EU Law of Economic and Monetary Union*. Oxford: Oxford University Press, pp. 214–258.

Afflatet, N. (2016). Deficit policy within the framework of the stability and growth pact: Empirical results and lessons for the fiscal compact. Diskussionspapier No. 168, Helmut-Schmidt-Universität – Universität der Bundeswehr Hamburg, Fächergruppe Volkswirtschaftslehre, Hamburg.

Afonso, A., Alves, J., and Balhote, R. (2019). Interactions between monetary and fiscal policies. *Journal of Applied Economics* 22(1), 132–151.

Amtenbrink, F. (1999). *The Democratic Accountability of Central Banks: A Comparative Study of the European Central Bank*. Oxford: Hart.

Amtenbrink, F. (2007). Continuation or reorientation. What future for European Integration, Erasmus Law Lectures 9, The Hague: Boom Juridische uitgevers.

Amtenbrink, F. (2014). New economic governance in the European Union: Another constitutional battleground? In K. Purnhagen and P. Roth (eds.), *Varieties of European Economic Law and Regulation: Liber Amicorum Hans W. Micklitz*. Cham: Springer, pp. 207–234.

Amtenbrink, F. (2018). A legal and political economy mapping of European Economic and Monetary Union. In G. Kalflèche, T. Perroud, and M. Ruffert (eds.), *L'avenir de l'Union économique et monétaire: une perspective franco-allemande*. Paris: LGDJ, Droit & économie, pp. 111–131.

Amtenbrink, F. (2019). The European Central Bank's intricate independence versus accountability conundrum in the post-crisis governance framework. *Maastricht Journal of European and Comparative Law* 26(1), 165–179.

Amtenbrink, F., and de Haan, J. (2003). Economic governance in the European Union: Fiscal policy discipline versus flexibility. *Common Market Law Review* 40, 1057–1106.

Amtenbrink, F., and van Duin, K. (2009). The European Central Bank before the European Parliament: Theory and practice after ten years of monetary dialogue. *European Law Review* 34, 561–583.

Amtenbrink, F., and Vedder, H. (2021). *European Union Law*. The Hague: Eleven International Publishing/Boom.

Amtenbrink, F., Repasi, R., and de Haan, J. (2016). Is there life in the old dog yet? Observations on the political economy and constitutional viability of common debt issuing in the euro area. *Review of Law and Economics* 12(3), 605–633.

Amtenbrink, F., and Repasi, R. (2017). Compliance and enforcement in economic policy coordination in EMU. In D. Kochenov and A. Jakab (eds.), *The Enforcement of EU Law and Values: Ensuring Member States' Compliance*. Oxford: Oxford University Press, pp. 145–181.

Amtenbrink, F., and Repasi, R. (2020). The German Federal Constitutional Court's decision in Weiss: A contextual analysis. *European Law Review* 45, 757–778.

Athanassiou, P. (2009). Withdrawal and expulsion from the EU and EMU. Some Reflections. ECB Legal Working Paper No. 10.

Beblavý, M., and Lenaerts, K. (2017). Feasibility and added value of a European unemployment benefits scheme. Report commissioned by DG EMPL of the European Commission. www.ceps.eu/ceps-publications/feasibility-and-added-value-european-unemployment-benefits-scheme/

Bellamy, R. (2006). Still in deficit: Rights, regulations, and democracy in the EU. *European Law Journal* 12(6), 725–742.

Bernanke, B. S. (2015). Monetary policy and inequality. Brookings Blog, 1 June 2015. www.brookings.edu/articles/monetary-policy-and-inequality/

Blichner, L.C., and Molander, A. (2008). Mapping Juridification. *European Law Journal* 14, 36–54.

Buiter, W., Corsetti, G., and Roubini, N. (1992). Excessive deficits: Sense and nonsense in the Treaty of Maastricht. *Economic Policy* 8(16), 57–100.

Calmfors, L., et al. (1997). The EMU as a political project. In *EMU: A Swedish Perspective*. Boston, MA: Springer.

Claeys, G. (2020). Building a euro-area budget inside the EU budget: Squaring the circle? In B. Laffan and A. De Feo (eds.), *EU Financing for Next Decade beyond the MFF 2021–2027 and the Next Generation EU*. Florence: European University Institute.

Collignon, S., and Diessner, S. (2016). The ECB's monetary dialogue with the European Parliament: Efficiency and accountability during the euro crisis? *Journal of Common Market Studies* 54, 1296–1312.

Council of the European Union (2016). Excessive deficit procedure: Council agrees to zero fines and new deadlines for Portugal and Spain. Press release, 9 August 2016. www.brookings.edu/articles/monetary-policy-and-inequality/

Craig, P. (2017). The Eurogroup, power and accountability. *European Law Journal* 23, 234–249.

Crum, B., and Merlo, S. (2020). Democratic legitimacy in the post-crisis EMU. *Journal of European Integration* 42(3), 399–413.

Committee for the Study of Economic and Monetary Union (Delors Report) (1989). Report on the Economic and Monetary Union in the European Communities.

De Haan, J. (1997). The European Central Bank: Independence, accountability and strategy: A review. *Public Choice* 93, 395–426.

De Haan, J., Amtenbrink, F., and Eijffinger, S. C. W. (1999). Accountability of central banks: Aspects and quantification. *BNL Quarterly Review* 52(209), 169–193.

De Jong, J. F. M., and Gilbert, N. D. (2019). Fiscal discipline in EMU? Testing the effectiveness of the Excessive Deficit Procedure. *European Journal of Political Economy* 61, 101822.

Delpla, J., and von Weizsäcker, J. (2010). The Blue Bond Proposal. Bruegel Policy Brief No. 2010/03.

Draghi, M. (2015). ECB press conference of 22 October 2015. Introductory statement to the press conference (with Q&A). www.ecb.europa.eu/press/pressconf/2015/html/is151022.en.html

Efstathiou, K. and Wolff, G. (2019). What drives national implementation of EU policy recommendations? Bruegel Working Paper No. 4, 24 April.

Eichengreen, B. and Frieden, J. (1993). The political economy of European monetary unification: An analytical introduction. *Economics & Politics* 5, 85–104.

Enderlein, H., Spiess, J., and Guttenberg, L. (2013). Blueprint for a cyclical shock insurance in the euro area. Studies & Reports No. 100. Jacques Delors Institute.

European Central Bank (2011). *The Monetary Policy of the ECB*. Frankfurt a.M.: ECB.

European Commission (2017a). Reflection Paper on the Deepening of the Economic and Monetary Union. COM(2017) 291.

European Commission (2017b). A European unemployment benefit scheme. The rationale and the challenges ahead. Directorate-General for Employment, Social Affairs and Inclusion, Directorate A – Employment & Social Governance, Unit A4 – Thematic analysis, January 2017.

European Commission (2019). *The EU Budget at a Glance*. Brussels: Publications Office of the European Union.

European Commission (2020). Economic governance review: Report on the application of Regulations (EU) No. 1173/2011, 1174/2011, 1175/2011, 1176/2011, 1177/2011, 472/2013 and 473/2013 and on the suitability of Council Directive 2011/85/EU, COM(2020) 55 final.

European Fiscal Board (2021). *Annual Report 2021*. Brussels: European Fiscal Board.

Ferejohn, J. (2002). Judicializing politics, politicizing law. *Law and Contemporary Problems* 65(3), 41–68.

Fromage, D. (2018). The European Parliament in the post-crisis era: An institution empowered on paper only? *Journal of European Integration* 40(3), 81–294.

Goldmann, M. (2020). The European economic constitution after the PSPP judgment: Towards integrative liberalism? *German Law Journal* 21(5), 1058–1077.

Gormley, L. W., and de Haan, J. (1996). The democratic deficit of the European Central Bank. *European Law Review* 21, 95–112.

Habermas, J. (1987). *The Theory of Communicative Action. Volume 2. Lifeworld and System: A Critique of Functionalist Reason* (Trans. T. McCarthy). Boston: Beacon Press.

Heidebrecht, S. (2019). Balancing independence and legitimacy. *Zeitschrift für Politikwissenschaft* 29, 393–410.

Heywood, A. (2019). *Politics*, 5th ed. London: Macmillan International Higher Education/Red Globe Press.

Hodson, D. (2020). EMU and political union revisited: What we learnt from the euro's second decade. *Journal of European Integration* 42(3), 295–310.

Ioannidis, M. (2020). The European Central Bank. In F. Amtenbrink and C. Herrmann (eds.), *The EU Law of Economic and Monetary Union*. Oxford: Oxford University Press, 353–388.

Karatzia, A., and Markakis, M. (2017). What role for the Commission and the ECB in the European Stability Mechanism? *Cambridge International Law Journal* 6(2), 232–252.

Keppenne, J.-P. (2020). Economic policy coordination: Foundations, structures, and objectives. In F. Amtenbrink and C. Herrmann (eds.), *The EU Law of Economic and Monetary Union*. Oxford: Oxford University Press, pp. 787–812.

Kröger, S. (2019). How limited representativeness weakens throughput legitimacy in the EU: The example of interest groups. *Public Administration* 97, 770–783.

Magnussen, A. M. and Banasiak, A. (2013). Juridification: Disrupting the relationship between law and politics? *European Law Journal* 19, 325–339.

Markakis, M. and Karatzia, A. (2020). The final act on the Eurogroup and effective judicial protection in the EU: Chrysostomides. EU Law Live (22.12.2020). eulawlive.com/op-ed-the-final-act-on-the-euro group-and-effective-judicial-protection-in-the-eu-chrysostomides-by-menelaos-markakis-and-anastasia-karatzia/

Philippon, T. (2015). The state of the monetary union. VOXEU, CEPR's Policy Portal, 31 August. https://voxeu.org/article/state-monetary-union

Praet, P. (2015). Public sector security purchases and monetary dominance in a monetary union without a fiscal union. Speech at the Conference The ECB and Its Watchers XVI, Contribution to the Panel on Low-interest-rate Policy and Non-standard Monetary Policy Measures: Effectiveness and Challenges, Frankfurt am Main.

Schnabel, I. (2020). The shadow of fiscal dominance: Misconceptions, perceptions and perspectives. Speech at the Centre for European Reform and the Eurofi Financial Forum, Berlin, 11 September.

Schmidt, S. K. (2018). *The European Court of Justice and the Policy Process: The Shadow of Case Law*. Oxford: Oxford University Press.

Schmidt, V. A. (2012). Democracy and legitimacy in the European Union revisited: Input, output and 'throughput'. *Political Studies* 61(1), 2–22.

Schmidt, V. A., and Wood, M. (2019). Conceptualizing throughput legitimacy: Procedural mechanisms of accountability, transparency, inclusiveness and openness in EU governance. *Public Administration* 97, 727–740.

Staudinger, I. (2021). The Court of Justice's self-restraint of reviewing financial assistance conditionality in the Chrysostomides case. *European Papers* 6(1), 177–188.

Teubner, G. (1987). Juridification concepts, aspects, limits, solutions. In G. Teubner (ed.), *Juridification of Social Spheres: A Comparative Analysis in the Areas of Labor, Corporate, Antitrust and Social Welfare Law*. Berlin: De Gruyter.

Tuori, K. (2020). Monetary policy (objectives and instruments). In F. Amtenbrink and C. Herrmann (eds.), *The EU Law of Economic and Monetary Union*. Oxford: Oxford University Press, pp. 615–698.

Vujčić, B. (2016). The role of central banks and how to insure their independence. Speech at the Symposium on 'Central Banking in Central and Eastern Europe: Policy Making, Investment and Low Yields', organized by the Czech National Bank and OMFIF, Prague, 10 June 2016.

Werner Report (1970). Report to the Council and Commission on the Realization by Stages of Economic and Monetary Union in the Community (OJ 1970, C 136/1).

Wyplosz, C. (1999). Economic policy coordination in EMU: Strategies and institutions. In Deutsch-Französisches Wirtschaftspolitisches Forum (ed.), *Financial Supervision and Policy Coordination in the EMU*. ZEI Working Paper, No. B 11-1999, Rheinische Friedrich-Wilhelms-Universität Bonn, Zentrum für Europäische Integrationsforschung (ZEI), Bonn.

5

Ideas, Interests, and Power

Germany's Complex Balancing Act in the Process of Economic and Monetary Union in Europe

Kenneth Dyson

5.1 INTRODUCTION

The issue of German power – its nature and its use – has remained at the heart of the Economic and Monetary Union (EMU) in Europe since its inception and has sparked much controversy. Quite simply, constructing EMU within the framework of European integration lacked serious economic and political credibility without Germany's willing and constructive participation. Germany occupied the pivotal position in launching the process, its agenda-setting power reflected in the tendency to deliberate and negotiate around German papers or papers co-authored by Germany (preferably with France). This pivotal position stemmed from Germany's role as the systemically significant net creditor state in the European integration process: a function of its relative size; the range and quality of its manufacturing exports; its large and persisting current account surpluses; its unmatched record of combining economic growth, price stability, and a strong currency; its prudent fiscal management; and, in consequence, its reputation for economic stability. European Union partners recognized that, to secure German participation, its governing elites had to be able to sell the new single currency domestically as 'at least as strong as the Deutschmark'.

Against this background, negotiating EMU, managing its crises, and reforming its institutional structures and policy mechanisms rested on asymmetric bargaining power. This asymmetry bedevilled the key strategic relationship with France as well as with other significant players such as Italy. German loyalty and voice – and listening to that voice – were key to the process of European monetary union. Conversely, a German exit, or its threat, raised the prospect of the end to any hope of establishing and retaining market and political credibility. In consequence, all roads to power over shaping EMU led to, and through, Germany – not least for the European Commission and European Central Bank (ECB) and for Member States like France, Italy, and the Netherlands. This context helps explain the choices of Frankfurt as the site for the new ECB, the Dutch central bank governor as its first president, the Bundesbank's chief economist as its first chief economist, as well as the term 'euro' rather than the French-sounding ecu for the new single currency. How Germany thought about its power, how it wished its power to be seen, and how it tried to use its power were clearly of decisive importance in shaping the character of EMU. If it was a hegemon, what kind?

This chapter draws on confidential interviews in the Federal Chancellor's Office, the federal finance ministry, the federal economics ministry, the Bundesbank, the European Central Bank, and DG2 of the European Commission.

EMU embodied two characteristics that helped to define the challenge facing Germany. First, it was an incomplete and evolving process, with an asymmetry between its pillar of monetary union and that of continuing Member State sovereignty in fiscal and economic policies. There was no agreement amongst Member States about final design. From the outset there had been opposed coalitions of Member States. In negotiating how EMU was to be constructed, the divide was between those advocating that economic convergence must precede monetary union (the 'economist' approach) and those maintaining that monetary integration could drive convergence (the 'monetarist' approach) (Dyson, 1994, pp. 66, 80, 345).

In thinking about the architecture of EMU and its reform, the divide was between those Member States committed to a 'stability union' and those committed to a 'fiscal union' (Hacker and Koch, 2017). Advocates of a 'stability union' prioritized an independent ECB with a narrow mandate to deliver price stability, clear and firm rules binding Member States' fiscal and structural policies, and no collective risk-sharing that rewarded irresponsible Member States by 'bail-outs'. EMU had to be proof against moral hazard. Proponents of a 'fiscal' union sought a fiscal stabilization mechanism involving transfers to Member States in serious difficulties, with Member States retaining their policy autonomy. They also backed unconventional monetary policies like quantitative easing, which advocates of a 'stability union' condemned as the monetary financing of deficits, inducing fiscal laxity.

German economic policy preferences placed the country firmly in the 'economist' and the 'stability union' camps, much closer to the New Hanseatic League, represented by the Netherlands, Denmark, Sweden, and Austria, than to France (Howarth and Schild, 2021; Wasserfallen et al., 2019). Moral hazard was to be avoided by robust defence of the independence of the ECB, by clear rules and attached sanctions in fiscal policies, by staunch opposition to transfers as an instrument of adjustment, and by strict conditionality for euro entry (the convergence criteria) and to accompany any forms of collective assistance to a euro area Member State in crisis. These policy positions represented what German EMU negotiators meant when, in 1971, in the wake of the Werner Report on EMU, they talked about a 'community of solidarity' (*Solidargemeinschaft*) as opposed to a 'community of risk' (*Risikogemeinschaft*) (Dyson and Featherstone, 1999, pp. 293–94) The operating assumption of EMU negotiators was that Germany would use its power to protect its interests by a leadership role on behalf of the 'economist' approach to EMU and of an architecture that sustained a 'stability union'. The question was how Germany would reconcile the pursuit of its interests with the challenge of managing the divisions about how to progress and to design EMU.

Secondly, the EMU process was punctuated by crises such as the tribulations of the 'Snake' exchange rate system in the 1970s; the Exchange Rate Mechanism (ERM) crises of 1983, 1987, and 1992–93; the post-2008 financial and then economic and sovereign debt crises; and the COVID-19 crisis in 2020–21. When such crises threatened to become existential for the whole European integration project, successive German federal chancellors were induced to act by the recognition that European integration was part of their state's *raison d'état* – Germany's ultimate insurance policy, written into the preamble of its Basic Law. As federal chancellor Angela Merkel reminded the Bundestag on 26 October 2011, at the height of the sovereign debt crisis: 'If the euro fails, Europe will fail' (Kornelius, 2013, p. 227). In such circumstances, though hedged by important qualifications and conditions, Germany revealed a willingness to make concessions – notably, in 2011 over the creation of the European Stability Mechanism (ESM) and in 2020, potentially more strikingly, over the creation of a European Union fiscal policy mechanism, albeit time-limited, with common debt issuance and substantial payments in grants to Member States, as part of the Next Generation EU (NGEU) (de la Porte and Jensen, 2021).

This chapter focuses on the nature and uses of German power in EMU over time. It analyses how German policymakers in EMU negotiations have handled the complex challenge of precariously balancing two intertwined sets of interests and ideas in which they are differentially embedded. On the one hand, they face an inheritance of a striking cross-party consensus on Germany's geopolitical and foreign and security policy interests and of foreign policy ideas about how best to pursue international cooperation. On the other, they are embedded in a powerful structure of German economic interests and economic policy ideas that are believed to best serve these interests (see Howarth and Schild, 2021). Within these strategic parameters, federal chancellors have characteristically sought to pursue tactical flexibility. They attempt to find a dynamic equilibrium between shaping the agenda on EMU on behalf of German economic interests and policy preferences; to hammer out common positions with the French government in a form of privileged bilateralism; to act more widely as a bridge-builder and avoid being identified as contributing to a split in the EU; and, in this way, to retain the reputation and soft power that comes from being a trusted player that is respected by all. The policy style of German federal chancellors in the context of the European Council inclines towards juggling tactical options within a constrained context.

5.2 THE EMBEDDEDNESS OF EMU IN GERMAN GEO-STRATEGY AND CONCEPTIONS OF FOREIGN AND SECURITY POLICY

Continuity and change in the geopolitical context and in role conceptions in foreign and security policy have played a major role in shaping German interests and use of power for developing EMU policy positions and engaging in EMU negotiations. Geopolitics and foreign and security policy have weighed most heavily on the strategic and tactical considerations of federal chancellors and foreign ministers. They shape the German approach to European Council and Euro Summit negotiations, above all in times of euro area crisis, and reflect the importance that diplomats play in the workings of the federal chancellor's office.

In the 1970s, two decades before the launch of the euro area, federal chancellor Helmut Schmidt's initiative to strengthen European economic and monetary integration through the European Monetary System (EMS) was framed through the lens of geopolitics and foreign and security policy as well as of German economic interests. Growing European criticism of the failures of Western leadership under then-US President Jimmy Carter, the decline of international economic coordination, and the strategic imbalance in Europe resulting from Soviet missile deployments created an opportunity to enhance Germany's international profile, and strengthen domestic support for the chancellor, by a leadership role in international summitry (Spohr, 2016). In Schmidt's narrative, used to persuade the Bundesbank, EMU was about avoiding the threat of German isolation and securing German security in a sense that transcended economics – and thus the responsibility of the central bank (Dyson, 2021, p. 408). Later, during debates about euro area reform from 2010, federal chancellor Angela Merkel prioritized the issue of Europe's global competitiveness and standing in an increasingly multipolar world, with the rise of China as a great power. Against the background of this global challenge, citing China and South-East Asia, she stressed that it was necessary to safeguard the EU and the euro as an economic counterweight by strengthening incentives for Member States to press ahead with economic reforms (Kornelius, 2013, pp. 189–98, 270–71). By 2020–21, mounting geostrategic worries about China, reinforced by the COVID-19 crisis, made Germany amenable to applying the concept of strategic autonomy to debates about external trade, the single market, and EMU.

German federal economics and finance ministers and their officials bear narrower responsibilities but ones that are vital to effective EMU governance. They are preoccupied with promoting German economic interests through technical fora such as the Eurogroup, the Economic and Financial Committee, and the Eurogroup Working Group. In a similar fashion, Bundesbank presidents are immersed in the affairs of the ECB. Even so, German finance ministers have recognized the importance of engaging with geopolitics and foreign and security policy interests. Successive Bundesbank presidents, even the most hawkish in monetary policy, are very aware of the limits of their authority over EMU. This recognition was evident when the French and German finance ministers, Pierre Bérégovoy and Theo Waigel, met in the Franco-German Economic Council on 24–25 August 1989 on the Tegernsee, joined by the president of the Bundesbank, Karl-Otto Pöhl (details in Dyson and Featherstone, 1999, pp. 190–94, 358–59). In the light of fast-moving events in eastern Europe, and new possibilities to reorder Europe, all three stressed the need for more intensive Franco-German collaboration to speed up progress on EMU. Federal finance ministry officials were pressed to review inherited views about EMU and to upgrade Franco-German cooperation (Dyson and Featherstone, 1999, pp. 359–62). Once the Intergovernmental Conference (IGC) on EMU had convened, and controversy sparked by the German draft treaty, Waigel backed the idea of top-secret Franco-German bilateral meetings, involving finance ministry and central bank officials, to try to narrow differences. They met six times between April and November 1990 (for details, see Dyson and Featherstone, 1999, pp. 412–17). Engaging in this way was seen as a means of keeping the federal chancellor and the foreign minister away from intervening in EMU business. The need to combine recognition of geopolitical and foreign and security policy interest with retaining control over the EMU process recurred in the post-2009 sovereign debt crisis. In 2011 the French and German finance ministers, Christine Lagarde and Wolfgang Schäuble, agreed to establish Franco-German working units in each other's ministries. Again, the signal to officials was to review inherited views about EMU.

The linkage between geopolitical interests and EMU remains the specialist domain of the intimate inner circle of diplomats around the federal chancellor, notably the chief foreign and European advisers. The definition of German geopolitical interests in European integration displayed a striking continuity from the chancellorship of Konrad Adenauer (1949–63) onwards. European integration, in close cooperation with France, was identified as providing the framework of security on which the successful pursuit of German economic interests and economic policy preferences depends. This principle represented a thread of continuity that connected the advisers to Adenauer (Herbert Blankenhorn, Felix von Eckhardt, and Walter Hallstein), to those of Helmut Kohl (Joachim Bitterlich and Horst Teltschik), and those of Merkel (Uwe Corsepius, Christoph Heusgen, and Nikolaus Meyer-Landrut). They helped to drive the 'embedded bilateralism' that privileged Franco-German discussions within the European integration process (Krotz and Schild, 2013). From the Elysée Treaty of 1963, through the creation of the Franco-German Economic Council as part of the twenty-fifth anniversary celebrations in 1988, to the Aachen Treaty of 2019, the institutional structures and working practices of Franco-German collaboration have been extended and deepened at political and official levels. The emphasis is on working to produce joint papers on EMU.

German policy on EMU was embedded in a foreign policy discourse that moulded together realistic analysis with a historically conditioned normative outlook that sharply constrained elite views on the nature and use of German power. Two lessons were drawn from Germany's traumatic experience as a unified state since 1871. First, Germany was a distinctively vulnerable state in the middle of Europe, with multiple neighbours, whose confidence and trust had to be cultivated if Germany was to live in peace and prosperity. Secondly, this confidence and trust building was an unprecedented challenge for Germany after the collapse of its moral authority by 1945. The politics of memory infected and constrained post-war German conceptions of how to use power. Against this background, German policy style became identified with the civilian power role concept (Maull, 2000). According to Hans Maull (2014, p. 9), this role concept had three characteristics: 'never again' (a rejection of Germany's past as a nationalist, expansionist, and militaristic great power), 'never alone' (a commitment to multilateralist foreign policies), and 'politics before force'. This role concept of civilian power was flexible enough to accommodate a 'shaping power' in EMU negotiations but as a 'cooperative hegemon', 'never alone' and 'never again' locked in power rivalry with France (Hellmann, 2016; Pedersen, 2002). German elites were reluctant to be seen as exercising hegemonic power in EMU (Bulmer and Paterson, 2019). Merkel, for instance, sought to present herself as the representative of a big Member State which enjoyed the best relations with the smaller EU states (Heckel, 2009, p. 231). She looked to other Member States with aligned economic interests, like the New Hanseatic League during the negotiations about the NGEU in 2020, to push hard for agreement on terms close to what she would like. Meanwhile, Germany worked closely with France and played its bridge-building role in the EU and between the EU and the euro area. The Dutch could be counted on to pursue a more abrasive policy style on behalf of closely aligned economic policy preferences.

5.3 THE EMBEDDEDNESS OF EMU IN GERMAN ECONOMIC INTERESTS AND ECONOMIC POLICY PREFERENCES

A striking continuity in German geopolitical interests and role conception in foreign policy has helped frame, guide, and constrain German approaches to the political economy of EMU, not least in policy style. It has been associated with a willingness to contemplate concessions. However, geopolitical interests and foreign policy role conception remain essentially contextual. Their presence and impact are less discernible in the more routinized, humdrum processes of economic governance, conducted in the complex and highly technical institutional milieus of EMU governance. Moreover, inclinations to make concessions on geopolitical and foreign policy grounds are constrained by the ongoing challenges of securing domestic institutional and political support. In defining the range of potentially acceptable outcomes at the domestic level, German EMU negotiators had to pay close attention to powerful domestic institutions, like the Bundesbank in negotiating the EMS and later the Maastricht Treaty, and the possibility of judicial review by the Federal Constitutional Court. They had also to take account of the structure of domestic party support for economic interests and economic policy ideas, of internal party and coalition dynamics, and of public opinion as expressed in media coverage, opinion polls, and federal and state elections. On occasion, the contrast between the seeming independence of action of a French president and the tortuous, slower-moving internal negotiations of a German federal chancellor proved a source of friction. This tension surfaced in 2008–9 over the coordinated EU fiscal stimulus in the wake of the Lehman Brothers collapse, with the attribution of the remark that 'France acts while Germany thinks' to Nicolas Sarkozy (Heckel, 2009, pp. 163–67, 173).

At the institutional level, the strategy of 'binding in' the Bundesbank became a decisive component in German EMU negotiations before 1999. In the case of the EMS agreement in 1978, Chancellor Schmidt made a special visit to the Bundesbank council to emphasize to its members that currency interventions to support the new ERM would not jeopardize its statutory obligation to 'safeguard the currency' (details in Dyson, 2021, p. 408). The strategy of 'binding in' the Bundesbank was even more evident in the process of negotiating the Maastricht Treaty. At the Hanover European Council in 1988, Chancellor Kohl ensured that central bank presidents were the majority presence in the membership of the Delors Committee. Later, Bundesbank officials were closely involved in the work of the IGC on EMU (Dyson and Featherstone, 1999, p. 42). Similarly, Chancellor Kohl asked for the Bundesbank's opinion on the EU Member States qualifying for stage three in 1998. The consent of the Bundesbank, even if only tacit, was essential for the German federal government to credibly claim that the new single currency would be at least as strong as the Deutschmark and that the government had given due care and attention to ensuring the euro area would be a 'stability community'. This consent was essential to secure and retain public and bipartisan party support.

However, the creation of the euro area, and the loss of its monetary policy responsibility, meant that from 1999 the Bundesbank ceded power as a privileged economic policy adviser to the federal government. Its relative loss of power vis-à-vis the federal finance ministry was soon demonstrated in 2003. Its opposition to the support of Chancellor Gerhard Schröder's government for a more flexible Stability and Growth Pact (SGP) to accommodate Germany's economic and financial problems proved ineffective (Dyson, 2009). This loss was further underlined during the post-2008 financial, economic, and sovereign debt crisis by its minority position as a 'hawk' on monetary policy in the governing council of the ECB. Merkel offered tacit support for the unconventional monetary policies of the ECB, including Draghi's famous commitment in July 2012 'to do whatever it takes' to safeguard the euro. She did so, in part, to stave off the existential crisis in the euro area and, in part, to divert pressure away from more politically sensitive and damaging demands for fiscal transfers. The Bundesbank was no longer the feared veto player that it had been in the federal chancellery and the federal finance ministry.

In addition, when contemplating possible concessions in EMU negotiations, federal chancellors faced major domestic electoral, party, and coalition constraints. Federal chancellors had to manage the dispersal of power in the federal system and take account of the frequency of state elections that could alter the balance of power in federal politics through change in the composition of the Bundesrat, the second chamber. In negotiations about the post-2009 sovereign debt crisis and reforms to euro area architecture, Merkel stressed these constraints in managing relations with French presidents, with presidents of the European Commission, and with other Member States, for instance, over the proposals for Eurobonds, for a European rescue fund for the financial sector, and for a euro area fiscal stabilization capacity. In 2010–12, she faced serious problems within her coalition partner, the liberal Free Democratic Party (FDP), about the ESM as a new financial support facility for euro area Member States in crisis, along with an appeal to the Federal Constitutional Court. In addition, leading German economists created anxieties about the way in which huge imbalances in the euro payment and settlement system (TARGET 2) were producing implicit liabilities for Germany (notably Sinn, 2012). These domestic problems enabled Merkel to stress the importance of attaching stringent conditions to the ESM and the need to link it to the 'fiscal compact' treaty that would reinforce Member States' fiscal discipline on the model of the German 'debt brake'. Similarly, following the election of President Macron in 2017, she was under great pressure to create a euro area fiscal capacity. In resisting she was mindful of the domestic electoral advances of the far-right Alternative for Germany (AfD) party, notably in the 2017 German federal elections, and the nervousness within her own Christian Democratic Union (CDU) and its sister party in Bavaria, the Christian Social Union (CSU). The rise of the AfD, worries about impending state elections, and the uncertainties created by repeated resort of critics to the Federal Constitutional Court narrowed the domestic room for manoeuvre in striking EU/euro area-level agreements on EMU.

German economic interests and the intellectual justification of their pursuit in German policy positions on EMU were the special responsibility of the federal economics and finance ministries – each possessing considerable individual independence under Article 65 of the Basic Law – and of the Bundesbank, one of the two most trusted German institutions and highly protective of its independence. German academic economists in a range of advisory councils provided intellectual legitimacy. In addition, leading German banks and industrial firms, along with employer and industrial organizations, were important in marshalling political support. The federal economics and finance ministries and the Bundesbank operated in their own domestic as well as EU technical-institutional milieus in which they sought to cultivate support.

In the early stages of EMU, German economic policy preferences were pursued in the context of the Council of Economic and Finance Ministers (ECOFIN), the EC Monetary Committee, and the Committee of EC Central Bank Governors. Participation in the Werner Group of 1970 offered the stimulus for German economics ministry officials to crystallize German commitment to the 'economist' approach to EMU, advocating convergence as the precondition for monetary union, with monetary union as the final coronation of EMU. They proved willing to settle on the principle of parallel progress in economic and monetary union, a way of inserting conditionality in any moves to monetary union and reflecting a deep-seated caution. Later, with the creation of the euro area, ECOFIN, the Eurogroup, the Economic and Financial Committee, the Eurogroup Working Group, and the ECB were central points of reference. In both stages, German finance ministry officials and central bankers exhibited an interest in institutional autonomy at this technical level, an interest that increased in times of pressure from the European Council, from the twice-yearly Euro Summits post-2011, and from the German foreign ministry. By striking agreements at this level, they sought to keep as much business as possible away from the European Council and the foreign ministry and thereby reduce the risks to German economic interests from high-level political concessions (Dyson and Featherstone, 1999). German concessions at technical level could be preferable to the uncertainties of marathon, late-night European Council sessions. Hence EU/euro area institutional factors created their own cross-national *esprit de corps* and technical-level pressures for German concessions. They were linked to a close interest of the German economics and finance ministries and of the Bundesbank in the design and control of the institutional venues in which EMU issues were negotiated, notably in a strong role for the Bundesbank (details in Dyson and Featherstone, 1999, pp. 57–59).

German policy positions on EMU rested on a fusion of realistic economic analysis of material interests with a distinctive set of economic policy ideas. These policy ideas combined an inherited native ordo-liberalism with a newly emerging internationally mainstream monetarist, credibility, and time-consistency literature by the 1980s. The definition of material economic interests was shaped by Germany's position from the early 1950s as Europe's most powerful net creditor state; as its most powerful manufacturing exporter, with often huge trade surpluses; as traditionally a European model of sound fiscal and monetary policies; and as the beneficiary of a consistently high sovereign creditworthiness rating. Germany's advantage in EMU negotiations was that these material interests were also strengths to deploy in shaping both the process and the content of EMU. In developing positions on EMU, German negotiators sought to protect and export these strengths: to upload the German model into the architecture of EMU and its working principles, perhaps most strikingly in the initial design of the ECB and in the transposition of Germany's constitutional 'debt brake' into the 'fiscal compact' treaty of 2012. In working closely with France on this architecture, German negotiators sought to negate concessions to France on *gouvernement économique* by filling the concept with German content. This strategy was evident in the contrast between Franco-German proposals for a eurozone budget in their Meseberg Declaration of June 2018 and their more detailed, modest proposal of November 2018. Franco-German relations in EMU remained close and privileged but, at the level of power over EMU, asymmetric.

For a Germany that was the trading power of the EU, the single European market was the crown jewel of European integration (on trade as the dominant interest of Germany's, see Kundnani, 2014). EMU was attractive to the extent that it could be justified as adding value to this jewel. The German export sector welcomed EMU as a means of reinforcing the gains of the single market through lower transaction costs, not least by ending the uncertainties of exchange rate instability. From this perspective, a larger EMU was preferable to a smaller. Evidence suggests that Germany was a significant beneficiary in trade terms from EMU in the period 1988–2009 (Wierts et al., 2014). Also, reinforcing the euro area through the creation of a 'core Europe', at cost to the integrity of the EU as a whole and its larger single market, posed economic risks for Germany as a trading power. This economic policy interest reinforced Merkel's preference for tying measures to strengthen the euro area to the EU. This strategy was pursued in the negotiations on the NGEU. The new fiscal capacity mechanism with its mix of grants and loans to Member States was linked to the EU's new Multiannual Financial Framework negotiations, giving all twenty-seven Member States a veto right.

German exporters recognized that the gains from the single market would be nullified if, in the process of reforming EMU, Germany's long-term strengths were to be impaired by unwise political concessions. They retained an interest in an EU-wide priority to convergence and competitiveness. A characteristic of EMU negotiations was that German banks, industrial companies, and employer and industrial associations retained trust in their economics and finance ministry officials and central bankers to construct and safeguard an institutional and policy structure that would protect their interests. German economic and finance ministry officials and central bankers enjoyed considerable latitude in matters of EMU architecture.

The intellectual justification for German positions in negotiating EMU from the 1970s onwards, and processes of cross-national consensus-building in the EU, was strengthened by a fortuitous convergence of developments in mainstream international economics with what had been regarded as idiosyncratic and outdated German ordo-liberal thinking in the earlier post-war age of the so-called Keynesian revolution. What had been German exceptionalism in a world of neo-Keynesian economic policy ideas became part of the new international mainstream. German arguments were more readily received, because they were consistent with the new conventional wisdom. Ordo-liberalism was not so much a technical economic theory as a set of principles about how best to design a sustainable and humane competitive market order (on which see Dyson, 2021, pp. 108–9). It gained domestic cultural resonance through cultivation of historical memory of the damage inflicted on Germany by hyperinflation, notably in 1923 and post-1945. The principles included the primacy of stable prices, open markets, unrestricted liability, and long-term continuity of economic policies (see the classic formulation in Eucken, 1952, pp. 254–337). The Bundesbank interpreted ordo-liberalism as providing useful legitimation of the principle of strict central bank independence, linked to the specific mandate of ensuring price stability. Uploading this model to the ECB was judged to be a major German negotiating success. According to ordo-liberalism, the principles had to be enshrined in a rule-based order, an 'economic constitution', and in reliance on market pressures, notably through bond markets, to enforce responsible fiscal behaviour (Issing, 2013). EMU required clear, firm rules governing the fiscal policies of Member States with respect to deficits and debt, enshrined in the SGP and enforced through the excessive deficit procedure; no monetary financing of deficits; a medium-term stability orientation in monetary policy that paid attention to a rule related to money-supply growth; and, more generally, avoidance of moral hazard, for instance through transfer payments.

Wilhelm Röpke was the ordo-liberal closest to Ludwig Erhard, federal economics minister 1949–63 and federal chancellor 1963–66 (Dyson, 2021, p. 358). He had argued that a stable European order must begin at home, in a 'bottom-up' fashion, with sound domestic policies of monetary and financial discipline on the German and Swiss models. The central danger to European integration arises when net creditor states become impotent in the face of demands from net debtor states (Röpke, 1954). This argument was reflected in Erhard's tough approach to the European Payments Union (EPU) in the 1950s: that the burden of adjustment must be undertaken by debtor states (Kaplan and Schleiminger, 1989). It resurfaced later in German attitudes to the crisis of the French franc in 1968, to successive ERM crises, to the architecture of the euro in the Maastricht Treaty, and to the sovereign debt crises post-2009, for instance in the design of the new macroeconomic imbalances procedure (MIP) of 2011. The MIP would trigger in-depth European Commission review, leading ultimately to sanctions, in cases of excessive current account imbalances. However, the rules of the MIP were more generous to surplus states like Germany than to deficit states: the surplus threshold was set at 6 per cent of GDP, the deficit threshold at 4 per cent. The issue of who bears the burden of adjustment to imbalances haunted European monetary integration across the decades (see the contribution by James, Chapter 3 in this volume) and, more than any other, exposed Germany to severe criticism.

The ordo-liberal emphasis on the responsible debtor as the foundation of economic stability was echoed in the principle advocated by Jens Weidmann, president of the Bundesbank, as the basis for euro area reforms (Maastricht 2.0) in the wake of the sovereign debt crises in the euro area – no liability without control (Weidmann, 2020). If Member States insist on retaining their fiscal sovereignty and sovereign rights with respect to structural economic reforms, they must remain liable for the consequences. Mutualization of risks, without a corresponding transfer of sovereignty in fiscal and economic policies to the European level, would increase moral hazard in euro area governance. Consistent with this argument, German negotiators resisted the call for Eurobonds and for the creation of a euro area fiscal capacity involving transfers. In negotiations on European banking union, they resisted calls for an early single resolution fund and empowerment of the ESM to recapitalize euro area banks until an effective independent single supervisory mechanism was in place. They worked to limit the financial capacity of the Single Resolution Fund and placed strong constraints on use of the ESM to recapitalize banks. And they helped to block collective deposit insurance, citing moral hazard (Howarth and Quaglia, 2016).

The persuasive force of these positions on EMU was reinforced not just by Germany's material power and status as a model but also by the synchronization of the design of EMU from the late 1970s with the capture of mainstream academic economics by monetarism and by credibility and time-consistency literature. Compliance with clear rules helped to stabilize long-term expectations. It meant binding the hands of governments to counter their political incentives to use discretion opportunistically, sacrificing the long-term to short-term party and electoral advantage.

Two factors, related to the structure and dynamics of EMU, posed problems for embedding German policy ideas in its evolution. In the first place, Germany was the one systemically significant net creditor power. Net creditor powers were numerically in a minority within the institutional structures of EMU. The other net creditor powers, like the Netherlands, looked to German leadership based on this affinity of economic interest. However, German preference for bridge-building to retain and foster trust within the EU and euro area meant that Germany opted for an external observer role in the New Hanseatic League of Austria, Denmark, Finland, the Netherlands, and Sweden – the so-called Frugals – in negotiations about the fiscal policy response to the COVID-19 crisis. Germany developed position papers with France rather than the New Hanseatic League, whilst seeking concessions from France that helped to appease the 'Frugals', which Germany tacitly supported (Howarth and Schild, 2021). The NGEU was testament to the tactical juggling that stemmed from the attempt to balance economic interest as a net creditor power with multilateral EU trust-building and the embedded bilateralism with France. Germany did not seek to replicate the attitudes and behaviour of the United States in the Bretton Woods system. It was a cautious and cooperative hegemon (Bulmer and Paterson, 2019).

Secondly, the structure and dynamics of EMU altered once the euro area was launched. Earlier, Germany's partners in the EU feared a German exit from negotiations, a threat that was existentially significant because German participation was a prerequisite of a sustainable monetary union. It was essential to keep Germany on board in negotiations by being prepared to make timely concessions. The work of both the Delors Committee and then of the IGC on EMU was shaped by German agenda-setting power. A notable example was the influence of the paper by Pöhl, the president of the Bundesbank, on the contents of the Delors Report of 1989 (details in Dyson and Featherstone, 1999, pp. 342–48). The SGP of 1997 showed that this German agenda-setting power continued after the Maastricht Treaty of 1993 (details in Heipertz and Verdun, 2010). The German finance ministry sought to appease domestic opinion by strengthening the conditionality requirements on fiscal policy in stage three.

However, with the launch of the euro area, the credibility of a German threat of exit was sharply diminished. Germany faced the sheer political sunk costs invested in EMU by its governing elite, the vastly complex web of financial and economic linkages that came with monetary union and increased German vulnerability to contagion, the technical complexities that would attend exit, and – not least – the costs that would be imposed on other Member States and in the process on German geopolitical and foreign and security policy interests. Germany hoped to rely on the institutional path dependencies that had been created by the Maastricht Treaty commitments, the constitution of the ECB, and the SGP. Its policymakers were fortified by the belief that the treaty had prohibited 'bailouts' of sovereigns. The euro area was to be stabilized without a 'transfer union'. Under the SGP, the euro area had the possibility of sanctions to punish fiscal irresponsibility. The ECB appeared to be constructed as the 'Bundesbank writ large' and located in Frankfurt. It was independent under the treaty (a stronger legal status than the Bundesbank had enjoyed in Germany) and had a strict commitment to the principle of price stability. The Bundesbank's chief economist was appointed as the ECB's first chief economist. As a last resort, the German Federal Constitutional Court (FCC) could police adherence to the treaties by the federal government and by the Bundesbank's participation in the ECB governing council.

The financial, economic, and sovereign debt crisis that unwound from 2008 and then the COVID-19 crisis from 2020 showed that these hopes had been disappointed. The ECB was no longer the Bundesbank writ large under presidents Mario Draghi and Christine Lagarde. The ECB began to introduce unconventional monetary policies to provide liquidity to the banks under Jean-Claude Trichet. In 2012, Draghi went much further by promising 'to do whatever it takes' to save the euro, followed by an expansion of central bank support measures to banks and sovereign bond markets. ECB policies in quantitative easing aligned it closely with mainstream international central banking practice. Attempts by German private plaintiffs to use the FCC to strike down or limit these measures proved unsuccessful by 2021 (Fontan and Howarth, 2021). In a sign of the sense of disappointment, after his retirement the first Bundesbank chief economist, Otmar Issing, became a forceful critic of unconventional ECB monetary measures (e.g. Issing, 2011). German dissatisfaction with ECB monetary policy was reflected in the resignation of Jürgen Stark in 2011 and Sabine Lautenschläger in 2019 from the directorate of the ECB, whilst the decision of Axel Weber to quit his post as Bundesbank president in 2011 was linked to his criticisms of the ECB's shift to unconventional monetary measures. The new monetary policy strategy in 2021 showed how far the ECB had shifted towards an asymmetric target that recognized inflation and deflation as equal dangers. Lagarde also championed the idea that monetary policy should address climate change and inequality, moving the ECB closer towards the political agenda.

5.4 A DYNAMIC EQUILIBRIUM: THE ROLE OF CRISIS IN GERMAN POLICY ON EMU

The use of German power in EMU has been intimately bound up with the complex interplay of, on the one hand, deeply entrenched economic interests and economic policy beliefs and, on the other, geopolitical and security interests and foreign policy role conceptions. Their enmeshing is captured in the concept of Germany as a cooperative hegemon in EMU. In EMU negotiations, all roads led to a Germany that combined support for the principles of a 'stability union' with both privileging the Franco-German relationship and acting as bridge-builder within the EU and between the EU and the euro area. This complex balancing act explains the mixture of continuity and change in German policy on EMU and the limited scope for heroic German leadership on EMU, even by a chancellor like Schmidt, who possessed an exceptional blend of intellectual self-confidence in both economic and security policies.

However, crisis creates the potential to punctuate the equilibrium in German EMU policy, to stimulate review of the balance of German interests and inherited policy ideas, to inject a new dynamism as a new constellation of forces emerges, and to lead to change in what might remain a routinized, humdrum technical milieu. Crisis can appear as geopolitical, as financial and economic, or as a combination of these two factors, both in cause and in implication. By 2021, the overall effect of crises had been to strengthen German elite perceptions of the geopolitical and economic importance of EMU, in particular the primacy of the relationship with France. Six crises and their legacies for EMU stand out: the crisis of distrust within the European Economic Community (EEC) that was provoked by the *Ostpolitik* of Chancellor Willy Brandt from 1969, alongside the mounting troubles and eventual collapse of the Bretton Woods system in 1971–73; German unification in 1989–90, and the end of the cold war in Europe; the SGP crisis of 2003; the euro area crisis from 2010; the crisis in transatlantic relations provoked by the US presidency of Donald Trump, 2017–21; and the COVID-19 crisis of 2020–21. Each left its imprint on the history of German policy towards EMU.

5.4.1 *Ostpolitik and the Bretton Woods Crisis*

As the EEC was provided with the public good of currency stability by the US dollar peg under the Bretton Woods system, EMU did not figure as a priority in German policy towards European integration in the 1950s and into the 1960s. Loyalty to the Bretton Woods system – however great the reservations about its operation, about US policy, and about risks of imported inflation – meant that the strategic relationship with the United States – and the international institutions in which the United States was engaged – trumped that with the EEC and France in ensuring economic and monetary cooperation. European Commission proposals to promote closer economic and monetary coordination within the EEC, notably the 1962 Action Programme for the Second Stage, were heavily diluted by German economics ministry negotiators. They stressed differences of economic policy belief with France and the virtues of international free trade over European market integration.

The period 1969–73 was a turning point. The tribulations of the Bretton Woods system in Europe came to a head in 1968–69 with the crisis of the French franc and initial firm German resistance to revaluation of the Deutschmark as part of the solution. Subsequent anger in French elite circles at the use of German power, represented by the combative figure of the economics minister Karl Schiller, was accompanied by distrust of the motives underpinning Germany's new *Ostpolitik*. Against this background, the new federal chancellor Brandt sought to mend relations with France and within the EEC by throwing his weight behind the proposal for a study group on EMU at the Hague Summit in 1969. Progress in implementing the proposals of the Werner Group was to prove very limited in the face of deep-seated differences of approach – the 'economist' versus the 'monetarist' approach – and adverse circumstances, notably the post-1973 oil crisis and the economic divergence that followed. Nevertheless, at the Paris Summit in 1972, Germany had signalled support for the principle of EMU and endorsed the proposal for a European Monetary Cooperation Fund.

The collapse of the Bretton Woods system proved of long-term significance in reshaping German views of EMU. Restoring the public good of currency stability inside the EEC was vital if Germany was to reap the economic rewards of European integration. Germany supported two mechanisms to help restore monetary stability in Europe: The Community mechanism for medium-term financial assistance, providing credits to Member States in balance-of-payments difficulties, in 1971; and a supplementary mechanism of Community loans in 1975 (Dyson and Quaglia, 2010, pp. 222–23, 257–58). More importantly, in 1977–78 Chancellor Schmidt took the initiative in working with the French government to negotiate the EMS. German negotiators were able to win important concessions. Pegging the ERM to the Deutschmark, instead of the ECU basket, symbolized a 'Deutschmark zone' in the EEC; the Bundesbank was able to gain assurance from the chancellor that it would not be required to intervene to support the ERM at cost to its domestic statutory obligation to 'safeguard the currency'; and a compensatory transfer mechanism to help adjustment by some other EEC states was averted.

Despite these concessions, an institutional mechanism involving EEC central bank cooperation, with German co-responsibility for exchange rate stability, had been created. Germany was drawn into fractious ERM crisis management that led to mounting pressures for reform towards more collective responsibility. The negotiation and speedy implementation of the European single market programme in 1985–87, notably freedom of capital movement, increased these pressures. New opportunities were opened to argue for EMU based on narratives linking the single market and the ERM. This opportunity was seized by the German foreign minister, Hans-Dietrich Genscher, in February 1988 to argue 'in a personal capacity' that EMU should be a priority for the current German EC presidency (details in Dyson and Featherstone, 1999, pp. 330–35; his memorandum in Dyson and Quaglia, 2010, pp. 367–69). As foreign minister, he was concerned to reduce the damage the ERM crises, like that of 1987, were doing to France and potentially to the single market. The German presidency culminated at the Hanover

Council in June 1988 with the appointment of the Delors Committee on EMU with a mandate to propose how EMU was to be realized – not to consider the principle.

5.4.2 *German Unification and the End of the Cold War*

German unification in 1989–90 and the end of the cold war altered the parameters of discussion and changed the balance of forces in negotiations about the EMU that were ongoing after the Delors Report in April 1989, but lacked firm commitment to a timeframe. The speed of events, and German reactions to them, reawakened the question of trust of German motives and fears about how Germany's increased power might in future be used in Europe. Kohl reacted decisively by stressing the principle that German unification and European unification were both 'sides of one and the same coin'. In another metaphor, he stressed that 'the German house must be built under a European roof'. Kohl gave new priority and urgency to implementing EMU in close collaboration with France (details in Dyson and Featherstone, 1999, pp. 363–69, 375–78). The Delors Report did not suffer the neglect of the Werner Report.

Kohl helped to drive the establishment of the two intergovernmental conferences on EMU and on political union in 1990 by fixing a clear timetable; to closely monitor progress; and crucially to emphasize German commitment by insisting that the principle of irreversibility must be written into the Maastricht Treaty – the final stage three was to start in 1996 or, at the latest, in 1999 (on Kohl and irreversibility, see Dyson and Featherstone, 1999, pp. 370–72, 440–48). This concession shocked many German economists and policymakers. It was freely entered into by Kohl as principal advocate. Kohl employed the instrument of strict timetable to discipline the EMU negotiations and their aftermath.

Then, to the surprise of German economists and policymakers who had expected the launch of stage three with five or six Member States, Kohl lent support to an initial membership of nine in the euro area. For many, the launch represented a German political concession based on a very flexible, 'lax' reading of the convergence criteria for euro entry. This suspicion seemed to be confirmed by the subsequent early entry of Greece and by later revelations about the quality of the process underlying this decision.

5.4.3 *The SGP Crisis of 2003*

The SGP crisis of November 2003 was extraordinary in having a German government criticizing and seeking to reform a set of fiscal rules that had been insisted on by German negotiators in 1995–97 as necessary to embed a 'stability culture' in EMU. A key part of its context was the long-term effects of German unification on Germany's economic performance, notably the fiscal burden, and the sense that Germany faced exceptional circumstances that needed to be recognized in EMU governance.

The crisis was precipitated by the European Commission's assessment of an excessive deficit in Germany. Strikingly, the French and German governments converged in demanding that the SGP change from a system of fixed rules to one of 'constrained discretion'. It should be an insurance arrangement for Member States, not just a disciplinary instrument. It should function as an anti-cyclical instrument that would focus on preventive measures in good times and strengthen long-term growth potential to support solid public finances. This convergence in Franco-German thinking was facilitated by a coalition government of Social Democrats and Greens under Chancellor Schröder. His government was better disposed to Keynesian ideas of stabilization policy and sought EU support for its domestically costly Agenda 2010 labour market and welfare state reforms (Schröder, 2005).

Domestic opposition was led by the CDU/CSU of Merkel, who came to power in 2005, and by the Bundesbank. The SGP reform of 2005 strengthened the preventive arm and introduced more flexibility by adopting country-specific medium-term objectives and greater discretion into the corrective arm. However, little was done to strengthen the authority of the European Commission in the excessive deficit procedure. Chancellor Merkel sought to restore German moral authority as a voice for stability culture by making fiscal consolidation an urgent priority and in 2009 by introducing the 'debt brake'. In this way, she hoped to contain and reverse the effects of the 2003 crisis on Germany's reputation. In Merkel's view, fiscal consolidation was essential to regain German power in Europe. It was a lesson that she returned to when faced with later, much bigger crises.

5.4.4 *The EU Financial and Economic Crisis and the Euro Area Sovereign Debt Crises*

From 2008, after the collapse of Lehman Brothers, the euro area became embroiled in a series of shocks that by 2010–11 generated an image of existential crisis. The tipping point was the Greek crisis from 2009. Financial and economic crisis morphed into sovereign debt crises that spread to Ireland, Portugal, Spain, and Italy. The scale of the crisis meant that the Franco-German relationship and the European Council became key venues. Germany accepted the case for strengthening European economic governance but resisted an enhanced role for the European Commission and the Community method.

Initially, Schäuble (2010), the German finance minister, was reluctant to support a rescue package for Greece other than on a voluntary bilateral basis; sought to depoliticize the process of providing emergency liquidity by his plan for a European Monetary Fund; called for mandatory sanctions under the excessive deficit procedure; and advocated withdrawal of voting rights as a sanction for non-compliance, including a procedure for expulsion from EMU. In practice, these ideas had little impact. German EMU negotiators came to recognize that EMU had created a new reality that induced reflection on German interests. Specifically, both French and German banks were heavily implicated in the Greek crisis, showing how EMU had led to greater financial integration and heightened risks of cross-national contagion. At the Deauville summit in October 2010, Merkel and Sarkozy proposed the creation of a permanent euro area financial support mechanism, to become the ESM, linked to a strengthening of the SGP (later to take the form of the 'fiscal compact' treaty). The EU 'Six Pack' reforms sought to strengthen European economic governance, but without mandatory sanctions, withdrawal of voting rights, or an exit procedure. More radically, by 2012, faced with the scale of bank crises, notably in Spain, euro area reforms went further than the initial German finance ministry's thinking in focusing on the European banking union, with three pillars – supervision, resolution, and common deposit insurance. The 'doom loop' between banks and sovereigns and the risks of financial contagion required bolder thinking.

German distrust of the European Commission was an integrating theme and was reinforced by its association with the idea of Eurobonds. German negotiators sought to limit the growth of the Commission's role in the expanding scope of European economic governance with the 'Six Pack' reforms of 2010–11. This objective had been reflected in Schäuble's EMF proposal. It also underpinned Merkel's insistence that the International Monetary Fund (IMF) and the ECB join the Commission in the new 'troika' arrangement for ensuring strict monitoring of compliance with the restructuring programmes that were attached to emergency financial support for

Member States in crisis. Drawing lessons from the protracted crisis over the European constitutional treaty and the eventual Lisbon Treaty, Merkel used her Bruges speech of 2010 to stress the limits of the Commission's role and of the Community method (Kornelius, 2013, pp. 240–41). She was above all keen to avoid any discussion of euro area reform that involved formal treaty change and precipitated a political crisis. Merkel looked to new intergovernmental arrangements that placed authority in the hands of the European Council and the Euro Summits.

In 2010–12, Merkel was under serious domestic threats from restive CDU/CSU Bundestag members, from incumbent CDU/CSU state governments which feared electoral defeat, from incipient revolt in her coalition partner the FDP, and from appeals to the Federal Constitutional Court. She sought to navigate these difficulties by persuading Sarkozy and EU Member States to accept strict conditions on the activities of the ESM, not least protecting the budgetary powers of the Bundestag; to link agreement of the ESM with the new 'fiscal compact' treaty that would reinforce fiscal discipline on German terms; to ensure that the MIP gave more discretion to Member States with current account surpluses than deficits; and to stress that effective measures for cross-national banking supervision were a necessary precondition for a bank resolution mechanism, which would apply strict conditions. She insisted that common deposit insurance was conditional on it not being a transfer mechanism.

Strikingly, over the course of the main phase of institutional reforms during the crisis, Sarkozy shifted French negotiating positions closer to those of Germany. He embraced both the debt brake and the diagnosis that France needed to act to strengthen its international competitiveness. However, the election of the Socialist President François Hollande in 2012 introduced new tensions. He sought common ground with the Italian and Spanish governments on collective support for the banks and for a new growth agenda. Merkel continued to be resistant to Hollande's calls for more collective liability. In 2015, Macron, the French economics minister, and Sigmar Gabriel, the German federal economics minister, proposed a euro area fiscal capacity, with common debt issuance. This initiative reflected the German Social Democratic Party's (SPD) attempt to construct an independent reform profile before the 2017 federal elections. Its importance resided in its rehearsal of ideas that were to form the priorities of Macron's engagement with Germany as French president from 2017.

The institution that gained the greatest accretion of power during the euro area crisis was the ECB, not the European Commission. It became the key player in the European Banking Union, both in cross-national banking supervision and in bank resolution. More strikingly, from 2010 onwards it began to engage in unconventional monetary policies that ran counter to the traditional thinking of the Bundesbank, culminating in Draghi's 'whatever it takes' speech in 2012. The Bundesbank found itself increasingly isolated in the ECB governing council. Merkel hesitated to offer public backing to the Bundesbank. She did not wish to be attacked for challenging the independence of the ECB, a cherished German principle. Also, the ECB's unconventional measures reduced the pressure on the federal chancellor to support collective fiscal action to sustain the euro area economy. The change was not just in the powers of the ECB. It was represented by the characters of its presidents and directors. Draghi and Lagarde were international in career background, very different from the last two presidents of the Bundesbank before 1999 – Helmut Schlesinger and Hans Tietmeyer. The ECB's chief economists came from different intellectual milieus to Issing, the first ECB chief economist. The Bundesbank's opposition to unconventional monetary policy measures was made public in the evidence that it gave in cases before the Federal Constitutional Court.

5.4.5 *The US Trump Presidency*

The Trump presidency from 2017 represented a frontal assault on traditional German commitment to multilateralism and a rule-based international order. It represented a geopolitical crisis that had been a long time in the making as US policy pivoted to Asia and Republican voices stressed the costs of multilateralism to the United States. To sharpen the sense of a radically changing geopolitical context, US President Donald Trump did not hide his contempt for the EU and his view of Germany as an economic power that was hostile to US interests. The presidency of Joe Biden from 2021 was welcome to Merkel. However, the domestic aggression of Trump supporters, the Republican Party's capture by Trumpism and its enduring public support, meant that the German foreign policy establishment had lost confidence in its future capacity to rely on the United States as a geopolitical partner in an increasingly uncertain world.

The combination of unpredictable Trumpism, renewed threats from Russia, economic and technological challenges from China, and Britain's exit from the EU accelerated Germany's turn to the EU and to the privileged relationship with France. Germany lent support to the emerging EU consensus about strategic autonomy. This support was strengthened by the COVID-19 crisis of 2020, the concern about EU vulnerability to supply chain disruption, and the potential for the single market to unravel in the absence of collective action. Against this background, strengthening EMU's resilience to shocks assumed a geopolitical as well as economic significance for German elites. Merkel sought to lead in arguing that the EU had to be more robust in promoting and defending its competitive strengths in a more fractured, multi-polar world and in capitalizing on the advantages of its large single market. In this context, protecting the euro area acquired increased geopolitical importance.

5.4.6 *The COVID-19 Crisis and Next Generation EU*

The changing geopolitical context, the legacy and lessons of the euro area crises that erupted in 2010, and Brexit played important roles in shaping how Germany responded to the COVID-19 crisis. Germany exhibited a greater willingness to make concessions to France on euro area reform, alongside a strengthened commitment to playing a bridging role within the EU and between the EU and the euro area in the interests of wider unity. The emphasis on this bridging role was reinforced by evidence of the harm that had been done to public trust in EU institutions and in the euro by the austerity measures that had been imposed on euro area Member States in the sovereign debt crises: both the intrusive surveillance and the harsh economic and social consequences. Rebuilding trust in an increasingly unpredictable world meant revisiting the architecture of European economic governance to make it more resilient to shocks and more effective in delivering prosperity.

Before the COVID-19 crisis, the incentive for strategic review of German interests was increased by a growing sense of a threat of European disintegration (Webber, 2019). It derived from the legacy of the euro area crises; the refugee crisis of 2015–16 and subsequent criticisms of Merkel; the shock of the Brexit referendum in 2016; the sharp deterioration in transatlantic relations from 2017; and the electoral successes of far-right parties, including in Germany. This heightened context of perceived threat created a sense of urgent need to protect German economic and security interest by reinforcing EU solidarity and purpose. This need was used by President Macron to intensify pressure on Merkel, above all to give the euro area its own fiscal stabilization capacity. As in 2010–11 with Sarkozy, the subliminal message was that 'France acts, Germany thinks'.

At technical levels, German policy reflection on European economic governance was caught up in lesson-drawing from the euro area sovereign debt crises. Neo-Keynesian critiques of German and EMU orthodoxy had gained increased traction within the ECB and other institutional milieus and opened space for fresh thinking. ECB chief economists and many central bank governors had serious doubts about the deflationary bias in the earlier ECB definition of price stability as inflation 'close to, but below' 2 per cent. Previous reforms failed to counter criticism of the excessive deficit procedure and the SGP, and the obligations to treat as reference values the fiscal rules of 3 per cent of GDP for deficits and 60 per cent for public debt. The 'fiscal compact' treaty was attacked as too restrictive, with a parallel growth of domestic criticism of the German 'debt brake'. By 2021, the emerging consensus was that EMU governance must do more to promote and protect physical and social investment to strengthen the long-term growth potential of the euro area, not least in facing the enormous challenges of digitalization and climate change. In addition, the pandemic drew attention to the need to reinforce social rights through the EU's social pillar. Pressure mounted to enshrine social policy targets and milestones, for instance in childcare spending, in the European Semester for coordinating Member States' economic policies with EU goals.

By 2020–21, the momentum of change had increased. The ECB announced a new symmetric medium-term target of 2 per cent, with flexibility to fluctuate above or below target in the short term. It also made clear that the unconventional monetary policies, like quantitative easing introduced over the previous decade, were here to stay. In addition, the EU suspended the SGP and launched a review of fiscal rules designed to increase public investment in the green and digital transitions in order to promote durable economic growth as well as stability.

The NGEU was the most high-profile reform and suggested a new German willingness to make concessions, above all to France. The German government agreed to accept a temporary EU fiscal capacity (€750 billion), involving grants (€390 billion) as well as loans (€360 billion). The recovery and resilience fund was supported by large-scale common debt issuance, managed by the European Commission. A vital role was played by the Franco-German relationship, which was active in agenda-setting, tabling proposals before the Commission, and shaping the negotiations (details in de la Porte and Jensen, 2021; Howarth and Schild, 2021).

The NGEU was controversial in the German finance ministry. A new generation of German officials, with a background in macroeconomics, proved more open to this kind of reform, as along with officials in the European division who were closely immersed in EU structures. This openness was accompanied by alarm at the huge public debt burdens that Member States had accumulated in fighting the COVID-19 crisis, at the risks of runaway inflation, and at the prospect that political pressure for permanent mutualization of debts would mount and prove difficult to resist. One solution, advanced by some German ordo-liberals, was a eurozone debt redemption pact. Highly indebted Member States would mutualize debt in excess of the 60 per cent of GDP threshold, deposit good collateral, practise fiscal discipline, and reduce their debts over a specific time period. Its intellectual and political appeal was in providing for orderly debt reduction without permanent mutualization (e.g. Schäuble, 2021). However, for many German ordo-liberals, the eurozone debt redemption pact proposal did not adequately address the issue of moral hazard.

German negotiators were at pains to distance themselves from the idea that they had colluded in a 'Hamiltonian moment' in European economic governance: the assumption of collective liability. They had made two major concessions: the recovery and resilience fund offered grants which amounted to a substantial transfer; and the EU was to issue common debt. However, Germany gained a number of concessions: the new fund was temporary; it was part of the EU framework and linked to the Multiannual Financial Framework (MFF) 2021–27 negotiations, hence not strictly a euro area fiscal capacity; linkage to the MFF enabled side-payments and rebates to be offered to the New Hanseatic League of 'Frugals'; German liability was limited to its share of ECB capital (27 per cent); the emphasis was on convergence and competitiveness, alongside stabilization; allocations depended on approval of Member State recovery and resilience plans, introducing conditionality and the possibility of withholding grants in cases of serious deviation from meeting milestones and targets; whilst Germany stood to benefit from the priority given to digital and green investments and from the change in the allocation key from low-income Member States to those most seriously hit by the pandemic. Overall, the relative scale of the NGEU allocations to GDP, problems of absorptive capacity and conditionality, and potential rule-of-law issues in some states begged questions about its adequacy as a crisis-response mechanism (Howarth and Quaglia, 2021).

The NGEU testifies to enduring German power in EMU. It illustrates the attempt to use the Franco-German relationship to fill French concepts with German content. At the same time, the NGEU represents a break with the way in which Germany responded in the aftermath of the 2008 crisis. German negotiators had redefined German interests. This process had been driven by the harsh lessons of the euro area crisis, by geopolitical challenges, and by the COVID-19 crisis. These three developments had heightened German appreciation of the interconnected values of the Franco-German relationship, the single market, EU unity, and the euro area and the need to keep them in balance with each other and with domestic political and legal constraints. When it came to safeguarding security and economic interests, these four interconnected values represented Germany's ultimate insurance policy. When it came to using German power, the pursuit of cooperative hegemony seemed more attractive than heroic leadership.

However, by 2021 redefining German interests did not amount to conceding a permanent euro area fiscal capacity mechanism or common debt issuance. The pivotal role of the FDP in the key federal finance ministry meant that the scope for the SPD to be more radical on euro area policy was highly constrained. In this key respect, Germany remained a brake rather than accelerator of euro area integration. There was a heightened sense of the need to build domestic, euro area, and EU resilience through greater investment in physical and social infrastructure, notably digital and green transition, in public health, and in supply chains. Given this constraint on building fiscal capacity and common debt issuance, the euro area seemed locked into a pattern of reliance on ad hoc emergency measures to deal with crises, seeking to tame financial markets and to keep voters onside. The outcome of this politically tortuous process was likely to be far removed from the kind of 'economic constitution' that had been sought by German ordo-liberals.

REFERENCES

Bulmer, S., and Paterson, W. (2019). *Germany and the European Union: Europe's Reluctant Hegemon?* London: Red Globe Press.

De la Porte, C. and Jensen, M. (2021). The Next Generation EU: An analysis of the dimensions of conflict behind the deal. *Social Policy and Administration* 55(2), 388–402.

Dyson, K. (1994). *Elusive Union: The Process of Economic and Monetary Union in Europe*. Harlow: Longman.

Dyson, K. (2009). German Bundesbank: Europeanization and the paradoxes of power. In K. Dyson and M. Marcussen (eds.), *Central Banks in the Age of the Euro: Europeanization, Convergence, and Power*. Oxford: Oxford University Press, pp. 131–160.

Dyson, K. (2021). *Conservative Liberalism, Ordo-liberalism, and the State: Disciplining Democracy and the Market*. Oxford: Oxford University Press.

Dyson, K., and Featherstone, K. (1999). *The Road to Maastricht: Negotiating Economic and Monetary Union*. Oxford: Oxford University Press.
Dyson, K., and Quaglia, L. (2010). *European Economic Governance and Policies. Volume 1: Commentary on Key Historical and Institutional Documents*. Oxford: Oxford University Press.
Eucken, W. (1952). *Grundsätze der Wirtschaftspolitik*. Tübingen: J. C. B. Mohr.
Fontan, C., and Howarth, D. (2021). The European Central Bank and the German Constitutional Court: Police patrols and fire alarms. *Politics and Governance* 9(2), 241–251.
Hacker, B., and Koch, C. (2017). *The Divided Eurozone: Mapping Conflicting Interests on the Reform of the Monetary Union*. Berlin: Friedrich Ebert Stiftung.
Heckel, M. (2009). *So Regiert die Kanzlerin*. Munich: Piper.
Heipertz, M., and Verdun, A. (2010). *Ruling Europe: The Politics of the Stability and Growth Pact*. Cambridge: Cambridge University Press.
Hellmann, G. (2016). Power and followership in a crisis-ridden Europe. *Global Affairs* 2(1), 3–20.
Howarth, D., and Quaglia, L. (2016). *The Political Economy of European Banking Union*. Oxford: Oxford University Press.
Howarth, D., and Quaglia, L. (2021). Failing forward in Economic and Monetary Union: Explaining weak eurozone financial support mechanisms. *Journal of European Public Policy* 28(10), 1555–1572.
Howarth, D. and Schild, J. (2021). Torn between two lovers: German policy on Economic and Monetary Union, the New Hanseatic League, and Franco-German bilateralism. *German Politics* 31(2), 323–343.
Issing, O. (2011). Perversion von Solidarität, interview. *Der Spiegel*, 12, 21 March.
Issing, O. (2013). Wir brauchen die Kontrolle durch die Märkte. *Handelsblatt*, 22 July.
Kaplan, J., and Schleiminger, G. (1989). *The European Payments Union*. Oxford: Clarendon Press.
Kornelius, S. (2013). *Angela Merkel: The Chancellor and Her World*. Richmond: Alma Books.
Krotz, U., and Schild, J. (2013). *Shaping Europe: France, Germany, and Embedded Bilateralism: From the Elysée Treaty to Twenty-First Century Politics*. Oxford: Oxford University Press.
Kundnani, H. (2014). *The Paradox of German Power*. London: Hurst.
Maull, H. (2000). Germany and the use of force: Still a civilian power. *Survival* 42(2), 56–80.
Maull, H. (2014). Germany's foreign policy travails: Germany's foreign policy 1955–2014: A fairy tale success. Unpublished manuscript.
Pedersen, T. (2002). Cooperative hegemony: Power, ideas, and institutions in regional integration. *Review of International Studies* 28(4), 677–696.
Röpke, W. (1954). *Internationale Ordnung – Heute*. Erlenbach bei Zürich: Eugen Rentsch.
Schäuble, W. (2010). Why Europe's monetary union faces its biggest crisis. *Financial Times*, 12 March.
Schäuble, W. (2021). Europe's social peace requires a return to fiscal discipline. *Financial Times*, 2 June.
Schröder, G. (2005). A framework for a stable Europe. *Financial Times*, 17 January.
Sinn, H.-W. (2012). *Die Target-Falle: Gefahren für Unser Geld und Unsere Kinder*. Munich: Carl Hanser.
Spohr, K. (2016). *The Global Chancellor: Helmut Schmidt and the Reshaping of the International Order*. Oxford: Oxford University Press.
Wasserfallen, F., et al. (2019). Analysing European Union decision-making during the eurozone crisis with new data. *European Union Politics* 20(1), 3–23.
Webber, D. (2019). *European Disintegration? The Politics of Crisis in the European Union*. London: Macmillan.
Weidmann, J. (2020). Ordnungspolitik im digitalen Zietalter. Auszüge aus Presseartikeln, 5 February, pp. 7–12. Frankfurt am Main: Deutsche Bundesbank.
Wierts, P., Van Kerkhoff, H., and de Haan, J. (2014). Composition of exports and export performance of eurozone countries. *Journal of Common Market Studies* 52(4), 928–941.

6

Coping with Economic Crises through Learning by Doing

An Evolving Policy Response

Iain Begg

6.1 INTRODUCTION

After a benign first decade, the euro has been through the turbulence of the Global Financial Crisis (GFC) and the ensuing sovereign debt crisis, followed by the economic disruption triggered by COVID-19. Initially, the events starting with the problems in the US subprime mortgage sector and the knock-on effects on US financial intermediaries, culminating in the collapse of Lehman Brothers and the rescues of AIG and leading UK banks, were seen as a problem of 'Anglo-Saxon' financial systems.

Subsequently, though, the recognition that there were problems inherent in both the design of EMU and its institutional architecture led to a succession of reform initiatives. These were aimed, as the titles of relevant reports and policy statements revealed, at transforming EMU to make it 'genuine' and 'complete'. Underlying objectives ranged from boosting the resilience of the eurozone economy to shocks, to creating new institutions able to cope with future shocks – whether asymmetric or symmetric. In doing so, Europe's leaders had to contend with tensions among, and the inconsistent preferences of, the participating Member States.

Many shortcomings in the eurozone's economic governance framework were exposed after 2007, but because the sovereign debt crisis was asymmetric in only affecting selected members, finding solutions proved to be both difficult and politically contested, pitting 'creditor' nations against 'debtors'. Nevertheless, numerous reforms were enacted and initiatives launched, with the aim of boosting the resilience of the euro area and establishing mechanisms to deal with future crises.

In spite of these reforms, the onset of the pandemic economic crisis again posed challenges for economic governance. The shock was initially symmetric insofar as all countries, though in differing ways, 'locked down' economic activity to contain infections. It brought forth extensive national policy packages aimed, first, at protecting jobs and viable firms and, second, at re-stimulating the economy as infection rates declined. In contrast to the GFC, key decisions at the European Union level included the suspension of supranational fiscal rules and controls on state aid, a massive European Central Bank (ECB) bond purchase programme, and an innovative package of grants and loans targeted at the worst-hit Member States.

The aim of this chapter is to trace the evolving policy responses to these crises and to assess whether they go far enough to underpin the sustainability and resilience of the euro area. Section 6.2 looks back to the debates, some dating from the 1960s, about how to achieve monetary integration in Europe, noting some of the ideas which, arguably, are now resurfacing.

How the crises of recent years arose and the policy responses they brought forth are then examined in Section 6.3. In Section 6.4, the key EU-level economic policy reforms prior to and since the start of the pandemic are assessed, exploring whether they create a (more) durable governance framework. Despite the policy activism, several gaps in the governance framework remain and these are analysed in Section 6.5, focusing on three areas: the future of EU fiscal rules, the need for and likely nature of a supranational fiscal capacity, and the consequences of economic divergence among euro area members. All three had already been under review in the run-up to the COVID-19 crisis, although the easing of the sovereign debt crisis saw a fall-off in the momentum of reform. Concluding comments complete the chapter.

6.2 THE LONG ROAD TO ECONOMIC AND MONETARY UNION IN THE EU

Although the decision to create the euro was formally taken in the early 1990s, with the negotiation and ratification of the Maastricht Treaty, and put into effect a decade later, monetary cooperation in Europe had, as James (Chapter 3 in this volume) explains, been under discussion from the start of European integration. It came more formally onto the agenda in the late 1960s. At that time, the post-war Bretton Woods system of fixed but flexible exchange rates was under growing stress before US President Nixon effectively ended it in 1971. Half a century later, the intensity of public anxiety about if or when devaluations or revaluations of currencies would take place seems arcane. Yet for Europe then, as would again be the case four decades later in the lead-up to the sovereign debt crisis, Germany's persistent trade surplus was seen in partner countries (with their counterpart deficits) as a destabilizing influence. Then, as now, there was tension between countries relying on export-led growth and those in which consumer demand was central.

In 1969, a report by Commission vice-president and future French prime minister, Raymond Barre (1969) proposed closer cooperation on monetary policy policies, alongside coordination of economic policies. A further report (Barre II) in early 1970 proposed three stages towards the creation of a common currency. It was quickly followed by the Werner Report (1970), which set out a ten-year schedule for moving to monetary union by 1980, also by stages, with an end goal of a single currency.

In a number of ways, the Werner blueprint was more integrative than the Delors Report (1989) (which paved the way for the Maastricht Treaty and the establishment of the euro), thirty years later. It stresses the need to establish free movement of goods, services, labour, and capital (well on the way to being realized by the time of the Delors Report, as a result of the single market programme launched in the mid-1980s) alongside monetary union. Noteworthy phrases include 'powers until then exercised by the national authorities will have to be transferred'; 'a process of fundamental political significance'; and a reference to EMU being a 'leaven for the development of political union which in the long run it cannot do without' (Werner, 1970, p. 12). The report, without specifying a level, calls for a higher Community budget. Subsequently, the MacDougall Report (European Commission, 1977) tried to calibrate the amounts needed to enable EMU to function, suggesting figures in the range 5 to 7 per cent of GDP, for a much less diverse membership than today's. Given the EU argued prior to COVID-19 about whether the budget should be 1.07 or 1.074 per cent of gross national income, such figures seem fanciful.

Although there was an attempt to curb exchange rate fluctuations (the 'snake in the tunnel') in the early 1970s, it foundered when oil prices rocketed following the Yom Kippur war, and the ensuing economic instability effectively put an end to the Werner timetable. Nevertheless, a more limited form of monetary integration was agreed in 1979 with the creation of the European Monetary System. Its centrepiece was the Exchange Rate Mechanism (ERM), designed – again – to limit fluctuations between the exchange rates of participating countries, together with some mechanisms to provide mutual support for currencies facing speculative attack.

The ERM faced a number of tensions during the 1980s, largely because of the relative strength of the Deutschmark, and latterly came to be seen as subject to German hegemony. Always reluctant to participate, the United Kingdom had joined in 1990 only to be ignominiously forced out less than two years later. However, the ERM survived until the launch of the euro and a version of it (ERM II) is still in existence, providing a staging-post for countries seeking to accede to the euro.

Despite political differences, the initiative for a renewed – ultimately successful – push for EMU came from the Delors Committee composed mainly of central bankers (Dyson and Featherstone, 1999). Indeed, it may be that an 'epistemic community' of central bankers, with support from some key politicians, came together to shape the proposals for EMU and to give momentum to the project, even though the most prominent among them, Bundesbank President Karl-Otto Pöhl (according to James, Chapter 3 in this volume) was expected to be hostile. Nevertheless, Delors played an important role, as did Helmut Kohl and a number of other prominent politicians (see Dyson, Chapter 5 in this volume).

Most strikingly, the form of monetary union decided upon was one that gave more weight to a rules-based system and sound money than to notions of 'gouvernement économique', with a stronger centralized fiscal policy, that French interests had sought. Indeed, these ideological differences have bedevilled EMU ever since. The choice made was, as McNamara (1998) argues, in part motivated by a paradigm shift away from the Keynesianism of the Bretton Woods era. Other cleavages have also been identified and commented on, such as between the interests of a 'core' and a 'periphery', or of large and small members. Brunnermeier et al. (2016, p. 4) portray the clash concisely: 'the basic elements of the contrasting philosophies can be delineated quite simply. The northern vision is about rules, rigor, and consistency, while the southern emphasis is on the need for flexibility, adaptability, and innovation. It is Kant versus Machiavelli'. However, core–periphery, North–South, Club Med, and similar labels can often be not just misleading, but also analytically dubious in implying that geography, per se, is a relevant, enduring, and central influence.

6.3 TWO EPISODES OF ECONOMIC CRISIS, TWO VERY DIFFERENT POLICY RESPONSES

Although there is some justification for attributing the blame for the GFC to the excesses of financial capitalism and lax regulation, above all in the United States, the spread to the EU and the metamorphosis of the initial shocks starting in August 2007 into the EU's sovereign debt crisis reflected home-grown pathologies (Pisani-Ferry, 2014). Several large European banks were badly hit by the financial crisis and public debt rose nearly everywhere.

6.3.1 *From Global to Eurozone Financial Crisis*

As the GFC evolved, seeming to abate in the course of 2009, the revelation by Greece of the true magnitude of its budget deficit shifted the focus to the soundness of public finances. However, the problems leading to the bailouts for Ireland in 2010, Cyprus in 2013, and the targeted support for Spain in 2012 arose in banking sectors which were revealed to have overextended their lending. Public guarantees, including deposit insurance, resulted in unsustainable pressures on these countries' public finances. At the same time, doubts arose about banks' holdings of their national sovereign debt amid worries that they could no longer be considered 'safe', as hitherto assumed in financial markets, because of fears of an unprecedented default. This 'doom-loop', as it came to be known, arose partly because large banks were considered too big to fail, obliging states to intervene to support them.

Monetary policy responses were rapid: in the early stages of the GFC, in August 2007, the ECB was quick to provide liquidity to the financial system and continued to do so when deemed necessary via long-term refinancing operations. It subsequently went further through a succession of purchasing programmes. These included:

- The securities market programme (SMP), launched in 2010 and ended in 2012 when the decision was taken to initiate outright monetary transactions (OMT), which, unlike the SMP, attached tough conditionality to its use. The OMT has not yet been used by the ECB.
- The asset purchase programme (APP), the Eurosystem's version of quantitative easing, launched in 2014. A veritable alphabet soup of components of this programme comprises purchases of public sector bonds (PSPP), corporate bonds (CSPP), and asset-backed securities (ABSPP).
- The pandemic emergency purchase programme (PEPP).

By contrast with monetary actions, the EU struggled to provide support through fiscal policy in response to the GFC. Although several Member States contributed to the 2009 round of fiscal stimulus packages orchestrated by the G20, others lacked the fiscal space to do so, and were constrained by the conjunction of fiscal rules and market pressures. The Stability and Growth Pact (see Eichengreen, Chapter 1 in this volume) was not suspended and, although the original threshold of a 2 per cent fall in GDP as an escape clause had been softened in 2005, the Commission continued to implement the excessive deficit procedure. In 2009, most Member States were subject to the procedure, and thus formally faced an obligation to consolidate their public finances.

The rationale for persevering with fiscal discipline goes back to the grand bargains needed to enable EMU to happen. Germany had insisted on a rules-based stability pact aimed at curbing fiscal profligacy and, although pressure from France (especially) led to the word 'Growth' being added to the pact's title when it was agreed in 1997, the thrust of it remained one of curbing excessive deficits in the interest of more coordinated fiscal policy. Without such a pact, Germany feared free-riding by Member States which would not face the same consequences of a looser fiscal policy, particularly in prompting a tightening of monetary policy. More broadly, the ordo-liberal ideology favoured by Germany prevailed over the preferences of France for greater discretion in fiscal policy. Nevertheless, the discipline was quickly undermined by the clash between the Commission, on the one hand, and Germany and France on the other, over attempts to impose sanctions on the latter in 2002. The resulting messy compromise effectively sent a signal to others that financial sanctions, as opposed to admonitions, were very unlikely to be imposed. It also allowed Member States to pay scant regard to the formal provisions of the Pact when it suited them – some would say with positive effects for economic prospects.

Thus, in 2009 and 2010, among the four largest Member States, Germany undertook discretionary fiscal measures worth 3.6 per cent of pre-crisis (2007) GDP, France 1.5 per cent, the United Kingdom 1.3 per cent, and Italy just 0.3 per cent. The corresponding figure for

China was 5.8 per cent, the USA 3.8 per cent, Canada 3.6 per cent, and Japan 4.2 per cent. The EU level made a limited contribution by delaying payments into its budget from its members and accelerating spending from Cohesion Policy, but the net effect was marginal compared with the national stimulus actions. On a limited scale, the EU also activated a mechanism for loans to three non-euro Member States facing balance-of-payments problems (Hungary, Latvia, and Romania). In part, the limited action by national governments in Europe reflected the tension between EU fiscal rules (and expectations implicit in policy narratives) and the desire to act. By 2011, the austerity turn in policymaking had become dominant (Blyth, 2013) and the attitude of creditor nations (mainly in the north) towards the debtor nations further south was that they needed to resolve their fiscal problems by much tighter fiscal policy.

For Greece, especially, this led to a deflationary spiral now widely recognized to have been unnecessarily severe (Alogoskoufis and Featherstone, 2021). Although there are quibbles about whether, or to what extent, the treatment of the other bailed out countries was qualitatively different, there would be little support now for this harsh medicine. Yet the extent of the support offered, especially to Greece, by other eurozone members should not be underestimated, even if it happened in a disjointed manner.

6.3.2 *The COVID-19 Economic Crisis*

When the COVID-19 crisis hit, the EU was much quicker to react. The immediate fiscal responses by EU governments mitigated the fall in GDP by 4.5 percentage points. In addition to the operation of automatic stabilizers, discretionary fiscal measures amounting to some 4 per cent of GDP were taken in 2020. According to the European Commission (2021, p. 4), governments' responses were 'facilitated by the early activation of the general escape clause of the Stability and Growth Pact in March 2020 and the use of the full flexibility foreseen under EU State Aid rules, in particular by means of a Temporary Framework also adopted in March 2020'. Coming just weeks after the magnitude of the pandemic was recognized, these measures were crucial.

To support action taken in most Member States to preserve jobs, the European instrument for temporary Support to mitigate Unemployment Risks in an Emergency (SURE) was set up to provide loans on favourable terms to EU members. Under SURE, the Commission is empowered to borrow from financial markets to lend to Member States in what are known as back-to-back loans. In essence, the EU's highly favourable credit rating means it can borrow on very keen terms and pass them on to Member States which might otherwise have to face tougher terms. The Commission borrowing is guaranteed by the EU budget and by what is known as a counter-guarantee by Member States for part of the amount borrowed. Unsurprisingly, SURE proved very popular with Member States and take-up was very rapid, absorbing most of the maximum of €100 billion allowed under the regulation setting up the scheme.

An altogether more ambitious policy development, finally agreed late in 2020 alongside a new Multi-annual Financial Framework (MFF) for the period 2021–27, was what has come to be known as Next Generation EU (NGEU). After an initial proposal in May 2020 by France and (arguably more surprisingly) Germany to create a new fund with €500 billion to provide support for investments intended to boost economies, the Commission proposed a still more ambitious amount of €750 billion. In this proposal, two-thirds would be grants to Member States (as in the Franco-German plan) and one-third would be back-to-back loans.

The simultaneous negotiation of the MFF and NGEU saw the customary acrimonious haggling that has long bedevilled settlements on EU finances, leading to a rebalancing to

€390 billion in grants and €360 billion in loans in the NGEU. Nevertheless, in a significant departure from previous orthodoxy, the money would be borrowed directly from financial markets to finance EU policies. NGEU is formally a temporary measure intended to support economic recovery from the pandemic, although some of the conditions that recipients have to fulfil point to wider ambitions. It is not a conventional fiscal stimulus package of the sort implemented in the United States in 2020 and 2021, both of which included direct payments to taxpayers aimed at encouraging them to spend. Instead, recipient countries have to present a medium-term plan for how the money will be used, and must meet minimum thresholds for the proportion of the money they receive to be spent on investments targeted at countering climate change, notably transitions to renewable energy, and supporting the digital economy.

Two-thirds of those responding to an expert survey on the future of the euro, conducted in the second semester of 2020, said they believed NGEU would pave the way for a permanent facility, with only 9 per cent saying it would not and the remainder answering it is too soon to tell (Begg, 2023). Amid much debate on whether or not it constituted a 'Hamiltonian moment', the consensus was that it did not. It is important also to be clear on the nature of the 1790 moment in the United States. As several of the contributors to a 'symposium of views' published by *The International Economy* attest, the crucial feature of Hamilton's plan (Hamilton, 1790) was to mutualize state debts at the federal level. Plainly, the new Fund does not envisage the assumption of the *existing* debts of the Member States by the EU level but, to employ a related metaphor, it may be seen as the crossing of a Rubicon by making such supranational borrowing seem doable in future.

Much will depend on whether the projects financed by the funding succeed. There is a substantial cross-border fiscal transfer from north-western Member States to those in the south and in central and eastern Europe in how the money has been allocated, and this is bound to reinforce the fears of the EU's net contributors about the money being squandered. To some extent the conditionality attached to the disbursement of the money can help, but the mixed track record of Cohesion Policy investments over several decades, despite increasingly intrusive monitoring from 'Brussels', invites caution (Bachtler et al., 2016).

At the heart of this debate are questions about the purpose of Cohesion Policy. The Delors Report (1989) made clear that moving to EMU could exacerbate regional disparities by encouraging concentration of economic activities, as predicted by new economic geography theorists (Fujita et al., 1999). A beefed-up Cohesion Policy was, therefore, introduced as a means of offsetting the centripetal forces. As the latest Cohesion Report shows, the net fiscal transfer to poorer EU Member States can exceed 2 per cent of GDP and, perhaps more tellingly, has come to dominate public investment in several of them: in Portugal, for example, the data presented show that EU transfers finance 90 per cent of public investment, and the proportion was over half for the 'cohesion' countries in aggregate (European Commission, 2022a, Chapter 8).

Another facet of NGEU could prove to be significant for the future governance of EMU. The eventual repayment of the loans taken out by the Commission will be split between the EU and Member State levels, the former to cover the grant component of the package, and the latter the back-to-back loan funding received by Member States, albeit with the EU level as the guarantor in the event of default. There will, in addition, be debt service payments. Rising interest rates to counter the surge in inflation after 2021 could make this burden more problematic than initially expected. An EU 'power to tax' has long been resisted by many Member States, but they agreed to hypothecate future revenues to the repayment of the NGEU borrowing.

Even with the caveat that NGEU is formally temporary, its effects on the EU's finances will be enduring because of the length of the repayment schedule, lasting over three decades, tacitly shifting the ground towards a power to tax. The moment may not have been Hamiltonian in relation to debt mutualization, but may be so in a different sense. Hamilton's proposition required federal taxes and, in this respect, the moment may be more significant than it first appears, by 'normalizing' EU revenue-raising. Part of the agreement on NGEU was to stipulate that new revenue streams would be tapped, entailing a rise in the ceiling for the size of EU revenue-raising as a proportion of EU gross national income (known as the own resources ceiling). Genuine EU taxes account for only a small proportion of the revenue accruing to the EU budget, most of which comes from national contributions. A small 'plastics tax' has already been introduced and a number of other candidates to add to revenue instruments have been put forward.

These arrangements for repaying the debt incurred to finance NGEU grants are novel and potentially contentious, because they are expected to stretch to 2058, implying that they will affect four, or possibly five, future EU multi-annual budgetary settlements, beyond the current one covering 2021–27. This, to put it mildly, is dubious politics because it implies that current provisions will bind future decisions in what is invariably one of the most acrimonious of EU decisions: agreeing the next multi-annual budgetary settlement.

Nevertheless, the modalities of the EU as a sovereign borrower are awkward, even if it widens its base of 'own' taxes. The EU Financial Regulation stipulates that the EU budget must balance every year and it is supposed to respect the principle of universality in not earmarking revenue for specific purposes. Moreover, the European Parliament has a more limited role than legislatures in most advanced economies in the EU's public finances. It co-decides expenditure, but is only consulted on revenue-raising, and has little power over the borrowing on the scale envisaged by the pandemic responses. There was evident dismay among MEPs in the manner in which NGEU was decided, despite it representing a major boost to spending on EU policies.

The implementation of NGEU took time with delays in submission of plans by some (Netherlands took until July 2022) and political objections to approving those of Hungary and Poland (end 2022). The funds now flowing will underpin the next stages of economic recovery from the pandemic. The focus on public investment contrasts with measures adopted elsewhere aimed at sustaining current spending, such as the cheques to all citizens with earnings below a certain threshold sent out by US Presidents Trump and Biden. For the most indebted Member States, especially, NGEU enables them to protect – and even enhance – public investment in circumstances where financing difficulties might have had the opposite effect. If NGEU realizes its ambition to facilitate growth-promoting structural transformation, at the same time as demonstrating the EU's capacity to act, the pandemic response will be doubly applauded – but it is a big 'if'.

6.4 A PROLIFERATION OF REFORMS

The turmoil after 2007 had exposed a plethora of shortcomings in the governance of the EU overall, and particularly of monetary union. Benign economic conditions in the years after the launch of the euro had disguised these shortcomings, but growing acknowledgment of their significance led to rapid (at least by EU standards) negotiation and adoption of extensive reforms. Obtaining agreement was, nevertheless, far from easy because of differing national priorities and disputes about the optimal sequencing of efforts to control and share risks.

Two EU level initiatives, the Four (2012) and Five (2015) Presidents' Reports, were at the heart of the reform agenda (European Council, 2012; Juncker et al., 2015). They set out proposals for reform of the governance of the eurozone under four broad headings. These were:

- An integrated financial framework with the aim of countering the problems associated with having fragmented, largely national banking systems, and thereby to ensure a financially stable system;
- An integrated budgetary framework with the dual aim of assuring fiscal discipline and developing new common fiscal policy instruments;
- An integrated economic policy framework able to promote growth, employment, and competitiveness in a manner consistent with the smooth functioning of EMU;
- Enhancement of democratic legitimation and channels of accountability, justified particularly by the loss of national autonomy in budgetary and other economic matters as a direct consequence of greater top-down constraints on national autonomy in economic decision-making.

These four headings provide a basis for reviewing the reforms of recent years and assessing the extent to which the evolution of the euro has been shaped by the crises of recent years. It is, however, worth starting by examining the conceptual reasoning behind focusing on these four headings, and what they reveal about the economic and political thinking on the directions for change. Above all, they point to the different ways in which the euro lacked attributes associated with a currency. Some of these derive from what Otmar Issing in a speech in 2006 called being 'a currency without a state' – reflecting the fact that the EU is far from a federal level of governance – but they also drew attention to the reluctance of policymakers to acknowledge the build-up of risks for which no entity was directly responsible or, indeed, accountable.

As James (Chapter 3 in this volume) explains in some detail, national preferences shaped, and limited, the scope for rapid financial integration, and have continued to do so. This had a number of repercussions. First, it meant that private channels of risk-sharing across national borders were lacking, inhibiting a means of adjustment to shocks. Second, opportunities for more efficiency in financial markets were not realized, and even today, plans for a capital markets union in the EU remain stalled. A third consequence of financial fragmentation was regulatory tension arising from the interplay between financial intermediaries with, in some cases, substantial cross-border activity and the largely domestic focus of the national regulators and prudential supervisors overseeing them, all in the context (for the euro area) of a single monetary policy. These tensions were exposed as the sovereign debt crisis deepened (Eichengreen, Chapter 1 in this volume) and an obvious inference is that financial stability was imperilled, partly because it was given insufficient attention, as monetary policy was directed predominantly at assuring price stability.

Fiscal union (sometimes also referred to as political union) was explicitly ruled out in the initial design of the euro (though not forever), with competence for fiscal policy left to the national level. The rationale was straightforward: faced with common monetary conditions, fiscal policy at the national level would enable adjustments to be made should asymmetric shocks arise (see de Haan and Gootjes, Chapter 18 in this volume). However, a second, more overtly political consideration was that taxes and public spending are at the heart of the compact between governments and citizens. Yet by having supranational constraints (the SGP) and adding further mechanisms to restrict national fiscal autonomy as part of the response to the sovereign debt crisis, both these considerations were diminished. Moreover, the political consequence was to kindle expectations of a supranational capability to compensate for what the national level was unable to deliver. The political problem with any such development, though, is that many Member States fear they will be locked into permanent fiscal transfers to EU partners they consider to be too profligate.

Closer integration of economic policy is seen as attractive because of the belief that the single market – still seen as the cornerstone of the EU 'project' – creates opportunities for all to boost prosperity. But it is also recognized that there will be economic dynamics which favour some over others. In the Delors Report (1989), the solution put forward was to boost Cohesion Policy aimed at boosting the development of more backward regions though targeted investments.

Many aspects of EMU are challenging for democracy because they shift power from governments to independent institutions. There is a wide-ranging debate in the political science literature about whether the EU does in fact suffer from a disproportionate democratic deficit (Moravcsik, 2002; Follesdal and Hix, 2006; Weiler, 2013; Schmidt, 2020). Regardless, faced with the rise of populism in many countries, EU decision-makers have manifestly taken the view that rules and institutions which distance voters from key decisions are becoming awkward, and legitimation has to be addressed.

6.4.1 *Financial Integration*

Following the publication of the de Larosière Report (2009), the initial emphasis in policy reform was on tightening the regulation and supervision of financial intermediaries. The main reforms were to boost banks' capital adequacy, rules on bankers' compensation, controls on hedge funds, and tighter regulation of ratings agencies. In addition, macro-prudential oversight of risks to financial stability – going beyond the supervision of individual financial entities, implicitly bringing together financial stability and fiscal sustainability – was formalized through the establishment at the end of 2010 of the European Systemic Risk Board. This board is dominated by central bankers and chaired by the president of the ECB, but its membership includes representatives of other bodies concerned with financial stability.

Initially, proposals to confer responsibility for supervision of financial intermediaries to the ECB, long on the agenda of monetary union (and provided for in Article 127(6) TFEU), were resisted. But as the sovereign debt crisis intensified in 2011, plans for a banking union took shape. These plans envisaged three components: common supervision; common resolution of failing banks; and common deposit insurance. The non-participation in the euro of a number of Member States – notably the United Kingdom, with its large and internationally orientated financial services sector – complicated the achievement of the banking union.

Even after Brexit, the largely voluntary arrangements through which the eight Member States not participating in the euro engage with banking union have made only limited headway. Bulgaria, now on a path to euro accession, is effectively inside banking union. The Danish and Swedish governments published studies on whether to join in 2019, but have not yet decided. The Danish study signals that membership is likely to be in the country's interest once certain features have been clarified, but it is also likely to be subject to a referendum. The Swedish study is more non-committal, confining itself to setting out the expected advantages and disadvantages. The issue appears not to be on the agenda for now in any of the other non-participating Member States.

A Single Supervisory Mechanism (SSM) covering the most significant eurozone banks was agreed in 2014 and the ECB was given overall responsibility for it through a new supervisory board, but pressure from some Member States (above all Germany) resulted in a continuing role for national supervisors in overseeing smaller banks. Shortly thereafter, a Single Resolution Mechanism (SRM) was established, again under the direction of a new institution, the Single Resolution Board, together with the setting up of a single resolution fund to which banks are obliged to contribute. The latter will, however, only reach its target level by 2023 at the earliest and proposals for a fiscal backstop have yet to be agreed. Though there have been undeniable achievements, problems remain (Angeloni, 2020) in the way both the SSM and the SRM function.

Common deposit insurance, though, has proven to be difficult. Various schemes have been mooted but divergent national sensitivities have prevented progress. In the medium term, the most likely form of European Deposit Insurance Scheme (EDIS) will be one which reinsures national schemes, rather than directly insuring depositors, as proposed by the European Commission (2015; see also Gros, 2015), at least during an extended transition.

More broadly, banking union has yet to realize some of its underlying aims. The painful saga of dealing with Monte dei Paschi di Siena, once among Italy's leading banks, has drawn attention to continuing tensions between national and eurozone-wide priorities. As Ignazio Angeloni (2021) puts it, it is 'only the latest sign demonstrating that the advent of the European banking union has not prevented massive waste of taxpayer money, nor guaranteed that unviable banks would exit the market'. Moreover, as Angeloni (2020) also observes, globally competitive cross-border banks have not emerged from banking union, an outcome that might have been expected. In addition, moves to establish a capital markets union have been proceeding at a glacial pace.

6.4.2 *Fiscal Arrangements*

The clear choice in setting up EMU to have fiscal policy at the national level and only a limited EU-level budget has had far-reaching consequences. It means, first, there is no easy way of arriving at a common fiscal stance for the eurozone, so long as national finance or budget ministers set their own budgets (see de Haan and Gootjes, Chapter 18 in this volume). Second, it effectively precludes the EU from using supranational fiscal policy for stabilization purposes: not only is the EU budget small – averaging 1 per cent of EU gross national income – but its composition does not offer more than minimal scope for discretionary fiscal action. Coordination of fiscal policy could have been a means of circumventing these limitations, but although the SGP was, in part, intended to fulfil this function, experience since it was established twenty-five years ago shows little sign of it achieving this aim.

On the contrary, one of the striking lessons from the crises of recent years is that national priorities have prevailed. To put it glibly, those with fiscal space have chosen not to use it for the benefit of the more constrained partner countries, while those most in need of using fiscal policy to stabilize their economies have lacked the fiscal space to do so. This dilemma flows, in large part, from the direction of reform of fiscal governance in the early 2010s. Broadly, the decisions taken on adapting the SGP, introducing new obligations on presenting budgets in advance for scrutiny by the Commission and strengthening domestic fiscal frameworks had one key goal: assuring the sustainability of fiscal policy. These orientations constrained the scope for fiscal policy to be used for stabilization purposes, especially for the eurozone as a whole. Instead, the main responsibility for countering downturns fell on the ECB, triggering increasing dismay about politicization of monetary policy and 'fiscal dominance' (Issing, 2021).

Some of the reforms, such as rebalancing the SGP to take account of public debt and not just the annual deficit, were welcome, but the overall thrust of the reforms was towards greater discipline, and, for some of the fiscally precarious Member States, pressure (however strongly resisted) to implement austerity policies. In some cases, notably Greece, these policies proved to be counterproductive by prolonging the economic distress. Other reforms, including the creation of the European Stability Mechanism (ESM, agreed as a separate intergovernmental treaty by the then members of the eurozone and thus outside the EU's legal order), manifestly filled gaps in the economic governance framework exposed during the years of crisis. Even so, the conditions attached to ESM support proved to be unsuited to dealing with the economic challenges of the pandemic.

Another development was the setting up of the European Fiscal Board with a mandate to analyse and report on the overall eurozone fiscal position and to monitor implementation of fiscal rules. However, as a purely advisory body, it has limited visibility. In parallel, all Member States were expected to establish independent national fiscal councils to provide assessments of budgetary policies. Nearly all did (a handful of Member States already had them in place) and some of these Councils rapidly acquired a pivotal position in the governance framework.

An analysis by Beetsma and Debrun (2016) suggested various ways in which the addition of independent fiscal 'watchdogs' could enhance the quality of policy-making, including by reducing the asymmetry of information between voters and decision-makers. Yet in several instances, especially where fiscal councils are poorly resourced and have more limited mandates, the jury remains out on whether they had a transformative effect (Beetsma and Debrun, 2018). Even so, a strengthened role for fiscal councils is widely regarded as important for better fiscal governance and is one of the key proposals for reform in current discourse.

Despite this swathe of reforms, eurozone fiscal policy still lacks the ability to deal with crises. A logical answer would be to have a supranational fiscal capacity to enable the sharing of risks to macroeconomic stability – NGEU could be a prototype – but the resistance to conferring such a capacity on the EU level remains profound (see Beetsma and Kopits, Chapter 21 in this volume). Similarly, the idea of jointly and severally guaranteed Eurobonds seem no closer to being acceptable than it was a decade ago.

An explanation is that the tensions between Member States over mechanisms likely to result in cross-border transfers of national taxpayers' money elicit strong objections and emotive language. Conceptually, the arguments can be interpreted as a contest between those worried about 'moral hazard' and those who believe an economic and monetary union devoid of 'solidarity' is unsustainable. Yet there are examples of measures able to accommodate both sides. Thus, according to a statement on the European Stabilisation Mechanism's website (since removed), the Greek public finances in 2017 were better off by as much as 6.7 percentage points of GDP because of the low interest rates payable on ESM loans. Was there an offsetting loss for the other Member States? Probably not, because their creditworthiness was not obviously damaged; in other words, there can be positive-sum outcomes.

6.4.3 *The Integrated Economic Framework*

For a monetary union to function well, even in the absence of cross-border fiscal flows, the extent of divergence among its members cannot be too great, as analysed in variants of optimal currency area theory (De Grauwe, 2020). There is some consensus that the euro fell some way short of meeting the criteria for optimality, but one of the more powerful arguments for pushing ahead with its creation was that it would act as a 'convergence machine'. Although in some respects it did, notably as portrayed in the now notorious chart showing sovereign interest rates converging in the years leading up to the Global Financial Crisis, its history since has shown that the initial convergence was illusory. As discussed in Section 6.5.3, divergent actual (and potential) growth rates are a major difficulty for which credible policy solutions are yet to be found.

Coordination of national economic policies – the 'E' in EMU – with the aim of coherence in eurozone-level policy positions is nevertheless important for the effective governance of the eurozone. The SGP and the various other forms of fiscal discipline provide mechanisms with at least some role in fiscal policy coordination, even if this original aim has faded. For other economic policies, there are two main approaches. The first is the succession of what might best be described as mega-strategies, beginning with the Lisbon Strategy at the start of the millennium, followed by the Europe 2020 Strategy, and now the Green Deal. Neither Lisbon nor Europe 2020 will go down in the economic history books as resounding successes and it is too early to pass judgement on the Green Deal.

Instead, the much shorter-term European semester should be regarded as the main process for coordinating economic policies. Belying the word 'semester', it has evolved through a succession of tweaks to its governance to become an annual process in which the Commission assesses Member State economies and proposes reforms. The latter are aimed simultaneously at improving the quality of national policy-making and their coherence with eurozone and Union-wide policy orientations and priorities. Recommendations from this surveillance are put to Member States with an expectation that they should either comply with them or explain why not. However, their impact on national policy-making appears to be limited, with low rates of compliance with the recommendations (Darvas and Leandro, 2015).

In recognition of the risks from economic imbalances other than fiscal, a new Macroeconomic Imbalances Procedure (MIP) was established in the same package of reforms (the 2011 'Six Pack') as the revisions to the SGP. Modelled on the latter, the MIP has preventive and corrective arms and is supposed to cover a wide range of indicators of potential sources of imbalance, including housing markets and balance-of-payments disequilibria. The MIP regulations include the possibility of financial sanctions, but the mechanism has been criticized for having no teeth and, in particular, for being powerless to curb the huge (and macroeconomically disruptive) external surpluses of a number of northern Member States, notably Germany and the Netherlands.

Despite these shortcomings, the semester remains at the heart of eurozone governance (see Eihmanis, Chapter 16 in this volume). As a press release from the Council secretariat notes, the semester was 'temporarily adjusted' in 2020 towards addressing the health emergency, and again in 2021 to concentrate on the recovery from the economic downturn. Questions therefore arise about when to revert to its previous priorities and procedures. Moreover, the semester has been assigned a pivotal role in the implementation of NGEU. In a communication aimed at restarting the debate on economic governance the European Commission (2021, p. 11) has acknowledged the flaws in the MIP, noting 'the persistence of imbalances in some cases warrants further reflection on how the implementation and design of the MIP'. As in other dimensions of euro governance, there is a divide between what the mechanism is meant to achieve and the practicalities of implementing it.

6.4.4 *Democratic Legitimation*

Although there have been repeated calls for better democratic oversight of key governance processes, it would not be unfair to say progress has been unimpressive. The dilemmas around legitimation are stark. Monetary policy, competition policy, and trade policy are seen as policy interventions to be judged on whether they work, and thus to be assessed on what has come to be known as 'output' legitimacy, whereas core choices about tax and spending are best legitimated by voters because they have more direct distributive effects. In practice, this division is fuzzy because there can be no doubt that all the former group of policies can have pronounced distributive effects, witness some of the complaints about how low interest rates penalize savers and favour borrowers.

The semester can constrain national policymakers and, although the analysis by Lord (2017) suggests the whole question needs to be looked at subtly, probably sidelines national parliaments in favour of executives. Schmidt (2020) has drawn attention to the difficulties associated with a lack of transparency in how decisions in semester and other processes are reached, casting doubt on what she calls the 'throughput' legitimacy. In addition, the limited role of the European Parliament in NGEU, described earlier, further detracts from legitimation. Moreover, as stressed by Schmidt (2020), some of the processes that led to obligations on Member States (Greece is the most egregious example) lack transparency, and are also bereft of 'throughput' legitimacy.

6.5 UNFINISHED BUSINESS

Just before the COVID-19 pandemic struck, fresh moves were being taken to restore momentum to the reform of eurozone governance, partly in reaction to the (inaccurate) perception that enough had been done and that difficult cases, such as Greece, were on the way to being resolved. A review launched by the European Commission (2020, p. 2) days before the magnitude of the pandemic became clear, noted how the economic governance 'framework has evolved in waves over time, with changes introduced in response to the emergence of new economic challenges, as well as based on the lessons gained in the implementation of the surveillance framework'.

The launch document of the review is candid in identifying flaws in the governance framework and, while claiming (p. 16) that the reforms discussed above in Section 6.3.2 'have led to a broader and more integrated approach to surveillance that better assures the overall consistency of policy advice within the European Semester', poses a series of questions about what can be improved. These range from how to achieve better integration of national and EU governance mechanisms to how to take the aggregate eurozone position better into account in the interest of a more effective and resilient euro. The word 'ownership' is much in evidence.

The review was held up by COVID-19, but in November 2022 the Commission (2022b) published its long-awaited proposals, triggering fresh debate on how to recast EU rules, guidance and expectations of Member States. The biggest proposed changes are to shift the focus to medium term debt sustainability and an expenditure rule. National ownership is also emphasized. As Begg (2023) notes, the proposals received a somewhat qualified welcome.

Many other facets of eurozone governance have attracted attention. Rehn (2020) also mentions the possibility of a new fiscal capacity, but expresses reservations about it becoming de facto a permanent transfer mechanism. An additional fiscal instrument, going beyond the limited competitiveness and convergence instrument proposed a decade ago, has been proposed by the current Commission. Others worry about how the divergence among Member States can be accommodated. The remainder of this section focuses on three dimensions of 'unfinished business'.

6.5.1 *From Ineffective Rules to a Credible Fiscal Framework*

EU fiscal rules have been heavily criticized from a variety of perspectives and the pandemic has triggered demands for a fresh approach to the fiscal framework. The SGP and the panoply of other EU and national rules surrounding it have been subject to four main criticisms: being too procyclical; too often being inappropriate while also relying too much on variables not easily measured; excessive complexity; and intractable problems of compliance and enforcement (Begg, 2017). A striking fact is the number of pages, some 200 of the *Vade Mecum*, the manual for how Member States implement the SGP (European Commission, 2019). There have been many proposals for reform, including by the European Fiscal Board members (Thygesen et al., 2021), and some commentators have argued both that the extent of the problem has been exaggerated and that viable solutions can be found. However, the political obstacles to reaching agreement remain daunting.

The resort to the general escape clause at the start of the pandemic allowed all EU Member States to use fiscal policy actively to cushion the economic downturn, but had the effect of raising public indebtedness. Rapid restoration of the rules would have been economically damaging and has, at the time of writing, been avoided. However, an 'exit' strategy will be needed, not just from this particular – admittedly, exceptionally severe – economic crisis, but also if the escape is triggered in future. Timing will be crucial, because even if there is a common shock, its incidence and duration is bound to be uneven among economies as diverse as those of the eurozone.

But if the existing rules are to be either scrapped or substantially modified, the question arises: in favour of what? There are three broad directions the fiscal framework could take:

- Modified EU-level fiscal rules offering answers to the main criticisms of existing rules;
- Reliance on national fiscal rules and associated constraints;
- A shift to the setting of fiscal standards, as recommended by Blanchard et al. (2021).

Prior to the pandemic, there was a lively, if ultimately inconclusive debate about how to proceed. One influential paper was produced by a group of fourteen leading French and German economists (Bénassy-Quéré et al., 2018) who argued: 'The current approach to fiscal discipline – an attempt to micromanage domestic policies through complex and often divisive fiscal rules – needs to be replaced by a combination of streamlined rules, stronger institutions, and market-based incentives, with the aim of strengthening national responsibility.' Their solution is to move away from rules on the structural deficit to an expenditure rule combined with targeting a long-term reduction in debt. The reasoning is that this would reduce the pro-cyclicality of rules and mean governments having to act on a variable they can decide on, based on the presumption that, in downturns, a fall in revenue is outside their direct control.

Blanchard et al. (2021) consider the time to be ripe to move away from numerical EU fiscal rules to what they call 'enforceable fiscal standards'. For various reasons, they argue against tweaking the parameters of existing fiscal rules. They maintain that the underlying macroeconomics of fiscal positions is 'a complex issue [... in which] there is no single, time-country-invariant, magic debt or deficit number'. Instead of looking for a revised approach to fiscal rules – they advocate a move to 'fiscal standards'. A simple observation lends weight to their standpoint: the two key ratios of a deficit of 3 per cent of GDP and a public debt of 60 per cent of GDP made some sense in the early 1990s when nominal growth (the increase in GDP at current prices, combining real growth and price increases) was 5 per cent; these three figures are a steady state. But when nominal growth is lower (as it was prior to the pandemic when, with inflation close to zero, nominal growth was barely 2 per cent) or higher (as seems likely after the pandemic, initially because of the rebound in economies and subsequently accentuated by rising prices), rigid ratios do not work well.

Gros and Corti (2021) offer a relatively sanguine analysis, arguing that even the more indebted countries should not struggle to meet their commitments to debt reduction under current fiscal rules, if they are restored. Moreover, if, as is plausible, low interest rates return after the inflation of 2022–23 falls, financing higher debt would be easier: Germany, in

2020–21could have invested in rebuilding its creaking infrastructure at zero capital cost by issuing long-term bonds. In addition, for countries with sustainable public finances, even a modest increase in debt would entail minor risks because inflation will erode the debt burden.

6.5.2 A *Supranational Fiscal Capacity*

Despite widespread agreement on the need for a more comprehensive macroeconomic stabilization capacity, agreement on how to achieve it is elusive. In essence, the conflicting views on the balance between risk control and risk-sharing are yet to be reconciled. One view, typically associated with Germany and other creditor countries, is that risk must first be substantially reduced by effective application of rules and other agreed instruments for constraining national policymakers to pursue sound macroeconomic policies. The other – which can be ascribed to France, Italy, and other southern Member States – is that risks need urgently to be shared to confer more room for manoeuvre on euro area members trapped in low growth trajectories. Without such risk-sharing, they will struggle to resolve their economic challenges and could aggravate divergence in macroeconomic performance, complicating euro area policy-making.

A key question about any new eurozone-level fiscal capacity is what it would be meant to achieve. The most obvious would be to correct the lack of a capacity to use fiscal interventions for macroeconomic stabilization, even if Member State policies are expected to do most of the heavy lifting. Nevertheless, as so many critiques from the other side of the Atlantic have emphasized, having no such capacity at the supranational level is a weakness.

A second broad function would be to deal with emergencies of different sorts, from coping with natural or other disasters to supporting economies hit by asymmetric shocks. The European Union Solidarity Fund, established in 2002, provides limited support for areas hit by natural disasters and was extended in scope (and folded into a new 'Solidarity and Emergency Aid Reserve') in 2020 to cover major health emergencies. But with an annual budget of €1200 million and typical payments in the tens of millions, its contribution (though undoubtedly welcome for the localities affected) is far from game changing. Solidarity is a word much bandied around, but even in the aftermath of the pandemic, there is little appetite for solidarity mechanisms.

Third, a fiscal capacity could be needed as a backstop for financial crises, even after the reforms of bank supervision and resolution which were intended to shift the burden away from the public finances. A fourth rationale would be funding major initiatives of pan-European significance. NGEU potentially paves the way for adopting more extensive EU or eurozone fiscal capacities. As commitments multiply in relation to moving to net zero carbon emissions, it is easy to see a justification for EU-level spending.

Much the most contentious function of a new fiscal capacity would be systematic cross-border transfers, especially for social policy purposes. Under Cohesion Policy, there are quite substantial net transfers from richer to poorer Member States, intended to bolster public investment, while payments to farmers can be regarded as a form of redistributive policy benefiting relatively poorer Member States, despite continuing high payments to a number of richer ones, notably France. Both, however, attract persistent criticism from net contributors to the EU budget and there would be strong opposition to further instruments along these lines.

That said, there has been no shortage of ideas of what form a new fiscal capacity could take. One of the papers accompanying the 2017 White Paper on the Future of Europe, reflecting on the deepening of EMU (European Commission, 2017), set out a range of options. The paper expressed what, even without the benefit of hindsight, many observers considered to be a highly optimistic 'view of concrete steps that could be taken by the time of the European Parliament elections in 2019'.

Some variation on an unemployment insurance fund has been repeatedly canvassed, including in the priorities for the 2019–24 Commission set out by its president, Ursula von der Leyen (2019). Any instrument of this sort would need to take account of potential design and implementation difficulties. Echoing thinking about deposit insurance, the most likely construction would be reinsurance of national unemployment funds, rather than direct transfers to claimants. Whether it is a loan (as in the SURE scheme described earlier) or a grant would also have to be resolved, although even if it is seen primarily as emergency cover, there would be pressure for the support to be repaid when the crisis abates.

Other ideas include a rainy-day fund which accumulates resources in 'good' times and allows contributors to draw from it in 'bad' times. This would confer a degree of automatic stabilization, but it is hard to see it being set up on a scale able to make a telling difference macroeconomically. Then there is the idea of a fund to enable Member States to maintain public investment in a downturn when the usual response of finance ministers is to cut it in order to protect social spending or avoid aggravating debt. NGEU could be seen through this lens: a hard-fought compromise, with a helpful though economically limited impact.

An open question about any new fiscal capacity would be its governance. NGEU comes with (limited) conditionality and, as noted above, largely bypasses the European Parliament. The Commission is charged with the associated debt management role, but yet another proposition to have surfaced is that the eurozone should establish a Treasury and – possibly as a direct corollary – a eurozone finance minister, the latter accountable to democratic bodies. Leaving aside the immediate difficulty that the Parliament is an EU27 body and the eurozone still has only nineteen members, unavoidably making accountability trickier, it is not obvious what mandate a finance minister would have or how it would differ from the presidency of the Eurogroup.

6.5.3 *The Challenges of Economic Divergence*

Economic divergence has, in many respects, been swept under the carpet since the run-up to the sovereign debt crisis. It is likely to resurface as a challenge for the euro if the trajectories out of the pandemic are unbalanced. Although widely differing economic performances were a feature of the euro from the outset, the ramifications of renewed divergence could threaten the stability of the euro and require new policy interventions.

Looking backwards, the facts are simple, if stark – see Figure 6.1, which shows cumulative growth since the launch of the euro (Croatia only joined in 2023). The Baltic countries, Ireland, Luxembourg, and Slovakia have managed robust economic growth despite significant hiccoughs during periods of crisis. At the other extreme, Italy's economy as it emerges from the COVID-19 recession is no bigger than it was in 1999, and neither Greece nor Portugal have fared much better after their struggles during the sovereign debt crisis. All of them currently have high public debt and are likely to face renewed structural difficulties if tourism, in particular, is slow to recover. In the middle are what many think of as the core eurozone countries.

The heterogeneity of public debt levels is emphasized in a European Commission (2021, p. 5) communication, noting that 'high debt ratios are expected to persist, remaining above pre-pandemic levels in about a third of member states over the next decade'.

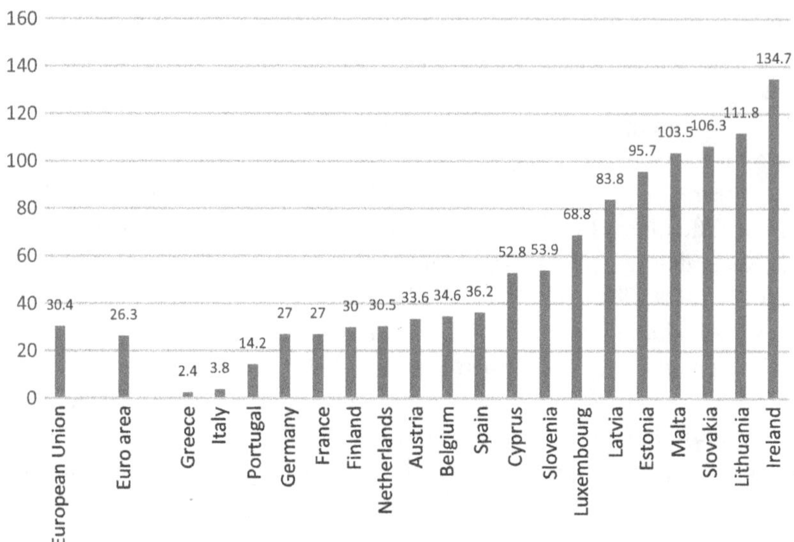

FIGURE 6.1. Aggregate GDP growth of eurozone members, 2000–19, % (Ameco database)

6.6 CONCLUDING REFLECTIONS

The euro is still a youthful currency, despite now being in its third decade. A relatively carefree childhood was followed by a turbulent adolescence and, as it contemplates adulthood, some of the scars of youth have yet to heal, but the extent of the reshaping of euro governance in the last decade should not be underestimated. Equally, difficult challenges stand between today's euro and one which can be regarded as complete and resilient enough to withstand future crises.

An abiding danger is of public finances being balkanized, with one strand of policy-making focusing on fiscal sustainability at the national level, a second dealing with the EU's own finances, and a third concerned with macroeconomic policy, while yet another dimension of policy is the microeconomics of tax and spending policies. The corollary is that seeking further to redesign or recalibrate rules as the cornerstone of EMU reform is likely to offer a false prospectus. Instead, what is needed is better definition of the EU's fiscal constitution and, within it, of how the different elements of public finances are brought together. Rules may still have a place but a more limited one and, because of the implicit contract between voters and taxpayers on one side, and decision-makers on the other, the political dimension of fiscal policy has to be centre-stage.

An obvious final remark is that more muddling through, despite it being almost the standard modus operandi of the EU, will no longer be sufficient. The matters in need of resolution are known and the options to resolve them have been extensively debated. What the eurozone needs now is decisive action, failing which the future resilience of the euro area cannot be taken for granted.

REFERENCES

Alogoskoufis, G., and Featherstone, K. (eds.) (2021). *Greece and the Euro: From Crisis to Recovery*. London: LSE Hellenic Observatory.

Angeloni, I. (2020). *Beyond the Pandemic: Reviving Europe's Banking Union*. London: CEPR Press. https://voxeu.org/content/beyond-pandemic-reviving-europe-s-banking-union

Angeloni, I. (2021) Three ways to fix European banking union. 3 September. www.omfif.org/2021/09/three-ways-to-fix-european-banking-union/

Bachtler, J., Begg, I., Charles, D., and Polverari, L. (2016). *EU Cohesion Policy in Practice: What Does It Achieve?* London: Rowman and Littlefield International.

Barre, R. (1969). Memorandum on Community action in the monetary field 12 February. Brussels: European Commission.

Beetsma, R. M. W. J., and Debrun, X. (2016). Fiscal councils: rationale and effectiveness. IMF Working Paper WP No. 16/86. Washington, DC: International Monetary Fund.

Beetsma, R. M. W. J., and Debrun, X. (eds.) (2018). *Independent Fiscal Councils: Watchdogs or Lapdogs?* VoxEU.org e-book. London: CEPR Press.

Begg, I. (2017). Fiscal and other rules in EU economic governance: Helpful, largely irrelevant or unenforceable. *National Institute Economic Review* 239, R3–13.

Begg, I. (2023) *Completing a Genuine Economic and Monetary Union.* Cambridge: Cambridge University Press.

Bénassy-Quéré, A., Brunnermeier, M. K., Enderlein, H., Farhi, E., Fratzscher, M., Fuest, C., Gourinchas, P.-O., Martin, P., Pisani-Ferry, J., Rey, H., Schnabel, I., Véron, N., Weder di Mauro, B., and Zettelmeyer, J. (2018). Reconciling risk sharing with market discipline: A constructive approach to euro area reform. CEPR Policy Insight No. 91. London: Centre for Economic Policy Research.

Blanchard, O., Leandro, A., and Zettlemeyer, J. (2021). Redesigning EU fiscal rules: From rules to standards. PIIE Working Paper No. 21-1. Washington, DC: Peterson Institute for International Economics.

Blyth, M. M. (2013). *Austerity: The History of a Dangerous Idea.* Oxford: Oxford University Press.

Brunnermeier, M. K., James, H., and Landau, J-P. (2016). *The Euro and the Battle of Ideas.* Princeton, NJ: Princeton University Press.

Darvas, Z., and Leandro, A. (2015). The limitations of policy coordination in the euro area under the European semester. *Bruegel Policy Contribution* No 2015/19, Policy Contribution. www.bruegel.org

De Grauwe, P. (2020). *Economics of Monetary Union*, 13th ed. Oxford: Oxford University Press.

De Larosière, J. [Chairman] (2009). The High-Level Group on Financial Supervision in the EU: Report. Brussels, 25 February.

Delors, J. (1989). Report on economic and monetary union in the European Community. Brussels, 17 April. http://aei.pitt.edu/1007/1/monetary_delors.pdf

Dyson, K., and Featherstone, K. (1999). *The Road to Maastricht: Negotiating Economic and Monetary Union.* Oxford: Oxford University Press.

European Commission (1977). *Report of the Study Group on the Role of Public Finance in European Integration.* Luxembourg: OOPEC.

European Commission (2015). Towards the completion of the Banking Union COM(2015) 587. Strasbourg, 24 November. http://aei.pitt.edu/1007/1/monetary_delors.pdf

European Commission (2017). Reflection paper on the deepening of the economic and monetary union. Brussels, 31 May. Reflection paper on the deepening of the economic and monetary union.

European Commission (2019). Vade mecum on the Stability and Growth Pact. Institutional Paper No. 101. Brussels: European Commission.

European Commission (2020). Economic governance review. COM(2020) 55, Brussels, 5 February. http://aei.pitt.edu/1007/1/monetary_delors.pdf.

European Commission (2021). The EU economy after COVID-19: Implications for economic governance. COM(2021) 662, Brussels. 19 October. https://ec.europa.eu/info/sites/default/files/economy-finance/economic_governance_review-communication.pdf.

European Commission (2022a). *Cohesion in Europe towards 2050: Eighth Report on Economic, Social and Territorial Cohesion.* Luxembourg: Publications Office of the European Union.

European Commission (2022b). 'Communication on orientations for a reform of the EU economic governance framework' COM (2022) 583, Brussels, 11.09.2022 https://economy.

European Council (2012). Towards a genuine economic and monetary union: report by President of the European Council, Herman van Rompuy. EUCO120/12, Brussels, 26 June.

Follesdal, A., and Hix, S. (2006). Why there is a democratic deficit in the EU: A response to Majone and Moravcsik. *Journal of Common Market Studies* 44(3), 533–562.

Fujita, M., Krugman, P., and Venables, A. J. (1999). *The Spatial Economy: Cities, Regions and International Trade*. Cambridge, MA: MIT Press.

Gros, D. (2015). Completing the Banking Union: Deposit insurance. CEPS Policy Brief No. 335, Brussels: CEPS, Download CEPS Publication.

Gros, D., and Corti, F. (2021). Fiscal rules in a post-Covid brave new world: No need to sprint. *Policy Insights* No. 2021-14. Brussels: CEPS. www.ceps.eu/download/publication/?id=34388&pdf=PI2021-14_Fiscal-rules-in-a-post-Covid-brave-new-world.pdf.

Hamilton, A. (1790). First report on the public credit. Communicated to the House of Representatives, 14 January. Treasury Department. https://archive.schillerinstitute.com/economy/2015/hamilton-first_report_on_the_public_credit.pdf.

Issing, O. (2006). The euro – a currency without a state. Speech by at an event organized by the Bank of Finland, Helsinki, 24 March.

Issing, O. (2021). An assessment of the ECB's strategy review. *Central Banking* XXXII(1), n.p.

Juncker, J.-C., with Tusk, D., Dijsselbloem, J., Draghi, M., and Schulz, M. (2015). Completing Europe's economic and monetary Union. European Commission, Brussels. 02.06.2015.

Lord, C. (2017). How can parliaments contribute to the legitimacy of the European Semester? *Parliamentary Affairs* 70, 673–690.

McNamara, K. R. (1998). *The Currency of Ideas: Monetary Politics in the European Union*. Ithaca, NY: Cornell University Press.

Moravcsik, A. (2002). Reassessing legitimacy in the European Union. *Journal of Common Market Studies*, 40(4), 603–624.

Pisani-Ferry, J. (2014). *The Euro Crisis and Its Aftermath*. Oxford: Oxford University Press

Rehn, O. (2020). *Walking the Highwire: Rebalancing the European Economy in Crisis*. Basingstoke: Palgrave Macmillan.

Schmidt, V. A. (2020). *Europe's Crisis of Legitimacy: Governing by Rules and Ruling by Numbers in the Eurozone*. Oxford: Oxford University Press.

Thygesen, N., Beetsma, R., Bordignon, M., Debrun, X., Szczurek, M., Larch, M., Busse, M., Gabrijelcic, M., Jankovics, L., and Malzubris, J. (2021). The EU fiscal framework: A flanking reform is more preferable than quick fixes. *Voxeu*. https://voxeu.org/article/eu-fiscal-framework-case-reform.

Von der Leyen, U. (2019). A Union that strives for more: My agenda for Europe. Political guidelines for the next European Commission, 2019–2024.

Weiler, J. (2013). In the face of crisis: Input legitimacy, output legitimacy and the political messianism of European integration. *Journal of European Integration* 34(7), 825–841.

Werner, P. (1970). Report to the Council and Commission on the realisation by stages of economic and monetary union in the Community. Supplement to Bulletin 11-1970 of the European Communities.

7

The Political Economy of Reinsurance

Waltraud Schelkle

7.1 OVERVIEW

The Economic and Monetary Union (EMU) and the experience of the euro area crisis have created expectations that the EU would act as an insurer of last resort to Member States. An insurer of last resort supports Member States when their national capacities to protect citizens are overwhelmed, but not in standard cyclical downturns, for example. Demand for mutual support was clearly expressed in the wake of the COVID-19 pandemic. The letter sent by nine heads of state to Council President Michel put it most clearly: '[The severity of the situation] requires the activation of all existing common fiscal instruments to support national efforts and ensure financial solidarity, especially within the eurozone' (Wilmès et al., 2020). The signatories proceeded to demand above all a common debt instrument, soon dubbed 'Coronabonds'. Even their most vocal opponent, Dutch prime minister Rutte, conceded in an interview with an Italian newspaper: 'We owe solidarity to the countries most affected by the pandemic, knowing, however, that we too have been seriously affected. This means that states that need and deserve help must also ensure that in the future they are capable of dealing with such crises on their own in a resilient way' (Valentino, 2020, Google translation). Surveys show that EU citizens endorse such a solidaristic response, though distinguishing between different types of crises and the nature of support requested (Cicchi et al., 2020; Ferrara et al., 2023). For instance, respondents are on average more willing to support other Member States in the case of natural disasters than when there is a surge in unemployment, presumably because natural disasters are shocks that cannot be attributed to past policy mistakes. If a crisis is common to all Member States, like a pandemic, this has a positive effect on solidaristic attitudes only if the mutual support does not consist of transfers but credit.

The expectation of EU support is remarkable in a policy area like public health in which the EU had hardly any mandate and Member States can still exercise protection, like border closure and discrimination against foreign suppliers, which are taboo elsewhere. Early in the pandemic, the Commission had limited legal and financial means to prevent this or come to the rescue of the hard-hit Member States that called for EU support (Herszenhorn and Wheaton, 2020). The EU encountered a typical 'capability–expectations gap' that Chris Hill (1993) noted in the EU's

I am grateful to the editors for their comments and amendments as well as to Deborah Mabbett (Birkbeck) for insightful discussions about reinsurance. This research was supported by the European Research Council under the Synergy Grant number ERC_SYG_2018 Grant no. 810356, in the scope of the project SOLID – *Policy Crisis and Crisis Politics. Sovereignty, Solidarity and Identity in the EU Post-2008*.

foreign policy many years ago. Many observers concluded that just like the reforms introduced during the euro-area crisis of 2010–14 (Matthijs and Blyth, 2015), measures taken during the COVID-19 pandemic in 2020–21 were incomplete and too little too late (Howarth and Quaglia, 2021; Jones et al., 2021).

This contribution will characterize these reforms as an evolving macroeconomic system of reinsurance. It is different from both fiscal federalism and optimal currency area ideal-type models that these critics have as implicit benchmarks.[1] Reinsurance compensates insurers for losses from a contingency for which they have to compensate their insurance holders but that could wreck their business. A standard example is private health insurance companies that seek such reinsurance against the risk that medical progress forces them to cover new high-cost treatments that they cannot finance out of regulated premia.

In the present context, we can look at the EU as reinsuring members' welfare states, as the ultimate social insurers of citizens, when crises overwhelm national policy capacities in a systemic crisis or a common shock like a pandemic (Schelkle, 2017, pp. 316–22; Bénassy-Quéré et al., 2018). Reinsurance is not merely a lowest common denominator policy that begs further steps towards fiscal integration until a complete set of co-insurance arrangements at the state and EU level does all the work of federal stabilization. Reinsurance is a form of fiscal integration in its own right. Moreover, it is a political compromise towards which a diverse union of democratic nation states has repeatedly gravitated. This chapter tries to explain how and why. The main argument will be that reinsurance for out-of-the-ordinary contingencies is democratically less demanding than a federal fiscal system and is therefore more pertinent for the present state of European political integration.

The Section 7.2 will analyse how new institutions were created and existing ones adapted since 2009 that can be understood as providing reinsurance. They constitute a system in the sense that the parts complement and respond to each other. This is all the more surprising since this recognizable system of reinsurance has not been designed by any identifiable collective of EU actors. Rather, it is the result of piecemeal reforms under the pressure of crisis escalation as well as the political imperative of keeping contingent liabilities of the insurance arrangement inconspicuous. We should therefore not be disappointed by realizing that this system of reinsurance has defects and does not fit a neofunctionalist account (Fabbrini and Capati, Chapter 20 in this volume). But any conceivable alternative also has defects, notably the US federation that is often the EU's implicit comparator (Rhodes, 2021). Section 7.3 shows why and how a reinsurance role for the EU constitutes a political compromise among Member State governments with very different views about how much fiscal integration is desirable and palatable. The conclusion is that we have to understand the EU not as an optimal currency area with a fiscal federation in the making but as an experimental union (Kriesi et al., 2021). Only time can tell whether European citizens recognize and appreciate that the EU provides mutual insurance, but only of last resort.

7.2 AN EMERGING SYSTEM OF REINSURANCE

This section briefly recalls how the major reforms followed each other and then interprets them as an emerging system of reinsurance for member states. Reinsurance is insurance for insurers,

[1] I come back to these models in Section 7,4. Fiscal federalism is a public finance theory that tries to determine which budgetary function, for instance stabilization or redistribution, should be financed and provided optimally by which level of government, federal, state, or local. Optimum Currency Area theory claims that only currency areas that are very similar in economic structure should forgo a flexible exchange rate, or have effective substitutes like labour mobility that can replace the exchange rate when an idiosyncratic shock hits one region but not others.

not individuals and communities directly (Ross, 2021). Typically, reinsurance is sought by the primary insurers in order to cover excess losses from tail risks,[2] which would overstretch their capacity of keeping their contractual promises to insurance policy holders. It can take many forms and can be categorically different from the primary insurance; notably, it is not confined to budgetary transfers.

7.2.1 *Evolution since 2009*

The reforms in the EU and in the euro area since 2009 evolved in response to the 'North Atlantic' financial crisis that started with the collapse of Lehman Brothers in September 2008. The European Central Bank (ECB) stepped up its liquidity operations massively from summer 2007 (ECB, 2007, pp. 30–34), before even the Federal Reserve Bank (Fed) became active in the USA, where worrying signals of the impending disaster were visible from 2006. European (or more precisely German) banks became early victims of imploding subprime US mortgage markets. The ECB had an early warning sign and was able to intervene so quickly because it was more directly active in money markets than the Fed, refinancing up to 2,000 banks on a daily basis compared to the twenty central counterparties with which the Fed interacts (Lenza et al., 2010, p. 298).

The first consequential reforms concerned the creation of a Single Rulebook for EU banks as well as sectoral regulatory authorities, as recommended by the de Larosière report of February 2009 (Report, 2009; see also Acharja, 2009). This legal harmonization later allowed a banking union to be built in an incredibly short time span of a few years that included elements of reinsurance for national banking systems.

The financial crisis entered its sovereign debt phase outside the euro area as early as 2008–9 with IMF–EU bailout programmes for non-euro countries in Hungary, Latvia, and Romania (Schelkle, 2017, pp. 167–70). Under EU rules, they could get credit as Balance of Payments Assistance. These bailouts went largely unnoticed until the crisis affected euro area members for which a no-bailout clause was in place. When the Greek government finally requested support, in May 2010, the call for tightening the existing fiscal rules became overwhelming. By late 2011, the so-called Six-Pack reforms came into force and were followed by an intergovernmental Fiscal Compact, signed in March 2012, meant to reinforce the message of fiscal discipline. Both intended to harden commitments to budgetary prudence and make sanctions for breaking the rules more automatic. While the latter did not happen, the reforms triggered a phase of pro-cyclical retrenchment ('austerity') that slowed down the recovery and may even have contributed to a double-dip recession in some countries (IMF, 2011; Heimberger, 2016).

This spooked financial markets. Between 2010 and 2013, five euro area countries needed extraordinary support because bond investors shunned national government debt denominated in the common currency. While the problems of Greece and Portugal could be seen as predominantly fiscal, the cause of sovereign debt crises in Ireland, Spain, and Cyprus was private debt, of households and banks, which governments underwrote or assumed before financial markets turned the table on them and effectively shut them out of affordable bond finance. Bailout capacity was built up in several stages, ending with a permanent European Stability Mechanism (ESM) that came into force in late 2012. The turning point of the euro area crisis came in mid-2012, with ECB President Draghi's famous speech to London

[2] Tail risks refer to realizations of a random outcome that are very unlikely and occur at the ends (in the tails) of a normal probability distribution.

investment bankers that the central bank would 'do whatever it takes to save the euro' (Draghi, 2012). His open-ended promise was underpinned by a new instrument, so-called Outright Monetary Transactions (OMT), but above all the decision of the European leaders' summit shortly before to introduce a banking union for the euro area.[3] By 2014, the core of the banking union, a Single Supervisory Mechanism, was in force and European economies had started to recover.

In 2020, the recovery ended abruptly. The COVID-19 pandemic was a public health crisis to which governments all over the world responded with shutdowns of entire sectors in the economy. The recessions that resulted were on average deeper than those during the financial sovereign debt crisis and nowhere deeper than in Europe. The fiscal fallout was dramatic. Governments compensated for their restrictions with massive job retention schemes, business subsidies, and guarantees vis-à-vis banks, while tax revenues imploded. The ECB accommodated the shock by stepping up its Quantitative Easing (QE) programme that had been in place from 2015 to stimulate recovery (De Grauwe and Diessner, 2020). The Pandemic Emergency Purchase Programme (PEPP) flooded the financial system with liquidity of up to €1.85 trillion, putting a floor under asset prices, in particular of government bonds. The innovation of PEPP was that the ECB could be more flexible in the amount of bonds it bought from each country, which gave it the flexibility to buy more issued by governments that were harder hit by the pandemic. Another instrument, the Targeted Long-term Refinancing Operations, made the lavish refinancing of banks conditional on their lending to business; a negative interest rate actually paid banks for doing so.

The Commission installed a hub-and-spoke system through which it coordinated the use of public health care resources in the EU, from repatriation flights to spare intensive care units and the procurement of vaccines. The landmark reform of the pandemic was a massive Recovery and Resilience Facility (RRF) that can hand out grants and loans to the tune of more than 6 per cent of the EU's 2018 GDP. Member States must submit detailed plans on how they want to spend the grants, of which a specified share must be for green and digital investments (Begg, Chapter 6 in this volume).

Other, less spectacular reforms were, first, the introduction of an ESM credit line of up to 2 per cent of each members' GDP, to a total of €240 billion. It is financed by bonds that the ESM issues and the Member States guarantee, which ensures extremely cheap financing costs. This ESM Pandemic Crisis Support prescribes a certain use of the loans at below market interest rates, notably to cover public health care costs. This is an innovation insofar as this contingent credit line does not require a government to fulfil 'strict conditionality' for drawing on it. Finally, the temporary 'Support to mitigate Unemployment Risks in an Emergency' (SURE) is a loan programme with an envelope of €100 billion by which EU Member States can finance job retention schemes, including support for self-employed businesses. SURE was mobilized very quickly while the ESM credit line has not been applied for by any Member State.

7.2.2 *The Building Blocks of a System*

The policy shift towards propping up overstretched Member States directly can be captured by the notion of reinsurance, defined as coverage of other insurers, to compensate for excessive or

[3] The banking union is arguably more important because the ECB cannot activate the OMT at short notice as it is predicated on an ESM programme. It is telling in this context that the ECB has not activated the OMT, not even in summer 2015 when market panic ensued during the discussions around the third bailout programme for Greece.

catastrophically high losses. In the euro area crisis, this tail risk was a fiscal collapse triggered by a sell-off of the government bonds that made debt issue or rollover prohibitively expensive. Even the Greek and Portuguese cases, which were on unsustainable fiscal trajectories before, can be seen as hit by a contingency eligible for reinsurance insofar as the unprecedented recession was a suddenly aggravating factor that pushed them over the edge. The catastrophic event was the drying up of affordable credit to national fiscal authorities that had huge deficits to finance. A bailout fund that can give affordable credit in such a situation amounts to reinsurance.

The contrast to reinsurance is co-insurance. Co-insurance is the principle on which a fiscal federation is typically based. The federal and the state level have complementary insurance schemes for residents and communities that come into play whenever contingencies materialize, simultaneously or in a division of labour, e.g. when transfers are largely financed by the federal budget while they are administered by the state. Co-insurance presupposes a budgetary system that links all levels of government.

To characterize a reform as reinsurance for catastrophic losses rather than co-insurance, the following features are relevant:

- The scheme that the reform introduced comes into play only as a secondary safety net to cover the downside tail risk, i.e. catastrophic or excess loss. It protects the primary scheme against overstretch or counterproductive responses like pro-cyclical expenditure cuts.
- The scheme does not require standardization of the primary insurance provision as it entails coverage of losses beyond a certain threshold only; the bulk of losses falls on the primary insurer. In turn, the reinsurance can also take a categorically different form and does not require harmonization with the primary insurance.
- The stipulations for receiving reinsurance should therefore also not reveal an overriding concern with moral hazard, i.e. risk-taking incentivized by available insurance. The primary (state) insurance is a stand-alone safety net and not merely a co-payment as in fiscal federations with a dominant centre.

The system that evolved has three relevant building blocks: (1) a supranational central bank, the ECB, that takes financial stability as seriously as price stability; (2) a banking union for the euro area; and (3) extension and differentiation of fiscal capacities like the ESM, the RRF, and SURE. All three elements are embedded in comprehensive regulation and legislation, including the ECB Statute, huge Directives on financial regulation, and the European Semester, an annual exercise in coordinating Member State policies through the Macroeconomic Imbalances Procedure and a complex set of fiscal rules. The latter were suspended in the pandemic[4] and are likely to be reformed again before their reactivation, officially planned in 2023.

7.2.3 *The European Central Bank as Reinsurer*

The ECB can produce liquidity in open-ended quantities and thus assume tail risks. It fulfilled this role from the start in 2007–8, as lender of last resort for the banking system. For instance, '[b]y relaxing collateral requirements for lending programs, central banks insure against the tail event in which the borrower and the collateral fail to cover the borrowed amount' (Brunnermeier and Sannikov, 2012, p. 3). But it took the ECB a while to acknowledge officially

[4] The suspension of fiscal rules means that no Excessive Deficit Procedure would be started if a Member State exceeded the 3 per cent deficit limit.

this role in a catastrophic financial collapse, more precisely a system-wide liquidity shortage. In fact, the early liquidity measures, which lent to banks at a fixed (low) rate as much as they wanted to borrow, took only the downside tail risk, with the collateral requirements determining the amount (Brunnermeier and Sannikov, 2012, p. 26). The previous holders of the collateralized assets, banks, were the main beneficiaries of this intervention because it put a floor under asset prices. By stopping the fall of asset prices that dragged even solid banks into the abyss, they were functionally equivalent to early bond purchasing programmes by other central banks.

The first programme of bond purchases in secondary markets, the Securities Market Programme, was adopted after the dramatic May 2010 summit that decided the bailout of Greece. While straight asset purchases still largely benefited their previous holders in that they put a floor under their price, it also benefited member state governments like Italy and Belgium. They were vulnerable to herding behaviour of bond investors that sold first the public debt of Greece, then Ireland and Portugal. Every ECB intervention brought down the risk spreads on their bonds and thus made new issues and the rollover of bonds considerably cheaper. If the catastrophic event is a self-fulfilling financial panic, the promise of reinsurance can prevent the need for its activation.

More importantly, the ECB's intervention took momentum out of the 'doom loop'. This is the popular term for a negative feedback mechanism by which weak banks require support from government that then leads to downgrading of government bonds, which, to the extent that a lot of bonds are still held on banks' balance sheets, further weakens even the previously sound banks; and a new round ensues. It drags the insurer, the national tax state, into the abyss and it is exactly such a situation that reinsurance is meant to prevent. The strings attached to any of the ECB programmes are soft and general, because the central bank wants to encourage ample use of liquidity to stabilize the system.

However, there were also features of the ECB's interventions that were incompatible with the provision of reinsurance. Above all, the participation of the ECB in the Troika was subject to a conflict of interest: its hard-line stance on fiscal conditionality in the negotiations of bailout programmes suggested that the reinsurer wanted to minimize its exposure. The ECB's constant lecturing of governments to return to the path of fiscal prudence as defined by the EU's fiscal rules created the impression that the ECB was a very reluctant reinsurer and asked the insured primary insurer to mend its ways and reduce tail risks in a counterproductive way. The significance of ECB President Draghi's commitment to do 'whatever it takes' is that it made the reinsurance promise less provisional and qualified.

7.2.4 *The Banking Union and Its Elements of Reinsurance*

The European Banking Union got reinsurance capacity for Member States with the Single Resolution Fund. Bank resolution is necessary when banks' solvency problems become manifest and do not go away with liquidity support. It is an emergency fund that can be called upon in times of crisis, i.e. after national resolution capacity has been deployed and becomes over-stretched. After its phasing in, this Fund is financed by the banking industry itself, which is also common in other jurisdictions such as the USA.

The fund is small, however, and covers only an amount equivalent to at least 1 per cent of the deposits that the member banks hold. Its negotiation took a long time since governments wanted to ensure that national bank supervisors have a say when called upon, that small domestic banks do not have to pay insurance for transnational banks, and that the fund really remains a secondary, exceptional safety net.[5] Too small a fund can precipitate crises because whenever it is called upon, panic may ensue for fear that it may run out soon. After much wrangling, it was decided in January 2021 that the ESM would provide an additional 'backstop' to the Fund from 2022 onwards. The ESM's contingent credit doubles the insured amount of the Single Resolution Fund by another 1 per cent of covered deposits, although it is capped at €68 billion.

This reinsurance is still very limited. A blog by ESM staff makes this obvious:

> The backstop will better shield governments from being forced to rescue failing banks, causing major disruption to their economies. Although it is tricky to draw parallels between crises, the last one saw governments inject around €360 billion into banks' capital over the ten years following the crisis, thus excluding asset relief interventions and guarantees (amounting to an additional €3.5 trillion in state aid. (Mascher et al., 2020)

While the ESM staff do not comment on this discrepancy, it is clear that the ability to reinsure governments when banks collapse is small.

The European Deposit Insurance Scheme (EDIS) is ready to be phased in but has not been finally approved by the EU Member States; in particular, Germany under finance minister Schäuble reneged on the promise to introduce such a backup for national deposit guarantee schemes. These schemes are already harmonized under EU legislation (Directive 2014/49/EU). The character of EDIS as a reinsurance scheme for national programmes is made quite clear in the Commission's justification of its proposal: 'EDIS would provide a stronger and more uniform degree of insurance cover in the euro area. This would reduce the vulnerability of national DGS to large local shocks, ensuring that the level of depositor confidence in a bank would not depend on the bank's location and weakening the link between banks and their national sovereigns' (European Commission, n.d.). The discussion is ongoing and it seems quite clear that EDIS will be introduced in the foreseeable future.

It is noteworthy that both reinsurance schemes, the SRF and EDIS, have to be paid for eventually by the financial industry itself. The EU's contribution to providing reinsurance is making it compulsory for banks operating in the euro area, i.e. as a regulator. Because of the limited amounts, however, the EU will have to back up the mandated private reinsurance with more tangible compensation, for instance with an ESM contingent credit line.

7.2.5 *Fiscal Capacities for Reinsurance*

The ESM (and its predecessors) was the first fiscal capacity that could help governments to sustain spending when they were shut out of bond markets. In 2010, it was not an *ex ante* insurance mechanism but risk-sharing *ex post*, which might explain the punitive strings attached as measures of deterrence. Even so, the support was massive, roughly three times as much as the IMF lent to countries at its peak in 2012. The Greek programme was the biggest in the history of sovereign bailouts (Pisani-Ferry et al., 2013; Schelkle, 2017, pp. 168–70). Yet the punitive conditionality tied to its low-cost loans has made the bailout fund so controversial that the Italian government, supported by a majority in parliament, pre-announced that it would not take the bailout with such conditions even if the pandemic hit them hard (Schelkle, 2021). The Pandemic Crisis Support, mentioned earlier, was the result, earmarking its use for high direct and indirect public health expenditures rather than making the receipt conditional on implementing far-reaching reforms.

[5] Nicolas Véron (2019) provides an insightful and informative account of the debate.

Earmarking is in line with a reinsurance contract. It tackles the vulnerability to the incident specifically, for instance by financing additional health-care capacities or training of additional staff. It assumes that the losses borne by the beneficiary are so high that excessive risk-taking can be excluded as a cause of the contingency. Strict conditionality, by contrast, is at odds with reinsurance in that the stipulated reforms effectively challenge the entitlement to reinsurance. Its proponents argue that the conditionality of reforms may reduce the need for reinsurance next time, but this insinuates typically that it was not (re)insurance for a catastrophic event beyond a government's control but self-inflicted harm.

The Recovery and Resilience Fund is a fund that promises support to those members that were either particularly hard hit by the pandemic or are too poor to finance an ambitious investment programme that can jump-start the recovery. The first eligibility criterion, but not the second, can be compatible with the interpretation of reinsurance. Its temporary and specific nature makes the RRF a reinsurance against the uncertainties of recovering from a pandemic that puts some countries at higher risk of lasting damage without some outside support. For Member States that are eligible on the second criterion, the RRF grants and loans resemble more co-insurance from a dominant federal centre. The primary insurance is hard to distinguish from a relatively small co-payment, e.g. in the guise of maintaining public expenditure, in some recipient Member States. The highly redistributive nature of the RRF in this case makes it also more like a transfer programme than insurance paid out when a particularly severe contingency arises.

SURE was from the start designed as reinsurance. It tries 'to address sudden increases in public expenditure for the preservation of employment'. The forced shut-down of entire sectors of the economy had no precedent; most unemployment schemes would have been overwhelmed and the uncertainty from unemployment would have made households consume even less, with further damaging effects on economies. In essence, SURE provides favourable loans to help finance job-retention schemes. Job preservation on this scale and with such a scope have never been financed by Member States before (OECD, 2020). SURE incentivized governments to introduce those schemes in the first place, thus preventing a massive rise in unemployment in countries that can predictably not afford it and would thus have raised the prospect of sovereign debt crises. SURE in turn is financed by bond issues of the Commission, guaranteed proportionally by each Member State.

7.2.6 *The System*

Table 7.1 summarizes the elements of reinsurance that developed from 2008, starting with the ECB. Financial markets are also considered as insurers, which they are supposed to be. They allow savers and investors to put their eggs in different baskets and thus diversify risks. This is not to deny that financial markets produce tail risk themselves, i.e. bring them about through their own failure (Brunnermeier and Sannikov, 2012). However, while this is true for the financial system as a whole, it is not true for every bank that got into trouble. In this, systemic financial failure is not categorically different from tail risks of climate change to which every consumer and producer contributes while becoming a victim of global warming and pollution at the same time.

It still remains to be seen that the three building blocks form a system in which the parts back each other up. The resolute interventions of the ECB created a loneliness problem in the Padoa–Schioppa sense (Mabbett and Schelkle, 2019): the central bank was forced to provide liquidity to banks indiscriminately because it could not force governments to recapitalize and

TABLE 7.1 *Reinsurance of tail risks of public and private insurers*

'Insurers' *Reinsurance providers*	Sovereign public finances	Financial markets
European Central Bank	Open-ended support (OMT announcement) in case of financial market panic	Lending and market making of last resort
Single Resolution Fund [European Deposit Insurance Scheme]	Circuit breaker for doom loop of bank-sovereign balance sheets; coverage of excessive losses to national schemes	Restructuring of too-big-to-fail banks, zombie banks
European Stability Mechanism	Bailout with conditionality, earmarked lending for pandemic	Backstop for an industry-financed resolution fund
Recovery and Resilience Facility, SURE	Substitute for bond market to finance public investments and job retention after major health crisis	n.a.

restructure national banking systems, which is fiscally costly. The collective of fiscal authorities in the Council could exploit their joint decision trap to free-ride on the ECB's stabilization efforts. The apparent cure of ever larger and bolder central bank interventions made the underlying problem of an oversized financial system, prone to boom–bust cycles, even more virulent. Asset bubbles, burgeoning shadow banking, and dubious financial innovations like crypto assets, chasing high yields with extremely speculative instruments, have been clear symptoms. In order to get out of this, the ECB insisted on institution-building that would ensure cooperation from fiscal authorities: both the bailout capacity that became the ESM and the banking union with its resolution capacity were stipulations by ECB Presidents Trichet and Draghi, respectively, in return for rolling out yet another programme (Mabbett and Schelkle, 2019).

The resolution capacity directly addresses the legacy problem of the euro area crisis, notably identifying and closing down so-called zombie banks. They are insolvent banks, in a commercial sense dead but still able to walk among the living, thanks to the central banks' liquidity support that put a floor under asset prices. The SRF (and EDIS, once in place) can help fiscal authorities to act by helping them with excess losses from bank restructuring.

The pandemic was a different crisis still labouring under this legacy problem. The RRF now provides respite for the ECB in that it is designed to reduce member states' need for national debt finance during their recovery and therefore their exposure to market panic. Despite its reform, the ESM has played only a secondary role, indicating that the legacy of its association with 'strict conditionality' has made it incompatible with reinsurance in the eyes of some governments.

But the ESM's Pandemic Crisis Support could still be useful for covering a tail risk of QE by the ECB (Schelkle, 2021). The ECB can buy government bonds from banks only after a prescribed time lag, so as not to encourage Member States to issue debt in the knowledge that the ECB will buy the bonds immediately; this would go against the prohibition of public debt monetization under Article 123 TFEU. Therefore, a situation could arise in which financial investors sell off a government's new bond issue soon afterwards, but the ECB could not stabilize the price of these bonds because they do not qualify for its asset purchase programme. Previously, such a government could only get a Troika programme from the ESM. Now, a government can avoid acute liquidity problems by drawing on the contingent credit line for

Pandemic Support, without the strict conditionality and lengthy negotiation of a Memorandum of Understanding that accompanies other precautionary ESM credit lines with similar purposes. The Pandemic Crisis Support is therefore a complementary reinsurer when the ECB cannot act in this way. This allows the ECB in turn to be more selective and robust in its reinsurance role if it is of the opinion that a fiscal authority is not cooperating.

In short, the reforms reduce the loneliness of the ECB as the reinsurer of first resort during a financial crisis. Some of these capacities act quite clearly as reinsurance, e.g. the ESM pandemic support, and the RRF for particularly hard-hit Member States, notably those with a large tourism sector. These public schemes are complemented by compulsory private reinsurance for national schemes in the banking union, although they are probably too small for a systemic crisis.

7.3 REINSURANCE AS A POLITICAL COMPROMISE

Why have reforms converged on a system of reinsurance, rather than incrementally introduced a budget that can be enlarged over time? Legal scholars would point out that there are considerable legal hurdles to introducing a federal budget into the EU Treaty (Tuori and Tuori, 2014, p. 255). This observation can be complemented with a political-economic argument about why reinsurance of Member States is so much more conducive to political agreement than co-insurance through a common budget. The main reasons are, first, the state of democratic development of the union and, second, the EU's diversity, not least between members of the euro area and EU members outside.

Reinsurance and co-insurance are forms of fiscal integration. Reinsurance is, first of all, a concession to those Member States, typically in the north and east of Europe, that do not wish to integrate fiscally via a central budget with taxing powers at the EU or euro area level and joint public debt management. They are in favour of more limited forms of fiscal integration, notably fiscal surveillance, a modicum of transfers for disadvantaged regions, and possibly minimum tax harmonization. The euro area crisis has demonstrated that, given integrated financial markets, this was not sufficient to prevent a financial crisis from morphing into a sovereign debt crisis for some, with the potential to affect a large number through a self-fulfilling bond market panic. A crisis resolution mechanism had to be added in the guise of the ESM. But Member States still resisted a full-fledged fiscal union as co-insurance through a federal budget as well as intertemporal pooling of fiscal powers through joint public debt management.

Reinsurance is democratically less demanding than co-insurance. Permanent co-insurance requires taxing powers for all levels of government and thus democratic legitimation at all those levels. Reinsurance can be financed by the pooling of guarantees that underpin the issue of debt at low interest rates. This is the principle of the ESM, analogous to the IMF for the world economy. Depending on whether the primary insurer in need of reinsurance receives low-cost loans or grants, the non-affected Member States may have to pay a greater or lesser share of the debt service. This can be done rather quietly and fiscal costs accrue only in a distant future. It works like any contribution to an international organization.

Reinsurance can be more targeted and bespoke than federal fiscal co-insurance. We have seen that the three fiscal schemes created over a decade address specific contingencies. The ESM is a permanent bailout fund when sovereign debtors lose access to euro-denominated bond markets, which threatens to become contagious. The RRF is a temporary fund to facilitate uncertain recovery from the deepest post-war recession that Europe has ever seen. Finally,

SURE helps Member States to finance job retention when unemployment and insolvency would affect so many workers and businesses that the political fallout would resemble the Great Depression. SURE could easily be recreated in future pandemics; after all, it has the politically attractive feature that it is self-terminating if and when public health measures like travel restrictions and lockdowns are eased.

As a secondary safety net, reinsurance does not require as much harmonization with the primary insurance scheme as a co-insurance arrangement. The latter has to have a complementary design so as to avoid free-riding and cumbersome administration, for instance the same categorical eligibility criteria for benefits. Reinsurance for tail risks, as in the EU, can be categorically different. Loans or grants to governments in exceptionally dire circumstances can be structured differently from the national income support system that it helps to finance. This is a significant advantage for a union that is extremely diverse and comprises members with very different (welfare) state traditions and generosity levels.

Closely related is the political advantage of reinsurance for the EU specifically, which comprises eight non-euro members. A common budget for the euro area would bring a membership crisis of the EU in its wake since it is inconceivable that Denmark, Sweden, Czechia, and Poland would accept this step. For instance, it would raise the question of how such a common euro area budget could be run alongside the Multi-Annual Financial Framework, which is the EU's budget. The European Parliament would have to get a new mandate that creates MEPs with different rights of representation for euro area and non-euro area citizens. By contrast, the reinsurance schemes can be flexibly extended to all, for which SURE is the most obvious example in practice.

This means that the Member States with a preference for the status quo, and thus a stronger bargaining position, can be moved towards more fiscal integration. They are assured that reinsurance operates only in exceptional circumstances and is specific to the contingency. In turn, those who favour more fiscal integration obtained large schemes that can quite significantly augment nation state capacities in a targeted way.

Last but not least, the primary insurers can claim political credit for any success of reinsurance. Reinsurance can act effectively as protection against contagion in those Member States which are not in the midst of the fire; the ESM is officially referred to as a 'firewall'. It can also act as the water and fuel supply to the fire brigade in countries which are directly affected. Reinsurance is only a backstop for those that are seen to come to the rescue, be it protecting residents from a crisis elsewhere or ameliorating the crisis at home; while not essential, it is reassuring to have.

Reinsurance therefore is not merely support of the lowest common denominator variety. This is an overly functionalist perspective that considers politics only as an obstacle to economically optimal solutions. That policies find political support is not merely a necessary condition; in democracies, it is more essential than finding a first-best solution, to the extent that they exist at all. Reinsurance has repeatedly proven to be a default position of interest constellations that can be captured by the battle of the sexes. While the partners, here democratically accountable governments, have quite different preferences on many policies, they prefer to do them together, even if it means at least for one side to make serious concessions on the preferred outcome. The problem of this game is to make sure that a consensus is reached, which is to determine who has to compromise this time. It requires trust that each side has to compromise from time to time. Scharpf (1997) argued that the battle of the sexes configuration is a more pertinent characterization of the 'games real actors [in the EU] play' than the overused prisoner's dilemma.

7.4 FISCAL INTEGRATION IN AN EXPERIMENTAL UNION

This chapter has outlined how a sequence of reforms, driven largely by unprecedented and rapidly spreading crises, led to institution-building that can be seen as a system for the reinsurance of Member States. These newly created institutions protect these Member States, i.e. the primary insurers of domestic residents, against extreme demands on their capacity to cope with a crisis. These reforms were not designed as a system but complemented each other in a systemic way. Notably, the ECB could not prevent sovereign default on its own but needed a fund to indemnify it if government bonds on its books fail. The ESM was eventually created as a permanent bailout fund for sovereign debt problems beyond the control of the affected government. But the prescribed reforms and budget consolidation made the post-crisis recovery a problem, even before the pandemic struck, with its temporary suspension of economic activity from which entire countries have to recover. A massive recovery package responded to this in summer 2020, although its immediate driver was the perceived need to have a politically conciliatory substitute for the Coronabond instrument. A scheme to support job preservation and a bank resolution fund provide reinsurance for short-term measures with long-term benefits.

This is an alternative to looking at reinsurance as covering up the incompleteness of the euro area in terms of an optimal currency area and a fiscal federation. The optimal currency area approach supports a homogenization and streamlining of Member States so as to prevent them being struck by 'asymmetric' (nation-specific) shocks for which they no longer have an exchange rate to deal with. Even its own starting point, shocks that need to be stabilized, do not justify this reasoning, as Asdrubali et al. (1996) argued long ago (see also Cimadomo et al., Chapter 22 in this volume). If shocks and crises are key problems, diversity is an advantage for the risk pool that a monetary union constitutes (Schelkle, 2017).

Fiscal federalism also acknowledges that a polity may benefit from the diversity of its constituent members and assigns an optimal division of labour in fulfilling the fiscal functions of stabilization, redistribution, and allocation (efficiency-enhancing public goods provision). But this literature has no interest in how one could get to such a division of labour if one does not start out with it. Or how optimal it still is if we consider Member States to act in their own interest and have incentives to exploit the centre's capacities. The comparative research of Rodden and Wibbels (2002, 2010) has cast doubt on the desirability of fiscal centralization. In the USA, states switch off their automatic stabilizers and shift the costs to the federal level, only then to complain about the reckless public finances of the centre.

Refraining from all centralization comes at a cost, however. The EU cannot and must not force fiscal centralization on Member States for which this would have very different consequences. Ultimately, there is no magic wand that can create the political integration required before a central budget can become a democratically viable institution. Reinsurance for extreme, contagious, and potentially EU-wide emergencies can strike a compromise between meaningful diversity and the ability to join forces in hard times. This is all the more important as some contingencies may include all EU members, while others affect primarily those in the euro area. And EU schemes widen the risk pool, which enlarges the insurance benefit.

Our research programmes therefore need adapting to the fact that the EU may constitute a new type of polity (Kriesi et al., 2021). Future research may want to explore the mechanisms at work that forge a system out of uncoordinated piecemeal reforms. It should solve the puzzle why the relatively well-off Member States and their governments are apparently less willing to reinsure massive bank resolutions for which they also might be eligible, compared to other contingencies, such as a bank panic during recovery. And research could explore the politics of reinsurance, which is missing in a literature that excels in the mathematics of insurance economics, ever since Karl Borch (1961) discovered reinsurance for academic study. The elected representatives of citizens so far seem to agree each time on schemes that do not provide an entry point into a centralized budget. But what about their voters? Do they resent that the EU only assists as a reinsurer, i.e. supporting their government when national losses are considerable and the situation has already become quite desperate? Or will voters in EU Member States appreciate that, with the recent reforms, the EU has committed to come to a Member State's rescue in the extreme but leaves it fiscal sovereignty otherwise? The prevailing attitudes of electorates towards risk-sharing in the EU are not necessarily aligned with those of executives in crisis-fighting mode (Cicchi et al., 2020). More research needs to be done, not least because the answers to these questions will decide the political success of experimental fiscal integration in the EU.

REFERENCES

Acharja, V. (2009). Some steps in the right direction: A critical assessment of the de Larosière report. *VoxEU blog*. 4 March.

Asdrubali, P., Sørensen, B. E., and Yosha, O. (1996). Channels of interstate risk sharing: United States 1963–90. *Quarterly Journal of Economics* 111(4), 1081–1010.

Bénassy-Quéré, A., Brunnermeier, M., Enderlein, H., Farhi, E., Fratzscher, M., Fuest, C., Gourinchas, P.-O., Martin, P., Pisani-Ferry, J., Rey, H., Schnabel, I., Véron, N., Weder di Mauro, B., and Zettelmeyer, J. (2018). How to reconcile risk sharing and market discipline in the euro area. *VoxEU blog*. 17 January.

Borch, K. (1961). Elements of a theory of reinsurance. *Journal of Insurance* 28(3), 35–43.

Brunnermeier, M. K., and Sannikov, Y. (2012). Redistributive monetary policy. Federal Reserve Bank of Kansas City Economic Conference Proceedings Jackson Hole Symposium, pp. 331–384.

Cicchi, L., Genschel, P., Hemerijck, A., and Nasr, M. (2020). EU solidarity in times of Covid-19. *Policy Briefs; 2020/34, European Governance and Politics Programme*. Fiesole: European University Institute. https://hdl.handle.net/1814/67755

De Grauwe, P., and Diessner, S. (2020). What price to pay for monetary financing of budget deficits in the euro area. *VoxEU blog*, 18 June.

Draghi, M. (2012). Speech by Mario Draghi, President of the European Central Bank at the Global Investment Conference in London 26 July [Press release]. www.ecb.europa.eu/press/key/date/2012/html/sp120726.en.html

ECB (2007). *Monthly Bulletin*. Box 3. September.

European Commission (n.d.). European Deposit Insurance Scheme. European Commission. https://ec.europa.eu/info/business-economy-euro/banking-and-finance/banking-union/european-deposit-insurance-scheme_en

Ferrara, F., Schelkle, W., and Truchlewski, Z. (2023). What difference does the framing of a crisis make to EU solidarity? Forthcoming in European Union Politics.

Heimberger, P. (2016). Did fiscal consolidation cause the double-dip recession in the euro area? WIIW Working Paper No. 130. Vienna: The Vienna Institute for International Economic Studies.

Herszenhorn, D., and Wheaton, S. (2020). How Europe failed the Coronavirus test. *Politico*, 7 April.

Hill, C. (1993). The capability–expectations gap, or conceptualizing Europe's international role. *Journal of Common Market Studies* 31(3), 305–328.

Howarth, D., and Quaglia, L. (2021). Failing forward in Economic and Monetary Union: Explaining weak eurozone financial support mechanisms. *Journal of European Public Policy* 28(10), 1555–1572.

IMF (2011). Slowing growth, rising risks. *World Economic Outlook*, September.

Jones, E., Kelemen, R. D., and Meunier, S. (2021). Failing forward? Crises and patterns of European integration. *Journal of European Public Policy* 28(10), 1519–1536.

Kriesi, H., Ferrera, M., and Schelkle, W. (2021). The theoretical framework of SOLID – A research agenda. SOLID Working Paper.

Lenza, M., Pill, H., and Reichlin, L. (2010). Monetary policy in exceptional times. *Economic Policy* 62, 295.

Mabbett, D., and Schelkle, W. (2019). Independent or lonely? Central banking in crisis. *Review of International Political Economy* 26(3), 436–460.

Mascher, N., Strauch, R., and Williams, A. (2020). A backstop to the Single Resolution Fund now! ESM blog, 3 December.

Matthijs, M., and Blyth, M. (eds.). (2015). *The Future of the Euro*. Oxford: Oxford University Press.

OECD (2020). Job retention schemes during the COVID-19 lockdown and beyond. Paris. 12 October.

Pisani-Ferry, J., Sapir, A., and Wolff, G. (2013). EU-IMF assistance to euro-area countries: An early assessment. Bruegel Blueprint series, XIX, Brussels: Bruegel. http://bruegel.org/2013/06/eu-imf-assistance-to-euro-area-countries-an-early-assessment/

Report (2009). De Larosière report. The High-Level Group on Financial Supervision in the EU. 25 February.

Rhodes, M. (2021). Failing forward: A critique in light of Covid-19. *Journal of European Public Policy* 28 (10), 1537–1554.

Rodden, J., and Wibbels, E. (2002). Beyond the fiction of federalism: Macroeconomic management in multitiered systems. *World Politics* 54(4), 494–531.

Rodden, J., and Wibbels, E. (2010). Fiscal decentralization and the business cycle: An empirical study of seven federations. *Economics & Politics* 22(1), 37–67.

Ross, S. (2021). The business model of reinsurance companies. Investopedia, 31 May.

Scharpf, F. W. (1997). *Games Real Actors Play: Actor-Centered Institutionalism in Policy Research*. Boulder, CO: Westview Press.

Schelkle, W. (2017). *The Political Economy of Monetary Solidarity: Understanding the Euro Experiment*. Oxford: Oxford University Press.

Schelkle, W. (2021). Fiscal integration in an experimental union: How path-breaking was the EU's response to the COVID-19 pandemic? *Journal of Common Market Studies* 59(S1), 44–55.

Tuori, K., and Tuori, K. (2014). *The Eurozone Crisis: A Constitutional Analysis*. Cambridge: Cambridge University Press.

Valentino, P (2020). Cara Italia, impara a farcela da sola. *Corriere della Sera* Weekly Newsmagazine '7', 3 July, 14–19.

Véron, N. (2019). Taking stock of the Single Resolution Board. Economic Governance Support Unit (EGOV). Directorate-General for Internal Policies of the Union. www.bruegel.org/wp-content/uploads/2019/04/IPOL_IDA2019634393_EN.pdf

Wilmès, S., Macron, E., Mitsotakis, K., Varadkar, L., Conte, G., Bettel, X., Costa, A., Janša, J., and Sánchez, P. (2020). [Letter to European Council President Charles Michel]. 25 March.

8

Euro Crises, the Productivity Slowdown, and the EMU

Nauro F. Campos

8.1 INTRODUCTION

In the past fifteen years, the world economy has experienced one of its most severe crises ever. The crisis started in the United States in 2007. It happened not only against the background of unprecedented financial deepening and globalization, but also in light of the very rapid rise of Chinese imports into the United States and Europe (Autor et al., 2016) and of the speedy diffusion of new manufacturing technologies (Acemoglu and Restrepo, 2020). The crisis that started in the United States was followed in 2010 by a sovereign debt crisis in Europe that shook the foundations of the European Economic and Monetary Union (EMU). In response to these crises, the eurozone has witnessed radical institutional innovations with a myriad of new structures put in place. Yet the crisis has left severe economic scars (productivity remains more than 10 percentage points below trend in the United States and in Europe) as well as important political scars, e.g. the rise of populism (Algan et al., 2017).

The objective of this chapter is to discuss the productivity implications of the sequence of financial and economic crises experienced by euro area (EA) economies since 2007. The argument is organized in three parts: Section 8.2 details the euro crises and the policy response (chiefly fiscal consolidation and structural reforms) to these crises over the post-2007 'long lost decade'. Our objective is to provide an up-to-date narrative of the crisis – a narrative that goes beyond the view that it was a localized series of events (first in the United States and then in Europe) that were basically independent of each other and yet that require similar solutions, namely improvements in financial regulation of private and public agents, respectively. This more recent narrative summarized here stresses a context of deep financial integration and globalization, of economic and political interdependence, and a need for coherent, massive, and coordinated policy action that did not happen in a timely (or synchronized) fashion, nor was it supported by a sufficient build-up of new institutions.

Section 8.3 focuses on the productivity slowdown in Europe and tries to establish three important facts. The first is that Europe experienced a successful and sustained convergence to US levels from 1950 until 1995 over a range of productivity measures. Since 1995, Europe as a whole has experienced divergence with heterogeneity across countries in this respect. The second fact is that there has been a severe slowdown in productivity in Europe that seems to

I would like to thank Dariusz Adamski and Jakob de Haan for detailed comments that helped hugely to improve this chapter. The responsibility for all remaining errors is mine.

have taken place after the slowdown in productivity in the United States was first observed. Third, and most importantly, econometric evidence suggests that the productivity slowdown in the United States and in Europe seem to have preceded the Global Financial Crisis (GFC). In short, there seems to be little evidence supporting the view that the crises in the euro area caused the productivity slowdown.

Section 8.4 discusses productivity convergence developments in the EMU. We use the synchronization of economic shocks framework to put forward evidence showing strong support for the endogenous optimal currency area hypothesis: the introduction of the euro accelerated the convergence process in the eurozone. Moreover, we find little evidence suggesting that neither the Global Financial Crisis of 2007 nor the sovereign debt crisis of 2011 has significantly disrupted this convergence process.

Finally, there seems to be little evidence for a significant uptick in structural reforms adoption following the crises. Although this may be because it is 'still too early to tell', the crises have had a significant dampening effect: the productivity rebound (or return to trend) that often follows recessions is yet to materialize in the euro area, raising grave concerns for convergence, integration, and welfare.

8.2 THE CRISES IN THE EURO AREA

Once a crisis erupts, its resolution depends, inter alia of course, on a common understanding of its causes. The quicker agreement emerges, the shorter and less severe the crisis should turn out to be. Moreover, the more quickly agreement spreads, the easier it is to identify the actors that drove the crisis and the easier it should be to spread or distribute the costs of the recovery. Such agreed narratives have deep intellectual, economic, and political implications (Shiller, 2019).

In this light, it is not surprising that a simple and compelling narrative quickly emerged after the 2007 Global Financial Crisis. It is also not unexpected that this narrative would be vigorously promoted and perpetuated by politicians, special interest groups, and the media. It is even less surprising that this narrative will be revisited, updated, improved, and corrected over the long run by scholars and academics. What perhaps is unexpected is that this work towards a deeper understanding of what happened is already taking place and that a rather different narrative has already started to materialize.

The original narrative that emerged from the GFC should by now be familiar. It states that the crisis surely did not originate in Europe, but in the United States, and was basically caused by a lack of financial supervision. The crisis started with problems in the United States, more specifically in its subprime mortgage sector, which spread to other parts of the financial system, culminating with the investment bank Lehman Brothers filing for bankruptcy. This led to a very sharp recession and an enormous and highly synchronized contraction in international trade. In this narrative, the potential solution suggests itself almost naturally: more rigorous banking supervision in the Anglo-Saxon financial systems (that is, the United States and United Kingdom) would be strongly called for. Indeed, in various EU capitals the prevailing view was that more robust supervisory practices in bank-based (not market-based) financial systems had to a large extent protected the euro area from the worst of the crisis.

The second part of this narrative centres on Europe. Sometime later, in 2010, the euro sovereign debt crisis started out with the disclosure, by the newly elected Greek government, that public debt was much higher than previously reported and in disregard of the euro area fiscal rules. This led unsurprisingly to a sharp turn in confidence and a severe 'sudden stop' of capital flows mostly to the periphery of the eurozone. This resulted in yet another severe recession, one that substantially curtailed the recovery from the 2007–8 crisis. The solution to these two crises could well be presented as similar: more and better supervision to private and public agents, respectively.

In short, the initial narrative was that the two crises started out in different places (the United States and Greece) and could be understood to a large extent as basically independent of each other, yet more supervision was the response to both. Obviously, this is not to ignore financial factors that were important, among other reasons, because recessions following financial crises tend to be deeper (De Haan et al., 2016). Our view here is that financial factors have been almost exclusively the early focus and the more recent literature tries to extend and complement this emphasis.

Although the original narrative still resonates, academics have been hard at work. This has led to a revision to the point that a different and better substantiated narrative is emerging, mainly because of enormous progress on at least three different complementary areas of inquiry: theory, history, and econometrics.

Firstly, on the theoretical side, the prevailing macroeconomic framework at the time was inadequate because it was mostly centred on the assumption of frictionless financial markets. This has been abandoned and, as a consequence, a flurry of new models motivated by the crisis have emerged (e.g. Gertler and Gilchrist, 2018). Secondly, using a myriad of just recently disclosed documents, revised data, memoirs, and accounts, the history of the crisis has been retold by bringing together these newly revised macroeconomic models, history, politics, as well as its important geopolitical dimensions (e.g. Tooze, 2018). And thirdly, there has been an enormous amount of new econometric evidence that has shed new light on the received narrative and has contributed to its revision (see, among others, Bordo and Meissner, 2016; Martin and Philippon, 2017; Griffin, 2021). These three areas buttress a different, more nuanced, and richer explanation of the financial crisis.

The revised and up-to-date narrative is different. The crisis did obviously start in the United States. Yet the extent of financial integration and the size of the financial system have both reached levels that were unseen and, to a large extent, were not fully appreciated at the time. By 2007, the largest purchaser of US assets and the largest foreign lender to the United States was not China, but Europe (Adrian et al., 2018). In this light, the crisis was never only financial. The degree of economic and financial interdependence would not allow it to be localized. It was to be a global economic crisis. It did turn out to be, in Ben Bernanke's words, 'the worst financial crisis in global history' even when compared to the Great Depression.

From the outset, the 2007 crisis was global: financial systems in continental Europe and in the Anglo-Saxon world (United States and United Kingdom) were extraordinarily large and interconnected. Hence its resolution could not be gradual, modest, or one-sided; it had to be coordinated on a large scale. It was simplistic to ask only for more supervision if that was not from the beginning part of a substantial and concerted effort involving commensurate monetary and fiscal responses. Although leadership and coordination were evident in 2007, they were already in short supply in 2009.

There are many dimensions that can be used to show the development of the crises but we think maybe unemployment does a particularly good job. One important observation is that, until the crisis, unemployment rates were not different in the euro area vis-à-vis the EU, but they were very different (i.e. higher) compared to those in the United States or Japan. The proportion of unemployed workers was about 9 per cent in Europe on average compared to about 5 per cent in the United States. The crisis can be seen to start in the United States in 2007 when unemployment begins to increase. By the same token, the crisis seems to start in Europe a year later.

The second feature worth highlighting is the speed with which the crisis develops: the US unemployment rate increases very rapidly and reaches European levels (after the 1970s oil shocks, a rare occurrence indeed) by the second half of 2009. These numbers also increase for Europe but not as much as for the United States. The point here is that this crisis is usually depicted based on figures of bond spreads over time and here we argue that, on the real side, unemployment tells an equally compelling story.

The third important feature is that, still focusing on unemployment rates, the US recovery, albeit slow by historical standards, reaches pre-crisis levels by 2014–15, while the recovery in Europe turns out to be completely different. Firstly, because there is a second moment of the crisis in Europe which corresponds to the euro sovereign debt crisis of 2011–13. In other words, European unemployment does not decline after 2011, it actually increases to an even higher plateau. It peaks at about 12 per cent in 2013 and only then starts to decline very slowly, reaching pre-crisis levels only around 2019, in what turns out to be the last quarters before the COVID-19 pandemic. Needless to say, Europe-wide averages conceal important differences both across and within countries.

A final important observation worth making is that, after 2011, the difference between the euro area and the overall EU unemployment rates seem to have increased and stabilized at around 1 per cent, a difference that has lasted until today.

Yet these unemployment figures do not show how contrasting the responses to the crisis within the euro area were (Blanchard, 2018.) The recovery in US real GDP was not as deep in comparison to Europe and was relatively swift, where it took until 2013 to regain momentum in Europe, that is, to again rise above pre-crisis levels. Although the 2008 recession was deeper in Europe than in the United States, by 2011 economic activity in both was back to pre-crisis levels. For all country groupings, the actual levels turn out to be significantly below the pre-crisis trend and especially so after 2011 for the United States and 2013 for Europe.

Even more importantly, we observe highly divergent behaviour of real GDP in the European periphery. The euro sovereign debt crisis turned out to be a major stress test for the EMU. Among other things, it turned into a recession for all euro area stressed countries, except Ireland of course. For the EA15 (excluding Portugal, Italy, Greece, and Spain), the recovery has followed a similar pattern as in the United States and Japan, albeit all below trend. The focus on euro area sovereign debt sometimes makes one forget that the crisis had actually already hit some of the periphery of Europe very hard in 2008, with the experiences of Latvia and Hungary here worth noting (Blanchard et al., 2013; Győrffy, 2015).

These last two arguments suggest that the policy response to the 2007 crisis seems to have been rather effective, while the same may not be said of the policy response to the sovereign debt crisis in 2011. Of course, these figures cannot reveal the full nature, extent, and circumstances in which the actual policy response took place. In the first moment, the reactions in the United States and China were swift and, when needed, involved the G20 and International Monetary Fund (IMF). In the United States, the Fed put in place a diversified set of liquidity facilities for private banks as well as substantial central bank liquidity swap lines (Adrian et al., 2018). In turn, China enacted in late 2008 a fiscal stimulus programme of more than 12 per cent of GDP (Bai et al., 2016). The European response was very different.

One view is that the insufficient recapitalization of European banks links the subprime to the sovereign debt episodes as the lack of confidence spread and deepened thanks, inter alia, to the lack of a consistent response. According to Tooze (2018, p. 270): ‘As the Germans and the French were determined to block talk of coordinated fiscal stimulus and there was something akin to a conspiracy of silence around the role that the Fed was playing in providing global liquidity, it was by the way of the IMF that Brown and Obama would deliver their expansive impulse.' Moreover, 'by comparison, despite the size of the EU's economy, Europe's fiscal response to the crisis was derisory, barely more than 10 percent on the most generous measure. It was a sign of things to come. The only Western fiscal stimulus that weighted seriously in the balance was that launched by the United States' (Tooze, 2018, p. 275).

In Europe, what was about to come was a coordinated response to the crisis but one based chiefly on fiscal consolidation and structural reforms. Three caveats are in order: this is the first or initial response; there has been substantial institutional innovation since; and the response changed later. There have been of course, as part of this response, considerable institutional innovations in Europe: the crisis and the consensus about the need to improve financial supervision propelled the de Larosière Report which resulted in a new European-wide supervisory framework that would lead to the creation of important new agencies such as the European Stability Mechanism (Korhonen, 2018). There have also been significant subsequent changes in the European macroeconomic policy response to the crisis, in particular following Draghi's 'whatever it takes' and the ensuing changes in monetary stance (see Koijen et al., 2021).

With these caveats in mind, there seems to be now an emerging consensus, at least among academic economists, that the crisis was deepened in Europe, and prolonged across the globe, because of a lack of initiative, urgency, and coordination that led to important policy mistakes, chiefly the turn to fiscal consolidation (or to 'austerity' according to Alesina et al., 2015). The IMF, which played a large role in the resolution of the crisis in Europe, has conducted an initial evaluation of its response that supports this view (IMF, 2014). At the time, support for the idea of immediate fiscal consolidation can be traced to the debt brake constitutional amendment to the German constitution of late 2009, the misreporting of budgetary figures by Greece, as well as to the influential research of Harvard economists Reinhart and Rogoff (2010). Our argument here is not that this is the only or the major cause of the crisis but that the austerity issue seems to be the one that experienced the greatest change in terms of understanding of what has so far occurred. Moreover, although there was an immediate realization of the economic costs, the political costs turned out to be perhaps even greater (e.g. the rise of populism across the EU and, more specifically, how it led to Brexit), although they only surfaced much later and their implications are still being felt today (Fetzer, 2019; Guiso et al., 2021).

In addition to austerity, the other leg of the immediate European policy response to the crisis was the implementation of structural reforms. Figure 8.1 presents indices of the strictness or rigidity of regulations in the product markets (PMR), the labour markets (LMR), and the financial markets (FMR) from 1971 to 2015. Higher numbers indicate more rigidity. The figure shows that in both product and financial markets, there was significant deregulation, especially from the early 1980s. This contrasts with the trend in labour market reform where regulation increased or became more rigid over the same period. It is rather difficult to identify a breaking point in these series around 2008 or 2011 which implies that in the European policy response to the crisis most of the work was done by the fiscal consolidation leg, perhaps not by reforms. These need not to be independent. De Haan and Wiese (2022, p. 746) study the relationship between structural reforms and fiscal stance and argue that 'that product market reforms mostly cause slightly negative growth. Labour market reforms hurt growth under restrictive and neutral fiscal policy but are conducive to economic growth if introduced during periods of expansionary fiscal policy'. Moreover, and providing a link with our argument in the next section, Cette et al. (2016) review evidence that Europe's relatively poor productivity performance may be due to remaining labour and product market rigidities.

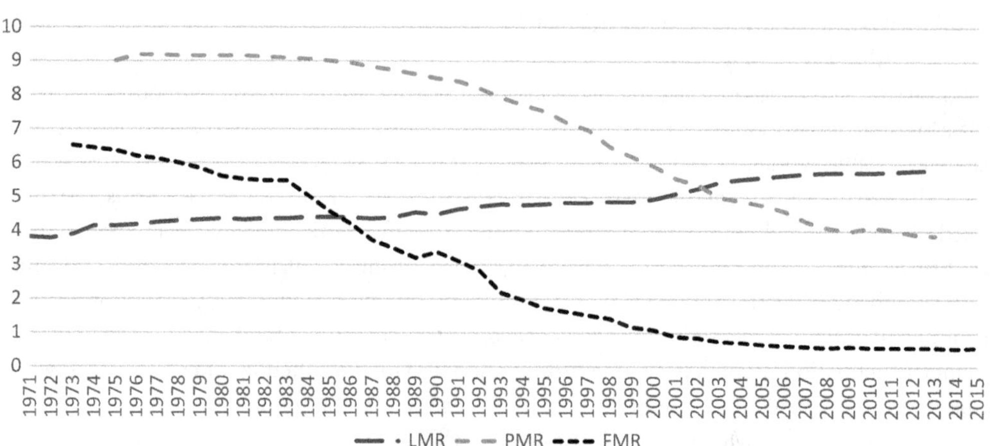

FIGURE 8.1. Structural reforms in OECD countries: 1971–2015.
Source: Constructed from OECD data using the methodology developed and explained in Campos et al. (2020).

8.3 THE PRODUCTIVITY SLOWDOWN

This section presents the basic stylized facts surrounding the slowdown in total factor productivity that has been observed over the last twenty years or so. It makes three main points. The first is that, taking the United States as the technological frontier, Europe between 1950 and 1995 was able to catch up in terms of output per worker and even more so when considering output per hour worked. Since 1995, we observe increasing divergence between Europe and the United States. Second, the onset of the productivity slowdown can be dated using modern structural break econometric techniques: such evidence overwhelmingly supports the view that the productivity slowdown precedes the Global Financial Crisis. The third important point we make in this section is that, despite the fact that productivity slowed down before the crisis, it has stagnated since 2008 and is now more than 10 per cent below trend.

Productivity matters. It is widely recognized that productivity is *the* key determinant of long-term prosperity (Jones, 2016). Productivity is normally defined as the ratio of the value of output (GDP) to inputs and is commonly understood as labour productivity (the value of output per worker or per hour worked) or as total or multifactor productivity (Syverson, 2011; Comin et al., 2020).

The first stylized fact about productivity we need to highlight is that, taking the United States as the technological frontier, between 1950 and 1995 Europe was able to catch up in terms of output per worker and, even more clearly, when considering output per hour worked. Since 1995, however, we observe an increasing divergence in productivity levels between Europe and the United States, as well as within Europe itself (Campos et al., 2019).

Van Ark et al. (2008) argue for three main phases in the evolution of Europe–US productivity differentials: the catch-up, the slowdown, and the left-behind periods. The first covers Europe catching up with the United States between 1950 and 1973. The second is the productivity slowdown in Europe and covers 1973 to 1995, at the end of which Europe closes the gap with the United States. The third is the period from 1995 until 2006, when the catch-up proved temporary and Europe started to fall behind again. That has continued to this day. Two important qualifications are as follows. The first is that although this overall pattern is clear, it is much stronger for output per hour worked than for output per capita. The second is

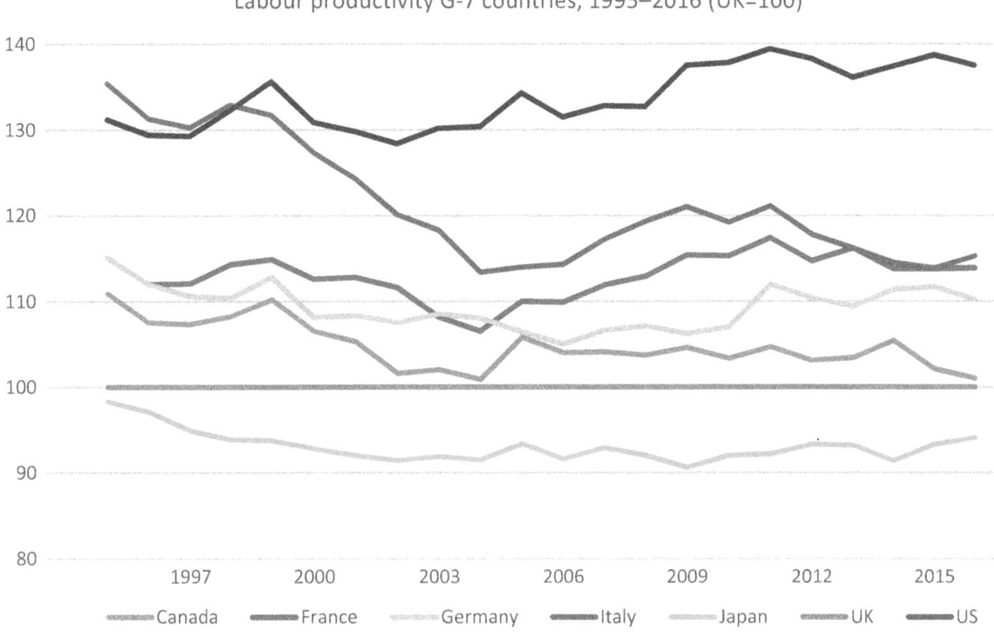

FIGURE 8.2. The productivity slowdown in advanced countries.
Source: Author's calculations using the latest available data from the Office of National Statistics.

that there are important differences within Europe that should not be downplayed. Some countries and some industrial sectors have done much better than others at different points in time.

The second important stylized fact about productivity we need to highlight is that the onset of the productivity slowdown has been dated using modern structural break econometric techniques: the evidence overwhelmingly supports the view that the productivity slowdown *precedes* the Global Financial Crisis. Fernald (2015) reports Bai–Perron multiple structural breaks evidence that indicates the existence of two main statistically significant breaks for US business sector labour productivity since 1973: a first one in the second quarter of 1997 that entails an acceleration of productivity growth and a second statistically significant structural break in the fourth quarter of 2003 that represents the beginning of the slowdown period. The exact break dates naturally depend on which data series is used (and to a lesser extent on the choice of the structural break test), but what is important to highlight is that in all cases the estimated dates precede the Global Financial Crisis, with confidence intervals typically excluding this event (Fernald, 2015).

The third important point we need to make in this section is that despite the fact that productivity clearly started to slow down before the crisis, since 2008 it has stagnated and is now more than 10 per cent below trend. Figure 8.2 shows that the productivity slowdown in advanced economies that seems to have started before the Global Financial Crisis is unmistakable, generalized, and severe. A slowdown of this magnitude in the United Kingdom, the country for which the longest available historical data series is available (although of course a country not in the EMU), has been qualified as historically unprecedented (Crafts and Mills, 2020). The figure also shows that these declines after 2009 in the United States and Germany (Italy and France) have been relatively smaller (larger).

8.4 CONVERGENCE

The crises in the euro area have brought to the fore the main shortcomings of its architecture. If one is searching for a measure of how widely recognized were the shortcomings of the euro area, one should look no further than Brussels' plan for a genuine economic and monetary union (Begg, 2014), with the word 'genuine' doing the heavy lifting. Agreement on the need for a solution coexists with apparently stark disagreement on the causes. One view is that 'design flaws' (De Grauwe, 2006) deepened imbalances, while another is that 'policy mistakes' (Sandbu, 2015) hindered convergence. Both views, however, rely upon 'asymmetries' (understood as different responses to shocks). The simple starting point of our argument in this section is that an increase in asymmetries in the distribution of output or productivity can be interpreted as divergence, while a decrease in asymmetries can be seen as convergence.

The main research question driving the scholarship on optimal currency areas (OCA) regards the costs and benefits of sharing a currency (Alesina and Barro, 2002). The main cost is the loss of monetary policy autonomy, while the main benefits are transaction costs and exchange rate uncertainty reductions, which may increase trade and competition. More recently, Chari et al. (2020) argue that what they call 'credibility shocks' should also be considered as criteria, and (b) there should be more consideration about how OCA criteria may be interrelated (Glick and Rose, 2016). De Haan et al. (2022) provide a broad and up-to-date overview of this literature.

The seminal paper here remains Bayoumi and Eichengreen (1993). They establish the existence of a highly asymmetric core–periphery pattern in the run-up to the EMU. Using pre-eurozone data, they convincingly argue that there is a core (Germany, France, Belgium, Netherlands, and Denmark) where supply shocks are highly correlated, and a periphery (Greece, Ireland, Italy, Portugal, Spain, and the United Kingdom) where synchronization is significantly lower. They correctly reason, in addition, that this pattern would undermine the eurozone project if persistent.

Bayoumi and Eichengreen's (1993) methodology develops Blanchard and Quah's (1989) procedure for decomposing permanent and temporary shocks. Based on the standard aggregate demand–aggregate supply (AD–AS) model, supply shocks have permanent effects on output while demand shocks have only temporary effects. Both are assumed to have permanent albeit opposite effects on prices.

The vast literature that follows Bayoumi and Eichengreen (1993) relies on static binary classifications. Further, for tractability purposes (i.e. exactly identified models) supply-related restrictions are seldom imposed (De Haan et al., 2008, 2022; Silva and Tenreyro, 2010).

Campos and Macchiarelli (2016) modify the Bayoumi–Eichengreen framework by bringing in an additional restriction on the effect of supply shocks on output. They devise a test for this overidentifying restriction that yields the probability of a country being classified as core. Specifically, the lower (higher) the percentage of times the test supports rejection, the more a country is said to be part of the core or centre (periphery). As dispersion has decreased compared to the pre-eurozone era, they conclude the core–periphery pattern has weakened since 1989. Another way of putting this is that the creation of the EMU had not, as feared, fostered divergence but instead instigated convergence among the member countries. Overall, the results support a reinterpretation of the core–periphery pattern: after Maastricht a new, smaller periphery emerges (Spain, Portugal, Ireland, and Greece) and its dynamics are systematically different from the rest.

In short, Bayoumi and Eichengreen (1993) is a seminal paper because, inter alia, it was one of the first to point out the risks of an entrenched core–periphery split to the then nascent

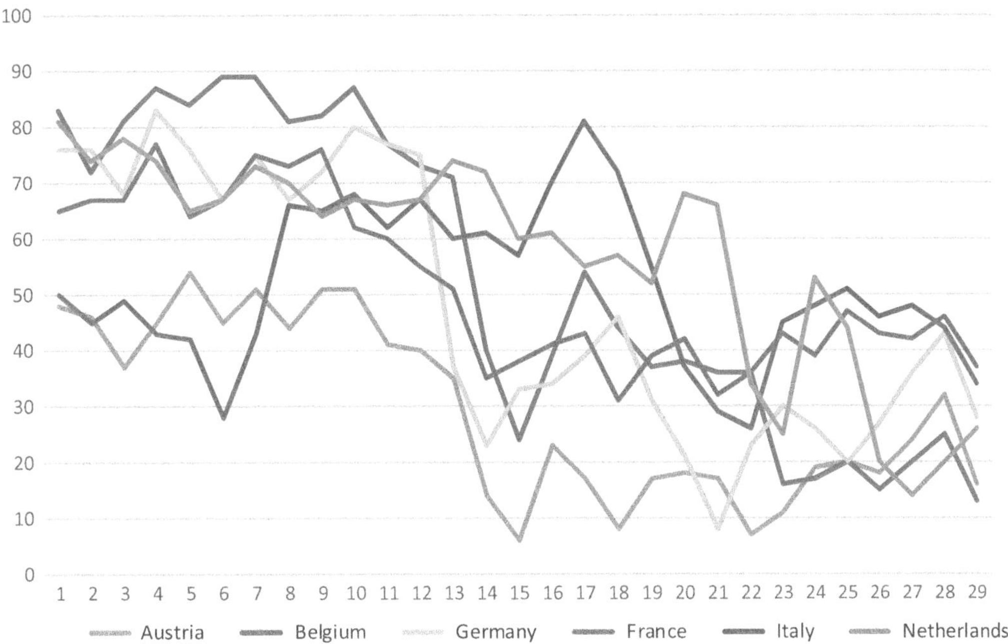

FIGURE 8.3. The formation of the eurozone core: 1987–2015.
Source: Constructed using Campos and Macchiarelli's (2021) data and methodology.

eurozone. Their influential diagnostics were based on data covering twenty-five years from 1963 to 1988. Using the same methodology, sample, and time window length, Campos and Macchiarelli (2016) revisit their results for 1989–2015. They ask whether the eurozone strengthened or weakened the core–periphery pattern and conclude for the latter.

Yet these results are based on a static framework. Campos and Macchiarelli (2021) put forward a dynamic framework to further study these asymmetries, generating a theory-based measure that is continuous and time-variant (i.e. it departs from static binary classifications of core and periphery). They estimate the probability of a country being classified as peripheral for a set of European countries yearly since 1989. Again, an increase in asymmetry is understood as divergence and a decrease as convergence.

Campos and Macchiarelli (2021) use this index to identify clusters and study convergence dynamics. As Figure 8.3 shows, the countries in the first cluster show a commonly sustained increase in the probability of being classified as core. Using the 50 per cent cut-off point for convenience, the first three countries to enter the core are Germany, France, and Austria, all by 1999, which is the year the euro was introduced. Belgium joined the core in 2000, while Italy and Netherlands did so in 2005 and 2007, respectively. These results suggest the formation over time of an endogenous OCA (Frankel and Rose, 1998) as countries only start joining the core after the currency union is in place.

The second set of countries is shown in Figure 8.4. As these countries have high levels in the index, they are identified as the periphery. Interestingly, notice that the series is trendless, reinforcing Bayoumi and Eichengreen's (1993) early warnings about the EMU, specifically about the possibility of an entrenched periphery. Note that neither Norway nor Switzerland are members of the eurozone, although Portugal, Finland, and Ireland are.

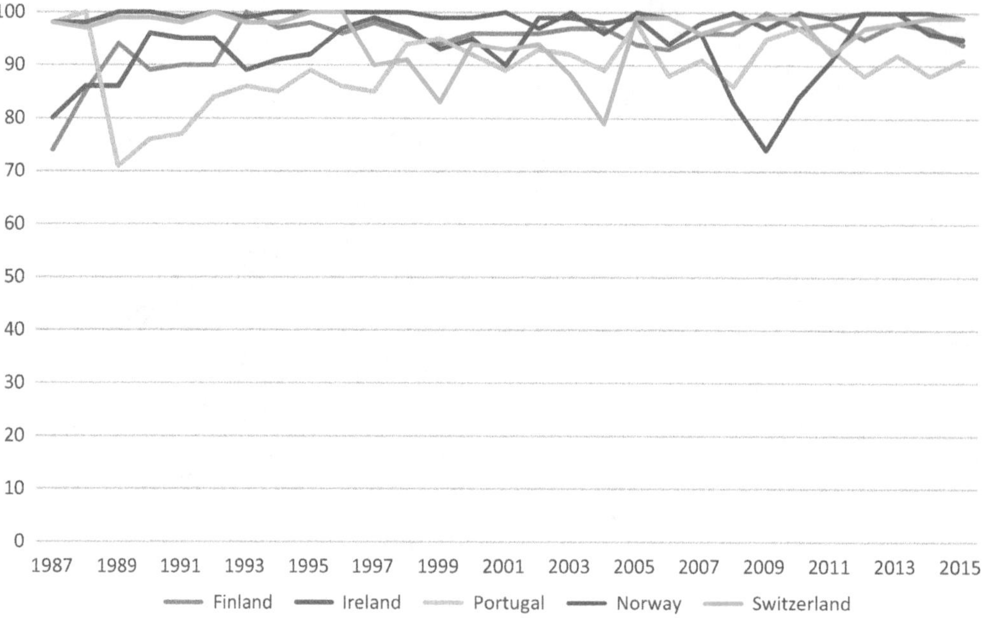

FIGURE 8.4. The persistence of the eurozone periphery: 1987–2015.
Source: Constructed using Campos and Macchiarelli's (2021) data and methodology.

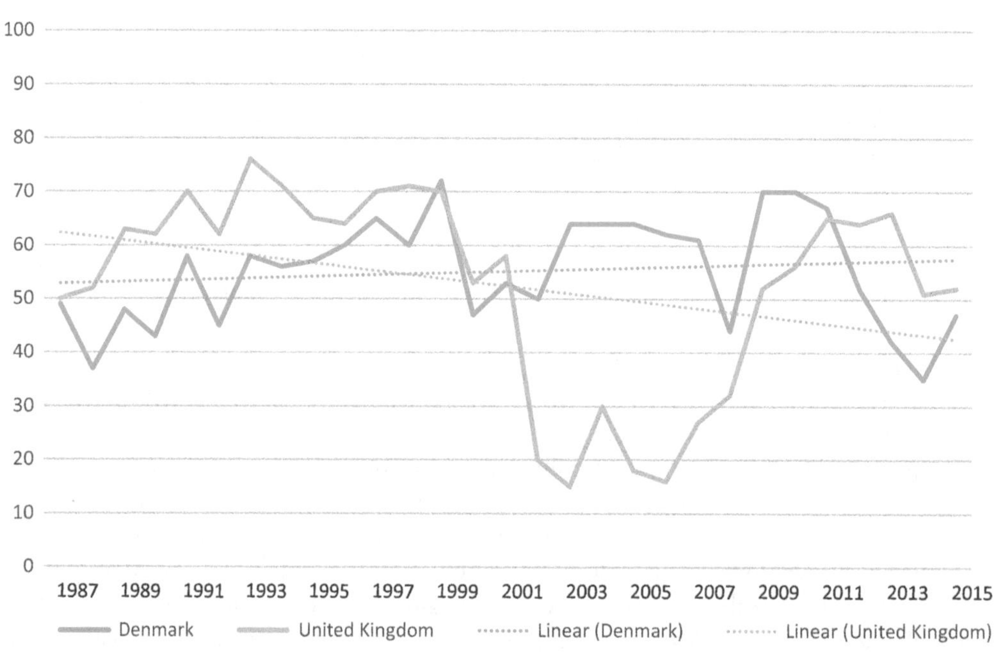

FIGURE 8.5. The intermittence of the eurozone centre ground: 1987–2015.
Source: Constructed using Campos and Macchiarelli (2021) data and methodology.

This analysis also identifies an intermediary set of countries, some for which the index is 'trendless' and others for which it is not ('trending'). In the former group, note figures for Denmark change little over time, while the opposite happens for the United Kingdom, where the high volatility means it moving in and out of the core (Figure 8.5).

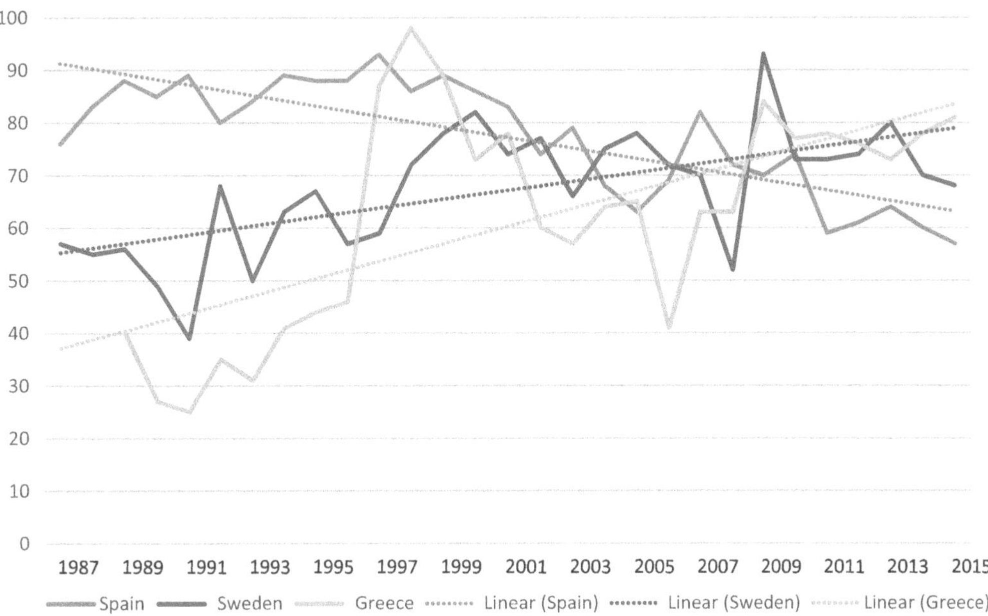

FIGURE 8.6. The joiners and leavers from the eurozone centre ground: 1987–2015.
Source: Constructed using Campos and Macchiarelli's (2021) data and methodology.

Among the intermediary trending cases, Spain's is flat until 1999 and starts to decline afterwards, moving towards the core (linear interpolation suggests it would join circa 2020) while Greece and Sweden move away from the core (Figure 8.6).

These results suggest that the core and periphery pattern in the EMU has changed considerably since 1989, in terms of relative strengths and distances between main groups of countries but also in terms of the trajectories of individual countries. This analysis shows that the convergence process within the eurozone has indeed taken place, albeit with important qualifications. The next question is what factors can throw light on this behaviour over time and across countries?

In order to shed light on this behaviour across countries and over time, Campos and Macchiarelli (2021) draw from OCA theory (De Grauwe, 2018) and identify a set of candidate explanatory variables. One first group refers to explanatory variables on the fiscal side (Martin and Philippon, 2017): debt-to-GDP ratios and cyclically adjusted budget balances. The second covers external links, including euro area membership, foreign direct investment (FDI), real effective exchange rate, and trade openness (Rose, 2000). The third group of explanatory variables focuses on financial links, for instance they study corporate and government bond spreads, interbank interest rate spreads, average consumer loan interest rate spreads, and returns on equity differential (ECB, 2017; Spiegel, 2009). The fourth and last main group of explanatory variables we draw upon regards structural reforms, chiefly employment protection legislation (EPL) and product markets regulation.

The main findings in Campos and Macchiarelli (2021) are that euro membership and looser product market regulations make countries more likely to be classified as core. Their results suggest a particularly strong role in explaining core–periphery dynamics for both membership in the eurozone and the strictness of product market regulation: euro membership is found to increase symmetry while a high degree of product market regulation decreases symmetry. The estimated effect of euro area membership implies as much as a 16 percentage point reduction in the probability of being classified as periphery. To further elaborate on the product market regulations result, they show that trade openness and foreign direct investment help to 'import competition' and in so doing substitute for product market regulations. Imports (but not exports) are found to increase the probability of a country being classified as core.

The second important result is that the emergence of the GFC does not substantially affect the stability of these estimates. The crisis that started in 2007 and affected all Europe in the first half of the 2010s (the eurozone sovereign debt crisis) by its very nature generated a similar response across countries. The extent of symmetry increased rapidly so one may be justifiably concerned that this would affect the results. Campos and Macchiarelli (2021) carry out a simple test for assessing this idea, namely whether splitting the sample in 2010 (or in 2007) substantially affects the baseline results. Their results show that their key results are robust with euro area membership and product market reforms (or imports) remaining the key factors.

8.5 CONCLUSIONS

The objective of this chapter was to bring together various elements that may be useful to understand the productivity implications of the crises in the euro area. One such element was an up-to-date interpretation of the crises themselves. Instead of focusing on the United States and insisting on banking supervision, the current narrative is richer, broader, and more consequential. The period from 2007 to 2019, from the subprime crash to the COVID-19 pandemic, witnessed a sequence of deep interrelated crises: global, financial, economic, and political emergencies that required large, coordinated, and considered policy responses that came late and hence extended the crises. COVID-19 presents a chance to bookend this period and start anew with Next Generation EU, hopefully a sign of things to come.

The second element was productivity. This chapter tries to put together three relevant stylized facts. Namely, that Europe did catch up with the United States, albeit briefly, in 1995, and that the productivity slowdown precedes the Global Financial Crisis (econometric evidence suggests it started in 2003: Q4), and that at least since 2008 it has stagnated and is now more than 10 per cent below trend.

The third important element or set of findings is that there seems to have been no effect of the crises on the pattern of increasing convergence in the eurozone. If one puts aside for a moment the below-trend performance of productivity, many effects of the crises are unexpectedly difficult to capture. Indeed, one sometimes has that Solow feeling: the crises seem to be everywhere except in the economic data. We saw that Campos and Macchiarelli (2021) had difficulty supporting the notion that the crises affected or increased divergence in EMU. Fernald (2015) argues that the crises did not cause the productivity slowdown. Bordignon et al. (2021) argue that the crises have also not had a discernible effect in terms of institutional development. And Campos et al. (2022) show that the crises did not significantly affect the relationship between growth and employment in Europe.

The main conclusion we offer is that the current available evidence suggests that the crises in the euro area caused neither the productivity slowdown nor severe disruptions in convergence patterns. Moreover, there is little evidence for any substantial uptick in structural reform adoption following the crises. Although this may well be because it is still too early to tell, the crises have had a significant dampening effect: the productivity rebound that often follows recessions is yet to materialize in the euro area, raising grave concerns for convergence, integration, and welfare.

There are at least three possibilities for this lack of effect. The first is severe heterogeneity: although the average effects are of zero change, for some countries (for some sectors and in some time periods) there are extremely large and counterweighting effects. The second is measurement error, and here we include the possibility that data series will be radically revised in the near future. The third is policy effectiveness: we have done just enough to avoid a major disaster, or another war. Future research would do well in pursuing these possibilities.

REFERENCES

Acemoglu, D., and Restrepo, P. (2020). Robots and jobs: Evidence from US labor markets. *Journal of Political Economy* 128(6), 2188–2244.

Adrian, T., Kiff, J., and Shin, H. S. (2018). Liquidity, leverage, and regulation 10 years after the global financial crisis. *Annual Review of Financial Economics* 10, 1–24.

Alesina, A., and Barro, R. (2002). Currency unions. *Quarterly Journal of Economics* 117(2), 409–436.

Alesina, A., Barbiero, O., Favero, C., Giavazzi, F., and Paradisi, M. (2015). Austerity in 2009–13. *Economic Policy* 30(83), 383–437.

Algan, Y., Guriev, S., Papaioannou, E., and Passari, E. (2017). The European trust crisis and the rise of populism. *Brookings Papers on Economic Activity* 2017(2), 309–400.

Autor, D. H., Dorn, D., and Hanson, G. H. (2016). The China shock: Learning from labor-market adjustment to large changes in trade. *Annual Review of Economics* 8, 205–240.

Bai, Chong-En, Hsieh, C. T., and Michael, S. Z. (2016). The long shadow of a fiscal expansion. *Brookings Papers on Economic Activity* 47(2), 129–181.

Bayoumi, T., and Eichengreen, B. (1993). Shocking aspects of European monetary integration. In F. Torres and F. Giavazzi (eds.), *Adjustment and Growth in the European Monetary Union*. Cambridge: Cambridge University Press.

Begg, I. (2014). Genuine economic and monetary union. In S. Durlauf and L. Blume (eds.), *The New Palgrave Dictionary of Economics*. London: Palgrave Macmillan.

Blanchard, O. (2018). Should we reject the natural rate hypothesis? *Journal of Economic Perspectives* 32(1), 97–120.

Blanchard, O., and Quah, D. (1989). The dynamic effects of aggregate demand and aggregate supply disturbances. *American Economic Review* 79, 655–673.

Blanchard, O. J., Griffiths, M., and Gruss, B. (2013). Boom, bust, recovery: Forensics of the Latvia crisis. *Brookings Papers on Economic Activity* 2013(2), 325–388.

Bordignon, M., Gatti, N., and Onorato, M. G. (2021). Getting closer or falling apart? Euro countries after the Euro crisis. University of Milan, Working Paper No. 105.

Bordo, M., and Meissner, C. M. (2016). Fiscal and financial crises. In J. B. Taylor and H. Uhlig (eds.), *Handbook of Macroeconomics*, Vol. 2. Amsterdam: Elsevier, pp. 355–412.

Campos, N., and Macchiarelli, C. (2016). Core and periphery in the European Monetary Union: Bayoumi–Eichengreen 25 years later. *Economics Letters* 147(3), 127–130.

Campos, N., and Macchiarelli, C. (2021). The dynamics of core and periphery in the European Monetary Union: A new approach. *Journal of International Money and Finance* 112, 102325.

Campos, N., Coricelli, F., and Moretti, L. (2019). Institutional integration and economic growth in Europe. *Journal of Monetary Economics* 103(1), 88–104.

Campos, N., Eichenauer, V., and Sturm, J. E. (2020). Close encounters of the European kind: Economic integration, sectoral heterogeneity and structural reforms. *European Economic Review* 129, 103511.

Campos, N., Macchiarelli, C., and Mitropoulos, F. (2022). Unemployment and growth before and after the Global Financial Crisis: New evidence from structural Okun estimates. LSE LEQS Discussion Paper No. 175.

Cette, G., Fernald, J., and Mojon, B. (2016). The pre-Great Recession slowdown in productivity. *European Economic Review* 88, 3–20.

Chari V., Dovis, A., and Kehoe, P. (2020). Rethinking optimal currency areas. *Journal of Monetary Economics* 111, 80–94.

Comin, D. A., Gonzalez, J. Q., Schmitz, T. G., and Trigari, A. (2020). Measuring TFP: The role of profits, adjustment costs, and capacity utilization. NBER Working Paper No. 28008.

Crafts, N., and Mills, T. (2020). Is the UK productivity slowdown unprecedented? *National Institute Economic Review* 251, R47–R53.
De Grauwe, P. (2006). What have we learnt about monetary integration since the Maastricht Treaty? *Journal of Common Market Studies* 44(4), 711–30.
De Grauwe, P. (2018), *The Economics of Monetary Unions*. Oxford: Oxford University Press.
De Haan, J., and Wiese, R. (2022). The impact of product and labour market reform on growth: Evidence for OECD countries based on local projections. *Journal of Applied Econometrics*, 37(4), 746–770.
De Haan, J., Inklaar, R., and Jong-A.-Pin, R. (2008). Will business cycles in the euro area converge? A critical survey of empirical research. *Journal of Economic Surveys* 22(2), 234–273.
De Haan, J., Hessel, J., and Gilbert, N. (2016). Reforming the architecture of EMU: Ensuring stability in Europe. In H. Badinger and V. Nitsch (eds.), *The Routledge Handbook of the Economics of European Integration*. New York: Routledge, pp. 408–432.
De Haan, J., Jacobs, J., and Zijm, R. (2022). Coherence of output gaps in the euro area: The impact of the COVID-19 shock. CESifo Discussion Paper No. 9654.
European Central Bank (2017). *Financial Integration in Europe*. Frankfurt: ECB.
Fernald, J. G. (2015). Productivity and potential output before, during, and after the Great Recession. *NBER Macroeconomics Annual* 29(1), 1–51.
Fetzer, T. (2019). Did austerity cause Brexit? *American Economic Review* 109(11), 3849–3886.
Frankel, J., and Rose, A. (1998). The endogeneity of the optimum currency area criteria. *Economic Journal* 108(449), 1009–1025.
Gertler, M., and Gilchrist, S. (2018). What happened: Financial factors in the Great Recession. *Journal of Economic Perspectives* 32(3), 3–30.
Glick, R., and Rose, A. (2016). Currency unions and trade: A post-EMU reassessment. *European Economic Review* 87, 78–91.
Griffin, J. M. (2021). Ten years of evidence: Was fraud a force in the financial crisis? *Journal of Economic Literature* 59(4), 1293–1321.
Guiso, L, Morelli, M., and T. Sonno (2021). The financial drivers of populism in Europe. Bocconi University, Working Paper No. 166.
Győrffy, D. (2015). Austerity and growth in central and eastern Europe: Understanding the link through contrasting crisis management in Hungary and Latvia. *Post-Communist Economies* 27(2), 129–152.
IMF (2014), IMF response to the financial and economic crisis. International Monetary Fund, Independent Evaluation Office.
Jones, C. (2016). The facts of economic growth. In J. Taylor and H. Uhlig (eds.), *Handbook of Macroeconomics*, Vol. 2. Amsterdam: Elsevier.
Koijen, R. S., Koulischer, F., Nguyen, B., and Yogo, M. (2021). Inspecting the mechanism of quantitative easing in the euro area. *Journal of Financial Economics* 140(1), 1–20.
Korhonen, K. (2018). An institutional innovation in the euro debt crisis: The ESM. In N. Campos and J. Sturm (eds.), *Bretton Woods, Brussels, and Beyond: Redesigning the Institutions of Europe*. London: CEPR Press.
Martin, P., and Philippon, T. (2017). Inspecting the mechanism: Leverage and the great recession in the eurozone. *American Economic Review* 107(7), 1904–1937.
Reinhart, C., and Rogoff, K. (2010). Growth in a time of debt. *American Economic Review* 100(2), 573–578.
Rose, A. K. (2000). One money, one market: The effect of common currencies on trade. *Economic Policy* 15(30), 8–45.
Sandbu, M. (2015), *Europe's Orphan: The Future of the Euro and the Politics of Debt*. Princeton, NJ: Princeton University Press.
Silva, J., and Tenreyro, S. (2010). Currency unions in prospect and retrospect. *Annual Review of Economics* 2(1), 51–74.
Shiller, R. J. (2019). *Narrative Economics: How Stories Go Viral and Drive Major Economic Events*. Princeton, NJ: Princeton University Press.
Spiegel, M. (2009). Monetary and financial integration in the EMU: Push or pull? *Review of International Economics* 17(4), 751–776.
Syverson, C. (2011). What determines productivity? *Journal of Economic Literature* 49(2), 326–365.
Tooze, A. (2018). *Crashed: How a Decade of Financial Crises Changed the World*. New York: Penguin.
Van Ark, B., O'Mahoney, M., and Timmer, M. P. (2008). The productivity gap between Europe and the United States: Trends and causes. *Journal of Economic Perspectives* 22(1), 25–44.

PART II

The Monetary Dimension

9

The Overburdened Monetary Policy Mandate of the ECB

Dariusz Adamski

9.1 INTRODUCTION

In a narrow sense, the term 'monetary policy mandate' covers statutory monetary policy objectives of a central bank. In a more comprehensive, broader sense it also encompasses other legal constraints imposed on the exercise of monetary powers.

The monetary policy objectives of the Eurosystem (the European Central Bank (ECB) and the national central banks of the Member States whose currency is the euro)[1] are two-tiered, hierarchical. Price stability comprises the primary objective. Supporting 'the general economic policies in the Union with a view to contributing to the achievement of the objectives of the Union as laid down in Article 3 of the Treaty on European Union' constitutes the secondary objective. Traditionally, the secondary objective has been side-lined almost to the extent of its irrelevance, with the primary objective overshadowing it entirely. More recently, it has been emphasized that the reference to the supporting role of monetary policy in the secondary objective betokens no authorization for the Eurosystem to decide on 'general economic policies in the Union' autonomously, detached from the priorities and actions of the political institutions in charge of these policies (Zilioli and Ioannidis, 2022). In practice, however, the ECB has a broad statutory leeway in pursuing the secondary objective as well, if only two conditions are met: first, its actions do not (palpably) contradict the primary objective and, second, they go in the same direction, reinforce, and facilitate the priorities of the political decision-makers in charge of 'the general economic policies in the Union.'

This has far-reaching implications, because Article 3 TEU is a cornucopia of various priorities which political institutions are routinely eager to achieve, yet often hesitate (or are unable) to fund from the treasury's chest, from 'sustainable development of Europe based on balanced economic growth, ... a highly competitive social market economy, aiming at full employment and social progress' to combating 'social exclusion' and promoting 'social justice and protection'. It should not therefore be particularly surprising that tackling climate change (Schoenmaker and Stegeman, Chapter 12 in this volume), increasing economic output and employment,

I would like to thank Jakob de Haan and Fabian Amtenbrink for their comments on an earlier draft. The usual disclaimer applies. I gratefully acknowledge the support of the National Science Centre, Poland (UMO-2015/18/M/HS5/00252).

[1] Monetary policy is managed in the euro area by the Eurosystem (the ECB and the national central banks of those Member States whose currency is the euro) – Art. 282(1) TFEU, but the Eurosystem itself is governed by the decision-making bodies of the European Central Bank: Art. 129(1) and Art. 282(2) TFEU. For this reason, the Eurosystem and the ECB will be used interchangeably throughout the chapter as the central bank of the euro area.

supporting debt sustainability of governments, or increasing the viability of national financial systems have all been pursued by the ECB, even if the institution has been at pains to avoid admitting the secondary objective characteristics of the more politically incendiary among them, instead highlighting their primary objective consequences only.

As will be further discussed in this chapter, the ECB's penchant for expressions like 'monetary transmission mechanism' and 'singleness of the monetary policy' to describe monetary policy actions with more implications for the secondary objective than for price stability is telling in this respect. From this perspective, the monetary policy mandate of the Eurosystem is not much narrower than the mandate of the US Federal Reserve System with its dual objective of maximum employment and stable prices,[2] even if it remains far less explicit and straightforward in endorsing objectives other than price stability. In fact, the mandate of the Eurosystem may be deemed even broader than of its counterpart on the other side of the Atlantic, due to more proper interactions between monetary policy and fiscal as well as macroeconomic policies in the United States, which absolves the Fed of the necessity to prevent the monetary union from falling apart.

More general legal constraints shaping the monetary policy mandate of the Eurosystem in the broader sense are specific not only in their original understanding, but – even more remarkably – because of their quite radical redefinition and repurposing under the pressure of practical exigencies. Two such constraints are particularly worth mentioning. One directs the central bank to act 'in accordance with the principle of an open market economy with free competition'.[3] It requires that monetary policy be 'market neutral',[4] which 'is understood to imply that the ECB should refrain from policy measures which would unduly disrupt the normal functioning of the markets or unduly restrict competition' (Ioannidis et al., 2021, pp. 27–28). Pursuant to the other, the Eurosystem is prohibited from monetary financing, i.e. from financing 'Union institutions, bodies, offices or agencies, central governments, regional, local or other public authorities, other bodies governed by public law, or public undertakings of Member States', as well as purchasing debt instruments directly from the issuers (Article 123(1) TFEU).

The case law of the Court of Justice of the European Union (CJEU) has shaped the understanding of the ECB's monetary policy mandate. In particular, according to an opinion of Advocate General Cruz Villalón[5] and a decision of the General Court,[6] the ECB is to strive for 'a higher objective' of 'maintaining the financial stability of the monetary union'. This phrase was used by the General Court in the context of the prohibition of monetary financing, to ensure 'that the Member States remain subject to the logic of the market when they enter into debt'. But its reach should arguably encompass the whole monetary policy, in line with the principle of market neutrality.

This contribution argues that all the constraints on the monetary policy mandate of the ECB have been gradually and profoundly relinquished. The role of the ECB has changed, from the narrow focus on the primary objective (restrained mandate) to the increasingly important role played by the secondary objective (more unrestrained mandate). While this process has helped

[2] Formally, the US Federal Reserve System has three monetary policy objectives: maximum employment, stable prices, and moderate long-term interest rates (Federal Reserve Act, 12 U.S. Code § 225a). Moderate long-term interest rates are not considered a distinct objective, however, because they should naturally follow if the other two – maximum employment and stable prices – are achieved (Mishkin, 2007).

[3] Art. 119(2), 127(1), Art. 2 Protocol No. 4.

[4] Opinion of AG Wathelet of 4 October 2018, Case C-493/17 *Weiss and Others* ECLI:EU:C:2018:815, [74].

[5] Opinion of Advocate General Cruz Villalón of 14 January 2015, Case C-62/14 *Gauweiler and others* ECLI:EU:C:2015:7 [219].

[6] Case T-868/16 *QI v. Commission and ECB* ECLI:EU:T:2022:58 [96].

achieve both the primary and the secondary objectives, it has also produced new risks and potential conflicts. In this sense, the monetary policy mandate has become overburdened.

Other central banks have also broadened their functions since the Global Financial Crisis (GFC), playing a much more important economic (and political) role when decreased inflation ushered in more accommodative monetary policy (Blinder et al., 2017). Concerns regarding the legitimacy and effectiveness of this process have been voiced in other major monetary unions as well (Jacobs and King, 2021). However, they are more acute in the euro area, due to the remaining serious divergences in actual and potential growth between the Member States (see also Begg, Chapter 6 in this volume), the lack of cross-border mechanisms allowing for cushioning of idiosyncratic output shocks (Cimadomo et al., Chapter 22 in this volume) and insufficient tools as well as virtually non-existent political appetite to remedy these fundamental shortcomings through viable political mechanisms established at the European level. Such an incomplete Economic and Monetary Union (EMU), where a uniform monetary policy is confronted with very loose economic coordination, or – to put it differently – the single currency is not matched by a fully fledged economic union (James, Chapter 3 in this volume), entails more complicated trade-offs for monetary policy than occurs in monetary unions closer to an optimum currency area.

To explain this argument, the remainder of this chapter will trace the functional change of the original restrained mandate of the ECB during and after the sovereign debt crisis (Section 9.2). Then it will concentrate on the short-term (Section 9.3) and more perplexing longer-term economic effects (Section 9.4) of the evolution. The often overlooked relationship between macroeconomic divergences and structural economic asymmetries in the euro area, on the one hand, and the increasingly overburdened monetary policy mandate of the ECB, on the other, will be dealt with in Section 9.5. This is followed by conclusions in Section 9.6.

9.2 THE TRANSITION OF THE EUROSYSTEM'S MONETARY POLICY MANDATE

The euro area was founded on a belief in a restrained monetary policy preoccupied exclusively with price stability (Adamski, 2020; Gordon, 2022). Pursuing other objectives than controlling inflation was considered a goal of other policies and other institutions. Hans Tietmeyer, who presided over the Deutsche Bundesbank in the period of the euro area's infancy, neatly expressed the underlying philosophy: 'if too many tasks were to be assigned to the European Central Bank this could complicate the conduct of monetary policy. The European System of Central Banks (ESCB) should therefore be free from responsibilities other than those for monetary policy' (quoted in Folkerts-Landau and Garber, 1992, p. 26).

Such an approach was buttressed not only by the idiosyncratically German hyperinflation woes, but also by the more imminent turbulent experiences of the 1970s and 1980s (James, Chapter 3 in this volume). Public choice theorists, who were swiftly gaining salience in the second half of the 1970s, argued that self-interest of political agents in charge of fiscal policy leads to a deficit spending bias and harmful resort to the printing presses of central banks for revenue purposes (Brennan and Buchanan, 1980; Buchanan and Wagner, 1977). Other scholars criticized the prevailing Keynesian approach to monetary policy from the standpoint of the emerging rational expectations model, more closely aligned with basic foundations of the neoclassical economics than its post-war predecessors (e.g. Barro, 1976; Cukierman, 1979).

Their work, too, implied the undesirability of political interference with monetary policy and made the case for a narrow, price-stability-oriented mandate of central banks.

The global wave of neoliberal financial deregulation (Campbell and Bakir, 2012), which occurred in the 1980s, and the expansion of financial markets, financial innovations, and liberalization of capital flows unfolding in parallel to the Maastricht process, forced central banks to broaden the scope of their monetary policy instruments and rendered them even more market-oriented (Laurens, 1994). Standing facilities providing overnight liquidity retained their role as a floor (deposit facility) and a ceiling (marginal lending facility) for overnight rates in the interbank market. But while another monetary policy instrument – reserve requirements – has lain practically unused in the ECB's toolbox,[7] open market operations – i.e. transactions with commercial banks involving government bonds, aimed to manage liquidity in the money market and steer short-term interest rates through liquidity-providing repo operations conducted as variable rate tenders – were of paramount importance. For them, the expanding debt markets were crucial.

The decline in the volatility of business cycle fluctuations and GDP growth since the mid-1980s, the so-called Great Moderation, corroborated the conceptual foundations on which this market-oriented, restrained ideology of the monetary policy mandate was built, nurturing price stability. As headline inflation for the euro area diminished, the original monetary strategy of the ECB based on 'a year-on-year increase in the Harmonised Index of Consumer Prices (HICP) for the euro area of below 2%' (ECB, 1998) was replaced by inflation 'below but close to 2% over the medium term' a few years later (ECB, 2003). Different to the changes undergone in the next decade, this modification left both the catalogue of the instruments deployed by the central bank and their intensity unaffected.

When, in the aftermath of the global financial meltdown in 2008, other major central banks grasped the point made by Krugman and his co-authors a decade earlier in the context of the Japanese liquidity trap – 'monetary policy will in fact be effective if the central bank can credibly promise to be irresponsible, to seek a higher future price level' (Krugman et al., 1998, p. 139) – the ECB refused to follow suit. It confined itself to a temporary provision of liquidity to the financial system through fixed-rate tenders with full allotment, to altering the maturity and the procedures of its main refinancing operations (MROs), and to cutting the policy rates (from 4.25 per cent in mid-2008 to 1 per cent since May 2009 for fixed rate MROs). It also enlarged the pool of collateral accepted for refinancing operations. Emergency liquidity in foreign currencies was provided and longer-term refinancing operations (LTROs) with maturities extended to one year were activated.

All these measures were falling into the sphere of lender of last resort for the banking sector. However, neither they nor the outright purchases of covered bonds within the Covered Bonds Purchase Programme (CBPP1) initiated in July 2009 seriously departed from the standard monetary policy toolbox. All of them, called Enhanced Credit Support Policies by the then ECB President Trichet (Trichet, 2009), were 'special and primarily bank-based measures . . . to enhance the flow of credit above and beyond what could be achieved through policy interest rate reductions alone'. In other words, they constituted transitory interventions intended to overcome confidence problems on the interbank market and help commercial banks manage

[7] Until January 2012, euro area banks had to hold a minimum of 2 per cent of certain liabilities (mainly customers' deposits) at their national central bank. Since then, this ratio has been lowered to just 1 per cent. At these levels the reserve requirements can hardly fulfil their main goal of mitigating the effects of unexpected short-term liquidity shocks.

the maturity mismatch between their assets and liabilities. They delivered liquidity drying out from the interbank market as uncertainties and counterparty risks erupted.

This approach changed when sovereign default and redenomination risks soon undermined the original belief in the benevolently corrective impact of financial markets on the governments. As financial instability and fiscal stress in the crisis countries were mutually reinforcing, the ECB reached for a non-standard monetary policy tool targeted precisely at the jurisdictions where redenomination risks were concentrated: the Securities Markets Programme (SMP), established in May 2010. From its outset, the programme was explained as a tool to restore the transmission of policy interest rate decisions to the real economy because government bonds play a very important role for bank balance sheets, for liquidity operations, and for benchmarking private sector lending rates. Seeking to achieve this goal, however, it was implicitly aimed at yet another objective, on which rebuilding the monetary transmission mechanism was contingent and which was far more significant systemically and politically: preventing the financial system from forcing sovereign defaults of the stressed countries.

For political reasons and due to legal doubts as to its relationship with the prohibition of monetary financing (Sester, 2012), the SMP was temporary and had its volumes capped, to demonstrate it would constitute a transitory relief rather than a permanent bailout of government debt. By design, the government bonds purchased under the programme (worth €218 billion by the end of 2012; EBC, 2013) would disappear from the balance sheet of the Eurosystem once they come to maturity. Furthermore, the interventions were sterilized – their effects on the monetary base were offset by sales of other assets.

The temporary and limited character of the non-standard monetary policy measures pursued when other major central banks went much further in their asset purchases can be explained by the rising inflation in the euro area from mid-2009. In May 2010, when the sovereign debt crisis erupted, it reached 1.7 per cent (subsequently it rose further, to 3 per cent in September–October 2011 – a level clearly above the policy target). But while inflation developments allowed the ECB to stick to its restrained monetary policy, they could not contribute to containing redenomination risks – i.e. the risks of a currency changeover from the euro into devalued national legal tenders – at a time when belated or inappropriate reactions of political leaders and national governments amplified these risks.

The same was true for the next exceptional liquidity measure: a new very Long-Term Refinancing Operation (vLTRO) with an extraordinarily long maturity of thirty-six months, triggered by the ECB in December 2011. Faced with the scarcity of assets with attractive risk-adjusted returns and therefore on the brink of a liquidity trap (Baldo et al., 2017), commercial banks in the vulnerable jurisdictions tended to use the liquidity available through vLTRO to invest in the low-priced bonds of the sovereigns whose yield spreads towards the German bund widened, rather than increasing lending to the real economy (Acharya and Steffen, 2015; Altunbas et al., 2014; Arnold and Soederhuizen, 2018). This carry-trade could not prevent risks from escalating further and spill-over effects additionally amplified them. A different measure was necessary to tackle the redenomination prospect.

The announcement of the Outright Monetary Transactions (OMT) programme (ECB, 2012) proved decisive in this respect (see also Chang, Chapter 10 in this volume). While it tackled redenomination risks, it did not increase inflation. At the point when the OMT was announced, this effect could have seemed laudatory.[8] Soon after, however, the downward path of inflation

[8] During the months prior to the announcement of the OMT, inflation in the euro area decreased moderately, from the high of 3.0 per cent in September 2011 to 2.6 per cent in August 2012.

became steeper and the policy of the ECB departed further from the approach of the other major central banks. In particular, while the asset side of the US Fed's balance sheet was growing throughout 2013 due to the QE3 programme announced in September 2012, in the euro area a reverse process took place, mainly due to early repayments of the vLTRO.

Instead of starting large-scale asset purchases, the ECB first deployed forward guidance on interest rates in July 2013. This new non-standard monetary policy instrument based on communication (de Haan, Chapter 11 in this volume) was originally expressed by the following statement by President Draghi (2013): 'the Governing Council expects the key ECB interest rates to remain at present or lower levels for an extended period of time'.

In the next step, the ECB introduced negative interest rates on the deposit facility (–0.10 per cent from June 2014, –0.20 per cent from September 2014, –30 per cent from December 2015, –0.40 per cent from March 2016, and –0.50 per cent between September 2019 and July 2022). Only in 2014, when inflation levels were constantly decreasing (they went below 0 per cent in December 2014), did the ECB become ready to launch a massive QE programme. The devotion to the restrained monetary policy mandate and concerns – expressed by various German central bankers in particular – about the legality of large-scale purchases of government bonds can help explain why the move took place only when the threat of deflation became imminent. As Bini Smaghi conjectured,

> most probably, in mid-2013 the Governing Council did not want to embark on another controversial decision, only twelve months after the divisive decision on OMT. It thus preferred to agree on a low hanging fruit, such as forward guidance, rather than dividing itself around quantitative easing. By mid-2014, the Governing Council might have expected that a decision to cut policy rates into negative territory would be less controversial and might stimulate monetary conditions to such an extent that it would avoid having to embark on QE, like other central banks had done a few years earlier. This expectation turned out to be wrong and the system cumulated the effects of QE with that of negative rates. (Bini Smaghi, 2020, pp. 8–9)

In late 2014, monetary policy of the ECB became seriously reprofiled. While previously it concentrated on emergency liquidity provision and improvements of the monetary policy transmission mechanism through suppression of sovereign spreads, subsequently it focused on asset purchases clearly related to inflation inducement.

On the one hand, non-standard targeted longer-term refinancing operations (TLTRO) were initiated in 2014 in order to increase credit supply. Their borrowing limits, and in the case of TLTRO-II (executed between 2016 and 2017) as well as TLTRO-III (taking place between 2019 and 2022) also the interest rates, depended on eligible net lending, in order to encourage commercial banks to extend loans to the non-financial sector.

On the other hand, in autumn 2014 the Eurosystem triggered the Asset Purchase Programme (APP). A part of it focused on private securities: the Covered Bond Purchase Programme 3 (CBPP3), launched in October 2014; the Asset-Backed Securities Purchase Programme (ABSPP), in force from November 2014; and the Corporate Sector Purchase Programme (CSPP), which started in June 2016. The main component of the APP – the Public Sector Purchase Programme (PSPP) – commenced in March 2015 (see also Chang, Chapter 10 in this volume). The APP had been accumulating securities (mainly government bonds) to the tune of €60–80 billion a month until December 2017. The purchases gradually declined to zero by the end of 2018 and underwent a period of principal payments reinvestments lasting until November 2019. Subsequently they saw a resumption of purchases until the end of June 2022, with reinvestment of redemptions taking place since July 2022.

Research suggests that until mid-2014 the monetary strategy of the ECB had been asymmetric, in the sense that it was responding more strongly to inflation above 1.9 per cent than below it (Maih et al., 2021). The underlying transition to a more symmetric – and hence more accommodative, anti-deflationary – logic was sealed in July 2019, when President Draghi announced the 'inflation aim' aspect to the monetary policy's target. Accordingly, 'if the medium-term inflation outlook continues to fall short of our aim, the Governing Council is determined to act, in line with its commitment to symmetry in the inflation aim. It therefore stands ready to adjust all of its instruments, as appropriate, to ensure that inflation moves towards its aim in a sustained manner' (Draghi, 2019).

This development was clearly related to the changing inflation trend. But it was also driven by a more profound discussion on the lowering of equilibrium real rates of interest taking place at that time (Ciccarelli et al., 2017). Accordingly, if – due to a decline in productivity growth, advancements in globalization and digitalization, demographic change, and high demand for liquid and safe assets – the equilibrium rates fall below 2 per cent, still more combatant actions of the central bank cannot lead to an inflationary spiral. As the ECB put it in mid-2021, turning the 'inflation aim' announced by President Draghi in 2019 into a key element of its new monetary strategy: 'when the economy is close to the lower bound, this requires especially forceful or persistent monetary policy measures to avoid negative deviations from the inflation target becoming entrenched. This may also imply a transitory period in which inflation is moderately above target' (ECB, 2021, p. 56). Such an accommodative, anti-deflationary approach to the monetary policy mandate of the ECB has far-reaching consequences for monetary policy. It demonstrates the willingness to tolerate headline inflation higher than 2 per cent, if the surge might be temporary and whenever it follows prolonged periods of lower inflation.

The eruption of the COVID-19 pandemic forced monetary policymakers to take an even more unrestrained approach. The ECB introduced additional LTROs and made the conditions of TLTRO-III still more favourable than before, especially for the counterparties maintaining their levels of credit provision (ECB, 2020a). It also instituted the Pandemic Emergency Purchase Programme (PEPP) of additional asset purchases.[9] Originally capped at €120 billion (ECB, 2020a), the programme was very soon expanded to €750 billion (ECB 2020c) and ultimately, in December 2020, elevated to €1,850 billion (ECB, 2020d). In the face of growing inflation, it was discontinued at the end of March 2022, with maturing principal payments from the securities purchased still planned to be reinvested at least for the next few years (ECB, 2022a).

Highlighting differences with the PSPP, a waiver of the eligibility requirements was granted for securities of the Greek government and a flexibility clause allowing in particular for deviations from the Eurosystem capital key as the benchmark for the allocation of the purchases across jurisdictions was introduced. In order to avoid bottlenecks in the supply of eligible assets, no issuer or issue share limits, previously established for the PSPP, were inherited by the PEPP, and the Governing Council even hinted it could reconsider these limits for the PSPP itself. As a result, 'the Eurosystem has, de facto, fully abandoned the issue and issuer limits for both programmes and now accepts the role of a strategic creditor with a blocking minority in future creditor negotiations' (Havlik and Heinemann, 2020, p. 2). The dividing line between government paper and commercial securities, previously purchased under two different schemes

[9] While net asset purchases under the PEPP were discontinued at this point, in December 2021 the ECB's Governing Council decided that the maturing principal payments from securities purchased under the PEPP would be reinvested until at least the end of 2024.

(PSPP and CSPP), was also blurred; the latter could be purchased under the PEPP as well. Finally, supply of the eligible paper was broadened by including assets with shorter remaining maturities: of at least twenty-eight days for private securities, instead of the previous six months under the CSPP, and at least seventy days, instead of one year for government bonds, as under the PSPP.

The surge of inflation in 2022 foreshadowed normalization of monetary policy. But it also demonstrated the embeddedness of the unrestrained monetary policy mandate. High inflation was met with moderate interest rate increases. In addition, growing spreads on government bonds forced the ECB to declare two specific measures. The first is flexibility in reinvesting redemptions coming due in the PEPP portfolio. Even more remarkably, in July 2022 the institution announced the second specific measure: 'a new anti-fragmentation instrument' (ECB, 2022b) called the Transmission Protection Instrument (TPI) and based on 'secondary market purchases of securities issued in jurisdictions experiencing a deterioration in financing conditions not warranted by country-specific fundamentals' (ECB, 2022c). In line with the previous non-standard instruments, both were explained in terms of the monetary policy transmission mechanism, even if in fact they were intended to achieve the price stability objective by discouraging bond markets from raising concerns about debt sustainability of the most vulnerable euro area Member States.

From this perspective it is telling that the new measures were announced when spreads on sovereign bonds were growing due to the expectations of higher debt servicing costs and the lack of other non-standard monetary policy instruments depressing them. The moment of their announcement demonstrates that for the TPI, just as for the SMP and the OMT programmes before it, the primary monetary policy objective is rather a corollary of pursuing a higher objective of maintaining the financial stability of the monetary union with market non-neutral tools.

9.3 SHORT-TERM EFFECTS OF NON-STANDARD MONETARY POLICY IN THE EURO AREA

Firstly and most noticeably, unconventional monetary policies of the ECB activated in 2014 and 2015 decreased long-term yields in general and yields on sovereign bonds in particular (Jäger and Grigoriadis, 2017; Krishnamurthy et al., 2018). As this effect was particularly strong in the euro area's periphery (Demir et al., 2022), sovereign spreads narrowed. It is important for the ECB's mandate, because elevated sovereign spreads have a negative impact on monetary policy transmission – they reduce the net worth of banks holding sovereign debt on their balance sheets, tighten funding constraints and reduce bank risk appetite (Bocola, 2016). Therefore, economists have concluded that the non-standard monetary policy aimed at easing refinancing conditions for sovereigns helped normalize the pass-through of monetary policy to bank lending rates, increased loan volumes, improved credit quality, and induced capital gains (Altavilla et al., 2019; Horvath et al., 2018). As another (side) effect, it alleviated the decline in net interest margins and net interest income of credit institutions produced by low and negative interest rates (Segev et al., 2021). All the positive effects of the OMT were reinforced by the TLTRO, which reduced the cost of credit and, as a result, increased annual net lending to the real economy (Afonso and Sousa-Leite, 2020).

The policy of negative interest rates could become contractionary, corroding profitability on bank capital, which could in turn reduce lending to the economy (Brunnermeier and Koby, 2017; Cavallino and Sandri, 2017). This apprehension, however, was not confirmed in the practice of the euro area. Some research (focusing on Spain) found that the ECB's non-standard monetary policy measures had no discernible impact on bank profitability (Tercero-Lucas, 2021), while others concluded that negative interest rates actually facilitated lending, as banks were striving to reduce their excess liquidity holdings in order to escape the penalty associated with the deposit facility charge (Demiralp et al., 2021; Heider et al., 2019). Hence, the non-standard monetary policy also improved the monetary policy transmission mechanism.

Reductions of sovereign spreads had positive effects on unemployment and output more generally. It was found that during the sovereign debt crisis the spreads on sovereign paper may have explained 20 per cent of the forecast error variance in the unemployment rate (Bahaj, 2020). In the same vein, ECB researchers concluded in 2018 that 'about one third of the 5 percentage points increase in the employment rate observed in the euro area as a whole since mid-2014 is estimated to be due to the ECB's measures. This is the equivalent of 2 to 3 million jobs' (Hartmann and Smets, 2018, p. 51).

The same research argued that during the period 2016–19 the non-standard monetary policies of the ECB raised GDP cumulatively by around 1.9 per cent. Without them, 'inflation would on average be almost half a percentage point lower than currently projected in each year over the 2016–2019 period' (Hartmann and Smets, 2018, p. 51). Studying the period 2015–18, Hohberger et al. (2019) also estimated the positive influence of the non-standard monetary policy measures on CPI inflation at 0.5 per cent on average, with only a slightly lower positive impact on the GDP growth (0.3 per cent annually).

In a large part, asset purchases impacted on the portfolio rebalancing channel. They pushed up prices of the targeted assets, so investors shifted their attention towards substitutes with higher expected returns, elevating their prices and reducing real interest rates, which is the prime goal of expansionary monetary policy. This relationship, which constitutes the very essence of non-standard monetary policy measures, may also cause certain undesired fallout effects. If prices of other assets – stocks or loans granted to the non-financial private sector – are artificially raised, the underlying policy may detach them from benchmark values, causing price bubbles and other imbalances. Research on this hypothesis has produced ambivalent results, however. While it has been concluded that the surprises of the ECB's monetary policy announcements do influence price imbalances on stock markets (Blot et al., 2020; Hudepohl et al., 2021), it has also been posited that growing house prices in the euro area – the main associated concern of the broader public – should not qualify as an imbalance caused by QE (Blot et al., 2020).

Research based on the experiences of conventional monetary policy shocks suggested that non-standard measures could increase income inequality (Furceri et al., 2018; Mumtaz and Theophilopoulou, 2017). However, empirical evidence has not corroborated these misgivings, either. Some researchers concluded that the main factor behind the QE spurring income inequality – increased valuations of financial assets benefiting high-income households – is likely to be offset by stimulating economic activity, which decreases income inequality (Colciago et al., 2019; Mäki-Fränti et al., 2022). The influence of unconventional monetary policies on wealth inequality is also mixed (Colciago et al., 2019; Mäki-Fränti et al., 2022).

While some concluded that the impact of non-standard monetary policy actions was very limited, others figured that the reduction of income inequality through the macroeconomic channel produced stronger outcomes than the opposite effects propogated through the financial channel (Lenza and Slacalekb, 2018; Samarina and Nguyen, 2019). In other words, QE affected the poorer parts of the population, as it reduced unemployment in this group and led to wage increases, lessening income inequality.

Diminished sovereign spreads and unemployment levels, along with increased lending to the real economy, translated into nominal interest rate adjustments and increased inflation expectations, ultimately lowering real interest rates, as intended. In this respect, the major asset purchase programmes – SMP, OMT, and APP – have proven much more effective than the main liquidity provision schemes (CBPP, ABSPP, LTRO, and TLTRO) (Ambler and Rumler, 2019), arguably because the latter were merely focused on (transitory) improvements of the banking sector's refinancing conditions.

Altogether, it may be argued that the actions taken by the ECB since the memorable 'whatever it takes' announcement of President Draghi in mid-2012 were crucial for moving the euro area from a bad equilibrium situation to a good equilibrium. As Dell'Ariccia et al. (2018, p. 148) noted (in the context of the euro area, the United Kingdom, and Japan), 'unconventional monetary policies have been quite effective in preventing further financial distress, restoring the functioning of financial markets, and providing additional monetary accommodation by compressing long-term interest rates. Furthermore, these policies likely had beneficial effects on macroeconomic variables such as real GDP growth and price stability, although these are more difficult to model and measure'.

All this is important from the perspective of statutory monetary policy objectives, which profoundly determine the mandate of the ECB. As long as the ECB's actions do not conflict with the primary objective of price stability, the institution is legally authorized to pursue the secondary objective of monetary policy. The research referred to in this section demonstrates that its non-standard monetary policies have helped reach this objective in the period of very low inflation, while also demonstrating their ability to bring inflation closer to the price stability objective. As a flipside of the same conclusion, arguably neither the primary nor the secondary objectives of the euro area's monetary policy could have been approximated by the original, restrained approach to the mandate of the central bank, at least until inflation throughout the euro area was boosted by a confluence of factors in late 2021.

9.4 LONGER-TERM EFFECTS OF THE NON-STANDARD MONETARY POLICY IN THE EURO AREA

The effectiveness of monetary policy is judged first and foremost by its influence on inflation. But especially in an incomplete monetary union, where political institutions in charge of economic and fiscal policies do not sufficiently contribute to the secondary objective of the monetary policy mandate, non-standard interventions for monetary purposes may have complicated effects in the realm of broader economic relations. These effects demonstrate how the burden imposed on monetary policy has increased, entailing serious new economic and political risks.

Uniform monetary policy tools inherently affect national economic systems differently in a community of sovereign states, even if the heterogeneity was found to be greater during the periods of conventional monetary policy than when non-standard monetary policies are applied (Dominguez-Torres and Hierro, 2020). It has also been observed that the portfolio rebalancing channel mainly affected the prices of securities issued by corporates in the more vulnerable countries of the euro area and mainly increased lending volumes to the real economy in the less vulnerable ones (Albertazzi et al., 2018). This suggests that QE augmented lending to economic agents – the main mechanism through which the monetary stimulus ought to increase economic output and inflation – in the core of the euro area, where otherwise the monetary transmission mechanism had not been seriously harmed at the outset of asset purchases and so monetary interventions were least requisite.

Weaker banks have been found more likely to extend credit to zombie firms, which would have to exit the market in a more competitive environment (Andrews and Petroulakis, 2019). More generally, enhanced risk-taking as a consequence of the monetary transmission mechanism operating through the portfolio rebalancing channel induced by QE was found to usher in lower lending standards for borrowers (Neuenkirch and Nöckel, 2018). Credit institutions with a more inferior capital structure were found to take on more risk as a result (Ioannidou et al., 2015), while asset purchases were less capable of improving output in the countries with lower capital ratio compared to those with well-capitalized banks (Altavilla et al., 2020; Boeckx et al., 2017, 2020). Similarly, research covering the period until the end of 2015 found that the pass-through of changes in money market rates was lower where and when the banking market concentration, the dependence on central bank financing, and the levels of non-performing loans were higher and bank asset quality lower than average, with particularly pronounced effects noted for smaller loans (Holton and d'Acri, 2018). Therefore, the process of stimulating the economy through the provision of new loans to the real economy was hindered in the more vulnerable countries by structural weaknesses of their banking systems and the real economy.

These weaknesses remained related to the demand for credit. If households and enterprises deleverage and the volumes of banks' non-performing loans remain high, demand for credit is weaker and of lower quality (higher risk). Not only does it have implications for the financial stability of these countries, but also for the monetary transmission mechanism. Where the propensity of credit institutions to grant credit is diminished by structural weaknesses and vulnerabilities in the real economy, the maximum amount of commercial bank money created with a certain amount of central bank money – the money multiplier – should be expected to decrease (Seghezza and Morelli, 2020). This is important because a diminished money multiplier reduces the amount of money with the public. It therefore has an adverse impact on both inflation and output, reducing economic activity and growth.

Therefore, while the non-conventional monetary policy measures reduced unemployment levels and increased lending to the real economy as well as output in the most vulnerable economies compared to the situation in which the central bank had not activated them, they also amplified economic divergences between the Member States. Because 'a weaker banking system amplifies the impact of monetary policy but also contributes to economic instability' (Cozzi et al., 2020, p. 10), the euro area's south became more vulnerable economically compared to the north, even if it benefited from the non-standard monetary policy in absolute terms, especially in the short term.[10] Burriel and Galesi (2018, p. 229) noted in this context that

> countries with more fragile banking systems benefit the least from unconventional monetary policy measures, and especially so in terms of output gains. Importantly, this heterogeneity has implications for the transmission of unconventional measures at the euro area level, as it substantially dampens the effects on real activity of the whole currency union.

The less vulnerable countries could thus take advantage of the accommodative monetary policy more easily and with fewer side effects than the vulnerable ones. Also, the risks produced

[10] In addition, non-standard monetary policy might have been positive for lending to the real economy and the macroeconomic aggregates, but research concluded that its effectiveness for bank lending and inflation decreases over time (Behrendt, 2017). It has also been argued that negative interest rates have proven expansionary in the short term, but they may undermine the effectiveness of the monetary transmission mechanism if maintained for a longer period (Horvath et al., 2018).

by non-standard monetary instruments tended to concentrate in the countries more vulnerable at the outset. Such instruments cannot therefore decrease divergences at the fundamental level between the two groups. If anything, the opposite can be expected.

In principle, macroprudential policy is intended to tackle the challenges to financial stability in countries particularly exposed to such a phenomenon. It is also worth heeding in this context that the ECB has the power to step in and apply more stringent macroprudential measures than those adopted nationally[11] and such an intervention would be by default tailored to the situation of a given Member State. In practice, however, increased macroprudential standards in the more vulnerable jurisdictions would have likely further dampened the risk-taking channel and the portfolio rebalancing channel of the monetary transmission mechanism. Financial stability would have increased in the more vulnerable jurisdictions as a result, yet more stringent standards for the banking sector should be expected to have constrained lending to the real economy, hampering the intended effects of non-standard monetary policies there, with no similar measures (and effects) witnessed in the less vulnerable Member States. This would have added to the finding of asymmetries in how the monetary policy transmission mechanism works in practice in different groups of the euro area Member States.

9.5 MONETARY POLICY CHALLENGES OF THE EURO AREA'S FRAGMENTATION

Political institutions in charge of macroeconomic and fiscal policies are the proper decision-making bodies to deal with euro area divergences. They ought to address perplexing productivity developments (ECB, 2017b; Campos, Chapter 8 in this volume), in order to effectively increase actual and potential GDP in the more vulnerable regions, as well as to decrease the propensity of those regions to undergo idiosyncratic shocks and to expedite post-crisis recovery.

However, European institutions have not been authorized to assume such far-reaching functions (see also Amtenbrink, Chapter 4 in this volume) and national authorities of the more vulnerable countries have not proven capable of delivering satisfying outcomes. The ensuing economic fragmentation has translated into additional public debt and economic imbalances. The yearly Macroeconomic Imbalance Procedure finds that a set of euro area countries persists either in excessive macroeconomic imbalances (Cyprus, Greece, Italy in 2022) or in macroeconomic imbalances (France, Germany, Netherlands, Portugal, Spain in 2022).[12] On the one hand, the monetary union allows Germany and the Netherlands to accumulate current account surpluses higher than what would be possible under monetary sovereignty, which in turn is key for their macroeconomic imbalance status. On the other, the single currency corrodes the price competitiveness of the other imbalanced countries. The dynamics of such centrifugal forces generated by the very participation in the euro area was reinforced by non-standard monetary policy interventions, as they facilitated euro depreciation (Dedola et al., 2021) and provided additional boost to the export-oriented economies. It therefore made the other shortcomings of the euro area's architecture – the lack of fiscal and macroeconomic policies capable of

[11] Art. 5(2) Council Regulation (EU) No 1024/2013 of 15 October 2013 conferring specific tasks on the European Central Bank concerning policies relating to the prudential supervision of credit institutions, OJ L 287, 29.10.2013, pp. 63–89.

[12] France, Italy, Spain, Greece, Portugal, and Cyprus have been found in either imbalance or excessive imbalance situation since the very beginning of the Macroeconomic Imbalance Procedure in 2012 (or since this procedure could be applied to them, as the countries receiving financial assistance have been excluded from the Macroeconomic Imbalance Procedure as long as they retain the status of a programme country). The Netherlands has been considered to be experiencing macroeconomic imbalances continuously since 2013 and Germany since 2014.

countering different amplitudes of business cycles (Franks et al., 2018) and the lack of meaningful risk-sharing mechanisms sufficient to cushion idiosyncratic economic shocks (Cimadomo et al., Chapter 22 in this volume) – still more ominous.

The fragmentation of the euro area stemming from structural fiscal and macroeconomic divergences has translated into disturbing financial developments. They, too, are enabled and facilitated by the very architecture of the euro area, in this case the payment system called TARGET2, used by both central banks and credit institutions for processing large-value payments.

Strictly speaking, the Eurosystem's management of TARGET2 does not belong to monetary policy, but to another Treaty task of the central bank: promoting 'the smooth operation of payment systems' (Article 127(2) TFEU). Moreover, increased TARGET2 imbalances do not entail any actual financial obligations on the side of the central banks accumulating liabilities towards those playing the role of creditors. However, a positive balance of each country in the TARGET2 system betokens capital flows towards the creditor jurisdictions through the banking system, while the opposite is true when the balance is negative. These financial movements may be caused by different degrees to which national banking systems rely on central bank liquidity or by perceptions of certain jurisdictions as safe havens – and others as risky investment locations – among economic agents (Hristov et al., 2020).

While such considerations determine whether TARGET2 balances of a national central bank are positive or negative, non-standard monetary policy measures deployed by the ECB since the onset of the GFC have influenced their magnitude. The speech of President Draghi in mid-2012, which paved the way for the OMT programme, reduced TARGET2 imbalances. The growth of the imbalances following the onset of the PSPP should be mainly associated with the international rebalancing facilitated by QE (ECB, 2017c). Because Germany and Luxembourg are the major financial centres of the euro area through which international portfolio rebalancing takes place (ECB, 2017a), their central banks recorded positive balances as foreign investors – the most important sellers of the securities purchased within the APP – were exchanging euro area assets for foreign instruments bearing higher yields (Koijen et al., 2021). Other researchers, however, have demonstrated that the asset purchases within the APP helped relocate the wealth of the non-financial private sector in vulnerable euro area countries from government bonds to financial vehicles registered in Luxembourg, the Netherlands, or Germany, which also contributed to TARGET2 developments (Minenna, 2022). Increased density of cross-border versus national relationships among TARGET2 banks (ECB, 2020b) likely facilitated them as well.

The ECB has been forced to assume an economic stabilization and anti-fragmentation function of managing the risks produced by all the macroeconomic, fiscal, and financial centrifugal processes. While the single currency has contributed to perplexing developments in domestic economies (captured by the Macroeconomic Imbalance Procedure), one of their side effects – increased public debt – was partly offloaded to the Eurosystem through QE. Removing a share of it from the market, the PSPP and the PEPP prevented the divergences and imbalances in the economic fundamentals from translating into starkly different borrowing costs for governments and hence precluded another sovereign debt crisis. But the balance sheet of the central bank has become more exposed to default risks in consequence of shifting a share of public debt from the private sector (financial institutions previously holding government bonds) to the public sector (Eurosystem).

Holdings of government securities on the balance sheet of the Eurosystem had increased moderately between the onset of the GFC and the launching of the PSPP, in January

2015 amounting to €575 billion (ECB, 2022d). Due to the PSPP they went up to €2.2 trillion in March 2020, then – as an effect of this programme combined with the PEPP – reached their apex in February 2022 (€3.9 trillion) and very slowly diminished thereafter. The stock of government securities thus absorbed by the central bank in September 2022 (€3.8 trillion) was a bit higher than the combined GDP of France (€2.50 trillion) and Spain (€1.21 trillion) in 2021. It was also only marginally lower than the combined GDP of Germany (€3.60 trillion) and Finland (€0.25 trillion) in the same year.

The sheer magnitude of the assets accumulated within QE has forced the ECB to de facto include debt management in its functions. Massive symmetric government bond purchases – while easy to reconcile with the price stability objective in the environment of very low inflation – attenuated consequences of macroeconomic imbalances, increased indebtedness in the most vulnerable countries and financial flows from the south to the north of the euro area.

When subsequently prices of goods and services increased, such interventions became more difficult to justify. It is remarkable, though, that even then the ECB came forth with the TPI, pushing the limits of the increasingly unrestrained monetary policy mandate. Explained in the usual monetary policy transmission mechanism terms (ECB, 2022b), it can be expected to be judicially vindicated by the CJEU if a question of its validity ever reaches the court. According to the legal standard developed in the case involving the most similar previous non-standard measure – the OMT – the TPI should not be considered as going 'manifestly beyond what is necessary to achieve' monetary policy objectives if it is tailored to achieve the familiar (very broad) goals of appropriate monetary policy transmission as well as the singleness of the monetary policy, and if its explanation relies on a careful and impartial examination of 'all the relevant elements of the situation in question'.[13] Following the same judicial interpretation, the TPI is compliant with the prohibition of monetary financing if four – not particularly demanding – conditions are met.[14] First, market participants should remain uncertain about the scope of bond purchases. Second, the interventions ought to be justified by the goals of improving the monetary transmission mechanism and the singleness of the monetary policy. Third, only bonds of governments with access to the market can be subject to interventions. And fourth, the Eurosystem ought to retain the option of selling the paper to the market at a later stage.

However, even with such an anti-fragmentation monetary mechanism in place, achieving the singleness of monetary policy is increasingly difficult in the face of centrifugal processes unleashed by the single currency's very architecture, as well as by insufficient coordination and a lack of burden sharing at the euro area level. In such a setup, maintaining the singleness of

[13] Case C-62/14 *Gauweiler* ECLI:EU:C:2015:400 [48-56, 69, 81]. As the CJEU emphasized, 'this programme is intended to rectify the disruption of the ESCB's monetary policy which arose as a result of the particular situation of government bonds issued by certain Member States. In those circumstances, the ESCB was fully entitled to take the view that a selective bond-buying programme may prove necessary in order to rectify that disruption, concentrating the ESCB's activity on the parts of the euro area which are particularly affected by that disruption and thereby preventing the scale of that programme from being needlessly increased, beyond what is necessary to achieve its objectives, or the programme's effectiveness from being diminished' [89].

[14] Case C-62/14 *Gauweiler* ECLI:EU:C:2015:400 [103, 106, 112, 116, 117]. The same ruling considered an activated assistance (bailout) programme as another justification for compliance of the OMT with the prohibition of monetary financing [120]. This factor was mentioned, however, only as one (last) among others, with no intimation by the Court that it must be met in each and every case. No activated assistance programme could therefore hardly be considered as an unsurmountable obstacle for considering an anti-fragmentation monetary policy instrument as congruent with the prohibition of monetary financing.

monetary policy becomes a byword for discouraging the markets from putting fiscally destabilizing pressure on costs of growing sovereign debt. In practical terms, market neutrality becomes distant from such monetary policy.

Paradoxically, because sources of the divergences contributing to the spreads on sovereign bonds are located in domestic macroeconomic, fiscal, and socioeconomic policies, as well as in the basic governance systems at the national level, the ECB has been forced to mitigate the effects of the processes it is not in a position to influence at their sources. In fact, its interventions may even exacerbate inter-state divergences. By alleviating the consequences for financial market of the deeper factors responsible for the fragmentation of sovereign debt markets, monetary policy actions intended to maintain the euro area's integrity discourage national policymakers from addressing deep sources of the divergence, in a self-reinforcing process increasing the pressure on the central bank to deal with the consequences of insufficient action by macroeconomic and fiscal policymakers.

Courts may be forced to broaden the interpretation of the monetary policy mandate in order to accommodate the anti-fragmentation interventions and prevent another sovereign debt crisis from occurring. But, if inappropriate coordination with (domestic) fiscal and macroeconomic policies makes government debt purchases impossible to significantly reverse – due to the expected negative effects it would entail for bond spreads and the basic integrity of the euro area – the debt management function can easily morph into de facto debt monetization: the ultimate manifestation of an overwhelmed monetary policy and an anathema to the original understanding of the ECB's mandate.

9.6 CONCLUSIONS

In the environment – prevailing in the 1990s and 2000s – of moderate inflation, relatively high economic growth and debt (both private and public) lower than subsequently, monetary policy may have remained solely focused on its primary objective of price stability. It could have been market neutral, leaving the possibility of pursuing the secondary monetary policy objective, also enshrined in the Treaty, but unexploited in practice. In the economic environment which followed the GFC and the sovereign debt crisis – marked by lower growth, interest rates at the ELB, and higher debt – monetary policy needed to change. The ECB's QE was making monetary policy less market neutral and entailed more intensive implications for the secondary objective of the monetary policy. Some central bankers argued that this development was unjustified, and that 'since its establishment, the ECB has taken on additional tasks that go way beyond its legal mandate' (Stark et al., 2020, p. 56). This chapter has argued, however, that the non-standard monetary policy instruments used during the decade 2012–22 were supportive of both the primary and the secondary objectives of the ECB. As a result, the monetary policy mandate of the ECB certainly became wider, but this development was justified by the economic developments to which monetary policy needed to respond.

At the same time, however, large purchases of debt instruments have non-monetary implications. Yield reductions on sovereign bonds induced by the QE facilitated the monetary transmission mechanism and increased valuations of assets (including the securities on the balance sheet of the Eurosystem). They also made debt servicing less expensive for national governments. In its 2021 Debt Sustainability Monitor the Commission noted this result, stating that 'the decisive ECB interventions and EU initiatives should ensure that sovereign financing conditions remain favourable going forward' (European Commission, 2021, pp. 9–10).

But the asset (public debt) management function, which has unavoidably become entangled in the operations of the ECB, puts it in an awkward position. Unable to control national fiscal or macroeconomic policies, the central bank can only deal with consequences of actions taken by other decision-makers. In the euro area this problem is more pressing than in other monetary unions simply because the effects of the divergences in national paths of factor accumulation – from different demography to different saving rates, technological progress, or actual and potential GDP – are magnified by the basic architecture of the EMU. In such an environment, monetary policy with positive short-term implications for the secondary objective of the monetary policy mandate entails risks of more serious negative longer-term consequences.

The growing number of functions assumed by the ECB remains in a particularly difficult relationship with the venerable Tinbergen rule, which states that the number of achievable policy goals cannot exceed the number of policy instruments at the disposal of the policymaker (Tinbergen, 1952). Otherwise, 'when central banks drift too far from being limited-purpose institutions and become independent multi-purpose institutions, they escape the checks and balances needed in a democratic system. This can lead to inappropriate interventions which may not have been approved by a legislative process or a vote of the people. It can also lead to poor economic performance' (Taylor, 2016, pp. 96–97). As the ECB does not possess tools and has no legitimacy (see also Bobić and Dawson, Chapter 14, as well as Diessner, Chapter 13 in this volume) to determine macroeconomic and fiscal policies of the euro area countries, and as it cannot properly fix gaps in risk-sharing produced by the incomplete political arrangements when the euro area was designed, its monetary policy interventions shift risks across sectors and Member States without putting the monetary institution in a position to effectively mitigate them beyond the short term.

In principle, the resulting economic and political tensions call for narrowing the mandate of the ECB to its price stability objective, which in turn requires that the secondary objective be effectively pursued by political decision-makers in charge of fiscal and economic policies. There are two conceivable paths leading to this outcome. One of them was constitutive for the European Semester and boils down to a decentralized system of fiscal and economic policies developed by national governments but corrected at the European level by positive and negative incentives aimed to motivate national policymakers to 'do the right thing'. The other is encapsulated by what Mario Draghi – as prime minister of Italy – said in early 2022: 'we need a pragmatic federalism that encompasses all areas affected by ongoing transformations' (quoted in Leali, 2022). In this latter scenario, (much) more powers in the fiscal and economic realms ought to be transferred from the national to the European level.

So far, the first solution has proven ineffective in delivering the expected results, while there has been little appetite for the other among the majority of national leaders and the euro area's societies. As long as the 'Economic' node of the 'Economic and Monetary Union' is seriously underdeveloped, though, the euro area's monetary policy is likely to remain overburdened by the task of mitigating consequences of actions beyond the control of the central bank, with negative effects for both its legitimacy and effectiveness.

REFERENCES

Acharya, V., and Steffen, S. (2015). The 'greatest' carry trade ever? Understanding eurozone bank risks. *Journal of Financial Economics* 115(2), 215–236.

Adamski, D. (2020). Objectives of the EMU. In *The EU Law of Economic and Monetary Union*. Oxford: Oxford University Press, 214–258.

Afonso, A., and Sousa-Leite, J. (2020). The transmission of unconventional monetary policy to bank credit supply: Evidence from the TLTRO. *The Manchester School* 88, 151–171.

Albertazzi, U., Becker, B., and Boucinha, M. (2018). Portfolio rebalancing and the transmission of large-scale asset programmes: Evidence from the euro area. ECB Working Paper No. 2125.

Altavilla, C., Andreeva, D., Boucinha, M., and Holton, S. (2019). Monetary policy, credit institutions and the bank lending channel in the euro area. ECB Occasional Paper No. 222.

Altavilla, C., Canova, F., and Ciccarelli, M. (2020). Mending the broken link: Heterogeneous bank lending rates and monetary policy pass-through. *Journal of Monetary Economics* 110, 81–98.

Altunbas, Y., Gambacorta, L., and Marques-Ibanez, D. (2014). Does monetary policy affect bank risk? *International Journal of Central Banking* 10(1), 95–136.

Ambler, S., and Rumler, F. (2019). The effectiveness of unconventional monetary policy announcements in the euro area: An event and econometric study. *Journal of International Money and Finance* 94, 48–61.

Andrews, D., and Petroulakis, F. (2019). Breaking the shackles: Zombie firms, weak banks and depressed restructuring in Europe. ECB Working Paper No. 2240.

Arnold, I. J. M., and Soederhuizen, B. (2018). Sovereign bond holdings and monetary policy operations in the euro area. *Journal of Policy Modeling* 14(6), 1243–1254.

Bahaj, S. (2020). Sovereign spreads in the euro area: Cross border transmission and macroeconomic implications. *Journal of Monetary Economics* 110, 116–135.

Baldo, L., et al. (2017). The distribution of excess liquidity in the euro area. ECB Occasional Paper No. 200.

Barro, R. (1976). Rational expectations and the role of monetary policy. *Journal of Monetary Economics* 2(1), 1–32.

Behrendt, S. (2017). Unconventional monetary policy effects on bank lending in the euro area. Jena Economic Research Paper No. 2017-002.

Bini Smaghi, L. (2020). Is the ECB at risk of becoming an underachiever? Luiss Policy Brief 1/2020.

Blinder, A., Ehrmann, M., de Haan, J., and Jansen, D.-J. (2017). Necessity as the mother of invention: Monetary policy after the crisis. *Economic Policy* 32(92), 707–755.

Blot, C., Hubert, P., and Labondance, F. (2020). Monetary policy and asset prices in the euro area since the global financial crisis. *Revue d'Economie Politique* 130(2), 257–281.

Bocola, L., 2016. The pass-through of sovereign risk. *Journal of Political Economy* 124(4), 879–925.

Boeckx, J., Dossche, M., and Peersman, G. (2017). Effectiveness and transmission of the ECB's balance sheet policies. *International Journal of Central Banking* 13(1), 297–333.

Boeckx, J., de Sola Perea, M., and Peersman, G. (2020). The transmission mechanism of credit support policies in the euro area. *European Economic Review* 124, 103403.

Brennan, G., and Buchanan, J. M. (1980). *The Power to Tax: Analytical Foundations of a Fiscal Constitution.* Cambridge: Cambridge University Press.

Brunnermeier, M. K., and Koby, Y. (2017). The 'reversal interest rate': An effective lower bound on monetary policy. https://scholar.princeton.edu/sites/default/files/markus/files/16f_reversalrate.pdf

Buchanan, J. M., and Wagner, R. E. (1977). *Democracy in Deficit: The Political Legacy of Lord Keynes.* New York: Academic Press.

Burriel, P., and Galesi, A. (2018). Uncovering the heterogeneous effects of ECB unconventional monetary policies across euro area countries. *European Economic Review* 101, 210–229.

Campbell, A., and Bakir, E. (2012). The pre-1980 roots of neoliberal financial deregulation. *Journal of Economic Issues* 46(2), 531–540.

Cavallino, P., and D. Sandri (2017). The Expansionary Lower Bound: A Theory of Contractionary Monetary Easing. Mimeographed, International Monetary Fund.

Ciccarelli, M., Osbat, C., Bobeica, E., Jardet, C., Jarocinski, M., Mendicino, C., … and Stevens, A. (2017). Low inflation in the euro area: Causes and consequences. ECB Occasional Paper No. 181.

Colciago, A., Samarina, A., and de Haan, J. (2019). Central bank policies and income and wealth inequality: A survey. *Journal of Economic Surveys* 33(4), 1199–1231.

Cozzi, G., Pariès, M. D., Karadi, P., Körner, J., Kok, C., Mazelis, F., … and Weber, J. (2020). Macroprudential policy measures: Macroeconomic impact and interaction with monetary policy. ECB Working Paper No. 2376.

Cukierman, A. (1979). Rational expectations and the role of monetary policy: A generalization. *Journal of Monetary Economics* 5(2), 213–229.

Dedola, L., Georgiadis, G., Gräb, J., and Mehl, A. (2021). Does a big bazooka matter? Quantitative easing policies and exchange rates. *Journal of Monetary Economics* 117, 489–506.

Dell'Ariccia, G., Rabanal, P., and Sandri, D. (2018). Unconventional monetary policies in the euro area, Japan, and the United Kingdom. *Journal of Economic Perspectives* 32(4), 147–172.

Demir, İ., Eroğlu, B. A., and Yildirim-Karaman, S. (2022). Heterogeneous effects of unconventional monetary policy on the bond yields across the euro area. *Journal of Money, Credit and Banking* 54 (5), 1425–1457.

Demiralp, S., Eisenschmidt, J., and Vlassopoulos, T. (2021). Negative interest rates, excess liquidity and retail deposits: Banks' reaction to unconventional monetary policy in the euro area. *European Economic Review* 136, 103745.

Dominguez-Torres, H., and Hierro, L. Á. (2020). Are there monetary clusters in the Eurozone? The impact of ECB policy. *Journal of Policy Modeling* 42(1), 56–76.

Draghi, M. (2013) Introductory statement to the press conference (with Q&A), 4 July. www.ecb.europa.eu/press/pressconf/2013/html/is130704.en.html

Draghi, M. (2019) Introductory statement to the press conference (with Q&A), 25 July. www.ecb.europa.eu/press/pressconf/2019/html/ecb.is190725~547f29c369.en.html

European Central Bank (ECB) (1998). A stability-oriented monetary policy strategy for the ESCB. www.ecb.europa.eu/press/pr/date/1998/html/pr981013_1.en.html

European Central Bank (2003). The ECB's monetary policy strategy. www.ecb.europa.eu/press/pr/date/2003/html/pr030508_2.en.html

European Central Bank (2012). Technical features of Outright Monetary Transactions. www.ecb.europa.eu/press/pr/date/2012/html/pr120906_1.en.html

European Central Bank (2013). Details on securities holdings acquired under the Securities Markets Programme. www.ecb.europa.eu/press/pr/date/2013/html/pr130221_1.en.html

European Central Bank (2017a). The ECB's asset purchase programme and TARGET balances: Monetary policy implementation and beyond. *Economic Bulletin* 3, 21–26.

European Central Bank (2017b). The slowdown in euro area productivity since the crisis in a global context. *Economic Bulletin* 3, 47–67.

European Central Bank (2017c). Distribution of excess liquidity in the euro area. Occasional Paper No. 200.

European Central Bank (2020a). Monetary policy decisions. 12 March. www.ecb.europa.eu/press/pr/date/2020/html/ecb.mp200312~8d3aec3ff2.en.html

European Central Bank (2020b). Financial Integration and Structure in the Euro Area.

European Central Bank (2020c). ECB announces €750 billion Pandemic Emergency Purchase Programme (PEPP). www.ecb.europa.eu/press/pr/date/2020/html/ecb.pr200318_1~3949d6f266.en.html

European Central Bank (2020d). Monetary policy decisions. 10 December. www.ecb.europa.eu/press/pr/date/2020/html/ecb.mp201210~8c2778b843.en.html

European Central Bank (2021). An overview of the ECB's monetary policy strategy. July. www.ecb.europa.eu/home/search/review/html/ecb.strategyreview_monpol_strategy_overview.en.html

European Central Bank (2022a). Account of the monetary policy meeting of the Governing Council of the European Central Bank held in Frankfurt am Main on Wednesday and Thursday, 15–16 December 2021. 20 January. www.ecb.europa.eu/press/accounts/2022/html/ecb.mg220120~7ed187b5b1.en.html

European Central Bank (2022b). Statement after the ad hoc meeting of the ECB Governing Council. 15 June. www.ecb.europa.eu/press/pr/date/2022/html/ecb.pr220615~2aa3900e0a.en.html

European Central Bank (2022c). The Transmission Protection Instrument. Press release, 21 July. www.ecb.europa.eu/press/pr/date/2022/html/ecb.pr220721~973e6e7273.en.html

European Central Bank (2022d). Statistical Data Warehouse: Holdings of debt securities issued by euro area general government reported by Eurosystem in the euro area (stock). https://sdw.ecb.europa.eu/quickview.do?SERIES_KEY=117.BSI.M.U2.N.C.A30.A.1.U2.2100.Z01.E

European Commission (2021). Debt Sustainability Monitor 2020, European Economy Institutional Paper No. 143.

Folkerts-Landau, D. F. I., and Garber, P. M. (1992). The European Central Bank: A bank or a monetary policy rule. National Bureau of Economic Research Working Paper No. 4016.

Franks, M. J. R., Barkbu, M. B. B., Blavy, M. R., Oman, W., and Schoelermann, H. (2018). Economic convergence in the euro area: Coming together or drifting apart? International Monetary Fund Working Paper No. 10.

Furceri, D., Loungani, P., and Zdzienicka, A. (2018). The effects of monetary policy shocks on inequality. *Journal of International Money and Finance* 85, 168–186.

Gordon, B. (2022). *The Constitutional Boundaries of European Fiscal Federalism*. Cambridge: Cambridge University Press.

Hartmann, P., and Smets, F. (2018). The first twenty years of the European Central Bank: Monetary policy. ECB Working Paper No. 2219.

Havlik, A., and Heinemann, F. (2020). Sliding down the slippery slope? Trends in the rules and country allocations of the Eurosystem's PSPP and PEPP (No. 21). EconPol Policy Report.

Heider, F., Saidi, F., and Schepens, G. (2019). Life below zero: Bank lending under negative rates. *Review of Financial Studies* 32, 3728–3761.

Hohberger, S., Priftis, R., and Vogel, L. (2019). The macroeconomic effects of quantitative easing in the euro area: Evidence from an estimated DSGE model. *Journal of Economic Dynamics and Control* 108, 103756.

Holton, S., and d'Acri, C. R. (2018). Interest rate pass-through since the euro area crisis. *Journal of Banking & Finance* 96, 277–291.

Horvath, R., Kotlebova, J., and Siranova, M. (2018). Interest rate pass-through in the euro area: Financial fragmentation, balance sheet policies and negative rates. *Journal of Financial Stability* 36, 12–21.

Hristov, N., Hülsewig, O., and Wollmershäuser, T. (2020). Capital flows in the euro area and TARGET2 balances. *Journal of Banking & Finance* 113, 105734.

Hudepohl, T., van Lamoen, R., and de Vette, N. (2021). Quantitative easing and exuberance in stock markets: Evidence from the euro area. *Journal of International Money and Finance* 118, 102471.

Ioannidis, M., Hlásková, S. J., and Zilioli, C. (2021). The mandate of the ECB: Legal considerations in the ECB's monetary policy strategy review. ECB Occasional Paper No. 276.

Ioannidou, V., Ongena, S., and Peydro, J.L. (2015). Monetary policy, risk-taking, and pricing: Evidence from a quasi-natural experiment. *Review of Finance* 19(1), 95–144.

Jacobs, L., and King, D. (2021). *Fed Power: How Finance Wins*. Oxford: Oxford University Press.

Jäger, J., and Grigoriadis, T. (2017). The effectiveness of the ECB's unconventional monetary policy: Comparative evidence from crisis and non-crisis euro area countries. *Journal of International Money and Finance* 78, 21–43.

Koijen, R. S., Koulischer, F., Nguyen, B., and Yogo, M. (2021). Inspecting the mechanism of quantitative easing in the euro area. *Journal of Financial Economics* 140(1), 1–20.

Krishnamurthy, A., Nagel, S., and Vissing-Jorgensen, A. (2018). ECB policies involving government bond purchases: Impact and channels. *Review of Finance* 22(1), 1–44.

Krugman, P. R., Dominquez, K. M., and Rogoff, K. (1998). It's baaack: Japan's slump and the return of the liquidity trap. *Brookings Papers on Economic Activity* 1998(2), 137–205.

Laurens, B. (1994). Refinance instruments: Lessons from their use in some industrialised countries. IMF Working Paper No. 51.

Leali, G. (2022). Draghi: EU needs 'pragmatic federalism', more integration. *Politico*, 3 May.

Lenza, M., and Slacalek, J. (2018). How does monetary policy affect income and wealth inequality? Evidence from quantitative easing in the euro area. ECB Working Paper No. 2190.

Maih, J., Mazelis, F., Motto, R., and Ristiniemi, A. (2021). Asymmetric monetary policy rules for the euro area and the US. *Journal of Macroeconomics* 70, 103376.

Mäki-Fränti, P., Silvo, A., Gulan, A., and Kilponen, J. (2022). Monetary policy and inequality: The Finnish case. Bank of Finland Research Discussion Paper No. 3.

Minenna, M. (2022). Target 2 determinants: The role of balance of payments imbalances in the long run. *Journal of Banking & Finance* 140: 106059.

Mishkin, F. (2007). Monetary policy and the dual mandate. Speech at Bridgewater College. www.federalreserve.gov/newsevents/speech/mishkin20070410a.htm

Mumtaz, H., and Theophilopoulou, A. (2017). The impact of monetary policy on inequality in the UK. An empirical analysis. *European Economic Review* 98, 410–423.

Neuenkirch, M., and Nöckel, M. (2018). The risk-taking channel of monetary policy transmission in the euro area. *Journal of Banking & Finance* 93, 71–91.
Samarina, A., and Nguyen, A. D. (2019). Does monetary policy affect income inequality in the euro area? DNB Working Paper No. 626.
Segev, N., Ribon, S., Kahn, M., and de Haan, J. (2021). Low interest rates and banks' interest margins: Does deposit market concentration matter? Bank of Israel Discussion Paper No. 16.
Seghezza, E., and Morelli, P. (2020). Why the money multiplier has remained persistently so low in the post-crisis United States? *Economic Modelling* 92, 309–317.
Sester, P. (2012). The ECB's controversial securities market program (SMP) and its role in relation to the modified EFSF and the future ESM. *European Company Finance Law Review* 9(2), 156–178.
Stark, J., Mayer, T., and Schnabl, G. (2020). The ECB needs to rediscover itself. *The International Economy* 34(3), 36–57.
Taylor, J. B. (2016). Independence and the scope of the central bank's mandate. *Sveriges Riksbank Economic Review* 3, 96–103.
Tercero-Lucas, D. (2021). Nonstandard monetary policies and bank profitability: The case of Spain. *International Journal of Finance & Economics*. https://doi.org/10.1002/ijfe.2535
Tinbergen, J. (1952). *On the Theory of Economic Policy*. Amsterdam: North-Holland.
Trichet, J. (2009). The ECB's enhanced credit support. Keynote address by Jean-Claude Trichet, President of the ECB at the University of Munich, 13 July.
Zilioli, C., and Ioannidis, M. (2022). Climate change and the mandate of the ECB: Potential and limits of monetary contribution to European green policies. *Common Market Law Review* 59(2), 363–394.

10

Government Bond Buying by the European Central Bank

Leadership versus Accountability

Michele Chang

10.1 INTRODUCTION

During the European Central Bank's (ECB) second decade, it faced numerous challenges which it was ill-prepared to handle. Designed as an institution to combat inflation, problems such as unprecedented financial instability and fragmentation, diverging sovereign bond yields, and the prospect of deflation left the ECB with constrained policy options. Through an array of non-standard monetary policy initiatives, the ECB helped to calm market speculation against the euro during the sovereign debt crisis (2010–12) and instil confidence in the EU's commitment to support the EU economy during the economic crisis caused by the COVID-19 pandemic.

Nevertheless, the largely unchanged legal and accountability framework raised questions on whether its policies fell within the ECB's mandate and were democratically legitimate. In particular, the successive bond-buying programmes elicited strong political reactions and even legal challenges. Their potential redistributive impact, questionable legal basis, and lack of accompanying accountability mechanisms indicated the political ramifications of the ECB's monetary policy for an institution that previously had been viewed as more technocratic than political.

This contribution analyses the politicization of the ECB's bond-buying programmes and its implications for the ECB's legitimacy. Section 10.2 looks at the creation of the ECB, one of the most independent central banks in the world. On the one hand, a consensus had developed on the role of independent central banks in achieving price stability. Section 10.2, however, notes that political economists put forward claims that central bank independence should also achieve political objectives that include locking in the conservative policy preferences and bridging conflicts in systems with multiple principals. Nevertheless, independent central banks came to be viewed as technocratic rather than political actors, and the ECB became one of the most independent central banks in the world, with a mandate of price stability and an accountability structure based mainly on reporting and engaging in a dialogue with the European Parliament.

Section 10.3 examines the bond-buying programmes of the ECB that began during the euro crisis. The ECB's high degree of independence in its pursuit of price stability initially constrained its response to the Global Financial Crisis (GFC) compared to other central banks instructed to pursue additional objectives, like the US Federal Reserve's mandate to also target full employment and moderate long-term interest rates. Indeed, the Federal Reserve engaged in large-scale government bond buying in order to revive the American economy after the GFC.

During the euro crisis, however, the ECB's Securities Market Programme (SMP) and the Outright Monetary Transactions (OMT) pushed back against some of these constraints. The ECB's bond-buying programmes continued with the launch of quantitative easing (QE) programmes, the Public Sector Purchase Programme (PSPP) and the Pandemic Emergency Purchase Programme (PEPP), to combat deflation.

While the official reasons for these programmes remained the pursuit of price stability, they also have redistributive effects that potentially constituted economic policymaking, over which the Member States retain competence. Section 10.4 looks at how political science alternately viewed these bond-buying programmes as an example of rising ECB leadership in the face of Member State inaction versus an ECB power grab. Such reflections on the legitimacy of the ECB's policies were not unique but were being conducted across the globe as analysts considered the implications of the rise of central banks more generally as 'the only game in town', because politicians did not respond quickly with the policies needed to combat the crisis. The redistributive nature of monetary policy, even when ostensibly pursued in the name of price stability, became clearer and fuelled political and legal backlash against central banks in general and the ECB in particular. Section 10.5 considers the extent to which the ECB's accountability framework has adjusted to its bond purchases in light of these consequences.

The final section considers the recent ECB strategy review and its implications for the political dimension of economic and monetary union. The increasing reliance on the ECB by euro area Member States to manage emergency situations has left the economic governance of the euro area in a precarious position regarding its legitimacy. While the ECB took pains to restrain its policies a decade ago, it has gradually allowed itself increasing discretion with little pushback from its political principals. The toolkit of the ECB has expanded substantially, but no additional accountability measures have been imposed upon it, only an expansion of transparency exercises initiated by and under the control of the ECB. The political expediency of allowing the central bank to become the major actor in mitigating economic crises clashes with the original rationale for the ECB's independence and minimal accountability scheme, and the latter should be updated to account for the ECB's new role.

10.2 FROM TECHNOCRATIC ACTOR TO POLITICAL PLAYER

10.2.1 *The Political Logic of Delegating Monetary Policy*

The original logic of delegating monetary policy to an independent central bank rested on a consensus shared by academics and policymakers of the superiority of independent central banks in achieving inflation objectives given the constraints and incentives such institutions provide (Cukierman et al., 1992; Grilli et al., 1991). Empirically, the success of independent central banks in the United States and Germany in combating inflation in the 1980s lent credence to this argument. A narrative emerged that portrayed central banks as technocratic actors pursuing the public good of price stability, contrasting with the inherently political nature of money and monetary politics (Kirshner, 2003). Indeed, a conservative coalition of actors with political power is a precondition for the creation of an independent central bank (Goodman, 1991; Posen, 1993). Delegation to an independent central bank thereby serves as a commitment device for the government to pursue price stability (Cukierman, 1992), though it comes at the cost of reduced government flexibility (Lohmann, 1992) and potentially democratic accountability and legitimacy (Elgie, 1998).

Politicians, however, may have additional incentives for granting independence to central banks besides controlling inflation. Internally, such institutions can alleviate conflicts between government ministers, backbench legislators and coalition partners in a multiparty government who may distrust one another but would allow an independent central bank to supply information on government policy choices and their consequences (Bernhard, 1998). Moreover, monetary policy has redistributive effects that can favour certain constituencies in the short term and constrain the choices of future governments in the long term (Bernhard et al., 2002). Indeed, the ability of an independent central bank to constrain political actors and rise above conflicts can help to explain their prevalence among countries governed by multiparty governments (Hallerberg, 2002), federal systems (Moser, 1999), and with multiple veto players (Keefer and Stasavage, 2003; see de Haan and Eijffinger, 2019 for a review).

Moreover, while granting central banks independence allowed them to pursue price stability without political interference, it also gave central banks significant latitude in how they did so and even how they interpreted their mandate. Critics warned of the redistributive nature of monetary policy and the political implications of central bank independence (Bowles and White, 1994; Kirshner, 2003), though many governments outside the EU also granted independence to their central banks.

The euro area Member States delegated monetary policy to an independent central bank that used its existing policy tools and created new ones in ways that would have been impossible to predict when it was first created. Analysts debated the merits and weaknesses of the ECB's accountability structures (Buiter, 1999; de Haan and Eijffinger, 2000; Issing, 1999), but the ECB became one of the world's most independent central banks (de Haan, 1997; de Haan et al., 2018; Dincer and Eichengreen, 2014).

10.2.1.1 Central Bank Independence in the Euro Area: ECB Accountability

A central bank's independence is constrained by factors including how the governing board of the central bank is appointed, their tenure, if the government must sign off on monetary policy decisions, and if price stability is written into the bank's statutes. Scholars have categorized this as political, economic (also referred to as financial), and personal independence (Alesina and Summers, 1993; Grilli et al., 1991; Howarth and Loedel, 2005).

Alesina and Summers (1993, p. 153) draw on the work of Bade and Parkin to define political independence as 'the ability of the central bank to select its policy objectives without influence from the government', based on the institutional relationship between the central bank and the government. Article 127.1 Treaty on the Functioning of the European Union (TFEU) imposed on the newly created ECB a primary mandate of price stability and Article 130 TFEU guaranteed its independence in pursuing its activities, as neither the ECB nor national central banks of the Member States could 'seek or take instructions from Union institutions, bodies, offices or agencies, from any government of a Member State or from any other body'. No fiscal counterweight like a euro area Treasury was created, and financial supervision remained a national competence until the start of the banking union. Although the Treaties established the ECB's mandate, defining price stability was left to the ECB itself, an important component of its political independence. In October 1998, the ECB Governing Council had defined price stability as 'a year-on-year increase in the Harmonised Index of Consumer Prices (HICP) for the euro area of below 2%'. This definition was refined in May 2003 to 'below but close to 2% over the medium term'. The ECB updated this definition again in 2021 to '2% inflation over the medium term' (see also de Haan, Chapter 11 in this volume).

Economic (Bowles and White, 1994) or financial (Eijffinger and de Haan, 1996) independence refers to the prohibition of the central bank to finance government deficits. Article 123 (1) TFEU prohibits monetary financing, thus granting the ECB economic independence. Due to personal (also known as 'personnel') independence, the government should not be involved in appointment procedures for central bank personnel, nor should it expect the personnel to conform to specific 'political, ideological, and/or national reasons' (Howarth and Loedel, 2005, p. 183). Nationality has played a role in the selection of the ECB's Executive Board; for example, there was some conflict on the selection of the first ECB president in 1998 when the French government tried to install its own candidate at the last minute (Chang, 2009, p. 57). Nevertheless, this has not been systematic, and research indicates practical difficulties in manipulating the appointment process to influence the ECB's policy outcomes (Chang, 2003).

Article 283 TFEU outlines the obligation for the ECB to submit annual reports to the European Council, the Council of the EU, the Commission and the European Parliament. In 2002, the ECB defined its accountability as 'being required to justify and explain' its policy (ECB, 2002, p. 48). This occurs through its interactions with the European Parliament, the main body ensuring its accountability through hearings known as the Monetary Dialogue that were created in the European Parliament's Rules of Procedure.

10.2.2 *Rethinking Monetary Policy after the Global Financial Crisis: Quantitative Easing*

While the objective of price stability still enjoyed widespread support among central bankers and academics after the GFC, expanding the central bank toolkit to include quantitative easing (in which the central bank purchases assets to reduce interest rates on savings and loans and to stimulate the economy) did not generate an immediate consensus (Blinder et al., 2017). Used by the Bank of Japan from 2001 to 2006, the US Federal Reserve announced its first QE programme in November 2008 and the Bank of England launched its QE programme in March 2009.

While central bankers emphasize that 'the distributional effects of monetary policy are complex and uncertain' (Bernanke, 2015), QE works through central bank asset purchases that inflate asset prices like stocks (see also Adamski, Chapter 9 in this volume). Economic criticism of the QE is based on three main charges:

- QE could threaten price stability (essentially creating more money in its purchase of assets). This, however, did not occur in practice, with studies showing only a modest impact on inflation in the United States (Engen et al., 2015), the United Kingdom (Churm et al., 2021), and the EU (Garcia Pascual and Wieladek, 2016);
- it interfered with market forces by blunting market discipline in creating additional demand for assets that otherwise might lose value, thereby creating moral hazard;
- and it had a stronger and more overt redistributive impact (in rewarding asset holders as other groups, like homeowners, lost considerable wealth during the crisis). Colciago et al. (2019) review this literature on the impact of monetary policy on inequality as well as how the transmission of monetary policy to the real economy is affected by inequality.

The ECB did not engage in QE in response to the GFC. On the one hand, the euro area's financial system was dominated by banks rather than capital markets, making QE a less attractive solution to aid the euro area's ailing banks. Moreover, the prohibition against monetary financing (Article 123 TFEU) also made the purchase of government debt legally problematic.

Rising inflation since mid-2009 and the potential inflationary consequences of QE also made it an unattractive option. Instead, the ECB engaged in successive rounds of longer-term refinancing operations (LTRO) that provided additional liquidity to banks, in addition to other unconventional monetary policies like covered bond purchases and fixed-rate full allotment.

10.3 GOVERNMENT BOND PURCHASES BY THE ECB

10.3.1 *The Sovereign Debt Crisis: SMP and OMT*

The revelation of the Greek government's true debt and deficit figures in 2009, coupled with market speculation on whether official help would be forthcoming, drove up Greek bond yields to unsustainable levels and threatened contagion to other euro area Member States with weak fiscal positions. In May 2010, the ECB announced its SMP, in which the ECB would purchase government debt on secondary markets. While ostensibly launched in defence of the monetary transmission mechanism (and therefore in line with the ECB's price stability mandate), it also had the effect of propping up prices in government bond markets. Nevertheless, the ECB distinguished SMP from QE and included a sterilization component for bond purchases to ensure that they would not threaten price stability.

The ECB's purchase of government debt, however, raised questions about the political motivations of the intervention, in particular the desire to keep bond yields for euro area governments at sustainable levels and preclude market speculation to force a country to leave the euro area, an option referred to at the time as 'Grexit' (Högenauer and Howarth, 2019; Macchiarelli et al., 2020). Such motivations could be interpreted as the monetary financing of governments by the central bank, something expressly prohibited by Article 123(1) TFEU.

The SMP marked an important shift for the ECB away from the traditional ordo-liberal roots of its predecessor, the German Bundesbank, to a central bank that viewed its mandate more broadly and was more tolerant of the prospect of some level of inflation. Over the years, we have seen several German members of the ECB Executive Board resign before the end of their mandate. In February 2011 German Bundesbank President Axel Weber, a vocal SMP opponent, resigned nearly a year before his term ended, effectively removing himself from the race to be the next ECB president despite enjoying the support of German Chancellor Angela Merkel. On 9 September 2011 ECB Chief Economist Jürgen Stark also resigned 'for personal reasons' nearly three years before the end of his mandate amid speculation over his opposition to ECB bond buying. These resignations were a harbinger for ongoing German discord within the ECB as Weber's successor Jens Weidmann (October 2020) and fellow ECB Executive Board Member Sabine Lautenschläger (September 2019) would find themselves in opposition to the ECB's loose monetary policy and resign before the end of their respective mandates.

The SMP, along with other measures announced in May 2010 to combat the burgeoning crisis, such as the rescue for Greece and creation of the European Financial Stability Facility as well as the European Financial Stabilisation Mechanism, provided only temporary respite for the euro area. The crisis spread across southern Europe and Ireland, eventually threatening Italy.

In July 2012, ECB President Mario Draghi vowed to do 'whatever it takes' to save the euro. This took the form of the Outright Monetary Transactions (OMT). As with the SMP, the ECB referenced the monetary transmission mechanism as the primary motivation (ECB, 2012). As under the SMP, the ECB pledged to purchase government debt on secondary markets, and any liquidity created would be sterilized. Unlike the SMP, however, these purchases would be unlimited. The ECB demanded that a Member State receiving support from the OMT also apply for a loan from the European Stability Mechanism, the permanent bailout mechanism that succeeded the EFSF, which would reduce concerns about monetary financing and improve the effectiveness of the programme that otherwise might be undermined by Member State policies.

The OMT programme has never been implemented, as the promise of the ECB to fully unleash a 'big bazooka' sufficed to ease market speculation and provided sufficient assurance of the integrity of the euro area (Chang and Leblond, 2015). This, combined with the announcement of the creation of the banking union in late June 2012, with the ECB as the direct supervisor for significant euro area banks as defined by the Single Supervisory Mechanism, marked a turning point for the euro crisis.

10.3.2 *Unleashing Quantitative Easing in the Euro Area: PSPP and PEPP*

The OMT announcement ended the speculation over redenomination risk and the intense phase of the euro crisis. Nevertheless, economic growth in the euro area remained weak. According to Eurostat, annual growth went from –0.9 per cent in 2012 to 1.4 per cent in 2014 compared to non-euro area countries enjoying more than double that growth rate: for example, Poland at 3.4 per cent, Hungary at 4.2 per cent, and the United Kingdom at 2.9 per cent growth in 2014. Moreover, by 2014 average euro area inflation dropped to 0.4 per cent, with countries like Greece and Spain in negative territory. The ECB's interest rates were very low, with one of the its main interest rates, the deposit facility, hitting 0 in July 2012 and going negative in June 2014.

On 22 January 2015, the PSPP, part of the Asset Purchase Programme (APP) begun in 2014, launched the ECB's QE programme. As with the previous bond-buying programmes, explicit links were drawn to its role in fostering price stability, since the PSPP would be 'aimed at fulfilling the ECB's price stability mandate … in order to address the risks of a too prolonged period of low inflation' (ECB 2015).

The ECB committed to purchasing bonds issued by euro area governments, agencies, and European institutions as part of the PSPP. Initially the PSPP was set to expire in September 2016 but was extended several times. On 9 June 2022, the ECB announced that it would end its net purchases under the APP on 1 July 2022.

Anticipating some of the criticism, ECB President Mario Draghi noted 'that each monetary policy always has some fiscal implication', and that the ECB, as a central bank without a corresponding treasury that could indemnify central bank losses, needed to balance monetary policy effectiveness with risk allocation. On the one hand, for a policy like OMT, Draghi argued that 'full risk sharing is fundamental for the effectiveness of that monetary policy measure'. In the case of the PSPP, however, the ECB enacted several measures to reduce risk sharing among euro area Member States. The Governing Council decided that only the purchase of securities issued by European institutions would be subject to loss sharing among national central banks, which would make up 12 per cent of the PSPP. In addition, the ECB would hold 8 per cent of the new asset purchases, making a total of 20 per cent of the PSPP subject to risk sharing. National central banks, however, would purchase the sovereign bonds of their own governments, and these would not be subject to risk sharing. Moreover, PSPP purchases would be allocated across issuers located in the euro area according to the ECB's capital key. An issuer limit of 33 per cent and an issue limit of 25 per cent would prevent the ECB from purchasing over 25 per cent of each issue or more than 33 per cent of each issuer's debt. The minimal conditionality requirements excluded only Greek bonds from the PSPP.

Despite the PSPP, the ECB struggled to achieve its inflation target of 'at or below 2 percent'. It created a Task Force on Low Inflation (LIFT) that conducted research from March 2015 to June 2016 and published its results as part of the ECB working papers series. Economic factors identified in the research emphasize the sharp drop in global energy prices and a series of negative shocks. The ECB's policies were deemed appropriate to the situation by the LIFT. The European Parliament (2016a) also commissioned experts to write on the effectiveness of the ECB's asset purchase programme as part of its Monetary Dialogue. The results also supported the ECB's unconventional policies in restoring the monetary transmission mechanism. These papers considered the impact on price stability, economic growth, and the provision of credit but did not examine political factors. For example, political economists pointed to economic growth models in which central banks are embedded (Reisenbichler, 2020), including the weakening of labour and the restrictive fiscal policies pursued by governments, as important factors in the persistence of low inflation and concomitant need for the ECB to respond with QE (Van Doorslaer and Vermeiren, 2021). These have important policy implications that point to the limits of monetary policy and how Member State policies and national institutions impact the efficacy of monetary policy, echoing earlier analyses on the political economy of central bank independence outlined in Section 10.2.

The onset of the COVID-19 pandemic in 2020 revived concerns that the EU would return to the fractured politics of the euro crisis, a fear that was exacerbated by ECB President Christine Lagarde's ill-timed comment that the ECB was 'not here to close the spreads' (Lagarde 2020). Nevertheless, the response of both the ECB and the Member States to the pandemic-induced economic crisis was swift. The ECB viewed its role during the pandemic as being to calm markets, preserve the credit supply, and minimize the pandemic's impact on the euro area's inflation trajectory (Lane, 2021a). Monetary policy was already accommodative, with the deposit facility rate negative. In addition to augmenting the APP by €120 billion and supporting the credit supply through a revised targeted longer-term refinancing operations programme (TLTRO III), in March 2020 the ECB launched the PEPP that, after increased envelopes in June and December, totalled €1.85 trillion and ran until the end of March 2022. The PEPP included all asset categories eligible under the APP, and a waiver on eligibility requirements was given to allow the purchase of government debt issued by Greece. While the benchmark allocation across jurisdictions would still follow the ECB capital key, the ECB granted itself 'flexibility of purchases over time, across asset classes and among jurisdictions' (ECB 2020).

The PEPP worked in conjunction with the strong fiscal policy response, unlike during the euro crisis. The PEPP and the Next Generation EU budget that included the Recovery and Resilience Facility helped prevent widening of the sovereign spreads (Lane, 2021b). The generous provision of liquidity has been judged favourably by economists (Boone and Rawdanowicz, 2021) and lawyers (Grund, 2020).

Nevertheless, the PEPP has political implications. Tooze (2020) argued that 'central banks now backstop the entire financial system on a near-permanent basis', going against the initial logic of euro area governance being predicated on market discipline (see also Adamski, Chapter 9 in this volume). Some academics have criticized the neoliberal turn implied by the blurring of monetary and fiscal policy by central banks during the crisis (Ban, 2021; Schelkle, 2013). With the PEPP, the ECB shifted away from the self-imposed restraint of its bond purchases found in the SMP, OMT, and PSPP, allowing itself maximum flexibility and discretion. No serious discussion has occurred among Member States or the European Parliament on how to ensure sufficient accountability and legitimacy in light of these developments.

10.4 THE POLITICAL ECONOMY OF THE ECB BOND PURCHASES: LEADERSHIP OR POWER GRAB?

As the Global Financial Crisis evolved into the euro crisis, the ECB played a role that some deemed more political. First, its monetary policy arguably became 'more distributive and targetable than previously thought' (Fernandez-Albertos, 2015, p. 230), as the economic crisis exacerbated the politicization of monetary policy through the expansion of its activities (see also Adamski, Chapter 9 in this volume). The channels through which conventional versus unconventional monetary policy operated and their impact on inequality, however, remain ambiguous. While a consensus exists among economists that inflation (above a certain threshold) increases inequality, studies of conventional and unconventional monetary policies on income and wealth inequality show 'mixed results' and 'are also not clear cut' (Colciago et al., 2019, p. 1199).

Second, ECB policies substituted for political actors unable or unwilling to enact the policies and institutional reforms necessary to restore market confidence. The euro area governance structure created under the Maastricht Treaty lacked a lender of last resort (LOLR) for sovereigns, integrated financial supervision, and the possibility of large-scale fiscal transfers for Member States in distress, which stoked concerns over the sustainability of EMU in the long term and over redenomination risks. Euro area governments acted slowly and reluctantly in filling these institutional lacunae: for example, the lender of last resort for sovereigns originally would be fulfilled by the EFSF, a temporary instrument designed to expire in three years. Policymakers finally instituted a permanent ESM in 2012, but this delay indicates the difficulty in reforming euro area governance as heads of state and government tried (without success) to calm markets in a series of high-profile summits advocating more piecemeal reforms such as strengthening fiscal policy coordination (Smeets and Zimmermann, 2013). Different preferences, domestic political ramifications entailed by institutional reforms, and the need to appeal to different political constituencies made it difficult for governments to agree on institutional reforms (Armingeon and Cranmer, 2018; Heins and de la Porte, 2015; Johnston and Regan, 2016; Pisani-Ferry, 2014; Walter et al., 2020) and often led to incomplete solutions (Jones et al., 2016). The ECB's policies calmed financial markets in the short term and encouraged further euro area economic integration (Yiangou et al., 2013), but it contributed to the rise of intergovernmental bargains (Bickerton et al., 2015; Schimmelfennig, 2015) favouring German interests. The ability of the central bank to provide a credible policy in the face of government inaction echoes earlier work done that emphasized the ability of an independent central bank to transcend 'conflicts over economic and monetary policy' (Bernhard, 2002, p. 9). Indeed, though the original work of Bernhard refers to rival political parties, the inability of the EU Member States to sort out their response to the crisis and the ECB stepping in echo these dynamics.

The ECB's actions during the euro crisis made it an indispensable player in euro area governance. Not only did its unconventional monetary policy instruments such as the OMT turn the tide during the euro crisis, the ECB left an indelible impact through its actions as government adviser (particularly as a member of the Troika) and in its selection as the euro area banking supervisor. How did the ECB make this transformation from an ostensibly technocratic actor to a political player, and what are the implications for euro area governance?

10.4.1 *Theorizing the ECB's Leadership*

The euro area Member States responded to the crisis in fits and starts. A leadership vacuum had emerged which ECB Presidents Trichet and then Draghi filled (Verdun, 2017). Germany, the euro area's largest economy that provided a model for euro area governance (including the ECB being modelled after the German Bundesbank), only went as far as being a 'reluctant hegemon' (Bulmer and Paterson, 2013), as the sceptical German electorate constrained the government's response. Particularly on the heels of a financial crisis that involved politically controversial bank bailouts, the prospect of bailing out euro area members that were portrayed as fiscally irresponsible was anathema.

The overall logic of independent central banks focused on price stability had already come under question during the Global Financial Crisis (Fontan et al., 2018), though central bankers remained committed to it (Blinder et al., 2017). The Federal Reserve, for example, became increasingly engulfed in providing liquidity in securities markets during a 'war, using every weapon at hand, including a number of new ones never used before', as competing views on economics and finance clashed (Mehrling, 2010). Belke (2010, p. 358) described the SMP as a potential threat to the ECB's financial independence if southern European countries were to be unable to pay off their debts (partly owned by the ECB), making it 'possible that the toxic bonds in the balance sheets of the ECB might eat up most of the Bank's reserves and equity capital if they were to fall in value by a sufficiently large amount'. Such concerns eventually gave way to ideational shifts within the ECB itself that moved from blaming fiscal policy for the euro crisis to systemic causes (Ferrara, 2020).

Political fragmentation within the euro area prevented bargains being struck between monetary and fiscal authorities during the euro crisis (Henning, 2016). The euro area institutional architecture was underdeveloped, and while the euro crisis provoked a series of reflections on the future of euro area governance that could include stronger fiscal and financial cooperation in the future (European Commission, 2017; Juncker et al., 2015; Van Rompuy et al., 2012), in the short term it left the ECB as the only institution that could respond quickly and credibly to the crisis, given the absence of political leadership from the Member States.

The governments of France, Italy, Spain, Portugal, and even Germany either advocated for or supported the ECB's decision to purchase bonds under the SMP (Bastasin, 2015; Ludlow, 2010). When the ECB prepared to restart the SMP in August 2011, the joint statement issued by German Chancellor Angela Merkel and French President Nicolas Sarkozy indicated that interventions would be based on ECB analyses, in which 'France and Germany are confident'. Similarly, the day after Draghi's 2012 speech came a joint communique from German Chancellor Merkel and French President Hollande supporting the defence of the integrity of the euro area by the Member States and European institutions: 'Germany and France are deeply committed to the integrity of the euro zone. They are determined to do everything to protect the euro zone' (Reuters 2012). The German finance minister, Wolfgang Schäuble, explicitly welcomed Draghi's intention to 'take the necessary measures to secure the euro in the framework of the existing ECB mandate' (Elliott and Tremlett 2012).

The European Parliament's annual resolutions on the ECB's annual report, the only institution giving a regular public response to the ECB's reporting requirement, also supported the ECB's bond-buying programmes. The European Parliament responded favourably, for example, to the SMP and the OMT in their resolutions on the ECB annual reports (European Parliament, 2013a, 2013b). On PSPP, the European Parliament was initially circumspect, noting the impact of reduced bond yields in most Member States (European Parliament, 2016b) but later crediting it with having 'contributed to the economic recovery' of the euro area (European Parliament, 2020), though a minority opinion criticized the PSPP for its disproportional impact across the euro area and for being outside of the ECB's mandate (European Parliament, 2021). On PEPP, the European Parliament 'invite[d] the ECB to continue purchases under the PEPP for as long as it deems necessary to meet its mandate' (European Parliament, 2022).

Drawing on the historical institutionalist framework that emphasizes path dependence and the constraints caused by EMU's legal framework, the ECB 'filled the gaps' of EMU governance (Yiangou et al., 2013) by providing a policy response that should have come from Member States. The ECB's actions allegedly blunted mass unrest in the euro area (Genovese et al., 2016). The credit given to saving the euro also indicates the ECB may have become a 'charismatic leader' whose 'authority hinges on the "attitudes of awe" that the leader inspires' that arguably compensated for longstanding complaints about the ECB's political legitimacy (Tortola and Pansardi, 2019, p. 100).

The portrayal of the ECB as a political actor found traction in neo-functionalist explanations that focus on the role of supranational institutions in driving European integration forward, taking advantage of transnational interests and spillovers. The extension of the ECB's power, and the role that OMT in particular played in stemming the euro crisis, led to arguments on the spillover of ECB power through its reinterpretation of the price stability mandate that included saving the euro (Heldt and Mueller, 2021; Nicoli, 2020). This contrasts with the type of integration through court cases that characterize the single market; the OMT marks the rise of a new form of integration in that it 'bolstered its capacity to stabilize the euro without having its mandate formally enlarged', which has a questionable basis for legitimacy, despite its short-term benefit in calming market speculation (Scicluna, 2018, p. 1874).

In contrast, other analyses viewed the ECB's activism as more ambivalent. The new intergovernmentalism literature stresses the importance of the EU Member States (not supranational institutions) acting within intergovernmental institutions like the European Council in the handling of the euro crisis and characterizes the ECB's entrepreneurship as more limited and strategic than neo-functionalist interpretations (Hodson, 2015). Similar analyses emphasize the reluctance of the ECB to take on such an active role during the euro crisis and view the OMT as an example of 'leadership by default' rather than an opportunistic power grab (Schoeller, 2018). Moreover, the introduction of conditionality in the OMT announcement arguably made the ECB more of an agent to the Member State principals rather than a proactive leader (Bernatavičius, 2021).

Finally, one can consider the interactions between the ECB and other euro area institutions. As noted in Section 10.2, central bank interactions with other institutions will influence the impact of its policies, particularly on whether monetary dominance prevails. Monetary dominance refers to the ability of the central bank to pursue price stability without being constrained by other policy considerations such as government bond yields or high government debt. When fiscal dominance prevails instead, such concerns drive central bank policy, often resulting in higher inflation rates or financial repression (Schnabel, 2020). The ECB has been portrayed as a strategic actor in its interactions with euro area Member States which can be likened to a game of chicken (Henning, 2016), with the ECB selectively launching its policy measures in a way that ultimately secured monetary dominance. The successive confrontations between the Member States and the ECB saw the ECB strategically declining to rescue Member States too quickly to make certain that they would undertake reforms and not free ride on ECB measures that would alleviate market pressure. These confrontations included: the pressure on the ECB by French President Nicolas Sarkozy in 2010 to purchase sovereign bonds; the 2011 inclusion of Spanish and Italian debt in SMP purchases in (tacit) exchange for structural reforms; the December 2011 introduction of three-year longer-term refinancing operations by the ECB and subsequent signing of the fiscal compact by the Member States; and the June 2012 banking union announcement followed by Draghi's 'whatever it takes' speech in July. Henning (2016) argues that the threat of deflation in 2014 indicates the success of monetary dominance, as this would not be consistent with fiscal dominance (though deflation was not a desirable monetary outcome either).

Others have indicated that the ECB's legal constraints have been used by it to strengthen its hand against financial markets, as market panic could force its hand to react in a way that would also threaten its independence. The need to act as a lender of last resort and create liquidity could trigger inflationary pressure. Markets may also expect a central bank to run a loose monetary policy if it is threatened with potential losses from its asset purchases. Finally, moral hazard could arise in markets that expect a central bank rescue (Mabbett and Schelkle, 2019).

Both interpretations contrast with traditional notions drawn from the principal–agent theory of agents trying to increase their own power, instead using their constraints in a strategic manner vis-à-vis other euro area actors. None of these interpretations of the ECB's actions, however, would negate the emergence of the ECB as a political actor during the euro crisis. Its policy entrepreneurship (reluctant or otherwise) and implementation of policies with a more marked redistributive effect than previous monetary policy tools gave the ECB a critical role with substantial discretion in determining the outcome of the euro crisis.

10.4.2 *Bond Buying as Fiscal Policy?*

Given that fiscal policy falls under the competence of governments rather than central banks, the charge that the PSPP constitutes fiscal policy through the backdoor is a serious one that potentially undermines QE's legitimacy. Whereas price stability had been accepted as a public good (albeit one that favours creditors over debtors), the redistributive implications of the ECB's use of its balance sheets were debated (Högenauer and Howarth, 2019). While research done after the Global Financial Crisis indicated the redistributive impact of QE in the United Kingdom, as 'holdings . . . heavily skewed with the top 5% of households holding 40% of these assets' (Bell et al., 2012, p. 254), more recent research questioned the redistributive character of QE (Colciago et al., 2019). The ECB's internal research goes so far as to suggest QE reduced income inequality and helped to reduce wealth inequality (Conti et al., 2017). NGOs such as Positive Money Europe, however, campaigned for the ECB to account for the inequality generated by its QE.

The redistributive nature of QE has drawn particular attention, as this would make it more akin to fiscal policy and made the ECB a quasi-lender of last resort to euro area sovereigns, a role not delegated to it in the Treaties. Some political scientists have viewed the ECB's policies as equivalent to 'fiscal integration through monetary policy' (Schelkle, 2013; see also Schlosser, 2019). Former ECB Executive Board member Jürgen Stark referred to the OMT as 'out of mandate transactions' (Stark, 2012). Moreover, the ECB's QE policy had a broader impact on environmental policy (Bolsinger et al., 2021; Hilmi et al., 2022), and central bank asset purchases are coming under increasing scrutiny for their impact on climate change.

Some economists and political scientists argued in favour of the ECB assuming the role of LOLR (De Grauwe and Ji, 2015; Gabor, 2014; Schlosser, 2019). This would allow the ECB to play a stabilizing role in financial markets, as concerns over the integrity of the euro area fuelled market speculation during the euro crisis (Chang and Leblond, 2015), and this speculation was pushing governments into a bad equilibrium through self-fulfilling crises that drove rising bond yield spreads away from underlying economic conditions (De Grauwe and Ji, 2013). Some have argued that the ECB already is a de facto LOLR working in conjunction with the European Stability Mechanism (Hu, 2014; Schlosser, 2019).

10.4.3 *Legal Challenges from the German Constitutional Court*

Legal challenges against ECB policies, specifically from the German Constitutional Court (BVerfG), argued that the ECB had exceeded its mandate and made economic policy decisions. The sequence of decisions between the BVerfG and the Court of Justice of the European Union (CJEU) is as follows:

1. A preliminary reference is made by the BVerfG;
2. The CJEU makes a decision;
3. The BVerfG makes a final decision in its main proceedings.

The Gauweiler case of 14 January 2014 against the OMT became the first challenge to the ECB's bond-buying programmes and was the first reference by the BVerfG to the CJEU. The legality of the OMT was questioned on the basis of whether the ECB would have exceeded its competence (*ultra vires*) and transgressed Article 123 TFEU on the prohibition of monetary financing. Craig and Markakis (2016) summarize how the BVerfG argued that the ECB acted against its mandate through: the conditionality provision linking OMT assistance to the ESM; selectivity in the purchase of government bonds; parallelism in purchasing government debt of countries in a European Stability Mechanism (ESM) – or European Financial Stability Facility (EFSF) – programme; and circumvention in that the OMT could undermine the limits and conditions of the ESM programme.

In 2015, the CJEU ruled that the OMT is compatible with EU law and a matter of monetary policy, accepting the ECB's justification of restoring monetary policy transmission mechanism (Court of Justice of the European Union, 2015). The ruling denied both claims that the ECB had exceeded its mandate and that it engaged in monetary financing. The CJEU did, however, insist on bond purchases being based on the principle of proportionality.

On 21 June 2016, the BVerfG followed up with a judgement on the participation of the German Bundesbank in the implementation of OMT requiring that purchases be unannounced, limited, not distort the initial issuance of government bonds, be limited to bonds of Member States with market access, bonds being held to maturity, and purchases ending or being restricted once intervention is no longer needed.

The PSPP also faced legal challenges from the BVerfG in the Weiss case that questioned if the PSPP constituted an *ultra vires* act that exceeded the ECB's mandate and infringed on the prohibition of monetary financing. In December 2018, the CJEU ruled that the PSPP neither exceeded the ECB's mandate nor contravened the prohibition of monetary financing. On 5 May 2020, however, the BVerfG ruled that the CJEU had overstepped in its December 2018 ruling, arguing that the CJEU had not applied the EU's principle of proportionality when analysing the broader economic effects of its monetary policy. The BVerfG demanded that the ECB demonstrate proportionality of the PSPP within three months for the Bundesbank to continue participating. The ECB took 'note' of the ruling but also noted its accountability to the CJEU (rather than national courts) which had ruled in 2018 that the ECB had acted within its mandate. Ultimately, the German Bundesbank provided the proportionality analysis and the German Bundestag accepted the results (Bundesbank, 2021, p. 22).

Though the legal challenges from Karlsruhe were largely unwelcome, Mody (2014) went so far as to argue that the BVerfG may have done the EU a favour by forcing a dialogue on the fuzziness between monetary and fiscal policy within the OMT. Nevertheless, the BVerfG's criticisms do represent the opinion of many economists, policymakers, and voters in Germany and should be taken seriously (Fratzscher, 2020). Moreover, they communicated to euro area leaders that 'decisions for which they ought to take ownership should not be delegated to an unelected body' (Pisani-Ferry, 2020). Indeed, national actors like the BVerfG could be viewed as 'fire alarms', in the absence of EU-level control mechanisms (Fontan and Howarth, 2021). Moreover, the German Federal Constitutional Court 'engaged in an open challenge to the ECJ as to whether it is willing to act consistently in reviewing ECB action' (Dawson and Bobić, 2019).

The EU Member States and the European Parliament accepted the ECB's arguments based on the monetary transmission mechanism and refrained from making any institutional changes that might alleviate the concerns raised by these cases. The CJEU accepted the ECB's discretion when making monetary policy. The official support from the ECB's member states and the European Parliament allowed it to avoid undertaking politically difficult reforms, thereby enabling the mission creep of the central bank (Binder and Spindel, 2017; Chang, 2018) without concomitant strengthening of accountability.

10.5 ECB LEGITIMACY: ACCOUNTABILITY VERSUS TRANSPARENCY

The official reflections on euro area governance that included the Four Presidents' Report (Van Rompuy et al., 2012), the Five Presidents' Report (Juncker et al., 2015), and proposals from the European Commission (2017) considered the legitimacy and democratic accountability of EMU, but none included any consideration of altering the ECB's accountability framework. Indeed, all of the actors to whom the ECB is officially accountable (Member States, European Parliament, CJEU) have accepted and supported the ECB's policies and its explanation of their need to restore the monetary transmission mechanism. Though issues of transparency were raised, and individual MEPS took the ECB to task during the Monetary Dialogue, there was only limited consideration of the ECB's accountability framework despite numerous proposals for reform (Claeys et al., 2014; Collignon and Diessner, 2016; Heidebrecht, 2019; Jourdan and Diessner, 2019; Whelan, 2014). The European Parliament noted 'the need to reflect on how scrutiny of the ECB by the European Parliament as well as through dialogue with national parliaments may be enhanced; calls for the negotiation of a formal interinstitutional agreement to formalise and go beyond the existing accountability practices regarding monetary functions' (European Parliament, 2021, p. 9), but no concrete actions were taken thereafter.

A 2018 ECB Economic Bulletin article acknowledged the challenges to the ECB's accountability framework due to the euro crisis, including its use of non-standard policy measures, its newly acquired role in the Single Supervisory Mechanism, and its role in the Troika institutions that designed and monitored the financial assistance programmes (Fraccaroli et al., 2018). The ECB responded to this accountability challenge mainly by increasing its interactions with the European Parliament and through additional transparency measures. While increased accountability should be welcome in light of the ECB's increased political role, should self-reporting and greater transparency on the initiative of the central bank itself be considered sufficient? The ECB has augmented both its policy toolkit and its own accountability measures.

For example, in 2011 the ECB voluntarily revealed the identity of those receiving \$638 billion in aid, in contrast to the Federal Reserve's decision to withhold this information (Jacobs and King, 2021, p. 34). ECB President Mario Draghi visited some national parliaments in order to enhance its legitimacy (Tesche, 2019). While welcome, these were one-off measures.

The ECB began publishing so-called monetary policy accounts in January 2015 in response to the longstanding criticism against its refusal to publish minutes of Governing Council meetings. The US Federal Reserve, the Bank of England, and the Bank of Japan had been publishing their minutes since the 1990s, though they did not contain market sensitive information (and nor do the ECB's monetary policy documents). Although the publication of monetary policy accounts was a welcome development, they do not provide an account of the discussions that took place, nor do they provide information on voting (Wyplosz, 2015).

The ECB's initial bond-buying programmes (SMP and the never-used OMT) occurred during a period of economic crisis in the euro area, which helped justify the measures taken and the continuation of the status quo accountability measures as necessary during an emergency. Indeed, the ECB was able to act quickly and with potentially unlimited funds (in the case of the OMT), depending on how it defined the parameters of the policy. Without these interventions during the euro crisis, the economic consequences from the crises that have beset the euro area could have been even more serious. Questioning what Heldt and Mueller (2021, p. 83) referred to as the ECB's 'self-empowerment' has not seemed to be in the interest of the other relevant actors in euro area governance (such as the Member States or European Parliament) that have come to rely upon, perhaps even expect, the ECB to be able to handle market instability.

Some political scientists have argued for a distinction to be drawn between normal times and crises. Arguments relating to the ECB's capacity for crisis management (Braun, 2013; Breuss, 2017; Brunnermeier et al., 2016; Howarth, 2009; Krampf, 2014; Schoeller, 2020; Schwarzer, 2012) and its role in 'emergency politics' (Rauh, 2022; Schmidt, 2022) developed, with the former tending to theorize how the ECB's crisis management function occurred and the latter tending to focus on longer-term implications of 'emergency politics'. For example, Rauh (2022, p. 966) references the use of 'alarmist language over and beyond objective crisis pressures when their competences are contested', which highlights how the context of near-constant economic crisis over the last decade has both incentivized and allowed the ECB to expand its policy toolkit. Schmidt (2022, pp. 1360–61) argues further that 'the ECB's persuasive rhetorical power ... ensured the normalization of the ECB's emergency politics of monetary easing'.

Can the euro area ensure greater accountability for the ECB without damaging its ability to act quickly during a crisis? One proposal would allow technocratic actors like central bankers to enjoy independence during normal periods but would require clear political support during crises (Jones and Matthijs, 2019). This acknowledges the broader remit of central banks, particularly during periods of crisis when financial stability poses a threat. If designed properly, such democratic validation could occur in a timely manner.

Political scientists have also offered numerous proposals for reforms that might improve accountability of the ECB. Most emphasized its relationship to the European Parliament and the ECB's participation in its Monetary Dialogue as the primary accountability mechanism (Collignon and Diessner, 2016; Heidebrecht, 2019; Jourdan and Diessner, 2019). The European Parliament's role and the ECB's accountability to it could be enhanced through the creation of a euro area subcommittee of the ECON (economic and monetary affairs) committee with a dedicated staff and standing committee of external experts to advise with a focus on oversight in Monetary Dialogue and Economic Dialogue (Chang and Hodson, 2018). The idea of a euro area parliament has also been raised (Maurer, 2013), but this could create rival mandates with the European Parliament and even depress voter turnout further.

The ECB successfully shifted the monetary discourse, with both Member States and public opinion, and justified its bond-buying programmes through its communication strategy, the tacit assent of Member States, and engaging in a discourse with an extensive network of experts to garner support (Schmidt, 2020). Market speculation quickly subsided after Draghi's OMT announcement, thereby ending the most dangerous phase of the euro crisis. While Draghi's move was widely praised, the legal ramifications received serious attention. This was not unique to the ECB, as central banks had been under increasing scrutiny since the global financial crisis (Tucker, 2018). The ECB, as a central bank without a political union behind it, was arguably more vulnerable to criticism for its legitimacy than other central banks and made frequent references to how its actions supported its primary objective of price stability. Regardless of all the academic and legal discussions, however, the ECB faced little political opposition, and the political actors that could hold the ECB to account (Member States and European Parliament) either remained silent or vocally supported its bond-buying programmes with no concerted attempt to impose additional accountability requirements.

And while the ECB's actions famously 'saved the euro', an uncomfortable precedent has been set on the flexibility of the ECB's mandate (for those who oppose this flexibility) and the unwillingness to set in place additional measures to guard against potential overreach by the ECB. Indeed, the euro area Member States should reconsider the ECB's accountability structure in light of the expanded role it has assumed in euro area governance (Amtenbrink, 2019; Bernatavičius, 2021; Dawson et al., 2019; Dietsch, 2020; Ferrara et al., 2021; Fromage et al., 2019; Giovannini and Jamet, 2020; Heldt and Müller, 2022; Lastra et al., 2020; Markakis, 2020).

10.6 REDEFINING UNCONVENTIONAL: THE ECB STRATEGY REVIEW

After all of the major central banks had undertaken some version of quantitative easing, analysts and policymakers questioned whether asset purchases would remain part of the central bank policy instruments. Research involving survey data of central bankers and academic economists noted that despite the lack of consensus regarding 'the usefulness of unconventional monetary policies, we expect most of them will remain in central banks' toolkits' (Blinder et al., 2017, p. 707). The Federal Reserve's 2020 monetary strategy review indicated that it was 'ready to use its full range of tools' to achieve its 2 percent inflation goal, which could include running above 2 percent after inflation had persistently run below this target. In June 2021 the Bank of England published its strategy, which included becoming 'the first central bank to propose greening a monetary policy portfolio'.

Analysts had commented on 'the high degree of discretion that it (the ECB) enjoys compared to other central banks when it comes to introducing new policy instruments' (Cohen-Setton et al., 2019, p. 5). This contrasts with the earlier narrative of the ECB's constraints given its narrow mandate and the lack of a euro area Treasury to back up its decisions.

In January 2020, the ECB announced it would undertake a strategy review, its first since 2003. Citing the changed economic environment that included historically low interest rates which reduced their room for manoeuvre, climate change, globalization, digitalization, and changing financial structures, the ECB could have added public opinion to the mix; indeed, the ECB opened an ECB Listens Portal on 24 February 2020 to allow a wider range of views.

In July 2021 the ECB Governing Council approved the new monetary policy strategy. First, the ECB's 'below but close to 2 per cent' inflation target was replaced with a symmetric 2 per cent inflation target over the medium term. And while interest rates would continue to serve as the primary policy tool, the unconventional monetary policy measures, including asset purchases and longer-term refinancing operations, would 'remain an integral part of the ECB's toolkit'. Homeownership costs would be phased in eventually to calculate inflation. Finally, the ECB developed an action plan in which climate change would factor into its monetary policy framework and possibly inform future asset purchases.

For those who applauded the ECB's bold policies, unconventional monetary policy instruments are now considered conventional. No mention was made in the strategy review whether any of the self-imposed limits on its use would continue or if the flexibility it allowed itself in the PEPP would be its new normal. The addition of asset purchases to its policy toolkit demonstrates the success of the ECB in both extending the interpretation of its mandate and fulfilling the functions for which it was delegated. As noted in Section 10.2, governments delegate to independent central banks for a host of political reasons that are not limited to the pursuit of price stability. Indeed, the ability of the ECB to accrue additional instruments (and competences) during the euro crisis indicate its relative success, as judged by its political principals. Central banks provide market credibility and can provide critical information in political systems characterized by diverse political interests, such as in multiparty and federal systems. The euro area suffered from relative paralysis during the crisis as northern and southern European governments sought to defend their respective interests, and only the ECB could provide a rapid policy response that was accepted by markets and ultimately by its political principals. Despite mixed academic research indicating redistributive effects of its bond-purchases, both within and across Member States, bond purchase programmes were considered monetary policy and not economic policy. The ECB accordingly turned its unconventional monetary policy instruments into conventional ones.

10.7 CONCLUSION

The use of unconventional monetary policy contributed to the rise of the ECB as one of the key players in euro area governance, well beyond what the drafters of the Maastricht Treaty could have envisioned. Part of this can be linked to the role that central banks have played in general since the Global Financial Crisis. Indeed, the willingness of governments to implicitly delegate to their central banks primary responsibility for dealing with the market turbulence that ensued had longer-term consequences. The ECB initially approached crisis management cautiously, eschewing QE and voluntarily imposing limits on itself to avoid accusations of overreach and illegality.

The ECB's initial reluctance to assume the mantle of leadership gradually shifted to increasingly bold policies that made fuller use of its independence. ECB leadership likely would not have arisen without the abdication of leadership on the part of the EU Member States during the euro crisis. The ECB thus alternatively provided the euro area with a convenient scapegoat and *deus ex machina* in alleviating market tensions. The ECB has gone from a timid, self-restrained bond-buying programme in the SMP to the PEPP, which lacks any constraints on the ECB's discretion. No attempts have been made to change the ECB's accountability mechanisms, and the measures undertaken over the last decade were at the behest of the ECB itself.

By 2022 the economic environment had changed substantially, as inflation in the euro area (and elsewhere) surged and the ECB ended its new asset purchases. Nevertheless, the legacy of these bond-buying programmes has left the ECB as an institution with the discretion to interpret its mandate and to develop additional tools that could have a redistributive impact. Contrary to the original rhetoric of independent central banks as technocrats pursuing the public good of price stability, central banks (including the ECB) make decisions with important political ramifications. Moreover, the wide range of factors that feed into the monetary policy transmission further complicates ECB policy choices. In 2022, for example, the euro area faced rising inflation as well as financial fragmentation, something that the ECB had cited as a reason for intervention during the euro crisis due to its impact on the monetary transmission mechanism.

While during the euro crisis, low inflation and financial fragmentation had similar policy prescriptions of monetary easing, financial fragmentation and high inflation pose a conundrum for policymakers. Choosing to tackle inflation implies tighter monetary policy, including higher interest rates and an end to asset purchases under the PEPP and the PSPP. Financial fragmentation and rising spreads of bond yields across the euro area, however, complicates such choices and threaten political stability in some of the more vulnerable euro area Member States. The ECB announced its intention to implement a new anti-fragmentation tool in July 2022. The GFC taught policymakers how interrelated monetary policy is with financial stability, and the political consequences of monetary policy decisions merit additional political scrutiny.

The challenges of altering the central bank's independence could require a formal treaty change, which would be anathema to the Member States. Moreover, allowing the ECB to take control over the emergency response to crises had the benefit of speed and avoiding difficult domestic political obstacles. As a result, the ECB has been relatively unimpeded, and even supported, in the expansion of its policy toolkit. The biggest critics have come internally (from the German Bundesbank) and externally (from the German Constitutional Court), while its political principals have shown remarkable complacency.

The ECB's actions have been evaluated mainly on their economic and financial impact. This will not hold forever as a basis for its legitimacy, and political actors must be willing to hold the ECB to account. Central banks require scrutiny above and beyond voluntary measures of transparency.

REFERENCES

Alesina, A., and Summers, L. H. (1993). Central bank independence and macroeconomic performance: Some comparative evidence. *Journal of Money, Credit and Banking* 25(2), 151–162.

Amtenbrink, F. (2019). The European Central Bank's intricate independence versus accountability conundrum in the post-crisis governance framework. *Maastricht Journal of European and Comparative Law* 26(1), 165–179.

Armingeon, K., and Cranmer, S. (2018). Position-taking in the euro crisis. *Journal of European Public Policy* 25(4), 546–566.

Ban, C. (2021). Central banking in pandemic times. *Global Perspectives* 2(1): 24188.

Bastasin, C. (2015). *Saving Europe: Anatomy of a Dream*. Washington, DC: Brookings Institution.

Belke, A. (2010). Driven by the markets? ECB sovereign bond purchases and the securities markets programme. *Intereconomics* 45(6), 357–363.

Bell, V., Joyce, M., Liu, Z., and Young, C. (2012). The distributional effects of asset purchases. *Bank of England Quarterly Bulletin* 52(3), 254–266.

Bernanke, B. (2015). Monetary policy and inequality. Brookings Institution blog, 1 June.

Bernatavičius, M. (2021). Independence of the ECB and the ECJ during the sovereign debt crisis: From active leadership to rubber-stamping? *Journal of Common Market Studies* 59(3), 483–496.

Bernhard, W. T. (1998). A political explanation of variations in central bank independence. *American Political Science Review* 92(2), 311–327.

Bernhard, W. T. (2002). *Banking on Reform: Political Parties and Central Bank Independence in the Industrial Democracies*. Ann Arbor: University of Michigan Press.

Bernhard, W. T., Broz, J. L., and Clark, W. R. (2002). The political economy of monetary institutions. *International Organization* 56(4), 693–723.

Bickerton, C. J., Hodson, D., and Puetter, U. (eds.) (2015). *The New Intergovernmentalism: States and Supranational Actors in the Post-Maastricht Era*. Oxford: Oxford University Press.

Binder, S., and Spindel, M. (2017). *The Myth of Independence: How Congress Governs the Federal Reserve*. Princeton, NJ: Princeton University Press.

Blinder, A. S., Ehrmann, M., de Haan, J., and Jansen, D. (2017). Necessity as the mother of invention: Monetary policy after the crisis. *Economic Policy* 32(92), 707–755.

Bolsinger, H., Hoffmann, J., and Villhauer, B. (2021). *The European Central Bank as a Sustainability Role Model: Philosophical, Ethical and Economic Perspectives*. Cham: Springer.

Boone, L., and Rawdanowicz, Ł. (2021). Assessment of monetary and financial policy responses in advanced economies to the Covid-19 crisis. In B. English, K. Forbes, and A. Ubide (eds.), *Monetary Policy and Central Banking in the Covid Era*. London: CEPR Press, pp. 325–340.

Bowles, P., and White, G. (1994). Central bank independence: A political economy approach. *Journal of Development Studies* 31(2), 235–264.

Bulmer, S., and Paterson, W. E. (2013). Germany as the EU's reluctant hegemon? Of economic strength and political constraints. *Journal of European Public Policy* 20(10), 1387–1405.

Braun, B. (2013). Preparedness, crisis management and policy change: The euro area at the critical juncture of 2008–2013. *British Journal of Politics & International Relations* 17(3), 419–441.

Breuss, F. (2017). The crisis management of the ECB. In N. da Costa Cabral, J. Renato Gonçalves, and N. Cunha Rodrigues (eds.), *The Euro and the Crisis: Perspectives for the Eurozone as a Monetary and Budgetary Union*. Heidelberg: Springer-Verlag, pp. 199–221.

Brunnermeier, M., James, H., and Landau, J.-P. (2016). *The Euro and the Battle of Ideas*. Princeton, NJ: Princeton University Press.

Buiter, W. H. (1999). Alice in Euroland. *Journal of Common Market Studies* 37(2), 181–209.

Bundesbank (2021). Annual Report 2020.

Chang, K. H. (2003). *Appointing Central Bankers: The Politics of Monetary Policy in the US and the EMU*. New York: Cambridge University Press.

Chang, M. (2009). *Monetary Integration in the European Union*. Houndmills: Palgrave Macmillan.

Chang, M. (2018). The creeping competence of the European Central Bank during the euro crisis. *Credit and Capital* 51(1), 41–53.

Chang, M., and Hodson, D. (2018). Reforming the European Parliament's monetary and economic dialogues: Creating accountability through a euro area oversight subcommittee. In O. Costa (ed.), *The European Parliament in Times of EU Crisis: Dynamics and Transformations*. London: Palgrave, pp. 343–364.

Chang, M., and Leblond, P. (2015). All in: Market expectations of eurozone integrity in the sovereign debt crisis. *Review of International Political Economy* 22(3), 626–655.

Churm, R., Joyce, M., Kapetanios, G., and Theodoridis, K. (2021). Unconventional monetary policies and the macroeconomy: The impact of the UK's QE2 and funding for lending scheme. *Quarterly Review of Economics and Finance* 80, 721–736.

Claeys, G., Hallerberg, M., and Tschekassin, O. (2014). European Central Bank accountability: How the monetary dialogue could be improved. Bruegel Policy Contribution.

Cohen-Setton, J., Collins, C. G., and Gagnon, J. E. (2019). Priorities for review of the ECB's monetary policy strategy. Peterson Institute for International Economics, 1 December.

Colciago, A., Samarina, A., and de Haan, J. (2019). Central bank policies and income and wealth inequality: A survey. *Journal of Economic Surveys* 33(4), 1199–1231.

Collignon, S., and Diessner, S. (2016). The ECB's monetary dialogue with the European Parliament: Efficiency and accountability during the euro crisis? *Journal of Common Market Studies* 54(6), 1296–1312.

Conti, A., Neri, S., and Nobili, A. (2017). Low inflation and monetary policy in the euro area. ECB Working Paper No. 2005.

Court of Justice of the European Union (2015). The OMT programme announced by the ECB in September 2012 is compatible with EU law. Press release No. 70/15.

Craig, P., and Markakis, M. (2016). Gauweiler and the legality of outright monetary transactions. *European Law Review* 41(1), 4–24.

Cukierman, A. (1992). *Central Bank Strategy, Credibility and Independence*. Cambridge, MA: MIT Press.

Cukierman, A., Webb, S. B., and Neyapti, B. (1992). Measuring central bank independence and its effect on policy outcomes. *World Bank Economic Review* 6(3), 353–398.

Dawson, M., and Bobić, A. (2019). Quantitative easing at the Court of Justice – Doing whatever it takes to save the euro: Weiss and others. *Common Market Law Review* 56, 1005–1040.

Dawson, M., Bobić, A., and Maricut-Akbik, A. (2019). Reconciling independence and accountability at the European Central Bank: The false promise of Proceduralism. *European Law Journal* 25(1), 75–93.

De Grauwe, P., and Ji, Y. (2013). From panic-driven austerity to symmetric macroeconomic policies in the eurozone. *Journal of Common Market Studies* 51, 31–41.

De Grauwe, P., and Ji, Y. (2015). Correcting for the eurozone design failures: The role of the ECB. *Journal of European Integration* 37(7), 739–754.

De Haan, J. (1997). The European Central Bank: Independence, accountability and strategy: A review. *Public Choice* 9(3–4), 395–426.

De Haan, J., and Eijffinger, S. C. W. (2019). The politics of central bank independence. In R. D. Congleton, B. Grofman, and S. Voigt (eds.), *The Oxford Handbook of Public Choice*, Vol. 2, Oxford: Oxford University Press.

De Haan, J., and Eijffinger, S. C. W. (2000). The democratic accountability of the European Central Bank: A comment on two fairy tales. *Journal of Common Market Studies* 38(3), 393–407.

De Haan, J., Bodea, C., Hicks, R., and Eijffinger, S. C. W. (2018). Central bank independence before and after the crisis. *Comparative Economic Studies* 60(2), 183–202.

Dietsch, P. 2020. Independent agencies, distribution, and legitimacy: The case of central banks. *American Political Science Review* 114(2), 591–595.

Dincer, N. N., and Eichengreen, B. (2014). Central bank transparency and independence: Updates and new measures. *International Journal of Central Banking* (March), 189–253.

ECB (2002). The accountability of the ECB. *Monthly Bulletin* (November), 45–57.

ECB (2012). Technical features of outright monetary transactions. 6 September.

ECB (2015). ECB announces expanded asset purchase programme. 22 January. Available at: www.ecb.europa.eu/press/pr/date/2015/html/pr150122_1.en.html. Last accessed on 25 June 2023.

ECB (2020). Pandemic Emergency Purchase Programme. Available at/ www.ecb.europa.eu/mopo/implement/pepp/html/index.en.html. Last accessed on 25 June 2023.

Eijffinger, S. C. W., and de Haan, J. (1996). *The Political Economy of Central-Bank Independence*. Princeton, NJ: Department of Economics, Princeton University.

Elgie, R. (1998). Democratic accountability and central bank independence: Historical and contemporary, national and European perspectives. *West European Politics* 21(3), 53–76.

Elliott, L., and Tremlett, G. (2012). Angela Merkel and Francois Hollande pledge to safeguard embattled euro. The Guardian 27 July. Available at: https://www.theguardian.com/business/2012/jul/27/debt-crisis-emu. Last accessed on 25 June 2023.

Engen, E. M., Laubach, T., and Reifschneider, D. L. (2015). The macroeconomic effects of the Federal Reserve's unconventional monetary policies. Finance and Economics Discussion Series 2015-5.

European Commission (2017). Reflection paper on the deepening of the economic and monetary union. Brussels, 31 May.

European Parliament (2013a). Report on 2011 Annual Report of the European Central Bank. 25 February.

European Parliament (2013b). Report on 2012 Annual Report of the European Central Bank. 13 November.

European Parliament (2016a). Effectiveness of the ECB Programme of Asset Purchases: Where do we stand? Monetary Dialogue, Compilation of Notes. June 2016.

European Parliament (2016b). Report on the European Central Bank Annual Report for 2015 (2016/2063 (INI)).

European Parliament (2020). Report on the European Central Bank Annual Report for 2018 (2019/2129 (INI)).

European Parliament (2021). Report on the European Central Bank Annual Report 2020 (2020/2123 (INI)).

European Parliament (2022). European Parliament resolution of 16 February 2022 on the European Central Bank – annual report 2021 (2021/2063 (INI)).

Fernández-Albertos, J. (2015). The politics of central bank independence. *Annual Review of Political Science* 18(1), 217–237.

Ferrara, F. M. (2020). The battle of ideas on the euro crisis: Evidence from ECB inter-meeting speeches. *Journal of European Public Policy* 27(10), 1463–1486.

Ferrara, F. M., Masciandaro, D., Moschella, M., and Romelli, D. (2021). Political voice on monetary policy: Evidence from the parliamentary hearings of the European Central Bank. *European Journal of Political Economy* art. no. 102143.

Fontan, C., and Howarth, D. (2021). The European Central Bank and the German Constitutional Court: police patrols and fire alarms. *Politics and Governance* 9(2). https://doi.org/10.17645/pag.v9i2.3888

Fontan, C., Carré, E., and L'Oeillet, G. (2018). Theoretical perspectives on the new era of central banking. *French Politics* 16, 453–470.

Fraccaroli, N., Giovannini, A., and Jamet, J.-F. (2018). The evolution of the ECB's accountability practices during the crisis. *ECB Economic Bulletin* (5/2018), 47–71.

Fratzscher, M. (2020). Taking the German Constitutional Court seriously. *Project Syndicate*, 12 May.

Fromage, D., Dermine, P., Nicolaides, P., and Tuori, K. (2019). ECB independence and accountability today: towards a (necessary) redefinition? *Maastricht Journal of European and Comparative Law* 26(1), 3–16.

Gabor, D. (2014). The ECB and the political economy of collateral. In C. Goodhart, D. Gabor, J. Vestergaard, and I. Ertürk (eds.), *Central Bank at a Crossroads: Europe and Beyond*. London: Anthem Press, pp. 157–176.

Garcia Pascual, A., and Wieladek, T. (2016). The European Central Bank's QE: A new hope. CEPR Discussion Papers.

Genovese, F., Schneider, G., and Wassmann, P. (2016). The Eurotower strikes back: Crises, adjustments, and Europe's austerity protests. *Comparative Political Studies* 49(7), 939–967.

Giovannini, A., and Jamet, J.-F. (2020). Matching accountability with independence: The ECB's experience. *Il Politico (Univ. Pavia)* 1, 103–121.

Goodman, J. B. (1991). The politics of central bank independence. *Comparative Politics* 23(3), 329–349.

Grilli, V., Masciandaro, D., and Tabellini, G. (1991). Political and monetary institutions and public financial policies in the industrial countries. *Economic Policy* (13), 342–391.

Grund, S. (2020). Legal, compliant and suitable: The ECB's Pandemic Emergency Purchase Programme (PEPP). Hertie School Policy Brief, 25 March.

Hallerberg, M. (2002). Veto players and the choice of monetary institutions. *International Organization* 56(4), 775–802.

Heidebrecht, S. (2019). Balancing independence and legitimacy. *Zeitschrift für Politikwissenschaft* 29(3), 393–410.

Heins, E., and de la Porte, C. (2015). The sovereign debt crisis, the EU and welfare state reform. *Comparative European Politics* 13(1), 1–7.

Heldt, E. C., and Mueller, T. (2021). The (self-)empowerment of the European Central Bank during the sovereign debt crisis. *Journal of European Integration* 43(1), 83–98.

Heldt, E. C., and Müller,. T. (2022). Bringing independence and accountability together: Mission impossible for the European Central Bank? *Journal of European Integration* 44(6), 837–853.

Henning, C. R. (2016). The ECB as a strategic actor: Central banking in a politically fragmented monetary union. In J. A. Caporaso and M. Rhodes (eds.), *Political and Economic Dynamics of the Eurozone Crisis*. Oxford: Oxford University Press, pp. 167–199.

Hilmi, N., Djoundourian, S., Shahin, W., and Safa, A. (2022). Does the ECB policy of quantitative easing impact environmental policy objectives? *Journal of Economic Policy Reform* 25(3), 259–271.

Hodson, D. (2015). De novo bodies and the new intergovernmentalism: The case of the European Central Bank. In C. J. Bickerton, D. Hodson, and U. Puetter (eds.), *The New Intergovernmentalism: States and Supranational Actors in the Post-Maastricht Era*. Oxford: Oxford University Press, pp. 263–285.

Högenauer, A.-L., and Howarth, D. (2019). The democratic deficit and European Central Bank crisis monetary policies. *Maastricht Journal of European and Comparative Law* 26(1), 81–93.

Howarth, D. (2009). The European Central Bank: The bank that rules Europe? In K. Dyson and M. Marcusen (eds.), *Central Banks in the Age of the Euro: Europeanization, Convergence, & Power*. Oxford: Oxford University Press, pp. 73–88.

Howarth, D. J., and Loedel, P. (2005). *The European Central Bank: The New European Leviathan?* New York: Palgrave.

Hu, K. (2014). The institutional innovation of the lender of last resort facility in the eurozone. *Journal of European Integration* 36(7), 627–640.

Issing, O. (1999). The Eurosystem: Transparent and accountable or 'Willem in Euroland'. *Journal of Common Market Studies* 37(3), 503–319.

Jacobs, L., and King, D. (2021). *Fed Power: How Finance Wins*, 2nd ed. New York: Oxford University Press.

Johnston, A., and Regan, A. (2016). European monetary integration and the incompatibility of national varieties of capitalism. *Journal of Common Market Studies* 54(2), 318–336.

Jones, E., and Matthijs, M. (2019). Beyond central bank independence: Rethinking technocratic legitimacy in monetary affairs. *Journal of Democracy* 30(2), 127–141.

Jones, E., Kelemen, D. R., and Meunier, S. (2016). Failing forward? The euro crisis and the incomplete nature of European integration. *Comparative Political Studies* 49(7), 1010–1034.

Jourdan, S., and Diessner, S. (2019). From dialogue to scrutiny: Strengthening the parliamentary oversight of the European Central Bank. *Positive Money Europe*, 9 April. www.positivemoney.eu/wp-content/uploads/2019/04/2019_From-Dialogue-to-Scrutiny_PM_Web.pdf

Juncker, J.-C., Tusk, D., Dijsselbloem, J., Draghi, M., and Schulz, M. (2015). Completing Europe's Economic and Monetary Union, 22 June. edited by European Commission. Brussels.

Keefer, P., and Stasavage, D. (2003). The limits of delegation: Veto players, central bank independence, and the credibility of monetary policy. *American Political Science Review* 97(3), 407–424.

Kirshner, J. (ed.) (2003). *Monetary Orders*. Ithaca, NY: Cornell University Press.

Krampf, A. (2014). From the Maastricht Treaty to post-crisis EMU: The ECB and Germany as drivers of change. *Journal of Contemporary European Studies* 22(3), 303–317.

Lagarde, C. (2020). Tweet on 12 March. Available at https://twitter.com/ecb/status/1238105175363129352?lang=en. Last accessed on 25 June 2023.

Lane, P. R. (2021a). The monetary policy response in the euro area. In B. English, K. Forbes and A. Ubide (eds.), *Monetary Policy and Central Banking in the Covid Era*. London: CEPR Press, pp. 81–91.

Lane, P. R. (2021b). The resilience of the euro. *Journal of Economic Perspectives* 35(2), 3–22.

Lastra, R., Wyplosz, C., Claeys, G., Dominguez, M., and Whelan, K. (2020). Accountability mechanisms of major central banks and possible avenues to improve the ECB's accountability. Study requested by the European Parliament's Committee on Economic and Monetary Affairs September www.europarl.europa.eu/RegData/etudes/STUD/2020/652748/IPOL_STU(2020)652748_EN.pdf

Lohmann, S. (1992). Optimal commitment in monetary policy: Credibility versus flexibility. *American Economic Review* 82(1), 273–286.

Ludlow, P. (2010). In the last resort: The European Council and the euro crisis. Spring 2010. *Eurocomment European Council Briefing Note* 7(7/8), 1–62.

Mabbett, D., and Schelkle, W. (2019). Independent or lonely? Central banking in crisis. *Review of International Political Economy* 26(3), 436–460.

Macchiarelli, C., Monti, M., Wiesner, C., and Diessner, S. (2020). *The European Central Bank between the Financial Crisis and Populisms*. London: Palgrave.

Markakis, M. (2020). *Accountability in the Economic and Monetary Union: Foundations, Policy, and Governance*. Oxford: Oxford University Press.

Maurer, A. (2013). From EMU to DEMU: The democratic legitimacy of the EU and the European Parliament. IAI Working Paper 13.

Mehrling, P. (2010). *The New Lombard Street: How the Fed Became the Dealer of Last Resort*. Princeton, NJ: Princeton University Press.

Mody, A. (2014). Did the German court do Europe a favour? Bruegel Working Paper 2014/09.

Moser, P. (1999). Checks and balances, and the supply of central bank independence. *European Economic Review* 43, 1569–1593.

Nicoli, F. (2020). Neofunctionalism revisited: integration theory and varieties of outcomes in the Eurocrisis. *Journal of European Integration* 42(7), 897–916.

Pisani-Ferry, J. (2014). *Utopia Untangled: The Euro Crisis and Its Aftermath*. Oxford: Oxford University Press.

Pisani-Ferry, J. (2020). The message in the ruling. Bruegel opinion, 12 May.

Posen, A. (1993). Why central bank independence does not cause low inflation: The politics behind the institutional fix. In R. O'Brien (ed.), *Finance and the International Economy*. Oxford: Oxford University Press, pp. 41–65.

Rauh, C. (2022). Supranational emergency politics? What executives' public crisis communication may tell us. *Journal of European Public Policy* 29(6), 966–978.

Reisenbichler, A. (2020). The politics of quantitative easing and housing stimulus by the Federal Reserve and European Central Bank, 2008–2018. *West European Politics* 43(2), 464–484.

Reuters. (2012). Merkel, Hollande vow to do everything to defend euro. 27 July. Available at https://www.reuters.com/article/us-eurozone-france-germany-idUSBRE86Q0GO20120727. Last accessed on 25 June 2023.

Schelkle, W. (2013). Fiscal integration by default. In P. Genschel and M. Jachtenfuchs (eds.), *Beyond the Regulatory Polity? The European Integration of Core State Powers*. Oxford: Oxford University Press, pp. 105–123.

Schimmelfennig, F. (2015). Liberal intergovernmentalism and the euro area crisis. *Journal of European Public Policy* 22(2), 177–195.

Schlosser, P. (2019). *Europe's New Fiscal Union*. London: Palgrave.

Schmidt, V. A. (2020). *Europe's Crisis of Legitimacy: Governing by Rules and Ruling by Numbers in the Eurozone*. Oxford: Oxford University Press.

Schmidt, V. A. (2022). European emergency politics and the question of legitimacy. *Journal of European Public Policy* 29(6), 979–993.

Schnabel, I. (2020). The shadow of fiscal dominance: Misconceptions, perceptions and perspectives. Speech by Isabel Schnabel, Member of the Executive Board of the ECB, at the Centre for European Reform and the Eurofi Financial Forum on 'Is the current ECB monetary policy doing more harm than good and what are the alternatives?' Berlin, 11 September.

Schoeller, M. G. (2018). Leadership by default: The ECB and the announcement of outright monetary transactions. *Credit and Capital Markets – Kredit und Kapital* 51 (1), 73–91.

Schoeller, M. G. (2020). Tracing leadership: The ECB's 'whatever it takes' and Germany in the Ukraine crisis. *West European Politics* 43(5), 1095–1116.

Schwarzer, D. (2012). The euro area crises, shifting power relations and institutional change in the European Union. *Global Policy* 3 (Supplement s1), 28–41.

Scicluna, N. (2018). Integration through the disintegration of law? The ECB and EU constitutionalism in the crisis. *Journal of European Public Policy* 25(12), 1874–1891.

Smeets, D., and Zimmermann, M. (2013). Did the EU summits succeed in convincing the markets during the recent crisis? *Journal of Common Market Studies* 51(6), 1158–1177.

Stark, J. (2012). The ECB's OMTs (out-of-mandate transactions). *International Economy* 26(4), 52–83.

Tesche, T. (2019). Instrumentalizing EMU's democratic deficit: The ECB's unconventional accountability measures during the eurozone crisis. *Journal of European Integration* 41(4), 447–463.

Tortola, P. D., and Pansardi, P. (2019). The charismatic leadership of the ECB presidency: A language-based analysis. *European Journal of Political Research* 58, 96–116.

Tooze, A. (2020). The death of the central bank myth. *Foreign Policy*, 13 May.

Tucker, P. (2018). *Unelected Power: The Quest for Legitimacy in Central Banking and the Regulatory State*. Princeton, NJ: Princeton University Press.

Van Doorslaer, H., and Vermeiren, M. (2021). Pushing on a string: Monetary policy, growth models and the persistence of low inflation in advanced capitalism. *New Political Economy* 26(5), 779–816.

Van Rompuy, H., Barroso, J. M., Juncker, J.-C., and Draghi, M. (2012). Towards a genuine economic and monetary union. Brussels, 5 December.

Verdun, A. (2017). Political leadership of the European Central Bank. *Journal of European Integration* 39 (2), 207–221.

Walter, S., Ray, A., and Redeker, N. (2020). *The Politics of Bad Options: Why the Eurozone's Problems Are So Hard to Resolve*. Oxford: Oxford University Press.

Whelan, K. (2014). The monetary dialogue and accountability for the ECB. Paper prepared for the European Parliament's Committee on Economic and Monetary Affairs, IP/A/ECON/NT/2014-01.

Wyplosz, C. (2015). ECB minutes: What they really tell us. voxEU, 2 March.

Yiangou, J., O'Keeffe, M., and Glöckler, G. (2013). 'Tough love': How the ECB's monetary financing prohibition pushes deeper euro area integration. *Journal of European Integration* 35(3), 223–237.

11

ECB Monetary Policies

The Increasing Importance of Communication

Jakob de Haan

11.1 INTRODUCTION

Over the past two decades, monetary policy has increasingly become the art of managing expectations (Svensson, 2006). As a consequence, central bank communication has become an important instrument in central banks' toolkits.[1] The European Central Bank (ECB) is no exception. Central bank communication can be defined as the provision of information by the central bank to the public on the objectives of monetary policy, the monetary policy strategy, the economic outlook, and the outlook for future policy decisions (Blinder et al., 2008). Central banks can choose from a large menu of communication instruments, such as press releases, speeches, official reports, and interviews, and each central bank uses its own mixture of these.

There are several reasons why central bankers talk a lot more than they used to do in the past. The first reason is the introduction of unconventional monetary policies. As these policies are more complex and controversial than conventional monetary policies, central banks needed to explain and justify them more extensively (Blinder et al., 2017). More communication was also required in view of the broader mandates of central banks (like maintaining financial stability through macroprudential policy). Central bank accountability is thus an important reason for increased central bank communication. As Goodhart and Lastra (2018, pp. 3–4) argue:

> While the initial legal basis "legitimizes" the establishment of the independent central bank, it cannot by itself legitimize on an ongoing basis the exercise of the powers delegated to such agency. It is then in the continuing life of that entity that accountability becomes necessary to ensure legitimacy. An accountable central bank must give account, explain and justify the actions or decisions taken, against criteria of some kind, and take responsibility for any fault or damage.

Communication enhances central bank transparency, which, in turn, is a key ingredient of (but not the same as) accountability, as argued in Section 11.4 of this chapter.

A second reason for increased central bank communication is the view that it may be used to manage expectations about interest rates and inflation. Even though central banks only have control over short-term interest rates, they can use communication to influence expectations

I would like to thank Dariusz Adamski and Fabian Amtenbrink for their feedback on a previous version of this chapter.

[1] In their survey among central bank heads, Blinder et al. (2017) find that more than 90 per cent of governors in advanced economies feel that communication had intensified since the financial crisis, and 60 per cent expect these changes to remain, or to go even further.

about future short-term interest rates, thereby affecting long-term interest rates. Long-term interest rates, reflecting expected future short-term interest rates, affect saving and investment decisions by households and firms. Therefore, the perception of future policy rates is critical for the effectiveness of monetary policy. In addition, central bank communication may affect inflation expectations. Inflation expectations are important, as they will affect actual inflation. Very simply, if economic agents expect an inflation rate of, say, 2 per cent and behave accordingly, actual inflation will move toward this rate. Anchoring of inflation expectations, i.e. inflation expectations that are in line with the inflation target of the central bank, prevents a fall in nominal short-term interest rates to be associated with a medium-term weakening of the economic situation and thus a decline in inflation expectations. Nowadays, many central bankers consider communication a potentially very effective instrument. However, Issing (2019, p. 69) argues: 'There is a risk that central banks ... regard communication as a priority. However, monetary policy comes first – the tail must not wag the dog.'

A final reason why central bankers talk more is that central bank communication may enhance credibility and trust. A survey among former members of the Governing Council of the ECB by Ehrmann et al. (2021) shows that, according to former ECB Governing Council members, the most important objective of monetary policy communication is enhancing credibility and trust. Some 70 per cent of respondents felt this was 'extremely important', while another 22 per cent answered 'very important'. This is quite remarkable, as academic research to date has hardly examined the impact of central bank communication on trust.

Central bank communication was initially primarily focused on financial markets. Recently, however, central banks started paying increasing attention to communication with the general public. ECB President Christine Lagarde even stated that the general public is the 'new frontier' for central bank communication, arguing: 'Central banks have to be understood by the people whom they ultimately serve. This is a key to rebuilding trust.'[2] Issing (2019, p. 69) is less optimistic: 'Expecting central banks to ever reach the general public in an all-encompassing way, using every information channel from town hall meetings to TV, is an illusion.'

This chapter discusses (research on) ECB communication. It first zooms in on the ECB's monetary policies, as this will help explain why communication has become so prominent. Section 11.3 examines ECB information policy, focusing on communication with the general public. Section 11.4 zooms in on how communication contributes to the accountability of the ECB. Section 11.5 summarizes research on trust in the ECB. Section 11.6 concludes.

11.2 THE ECB'S MONETARY POLICIES

11.2.1 *The Same Legal Primary Objective but Different Definitions*

The primary objective of the ECB is maintaining price stability in the euro area. As a subordinated – secondary – objective, the Eurosystem, i.e. the ECB and the national central banks of the countries in the euro area, is supposed to support the general economic policies in the EU, with a view to contributing to the achievement of the Union's objectives as laid down in Article 3 of the Treaty on European Union. These objectives include balanced economic growth, a highly competitive social market economy aiming at full employment and social

[2] See www.europarl.europa.eu/doceo/document/A-9-2019-0008_EN.html#title. The importance of trust was already stressed by Issing in 2000: 'a culture of openness and dialogue should help central banks to earn the trust of the wider public, which is particularly important for a central bank that is both new and independent' (Issing, 2000).

progress, a high level of protection, and improvement of the quality of the environment. The Treaty nevertheless falls short of providing a well-defined monetary objective the fulfilment of which could become subject to review. In fact, it is up to the ECB to define the objective of price stability.

One of the outcomes of the recent ECB monetary policy strategy review, as published in July 2021, is that the ECB's inflation objective has been changed. Before, i.e. since the previous strategy review of 2003, the ECB aimed for an inflation rate of close to, but below 2 per cent in the euro area in the medium term, where inflation is measured using the Harmonised Index of Consumer Prices (HICP).[3] Now the ECB Governing Council considers that price stability is best maintained by aiming for 2 per cent inflation over the medium term. So, the target is 'symmetric', which means that the Council considers negative and positive deviations from 2 per cent as equally undesirable. Furthermore, 'forceful or persistent monetary policy measures' have been announced, in particular when the economy is close to the so-called effective lower bound (ELB), to 'avoid negative deviations from the inflation target becoming entrenched'. This may also imply 'a transitory period in which inflation is moderately above target'.[4]

According to the ECB Governing Council, the 'primary monetary policy instrument is the set of ECB policy rates. In recognition of the effective lower bound on policy rates, the Governing Council will also employ in particular forward guidance, asset purchases and longer-term refinancing operations, as appropriate'.[5] Finally, the Council has confirmed that the HICP remains the appropriate measure for assessing the achievement of the price stability objective. However, it recognizes that the inclusion of the costs related to owner-occupied housing in the HICP would better represent the inflation rate that is relevant for households. It will be a number of years before Eurostat will revise the HICP by including owner-occupied housing. In the meantime, the Council will take into account inflation measures that include initial estimates of the cost of owner-occupied housing in its wider set of supplementary inflation indicators. The ECB acknowledges that including owner-occupied housing would have an impact of on average 0.2–0.3 percentage points (Issing, 2021).

How should these changes be assessed? Issing (2021) argues that 'The decision in favour of a symmetric target of 2% is a distinct signal that the ECB will tolerate – if not aim for – higher inflation. The concrete outcome remains to be seen, as do the consequences in terms of anchoring inflation expectations, the credibility of the ECB and public trust in the stability of the euro'. It seems likely that the new objective implies a higher inflation target. Under the previous formulation, 2 per cent was a threshold, while it is now a target. One can have serious doubts about this decision. How credible is it to raise the inflation target, while the ECB failed for many years to reach its previous target? Although the 'symmetry' is often regarded as a new element, it is not. For example, at the March 2016 press conference, then-ECB President Mario Draghi said that 'our mandate is defined as reaching an inflation rate which is close to 2% but below 2% in the medium term, which means that we'll have to define the medium term in a way that, if the inflation rate was for a long time below 2%, it will be above 2% for some time. The key point is that the Governing Council is symmetric in the definition of the objective of price stability over the medium term'.[6]

[3] Before the 2003 review, the ECB described price stability as a year-on-year increase in the HICP for the euro area of below 2 per cent, adding that price stability had to be maintained over the medium term.

[4] www.ecb.europa.eu/home/search/review/html/ecb.strategyreview_monpol_strategy_statement.en.html

[5] Ibid.

[6] www.ecb.europa.eu/press/pressconf/2016/html/is160310.en.html

Leaving the issue of raising the inflation target aside, perhaps more important is whether the new definition of price stability is sufficiently clear. That the target is now 2 per cent (instead of below but close to 2 per cent) may be considered a step in the right direction, as it makes the yardstick against which the ECB should be held accountable clearer (see Section 11.4). The same holds true for the inclusion of owner-occupied housing in the HICP. However, as argued by Angeloni and Gros (2021), the 'new central target – 2% with a symmetric but unspecified range around it – offers no clue to what deviation the ECB is willing to tolerate'. Furthermore, it is not clear how precisely the ECB will take owner-occupied housing into account until the HICP has been revised.

11.2.2 *Policy Instruments: Overview*

Under normal circumstances, the ECB's main instrument is its interest rate policy. Simply put, the ECB raises or lowers money market rates through the use of its instruments if inflation and economic developments so require (see chapter 4 in de Haan et al., 2020 for more details). In June 2014 and again in September 2014, the ECB lowered its deposit facility rate (the interest rate banks receive on their account at the ECB) by 10 basis points each time to –0.2 per cent. A negative deposit interest rate means that the ECB will charge banks for depositing their surplus liquidity with it. The ECB was the first major central bank to introduce negative interest rates, even if those from a few smaller countries, such as Denmark and Switzerland, had taken this step earlier.

However, there is a limit as to how low central banks' interest rates can go. This is because the nominal short-term interest rate cannot be lowered much below zero. This lower bound reflects that people will prefer to keep funds in the form of cash rather than to deposit them at a bank that charges negative rates on deposits. But central banks have more instruments at their disposal, such as asset purchase programmes, often referred to as quantitative easing (QE). As pointed out by Borio and Disyatat (2010), the distinguishing feature of these measures is that central banks actively use their balance sheets by purchasing securities (mainly government bonds) to affect market prices and conditions beyond a short-term interest rate.

The ECB introduced QE much later than other major central banks. Initially, its unconventional policies during the financial crisis mainly focused on sustaining the banking sector by providing liquidity to banks. The main reason is that the banking sector plays a fundamental role in the monetary transmission mechanism in the euro area, because non-financial corporations are highly dependent on bank credit. For instance, the ECB provided unlimited liquidity through 'fixed rate tenders with full allotment'. Thus, contrary to normal practice, banks had unlimited access to central bank liquidity at the main refinancing rate, subject to adequate collateral. After inflation in the euro area had dropped below 0 per cent, in January 2015 the ECB launched an expanded asset purchase programme (APP), encompassing its existing purchase programmes for asset-backed securities and covered bonds.

Apart from negative interest rates and QE, the ECB introduced other unconventional monetary policy instruments, such as targeted longer-term refinancing operations (TLTROs). Under this scheme, the amount banks can borrow from the central bank is linked to their loans to non-financial corporations and households. These operations offer banks long-term funding at attractive conditions to further ease private sector credit conditions and stimulate bank lending to the real economy.

The ECB also introduced forward guidance. The idea behind forward guidance can be explained as follows. Monetary policy works not only through the current setting of policy instruments, but also through expectations about the future course of policy, which affects, among other things, the yield curve, which relates the yield on a security to its time to maturity. Management of these expectations can therefore be a powerful tool once the central bank has already lowered short-term rates as much as it can (or wants to). If a central bank can commit to future values of the policy rate, it can work around the ELB constraint by promising to keep interest rates low in the future, i.e. once the ELB ceases to bind. However, there is a time-inconsistency problem. Once the ELB ceases to bind, the central bank's preferred policy is to have a positive interest rate, whereas the bank had promised to keep the interest rate at zero (or even below zero) during this period. Thus the central bank has an incentive to break its promise. And if markets believe the central bank will not stick to its promise, they may not adjust their expectations of future policy rates downward so that long-term rates will not come down. In other words, forward guidance is most effective if the central bank can convince markets that – like Odysseus who tied himself to the mast to withstand the song of the Sirens – it is committed to this policy and will not change course. Apart from *Odyssean forward guidance*, central banks may apply *Delphic forward guidance*. This means that they publish their forecasts of macroeconomic developments and their likely monetary policy actions without any commitment, reserving the right to re-optimize their plans in every future period. So the central bank acts in a similar way to the Delphic oracle, hence its name. However, this type of forward guidance may also affect private sector expectations. As long-term rates are more relevant for economic decisions than the current level of the overnight rate, any action by the central bank that influences interest rate expectations could be a potential tool of monetary policy, even if current short-term rates cannot be reduced any further (Blinder et al., 2008). Note that forward guidance can be applied for different policy instruments. Most frequently, it has been related to the future course of policy rates, but the ECB has also provided forward guidance in relation to its asset purchases (Coenen et al., 2017).

Central banks may apply three forms of forward guidance: (1) *qualitative* (or open-ended) *forward guidance*, where the central bank does not provide detailed quantitative information about the envisaged time frame for its policy intentions; (2) *calendar-based* (or time-contingent) *forward guidance*, where the central bank refers to a clearly specified time horizon for its policies; and (3) *threshold-based* (or data-based, state-contingent) *forward guidance*, where the central bank links future rates to specific quantitative economic thresholds. In practice, central banks often use more than one type of forward guidance (Moessner et al., 2017). This also holds for the ECB, as will be explained in more detail in the next section.

Finally, in response to the COVID-19 pandemic, central banks introduced several new measures, including unprecedented asset purchase programmes. The ECB's pandemic emergency purchase programme (PEPP) was initiated in March 2020 to counter the serious risks to the economic outlook for the euro area posed by the COVID-19 outbreak. The PEPP is a temporary asset purchase programme of private and public sector securities. The Governing Council decided to increase the initial €750 billion envelope for the PEPP by €600 billion on 4 June 2020 and by €500 billion on 10 December 2020, for a new total of €1,850 billion. All asset categories eligible under the existing APP are also eligible under the PEPP, while a waiver of the eligibility requirements has been granted for securities issued by the Greek government.

The ECB announced that for the purchases of public sector securities under the PEPP, the benchmark allocation across jurisdictions will be the Eurosystem capital key of the national central banks. At the same time, purchases will be conducted in 'a flexible manner on the basis of market conditions'. In practice, accumulated actual purchases hardly deviate from this benchmark (Mendez-Barreira, 2021). On 16 December 2021, the Governing Council decided to discontinue net asset purchases under the PEPP at the end of March 2022. The maturing principal payments from securities purchased under the PEPP will be reinvested until at least the end of 2024. The ECB decided to discontinue reinvestments under the APP as of July 2023.

11.3 ECB COMMUNICATION POLICIES

11.3.1 *Communication Instruments*

As Table 11.1 shows, ECB communication takes many forms, from policy statements and press conferences immediately after policy meetings, economic forecasts, and monetary policy (or inflation) reports, to speeches, interviews, and testimonies before parliament.

No doubt, the ECB policy statements and the president's introductory statements at the press conferences following Governing Council (GC) meetings about monetary policy receive most attention. Still, they are not easy to read. Coenen et al. (2017) report that ECB statements receive a Flesch–Kincaid score between 13 and 15. This score indicates how many years of formal training are required to understand the text, based on the length of its sentences and words used. Speeches of ECB Executive Board members have become more important. The average number of speeches per year increased from 88 before the crisis to 126 since 2007 (Bernoth and Dany-Knedli, 2020). Since 2015, the ECB has published the 'accounts' (minutes) of the Governing Councils' meetings. However, these minutes contain neither voting results on

TABLE 11.1 *Communication about monetary policy by the ECB*

Type	Communicator	Frequency	Release time
Policy statement	GC	After every GC meeting about monetary policy	Press release at 13.45
Press conference	President and vice president	Every six weeks	Starts at 14.30 after GC meeting
Minutes ('accounts')	GC	Every six weeks	About a month after GC meeting
Economic forecasts	ECB	Four times per year	In Economic Bulletins of March, June, September, and December
Economic Bulletin	GC	Eight times per year	Two weeks after GC meeting
Financial statement[a]	ECB	Weekly	
Testimony in European Parliament	President and vice president	Present annual report by vice president in ECON committee and by president in plenary debate; monetary dialogue with ECON;[b] ad hoc meetings	Yearly; quarterly
Speeches and interviews	All GC members	Infrequent	Not seven days before GC meeting

[a] The consolidated financial statement of the Eurosystem provides information on monetary policy operations, foreign exchange operations, and investment activities.
[b] Other ECB Executive Board members may also participate. ECON is the European Parliament's committee on Economic and Monetary Affairs. MPs can also address written questions to the ECB.

policy decisions nor individual statements of the Governing Council members in the decision process.

One of the challenges that the ECB communication faces is that the euro area is a multicultural and multilingual monetary union. As Issing (2000) puts it:

> Communication requires a common language. Now this already raises some particular issues to do with translation and the meaning of words in a multi-lingual context and, more generally, due to the diverse monetary policy and communication traditions that prevailed in the euro area. It is striking how the reporting in the media on the ECB continues to differ across countries and how often even identical information is interpreted very differently.

11.3.2 *Forward Guidance*

As pointed out in the previous section, the ECB provided forward guidance about its policies. Initially, this forward guidance was open ended. For a while, the Governing Council stated that monetary policy would be accommodative 'for as long as necessary'. However, in July 2013 the ECB announced that interest rates would remain at present or lower levels for 'an extended period of time'. This statement was used until January 2016 (Coenen et al., 2017). Later, the ECB's forward guidance on interest rates has become state (inflation) and time dependent (horizon). For instance, on 10 March 2016 the ECB stated that it 'expects the key ECB interest rates to remain at present or lower levels for an extended period of time, and well past the horizon of our net asset purchases'.[7] This statement links the future path of policy rates to the ECB's APP, which, at that time, was 'intended to run until the end of March 2017, or beyond, if necessary, and in any case until the Governing Council sees a sustained adjustment in the path of inflation consistent with its inflation aim'.[8] Likewise, when the Governing Council announced on 14 June 2018 that it would stop QE, it also stated that it expected policy rates to remain at their then-present levels at least through the summer of 2019 and, in any case, for as long as necessary to ensure the sustained convergence of inflation to levels that are below, but close to, 2 per cent (Hartmann and Smets, 2018). A similar statement was issued in September 2019: 'We now expect the key ECB interest rates to remain at their present or lower levels until we have seen the inflation outlook robustly converge to a level sufficiently close to, but below, 2% within our projection horizon, and such convergence has been consistently reflected in underlying inflation dynamics.'[9]

The ECB's strategy review (as discussed earlier) led to a new formulation of the ECB's forward guidance (Lane, 2021):

> In support of its symmetric two per cent inflation target and in line with its monetary policy strategy, the Governing Council expects the key ECB interest rates to remain at their present or lower levels until it sees inflation reaching two per cent well ahead of the end of its projection horizon and durably for the rest of the projection horizon, and it judges that realised progress in underlying inflation is sufficiently advanced to be consistent with inflation stabilising at two per cent over the medium term. This may also imply a transitory period in which inflation is moderately above target.

[7] www.ecb.europa.eu/press/pressconf/2016/html/is160310.en.html
[8] Ibid.
[9] www.ecb.europa.eu/press/pressconf/2019/html/ecb.is190912~658eb51d68.en.html

As pointed out by Lane (2021), this statement implies policy rates should not be lifted unless underlying inflation is also judged to have made satisfactory progress towards the target. 'This condition … provides an extra safeguard against a policy tightening in the face of cost-push shocks that might elevate headline inflation temporarily but fade quickly.' In other words, if inflation increases because of temporary factors, a lift-off is out of sight for the time being. This became relevant as inflation in the euro area started to rise in the second half of 2021. In October 2021, the ECB expected that inflation would be 'rising further in the near term, but then declining in the course of next year'. So, an interest rate lift-off was not to be expected soon. At the time, financial markets were not convinced by the ECB's forward guidance. This also worried members of the ECB Governing Council. According to the accounts of the meeting of 27–28 October 2021,

> Concerns were voiced that expectations regarding the future path of short-term money market interest rates were difficult to reconcile with the Governing Council's forward guidance on interest rates, with market participants anticipating a much earlier date for the first rate increase than at the time of the Governing Council's September meeting. The question was raised as to whether market participants might misunderstand the three conditions laid out in the Governing Council's forward guidance that had to be satisfied before the first increase in policy rates.[10]

At the beginning of 2022, inflation in the euro area increased further. In January 2022, the HICP increase stood at 5.1 per cent (year-on-year), while in April inflation was 7.5 per cent. Whereas some other central banks in advanced economies facing similar inflation hikes decided to increase their policy rates, the ECB Governing Council's monetary policy statement after the February 2022 meeting was almost identical to the statement issued after the December meeting, stressing that the ECB expected higher inflation to be temporary. However, later on, the ECB changed its view. In a speech in May 2022, Lagarde expected that inflation will 'likely to remain high for some time' and that therefore the ECB would end net asset purchases early in the third quarter of 2022 (although PEPP was stopped, under the APP the ECB was still purchasing assets).[11] Within 'only a few weeks thereafter' an interest rate hike was likely. Indeed, since then, the ECB has increased its policy rates several times in view of the persistently high inflation and stopped providing forward guidance; future policy rate decisions will be 'data-dependent' and the ECB will follow 'a meeting-by-meeting approach'.[12]

11.3.3 *Communicating with the General Public: Doomed to Fail?*

The ECB provides a lot of information on its policies, but providing information is not the same as effective communication with the general public (Blinder et al., 2022). What does the ECB do to reach out to the general public?

Although its policy statements may be too difficult to understand for most people, the ECB publishes so-called explainers on its website, i.e. short and clear explanations on specific issues related to the ECB's tasks and activities. Apart from their websites, central banks also increasingly use social media in their communication with the general public. The Eurosystem is no exception. In their analysis of the use of Twitter among European central banks, Korhonen and Newby (2019) show that disseminating official statements was the most common motivation

[10] www.ecb.europa.eu/press/accounts/2021/html/ecb.mg211125~ca9833f9a9.en.html

[11] www.ecb.europa.eu/press/key/date/2022/html/ecb.sp220511~4c8d4500f6.en.html

[12] www.ecb.europa.eu/press/pr/date/2023/html/ecb.mp230202~08a972ac76.en.html

for central banks for using Twitter, followed by promoting publications and research, media appearances of personnel and job opening announcements. Although emerging-market central banks, and particularly those from Latin America, appear to be the most active on Twitter (Kyriakopolou and Ortlieb, 2019), the ECB is also in the top five of most active central banks. The ECB tries to engage with its audience by participating in Q&As (#AsktheECB#). Ehrmann and Wabitsch (2021) analyse ECB-related Twitter traffic, where they are able to differentiate tweets issued by experts and by non-experts. They provide evidence that Twitter traffic by non-experts is responsive to the ECB's communication. In general, following communication events by the ECB, the discussion on Twitter becomes more factual. However, these authors also report that tweets are more likely to get retweeted if they express strong views about the ECB and if they are less factual.

When she explained the ECB's monetary policy strategy review to the European Parliament, the ECB president said that 'to further enhance our transparency and ensure that we are aware of citizens' expectations and concerns in relation to our policies, we have modernised our communication policy and we will make outreach events a structural feature of our interaction with the public' (Lagarde, 2021). The president refers to the listening events across the euro area that the ECB organized as part of its strategy review. As the website of the ECB explains: 'During our Listening events, we heard and discussed the concerns of civil society and people at large. Learning directly from people about their worries and what they expect from their central bank has expanded our views of how to conduct our policy. That is why we are making listening a regular feature of our communication.'[13] One of the outcomes of the strategy review is that the ECB 'will make greater efforts to explain our monetary policy in less technical and more understandable terms, so that people can see why we are taking our decisions and what that means for their lives. ... That is why the Governing Council agreed to modernise our communication and make it more understandable'.[14]

The ECB also launched the 'ECB Listens Portal' as part of its strategy review, encouraging the general public to express their views on a range of issues. When asked about ways to improve communication with the public, nearly 40 per cent of respondents suggested explaining policies in simple language and with relatable, concrete examples. This percentage was remarkably constant across different socio-demographic groups. When asked whether they felt well informed about the ECB, almost 50 per cent of respondents affirmed they were inadequately informed or not informed at all.

The latter finding suggests the need for better communication. There seems to be consensus in the literature that communication with the general public should be less technical than communication with experts. Simple messages – as simple as one sentence informing agents about the central bank's inflation target or recent inflation – can be much more effective in influencing beliefs than complex statements (Candia et al., 2020). Based on a large-scale online experiment with a sample representative of the UK population, Bholat et al. (2019) report that the simplification of central bank communication increases public comprehension more than the inclusion of visuals, and that public comprehension can be improved by making monetary policy messages relatable to people's lives. Likewise, Haldane et al. (2020) argue that simplifying communication in itself is not enough. They propose that central banks invest in what they call the three E's: Explanation, Engagement, and Education. Haldane and McMahon (2018) report supportive evidence for this approach. They conclude that a layered set-up of the Bank of

[13] www.ecb.europa.eu/home/search/review/html/monpol-communication.en.html

[14] Ibid.

England's Inflation Report, where some of these layers are targeted to less specialist audiences, improves understanding.

But even if the ECB's communication were to change in this direction, there is serious doubt whether it will reach the general public. The reason is that, in contrast to financial market participants and professional forecasters, households and firms seem to have a low desire to be informed by the ECB (Van der Cruijsen et al., 2015) and are relatively inattentive to information concerning monetary policy and inflation dynamics. Consequently, if the public ignore central bank information and thus do not process it, communication cannot be effective. As Blinder (2018, p. 569) puts it, 'in truth, the part of central bank communication that matters most is the way policymakers communicate with markets – and for a simple reason: market participants listen'.

This can also be explained by theory (Blinder et al., 2022). It may be rational for the public not to pay attention to the central bank. According to the rational inattention theory, households and firms are more likely to pay attention to communication if they believe that this will benefit them and if they find it not very costly to do so. On the benefits side, households and firms are more likely to pay attention to central bank communications if they believe these communications will improve their ability to make decisions. However, if households and firms do not understand what the central bank is aiming for, how its policies affect economic conditions, and how these conditions, in turn, affect them personally, they will be less attentive (Binder, 2017). The public generally have a low understanding of central banks' objectives and policies (Van der Cruijsen et al., 2015), making it hard for the public to understand how information communicated will affect them personally, thus lowering the perceived benefits of engaging in the communication. Likewise, consumers may not consider the central bank responsible for economic developments, so that they may not pay attention to the central bank when gathering input for economic decision-making (Binder, 2017). Furthermore, as pointed out by Coibion et al. (2020), successful monetary policy breeds inattention to monetary policy: economic agents in countries with long histories of low and stable inflation have little incentive to track inflation and monetary policy decisions and tend to be systematically less well informed about these than those living in countries with high or volatile inflation.

Still, several studies report that central bank communication with the general public helps anchor inflation expectations. This evidence suggests that inflation expectations shift towards the central bank's inflation target when people receive information about: the ECB's inflation target (Baerg et al., 2020) and the ECB's monetary policy instruments (Brouwer and de Haan, 2022). However, this evidence is based on *randomized controlled trials* (RCTs) and therefore *assumes* that the central bank's signal is received. Participants are confronted with a message (or deliberately do not receive this message, to generate a control group), and then can react to it (or not). However, it is very likely that the public will not receive the information from the central bank or will not understand it properly, so that central bank communication may not affect expectations.

A few studies examining the impact of central bank communication on households' or firms' expectations rely on other methodologies than RCTs. For instance, Enders et al. (2019) find that ECB surprises about unconventional monetary policy hardly affect expectations of German manufacturing firms and to the extent that they do, they *lowered* expectations of their own prices and production. However, interest rate surprises impact firm expectations significantly, but the strength of the effect declines as the surprise becomes bigger, both for positive and negative surprises. Enders et al. also find that favourable central bank news about the economy raises price expectations but does not affect output expectations.

11.4 ACCOUNTABILITY

11.4.1 *Objective as Yardstick for Accountability*

Among monetary policymakers there is a broad consensus that central banks should have instrument independence, i.e. they should be able to decide on the use of monetary policy instruments without political interferences. This view is based on the belief that central bank independence leads to superior macroeconomic outcomes.

Economists consider delegating monetary policy to an independent central bank that has a clear mandate to strive for price stability as a commitment device. With an independent and inflation-averse central bank in charge of monetary policy, the inflation bias due to the so-called time-inconsistency problem is much less than when the government is in charge of monetary policy (Rogoff, 1985). The time-inconsistency problem arises due to the short-term benefits that surprise inflation has, like lowering unemployment and reducing the real value of government debt. The government may be tempted to reap the short-term benefits of surprise inflation even if the long-term costs of such a policy may be high. In the words of Bernanke (2010):

> a central bank subject to short-term political influences would likely not be credible when it promised low inflation, as the public would recognize the risk that monetary policymakers could be pressured to pursue short-run expansionary policies that would be inconsistent with long-run price stability. When the central bank is not credible, the public will expect high inflation and, accordingly, demand more-rapid increases in nominal wages and in prices. Thus, lack of independence of the central bank can lead to higher inflation and inflation expectations in the longer run, with no offsetting benefits in terms of greater output or employment.

At the same time, it is widely believed that independence requires accountability. This can be explained as follows. In a principal–agent set-up, the essence of accountability is that once a principal has delegated a particular task to an agent and has given the agent instruments to perform this task, the agent must be held accountable for achieving the objective. This means that the principal must form an opinion of the agent's performance. In other words, a central bank must be transparent. Transparency is an important element of accountability (Amtenbrink and Lastra, 2008; Lastra, 2020), but accountability is more than transparency (in contrast to what many central bankers seem to believe; see next section). The evaluation of central bank performance is the central element in a principal–agent framework and a clearly stated objective, which forms the basis for such an assessment, is therefore essential (Amtenbrink and de Haan, 2002).

11.4.2 *Accountable to Whom?*

Central bankers often consider accountability to be the same as transparency. For instance, in a contribution in the ECB's *Economic Bulletin*, Fraccaroli et al. (2018) define accountability as 'the legal and political obligation of an independent central bank to explain and justify its decisions to citizens and their elected representatives'. In fact, for the case of the ECB, mechanisms of accountability are limited to the exchange of information in the form of a dialogue with EU institutions, notably the European Parliament (see below), and certain reporting requirements (Amtenbrink and van Duin, 2009). Others (e.g. Amtenbrink, 2019) add that the principal should have the possibility to take steps based on its assessment of the policies of the central bank (such as changing the mandate of the central bank, the possibility for the government and/or parliament to override the central bank under certain conditions, and a performance-based dismissal of the central bank governor).[15] No matter how it is defined, a key question is to whom the central bank is accountable, i.e. who is the principal.

On the one hand, the legislature may be considered as the main or even only principal. Indeed, according to Bernanke (2007), accountability implies that central banks provide '*elected representatives* a full and compelling rationale for the decisions they make'.[16] This makes sense. After all, in most countries the legislature decides on (changing) the mandate of the central bank (but not in the euro area where the mandate is defined by the TFEU, so that changing the mandate requires a Treaty amendment). This mandate determines what central banks are supposed to do. That is why central bank communications frequently refer to these mandates. It also implies that politicians are a key target audience of central bank communications.[17] As Amtenbrink and de Haan (2002, pp. 65–66) argue:

> Parliament should always hold the ultimate responsibility for monetary policy. Parliament should set the rules with which the central bank must comply. Moreover, Parliament should be able to decide to change the legal basis of the bank as a reaction to certain behaviour. Monetary policy is, in our view, just one form of economic policy, albeit an important one. Ultimately, it should be treated like other elements of economic policy (such as decisions on tax policy, or government spending, or regulation), even if its institutional set-up is arranged differently, in the sense that the implementation of monetary policy is – for convincing reasons of political-economy – delegated to a central bank with instrument independence.

In the case of the ECB, the European Parliament (EP) is the only European institution whose members are directly elected by the citizens of the Member States, so it makes sense that the ECB is accountable vis-à-vis the EP, even though the EP cannot change the ECB's mandate. Several papers have analysed the so-called monetary dialogue, i.e. the regular hearings of the EP committee on economic and monetary affairs, which, according to Diessner (2022), has become the cornerstone of the ECB's accountability framework. Amtenbrink and van Duin (2009, p. 578) pose that 'the monetary dialogue has not only functioned as an instrument for MEPs to review the performance of the ECB related to its primary and secondary objective, but also as a means to gradually convince the ECB of the need to structurally increase the level of transparency in its operations to a degree that surpasses the legal requirements under primary Community law'. At the same time, they conclude that 'the quality of accountability of the ECB could be significantly increased if the monetary dialogue would focus more than is presently the case on monetary policy issues, with more intensive use in the preparatory phase of the monetary expert panel, and more time during the dialogue for discussion and follow up questions' (Amtenbrink and van Duin, 2009, p. 582). In a later analysis, Collignon and Diessner (2016, p. 1297) conclude that, 'while the exchanges between the two institutions seem to have done very little to improve the stability of financial markets, they do play a role in informing and involving members of the parliament and thus further the ECB's democratic accountability'.

[15] The current legal set-up provides no opportunities for this. The ECB cannot be overridden on monetary policy decisions, nor can a member of the Governing Council be dismissed on grounds of bad performance. Changing the legal basis of the ECB and thus also its independent status and/or its mandate through a Treaty change is very unlikely, as all Member States have to agree on such an amendment. See Diessner (2022) for a further discussion.

[16] In the case of the ECB, according to Article 284 (3) TFEU and Article 15 of the ESCB Statute, this is the European Parliament; see also Lastra (2020).

[17] Alternatively, the central bank may also be accountable to the government, which provides the central bank's inflation target on the basis of the general objective(s) of the central bank as decided upon by parliament. The government, in turn, is also accountable to parliament. This system is in place in the United Kingdom (see Lastra, 2020).

Amtenbrink and van Duin (2009) have already pointed to the EP members' interest in the ECB's secondary objective, while Amtenbrink and Markakis (2019) show that monetary policy issues are discussed in the context of the EP's dialogue with the Single Supervisory Mechanism, which suggests that Members of the European Parliament (MEPs) have difficulties in keeping different tasks of the ECB apart. In a recent analysis, Ferrara et al. (2022) show that MEPs do not always keep the ECB accountable for its primary objective of price stability. Instead, MEPs also attempt to keep the central bank accountable for a broader set of issues, notably unemployment in their constituencies: the higher the domestic unemployment rate in the country where they have been elected, the lower the MEPs' attention to price stability.

Instead of parliament, it is often argued that the central bank should be accountable to the *general public*, suggesting that the general public is the central bank's principal (Bernanke, 2010). Even though the general public does not give the central bank its mandate and cannot change it, it can be considered as the ultimate sovereign. As former ECB President Mario Draghi (2014) puts it: 'A transparent central bank serves the general public, by improving understanding of its actions and accountability for its decisions.'

Some recent studies address the question of why central banks increasingly refer to accountability to the general public (see also Diessner, Chapter 13 in this volume). Lokdam (2020) argues that the ECB increasingly refers to the political will of the people of Europe to legitimize its actions. According to Lokdam (2020, p. 979),

> this permits a more discretionary governing philosophy and the notion that acts of the ECB are implicitly authorized, and thereby legitimate, unless political will is explicitly and effectively expressed against them. An organic link between the ECB and the people of Europe thus provides a justification for the ECB's expanded mandate and role in Eurozone governance in and following the Eurozone crisis.

In a similar vein, Binder (2021) refers to dissatisfaction with representative democracy in the United States in combination with the growth of online digital technologies to explain why the Federal Reserve System and other central banks have put more emphasis on accountability towards the general public. According to Binder (2021, p. 9), this

> dissatisfaction implies that central bankers face pressure to use their expertise to do *more* to serve "the people." Some of this pressure ... comes from the public, who can more effectively translate their causes into policy by influencing technocratic agencies than by working through nominally democratic, but unresponsive, institutions like Congress ... Central banks face pressure to be *directly* responsive to public wishes as a form of unmediated accountability to the people. To gain legitimacy, central banks combine appeals to expertise with appeals to the people. In exchange for greater responsiveness, central banks are granted greater power and discretion.

11.5 PUBLIC TRUST IN THE ECB

Central banks increasingly refer to public trust to motivate their communication with the general public. The website of the ECB, for instance, states that

> Communication helps people to better understand what we do. And this also helps to build trust. Trust means that people have confidence in what we say and do. That makes our monetary policy more effective. But not only that: trust is especially important because we are an

> independent institution. We need to explain in very clear terms what we are doing to achieve our goal so that we can be held to account by the people and their elected representatives.[18]

Ehrmann et al. (2013, p. 782) define citizens' trust in the central bank as 'a belief that the central bank, as the agent in a principal-agent relationship, will deliver on its stated goals – in the case of the European Central Bank (ECB), price stability – to its principal (i.e., citizens)'. After the Global Financial Crisis, trust in the ECB declined substantially, recovering only slowly (Bergbauer et al., 2020).

Why is public trust so critically important for central banks? No doubt, public trust in policy-making institutions, not only central banks, is of fundamental importance for their long-term success. Central bankers often add that public trust is even more important for independent central banks, arguing that central banks ultimately derive their democratic legitimacy from the public's trust in them (Ehrmann et al., 2013; see Diessner, Chapter 13 in this volume, for a different perspective). According to Schnabel (2020),

> Money is a credence good. The euro bills and coins in our wallets, like deposits at the bank, are so-called fiat money. That is, they are not backed by an intrinsic value such as gold. Our money is a social convention, the value of which depends on trust in the money-issuing institution – i.e. the central bank. Public trust is therefore the cornerstone for fulfilling the ECB's primary mandate – maintaining price stability. Recent studies show that a high degree of trust is crucial for anchoring the inflation expectations of private households near the level that the central bank defines as price stability. Stable inflation expectations in turn ensure that short-term deviations in inflation from the ECB's medium-term target do not take hold in the price and wage decisions of companies and households. This mechanism can be self-reinforcing, as the achievement of our monetary policy mandate may in turn strengthen trust in the ECB. Furthermore, stable money and public trust in central banks are essential to generate broad acceptance of their independence in the population at large. Independence protects central banks against political interference and thus underpins the credibility of monetary policy. By contrast, a lack of public trust can render the central bank more vulnerable to political pressure. In a worst-case scenario, such a development can call into question the central bank's independence.

Schnabel (2020) refers to evidence suggesting that trust is related to anchoring inflation expectations. Indeed, some studies report that individuals who trust central banks tend to have inflation expectations which are closer to the ECB's inflation target (Christelis et al., 2020; Rumler and Valderama, 2020). So, if central bank communication is able to increase trust, it may indirectly affect inflation expectations.

According to Haldane (2017), central banks face a 'twin deficits problem', i.e. a deficit of public understanding and a deficit of public trust. These deficits are related. There is quite some evidence suggesting that better knowledge about the central bank enhances trust (Hayo and Neuenkirch, 2014; Mellina and Schmidt, 2018; van der Cruijsen and Samarina, 2021). This implies that informing the population on monetary policy matters may be a promising way of increasing central bank trust. So much for the good news. The bad news is that there is little evidence that communication to the public increases their knowledge about the central bank. Van der Cruijsen et al. (2015) and Brouwer and de Haan (2022) used the same survey method to test individuals' knowledge about the mandate of the ECB, but at very different points in time (2009 and 2020, respectively). Both studies find very similar results, suggesting that knowledge about the ECB has remained stable despite the ECB's increased focus on communication to the public.

[18] www.ecb.europa.eu/home/search/review/html/monpol-communication.en.html

In view of the importance that central banks attach to public trust, it is quite remarkable that there is very limited research on the effect of central bank transparency and communication on trust in the central bank (Blinder et al., 2022). Zooming in first on studies about the impact of transparency on trust in the ECB, these studies suggest (but not unequivocally) that central bank transparency enhances trust in the central bank. Using data from a Dutch household survey, van der Cruijsen and Eijffinger (2010) focus on the relationship between perceived transparency on citizens' trust in the ECB. Their evidence suggests that higher perceived transparency is positively associated with trust, but the link between perceived and actual transparency is rather weak. Horvath and Katuscakova (2016) examine the effect of actual central bank transparency on trust in the ECB (based on Eurobarometer data) and conclude that greater transparency improves citizens' trust in the ECB, but only up to a certain point; too much transparency is not conducive to trust.

Brouwer and de Haan (2022) use an experiment in a survey among Dutch households in which the treatment groups received information about the ECB's price stability objective and about a particular monetary policy instrument (interest rate policy, negative interest rate policy, and asset purchasing programme) of the ECB. The control group only received information about the ECB's primary objective. Their results suggest that communicating about how the ECB tries to achieve price stability has no impact on trust in the ECB.

11.6 CONCLUSIONS

Although communicating with the general public is important, it is not clear whether non-experts are within reach of the ECB. Even if they receive the communications, it cannot be taken for granted that they process them, and do so appropriately, because non-experts might lack the relevant background, or the communication by the central banks is too complex. Observations of this nature caused Blinder (2018) to predict that 'central banks will keep trying to communicate with the general public, as they should. But for the most part, they will fail'. This scepticism seems to be supported by most research. Survey evidence suggests that the public has little knowledge about central banks, and that the situation has not improved despite central banks' efforts. Still, central banks only recently started to pay attention to the general public as a target audience, so it may be too early for this pessimism. Furthermore, even if central bank communication with the general public may have limited impact on inflation expectations, central bank accountability simply requires that central banks talk (and listen) to the general public. Although the European Parliament should be considered as the ECB's principal (despite its very limited abilities to really hold the ECB to account), clear and easy-to-understand communication to the general public is essential for the ECB's legitimacy. The ECB should primarily focus on explaining its price stability mandate in communicating to the general public, and do so in a relatable manner. The recent change of the inflation target is probably easier to explain to non-experts than the previous close to but below 2 per cent target. At the same time, the new target is still not specific enough as it is not clear what deviation from the 2 per cent target the ECB is willing to tolerate.

REFERENCES

Amtenbrink, F. (2019). The European Central Bank's intricate independence versus accountability conundrum in the post-crisis governance framework. *Maastricht Journal of European and Comparative Law* 26(1), 165–179.

Amtenbrink, F., and de Haan, J. (2002). The European Central Bank: An independent specialized organization of community law – A comment. *Common Market Law Review* 39, 65–76.

Amtenbrink, F., and Lastra, R. M. (2008). Securing democratic accountability of financial regulatory agencies. A theoretical framework. In R. V. De Mulder (ed.), *Mitigating Risk in the Context of Safety and Security: How Relevant Is a Rational Approach?* Rotterdam: OMV, pp. 115–132.

Amtenbrink, F., and Markakis, M. (2019). Towards a meaningful prudential supervision dialogue in the euro area? A study of the interaction between the European Parliament and the European Central Bank in the Single Supervisory Mechanism. *European Law Review* 44(1), 3–23.

Amtenbrink, F., and van Duin, K. (2009). The European Central Bank before the European Parliament: Theory and practice after ten years of Monetary Dialogue. *European Law Review* 34(4), 561–583.

Angeloni, I., and Gros, D. (2021). The ECB's new monetary policy strategy: Unresolved issues rather than clarification. VoxEU, 16 July. https://voxeu.org/article/ecb-s-new-monetary-policy-strategy

Baerg, N., Duell, D., and Lowe, W. (2020). Central bank communication as public opinion: Experimental evidence. Mimeo.

Bergbauer, S., Hernborg, N., Jamet, J.-F., and Persson, E. (2020). The reputation of the euro and the European Central Bank: Interlinked or disconnected? *Journal of European Public Policy* 27(8), 1178–1194.

Bernanke, B. (2007). Federal Reserve communications. Speech at the Cato Institute 25th Annual Monetary Conference, Washington, DC.

Bernanke, B. (2010). Central bank independence, transparency, and accountability. Speech at the Institute for Monetary and Economic Studies International Conference, Bank of Japan, Tokyo, Japan.

Bernoth, K., and Dany-Knedlik, G. (2020). The ECB's communication strategy: Limits and challenges after the financial crisis. Study requested by the ECON committee, Monetary Dialogue, February 2020.

Bholat, D., Broughton, N., Ter Meer, J., and Walczak, E. (2019). Enhancing central bank communications using simple and relatable information. *Journal of Monetary Economics* 108, 1–15.

Binder, C. (2017). Fed speak on main street: Central bank communication and household expectations. *Journal of Macroeconomics* 52, 238–251.

Binder, C. (2021). Technopopulism and central banks. CMFA Working Paper 004-2021.

Blinder, A. (2018). Through a crystal ball darkly: The future of monetary policy communication. *American Economic Association Papers and Proceedings* 108, 567–571.

Blinder, A. S., Ehrmann, M., Fratzscher, M., de Haan, J., and Jansen, D. (2008). Central bank communication and monetary policy: A survey of theory and evidence. *Journal of Economic Literature* 46, 910–945.

Blinder, A. S., Ehrmann, M., de Haan, J., and Jansen, D. (2017). Necessity as the mother of invention: Monetary policy after the crisis. *Economic Policy* 32(92), 707–755.

Blinder, A. S., Ehrmann, M., de Haan, J., and Jansen, D. (2022). Central bank communication with the general public: Promise or false hope? DNB Working Paper 744, forthcoming in the *Journal of Economic Literature*.

Borio, C. E. V., and Disyatat, P. (2010). Unconventional monetary policies: An appraisal. *The Manchester School* 78(1), 53–89.

Brouwer, N., and de Haan, J. (2022). The impact of providing information about instruments on inflation expectations and trust in the ECB: Experimental evidence. *Journal of Macroeconomics* 73, 103430.

Candia, B., Coibion, O., and Gorodnichenko, Y. (2020). Communication and the beliefs of economic agents. Paper presented at the Jackson Hole Economic Symposium, August 2020.

Christelis, D., Georgarakos, D., Jappelli, T., and van Rooij, M. (2020). Trust in the central bank and inflation expectations. *International Journal of Central Banking* 65, 1–37.

Coenen, G., Ehrmann, M., Gaballo, G., Hoffmann, P., Nakov, A., Nardelli, S., Persson, E., and Strasser, G. (2017). Communication of monetary policy in unconventional times. ECB Working Paper 2080.

Coibion, O., Gorodnichenko, Y., Kumar, S., and Pedemonte, M. (2020). Inflation expectations as a policy tool. *Journal of International Economics* 124(May), 103297.

Collignon, S., and Diessner, S. (2016). The ECB's monetary dialogue with the European parliament: efficiency and accountability during the euro crisis? *Journal of Common Market Studies* 54(6), 1296–1312.

De Haan, J., Schoenmaker, D., and Wierts, P. (2020). *Financial Markets and Institutions: A European Perspective*, 4th ed. Cambridge: Cambridge University Press.

Diessner, S. (2022). The promises and pitfalls of the ECB's 'Legitimacy-as-Accountability' towards the European Parliament post-crisis. *Journal of Legislative Studies* 28(3), 402–420.

Draghi, M. (2014). Monetary policy communication in turbulent times. Speech at the Conference De Nederlandsche Bank 200 Years: Central Banking in the Next Two Decades, Amsterdam, 24 April. www.ecb.europa.eu/press/key/date/2014/html/sp140424.en.html

Ehrmann, M., and Wabitsch, A. (2021). Central bank communication with non-experts – A road to nowhere? CEPR Discussion Paper 16526.

Ehrmann, M., Soudan, M., and Stracca, L. (2013). Explaining European Union citizens' trust in the European Central Bank in normal and crisis times. *Scandinavian Journal of Economics* 115(3), 781–807.

Ehrmann, M., Holton, S., Kedan, D., and Phelan, G. (2021). Monetary policy communication: perspectives from former policy makers at the ECB. CEPR Discussion Paper 16816.

Enders, Z., Hünnekes, F., and Müller, G. J. (2019). Monetary policy announcements and expectations: Evidence from German firms. *Journal of Monetary Economics* 108, 45–63.

Ferrara, F. M., Masciandaro, D., Moschella, M., and Romelli, D. (2022). Political voice on monetary policy: Evidence from the parliamentary hearings of the European Central Bank. *European Journal of Political Economy*, 74, art. nr. 102143.

Fraccaroli, N., Giovannini, A., and Jamet, J.-F. (2018). The evolution of the ECB's accountability practices during the crisis. *ECB Economic Bulletin*, Issue 5/2018.

Goodhart, C. and Lastra, R. (2018). Central bank accountability and judicial review. SUERF Policy Note 32, May 2018.

Haldane, A. (2017). A little more conversation, a little less action. www.bankofengland.co.uk/-/media/boe/files/speech/2017/a-little-more-conversation-a-little-less-action.pdf?la=en&hash=E49F87ECF3D5A52A5E17349026B1CFAC18E2B78F

Haldane, A., and McMahon, M. (2018). Central bank communications and the general public. *American Economic Association Papers and Proceedings* 108, 578–583.

Haldane, A., Macauly, A., and McMahon, M. (2020). The 3 E's of central bank communication with the public. Bank of England Staff Working Paper 847.

Hartmann, P., and Smets, F. (2018). The first twenty years of the European Central Bank: Monetary policy. CEPR Discussion Paper 13411.

Hayo, B., and Neuenkirch, E. (2014). The German public and its trust in the ECB: The role of knowledge and information search. *Journal of International Money and Finance* 47, 286–303.

Horvath, R., and Katuscakova, D. (2016). Transparency and trust: The case of the European Central Bank. *Applied Economics* 48(57), 5625–5638.

Issing, O. (2000). Communication challenges for the ECB. *Speech*. www.ecb.europa.eu/press/key/date/2000/html/sp000626_2.en.html

Issing, O. (2019). *The Long Journey of Central Bank Communication*. Cambridge, MA: MIT Press.

Issing, O. (2021). An assessment of the ECB strategy review. Central Banking, 10 August. www.centralbanking.com/central-banks/monetary-policy/operating-framework/7864761/an-assessment-of-the-ecbs-strategy-review

Korhonen, I., and Newby, E. (2019). Mastering central bank communication challenges via Twitter. BoF Economics Review 7/2019, Bank of Finland, Helsinki.

Kyriakopoulou, D., and Ortlieb, P. (2019). Central banks take on social media. OMFIF Special Report.

Lagarde, C. (2021). Introductory statement (via videoconference) by Ms Christine Lagarde, President of the European Central Bank, before the Hearing at the Committee on Economic and Monetary Affairs of the European Parliament, Frankfurt am Main, 18 March.

Lane, P. (2021). The new monetary policy strategy: Implications for rate forward guidance. ECB blog. www.ecb.europa.eu/press/blog/date/2021/html/ecb.blog210819~c99d1b768d.en.html

Lastra, R. (2020). Accountability mechanisms of the Bank of England and the European Central Bank. In *Accountability Mechanisms of Major Central Banks and Possible Avenues to Improve the ECB's Accountability*. Study requested by the ECON committee, Monetary Dialogue, September.

Lokdam, H. (2020). 'We serve the people of Europe': Reimagining the ECB's political master in the wake of its emergency politics. *Journal of Common Market Studies* 58(4), 978–998.

Mellina, S., and Schmidt, T. (2018). The role of central bank knowledge and trust for the public's inflation expectations. Deutsche Bundesbank Discussion Paper 32.

Mendez-Barreira, V. (2021). Is the ECB's strategy review enough? Central Banking, 26 August. www.centralbanking.com/central-banks/monetary-policy/operating-framework/7867576/is-the-ecb-strategy-review-enough

Moessner, R., Jansen, D., and de Haan, J. (2017). Communication about future policy rates in theory and practice: A survey. *Journal of Economic Surveys* 31(3), 678–711.

Rogoff, K. (1985). The optimal degree of commitment to an intermediate monetary target. *Quarterly Journal of Economics* 100, 116–989.

Rumler, F., and Valderrama, M. T. (2020). Inflation literacy and inflation expectations: Evidence from Austrian household survey data. *Economic Modelling* 87, 8–23.

Schnabel, I. (2020). The importance of trust for the ECB's monetary policy. Speech by Isabel Schnabel, Member of the Executive Board of the ECB, at the Hamburg Institute for Social Research. www.ecb.europa.eu/press/key/date/2020/html/ecb.sp201216_1~9caf7588cd.en.html

Svensson, L. E. O. (2006). The instrument-rate projection under inflation targeting: The Norwegian example. In *Stability and Economic Growth: The Role of Central Banks*. Mexico City: Banco de Mexico, pp. 175–198.

Van der Cruijsen, C. A., and Eijffinger, S. C. W. (2010). From actual to perceived transparency: The case of the European Central Bank. *Journal of Economic Psychology* 31(3), 388–399.

Van der Cruijsen, C., and Samarina, A. (2021). Trust in the ECB in turbulent times. DNB Working Paper 722.

Van der Cruijsen, C., Jansen, D., and de Haan, J. (2015). How much does the public know about the ECB's monetary policy? Evidence from a survey of Dutch households. *International Journal of Central Banking* 11, 169–218.

12

From Market to Green Economics

Impact on Monetary and Financial Policies

Dirk Schoenmaker and Hans Stegeman

12.1 INTRODUCTION

Central banks are 'a child of their own time'. The Bank of England was founded to help finance the war against France and to stabilize financial activity in London in the late seventeenth century. This explains the broad remit of the Bank of England, combining monetary and financial stability. The (predecessor of the) Bundesbank was founded after the Interbellum hyperinflation and the subsequent Second World War (de Haan, 2018). This explains the narrow central banking model of the Bundesbank with the singular objective of monetary stability and full independence to achieve that objective (Capie et al., 1994).

In a similar way, the European Central Bank (ECB) is a construct of the Great Moderation from the mid-1980s until 2007. The prevailing paradigm at that time was a strong belief in the working of markets. This 'market economics' thinking combined with strong German ordo-liberal influence led to a narrow central bank aimed at monetary policy. The ECB did not get primary responsibility for financial stability and supervision, as financial markets were thought to be self-equilibrating without a need for government intervention.

In the aftermath of the Global Financial Crisis (GFC), when financial markets appeared not to be self-equilibrating and fiscal policy did not come to the rescue, the ECB's remit was expanded to being a broad central bank, with responsibility for financial stability and banking supervision, alongside its original monetary policy mandate (see also Adamski, Chapter 9 in this volume). Several observers (e.g. Folkerts-Landau and Garber, 1992; Schoenmaker, 1997) already stressed the need for a broad central bank before the Economic and Monetary Union (EMU) started in 1999. In a narrower sense, Bagehot (1873) set out the case for a stabilizing central bank in the late nineteenth century.

The contemporary challenge for Europe (and the broader world) is to deal with the sustainability challenges that we are facing. 'Green' economics, also called ecological economics (Daly, 1996), stresses the need to operate within planetary boundaries (Steffen et al., 2015). In this chapter, we argue that new economic thinking should respect this ecological constraint.

The government is in the driving seat for 'greening' the economy. In Europe, the political bodies – the European Commission, the Council, and the European Parliament – have

The authors would like to thank the editors, Dirk Bezemer, Diego Valiante, Sjoerd van der Zwaag and participants at the ECB Green Seminar Series for very useful comments.

endorsed the European Green Deal, which sets ambitious policy targets for greening the economy (European Commission, 2019). Given the primary role of the political bodies, the question is, what is the appropriate role for the ECB to address the emergent sustainability risks? There is consensus that the ECB should help with 'de-risking the financial system' in its financial policy roles. In sustainability language, this is called 'do no harm' by avoiding negative impact. But there is no consensus on the ECB's role in monetary policy (ECB, 2021a; Schoenmaker, 2021). Should the ECB aim for positive impact by allocating its monetary policy operations more to low-carbon assets and less to high-carbon assets in order to operate within planetary boundaries?

This chapter sets out the sustainability challenges for monetary and financial policies. How do these sustainability challenges – with a complex nature and long horizon – affect the ECB's policies? The next step is to explore new instruments and recalibrate existing instruments to address the challenges. The final step is a detailed discussion of the ECB's role in applying these instruments.

This chapter is organized as follows. Sections 12.2 and 12.3 discuss the paradigms of market and green economics, respectively, and how these paradigms apply to the ECB's policies. The next sections deal subsequently with the policy areas: green monetary policy, green financial stability, and green financial supervision. The final section concludes.

12.2 DOMINANCE OF MARKET ECONOMICS

EMU was designed and built in the 1980s and 1990s. Landmark publications are the Delors Report in 1989 (Committee for the Study of Economic and Monetary Union, 1989) and the Maastricht Treaty in 1992 (Council of European Communities, Commission of the European Communities, 1992). In the 1980s, the deregulation of the economy reached momentum as part of the broader agenda of the leading politicians of that day, US President Ronald Reagan and UK Prime Minister Margaret Thatcher, who reduced the influence of the government on economic processes and promoted private markets. The political setting underpinned the prevalence of market economics thinking in the late twentieth century.

In market economics, the economy is considered a self-contained 'structure of production, distribution and consumption of goods and services within a given country or region' (Mitchell, 1998, p. 84). Ecology and/or sustainability are missing from the economy's definition. This idea can be seen as the preanalytical vision of market economics: It excludes sustainability from the framework of analysis. 'Since analysis cannot supply what the preanalytical vision omits, it is only to be expected that macroeconomic texts would be silent on the environment, natural resources, depletion and pollution' (Daly, 1996, p. 47). That makes it challenging to solve sustainability problems if it is not a part of the system.

The central yardstick for measuring progress in market economies is GDP growth. Robinson (1972) argues that economic theory does not look at the composition or distribution of GDP. GDP indicators fail to distinguish between desirable and undesirable economic activities. In the calculation of GDP, all market transactions count, and the idea is that the higher the value of market transactions, the better it is (higher economic growth). Consequently, welfare-reducing or restoring activities (mining activities that destroy the environment, selling cigarettes, clean-up activities after a hurricane, prisons' costs) are treated in the same way as welfare-enhancing activities (public education, building a dam, research on vaccines).

Market economics' core values are utility maximising combined with strict economic analysis assumptions, which Dennis Snower (2021) called 'invisible hand conditions', such as perfect knowledge, independence of decisions, perfect foresight, and perfect markets with no externalities and perfect competition (Moos, 2019). The neoclassical definition determines the economic system's underlying values: valuation depends on the relative scarcity of aggregate capital regardless of whether it is natural capital or manufactured capital (Zaman, 2012). It is also assumed that depletion of natural resources is considered most optimally by assuming perfect information (including perfect foresight) and substitutability between natural resources and other production factors (Solow, 1974). Value is implicitly measured in terms of a subjective mental metric, often referred to as preference satisfaction, pleasure/pain or happiness/suffering (McShane, 2017). These definitions have in common that the valuation of goods and services is centred on their impact on subjective human preferences rather than their impact on ecosystems or socioeconomic reproduction.

At the societal level, utility maximization translates into increasing GDP per capita as the argument for economic growth as a reflection of society's perceived underlying values (Temesgen et al., 2021). Market prices are the correct reflection of economic actors' subjective valuations of products and services. Hence, the way to aggregate all different kinds of preferences can be done by the monetized value through market transactions.

Market economies centralize markets as an interaction mechanism, being the most efficient and therefore delivering optimal value (Debreu, 1959). They declare market exchange as the natural state, often referring to the invisible hand of Adam Smith. Over recent decades, we have often seen markets used as an interaction mechanism for more than just private commodities: ranging from nature to informal work to government tasks. The central measurement of outcomes in the market view is expressed in terms of GDP, as measured in the national accounts.

In sum, an economic system that only values the utility of 'material goods and services', organizes interaction via markets, and registers only goods and services, leads to expansion of production and consumption of these goods and services (economic growth), ignoring social and environmental factors by excluding them in its preanalytical vision of 'the economy'. Market economics does not provide for the maintenance of the 'commons' for current and future generations (Schoenmaker and Stegeman, 2023).

12.2.1 *Market Economics in Policy*

The prevailing thinking in terms of market economics had an impact on all EMU's policy areas:

1. Market neutrality in the application of monetary policy;
2. Self-equilibrating markets for financial stability;
3. Capital adequacy rules based on historical loss rates and market volatility for banking supervision.

For each policy area, the influence of market economics at the time of establishing EMU is discussed. In short, the ECB was based on a narrow concept of central banking, as the economy and markets needed little guidance. The narrow concept focuses on the role of monetary policy. Next, the financial crisis and the euro-sovereign crisis led to a fading trust in market economics to deliver financial stability. The ECB took a more hands-on role to interfere in the economy and markets, moving to a broad concept of central banking, which included financial stability and supervision. The emergence of green economics, and its impact on the role of the ECB, is discussed in Section 12.3.

12.2.1.1 Policy Area 1: Market Neutrality in Monetary Policy

The guiding principle in the implementation of monetary policy has been 'market neutrality', whereby the central bank buys sovereign, corporate, and bank bonds proportionally to outstanding debt with the idea that such a 'market-neutral' approach will not disturb (relative) prices. An asset purchase or collateral framework and its criteria and/or requirements should not lead to the preferential treatment of distinct asset classes, issuers, or sectors and should avoid market distortion (Bindseil et al., 2017).

From a legal point of view, the principle of market neutrality as such is not present in the EU Treaties (Dikau and Volz, 2021; Van Tilburg and Simić, 2021). There is only a reference in Article 127(1) Treaty on Functioning of the European Union (TFEU) that 'The ESCB [European System of Central Banks] shall act in accordance with the principle of an open market economy with free competition, favouring an efficient allocation of resources'. It has also been also argued that non-standard monetary operations of the ECB have made its policy stance increasingly more market non-neutral (Adamski, Chapter 9 in this volume). Nevertheless, the current operationalization – to buy assets or take collateral in proportion to the market – follows from a belief that the prevailing market allocation is efficient and should not be distorted (Schoenmaker, 2021).

Market neutrality can be discussed in the context of the appropriate remit of central banks. Tucker (2018) raises the valid point of delegation of economic policy powers from elected policymakers to unelected, albeit democratically appointed, technocratic central bankers. He argues that a central bank can be seen as a co-manager of the government's consolidated balance sheet, as the profits and losses from central bank operations (seigniorage) largely fall to the government.[1] Allocation decisions on assets and collateral thus have a bearing on the riskiness of the government's consolidated balance sheet and on the seigniorage income for the government. At the same time, central banks are independent in the setting and implementation of monetary policy, which forbids them from taking government instructions on their monetary policy operations. So, how far should central banks go in their operations?

A minimalist approach is to restrict monetary policy operations to open-market operations with short-term treasury paper (Goodfriend, 2011). In that way, the central bank remains fully neutral towards the private sector. By contrast, in a maximalist approach, the central bank would be given free rein to manage the consolidated balance sheet, which would involve risks related to a different group of companies and households. Tucker (2018, p. 57) argues that the maximalist approach would 'take central banks close to being the fiscal authority and cannot be squared with any mainstream ideas of central banking competences in democracies'.

The Eurosystem's current policy of market neutrality (Bindseil et al., 2017; Wuermeling, 2018) is theoretically consistent with the minimalist conception of monetary policy operations. In practice, however, it seems to be a hybrid system, since the Eurosystem already accepted private sector paper (corporate bonds, bank bonds, and bank loans) for asset purchases and collateral prior to the GFC. This credit policy practice has been intensified under quantitative easing following the Global Financial Crisis. The Eurosystem's asset purchase programme (APP) includes all programmes under which private sector securities and public sector securities

[1] In most countries, the government holds the shares in the national central bank. The central bank is typically allowed to add a small fraction of profits (say 1 to 5 per cent) to its reserves with the remainder paid-out as dividends to the (ultimate) shareholders (the government) – to reflect the Eurosystem situation where the national central banks own the ECB, not the governments directly.

are purchased in order to address the risks of too prolonged a period of low inflation. The APP shows that the Eurosystem is not following the minimalist approach, but already conducts credit operations with the private (and public) sector to foster economic growth[2] (although the stated aim is to address the risk of prolonged low inflation).

The ECB overlooks the broader consequences of market interference on sustainability. There is evidence that the current 'market neutral' approach towards private companies (just buying private securities in proportion to the market index) is not carbon neutral. As carbon-intensive companies, such as fossil fuel companies, utilities, car manufacturers, and airlines, are typically capital intensive (Doda, 2018), market indices for equities and corporate bonds are overweight in high-carbon assets. The ECB's application of market neutrality thus leads to the Eurosystem's private sector asset and collateral base being relatively carbon intensive (Matikainen et al., 2017; Schoenmaker, 2021). Investment in carbon-intensive companies reinforces the long-term lock-in of carbon in production processes and infrastructure. Maintaining the current application of market neutrality would therefore be a decision that undermines the general policy of the EU to achieve a low-carbon economy (see Section 12.3).

12.2.1.2 Policy Area 2: Self-Equilibrating Markets for Financial Stability

At the time when EMU was designed in the 1990s, Folkerts-Landau and Garber (1992) published a paper titled: 'The European Central Bank: A Bank or a Monetary Policy Rule?' in which they introduce two concepts of central banking. The narrow concept only includes monetary stability (monetary policy rule), while the broad concept includes financial as well as monetary stability. Examples of the financial stability task are the lender of last resort (LOLR) function and supervision of financial institutions. The original ECB is largely modelled after the Bundesbank and follows the narrow central banking concept focusing on monetary stability. The Treaty defines maintaining of price stability as the primary objective (Article 127(1) TFEU) of the European System of Central Banks (ESCB) and specifies that the ESCB should only contribute to the supervision and financial stability policies of the national authorities (Article 127(5) TFEU).

The narrow mandate is consistent with the prevailing free market ideology in the 1990s and early 2000s that markets are best left to themselves. Markets are self-equilibrating and should not be (over)regulated. The free market ideology was promoted by leading politicians (e.g. Reagan and Thatcher) as well as leading central bankers (e.g. former Fed chair Greenspan). After the Global Financial Crisis of 2008, Greenspan admitted in a congressional hearing that the free market ideology may be flawed (Naylor, 2008).

By contrast, Folkerts-Landau and Garber (1992) argued that the narrow mandate for the ECB may hamper effective crisis management. The ECB has slowly moved to become a full-fledged central bank by developing its 'banking' functions. It has been publishing a Financial Stability Review since 2004. During the GFC and the subsequent euro-sovereign debt crisis, the ECB adopted the role of a central crisis manager. By its generous provision of liquidity to all banks (and a broader range of eligible collateral), the ECB has come close to becoming a LOLR for ailing individual banks (Schoenmaker, 2013). However, the ECB adopted its LOLR function only for the euro area banking system as a whole – this is called general LOLR. Decisions to provide emergency liquidity assistance to individual banks (individual LOLR) are still up to the

[2] Ampudia et al. (2018) analysed the effects of unconventional monetary policy. An important finding is that the Asset Purchase Programme has contributed to a reduction in unemployment.

national central banks in the respective countries where banking groups are licensed and operate (Padoa-Schioppa, 1999). This individual LOLR function of national central banks is subject to ECB approval to safeguard the overall liquidity of the euro area banking system. Finally, the ECB has been chairing and hosting the European Systemic Risk Board (ESRB) since its conception in 2010. The role of the ESRB is to oversee risk in the EU financial system from a macro-prudential perspective.

In sum, as financial markets appeared not to be self-equilibrating, the ECB has moved from the narrow concept to the broad concept of central banking. The next question is what the ECB's role should be in addressing climate risk as a source of systemic risk.

12.2.1.3 Policy Area 3: Capital Adequacy Rules Based on Market Principles

For banking supervision, the ECB also followed the Bundesbank model of separating monetary policy and banking supervision (Goodhart and Schoenmaker, 1995). The key idea is that the reputation of the central bank should not be tarnished by supervisory failures, which are bound to happen when the central bank is responsible for banking supervision. Moreover, monetary policy decisions should not be contaminated by financial stability or banking supervisory considerations.

Sometimes the 'conflict of interest' argument is mentioned, as monetary and financial stability may have different interests. However, Goodhart and Schoenmaker (1995) argue that a central bank has to deal with a weak banking system anyway during times of crisis, whether it is the banking supervisor or not. A responsible central bank would not just increase interest rates, if needed for monetary policy purposes, when the banking system is at the brink for two related reasons. First, the transmission of monetary policy happens through the banking system, in particular in Europe with its large banking system relative to financial markets. A malfunctioning banking system hampers an effective transmission of monetary policy. Second, potential financial instability (due to higher interest rates) may hamper the economy.

The 'clean hands' approach shifted in the aftermath of the euro-sovereign crisis, when the ECB assumed the role of banking supervisor in the Banking Union (Schoenmaker and Véron, 2016). The ECB has by now become a broad central bank with full-fledged monetary and financial stability responsibilities. This is a recognition of the idea that monetary stability and financial stability are two sides of the same coin. A stable financial system is a precondition for both.

Capital adequacy policies for banks are set by the Basel Committee on Banking Supervision. The capital adequacy rules for credit risk are based on historical loss rates and those for market risk on historical market volatility (see also Parchimowicz, Chapter 23 in this volume). The underlying assumption is that historical default patterns or market movements are a good indicator or proxy of future risk. However, structural changes in the economy, including sustainability transitions, violate this assumption. This is the so-called Lucas critique. Lucas (1976) basically argues that the structure of the historical relationships will change when the nature of the assets changes due to structural and policy changes. So historical relationships are not always a good guide for the future. Government policies (or stakeholder pressure) to address sustainability challenges may well turn the tables on companies. Profitable companies in the past may become stranded assets in the future (often quoted examples are oil and tobacco companies), while new companies providing solutions to the sustainability challenges rise in value (e.g. electric car manufacturers).

Another issue is the time horizon. The Basel capital adequacy rules assume a one-year holding period for credit risk and a ten-day holding period for market risk. The underlying assumption is that banks can mitigate the credit or market risk within this period. Less liquid assets (e.g. companies or funds without a listing and thus without readily available stock prices) face higher capital charges.

In sum, capital adequacy rules are based on market principles not taking into account emerging risks and concentrating on a short horizon. This is at odds with the nature of sustainability risks. The question at hand is whether climate risk should be included in the capital adequacy framework. Earlier discussions have centred on the adoption of a green support factor or a brown capital surcharge (Boot and Schoenmaker, 2018). Another question is whether capital charges should continue to favour liquid, tradable assets with lower capital charges, as sustainable lending is more focused on stewardship (building a relationship with clients) than on transaction-based banking (Boot and Thakor, 2000).

12.3 EMERGENCE OF GREEN ECONOMICS

Green economics follows different dynamics than market economics. In market economics, the intersection of supply and demand leads to transactions. The resulting clearing or market price reveals the scarcity of the good and service. By contrast, scientists model climate change, biodiversity losses, and freshwater shortages as boundaries which should not be trespassed.

The planetary boundaries framework of Steffen et al. (2015), which is updated by Persson et al. (2022), defines a safe operating space for humanity within the boundaries of nine productive ecological capacities of the planet. The framework is based on the intrinsic biophysical processes that regulate the stability of the Earth system on a planetary scale. The green zone in Figure 12.1 is the safe operating space, light orange represents the zone of uncertainty (increasing risk) and dark orange indicates the high-risk zone.

Applying the *precautionary principle*, the *planetary boundary* itself lies at the intersection of the green and light orange zones. To illustrate how the framework works, we look at the control variable for climate change, the atmospheric concentration of greenhouse gases. The zone of uncertainty ranges from 350 to 450 parts per million (ppm) of carbon dioxide. We crossed the planetary boundary of 350 ppm in 1988, with a level of 420 ppm in early 2023 and currently adding at a rate of around 2 ppm every year. The upper limit of 450 ppm is consistent with the goal (at a fair chance of 66 per cent) to limit global warming to 2° Celsius above the pre-industrial level and lies at the intersection of the light orange and dark orange zones. At the current rate of emissions, the upper limit of 450 ppm may be reached around 2038.

Another example in the light orange zone of increasing risk is land-system change. The control variable is the area of forested land as a proportion of forest-covered land prior to human alteration. The planetary boundary is at 75 per cent forest-covered land, while we are currently at 62 per cent and the percentage is falling.

The current linear production and consumption system is based on extraction of raw materials (take), processed into products (make), consumption (use), and disposal (waste). Traditional business models centred on a linear system assume the ongoing availability of unlimited and cheap natural resources. This is increasingly risky because non-renewable resources, such as fossil fuels, minerals, and metals, are increasingly under pressure, while potentially renewable resources, such as forests, rivers, and prairies, are declining in their extent and regenerative capacity. Moreover, the use of fossil fuels in the linear production and consumption system overburdens the Earth system as natural sink (absorbing pollution).

With this linear economic system, we are crossing planetary boundaries beyond which human activities might destabilize the Earth system. In particular, the planetary boundaries of climate

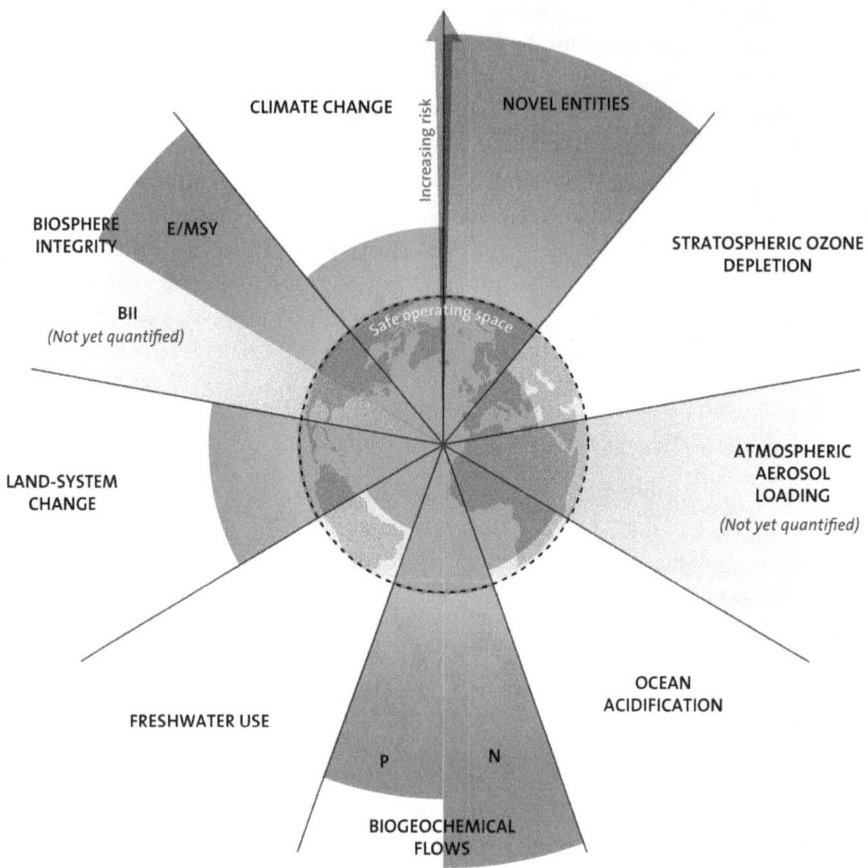

FIGURE 12.1. The planetary boundaries.
Credit: Azote for Stockholm Resilience Centre, based on analysis in Persson et al. (2022) and Steffen et al. (2015).

change, land-system change (deforestation and land erosion), biodiversity loss (terrestrial and marine), and biochemical flows (nitrogen and phosphorus, mainly because of intensive agricultural practices) have been crossed (see Figure 12.1). A timely transition towards an economy based on sustainable production and consumption, including use of renewable energy, reuse of materials, and land restoration can mitigate these risks to the stability of the Earth system.

12.3.1 *Greening Policies*

A key question is the relationship between green and market economics. As explained in Section 12.2, the interaction mechanism for market economics is market exchange of goods and services. The interaction mechanism for green economics is regeneration to preserve ecosystems. As the economy is a sub-part of the broader Earth ecosystem, this suggests that economic activity has to take place within the planetary boundaries (Daly, 1996; Holling, 2001). The ecological constraint should thus be included in production and consumption functions (Dasgupta, 2021).

Recognizing the ecological constraints, the European Commission (2019) has adopted the European Green Deal as the cornerstone of its economic policies. The Green Deal sets ambitious targets for carbon reduction, healthy food, and recycling resources, which will transform the EU economy. The Green Deal has been endorsed by the European Council and the European Parliament. The EU political bodies are the prime mover on green policies. Where does this leave other operators in the economy, such as companies, financial institutions, central banks, and financial supervisors? The ecological constraint is relevant for all economic operators. While market economics simply equates demand and supply to set prices and facilitate transactions, green economics starts with the ecological constraint and from there operates in the most efficient way.

The ECB plays an important role in the economy. At the meta level, the ECB, like any central bank, aims for sustainable development of the economy. This means healthy development of the economy in the long run. Sustainable development is usually discussed in impact terms. The starting point is a requirement to do no harm by avoiding negative impact. The ECB should thus at a minimum avoid negative impacts by correcting a biased allocation in monetary policy and de-risking the financial system in financial policies. At a more ambitious level, the ECB can also look for positive impact (in its monetary policy role) to move the economy within planetary boundaries. The next sections show how the ECB can green its policies instead of relying on self-correcting markets, which ignore the ecological constraints.

There may be concerns that the Tinbergen rule is violated. Tinbergen (1952) argued that at least one independent policy instrument is required for each policy objective. As Section 12.4.3 shows, the ECB can change its operational procedures to correct its over-allocation to high-carbon companies, while keeping its monetary policy instrument (i.e. setting interest rates) intact. The Tinbergen rule would then not be violated.

12.4 GREEN MONETARY POLICY

Current monetary policy operations have a bias towards high-carbon companies in its asset and collateral framework, as explained in Section 12.2. We discuss the legal mandate, coordination between fiscal and monetary policy and methods to counter the carbon bias.

12.4.1 *Legal Mandate*

Across the world, the core task of central banks is to maintain price stability. In addition, central banks are often asked to support economic growth. The precise division and wording of these functions is different in different countries. In the United States, the Federal Reserve has a dual mandate to stabilize prices and maximize employment. In the European Union, Article 127(1) TFEU clearly prioritizes price stability:

> The primary objective of the European System of Central Banks (hereinafter referred to as 'the ESCB') shall be to maintain price stability. Without prejudice to the objective of price stability, the ESCB shall support the general economic policies in the Union with a view to contributing to the achievement of the objectives of the Union as laid down in Article 3 of the Treaty on European Union.

The reference to general economic policies means the ESCB's actions cannot be measured in terms of specific policies, but rather by its support for the underlying trends in economic policy (Smits, 1997).

Article 3(3) TEU, meanwhile, specifies that the EU should 'work for the sustainable development of Europe based on balanced economic growth and price stability, a highly competitive social market economy, aiming at full employment and social progress, and a high level of protection and improvement of the quality of the environment'. This wording leaves room for the greening of monetary policy, as long as it does not contradict the primary objective. It supports a broad definition of economic growth which recognizes that economic policies also affect society and the environment, and that sustainability considerations should be included in financial decision-making (see, for example, Stiglitz, 2009).

Following Smits (1997) and Tucker (2018), we argue that the Eurosystem should refrain from favouring assets of particular sustainable projects, agencies, or companies. Such individual choices are the domain of elected policymakers. But should the ECB adopt a general approach towards low-carbon assets in support of the EU's general policies on reducing carbon emissions?

As long as the Eurosystem followed a general approach, it would not assume an active policy role. It would only support (instead of hinder) the EU's policy decision to move to a low-carbon economy. In that way, the risk that appointed technocrats take policy decisions with distributional consequences, as highlighted by Tucker (2018), would be minimized. Nevertheless, even a general approach towards low-carbon assets would have distributional consequences for the economy, because assets from low-carbon sectors would become 'more' eligible than those from high-carbon sectors. But these are exactly the kind of distributional consequences that are intended by the EU's policies on reducing carbon emissions.

Particularly since the ECB's strategic review in summer 2021 (for more details see de Haan, Chapter 11 and Chang, Chapter 10 in this volume), the ECB seems to be ready to move away from a strict interpretation of market neutrality. Schnabel (2021, p. 55) argues that 'it seems appropriate, then, to replace the market neutrality principle with one of market efficiency that more fully incorporates the risks and societal costs associated with climate change ... taking into account the alignment of issuers with EU legislation implementing the Paris Agreement'.

There is a need for political space for the ECB to avoid central bankers making policy decisions countering policies of political decision-makers (provided they do not conflict with the primary monetary policy objective of price stability). As climate policy is a real concern and consistently a top priority of European policy, the ECB can contribute to this secondary objective in its asset and collateral framework for monetary policy operations. The European Commission and Council have repeatedly stated their aim to combat climate change by reducing carbon emissions. This climate framework can be considered as the EU's general economic policies to protect the environment (in the context of Article 3(3) TEU). European Parliament members have repeatedly asked questions to the ECB president about the ECB's (lack of) carbon policies.[3]

12.4.2 *Coordination between Fiscal and Monetary Policy*

The first-best solution to climate concerns is to tax the climate change externality caused by carbon emissions. An appropriate carbon tax provides an 'official' price for carbon risk and would spur the move from high- to low-carbon investments. The good news is that the European carbon price – based on emissions trading – has started to rise, from about €8 per tonne CO_2-equivalent in 2016/2017 to about €80 in early 2022 (see Figure 12.2). Emissions trading is a market-based approach to controlling pollution. Under the emissions trading scheme (ETS), companies buy or receive emissions allowances, which they can trade with one another as needed.

[3] It could be argued that the ECB's carbon policy in the asset and collateral framework for its monetary policy operations should be discussed (and perhaps also approved) by the European Parliament.

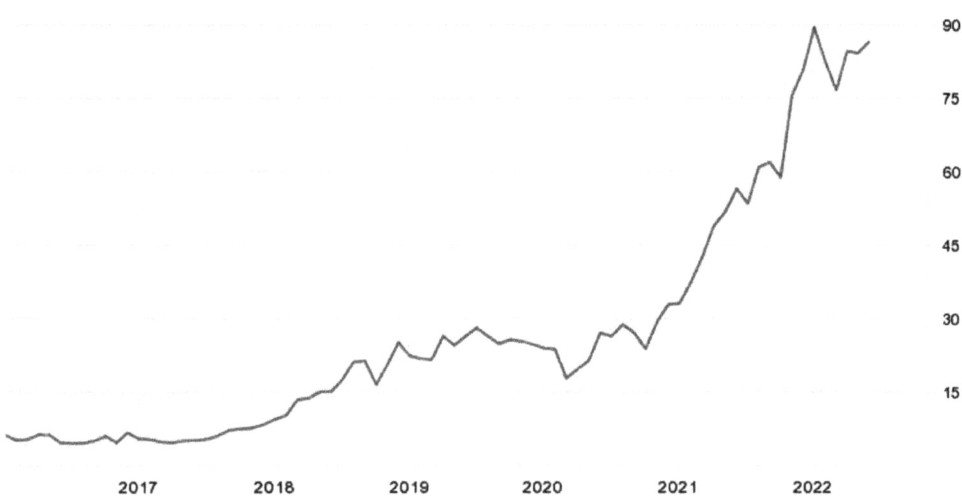

FIGURE 12.2. European carbon price in euros (2017–22).
Source: Tradingeconomics.com.

Nevertheless, this market price is still below the shadow price of €157, which reflects the abatement cost at which carbon emissions can be reduced to meet the 2°C limit (True Price, 2021). In this second-best world which lacks a sufficiently high carbon tax, the question is what private companies, investors, and public sector bodies (like central banks) can contribute to reducing carbon emissions.

Coordination between the fiscal and monetary authorities is needed to come to an 'appropriate' carbon tax for the euro area. What is the optimal fiscal–monetary policy mix? On the monetary policy side, the institutional framework of the ECB allows, in principle, for adoption of the monetary policy stance most appropriate for the euro area as a whole, taking into account the fiscal policy stance for the euro area as a whole (Orphanides, 2017). In the case of the transition to a low-carbon economy, this means the lower the carbon tax, the stronger the low-carbon allocation in monetary policy (and the higher the tax, the looser the low-carbon allocation). It should be noted that fiscal policy (i.e. setting the carbon tax) and regulatory policy under the Green Deal are far more powerful in mitigating climate change than any monetary policy low-carbon allocation can ever be.

There are fears of carbon leakage when companies move their production outside the euro area and/or European Union in response to regulatory, fiscal, and/or monetary carbon instruments. This could be reinforced by a cumulation of fiscal and monetary instruments affecting carbon-intensive investments, when other countries and central banks are not adopting these instruments. As argued, fiscal policy is more important. The European Commission has proposed a Carbon Border Adjustment Mechanism (CBAM) to reconcile the EU's climate and trade interests. CBAM introduces a cross-border tax – in proportion to a product's carbon intensity – for imports. In that way, a lack of a foreign carbon price is neutralized. On the monetary side, the ECB could cooperate with other central banks within the Network for Greening the Financial System on adopting 'similar' monetary carbon instruments.

12.4.3 *Methods to Decarbonize*

Schoenmaker (2021) derives two main conditions for greening monetary policy. These conditions are a general approach (as discussed in Section 12.4.1) and a broad asset and collateral base. The latter is important to avoid distortions in the transmission of monetary policy to the economy (monetary policy should ideally get in all the cracks of the economy). To satisfy both conditions, we propose a tilting approach for a central bank's direct asset holdings (related to official reserves or asset purchases under quantitative easing) and collateral holdings (related to monetary policy operations). The basic idea of the tilting approach is to shift the composition of the ECB's asset and collateral portfolio towards low-carbon assets. The ECB can do that by increasing the proportion of low-carbon and transitional assets and at the same time reducing the proportion of high-carbon assets (see Schoenmaker, 2021, for details).

To give an idea of size, Tables 12.1 and 12.2 show the ECB's asset and collateral holdings. Table 12.1 breaks down the securities holdings under the Asset Purchases Programme (APP). The first column indicates the eligible market securities, the second column the ECB holdings under the APP and the third column the holdings as percentage of eligible market securities. Government securities (€2,157 billion) form the vast majority of these securities at more than 80 per cent. The carbon factors are only relevant for the private securities at 18.5 per cent, which amount to €483 billion. These comprise covered bank bonds (10.3 per cent of total securities holdings), corporate bonds (7.1 per cent), and other assets (1.1 per cent).

Table 12.2 provides the collateral data of the Eurosystem taken from the ECB. The first column indicates the eligible market assets, the second column the amount used as collateral in the Eurosystem and the third column the collateral holdings as a percentage of eligible market assets. Table 12.2 shows that banks keep the most liquid and high-quality assets, like government bonds, on their own balance sheet, and pledge covered bonds (€381 billion), asset-backed securities (€359 billion), and bank loans (€380 billion) as collateral at the Eurosystem. The tilting factors can be applied to slightly over 80 per cent of the Eurosystem's collateral holdings

TABLE 12.1 *Outstanding holdings under the Asset Purchases Programme, 20 December 2019*

Securities	1. Eligible market securities (in € billions)	2. ECB holdings (in € billions)	3. Holdings as share of market (2. as % of 1.)	4. Carbon factors applicable (2. as % of total)
Government securities	7,903.5	2,156.9	27.3%	n.a.
Covered bank bonds	1,515.3	268.8	17.7%	10.3%
Corporate bonds	1,558.9	184.8	11.9%	7.1%
Asset-backed securities	596.8	29.0	4.9%	1.1%
Total	**11,574.5**	**2,639.4**	**22.8%**	**18.5%**

Note: The second column presents marketable securities that are eligible under the APP. The third column presents the holdings under the APP. The fourth column presents APP holdings as share of eligible market securities. The fifth column indicates whether the carbon factor would be applicable to the respective collateral category and measures the percentage of total holdings.
Source: Schoenmaker (2021) based on ECB EURO outright operations.

TABLE 12.2 *Collateral data of the Eurosystem, 20 December 2019*

Collateral categories	1. Eligible market assets (in € billions)	2. Use of collateral in Eurosystem (in € billions)	3. Collateral as share of market (2. as % of 1.)	4. Carbon factors applicable (2. as % of total)
Central government securities	7,432.8	225.2	3.0%	n.a.
Regional government securities	470.7	59.6	12.7%	n.a.
Uncovered bank bonds	1,679.6	81.2	4.8%	5.1%
Covered bank bonds	1,515.3	380.8	25.1%	23.9%
Corporate bonds	1,558.9	54.2	3.5%	3.4%
Asset-backed securities	596.8	359.1	60.2%	22.5%
Other marketable assets	874.3	36.8	4.2%	2.3%
Bank loans		379.9		23.8%
Total	**14,128.4**	**1,576.8**	**8.5%**	**81.0%**
Central bank operations				
Monetary policy operations		619.0		
Other operations		957.8		

Note: The second column presents marketable assets that are eligible as collateral. The third column presents the collateral holdings in the Eurosystem at market values after haircuts applied. The fourth column presents collateral as share of eligible market assets. The fifth column indicates whether the additional carbon haircut would be applicable to the respective collateral category. The bottom rows specify for which central bank operations collateral is used. Other operations include large-value payment system operations.
Source: Schoenmaker (2021) based on ECB Eurosystem collateral data.

(see last column of Table 12.2). This indicates that the tilting approach has a bigger impact on collateral (81.0 per cent) than on asset purchases (18.5 per cent).

As asset purchases are 'officially' temporary under quantitative easing, the lasting impact of tilting is on collateral. The tilting factors should be separately modelled to tilt the portfolio towards low-carbon assets, because the ecological constraint is binding. Currently, collateral haircuts are based on credit risk.

In a detailed roadmap of climate-related action as part of its strategic review (ECB, 2021a), the ECB aims to correct the credit risk assessment of the collateral framework for carbon risk. The ECB encourages credit rating agencies to be more transparent about how climate risks are incorporated in credit ratings (Lagarde, 2022). Moreover, the Eurosystem has adopted common minimum standards for climate risks in national central banks' in-house credit assessment systems. Boneva et al. (2021, p. 12) describe the problem of credit risk assessment in terms of market failures which 'may drive a wedge between market prices and efficient asset values that reflect externalities'. This analysis is still cast within the prevailing paradigm of market economics. But the key issue is not whether credit risk assessments or credit ratings 'properly' incorporate carbon risk – point 8 of the ECB's roadmap (ECB, 2021a).

By contrast, the green economics paradigm argues that policies should recognize the ecological constraint. In this context, the rationale for green monetary policy is that central banks reduce their allocation towards high-carbon assets and increase their allocation towards low-carbon assets – point 4 of the ECB's roadmap (ECB, 2021a). The ECB has decided on the first steps towards such an allocation approach (Lagarde, 2022). The ECB aims for a gradual decarbonization of the corporate bond portfolio held under the Asset Purchases Programme. From October 2022, reinvestments will be tilted towards issuers with better climate performance (measured in terms of lower carbon emissions, more ambitious reduction targets, and better climate-related disclosures). On the collateral front, the ECB will limit the share of high-carbon assets that banks can mobilize as collateral when borrowing from the Eurosystem. This limit is applicable to bonds issued by non-financial companies from end-2024; additional asset classes may be included once data quality improves.

Central bank efforts to green monetary policy operations give a powerful signalling effect to other financial market participants (Braun, 2018), boosting the case for greening the financial system and thereby the economy.

12.4.4 *Decarbonizing in Times of Energy Crisis*

At the time of writing, the Russo-Ukrainian war has increased energy prices. This would ultimately lead to a further increase of prices, considering that – apart from just a few exceptions, Sweden first and foremost – all EU economies are carbon-intensive. Higher capital costs through monetary and financial policy instruments for carbon-intensive assets would raise (otherwise high) inflation, which would conflict with the primary objective of the ECB.

Broadly speaking, two opposite policy responses are possible. The first is to slow down the phasing in of monetary and financial policy instruments for carbon-intensive assets. The industry is also lobbying for a slowdown of the energy transition. However, that is just a postponement of the inevitable energy transition. Moreover, outperforming fossil fuel companies currently experience lower costs of capital, while renewables face higher costs of capital due to higher interest rates and rising material costs.

The second is to implement monetary and financial policy instruments for carbon-intensive assets, as scheduled, in line with other EU Green Deal regulatory policies. To soften the impact on inflation and speed up the energy transition (reducing the reliance on fossil fuels), the ECB can incentivize private banks to lend more money for green investments. By tweaking its Targeted Longer-Term Refinancing Operations (TLTROs) programme, the ECB can make green lending much more affordable for businesses and households through lower rates (Van 't Klooster and Van Tilburg, 2020).

12.5 GREEN FINANCIAL STABILITY POLICY

Climate change can create financial instabilities. Central banks have started to conduct system-wide climate stress tests to detect vulnerabilities. On the policy instruments side, we explore the use of large exposure limits.

12.5.1 *Green Swan*

Climate change is inherently uncertain. The Intergovernmental Panel on Climate Change (IPCC) therefore works with confidence intervals to assess the impact of carbon emissions on global warming. Bolton et al. (2020) consider climate risk as a tail risk for the financial system. In their typology, green swans, or 'climate black swans', typically fit fat-tailed distributions: both physical and transition risks are characterized by deep uncertainty and non-linearity, their chances of occurrence are not reflected in past data, and the possibility of extreme values cannot be ruled out.

Climate risk has a physical and transition component. On the physical side, global warming can lead to droughts and rising sea levels as well as more adverse weather patterns with intensified rainfall. The latter happened in the summer of 2021 in Europe with major river floodings in Germany and Belgium. On the transition side, there is the risk of intensifying carbon policies. The Advisory Scientific Committee of the European Systemic Risk Board (ASC, 2016) warned against the scenario of policies that are too late and too sudden. The longer politicians wait to implement serious carbon taxes and thus let carbon emissions continue, the higher carbon taxes will have to be to curb carbon emissions sufficiently to stay within the 1.5° or 2° Celsius limit of global warming.

When pricing of the externalities and/or reputation damage materialize in the medium term, the old production process becomes obsolete and the new production process becomes more favourable. Welsby et al. (2021) estimate that 58 per cent of oil, 59 per cent of gas, and 89 per cent of coal reserves may be unextractable in 2050 to achieve a 50 per cent probability of keeping the global temperature increase to 1.5° C. This means that very high shares of reserves considered economic today would not be extracted under a global 1.5° C limit.

In the case of medium- to long-term investments, the assets used in the original production process might become stranded assets resulting in a loss of financial value. Caldecott et al. (2014) introduced this term for fossil fuel assets, which may become stranded due to government regulation (e.g. carbon pricing) or technological change (e.g. reduced cost of solar photovoltaic panels or wind turbines). It is applicable more widely to carbon-intensive assets, such as real estate or traditional cars. Real estate with a low energy-efficiency label may lose its (collateral) value if measures to improve the energy efficiency are not cost-efficient. Diesel cars are, for example, losing their value, as cities have started to ban them from entering the city centre to reduce pollution levels.

While the focus of green policies is currently on climate change, biodiversity loss poses a similar, if not more severe, tail risk (Kennedy et al., 2022). The dynamic complexity of ecosystem functioning can cause abrupt ecosystem change. Transformational change of ecosystems may occur and changes to biodiversity may influence its likelihood. A widespread collapse of ecosystems has a major impact on food production with subsequent impacts on the economy and wider society, with related financial instabilities. Climate change and biodiversity loss are connected, as a change in climate can destabilize ecosystems. Climate change is thus one of the direct drivers of biodiversity loss (CISL, 2021).

12.5.2 *Climate Stress Tests*

Central banks and supervisors have started to conduct stress tests of the financial sector, using extreme scenarios to identify tail risks in the financial system. Traditional stress tests based on macroeconomic scenarios and a three-year horizon underestimate the transition risk to a carbon-neutral economy. Thomä and Dupre (2017) rightly argue that the impact of climate factors needs to be analysed at the sector level and with longer horizons.

The ECB is at the forefront of developing climate stress tests (Alogoskoufis et al., 2021). A climate stress test typically has three pillars: (1) climate-specific scenarios which identify future projections of climate and macroeconomic conditions over the next thirty years; (2) a comprehensive dataset that combines climate and financial information for companies worldwide and maps them to the loan and trading book of banks; and (3) climate-specific models that capture transmission channels of climate risk drivers for companies and banks.

It is no surprise that the ECB's economy-wide stress tests show that there are clear benefits to acting early (Alogoskoufis et al., 2021). The costs of transition are far less than the costs of climate change in the medium to long term. By contrast, in the case of no climate change mitigation, the effects of climate risks are concentrated in certain geographical areas and sectors. Physical risks become increasingly higher over time. This reinforces the message of transition, including the earlier mentioned scenario of 'too late and too sudden' (ASC, 2016).

Biodiversity loss is also a threat to financial stability (Joint NGFS-INSPIRE Study Group, 2022). As with climate change, biodiversity loss poses physical and transition risks which could aggregate to generate systemic risks. A considerable amount of economic activity is either directly dependent upon ecosystem services provided by nature or impacts biodiversity to an extent that it is at risk of being misaligned with the required move to a nature-positive global economy.

Kennedy et al. (2022) argue for using resilience thinking from the natural sciences. Resilience thinking focuses on measuring how biodiversity contributes to an ecosystem's capacity to adapt to disturbances and avoid sudden, transformative change. They propose a set of seven key mechanisms that can inform measurement development across three biodiversity attributes: abundance, composition, and distribution of species. It would be a next logical step for central banks to prepare the instruments needed for stress tests on biodiversity, starting with scenarios and data.

12.5.3 *Large Exposure Limits*

The policy question is which macroprudential instruments can be used to reduce the financial sector's exposure to climate risk. Schoenmaker and Van Tilburg (2016) advocate large exposure limits to reduce the impact on banks. Current large exposure rules limit a bank's exposure to individual counterparties to 25 per cent of a bank's eligible capital. Their rationale is to protect the bank against specific shocks, such as the failure of a large counterparty.

In the case of climate change, large exposure limits could be set to protect banks against transition shocks and physical shocks. To calibrate large climate exposure limits, we need to identify the appropriate size of the limit and the shocks. While large exposure rules in banking supervision are set at the micro level against individual companies, large climate exposure rules for macroprudential purposes are set at the macro level against aggregate exposures. Higher limits, such as 50 or 75 per cent of a bank's eligible capital, are warranted.

Moving to the shocks, carbon-intensive assets would be affected by a transition shock that imposes high carbon taxes and/or limits on the use of fossil fuels. The exposures could be calibrated with a weighting scheme aligned with the carbon intensity of assets. In a similar way, assets that are subject to physical risk (as reported in the climate stress test) can be aggregated to determine a bank's physical exposure. Such large climate exposure limits force banks to proactively manage their climate exposures and, where necessary, to reduce them. Moreover, these limits also speed up the allocation towards low-carbon assets (promoting climate mitigation) and physically protected assets (promoting climate adaptation).

12.6 GREEN FINANCIAL SUPERVISION

Planetary boundaries are directly relevant for financial supervision. Banks are fully exposed to the transition and physical risks in the real economy. Transition metrics are being developed to assess the transition preparedness of borrowing companies. As supervisory tools are also in development, we suggest reviewing the underlying principles of the capital adequacy framework.

12.6.1 *Banks Are Centre Stage*

As banks are the main financier of the European corporate sector, they are fully exposed to climate change risks in the real economy. While some banks are getting involved in sustainable lending, they tend to keep their exposure to the old economy, such as fossil fuel companies, other carbon-intensive companies, and food-processing and production companies depending on intensive agriculture. The old economy assets can turn into stranded assets, as discussed in Section 12.5.1.

Banks are exposed to several shocks. The largest exposure in the short to medium term is to transition risk, when their borrowing companies appear not to be prepared for a possibly accelerating transition. Next, there is exposure to physical risk on the medium to long time horizon. In a recent review, the ECB (2021b) concludes that banks are mostly aware of transition risks, but far less so of physical risks of climate change and other environmental risks, such as biodiversity loss and pollution. Finally, there is also the risk of a green asset bubble, when there is overinvestment and/or innovation risk. Nevertheless, the dominant risk is transition risk.

12.6.2 *Transition Metrics*

Transition metrics are introduced to assess banks' lending portfolios. The European Banking Authority (EBA) (Eley, 2021) developed a transition tool, which builds on the EU's taxonomy for sustainability activities. The EU taxonomy is a classification system, establishing a list of environmentally sustainable economic activities. It helps the EU to scale up sustainable investment and implement the European Green Deal. The EU taxonomy provides companies, investors, and policymakers with appropriate definitions for which economic activities can be considered environmentally sustainable. The technical screening criteria of the taxonomy include economic activities that (1) make a substantive contribution to one of the six environmental objectives of the taxonomy regulation; (2) do not significantly harm the other five; and (3) meet minimum social safeguards. It should be noted that at the time of writing only the first two environmental objectives of climate mitigation and climate adaptation are defined.

EBA's transition capacity testing ratio is defined as follows:

$$\text{Transition capacity testing ratio} = \frac{\text{Taxonomy aligned exposures} + \text{x\%} * \text{partially aligned exposures}}{\text{Taxonomy eligible exposures}}$$

The ratio thus includes taxonomy aligned or expected to be fully aligned exposures in full and partially aligned exposures only partly. This part is x per cent and is to be assessed by the bank. The default setting is 50 per cent in the absence of information.

By contrast, the remaining exposures are not likely to be in transition:

Not likely to transition ratio = (1 − transition capacity testing ratio)

These metrics could potentially be useful for banks (and their supervisors) to monitor. But concessions are currently being negotiated. If and when, for example, gas and nuclear energy are labelled as green, then one gets the strange situation that green-labelled assets can also become stranded assets with tightening greening policies (as these assets are not green). The EU taxonomy would then no longer be science-based and aligned with sustainability. Moreover, the taxonomy criteria are static (and can only be adjusted with some delay) and partial (only two out of six defined), while innovation is adding to the universe of green assets.

To calculate these ratios, banks need to be able to classify a company's activities. The Corporate Sustainability Reporting Directive (EU/2022/2464) requires companies to disclose sustainability-related information in their annual report. The Sustainable Finance Disclosure Regulation (EU/2019/2088) requires financial institutions to report their sustainability profile.

Notwithstanding these recent disclosure standards, transitions and the transition preparedness of companies are difficult to measure in practice. Forward-looking data, such as the type of capital expenditures (in low-carbon versus high-carbon technologies), are needed, as historical data provide no guide for future transitions.

12.6.3 *Supervisory Instruments*

The starting point for banking supervisors is the SREP – supervisory review and evaluation process – instrument. The SREP allows supervisors to assess banks' capital and risk-control procedures. Severe shortfalls that are observed by the supervisor are translated into so-called pillar 2 capital requirements. So, when banks do not have appropriate procedures to assess climate risks and/or appear to have a high 'not likely to transition ratio', the supervisor can apply an extra pillar 2 capital requirement. These pillar 2 capital charges are incentive compatible: they provide banks with the carrot of less extra capital when they improve and the stick of more extra capital when they fall behind.

Adjusting the pillar 1 minimum capital requirements for climate risk is more fundamental. To discourage lending to brown assets, a differentiated capital treatment of green and brown assets would be helpful. The question is whether green assets should get a lower risk weight or brown assets a higher risk weight. We argued earlier that a green support factor is not warranted (Boot and Schoenmaker, 2018). It is a bad idea to grant banks extra-low levels of capital if something is 'green'; realizing the extra risk of 'brown' does not make 'green' extra safe. Endorsing lower capital requirements for certain climate-friendly investments, such as energy-efficient mortgages or electric cars (D'Orazio and Popoyan, 2019), is asking banks to turn a blind eye on proper risk management, as it is not clear which green technologies will win (i.e. business and innovation risk). Instead of the 'green supporting factor', Boot and Schoenmaker (2018) argue that a much stronger case can be made for a 'brown penalizing factor' for fossil-fuel-intensive and dependent assets. Not only does it give lenders the capacity to withstand losses when the energy transition accelerates, a brown penalizing factor will also discourage further investments that contribute to climate change. Thus, the risk of stranded assets would be reduced.

Preferably this is done through the first pillar of the capital regulation framework that sets minimum capital requirements (Boot and Schoenmaker, 2018). Climate exposures – proxied by the carbon intensity of assets – should be translated into credit risk. This cannot be done using risk models that are based on historical data, as the energy transition is an unprecedented development. Rather, scenario studies should be used to quantify the impact of transition.

A final element is the implied horizon for capital requirements. In Section 12.2.1, we showed that credit risk is based on a one-year holding period and market risk on a ten-day holding period. These holding periods assume that banks can and should reduce their exposure in a timely fashion when problems emerge. This is founded on a transaction-based banking view (Boot and Thakor, 2000).

By contrast, there is an emerging view that financial institutions should engage with their client companies on the sustainability transition (Schoenmaker and Schramade, 2019, 2022). This stewardship role is based on a relation-based banking view, whereby banks help their clients through the transition instead of running away at the first sight of problems. This relation-based engagement is not open-ended; banks should set and monitor clear pathways and targets for their client companies to move to a sustainable business model (including production technologies) and products/services. Then the quality and transition preparedness of borrowing companies become more important indicators for credit risk than a short holding period.

Financial regulations favour short-term and exchange-listed assets. New rules are needed that enable investment in illiquid, long-term assets, such as energy and transport infrastructure, and land restoration. These investments currently receive higher capital charges because of their supposedly inferior market liquidity. However, sustainable investing and lending is more focused on stewardship than on trading.

12.7 CONCLUSIONS

This chapter reviewed the evolution of the ECB. Starting from a light touch – just setting monetary policy in well-functioning markets – the scope of the ECB has expanded rapidly over recent decades. The first expansion was towards heavy-handed financial policies to stabilize financial markets and supervise the soundness of banks. For the latter task, the ECB established the Supervisory Board for the supervision of euro area banks, which is executed in close collaboration with national supervisors. The current expansion is towards greening its monetary and financial policies. The ECB has recently launched a climate change centre with an ECB-wide remit.

On the financial side, there is broad consensus that the ECB has a major role to play in 'de-risking the financial system'. As sustainability risks are complex and have a long horizon, these risks pose major challenges for the conduct of financial policies. We explain how the main instruments, such as stress tests and capital adequacy rules, can be adjusted to incorporate sustainability risks. It is reassuring to conclude that the ECB is at the forefront of designing and implementing these new instruments. The climate stress tests have been designed and are currently being run. While the impact of climate risks on the banking system has already been reviewed (ECB, 2021b), the overhaul of the banking capital adequacy framework still has to start. This is a task for the Basel Committee on Banking Supervision, where we expect the ECB to play a leading role.

On the monetary side, the ECB is still following a two-pronged strategy in its strategic review (ECB, 2021a). The ECB is adopting both a defensive, risk-based approach and a proactive, allocation-based approach. Pursuing the first of the two approaches, the ECB recommends that credit rating agencies incorporate climate risk in their credit ratings. This risk approach is still cast within the leading market economics paradigm and will not address the current bias towards high-carbon assets in monetary policy operations. Following the second approach, the ECB takes the first steps to implementing an allocation approach by tilting its corporate bond holdings towards low-carbon companies and by putting limits on the share of high-carbon assets in its collateral pool. This is in the realm of the emerging green economics paradigm. The ECB has crossed the Rubicon by acknowledging its allocational role in the economy and countering the current carbon bias.

REFERENCES

Advisory Scientific Committee (ASC) (2016). Too late, too sudden: Transition to a low-carbon economy and systemic risk. Report No. 6 of the Advisory Scientific Committee of the European Systemic Risk Board, Frankfurt.

Alogoskoufis, S., Dunz, N., Emambakhsh, T., Hennig, T., Kaijser, M., Kouratzoglou, C., Muñoz, M., Parisi, L., and Salleo, C. (2021). ECB economy-wide climate stress test: Methodology and results. Occasional Paper Series No. 281, European Central Bank.

Ampudia, M., Georgarakos, D., Slacalek, J., Tristiani, O., Vermeulen, P., and Violante, G. (2018). Monetary policy and household inequality. ECB Working Paper No. 2170.

Bagehot, W. (1873). *Lombard Street: A Description of the Money Market*. London: HS King & Company.

Bindseil, U., Corsi, M., Sahel, B., and Visser, A. (2017). The Eurosystem collateral framework explained. ECB Occasional Paper Series 189.

Bolton, P., Despres, M., Pereira Da Silva, L., Samama, F., and Svartzman, R. (2020). *The Green Swan: Central Banking and Financial Stability in the Age of Climate Change*. Basel: Bank for International Settlements.

Boneva, L., Ferrucci, G., and Mongelli, F. (2021). To be or not to be 'green': How can monetary policy react to climate change? ECB Occasional Paper No. 285.

Boot, A., and Schoenmaker, D. (2018). Climate change adds to risk for banks, but EU lending proposals will do more harm than good. Bruegel blog post, Brussels.

Boot, A., and Thakor, A. (2000). Can relationship banking survive competition? *Journal of Finance* 55(2), 679–713.

Braun, B. (2018). Central banking and the infrastructural power of finance: The case of ECB support for repo and securitization markets. *Socio-Economic Review* 16, 1–24.

Caldecott, B., Tilbury, J., and Carey, C. (2014). Stranded assets and scenarios. Discussion Paper, Smith School of Enterprise and the Environment, University of Oxford, Oxford.

Cambridge Institute for Sustainability Leadership (CISL) (2021). Handbook for nature-related financial risks: Key concepts and a framework for identification. Cambridge.

Capie, F., Goodhart, C., Fisher, S., and Schnadt, N. (1994). *The Future of Central Banking*. Cambridge: Cambridge University Press.

Committee for the Study of Economic and Monetary Union (1989). Report on economic and monetary union in the European Community. Delors Report, Brussels.

Council of European Communities, Commission of the European Communities (1992). *Treaty on European Union*. Maastricht Treaty. Luxembourg: Office for Official Publications of the European Communities.

Daly, H. (1996). *Beyond Growth: The Economics of Sustainable Development*. Boston: Beacon Press.

Dasgupta, P. (2021). *The Economics of Biodiversity: The Dasgupta Review*. London: HM Treasury.

Debreu, G. (1959). *Theory of Value: An Axiomatic Analysis of Economic Equilibrium*. New York: John Wiley and Sons.

De Haan, J. (2018). The struggle of German central banks to maintain price stability. In R. Edvinsson, T. Jacobsen, and D. Waldenström (eds.), *Sveriges Riksbank and the History of Central Banking*. Cambridge University Press, pp. 388–417.

Dikau, S., and Volz, U. (2021). Central bank mandates, sustainability objectives and the promotion of green finance. *Ecological Economics* 184, 107022.

Doda, B. (2018). Tales from the tails: Sector-level carbon intensity distribution. *Climate Change Economics* 9(4), 1850011.

D'Orazio, P., and Popoyan, L. (2019). Fostering green investments and tackling climate-related financial risks: Which role for macroprudential policies? *Ecological Economics* 160, 25–37.

Eley, S. (2021). Testing capacity of the EU banking sector to finance the transition to a sustainable economy. EBA Staff Paper No. 13, Frankfurt.

European Central Bank (2021a). *Detailed Roadmap of Climate-Change Related Actions*. Frankfurt: ECB.

European Central Bank (2021b). *The State of Climate and Environmental Risk Management in the Banking Sector: Report on the Supervisory Review of Banks' Approaches to Manage Climate and Environmental Risks*. Frankfurt: ECB.

European Commission (2019). The European Green Deal. Communication from the Commission to the European Parliament and the European Council. COM(2019) 640 final, Brussels.

Folkerts-Landau, D., and Garber, P. (1992). The ECB: A bank or a monetary policy rule? In M. Canzoneri, V. Grilli, and P. Masson (eds.), *Establishing a Central Bank: Issues in Europe and Lessons from the US*. Cambridge: Cambridge University Press, pp. 86–110.

Goodfriend, M. (2011). Central banking in the credit turmoil: An assessment of Federal Reserve practice. *Journal of Monetary Economics* 58(1), 1–12.

Goodhart, C., and Schoenmaker, D. (1995). Should the functions of monetary policy and banking supervision be separated? *Oxford Economic Papers* 47(4), 539–560.

Holling, C. S. (2001). Understanding the complexity of economic, ecological, and social systems. *Ecosystems* 4(5), 390–405.

Joint NGFS-INSPIRE Study Group on Biodiversity and Financial Stability (2022). Central banking in the biosphere: Biodiversity loss, financial risk and system stability – an agenda for action. Final Report, NGFS Occasional Paper.

Kennedy, S., Fuchs, M., van Ingen, W., and Schoenmaker, D. (2022). A resilience approach to corporate biodiversity impact measurement. *Business Strategy and the Environment*, 1–16. https://doi.org/10.1002/bse.3140

Lagarde, C. (2022). Further steps to incorporate climate change into ECB's monetary policy operations. Letter of the ECB president to the European Parliament, Frankfurt.

Lucas, R. (1976). Econometric policy evaluation: A critique. In K. Brunner and A. Meltzer (eds.), *The Phillips Curve and Labor Markets*. Carnegie-Rochester Conference Series on Public Policy. New York: American Elsevier, pp. 19–46.

Matikainen, S., Campiglio, E., and Zenghelis, D. (2017). The climate impact of quantitative easing. Grantham Research Institute on Climate Change and the Environment, Policy Paper.

McShane, K. (2017). Intrinsic values and economic valuation. In C. Spash (ed.), *Routledge Handbook of Ecological Economics*. Abingdon: Routledge, pp. 237–245.

Mitchell, T. (1998). Fixing the economy. *Cultural Studies* 12(1), 82–101.

Moos, K. A. (2019). The facts and the values of the Lucas critique. *Review of Political Economy* 31(1), 1–25.

Naylor, B. (2008). Greenspan admits free market ideology flawed. NPR. www.npr.org/templates/story/story.php?storyId=96070766&t=1633282765725

Orphanides, A. (2017). The fiscal-monetary policy mix in the euro area: Challenges at the zero lower bound. CEPR Discussion Paper No. 12039.

Padoa-Schioppa, T. (1999). EMU and banking supervision. *International Finance* 2(2), 295–308.

Persson, L., Carney Almroth, B., Collins, C., Cornell, S., de Wit, C., Diamond, M., Fantke, P., Hassellov, M., MacLeod, M., Ryberg, M., Sogaard Jorgensen, P., Villarrubia-Gomez, P., Wang, Z., and Hauschild, M. (2022). Outside the safe operating space of the planetary boundary for novel entities. *Environmental Science & Technology* 56(3), 1510–1521.

Robinson, J. (1972). The second crisis of economic theory. *American Economic Review* 62(1/2), 1–10.

Schnabel, I. (2021). Climate change and monetary policy: Central banks must do their part in fighting global warming. Finance & Development, International Monetary Fund, September, pp. 53–55.

Schoenmaker, D. (1997). Banking supervision and lender of last resort in EMU. In M. Andenas, L. Gormley, C. Hadjiemmanuil, and I. Harden (eds.), *European Economic and Monetary Union: The Institutional Framework*. London: Kluwer International.

Schoenmaker, D. (2013). Central banks role in financial stability. In G. Caprio (ed.), *Handbook of Safeguarding Global Financial Stability*, Vol. 2. Amsterdam: Elsevier, pp. 271–284.

Schoenmaker, D. (2021). Greening monetary policy. *Climate Policy* 21(4), 581–592.

Schoenmaker, D., and Schramade, W. (2019). *Principles of Sustainable Finance*. Oxford. Oxford University Press.

Schoenmaker, D., and Schramade, W. (2022). Valuing companies in transition. *Sustainability Letters* 1(1), 1–12.

Schoenmaker, D., and Stegeman, H. (2023). Can the market economy deal with sustainability? *De Economist* 171(1), 25–49.

Schoenmaker, D., and van Tilburg, R. (2016). What role for financial supervisors in addressing environmental risks? *Comparative Economic Studies* 58(3), 317–334.

Schoenmaker, D., and Véron, N. (2016). *European Banking Supervision: The First Eighteen Months.* Blueprint 25. Brussels: Bruegel.

Smits, R. (1997). *The European Central Bank: Institutional Aspects.* The Hague: Kluwer Law International.

Snower, D. J. (2021). Capitalism recoupled. CEPR Discussion Paper DP16302.

Steffen, W., Richardson, K., Rockström, J., Cornell, S., Fetzer, I., Bennett, E., Biggs, R., Carpenter, S., de Vries, W., de Wit, C., Folke, C., Gerten, D., Heinke, J., Mace, G., Persson, L., Ramanathan, V., Reyers, B., and Sörlinet, S. (2015). Planetary boundaries: Guiding human development on a changing planet. *Science* 347(6223), 736–747.

Stiglitz Report (2009). Report by the Commission on the measurement of economic performance and social progress. Paris.

Solow, R. M. (1974). Intergenerational equity and exhaustible resources. *Review of Economic Studies* 41(5), 29–45.

Temesgen, A., Storsletten, V., and Jakobsen, O. (2021). Circular economy – Reducing symptoms or radical change? *Philosophy of Management* 20, 37–56.

Thomä, J. and Dupre, S. (2017). Right direction, wrong equipment: Why transitions risks do not fit into regulatory stress tests. Discussion Paper, 20 Investing Initiative, London.

Tinbergen, J. (1952). *On the Theory of Economic Policy*. Amsterdam: North-Holland Publishing Company.

True Price (2021). Monetisation factors for true pricing: Version 2.0.3. Amsterdam.

Tucker, P. (2018). Pristine and parsimonious policy: Can central banks ever get back to it and why they should try. In P. Hartmann, H. Huang, and D. Schoenmaker (eds.), *The Changing Fortunes of Central Banking*. Cambridge: Cambridge University Press, pp. 48–64.

Van 't Klooster, J., and van Tilburg, R. (2020). *Targeting a Sustainable Recovery with Green TLTROs.* Brussels: Positive Money Europe.

Van Tilburg, R., and Simić, A. (2021). Legally green: Climate change and the ECB mandate. Sustainable Finance Lab Policy Paper, Utrecht.

Welsby, D., Price, J., Pye, S., and Ekins, P. (2021). Unextractable fossil fuels in a 1.5° C world. *Nature* 597 (7875), 230–234.

Wuermeling, J. (2018). Prospects for monetary policy implementation. Speech at the 2018 Banking Evening at the Deutsche Bundesbank's Regional Office in Baden-Württemberg, Stuttgart, 6 February.

Zaman, A. (2012). The normative foundations of scarcity. *Real-World Economics Review* 61, 22–39.

13

The Politics of Monetary Union and the Democratic Legitimacy of the ECB as a Strategic Actor

Sebastian Diessner

13.1 INTRODUCTION

Any take on the politics of monetary policy starts from the recognition that a *de facto* separation of central banking from democratic processes is impossible to achieve fully in a democratic society, even if it is mandated *de iure* in the form of central bank independence (Adolph, 2013, 2018; Kirshner, 2003). This implies that monetary authorities, like the European Central Bank (ECB), can and should be evaluated not only in terms of how well they perform according to their own mandates, but also in terms of wider normative criteria of democratic legitimation (Dietsch, 2020; van 't Klooster, 2020). This chapter thus submits that to make sense of the *politics* of Europe's *monetary* union we need to focus on the *legitimacy* of the *ECB*.

European political science and political economy debates have traditionally revolved around the dimensions of input, output, and – more recently – throughput legitimacy (Scharpf, 1999; Schmidt, 2013).[1] However, the literature has had far less to say about the ways in which policymakers navigate and draw upon these different dimensions to legitimate their policies. Normative accounts of democratic legitimation stress that input and output legitimacy 'coexist side by side, reinforcing, complementing, and supplementing each other' (Scharpf, 1999, p. 12) and that throughput legitimacy 'cannot be a substitute' for either or both of them (Schmidt, 2013, p. 18). In contrast, this chapter argues and demonstrates that strategic actors who seek to legitimate their policies at minimal cost and within given institutional constraints *will* try to substitute the dimensions for one another in a way which suits their interests. There is little doubt that the ECB qualifies for the title of strategic actor. Despite its technocratic credentials as an independent agent, the supranational central bank has by no means remained a disinterested bystander within Europe's Economic and Monetary Union (EMU).[2] To the contrary, it has communicated and pursued its interests with a high capacity for strategic action before, during, and after the Global Financial Crisis (GFC) (Heldt and Müller, 2021; Henning, 2016;

[1] *Input* legitimacy refers to participation by the citizens as well as responsiveness to their concerns; *output* legitimacy refers to the effective achievement of policy outcomes (on both, see Scharpf, 1970); and *throughput* legitimacy refers to the quality of governance processes in terms of four dimensions: accountability, transparency, inclusiveness, and openness to consultation (see Schmidt, 2013, p. 2). While political scientists and political economists have discovered and debated throughput legitimacy only more recently, legal scholars have long been grappling with procedural types of legitimation in general, and the conditions and instruments that underpin accountability in particular (see, for example, Amtenbrink, 1999, 2019).

[2] As former ECB president Mario Draghi (2012) aptly reminded the audience of his now-notorious 'whatever it takes' speech: 'I don't think we are unbiased observers in Frankfurt.'

Howarth, 2004; Jones, 2019; Mabbett and Schelkle, 2019; Macchiarelli et al., 2020a; Müller and Braun, 2021; and see Chang, Chapter 10 in this volume).

Against that backdrop, this chapter seeks to shed light on the ECB's *legitimation strategies* throughout the first two decades of EMU. It shows that the central bank has – for both organizational and systemic reasons – over-prioritized output legitimacy throughout much of its existence. This lop-sided legitimation strategy became unviable during the protracted crisis of the eurozone, however, which forced monetary policymakers to belatedly take steps towards strengthening the ECB's throughput legitimacy as well. Whether this new strategy will suffice to sustain the central bank's democratic legitimacy in the long run is questionable.

The remainder of the chapter is organized as follows. Section 13.2 briefly discusses the key dimensions of input, output, and throughput legitimacy in EMU and develops a theory of when and how the ECB can be expected to draw on these strategically. Section 13.3 traces the central bank's legitimation strategies empirically in light of its pre-crisis and post-crisis monetary policy-making. Section 13.4 compares the ECB's democratic legitimacy to that of other major central banks and discusses whether the politics of monetary policy in Europe are special. Section 13.5 reflects on what lies ahead for the ECB's legitimacy in the future.

13.2 THE DEMOCRATIC LEGITIMACY OF THE ECB

The legitimacy of the ECB is, first and foremost, based on an act of delegation of policy autonomy which is codified in the European Treaties.[3] The Treaties are derived from citizens' 'input' insofar as they are concluded by the EU's heads of state or government who, in turn, are voted into office by their citizens or parliaments (see Majone, 1999, p. 7). While this could be seen as a form of input legitimation on behalf of EU citizens via elected governments (and/or via popular referenda in several Member States), such inputs were effectively designed to remain a one-off in order to safeguard the far-reaching independence conferred upon the ECB. The Treaties stipulate in no uncertain terms that the supranational central bank shall not 'seek or take instructions from Union institutions, bodies, offices or agencies, from any government of a Member State or from any other body' (Article 130 TFEU) – or, put differently, that it shall not receive substantive inputs from anyone. For proponents of Europe's 'unprecedented divorce between the main monetary and fiscal authorities', this strict separation was seen as 'all to the good; indeed, it [was] largely the purpose of the exercise' (Goodhart, 1998, p. 410). Other observers have been less sanguine and have instead placed the ECB's unprecedented autonomy in the wider context of the EU's democratic deficit (Berman and McNamara, 1999; Majone, 1999; Sánchez-Cuenca, 2017; Verdun, 1998). In particular, the literature has pointed to an excessive reliance on output legitimation in EMU, rendering the legitimacy of macroeconomic policy overly dependent on the effective achievement of policy outcomes (Auer and Scicluna, 2021; Enderlein and Verdun, 2009; Jones, 2009; Sadeh, 2018).

To try and redress this imbalance, Europe's monetary policymakers have resorted to more procedural forms of legitimation. The clearest manifestation of this is the ECB's emphasis on accountability as the 'necessary counterpart' to its independence (ECB, 2021; and see Braun, 2017), a precondition for which is monetary policy transparency (Curtin, 2017; de Haan et al.,

[3] This sub-section draws substantively on Macchiarelli et al. (2020a).

2004).[4] The ECB's accountability, in turn, has come to revolve around a host of different practices, the most important of which is oversight by the input-legitimated European Parliament (EP). While also reporting to the Council of the EU, the European Commission, and the European Council (Article 284(3) TFEU), the quarterly hearings between the ECB president and the EP's Committee on Economic and Monetary Affairs (ECON), known as the Monetary Dialogue, have inarguably become the cornerstone of the central bank's accountability framework.

At the same time, the ECB's accountability in general, and the Monetary Dialogue in particular, have long been subject to controversial debate (Buiter, 1999; de Haan and Eijffinger, 2000; Issing, 1999) and have been faced with growing criticism from academics and think tanks in recent years (Chang and Hodson, 2019; Claeys et al., 2014; Jourdan and Diessner, 2019). Those critiques have centred around the non-substantive, and thus mostly procedural, nature of the ECB's accountability towards the European Parliament, which has no means at its disposal to reward or sanction the supranational central bank (Schmidt and Wood, 2019, p. 8).[5] How, then, has the ECB navigated the tensions stemming from its limited input legitimacy, overstretched output legitimacy, and non-substantive throughput legitimacy over time?

13.2.1 *A Theory of Legitimation Strategies*

The political science and political economy literature on the EU has established and debated the relative importance of input, output, and throughput legitimacy at length (see Scharpf, 1999; Schmidt, 2020). It has paid less attention, however, to the question of when and why one type of legitimation may come to trump either or both of the others.[6] In the case of EMU, it would seem that part of this question is predetermined *de iure*, due to the Treaty prohibition for the ECB to receive instructions or 'inputs'.[7] Yet the ways in which the central bank has sought to balance the remaining two dimensions of output and throughput legitimacy is far from self-evident and arguably lies to some extent within its own discretion. This requires a closer look at

[4] Scholars have observed a tendency for the ECB to equate accountability with transparency, which, albeit overlapping, are conceptually distinct categories (Buiter, 2006; Collignon and Diessner, 2016). For instance, the ECB is keen to highlight 'other information channels' as part of its accountability framework, including press conferences, accounts (i.e., minutes) of monetary policy meetings, economic bulletins, weekly financial statements, and media as well as research outputs (interviews, articles, and speeches) (see ECB, 2021; Fraccaroli et al., 2018).

[5] For critiques of proceduralism, and hence of throughput legitimacy, see Dawson and Maricut-Akbik (2021), Klein (2021), and Steffek (2019). Beyond this, note also the role which has been attributed to judicial review by the Court of Justice of the EU and the national courts, especially in the context of the ECB's crisis policy-making. On the interplay between judicial review and accountability, see Bobić and Dawson (Chapter 14 in this volume); on judicial review and democratic legitimacy, see de Boer and van 't Klooster (2020); and on both, see Markakis (2020). On the distinction between legal and other types of accountability in public administration research, see Romzek (2000) and van Osch et al. (2023).

[6] This sub-section draws substantively on an earlier version of Braun et al. (2022), which elaborated on the distinction between organizational and systemic interests in more depth. For a recent study of the ECB's legitimation strategies in times of crisis, see Christensen and Nedergaard (2023). On the (self-)legitimation strategies of independent agencies in the EU, see Rimkutė (2019). On strategic and institutional approaches to legitimacy in sociology and organizational studies, see Suchman (1995).

[7] Note, however, that Article 284(1)–(2) TFEU foresees the participation of the Council president in ECB meetings and of the ECB president in Council meetings. Moreover, it has been suspected that the ECB could seek or obtain inputs informally – as it supposedly did ahead of launching the Outright Monetary Transactions programme – which is harder to ascertain, however. This chimes with the often-highlighted vagueness of the ECB's mandate, as a result of which the central bank not only enjoys instrument and target independence, but also a degree of goal independence (Debelle and Fischer, 1994; De Grauwe, 2020). On the extent to which the mandate has become stretched, see Adamski (Chapter 9 in this volume).

TABLE 13.1 *The ECB's legitimation strategies*

Economic context	Dominant interest	Dominant legitimation strategy
Normal/pre-crisis	Organizational	**Output** (Mandated) > Throughput
Acute crisis	Systemic	**Output** (Reinterpreted) > Throughput
Non-acute/post-crisis	Organizational	Output (Diminished) < **Throughput**

Source: Author's elaboration, based on Braun et al. (2022).

the ECB's *de facto* legitimation strategies and, in particular, the varying interests behind its emphasis on output and throughput legitimation at different points in time.

A straightforward way to think about the ECB's strategic agency is to make a distinction between its organizational and systemic interests. While organizational interests inform the ECB's actions in non-crisis times, they are superseded by systemic interests in moments of crisis. Moreover, crisis times can usefully be subdivided into acute (fast-burning) and non-acute (slow-burning) crises (Boin et al., 2005; Seabrooke and Tsingou, 2019). In normal, non-crisis times central banks' organizational interests are shaped by their interactions with two main audiences: on the one hand, central banks seek to establish and maintain *credibility* in the eyes of market audiences (Lohmann, 2003) while, on the other hand, seeking to establish and maintain *legitimacy* in the eyes of political audiences (Mair, 2011; Moschella et al., 2020). Both of these efforts ultimately boil down to achieving and defending 'outputs' in the form of accomplishing mandated policy goals (Scharpf, 1999).[8]

Organizational interests cannot, however, account for central bank actions during crisis times, especially if the crisis is acute. Severe financial distress invariably forces central banks to step in as lenders of last resort, irrespective of the consequences for their credibility and legitimacy. The distinction between normal and crisis times applies with particular force to the ECB, which, in an acute crisis, is confronted with the very real possibility of a disorderly break-up of the monetary union over which it presides.[9] Avoiding such a breakdown – and, by implication, its own obsolescence – then becomes a systemic interest or 'grim necessity' (Dyson, 2013) for the ECB. Central banks whose lender-of-last-resort function is ambiguous, such as the ECB (Buiter, 1999), will then find that the only viable way to justify their actions is to reinterpret their mandates in order to argue that acute crisis-fighting is a precondition for achieving their mandated policy outputs.

Whether this legitimation strategy can suffice beyond the immediate emergency of an acute crisis is questionable, however. As the discrepancy between (original) mandate and (reinterpreted) policy outputs becomes visible to an ever-broader audience over time, it risks bringing about a growing loss in public trust and popularity for the central bank (Macchiarelli et al., 2020c). It is only at this point that the focus can be expected to shift more decisively towards improving the central bank's throughput legitimacy, as an imperfect substitute to fill the gaps that have been left not only by missing inputs, but also by diminished outputs.

In sum, and with regard to the question of which legitimation strategy will prevail over the others and when, the preceding discussion suggests a three-fold sequence in theory (summarized in Table 13.1). First, a near-exclusive focus by central bankers on output legitimacy in normal

[8] The perception of both efforts also rests on the ECB's epistemic authority on matters of macroeconomic policy (Dietsch et al., 2018; Mudge and Vauchez, 2016).

[9] While central bankers across the globe habitually stress that public trust in their currencies is vital to their own legitimacy (Braun, 2016), the ECB is perhaps the one major central bank that faced the most acute risk of unravelling of (trust in) the currency it governed in the aftermath of the Global Financial Crisis of 2008.

(i.e., pre-crisis) times. Second, a reinterpretation of said output legitimacy in acute crisis times. And third, an emphasis on throughput legitimacy in non-acute (i.e., post-)crisis times. The chapter now turns to illustrating this sequence empirically.

13.3 THE DEMOCRATIC LEGITIMACY OF THE ECB AS A STRATEGIC ACTOR, 1998–2020

Equipped with the above toolkit, this section sheds light on the varying relevance of input, output, and throughput legitimation in the ECB's monetary policy-making pre- and post-crisis.

13.3.1 *Normal, Pre-crisis Times: Business-as-(Un)Usual, 1998–2008*

Throughout the early years of EMU, the ECB was preoccupied with business as usual – or rather, with establishing what business as usual ought to look like for an unusual monetary authority which had been tasked with setting monetary policy for a union of initially twelve (and nowadays twenty) Member States. Modelled 'largely' on the German Bundesbank (Schmid, 1997) and situated nearby its 'boring older brother' in Frankfurt am Main (Schelkle, 2018), the young ECB seemed poised to develop its own version of one of the key mantras of the German central bank – namely, that independence should come with as little accountability as possible.[10] For instance, when confronted with proposals to create a 'dialogue between monetary policy and other policy areas', the ECB's first president, Wim Duisenberg, declared to the European Parliament early on that 'such a dialogue should be clearly distinguished from any attempts to coordinate policies *ex ante*', as this would only serve to 'increase uncertainty about policy actions' (Duisenberg, 1999; and see Braun et al., 2022). Instead, the ECB's approach to democratic legitimation became one of *ex post* answerability – or, in Duisenberg's half-joking words to Members of the European Parliament (MEPs): 'I will fully inform you *after* the event' (Adams and Osborn, 2001, emphasis added; see Akbik, 2022; Diessner, 2022).

As such, concerns about throughput legitimacy – and about democratic accountability in particular – seem to have played a subordinate role for the ECB during the first years of EMU.[11] Rather, the central bank's predominant concern lay with achieving output legitimacy by meeting its mandated primary objective of price stability. This entailed a lengthy process of defining its own price stability target, which culminated in the 2003 monetary policy strategy review, so as to cement a yardstick against which to measure 'outputs' in the first place. Duisenberg's successor, Jean-Claude Trichet, who took the helm of the central bank shortly after the completion of the review, built on these foundations and painstakingly sought to make the price stability target the be-all and end-all of debates about the ECB's policymaking. For instance, in his regular exchanges with the ECON Committee, Trichet 'frequently stopped technical questions by referring to the ECB's mandate', which meant that debates 'covered broad macroeconomic issues and remained more superficial' (Collignon and Diessner, 2016,

[10] Paul Tucker (2018, p. 2) summarizes this 'German view', to which he objects, as follows: 'We testify on other things, other people's affairs, but we do not testify on monetary policy, and nor should we, because it would undermine our independence', implying that independent monetary policymakers should be 'protected from accountability' (Helmut Schlesinger quoted in Tucker, 2018, p. 9).

[11] In Willem Buiter's (1999, p. 207) words, it was 'do[ing] no good either to the European Parliament or to the ECB to have the President of the ECB walk all over the MEPs'. See, however, Issing (1999).

p. 1305).[12] This state of affairs would change eventually, but only gradually, after the eurozone crisis.

13.3.2 *Acute Crisis Times: Preserving the Euro, 2009–2014*

It is fair to say that the story of the eurozone crisis, and the ECB's pivotal role in resolving it, has become so familiar that it hardly requires reiterating in depth. In the collective memory of lay and expert observers in Europe and beyond, the ECB's crisis management essentially boils down to three vital – if not magic – words: 'whatever it takes' (Bloomberg, 2018). Yet at least as important as the ECB's policy interventions, including said promise of flexible and quasi-unlimited government bond purchases, were the legitimation strategies for these interventions as well as their wider political implications.

At closer inspection, there is a technical and a more substantial side to those legitimations, reflecting not merely the organizational but rather the systemic interests of the central bank. In terms of technicalities, the ECB was at pains to point out that interventions in sovereign bond markets were reconcilable with its mandated objective of price stability. It argued that this was the case as long as sovereign risk premia did 'not have to do with factors inherent to' eurozone sovereigns themselves and '[t]o the extent that the size of these sovereign premia hampers the functioning of the monetary policy transmission channel' (Draghi, 2012).[13] This legitimation strategy amounted to a subtle reinterpretation of the ECB's mandate in terms of elevating the auxiliary objective of financial stability to achieve the primary objective of price stability (Adamski, Chapter 9 in this volume).

The subtlety of the technical argument notwithstanding, it did little to avert a political backlash across parts of the monetary union, let alone protracted legal battles in European and national constitutional courts (Saurugger and Fontan, 2019; Chang, Chapter 10 in this volume). The fact that these repercussions, as well as their negative impact on the ECB's perceived legitimacy, were largely foreseeable strongly suggests that they were deemed a risk worth taking in light of the systemic threat to the single currency as a whole (Braun et al., 2022; Ferrara, 2020). The same can be said of the ECB's advocacy for fiscal consolidation and structural reform, and its ill-fated participation in the Troika (Lütz et al., 2019), all of which provoked predictable pushback across other parts of the monetary union (Kentikelenis, 2018; Schmidt, 2020).

However, the more significant reinterpretation which took place was in terms of the ECB's role within EMU as a whole. Consciously or not, the supranational central bank would rise to become the guarantor of the stability not only of prices and financial markets in the euro area, but of the euro area itself (Nicoli, 2019). This was most evident in president Mario Draghi's (2012) famed pledge that the ECB would do whatever it took to 'preserve the euro'. When confronted with another acute and equally systemic crisis in March 2020, his successor Christine Lagarde would make recourse to the very same legitimation strategy, pledging that there were 'no limits to our commitment to *the euro*' (Lagarde, 2020, emphasis added).

[12] During his penultimate appearance before the EP, the outgoing ECB president expressed surprise at the fact that ECON members had not been inquiring exclusively about inflation and interest rates, contrary to what he 'would have expected' (Trichet, 2011, p. 15, quoted in Claeys and Domínguez-Jiménez, 2020, p. 21).

[13] This implied a belated recognition of the argumentation that had been championed by observers like Paul De Grauwe (2011; see Wolf, 2012).

13.3.3 *Non-Acute, Post-Crisis Times: Throughput Legitimacy to the Rescue, 2015–2020*

Beyond the reinterpretation of its mandate, a final legitimation strategy which became apparent towards the end of the crisis was the ECB's attempt to improve its throughput legitimacy. This manifested itself in the form of a 'strategic partnership' between the ECB and the ECON Committee (Torres, 2013), with exchanges becoming reflective of a 'more emancipated' accountability relationship between the two institutions and with president Draghi displaying an increased 'willing[ness] to answer even hypothetical questions' by MEPs compared to his predecessors (Collignon and Diessner, 2016, p. 1305). However, it would take several years and an intensifying political backlash for these and other throughput legitimation efforts to be pursued more seriously.

Despite being perceived as the saviour of the eurozone in academic circles and beyond (Bloomberg, 2018; Iversen and Soskice, 2013, p. 15; Wallace, 2015, p. 175), the post-crisis period proved to be anything but smooth sailing for the ECB. The protracted nature of the crisis and a decidedly sluggish recovery across large parts of the monetary union meant that growth remained well below – and unemployment well above – their pre-crisis trajectories. Accordingly, anti-establishment parties mushroomed and eventually found their way into coalition governments in several Member States (Hopkin, 2020). Maintaining output legitimacy in the sense of keeping the eurozone just about afloat, while no mean feat, did not turn out to be enough for the ECB. To make things worse, the central bank also began to underperform on its traditional yardstick for 'output'– i.e., price stability – as it faced the threat of deflation from late-2014 onwards (Rostagno et al., 2019).

The fateful combination of limited input legitimacy, neglected throughput legitimacy, and diminished output legitimacy can explain the broad-based backlash against the ECB post-crisis (Macchiarelli et al., 2020b). In short, two disparate but interlinked groups of critics came to voice their discontent in strange unison. Those – mainly from Europe's north – who thought the ECB was doing *too much* given its limited mandate, were joined by those – mainly from Europe's south – who thought it was doing *too little* given the meagre post-crisis recovery (Macchiarelli et al., 2020c; Walter et al., 2020). Among the latter, one may also count those who thought the ECB was asking too much *of them* in terms of fiscal restraint and structural reform, with too little democratic legitimation for doing so (Braun et al., 2022). The resulting deterioration in public trust has been amply documented, including by the central bank itself (see e.g. Bergbauer et al., 2020).

In response to these growing threats to its legitimacy, the ECB has ramped up its communication strategy, including towards the general public (Ehrmann and Wabitsch, 2021; Gardt et al., 2021; Lokdam, 2020; de Haan, Chapter 11 in this volume). It has started to publish minutes or 'accounts' of its monetary policy meetings (Heidebrecht, 2015) and has reacted to calls for more transparency in its asset-purchasing programmes. Moreover, the central bank launched a series of 'ECB Listens' events, starting with civil society organizations in 2019, which fed into its second monetary policy strategy review of 2021 (Begg, 2021). Despite these belated efforts to strengthen the ECB's throughput legitimacy, whether we can 'believe [that] it will be enough', to paraphrase Draghi's 2012 speech, remains an open question to date (which I shall return to in the concluding section).

13.4 IS THE ECB'S DEMOCRATIC LEGITIMACY SPECIAL?

This section discusses whether the ECB's legitimacy is comparable to that of other major central banks. It argues that the ECB's democratic legitimacy is undoubtedly special, but not in the way we tend to think, and that being special does not amount to being incomparable, as opposed to the often-stressed notion that the monetary union is *sui generis* and thus beyond comparison.

13.4.1 *Same Same, but Different*

It is frequently said of Europe's Economic and Monetary Union that it is a unique construct and that its monetary authority, the ECB, is the most independent central bank in the world. While both statements are true, neither can be taken to imply that the ECB's actions are predetermined or that the politics surrounding its monetary policy-making are incomparable to other major central banks – many of which face similar challenges to those faced by the ECB (Sandbu, 2021). In particular, two salient features of EMU are typically highlighted to suggest that Europe's monetary union is unique. The first points to the sheer heterogeneity among the members of the union (Eichengreen, 1990; Scharpf, 2012), which leads to a situation in which the ECB is confronted with a diverse set of twenty national economies and societies, all of which are represented on the ECB's Governing Council through their national central bank governors. The second stresses the fact that this supranational central bank does not have a unified fiscal counterpart, which has led to an unprecedented divorce (read, degree of independence) between the monetary and fiscal authorities in any given polity (Goodhart, 1998).[14]

While both suggestions are correct, neither of them renders EMU, or its legitimation, incomparable. First, heterogeneity is by no means exclusive to Europe: there is little doubt about the diversity among regions in the United States monetary union, for example (Krugman, 1993; Schelkle, 2017).[15] This diversity has meant that the Federal Reserve System is a more 'decentralized central bank' than is commonly assumed (Ainsley, 2021), even if less so than the Eurosystem (Cohen-Setton and Vallée, 2018). Thus, the key features of centralized agenda-setting (on behalf of a federal executive board) and of decentralized monetary policy *inputs* (on behalf of sub-federal central banks) are not all that different between the two monetary unions. Second, it is obvious that the ECB does not have a unified fiscal counterpart at the supranational level. However, evidence from the GFC suggests that this circumstance is not decisive for the achievement of policy *outputs* either, as Mabbett and Schelkle (2019) demonstrate for the case of financial stabilization (see also Diessner, 2018, 2019).

Yet what is truly special about the ECB's democratic legitimacy is that it has become inextricably linked to the legitimacy – and essentially the continued integration – of the EU polity as a whole (Lokdam, 2019).[16] Since the eurozone crisis at the latest, it has become apparent that the central bank not only serves to resolve the commitment problems of its Member State principals and thereby furthers the integration of EMU, which is in line with the standard logic of delegation that runs through both the liberal-intergovernmental and neo-functionalist traditions of EU scholarship (Franchino, 2007; Moravcsik, 1998; Pierson, 1996; Sandholtz and Stone Sweet, 2012; Stone Sweet and Sandholtz, 1997; Tallberg, 2002; Thatcher

[14] What is less appreciated in the literature is the fact that the ECB also boasts one of the most autonomous administrations of any international organization, second only to the World Bank, according to Bauer and Ege (2016, pp. 1031–33).

[15] On the heterogeneity of the US 'dollarzone' and the UK 'poundzone', see Schelkle (2014, 2017b).

[16] One other broadly comparable example that comes to mind is that of the Bank of England's brief and controversial involvement in quasi-constitutional debates around the British referendum on membership in the European Union as well as the Scottish referendum on independence from the United Kingdom. The Bank appeared to articulate a strong preference for the United Kingdom to remain a member of the EU during the former, while the question of whether an independent Scotland would be able to continue to use the British pound sterling as its official currency became a salient topic during the latter.

and Stone Sweet, 2002). Instead, it has come to resolve the *de*-commitment problems of its principals as well, by reinterpreting incomplete Treaty requirements in order to avert a disorderly *dis*integration of the union (Diessner and Genschel, 2021; Genschel and Tesche, 2020; Schulz and Verdun, 2022). This shift is reflective of a broader transformation of EU politics after the global financial crisis. Whereas previously the main political cleavages at the European level had run along the same lines as those within national democracies – including the traditional left–right cleavage – this has given way to a new dominant divide, namely of being either in favour of or against the European Union and its integration per se (see Hix et al., 2007, 2019; Hooghe and Marks, 2009).

These factors uniquely complicate the politics of central bank legitimacy in the case of EMU. Like other supranational institutions, the ECB has a systemic interest in maintaining the union (Pollack, 2003, p. 384; Scharpf, 1999, p. 62; Spielberger, 2023). Unlike other supranational institutions, however, it also has the necessary financial power to preserve the union in the short to medium term. Moreover, the ECB's 'dependence' on the existence of EMU extends beyond the mere preservation of its institutional status quo. If we accept the argument that EMU is 'unfinished' and 'incomplete' and thus remains 'fragile' unless complemented with more deeply integrated fiscal and financial unions, then the ECB is not only dependent on the continued existence but also on the eventual completion of the union (Begg, 2023; De Grauwe, 2011; Macchiarelli et al., 2019). This helps explain its strong preference for said completion (Jones, 2019; Schulz et al., 2020), as expressed through regular participation in the 'presidents' reports' as well as explicit calls on Member State governments to engage in much-needed institution-building (Diessner and Lisi, 2020; but see Hodson, 2011).

13.5 CONCLUSION

This chapter started from the proposition that the politics of Europe's monetary union are inextricably linked to the question of the legitimacy of the ECB. It then identified a gap in the literature on democratic legitimation in the EU, which has focused predominantly on input, output, and throughput legitimacy thus far, but which has told us little about how strategic actors navigate these dimensions in the pursuit of their own interests. To fill this gap, the chapter has put forward a theory of the ECB's legitimation strategies based on distinctions between normal and crisis times as well as between the organizational and systemic interests of a central bank. A closer look at the ECB's pre-crisis and post-crisis actions reveals that Europe's monetary policymakers have sought to enhance their throughput legitimacy only as a measure of last resort, once their policy outputs were increasingly called into doubt. It also reveals that the ECB's legitimacy has become closely tied to the existence and continued integration of the monetary union as a whole, which is what sets it apart from other major central banks.

Yet a vexing question remains. Can the ECB's current legitimation strategy be enough to sustain its democratic legitimacy in the future? That the central bank's fortunes have become tied to those of the euro area itself is a reason for both optimism and pessimism in this regard. On the optimistic side, one may note that while public trust in the ECB has remained subdued ever since the eurozone crisis, support for the single currency has held up relatively strongly (Bergbauer et al., 2020). One simple answer to the question whether the ECB's throughput legitimacy will be enough could thus be that it does not have to be enough, as long as it is the output legitimacy of EMU – or the sheer perception thereof (Jones, 2009) – that matters.

On a more pessimistic note, however, this state of affairs also gives rise to a unique risk to the ECB's democratic legitimacy. If the central bank openly takes responsibility for preserving the monetary union, as it has done throughout successive crises, then it will be difficult, if not impossible, for the ECB to disentangle its legitimacy from that of the union when need be. As a result, Europe's monetary policymakers run the risk of taking the blame, even more than other actors, for the perceived outputs of EMU in areas for which they bear little to no responsibility and over which they can exert little to no influence on their own (Adamski, Chapter 9 in this volume). This helps explain the ECB's striking loss of popularity not merely in and as of itself, but also to an extent which exceeds that of other EU institutions (Macchiarelli et al., 2020a). Normative accounts of democratic legitimation have long cautioned us that any attempt at substituting input, output, and throughput legitimacy for one another is ultimately bound to fail. The ECB, and the monetary union more broadly, are poised to remain suitable test cases for these normative claims in the future.

REFERENCES

Adams, R., and Osborn, A. (2001). ECB defends U-turn. *The Guardian*, 29 May. https://amp.theguardian.com/business/2001/may/29/emu.theeuro.

Adolph, C. (2013). *Bankers, Bureaucrats, and Central Bank Politics: The Myth of Neutrality*. New York: Cambridge University Press.

Adolph, C. (2018). The missing politics of central banks. *PS: Political Science & Politics* 51(4), 737–742.

Ainsley, C. (2021). Decentralized central banks: Political ideology and the Federal Reserve system of regional banks. *Governance* 34(2), 277–294.

Akbik, A. (2022). *The European Parliament as an Accountability Forum: Overseeing the Economic and Monetary Union*. Cambridge: Cambridge University Press.

Amtenbrink, F. (1999). *The Democratic Accountability of Central Banks: A Comparative Study of the European Central Bank*. Oxford: Hart Publishing.

Amtenbrink, F. (2019). The European Central Bank's intricate independence versus accountability conundrum in the post-crisis governance framework. *Maastricht Journal of European and Comparative Law* 26(1), 165–179.

Auer, S., and Scicluna, N. (2021). The impossibility of constitutionalizing emergency Europe. *Journal of Common Market Studies* 59, 20–31.

Bauer, M. W., and Ege, J. (2016). Bureaucratic autonomy of international organizations' secretariats. *Journal of European Public Policy* 23(7), 1019–1037.

Begg, I. (2021). The European Central Bank's revised monetary policy strategy, *LSE EUROPP*. https://blogs.lse.ac.uk/europpblog/2021/08/20/the-european-central-banks-revised-monetary-policy-strategy/.

Begg, I. (2023). *Completing a Genuine Economic and Monetary Union*. Elements in Economics of European Integration. Cambridge: Cambridge University Press.

Bergbauer, S., Hernborg, N., Jamet, J.-F., and Persson, E. (2020). The reputation of the euro and the European Central Bank: Interlinked or disconnected? *Journal of European Public Policy* 27(8), 1178–1194.

Berman, S., and McNamara, K. R. (1999). Bank on democracy: Why central banks need public oversight. *Foreign Affairs* 78(2), 2–8.

Bloomberg (2018). 3 words and $3 trillion: The inside story of how Mario Draghi saved the euro. www.bloomberg.com/news/features/2018-11-27/3-words-and-3-trillion-the-inside-story-of-how-mario-draghi-saved-the-euro

Boin, A., 't Hart, P., Stern, E., and Sundelius, B. (2005). *The Politics of Crisis Management: Public Leadership under Pressure*. Cambridge: Cambridge University Press.

Braun, B. (2016). Speaking to the people? Money, trust, and central bank legitimacy in the age of quantitative easing. *Review of International Political Economy* 23(6), 1064–1092.

Braun, B. (2017). *Two Sides of the Same Coin? Independence and Accountability of the European Central Bank*. Brussels: Transparency International EU.

Braun, B., Di Carlo, D., Diessner, S., and Düsterhöft, M. (2022). Between governability and legitimacy: The ECB and structural reforms. *SocArXiv*. https://osf.io/preprints/socarxiv/dp3nv/.

Buiter, W. H. (1999). Alice in Euroland. *Journal of Common Market Studies* 37(2), 181–209.

Buiter, W. H. (2006). How robust is the new conventional wisdom in monetary policy? The surprising fragility of the theoretical foundations of inflation targeting and central bank independence. CEPR Discussion Paper No. 5772.

Chang, M., and Hodson, D. (2019). Reforming the European Parliament's monetary and economic dialogues: Creating accountability through a euro area oversight subcommittee. In O. Costa (ed.), *The European Parliament in Times of EU Crisis: Dynamics and Transformations*. London: Palgrave Macmillan, pp. 343–364.

Christensen, S. E., and Nedergaard, P. (2023). All along the watch tower: The European Central Bank and legitimation strategies in times of crisis. *Journal of Common Market Studies*.

Claeys, G., and Domínguez-Jiménez, M. (2020). How can the European Parliament better oversee the European Central Bank? EP Monetary Dialogue Papers, September.

Claeys, G., Hallerberg, M., and Tschekassin, O. (2014). European Central Bank accountability: How the Monetary Dialogue could evolve. Bruegel Policy Contribution. Issue 2014/04.

Cohen-Setton, J., and Vallée, S. (2018). Federalizing a central bank: A comparative study of the early years of the Federal Reserve and the European Central Bank. In J. F. Kirkegaard and A. S. Posen (eds.), *Lessons for EU Integration from US History*. Washington, DC: Peterson Institute for International Economics, pp. 108–142.

Collignon, S., and Diessner, S. (2016). The ECB's monetary dialogue with the European Parliament: Efficiency and accountability during the euro crisis? *Journal of Common Market Studies* 54(6), 1296–1312.

Curtin, D. (2017). Accountable independence of the European Central Bank: Seeing the logics of transparency. *European Law Journal* 23(1–2), 28–44.

Dawson, M., and Maricut-Akbik, A. (2021). Accountability in the EU's para-regulatory state: The case of the Economic and Monetary Union. *Regulation & Governance* 17(1), 142–157.

Debelle, G., and Fischer, S. (1994). How independent should a central bank be? Federal Reserve Bank of San Francisco Working Papers in Applied Economic Theory, 94-05.

De Boer, N., and van 't Klooster, J. (2020). The ECB, the courts and the issue of democratic legitimacy after Weiss. *Common Market Law Review* 57(6), 1689–1724.

De Grauwe, P. (2011). The governance of a fragile eurozone. CEPS Working Document, 346.

De Grauwe, P. (2020). *Economics of Monetary Union*, 13th ed. Oxford: Oxford University Press.

De Haan, J., and Eijffinger, S. C. W. (2000). The democratic accountability of the European Central Bank: A comment on two fairy-tales. *Journal of Common Market Studies* 38(3), 393–407.

De Haan, J., Amtenbrink, F., and Waller, S. (2004). The transparency and credibility of the European Central Bank. *Journal of Common Market Studies* 42(4), 775–794.

Diessner, S. (2018). The spectre of central bankruptcy in Europe and Japan: Towards a political economy of central bank capital. SASE 30th Annual Meeting, 23–25 June.

Diessner, S. (2019). Essays in the political economy of central banking. PhD Dissertation, London School of Economics and Political Science.

Diessner, S. (2022). The promises and pitfalls of the ECB's 'legitimacy-as-accountability' towards the European Parliament post-crisis. *Journal of Legislative Studies* 28(3), 402–420.

Diessner, S., and Genschel, P. (2021). The ECB during the COVID-19 and eurozone crises: Supranational agency, de-commitment, and principal loss. Unpublished manuscript.

Diessner, S., and Lisi, G. (2020). Masters of the 'Masters of the Universe'? Monetary, fiscal and financial dominance in the eurozone. *Socio-Economic Review* 18(2), 315–335.

Dietsch, P. (2020). Independent agencies, distribution, and legitimacy: The case of central banks. *American Political Science Review* 114(2), 591–595.

Dietsch, P., Claveau, F., and Fontan, C. (2018). *Do Central Banks Serve the People?* Cambridge: Polity Press.

Draghi, M. (2012). Verbatim of the Remarks by Mario Draghi at the Global Investment Conference, London, 26 July. www.ecb.europa.eu/press/key/date/2012/html/sp120726.en.html

Duisenberg, W. (1999). Introductory statement at the European Parliament, Strasbourg, 26 October.

Dyson, K. (2013). Sworn to grim necessity? Imperfections of European economic governance, normative political theory, and supreme emergency. *Journal of European Integration* 35(3), 207–222.

ECB (2021). Accountability. www.ecb.europa.eu/ecb/orga/accountability/html/index.en.html

Eichengreen, B. (1990). Is Europe an optimal currency area? CEPR Discussion Paper No. 478.

Ehrmann, M., and Wabitsch, A. (2021). Central bank communication with non-experts: A road to nowhere? ECB Working Paper No. 2594.
Enderlein, E., and Verdun, A. (2009). EMU's teenage challenge: What have we learned and can we predict from political science? *Journal of European Public Policy* 16(4), 490–507.
Ferrara, F. M. (2020). The battle of ideas on the euro crisis: Evidence from ECB intermeeting speeches. *Journal of European Public Policy* 27(10), 1463–1486.
Fraccaroli, N., Giovannini, A., and Jamet, J.-F. (2018). The evolution of the ECB's accountability practices during the crisis. *ECB Economic Bulletin*, Issue 5/2018.
Franchino, F. (2007). *The Powers of the Union: Delegation in the EU*. Cambridge: Cambridge University Press.
Gardt, M., Angino, S., Mee, S., and Glöckler, G. (2021). ECB communication with the wider public. *ECB Economic Bulletin*, Issue 8/2021.
Genschel, P., and Tesche, T. (2020). Supranational agents as de-commitment devices: The ECB during the eurozone crisis. ACES Research Paper No. 2020/02.
Goodhart, C. A. E. (1998). The two concepts of money: Implications for the analysis of optimal currency areas. *European Journal of Political Economy* 14(3), 407–432.
Heidebrecht, S. (2015). Wie transparent ist die Europäische Zentralbank? Eine international vergleichende Betrachtung vor dem Hintergrund der weitreichenden Neuerungen zum Januar 2015. *Zeitschrift für Politikwissenschaft* 25(4), 501–526.
Heldt, E. C., and Müller, T. (2021) The (self-)empowerment of the European Central Bank during the sovereign debt crisis. *Journal of European Integration* 43(1), 83–98.
Henning, C. R. (2016). The ECB as a strategic actor: Central banking in a politically fragmented monetary union. In J. A. Caporaso and M. Rhodes (eds.), *The Political and Economic Dynamics of the Eurozone Crisis*. Oxford: Oxford University Press, pp. 167–199.
Hix, S., Noury, A., and Roland, G. (2007). *Democratic Politics in the European Parliament*. Cambridge: Cambridge University Press.
Hix, S., Noury, A., and Roland, G. (2019). Changing political cleavages in advanced democracies: Evidence from the European Parliament. Unpublished manuscript.
Hodson, D. (2011). *Governing the Euro Area in Good Times and Bad*. Oxford: Oxford University Press.
Hopkin, J. (2020). *Anti-System Politics: The Crisis of Market Liberalism in Rich Democracies*. Oxford: Oxford University Press.
Hooghe, L., and Marks, G. (2009). A postfunctionalist theory of European integration: From permissive consensus to constraining dissensus. *British Journal of Political Science* 39(1), 1–23.
Howarth, D. (2004). The ECB and the Stability Pact: Policeman and judge? *Journal of European Public Policy* 11(5), 832–853.
Issing, O. (1999). The Eurosystem: Transparent and accountable or 'Willem in Euroland'. *Journal of Common Market Studies* 37(2), 503–519.
Iversen, T., and Soskice, D. (2013). A structural-institutional explanation of the eurozone crisis. Unpublished manuscript.
Jones, E. (2009). Output legitimacy and the Global Financial Crisis: Perceptions matter. *Journal of Common Market Studies* 47(5), 1085–1105.
Jones, E. (2019). Do central bankers dream of political union? From epistemic community to common identity. *Comparative European Politics* 17(4), 530–547.
Jourdan, S., and Diessner, S. (2019). *From Dialogue to Scrutiny: Strengthening the Parliamentary Oversight of the European Central Bank*. Brussels: Positive Money Europe.
Kentikelenis, A. (2018). The social aftermath of economic disaster: Karl Polanyi, counter-movements in action, and the Greek crisis. *Socio-Economic Review* 16(1), 39–59.
Kirshner, J. (2003). The inescapable politics of money. In J. Kirshner (ed.), *Monetary Orders: Ambiguous Economics, Ubiquitous Politics*. Ithaca, NY: Cornell University Press, pp. 3–24.
Klein, S. (2021). Democracy against proceduralism. *LPE Project*. https://lpeproject.org/blog/democracy-against-proceduralism/
Krugman, P. (1993). Lessons of Massachusetts for EMU. In F. Torres and F. Giavazzi (eds.), *Adjustment and Growth in the European Monetary Union*, Cambridge: Cambridge University Press, pp. 241–261.
Lagarde, C. (2020). Twitter, @Lagarde. twitter.com/lagarde/status/1240414918966480896

Lohmann, S. (2003). Why do institutions matter? An audience-cost theory of institutional commitment. *Governance* 16(1), 95–110.
Lokdam, H. (2019). Banking on sovereignty: A genealogy of the European Central Bank's independence. PhD Dissertation, London School of Economics and Political Science.
Lokdam, H. (2020). 'We serve the people of Europe': Reimagining the ECB's political master in the wake of its emergency politics. *Journal of Common Market Studies* 58(4), 978–998.
Lütz, S., Hilgers, S., and Schneider, S. (2019). Accountants, Europeanists and monetary guardians: Bureaucratic cultures and conflicts in IMF-EU lending programs, *Review of International Political Economy* 26(6), 1187–1210.
Mabbett, D., and Schelkle, W. (2019). Independent or lonely? Central banking in crisis. *Review of International Political Economy* 26(3), 436–460.
Macchiarelli, C., Gerba, E., and Diessner, S. (2019). The ECB's unfinished business: Challenges ahead for EMU monetary and fiscal policy architecture. Note for the European Parliament's Committee on Economic and Monetary Affairs, PE 638.423.
Macchiarelli, C., Monti, M., Wiesner, C., and Diessner, S. (2020a). *The European Central Bank between the Financial Crisis and Populisms*. Cham: Palgrave Macmillan.
Macchiarelli, C., Monti, M., Wiesner, C., and Diessner, S. (2020b). The growing challenge of legitimacy amid central bank independence. In *The European Central Bank between the Financial Crisis and Populisms*. Cham: Palgrave Macmillan, pp. 103–121.
Macchiarelli, C., Monti, M., Wiesner, C., and Diessner, S. (2020c). How popular has the ECB been? Popularity, protest, and populism post-crisis. In *The European Central Bank between the Financial Crisis and Populisms*. Cham: Palgrave Macmillan, pp. 123–143.
Mair, P. (2011). Bini Smaghi vs. the parties: Representative government and institutional constraints. EUI Working Paper, RSCAS 2011/22.
Majone, G. (1999). The regulatory state and its legitimacy problems. *West European Politics* 22(1), 1–24.
Markakis, M. (2020). *Accountability in the Economic and Monetary Union: Foundations, Policy, and Governance*. Oxford: Oxford University Press.
Moravcsik, A. (1998). *The Choice for Europe: Social Power and State Purpose from Messina to Maastricht*. Ithaca, NY: Cornell University Press.
Moschella, M., Pinto, L., and Martocchia Diodati, N. (2020). Let's speak more? How the ECB responds to public contestation. *Journal of European Public Policy* 27(3), 400–418.
Mudge, S. L., and Vauchez, A. (2016). Fielding supranationalism: The European central bank as a field effect. *Sociological Review Monographs* 64(2), 146–169.
Müller, M., and Braun, C. (2021). Guiding or following the crowd? Strategic communication as reputational and regulatory strategy. *Journal of Public Administration Research and Theory* 31(4), 670–686.
Nicoli, F. (2019). Neofunctionalism revisited: Integration theory and varieties of outcomes in the Eurocrisis. *Journal of European Integration* 42(7), 897–916.
Pierson, P. (1996). The path to European integration: A historical institutionalist analysis. *Comparative Political Studies* 29(2), 123–163.
Pollack, M. A. (2003). *The Engines of European Integration: Delegation, Agency, and Agenda Setting in the EU*. Oxford: Oxford University Press.
Rimkuté, D. (2019). Building organizational reputation in the European regulatory state: An analysis of EU agencies' communications. *Governance* 33, 385–406.
Romzek, B. (2000). Dynamics of public sector accountability in an era of reform. *International Review of Administrative Sciences* 66(1), 21–44.
Rostagno, M., Altavilla, C., Carboni, G., Lemke, W., Motto, R., Saint Guilhem, A., and Yiangou, J. (2019). A tale of two decades: The ECB's monetary policy at 20. ECB Working Paper No. 2346.
Sadeh, T. (2018). How did the euro area survive the crisis? *West European Politics* 42(1), 201–226.
Sánchez-Cuenca, I. (2017). From a deficit of democracy to a technocratic order: The postcrisis debate on Europe. *Annual Review of Political Science* 20, 351–369.
Sandbu, M. (2021). The European school of central banking is no more. *Financial Times*, 13 July. www.ft.com/content/435e9652-96f3-4c8c-94c3-7863362688e1

Sandholtz, W., and Stone Sweet, A. (2012). Neo-functionalism and supranational governance. In E. Jones, A. Menon, and S. Weatherill (eds.), *The Oxford Handbook of the European Union*. Oxford: Oxford University Press, pp. 18–33.

Saurugger, S., and Fontan, C. (2019). The judicialisation of EMU politics: Resistance to the EU's new economic governance mechanisms at the domestic level. *European Journal of Political Research* 58 (4), 1066–1087.

Scharpf, F. W. (1970). *Demokratietheorie zwischen Utopie und Anpassung*. Konstanz: Universitätsverlag.

Scharpf, F. W. (1999). *Governing in Europe*. Oxford: Oxford University Press.

Scharpf, F. W. (2012). Legitimacy intermediation in the multilevel European polity and its collapse in the euro crisis. MPIfG Discussion Paper No. 12/6.

Schelkle, W. (2018). The ECB at 20: Not Like Its Boring Older Brother. In P. De Grauwe, W. Schelkle, S. Diessner, H. Lokdam and S. Vallée, *Five Views: What We've Learned from 20 Years of the European Central Bank*. LSE EUROPP. https://blogs.lse.ac.uk/europpblog/2018/06/01/four-views-what-weve-learned-from-20-years-of-the-european-central-bank

Schelkle, W. (2014). The 'poundzone' is just as sub-optimal a currency area as the Eurozone, LSE EUROPP. https://blogs.lse.ac.uk/europpblog/2014/07/30/the-poundzone-is-just-as-sub-optimal-a-currency-area-as-the-eurozone/

Schelkle, W. (2017a). *The Political Economy of Monetary Solidarity: Understanding the Euro Experiment*. Oxford: Oxford University Press.

Schelkle, W. (2017b). Listening to the experts on European monetary integration: Comment on Noah Carl. *Political Quarterly* 88(4), 684–688.

Schmid, J. (1997). Bundesbank chief says euro could spawn wage conflicts. *International Herald Tribune*. www.nytimes.com/1997/02/28/business/worldbusiness/IHT-bundesbank-chief-says-euro-could-spawn-wage.html

Schmidt, V. A. (2013). Democracy and legitimacy in the European Union revisited: Input, output and 'throughput'. *Political Studies* 61(1), 2–22.

Schmidt, V. A. (2020). *Europe's Crisis of Legitimacy: Governing by Rules and Ruling by Numbers in the Eurozone*. Oxford: Oxford University Press.

Schmidt, V. A., and Wood, M. (2019). Conceptualising throughput legitimacy: Procedural mechanisms of accountability, transparency, inclusiveness and openness in EU governance. *Public Administration* 97 (4), 727–740.

Schulz, D., and Verdun, A. (2022). The European Central Bank: A bulwark against (differentiated) disintegration? In B. Leruth, S. Gänzle, and J. Trondal (eds.), *The Routledge Handbook of Differentiation in the European Union*. London: Routledge.

Schulz, D., Gardt, M., and da Conceição-Heldt, E. (2020). What European Union do central bankers want? Preference formation in the European Central Bank. Paper prepared for the 10th Conference of the ECPR-SGEU.

Seabrooke, L., and Tsingou, E. (2019). Europe's fast- and slow-burning crises. *Journal of European Public Policy* 26(3), 468–481.

Spielberger, L. (2023). The politicisation of the European Central Bank and its emergency credit lines outside the euro area. *Journal of European Public Policy* 30(5), 873–897.

Steffek, J. (2019). The limits of proceduralism: Critical remarks on the rise of 'throughput legitimacy'. *Public Administration* 97(4), 784–796.

Stone Sweet, A., and Sandholtz, W. (1997). European integration and supranational governance. *Journal of European Public Policy* 4(3), 297–317.

Suchman, M. C. (1995). Managing legitimacy: Strategic and institutional approaches. *Academy of Management Review* 20(3), 571–610.

Tallberg, J. (2002). Delegation to supranational institutions: Why, how, and with what consequences? *West European Politics* 25(1), 23–46.

Thatcher, M., and Stone Sweet, A. (2002). Theory and practice of delegation to non-majoritarian institutions. *West European Politics* 25(1), 1–22.

Torres, F. (2013). The EMU's legitimacy and the ECB as a strategic political player in the crisis context. *Journal of European Integration* 35(3), 287–300.

Tucker, P. (2018). Opening remarks at New City Agenda Event on Unelected Power: The Quest for Legitimacy in Central Banking and the Regulatory State, London, 12 June.

Van Osch, D., de Ruiter, R., and Yesilkagit, K. (2023). An accountability deficit? Holding transgovernmental networks to account. *Journal of European Public Policy* 30(2), 315–333.
Van't Klooster, J. (2020). The ethics of delegating monetary policy. *Journal of Politics* 82(2), 587–599.
Verdun, A. (1998). The institutional design of EMU: A democratic deficit? *Journal of Public Policy* 18(2), 107–132.
Wallace, P. (2015). *The Euro Experiment*. Cambridge: Cambridge University Press.
Walter, S., Ray, A., and Redeker, N. (2020). *The Politics of Bad Options: Why the Eurozone's Problems Have Been So Hard to Resolve*. Oxford: Oxford University Press.
Wolf, M. (2012). Draghi alone cannot save the euro. *Financial Times*, 11 September. www.ft.com/content/e6bb0966-fb41-11e1-87ae-00144feabdc0

14

How Can Courts Contribute to Accountability in EU Monetary Policy?

Ana Bobić and Mark Dawson

14.1 INTRODUCTION

It is by now well established that monetary policy as set out in European Union primary law is a paradoxical field. On the one hand, it is a self-contained regime, governed in the euro area exclusively by a single institution, the European Central Bank (ECB), which also has wide discretion in defining this mandate through setting the inflationary target (Mendes, in press). Article 119(2) TFEU states that the ECB's competence includes 'the *definition* and conduct of a single monetary policy' (see also, Article 127(2) TFEU). In other words, the very *existence* of monetary policy is almost impossible to separate from and already forms part of its *exercise*: in order to find out whether the ECB acted *within* its mandate, we need to find out *how* it has decided to define its mandate (de Boer and van 't Klooster, 2020).[1] That this self-defined and specific price stability mandate has important consequences for the accountability of the ECB has been highlighted by the Court of Justice,[2] the Bundesverfassungsgericht,[3] as well as in the literature (Dawson et al., 2019, pp. 77–80; de Haan and Effinger, 2000, p. 395; Violante, 2020, pp. 1053–56). The ECB seems thus to act as a specialized or self-contained regime, where accountability to judicial institutions should be limited.

On the other hand, monetary policy has developed into a core example of judicialization (see also Amtenbrink, Chapter 4 in this volume). The boundaries of the field are increasingly set through judicial interactions between high courts at the national and EU levels. The accountability of the ECB has become increasingly bound up with discussions about the accountability of the EU more broadly, with the ECB's lack of political accountability placing even greater emphasis on its accountability through law and legal processes. How should we see this constitutional paradox from an accountability perspective? In this contribution we will thus attempt to determine to what extent the process of judicialization of ECB activity improves or frustrates accountability in the monetary field.

In addressing this accountability conundrum, the chapter will rely on the framework of accountability goods (Dawson and Maricut-Akbik, 2020) to provide a descriptive and normative appraisal of the role of law and courts in the monetary policy of the EU. In so doing, we will first

[1] They argue that the crisis has changed the operation of the ECB in such a way that judicial review has shifted from assessing the limits of its mandate, to reviewing measures with significant choices even within its mandate that might still lack democratic legitimacy.

[2] Case C-11/00 *Commission* v. *ECB* EU:C:2003:395 [134], [137].

[3] Case 2 BvR 2728/13 *Gauweiler*, Order of 14 January 2014 [187].

outline the theoretical framework for analysing accountability in the monetary field, namely by looking at the four goods that accountability serves to deliver in democratic polities (Section 14.2). In the subsequent four sections (14.3–14.6), we will analyse to what extent courts (both national and European) deliver individual accountability goods, offering a normative appraisal as to the possible contributions of courts to improving accountability in the monetary field. Section 14.7 will then summarize the findings regarding the four accountability goods and offer some conclusions. As we will argue, judicial intervention (in the absence of meaningful channels of political accountability) has made a modest contribution to improving the accountability of the EU's monetary policy.

14.2 THEORETICAL FRAMEWORK

Assessing whether courts and EU law can contribute to improving the accountability of monetary policy requires a benchmark of assessment. Monetary policy, by its very nature, poses problems for traditional definitions of accountability. Most definitions in the literature are relational, i.e. they see accountability in terms of a relationship between an actor and a forum (or alternatively, an 'agent' and a 'principal' to whom they must answer) (see, for example, Bovens, 2007). In the case of the ECB, however, who is the principal and who is the agent? While the ECB has some account-giving duties towards EU institutions and the European Parliament, it is intentionally insulated from political decision-making (Maricut-Akbik, 2022, pp. 27–32). While political institutions have the tools to engage in a dialogue with the ECB concerning its activities, they decidedly lack the ability to impose on the ECB any obligation to change its policies. It cannot therefore meaningfully be seen as the agent of any other institution. If anything, the ECB is accountable for fulfilling a norm, namely its mandate as laid out in the Treaties (and, ultimately, accountable to a diffuse and weakly institutionalized European public in implementing that norm). There is a basic mismatch between a strong duty on the ECB (to pursue its mandate) and a weak set of institutions to ensure compliance with this duty. Monetary policy therefore requires an additional dimension when assessing accountability.

A fruitful way forward (one advanced in, for example, Goodhart, 2011) is to think about accountability not solely in terms of *to whom* an actor is accountable but *for what*? For what purpose is an actor accountable and to which normative ends? This approach may be particularly valuable in a trans-national or 'multi-level' context where clear lines of accountability (e.g. to a set group of institutions or citizens) are blurred. Accountability studies of the ECB tend to focus strongly on inter-institutional relations, e.g. whether the European Parliament is sufficiently empowered in relation to the ECB (Collignon and Diessner, 2016; Markakis, 2020). Of equal interest, however, is surely the uses and purposes for which the Parliament employs its accountability functions.

Our conceptual framework, drawing on other work (Dawson and Maricut-Akbik, 2020), therefore assesses accountability through asking a foundational question – what is accountability *for*? The idea of a norm-based approach to accountability is used by Goodhart as an alternative to principal–agent approaches, but it can just as easily act as a complement to them (by shifting attention from a focus on actors – who is the principal and who the agent – towards the normative duties these actors in fact carry). By drawing on literature in public administration and political theory, accountability might be boiled down to four basic normative goods it advances in modern societies. These normative goods are not specific to monetary policy or the ECB but apply to *all* institutions wielding public power (whether 'independent' or otherwise). However, we argue that the perspective of normative goods is particularly useful in the paradoxical context of the ECB, where the constitutional organization of its powers makes it difficult to subject it to traditional routes of principal–agent accountability.

The first good is openness. Liberal thinkers from Bentham onwards have long argued that public confidence in official action is likely to be increased where public policy is conducted under the public gaze (what he termed 'publicity'). The openness of public policy has thus been linked to a number of public goods such as the avoidance of corruption, the improvement of public knowledge, and the republican demand that free citizens should enjoy 'non-domination' through the ability to question and contest official action. We might therefore want accountability because we see it as a device to ensure that public action is open, transparent, and contestable. This accountability good is already ubiquitous in ECB discourse in so far as ECB actors frequently emphasize the need to guarantee basic levels of transparency in monetary policy (as well as in other ECB activities discussed in this volume) (Curtin, 2017).

The second such good is non-arbitrariness. There is a deep tradition in accountability research of tying accountability to notions of principal–agent theory in which accountability is a device for (political) principles to control (administrative) agents to whom they have delegated powers. This is a narrower instance in the service of achieving a broader accountability good, namely that those who wield public power should do so in a limited manner and that they should exercise coercion only to the degree necessary to achieve their goals. Non-arbitrariness is therefore also linked to more general limits on public action such as human rights or due process guarantees, which seek to regulate the relationship between the individual and the state. Accountability – by making officials answer for conduct – provides a means by which arbitrary distinctions or applications of power can be identified, and later remedied. Once again, it is hardly controversial to apply this category to the ECB – as a body established via the EU Treaties, it is also at the same time limited by them, and by the many due process and non-arbitrariness standards EU primary law establishes.[4]

The third good which accountability seeks to render concerns effectiveness. While openness and non-arbitrariness seem highly normative values, accountability may be sought for more utilitarian reasons, namely that accountable officials are more likely to deliver high-quality services. From this perspective, accountability holds the promise of performance. By making an official answer for their conduct, and by offering the possibility to correct potential errors, accountability is a mechanism to improve the efficacy and responsiveness of public policy. Here, the premise is that the need to justify and even correct conduct will likely improve, and encourage reflection upon, the design of policy-making or implementation. For the ECB, while its accountability to institutions like the Parliament can be seen as a form of inter-institutional oversight, that oversight is also conducted with a functional goal in mind – improving the ECB's ability to meet its policy goals (with the majority of questions focused on whether it really does so or *how it could do better*) (Maricut-Akbik, 2020).

The final such good is one of publicness: official action should be oriented towards the common good. The common good in this context is one justified by public or universal reasons, but crucially, not by the actor itself. Whereas non-arbitrariness concerns examining whether public action is limited, publicness concerns *the interests on whose behalf public power is wielded*. This involves demonstrating both that officials were not personally enriched and that their decisions are fairly balanced, taking into account different societal interests and perspectives. Once again, accountability is a key device for ensuring the publicness of official action in this sense – when parliamentarians scrutinize government agencies, or courts conduct judicial

[4] For an early case addressing these points, see Case C-11/00 *Commission* v. *ECB* EU:C:2003:395.

review, a key demand is that actors show how their activities forwarded the national or collective interest (with different accountability forums likely to disagree on what a fair balancing of societal interests would entail). Accountability is thus a device to advance the normative good of public policy grounded in the public interest. In the context of the ECB, thus, the self-defined nature of its mandate is restrained by the common good that is more generally pursued by the Treaties. To return to the example of parliamentary oversight of the ECB, while we might expect MEPs to focus on the Bank's performance, they also do so from the perspective of their constituents, seeking to ensure that the ECB forwards monetary policies in the interests of all Europeans and not just some.

These four goods of accountability can be used as an analytical device, tracking the performance of different institutions across different policy fields. It is also necessary to note that the four goods do not operate in isolation but rather influence each other. For example, the demand for openness of an institution may have effects on its effectiveness, in situations when the success of delegated powers depends on the extent of information it should or is able to share with the public. In the ECB context, this may be seen in one particular example. The CJEU has insisted that blackout periods under the Public Sector Purchase Programme (PSPP) mechanism be made secret in order not to influence market price formation of bonds. This speaks to 'effectiveness' in the sense that it is a condition insisted upon by the Court in order to ensure bond-buying does not violate the Treaty prohibition on monetary financing. Yet the same demand contradicts the criteria of openness for the purposes of judicial review (by making it impossible for courts to know the extent of these periods and therefore assess whether legal conditions are de facto complied with).[5] Thus, in our analysis of the four accountability goods, their interconnectedness will be an important consideration.

Ultimately, then, when considered in the ECB context, the main use of accountability goods is to allow us to disaggregate claims that the ECB is or is not accountable. While a given institution may, for example, experience deficits in relation to transparency and openness, this can easily distort an assessment of the overall accountability of an institution or policy field if other elements of accountability are overlooked. Applying these categories to the field of monetary policy, monetary decision-makers are therefore more or less accountable depending on the extent to which their activities demonstrate the qualities of openness, non-arbitrariness, effectiveness, and publicness. The next sections will apply each category to EU monetary policy in turn, focusing on a more limited element of each, i.e. the role of *law* in improving the accountability of the ECB in each dimension.

14.3 OPENNESS

When assessing how courts deliver openness as an accountability good, and how they should do so in the future, one must examine the type, amount, and quality of information delivered by the ECB. Of relevance, in addition, is the understandability of information, i.e. is it accessible in a manner that can allow the public to understand and scrutinize ECB activity? 'Openness' is not therefore exhausted by formal transparency and the availability of documents – it implies that the public have genuine opportunities to engage with a given policy and understand its functioning (Blinder et al., 2022).

[5] German Bundesverfassungsgericht Cases 2 BvR 859/15, 2 BvR 980/16, 2 BvR 2006/15, 2 BvR 1651/15 *Weiss and Others*, Order for reference of 18 July 2017 at [95].

As is well known, the ECB has made significant efforts to strengthen the transparency of monetary policy-making. The ECB publishes summaries ('accounts') of the meetings of the Governing Council, allowing some sense of the substantive discussions underlying monetary decisions. This is accompanied by regular press conferences and guidelines setting out principles for ECB policymakers to follow during public appearances (designed for example to limit the unauthorized release of market-sensitive information) (ECB, 2022). These commitments are largely of the ECB's own making, however, leaving limited room for courts in enforcing their terms. They are also limited by the nature of the ECB's tasks: an example being the requirement that the Bank not reveal the exact timing of bond-buying purchases (in order to produce a degree of uncertainty as to when government bonds will be bought and therefore respect the prohibition of monetary financing laid down in Article 123 TFEU).

One important accountability obligation in terms of openness is laid down in Decision 2004/258/EC, which lays out the ECB's document access regime (ECB, 2004). Analogous to other document access instruments in EU law, it lays out a general right of access while carving out significant public interest exceptions, including where the confidentiality of the proceedings of decision-making bodies are concerned. The CJEU has interpreted this provision broadly; for example, in October 2020 it overturned a General Court decision that the ECB had insufficiently justified the refusal to disclose information discussed when the Governing Council decided to freeze emergency liquidity assistance to a Portuguese bank.[6] For the CJEU, 'the Director-General Secretariat of the ECB is required to refuse to grant access to the outcome of deliberations of the Governing Council, unless the latter has decided to make that outcome public in whole or in part'.[7] Decision 2004/258 thus allows a general refusal of access to information discussed in the Governing Council, without any need for the ECB to give specific reasons to the individual seeking access (or to 'verify how, specifically and actually, access to that information would have undermined the public interest as regards the confidentiality of proceedings of the ECB's decision-making bodies').[8] Openness is often seen in terms of its relation to the ECB's independence. In *Commission* v. *Slovenia*, for example, the CJEU criticized the decision of national police to enter and obtain access to documents of the national central bank, arguing that this violated the independence of the European System of Central Banks (ESCB) as a system of both national and EU central banks.[9] What is noticeable in the (limited) case law on ECB transparency is the lack of reference to general provisions of EU law, such as Article 15 TFEU or the Charter of Fundamental Rights of the European Union: the relevant standards used by the Court are provisions adopted by the ECB itself.[10]

A similar type of deference to the ECB in terms of the information it may use to justify its decisions concerns more general judicial review of ECB activity. In *Weiss*, the Court of Justice was arguably one-sided in the choice of information that it found relevant for assessing the proportionality of the PSPP, accepting the information provided by the ESCB as the only

[6] Case C-396/19 P *ECB* v. *Insolvent Estate of Espírito Santo Financial Group SA* EU:C:2020:845.

[7] Ibid. at [51].

[8] Ibid. at [54].

[9] Case C-316/19 *Commission* v. *Slovenia* EU:C:2020:845. 'In order to have access to documents in the archives of the Union, the national authorities require the agreement of the institution concerned or, if access is refused, a decision of authorisation from the EU judicature forcing that institution to provide access to its archives. Indeed, it would make no sense not to make access to such documents subject to the agreement of the institution concerned or to authorisation by the EU judicature in the event that the national authorities choose to act unilaterally, since such agreement or authorisation enables the inviolability of the archives of the Union to fulfil its function, namely that of preventing unjustified interference in its functioning and independence, to be safeguarded' [104].

[10] See also Case C-442/18 P *ECB* v. *Espírito Santo Financial (Portugal)* EU:C:2019:1117.

relevant one.[11] In essence, the Court of Justice does not demand a pluralist peer review of the duty to state reasons on the part of the ESCB (Dawson and Bobić, 2019, p. 1023). This criticism has been picked up directly by the Bundesverfassungsgericht,[12] demanding that less burdensome alternatives be considered, and a wider array of interests included in such considerations. The ECB complied with this request to the satisfaction of the Bundesverfassungsgericht, by providing a compilation of its assessment of the programme in the form of a proportionality analysis (Lagarde, 2020).

Procedurally, we may conclude that the decision of the ECB to comply with this request of the Bundesverfassungsgericht and present its proportionality analysis in a manner accessible to the public constitutes a contribution of judicial interactions to the accountability good of openness. Yet this approach seems to contribute little to substantive 'accountability as openness' in that the decision over how the ECB should make decisions, and which information it should rely upon, is left largely to the institution itself. A strong notion of accountability as openness would conceptualize openness as a constitutional limit on public institutions, the definition of which should be shaped by public engagement, and which ultimately would require courts to balance public and institutional interests. The CJEU's significant deference to the ECB to date in defining how its monetary policy is communicated does not seem to reflect this. Many would reject such a strong notion of openness as allowing both courts and the public to delve too deeply into central bank deliberations, thus ultimately undermining the effectiveness of central bank intervention. This returns to a comment made earlier, and that will be repeated in later sections – accountability goods have the capacity to interrelate, and also to constrain, each other.

14.4 NON-ARBITRARINESS

As was outlined in the introduction, the way that monetary policy is regulated by the Treaties creates contradictions for judicial review, and in particular the traditional manner of reviewing administrative action. The Court of Justice has developed its jurisprudence by looking at the duty to state reasons in technical bodies exercising discretion, using those reasons to insist that EU institutions explain the rationale of their policies to those affected by them (particularly so that those individuals can exercise their judicial review rights). In doing so, however, the Court has created an inversely proportional relationship between discretion and the expertise of the institution in question. In other words, the more expertise the institution possesses in carrying out its tasks, the higher degree of discretion is granted to it. For the ECB specifically, this has meant that the Court of Justice has usually assessed only whether a manifest error of judgement by the ECB has taken place (Dawson et al., 2019). In our opinion, this is not a satisfactory way of ensuring that the ECB acts in a non-arbitrary manner.

Let us take a closer look at how the Court of Justice separates the analysis of existence and exercise of monetary policy competence for the ECB. In both *Gauweiler* and *Weiss*, 'delimitation of monetary policy' and 'proportionality' are separate headings, in line with the division laid out in Article 5(1) TEU (Wendel, 2020, p. 985). Many EU lawyers have argued, therefore, that while EU institutions may be under proportionality duties in how they exercise their competences, the delimitation of competence is a separate step, for which proportionality is not applicable (Editorial Comments, 2020).

[11] Case C-493/17 *Weiss* EU:C:2018:1000 [81]. This was even more pronounced in the Opinion of Advocate General Wathelet in Case C-493/17 *Weiss* EU:C:2018:815 [135]–[138].

[12] Cases 2 BvR 859/15, 2 BvR 980/16, 2 BvR 2006/15, 2 BvR 1651/15, *Weiss II* [184], [190].

However, in substance, a proportionality analysis can be discerned under both headings. In the proportionality section in *Gauweiler*, the Court of Justice defined it as requiring that acts of EU institutions be appropriate for attaining the objectives pursued and not go beyond what is necessary in achieving those objectives.[13] Back in the section on delimiting monetary policy, however, the Court of Justice also analysed whether the Outright Monetary Transactions (OMT) mechanism *contributes to* achieving the objective of singleness of monetary policy and maintaining price stability.[14] Furthermore, the Court went on to assess whether the *means* to achieve the objectives of the OMT are in line with the objectives of monetary policy[15] – finding itself on the thin line separating existence from exercise of monetary policy. Precisely because a measure may have both monetary policy and economic policy effects,[16] and these are difficult to separate,[17] the Court is inevitably engaging in an assessment of whether the decision-maker (the ECB) by enacting its measures (the OMT, the PSPP) exceeded the scope of its mandate (monetary policy) (Craig, 2012, p. 656; Harbo, 2010, pp. 177–80). The inability of separating the question of existence versus exercise is more explicit in *Weiss*, when the Court of Justice analysed the delimitation of monetary policy:

> It does not appear that the specification of the objective of maintaining price stability as the maintenance of inflation rates at levels below, but close to, 2% over the medium term, which the ESCB chose to adopt in 2003, is *vitiated by a manifest error of assessment and goes beyond* the framework established by the FEU Treaty.[18]

A manifest error of assessment is a well-established standard for assessing the proportionality of exercise of competence of EU institutions in EU law (Harbo, 2010, p. 177). Even more directly, going 'beyond' what is necessary is the explicitly stated third step of the proportionality test (Craig, 2012, pp. 656–57). This approach is in fact no different from the way in which the Bundesverfassungsgericht phrased its standard in its Order for reference in *Weiss*: was there a manifest and structurally significant exceeding of competences.[19]

The argument here is not that the two tests correspond to each other in their precise content, but that both carry a logic of proportionality in assessing the ECB's compliance with its monetary policy mandate. From the perspective of ensuring the non-arbitrariness of the ECB in a set-up where it is empowered to define its own mandate, it thus seems inherently impossible to separate the existence and the exercise stage of competence control. The ECB, when determining the inflation target – which arguably should act as the outer limit of that primary monetary policy competence – is in fact already also *exercising* that competence.[20]

A somewhat positive consequence of applying the principle of proportionality to the existence of competence in monetary policy is an increased standard in monitoring non-arbitrariness. This has arguably been at the source of the preliminary references in both *Gauweiler* and *Weiss*. Once applied to the PSPP, proportionality does have the ability to decrease the potential arbitrariness of ECB decisions through a more stringent obligation of giving account, even in the stage of defining the Bank's inflation target. The Court of Justice has been subject to ample

[13] Case C-62/14 *Gauweiler* EU:C:2015:400 [67].
[14] Ibid., [48], [49].
[15] Ibid., [53].
[16] Ibid., [51], [52].
[17] Ibid., [110]. See also Case C-493/17 *Weiss* EU:C:2018:1000 [60], [64].
[18] Case C-493/17 *Weiss* EU:C:2018:1000 [56] (emphasis added).
[19] German Bundesverfassungsgericht Cases 2 BvR 859/15, 2 BvR 980/16, 2 BvR 2006/15, 2 BvR 1651/15 *Weiss and Others*, Order for reference of 18 July 2017 [64].
[20] Case C-493/17 *Weiss* EU:C:2018:1000 [56].

critique concerning its light-touch proportionality review in both *Gauweiler* (Steinbach, 2017, p. 145; Tridimas and Xanthoulis, 2016, p. 31) and *Weiss* (Dawson and Bobić, 2019, pp. 1022–28), reducing its review to the duty to state reasons, and accepting any and all reasons provided by the ESCB as sufficient. The proportionality analysis in *Gauweiler* did not properly engage in the assessment of less burdensome alternatives, and was reduced to the Court of Justice analysing and ultimately accepting solely the information provided by the ESCB. The Court thus concluded that 'the ESCB weighed up the various interests in play so as to actually prevent disadvantages from arising, when the programme in question is implemented, which are manifestly disproportionate to the programme's objectives'.[21]

The lesson learned from *Gauweiler* and *Weiss* may well be that the structure of Article 5 TEU (Steinbach, 2021) does not operate as well in the context of self-defined mandates, where judicial review would need to be confined to accepting any and all reasons provided by the institution in question.[22] Rather, a substantive appraisal of non-arbitrariness would require the ECB to provide a 'literature review' of sorts: what are the different options available to it, what are their advantages and drawbacks, and what interests have been guiding the ECB in ultimately making its choice for one solution or another? Non-arbitrariness requires, in short, an institution not just to carry formal limits on its activities but to show how it acts upon those limits, using it to weigh and discard policies that negatively affect others (the core of the Bundesverfassungsgericht's initial objection to the PSPP programme). The interaction between courts at the national and EU levels has circuitously pushed EU monetary policy in this direction over the last half decade.

14.5 EFFECTIVENESS

The third accountability good is 'effectiveness', which is the notion that accountability allows for the correction of error and thereby the improvement of institutional performance. There once again seems something inherently problematic about courts checking whether a central bank has done its job 'properly': the question of substituting legal for economic judgement returns.

At the same time, one of the interesting features of the Economic and Monetary Union (EMU) chapters of the Treaty is the heavy substantive principles they contain. The Treaty anchors the ECB and other EU economic decision-makers in certain principles (such as in Article 119 TFEU, 'stable prices, sound public finances and monetary conditions and a sustainable balance of payments') that are meant to orient the EMU in the long term and provide a basis for assessing whether economic policy is being conducted properly. At the same time, it is not entirely clear who is responsible (apart from the decision-makers themselves) to ensure that these principles are effectively complied with.

We might make at least two preliminary conclusions in this regard. The first is that there is little indication that judicial review has limited or narrowed the ability of the ECB to deliver its primary mandate effectively. The CJEU is yet to annul a monetary policy measure. In addition, although the much-discussed ruling of the German Constitutional Court found the quantitative easing (QE) programmes outside its monetary policy mandate, the ECB has mostly proceeded on its course unhindered.

[21] Case C-62/14 *Gauweiler* EU:C:2015:400 [91].

[22] Arguably this seems to be the case in Case C-62/14 *Gauweiler* EU:C:2015:400 [60] and Case C-493/17 *Weiss* EU:C:2018:1000 [56].

There is, however, evidence of judicial review significantly structuring how programmes are designed. To give an example, several conditions laid out in the *Gauweiler* decision of the CJEU – such as the need to observe a minimum period between the purchase of a bond on the primary market and its resale on the secondary one, or the ability of the ECB to at any time terminate purchases – found their way into subsequent QE programmes, such as the PSPP.[23] This effect of judicial review recalls Stephen Weatherill's (2011) well-known argument that the Court's case law on Article 114 TFEU operated as a legislative 'drafting guide'. By indicating conditions for compliance with substantive principles, judicial review seems to narrow the range of policy responses without ever risking ruling *any* substantive instrument 'out'.

Another consideration is the role of courts in assessing the effectiveness of measures of institutions with specific expertise. The criticism that the courts are not experts in monetary policy is valid, but that does not mean that they cannot check the coherence and consistency of such a decision-making process.[24] The Court of Justice is furthermore able to order expert reports as well as question them in the hearings before it.[25] This is also standard practice before national courts (e.g. Grashof, 2018). The courts therefore do not need to become experts in the field in order to ensure that a proper peer review of decisions such as the ECB's is subject to a more detailed obligation of justification resulting in the substantive good of effectiveness.

The second conclusion may be that once again judicial review's consequences in terms of effectiveness may be indirect rather than direct. While the judicial interactions between national courts and the CJEU on QE did not render it unusable, they did signal the existence of potential limits on the use of this instrument. More specifically, it laid open for all to see a feature of EMU long recognized by academics, namely the 'loneliness' of the Bank (Mabbett and Schelkle, 2019). Unlike other currency unions, the ECB was operating monetary policy in the absence of a fiscal counterpart, forcing it to take certain actions in defence of the larger eurozone economy that arguably would have been shouldered better by political actors (which had inevitable effects on its own ability to ensure stable prices). It was therefore in the context of the *PSPP* ruling, and the surrounding COVID-19 crisis, that the German government's long-held opposition to greater fiscal sharing in the eurozone began to erode, resulting in its eventual support for the Next Generation EU fund, and its Own Resources Decision.

This in fact is one of the ironies of the Bundesverfassungsgericht's jurisprudence. While it has persistently questioned whether fiscal sharing might trigger Germany's constitutional identity, the very limits it placed on ECB activity also acted as a push for German institutions to reconsider the effectiveness of EMU's existing institutional set-up (thus nudging German policymakers towards the embrace of an explicit debt-sharing instrument). While it is therefore difficult to assess whether legal accountability contributed to effectiveness directly, the indirect consequence of judicial interaction has been to shine an increasing spotlight on EMU's fiscal and political deficiencies.

[23] Case C-62/14 *Gauweiler* EU:C:2015:400 [107]–[113].

[24] See for example the approach of the General Court in T-783/17 *GE Healthcare* v. *Commission* [2019] EU:T:2019:624 [50]: 'the courts may only examine whether the opinion contains a statement of reasons from which it is possible to ascertain the considerations on which the opinion is based, and whether it establishes a comprehensible link between the medical or scientific finding and their conclusions'. This approach was earlier confirmed by the Court of Justice in Case C-269/13 P *Acino AG* v. *European Commission* EU:C:2014:255 [62].

[25] Article 70 of the Rules of Procedure of the Court of Justice.

14.6 PUBLICNESS

Does judicial review contribute to the final accountability good: publicness? Publicness concerns the ability of public policy to reflect the common (rather than factional) good. In the EU case, this concerns the distributive impact of decisions across states and societal interests, i.e. do quantitative easing and other ECB programmes serve the common interest and not simply the interests of selected sectors or states (see Colciago et al., 2019)? The PSPP litigation, and widespread concern over the distributive impact of monetary decisions, seems a test case of divided national responses to this question. In this sense, while effectiveness speaks to the ability of the ECB to achieve its mandate (and the role of law in relation to this), publicness refers to the broader ability of monetary policy to forward the public good (which may involve weighing other goals and effects of monetary policy, and which does not concern the effectiveness of monetary policy per se).

Who is in the best position to assess whether the distributive effects of ECB programmes contribute to the common interest? One answer, due to its Treaty role as well as its necessary expertise, is that the ECB should be the main actor to weigh the suitability of monetary policies. From a legal perspective, however, this leaves us with the question of which court is in the best position to review such an assessment. Here, three different positions present themselves. The first is that this review should be conducted exclusively by the Court of Justice as an institution presumed to safeguard EU-wide considerations, as opposed to a single national court (and using a deferential standard of review) (for a criticism, see Marzal, 2020). The Bundesverfassungsgericht has received heavy criticism, for example, for focusing its proportionality analysis on a set of stakeholders heavily skewed by the German perspective (most notably pensioners and savers potentially losing out via the impact of QE programmes). Looking at both the phrasing employed[26] as well as the fact that a general proportionality assessment submitted by the ECB was ultimately accepted, a monopoly of the Court of Justice to review decisions of the ECB, without considering input from national courts via the preliminary reference procedure, does not appear to us warranted. At the same time, by requiring the ECB to publish a proportionality analysis, the German jurisprudence also opened the door for the ECB to take into account redistributive effects on all Member States/societal groups when designing monetary policy.

The second is that judicial review of monetary policy decisions (de Boer and van 't Klooster, 2020) is structurally impossible: judges face inherent difficulties in making complex economic assessments, as explicitly acknowledged by the Bundesverfassungsgericht, limiting their ability to truly assess the robustness of the information the ECB relies upon (Goldmann, 2014).[27] 'Publicness' can therefore be assessed by the ECB alone (a conclusion that some would see as

[26] 'Relevant economic policy effects of the PSPP furthermore include the risk of creating real estate and stock market bubbles as well as the economic and social impact on virtually all citizens, who are at least indirectly affected inter alia as shareholders, tenants, real estate owners, savers or insurance policy holders. For instance, there is a considerable risk of losses for private savings. This has direct consequences for (private) pension schemes and the returns they generate ... Both factors lead to, in part excessive, portfolio shifts ... while risk premiums are in decline. Real estate prices are on the rise with trends of sometimes particularly sharp increases – especially regarding residential property in major cities – ... which possibly already come close to creating a "market bubble", as the oral hearing confirmed. It is not for the Federal Constitutional Court to decide in the current proceedings how such concerns are to be weighed exactly in the context of a monetary policy decision; rather, the point is that such effects, which are created or at least amplified by the PSPP, must not be completely ignored': Cases 2 BvR 859/15, 2 BvR 980/16, 2 BvR 2006/15, 2 BvR 1651/15, *Weiss II* [173].

[27] Cases 2 BvR 859/15, 2 BvR 980/16, 2 BvR 2006/15, 2 BvR 1651/15, *Weiss II* [173].

appropriate and by some as pointing to a more fundamental democratic dilemma, perhaps questioning the vesting of such significant powers in central banks to begin with) (Joerges, 2019).

A third alternative is to use national courts as intermediaries to nudge the ECB into greater justification of how common interest is to be achieved by its programmes. This strategy carries its own risks – a possible consequence of the German PSPP litigation is that other national courts follow the German example and begin imposing their own standards and demands for justification on part of the ECB. This could lead to a proliferation of diverging national standards, resulting in the creation of an unrealistic burden for the ECB. National rulings have the potential of blurring the pursuit of an EU-wide common interest by the ECB.

To remedy this risk, a more substantial improvement in the accountability of the ECB may ultimately necessitate a change that would devise novel accountability arrangements in the way that the ECB presents and justifies its decisions (for a proposal concerning Article 48(6) TEU, see de Boer and van 't Klooster, 2020). However, as long as ('solange') this does not take place, national courts demanding more of the ECB in terms of assessing the redistributive effects of large-scale purchase programmes such as the PSPP does not appear to us controversial, so long as this is done in a comprehensive manner, and at the EU level. In fact, the ECB, despite Article 130 TFEU explicitly prohibiting it from taking instructions from Member States, complied with the request of the Bundesverfassungsgericht to better explain the proportionality of the PSPP. The ECB has, 'in line with the principle of sincere cooperation[,] ... decided to accommodate this request' (Lagarde, 2020). The cascade of diverging national litigation is yet to appear (and can be limited by institutional features of the EU system, such as the duty to submit a preliminary reference when assessing the validity of EU law). National courts may, therefore, still play an indirect role in inducing monetary policy-making that is better able to account for its role in forwarding the common interest.

At present, the EU's 'Next Generation EU' pandemic programme that forms part of the EU's Own Resources Decision (European Council, 2020) is being challenged before the Bundesverfassungsgericht by the founder of the Alternative für Deutschland (AfD) on the basis of constitutional identity. On 26 March 2021, the Bundesverfassungsgericht issued an unreasoned decision to the federal president to hold off signing the bill until it decides whether to grant the applicants interim relief (Repasi, 2021). The central argument of the applicants revolves around the possibility that Germany becomes liable for the entire amount of the pandemic fund, effectively introducing risk-sharing into EU law. Afterwards, the Bundesverfassungsgericht rejected the interim relief request, allowing the Own Resources Decision to be ratified by Germany.[28] It nevertheless continued the proceedings on merits that might subsequently find that the Decision is either *ultra vires* or breaches Germany's constitutional identity. In such a scenario, the Order itself envisages a preliminary reference to be submitted to the Court of Justice on the interpretation of the risk-sharing elements of the Own Resources Decision. It is important to underline that the Bundesverfassungsgericht acknowledged that, although it is possible that constitutional identity is engaged, the consequences of stopping the ratification of the Decision are too great to trigger it before a full review is undertaken. An interesting debate concerning the Own Resources Decision is also taking place in Finland in relation to contesting what is the common interest and to what extent the legal framework allows for it (by the Constitutional Committee of the Parliament that effectively conducts constitutional review there in the absence of a constitutional court) (Leino-Sandberg, 2021).

[28] German Bundesverfassungsgericht Case 2 BvR 547/21 Order of the Second Senate of 15 April 2021 www.bundesverfassungsgericht.de/SharedDocs/Entscheidungen/DE/2021/04/rs20210415_2bvr054721.html.

These developments point to a subtle role for national courts in forwarding 'publicness' in terms of reasserting the place of 'the public' in the construction of EMU. The dominance of the Court of Justice as the central judicial body in the EU (Rodin, 2011, p. 315) does not sit easily with its ability to properly scrutinize measures of economic governance, given the strictness of its admissibility threshold (in order to manage docket control) (Rodin, 2015). Moreover, once the admissibility threshold is met, the Court usually defers to expertise, maintaining limited review of the use of discretion by the ECB, as we have seen in the review of the Bank's monetary policy mechanisms (Dawson and Bobić, 2019; Goldoni, 2017). Judicial review and parliamentary scrutiny at both the national and EU levels rely heavily on the principle of equality of sovereign Member States, ensuring budgetary autonomy of national parliaments through an emphasis on conditionality in financial assistance. There is some irony therefore that while EU law is often legitimated in terms of its historic use to enhance the rights of individuals and forge a new conception of the public good, the structure of EMU means that national courts are the main fora through which individual contestation of EMU (often on the grounds that it damages the national or European public good) can reach the EU level.

This role of national courts is a double-edged sword. National courts focus on the need for majoritarian representation to be ensured for decision-making in budgetary matters. Such a focus, particularly during the euro crisis, influenced the division of competences between the EU and the national level in a way that decreased emphasis on solidarity. The almost universal common denominator of national jurisprudence is that sovereignty is preserved so long as the constitutionally granted powers of the legislature in budgetary matters on the national level remains intact. The individual is mentioned only in the context, most prominently in the German decisions, where the right to vote and the ensuing parliamentary budgetary sovereignty were considered a fundamental right, warranting the direct interest necessary for the submission of a constitutional complaint.[29] This means that the variety of societal interests implicated in monetary decisions end up being conflated to a single one – that of participating in national elections. Thus there remain limits in the role of national courts in contributing to the development of an EU-wide 'common interest', reflective of the wide range of individuals affected by monetary decision-making.

On the other hand, accountability as publicness ultimately requires mechanisms for issues reflective of the public good, and capturing public discourse, to reach and influence EU monetary policy. An example might be the current discussion over 'greening' the ECB's monetary mandate (de Grauwe, 2019; Schoenmaker and Stegeman, Chapter 12 in this volume). A wave of climate-induced litigation is currently sweeping Europe – it is difficult to imagine such contestation reaching the EU legal order apart from through the intermediary of national courts (where climate groups can more easily litigate and raise claims than they can do via EU law directly). As often in the history of integration, national judiciaries have an important role to play in defining EU law and in carrying into EU monetary policy new understandings of the public good (Bobić, 2020, 2022).

14.7 CONCLUSION

This chapter has considered monetary policy using the frame of accountability, and more particularly the normative goods implicit in accountability claims. By definition, such accountability is meant to be achieved by multiple forums – there is no reason to think (and many

[29] Case 2 BVerfG 1390/12, *ESM Treaty*, Judgment of the Second Senate of 12 September 2012 [92].

reasons to doubt) that courts should be the sole or primary bodies to ensure accountability for monetary decisions. This is reflected in the accountability system of the ECB, which primarily sees accountability duties as flowing to political institutions (principally the European Parliament).

At the same time, political accountability for monetary policy remains underdeveloped, placing more emphasis and strain on the use of 'legal accountability' as its counterpart. As this chapter has argued, judicial interactions have moderately improved accountability along the four observed dimensions (in the absence of political institutions able to fulfil these goals themselves). The contribution of courts remains, however, largely procedural in nature, nudging monetary decision-makers to alter their process of decision-making without obvious effects on substantive decisions.

The EU courts largely respect the ECB's operational independence, in particular its wide discretion to define its own mandate. This is in keeping with the wider approach of the CJEU to the review of EU institutions exercising discretion based on expertise. We can observe more serious challenges to the accountability structure of monetary policy emerging mainly from national institutions. This has triggered subtle changes in the EMU's larger architecture and in the applicable standard of judicial review, without strong evidence that political means of steering EMU's future have been foreclosed. In this sense, for all the extensive academic concern that judicialization would do harm to the basic economic structure of EMU, this chapter finishes with a more modest conclusion: Courts have made EU monetary policy more accountable without fundamentally transforming its operation.

REFERENCES

Blinder, A. S., Ehrmann, M., de Haan, J., and Jansen, D.-J. (2022). Central bank communication with the general public: Promise or false hope? Griswold Center for Economic Policy Studies Working Paper No. 291.

Bobić, A. (2020). Constructive versus destructive conflict: Taking stock of the recent constitutional jurisprudence in the EU. *Cambridge Yearbook of European Law and Policy* 22, 60–84.

Bobić, A. (2022). *The Jurisprudence of Constitutional Conflict in the European Union*. Oxford: Oxford University Press.

Bovens, M. (2007). Analysing and assessing accountability: A conceptual framework. *European Law Journal* 13(4), 447–468.

Colciago, A., Samarina, A., and de Haan, J. (2019). Central bank policies and income and wealth inequality: A survey. *Journal of Economic Surveys* 33(4), 1199–1231.

Collignon, S., and Diessner, S. (2016). The ECB's monetary dialogue with the European Parliament: Efficiency and accountability during the euro crisis? *Journal of Common Market Studies* 54(6), 1296–1312.

Craig, P. (2012). *EU Administrative Law*. Oxford: Oxford University Press.

Curtin, D. (2017). 'Accountable independence' of the European Central Bank: Seeing the logics of transparency. *European Law Journal* 23(1–2), 28–44.

Dawson, M., and Bobić, A. (2019). Quantitative easing at the Court of Justice – Doing whatever it takes to save the euro: Weiss and others. *Common Market Law Review* 56, 1005–1040.

Dawson, M., and Maricut-Akbik, A. (2020). Procedural vs substantive accountability in EMU governance: Between payoffs and trade-offs. *Journal of European Public Policy* 28(11), 1707–1726.

Dawson, M., Bobić, A., and Maricut-Akbik, A. (2019). Reconciling independence and accountability at the European Central Bank: The false promise of proceduralism. *European Law Journal* 25(1), 75–93.

De Boer, N., and van 't Klooster, J. (2020). The ECB, the courts and the issue of democratic legitimacy after Weiss. *Common Market Law Review* 57(6), 1689–1724.

De Grauwe, P. (2019). Green money without inflation. *Vierteljahrshefte zur Wirtschaftsforschung* 88(2), 51–54.

De Haan, J., and Eijffinger, S. C. W. (2000). The democratic accountability of the European Central Bank: A comment on two fairy-tales. *Journal of Common Market Studies* 38(3), 393–407.

Editorial Comments (2020). Not mastering the Treaties: The German Federal Constitutional Court's PSPP judgment. *Common Market Law Review* 57, 965.

European Central Bank (2004). Decision 2004/258/EC of the European Central Bank of 4 March 2004 on public access to European Central Bank documents.

European Central Bank (2022). Guiding principles for external communication for high-level officials of the European Central Bank. www.ecb.europa.eu/ecb/orga/transparency/html/eb-communications-guidelines.en.html

European Council (2020). European Council Conclusions, 10–11 December, EUCO 22/20.

European Court of Justice (2015). *Gauweiler and Others* v. *Deutscher Bundestag*, Case C-62/14, Judgment of 16 June.

European Court of Justice (2018). *Heinrich Weiss and Others*. Case C-493/17, Judgment of 11 December.

Goldmann, M. (2014). Adjudicating economics? Central bank independence and the appropriate standard of judicial review. *German Law Journal* 15(2), 265–280.

Goldoni, M. (2017). The limits of legal accountability of the European Central Bank. *George Mason Law Review* 24(2), 595–616.

Goodhart, M. (2011). Democratic accountability in global politics: Norms, not agents. *Journal of Politics* 73(1), 45–60.

Grashof, F. (2018). The 'you know better' dilemma of administrative judges in environmental matters: A note on the German legal context. *European Energy and Environmental Law Review* 27, 151

Harbo, T.-I. (2010). The function of the proportionality principle in EU law. *European Law Journal* 16(2), 158–185.

Joerges, C. (2019). Where the law runs out: The overburdening of law and constitutional adjudication by the financial crisis and Europe's new modes of economic governance. In S. Garben, I. Govare, and P. Nemitz (eds.), *Critical Reflections on Constitutional Democracy in the European Union*, Oxford: Hart Publishing, pp. 167–178.

Lagarde, C. (2020). Response to Letter QZ-036 by MEP Mr Sven Simon (2020). www.ecb.europa.eu/pub/pdf/other/ecb.mepletter200629_Simon~ece6ead766.en.pdf

Leino-Sandberg, P. (2021). Between European commitment and taking the law seriously. The EU Own Resources decision in Finland. Verfassungsblog 29 April 2021. https://verfassungsblog.de/between-european-commitment-and-taking-the-law-seriously/

Mabbett, D., and Schelkle, W. (2019). Independent or lonely? Central banking in crisis. *Review of International Political Economy* 26(3), 436–460.

Maricut-Akbik, A. (2020). Contesting the European Central Bank in banking supervision: Accountability in practice at the European Parliament. *Journal of Common Market Studies* 58(5), 1199–1214.

Maricut-Akbik, A. (2022). *The European Parliament as an Accountability Forum*. Cambridge: Cambridge University Press.

Markakis, M. (2020). *Accountability in the Economic and Monetary Union: Foundations, Policy, and Governance*. Oxford: Oxford University Press.

Marzal, T. (2020). Is the BVerfG PSPP decision 'simply not comprehensible'? A critique of the judgement's reasoning on proportionality. Verfassungsblog, 9 May 2020. https://verfassungsblog.de/is-the-bverfg-pspp-decision-simply-not-comprehensible/

Mendes, J. (in press). Constitutive powers and justification: The duty to give reasons in EU monetary policy. In M. Dawson (ed.), *Substantive Accountability in Europe's New Economic Governance*. Cambridge: Cambridge University Press.

Repasi, R. (2021). Karlsruhe, again: The interim-interim relief of the German Constitutional Court regarding Next Generation EU. EU Law Live 29 March 2021. https://eulawlive.com/analysis-karlsruhe-again-the-interim-interim-relief-of-the-german-constitutional-court-regarding-next-generation-eu-by-rene-repasi/

Rodin, S. (2011). Back to the square one: The past, the present and the future of the Simmenthal mandate. In J. M. Beneyto and I. Pernice (eds.), *Europe's Constitutional Challenges in the Light of the Recent Case Law of National Constitutional Courts – Lisbon and Beyond*. Berlin: Nomos, pp. 297–326.

Rodin, S. (2015). A metacritique of the Court of Justice of the EU. Bingham Centre talk, London, 2015. www.biicl.org/documents/772_rodins_paper_2015.pdf?showdocument=1

Steinbach, A. (2017). All's well that ends well? Crisis policy after the German constitutional court's ruling in Gauweiler. *Maastricht Journal of European and Comparative Law* 24(1), 140–149.

Steinbach, A. (2021). The federalism dimension of proportionality. *European Law Journal*. https://dx.doi.org/10.2139/ssrn.3808648

Tridimas, T., and N. Xanthoulis (2016). A legal analysis of the *Gauweiler* case: Between monetary policy and constitutional conflict. *Maastricht Journal of European and Comparative Law* 23(1), 17–39.

Violante, T. (2020). Bring back the politics: The PSPP ruling in its institutional context. *German Law Journal* 21, 1045–1057.

Weatherill, S. (2011). The limits of legislative harmonization ten years after tobacco advertising: How the court's case law has become a 'drafting guide'. *German Law Journal* 12(3), 827–864.

Wendel, M. (2020). Paradoxes of ultra-vires review: A critical review of the PSPP decision and its initial reception. *German Law Journal* 21, 979–994.

PART III

The Economic and Fiscal Dimensions

15

Reviving the Case for Policy Coordination in EMU

Maria Demertzis, Marta Domínguez Jiménez, and Nicola Viegi

15.1 INTRODUCTION

This chapter reviews the way fiscal–monetary policy interactions have played out in the single currency area, in light of the two global shocks of the last decade, the financial and the pandemic crises. These shocks have put extraordinary pressure on the Union's macroeconomic framework and have required many adjustments. However, such adjustments were mainly guided by political feasibility and were largely piecemeal. We will show how they did not respond to an optimal economic coordination set-up, between fiscal and monetary and amongst member states.

The Economic and Monetary Union (EMU) architecture was originally designed to deal with one important problem, that of potential fiscal free-riding on the common monetary standard. It was designed to stop countries from fiscally expanding, taking advantage of the monetary credibility the single currency brought, in ways that would jeopardize their fiscal sustainability. Two institutional features were applied: first the European Central Bank (ECB) was given the highest possible level of independence, being freed from political pressures, and second, national fiscal policies were constrained with simple and, in principle, enforceable numerical limits.

Although the Maastricht rationale was right, the set-up did not actually meet its objective of providing for fiscal coordination. Aimed at constraining rather than promoting coordination between countries, the Maastricht criteria led to fiscal policy being mostly underused. The two global crises have shown the technical and economic limits of monetary policy, especially at the zero–lower bound, and the importance of discretionary fiscal policy as a stabilization instrument. Monetary policy has played an outsized role during the Global Financial Crisis (GFC), when policies aimed to achieve economic stabilization and to protect the common currency from the risk of fiscal default in large countries. As the COVID-19 shock unravelled, monetary policy could only play an ancillary role to a fiscal response, aiming to prevent financial fragmentation rather than actually counteracting the shock. It was fiscal policy that had to come to the rescue. But coming into the shock, fiscal policy at the euro area level was only partially coordinated and is still limited by its initial architectural design based on the strategic bargain between autonomous but interdependent national authorities that need to respond to an emergency.

To the memory of Professor Andrew Hughes Hallett, who has taught us all we know about policy coordination.

This chapter contributes to that debate by focusing on the necessity to build cooperative solutions to the EMU policy game. In fact, all institutional changes that we have seen in the EMU in the past ten years, as a response to the shocks, have indeed been attempts to move the policy framework closer to a cooperative solution. First, a cooperative solution between fiscal authorities that provides flexibility in responding to shock while limiting the discretionary nature of fiscal policy at the national level. Second, a cooperative solution between monetary and fiscal authorities, with responsibility moved away from the ECB to other 'quasi-fiscal' institution at the European level providing resources for financial and economic stability.

This development has created a hybrid model, where monetary policy is committed to do 'whatever it takes' to preserve the EMU while the underlying fiscal compromise is constantly under threat from centrifugal political developments. While the institutional development in the EMU goes in the right direction, it does not induce an efficient use of the instruments and it is not robust to policy shocks in big countries (and arguably also small countries).

Indeed, it took a second 'once in lifetime shock' – in other words a very extreme shock – in the space of ten years to realize the fundamental role fiscal policy can play in response to economic shocks. After the COVID-19 pandemic, the Maastricht criteria were immediately suspended and efforts were made to 'centralize' the response that came in the form of Next Generation EU (NGEU) funds. Although not a fiscal stabilization tool in itself, the NGEU fund is an attempt to coordinate national fiscal policies at least at the level of investments needed to prepare next generations for the challenges that lie ahead. This also signals a focus on public investment for putting Europe back on a growth trajectory. As we do not start with a clean slate, there will be varied ability among Member States to cover their investment needs. This is of particular relevance for the European Union's climate objectives. It is in the nature of public goods that if one country does not invest sufficiently, other countries will also be unable to meet their climate objectives.

We revisit the economic policy coordination literature to help inform how to travel the road from Nash uncooperative suboptimal outcomes to outcomes that are closer to the contract curve between the different players. We appreciate the political constraints that come with a Union of twenty-seven sovereign states. But economic instability and policy inaction are a real threat to the future of the Union, and of course to the ability of the EU to exert global influence in light of the major challenges ahead.

15.2 THE MAASTRICHT TREATY AND THE ROLE OF FISCAL POLICY

The Maastricht framework was driven by the economic thinking at the time, mainly concerned with the inflationary consequences of large ('excessive') deficits. This was considered particularly pertinent within a monetary union, where the fiscal decisions of one Member State would result in non-negligible externalities for other members. There was also a legitimate fear that monetary union by itself would cause excessive deficits that would stem from the credibility gains of tying one's hands in the form of lower borrowing costs. These underlying views doubtless had an effect on the development of the eurozone's fiscal framework, namely the Maastricht criteria, and are reflected in the 1989 Delors Report (formally the Report on Economic and Monetary Union in the European Community) that formed the basis of the EMU.

15.2.1 *The Role of Fiscal Policy Back Then*

The effectiveness of fiscal policy as a demand management and stabilization tool became increasingly questioned in the 1970s. In an early paper Barro (1974) shows that the effect of fiscal policy on consumption is effectively null as consumers anticipate future tax hikes required to service the spending and save accordingly (commonly known as Ricardian equivalence). While full Ricardian equivalence relies on a particularly strong set of assumptions, most economists agreed on intertemporal sustainability and tax smoothing (Barro, 1979; Buti and van der Noord, 2004). Further, the early 1980s saw the rise of real business cycle theory, which assumed economic fluctuations were driven by real (supply-side) shocks, and thus considered fiscal policy at best ineffective and, at worst, potentially damaging.

More specific to the policy debate surrounding EMU in Europe, Sargent and Wallace (1981) introduced a model that established the inflationary risks posed by excessive deficits. This involved a game of chicken between the monetary and fiscal authorities in which the latter ran persistent and unsustainable deficits. The model relies in part on Blinder and Solow (1973) who present a case of instability under debt-financed fiscal stimulus. Given certain assumptions and in such a case, Sargent and Wallace (1981) show the monetary authority could ultimately lose the ability to control inflation. Continued fiscal imbalances and spiralling debt would place substantial pressure on the monetary authority to monetize the latter.

While Sargent and Wallace (1981) relied on monetarist assumptions and fiscal dominance, Leeper (1991) showed that inflationary pressure from excessive deficits existed even when monetization is ruled out credibly by central bank commitment. Under his model, if a government runs a persistent structural deficit, i.e. has an unsustainable fiscal policy that violates its intertemporal budget constraint, then inflation is the only credible outcome. This approach is typically referred to as the fiscal theory of the price level, and was additionally developed by Sims (1994) and Woodford (1994, 1995, 2001). It considers fiscal sustainability to be a prerequisite for the monetary authority to be able to keep the price level low and stable. Public solvency constraints would thus be necessary to contain inflationary pressures.

In parallel, much of the academic literature at the time showed the existence of an apparent tendency towards fiscal laxity. An early model by Blinder (1982) showed that differing objectives between monetary and fiscal authorities would result in a sub-optimal policy mix, with excessive fiscal laxity and monetary tightness. Beetsma and Uhlig (1999) showed, in an intertemporal set-up, that governments have an incentive to issue a sub-optimally high level of debt in the first period for fear of being voted out, constraining monetary policy in the second period.

In this context, the construction of the EMU was heavily influenced by the belief that strict budgetary discipline was desirable to ensure monetary dominance and effective inflation control and avoid undesirable, policy-induced shocks (Buti and van der Noord, 2004). Financial soundness was considered necessary to ensure the appropriate conditions for price stability, with fiscal policy supporting monetary policy. The Delors Report (1989), which formed the underlying basis for EMU, reflected much of the aforementioned academic thought.

15.2.2 *The Existence of Externalities within a Monetary Union*

The general need for budgetary discipline laid out in the previous section was considered even more relevant in a monetary union.

The theoretical literature widely supported the benefits of fiscal coordination (or a cooperative solution) in the case of interdependence, which can be quite substantial within a monetary union (e.g. De Grauwe, 1990; Krugman, 1987). With monetary policy delegated to a supranational level, fiscal coordination would help improve the overall policy mix and ensure fiscal policy that is appropriate for the aggregate currency area. In the construction of the

Maastricht framework, fiscal coordination was primarily concerned with avoiding excessive deficits, and thus negative externalities from one Member State to another, described in Lamfalussy (1989).

First, there was the threat of sovereign default and the pressure that that would create for either a monetary or a fiscal bail-out. Monetary financing is explicitly ruled out in the EU treaties (Article 123 Treaty on the Functioning of the European Union – TFEU, and there is an explicit no-bail-out clause (Article 125 TFEU). Demertzis and Viegi (2011) argue that in a monetary union, low-debt countries have an incentive to bail out those debt countries that are at risk of default, effectively pointing to the non-credibility of the no-bail-out clause. Budgetary discipline is then the other layer that can protect from excessive fiscal spending.

Additionally, negative externalities could arise even without a risk of insolvency in one Member State. By borrowing in the capital markets, a sovereign state increases demand for capital and thus puts upward pressure on interest rates for other Member States, to be serviced with distortionary taxation (Canzoneri and Diba, 1991). A Member State that runs an excessive deficit would, in effect, absorb a disproportionate amount of union savings. This could raise interest rates throughout and crowd out investment in countries where rates would have otherwise been lower. Finally, markets may not accurately or sufficiently differentiate between Member State risk premiums. This links directly with the earlier argument on fiscal bail-outs: market confidence in a certain solidarity between Member States could affect evaluation of risk for states on both sides of the deficit spectrum.

Finally, there is the question of a possible bias towards excessive deficits within a monetary union. Beetsma and Uhlig (1999) show that short-sighted governments become sub-optimally highly indebted, constraining future monetary policy. In the case of a European monetary union, this effect would only increase, as the relative constraint each Member State can place on future monetary policy is smaller (Buti and van der Noord, 2004). Ample literature further sought to identify political explanations for excessive deficits, attributed, for example, to political instability (Grilli et al., 1991), weak governments (Roubini and Sachs, 1989), and even government ideology (Alesina et al., 1993). The existence of this bias towards excessive deficits provided a theoretical basis for external budgetary rules to act as a constraint, especially for Member States where some of the identified markers (e.g. high government turnover, instability) were more prevalent.

There were, however, critics of the Maastricht framework right from the start. For example, Sims (1999), a major proponent of the fiscal theory of the price level, considered the Maastricht criteria insufficient to credibly avoid a downward spiral of deficits and inflationary pressure. Other authors held the opposite view: Canzoneri and Diba (2001) saw the criteria as too stringent and considered the need for cyclically adjusted measures so as not to constrain available policy tools too severely. Buti and van der Noord (2004) made a lengthy case for the need to ensure discipline and the broad principles behind the Maastricht criteria, but argued for a shift in the execution of fiscal policy and a bigger role for automatic stabilizers.

However, some questioned not only the stringency but even the underlying premise of the Maastricht criteria immediately after these were announced. For example, Buiter et al. (1993) argued that implementing these would lead to excessive fiscal retrenchment and questioned the lack of flexibility allowed for higher-return public sector investment. Buiter, it should be noted, was a strong critic of the fiscal theory of the price level.[1]

[1] For example, Buiter (2002). McCallum (1999, 2001, 2003) is another of its major critics.

15.2.3 *Strategic Conflicts in EU Policy-Making*

It is fair to say that the rationale behind the Maastricht Treaty was driven by the fear that uncoordinated fiscal policies would generate excessive use of the instrument in response to external shocks, compromising the long-term stability of the Union. The framework's intention, therefore, was very much to prevent these excesses from happening.

In reality, however, as we will show in the next section and as is in fact common knowledge by now, the Maastricht architecture has led to the underuse of the fiscal instrument. A set-up that aimed to prevent negative spillovers produced a strategic environment where the non-cooperative equilibrium minimized the use of the instrument not just for the high-debt countries but for all the countries in the union. We describe this strategic interaction in the context of EMU based on the framework of Hamada (1976) described in Demertzis et al. (2004).

Consider the fiscal policy game between two countries in a monetary union, one with high levels of debt (country A) and one with low levels of debt (country B), that face a common negative shock. If the high debt country uses fiscal policy to counteract the shock, it will induce an increase in its spreads, which will damage not only itself but also the other country. This is the 'fear' behind the Maastricht criteria. On the other hand, when the low-debt country uses its fiscal policy to counteract the shock, it benefits both itself and the other country in a way that it would when countries are closely integrated. The high-debt country therefore imposes a negative externality on the Union when it uses its fiscal policy, whereas the low-debt country imposes a positive one.

The asymmetry in the way that the two countries affect each other is reflected in the opposite slopes of their reaction functions (RFs) in Figure 15.1. Faced with a negative shock, the high-debt country can benefit from the other country's fiscal expansion and therefore reduce the pressure on its own budget (negative slope RF). The low-debt country on the other hand will have to make a stronger fiscal response to counteract the negative spillover effect of the high-debt country (hence positive sloped RF).

Points A and B reflect the optimal response to the shock for the two countries, absent of any strategic interaction. There is a deficit bias in the high-debt country, A_b, and a preference for fiscal stability in the low-debt country (i.e. it wants the high-debt country to do nothing, so point B is on the x-axis at value B_b).

Point N reflects the uncooperative outcome, when both players have accounted for each other's actions, i.e. the Nash equilibrium of this policy game. The overall fiscal response to the external shock is too small ($A_{nash} + B_{nash}$), and certainly by comparison to the cumulative response of both countries absent the strategic interaction ($A_b + B_b$, identified at respective bliss points). The high-debt country's response to the shock is actually pro-cyclical, as it ends up having a surplus.

This shows that in response to a negative shock, the absence of explicit fiscal coordination between the two countries leads to a response that is much less expansionary than optimal, and even procyclical for the high-debt country. This is the result of each country using fiscal policy independently, but within a framework where there are interdependencies.[2]

[2] If fiscal policy response is linear, such that its size is the same irrespective of whether the shock is positive or negative (and of course opposite in sign), then the picture is entirely symmetric across both axes, for a positive shock. Graph available upon request.

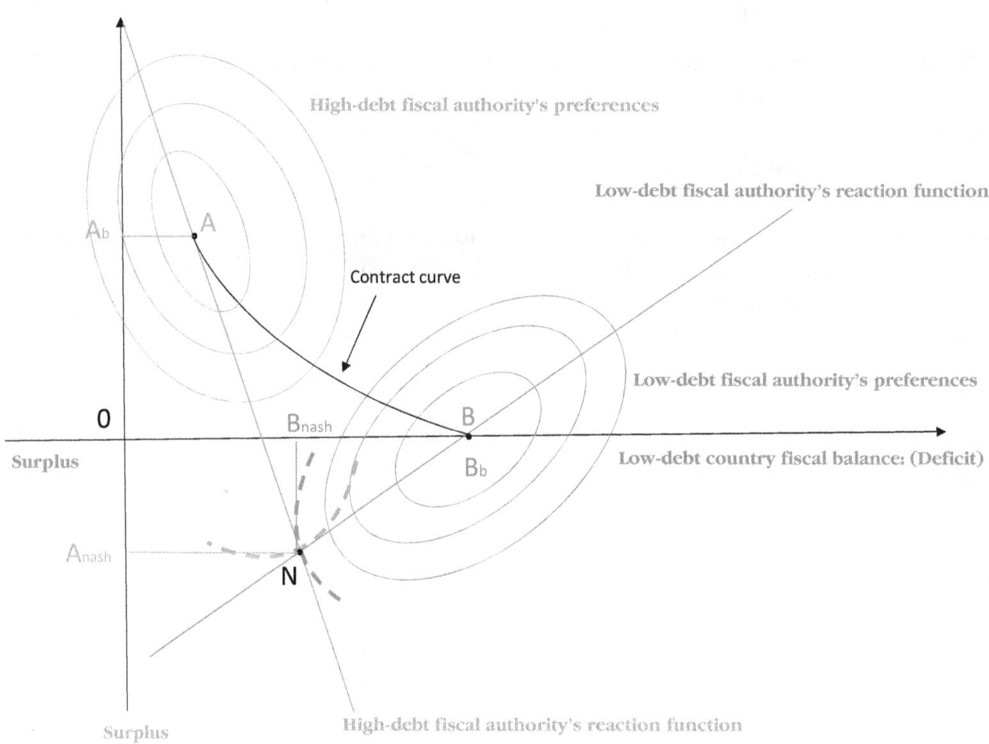

FIGURE 15.1. Fiscal policies strategic interactions in a monetary union (negative shocks)

The contract curve tracks the pairs of fiscal responses when policies are coordinated (with different weights). There exists a coordinated fiscal policy response, as at point C in Figure 15.2, where both do better in welfare terms by comparison to Nash (indifference curves that go through C are closer to respective bliss points). The fiscal response of the high-debt country is now counter-cyclical but not as big as it would have been, had the country not considered the negative spillovers it imposes.

Exactly where C will lie in the F_1F_2 part of the contract curve (where both countries do better than Nash) will depend on the bargaining power of the two players, and is indeed known as the area of feasible policy bargain (Holly and Hughes Hallet, 1989).

We discuss next how the lack of cooperation between the independent fiscal authorities affects monetary policy. The suboptimal fiscal policy outcome captured by the Nash equilibrium, point N in Figure 15.1, is conditional on monetary policy, in other words for a given interest rate level. For a higher interest rate, both fiscal authorities would wish to have a more expansionary fiscal position (i.e. higher fiscal deficit) to counteract the contractionary effect coming from monetary policy. This means that both actors' reaction functions move to the right as interest rates increase and so the respective Nash equilibria move north-east, as shown in Figure 15.3. The collection of all Nash equilibria depicts the aggregate European fiscal reaction function to the common monetary policy.

But we can also derive the equivalent aggregate EU fiscal reaction function to monetary policy when fiscal policies are coordinated, equivalent to the collection of all coordinated equilibria captured by the dashed green line. This line moves upwards, and the coordinated equilibria move to the north-east of the Nash equilibria equivalent shown in Figure 15.2.

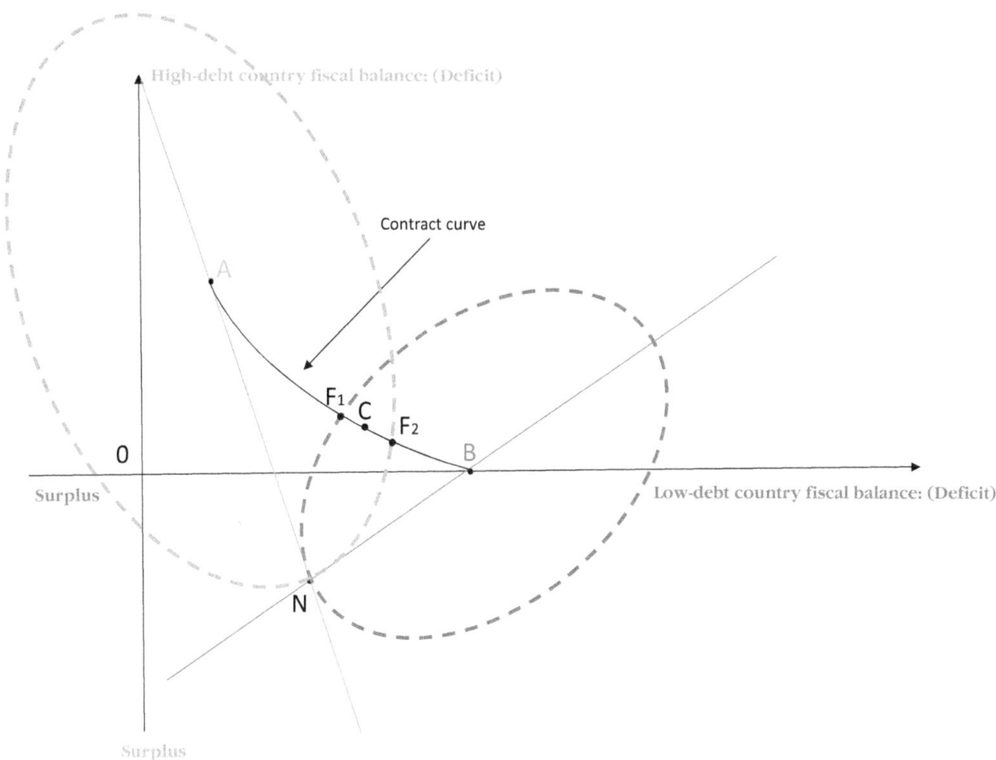

FIGURE 15.2. The benefits of Member States' fiscal policy coordination

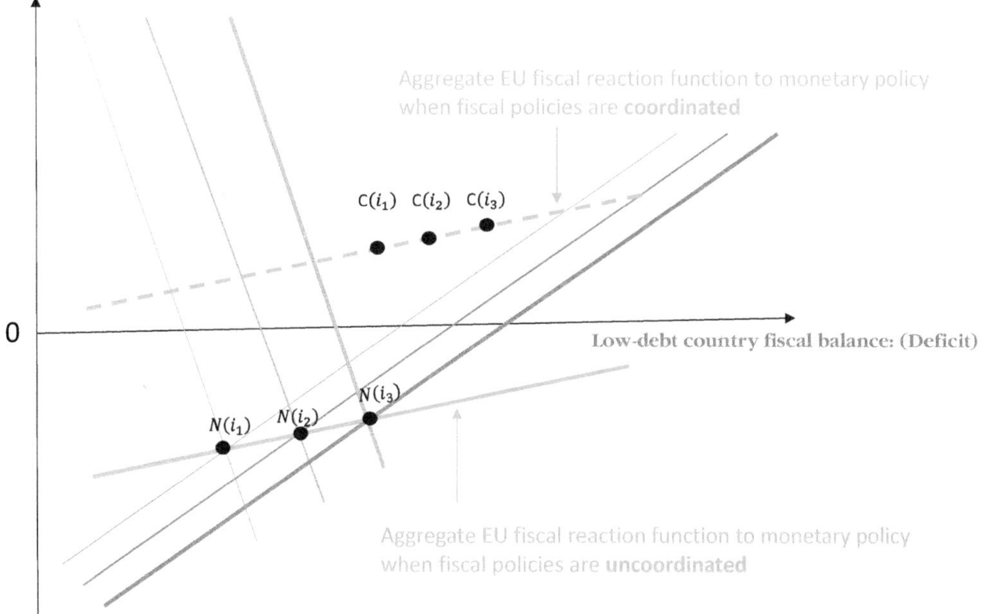

FIGURE 15.3. Fiscal policy expands as monetary policy contracts

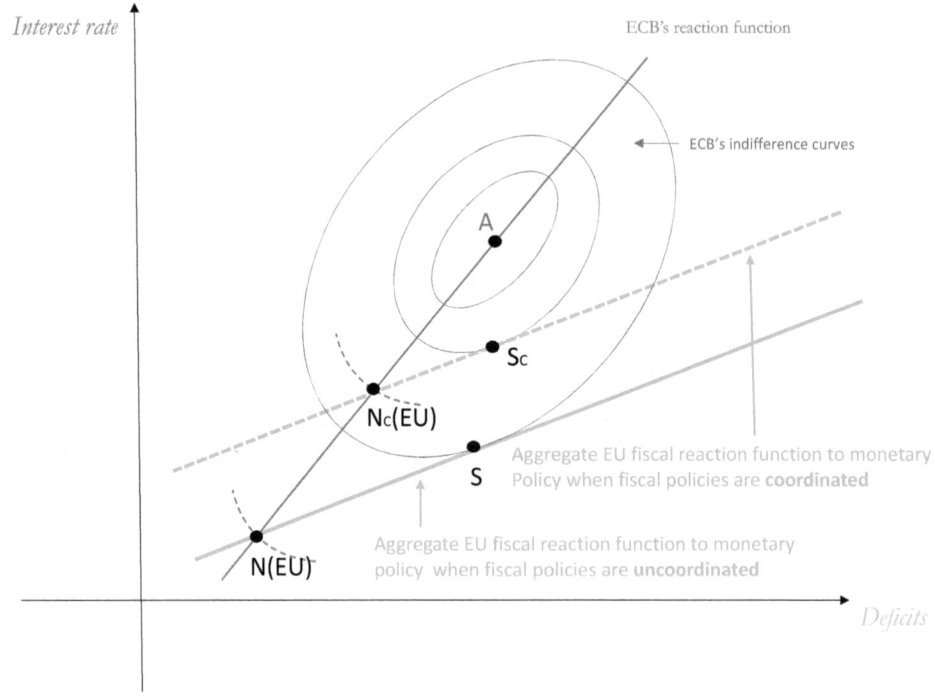

FIGURE 15.4. Monetary–fiscal interactions in monetary union: the overuse of monetary policy (negative shock)

We can now consider the fiscal–monetary policy game in their respective instrument space, interest rate and deficits (Figure 15.4), for a given negative shock. The ECB's RF and the collective fiscal response are positively sloped. For any fiscal expansion, the ECB will increase the interest rate, and similarly fiscal policy will be more expansionary the more contractionary monetary policy is.

Point A indicates the pair of values for the interest rate and deficit preferred by the ECB to deal with the shock (bliss point). In this graph we do not have a bliss point for the fiscal authorities as the fiscal reaction function is the set of equilibria for different levels of the interest rate. This also means that we cannot have a cooperative solution between the ECB and fiscal authorities (i.e. we cannot have a contract curve) unless we first identify a cooperative solution among fiscal authorities that defines European-wide fiscal preferences.

When monetary and fiscal policies are decided independently of each other, then the only credible outcome is the Nash equilibrium, point N(EU). We have shown that fiscal policy is underused in response to the shock, and it is now monetary policy that is having to be more expansionary (lower interest rate) than it would have been otherwise.

Even if we assume that the monetary authority is a Stackelberg leader where the ECB autonomously decides its policy having taken into consideration the aggregate fiscal response, (point S in Figure 15.4), monetary policy is still more expansionary than the shock would dictate (at point A). Had fiscal authorities been able to strike a bargain and coordinate, then fiscal policy would have been more active. The ECB would have had to react by less, shown by the points N_C(EU) and S_C for the Nash and Stackelberg game respectively, which are moved in a north-easterly direction.

Figures 15.1–15.4 show that the lack of coordination between fiscal authorities induces an aggregate outcome where the instrument is underused and monetary policy is too expansionary.

So, for monetary policy to be able to do less, there must be greater fiscal cooperation between countries and an appreciation of the fact that the monetary union imposes strategic interdependencies that need to be dealt with.

15.3 THE LEGACY OF MACRO POLICY UNDER MAASTRICHT

Beyond theory, we observe that the way fiscal policy was implemented in the EU, and in particular in the eurozone, was at best inadequate. We observe this in three ways.

15.3.1 *Fiscal Policy Was by and Large Procyclical*

The underuse of fiscal policy as a demand management instrument is evident in the data. We plot the yearly change in structural balance against the yearly change in the output gap for selected years since 2000 for euro area countries.

There are two observations to make. First, each country's position within the four quadrants is relevant. A traditional Keynesian view of fiscal policy would place countries in one of two quadrants: the first (++) or the third (—). In times of increase in the output gap (i.e. times of economic growth) an increase in the structural balance is associated with a decrease in discretionary fiscal measures. Similarly, in the third quadrant, when the output gap is negative, the structural balance should decrease as a result of the corresponding discretionary measures to stimulate demand. This was the case in 2020, with every single country in the third quadrant. However, since 1992, only around half of the euro area countries were in one of those two quadrants in any given year, and in 2012 (at the height of the sovereign debt crisis) only three were: Estonia, Finland, and Malta.

Second, is the analysis of the correlation between the change in the output gap and the structural balance. We would expect this correlation to be positive, or – in other words – the greater the fall (rise) in the output gap, the greater the change in the structural balance in the same direction. Figure 15.5 plots this relation for a selected group of years, including some when the two values were especially strongly correlated (2005, 2010). This relation was weak and ambiguous before the introduction of the euro, but after 2002 only in 2007 and 2008 is the relation between those two changes positive. That is, only in those two years did countries with the greatest deterioration in their output gap on average also reduce their structural balance more (indicating an increase in discretionary fiscal measures). In all other years between 2003 and 2020, countries with a greater annual fall in their output gap on average undertook less discretionary fiscal policy than those with an increase (or smaller decrease) in their output gap. This implies a highly imperfect use of fiscal policy for countercyclical purposes in the euro area, with individual Member States seemingly not particularly responding to needs (see also de Haan and Gootjes, Chapter 18 in this volume). This entailed a certain disregard for fiscal norms in the boom period (pre-crisis), as well as worst-hit Member States being heavily constrained during the bust and unable to respond. The countercyclical measures adopted in 2008 are perhaps encouraging and unsurprising given the economic context, yet the situation reverted quickly and by 2010 the relationship had been strongly inverted.

Even in 2020, when every single euro area country saw a negative change in their structural balance in response to the COVID-19-induced economic downturn and a shift in attitudes on the need for expansive fiscal policy was evident throughout the EU, we see a negative correlation. Countries where the economic impact of COVID-19 was comparatively lower (with a

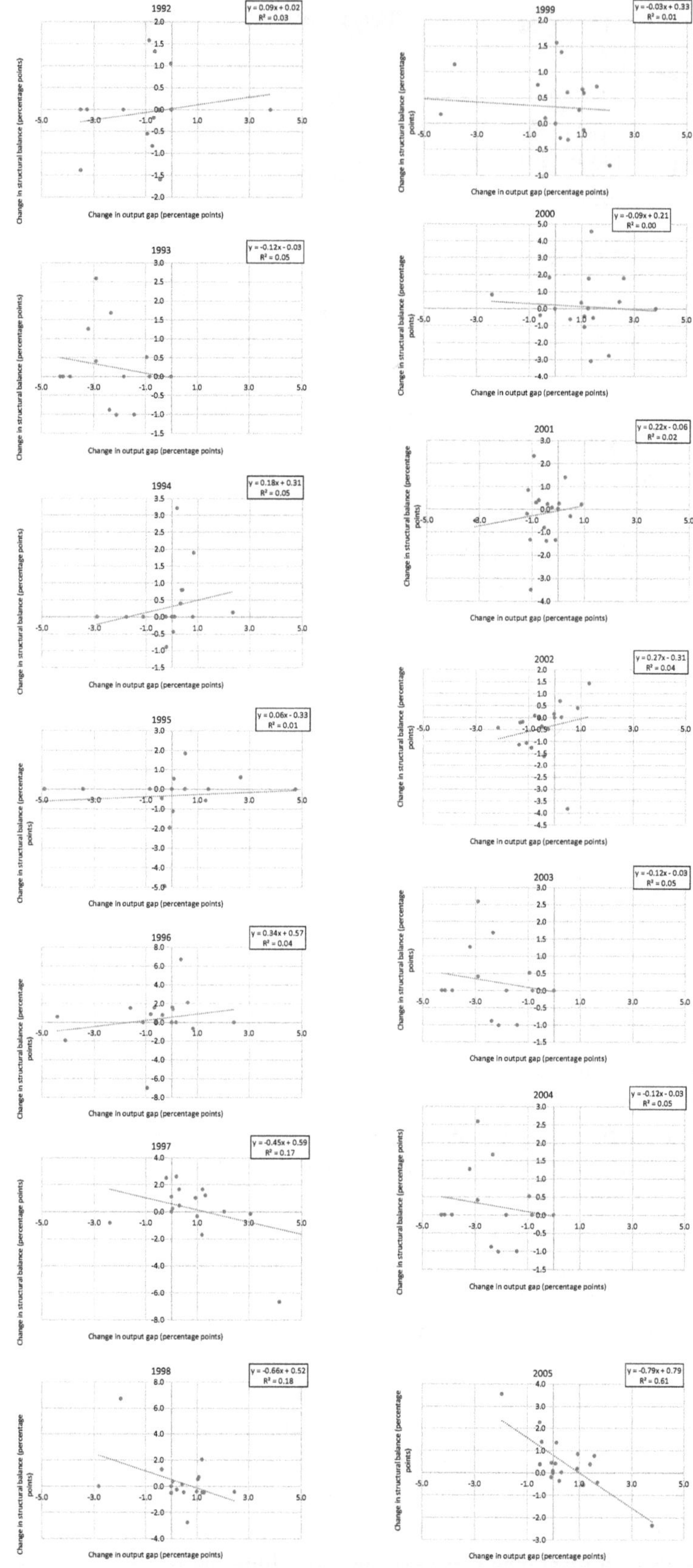

FIGURE 15.5. The procyclicality of fiscal policy: change in structural balance and output gap (percentage points).
Source: Bruegel via IMF World Economic Outlook.

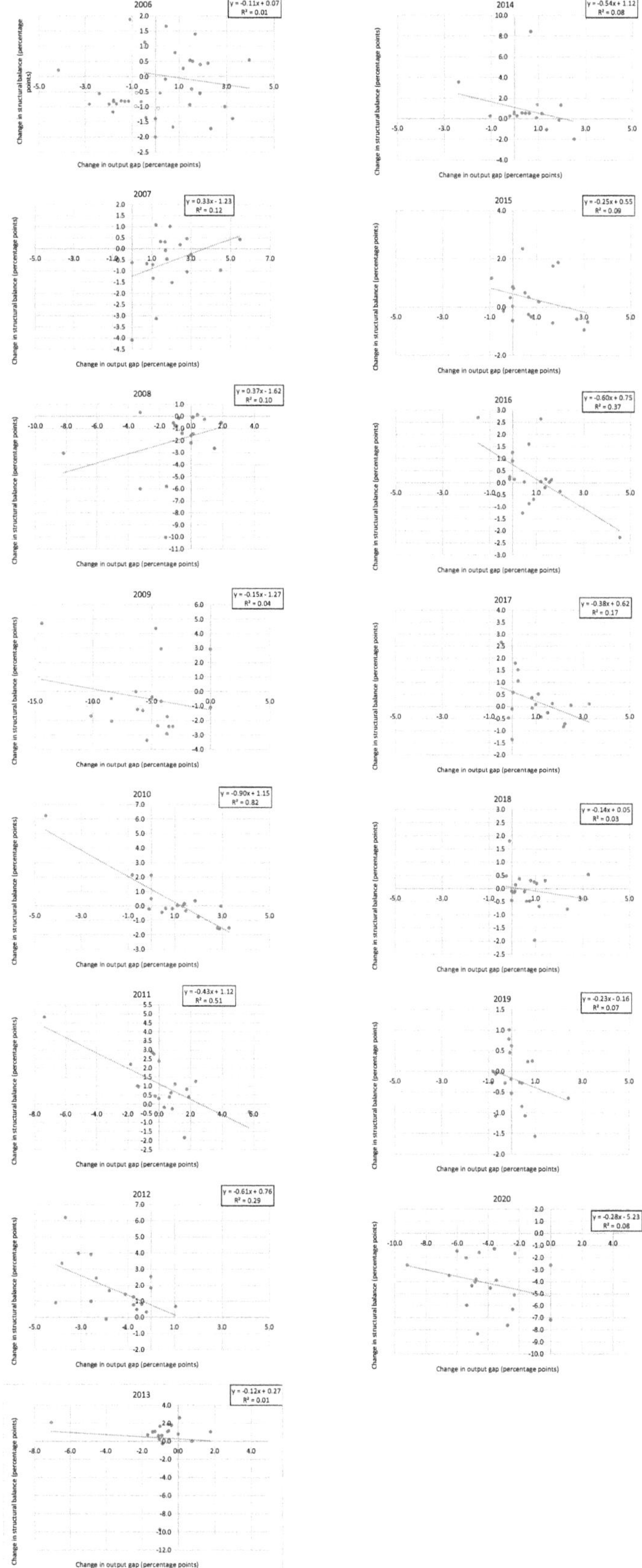

FIGURE 15.5. *(cont.)*

smaller decrease in their output gap vis-à-vis 2019) also generally implemented greater discretionary fiscal measures, evident in the deterioration of their structural balance.

15.3.2 *Investment Is the First to Suffer*

A key distinction to be made, and which should lie at the core of European fiscal decisions, is that between public investment and other forms of fiscal spending. Public investment concerns general government net fixed capital formation, and unlike other forms of public spending, this has a direct effect on potential output and growth more generally. And yet, public investment in many European countries remains very low compared to other developed economies, especially since the financial crisis of 2008.

Ample academic research has shown public investment to be the first victim of fiscal tightening programmes. The following paragraphs review this literature, and then discuss the current situation in Europe and various proposals aimed at introducing special consideration for this type of investment within fiscal norms.

The popularity of balanced-budget rules in the 1980s and 1990s spawned a series of academic studies on the effects of fiscal consolidation on government fixed capital formation. This research consistently shows that consolidation programmes have a particularly strong negative effect on the level of public investments, which often falls consistently more than other types of public expenditure. Roubini and Sachs (1989) noted that capital expenditures are the first to be reduced, often drastically, during periods of restrictive fiscal policy given they are the least rigid component of fiscal policy. Similarly, de Haan et al. (1996) explained the decline of government capital formation by its disproportionate decline in times of fiscal tightening. Peletier et al. (1999) showed that a balanced-budget rule caused below-optimal levels of investment, even as they conceded that exceptions for public investment are hard to introduce, primarily given difficulties classifying investment and government propensity to exploit such exceptions. They demonstrate how balanced-budget rules can reduce *ex ante* utility.

Data on fiscal adjustment programmes between 1960 and 1994 exposes a similar pattern: Alesina and Ardagna (1998) show public investment as a share of GDP to be 16 per cent lower in the two years following a successful adjustment programme. This was found to be even higher in countries which had high debt levels at the time: for example, public investment fell by 40 per cent in Belgium (1986–87) and 29 per cent in Ireland (1985–86), and did not recover in the years following the adjustment. More generally, Blanchard and Leigh (2013) found that not only is fiscal consolidation associated with lower investment growth, this decline is three times the size of the fall in consumption. Similarly, Romer and Romer (2010) showed that investment growth declines four times faster than consumption following a tax increase. That said, Wiese et al. (2018) show that the composition of fiscal adjustment (spending cuts vs. tax hikes) is largely unrelated to their success, and a focus on the latter should reduce the damaging effects to public investment.

Some disagreement remains on the desirability of fiscal laxity or simply exceptions to budgetary prudence when it comes to public investment. For example, Kellermann (2007) found the social opportunity cost of debt-finance public investment was higher than that financed by taxes, indicating a benevolent government would raise the latter to fund investment.

In light of this literature, EU fiscal norms have received attention for their possible role in stifling public investment. Turrini (2004) found some evidence of this, especially in the early days of the Maastricht criteria (although his results leave room for ambiguity). Generally low levels of public investment in most EU countries can be identified in Figure 15.6, which

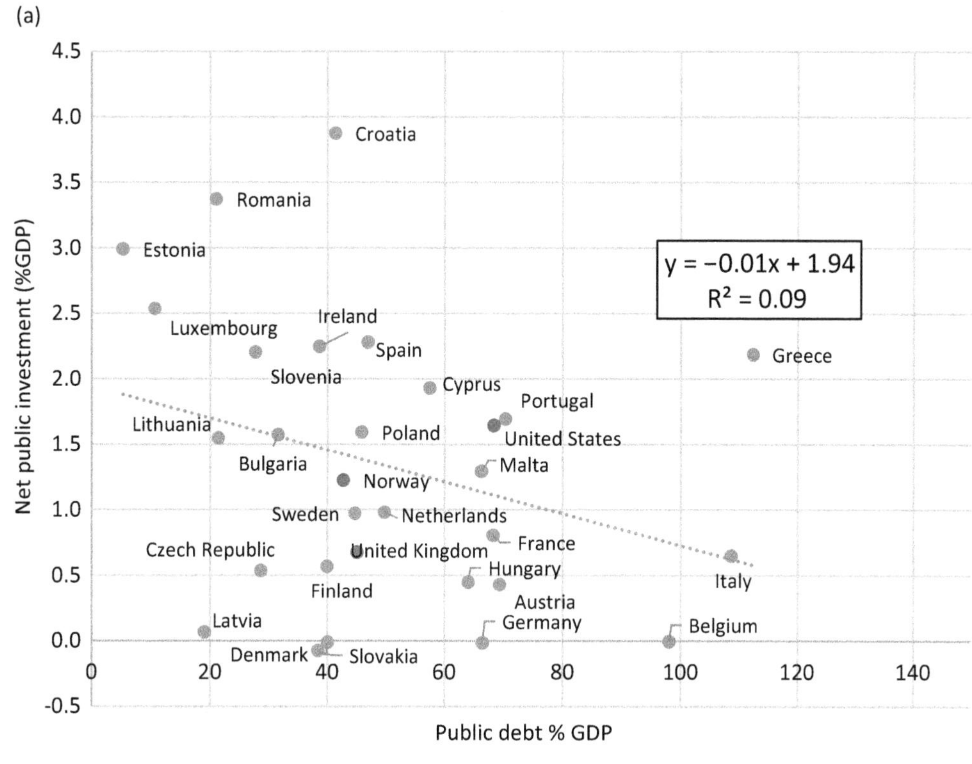

(A) In 2001–10

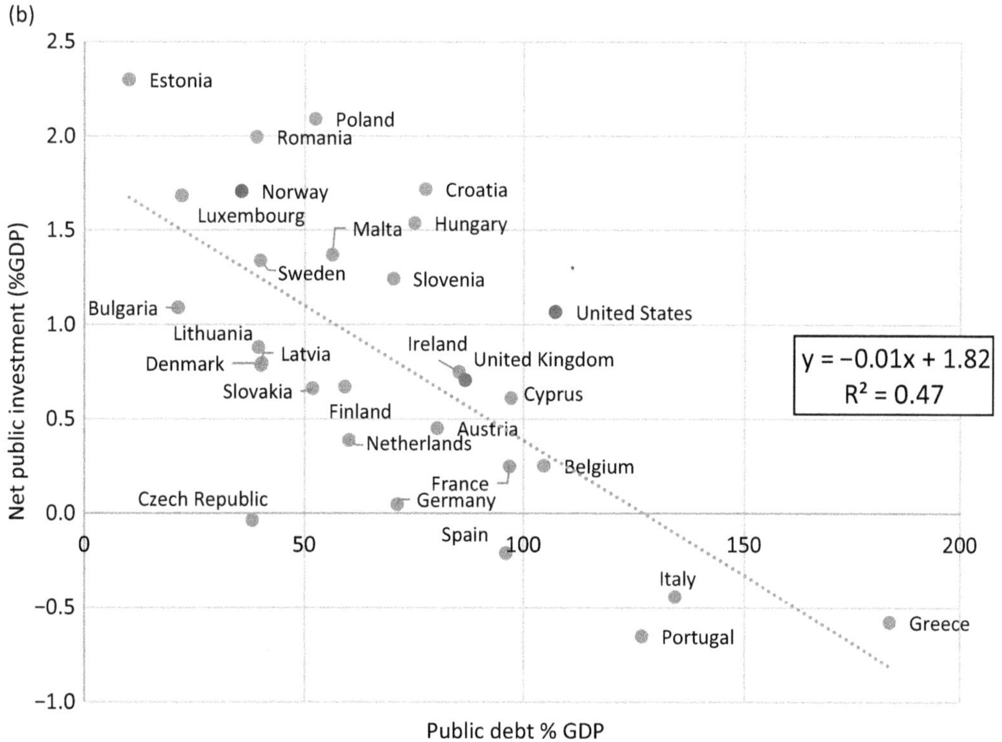

(B) In 2011–20

FIGURE 15.6. Net public investment and public debt, percentage of GDP
Source: Bruegel via European Commission AMECO database, Eurostat, IMF World Economic Outlook.

exhibits an evident negative relation between levels of public debt and net public investment (gross investment minus the depreciation of capital stock). Not only did investment not recover following the GFC, in 2019 net public investment was negative in Italy, Spain, Greece, and Portugal, for a whole decade on average. More generally, most large EU countries lie far below other large economies such as the United States or the United Kingdom.

As a result, there are many calls for reforming the fiscal rules to allow Member States to undertake necessary investments, with numerous proposals emerging in the aftermath of the sovereign debt crisis and especially following the COVID-19 pandemic.

The sovereign debt crisis and poor recovery of European public investment, in the periphery especially but generally throughout the Union, resulted in several proposals. Truger (2015) calls for a golden rule that allows for deficit-financed public investment to be included in the EU's fiscal norms, for both growth and intergenerational fairness purposes. He proposes a simple calculation that subtracts military expenditure and adds investment grants for the private sector to current net public investment calculations. This measure would be refined over time. Barbiero and Darvas (2014) similarly examine how net public investment recovered elsewhere but not in the EU following the 2008 crisis, and was particularly poor in fiscally constrained countries. They similarly lay out a set of proposals for an asymmetric golden rule to protect and incentivize public investment, to go hand in hand with improvements in budgeting, transparency, and project assessment. Bogaert (2016) proposes a change in accounting within the Stability and Growth Pact (SGP) so that public investment becomes a core aspect of structural policy (and not a cyclical instrument) while maintaining much of the remaining current structure. It should be noted that other papers have emerged arguing against a golden rule, including Bundesbank (2019), which examines Germany's unsuccessful experience (this golden rule was removed in 2011).

The COVID-19 pandemic has laid bare the need for a reform in EU fiscal rules, before their current suspension ends. In light of the accelerated shift in consensus over the merits of fiscal policy, it is unsurprising that calls for a bigger role for public investment have also grown. Darvas and Anderson (2020) present many of the arguments in favour of changing how public investment is treated in EU fiscal rules: intergenerational fairness, avoiding strategic underinvestment due to deficit limits, improved medium-term fiscal sustainability with higher potential growth, and the spread of the cost of public investment across years of use (as is done in corporate accounting). They also acknowledge some of the issues around a golden rule (difficulties classifying expenditure, possible spending distortions, protracted deficits). They propose a multi-year forward expenditure rule, augmented with an asymmetric golden rule in times of recession. Thygesen et al. (2020) call for growth-enhancing expenditure to be protected, after decades of decline in this kind of expenditure, necessary for improving economic resilience. Bofinger (2020) similarly proposes the introduction of a golden rule in EU fiscal norms that excludes public investment from deficit targets and thus eases 'the EU fiscal straitjacket'. Finally, Martin et al. (2021) do not support a golden rule, given possible distortions in the mix of investment expenditure and other growth-enhancing expenditure, but consider International Financial Institutions (IFIs) and the EU should account for the impact of different kinds of expenditure of potential output and ensure climate investments are not postponed.

15.3.3 *Monetary Policy as the 'Only Game in Town'*

The cost of the Maastricht policy architecture became evident in the response of Europe to the GFC. Once the crisis morphed into a sovereign debt crisis Europe didn't have instruments to deal with the aggregate cyclical fluctuations. Monetary policy found itself fighting on two fronts:

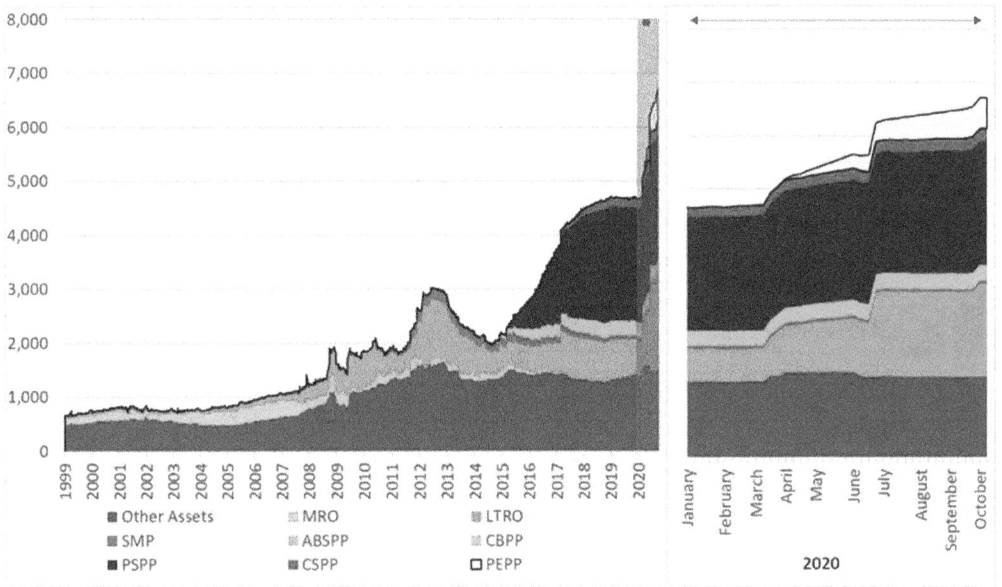

FIGURE 15.7. ECB balance sheet (billion euros).
Note: Main Refinancing Operations (MRO), Longer-Term Refinancing Operations (LTROs), Securities Market Programme (SMP), Asset-Backed Securities Purchase Programme (ABSPP), Covered Bond Purchase Programme (CBPP), Public Sector Purchase Programme (PSPP), Corporate Sector Purchase Programme (CSPP), Pandemic Emergency Purchase Programme (PEPP).
Source: Bruegel via Bloomberg.

on one side the cyclical fluctuations required a drastic reduction in the policy rate close to and beyond the zero–lower bound; on the other side, the fiscal crisis required firm intervention to stabilize increasingly fragmented bond markets.

The Maastricht framework did not provide any help either in preventing the crisis or in dealing with the consequences. The rules were not robust to a sizable external shock. As argued by Draghi (2014), 'since 2010 the euro area has suffered from fiscal policy being less available and effective, especially compared with other large advanced economies'.

Fiscal policy inaction implied that monetary policy had to overstretch. Once interest rates were at the zero–lower bound, monetary policy resorted to unconventional tools, namely quantitative easing (QE). Figure 15.7 shows the balance sheet of the ECB as it stands now, including with the pandemic programme.

It is also the fact that interest rates have been at the lower bound that required the applications of other tools, like QE. But while the effects of such a sizable balance sheet for the functioning of the economy are not known, monetary policy has become a little more like fiscal policy. And in the same way as the existence of high debt constrains the use of fiscal policy, the sizable balance sheet limits the central bank's capacity to do more.

What will happen if inflation becomes sustained and the ECB is obliged to respond? There are two issues that, unlike other central banks, make the ECB's response to an inflationary shock particularly hard.

First, an increase in inflation could put the ECB in an awkward position. Inflationary pressures would require putting a stop to quantitative easing and an increase in policy rates. The ECB has a crucial role to play in enabling euro area sovereigns to borrow in order to finance spending. This role could be jeopardized if its price-stability objective was pitted against its desire to help sovereigns access affordable financing to avoid dangerous spirals due to financial fragmentation (whereby strong links remain between national banks and sovereigns threatening governments' access to financing in countries with deeper financial crises). There are many discussions about 'fiscal dominance' being a risk to the ECB's standing. However, the last thing that we needed as we managed the recovery in the middle of the COVID-19 pandemic was an attack on sovereign spreads that would jeopardize the integrity of the euro. The dilemma between preventing financial fragmentation and pursuing its inflation mandate may become very real for the ECB.

The proportionality of ECB policies has been challenged by the German constitutional court, setting a dangerous precedent that could undermine the ECB's reputation and ability to achieve its objectives – especially if confronted with the policy conflict – avoiding financial fragmentation and controlling inflationary pressures.

15.4 FISCAL POLICY AT THE HEART OF THE NEED FOR GREATER COORDINATION

There are two problems to fix as we move forward: first, fiscal policies need to revert to countercyclical behaviour as the only way to manage shocks effectively, and secondly, there need to be ways of ensuring that investments, particularly in European public goods, are not jeopardized through lack of coordination. If fiscal policy were to assume such a renewed role, then monetary policy would not have to carry the burden of macroeconomic management.

With the Maastricht criteria suspended during the pandemic crisis, there is a great urgency to rethink the whole framework to adapt to the post-pandemic reality of high debt and significant investment needs. The rationale for fiscal coordination remains but, as we showed in the previous section, the Maastricht framework effectively led to non-cooperative outcomes. There are many who have argued about how to reform the fiscal rules in order to correct for these two problems (see Claeys and Demertzis, 2022 for a summary). Indeed, measurement issues (like output gap vs. unemployment), as well as which variables to target (expenditure vs. debt rules), aim to achieve more effective coordination of fiscal policy at the business cycle frequency. But some efforts to reform the rules also look beyond the business cycle frequency and aim to ensure that investments are sustained particularly to deal with climate.

However, reforming the rules alone will not deal with the fact that the role of fiscal policy in the future will be different than what it was when the Maastricht framework was constructed. Back then the EU framework was intended to prevent fiscal indiscipline by Member States and to stop it spreading across the eurozone. Its design reflected the prevailing economic orthodoxy in the 1990s on the role of fiscal policy. This emphasized automatic adjustments in tax revenues and spending to stabilize income, consumption, and business activity over the business cycle. Any fiscal policy that attempted to go beyond these 'automatic stabilizers' was likely to cause inflation. Consequently, politicians, who have an incentive to overspend, ought to be institutionally constrained.

Today, however, after the GFC and a global pandemic, two once-in-a-lifetime shocks in the space of just over a decade, the economic context is very different. Both these episodes show that fiscal policy is about more than just automatic stabilization, although at first policymakers in Europe were slow to recognize this – partly because of the grip exerted by the old orthodoxies, but mostly because of the fear of fiscal spillovers across borders.

But we do not start with a clean slate. The past twelve years have left countries with large debts. This implies that the space for countries in the euro area to use fiscal policy will not be the same. The most obvious place where this problem will manifest is in the way public authorities will have to contribute to our future investment needs. While countries will have to continue to use fiscal policy to manage shocks at the business cycle frequency, they will also need funds to manage the green and digital transitions.

Darvas and Wolff (2021) estimate that between 0.5 and 1 per cent of GDP of additional public investment will be required annually during this decade to meet EU climate goals. They advocate for a green golden rule that excludes net green investment from the EU fiscal indicators used to measure fiscal rule compliance, and thus avoid underinvestment due to deficit constraints. Other global estimates of investment needs are summarized in Lenaerts et al. (2021) and include those recently developed by the International Energy Agency (IEA), which estimates annual investments globally stand at $2 trillion per year or 2.5 per cent of global GDP and should rise to $5 trillion by 2030 (and remain so at least until 2050). The International Renewable Energy Agency (IRENA) frontloads these investments, considering $5.7 trillion is required annually until 2030, while Bloomberg New Energy Finance (BNEF) estimates yearly investment requirements of between $3.1 and 5.8 trillion up to 2050. Finally, the European Commission estimates, only in the EU, meeting 2030 targets will require €360 billion in additional investment annually.

But while most of the discussion on handling future investments is done in the context of reforming the fiscal rules to exclude them one way or another, this does not solve the problem of huge legacy debts, at least for some countries. Whether investments are part of a new rule or not, a good number of countries will not have the space to invest the necessary funds without raising debt sustainability concerns.

How can we ensure that enough funds are available to provide particularly for those investments that pertain to crucial public goods, like climate? It is the public nature of climate that, unless everyone invests, nobody will achieve their climate goals.

Given legacy debts and the public nature of these investment needs, the only other option available is to mutualize some of the fiscal policy. There are a few principles that can help guide the extent to which this mutualization could or indeed should be attained.

The most obvious starting point is that the mutualization of fiscal risk cannot be about past liabilities. Therefore, the legacy issues still need to be resolved at the national level. And indeed, common fiscal policy needs to be about investing in those items that are of equal relevance to all countries, but also across generations. The decision on what qualifies as an investment item to be financed centrally needs to be removed from national control.

Here the Recovery and Resilience Fund (RRF) provides a very useful template on how to proceed. This is because:

1. It has a clear and limited purpose. It has a very clear purpose, primarily to fund the energy and digital transition, common to all countries. It will finance no other expenditure or investment;
2. It reduces the opportunity for greenwashing. It may be put together at the national level but it requires the approval of centralized European institutions. While this may not remove the temptation to oversubscribe, it will reduce it. As such, it will provide better protection against greenwashing, the temptation to put all investments under the green label, and therefore promote more effectively the right types of investment;
3. It increases coordination implementability. As it is monitored centrally, implementation of plans will have better chances of providing the necessary policy coordination and hence succeeding;
4. It helps deal with legacy problems. The debt issued will be self-financed, and at least the grant component will not be a part of national debts. This will help those countries that have legacy problems also advance with green and digital investments;

5. It is an accepted instrument among Member States. The RRF is not a stabilization tool[3] and does not therefore suffer from the main political-economic problem of required representation for any new taxation. As a template, it is incentive-compatible in that it has been accepted by national authorities as a legitimate tool to deal with long-term investment needs. There is no need to discuss the issue of how to pull risks together any further, an effort that is very difficult from a political-economic perspective.

With an instrument like the RRF the EU can make progress on advancing with the green and digital agenda at a minimum speed that is common to all, and help counteract the poor levels of public investment of the last decade of more restrictive fiscal policy. There are other suggestions that aim to address this issue, such as that by Garicano (2022), who talks about a European Climate Facility. His suggestion, which is less ambitious than the RRF, bypasses the political obstacle that the RRF is a one-off instrument that requires a treaty change to become permanent. True though this is, it is difficult to solve an emergency of the scale and importance of climate without making deep adjustments, including in changing our current treaties. The RRF offers a good template to think about a future instrument that can help deal more effectively with the green transition.

15.5 CONCLUSIONS

The Maastricht framework was created at a time when fiscal policy was not expected to play a significant role in managing demand. Almost thirty years and two global crises later we can expect fiscal policy to have a much more active role in the future that goes beyond automatic stabilization. Moreover, our climate and digital ambitions will demand big public investments in order to attract the private funds that are necessary.

At the same time, however, we observe that the Maastricht framework failed in its efforts to coordinate fiscal policies in the EU. By putting the emphasis on constraining the use of the instrument, fiscal policy was underused as a stabilization tool, so much so that fiscal policy was by and large procyclical for most of the period considered.

At the same time, this implied that monetary policy had to deal with negative shocks. As the only game in town and with little space for using its conventional tools, monetary policy had to resort to unconventional measures and land on a point that is much further away from what it would consider optimal. This overuse of the monetary instrument also means that the ECB now has a large balance sheet, as a stock position, that might constrain its ability to act in the future. In this respect, monetary policy has become more like fiscal policy.

As we move forward, fiscal policy will play a bigger role. This is not without problems as we do not start with a clean slate. Not all countries have the same fiscal capacity and therefore their ability to use fiscal policy will vary. Just reforming the fiscal rules, say by excluding certain types of investment, will not suffice.

We argue that with particular reference to the global public goods, primarily climate, a failure of any given member state to undertake the necessary investments will prevent others in the EU from meeting their objectives. To avoid this happening we argue that the investments that pertain to common public goods should be centralized to ensure a sufficient investment to progress with the green transition. This would involve centralizing some fiscal policy. There is no talk of federalism but rather of following the template of Next Generation EU.

[3] Although by allocating funds to long-term investments it does release budgetary resources for stabilization purposes.

Appendix A

We describe the strategic interaction and outcome of the lack of fiscal policy coordination for a positive (expansionary) shock. The graph in Figure 15.A1 is simplified by displaying only the Reaction Functions for the two players in the two states of the world (n for negative and p for positive) and the contract curves.

1. Points B_n and B_p are equal and opposite in sign. In absence of any policy response from country A, the response of country B to shock is linear and therefore symmetric.
2. Point B_p is the bliss point for the low-debt country, because the bliss point shows the case where low-debt country wants to minimize the negative spillover of high-debt country policies on itself. When we have a positive shock, country B wants to stabilize by running a surplus (therefore contract), but if country A also runs a surplus, then country risk will reduce and that will have an expansionary spillover effect on country B, which goes against its policies. So country B would prefer country A to do nothing at all, and that is why its bliss point is on the axis (don't react to the cycle – only deal with stability of budget).

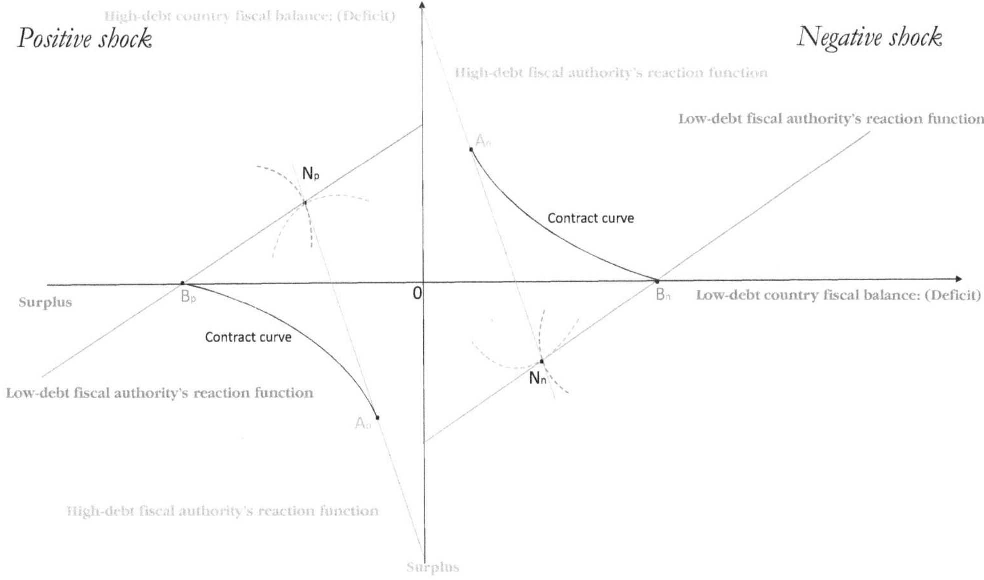

FIGURE 15.A1. Fiscal policies' strategic interaction in a monetary union (positive shock)

3. Similar arguments hold for country A. The intercept when B = 0 (reflecting no policy action from country B) should be symmetric around the zero point.
4. The slope of the reaction functions cannot change, as the shock does not affect preferences, just the position in space. So the reaction functions are drawn symmetrically.
5. Again, the Nash equilibrium has country A expanding to a positive shock but much less than it would do left to itself, and country B actually expands. So the cumulative fiscal policy is much less contractionary than would have been achieved if countries have a collective (cooperative policy on the contract curve) fiscal response.

REFERENCES

Alesina, A., and Ardagna, S. (1998). Tales of fiscal adjustment. *Economic Policy* 13(27), 488–545.

Alesina, A., Cohen, G. D., and Roubini, N. (1993). Electoral business cycle in industrial democracies. *European Journal of Political Economy* 9(1), 1–23.

Barbiero, F., and Darvas, Z. (2014). In sickness and in health: Protecting and supporting public investment in Europe. Bruegel Policy Contribution. www.bruegel.org/policy-brief/sickness-and-health-protecting-and-supporting-public-investment-europe

Barro, R. J. (1974). Are government bonds net wealth? *Journal of Political Economy* 82(6), 1095–1117.

Barro, R. J. (1979). On the determination of the public debt. *Journal of Political Economy* 87(5, Part 1), 940–971.

Beetsma, R., and Uhlig, H. (1999). An analysis of the Stability and Growth Pact. *Economic Journal* 109 (458), 546–571.

Blanchard, O. J., and Leigh, D. (2013). Growth forecast errors and fiscal multipliers. *American Economic Review* 103(3), 117–120.

Blinder, A. S. (1982). Issues in the coordination of monetary and fiscal policy. NBER Working Paper No. 982. Cambridge, MA: National Bureau of Economic Research.

Blinder, A. S., and Solow, R. M. (1973). Does fiscal policy matter? *Journal of Public Economics* 2(4), 319–337.

Bofinger, P. (2020). Easing the EU fiscal straitjacket. *Social Europe*, 14 December. https://socialeurope.eu/easing-the-eu-fiscal-straitjacket?msclkid=32e04d8ed0f511ec90de9a355e0191ed

Bogaert, H. (2016). *Improving the Stability and Growth Pact by Integrating a Proper Accounting of Public Investments: A New Attempt*. Brussels: Federal Planning Bureau.

Buiter, W. H. (2002). The fiscal theory of the price level: A critique. *The Economic Journal* 112(481), 459–480.

Buiter, W., Corsetti, G., and Roubini, N. (1993). Excessive deficits: Sense and nonsense in the Treaty of Maastricht. *Economic Policy* 8(16), 57–100.

Bundesbank, D. (2019). European Stability and Growth Pact: Individual reform options. *Monthly Report*, April, 77–90.

Buti, M., and Van den Noord, P. (2004). *Fiscal Policy in EMU: Rules, Discretion and Political Incentives*. Brussels: Directorate General Economic and Financial Affairs (DG ECFIN), European Commission.

Canzoneri, M. B., and Diba, B. T. (1991). Fiscal deficits, financial integration, and a central bank for Europe. *Journal of the Japanese and International Economies* 5(4), 381–403.

Canzoneri, M. B., and Diba, B. T. (2001). The Stability and Growth Pact: A delicate balance or an albatross? In A. H. Hallett, P. Mooslechner, and M. Schuerz (eds.), *Challenges for Economic Policy Coordination within European Monetary Union*. Boston, MA: Springer, pp. 127–142.

Claeys, G., and Demertzis, M. (2022). A return to what fiscal rules? In *Good Policies, a Gap Year on Reforms, A Yearbook on the Euro 2022*. Madrid: Fundación de Estudios Financieros and Fundación ICO.

Darvas, Z., and Anderson, J. (2020). *New Life for an Old Framework: Redesigning the European Union's Expenditure and Golden Fiscal Rules*. Strasbourg: European Parliament.

Darvas, Z., and Wolff, G. (2021). A green fiscal pact: Climate investment in times of budget consolidation. Bruegel Policy Contribution, Brussels.

De Grauwe, P. (1990). *Fiscal Policies in the EMS: A Strategic Analysis*. Leuven: Katholieke Universiteit, Centrum voor Economische Studien.

De Haan, J., Sturm, J. E., and Sikken, B. J. (1996). Government capital formation: Explaining the decline. *Weltwirtschaftliches Archiv* 132(1), 55–74.

Delors, J. (1989). *Report on Economic and Monetary Union in the European Community* (Delors Report). Brussels: Committee for the Study of Economic and Monetary Union.

Demertzis, M., and Viegi, N. (2011). Interdependence of fiscal debts in EMU. De Nederlandsche Bank Working Paper No. 309.

Demertzis, M., Hughes Hallett, A., and Viegi, N. (2004). An independent central bank faced with elected governments. *European Journal of Political Economy* 20(4), 907–922.
Draghi, M. (2014). Unemployment in the euro area. Speech at the Annual Central Bank Symposium in Jackson Hole, 22 August. www.ecb.europa.eu/press/key/date/2014/html/sp140822.en.html
Garicano, L. (2022). Combining environmental and fiscal sustainability: A new climate facility, an expenditure rule, and an independent fiscal agency. *VoxEU.org*. https://cepr.org/voxeu/columns/combining-environmental-and-fiscal-sustainability-new-climate-facility-expenditure
Grilli, V., Masciandaro, D., and Tabellini, G. (1991). Political and monetary institutions and public financial policies in the industrial countries. *Economic Policy* 6(13), 341–392.
Hamada, K. (1976). A strategic analysis of monetary interdependence. *Journal of Political Economy* 84(4, Part 1), 677–700.
Holly, S., and Hughes Hallet, A. (1989). *Optimal Control, Expectations and Uncertainty*. Cambridge: Cambridge University Press.
Kellermann, K. (2007). Debt financing of public investment: On a popular misinterpretation of 'the golden rule of public sector borrowing'. *European Journal of Political Economy* 23(4), 1088–1104.
Krugman, P. (1987). European economic integration: Conceptual problems. In *Efficiency, Stability and Equity (Padoa–Schioppa Report)*. Brussels: European Commission.
Lamfalussy, A. (1989). Macro-coordination of fiscal policies in an economic and monetary union in Europe. In *Report on Economic and Monetary Union in the European Community*. Brussels: Committee for the Study of Economic and Monetary Union.
Leeper, E. M. (1991). Equilibria under 'active' and 'passive' monetary and fiscal policies. *Journal of Monetary Economics* 27(1), 129–147.
Lenaerts, K., Tagliapietra, S., and Wolff, G. B. (2021). How much investment do we need to reach net zero? *Bruegel Blog*. www.bruegel.org/2021/08/how-much-investment-do-we-need-to-reach-net-zero/
Martin, P., Pisani-Ferry, J., and Ragot, X. (2021). A new template for the European fiscal framework. *VoxEU.org*. https://cepr.org/voxeu/columns/new-template-european-fiscal-framework
McCallum, B. T. (1999). Issues in the design of monetary policy rules. *Handbook of Macroeconomics* 1, 1483–1530.
McCallum, B. T. (2001). Indeterminacy, bubbles, and the fiscal theory of price level determination. *Journal of Monetary Economics* 47(1), 19–30.
McCallum, B. T. (2003). Is the fiscal theory of the price level learnable? NBER Working Paper No. 9961. Cambridge, MA: National Bureau of Economic Analysis.
Peletier, B. D., Dur, R. A., and Swank, O. H. (1999). Voting on the budget deficit: Comment. *American Economic Review* 89(5), 1377–1381.
Romer, C. D., and Romer, D. H. (2010). The macroeconomic effects of tax changes: Estimates based on a new measure of fiscal shocks. *American Economic Review* 100(3), 763–801.
Roubini, N., and Sachs, J. (1989). Government spending and budget deficits in the industrial countries. *Economic Policy* 4(8), 99–132.
Sargent, T. J., and Wallace, N. (1981). Some unpleasant monetarist arithmetic. *Federal Reserve Bank of Minneapolis Quarterly Review* 5(3), 1–17.
Sims, C. A. (1994). A simple model for study of the determination of the price level and the interaction of monetary and fiscal policy. *Economic Theory* 4(3), 381–399.
Sims, C. A. (1999). The precarious fiscal foundations of EMU. *De Economist* 147(4), 415–436.
Thygesen, N., Beetsma, R., Bordignon, M., Debrun, X., Szczurek, M., Larch, M., Busse, M., Gabrijelcic, M., Orseau, E., and Santacroce, S. (2020). Reforming the EU fiscal framework: Now is the time. *VoxEU.org*. https://cepr.org/voxeu/columns/reforming-eu-fiscal-framework-now-time
Truger, A. (2015). Implementing the golden rule for public investment in Europe: Safeguarding public investment and supporting the recovery. WIFO Studies Policy Paper No. 22. www.wifo.ac.at/wwa/pubid/57898
Turrini, A. (2004). *Public Investment and the EU Fiscal Framework*. Brussels: Directorate General Economic and Financial Affairs (DG ECFIN), European Commission.
Wiese, R., Jong-A-Pin, R., and de Haan, J. (2018). Can successful fiscal adjustments only be achieved by spending cuts? *European Journal of Political Economy* 54, 145–166.
Woodford, M. (1994). Monetary policy and price level determinacy in a cash-in-advance economy. *Economic Theory* 4(3), 345–380.
Woodford, M. (1995). Price-level determinacy without control of a monetary aggregate. *Carnegie-Rochester Conference Series on Public Policy* 43, 1–46.
Woodford, M. (2001). Fiscal requirements for price stability. *Journal of Money, Credit and Banking* 33, 669–728.

16

Ten Years of the European Semester

From the Sovereign Debt Crisis to the COVID-19 Crisis

Edgars Eihmanis

16.1 INTRODUCTION

Over the last decade, European Union economic governance has undergone major changes, and become increasingly complex. To tackle fiscal, economic, and social imbalances during the sovereign debt crisis (SDC), the EU developed a series of new governance tools, tied together by the European Semester (Semester), the EU's main economic policy coordination framework launched in 2011 (D'Erman and Verdun, 2022; Verdun and Zeitlin, 2018). For most of the last decade, the European Commission has annually identified key challenges for each Member State, drawing on inputs from a variety of national and European actors, and, together with the Council issues, Country Specific Recommendations (CSRs) on how to tackle them. The COVID-19 pandemic further enhanced the significance of the European Semester, which will also serve to monitor and assess Member States' use of EU financial support under the Recovery and Resilience Facility (RRF) (Vanhercke and Verdun, 2022).

This chapter accounts for a decade (2011–21) of the Semester's changing policy goals, institutions, and legitimacy from its inception in the aftermath of the euro crisis to its transformation during the COVID-19 crisis. The basic research question is: How has the EU adjusted the goals and institutions of socioeconomic policy coordination in response to a decade of crises, and what explains these evolving policy measures? To map the changing politics and governance of the Semester in a longer-term perspective, the chapter traces the Semester's development over three phases that are commonly identified in the state-of-the-art political science literature: the initial focus on competitiveness, the gradual socialization post-2014, and the Semester's institutional adaptation to the RRF post-pandemic (D'Erman and Verdun, 2022; Verdun and Zeitlin, 2018).

Theoretically, the chapter draws on various strands of political science scholarship, such as Europeanization, policy coordination and learning, experimentalism, agenda-setting, national ownership, and representative democracy. Analytically, the chapter builds on three premises. First, I contend that in order to evaluate the EU's socioeconomic policy coordination over time, one must pay attention to the leadership of the Commission and its policy goals, articulated via various planning documents and the Semester's CSRs. EU policy goals change regularly, depending on previous policies, political context, and leadership of the Commission (Corti,

Funded by the National Science Centre, Poland. Grant number 2020/37/B/HS5/00328, project webpage: www.pandemo.eu. The author would like to thank Jonathan Zeitlin for helpful comments.

2022; Schmidt, 2019; Vesan and Pansardi, 2021; Zeitlin and Vanhercke, 2018). Second, I contend that to comprehensively evaluate the impact of the Semester, one must depart from a narrow conceptualization of effectiveness, which assesses the extent to which a country-specific recommendation is implemented over a single year. Such a restricted conceptualization of 'effectiveness' has often resulted in conclusions that implementation of the CSRs across Member States has been extremely limited (Darvas and Leandro, 2015; Efstathiou and Wolff, 2018). Borrowing from the rich body of scholarship on the Open Method of Coordination (OMC), the EU's pioneering framework for coordinating social and employment policy, I contend that CSRs can have variegated – short- and long-term – effects, if not immediately materializing in national reforms, then reshaping the policy process itself, for instance through setting the political agenda or providing external legitimacy for reforms (Barcevicius et al., 2014; Bokhorst, 2022; Eihmanis, 2018; Munta, 2021; Zeitlin, 2009). Third, to understand the democratic legitimacy of EU economic governance, one must look at a broad set of actors – such as parliaments, EU committees, social partners and civil society organizations – at both the national and European levels. Involvement of social actors can take different forms. It has varied markedly throughout different crises, with large implications for different types of legitimacy (Crum, 2018; Maatsch, 2016; Maatsch and Cooper, 2017; Zeitlin and Vanhercke, 2018).

By comparing how the Semester's policy goals and reception have changed over time, the chapter develops a three-fold argument. First, I argue that the European Commission has experimented with governance tools to address different crises as they emerge, in line with the ruling ideas at the time. Over the decade of the Semester, the Commission has travelled a long way from pushing fiscal consolidation and structural reforms through enforced fiscal and macroeconomic policy surveillance to emphasizing social investment. This trend has become even more salient with the RRF.

Second, I argue that the Semester's CSRs, while often failing to change national policy in a single year, can have significant 'indirect' effects in the longer term, such as putting new issues on the agenda and shaping national policy debate. Furthermore, I expect that the Commission's influence over national policy processes will rise in the post-pandemic period, via the RRF conditionality regarding 'green' and 'digital' transitions but also the CSRs. Notwithstanding the temporary character of the RRF, this will occur not only because of the increased powers of the Commission as the administrator of the RRF funds, alongside the Council acting through Implementing Decisions. It will also occur because of the expectedly higher national ownership due to increased national involvement in formulating and implementing the Recovery and Resilience Plans (RRPs).

Third, I argue that representation of broad social interests changes over time, depending on how such representation adapts to changing institutions of EU economic governance. During emergency situations, social partners and civil society tend to be excluded from EU economic governance processes. However, over time these social representatives may adapt to EU institutional changes and reinstate their roles, although their success in doing so varies across different social groups and countries. Building on recent literature, the chapter shows that similar dynamics can be observed regarding national parliaments.

The chapter is structured as follows. First, after briefly introducing the background against which the Semester was adopted in 2010, I discuss its basic institutions, procedures, and actors. Second, I discuss the Semester's political reception, social involvement, and variegated effects on national policy. Then, I review the literature on how the Semester's policy goals and reception have changed post-pandemic, paving the way for it to become the main framework to administer the RRF funds. The chapter concludes by situating the arguments in a broader narrative of EU economic governance and indicating potential future developments.

16.2 THE EU'S 'NEW ECONOMIC GOVERNANCE' AND THE EUROPEAN SEMESTER

Since the launch of the euro in 1999, the EU has tried various ways to coordinate Member States' fiscal, economic, and social policies which have a major impact on the functioning of the Economic and Monetary Union (EMU) as a whole. The goals of economic stability and social solidarity have always had an uneasy relationship (Ferrera, 2017). In fiscal policy, the EU has – at least on paper – resorted to a 'hard' governance approach of universal budget deficit and public debt targets, with uniform rules and sanctions in case of non-compliance. By contrast, in social and labour market policy, the EU has tried to respect the diversity of national welfare regimes by resorting to 'soft' modes of governance (Zeitlin et al., 2005). In practice, however, the difference between these types of governance is not clear-cut and has further blurred over the past decade (Schmidt, 2020; Trubek and Trubek, 2005).

As the EU framework for policy coordination, the Semester is an extension of earlier EU frameworks for governing fiscal and social policy. In the context of increased economic integration and the launch of the single currency in 1999, coordination of Member States' budgetary, labour market, and social protection systems became necessary (Heidenreich and Zeitlin, 2009; Howarth and Verdun, 2020). Regarding fiscal policy, the Semester built on the 1998 Stability and Growth Pact (SGP), operationalizing the Maastricht criteria that limited the level of debt to 60 per cent and budget deficits to 3 per cent of GDP respectively). Regarding social and employment policy, the Semester builds on the 1997 European Employment Strategy (EES) and the 2000 Open Method of Coordination – path-setting governance processes for EU employment and social policy, based on iterative benchmarking of national progress towards common European objectives and organized mutual learning. Altogether these initiatives put a stronger emphasis on social rights and solidarity, taking baby steps toward a 'Social Europe' (Barcevicius et al., 2014; Zeitlin, 2009).

However, by the mid-2000s it became obvious that these infant attempts to coordinate Member States' economic policies did not work as expected. The infamous breaches of the 3 per cent budget deficit limit by France and Germany only confirmed the built-in asymmetry between economic and monetary policies, where the former were governed in a decentralized way, while the latter were governed supranationally (Howarth and Verdun, 2020; Verdun, 1996). Similar criticisms have been made about the Open Method of Coordination, although social policy coordination was significantly streamlined and made more effective post-2006 (Barcevicius et al., 2014).

The sovereign debt crisis exposed the shortcomings of the EU's coordination of national economic policies which subsequently were also remedied by the Semester. After it became clear that Greece had systematically falsified its budget deficit figures, the cost of Greek borrowing sharply increased to unsustainable levels (de Haan et al., 2015). The possibility of Greece's default and exit from the eurozone then entailed fears of financial contagion to other southern European countries. As investors bet against the weaker EU Member States, their fiscal sustainability became less likely. This self-fulfilling prophecy was further aggravated by the feedback loop between sovereigns and the banking sector (de Haan et al., 2015). In this context, the Barroso Commission launched the European Semester – a more systematic, streamlined, and forceful policy coordination than its predecessors, integrating the SGP, the Broad

Economic Policy and Employment Guidelines, and (more implicitly) the Social OMC. The Semester represented a major step forward regarding the EU's capacity to shape national policy-making processes in 'core state powers' (Genschel and Jachtenfuchs, 2014), such as budgeting and welfare (Heins and de la Porte, 2015; Vesan et al., 2021).

Since its inception in 2011, the Semester has been subject to a series of changes regarding its procedures and actors involved. However, for most of the decade (2014–20), the Semester operated as follows. In October, the Commission's Annual Growth Survey (AGS) provides reform priorities and reform guidance for the coming year. As part of the 'autumn package', the Commission also issues an Alert Mechanism Report, designating Member States for In-Depth Reviews (IDR) of the Macro-Imbalances Procedure (MIP), and proposes recommendations for the euro area, as well as the Joint Employment Report. In February, after intensive dialogue with national governments and stakeholders, the Commission publishes Country Reports, laying out conclusions of the MIP IDRs, and identifying reform progress and key reform challenges in each Member State. Based on these assessments, the Commission proposes country-specific recommendations (CSRs) – except for Member States under financial assistance programmes – that are later endorsed by the European Council. In April, Member States submit their National Reform Programmes (NRPs) and fiscal stability or convergence programmes. In May, having assessed these programmes, the Commission proposes CSRs on a wide range of policy fields. After being reviewed and amended by committees of Member State officials preparing the work of the Council, CSRs are then endorsed by the European Council and adopted by the Council. Finally, it is up to Member States whether to implement the CSRs or not (Verdun and Zeitlin, 2018).

However, the Commission's assessments of Member States' socioeconomic outlook and reforms needed in the context of the Semester have varied over time, reflecting changing politics at the national and European level. Against the backdrop of the Greek crisis, the Barroso Commission saw the eurozone crisis through a 'fiscal lens', where economic imbalances were caused by a lack of discipline in public finances (Buti, 2020, 2021). While steering clear of bold integrationist moves that could be contested by powerful Member States, the Barroso Commission instead pursued strict adherence to budget discipline (Hodson, 2013; Warren et al., 2017). Within the Semester framework, Member States had to submit their budgetary plans to the Commission even before they were approved in national parliaments. In line with neoclassical economics, it was argued that public spending cuts – combined with increased labour market flexibility and reduction of social welfare costs – would result in economic growth (Alesina et al., 2020; Helgadóttir, 2016).

In parallel with the Semester procedures, a number of new governance frameworks were launched to enforce budgetary surveillance. Although these frameworks are legally independent from the Semester, in practice they complement the Semester processes. First, the 2011 Six-Pack consolidated the SGP provisions on medium-term objectives (MTOs) in budget consolidation. To detect and correct macroeconomic imbalances in the economy, it also included the Macroeconomic Imbalance Procedure, based on a scoreboard of indicators. Second, the 2013 Two-Pack provided another layer of fiscal surveillance to euro area countries by introducing a procedure for assessment of Member States' budgetary plans by the Commission, even before they are submitted to national parliaments (de la Porte and Heins, 2016). Third, the intergovernmental Treaty on Stability, Coordination and Governance of EMU (2012), the so-called Fiscal Compact, enshrined the 'balanced budget' rule, requiring that Member States' structural (cyclically adjusted) budget deficits converged toward 0.5 per cent of GDP (Member States with public debt below 60 per cent are allowed to have a structural deficit of 1 per cent of GDP) (Laffan and Schlosser, 2016; Schlosser, 2019).

However, the reinforced fiscal surveillance did little to calm down market sentiment before the ECB President Draghi's 2012 promise to 'do whatever it takes' to save the euro (Copelovitch et al., 2016). Besides the harsh conditionality of the financial assistance programmes, the Semester's focus on fiscal consolidation and structural reforms also significantly curtailed national capabilities to deal with economic and social challenges. Poverty, inequality, and unemployment, which were rising to record highs not only in Member States under Macroeconomic Adjustment Programmes (MAP) but also in those at risk of becoming subject to them (Cantillon and Vandenbroucke, 2014; Costamagna, 2018; Vesan et al., 2021). It was the combination of reinforced fiscal surveillance and its failure to deliver which, amidst increased politicization at the national level, led to a rise in socialization of EU economic governance around the mid-2010s. As will be demonstrated in Section 16.3, this socialization resulted not only in a higher proportion of social CSRs but also in more social involvement and monitoring.

16.3 THE SEMESTER'S RECEPTION AND EFFECTS

The EU's 'new economic governance' (NEG) post-Global Financial Crisis (GFC) has been widely criticized for subordinating 'softly' governed social objectives to 'harder' and more strictly enforced fiscal and macroeconomic policy targets (Crespy and Menz, 2015; Daly, 2012; Dawson, 2018; Schmidt, 2015). Some have even argued that the national space for social policy has been turned into a mere 'adjustment variable' in the pursuit of EMU-related objectives (Costamagna, 2018; Pochet and Degryse, 2013). National political parties increasingly blamed the EU for their socioeconomic (but also cultural) grievances, thus creating a politics trap (Hooghe and Marks, 2019; Hutter and Kriesi, 2019; Zeitlin et al., 2019). Criticisms of the NEG have been particularly pronounced in the parliamentary arena. It has been argued that the increasing 'executive dominance' of the Troika and the Council, particularly in negotiating EU financial assistance programmes (Bauer and Becker, 2014; Fabbrini and Puetter, 2016), has come at the cost of side-lining national parliaments and the European Parliament (Crum, 2013; Fasone, 2014; Rittberger, 2014). The increasingly powerful Commission and the Council have not been matched by appropriate increases in parliamentary control, creating an 'accountability gap' (Crum, 2018; Lord, 2017).

However, while these accounts rightly problematize the Commission's focus on fiscal consolidation and structural reforms, particularly in the initial Semester cycles, they tend to ignore gradual changes in the Semester's goals, procedures, and substance over time. A burgeoning literature suggests that over the last decade the Semester has become more socially oriented not only in policy substance, but also in the involvement of social actors and in surveillance capacity under the Juncker Commission (see later in this section). If the Semester's original sin was its orientation toward fiscal austerity and competitiveness, mounting evidence suggests a 'partial but progressive socialization' (Zeitlin and Vanhercke, 2018).

This socialization trend was rooted in changing national and EU politics, before materializing in EU programmatic documents and the Semester procedures. Against the backdrop of socioeconomic grievances in Europe's different peripheries, a salient EU-level political debate on the need for a social dimension emerged, initiated by the then President of the European Council Herman van Rompuy (Zeitlin and Vanhercke, 2018). At the Commission, the need for a market-correcting approach was first raised by László Andor, the Commissioner for Employment, Social Affairs and Inclusion under Barroso (Andor, 2013; Copeland and Daly, 2018). At the EU level, the emphasis on social affairs was further increased by the incoming

Juncker Commission as of late 2014. If Barroso went to great lengths to maintain the image of an 'apolitical' Commission, Juncker explicitly emphasized from the start that he was a 'political' leader who took EU citizens' social concerns seriously (Schmidt, 2019; Vesan and Pansardi, 2021). An increasing range of EU documents, initiatives, and policies subsequently aimed to tackle various social imbalances, even if these measures did not have immediate effects (Graziano and Hartlapp, 2019).

Between 2011 and 2016, the main focus in the Annual Growth Strategy (AGS), the primary agenda-setting document, shifted to 'upward convergence' and social investment (Crespy and Vanheuverzwijn, 2019; Zeitlin and Vanhercke, 2018). Over successive Semester cycles, CSRs increasingly emphasized employment and social issues, regarding health care, the fight against poverty, and social exclusion (Bekker, 2013; Bekker and Klosse, 2014). Using a coding scheme that classifies CSRs promoting 'social investment' vis-à-vis 'social retrenchment', Crespy and Vanheuverzwijn (2019) find that the share of the former increased from 50 to 64 per cent between 2011 and 2015. Using a coding scheme that further distinguishes between 'social retrenchment', 'social investment', and 'social protection' to analyse all CSRs between 2011 and 2019, Vesan et al. (2021) find a sharp reduction in social retrenchment prescriptions (from 48 to 4 per cent), a steady increase in social protection prescriptions (from 3 to 40 per cent), and relatively stable social investment prescriptions.

Another dimension of 'socialization' concerned the intensification of social monitoring, multilateral surveillance, and an enhanced role for social and employment policy actors. Between 2011 and 2014, the drafting process at the Commission increasingly relied on bottom-up input from country desk officers and involved a wider range of Directorates-General beyond Economic and Financial Affairs (ECFIN), particularly DG Employment, Social Affairs and Inclusion (EMPL). Council advisory committees of Member State officials, such as the Social Protection Committee (SPC) and Employment Committee (EMCO), have also played an enhanced role in monitoring, reviewing, and assessing national reforms (Zeitlin and Vanhercke, 2014).

To increase national 'ownership' of the CSRs, the Juncker Commission implemented a further series of major procedural changes: simplifying and streamlining the process by reducing the number and scope of the CSRs, leaving more room for Member States to determine implementation modalities, and intensifying exchanges with national actors through country missions and local European Semester Officers (Munta, 2020; Vanhercke et al., 2015; Zeitlin and Vanhercke, 2018). The 2017 European Pillar of Social Rights (EPSR), a flagship agenda-setting tool of the Juncker Commission, further consolidated the social dimension of EU economic governance and increased attention to social and employment issues. The Commission's newly launched Social Scoreboard made monitoring of social imbalances more structured, thus partially matching the MIP's focus on macroeconomic imbalances (Vesan et al., 2021).

How did the changing EU economic governance shape the opportunities of national parliaments? Apart from the states under EU financial assistance programmes which by design suspend the Semester's CSRs, 'executive dominance' has turned out to be more limited and less widespread than initially expected. On the one hand, the reinforced fiscal governance enabled the Commission to examine national budgetary plans and suggest recommendations, even before approvals of national parliaments. Another threat to parliamentary powers in budgeting and public debt stemmed from Reverse Qualified Majority Voting (RQMV) in the Economic and Financial Affairs Council (ECOFIN), even if the mechanism has never been used in practice (Schlosser, 2019).

On the other hand, the more structured processes of fiscal surveillance have also provided parliamentary actors with new opportunities, whose use largely depended on a number of factors, including parliamentary capacity, ownership, and the interests of the ruling parties (Kreilinger, 2018). In some cases, the Semester has allowed parliamentary parties to 'domesticate' European economic governance (Kröger and Bellamy, 2016). In other cases, parliaments have effectively contested EU economic governance, thus fulfilling their constitutive representative role (Jančić, 2016, 2017; Maatsch, 2017). Nevertheless, such dynamics have not necessarily led to increased parliamentary scrutiny and accountability (Borońska-Hryniewiecka, 2021; Skazlic, 2021), just as the intensification of contacts between the Commission and parliaments did not entail higher implementation of CSRs (Woźniakowski, 2021). If anything, this raises important questions regarding the extent to which national parliamentarians as broad popular representatives are able and/or willing to meaningfully engage in rather technical 'low salience' policy issues that are often raised by the CSRs.

However, in practice, the changing policy goals of the Semester matter only as far as the CSRs can actually shape national policies, which remain at the discretion of Member States. Paradoxically, amidst intense debates between those who think that the CSRs intervene too assertively in national social policy and those who think that they are not assertive enough, effects of the Semester have been subject to surprisingly little empirical research. Standard accounts of the Semester's effects are based on the Commission's self-assessments of CSRs' compliance. Each year, the Commission assesses to what extent its recommendations have been addressed and gives an implementation score (i.e. full implementation or substantial progress, some progress, limited progress, or no progress). Quantitatively oriented researchers using these scores agree that compliance of the CSRs is on average low (Darvas and Leandro, 2015) and has been declining over time (Efstathiou and Wolff, 2018). The Commission itself has concluded that implementation of the CSRs across Member States has been 'uneven' and 'limited' (European Commission, 2015, p. 3).

Yet such quantitative accounts are based on an overly narrow conceptualization of 'effectiveness'. In practice, European influence on national policy can be substantial, even if indirect and slow. Because reform progress is *cumulative* over numerous years, 'some progress' in a particular year can mark a breakthrough in the longer term (Bokhorst, 2019; van der Veer and Haverland, 2018). Second, as demonstrated by the literature on OMC, EU economic governance processes can not only *directly* result in implementation of the Commission's recommendations, but significantly shape the policy process itself (Barcevicius et al., 2014; Heidenreich and Zeitlin, 2009). Such *indirect* effects may concern substantive changes in national policy ideas, agendas, programmes, procedural changes in national steering capacities, coordination, and involvement of actors (Bokhorst, 2022).

Recent empirical research confirms that in several countries the Semester has significantly shaped national policy process even in sensitive areas such as budgeting, taxation, and welfare. For instance, Bokhorst (2022) finds that the Semester had significant 'issue salience' and 'agenda-setting' effects in the liberalization of professions in Italy and wage indexation in Belgium. Similarly, Munta (2021) has established the effect of 'creative appropriation', as national governments strategically use EU stimuli which fit their domestic agenda. Eihmanis (2018, 2020) demonstrates that the Semester has played a major role in shaping anti-poverty policy debate in Latvia. This not only changed public discourse on inequality and poverty but also resulted in increased social benefits and progressive tax credits. Furthermore, recent literature suggests that the NEG not only centralized national budgetary processes but also improved access to national budgetary decision-making and enhanced executive monitoring capacities (Csehi and Schulz, 2022; Fasone, 2021; Raudla et al., 2020).

16.4 REFORMING THE SEMESTER AFTER THE COVID-19 CRISIS

The COVID-19 crisis marked a rapid turn in EU economic governance, with large implications to the functioning of the European Semester. In the favourable political context of a newly elected European Parliament and a new Commission, various EU actors demonstrated significant learning from the lessons of the previous financial crisis and took bold policy measures to avoid, in Mario Draghi's (2020) words: 'a human tragedy of potentially biblical proportions' (D'Erman and Verdun, 2022; Tesche, 2022; Wolff and Ladi, 2020). The Commission's bold responses to crises were subsequently able to overcome the differences between the south and north of the EU. To enable fiscal responses at the national level, the Commission, among other things, lifted state aid rules to support the economy and businesses and put on hold EU fiscal rules, thus temporarily suspending EU restrictions on national spending and borrowing (Fabbrini, 2022; Ladi and Tsarouhas, 2020). In addition, building on the Franco-German compromise regarding an EU recovery fund, the Commission proposed a series of new spending initiatives, under the umbrella of Next Generation EU (NGEU). Unprecedentedly in the history of European integration, this very generous package has been financed by commonly issued debt (de la Porte and Jensen, 2021; Schelkle, 2021). Setting a historical precedent of joint borrowing which allows the Commission to raise its 'own resources', the NGEU constitutes a 'paradigm change' in the NEG and EU integration (Fabbrini, 2022; Jones, 2021).

Ambitiously, the RRF aimed to facilitate the green and digital transitions, while also tackling long-standing economic, political, and social divides (Jones, 2021; Pisani-Ferry, 2020b; von der Leyen, 2021). Effectively, the COVID-19 crisis served as a window of opportunity to accelerate the industrial shifts that the Commission had envisaged before the pandemic. Incoming Commissioner von der Leyen launched the European Green Deal (EGD) as 'Europe's man on the moon moment' less than two weeks after taking the helm of the Commission in late 2019 (Mazzucato, 2018; von der Leyen, 2019). To achieve net zero emissions of greenhouse gases in the EU by 2050, the EGD planned a broad roadmap of cutting emissions, investing in green technologies, and protecting the natural environment (Bongardt and Torres, 2022). In early 2020, the Commission's 'New Industrial Strategy for Europe' provided for 'twin' green and digital transitions, which would go hand-in-hand with high social and living standards in line with the EPSR (European Commission, 2020; Renda, 2021). These policy goals then directly informed the content of the RRF/RRPs.

The renewed emphasis on economic and social upgrading ensued major institutional changes in the Semester. Regarding the subject of this chapter, the key development was that the governance of the RRF was integrated into the institutional infrastructure of the Semester (Vanhercke and Verdun, 2022). Building on the established policy coordination cycle of the Semester, Member States could qualify for the RRF support by submitting RRPs which set reform and investment agendas. The RRPs had to be in line with the Commission's objectives for 'green' and 'digital' investment (of 37 and 20 per cent, respectively), on the one hand, and a 'significant subset' of the CSRs, on the other (European Commission, 2021; Pisani-Ferry, 2020a). Another key criterion, inserted by the EP, was that the RRPs must show how they address the principles of the European Pillar of Social Rights (Closa Montero et al., 2021; Vesan et al., 2021). Some scholars have argued that the Commission used the institutional setting of the Semester to administer the RRF, because of the Semester's unique 'Goldilocks' combination of structural rigour and flexibility (Vanhercke and Verdun, 2022). Complementarily, the new arrangement allowed the Commission to increase compliance with CSRs and counter the impression of a top-down approach (Bekker, 2021; Tesche, 2022). However, by and large, the integration of the RRF within the Semester significantly changes not only the Semester's process but also its policy goals.

To cater to the needs of the RRF, important functions of the Semester's procedures have been overhauled, while others have been eliminated altogether. First, as of 2021 the Commission issues no new CSRs, except for fiscal policy in the light of the SGP. Instead, Member States are supposed to follow earlier CSRs, particularly – but not limited to – those issued in the 2019 and 2020 cycles. Second, there is a significant change regarding the Semester's documents. National Reform Programmes – previously, Member States' reporting obligation within the annual Semester cycle – have been integrated with National Recovery and Resilience Plans (NRRPs), whose significance and role has notably increased. In addition, Country Reports – central analytical documents that indicate how the Commission assessed national reform progress – have been replaced by the Commission's assessment of the NRRPs. Meanwhile, the role of multilateral surveillance, a central feature of the Semester, has been significantly narrowed, to give more space for bilateral discussions between the Commission and individual Member States.

As a result of these post-pandemic changes, the power of the Commission vis-à-vis Member States has significantly increased. For most of the first decade of the Semester's operation, the Commission issued country-specific recommendations for reforms, while leaving implementation at the discretion of the individual countries (Haas et al., 2020). However, as the Commission has become the chief administrator of RRF funds, its potential ability to shape national reforms has significantly increased, even beyond the fiscal realm (Bekker, 2021; Moschella, 2020). The most politically salient example of this is the rule of law and judicial independence in Hungary and Poland (Baraggia and Bonelli, 2021; Nguyen, 2021; de la Porte and Jensen, 2021), as illustrated by the delayed approval of their RRPs (at the time of writing, only the Polish RRP has been endorsed by the Commission). An important role will be played by the Commission's Recovery and Resilience Task Force (RECOVER), a newly established unit within the DG Secretariat-General responsible for steering the implementation of the RRF and coordinating the Semester. Disbursement of the RRF funds every six months until 2026 is conditioned on the achievement of the intermediate milestones set. In principle, the Commission can withhold funding whenever it thinks a pre-agreed milestone is missed (Corti and Ferrer, 2021).

The power asymmetry between the Commission and Member States will be complicated by the large variation in relative significance of RRPs to national economies, which varies from more than 10 per cent of 2020 GDP in Croatia, Bulgaria, and Greece, to less than 1 per cent in Austria, Finland, Germany, the Netherlands, Denmark, and Ireland (Nguyen and Redeker, 2022). As noted by Nguyen and Redeker (2022), there is a risk that the Commission uses this leverage to scrutinize the less advanced Member States with relatively larger RRPs (in both absolute and relative terms). Since these less developed peripheral countries also tend to suffer from low state capacity and governance problems, the process could echo the centre–periphery dynamics of the post-GFC era.

Relatedly, the increasing importance of bilateral negotiations between the Commission and national governments has come at the cost of reduced representation of various social interests, including parliaments. As a co-legislator of the RRF regulation, the EP's role was mixed. While continuing in its usual progressive role and adding 'social cohesion' and 'institutional resilience' to the RRF policy goals, the EP obtained only limited gains in terms of RRF accountability and scrutiny capacities, notably regarding the rule of law (Closa Montero et al., 2021). Moreover, in the post-pandemic context of executive dominance, the role of national parliaments in negotiating the RRPs seems to be marginal, though more research is needed to confirm this (Bekker, 2021).

A similarly mixed picture regards various kinds of social actors. Although the RRF regulation by the EP and the Council of the EU requires Member States to report not only on the social consultation process but also how the stakeholders' input is reflected in RRPs, most social actors have been side-lined during the initial phase of the crisis. Positively, European institutional actors, such as the Employment Committee (EMCO), Employment, Social Policy, Health and Consumer Affairs (EPSCO) Council and Social Protection Committee (SPC), have successfully pushed back and regained much of their former role in the European Semester (Vanhercke and Verdun, 2022). However, the jury is still out as to what extent national social actors have been involved in drafting and implementation of the RRPs. Initial survey evidence suggests that involvement of national social actors in formulating RRPs has been mixed across MS (EESC, 2021; ICNL, 2021).

16.5 CONCLUSIONS

The chapter has traced how the Semester's policy goals, institutions, and processes have changed over the last decade, depending on changing national and supranational politics. If during the initial years the Semester prioritized macroeconomic and fiscal over social goals, the increased politicization of the NEG as of 2013–14 has led to a relative socialization not only of the ideological content of the CSRs, but also regarding increased involvement of various social actors and social surveillance. More recently, the COVID-19 crisis has disrupted involvement of national social actors in the NEG, albeit to a different extent across the EU. Relatedly, the chapter has reviewed the available evidence showing that the Semester can significantly shape national debates and at times national policy outcomes. Finally, it has argued that during the 'socialization' phase before the pandemic, the Semester has not only constrained policy space, but also provided parliaments and social actors with new opportunities and increased their capacities. However, further research needs to be done on social actor involvement in the formulation and implementation of the RRPs from 2020 to 2026.

Considering the rapid evolution of its goals, institutions, and processes over the last ten years, the Semester is very likely to change in the future. Although it is impossible to predict the future directions of development, they will clearly be shaped by the institutional precedents set by the GFC and the COVID-19 crisis. Below we identify a couple of junctures where future developments will have important implications for the Semester over the coming years. First, the post-pandemic precedent of joint EU debt might be extended to tackle the ongoing challenges, including those related to climate change, the energy crisis, and Russia's invasion of Ukraine (Fabbrini, 2022; Jones, 2021). Besides the broader implications for the integration of the EU, it would have direct implications for the Semester as the institutional framework in which such extraordinary spending and lending is currently administered on the part of the EU. For this reason, it is likely that the Semester will not return to its pre-pandemic operations once the RRF is finished in 2026.

Second, the ongoing uncertainty regarding the EU's fiscal rules carries massive implications for the Semester's fiscal surveillance function as established post-2011. To allow Member States to support their economies, the Commission has suspended not only the state-aid restrictions, but the entire architecture of EU fiscal surveillance as enforced since the SDC. However, in the light of the slow recovery from the SDC and the lessons of the pandemic, there is increasing consensus that the EU fiscal rules as consolidated since the financial crisis must be reformed to deliver reasonable outcomes across the full range of countries and circumstances. Possible reform options range from revised debt and spending rules to continuing the existing focus on the structural budget balance (Barnes and Oliinyk, 2021; ESM, 2021; EUIFI, 2021). They will likely lead to exacerbated political clashes between EU's northern creditor and southern debtor Member States. A need for fiscal flexibility and space at the European level will only increase, considering Europe's mounting security, energy, and migration challenges.

The RRF has massively transformed the Semester's goals and processes, and for a foreseeable future has become an integral part of EU socioeconomic governance. Until 2026, the RRF/Semester nexus will be the main framework for policy coordination between the Commission and Member States, though it is not entirely clear how national and EU actors will operate within this framework. For the RRF to be a success, it must satisfy a number of conditions – tackle key socioeconomic vulnerabilities of the Member States, enhance green and digital transformations in line with the Commission's long-term vision, and, not least, provide democratic legitimacy through involvement of diverse social actors. Achieving these conditions will require a significant effort from all parties involved. If the recent history of the Semester teaches us anything, it is that it is rarely possible to get things right from the start, but it is the flexibility to change approach when facing challenges that matters in the longer term.

REFERENCES

Alesina, A., Favero, C., and Giavazzi, F. (2020). *Austerity: When It Works and When It Doesn't*. Princeton, NJ: Princeton University Press.

Andor, L. (2013). *Developing the Social Dimension of a Deep and Genuine Economic and Monetary Union*. Brussels: European Policy Centre.

Baraggia, A., and Bonelli, M. (2021). Linking money to values: The new rule of law conditionality regulation and its constitutional challenges. *German Law Journal* 23(2), 131–156.

Barcevicius, E., Weishaupt, T., and Zeitlin, J. (eds.) (2014). *Assessing the Open Method of Coordination: Institutional Design and National Influence of EU Social Policy Coordination*. New York: Palgrave Macmillan.

Barnes, S., and Oliinyk, I. (2021). *Policy Insight | The EU's economic governance review. Road-testing alternative fiscal rules? | CEPS | PubAffairs Bruxelles*. www.pubaffairsbruxelles.eu/policy-insight-the-eus-economic-governance-review-road-testing-alternative-fiscal-rules-ceps/

Bauer, M. W., and Becker, S. (2014). The unexpected winner of the crisis: The European Commission's strengthened role in economic governance. *Journal of European Integration* 36(3), 213–229.

Bekker, S. (2013). The EU's stricter economic governance: A step towards more binding coordination of social policies. WZB Discussion Paper SP IV 2013–501. Berlin: Social Science Research Center.

Bekker, S. (2021). The EU's recovery and resilience facility: A next phase in EU socioeconomic governance? *Politics and Governance* 9(3), 175–185.

Bekker, S. and Klosse, S. (2014). The changing legal context of employment policy coordination: How do social policy issues fare after the crisis? *European Labour Law Journal* 5(1), 6–17.

Bokhorst, D. (2019). Governing imbalances in the economic and monetary union: A political economy analysis of the macroeconomic imbalance procedure. PhD diss., University of Amsterdam. https://dare.uva.nl/search?identifier=85d7b956-00d5-47ac-95d2-284115ca9bbf

Bokhorst, D. (2022). The influence of the European Semester: Case study analysis and lessons for its post-pandemic transformation. *Journal of Common Market Studies* 60(1), 101–117.

Bongardt, A., and Torres, F. (2022). The European Green Deal: More than an exit strategy to the pandemic crisis, a building block of a sustainable European economic model. *Journal of Common Market Studies* 60(1), 170–185.

Borońska-Hryniewiecka, K. (2021). Accountability revisited: Parliamentary perspectives on the Inter-Parliamentary Conference on Stability, Economic Coordination, and Governance. *Politics and Governance* 9(3), 145–154.

Buti, M. (2020). Economic policy in the rough: A European journey. Centre for Economic Policy Research. https://cepr.org/events

Buti, M. (2021). *The Man Inside: A European Journey through Two Crises*. Milan: EGEA Spa – Bocconi University Press.

Cantillon, B., and Vandenbroucke, F. (2014) *Reconciling Work and Poverty Reduction: How Successful Are European Welfare States?* Oxford: Oxford University Press.

Closa Montero, C., de León, F. G., and González, G. H. (2021). Pragmatism and the limits to the European Parliament's strategies for self-empowerment. *Politics and Governance* 9(3), 163–174.

Copeland, P., and Daly, M. (2018). The European Semester and EU social policy. *Journal of Common Market Studies* 56(5), 1001–1018.

Copelovitch, M., Frieden, J., and Walter, S. (2016). The political economy of the euro crisis. *Comparative Political Studies* 49(7), 811–840.

Corti, F. (2022). *The Politicisation of Social Europe: Conflict Dynamics and Welfare Integration*. Cheltenham: Edward Elgar.

Corti, F., and Ferrer, J. N. (2021). *Steering and Monitoring the Recovery and Resilience Plans: Reading between the Lines*. Brussels: CEPS.

Costamagna, F. (2018). National social spaces as adjustment variables in the EMU: A critical legal appraisal. *European Law Journal* 24(2–3), 163–190.

Crespy, A., and Menz, G. (2015). Commission entrepreneurship and the debasing of social Europe before and after the eurocrisis. *Journal of Common Market Studies* 53(4), 753–768.

Crespy, A., and Vanheuverzwijn, P. (2019). What 'Brussels' means by structural reforms: Empty signifier or constructive ambiguity? *Comparative European Politics* 17(1), 92–111.

Crum, B. (2013). Saving the euro at the cost of democracy? *Journal of Common Market Studies* 51(4), 614–630.

Crum, B. (2018). Parliamentary accountability in multilevel governance: What role for parliaments in post-crisis EU economic governance? *Journal of European Public Policy* 25(2), 268–286.

Csehi, R., and Schulz, D. F. (2022). The EU's New Economic Governance Framework and budgetary decision-making in the Member States: Boon or bane for throughput legitimacy? *Journal of Common Market Studies* 60(1), 118–135.

Daly, M. (2012). Paradigms in EU social policy: A critical account of Europe 2020. *Transfer: European Review of Labour and Research* 18(3), 273–284.

Darvas, Z., and Leandro, Á. (2015). The limitations of policy coordination in the euro area under the European Semester. Bruegel Policy Contribution. www.econstor.eu/handle/10419/126693

Dawson, M. (2018). New governance and the displacement of social Europe: The case of the European Semester. *European Constitutional Law Review* 14(1), 191–209.

De Haan, J., Hessel, J., and Gilbert, N. (2015). Reforming the architecture of EMU: Ensuring stability in Europe. In H. Badinger and V. Nitsch (eds.), *Handbook of the Economics of European Integration*. New York: Routledge.

De la Porte, C., and Heins, E. (2016). A new era of European integration? Governance of labour market and social policy since the sovereign debt crisi. In C. De La Porte and E. Heins (eds.), *The Sovereign Debt Crisis, the EU and Welfare State Reform*. London: Palgrave Macmillan UK, pp. 15–41.

De la Porte, C., and Jensen, M. D. (2021). The Next Generation EU: An analysis of the dimensions of conflict behind the deal. *Social Policy & Administration* 55(2), 388–402.

D'Erman, V., and Verdun, A. (2022) An introduction: Macroeconomic policy coordination and domestic politics: Policy coordination in the EU from the European Semester to the Covid-19 crisis. *Journal of Common Market Studies* 60(1), 3–20.

Draghi, M. (2020) Draghi: We face a war against coronavirus and must mobilise accordingly. *Financial Times*, 25 March. www.ft.com/content/c6d2de3a-6ec5-11ea-89df-41bea055720b

EESC (2021) *Involvement of Organised Civil Society in the National Recovery and Resilience Plans – What Works and What Does Not?* Brussels: European Economic and Social Committee.

Efstathiou, K., and Wolff, G. B. (2018) Is the European Semester effective and useful? Bruegel Policy Contribution. www.econstor.eu/handle/10419/208014

Eihmanis, E. (2018). Cherry-picking external constraints: Latvia and EU economic governance, 2008–2014. *Journal of European Public Policy* 25(2), 231–249.

Eihmanis, E. (2020). *Between Democracy, Business Power and International Organisations: Explaining Redistributive Tax Reforms in Central and Eastern Europe.* Florence: European University Institute.

ESM (2021). EU fiscal rules: Reform considerations. European Stability Mechanism.

EUIFI (2021). EU fiscal and economic governance review: A contribution from the Network of Independent EU Fiscal Institutions. EU Independent Fiscal Institutions.

European Commission (2015). Communication from the Commission to the European Parliament, the Council and the European Central Bank: On steps towards completing Economic and Monetary Union. Brussels. https://ec.europa.eu/transparency/regdoc/rep/1/2015/EN/1-2015-600-EN-F1-1.PDF

European Commission (2020). A new industrial strategy for Europe. https://eur-lex.europa.eu/legal-content/EN/TXT/PDF/?uri=CELEX:52020DC0102&from=EN

European Commission (2021). Questions and answers: The Recovery and Resilience Facility, 2021. European Commission. https://ec.europa.eu/commission/presscorner/detail/en/qanda_21_1870

Fabbrini, F. (2022). The legal architecture of the economic responses to COVID-19: EMU beyond the pandemic. *Journal of Common Market Studies* 60(1), 186–203.

Fabbrini, S., and Puetter, U. (2016). Integration without supranationalisation: Studying the lead roles of the European Council and the Council in post-Lisbon EU politics. *Journal of European Integration* 38(5), 481–495.

Fasone, C. (2014). European economic governance and parliamentary representation: What place for the European Parliament? *European Law Journal* 20(2), 164–185.

Fasone, C. (2021). Do independent fiscal institutions enhance parliamentary accountability in the eurozone? *Politics and Governance* 9(3), 135–144.

Ferrera, M. (2017). The Stein Rokkan Lecture 2016: Mission impossible? Reconciling economic and social Europe after the euro crisis and Brexit. *European Journal of Political Research* 56(1), 3–22.

Genschel, P., and Jachtenfuchs, M. (2014). *Beyond the Regulatory Polity? The European Integration of Core State Powers.* Oxford: Oxford University Press.

Graziano, P., and Hartlapp, M. (2019). The end of social Europe? Understanding EU social policy change. *Journal of European Public Policy* 26(10), 1484–1501.

Haas, J. S., D'Erman, V. J., Schulz, D. F., and Verdun, A. (2020). Economic and fiscal policy coordination after the crisis: Is the European Semester promoting more or less state intervention? *Journal of European Integration* 42(3), 327–344.

Heidenreich, M., and Zeitlin, J. (eds.) (2009). *Changing European Employment and Welfare Regimes: The Influence of the Open Method of Coordination on National Reforms*, 1st ed. London: Routledge.

Heins, E., and de la Porte, C. (2015). The sovereign debt crisis, the EU and welfare state reform. *Comparative European Politics* 13(1), 1–7.

Helgadóttir, O. (2016). The Bocconi boys go to Brussels: Italian economic ideas, professional networks and European austerity. *Journal of European Public Policy* 23(3), 392–409.

Hodson, D. (2013). The little engine that wouldn't: Supranational entrepreneurship and the Barroso Commission. *Journal of European Integration* 35(3), 301–314.

Hooghe, L., and Marks, G. (2019). Grand theories of European integration in the twenty-first century. *Journal of European Public Policy* 26(8), 1113–1133.

Howarth, D., and Verdun, A. (2020). Economic and Monetary Union at twenty: A stocktaking of a tumultuous second decade: Introduction. *Journal of European Integration* 42(3), 287–293.

Hutter, S., and Kriesi, H. (2019). Politicizing Europe in times of crisis. *Journal of European Public Policy* 26(7), 996–1017.

ICNL (2021). Participation of civil society organisations in the preparation of the EU National Recovery and Resilience Plans. https://civilsocietyeurope.eu/wp-content/uploads/2021/01/CSE-ECNL-Participation-of-CSOs-in-the-preparation-of-the-EU-NRRPs_spread.pdf

Jančić, D. (2016). National parliaments and EU fiscal integration. *European Law Journal* 22(2), 225–249.

Jančič, D. (2017). *National Parliaments after the Lisbon Treaty and the Euro Crisis: Resilience or Resignation?* Oxford: Oxford University Press.

Jones, E. (2021). Did the EU's crisis response meet the moment? *Current History* 120(824), 93–99.

Kreilinger, V. (2018). Scrutinising the European Semester in national parliaments: What are the drivers of parliamentary involvement? *Journal of European Integration* 40(3), 325–340.

Kröger, S., and Bellamy, R. (2016). Beyond a constraining dissensus: The role of national parliaments in domesticating and normalising the politicization of European integration. *Comparative European Politics* 14(2), 131–153.

Ladi, S., and Tsarouhas, D. D. (2020). EU economic governance and Covid-19: Policy learning and windows of opportunity. *Journal of European Integration* 42(8), 1041–1056.

Laffan, B., and Schlosser, P. (2016). Public finances in Europe: Fortifying EU economic governance in the shadow of the crisis. *Journal of European Integration* 38(3), 237–249.

Lord, C. (2017). How can parliaments contribute to the legitimacy of the European Semester? *Parliamentary Affairs* 70(4), 673–690.

Maatsch, A. (2016). *Parliaments and the Economic Governance of the European Union: Talking Shops or Deliberative Bodies?* London: Taylor & Francis.

Maatsch, A. (2017). Effectiveness of the European Semester: Explaining domestic consent and contestation. *Parliamentary Affairs* 70(4), 691–709.

Maatsch, A., and Cooper, I. (2017). Governance without democracy? Analysing the role of parliaments in European economic governance after the crisis: Introduction to the special issue. *Parliamentary Affairs* 70(4), 645–654.

Mazzucato, M. (2018). *Mission-Oriented Research & Innovation in the European Union: A Problemsolving Approach to Fuel Innovation Led Growth.* Leuven: Directorate-General for Research and Innovation, European Commission. https://data.europa.eu/doi/10.2777/360325

Moschella, M. (2020). What role for the European Semester in the recovery plan? European Parliament. www.europarl.europa.eu/RegData/etudes/IDAN/2020/651377/IPOL_IDA(2020)651377_EN.pdf

Munta, M. (2020). Building national ownership of the European Semester: The role of European Semester officers. *European Politics and Society* 21(1), 36–52.

Munta, M. (2021). *EU Socio-Economic Governance in Central and Eastern Europe: The European Semester and National Employment Policies*, London: Routledge.

Nguyen, T. (2021). How much money is a lot of money? Verfassungsblog. https://verfassungsblog.de/how-much-money-is-a-lot-of-money/

Nguyen, T., and Redeker, N. (2022). How to make the marriage work: Wedding the Recovery and Resilience Facility and European Semester, 2022. Hertie School. www.delorscentre.eu/en/publications/detail/publication/how-to-make-the-marriage-work

Pisani-Ferry, J. (2020a). European Union recovery funds: strings attached, but not tied up in knots. Bruegel Policy Contribution. www.bruegel.org/2020/10/european-union-recovery-funds-strings-attached-but-not-tied-up-in-knots/

Pisani-Ferry, J. (2020b). Europe's recovery gamble | Bruegel. www.bruegel.org/2020/09/europes-recovery-gamble/

Pochet, P., and Degryse, C. (2013). Monetary union and the stakes for democracy and social policy. *Transfer: European Review of Labour and Research* 19(1), 103–116.

Raudla, R., Bur, S., and Keel, K. (2020). The effects of crises and European fiscal governance reforms on the budgetary processes of Member States. *Journal of Common Market Studies* 58(3), 740–756.

Renda, A. (2021). The EU industrial strategy: Towards a post-growth agenda? *Intereconomics* 56(3), 133–138.

Rittberger, B. (2014). Integration without representation? The European Parliament and the reform of economic governance in the EU. *Journal of Common Market Studies* 52(6), 1174–1183.

Schelkle, W. (2021). Fiscal integration in an experimental union: How path-breaking was the EU's response to the COVID-19 pandemic? *Journal of Common Market Studies* 59(S1), 44–55.

Schlosser, P. (2019). *Europe's New Fiscal Union*. Cham: Palgrave Macmillan.

Schmidt, V. (2015). Changing the policies, politics, and processes of the Eurozone in crisis: Will this time be different? In D. Natali and B. Vanhercke (eds.), *Social Policy in the European Union: State of Play 2015*. Brussels: European Trade Union Institute, European Social Observatory, pp. 33–64.

Schmidt, V. A. (2019). Politicization in the EU: Between national politics and EU political dynamics. *Journal of European Public Policy* 26(7), 1018–1036.

Schmidt, V. A. (2020). *Europe's Crisis of Legitimacy: Governing by Rules and Ruling by Numbers in the Eurozone*. Oxford: Oxford University Press.

Skazlic, I. (2021). Routine or rare activity? A quantitative assessment of parliamentary scrutiny in the European Semester. *Politics and Governance* 9(3), 112–123.

Tesche, T. (2022). Pandemic politics: The European Union in times of the coronavirus emergency. *Journal of Common Market Studies* 60(2), 480–496.

Trubek, D., and Trubek, L. (2005). Hard and soft law in the construction of social Europe: The role of the Open Method of Co-ordination. *European Law Journal* 11(3), 343–364.

Van der Veer, R., and Haverland, M. (2018). Bread and butter or bread and circuses? *European Union Politics*, 19(3), 524–545.

Vanhercke, B., and Verdun, A. (2022). The European Semester as Goldilocks: Macroeconomic policy coordination and the Recovery and Resilience Facility. *Journal of Common Market Studies* 60(1), 204–223.

Vanhercke, B., Zeitlin, J., and Zwinkels, A. (2015). Further socializing the European Semester. www.accesseurope.org/research/publications/5-policy-report/15-further-socializing-the-european-semester

Verdun, A. (1996). An 'asymmetrical' economic and monetary union in the EU: Perceptions of monetary authorities and social partners. *Journal of European Integration* 20(1), 59–81.

Verdun, A., and Zeitlin, J. (2018). Introduction: the European Semester as a new architecture of EU socioeconomic governance in theory and practice. *Journal of European Public Policy* 25(2), 137–148.

Vesan, P., and Pansardi, P. (2021). Speaking social Europe: A paradigmatic shift in the European Commission Presidents' social policy discourse? *Journal of European Social Policy* 31(4), 365–379.

Vesan, P., Corti, F., and Sabato, S. (2021). The European Commission's entrepreneurship and the social dimension of the European Semester: From the European Pillar of Social Rights to the Covid-19 pandemic. *Comparative European Politics* 19(3), 277–295.

Von der Leyen, U. (2019). President von der Leyen on the European Green Deal. https://ec.europa.eu/commission/presscorner/detail/en/speech_19_6749

Von der Leyen, U. (2021). Speech by President von der Leyen at the European Parliament Plenary on the European Parliament's scrutiny on the ongoing assessment by the Commission and the Council of the national recovery and resilience plans. European Commission, Brussels. https://ec.europa.eu/commission/presscorner/detail/en/speech_21_2887

Warren, T., Holden, P., and Howell, K. E. (2017). The European Commission and fiscal governance reform: A strategic actor? *West European Politics* 40(6), 1310–1330.

Wolff, S., and Ladi, S. (2020). European Union responses to the Covid-19 pandemic: Adaptability in times of permanent emergency. *Journal of European Integration* 42(8), 1025–1040.

Woźniakowski, T. P. (2021). Accountability in EU economic governance: European commissioners in Polish parliament. *Politics and Governance* 9(3), 155–162.

Zeitlin, J. (2009). The Open Method of Coordination and reform of national social and employment policies: Influences, mechanisms, effects. In M. Heidenreich and J. Zeitlin (eds.), *Changing European Employment and Welfare Regimes: The Influence of the Open Method of Coordination on National Reforms*. London: Routledge, pp. 214–245.

Zeitlin, J., and Vanhercke, B. (2014). *Socializing the European Semester? Economic Governance and Social Policy Coordination in Europe 2020*. Stockholm: Swedish Institute for European Policy Studies.

Zeitlin, J., and Vanhercke, B. (2018). Socializing the European Semester: EU social and economic policy co-ordination in crisis and beyond. *Journal of European Public Policy* 25(2), 149–174.

Zeitlin, J., Nicoli, F., and Laffan, B. (2019). Introduction: The European Union beyond the polycrisis? Integration and politicization in an age of shifting cleavages. *Journal of European Public Policy* 26(7), 963–976.

Zeitlin, J., Pochet, P., and Magnusson, L. (eds.) (2005). *The Open Method of Co-ordination in Action: The European Employment and Social Inclusion Strategies*. Bern: Peter Lang.

17

The EU Fiscal Rules

Principle, Policy, and Reform Prospects

Menelaos Markakis

17.1 INTRODUCTION

The Economic and Monetary Union (EMU) and the euro have been the battleground of varying (economic) ideas (see generally Brunnermeier et al., 2016). Unsurprisingly, the future direction of EMU has equally been the subject of heated debate (Craig and Markakis, 2020). Among those features pertaining to its future evolution, this chapter focuses on one particular aspect of the EMU, namely the reform of the EU fiscal rules. In doing so, it complements the other chapters in this volume. The key objective is to shed light on the legal mechanics of reforming the EU framework for fiscal coordination and surveillance.

There is a growing consensus that the EU's fiscal and economic governance framework, notably the fiscal rules, should be reformed. This is due to a variety of reasons, either pertaining to the past performance of the framework or to the ever-changing macroeconomic environment. Moreover, one should not lose sight of the fresh challenges brought about by the COVID-19 pandemic. 'Furthermore, it should be considered to what extent the framework can support economic, environmental and social policy needs related to the transition towards a climate-neutral, resource efficient and digital European economy, complementing the key role of the regulatory environment and structural reforms' (European Commission, 2020, p. 17). According to many commentators, a rare window of opportunity for reform seems to be open (see e.g. Dermine, 2022a). However, the direction of travel is still unclear. There has been a large number of reform proposals, working papers, roadmaps, and blueprints from the EU institutions and bodies, national governments, international institutions, academics, think tanks, and so on. Notwithstanding the various points of convergence among these proposals, which undoubtedly do exist, there is still significant disagreement among commentators and, perhaps most crucially, among the Member States. The economic sensibility and political feasibility of any proposed reforms are key factors in this debate. And so should be their legal feasibility, which is the principal focus of this chapter.

The chapter is structured as follows. The discussion begins with an overview of the existing EU framework for fiscal and economic governance, its economic rationale, and the reforms adopted in response to the eurozone crisis. This is followed by analysis of the preventive and

The author is the recipient of the EUR Fellowship at Erasmus University Rotterdam. He is grateful to Dariusz Adamski, Fabian Amtenbrink, Roel Beetsma, Francesco Costamagna, Paul Dermine, Diane Fromage, Jakob de Haan, René Repasi, as well as the participants of the authors' workshop and the ICON panel held on 15 December 2021 and 5 July 2022, respectively, for their valuable feedback. The usual disclaimer applies. The manuscript was completed on 22 August 2022.

corrective arms of the Stability and Growth Pact, on which this contribution principally focuses. We then turn to consider the criticism to which the existing EU framework for fiscal and economic surveillance has been subjected, as well as the Commission's economic governance review. The focus then shifts to the various proposals on the future evolution of the EU's fiscal and economic governance framework. More specifically, the chapter looks at the European Fiscal Board proposals, the proposal by the European Stability Mechanism, as well as other proposals by national governments, academics, think tanks, and policymakers where appropriate. It should be stressed from the outset that the focus in this chapter is on the EU's fiscal rules (and their interaction with other aspects of the economic governance framework), and that aspects pertaining to increased risk sharing, common borrowing, and the size and use of the EU budget are beyond the scope of this contribution (on which, see however Amtenbrink and Markakis, in press, with further references; and the contributions by Beetsma and Kopits, Chapter 21 and Wasserfallen, Chapter 19 in this volume). The penultimate section provides a legal assessment of the proposed reforms, thereby setting out what would be required, from a legal perspective, in order to amend, replace, or repeal the various aspects of the EU framework for fiscal coordination and surveillance that are relevant for the purposes of our discussion. The final section concludes by driving the point home that the (potential) reform of the EU fiscal rules is but a key piece of the broader puzzle of EMU reform. We should be mindful of what can (or cannot) be achieved by fiscal rules and hence not neglect other aspects of EMU reform.

17.2 AN OVERVIEW OF THE EXISTING EU FRAMEWORK FOR FISCAL AND ECONOMIC GOVERNANCE AND THE REFORMS ADOPTED IN RESPONSE TO THE EUROZONE CRISIS

Given the original architecture of EMU, national fiscal policies were meant to be 'the predominant macroeconomic stabilisation instrument' (European Stability Mechanism, 2021, p. 5). It is explained by economists that, 'With the exchange rate and monetary policy no longer being handled domestically, a low labour mobility and strong price and wage rigidities, national fiscal policy is indeed bound to take centre stage when it comes to buffer[ing] shocks in monetary union' (Thirion, 2017, p. 4). Fiscal rules are needed in the EMU in order to 'prevent negative spillovers, inflation risks stemming from diverging fiscal positions, and potential overburdening of the European Central Bank' (European Stability Mechanism, 2021, p. 5). The rationale for fiscal rules was, in other words, to reduce the risk of shocks stemming from weak fiscal and unbalanced macroeconomic positions, which could lead to adverse spillover effects for other Member States (Thirion, 2017, p. 5). Imprudent economic and fiscal policies could give rise to inflationary pressures across the euro area and threaten the sustainability of the monetary union. The euro area Member States were expected to conduct their fiscal policies in a countercyclical fashion, thereby building fiscal buffers during good times used to stabilize the economy during bad times. This would also permit the ECB to focus on its core mandate of maintaining price stability (European Stability Mechanism, 2021, p. 5; Thirion, 2017, pp. 4–6).

There is a rich body of literature on the EU's fiscal and economic governance framework and the various changes effectuated thereto in order to address the eurozone crisis (see among many others Adamski, 2018, ch. 2; Amtenbrink, 2014; Amtenbrink and Repasi, 2017; Dermine, 2022b; Flynn, 2020; Hinarejos, 2020a; Keppenne, 2014, 2020a, 2020b; Markakis, 2020a, chs. 2–3). In what follows, we will briefly set out the core legal provisions and outline the key changes that were made to this framework in response to the eurozone crisis, so as to situate the ensuing discussion on the reform of those rules.

The EU Treaties lay down the core provisions on economic policy coordination in the Union. First of all, Article 3(4) of the Treaty on European Union (TEU) provides that, 'The Union shall establish an economic and monetary union whose currency is the euro'. Article 2(3) of the Treaty on the Functioning of the European Union (TFEU) provides that, 'The Member States shall coordinate their economic and employment policies within arrangements as determined by this Treaty, which the Union shall have competence to provide'. Article 5(1) TFEU focuses sharply on economic policy: 'The Member States shall coordinate their economic policies within the Union. To this end, the Council shall adopt measures, in particular broad guidelines for these policies.' It is further provided in Article 5(1) TFEU that specific provisions shall apply to euro area Member States, these being Articles 136–138 TFEU.

Part Three, Title VIII of the TFEU is specifically dedicated to 'Economic and Monetary Policy'. Article 119(1) TFEU provides that, for the purposes set out in Article 3 TEU (namely, the core Treaty provision on the objectives pursued by the Union), the activities of the Member States and the Union shall include, as provided in the Treaties, the adoption of an economic policy which is based on the close coordination of Member States' economic policies, on the internal market, and on the definition of common objectives, and conducted in accordance with the principle of an open market economy with free competition. The activities of the Member States and the Union shall entail compliance with the following guiding principles: stable prices, sound public finances and monetary conditions, and a sustainable balance of payments (Article 119(3) TFEU). Article 120 TFEU provides, inter alia, that Member States shall conduct their economic policies with a view to contributing to the achievement of the objectives of the Union, as defined in Article 3 TEU, and in the context of the broad guidelines referred to in Article 121(2) TFEU. Member States shall regard their economic policies as a matter of common concern and shall coordinate them within the Council (Article 121(1) TFEU). Article 126 TFEU shifts the focus to fiscal surveillance and provides that the Member States shall avoid excessive government deficits (Article 126(1) TFEU). The remainder of this article sets out the various stages of the Excessive Deficit Procedure, which aims to ensure compliance with budgetary discipline on the basis of deficit and debt criteria. As explained in Section 17.3, the reference values necessary for the application of the Excessive Deficit Procedure are set out in Protocol (No. 12) on the Excessive Deficit Procedure, which is annexed to the EU Treaties and forms part of primary EU law.

The Stability and Growth Pact (SGP) adds the flesh to the bare bones of these primary EU law provisions. It would not be an exaggeration to suggest that EU fiscal governance is principally based on the SGP. The Pact initially consisted of Council Regulation 1466/97 on the strengthening of the surveillance of budgetary positions and the surveillance and coordination of economic policies, Council Regulation 1467/97 on speeding up and clarifying the implementation of the excessive deficit procedure, and the Resolution of the European Council on the Stability and Growth Pact. The SGP implements – and reinforces – the relevant Treaty provisions (Articles 121 and 126 TFEU). It has been amended twice since its inception, in 2005 and in 2011. The Pact has two arms. Article 121 TFEU and Regulation 1466/97 form *the preventive arm* of the SGP. The preventive arm aims to ensure sound budgetary policies over the medium term by setting parameters for the Member States' fiscal planning and policies during normal economic times, while taking into account the ups and downs of the economic cycle. Article 126 TFEU and Regulation 1467/97 form *the corrective arm* of the SGP. This arm aims to ensure that Member States adopt appropriate policy responses to correct excessive deficits (and/or debts) by implementing the Excessive Deficit Procedure. Protocol No. 12 gives further details on the Excessive Deficit Procedure, including the reference values on deficit and debt (see also European Commission, n.d.b).

The perceived failure of the EU fiscal and economic governance framework to prevent the sovereign debt crisis and/or to mitigate its effects led to various important changes.[1] They range from the fine-tuning of existing instruments to the adoption of new rules and were effectuated both within ('six-pack' and 'two-pack' legislation) and outside the framework of EU law (Treaty on Stability, Coordination and Governance in the Economic and Monetary Union (TSCG), also known as the Fiscal Compact). Regardless of the legal form through which change was effectuated in the EU during the crisis, the overarching objective was to enhance EU oversight of national fiscal and economic policies and, lest we forget, 'to address the imbalance between the strong monetary union and the weak economic coordination between the members of the euro area' (Hinarejos, 2020a, p. 598). In terms of substance, the instruments adopted in response to the crisis amended the SGP; created a new macroeconomic imbalances procedure; introduced uniform requirements for budgetary frameworks; and sought to enhance economic coordination and surveillance in the euro area. It should be stressed that some of these rules apply to all twenty-seven EU Member States, whereas others only apply to the twenty Member States that have adopted the single currency. This was due to the fact that additional measures were felt to be needed for euro area Member States so as to strengthen the coordination and surveillance of their budgetary and economic policies. The adoption of specific measures for the euro area was made possible thanks to the Treaty provisions for euro area Member States mentioned earlier (in particular Article 136 TFEU in combination with Article 121(6) TFEU).

The norms applicable to all EU Member States may be divided into three categories. First, the preventive and corrective arms of the SGP were amended through two Regulations forming part of the 'six-pack' legislation. Regulation 1175/2011 aims to provide for 'more stringent forms of surveillance' and an 'improved economic governance in the Union', built upon 'a stronger national ownership of commonly agreed rules and policies' and 'a more robust framework at the level of the Union for the surveillance of national economic policies' (preamble recitals 4 and 8). In turn, Regulation 1177/2011 aims to strengthen the rules on budgetary discipline, 'in particular by giving a more prominent role to the level and evolution of debt and to overall sustainability', and to strengthen the mechanisms to ensure compliance with, and enforcement of, those rules (preamble recital 12). Second, Regulation 1176/2011 created a new Macroeconomic Imbalance Procedure to prevent and correct macroeconomic imbalances in the Member States, thereby broadening the surveillance of their economic policies beyond budgetary surveillance. Third, Directive 2011/85, also forming part of the 'six pack', governs national budgetary frameworks and aims to ensure the Member States' compliance with the Treaty obligation to avoid excessive government deficits (Article 126(1) TFEU).

As regards the rules which only apply to the euro area Member States, the 'six-pack' legislation sets out a system of sanctions for enhancing the enforcement of the preventive and corrective parts of the SGP in the euro area (Regulation 1173/2011). It further provides for sanctions for excessive macroeconomic imbalances (Regulation 1174/2011). Moreover, the TSCG lays down the balanced budget rule and provides for the adoption of a correction mechanism at national level, which entails the obligation to implement measures to correct deviations from fiscal targets over a defined period of time. This part of the treaty only applies to euro area Contracting Parties, unless non-euro area Contracting Parties declare their intention to be bound by it

[1] To be sure, it is not suggested that the relevant rules failed to have any impact whatsoever. See also De Haan and Gootjes, Chapter 18 in this volume; and EU Independent Fiscal Institutions (2021), p. 6, with further references.

(Article 14).[2] Furthermore, the 'two-pack' legislation provides for enhanced economic and budgetary surveillance in the euro area. More specifically, Regulation 472/2013 lays down provisions for strengthening the economic and budgetary surveillance of euro area Member States experiencing or threatened with serious difficulties with respect to their financial stability or the sustainability of their public finances, and of euro area Member States which request or receive financial assistance (Article 1(1)). Regulation 473/2013 sets out provisions for enhanced monitoring of budgetary policies in the euro area and for ensuring that national budgets are consistent with the economic policy guidance issued in the context of the SGP and the European Semester for economic policy coordination (Article 1(1)).

17.3 THE PREVENTIVE AND CORRECTIVE ARMS OF THE STABILITY AND GROWTH PACT

The discussion thus far has focused on the core rules and instruments in the EU fiscal and economic governance framework. This section zooms in on the EU fiscal rules as currently in force, following their amendment in 2005, 2011, and – for euro area Member States – 2013. In what follows, the emphasis will be on the preventive and corrective arms of the SGP. Due to space constraints, we will principally focus on the *substance* of the relevant rules, as opposed to the *procedure(s)* by means of which they are applied and enforced.

The preventive part of the SGP requires that Member States achieve and maintain *a medium-term budgetary objective* and submit stability and convergence programmes to that effect. According to Regulation 1466/97, as currently in force, each Member State shall have a differentiated medium-term objective for its budgetary position (MTO). The MTOs shall ensure the sustainability of public finances or rapid progress towards such sustainability while allowing room for budgetary manoeuvre, considering in particular the need for public investment. They may diverge from the requirement of a close-to-balance or in-surplus position, while providing a safety margin with respect to the 3 per cent of GDP government deficit ratio (first paragraph of Article 2a). For euro area Member States and Member States participating in the European Exchange Rate Mechanism II (ERM II),[3] the country-specific MTOs shall be specified within a defined range between –1 per cent of GDP and balance or surplus, in cyclically adjusted terms, net of one-off and temporary measures (second paragraph of Article 2a).[4] The MTO shall be revised every three years. A Member State's MTO may be further revised in the event of the implementation of a structural reform with a major impact on the sustainability of public finances (third paragraph of Article 2a).

Each euro area Member State shall submit to the Council and the Commission the information necessary for the purpose of multilateral surveillance at regular intervals under Article 121 TFEU in the form of a stability programme (Article 3(1)).[5] This programme shall present inter alia the MTO and the adjustment path towards that objective for the general government balance as a percentage of GDP (Article 3(2)(a)). Based on assessments by the Commission and

[2] The Fiscal Compact (Title III of the TSCG) currently formally binds twenty-two EU Member States: the nineteen euro area Member States, as well as Bulgaria, Denmark, and Romania, which have decided to opt in.

[3] Currently, these countries are Bulgaria and Denmark. Croatia joined the euro area on 1 January 2023.

[4] The balanced budget rule in the Fiscal Compact provides for a lower limit of a structural deficit of 0.5 per cent of the GDP at market prices (Article 3(1)(b)). However, where the ratio of the general government debt to GDP at market prices is significantly below 60 per cent and where risks in terms of long-term sustainability of public finances are low, the lower limit is 1.0 per cent (Article 3(1)(d)).

[5] Non-euro area Member States instead submit a convergence programme, and Regulation 1466/97 lays down separate rules for them in Articles 7–10.

the Economic and Financial Committee, the Council examines the MTOs presented by the Member States concerned in their stability programmes, assesses whether the economic assumptions on which the programme is based are plausible, whether the adjustment path towards the MTO is appropriate, including consideration of the accompanying path for the debt ratio, and whether the measures being taken or proposed to respect that adjustment path are sufficient to achieve the MTO over the cycle (first subparagraph of Article 5(1)). When assessing the adjustment path towards the MTO, the Council and the Commission shall examine if the Member State concerned is pursuing an appropriate annual improvement of its cyclically adjusted budget balance, net of one-off and other temporary measures, required to meet its MTO, with 0.5 per cent of GDP as a benchmark. For Member States faced with a debt level exceeding 60 per cent of GDP or with pronounced risks of overall debt sustainability, the annual improvement must be greater than 0.5 per cent of GDP. The Council and the Commission shall take into account whether a higher adjustment effort is made in economic good times, whereas the effort might be more limited in economic bad times. In particular, revenue windfalls and shortfalls shall be considered (second subparagraph of Article 5(1)).[6]

Whether the Member State concerned is making sufficient progress towards its MTO shall be evaluated on the basis of an *overall assessment* with the structural balance as the reference, including an analysis of expenditure net of discretionary revenue measures. This brings us to the so-called *expenditure benchmark*. The Council and the Commission shall assess whether the growth path of government expenditure, taken in conjunction with the effect of measures being taken or planned on the revenue side, is in accordance with the following conditions:

- for Member States that have *achieved* their MTO, annual expenditure growth does not exceed a reference medium-term rate of potential GDP growth, unless the excess is matched by discretionary revenue measures;
- for Member States that have *not yet reached* their MTO, annual expenditure growth does not exceed a rate below a reference medium-term rate of potential GDP growth, unless the excess is matched by discretionary revenue measures;
- for Member States that have not yet reached their MTO, discretionary reductions of government revenue items are matched either by expenditure reductions or by discretionary increases in other government revenue items or both (third subparagraph of Article 5(1)).

It is legally possible for a Member State to *deviate* from the adjustment path towards its MTO in two cases. First, there is the so-called *structural reform clause* (seventh subparagraph of Article 5(1)). When defining the adjustment path to the MTO for Member States that have not yet reached this objective, and in allowing a temporary deviation from this objective for Member States that have already reached it, the Council and the Commission shall take into account the implementation of major structural reforms which have direct long-term positive budgetary effects, including by raising potential sustainable growth, and therefore a verifiable impact on the long-term sustainability of public finances. It is however required that an appropriate safety margin with respect to the 3 per cent of GDP deficit reference value be

[6] For a detailed breakdown of the required annual adjustment – the so-called matrix of requirements – according to which the speed of adjustment to the MTO varies in accordance with the size of the output gap and the debt level, see the 'Commonly agreed position on flexibility within the Stability and Growth Pact' endorsed by the ECOFIN Council of 12 February 2016 (see Council of the European Union, 2017, Annex 5).

preserved and that the budgetary position be expected to return to the MTO within the programme period.[7] Second, the Commission and the Council may take into account *the impact of adverse economic events*. In the case of an unusual event outside the control of the Member State concerned which has a major impact on the financial position of the general government ('unusual events clause') or in periods of severe economic downturn for the euro area or the Union as a whole ('general escape clause'), Member States may be allowed temporarily to depart from the adjustment path towards the MTO, provided that this does not endanger fiscal sustainability in the medium term (tenth subparagraph of Article 5(1)).

After its submission, the stability programme is examined by the Council and the Commission. Where the Council considers that the objectives and content of the programme should be strengthened, with particular reference to the adjustment path towards the MTO, it shall invite the Member State concerned to adjust its programme (Article 5(2)). In practice, this is done within the confines of the fiscal recommendation which forms part of the country-specific recommendations adopted in the context of the European Semester. 'Through the adoption of the [country-specific recommendations], the Commission and the Council make an overall assessment of compliance of the Member States for the past and for the future (the so-called "*ex ante* and *ex post* analysis"), using the criteria mentioned in Regulation (EC) 1466/97' (Keppenne, 2020b, p. 826).

The Council and the Commission monitor the implementation of stability programmes, on the basis of information provided by the Member States and of assessments by the Commission and the Economic and Financial Committee (Article 6(1)). In the event of a significant observed deviation from the adjustment path towards the MTO, the Commission shall address a warning to the Member State concerned. The Council shall examine the situation and adopt a recommendation for the necessary policy measures, on the basis of a Commission recommendation. In turn, the Member State concerned shall report to the Council on action taken in response to the recommendation. If the Member State concerned fails to take appropriate action within the deadline specified in the Council recommendation, the Commission shall immediately recommend to the Council to adopt a decision establishing that no effective action has been taken. At the same time, the Commission may recommend to the Council to adopt a revised recommendation on necessary policy measures (Article 6(2)). The same procedure (known as '*the significant deviation procedure*') is followed for monitoring the implementation of convergence programmes submitted by non-euro area Member States (Article 10(2)),[8] except for *euro area* Member States there is the possibility of *sanctions* in case the Council adopts a decision establishing that a Member State failed to take action in response to its recommendation. The Member State concerned may be required to lodge with the Commission an interest-bearing deposit amounting to 0.2 per cent of its GDP in the preceding year (Regulation 1173/2011, Article 4).

As regards the corrective arm of the SGP, Article 126(1) TFEU provides that Member States shall avoid excessive government deficits. According to Article 126(2) TFEU, compliance with budgetary discipline is examined on the basis of a deficit criterion and a debt criterion. The assessment is based on the reference values laid down in Protocol (No. 12) on the excessive deficit procedure, which is annexed to the EU Treaties. These are the famous 3 per cent and

[7] Further guidance is provided in the Commission's Communication on 'Making the best use of the flexibility within the existing rules of the Stability and Growth Pact' and the 'Commonly agreed position on flexibility within the Stability and Growth Pact'.

[8] So far, this procedure has been triggered against Romania and Hungary. See further European Commission (n.d.a).

60 per cent rules: 3 per cent for the ratio of the planned or actual government deficit to GDP at market prices; and 60 per cent for the ratio of government debt to GDP at market prices. It should be stressed that there is no automaticity, in the sense that breaching these values does not necessarily lead to the Member State concerned being subject to an Excessive Deficit Procedure; other factors, too, may be considered (see Article 126(3)–(6) TFEU and Regulation 1467/97, esp. Article 2(3)–(7)). There is 'a large margin of discretion as regards the relevant factors to be taken into account' (Keppenne, 2020b, p. 833). A link is also established with Regulation 1176/2011, insofar as Article 2(3) of Regulation 1467/97 also refers, among other factors, to 'the implementation of policies in the context of the prevention and correction of excessive macroeconomic imbalances'. As explained later in this section, it is ultimately up to the Council to decide whether an Excessive Deficit Procedure should be opened.

A Member State's deficit is considered excessive when it exceeds the reference value of 3 per cent, unless 'the ratio has declined substantially and continuously and reached a level that comes close to the reference value' or 'the excess over the reference value is only exceptional and temporary and the ratio remains close to the reference value' (Article 126(2)(a) TFEU). 'There is no formal definition of the meaning of a level being "close to three per cent" but according to a constant practice, a difference of more than 0.5 per cent is no longer close' (Keppenne, 2020b, p. 829 fn 84). The excess of a government deficit over the reference value shall be considered exceptional 'when resulting from an unusual event outside the control of the Member State concerned and with a major impact on the financial position of general government, or when resulting from a severe economic downturn' (Regulation 1467/97, as currently in force, first subparagraph of Article 2(1)). It shall be considered temporary 'if budgetary forecasts as provided by the Commission indicate that the deficit will fall below the reference value following the end of the unusual event or the severe economic downturn' (second subparagraph of Article 2(1)).

A Member State's public debt is considered excessive when its ratio to GDP exceeds the 60 per cent reference value, 'unless the ratio is sufficiently diminishing and approaching the reference value at a satisfactory pace' (Article 126(2)(b) TFEU). According to secondary legislation, it shall be considered as sufficiently diminishing and approaching the reference value at a satisfactory pace 'if the differential with respect to the reference value has decreased over the previous three years at an average rate of one twentieth per year as a benchmark, based on changes over the last three years for which the data is available' (Regulation 1467/97, Article 2(1a)). This is the so-called *debt-reduction benchmark*.

As regards the procedural steps to be taken, these are set out in Article 126 TFEU and further fleshed out in Regulation 1467/97. If a Member State does not fulfil the requirements under one or both of the deficit and debt criteria, the Commission shall prepare a report, taking into account, as noted earlier, all relevant factors (Article 126(3) TFEU). The Economic and Financial Committee shall formulate an opinion on the report of the Commission (Article 126(4) TFEU). If the Commission considers that an excessive deficit in a Member State exists or may occur, it shall address an opinion to the Member State concerned (Article 126(5) TFEU). The Council shall, on a proposal from the Commission, and having considered any observations which the Member State concerned may wish to make, decide after an overall assessment whether an excessive deficit exists (Article 126(6) TFEU). Where the Council decides that an excessive deficit exists, it shall adopt, on a recommendation from the Commission, recommendations addressed to the Member State concerned with a view to bringing that situation to an end within a given period (Article 126(7) TFEU). Following the expiry of the deadline set by the Council, the Commission assesses whether the Member State concerned is on track to correct its excessive deficit. The Commission and the Council have agreed a methodology for assessing whether a Member State has taken effective action, which includes a 'careful analysis'.[9] If the Commission considers that the Member State concerned has not taken effective action, it recommends to the Council to adopt a decision establishing that there has been no effective action in response to its recommendations within the period laid down (Article 126(8) TFEU).[10]

For non-euro area Member States, the procedure stops with the Council decision based on Article 126(8) TFEU. Where the Council decides, in accordance with Article 126(8) TFEU, that a non-euro area Member State has not taken effective action, it may only address to it a revised recommendation under Article 126(7) TFEU. Any further steps outlined in Article 126 TFEU – 'the coercive means of remedying excessive deficits', as the Treaty puts it – do not apply to non-euro area Member States (Article 139(2)(b) TFEU). By contrast, if a euro area Member State persists in failing to put into practice the recommendations of the Council, the latter may decide to give notice to it to take, within a specified time limit, measures for the deficit reduction which is judged necessary in order to remedy the situation (Article 126(9) TFEU). Although it is not legally possible to bring infringement proceedings under Articles 258–259 TFEU within the framework of the Excessive Deficit Procedure (Article 126(10) TFEU), if a euro area Member State fails to comply with an Article 126(9) TFEU decision, the Council may decide to apply or, as the case may be, intensify one or more of the measures listed in Article 126(11) TFEU. Following the 2011 reform of the SGP, whenever the Council decides to impose sanctions, a fine is, as a rule, required, which can be up to 0.5 per cent of the Member State's GDP (Regulation 1467/97, as currently in force, Articles 11–12). In addition, Regulation 1173/2011 provides for financial sanctions at earlier stages of the Excessive Deficit Procedure. More specifically, if the Council, acting under Article 126(6) TFEU, decides that an excessive deficit exists in a Member State which has lodged an interest-bearing deposit under the preventive arm of the SGP, or in case of particularly serious non-compliance with the budgetary policy obligations laid down in the SGP, Regulation 1173/2011 provides for a non-interest-bearing deposit amounting to 0.2 per cent of the Member State's GDP in the preceding year (Article 5). If the Council, acting under Article 126(8) TFEU, decides that a Member State has not taken effective action to correct its excessive deficit, Regulation 1173/2011 provides for a fine, amounting to 0.2 per cent of the Member State's GDP in the preceding year (Article 6). 'However, in practice, the Council has not activated such sanctions, nor the ultimate steps of the [Excessive Deficit Procedure] also leading to sanctions on the Member States concerned, because the Commission has never submitted such proposals to the Council' (Keppenne, 2020b, p. 831).[11]

At the time of writing, the EU has activated, for the first time, the 'general escape clause' in the SGP in response to the COVID-19 pandemic so as to enable increased spending from the Member States. This clause, which has been part of its arsenal since the 'six-pack' reform of 2011, allows for a coordinated and orderly temporary deviation from the budgetary requirements that would normally apply to Member States, in a situation of generalized crisis caused by a

[9] If the 'careful analysis' concludes that the Member State concerned has delivered on its policy commitments, the assessment will conclude that effective action has been taken, with a possibility to extend the deadline, even if the headline deficit target has not been met. See further European Commission (2019), pp. 62–65; Council of the European Union (2016).

[10] The seminal Case C-27/04 (Full Court), *Commission of the European Communities* v. *Council of the European Union*, EU:C:2004:436, concerning excessive deficit procedures with respect to Germany and France, illustrates the discretion enjoyed by the Council.

[11] In the past, the Commission proposed that fines be imposed on Portugal and Spain for failure to take effective action to address their excessive deficit, which it then recommended that they be cancelled. The Council followed the Commission's recommendation and cancelled the fines. See further European Commission (2016).

severe economic downturn for the euro area or the Union as a whole.[12] More specifically, this clause allows the Member States to depart from the adjustment path towards their respective MTO (see Regulation 1466/97, as is currently in force, Articles 5(1), 6(3), 9(1), and 10(3)). In case an excessive deficit exists, a revised fiscal trajectory may be charted (see Regulation 1467/97, as is currently in force, Articles 3(5) and 5(2)). The 'general escape clause' allows the Commission and the Council to undertake the necessary policy coordination measures within the framework of the SGP, while departing from the budgetary requirements that would normally apply, in order to tackle the economic consequences of the pandemic (Dermine, 2020, pp. 338–341; on the implementation of the SGP in pandemic times see Hagelstam and De Lemos Peixoto, 2022).

17.4 THE CRITIQUE OF THE EXISTING FRAMEWORK AND THE COMMISSION'S ECONOMIC GOVERNANCE REVIEW

The EU's fiscal and economic governance framework has received mostly brickbats and barely any bouquets. It has been subject to criticism even from within the EU's institutional core (see notably the European Parliament resolutions of 24 June 2015 and 8 July 2021; European Court of Auditors, 2016, 2018a, 2018b, 2019; European Fiscal Board, 2019a). We will refer to some of the most prominent criticisms levelled against the EU's fiscal rules, which are also relevant for reform purposes. This is merely an aggregation of the relevant issues, as different versions of the framework have given rise to different problems over time. First of all, notwithstanding the fact that the EU fiscal rules are based on cyclically adjusted variables, they did not always manage to prevent procyclical fiscal policies (European Stability Mechanism, 2021, pp. 7–10). Due to insufficient fiscal consolidation in good economic times, countries did not build up adequate fiscal buffers which could be used to stabilize the economy during downturns without jeopardizing the long-term sustainability of public finances (see also the contributions by De Haan and Gootjes, Chapter 18 and Demertzis et al., Chapter 15 in this volume). 'Not only were they strongly asymmetric – i.e. only binding to restrict deficits and not to impose surpluses, but they also too often went unenforced, which wiped out the credibility of future sanctions' (Thirion, 2017, p. 5; on the framework's emphasis on enforcement, rather than on achieving compliance, see Amtenbrink and Repasi, 2017). The rules are incredibly complex and difficult to apply, and the revisions made in response to the eurozone crisis further increased that complexity. A key source of that complexity is 'the heavy reliance on unobservable indicators of fiscal performance in all stages of fiscal surveillance' (European Fiscal Board, 2019b, p. 74). It is often noted that, under the existing framework, the potential GDP and growth needed to determine the adjustment requirements in terms of structural balance are hard to measure and frequently subject to substantial revisions. Essentially, the current framework relies on a variable (output gap) that is 'unobservable … and estimating it is fraught with uncertainty' (European Court of Auditors, 2016, p. 59).[13] 'Frequent revisions of potential GDP and output gap undermined the credibility and enforceability of fiscal rules' (European Stability Mechanism, 2021, p. 7). It is rightly noted that the problems adumbrated above are interrelated in various ways: 'Complexity for example

[12] See the Communication from the Commission to the Council on the activation of the general escape clause of the Stability and Growth Pact COM(2020) 123 final (Brussels, 20 March 2020), endorsed by the Council of the European Union (2020).

[13] 'The output gap is an economic measure of the difference between the actual output of an economy and its potential output. Potential output is the maximum amount of goods and services an economy can turn out when it is most efficient – that is, at full capacity' (Jahan and Saber Mahmud, 2013, p. 38).

contributes to weak compliance and ineffective enforcement, which can lead to procyclicality. The combination of these problems reduces buy-in from Member States, key stakeholders and citizens' (EU Independent Fiscal Institutions, 2021, p. 6).

In its February 2020 Communication, the Commission reviewed the extent to which the different elements of the current framework for fiscal and economic surveillance, as introduced or amended by the 'six-pack' and 'two-pack' reforms, have been effective in achieving the key objectives, namely (i) ensuring sustainable government finances and growth, as well as avoiding macroeconomic imbalances, (ii) providing an integrated surveillance framework that enables closer coordination of economic policies, in particular in the euro area, and (iii) promoting the convergence of economic performances among Member States (European Commission, 2020, p. 5). It being the institution in charge of applying the relevant framework, together with the Council, the Commission's views are arguably extremely interesting for present purposes.

The Commission notes that the economic context has materially evolved, such that the challenges facing the Member States are different from the prevailing economic conditions when these reforms were initially agreed upon. More specifically, it draws attention, inter alia, to the decline in potential growth and interest rates, in a context of an ageing population, which has gone hand in hand with persistently low inflation. What is more, as regards structural reforms to strengthen potential growth and support economic adjustment, the reform momentum has faded and progress has become uneven across Member States and policy areas. These developments should be seen against the EU's broader ambitions to pursue a sustainable growth strategy that would render it the world's first climate-neutral continent, resource efficient and fit for the digital age, while ensuring social fairness. Achieving such goals would require significant additional private and public investment over a sustained period of time (European Commission, 2020, p. 7).

The Commission's review reveals strengths as well as possible areas for improvement. On the positive side, it is argued that the 'six-pack' and 'two-pack' reforms, together with the European Semester, have strengthened the framework for economic surveillance and guided the Member States in achieving their economic and fiscal policy objectives. They have also led to a broader and more integrated approach to surveillance that better ensures the overall consistency of policy advice within the European Semester. The measures introduced have contributed to ensuring closer coordination of economic policies. It is further claimed that the 'six-pack' and 'two-pack' reforms have contributed to achieving the Union's strategy for growth and jobs, and that they have fostered convergence in the economic performance of the Member States (European Commission, 2020, p. 16).

On the negative side, the Commission readily acknowledges that public debt levels remain high in some Member States, which are also far from their MTOs while their reform efforts are waning. The fiscal stance at the national level has frequently been pro-cyclical. Combined with the absence of a central stabilization capacity, this hampers the ability to steer the fiscal stance for the euro area as a whole in the event of large shocks. The current framework and its implementation have not fostered macroeconomic stabilization. Moreover, it is argued that the current surveillance framework and its implementation did not sufficiently differentiate between Member States that have markedly different fiscal positions, sustainability risks, or other vulnerabilities. Furthermore, the fiscal framework has grown excessively complex, hence the rules have become less transparent, thereby hampering predictability, communication, and political buy-in. Further, while the interaction between the specific surveillance strands has been adequate, there is further scope to make them work better together. Finally, it is rightly claimed that more thought should be given to the need for the surveillance framework to assist in tackling pressing economic, demographic, and environmental challenges (European Commission, 2020, pp. 16–17).

In October 2021, the Commission relaunched the public debate on the review of the EU economic governance framework, with the aim of building a broad-based consensus on the way forward (European Commission, 2021). Whilst stating that the main conclusions from the February 2020 Communication remained valid and relevant, the Commission underlined the need to combine these findings with the lessons drawn from the COVID-19 crisis. In the Commission's view, the COVID-19 crisis has shed light on the challenges facing the EU's economic governance framework and rendered several of them even more relevant. It is further argued that the review of the economic governance framework could draw useful lessons from the EU policy response to the COVID-19 crisis, in particular the Recovery and Resilience Facility framework and its governance. The stated aim of the public debate is to reflect on how the EU economic governance framework can support the Member States in tackling post-COVID macroeconomic challenges. Accordingly, the key issues that had been earlier identified for public debate were slightly reformulated and complemented by additional questions.[14]

17.5 PROPOSALS FOR THE FUTURE EVOLUTION OF THE EU'S FISCAL AND ECONOMIC GOVERNANCE FRAMEWORK

In light of the developments and trends outlined above, there has been a large number of proposals on the reform of the EU fiscal and economic governance framework, as well as studies examining the legal and economic feasibility of those proposals (see, among a myriad of other proposals, Bénassy-Quéré et al., 2018; Blanchard et al., 2021; Martin et al., 2021). There have further been studies that straddle the divide, such that not only do they examine the legal feasibility and economic desirability of other studies but they also put forward their own suggestions (see e.g. Dullien et al., 2021; Maduro et al., 2021). In what follows, we will principally focus on the European Fiscal Board proposals (2018, 2019b, 2020, 2021) and the proposal by the European Stability Mechanism (2021). Examining these proposals in depth will also allow us to appreciate more fully the challenges facing the existing framework, as well as the additional challenges brought about by the COVID-19 crisis. We will further look at other proposals from national governments, academics, think tanks, and policymakers where appropriate.[15] The existing proposals share common elements (notably, in so far as they rely on expenditure rules with a debt anchor)[16] but also exhibit important differences.

The latest report of the European Fiscal Board (2021) helpfully sets out the key elements of this 'new generation of reform proposals'. These will only be summarized here. First of all, there is a focus on '[d]eclining debt trajectories when possible and desirable (that is by avoiding procyclicality in good times)', and on expenditure ceilings as the core operational rule so as to 'provide short-to-medium term guidance tying annual budgets to the debt anchor' (European Fiscal Board, 2021, pp. 76–77). That approach not only relies on observable indicators (e.g. expenditure growth) rather than estimated ones (e.g. the structural budget balance), but also

14 On the state of play of the economic governance review, see European Commission (2022a). For the report summarizing the results of the online public survey on the future of the EU's economic governance framework, see European Commission (2022b).

15 Although harder to cite, conferences and webinars certainly deserve a mention. See notably CEPS Think Tank (2021).

16 Expenditure rules aim to limit increases in current expenditure, the latter being adjusted in accordance with a narrowly set definition that excludes certain spending items (European Stability Mechanism, 2021, p. 15).

'provides short-term flexibility by letting automatic stabilisers play in real time and in a fully symmetric manner (allowing the organic regeneration of fiscal space during good times)' (European Fiscal Board, 2021, pp. 76–77). This greater focus on debt is also accompanied by an acknowledgement of 'the diversity of situations across countries and possibly different degrees of exposure to the realisation of contingent liabilities', with many proposals arguing in favour of tailoring the implementation of the rules to individual country circumstances (European Fiscal Board, 2021, p. 77). Last but not least, many proposals argue for a greater role for independent fiscal institutions in the monitoring and implementation of the fiscal rules (European Fiscal Board, 2021, p. 77).

As regards the main differences between the existing proposals, these 'relate to operational rules, debt targets, benchmarks for expenditure growth, debt correction speed, and the selected expenditure aggregate' (European Stability Mechanism, 2021, p. 15). Maduro et al. helpfully provide a typology of the reform options put forward thus far. The common thread running through these reform scenarios is that the deficit and debt reference values, and the speed at which they are reached, do not need to be the same across all countries and at all times:

> Arguably the most radical idea is to give up on numerical fiscal rules altogether (Blanchard et al., 2021). … An alternative, less radical approach would be to maintain debt (and possibly deficit) reference values, as well as a fiscal rule governing adjustment toward those values, but to give up the principle that they must be the same for all countries and at all times (Martin et al., 2021). … The third variant, which includes proposals by the European Fiscal Board (EFB), would be to maintain the existing debt and deficit reference values … but to allow more flexibility along the path of convergence towards these objectives… (Maduro et al., 2021, p. 12)

The latter option could be achieved 'by setting country-specific speeds of adjustment toward the debt reference value and regularly revising this speed'; 'by giving debt sustainability analysis a central role in deciding whether … the members comply with budgetary discipline'; or 'by broadening and providing more structure to the "general escape clause"' (Maduro et al., 2021, pp. 12–13).

In its 2021 annual report, the European Fiscal Board (EFB) sought to outline an intermediate position between the views of those Member States that regard an early return to the pre-pandemic framework, more rigorously complied with, as desirable; and those Member States that find that framework outdated to such an extent that radical reform, including legislative steps, has become a prerequisite for a return to rules-based governance. It did so in light of what it believes the current perspectives on the role of fiscal policies to be, as well as the experience accumulated over the past three decades. 'That experience inspires a degree of humility in two dimensions: above all recognition of the limits to what a rules-based fiscal framework can achieve in a European Union that remains economically and politically very heterogeneous; but also the need to discard policy recommendations based on indicators too uncertain to rely on' (European Fiscal Board, 2021, p. 72).

The EFB argues that reforming the fiscal framework remains a far better approach than discretionary and hard-to-predict tweaks in the implementation of the existing rule book. Reforming the framework in time would serve the interests of *both* Member States which are keen to avoid a further erosion of the rules-based system and those willing to exploit flexibility in a productive manner (European Fiscal Board, 2021, pp. 71, 84–86). However, despite significant convergence in published policy advice, there is no consensus among Member States, leaving the prospect for and the scope of potential improvements in doubt (European Fiscal Board, 2021, pp. 74–75). Yet it is forcefully argued that 'the legacy of historically high public debt combined with the persistence of low borrowing costs and increased spending pressures (on public investment, healthcare, and other social spending) call for a bold rethinking of the institutional setup imagined more than 30 years ago' (European Fiscal Board, 2021, p. 78).

The proposal advanced by the EFB was fleshed out initially in its 2018 annual report and further refined in subsequent reports. It forms part of a growing class of proposals and plans that share the goal of refocusing the surveillance framework on the prevention of gross policy errors that are likely to jeopardize debt sustainability, rather than micromanaging national affairs. In a nutshell, the EFB proposal rests on a single fiscal anchor (debt), a single operational rule to guide fiscal policies (net expenditure growth), and a single escape clause triggered on the basis of independent economic analysis (European Fiscal Board, 2021, p. 77). Instead of two separate anchors (deficit and debt), the debt-to-GDP ratio would be the anchor of the new simplified fiscal framework. The ceiling for the debt ratio would remain at 60 per cent of GDP. To achieve the objective of the framework, as defined by the fiscal anchor, a ceiling on net expenditure growth is proposed as the operational target.[17] More specifically, for Member States whose debt is above 60 per cent of GDP, fiscal requirements would take the form of a ceiling on the growth rate of primary expenditure at current prices, net of discretionary revenue measures. The growth rate of the expenditure ceiling would be capped by the trend rate of potential output growth. This ceiling would be fixed for a three-year period, in order to provide a medium-term orientation to fiscal policies, and recalculated thereafter so as to ensure that the debt ratio is brought within the range of its long-run objective in a given maximum number of years. The framework proposed may be (principally) designed for Member States with high debt, but it further aims to contain the deficits of low-debt countries through the 3 per cent reference value for the headline deficit (European Fiscal Board, 2018, p. 79). The adjustment of government debt could be made country-specific, either by opting for differentiated debt reference values and/or by differentiating the speed of adjustment towards the debt reference value. Member States with strong fiscal positions could be required to commit to a binding net expenditure path, which would include growth-enhancing public investments with cross-border effects (European Fiscal Board, 2019b, pp. 77–79; European Fiscal Board, 2020, pp. 85–92).

In contrast to the current framework, which relies on an overall assessment on the basis of multiple indicators (structural balance, expenditure rule) in the preventive arm or a 'careful analysis' in the corrective arm, the assessment of compliance with the expenditure rule would be based on a single indicator of fiscal performance (net expenditure), which would not be complemented by any additional information (European Fiscal Board, 2018, pp. 79–80). Moreover, the EFB proposes a more effective system of sanctions for both arms of the SGP, as well as a streamlined surveillance cycle with fewer steps.[18] Notably, a compensation account would track deviations from fiscal requirements. To provide additional flexibility in the framework, beyond the countercyclical effect of the proposed expenditure rule, a general escape clause would replace the existing system of waivers and derogations. It would be triggered, at the request of the Member State concerned or by the Commission and the Council, only in

[17] 'In line with the current methodology used in the expenditure benchmark of the SGP, net expenditure is defined as overall government expenditure net of interest payments, cyclical unemployment benefits, EU-funded investments and discretionary revenue measures, with gross fixed capital formation smoothed over four years' (European Fiscal Board, 2018, pp. 79–80).

[18] The emphasis on sanctions was toned down in subsequent reports, as 'in the present crisis context, following the unprecedented economic shock resulting from the Covid-19 pandemic, financial sanctions would be very difficult to justify let alone enforce' (European Fiscal Board, 2020, p. 94). Another option explored is whether financial sanctions should be substituted with an incentive to maintain or obtain access to joint facilities.

exceptional circumstances and would cover events that are outside the control of the Member State concerned, subject to an independent verification that the eligibility criteria are satisfied (European Fiscal Board, 2018, pp. 79–83). It is further argued in the EFB proposals that three additional elements are needed in the EU fiscal and economic governance framework for ensuring the long-term sustainability of public finances, stabilizing economic activity, and improving the quality of public finances in a post-pandemic EU. These are a central fiscal capacity for stabilization; a safeguard against counterproductive spending cuts, i.e. cuts in public investment; and a greater focus on macroeconomic imbalances (notably, current account surpluses), given the link between the SGP and the Macroeconomic Imbalance Procedure (European Fiscal Board, 2021, pp. 82–84).

Looking at other proposals, we can identify a similar emphasis on expenditure rules. The so-called Dutch–Spanish proposal (Government of the Netherlands, 2022) also proposes the transformation of medium-term objectives into a simple expenditure rule, coupled with well-defined escape clauses for extraordinary events outside the control of governments. It also proposes strengthening national fiscal frameworks, including through a greater role for independent fiscal institutions. Bénassy-Quéré et al. (2018) propose replacing the current system of fiscal rules focused on the structural deficit by a simple expenditure rule guided by a long-term debt-reduction target. Monitoring compliance with the fiscal rule would be devolved to national fiscal councils supervised by an independent euro area fiscal watchdog. Dullien et al. (2021) recommend replacing the current operational target of structural balances with expenditure rules and introducing a golden rule that safeguards public investment.[19]

The European Stability Mechanism (ESM) proposal is different in important respects. It is premised on the realization that 'the original link between the deficit and debt anchor is no longer valid' (European Stability Mechanism, 2021, p. 24). The economic thinking behind the famous 3 per cent and 60 per cent rules was that a 3 per cent deficit was sufficient to stabilize the economy during downturns. Assuming a nominal growth of 5 per cent and inflation of 2 per cent, debt would stabilize at around 60 per cent of GDP, which was also close to the EMU average at the time (European Stability Mechanism, 2021, pp. 5, 24–25, Box 3). The economic situation has changed, with lower growth and a low interest rate environment now being the norm.

The ESM paper adduces two main arguments as to why *the debt reference value should be raised to 100 per cent of GDP*. First, higher debt levels are considered serviceable, even though the expected nominal growth is lower. It is argued that interest rates and the debt servicing burden, which were already steadily declining prior to the pandemic, are likely to remain below the levels witnessed during the 1990s when the EU fiscal framework was devised (European Stability Mechanism, 2021, p. 24). Second, it is argued that 'requiring all euro area Member States to converge to the current 60% debt-to-GDP reference value appears unrealistic, and risks undermining fiscal framework credibility ... thus impairing the market discipline channel and causing countries to adopt inappropriately tight and unsustainable policies' (European Stability Mechanism, 2021, p. 15). Post-pandemic debt levels are higher, thereby widening the distance to the 60 per cent reference value and requiring a longer period during which Member States

[19] For their part, the most recent proposals by the German government suggest placing a stronger focus on the 'expenditure benchmark' but also keeping the structural balance as the parameter of the MTO in the preventive arm of the Pact. They further propose limited adjustments to the clauses in the SGP, including through clear(er) criteria for the 'general escape clause', as well as reviewing the possibility of making the EFB institutionally and organizationally independent from the Commission (Federal Ministry for Economic Affairs and Climate Action, 2022). On whether these proposals help to move the needle, both domestically and at EU level, see Vallée (2022).

would need to maintain high primary surpluses in order to reach this threshold. What is more, these surpluses would need to be achieved under conditions of lower economic growth. Maintaining such high surpluses for an extended period would work against the need for investment in modernizing and greening European economies, thereby inhibiting growth (European Stability Mechanism, 2021, p. 15).

How one infers a debt limit of 100 per cent of GDP is, according to the ESM paper, 'a practical question' (European Stability Mechanism, 2021, p. 15). 'In the foreseeable future with lower growth and a low interest rate environment, the 3% deficit limit would be consistent with a debt anchor at 100% of GDP' (European Stability Mechanism, 2021, p. 24). Assuming a 3 per cent deficit limit (which, according to the argument, 'has proven a good fiscal policy anchor, and general agreement suggests it has been effective and should be kept') and nominal growth at 3 per cent (1 per cent real growth and 2 per cent inflation), debt would stabilize at 100 per cent of GDP (European Stability Mechanism, 2021, pp. 15, 24). It is fortuitous that this new reference value would also be close to the current euro area average, as was the 60 per cent limit when it was adopted (European Stability Mechanism, 2021, pp. 15–16).

According to the ESM proposal, the 3 per cent deficit-to-GDP and the 100 per cent debt-to-GDP reference values would be complemented by *an expenditure rule*. Yearly expenditure ceilings that track trend growth would replace existing MTOs expressed in structural balance terms. For all Member States, the growth in expenditure – net of EU funds co-financing, the cyclical impact of automatic stabilizers, and one-offs – would not be higher than the potential growth or trend growth rate. For states experiencing an investment gap, expenditure growth could temporarily be higher than the trend GDP growth rate. The expenditure path for the following three years would be expressed in terms of annual spending ceilings, to be revised yearly on a rolling basis alongside the projected growth path. For countries breaching the deficit or debt rule, expenditure growth could also be held below trend, leading to a faster pace of debt reduction (European Stability Mechanism, 2021, p. 25).

Countries with debt below 100 per cent of GDP would only be bound by the expenditure rule. The ESM proposal does not envisage a debt-reduction pace for those states, and the expenditure rule would act as an implicit debt brake. According to the ESM, this would also support domestic demand in those states and external demand in higher-debt states. On the contrary, *countries with debt above 100 per cent of GDP* would also need to follow *a primary balance rule* implying a debt reduction of one-twentieth per year. The Commission would calibrate the primary balance needed for the targeted debt reduction across a rolling three-year horizon in order to ensure continuous convergence towards the debt anchor. The required debt reduction pace would reflect economic circumstances, and deviations would be possible in exceptional circumstances, namely in case of a severe downturn or a productive investment gap (European Stability Mechanism, 2021, p. 25).

According to the proposal, an Excessive Deficit Procedure could be triggered if the 3 per cent deficit limit, expenditure limits, or primary balance targets were breached, unless this was justified given the circumstances. Such exceptional circumstances justifying the breach of the rules could also allow the activation of European safety nets, which do not yet exist, such as a new fiscal stabilization instrument. The enforcement of the EU fiscal framework would also be altered significantly. It is proposed by the ESM that a breach of the expenditure or deficit limits should *not* lead to sanctions, but that it be registered in an adjustment account that keeps track of repeated non-compliance (European Stability Mechanism, 2021, p. 26). Nevertheless, it should not readily be assumed that compliance would suffer as a result: 'a country's past track record of sufficient compliance with the rules would be an important determinant to access the funds, also supporting fiscal discipline in normal times' (European Stability Mechanism, 2021, p. 30). 'Cumulative deviations could serve as a starting point for discussions about conditions to be attached to financial support, for example in the context of the subsequent EU's Multiannual Financial Framework' (European Stability Mechanism, 2021, p. 26).

The ESM proposal differs a great deal from the EFB proposal examined earlier.[20] Whilst it is not the aim of this chapter to assess the reform proposals other than in terms of their legal feasibility, a few comments are warranted at this juncture. It is explicitly stated in the ESM proposal that there is a need – and indeed the intention is – to simplify the existing EU fiscal framework. Nevertheless, *the ESM proposal itself* is complicated, at the very least in the eyes of an EMU lawyer. Moreover, the ESM paper clearly seeks to assuage the (not necessarily illegitimate) concerns of 'hawkish' Member States and at times it feels almost as if it speaks to a German audience. At the same time, the proposal put forward clearly seeks to take the economic conditions in highly indebted Member States into account, with hypothetical examples that are not far removed from the actual situation in the EU periphery (see e.g. European Stability Mechanism, 2021, Box 4). Furthermore, the changes from the perspective of compliance and enforcement would also be significant. Admittedly, an assessment from this viewpoint is not easy, as the proposals made by the ESM are somewhat less detailed in that regard. Though the importance of independent fiscal councils and statistical offices is duly noted, the ESM paper forcefully argues in favour of 'additional compliance incentives and enforcement' (European Stability Mechanism, 2021, p. 29). 'Incentives could be strengthened by linking the EU financial support to the prior compliance with fiscal rules or tightening the policy conditions when financial support is provided' (European Stability Mechanism, 2021, p. 29). This could be seen as problematic, if the fiscal rules themselves (or the policy conditions attached to such support) remained unchanged. This is more especially so since 'financial support' is conceived fairly broadly, and is not equated with financial support *stricto sensu*, namely from financial assistance mechanisms such as the ESM itself. It encompasses not only the EU budget but also other 'EU financial instruments' serving stabilization, structural support, or crisis resolution objectives, which are not named specifically in the proposal. The ESM proposal further refers to instruments that do not yet exist, thereby echoing 'discussions about deeper fiscal integration, including the establishment of a stronger central European budget and about a fiscal stabilisation function' (European Stability Mechanism, 2021, p. 29; see generally Hinarejos and Schütze, in press). This stabilization instrument, references to which have featured almost invariably in post-crisis EMU reform proposals emanating from the EU institutions, 'could take the form of unemployment insurance or reinsurance fund, macroeconomic stabilisation fund, rainy day fund or an ESM credit line' (European Stability Mechanism, 2021, p. 29 fn 76). As regards the latter option, it is interesting to note that the ESM paper suggests that 'the ESM could provide a loan-based fiscal stabilisation facility to be repaid over the business cycle, subject to economic conditions and forecast-based eligibility criteria, and [that] this could replace the temporary Pandemic Crisis Support instrument' (European Stability Mechanism, 2021, p. 30; for a similar proposal see Markakis, 2020b, p. 382).[21]

Another strand of proposals does not define *ex ante* the reference values and the pace at which countries should adjust to them. Instead, it proposes looking at each case individually, taking

[20] For its key differences from the EFB proposals, see European Stability Mechanism (2021), p. 28.

[21] Various contributions to the ESM Conference on the Future of Europe (held on 24 January 2022), including from the ESM's Managing Director himself, argued that the permanent fiscal stabilization mechanism for the euro area could be an ESM facility taking the form of a revolving fund drawing on the ESM's existing lending capacity, with no need for additional taxpayer money (see European Stability Mechanism, 2022).

into account country and context specificities, in order to judge whether fiscal policy needs to be adjusted. Blanchard et al. (2021) recommend abandoning fiscal rules in favour of fiscal standards, i.e. qualitative prescriptions that leave room for judgement together with a process to decide whether the standards are met.[22] There would be country-specific assessments using stochastic debt sustainability analysis, led by national independent fiscal councils and/or the European Commission. This analysis would generate a distribution of paths of the debt ratio based on forecasts for the drivers of the debt dynamics, which are themselves stochastic: the path of primary balances, one-off liabilities (e.g. related to ageing or the retirement system), growth, interest rates, and the maturity structure of the debt. The forecasts would also take into account the policy intentions of the authorities as well as the interactions between growth and fiscal policies. The probability that the debt-stabilizing primary balance exceeds the actual primary balance would indicate risks to debt sustainability. If this probability were low, the primary fiscal standard – debt sustainability with high probability, conditional on baseline policies – would be considered satisfied. The fiscal standards would not prescribe behaviour where debt sustainability is not at risk. On the contrary, if this probability were high, the country would need to adjust, with the speed of adjustment depending on the risks to sustainability, the state of the economic cycle, and the capacity of monetary policy to offset the contractionary impact of adjustment on the EU as a whole. Changes in the pattern of enforcement would also be significant. More specifically, disputes between Member States and the European Commission on the application of the fiscal standards should preferably be adjudicated by an independent institution, such as the European Court of Justice (or a specialized chamber). Restoring this judicial enforcement channel would allow, according to Blanchard et al. (2021), not only the Commission but also other Member States to bring infringement proceedings against the Member State concerned (Articles 258–259 TFEU). In case EU-level judicial enforcement is considered politically unfeasible, Blanchard et al. (2021) propose that independent fiscal institutions or the Commission obtain the power to block (or at least delay) the adoption of the national budget, with the Council of the EU having the final say.

In a similar vein, Martin et al. (2021) agree with Blanchard et al. (2021) on giving a central role to the analysis of debt sustainability and on giving up the uniform numerical values for the deficit and debt in the EU fiscal framework. However, they regard as 'unrealistic a complete break with the Pact and the substitution of Council decisions with judicial procedures' (Martin et al., 2021, p. 6). More specifically, based on a common methodology, each Member State would set a medium-term debt target, the relevance of which would be assessed by the national independent fiscal institution and by the Commission and Council. Once this debt target has been set, it would serve as an anchor for the medium-term programming of public finances through a corresponding expenditure rule, also to be assessed by the EU institutions.

Last but definitely not least, various reform proposals focus on the relationship between the fiscal rules and the macroeconomic imbalance procedure (see e.g. Bénassy-Quéré and Wolff, 2020; Dullien et al., 2021, pp. 12–13, 26–30, with further references; European Fiscal Board, 2019a). Neither in law nor in practice are the processes of fiscal monitoring and of monitoring macroeconomic imbalances hermetically sealed from one another. Not only are fiscal and non-fiscal surveillance, including the surveillance to prevent and correct macroeconomic

[22] It should be noted that Blanchard et al. (2021), p. 28, also argue that: 'Retaining the reference values of 3 percent deficit and 60 percent debt-to-GDP ratio, anchored in the Treaty, might conceivably be consistent with the fiscal standards approach proposed in this paper, so long as the decisions on whether the deficit ratio is "close" (enough) to the reference value and on whether the debt ratio is "sufficiently diminishing and approaching the reference value at a satisfactory pace" are governed by the type of stochastic debt sustainability analysis and other methods discussed in this paper'.

imbalances under Regulation 1176/2011, brought together in the European Semester, which is the EU's cycle of economic, fiscal, labour, and social policy coordination (on the European Semester, see Eihmanis, Chapter 16 in this volume), but there are also normative cross-references in the texts of the respective Regulations. At a broader level, it should be noted that the main fiscal externalities in the EMU are demand and debt (or insolvency) externalities. However, the EU fiscal rules principally focus on debt externalities. 'Demand externality has been less prominent, although it becomes more relevant when the ECB's policy rate is close to its effective lower bound, leading to clearer effects through the overall fiscal stance' (EU Independent Fiscal Institutions, 2021, p. 7; see also Martin et al., 2021, p. 5). Regulation 1176/2011 could play a useful role in targeting demand externalities. There are limits to what the EU fiscal rules in and of themselves can do, and their interaction with other instruments in the EU fiscal and economic governance framework is arguably very important. To be sure, it should be noted that demand externalities may also be addressed by common borrowing at EU level (see also Blanchard et al., 2021, p. 23). This is precisely what is happening with Next Generation EU, which also aims to avoid an insuperable increase in national debt levels.

17.6 REFORMING THE EU FISCAL RULES: THE LEGAL DIMENSION

Having examined some of the key reform proposals, we now turn to consider what would be required from a legal perspective in order to reform the EU framework for fiscal coordination and surveillance. As has been the case throughout this contribution, the main emphasis will be on the reform of the EU fiscal rules, as the core element of the EU fiscal and economic governance framework on which the ongoing policy debate principally focuses.

The following considerations are informed by an understanding of what would be politically feasible in the current environment. From a legal standpoint, the key elements to consider with respect to the reform of the EU fiscal and economic governance framework are as follows:

(i) There must be a legal basis (or legal bases) on the basis of which the desired changes could be made to secondary EU law.
(ii) The desired precepts to be laid down in secondary law must be in conformity with primary EU law.
(iii) Wherever changes to primary EU law are needed, it should ideally be possible to amend primary EU law without an ordinary Treaty revision, due to the legal and political constraints that the latter option would entail.
(iv) The changes to be made to the EU fiscal and economic governance framework should ideally not require an amendment of intergovernmental treaties signed by the EU Member States, such as the Fiscal Compact. Alternatively, such instruments could be incorporated into EU law and then amended on that occasion.

As regards points (i) and (ii), changes to the relevant rules and procedures are legally possible by means of amending secondary EU law, insofar as the relevant rules and procedures are not enshrined in the EU Treaties. As a general remark, it is rightly argued that:

> a lot is already feasible by mere legislative reform under the current framework of the Treaties, relying on the legal bases of the SGP, namely Articles 121(6) and 126(14) of the ... TFEU... Primary law is less a constraint than it is often depicted as being, and the comprehensive reform of the SGP passed in the aftermath of the euro area crisis with the Six-Pack and Two-Pack is clear testament to this. (Dermine, 2022a, p. 411)

More specifically, as regards the preventive arm of the SGP, the rules (and procedures) on both the MTO and the 'expenditure benchmark' could be amended or replaced by means of the ordinary legislative procedure. When Regulation 1466/97 was last amended, the relevant Regulation (Regulation 1175/2011) was based on Article 121(6) TFEU, which provides that the European Parliament and the Council of the EU, acting by means of regulations in accordance with the ordinary legislative procedure, may adopt detailed rules for the multilateral surveillance procedure referred to in Article 121(3)–(4) TFEU. The same legal basis could be utilized, and the same procedure would be followed, for any future amendments to the preventive arm of the SGP.

As regards the corrective arm of the SGP, it will be recalled that Regulation 1467/97 lays down inter alia the 'debt reduction benchmark' which determines whether the ratio of the government debt to GDP shall be considered as sufficiently diminishing and approaching the reference value at a satisfactory pace in accordance with Article 126(2)(b) TFEU. Various reform proposals have highlighted the need that this rule be adjusted. In terms of the legal basis to be utilized for changes to the corrective arm of the SGP, it should be noted that:

> Regulation 1467/97 was adopted on the basis of the second subparagraph of Article 104c of the Treaty establishing the European Community (TEC) (now Article 126 TFEU) even though it was not formally replacing the Protocol but only 'speeding up and clarifying the implementation of the excessive deficit procedure'. The Council took the view that this Regulation constitute[d] a kind of supra-legislative act whose provisions 'constitute, together with those of Protocol (No 5) [today: Protocol No 12] to the Treaty, a new integrated set of rules'. For that reason, when as part of the 'six-pack' it was decided to amend this regulation, the same procedure requiring unanimity with the Council was followed. (Keppenne, 2020b, pp. 828–829)

And indeed, Regulation 1177/2011, which amended Regulation 1467/97, was based on the *second* subparagraph of Article 126(14) TFEU, which requires that the Council of the EU act unanimously in accordance with a special legislative procedure and after consulting the European Parliament and the ECB. The *third* subparagraph of Article 126(14) TFEU, according to which, 'Subject to the other provisions of this paragraph, the Council shall, on a proposal from the Commission and after consulting the European Parliament, lay down detailed rules and definitions for the application of the provisions of the said Protocol', was not used for the adoption of Regulation 1177/2011. Accordingly, the decisional hurdles involved in making changes to Regulation 1467/97, as is currently in force, would be high.

Any changes to Regulation 1176/2011 on the prevention and correction of macroeconomic imbalances, notably in order to strengthen the macroeconomic imbalance procedure and/or its link with the remainder of the fiscal and economic governance framework, could also be accommodated within secondary EU law, provided that point (ii) above is kept well in mind, namely that the relevant precepts would be in conformity with primary EU law (on the latter point, see also Dullien et al., 2021, p. 29). Regulation 1176/2011 was adopted on the basis of Article 121(6) TFEU, which provides, as we have seen, that the European Parliament and the Council of the EU, acting by means of regulations in accordance with the ordinary legislative procedure, may adopt detailed rules for the multilateral surveillance procedure referred to in Article 121(3)–(4) TFEU. The European Parliament and the Council of the EU could draw on the same legal basis in order to amend Regulation 1176/2011. As regards the scoreboard of indicators and their indicative thresholds (where these exist) used by the Commission for the identification and monitoring of imbalances, these could be changed by the Commission, in close cooperation with the European Parliament and the Council (see Regulation 1176/2011,

Article 4(7) and preamble recital 12; see also Flynn, 2020, p. 859 fn 39), without the need to amend Regulation 1176/2011, provided that the changes to the indicators, thresholds, and methodology used would not contradict the provisions of Regulation 1176/2011. If the latter was not true, it would also be necessary to modify Regulation 1176/2011 accordingly. Depending on the nature of the proposed changes, strengthening the relationship between the SGP and Regulation 1176/2011 may of course also require changes in the SGP itself (and not only in Regulation 1176/2011), in line with the procedures that were described earlier. For example, we have seen that the Commission, when preparing a report under Article 126(3) TFEU, shall take into account, inter alia, 'the implementation of policies in the context of the prevention and correction of excessive macroeconomic imbalances' (Regulation 1467/97, Article 2(3)(b)). However, there is no similar explicit reference in the preventive arm of the SGP: 'The preventive arm of the SGP does not contain a comparable obligation to consider efforts to implement the [macroeconomic imbalance procedure] when assessing the compliance with the MTO and the adjustment path towards it' (Dullien et al., 2021, p. 30).[23]

As regards point (iii) above, not all changes to primary EU law would require following an arduous process of Treaty revision (see Article 48 TEU). Protocol (No.12) on the excessive deficit procedure, which contains the reference values on which the deficit and debt criteria are based, may be replaced by provisions adopted by the Council of the EU, acting unanimously in accordance with a special legislative procedure and after consulting the European Parliament and the ECB (second subparagraph of Article 126(14) TFEU). In other words, there is no need for an ordinary or simplified revision of the EU Treaties in order to replace the Protocol, notwithstanding the fact that it forms part of primary EU law. It would obviously not be an easy feat to overcome these decisional hurdles, but at the very least the Pandora's box of treaty revision would not be opened.

Other changes to EU primary law not covered by the possibilities outlined above would presumably require a treaty revision. For example, depending on the precise modalities (including the enforcement of the proposed norms, for that matter), the implementation of the proposal made by Blanchard et al. (2021) would require a revision of the EU Treaties. It will be recalled that Blanchard et al. (2021) propose the abandonment of fiscal rules in favour of fiscal standards, i.e. qualitative prescriptions that leave room for judgement, together with a process to decide whether the standards are met. According to their proposal, there would be country-specific assessments using stochastic debt sustainability analysis, led by national independent fiscal councils and/or the European Commission. According to their preferences, disputes between Member States and the European Commission on the application of these standards should be adjudicated by an independent institution such as the Court of Justice of the EU (CJEU) or by a new, designated body, rather than by the Council of the EU. They explicitly propose removing paragraphs 3–10 from Article 126 TFEU and allowing for infringement proceedings (currently not permitted by Article 126(10) TFEU). Some aspects of the proposed reforms may even

[23] In turn, Regulation 1176/2011 provides that the Commission's in-depth review for Member States that it considers may be affected by, or may be at risk of being affected by, imbalances shall, in particular, take into account Council recommendations or invitations addressed to the Member State concerned within the framework of the European Semester (adopted in accordance with Articles 121, 126, and 148 TFEU and under Articles 6, 7, 8, and 10 of this Regulation), as well as the policy intentions of the Member State concerned, as reflected in its national reform programmes and, where appropriate, in its stability or convergence programme (Regulation 1176/2011, Article 5(2)(a)–(b)). In practice, instruments adopted under the Excessive Deficit Procedure may refer to guidance received in the context of non-fiscal surveillance (see e.g. Flynn, 2020, pp. 868–869, who refers to the example of the Article 126(9) TFEU notice to Portugal in 2016). 'Thus economic policy guidance provided under Article 121 TFEU and under Regulation (EU) 1176/2011 ties back to the fiscal surveillance mechanisms' (Flynn, 2020, p. 869).

require changes in *national constitutions*. This would be if, for example, according to their assessment, a specific independent entity – either a national independent fiscal institution or an EU entity – is given significant power in the national budget approval process (Blanchard et al., 2021, pp. 26–27). It is naturally beyond the scope of this contribution to assess the constitutional constraints that would be involved in making changes to the EU fiscal and economic governance framework in all twenty-seven EU Member States, which could nevertheless only be judged on the basis of the precise modalities of the proposed reforms.

A *simplified* Treaty revision remains an option for amending provisions of Part Three of the TFEU relating to the internal policies and action of the Union (Articles 26–197 TFEU), which includes the provisions on EMU (Articles 119–144 TFEU) (see also Maduro et al., 2021, p. 14 fn 24). More specifically, Article 48(6) TEU provides that the government of any Member State, the European Parliament, or the Commission may submit to the European Council proposals for revising all or part of the provisions of Part Three of the TFEU relating to the internal policies and action of the Union. The European Council may adopt a decision amending all or part of the provisions of Part Three of the TFEU. It shall act by unanimity after consulting the European Parliament and the Commission, and the ECB in the case of institutional changes in the monetary area. That decision shall not enter into force until it is approved by the Member States in accordance with their respective constitutional requirements. Apart from these procedural hurdles, there is further a number of strings attached to the possibility of a simplified treaty revision. As Article 48(6) TEU provides, that European Council decision must not increase the competences conferred on the Union in the Treaties. The CJEU has also stressed in its case law that the amendments decided upon must concern only Part Three of the TFEU, which implies that they do not entail any amendment of provisions of another part of the Treaties on which the EU is founded; and that they must not increase the competences of the Union. A simplified revision of the EU Treaties must therefore not affect other parts of the TFEU or encroach on competences of the Union as laid down in those other treaty parts. The CJEU has jurisdiction to examine compliance with these conditions (Case C-370/12, *Pringle*, paras. 29–76).

As regards point (iv) above, it is certainly legally possible to amend the Fiscal Compact (see also the assessment by the European Stability Mechanism, 2021, pp. 22–23), although the recent experience with the reform of the ESM Treaty shows that this could lead to a protracted negotiation and ratification process that is, in the case of the ESM reform, still pending. It is further possible to integrate the Fiscal Compact into EU law, as already envisaged by that treaty (Article 16), and then amend it on this occasion. The Commission had in the past submitted a legislative proposal to that end (European Commission, 2017; see Craig and Markakis, 2020, pp. 1409–13). It will be recalled that the Fiscal Compact provides for a 'balanced budget rule' that is in some cases stricter than the preventive arm of the SGP (Article 3(1)). It 'shall take effect in the national law of the Contracting Parties ... through provisions of binding force and permanent character, preferably constitutional, or otherwise guaranteed to be fully respected and adhered to throughout the national budgetary processes' (Article 3(2)). The Contracting Parties are also required to put in place at national level a correction mechanism to be triggered automatically in the event of significant observed deviations from the MTO or the adjustment path towards it, which shall include the obligation to implement measures to correct the deviations over a defined period of time (Article 3(2)). In case changes were made to the Fiscal Compact, those national provisions would need to be amended accordingly. The Fiscal Compact also mentions (and overlaps with) other provisions of the EU fiscal and economic governance framework, such as the 'debt reduction benchmark' (Article 4).

Incorporating such provisions into EU law and then amending them – as the case may be – on that occasion would be the current author's preferred option, as it would strengthen the internal consistency, transparency, and simplicity of the framework (on the desirable features of fiscal rules, see further European Fiscal Board, 2018, pp. 74–77; Kopits and Symansky, 1998). In case the Fiscal Compact was not modified in accordance with any changes that would be made to the EU fiscal and economic governance framework, the relevant treaty provides that it shall be applied and interpreted in conformity with the EU Treaties and law (Article 2(1)); and that it shall apply insofar as it is compatible with the EU Treaties and law (Article 2(2)). It is further provided that the balanced budget rule and the correction mechanism shall be applied in addition and without prejudice to the Contracting Parties' obligations under EU law (Article 3 (1)) (for a view on this, see also Dullien et al., 2021, pp. v–vi, 5, 20).

Last but definitely not least, the possibility of *legal challenges* brought before the EU (or even national) courts against any reforms implemented in the future, whether to EU or non-EU rules, should not be neglected either. After all, the various legal challenges brought against the EU's response to the financial and sovereign debt crisis (on which, see e.g. Hinarejos, 2020b; Markakis, 2020a, esp. chs. 8–9) are 'exhibit a' in our case. 'Whilst so far these legal disputes have, for the most part, been resolved in a manner that allowed those initiatives to be preserved, their recurrence signals that the process of adapting the EU policy system within the framework of the existing Treaties may be close to reaching its limits' (Maduro et al., 2021, p. 2). Any reform efforts in the future have to be mindful of those legal limits.

17.7 CONCLUDING REMARKS

This chapter has traced the evolution of the EU fiscal and economic governance framework since the eurozone crisis and outlined the key provisions of the EU Treaties and secondary law (notably, the SGP). We have seen that this framework has been subject to various criticisms. The existing rule book has grown excessively complex. Key features of the current framework were designed for a different macroeconomic environment and, dare we say, for a much different world. This framework has often given rise to procyclical effects (and/or not prevented procyclicality in national fiscal policies) and, especially after the COVID-19 crisis, the fiscal targets it sets could be said to be economically unrealistic. There is further a need to incentivize public investment, also in light of the EU's priorities regarding the green and digital twin transition. Depending on one's perspective, this list of 'flaws' or challenges facing the existing framework could go on. The proposals put forward thus far seek to achieve multiple objectives. To be sure, this is not a criticism of the proposals. It is instead meant to highlight that the various reform blueprints acknowledge the complexity of the world we currently live in and seek to address the various challenges facing the EU fiscal and economic governance framework as well as national fiscal and economic policies. Another key aspect is that whilst the various reform proposals advanced often converge on their diagnosis of the current macroeconomic environment and the weak points of the existing legal and institutional framework, they can diverge quite considerably when it comes to the nature of the proposed solution. The extent of their reform ambition is also determinative of the legal difficulties that would obtain when implementing the desired precepts.

This chapter has sought to shed light on the legal engineering that would be required to reform the EU's fiscal and economic governance framework, whether the relevant rules are enshrined in primary or secondary EU law or in international treaties. We have advanced the view that the legal complexities involved are not prohibitive of those reform ambitions, although in some cases the decisional hurdles involved would be quite high. Last but definitely not least, it should not be forgotten that a reform of the EU fiscal rules is only part of the puzzle of 'completing' or 'deepening' the EMU. It is rightly noted that 'we should be mindful of the limitations of any fiscal framework that relies exclusively on co-ordination of national fiscal policies in the absence of a meaningful fiscal capacity at the central level', and that 'arrangements for surveillance and co-ordination of national fiscal policies will always be limited in what they can achieve; their reform should be part of a more ambitious EMU reform that includes the creation of a permanent fiscal capacity for the EU or the euro area' (Hinarejos, 2021, p. 128). This aspect is not lost on the (vast majority of) reform proposals adumbrated above. A comprehensive reform of EMU should further include other key elements, such as the completion of the Banking Union and making progress towards the Capital Markets Union (Craig and Markakis, 2020; Markakis, 2020a, ch. 9).

REFERENCES

Adamski, D. (2018). *Redefining European Economic Integration*. Cambridge: Cambridge University Press.

Amtenbrink, F. (2014). General report. In U. Neergaard, C. Jacqueson, and J. Hartig Danielsen (eds.), *The Economic and Monetary Union: Constitutional and Institutional Aspects of the Economic Governance within the EU. The XXVI FIDE Congress in Copenhagen 2014, Congress Publications Vol. 1*. Copenhagen: Djøf Publishing, pp. 73–178.

Amtenbrink, F., and Markakis, M. (in press). Never waste a good crisis: On the emergence of an EU fiscal capacity. In A. Hinarejos and R. Schütze (eds.), *EU Fiscal Federalism: Past, Present, Future*. Oxford: Oxford University Press.

Amtenbrink, F., and Repasi, R. (2017). Compliance and enforcement in economic policy coordination in EMU. In A. Jakab and D. Kochenov (eds.), *The Enforcement of EU Law and Values: Ensuring Member States' Compliance*. Oxford: Oxford University Press, pp. 145–181.

Bénassy-Quéré, A., and Wolff, G. (2020). How has the macroeconomic imbalances procedure worked in practice to improve the resilience of the euro area? (Study for the European Parliament's Committee on Economic and Monetary Affairs). www.europarl.europa.eu/RegData/etudes/STUD/2020/645710/IPOL_STU(2020)645710_EN.pdf

Bénassy-Quéré, A., Brunnermeier, M., Enderlein, H., Farhi, E., Fratzscher, M., Fuest, C., Gourinchas, P.-O., Martin, P., Pisani-Ferry, J., Rey, H., Schnabel, I., Véron, N., Weder di Mauro, B., and Zettelmeyer, J. (2018). Reconciling risk sharing with market discipline: A constructive approach to euro area reform (Centre for Economic Policy Research Policy Insight No. 91). https://cepr.org/publications/policy-insight-91-reconciling-risk-sharing-market-discipline-constructive-approach

Blanchard, O., Leandro, Á., and Zettelmeyer, J. (2021). Redesigning EU fiscal rules: From rules to standards (Peterson Institute for International Economics Working Paper No. 21-1). www.piie.com/publications/working-papers/redesigning-eu-fiscal-rules-rules-standards

Brunnermeir, M. K., James, H., and Landau, J.-P. (2016). *The Euro and the Battle of Ideas*. Princeton, NJ: Princeton University Press.

CEPS Think Tank. (2021). CEPS/Intereconomics conference: Redesigning EU Fiscal Rules after COVID-19 [Video file]. 30 November. www.youtube.com/watch?v=Rj7mE-GIdAM&ab_channel=CEPSThinkTank

Council of the European Union (2016). Improving the assessment of effective action in the context of the excessive deficit procedure – A specification of the methodology (Opinion of the Economic and Financial Committee). https://data.consilium.europa.eu/doc/document/ST-14813-2016-INIT/en/pdf

Council of the European Union (2017). Revised specifications on the implementation of the Stability and Growth Pact and Guidelines on the format and content of Stability and Convergence Programmes (Code of Conduct of the Stability and Growth Pact). https://data.consilium.europa.eu/doc/document/ST-9344-2017-INIT/en/pdf

Council of the European Union (2020). Statement of EU Ministers of Finance on the Stability and Growth Pact in light of the COVID-19 crisis. 23 March. www.consilium.europa.eu/en/press/

press-releases/2020/03/23/statement-of-eu-ministers-of-finance-on-the-stability-and-growth-pact-in-light-of-the-covid-19-crisis/

Craig, P., and Markakis, M. (2020). EMU reform. In F. Amtenbrink and C. Herrmann (eds.), assisted by R. Repasi, *The EU Law of Economic and Monetary Union*. Oxford: Oxford University Press, pp. 1400–1448.

Dermine, P. (2020). The EU's response to the COVID-19 crisis and the trajectory of fiscal integration in Europe: Between continuity and rupture. *Legal Issues of Economic Integration* 47(4), 337–358.

Dermine, P. (2022a). Fiscal surveillance and coordination in post-pandemic times – between uncertainty and opportunity. www.ecb.europa.eu/pub/pdf/other/ecb.ecblegalconferenceproceedings202204~c2e5739756.en.pdf

Dermine, P. (2022b). *The New Economic Governance of the Eurozone: A Rule of Law Analysis*. Cambridge: Cambridge University Press.

Dullien, S., Paetz, C., Repasi, R., Watt, A., and Watzka, S. (2021). Between high ambition and pragmatism: Proposals for a reform of fiscal rules without treaty change (Study for the European Economic and Social Committee). www.eesc.europa.eu/fi/our-work/publications-other-work/publications/between-high-ambition-and-pragmatism-proposals-reform-fiscal-rules-without-treaty-change

EU Independent Fiscal Institutions (2021). EU Fiscal and Economic Governance Review: A contribution from the Network of Independent EU Fiscal Institutions. www.euifis.eu/publications/6

European Commission (2016). Stability and Growth Pact: Council adopts recommendations on Spain and Portugal. https://ec.europa.eu/commission/presscorner/detail/en/IP_16_2761

European Commission (2017). Proposal for a Council Directive laying down provisions for strengthening fiscal responsibility and the medium-term budgetary orientation in the Member States (COM(2017) 824 final). https://ec.europa.eu/info/sites/default/files/economy-finance/com_824_0.pdf

European Commission (2019). Vade Mecum on the Stability & Growth Pact – 2019 Edition (Institutional Paper No. 101). https://economy-finance.ec.europa.eu/publications/vade-mecum-stability-and-growth-pact-2019-edition_en

European Commission (2020). Economic governance review: Report on the application of Regulations (EU) No 1173/2011, 1174/2011, 1175/2011, 1176/2011, 1177/2011, 472/2013 and 473/2013 and on the suitability of Council Directive 2011/85/EU (COM(2020) 55 final). https://ec.europa.eu/info/sites/default/files/economy-finance/com_2020_55_en.pdf

European Commission (2021). Questions and answers: Commission relaunches the review of EU economic governance. https://ec.europa.eu/commission/presscorner/detail/en/qanda_21_5322

European Commission (2022a). Commission presents fiscal policy guidance for 2023. https://ec.europa.eu/commission/presscorner/detail/en/ip_22_1476

European Commission (2022b). Economic Governance Review – Summary report of the public consultation. https://ec.europa.eu/info/files/economic-governance-review-summary-report-public-consultation_en

European Commission (n.d.a). Significant Deviation Procedure. https://economy-finance.ec.europa.eu/economic-and-fiscal-governance/stability-and-growth-pact/preventive-arm/significant-deviation-procedure_en

European Commission (n.d.b). Stability and Growth Pact. https://ec.europa.eu/info/business-economy-euro/economic-and-fiscal-policy-coordination/eu-economic-governance-monitoring-prevention-correction/stability-and-growth-pact_en

European Court of Auditors (2016). Further improvements needed to ensure effective implementation of the Excessive Deficit Procedure (Special Report No. 10/2016). www.eca.europa.eu/Lists/ECADocuments/SR16_10/SR_EDP_EN.pdf

European Court of Auditors (2018a). Audit of the Macroeconomic Imbalance Procedure (MIP) (Special Report No. 03/2018). www.eca.europa.eu/Lists/ECADocuments/SR18_03/SR_MIP_EN.pdf

European Court of Auditors (2018b). Is the main objective of the preventive arm of the Stability and Growth Pact delivered? (Special Report No. 18/2018). www.eca.europa.eu/Lists/ECADocuments/SR18_18/SR_EUROPEAN_SEMESTER_EN.pdf

European Court of Auditors (2019). EU requirements for national budgetary frameworks: need to further strengthen them and to better monitor their application (Special Report No. 22/2019). www.eca.europa.eu/Lists/ECADocuments/SR19_22/SR_Fiscal_Stability_EN.pdf

European Fiscal Board (2018). Annual Report 2018. https://ec.europa.eu/info/sites/default/files/2018-efb-annual-report_en.pdf

European Fiscal Board (2019a). Assessment of EU fiscal rules with a focus on the six and two-pack legislation. https://ec.europa.eu/info/sites/default/files/2019-09-10-assessment-of-eu-fiscal-rules_en.pdf

European Fiscal Board (2019b). Annual Report 2019. https://ec.europa.eu/info/sites/default/files/2019-efb-annual-report_en.pdf

European Fiscal Board (2020). Annual Report 2020. https://ec.europa.eu/info/sites/default/files/efb_annual_report_2020_en_1.pdf

European Fiscal Board (2021). Annual Report 2021. https://ec.europa.eu/info/sites/default/files/annual_report_2021_efb_en_1.pdf

European Stability Mechanism. (2021). EU fiscal rules: Reform considerations. ESM Discussion Paper No. 17. www.esm.europa.eu/publications/eu-fiscal-rules-reform-considerations

European Stability Mechanism (2022). ESM conference on deepening EMU. Summary of proceedings. www.esm.europa.eu/system/files/document/2022-02/2022-01-24%20ESM%20conference%20summary%20of%20proceedings.pdf

Federal Ministry for Economic Affairs and Climate Action (2022). Proposed principles to guide the German government in deliberations on the reform of EU fiscal rules. www.bmwk.de/Redaktion/EN/Downloads/P/proposed-principles-to-guide-the-german-government-in-deliberations-on-the-reform-of-eu-fiscal-rules.html

Flynn, L. (2020). Non-fiscal surveillance of the Member States. In F. Amtenbrink and C. Herrmann (eds.), assisted by R. Repasi, *The EU Law of Economic and Monetary Union*. Oxford: Oxford University Press, pp. 850–877.

Government of the Netherlands (2022). Spain and The Netherlands call for a renewed EU Fiscal Framework fit for current and future challenges. www.government.nl/latest/news/2022/04/04/spain-and-the-netherlands-call-for-a-renewed-eu-fiscal-framework-fit-for-current-and-future-challenges

Hagelstam, K., and De Lemos Peixoto, S. (2022). Implementation of the Stability and Growth Pact under pandemic times. European Parliament, Economic Governance Support Unit. www.europarl.europa.eu/RegData/etudes/IDAN/2022/699510/IPOL_IDA(2022)699510_EN.pdf

Hinarejos, A. (2020a). Economic and Monetary Union. In C. Barnard and S. Peers (eds.), *European Union Law*, 3rd ed. Oxford: Oxford University Press, pp. 583–611.

Hinarejos, A. (2020b). The legality of responses to the crisis. In F. Amtenbrink and C. Herrmann (eds.), assisted by R. Repasi, *The EU Law of Economic and Monetary Union*. Oxford: Oxford University Press, pp. 1363–1399.

Hinarejos, A. (2021). Economic governance and the pandemic: A year on. *European Law Review* 46(2), 127–128.

Hinarejos, A., and Schütze, R. (eds.) (in press). *EU Fiscal Federalism: Past, Present, Future*. Oxford: Oxford University Press.

Jahan, S., and Saber Mahmud, A. (2013). What is the output gap? *Finance & Development* 50(3), 38–39.

Keppenne, J.-P. (2014). Institutional report. In U. Neergaard, C. Jacqueson, and J. Hartig Danielsen (eds.), *The Economic and Monetary Union: Constitutional and Institutional Aspects of the Economic Governance within the EU. The XXVI FIDE Congress in Copenhagen 2014, Congress Publications Vol. 1*. Copenhagen: Djøf Publishing, pp. 179–257.

Keppenne, J.-P. (2020a). Economic policy coordination: Foundations, structures, and objectives. In F. Amtenbrink and C. Herrmann (eds.), assisted by R. Repasi, *The EU Law of Economic and Monetary Union*. Oxford: Oxford University Press, pp. 787–812.

Keppenne, J.-P. (2020b). EU fiscal governance on the Member States: The Stability and Growth Pact and beyond. In F. Amtenbrink and C. Herrmann (eds.), assisted by R. Repasi, *The EU Law of Economic and Monetary Union*. Oxford: Oxford University Press, pp. 813–849.

Kopits, G., and Symansky, S. A. (1998). Fiscal policy rules. IMF Occasional Paper No. 1998/011. www.imf.org/en/Publications/Occasional-Papers/Issues/2016/12/30/Fiscal-Policy-Rules-2608

Maduro, M., Martin, P., Piris, J.-C., Pisani-Ferry, J., Reichlin, L., Steinbach, A., and Weder di Mauro, B. (2021). Revisiting the EU framework: Economic necessities and legal options. Centre for Economic Policy Research Policy Insight No. 114. https://cepr.org/active/publications/policy_insights/viewpi.php?pino=114

Markakis, M. (2020a). *Accountability in the Economic and Monetary Union: Foundations, Policy, and Governance*. Oxford: Oxford University Press.

Markakis, M. (2020b). The reform of the European Stability Mechanism: Process, substance, and the pandemic. *Legal Issues of Economic Integration* 47(4), 359–384.
Martin, P., Pisani-Ferry, J., and Ragot, X. (2021). Reforming the European Fiscal Framework (Les notes du conseil d'analyse économique, no. 63, April 2021). www.cae-eco.fr/en/pour-une-refonte-du-cadre-budgetaire-europeen
Thirion, G. (2017). European Fiscal Union: Economic rationale and design challenges. CEPS Working Document No. 2017/01. www.ceps.eu/ceps-publications/european-fiscal-union-economic-rationale-and-design-challenges/
Vallée, S. (2022). A German Proposal That May Finally Break the EU Fiscal Rules Stalemate. https://dgap.org/en/research/publications/german-proposal-may-finally-break-eu-fiscal-rules-stalemate.

Council Regulation (EC) 1466/97 of 7 July 1997 on the strengthening of the surveillance of budgetary positions and the surveillance and coordination of economic policies [1997] OJ L209/1.
Council Regulation (EC) 1467/97 of 7 July 1997 on speeding up and clarifying the implementation of the excessive deficit procedure [1997] OJ L209/6.
Resolution of the European Council on the Stability and Growth Pact Amsterdam, 17 June 1997 [1997] OJ C236/1.
Regulation (EU) 1173/2011 of the European Parliament and of the Council of 16 November 2011 on the effective enforcement of budgetary surveillance in the euro area [2011] OJ L306/1.
Regulation (EU) 1174/2011 of the European Parliament and of the Council of 16 November 2011 on enforcement measures to correct excessive macroeconomic imbalances in the euro area [2011] OJ L306/8.
Regulation (EU) 1175/2011 of the European Parliament and of the Council of 16 November 2011 amending Council Regulation (EC) No 1466/97 on the strengthening of the surveillance of budgetary positions and the surveillance and coordination of economic policies [2011] OJ L306/12.
Regulation (EU) 1176/2011 of the European Parliament and of the Council of 16 November 2011 on the prevention and correction of macroeconomic imbalances [2011] OJ L306/25.
Council Regulation (EU) 1177/2011 of 8 November 2011 amending Regulation (EC) No 1467/97 on speeding up and clarifying the implementation of the excessive deficit procedure [2011] OJ L306/33.
Council Directive 2011/85/EU of 8 November 2011 on requirements for budgetary frameworks of the Member States [2011] OJ L306/41.
Regulation (EU) 472/2013 of the European Parliament and of the Council of 21 May 2013 on the strengthening of economic and budgetary surveillance of Member States in the euro area experiencing or threatened with serious difficulties with respect to their financial stability [2013] OJ L140/1.
Regulation (EU) 473/2013 of the European Parliament and of the Council of 21 May 2013 on common provisions for monitoring and assessing draft budgetary plans and ensuring the correction of excessive deficit of the Member States in the euro area [2013] OJ L140/11.
Communication from the Commission, Making the best use of the flexibility within the existing rules of the Stability and Growth Pact. COM(2015) 12 final.
Communication from the Commission to the Council on the activation of the general escape clause of the Stability and Growth Pact. COM(2020) 123 final.
European Parliament resolution of 24 June 2015 on the review of the economic governance framework: stocktaking and challenges (2014/2145(INI)) [2016] OJ C407/86.
European Parliament resolution of 8 July 2021 on the review of the macroeconomic legislative framework for a better impact on Europe's real economy and improved transparency of decision-making and democratic accountability (2020/2075(INI)) [2022] OJ C99/191.
Treaty on Stability, Coordination and Governance in the Economic and Monetary Union. https://eur-lex.europa.eu/legal-content/EN/TXT/PDF/?uri=CELEX:42012A0302(01)&from=EN
Case C-27/04 (Full Court), *Commission of the European Communities* v. *Council of the European Union*, EU:C:2004:436.
Case C-370/12 (Full Court), *Thomas Pringle* v. *Government of Ireland and Others*, EU:C:2012:756.

18

National Fiscal Policy in EMU

Insufficient Sustainability and Stabilization?

Jakob de Haan and Bram Gootjes

18.1 INTRODUCTION

Whereas monetary policy in the European Economic and Monetary Union (EMU) is conducted at the supranational level, fiscal policy has remained the competence of national governments. Still, EMU implies constraints on national fiscal policy. According to the European Central Bank (ECB), a well-functioning monetary union requires Member States to maintain fiscal discipline (ECB, 2011). Large deficits can give rise to inflationary pressures that may force the ECB to keep short-term interest rates higher than would otherwise be necessary. Furthermore, unsustainable fiscal policies may undermine confidence in the ECB's monetary policy if markets come to expect that excessive government borrowing will ultimately be financed through money creation. In such a fiscal dominance regime, the central bank has to adjust its policies to the financial position of the government, thus abandoning price stability. Another rationale for constraints on national fiscal policies in a monetary union is that unsustainable fiscal dynamics in one Member State may entail costs borne by all Member States (Buti and Carnot, 2012).

Apart from maintaining sustainability, fiscal policymakers may aim for economic stabilization. That is, it should be contractionary in good times and expansionary in bad times to dampen business cycle fluctuations. With the creation of EMU, Member States abandoned domestic monetary and exchange rate policies to respond to country-specific shocks, so that fiscal policy is the only tool available for macroeconomic stabilization at the national level. In practice, however, fiscal policies often amplified business cycle fluctuations, i.e. these policies were procyclical. This experience meant that the reputation of countercyclical fiscal policy in the economics profession reached a low point around 1990. However, nowadays, economists have a much more positive view about the use of fiscal policy for stabilization purposes (EFB, 2019), no doubt also because of the experiences during the recent COVID-19 pandemic. Notably, in a situation where monetary policy increasingly runs out of steam due to the effective lower bound (ELB)[1] on interest rates and the decreasing effectiveness of unconventional policies (Blinder

We would like to thank Dariusz Adamski, Fabian Amtenbrink, and George Kopits for their feedback on a previous version of this chapter and Fleming Zimbalski for his assistance.

[1] Sometimes the lowest possible interest rate level is referred to as zero lower bound (ZLB). However, as the lowest possible policy rate may be negative, we prefer the term effective lower bound. Cutting the interest rate further than the ELB is impossible, as the public would otherwise switch to cash. If the interest rate on a savings account turns negative, i.e. clients have to pay interest for keeping the money at their bank account, at some point it becomes cheaper to keep the money as cash.

et al., 2017), several policymakers have called upon fiscal policy to bring the economy back on track. For instance, then-ECB President Draghi argued in his speech at Jackson Hole in 2014 that: 'it would be helpful if fiscal policy could play a greater role alongside monetary policy, and I believe there is scope for this' (Draghi, 2014). Likewise, in the letter of intent accompanying his 2016 State of the Union address, then-President of the European Commission Juncker endorsed 'a positive fiscal stance for the euro area, in support of the monetary policy of the European Central Bank'. Recent research suggests that fiscal policy is more effective at the ELB than under normal circumstances. For instance, Bonam et al. (2022) find that both the cumulative government consumption and investment multipliers are significantly higher when interest rates are persistently low.

Until recently, the economic stabilization function of national fiscal policy received scant attention among European Union policymakers. Instead, priority was given to maintaining fiscal sustainability. The Maastricht Treaty contains provisions for monitoring and coordinating EU Member States' fiscal policies, which were further specified in the Stability and Growth Pact (SGP) that was adopted in 1997. The SGP contains a preventive arm that prescribes the path for sound fiscal policies, and a corrective arm requiring correction in case of an excessive deficit (initially defined as a budget deficit above the 3 per cent of GDP threshold). Under the preventive arm of the SGP, Member States submit stability or convergence programmes in which they detail their medium-term budgetary plans. Under the original SGP, Member States were required to pursue the medium-term objective of budgetary positions that were 'close to balance or in surplus' (this was changed later; see Section 18.3), thereby allowing automatic stabilizers to operate, with some room for a discretionary countercyclical stance (Kopits, 2018a).[2] The SGP's corrective arm specifies the Excessive Deficit Procedure (EDP). When the Economic and Financial Affairs Council (ECOFIN) decides that a Member State has an excessive deficit, the procedure stipulates a sequence of steps to be taken to intensify pressure on the Member State to take effective action to correct the problem. If a Member State did not take (sufficient) action to redress its deficit, sanctions could be imposed (although this has never happened).

The SGP has been much criticized. One of the main concerns was that these fiscal rules might restrain governments from implementing expansionary policies during downturns, which would make fiscal policy procyclical (Buiter, 2004). In turn, procyclical fiscal policy in one Member State may undermine the sustainability of public finances in other EU members. As EU economies are heavily integrated, fiscal policy in one EU country may have large spillovers to other Member States' economies;[3] these spillovers are generally not internalized (Eyraud et al., 2017). At the same time, the SGP has been criticized for being toothless so that countries do not adhere to its rules (de Haan et al., 2004; Eyraud et al., 2017). But, of course, for corrective fiscal policy measures to be procyclical, Member States have to comply with the rules, to begin with. Therefore, the voiced criticisms do not seem to be completely consistent and warrant further consideration.

[2] Automatic stabilizers are mechanisms built into government budgets that automatically increase government spending or decrease taxes when the economy goes into a recession. For instance, households' tax bills decrease automatically without changes in the tax law or any other new legislation if their incomes drop. Additionally, when people become unemployed, they are eligible for unemployment benefit. As a consequence, households' consumption does not drop substantially due to the recession.

[3] For instance, if government spending drops in one Member State, this will cause a decline in its imports from other Member States.

This chapter reviews the discussion on the effectiveness and reform of the SGP, focusing on fiscal policy sustainability and fiscal policies' contribution to economic stabilization. Section 18.2 provides an overview of the lessons learned from academic research about the design of fiscal rules. Section 18.3 briefly outlines how the European fiscal rules have evolved, while Section 18.4 discusses their effectiveness in maintaining fiscal policy sustainability. Section 18.5 assesses the stance of fiscal policy in EU Member States, also discussing whether fiscal rules imply more procyclical fiscal policies. The final section briefly touches upon the reform of the European fiscal rules (discussed in more detail by Markakis, Chapter 17 in this volume).

18.2 DESIGN OF EFFECTIVE FISCAL RULES

When fiscal policy is left unconstrained, governments tend to run budget deficits and accumulate public debt beyond socially desirable levels (Begg, 2017). This may be caused by a myriad of factors, such as distributional conflicts over government resources, leading to political pressure for increasing public spending (Velasco, 2000). Likewise, incumbents may use fiscal policy to increase their re-election chances (Shi and Svensson, 2006). The incumbent may also incur public debt strategically to tie the hands of its successor (Alesina and Tabellini, 1990; Persson and Svensson, 1989). Such distortions provide a rationale for imposing restrictions on fiscal policy. As pointed out in Section 18.1, in the context of the EMU, fiscal rules are also important because of spillover effects of fiscal imbalances and the risk of fiscal dominance.

Kopits and Symanski (1998, p. 2) describe a fiscal rule as 'a permanent constraint on fiscal policy, typically defined in terms of an indicator of overall fiscal performance', usually relating to the budget balance, government debt, or both, or to aggregate public spending. They go on to stress that a rule 'is intended for application on a permanent basis by successive governments ... [and] to be credible, it must involve commitment over a reasonably long period of time' (see also Schaechter et al., 2012).

There is ample evidence that fiscal rules improve fiscal performance. In a sample of 142 countries, Caselli and Reynaud (2020) find that fiscal rules are associated with lower government budget balances. Gootjes et al. (2021) show that fiscal rules constrain election-motivated manipulation of fiscal policy. However, these studies only find a statistically significant impact of the rules when they are well designed; they should, for example, cover the entire public sector. Asatryan et al. (2018) present evidence that constitutional fiscal rules significantly reduce the probability of experiencing a sovereign debt crisis, but rules with a lower statutory basis do not. Using Monte Carlo simulations, Landon and Smith (2017) find that fiscal rules that set ceilings in cyclically adjusted terms have the highest welfare improving effects compared to baseline discretionary fiscal policy. Guerguil et al. (2017) confirm that fiscal rules that include cyclical adjustment features result in fiscal policy being more countercyclical.

A proper design of fiscal rules is clearly important, but (as the European experience with the SGP has shown) a problem is that the fiscal rules framework may become overly complex (Debrun and Jonung, 2019). In general, the complexity of fiscal rules makes it harder to monitor whether fiscal policy is in line with these rules. For instance, Burret and Feld (2018) show that the effect of the Swiss cantonal fiscal rules is stronger when the budget components targeted by the rules are more specific. Furthermore, as the political system is full of distortive incentives, (complicated) rules may provoke window-dressing measures instead of real budgetary adjustments (Milesi-Ferretti, 2004). Indeed, Koen and van der Noord (2005) and von Hagen and Wolff (2006) discuss early experiences with the SGP criteria and show that EU countries that were about to breach the 3 per cent deficit limit tried to circumvent the rule by one-off measures and creative accounting. The likelihood that governments will not adhere to fiscal rules depends on the punishment for violating the rules (e.g. financial, political, or reputational costs) and the ability to detect such violations. The latter, in turn, depends on the size of creative accounting and the degree of fiscal transparency (Milesi-Ferretti, 2004). Some studies indeed suggest that the transparency of fiscal policy enhances the effectiveness of fiscal rules. Alt et al. (2014) show that the SGP rules induced gimmicks in public finance statistics (attempts to improve the government budget that do not have a real effect on the underlying fiscal position), but only in low-transparency environments. Therefore, the appeal of gimmicks seems conditional on the degree of budget transparency, as more transparency increases the probability of detection by auditors, bond markets, and society. Gootjes and de Haan (2022b) report that the effect of fiscal rules is dependent on budget transparency. Using a panel of seventy-three advanced and developing economies, these authors find that fiscal rules need budget transparency to lower budget deficits. In addition, they show that fiscal rules trigger fiscal consolidations and make the success of these fiscal adjustments more likely, but only in countries with sufficiently high levels of transparency.

Finally, empirical evidence suggests that independent fiscal councils – institutions entrusted with a watchdog role over public finances – foster compliance with fiscal rules (Beetsma et al., 2019) and improve the effect of fiscal rules on the government budget (Maltritz and Wüste, 2015).

18.3 EUROPEAN FISCAL RULES

In the original Maastricht set-up of EMU, the single monetary policy is complemented by decentralized fiscal policies that are governed by fiscal rules and a no-bailout clause as a further deterrent to lack of fiscal discipline. However, the Maastricht Treaty is not specific on the definition of fiscal imbalances and the targets for fiscal policy. These issues were arranged in the SGP that consists of two regulations: (i) *the preventive arm* (Council Regulation (EC) No. 1466/97), which aims to ensure sound budgetary policies over the medium term; and (ii) *the corrective arm* (Council Regulation (EC) No. 1467/97), which details the excessive deficit procedure enshrined in Article 126 of the Treaty on the Functioning of the European Union (TFEU) (see Amtenbrink et al., 1997).

In 2005, the SGP was amended to introduce more discretion and flexibility into the surveillance procedures and make the corrective arm slightly more stringent. The amendments included requiring each Member State to present its own country-specific medium-term objective (MTO) in its stability programme. These country-specific objectives may diverge from the 'close to balance'/'in surplus' requirement depending on the current debt ratio and potential growth. The adjustment effort should be greater in good times (i.e. periods where output exceeds its potential level) and could be more limited in bad times. As a benchmark, Member States should pursue an annual adjustment in cyclically adjusted terms, net of one-off and temporary measures, of 0.5 per cent of GDP. Focusing on the cyclically adjusted budget balance was considered necessary to make the rules less procyclical (Larch and Santacrose, 2020).[4] The

[4] The cyclically adjusted budget balance is not directly observable but has to be estimated using the output gap and (semi-)elasticities of various revenue and expenditure categories. The errors in real-time estimates of the output gap can be quite large (Reuter, 2020). Kamps and Leiner-Killinger (2019) show that the euro area aggregate output gap was more favourable than initially forecast in nine of the fourteen years under consideration. Consequently, fiscal consolidation efforts in the euro area proved too low compared to what was identified *ex post* to have been better economic times than thought in real-time. See Reuter (2020) for a further discussion.

amended SGP also places more emphasis on the government debt ratio. This was important, as the ECOFIN had previously only focused on the government budget deficit. In the early days of the SGP, the debt rule did not play much of a role as nominal GDP growth of around 5 per cent per year would imply that countries complying with the deficit rule would eventually also be in line with the debt rule, i.e. a debt-to-GDP ratio of less than 60 per cent (Larch and Santacrose, 2020).

In an attempt to improve the functioning of the SGP, the 'Six-Pack', 'Two-Pack', and 'Fiscal Compact' have amended it. The 'Six-Pack' entered into force in 2011, one of its aims being to strengthen fiscal policy coordination. Under the 'Six-Pack', a Member State will be put in the EDP if the gap between its debt level and the 60 per cent reference is not reduced by one-twentieth annually on average over three years (even if its deficit is below 3 per cent). Due to the lower nominal GDP growth rates, keeping the deficit below 3 per cent of GDP was no longer sufficient to keep the government debt-to-GDP ratio on a downward path (Larch and Santacrose, 2020). Furthermore, an expenditure rule was introduced that puts a maximum on public expenditure growth for Member States that have not reached their MTO. Finally, and perhaps most importantly, Reverse Qualified Majority Voting (RQMV) was introduced. RQMV implies that a Commission recommendation or proposal is considered adopted by the Council unless a qualified majority of Member States votes against it. Whereas the ECOFIN previously had to agree to sanctions by means of a qualified majority, RQMV only allows Member States to oppose the proposed sanctions.

The 'Two-Pack' entered into force in 2013. It consists of two regulations that build on and complement the regulations laid down under 'Six-Pack'. Under the regulations, Member States are required to publish their draft budgetary plans for the coming year. The Commission thereafter has the opportunity to review them and, if necessary, provide guidance on how to alter them to be in line with the requirements of the SGP.

Finally, the 'Fiscal Compact' entered into force on 1 January 2013. Its most important feature is that the signatory countries are committed to implementing the introduction of a close-to-balance or in-surplus fiscal rule in their national legislation. The balanced budget rule can be considered respected if Member States achieve their MTO. The 'Fiscal Compact' establishes a floor for the MTO of a structural budget balance of –0.5 per cent of GDP for countries with debt above 60 per cent of GDP and of –1 per cent of GDP for countries with debt significantly below 60 per cent of GDP. The 'Fiscal Compact' also foresees that Member States commit themselves to proposals or recommendations by the European Commission unless a qualified majority in the ECOFIN opposes them.

In 2015, a matrix of fiscal effort requirements was introduced to apply for countries that have not achieved their MTOs. This matrix granulates the fiscal adjustment needs towards sound fiscal positions according to the size of the country's output gap as well as its debt level. Beyond this, the implementation of the SGP's preventive arm now entails the possibility of lower structural fiscal adjustment requirements in exchange for structural reforms or additional public investment.

In 2017, the European Commission introduced a 'margin of discretion' or 'margin of appreciation' that would further lower structural adjustment requirements under the preventive arm below what the above-mentioned matrix would imply. For 2019, the ECOFIN endorsed Commission recommendations that for some countries lower the structural adjustment requirements below the matrix requirements (Kamps and Leiner-Killinger, 2019).

In view of the COVID-19 pandemic, the European Commission has activated the general escape clause of the SGP for the first time ever. This allowed Member States to implement fiscal stimulus measures to adequately deal with the crisis while departing from the budgetary requirements that would normally apply under the European fiscal framework. The escape clause will last until 2024.

18.4 EFFECTIVENESS OF EUROPEAN FISCAL RULES

Critics of the original SGP pointed to a major weakness of the rules in place, namely that the ECOFIN is responsible for enforcement (Amtenbrink and de Haan, 2003). The ECOFIN ministers will tend to cover their colleagues in order to build credit in case they breach the rules themselves in the future. Furthermore, apart from peer pressure, there is little the ECOFIN can do as financial sanctions are likely to be counterproductive because they will only worsen the economic situation in countries that breached the rules and there may be negative spillovers. And the ECOFIN can only take decisions based on a proposal of the European Commission, which, for political reasons, may decide not to come up with a proposal. A complicating problem is that the European Commission's fiscal forecasts on which ECOFIN decisions are based, turn out to be upward biased if the deficit limit is expected to be binding (Gilbert and de Jong, 2017).

Lack of enforcement is especially problematic in the preventive arm of the framework. Instead of targeting the close-to-balance objective or MTO, it appears that the 3 per cent of GDP deficit reference value has acted as a guidepost for fiscal policies since the SGP took effect (Caselli and Wingender, 2018; Kamps and Leiner-Killinger, 2019). The nominal deficit reference value is a transparent benchmark that is well anchored in public communication and can be monitored rather easily by financial markets and the general public. However, as the deficit hovered around the reference value even in economic good times, cyclical improvements in the budget balance were eaten up by discretionary fiscal loosening. According to Kamps and Leiner-Killinger (2019), several countries aimed to reach the 3 per cent of GDP deficit reference value by the EDP deadline, irrespective of whether they complied with the required structural efforts under the EDP recommendation. 'By allowing for such nominal strategies, the EU's fiscal framework thus inherently favours the 3% of GDP deficit reference value over the fiscal compact's MTO under the SGP's preventive arm, which would call for stronger progress towards achieving sound underlying budgetary positions' (Kamps and Leiner-Killinger, 2019, p. 11).

As they did not create sufficient fiscal space for bad times, Member States regularly exceeded the 3 per cent of GDP deficit reference (see Figure 18.1). In 2003, three large euro area countries (Germany, France, and Italy) were running deficits above the reference value. By the end of 2003, it became clear that especially France and Germany did not manage to reduce their deficit sufficiently. The European Commission therefore proposed to ratchet up the excessive deficit procedure, going to the last stage before a fine could be imposed. However, the Commission's proposal was subsequently voted down by the ECOFIN. According to Gros (2016), this was the first time the SGP died. The second time was in 2016 when the European Commission, despite non-compliance with the rules, cancelled fines for Portugal and Spain. In a press release of 8 August, the ECOFIN stated that it agreed (Begg, 2017). Still, the situation in 2016 was different than in 2003. Under the revised SGP, the Commission had the right to recommend fines of up to 0.2 per cent of GDP on any Member State that had failed to reduce its budget deficit and to bring it gradually back down, to below 3 per cent of GDP. The ECOFIN never voted about this proposal, as the Commission decided to 'cancel' the fine against both countries.

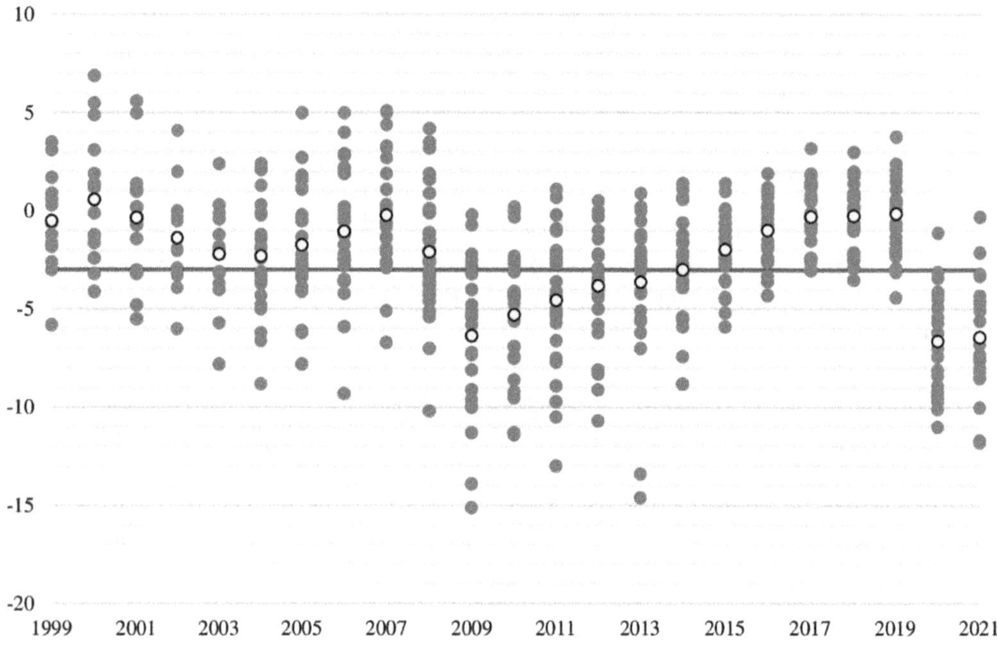

FIGURE 18.1. Dispersion of general government budget balances (in % of GDP) in the EU, 1999–2021.

Note: The blue dots show the dispersion of the government budget balances of EU Member States; the yellow dots show the EU average. The red line shows the 3 per cent deficit limit. The outlier for Ireland in 2010 (–32 per cent) has been dropped.
Source: AMECO database.

The previous analysis might suggest that the European fiscal rules had no impact on Member States' fiscal policies. That conclusion is not fully warranted. The European Fiscal Board (EFB) provides information on how well Member States complied with the rules of the SGP (Larch and Santacroce, 2020). Table 18.1 presents a summary. It should be pointed out that the EFB database assesses whether in purely quantitative terms the relevant fiscal aggregates evolved within or outside the perimeters defined by the fiscal rules. The assessment is backward looking, based on actual data, and does not consider compliance in the planning process. Although the definitions used for the assessment (see the note to Table 18.1) do not have an official, let alone legal, status, they 'nevertheless represent an accurate description of the main features the EU fiscal rules as set out in primary and secondary EU legislation' (Larch and Santacroce, 2020, p. 4). It should also be noted that the assessment of the rules covers the entire period, also in years when the SGP had not yet been reformed. For instance, the expenditure rule was only introduced with the 2011 reform of the SGP. Larch and Santacroce (2020) conclude that the overall compliance record was slightly above 50 per cent, but this number masks stark cross-country differences as shown in Table 18.1.[5] Remarkably, euro area countries have a slightly lower compliance score than non-euro area countries. Larch and Santacroce (2020) show that in 2007, more than 80 per cent of the EU Member States complied with the deficit and the debt

[5] Likewise, Reuter (2019) finds that average compliance with fiscal rules was around 50 per cent between 1995 and 2015. Using somewhat different definitions of EU fiscal rules and a narrower definition of compliance, Eyraud et al. (2017) conclude that non-compliance has been the rule rather than the exception in the EU.

TABLE 18.1 *Compliance with SGP rules (percentage share of years), 1998–2020*

	Deficit rule	Debt rule	Structural balance rule	Expenditure
Austria	83	30	26	22
Belgium	70	48	17	17
Bulgaria	83	100	65	52
Croatia	43	74	37	42
Cyprus	43	48	65	35
Czech Rep.	57	100	57	52
Denmark	100	100	65	70
Estonia	96	100	52	48
Finland	96	87	52	57
France	35	22	17	17
Germany	65	52	61	43
Greece	17	0	57	48
Hungary	35	57	35	30
Ireland	65	78	65	70
Italy	65	4	22	13
Latvia	74	100	30	30
Lithuania	61	100	52	48
Luxembourg	96	100	91	78
Malta	57	57	43	30
Netherlands	74	83	48	43
Poland	30	100	35	30
Portugal	22	26	39	35
Romania	52	100	39	22
Slovakia	48	96	22	39
Slovenia	61	78	22	13
Spain	52	52	30	22
Sweden	96	100	83	83

Notes: A country is considered compliant if (i) the general government budget balance is at or above −3 per cent of GDP or if (ii) an excess below −3 per cent of GDP is limited to one year. A country is considered compliant if the debt-to-GDP ratio is below 60 per cent of GDP or if the excess above 60 per cent of GDP has been declining by 1/20 on average over the past three years. A country is compliant if the structural budget balance is at or above the medium-term objective (MTO) or, if it is below the MTO, its structural fiscal effort (i.e. the change in the structural balance) is equal or higher than the benchmark requirement of 0.5 per cent of GDP. A country is compliant if the annual rate of growth of primary government expenditure, net of discretionary revenue measures and one-offs, is at or below the ten-year average of the nominal rate of potential output growth minus the convergence margin necessary to adjust towards the MTO.
Source: EFB.

rules of the SGP, but compliance with the other rules was much lower. A similar pattern emerged in the years before the COVID-19 pandemic: compliance with rules that exhibit a cyclical pattern improved, while compliance with rules designed to cut through cyclical swings deteriorated. They also conclude that the flexibility introduced by the Six-Pack reform of 2011 (a country is considered broadly compliant if the observed adjustment deviates by up to 0.5 per cent of GDP in one year or in cumulative terms over two successive years) meant that the margin of broad compliance produced a 'magnet' effect, i.e. countries aim for it.

In properly interpreting these findings, it is important to note that 'just testing whether rules are complied with neglects the fact that they often tug fiscal policy towards the target enshrined in the rule: the speed limit on the road may be 120 kilometres per hour (kph), the observed average speed may be 130 kph, but the instances of 150 kph or more are rare. In this sense, the presence of the rule has an impact missed by looking only at full compliance' (Begg, 2017,

p. R11). In other words, in the absence of the counterfactual, i.e. what would have happened without the fiscal rules, non-compliance does not necessarily imply that fiscal rules are ineffective.

Furthermore, the analysis of De Jong and Gilbert (2020) suggests that compliance with the EDP recommendations is actually quite satisfactory. These authors constructed a real-time database of country-specific Excessive Deficit Procedure recommendations from the introduction of the euro until 2017, tracking all revisions and changes in these recommendations. In total, twenty-two Excessive Deficit Procedure recommendations were launched for the EMU Member States, yielding eighty-eight individual country-year targets in the sample period considered. Although not all of these recommendations were fully implemented, most Member States improved their structural budget balance in line with the recommended changes under the 'corrective arm'.

18.5 STANCE OF FISCAL POLICY

As pointed out before, national fiscal policy is the only instrument available to deal with idiosyncratic shocks at the national level in the EMU (Begg, 2017). Whereas common shocks hit all Member States (although their transmission may be asymmetric, as the COVID-19 pandemic has illustrated), idiosyncratic shocks are asymmetric in nature (i.e. not all Member States of the monetary union are affected by them). Under normal circumstances, common shocks can be countered by the monetary policy of the ECB, while fiscal policy could be used to stabilize idiosyncratic shocks and the asymmetric effects of common shocks. This requires that fiscal buffers are built up during economic expansions so that fiscal support can be provided during serious downturns without jeopardizing the long-term sustainability of public finances (EFB, 2019).

National fiscal policy can be quite effective for stabilization purposes. Empirical estimates of Bayoumi and Masson (1995) suggest that (at that time) national fiscal policies in the euro area were able to deliver a similar degree of stabilization as the fiscal transfer systems in the United States and Canada. This evidence suggests that properly executed national fiscal policy may reduce the need for a European fiscal capacity (which is discussed in more detail by Beetsma and Kopits in Chapter 21 of this volume). Likewise, Dolls et al. (2012) show that a larger percentage of both income and unemployment shocks is absorbed by automatic stabilizers in the euro area compared to the United States, although the heterogeneity between Member States is considerable.

A potential problem when it comes to fiscal policy's stabilizing role is that fiscal policy is decided at the national level. As a consequence, it is likely that national fiscal policies do not take the euro area output gap and spillover effects of national fiscal policy into account (Pogoshyan, 2017 provides evidence for these spillovers). From a euro area perspective, failing to internalize these externalities leads to a suboptimal aggregate fiscal stance (Beetsma et al., 2001; Gali and Monacelli, 2008).

We leave the issues of a European fiscal policy capacity and the optimal European fiscal policy stance aside and take a purely national perspective in the remainder of this section. One straightforward way to assess whether national fiscal policies were able to deal with the consequences of idiosyncratic shocks or asymmetric common shocks is to look at the stance of fiscal policy. Here we follow Golinelli and Momigliano (2009) and examine the change of the cyclically adjusted primary budget balance (as a percentage of GDP) pertaining to the level of the output gap. When the change of the government budget and the output gap have opposite

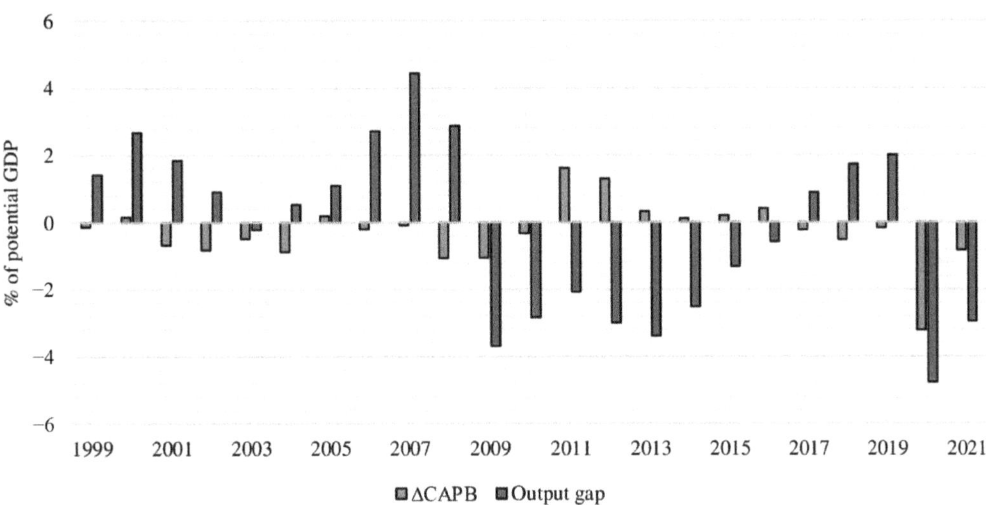

FIGURE 18.2. The average fiscal stance in the euro area, 1999–2021.
Note: The output gap and the change in the cyclically adjusted primary budget balance (ΔCAPB) are measured in percentage of GDP. When the output gap and the ΔCAPB have opposite signs, fiscal policy is considered procyclical.
Source: own calculations using updates of the database used by Gootjes and de Haan (2022a).

signs, the reaction of fiscal policy is considered procyclical. Figure 18.2 plots the EU averages for the years 1999–2021. It shows that fiscal policy was most often procyclical (see also Demertzis et al., Chapter 15 in this volume). Only two clear-cut episodes of countercyclical fiscal policy can be identified: the European Economic Recovery Plan of 2009 and the fiscal response to the COVID-19 pandemic. The figure does not indicate that after more flexibility had been introduced into the rules of the SGP in 2005 fiscal policy became less procyclical. Likewise, the changes introduced in 2011 did not make fiscal policy more anticyclical.

Larch et al. (2021) also conclude that national fiscal policy was often procyclical. Their results suggest that the failure to deliver countercyclical fiscal policies is not due to the volatility of real-time output gap estimates. Procyclicality is confirmed when alternative indicators of the business cycle are used.

> Consequently, procyclicality is first and foremost a political economy rather than a measurement issue. We find that procyclicality tends to be an issue when debt is very high and/or fiscal rules are not followed. In fact, the stock of government debt signals successive deviations from commonly agreed rules. In the presence of very high debt, and barring help from a superordinated level of macroeconomic policymaking, sustainability concerns can trump stabilisation needs. Compliance with EU fiscal rules reduces the likelihood of running procyclical policies. (Larch et al., 2021, p. 2)

Reuter (2020) reaches a similar conclusion.

Although the conclusion may come as a surprise to some readers, it is consistent with the findings of several other studies which report that well-designed fiscal rules reduce procyclicality (Combes et al., 2017; Guerguil et al., 2017; Nerlich and Reuter, 2015). A drawback of these studies, however, is that they are based on *ex post* fiscal data, which has often been revised, and therefore almost certainly gives misleading inferences about policy intentions. As governments generally base their policy decisions on highly uncertain estimates about the state of the economy, the actual budgetary policy may be significantly different from the *ex ante* intentions of policymakers (Cimadomo, 2016). Gootjes and de Haan (2022a) analyse the cyclical stance of discretionary fiscal policy in EU countries across its various stages. They use real-time data, i.e. data available to policymakers at the time they made their budgetary decisions (the planning phase) and when they implemented their plans (the implementation phase), and compare these with *ex post* fiscal policy data (fiscal outcomes). The authors find that over the 2000–2015 period, the fiscal plans of EU countries have an acyclical stance on average. However, the cyclical stance weakens during the implementation phase of fiscal policy, whilst fiscal outcomes end up being procyclical. Consistent with the results of studies discussed above, they also find that sufficiently stringent fiscal rules reduce procyclical fiscal policies.

18.6 REFORM OF THE EUROPEAN FISCAL RULES

Our analysis suggests that (1) Fiscal rules to maintain the sustainability of fiscal policy are needed in EMU; (2) The rules in place have only been partly successful, notably, the preventive arm of the SGP has failed; (3) Oftentimes, fiscal policy in the euro area was procyclical; (4) Fiscal rules as such do not imply that fiscal policy becomes procyclical; (5) The EU's fiscal framework has become overly complex and incoherent.

What do these findings imply for the future of the European fiscal framework, considering the experiences during the COVID-19 pandemic? During the COVID-19 crisis, very large budget deficits led to much higher levels of debt in most EU Member States, far beyond the 60 per cent target (see Figure 18.3). Low interest rates (to levels even below economic growth) make debt more likely to be sustainable. However, this is no reason to ignore the risks of rising national debt

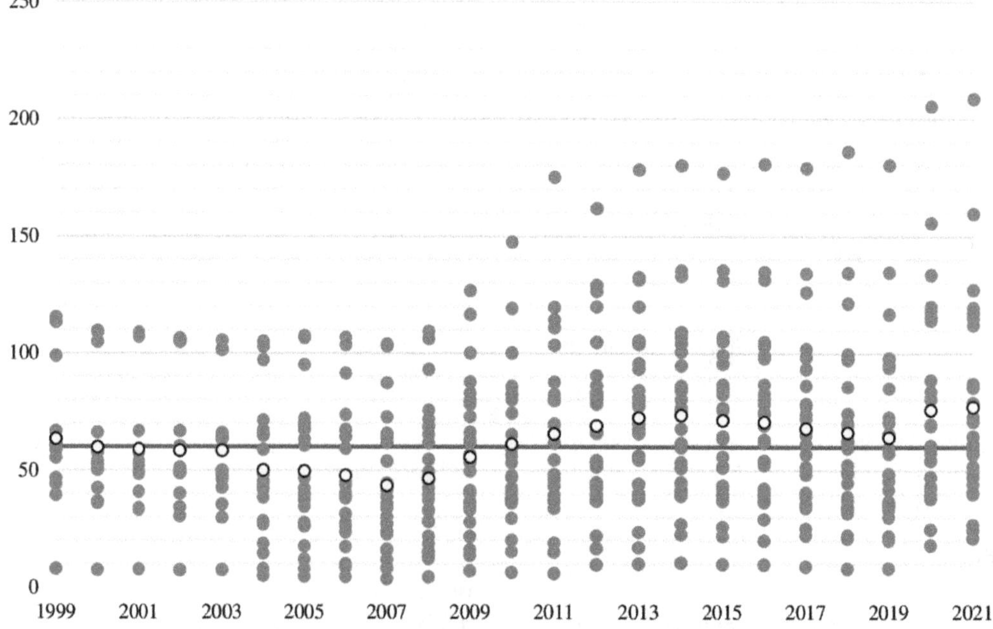

FIGURE 18.3. Dispersion of government debt ratios (in % of GDP) in the EU, 1999–2021.
Note: The blue dots show the dispersion of the public debt ratios of EU Member States; the yellow dots show the EU average. The red line shows the 60 per cent debt limit.
Source: AMECO database.

levels. As recent developments have shown, interest rates may not always be lower than the growth rate so that debt sustainability will become a problem. The adverse consequences of unsustainable public debt are considerable. Therefore, precaution is desirable. Prudent macroeconomic risk management requires taking into account circumstances in the future in which the interest rate will be higher than the GDP growth rate. After all, this has happened before. Such a policy would also create room for the ECB to raise interest rates, should the development of inflation call for it. Excessive government debt hinders the central bank in its core task of maintaining price stability.

The COVID-19 crisis has shown how important it is to build up fiscal buffers in economic good times. For instance, the Netherlands was in a much better position than many other European countries to absorb the economic shock caused by the COVID-19 crisis. Although rising, the Dutch public debt-to-GDP ratio is at the time of writing not in the danger zone despite a huge increase in government spending during the crisis. This suggests that a structurally low level of debt is desirable. It creates room to implement decisive measures during a crisis without having to worry about an excessively high debt ratio. Moreover, research shows that the effectiveness of an expansionary fiscal policy stance, which may be needed at the time of crisis (and only then), is much lower when public debt is high. Huidrom et al. (2019) find that the multiplier of expansionary fiscal policy is systematically smaller when public debt is high. This is due to two mechanisms. When a government with a weak financial position implements stimulus policies, households are more likely to expect a future tax increase (to keep the debt sustainable). Moreover, a fiscal stimulus may increase lenders' concerns about credit risk in this situation.

Kamps and Leiner-Killinger (2019) nicely illustrate the argument that cautious fiscal policy may create fiscal space when needed. As these authors point out, as part of the Two-Pack regulations, euro area countries have to submit draft budgetary plans for the subsequent year to the European Commission and the Eurogroup. Table 18.2, taken from their study, shows that one group of countries have planned sound budgetary policies for most of the years since this exercise was established. This group includes Cyprus, Estonia, Germany, Lithuania, Luxembourg, and the Netherlands. Another group includes countries that have not once delivered a draft budgetary plan in full compliance with the SGP. This group covers, inter alia, all countries with high levels of debt, including notably Belgium, France, Italy, Spain, and Portugal.

The EFB (2019) identifies the weaknesses of the current regime as follows. First, there is an excessive reliance on unobservable indicators and real-time data, which are often subject to major revisions *ex post*. Second, flexibility was often badly timed, also due to political considerations, thus facilitating procyclicality. Third, there is a tendency to rely on annual rather than longer-term plans. Member States continue to postpone adjustments to the outer years in their stability and convergence programmes.

What to do? Broadly speaking, two options have been proposed. The first is to decentralize the responsibility for fiscal discipline to the national level as suggested by Wyplosz (2019). National rules might fare better than supranational rules as they stand a greater chance of securing a consensus among national actors. Wyplosz (2019) proposes to adopt the debt-to-GDP ratio as a target and annual budget balances as the instrument. This would allow for the countercyclical use of fiscal policy while constraining the path of the debt ratio. In his proposal, independent fiscal councils must be empowered to compute the long-term evolution of the debt and to determine whether fiscal discipline is respected. More specifically, the council must be in charge of translating the government's budgetary decisions into numbers for the budget and the

TABLE 18.2 *Assessments under the review of draft budgetary plans 2011–18*

	2011	2012	2013	2014	2015	2016	2017	2018
Belgium	–4.5	–4.0	–3.8	–3.7	–3.0	–2.1	–1.3	–1.4
Germany	–0.6	0.4	0.8	1.6	1.6	1.6	2.0	1.7
Estonia	0.1	0.0	–0.6	0.0	0.0	–0.4	–0.7	–0.8
Ireland	–7.6	–6.0	–3.9	–3.6	–1.5	–0.3	0.4	–0.1
Spain	–6.3	–3.1	–1.7	–1.5	–2.4	–3.3	–3.0	–3.3
France	–5.0	–4.3	–3.4	–3.0	–2.3	–2.2	–1.7	–1.7
Italy	–3.3	–1.3	–0.7	–0.8	–0.6	–1.4	–1.7	–1.7
Cyprus	–4.9	–3.9	–0.7	3.3	1.7	1.2	1.4	0.8
Latvia	–1.1	0.1	–0.4	–0.1	–0.5	0.7	–0.2	–0.9
Lithuania	–3.8	–2.8	–0.9	–0.4	0.3	0.7	0.4	0.3
Luxembourg	1.1	2.1	2.3	1.4	1.1	2.3	2.3	1.3
Malta	–1.9	–2.7	–1.7	–2.6	–2.5	0.5	3.5	0.6
Netherlands	–2.9	–1.5	–0.2	0.1	–0.4	1.3	1.0	0.4
Austria	–2.6	–1.9	–1.3	–0.3	0.4	–0.4	–0.1	–0.3
Portugal	–6.2	–3.1	–2.6	–1.3	–1.8	–2.2	–1.4	–1.4
Slovenia	–4.5	–1.6	–1.2	–2.1	–1.3	–1.1	–0.9	–1.4
Slovakia	–4.2	–3.6	–1.1	–1.6	–1.7	–1.5	–0.5	–0.7
Finland	–1.3	–1.6	–0.6	–1.0	–0.4	–0.2	0.4	–0.3

Notes: The table reflects the opinions of the European Commission on the draft budgetary plans as delivered in autumn of year t–1 for year t (e.g. the entry for '2014' gives the Commission's opinion in November 2013 on the Draft Budgetary Plan for 2014). The numbers refer to the distance of the the structural balance from the country-specific MTO. Green bars relate to countries whose draft budgetary plan is considered by the European Commission to be (broadly) compliant with the SGP. Red bars relate to countries whose draft budgetary plan is considered by the European Commission to be at risk of non-compliance with the SGP.
Source: Kamps and Leiner-Killinger (2019).

public debt path. Furthermore, the council must be tasked to determine whether the government's choices are compatible with fiscal discipline. Larch and Braendle (2018) go a step further and propose to separate stabilization from the other functions of fiscal policy and delegate this task to national fiscal councils. The council would first set a ceiling for the budget deficit for a given period subject to fiscal sustainability while politicians would then decide how to allocate available budgetary resources. In such a set-up, politicians would still be able to choose any amount of redistribution and public goods as long as corresponding revenues or compositional changes of public expenditures funded new measures. However, it is doubtful that delegating decisions about fiscal policy to non-elected technocrats, in a similar fashion as monetary policy has been delegated, is feasible. Existing fiscal councils are strictly monitoring entities, without any policymaking function (Kopits, 2018b): they bark but they don't bite.

The second option, which seems more likely to be implemented, is to reform the current fiscal framework. Several reform proposals have been put forward and most of them take the TFEU as a starting point. As argued by Blanchard et al. (2021), this seems a realistic way to proceed because modifying or abolishing existing limits would require Treaty change. Within the Treaty framework, Darvas et al. (2018), Feld et al. (2018), and the EFB (2019) propose an expenditure rule and a debt anchor. To be more specific, the EFB (2019) has made a proposal that relies on a simple medium-term debt ceiling and a ceiling on the growth rate of primary expenditure (net of discretionary revenue measures), augmented with an escape clause triggered based on independent economic judgement. 'This proposal would focus more clearly on underpinning sustainability, improve observability, simplify the rules and reduce procyclicality. This latter effect is due to the fact that net primary expenditure growth is linked to potential growth and thus would have an implicit stabilising effect on the economy' (EFB, 2019, p. 7). In our view, this proposal makes perfect sense. Feld et al. (2018) motivate the use of an expenditure rule because governments can directly influence the majority of their own expenditures. Instead, balanced budget rules constrain fiscal policy variables that for a large part are not directly controlled by the government. Moreover, public spending is less dependent on the business cycle than the budget balance and its forecast errors are therefore relatively smaller (Christofzik et al., 2018). Still, as pointed out by Reuter (2020), expenditure rules are also associated with significant challenges when forecasting and estimating the variables needed for implementation, including discretionary revenue measures, which are associated with a high degree of uncertainty. Recently, the European Commission has put forward its ideas about reform.[6] The centrepiece of the proposal is the introduction of so-called national medium-term fiscal plans (NMFPs) that would replace the current annual Convergence and Stability Programmes. The key variable in the NMFPs should be a time path for nationally financed net primary expenditure that is supposed to be set so to ensure that debt is put or kept on a downward path or stays at prudent levels, while ensuring that the budget deficit is maintained below 3 per cent of GDP over the medium term.

Some proposals also discuss measures if countries do not adhere to the rules. Instead of relying only on sticks (sanctions), carrots should be introduced to incentivize Member States to comply with the rules. If a common fiscal capacity at the European level was introduced, one of the eligibility criteria to access funds could be compliance with the EU fiscal rules (EFB, 2019). Promoting adherence to the fiscal rules in this way might be more effective than sanctions.

Despite our positive assessment of these proposals, they do not address some of the shortcomings we have identified, notably the pivotal role of the ECOFIN. Although the EFB (2019) argues that RQMV should be abolished, going back to the old situation may not be an improvement. As Begg (2017, p. R12), referring to the 2003 and 2016 episodes, writes:

> [I]n the absence of unambiguous automaticity in implementation, even the most cleverly conceived rules will not achieve their aims. If, in addition, governments actively search for ways around rules, be it through statistical fudging, redefinitions of coverage or the meaning of a cycle, let alone explicit use of escape clauses, the very philosophy of rules as an approach to tie the hands of governments will progressively lose conviction.

Although we support proposals for an expenditure rule, we would like to stress that when fiscal adjustments are necessary, they should not rely only on expenditure cuts. Despite a very popular view that in order to be successful fiscal adjustments should be based on spending cuts, recent research has shown that consolidation efforts based on increasing revenues can be equally effective as consolidations based on cutting spending (see Schaltegger and Weder, 2015 and Wiese et al., 2018).

Finally, as we have discussed in this chapter, research has also shown that the effectiveness of fiscal rules depends on the ability to observe their effects. Strengthening the role of supporting institutions (*fiscal councils*) and procedures (*budget transparency*) is therefore warranted.

[6] Communication from the Commission to the European Parliament, the Council, the European Central Bank, the European Economic and Social Committee and the Committee of the Regions, Brussels, 9.11.2022, COM (2022) 583.

REFERENCES

Alesina, A. and Tabellini, G. (1990). A positive theory of fiscal deficits and government debt. *Review of Economic Studies* 57, 403–414.

Alt, J. E., Lassen, D. D., and Wehner, J. (2014). It isn't just about Greece: Domestic politics, transparency, and fiscal gimmickry. *British Journal of Political Science* 44, 707–716.

Amtenbrink, F., and de Haan, J. (2003). Economic governance in the European Union: Fiscal policy discipline versus flexibility. *Common Market Law Review* 40, 1075–1106.

Amtenbrink, F., de Haan, J., and Sleijpen, O. C. H. M. (1997). Stability and Growth Pact: Placebo or panacea? *European Business Law Review* 8 and 9/10, 202–210; 223-238.

Asatryan, Z., Castellón, C., and Stratmann, T. (2018). Balanced budget rules and fiscal outcomes: Evidence from historical constitutions. *Journal of Public Economics* 167, 105–119.

Bayoumi, T., and Masson, P. R. (1995). Fiscal flows in the United States and Canada: Lessons for Monetary Union in Europe. *European Economic Review* 39(2), 253–274.

Beetsma, R., Debrun, X., Fang, X., Kim, Y., Lledó, V., Mbaye. S., and Zang, X. (2019). Independent fiscal councils: Recent trends and performance. *European Journal of Political Economy* 57, 53–69.

Beetsma, R., Debrun, X., and Klaassen, F. (2001). Is fiscal policy coordination in EMU desirable? *Swedish Economic Policy Review* 8, 57–98.

Begg, I. (2017). Fiscal and other rules in EU economic governance: Helpful, largely irrelevant or unenforceable? *National Institute Economic Review* No. 239, R3–R13.

Blanchard, O., Leandro. A., and Zettelmeyer, J. (2021). Redesigning EU fiscal rules: From rules to standards. *Economic Policy* 36(106), 195–236.

Blinder, A., Ehrman, M., de Haan, J., and Jansen, D. (2017). Necessity as the mother of invention: Monetary policy after the crisis. *Economic Policy* 32(92), 707–755.

Bonam, D., de Haan, J., and Soederhuizen, B. (2022). The effects of fiscal policy at the effective lower bound. *Macroeconomic Dynamics* 26(1), 149–185.

Buiter, W. H. (2004) Two naked emperors? Concerns about the Stability & Growth Pact and second thoughts about central bank independence. *Fiscal Studies* 25, 249–277.

Burret, H. T., and Feld, L. P. (2018). (Un-)intended effects of fiscal rules. *European Journal of Political Economy* 52, 166–191.

Buti, M., and Carnot, N. (2012). The EMU debt crisis: Early lessons and reforms. *Journal of Common Market Studies* 50(6), 899–911.

Caselli, F., and Reynaud, L. (2020). Do fiscal rules cause better fiscal balances? A new instrumental variable strategy. *European Journal of Political Economy* 63, 101873.

Caselli, F., and P. Wingender (2018). Bunching at 3 percent: The Maastricht fiscal criterion and government deficits. IMF Working Paper No. 18/182.

Christofzik, D. I., Feld, L. P., Reuter, W. H., and Yeter, M. (2018). Uniting European fiscal rules: How to strengthen the fiscal framework. German Council of Economic Experts Working Paper No. 04.

Cimadomo, J. (2016). Real-time data and fiscal policy analysis: A survey of the literature. *Journal of Economic Surveys* 30, 302–326.

Combes, J., Minea, A., and Sow, M. (2017). Is fiscal policy always counter- (pro-)cyclical? The role of public debt and fiscal rules. *Economic Modelling* 65, 138–146.

Darvas, Z., Martin, P., and Ragot, X. (2018). European fiscal rules require a major overhaul. Policy Contribution No. 18. Brussels: Bruegel.

De Haan, J., Berger, H., and Jansen, D. (2004). Why has the Stability and Growth Pact failed? *International Finance* 7(2), 235–260.

De Jong, J. F. M., and Gilbert, N. D. (2020). Fiscal discipline in EMU? Testing the effectiveness of the Excessive Deficit Procedure. *European Journal of Political Economy* 61, 101822.

Debrun, X., and Jonung, L. (2019). Under threat: Rules-based fiscal policy and how to preserve it. *European Journal of Political Economy* 57, 142–157.

Dolls, M., Fuest, C., and Peichl, A. (2012). Automatic stabilizers and economic crisis: US vs. Europe. *Journal of Public Economics* 96(3–4), 279–294.

Draghi, M. (2014). Unemployment in the euro area. Speech by Mario Draghi, President of the ECB, Annual central bank symposium in Jackson Hole, 22 August. www.ecb.europa.eu/press/key/date/2014/html/sp140822.en.html

European Central Bank (2011). The reform of economic governance in the Euro Area – Essential elements. *ECB Monthly Bulletin*, March 2011, 99–119.

European Fiscal Board (2019). Assessment of EU fiscal rules with a focus on the six and two-pack legislation. August 2019.

Eyraud, L., Gaspar, V., and Poghosya, T. (2017). Fiscal politics in the euro area. In V. Gaspar et al. (eds.), *Fiscal Politics*. Washington, DC, International Monetary Fund.

Feld, L., Schmidt, C., Schnabel, I., and Wieland, V. (2018). Refocusing the European fiscal framework. *VoxEU.org*, 12 September.

Gali, J., and Monacelli, T. (2008). Optimal monetary and fiscal policy in a currency union. *Journal of International Economics* 76, 116–132.

Gilbert, N. D., and de Jong, J. F. M. (2017). Do the European fiscal rules induce a bias in fiscal forecasts? Evidence from the Stability and Growth Pact. *Public Choice* 170(1), 1–32.

Golinelli, R., and Momigliano, S. (2009). The cyclical reaction of fiscal policies in the euro area: The role of modelling choices and data vintages. *Fiscal Studies* 30, 39–72.

Gootjes, B., and de Haan, J. (2022a). Procyclicality of fiscal policy in European Union countries. *Journal of International Money and Finance* 120, 102276.

Gootjes, B., and de Haan, J. (2022b). Do fiscal rules need budget transparency to be effective? *European Journal of Political Economy* 120, 102210.

Gootjes, B., de Haan, J., and Jong-A-Pin, R. M. (2021). Do fiscal rules constrain political budget cycles? *Public Choice* 188, 1–30.

Gros, D. (2016). The second death of the Stability Pact and the birth of an inter-governmental Europe. Centre for European Policy Studies commentary, 28 July. www.ceps.eu/ceps-publications/second-death-stability-pact-and-birth-inter-governmental-europe/

Guerguil, M., Mandon, P., and Tapsoba, R. (2017). Flexible fiscal rules and countercyclical fiscal policy. *Journal of Macroeconomics* 52, 189–220.

Huidrom, R., Kose, M. A., Lim, J. J., and Ohnsorge, F. L. (2019). Why do fiscal multipliers depend on fiscal positions? CAMA Working Paper No. 28/2019.

Kamps, C., and Leiner-Killinger, N. (2019). Taking stock of the functioning of the EU fiscal rules and options for reform. ECB Occasional Study No. 231.

Koen, V., and van den Noord, P. (2005). Fiscal gimmickry in Europe: One-off measures and creative accounting. OECD Economics Department Working Paper No. 417.

Kopits, G. (2018a). How could the Stability and Growth Pact be simplified? Directorate-General for Internal Policies of the Union, Economic and Monetary Committee, European Parliament. www.europarl.europa.eu/RegData/etudes/IDAN/2018/614509/IPOL_IDA(2018)614509_EN.pdf

Kopits, G. (2018b). Some myths about independent fiscal institutions. In R. Beetsma and X. Debrun (eds.), *Independent Fiscal Councils: Watchdogs or Lapdogs?* London: Centre for Economic Policy Research.

Kopits, G., and Symansky, S. A. (1998). Fiscal policy rules. IMF Occasional Paper No. 162.

Landon, S., and Smith, C. (2017). Does the design of a fiscal rule matter for welfare? *Economic Modelling* 63, 226–237.

Larch, M., and Braendle, T. (2018). Independent fiscal councils: Neglected siblings of independent central banks? An EU perspective. *Journal of Common Market Studies* 56(2), 267–283.

Larch, M., and Santacroce, S. (2020). Numerical compliance with EU fiscal rules: The compliance database of the Secretariat of the European Fiscal Board. https://commission.europa.eu/business-economy-euro/economic-and-fiscal-policy-coordination/european-fiscal-board-efb/compliance-tracker_en

Larch, M., Orseau, E., and van der Wielen, W. (2021). Do EU fiscal rules support or hinder counter-cyclical fiscal policy? *Journal of International Money and Finance* 112, art. 102328.

Maltritz, D., and Wüste, S. (2015). Determinants of budget deficits in Europe: The role and relations of fiscal rules, fiscal councils, creative accounting and the Euro. *Economic Modelling* 48, 222–236.

Milesi-Ferretti, G. M. (2004). Good, bad or ugly? On the effects of fiscal rules with creative accounting. *Journal of Public Economics* 88, 377–394.

Nerlich, C., and Reuter, W. H. (2015). Fiscal rules, fiscal space and procyclical fiscal policy. ECB Working Paper 1872.

Persson, T., and Svensson, L. E. O. (1989). Why a stubborn conservative would run a deficit: Polity with time-inconsistent preferences. *Quarterly Journal of Economics* 104, 325–345.

Poghosyan, T. (2017). Cross-country spillovers of fiscal consolidations in the euro area. IMF Working Paper No. 17/140.

Reuter, W. H. (2020). Benefits and drawbacks of an 'expenditure rule', as well as of a 'golden rule', in the EU fiscal framework. IPOL Economic Governance Support Unit, PE 645.732.

Schaechter, A., Kinda, T., Budina, N., and Weber, A. (2012). Fiscal rules in response to the crisis – Toward the 'next-generation' rules. A new dataset. IMF Working Paper No. 12/187.

Schaltegger, C. A., and Weder, M. (2015). Fiscal adjustments and the probability of sovereign default. *Kyklos* 68, 81–110.

Shi, M., and Svensson, J. (2006). Political budget cycles: Do they differ across countries and why? *Journal of Public Economics* 90, 1367–1389.

Velasco, A. (2000). Debts and deficits with fragmented fiscal policymaking. *Journal of Public Economics* 76, 105–125.

Von Hagen, J., and Wolff, G. (2006). What do deficits tell us about debt? Empirical evidence on creative accounting with fiscal rules in the EU. *Journal of Banking & Finance* 30, 3259–3279.

Wiese, R., Jong-A-Pin, R., and de Haan, J. (2018). Can successful fiscal adjustments only be achieved by spending cuts? *European Journal of Political Economy* 54, 145–166.

Wyplosz, C. (2019). Fiscal discipline in the Eurozone: Don't fix it, change it. Ifo DICE Report, Summer 2019, 17, 3–6.

19

The Politics of Fiscal Integration in Eurozone Reforms and Next Generation EU

Fabio Wasserfallen

19.1 INTRODUCTION

The introduction of the Economic and Monetary Union (EMU) with the euro as a common currency is the deepest form of integration among EU Member States. From the beginning, the institutional setting of the common currency area was contested – not least because the basic goal of the EMU was controversial: for some, the euro was a rather technical and incremental extension of economic integration, while others saw in the common currency a big step towards a closer political union. To date, the key question remains how strongly the members of the eurozone, who gave up national authority in monetary policy, have to pool fiscal and economic policymaking on the European level. At the 1991 Maastricht summit, the EU leaders discussed the need for a deeper political union with pooled fiscal and economic authority, which was supposed to complement the monetary union. Eventually, the heads of state and government created in Maastricht the EMU, but they could not agree on a common approach for deeper political and fiscal integration – and this discussion has remained conflictual ever since (Wasserfallen, 2014; Woolley, 1994).

Stepwise, the EMU's institutional setting was introduced and extended, for example, with the deficit and debt criteria and the Stability and Growth Pact (SGP). The approach to governing the eurozone with fiscal rules remains controversial, and the non-sanctioning of Germany and France, which violated the deficit criteria in 2003, weakened the pact's credibility. The institutional framework of fiscal integration is still a work in progress, whereas the crises of the eurozone and COVID-19 triggered multiple fiscal integration steps. This chapter seeks to analyse the recent trends and remaining challenges of fiscal integration by asking the following guiding questions: Who is in conflict with whom over what? Why and how did the EU Member States agree to deepen fiscal integration further? What are the key challenges of fiscal integration? To provide some answers to these questions, the following analysis draws on political science research and investigates how the EMU's institutional framework was established and how it was updated in the last few years during the eurozone crisis and in reaction to the COVID-19 pandemic. The focus lies on the political conflicts, which shape the EMU's governance structure. This chapter also addresses the more general questions of democratic legitimacy and the varying degrees to which EU Member States are fiscally integrated.

The EMU's fiscal cornerstones are the no-bailout clause and sustainable fiscal policy. Building on this institutional legacy, the reforms enacted during the eurozone crisis between 2010 and 2015 further deepened the monetary union. As often in European integration, a crisis opened the window of opportunity for accomplishing more integration among EU Member States (Ioannou et al., 2015; Jones et al., 2021). In essence, the EU Member States agreed on further strengthening the fiscal discipline criteria with the Two- and Six-Pack legislation, and they created rescue funds in the form of the European Stability Mechanism. A further key element of the reforms was the Banking Union comprising the Single Supervisory Mechanism and the Single Resolution Mechanism (Howarth and Quaglia, 2016; Wasserfallen et al., 2019). Not on the negotiation table was the common financing of debts through Eurobonds, which would have been a more explicit step in the direction of a fiscal federal EMU set-up.

All the mentioned reforms were negotiated under the context of highly conflictual politics. Political science research sheds light on the political conflicts and power constellations in the EMU's reform negotiations. Four broader findings stand out: (a) the dominance of intergovernmental conflicts among rather stable coalitions of Member States, often simplified as the north–south divide (Armingeon and Cranmer, 2018; Brunnermeier et al., 2016; Lehner and Wasserfallen, 2019); (b) the importance of the French–German partnership in accommodating this intergovernmental conflict with compromises, particularly in the preparatory stage, where the potential options for reform are defined (Bulmer, 2014; Degner and Leuffen, 2019; Schild, 2013); (c) the important role of smaller coalitions of Member States at the spectrum's polarized ends (Armingeon et al., 2021; Morlino and Sottilotta, 2019); and (d) the Commission's influence in policy preparation and the final bargaining stage (Carstensen and Schmidt, 2021; Kudrna and Wasserfallen, 2021; Lundgren et al., forthcoming).

The COVID-19 pandemic led again to deeper fiscal integration in the form of the Next Generation EU (NGEU) programme. From a fiscal point of view, the NGEU programme is remarkable because it extends the EU's fiscal capacity by adding €806 billion to the regular budget of €1,074 billion, known as the multiannual financial framework of 2021–27. Moreover, the Member States jointly finance the NGEU by issuing bonds on the financial market (European Commission, 2021). Overall, we find continuity and change from the EMU reforms to the NGEU programme. On the one hand, both reforms were triggered by crises, and in both cases, we find a similar divide between fiscally more hawkish countries and proponents of more fiscal transfers. On the other hand, Germany took a more accommodating stance in the case of NGEU, which made it possible to move in the direction of joint financial responsibility. NGEU's novelty is that the Commission borrows on a large scale, on the EU's behalf, within the capital markets for the programme's financing, which is a strong development towards more fiscal federalism from EMU reforms to NGEU (Armingeon et al., 2021; Schelkle, 2021).

Among other reasons, this step towards substantial joint borrowing was politically feasible because the NGEU programme is supposed to be exceptional and is thus not anticipated to become a regular tool of fiscal policymaking. It remains to be seen whether that will be the case. A key challenge of fiscal integration is the demarcation between the EMU and EU-27. The NGEU programme is designed for the EU-27, not the eurozone with its twenty members, and was a reaction to the economic and social consequences of the COVID-19 pandemic. On a more general level, the comparison between the eurozone reforms and NGEU illustrates that the EU Member States are fiscally integrated to varying extents.

The scholarship on differentiated integration investigates precisely these varying degrees of integration across policies and Member States (Leuffen et al., 2013; Schimmelfennig and Winzen, 2020). This literature is particularly relevant in the fiscal, financial, and economic fields, where some reforms include all EU Member States (e.g. NGEU) and others include only the EMU members (e.g. European Stability Mechanism). Some policies are legislated according to the EU's ordinary or special legislative procedure (e.g. the banking regulations) and others as intergovernmental agreements (e.g. the fiscal compact). Against this backdrop of large integration heterogeneity, some researchers advocate deeper integration among a subset of Member States within the EMU (De Vries, 2018; Fabbrini, 2019).

Another key challenge is the extent to which authority transfers to the EU level are democratically anchored and legitimized. The literature on the EU's so-called democratic deficit is abundant (Follesdal and Hix, 2006; Hix, 2008; Majone, 1998; Moravcsik, 2002). One concern is the substantial power shift from parliaments to the national executives. In the area of fiscal and economic policymaking, there is limited involvement of the European Parliament and, on the domestic level, Member State governments only marginally integrate their national parliaments in EU fiscal politics (Târlea et al., 2023). Consequently, the national executives take up a dominant role on the EU level and interfere directly with the prerogative of national parliaments, namely the legislative authority in taxation and spending (Genschel and Jachtenfuchs, 2018). This power shift to the national executives raises concerns that fiscal policymaking on the EU level lacks democratic anchoring and legitimacy.

Within this broader context of recent reforms and the remaining key challenges of fiscal integration, this chapter discusses the politics of fiscal integration in four parts. Section 19.2 identifies the main political conflicts, with a focus on the EMU reforms enacted as a reaction to the eurozone crisis. Section 19.3 investigates the NGEU programme, highlighting similarities and changes compared to EMU politics. Based on the EMU and NGEU analyses, Section 19.4 identifies the scope conditions for fiscal reforms, as well as the general power structure of fiscal integration politics. Section 19.5 highlights two remaining key challenges, namely the difficulty of integration in a highly differentiated area with unclear demarcation lines between the EU-27 and eurozone, as well as the limits of democratic legitimacy in fiscal politics.

19.2 THE POLITICS OF THE EUROZONE REFORMS

More than thirty years ago, when the EMU was founded in Maastricht, the heads of state and government were in conflict with one another over the scope and scale of fiscal integration, which was required to complement and stabilize a common currency area. At the Maastricht summit, the EU leaders could not agree on a common approach for deeper political and fiscal integration but, nevertheless, created the EMU (Woolley, 1994). A main building block of EMU governance in the fiscal realm became the 1997 SGP, with its attempt to operationalize the fiscal deficit and debt rules. In 2003, the SGP framework was severely undermined when no sanctions were enacted against Germany and France, which violated the deficit criteria. A rather fundamental critique of the SGP was that, instead of building on fiscal discipline, a system of burden-sharing and automatic fiscal transfers within the eurozone was required to stabilize the common currency area.

Triggered by the financial crisis, the eurozone's stability was then severely challenged starting in late 2009, even to the point where some economists speculated about a breakdown of the common currency. With the benefit of hindsight, this gloom and doom scenario was exaggerated, but the eurozone crisis showed that the EMU's institutional framework was not resilient enough to absorb imbalances and shocks (Alesina and Wacziarg, 1999; Schelkle, 2017; Sinn, 2014; Stiglitz, 2016). The perspective of economists on the eurozone is strongly influenced by concerns that the EMU is not an optimal currency area, mainly because asymmetries in macroeconomic conditions are not sufficiently equalized with automatic stabilizers, such as labour mobility or fiscal transfers (Mundell, 1961; Obstfeld et al., 1997). This economic analysis points to the risks of a monetary union and highlights the eurozone's institutional deficiency with respect to missing fiscal stabilizers (Feldstein, 2012; Krugman, 2013; de Haan and Gootjes, Chapter 18 in this volume).

Along these lines, a large literature on fiscal federalism explores which institutional settings and fiscal stabilizers could make the EMU more resilient. One proposal is the adoption of European-level unemployment insurance, which would automatically provide transfers to economically weaker regions and thus equalize the differences in economic conditions across the eurozone (Dolls et al., 2018). Another policy option is a permanent EU-wide stabilization facility (Beetsma and Kopits, Chapter 20 in this volume). This literature serves as a relevant point of orientation for understanding the eurozone's struggles because the core reason for the crisis was that eurozone members accumulated imbalances, which turned into a balance-of-payments and debt crisis (Copelovitch et al., 2016; Frieden and Walter, 2017). A further strand of studies draws lessons from the United States' fiscal and monetary integration history (Bordo et al., 2013; Sala-i-Martin and Sachs, 1991).

For EMU leaders, the key political question in the reaction to the crisis was the same as twenty years before in the Maastricht summit: How much emphasis should they put on fiscal discipline and what type of fiscal transfers are needed to make the common currency area more resilient? The EU Member States agreed on a large set of reforms from 2010 to 2015. One part of these reforms further strengthened the EMU's fiscal discipline side with the legislation of the Two-Pack, Six-Pack, and Fiscal Compact. In addition, the fiscal transfers of the EMU architecture expanded with rescue funds in the form of the European Financial Stability Facility, the European Stability Mechanism, and assistance packages to Greece. The final key elements of the EMU reforms brought about the Banking Union (i.e. the Single Supervisory Mechanism and the Single Resolution Mechanism and Fund; see Kudrna and Puntscher Riekmann, 2021; Wasserfallen et al., 2019). All of these EMU reforms were negotiated in the context of highly conflictual policymaking. The research of political scientists points to four broader characteristics that define and explain the fiscal politics of EMU reforms.

First, the politics of EMU reforms were *dominated by intergovernmental conflicts* with Member States' governments as central actors. Although there are interesting nuances in respect to the involvement of domestic national actors and national legal constraints across Member States (Griller and Lentsch, 2021; Kassim et al., 2020), the dominant role of national executives in EU decision-making is a striking feature of EMU politics (Târlea et al., 2023). This dominant role of governments was amplified by the intergovernmental nature of the reform politics (Csehi and Puetter, 2021). The policymaking of the EMU reforms involved several institutional procedures, from intergovernmental treaties to legislation according to the ordinary legislative procedure, as well as involving the Commission and partly the European Parliament. Overall, however, the reforms generally were decided in intergovernmental negotiations.

Second, the conflict among Member States is often simplified as the *north–south divide* (Armingeon and Cranmer, 2018; Brunnermeier et al., 2016; Lehner and Wasserfallen, 2019). On one side are the northern countries of the eurozone, including Germany and the frugal four (i.e. Austria, Denmark, the Netherlands, and Sweden), which emphasize the need for strict fiscal discipline rules. On the other side are the Mediterranean countries, such as Greece, Italy, France, Spain, and Portugal, which demand greater fiscal burden-sharing and fiscal equalization in the form of transfers. This conflictual structure between the two groups of Member States advocating two fundamentally different approaches to the eurozone's institutional governance is a rather stable feature of EMU politics. Overall, neither side of this political divide dominated the bargaining of the recent EMU reforms. The reform outcomes between 2010 and 2015 accommodated the core demands of both sides. Accordingly, the analysis of the intergovernmental bargaining shows that the negotiation outcomes were the result of compromises and reciprocity between these two opposing camps of Member States (Lundgren et al., 2019).

Third, the *partnership between France and Germany*, which is well-known as the European integration engine, played a key role in the pre-bargaining stage, that is, the agenda-setting of policymaking (Degner and Leuffen, 2019). Agenda-setting refers to the pre-negotiation period, during which decision-makers define the options to be negotiated among all EU Member States. An important power at this stage is the blockage of certain proposals (Bachrach and Baratz, 1962). France and Germany, as northern and southern coalition representatives, could broker compromises in advance and keep certain proposals off the agenda. For example, the Germans blocked the proposal for Eurobonds. The joint agenda-setting power of France and Germany, however, did not translate into the final bargaining among all EU Member States – neither of the two was remarkably successful, compared to the other EU Member States, in influencing the final bargaining outcome (Lundgren et al., 2019). This summarizes the broader picture. Depending on the context and specific initiatives, we also observe additional coalitions and cooperation among countries that go beyond this stylized and general pattern.

Finally, two *supranational institutions*, the European Central Bank (ECB) and the Commission, played a key role in further deepening the eurozone. The ECB's decisive actions, such as the outright monetary transactions that followed the famous dictum of Mario Draghi that the ECB will do 'whatever it takes' to preserve the euro, have been broadly discussed. Less emphasis has been put on the Commission's role, not least because the EMU reforms have been analysed primarily through the lens of intergovernmental conflicts among the Member States, as mentioned earlier. The Commission, however, was an influential actor during the legislation of EMU reforms, such as the Two- and Six-Pack. For starters, the Commission carefully prepared the ground for new reforms, waiting for the political window of opportunity to open (Kudrna and Puntscher Riekmann, 2021). In addition, the Commission was remarkably successful in influencing the final bargaining in the negotiations among the Member States. The Commission pulled the negotiation outcomes to its preferred option by exerting influence on Member States, which were less exposed to the EMU policy reforms, less integrated in intergovernmental politics, and attached lower salience to the negotiated policies (Lundgren et al., forthcoming).

19.3 BREAKING NEW GROUND WITH NEXT GENERATION EU

If we extend the analysis from EMU reforms to NGEU, which is a financial programme set up in reaction to the COVID-19 pandemic, we observe a continuation of EMU politics, as well as remarkable shifts. The COVID-19 pandemic led to a substantial economic contraction in several EU Member States. To address this economic hardship, the NGEU package was negotiated as a supplement to the new EU budget (i.e. the multiannual financial framework). The NGEU programme substantially extends the EU budget and breaks new ground in respect to both the financing and spending.

In terms of its size, the NGEU's volume is approximately €806 billion for the period 2021–26 (compared to the regular budget of €1,074 billion for 2021–27). All EU Member States together are entitled to receive €386 billion in loans, €407.5 billion in grants, and €12.5 billion for allocation through competitive programmes (European Commission, 2021). The NGEU's spending mechanism is that every Member State has a certain proportion of the programme assigned and submits investment plans, which are supposed to rebuild the EU countries' economies after the COVID-19 pandemic with a specific emphasis on programmes fostering green and digital transitions.

Even more remarkable than the spending side is that NGEU is funded through jointly raised capital on the financial markets. The EU has issued bonds on the financial markets since the 1970s, but never at the scale of NGEU (European Commission, 2021). For example, the EU raised almost €100 billion between 2020 and 2022 for temporary support to mitigate unemployment risks caused by the COVID-19 pandemic (this emergency measure is abbreviated as SURE). The SURE programme was designed as a labour market stabilizer, allowing for the financing of a crisis unemployment insurance scheme with low-interest rate loans (Schelkle, 2021). Thus, although the EU has issued bonds with other programmes, the case of NGEU is unique because of its substantial financing capacity. The Commission has a wide range of funding instruments and techniques at its disposal to borrow on capital markets for the NGEU on the EU's behalf, using the EU budget as security. That the EU Member States jointly raise capital on the financial markets at this scale is a new level of joint financial responsibility, which makes capital for some members available at better conditions. Stabilizing and developing the EU economy by issuing long-term bonds on the capital markets is a policy instrument which was, in this form and scale, out of reach in the EMU reform discussions, during which Eurobonds did not even make it to the negotiation table.

A striking similarity between the EMU reforms and NGEU politics is that both fiscal integration steps were triggered by economic crises. Thus, the updating and advancing of the institutional architecture in fiscal and economic policymaking are highly reactive to crises. In addition, the lines of conflict in EMU and NGEU politics were similar, with the frugal four forming the most sceptical group of EU Member States (i.e. Austria, Denmark, the Netherlands, and Sweden; see Armingeon et al., 2022). The heads of state and government of these countries asked for a downsizing of NGEU programmes, opposing the joint financing of public spending and asking for strict spending conditionality. A major change in NGEU negotiations, compared to EMU politics, was that Germany supported the joint raising of capital at this scale, which made the collective sharing of financial responsibility possible in the NGEU programme. Germany's accommodative stance substantially weakened the northern coalition of Member States and isolated the frugal four, which then could successfully negotiate concessions on the size of the NGEU programme, but they could not block the basic design of this new financing instrument.

Why, then, was this deeper form of collective financing possible in NGEU but not in EMU politics? The major difference between EMU and NGEU was the framing of the causes of the two crises. In NGEU, the asymmetric shock that the pandemic exerted across EU Member States was seen as completely exogenous. Thus, the heavy exposure of some countries to the COVID-19 pandemic was not perceived as a self-inflicted problem. This stands in strong contrast to the narrative in EMU politics, where politicians in fiscally hawkish Member States argued that the countries in need of financial assistance were responsible for their crisis conditions (Matthijs and McNamara, 2015).

This difference in interpretation of the crisis matters. In the case of the eurozone crisis, the narrative of self-inflicted problems laid the ground for strong conditionality and blocked burden-sharing in the form of Eurobonds. An opposing narrative focused on the systemic elements of the crisis. The argument from this perspective is that the EMU's institutional deficiency led to an accumulation of imbalances within the eurozone and exposed the eurozone's less competitive countries to the shocks of the financial crisis (Frieden and Walter, 2017). Following this persuasive analysis, the crisis conditions of some eurozone countries were not primarily self-inflicted. Rather, they were largely a function of the EMU's institutional deficiency.

The broader point for the purpose of this analysis is that the interpretation of how exogenous or self-inflicted an economic crisis is for an EU Member State influences the extent to which the other Member States are willing to agree to fiscal solidarity in the form of fiscal transfers and common debts. A further important element in the discourse about COVID-19 is that the pandemic is regarded as exceptional, and the NGEU programme was designed as a one-time fiscal intervention. The big question is, thus, whether the NGEU instrument of jointly raising credit on the financial markets at this scale becomes a new blueprint in EU fiscal integration in the direction of fiscal federalism or whether this instrument will remain a one-time exception. More broadly speaking, it remains to be seen how fiscal discipline with the SGP, which was suspended because of the pandemic, will be modified in the years ahead.

19.4 SCOPE CONDITIONS AND POWER STRUCTURE IN FISCAL INTEGRATION

The analysis of the EMU reforms and NGEU politics highlights the potential, limits, and scope conditions of fiscal integration in the EU and the eurozone. In the last decade, the two crises have led to various fiscal, financial, and economic reforms with new collective financing mechanisms. The two cases suggest that an economic crisis is a necessary condition for deeper fiscal and economic integration. Although the conflict constellation among EU Member States in the politics of the EMU and NGEU was rather stable, we also observe remarkable shifts, especially regarding Germany's willingness to agree to the new financing instrument in NGEU, which is a substantial development compared to EMU reform politics between 2010 and 2015.

Besides the stable conflict constellations among EU Member States in fiscal integration, it matters how a crisis is framed, particularly whether a crisis is treated as exceptional or the hardship of exposed countries is perceived to be self-inflicted. So far, we have focused on the analysis of the scope conditions and differences in the narratives of the two fiscal integration steps. Another question is who was most powerful and influential in EMU and NGEU politics. In respect to power and influence in fiscal integration politics, we can draw five key conclusions.

First, the politics of fiscal transfers and discipline in the EU are structurally shaped by a rather stable conflict between predominantly northern and southern Member States on both sides. This divide stems from profound differences in economic interests and ideational paradigms of economic and fiscal policymaking (Brunnermeier et al., 2016; Hall, 2018). Of course, there are important nuances across Member States, but this broader divide defines the structure of political conflict among EU Member States. Second, Franco-German cooperation plays a key role in how this structural conflict among Member States translates into policymaking. Both countries play an influential role in defining the policy options that are eventually negotiated (and blocked from the policy choice set), and they both can change the power balance when they take an accommodating stance in the other side's direction, as Germany did in the case of NGEU. Third, smaller coalitions, such as the frugal four, can shape the scope of fiscal integration programmes if they coordinate with one another, but they cannot block the basic design and direction of a fiscal integration step. Fourth, the Commission plays an influential role in the preparation and the final bargaining stage, even when the negotiations are predominantly intergovernmental among Member States.

Finally, the power of ideas and narratives is critical for understanding the politics of fiscal integration (Brunnermeier et al., 2016; McNamara, 1998). Crises may be necessary for further integration, but the way an economic crisis is framed is decisive in respect to how much fiscal solidarity and burden-sharing are part of a new fiscal integration step. The main question in that respect is whether exposure to an economic shock is perceived to be self-inflicted. If not, the odds are much better that the fiscal response of the EU puts more emphasis on burden-sharing and transfers – and is not dominated by the principles of fiscal discipline and conditionality.

Summing up these key findings, we find great continuity since the EMU's creation in Maastricht in 1992. Essentially, two models of integration compete with one another: one is built on fiscal discipline and the other on fiscal transfers and joint debts. Simplifying the politics of fiscal integration, the northern coalition of Member States advocates the former model, the southern coalition the latter. New fiscal reforms and programmes, developed as reactions to crises, are built to varying degrees on the two competing models, while the problems of enforceability and the suspension of fiscal discipline criteria have shown the limits of the fiscal discipline approach. By putting more or less emphasis on the former or the latter model, the new elements of fiscal integration change the fiscal architecture of the EU. Besides the discussed shifts and changes in NGEU and EMU politics, the larger picture points to a remarkably stable political setting since Maastricht. The experience of the last decade also suggests that crises lead to deeper integration – not disintegration, as some may fear – but how the fiscal and economic reform programmes incrementally advance the fiscal architecture of the EU and EMU is heavily dependent on the interpretation of the crisis to which they are designed as a reaction.

19.5 DIFFERENTIATED INTEGRATION AND DEMOCRATIC LEGITIMACY

The NGEU and EMU reforms deepened fiscal integration, and they added new layers of complexity to the model of how Member States are integrated in the fiscal and economic structures of the EU-27 and EMU. An abundance of literature on differentiated integration studies the phenomenon that EU Member States are, to varying extents, integrated in the EU by analysing how and why some Member States integrate further, while others opt-out of certain EU policies (Leuffen et al., 2013; Schimmelfennig and Winzen, 2020; Schimmelfennig et al., 2015). Fiscal, monetary, and financial integration is a crucial case in point. For example, the eurozone includes twenty EU Member States. Denmark has opted out after the Maastricht Treaty was rejected in a referendum, and Sweden does not want to adopt the euro either. At the same time, some Central and Eastern European Member States are waiting for the next steps in the euro accession process, while others have no such plans.

Overall, integration in EU fiscal policy is highly fragmented, which complicates reforms. As previously discussed, NGEU is designed as a fiscal reaction for the EU-27 to the pandemic and as a complement to the EU budget. In that sense, NGEU is not connected to the challenges of EMU, although the fiscal programme of NGEU includes – with the joint raising of credits – a tool of fiscal solidarity, which is, as a policy instrument, highly relevant for the challenges of the eurozone. Moreover, regarding the spending side, the investment programmes of NGEU address a core challenge of the eurozone, as they are supposed to increase the competitiveness of EU Member States. The imbalances in competitiveness across the eurozone countries are a main source of instability within the currency area (Frieden and Walter, 2017). The broader point is that the existing fiscal and economic programmes of the EU and EMU do not define clear demarcation lines between the policies and competences of the eurozone and EU-27, which complicates the targeted improvement of the fiscal architecture in the monetary union and the full EU-27.

Zooming into the eurozone's governance structure, we observe high levels of differentiation and complexity. Fiscal and economic policies apply to varying sets of Member States and are to different extents implemented. Also, the decision-making processes vary, from legislation according to the ordinary or special legislative procedure (e.g. banking regulations) to intergovernmental agreements (e.g. fiscal compact). One example of differentiated integration is the fiscal compact, which was signed in 2012 as an intergovernmental treaty by all EU Member States, except the Czech Republic and the United Kingdom (Smeets and Beach, 2021). The intergovernmental treaty was signed outside the EU legal framework, and some parts are only binding for eurozone Member States. The institutional architecture of the banking regulations stands in contrast to the fiscal compact. The banking union policies (i.e. the Single Supervisory Mechanism and the Single Resolution Mechanism and Fund) were adopted according to the community method of special and ordinary legislative procedure, which involves the European Parliament in decision-making, and the policies cover all EU countries (Howarth and Quaglia, 2016).

These examples illustrate that fiscal, economic, and financial policies apply to different compositions of Member States and follow different decision-making procedures. As an additional level of heterogeneity, we also observe variation in compliance across countries (e.g. as far as adherence to the fiscal debt and deficit criteria is concerned; see de Haan and Gootjes, Chapter 18 in this volume). In sum, the levels of fiscal integration across Member States and policy fields, as well as the governance structure, are highly differentiated. This institutional structure becomes even more complex when including the involvement of the different institutions, such as the ECB, the Commission, and the European Parliament, or more specialized bodies, such as the Boards of Governors and Directors of the European Stability Mechanism, which conducts the task of providing conditional financial assistance to eurozone countries in need.

Overall, this complex and differentiated set-up complicates the search for reforms aiming to clarify integration in the fiscal and economic area. Such a clarification should be done by a Treaty revision, but there has been no Treaty update since the Lisbon amendment was signed in 2007. Thus, the structure of fiscal and economic policymaking in the EU remains somewhat ambiguous on the question of which type of fiscal coordination and fiscal burden-sharing ought to be organized on the level of the EMU or EU-27. The differentiated nature of the fiscal policy area eventually raises questions about the desirability of fragmentation and on the democratic legitimacy of EU fiscal policymaking.

Several scholars have identified the need for deeper fiscal and economic integration (De Grauwe and Ji, 2014; Genschel and Jachtenfuchs, 2018). The approach towards deeper integration, however, is contested. Some analyses have identified more differentiated integration as a path forward because this allows a subset of Member States that are willing and able to move ahead with further fiscal integration. The argument for this integration model is that more flexibility in the composition of Member States helps overcome conflicts and is conducive to achieving deeper integration among some Member States (De Vries, 2018; Fabbrini, 2019). Accordingly, more differentiation with deeper integration within the EMU is supposed to make the institutional framework of the eurozone more resilient. The Commission, however, is critical towards more differentiation (although the White Paper of the Commission from 2017 mentions this as a possible scenario; see European Commission, 2017). Also, the EU Member States that want to adopt the euro, but are not yet members of the eurozone, are critical as well. They fear that more flexibility will eventually make it more difficult for them to enter the eurozone.

A final and related key challenge of fiscal integration is the democratic anchoring of decision-making on the European level. An abundant literature in political science has analysed the so-called democratic deficit of the EU (Follesdal and Hix, 2006; Hix, 2008; Majone, 1998; Moravcsik, 2002). In the case of fiscal and economic integration, three dimensions are particularly relevant in this debate: (a) the substantial power shift to national governments discussed earlier, (b) the vertical separation of authority between the national and European levels, and (c) the extent to which decision-making is democratically legitimized (Scharpf, 2011).

A defining characteristic of fiscal integration in the EU is that national governments take a central role. The Council of the EU and the European Council, composed of representatives of national governments, are the key institutions (Smeets and Beach, 2021; Târlea et al., 2023). In these institutions, the governments formulate policies to which they are then held accountable. This elevates the national executives to legislators on the European level and, consequently, limits the room of national parliaments to manoeuvre in fiscal policymaking (Scharpf, 2011). One remedy to this problem is the empowerment of the European Parliament, which, however, also raises questions in respect to authority transfers to the European level and the capacity of the European Parliament to provide this democratic anchoring within the institutional structure of the EU.

In any case, the shift of power from national parliaments to national governments is particularly sensitive in the area of fiscal integration because the power to tax and spend is a core state power. As such, fiscal policymaking is a prerogative of national parliaments in parliamentary democracies, which makes it difficult to transfer authority in this field to the EU level. The policy authority on the European level recalibrates this separation of power between executives and legislators on the national level. One way to address this problem is the systematic involvement of national parliaments in EU fiscal and economic policymaking (Beukers, 2013; Puntscher Riekmann and Wydra, 2013; Winzen, 2022).

A related critique is that the EU's economic and fiscal policies, most notably the conditionality policies of the eurozone reforms, confront 'national democratic choice' (Featherstone, 2016, p. 48), and may lead to 'a crisis of democratic legitimacy' (Scharpf, 2011, p. 165). The basic concern is that EMU governance puts constraints on national policy options and lacks democratic mechanisms for managing crisis politics. Consequently, citizens may become detached from national and EU democracy. Several studies have observed this phenomenon in countries that were exposed to the eurozone crisis (Armingeon et al., 2016; Matthijs, 2017), while others have identified this effect as a temporary problem rather than as a systemic threat to the legitimacy of democratic governance (Schraff and Schimmelfennig, 2019).

Finally, Scharpf (2011) approaches the democratic challenge of fiscal integration with the conceptual distinction between input and output legitimacy. His analysis elucidates the limits and challenges of input legitimacy (i.e. governance by the people) based on a complex chain of delegation and representation in the EU's multilevel structure. Output legitimacy (i.e. governance for the people) refers to the requirement of providing welfare and prosperity to EU citizens. The eurozone crisis has shown that output legitimacy is lacking when citizens in countries exposed to economic hardship, such as Greece or Italy, do not experience the euro as a source of welfare and prosperity, particularly when EMU fiscal policies involve austerity (Baccaro et al., 2021; Franchino and Segatti, 2019; Jurado et al., 2020). Without output legitimacy, the governance of the eurozone becomes challenging because the EMU institutional framework lacks a strong foundation on the principle of input legitimacy.

19.6 CONCLUSION

Building on the political science scholarship, this contribution has analysed the politics of fiscal integration. From a long-term perspective, the politics of fiscal integration are characterized by a strong continuity in the basic set-up since the EMU's creation in Maastricht approximately thirty years ago. The core political conflict is between predominantly northern and southern Member States, and the basic conflict is between those who emphasize fiscal discipline measures versus those who advocate a system of fiscal transfers (Brunnermeier et al., 2016; Lehner and Wasserfallen, 2019). This conflict constellation is conducive to a standstill and gridlock, but the recent crises of the eurozone and the COVID-19 pandemic have also led to several fiscal, financial, and economic reforms. Overall, both crises were addressed with a deepening of fiscal integration. Whereas the banking union stands out in the case of the EMU as a reform achievement, the NGEU introduced an investment programme that is financed through joint borrowing on the capital markets (Armingeon et al., 2022; Howarth and Quaglia, 2016; Schelkle, 2021).

Besides the progress on integration, this reactive mode of crisis-induced fiscal integration has further increased the complexity of the EU's fiscal architecture. As a result, fiscal policy is a textbook case of differentiated integration in the EU: different fiscal and economic policies apply to different compositions of Member States, which are shaped and administered by different decision-making procedures and institutions and implemented to varying extents by Member States. On a more general level, the demarcation line between fiscal policies of the EU-27 and the EMU is ambiguous. Against this backdrop, a key question is whether a more distinct differentiation in the form of deeper fiscal integration among a core group of Member States in the eurozone is a promise or peril for the future of European integration. While this approach may have clear advantages, as willing and able Member States could move ahead, proposals in that direction meet strong resistance, questioning the political feasibility of such initiatives.

Given the ad hoc and crisis-induced extension of fiscal integration and the high level of differentiation, clarifications about the approach to fiscal integration and the institutional responsibilities would be a reasonable next ambition. Instead of adding new layers of complexity to the fiscal architecture, a basic reform should clarify the model of fiscal integration. Ideally, such a constitutional reform would (a) define the balance between the principles of fiscal discipline and transfer, (b) distinguish between the fiscal policies of the eurozone and the EU-27, and (c) separate authority between the national and EU levels more distinctively. Only such a reform, which requires a Treaty change, can address concerns about the democratic legitimacy of fiscal policymaking in the EU (Auer and Scicluna, 2021). The governments of EU Member States have been too powerful in the fiscal politics of crisis management during the last decade. From a democratic point of view, this executive dominance should be better balanced by either domestic parliaments or the European Parliament. A constitutional reform in this direction would eventually foster the democratic anchoring of fiscal integration.

This may all be desirable, but the unanimity requirement of Treaty amendments makes such constitutional reforms unlikely when there is a high level of political contestation about basic principles, as is the case with fiscal integration. Thus, more realistic is further crisis-induced and incremental reform with a central role played by the Franco-German partnership in the basic conflict constellation between northern and southern Member States (Kudrna and Puntscher Riekmann, 2021). A further reality is that the EU has to tackle one crisis after another and that the next fiscal conflict is already on the agenda. Because of the COVID-19 pandemic, the fiscal deficit and debt rules have been suspended and will most likely be modified. Several Member States have called for an easing of the fiscal rules, and Germany reacted sceptically but signalled some flexibility. Thus, the basic conflict among advocates of fiscal discipline and supporters of more fiscal transfers will continue, and time will tell whether the EU Member States will recalibrate fiscal integration by designing a more distinct and stable model. The alternative is that ad hoc and crisis-induced reactions will continue to add new layers of complexity to the EU fiscal architecture.

REFERENCES

Alesina, A., and Wacziarg, R. (1999). Is Europe going too far? *Carnegie-Rochester Conference Series on Public Policy* 51(1), 1–42.

Armingeon, K., and Cranmer, S. (2018). Position-taking in the euro crisis. *Journal of European Public Policy* 25(4), 546–566.

Armingeon, K., Guthmann, K., and Weisstanner, D. (2016). How the euro divides the Union: The effect of economic adjustment on support for democracy in Europe. *Socio-Economic Review* 14(1), 1–26.

Armingeon, K., de la Porte, C., Heins, E., and Sacchi, S. (2022). Voices from the past: Economic and political vulnerabilities in the making of next generation EU. *Comparative European Politics* 20, 144–165.

Auer, S., and Scicluna, N. (2021). The impossibility of constitutionalizing emergency Europe. *Journal of Common Market Studies* 59(1), 20–31.

Baccaro, L., Bremer, B., and Neimanns, E. (2021). Till austerity do us part? A survey experiment on support for the euro in Italy. *European Union Politics* 22(3), 401–423.

Bachrach, P., and Baratz, M. S. (1962). Two faces of power. *American Political Science Review* 56(4), 947–952.

Beukers, T. (2013). The eurozone crisis and the legitimacy of differentiated integration. EUI Working Paper, Max Weber Programme 2013/36.

Bordo, M. D., Jonung, L., and Markiewicz, A. (2013). A fiscal union for the euro: Some lessons from history. *CESifo Economic Studies* 59(3), 449–488.

Brunnermeier, M. K., James, H., and Landau, J.-P. (2016). *The Euro and the Battle of Ideas*. Princeton, NJ: Princeton University Press.

Bulmer, S. (2014). Germany and the eurozone crisis: Between hegemony and domestic politics. *West European Politics* 37(6), 1244–1263.

Carstensen, M. B., and Schmidt, V. A. (2021). Between power and powerlessness in the euro zone crisis and thereafter. *Journal of European Public Policy* 28(6), 922–929.

Copelovitch, M., Frieden, J., and Walter, S. (2016). The political economy of the euro crisis. *Comparative Political Studies* 49(7), 811–840.

Csehi, R., and Puetter, U. (2021). Who determined what governments really wanted? Preference formation and the euro crisis. *West European Politics* 44(3), 463–484.

De Grauwe, P., and Ji, Y. (2014). The future of the eurozone. *The Manchester School* 82(S1), 15–34.

De Vries, C. E. (2018). *Euroscepticism and the Future of European Integration*. Oxford: Oxford University Press.

Degner, H., and Leuffen, D. (2019). Franco-German cooperation and the rescuing of the eurozone. *European Union Politics* 20(1), 89–108.

Dolls, M., Fuest, C., Neumann, D., and Peichl, A. (2018). An unemployment insurance scheme for the euro area? A comparison of different alternatives using microdata. *International Tax and Public Finance* 25(1), 273–309.

European Commission (2017). *White Paper on the Future of Europe: Reflections and Scenarios for the EU27 by 2025*. COM(2017) 2025. Brussels: European Commission.

European Commission (2021). *Communication from the Commission to the European Parliament and the Council: On a New Funding Strategy to Finance Next Generation EU*. COM(2021) 250 final. Brussels: European Commission.

Fabbrini, S. (2019). *Europe's Future: Decoupling and Reforming*. Cambridge: Cambridge University Press.

Featherstone, K. (2016). Conditionality, democracy and institutional weakness: the euro-crisis trilemma. *Journal of Common Market Studies* 54(1), 48–64.

Feldstein, M. (2012). The failure of the euro: The little currency that couldn't. *Foreign Affairs* 91(1), 105–116.

Follesdal, A., and Hix, S. (2006). Why there is a democratic deficit in the EU: A response to Majone and Moravcsik. *Journal of Common Market Studies* 44(3), 533–562.

Franchino, F., and Segatti, P. (2019). Public opinion on the eurozone fiscal union: Evidence from survey experiments in Italy. *Journal of European Public Policy* 26(1), 126–148.

Frieden, J., and Walter, S. (2017). Understanding the political economy of the eurozone crisis. *Annual Review of Political Science* 20(1), 371–390.

Genschel, P., and Jachtenfuchs, M. (2018). From market integration to core state powers: The eurozone crisis, the refugee crisis and integration theory. *Journal of Common Market Studies* 56(1), 178–196.

Griller, S., and Lentsch, E. (2021). *EMU Integration and Member States' Constitutions*. Oxford: Hart Publishing.

Hall, P. A. (2018). Varieties of capitalism in light of the euro crisis. *Journal of European Public Policy* 25(1), 7–30.

Hix, S. (2008). *What's Wrong with the European Union and How to Fix It*. Cambridge: Polity Press.

Howarth, D., and Quaglia, L. (2016). *The Political Economy of European Banking Union*. Oxford: Oxford University Press.

Ioannou, D., Leblond, P., and Niemann, A. (2015). European integration and the crisis: Practice and theory. *Journal of European Public Policy* 22(2), 155–176.

Jones, E., Kelemen, D. R., and Meunier, S. (2021). Failing forward? Crises and patterns of European integration. *Journal of European Public Policy* 28(10), 1519–1536.

Jurado, I., Walter, S., Konstantinidis, N., and Dinas, E. (2020). Keeping the euro at any cost? Explaining attitudes toward the euro–austerity trade-off in Greece. *European Union Politics* 21(3), 383–405.

Kassim, H., Saurugger, S., and Puetter, U. (2020). The study of national preference formation in times of the euro crisis and beyond. *Political Studies Review* 18(4), 463–474.

Krugman, P. (2013). Revenge of the optimum currency area. *National Bureau of Economic Research Macroeconomics Annual* 27(1), 439–448.

Kudrna, Z., and Puntscher Riekmann, S. (2021). Eurozone politics and its implications for further reforms. In K. Zdenek, S. Puntscher Riekmann, and F. Wasserfallen (eds.), *The Politics of Eurozone Reforms*. Colchester: Rowman and Littlefield, pp. 123–152.

Kudrna, Z., and Wasserfallen, F. (2021). Conflict among Member States and the influence of the Commission in EMU politics. *Journal of European Public Policy* 28(6), 902–913.

Lehner, T., and Wasserfallen, F. (2019). Political conflict in the reform of the eurozone. *European Union Politics* 20(1), 45–64.

Leuffen, D., Rittberger, B., and Schimmelfennig, F. (2013). *Differentiated Integration: Explaining Variation in the European Union*. London: Palgrave Macmillan.

Lundgren, M., Bailer, S., Dellmuth, L. M., Tallberg, J., and Târlea, S. (2019). Bargaining success in the reform of the eurozone. *European Union Politics* 20(1), 65–88.

Lundgren, M., Tallberg, J., and Wasserfallen, F. (forthcoming). Differentiated influence by supranational instititutions: Evidence from the European Union. *European Journal of Political Research*.

Majone, G. (1998). Europe's 'democratic deficit': The question of standards. *European Law Journal* 4(1), 5–28.

Matthijs, M. (2017). Integration at what price? The erosion of national democracy in the euro periphery. *Government and Opposition* 52(2), 266–294.

Matthijs, M., and McNamara, K. R. (2015). The 'euro crisis' theory effect: Northern saints, southern sinners, and the demise of the Eurobond. *Journal of European Integration* 37(2), 229–245.

McNamara, K. R. (1998). *The Currency of Ideas: Monetary Politics in the European Union*. Ithaca, NY: Cornell University Press.

Moravcsik, A. (2002). In defense of the 'democratic deficit': Reassessing legitimacy in the European Union. *Journal of Common Market Studies* 40(4), 603–634.

Morlino, L., and Sottilotta, C. E. (2019). *The Politics of the Eurozone Crisis in Southern Europe: A Comparative Reappraisal*. London: Palgrave Macmillan.

Mundell, R. A. (1961). A theory of optimum currency areas. *American Economic Review* 51(4), 657–665.

Obstfeld, M., Alesina, A., and Cooper, R. N. (1997). Europe's gamble. *Brookings Papers on Economic Activity* 1997(2), 241–317.

Puntscher Riekmann, S., and Wydra, D. (2013). Representation in the European state of emergency: Parliaments against governments? *Journal of European Integration* 35(5), 565–582.
Sala-i-Martin, X., and Sachs, J. (1991). Fiscal federalism and optimum currency areas: Evidence for Europe from the United States. NBER Working Paper No. 3855.
Scharpf, F. W. (2011). Monetary Union, fiscal crisis and the pre-emption of democracy. *Zeitschrift für Staats- und Europawissenschaften (ZSE)/Journal for Comparative Government and European Policy* 9 (2), 163–198.
Schelkle, W. (2017). *The Political Economy of Monetary Solidarity: Understanding the Euro Experiment*. Oxford: Oxford University Press.
Schelkle, W. (2021). Fiscal integration in an experimental union: How path-breaking was the EU's response to the COVID-19 pandemic? *Journal of Common Market Studies* 59(S1), 44–55.
Schild, J. (2013). Leadership in hard times: Germany, France, and the management of the eurozone crisis. *German Politics and Society* 31(1), 24–47.
Schimmelfennig, F., and Winzen, T. (2020). *Ever Looser Union? Differentiated European Integration*. Oxford: Oxford University Press.
Schimmelfennig, F., Leuffen, D., and Rittberger, B. (2015). The European Union as a system of differentiated integration: Interdependence, politicization and differentiation. *Journal of European Public Policy* 22(6), 764–782.
Schraff, D., and Schimmelfennig, F. (2019). Eurozone bailouts and national democracy: Detachment or resilience. *European Union Politics* 20(3), 361–383.
Sinn, H.-W. (2014). *The Euro Trap: On Bursting Bubbles, Budgets and Beliefs*. Oxford: Oxford University Press.
Smeets, S., and Beach, D. (2021). Political and instrumental leadership in major EU reforms. The role and influence of the EU institutions in setting-up the fiscal compact. *Journal of European Public Policy* 27 (1), 63–81.
Stiglitz, J. E. (2016). *The Euro: How a Common Currency Threatens the Future of Europe*. New York: W. W. Norton.
Târlea, S., Kudrna, Z., Bailer, S., and Wasserfallen, F. (2023). Executive power in European Union politics. *Governance*, Early View, 1–18. https://doi.org/10.1111/gove.12761
Wasserfallen, F. (2014). Political and economic integration in the EU: The case of failed tax harmonization. *Journal of Common Market Studies* 52(2), 420–435.
Wasserfallen, F., Leuffen, D., Kudrna, Z., and Degner, H. (2019). Analysing European Union decision-making during the eurozone crisis with new data. *European Union Politics* 20(1), 3–23.
Winzen, T. (2022). The institutional position of national parliaments in the European Union: Developments, explanations, effects. *Journal of European Public Policy* 29(6), 994–1008.
Woolley, J. T. (1994). Linking political and monetary union: The Maastricht agenda and German domestic politics. In B. Eichengreen and J. Frieden (eds.), *The Political Economy of European Monetary Unification*. Boulder, CO: Westview Press, pp. 67–86.

20

Adjustments in Economic Crises

The Different Outcomes of the Sovereign Debt and Pandemic Crises in Europe

Sergio Fabbrini and Andrea Capati

20.1 INTRODUCTION

This chapter's aim is to investigate *economic* adjustment in Europe. By economic adjustment we mean the logic of the institution created to support Member States in need of financial help. The European Union introduced two different financial institutions for helping Member States to adjust to two crises with similar systemic implications, the sovereign debt crisis of the early 2010s and the pandemic crisis of the early 2020s. That is, the European Stability Mechanism (ESM) for adjusting to the sovereign debt crisis and the Recovery and Resilience Facility (RRF) for recovering from the pandemic crisis. Apparently, the two financial instruments have different aims, the ESM having a crisis management role and the RRF the role of helping the post-pandemic recovery of Member State economies. However, through its conditionality system, the ESM too aims to influence the post-crisis adjustment of the budgetary framework of Member States receiving ESM help. In less than a decade, facing two crises with similar economic implications, the EU moved from an approach of 'unconstrained intergovernmentalism' (ESM) to one of 'constrained supranationalism' (RRF), although the ESM is a permanent institution while RRF is a *pro-tempore* one (lasting until December 2026).

The focus on post-crisis *economic* adjustment does not imply an undervaluation of the role of monetary instruments. Indeed, in both crises, the European Central Bank (ECB) played a crucial role in managing them, giving time to national governments (coordinated through the Council and European Council) and supranational actors (represented mainly by the European Commission) to devise the financial instrument for helping Member States hit by the crisis to economically adjust in the post-crisis period. The chapter distinguishes between economic and monetary instruments, on the assumption that the ECB has been a crucial crisis manager (as we show in detail), while the Council of the EU/European Council and the European Commission have been the crucial actors for devising the post-crisis economic adjustment.

The chapter is organized as follows. Section 20.2 analyses the mixed decision-making structure that has characterized the EU since the 1992 Maastricht Treaty with special attention to the governance of the EMU. Section 20.3 examines the institutional features and decision-making procedures of the ESM, showing its unconstrained intergovernmental nature. Section 20.4 considers the institutional features and decision-making procedures of the RRF, showing its constrained supranational nature. Section 20.5 uses the policy learning paradigm to explain why the EU moved from the ESM to the RRF governance logic to economically adjust to the pandemic crisis. The conclusion sums up the chapter's argument.

20.2 EU DECISION-MAKING OR GOVERNANCE REGIMES

20.2.1 *The Post-Maastricht Governance Framework*

What has come to characterize the post-1992 Maastricht EU has been the institutionalization of different decision-making regimes. In a pioneering work, Helen Wallace (2000, pp. 28–35) identified five policy modes (community method, regulatory model, multi-level governance, policy coordination, and intensive transgovernmentalism) for dealing with different policy issues. The subsequent development of the EU policy-making system (Richardson and Mazey, 2015) led Fabbrini (2020), twenty years later, to identify four policy modes, two organized through a supranational governance regime (community method and centralized regulation) and two through one of two intergovernmental regimes (policy coordination and intergovernmental method) for deciding different policy issues.

One might argue that, from a governance regime perspective, the post-Maastricht EU has come to adopt (heuristically) two different logics. On the one hand, it consolidated the supranational logic, inaugurated by the 1957 Rome Treaties, for dealing with regulatory policies of the common and then single market. On the other, it institutionalized an intergovernmental logic for dealing with the strategic policies that entered its agenda with the end of the cold war. As different as the four policy modes may be, their decision-making processes stress the predominance of either a supranational or an intergovernmental logic. While the supranational logic typically concerns issues of low domestic political salience (the regulatory policies of the single market) (Egan, 2020; Dehousse, 2011), the intergovernmental logic deals with issues of high domestic political salience (the Core State Power or CSP policies traditionally close to national sovereignty, Genschel and Jachtenfuchs, 2014; see also Bickerton et al., 2015).

The current 2009 Lisbon Treaty constitutionalized the distinction between different decision-making regimes in relation to distinct policies (Fabbrini, 2015), although it abolished the pillar structure devised in Maastricht for organizing them. Particularly, acknowledging (for the first time) the European Council as an EU institution without a legislative role (thus distinct from the Council, specifically the Economic and Financial Affairs (ECOFIN) Council) and acting as a collegial executive (Bickerton et al., 2015), it created the conditions for making the management of a future crisis a *Chefsache*, a matter for the bosses (Fabbrini and Puetter, 2016; Puetter, 2014). Thanks to the Lisbon Treaty, in a crisis (Borzel, 2016) the European Council could give not only political orientation to the EMU, but it could also be involved in designing the policy instruments to deal with the crisis (Wessels, 2016). This is exactly what happened.

20.2.2 *The Economic Governance of the EMU*

Although governance differentiation has come to constitute a structural feature of the post-1992 EU decision-making process, it cannot be understood as a rigid separation between the two decision-making logics. Institutional innovation has not only been tested in interstitial policy fields (Batòra, 2020; Heritier, 2007), but particularly with the start of the Economic and Monetary Union (EMU) in 1999 the two decision-making logics were combined. The EMU economic policy side was put under the control of intergovernmental institutions (the ECOFIN Council and then the Eurogroup of the economic and financial ministers of EMU Member States), whereas the monetary policy side was assigned to the full control of a supranational and independent institution, i.e. the European Central Bank or ECB (Fabbrini, 2016; Tuori and Tuori, 2014). The EMU is thus an institutionally mixed policy regime, decentralized in the management of economic (i.e. fiscal, budgetary) policies but centralized in the management of monetary policy (Jones, 2020a; Enderlein and Verdun, 2013). Thus, the twenty (from 1 January 2023) national governments have agreed to share a single currency but not a single fiscal policy. Instead of creating an autonomous Brussels fiscal capacity, fiscal policy has in fact remained in the hands of national governments. However, through the 1997 Stability and Growth Pact (SGP), consisting of a Resolution and two Council regulations (the 'preventive arm' entered into force in 1998 and the 'dissuasive arm' in 1999), the national fiscal policies of the EMU Member States have come to be highly regulated, placed as they were under macroeconomic parameters (national public debt should not be higher than 60 per cent and public deficit should not be higher than 3 per cent of national GDP) constraining their fiscal sovereignty. Thus, with the single currency the EMU adopted a model of coordination of national fiscal policies rather than the model of central fiscal capacity adopted by other monetary unions (Hallerberg, 2014). The EMU is the outcome of an interstate compromise (Fabbrini, 2015) which generated an incomplete contract or unsettled equilibrium between two different decision-making logics (on incomplete contracts see Farrell and Heritier, 2007).

Moreover, the Maastricht Treaty and the SGP rules are asymmetric in their call to avoid excessive government deficits without any constraint on the corresponding budget surpluses. The rules proscribe excessive government deficits even if this entails pro-cyclical fiscal behaviour, but do not have any prescribing power over policies by countries with fiscal space. This asymmetry reflected the Brussels–Frankfurt consensus prevailing at the time of the negotiations on the Maastricht Treaty and the SGP: the focus was on the risk of government deficits aggravated by the common pool problem (Buti and Gaspar, 2021). For the European Commission and the Council to credibly enforce the Excessive Deficit Procedure in the absence of a central fiscal capacity, monetary policy should have an unconstrained space to respond to shocks, i.e. monetary policy cannot be limited by an Effective Lower Bound (ELB) on interest rates (Buti and Fabbrini, 2023). During the EMU's first decade (2000s), the lack of a central fiscal capacity combined with a weak monetary dominance led some Member States' governments to ask for temporary exemption (obtaining it, in the cases of Germany and France in 2003) and thus a reform in 2005 for making respect for the requirements of the SGP less discretionary (Verdun and Zimmermann, 2006). The revision, however, did not affect the large 'convergence bonus' benefiting the Member States, arising from a substantial fall in their interest burden and the automatic benefits of sustained growth. Their combined effect allowed euro area Member States to reduce deficits without underlying adjustment and structural reforms.

20.2.3 *The EMU and the Sovereign Debt Crisis*

When the Global Financial Crisis (GFC) started in 2007–8, becoming an economic crisis and thus, in Europe, a sovereign debt crisis in 2010–11, the EMU compromise did not stand. The order and magnitude of the Greek violation of the SGP rules made it difficult to identify a solution (although many were considered), also because the EU lacked a central budget or other funds to be used during a time of a crisis. A decision-making structure (the Eurogroup, see Puetter, 2006) aggregating different national preferences and dependent on the approval of different national parliaments did not help. With the emergence of the sovereign debt crisis in 2009, the EU tried to overcome the shortcomings of the EMU compromise, creating first the European Financial Stabilisation Mechanism (EFSM), an emergency funding programme (based on Council Regulation No. 407/2010 of 11 May 2010) raising funds on the financial markets and guaranteed by the European Commission using the EU budget as collateral; then the European Financial Stability Facility (EFSF) in May 2010, a special purpose vehicle based on an international treaty, financed by members of the EMU, and located in Luxembourg; and, finally, the European Stability Mechanism in October 2012, based on an intergovernmental treaty external to the EU legal order, thus advancing towards further economic integration through the programme of the banking union (Howarth and Quaglia, 2016).

However, because the Greek crisis was left without a clear solution, the sovereign debt crisis escalated, leaving to the ECB the role of stabilizing markets (Verdun, 2017). Already in August 2007, the ECB made credit available; in the autumn of 2008, it cooperated actively with the other central banks to respond to the financial crisis; in May 2010, it participated as a member of the Troika to assist needy countries and inaugurated the Security Market Programme (SMP) to restore an appropriate functioning of the monetary policy transmission mechanism; in December 2011, it enabled long-term refinancing to 500 banks, extended in February 2012 to 800 banks in its second long-term refinancing operation; in summer 2012, in order to control yield spreads between countries at the periphery and at the core of the euro area, it introduced the unprecedented programme of Outright Monetary Transactions (OMT), which would allow it to buy unlimited quantities of bonds from a country under market speculation. Although the OMT has never been used, it epitomized the commitment taken by the then ECB president, Mario Draghi, in his 2012 July speech in London, 'to do whatever it takes to preserve the euro'. In June 2014, the ECB introduced negative interest rates, then launched quantitative easing (QE), intended to stave off the risk of deflation. The ECB, particularly during the presidency of Mario Draghi (Verdun, 2017), took innovative decisions to manage the sovereign debt crisis, but also to promote growth (injecting liquidity into the economy), going much beyond its statutory assignment to take care only of price stability (Heldt and Mueller, 2019). If it is true that monetary policy was the only game in town (El-Erian, 2016), it was a very unconventional one.

The euro area crisis management by the ECB allowed the time necessary for national governments of the euro area to devise the budgetary adjustment strategy (the 'E' of EMU) to achieve EMU stability (Van Middelaar, 2019; Verdun, 2015). Because the crisis affected mainly the sovereign debt of some EMU Member States, the Eurogroup (within the ECOFIN Council) and the Euro Summit of national leaders (within the European Council) became the main arenas for devising that strategy (Fabbrini, 2015). In particular, the European Council/ Euro Summit came to exercise executive power to define the direction to be followed by national legislatures in implementing its policy decisions (the so-called austerity measures). It transformed itself into an international arena for setting up new intergovernmental instruments, outside of the EU legal order, when necessary for circumventing internal resistance (Fossum, 2020), as was the case with the 2012 ESM, the 2012 Treaty on Stability, Coordination and Governance in EMU (or Fiscal Compact), and the 2016 Single Resolution Fund (SRF). At the same time, the Single Resolution Mechanism was enacted through both a Regulation (of the European Parliament and the Council establishing uniform rules and a uniform procedure for the resolution of credit institutions) and an intergovernmental agreement (on the transfer and mutualization of contributions to the Single Resolution Fund), and the Single Supervisory Mechanism (SSM), to supervise banks in the euro area and other participating EU countries, was enacted through two regulations (No. 1022/2013 and No. 1024/2013) with significant influence from the EP. The mixed institutional nature of the various pillars of the banking union (Howarth and Quaglia, 2016) is a testament to the mixed character of EMU. While the supranational ECB emerged from the crisis with new policy instruments, the intergovernmental

Eurogroup and Euro Summit devised new financial instruments for economic adjustment, the majority of which are invariably intergovernmental. The ESM was at the centre of this new intergovernmental order.

20.3 THE ESM AND THE ECONOMIC ADJUSTMENT OF THE EURO AREA

Entered into force in 2012 and established as an international treaty external to the EU legal framework in 2013 (Fabbrini, 2016; ESM Treaty, 2012), the ESM applies to its signatory states (i.e. EMU Member States). It was created as a permanent institution for financing those EMU Member States in need of help (during the sovereign debt crisis and afterwards). Based on national financial quotas, the ESM support is predicated on respect for strict conditionalities (see Matthijs and Blyth, 2015) by the receiving Member State.

The ESM has its own set of decision-making bodies and voting rules, but ultimately the decision-making pattern is that the EMU Member States provide an initial capital contribution (in proportion to their GDP) and receive voting rights in line with their share in the total capital stock of the instrument. Its institutional structure consists of a Board of Governors, a Board of Directors, and a Managing Director. The Board of Governors and the Board of Directors come from Member State governments. The Board of Governors is the highest decision-making institution of the ESM. It is made up of the ministers of finance of the ESM members, thus featuring the same composition as the Eurogroup. Representatives of the European Commission and the ECB may participate in meetings of the Board of Governors but only as observers. The Board of Directors consists of senior officials from the ESM Member States appointed by the Board of Governors and revocable at any time. The European Commission and the ECB may appoint one representative each with the right to participate in meetings of the Board of Directors, but only as observers. The Managing Director is appointed by the Board of Governors for a five-year term, renewable once, and can be dismissed at any time by the same Board. The Managing Director acts under the Board of Directors' control, which operates under the Board of Governors' political will, thus reflecting the interests of Member State governments, according to the quota of their share in the ESM treasury. In this decision-making framework, the European Commission plays a technical role for the Board of Governors and the ECB as the latter's financial adviser, a highly problematic role since both institutions are part of the EU institutional structure while the ESM represents a different international organization.

Regarding voting rules, the Board of Governors and the Board of Directors take decisions by mutual agreement, qualified majority, or simple majority. Decisions by mutual agreement require the unanimity of all members, net of abstentions; the adoption of a decision by qualified majority requires 80 per cent of the votes cast; while decisions by simple majority require 50 per cent plus 1 of the votes cast. The voting rights of each ESM member in the Board of Governors and the Board of Directors equal the number of their shares in the capital stock of the instrument. Through such a procedure, the adoption of a decision by mutual agreement requires a qualified majority of 85 per cent of the votes cast rather than unanimity. This might outvote smaller member states, although that possibility was challenged by Estonia's constitutional court (Judgement 3-4-1-6-12). The Board of Governors decides, by mutual agreement, whether the ESM should provide financial assistance to any ESM member based on a conditionality scheme. It thus mandates the European Commission and the ECB to design the terms of the economic policy conditionality of each financial assistance programme. The Board of Directors takes decisions mostly by qualified majority, while adopting the same voting rules as the Board of Governors for decisions delegated to it by the latter. By qualified majority, the Board of Directors approves the financial assistance facility agreement. Through the composition of its decision-making bodies and their voting rules, the intergovernmental logic permeates the entire governance of the ESM.

In sum, the ESM provides stability support to the EMU but on condition of pursuing macroeconomic adjustment programmes. The decision-making process for granting support and disbursement of the tranches of financial assistance is spearheaded by the Board of Governors and formally completed by the Board of Directors. While relying on the technical support of EU institutions – such as the European Commission and the ECB – for negotiating and monitoring compliance with the terms of financial assistance, the final decision is taken by the Board of Governors, directly expressing the views of the Member State governments participating in the facility. The national governments transfer the financial resources and decide how to use them. That is why the ESM has the features of unconstrained intergovernmentalism.

20.4 THE COVID-19 CRISIS AND THE RRF

20.4.1 *Addressing the Pandemic*

The COVID-19 crisis of the early 2020s had dramatic transnational economic consequences, although it hit southern Member States (such as Italy and Spain) first and entailed different consequences depending on the economic situation of Member States prior to the pandemic (Jones, 2020b).

Again, the monetary strategy was crucial for immediately containing the pandemic's economic effects (Quaglia and Verdun, 2021). Although on 12 March the ECB's new president, Christine Lagarde, stated that it was not the ECB's duty to close the spread between the sovereign debt instruments of the various national governments (particularly between German and Italian bonds) caused by the spread of the pandemic, the ECB dramatically changed its policy position a few days later. On 18 March, the ECB promoted a new Pandemic Emergency-Purchase Programme (PEPP) of private and public sector securities, originally consisting of €750 billion. On April 2020, it also introduced the Pandemic Emergency Longer-Term Refinancing Operations (PELTROs) to serve as a liquidity backstop to the euro area banking system. On June 2020, it increased the €750 billion envelope for the PEPP by €600 billion to a total of €1,350 billion and by another €500 billion the following December. The aim of this non-standard monetary programme was 'to counter the serious risks to the monetary policy transmission mechanism and the outlook for the euro area posed by the coronavirus (COVID-19) outbreak' (as declared in the ECB's official statement).

Using also the Asset Purchase Programme already established in 2014, it reduced the yield spread between government bonds of the Member States with different fiscal stances. Moreover, it used the Targeted Longer-Term Refinancing Operations (TLTROs) inaugurated in 2014 to provide financing to credit institutions, thus preserving favourable borrowing conditions for banks engaged in supporting the real economy. The ECB thus strengthened the policy path tested during the sovereign debt crisis.

On the economic side (which primarily matters for this chapter), this time national governments were more responsive to the crisis than in the early 2010s. Already on 23 March 2020, the ECOFIN Council temporarily suspended the SGP with a view to providing the Member States with greater fiscal space to withstand the economic shock. It was the first time that the SGP had been formally suspended, just as it was the first time that the rules restricting state aid to failing companies in the real economy had been eased. Moreover, in those very first months of the pandemic, the ESM immediately set up the Pandemic Crisis Support programme of €240 billion, based on its Enhanced Conditions Credit Line (ECCL), available to all EMU countries, with the only condition being to use the money for 'direct or indirect health expenditure'. Also, the intergovernmental European Investment Bank (EIB) mobilized €200 billion to support small and medium-size enterprises, while a new and limited EU instrument (Support to mitigate Unemployment Risks in an Emergency, SURE, of €100 billion) was activated.

Nevertheless, these measures were perceived as inadequate for dealing with the diffusion of the pandemic and (above all) with its dramatic economic effects. Already on 25 March 2020 the governments of nine EMU Member States (Italy and Spain, the worst hit countries, and then France, Portugal, Greece, Ireland, Belgium, Luxembourg, and Slovenia) sent a letter to European Council President Charles Michel (Letter of the nine, 2020) advancing a different paradigm to deal with the economic consequences of the pandemic. According to the signatories, the pandemic, which epitomizes a symmetric crisis – although with asymmetric effects, for which 'none of the Member States could be considered responsible' – had to be faced through a unified approach rather than through the perception of moral hazard used during the sovereign debt crisis. According to the nine national leaders, later joined by the German chancellor but abandoned by the Slovenian premier, the pandemic urged a common European response, such as issuing common debt. This proposal was thus specified in a Franco-German meeting held on 18 May 2020 (Fleming, 2020). The leaders of the two countries came out of that meeting with a proposal for a Recovery Fund consisting 'of €500 billion to provide EU budgetary expenditure – not loans but budgetary expenditure – for the regions and sectors most affected by the pandemic' (Elysee, 2020), inviting the European Commission to borrow money on the financial markets to fill the €500 billion cash pot and distribute it to governments through the EU budget. The European Commission followed suit (European Commission, 2020). It took the proposal upon itself, renaming it as Next Generation EU (NGEU) and increasing it to €750 billion (two-thirds as grants, one-third as loans). It took five days (17–21 July) of bitter discussions for the European Council to agree on the European Commission's NGEU as the agreement implied changes in the composition of the programme (which however remained at €750 billion) and in the size of the EU budget (to which the NGEU had to be attached) (European Council, 2020). The policy-making process, which led to the 'political' approval of NGEU and then to the regulation of 16 December 2020 formalizing it, was characterized by unusual contrasts between coalitions of Member States regarding the interpretation of the crisis, the resources to use for dealing with it, and the governance model for managing those resources (Fabbrini, 2023).

The Recovery and Resilience Facility, the NGEU's major financial programme, would provide a total of €672.5 billion to support Member State investments and reforms. Grants worth a total of €312.5 billion would be provided to Member States under the RRF and the remaining €360 billion would be provided in loans. In the end, the €750 billion NGEU was split into €390 billion in grants and €360 billion in loans, thus attached to the Multiannual Financial Framework or MFF 2021–27 (Council of the EU, 2020). In the same July meeting, it was also agreed that the financing of NGEU could not come from national transfers but would be guaranteed through EU debt assured by the EU budget, getting the resources to pay back interest on funds for the NGEU from new European taxes (European Parliament, 2020).

With monetary policy at the ELB and the explosion of national public debt, the pressure increased for the EU to move towards building a fiscal capacity at the centre, although it was agreed that the SGP rules, temporarily suspended, would be reactivated by January 2024, in a revised form, because of the economic consequences of the February 2022 Russian aggression towards Ukraine. In order to access the RRF funds, Member States needed to submit Recovery and Resilience Plans (RRPs) to the European Commission. The latter was given the power to evaluate these together with the ECOFIN Council (under the shadow of the European Council). Connecting NGEU to the MFF was instrumental for also bringing the EP onboard, although the latter's power has remained marginal.

20.4.2 *The Governance of the Post-Pandemic Adjustment*

The RRF constitutes a significant departure from the ESM's model. If the ESM is based on an international treaty external to the EU, the RRF is internal to the EU legal order (RRF Regulation 2021; Truchlewski et al., 2021). As a result, its governance relies exclusively on the formal EU institutional structure. Two decision-making procedures arise from the RRF: one for the disbursement of financial contributions and the other for the suspension (and lifting thereof) of financial commitments and payments. Both procedures revolve around the European Commission and the Council, with shifting power relations between the former (disbursement) and the latter (suspension and lifting of suspension) procedures. In both procedures, the European Commission's decision-making role is crucial.

It is the European Commission that establishes whether the RRPs meet the goals of the RRF and the country-specific recommendations issued in the framework of the European Semester. It is the European Commission that decides whether the plans have the potential for a long-lasting impact on the Member States and whether they include the milestones, targets, and related indicators to ensure effective monitoring and implementation. It is the European Commission that should agree on the amount of the total costs of the programmes as estimated by the Member States and it should establish whether the Member States have done enough to prevent corruption, fraud, and conflicts of interest when making use of the funds under the RRF. Finally, it is the European Commission that checks whether the structural reforms and public investment programmes represent a coherent and long-term project. The single RRPs are then submitted to the Council (and defended before the Council) by the European Commission (and not by the minister of the Member State concerned).

In the procedure for the disbursement of financial assistance, the European Commission assesses the RRPs and makes proposals for the Council, which approves the RRPs on a case-by-case basis and in the form of an implementing decision by qualified majority. The Council decision formalizes the amount of financial contributions to the Member States. On a proposal from the European Commission, the Council can, at any time, amend its implementing decisions by qualified majority. Before authorizing the payment, however, the European Commission should ask for the technical opinion of the Economic and Financial Committee (constituted by the technical experts of the Member States), which decides by consensus. In that context, if any Member State finds a RRP in a serious deviation from the relevant milestones and targets, they may activate an emergency brake to postpone the provision of financial assistance by referring the matter to the next European Council meeting. When this happens, the European Commission cannot authorize the payment until the European Council has discussed the matter. Within the European Council no national leader has a veto power over the deliberation. The final decision on authorizing the disbursement lies with the European Commission.

In the procedure for the suspension (or lifting thereof) of financial assistance, the European Commission informs the EP, providing a detailed account of the commitments and payments which should be suspended or whose suspension should be lifted, although it is not formally

TABLE 20.1 *Governance logic of the ESM and RRF*

	Governance		
	Decision-making institutions	Voting rules	Outcome
European Stability Mechanism	ESM Board of Governors, ESM Board of Directors, ESM Managing Director	Unanimity (Board of Governors) and qualified majority (Board of Directors)	Unconstrained intergovernmentalism
Recovery and Resilience Facility	European Commission and Council	Disbursement: QM in the Council on a proposal from the European Commission; Suspension: RQM in the Council on a proposal from the European Commission.	Constrained supranationalism

constrained by the position of the EP, whose role remains very limited throughout. The European Commission's suspension proposal is considered adopted 'unless the Council decides, by means of an implementing act, to reject such a proposal by qualified majority within one month of the submission of the European Commission proposal' (RRF Regulation, 2021, Art. 24). By the same token, the Council adopts the European Commission proposal unless it is able to vote it down through a Reverse Qualified Majority (RQM). This further diminishes the Council's decision-making role to the advantage of the European Commission as compared to the procedure for the disbursement of funds.

To conclude, the RRF, the financial instrument for supporting Member States' post-pandemic recovery, differs significantly from the ESM. It is internal to the EU legal order and, above all, it acknowledges a crucial role for the European Commission, together with the Council. Yet the Council's RQM voting mechanism enhances the European Commission's power. To be sure, a fully supranational procedure (definable as co-legislative procedure after the 2009 Lisbon Treaty) would entail the Council and EP sharing decision-making powers on a European Commission proposal, with the Council acting by qualified majority and the EP by simple or absolute majority (as per Article 294 TFEU). Under the RRF, the European Commission has the monopoly on policy initiative, while the Council decides on a European Commission proposal, with no or limited involvement of the EP. The European Council is only allowed to discuss a single RRP before the European Commission can authorize the payment when requested by the Economic and Financial Committee. Moreover, national governments within the Council and, even more so, within the European Council can exercise no formal veto power. Hence, the governance of the RRF constitutes a form of constrained supranationalism significantly different from the unconstrained intergovernmentalism of the ESM (see Table 20.1).

20.4.3 *From One Crisis to Another: The Role of Policy Learning*

The EU adopted two different economic adjustment schemes for dealing with the economic consequences of the sovereign debt and pandemic crises. In both crises, the ECB played a central role in managing them, adopting (during the former crisis) and then fine-tuning (during the latter crisis) unprecedented innovative policies, thus giving national governments and EU actors the time for devising the post-crisis institutions for economic adjustment. In terms of the governance of those institutions, the EU has moved from the unconstrained intergovernmental adjustment of the response to the sovereign debt crisis (epitomized by the ESM) to the constrained supranational adjustment of the response to the economic consequences of the pandemic (epitomized by the RRF). In the former case, the adjustment concerned EMU Member States, in the latter case the entire EU.

During the COVID-19 pandemic, the answer to the sovereign debt crisis was necessarily the benchmark experience, also because it was very recent. When the pandemic broke out in March 2020, the ESM was (on the economic governance side) the single major crisis-resolution tool at the EU's disposal. The ESM, however, struggled to maintain its previous pivotal role, although the ESM members did agree to reform it (without altering its international/intergovernmental nature). Even if the ESM inaugurated the Pandemic Crisis Support financial programme devoid of any conditionality (except for the use of the funds for purely sanitary purposes), no Member State has ever applied for it. The political consequences of the economic management of the sovereign debt crisis were still felt in the southern Member States (Jacoby and Hopkin, 2020), where populist and Eurosceptic parties and movements continued to affect the domestic agenda (Matthijs, 2020). The ESM failed to mend the fracture between creditor and debtor Member States, in fact it institutionalized that fracture.

After all, ESM decisions, despite having implications for the EMU as a whole, have been taken without the institution (the EP) representing EU citizens or the institution (the European Commission) representing the 'European interest', highlighting the lack of counterbalancing mechanisms of national governments' power and hierarchies (Howarth and Spendzharova, 2019). In general, the ESM has been perceived as the culprit for the austerity measures adopted during and after the sovereign debt crisis (Schmidt, 2019). It is not surprising that, given these factors, the ESM was not considered by several national and supranational leaders a viable option for tackling the pandemic crisis or a plausible pivot for the post-pandemic adjustment framework.

That explains why, soon after the outbreak of the pandemic, nine national governmental leaders (representing some of the Member States that suffered most from the sovereign debt crisis), supported by relevant supranational actors (European Commissioners and the EP party groups), advanced a different approach than the one adopted in the early 2010s. Based on an interpretation of the pandemic as a 'symmetric external shock, for which no country bears responsibility', they demanded that the ECB monetary policy be accompanied by a common debt instrument issued by the European Commission, an instrument of sufficient size and long maturity (Ferrera et al., 2021). Although the proposal was contested by a rival coalition of national leaders (the Netherlands, Austria, Denmark, Sweden, and Finland), who reiterated the moral hazard paradigm, the European Council finally decided in favour of a common debt instrument. The letter from the nine national leaders signalled the start of a policy learning process through contrasts (Crespy and Schramm, 2021).

While learning through confrontation might sound odd, hard negotiations can produce information and shed light on alternative courses of action which would otherwise remain uncharted (Dunlop and Radaelli, 2016). Thus, during the pandemic crisis, while the supranational ECB strengthened and fine-tuned many of the policy innovations tested in the previous sovereign debt crisis, the intergovernmental European Council (under pressure from the European Commission) decided to set up instead a different financial instrument than the ESM for post-pandemic adjustment. Faced with the threat of an economic collapse and concerned about a new populist reaction, national and supranational actors devised a new approach (compared to the previous decade) for the recovery and transformation of the national economies (Ladi and Tsarouhas, 2020). The RRF epitomizes the new approach, with the formation of a (limited) central fiscal capacity and the establishment of a decision-making system based on the centrality of the European Commission checked by the Council (Fabbrini, 2022). Those leaders proved to have learned from the experience of the 2010s (Buti, 2020; Morelli and Seghezza, 2021).

The literature on policy learning (Quaglia and Verdun, 2021; Dunlop and Radaelli, 2016) distinguishes between two types, depending on when the process occurs. Policy learning can take place between one crisis and the next (*inter-crisis*) or within a single crisis episode (*intra-crisis*). Inter-crisis policy learning tends to produce a muddling-through adaptation of the established paradigm through a series of piecemeal reforms (the policy bias is in favour of path dependency). Because those reforms are relatively small and incremental, they benefit from a passive or active consensus. On the contrary, intra-crisis policy learning has a bias favouring path reversal, through unconventional reforms, activating adversarial behaviour between policy actors, especially if those reforms prefigure a change of paradigm. The EU generally advances by muddling through or piecemeal reforms, which guarantees the consensus of the plurality of actors involved and whose outcome consists in the lowest common denominator of gradual change (Dunlop and Radaelli, 2016; Jones et al., 2016).

When the economic consequences of the pandemic became apparent, having the knowledge of the political consequences of the previous crisis, influential national and supranational actors felt the pressure to move beyond the current paradigm. The search for a new approach increased the contrasts between policy actors. Because national governments interpreted the solution to the previous crisis differently (some defending it and others criticizing it), the identification of a new paradigm was not consensual. Thus, muddling through was substituted by confrontation and business as usual by hard bargaining. The outcome (the shift from paradigm adaptation to paradigm change) was the result of the successful agency of crucial policy actors.

20.5 CONCLUSION

The chapter has compared the different economic adjustments pursued by the EU in the sovereign debt crisis of the 2010s and the pandemic crisis of the 2020s. The ECB was crucial for managing both crises, allowing time for political leaders to devise the economic adjustment framework, which was significantly different in one crisis (the ESM in the sovereign debt crisis) and in the other (the RRF in the pandemic crisis). To conceptualize this difference, the chapter started from an analytical reconstruction of the EU institutional setting developed after the 1992 Maastricht Treaty, showing the two different governance logics (supranational and intergovernmental) characterizing it and their combination in the case of the EMU (supranational on the monetary side and intergovernmental on the economic side).

Facing crises with severe economic consequences, the two sides reacted differently. Regarding the monetary side, the supranational ECB asserted its management role in the sovereign debt crisis, strengthening it during the following pandemic crisis. Regarding the economic side, the intergovernmental European Council and ECOFIN Council pursued different solutions during the two crises. They created an international financial institution (ESM) to deal with the sovereign debt crisis, based on national financial quotas, with support subject to strict conditionality criteria – a model of 'unconstrained intergovernmentalism'. On the other hand, to deal with the economic consequences and help EU Member States recover from the pandemic crisis, they set up an EU financial institution (RRF), based on new resources and managed by both the European Commission and the Council – a model of 'constrained supranationalism'.

Thus, during the pandemic, national and supranational actors moved the EU from the unconstrained intergovernmentalism of ESM to the constrained supranationalism of RRF. The reaction to the economic effects of the pandemic did not follow the intergovernmental path, as one might have expected. The European Council's majority acknowledged the implausibility of relying on the ESM (or of setting up a similar international institution involving the non-EMU Member States) to deal with the economic consequences of the pandemic. The RRF is the outcome of an intra-crisis policy-learning process leading up to contrasting policymaking, within which the European Commission plays a crucial role (indeed, it formulated the proposal of NGEU). Moreover, NGEU was located within the EU legal order and linked to the MFF 2021–27.

This change has been justified by the different nature of the pandemic crisis (exogeneous and symmetric) and favoured by policy actors who learned from the political consequences of the response to the sovereign debt crisis. However, while the ESM is a permanent economic adjustment financial institution, the RRF is a *pro-tempore* one (operative until December 2026). It is thus an open question whether the RRF will remain an ad hoc and temporary model or will evolve towards the institutionalization of a new paradigm for dealing with the consequences of economic crises deriving from exogeneous shocks for which no member state could be considered responsible.

REFERENCES

Batora, J. (2020). Interstitial organisations and segmented integration in EU Governance. In J. Bátora and J. E. Fossum (eds.), *Towards a Segmented European Political Order: The European Union's Post-Crises Conundrum*. London: Routledge, pp. 152–174.

Bickerton, C. J., Hodson, D., and Puetter, U. (eds.) (2015). *The New Intergovernmentalism: States and Supranational Actors in the Post-Maastricht Era*. Oxford: Oxford University Press.

Borzel, T. A. (2016). From EU governance of crisis to crisis of EU governance: Regulatory failure, redistributive conflict and Eurosceptic public. *Journal of Common Market Studies* 54, 8–31.

Buti, M. (2020). A tale of two crises: Lessons from the financial crisis to prevent the Great Fragmentation. *VoxEU*, July.

Buti, M., and Gaspar, V. (2021). Maastricht values. *VoxEU*, July. https://cepr.org/voxeu/columns/maastricht-values

Buti, M., and Fabbrini, S. (2023). Next Generation EU and the future of economic governance: Towards a paradigm change or just a big one off? *Journal of European Public Policy* 30(4), 676–695.

Council of the EU (2020). Next multiannual financial framework and recovery package: Council presidency reaches political agreement with the European Parliament. Brussels, 10 November. www.consilium.europa.eu/en/press/press-releases/2020/11/10/next-multiannual-financial-framework-and-recovery-package-council-presidency-reaches-political-agreement-with-the-european-parliament/

Crespy, A., and Schramm, L. (2021). Breaking the budgetary taboo: German preference formation in the EU's response to Covid-19. Paper presented at the Governance and Politics Programme seminar series, EUI, 13 January.

Draghi, M. (2012). Speech at the Global Investment Conference in London, 26 July. www.ecb.europa.eu/press/key/date/2012/html/sp120726.en.html

Dehousse, R. (ed.) (2011). *The 'Community Method': Obstinate or Obsolete?* New York: Palgrave Macmillan.

Dunlop, C. A., and Radaelli, C. M. (2016). Policy learning in the eurozone crisis: Modes, power and functionality. *Policy Sciences* 49, 107–124.

Egan, M. (2020). The internal market: Increasingly differentiated? In R. Coman, A. Crespy and V. A. Schmidt (eds.), *Governance and Politics in the Post-Crisis European Union*, Cambridge: Cambridge University Press, pp. 159–178.

El-Erian, M. (2016). *The Only Game in Town*. New York: Random House.
Elysee (2020). *French-German Initiative for the European Recovery from the Coronavirus Crisis*. www.elysee.fr/en/emmanuel-macron/2020/05/18/french-german-initiative-for-the-european-recovery-from-the-coronavirus-crisis
Enderlein, H., and Verdun, A. (eds.) (2013). *EMU and Political Science: What Have We Learned?* London: Routledge.
ESM Treaty (2012). Available at www.esm.europa.eu/sites/default/files/20150203_-_esm_treaty_-_en.pdf
European Commission (2020). Proposal for a Regulation of the European Parliament and of the Council establishing a Recovery and Resilience Facility. Brussels, 28 May. https://eur-lex.europa.eu/legal-content/FR/TXT/?uri=CELEX:52020PC0408
European Council (2020). Conclusions. Brussels, 17–21 July. www.consilium.europa.eu/media/45109/210720-euco-final-conclusions-en.pdf
European Parliament (2020). European Parliament resolution of 23 July 2020 on the conclusions of the extraordinary European Council meeting of 17–21 July 2020. Brussels, 23 July. www.europarl.europa.eu/doceo/document/TA-9-2020-07-23_EN.html
Fabbrini, F. (2016). *Economic Governance in Europe: Comparative Paradoxes and Constitutional Challenges*. Oxford: Oxford University Press.
Fabbrini, S. (2015). *Which European Union? Europe after the Euro Crisis*. Cambridge: Cambridge University Press.
Fabbrini, S. (2020). Institutions and decision-making in the EU. In R. Coman, A. Crespy, and V. Schmidt (eds.), *Governance and Politics in the Post-Crisis European Union*. Cambridge: Cambridge University Press, pp. 54–73.
Fabbrini, F. (2022). *The EU Fiscal Capacity: Legal Integration After Covid-19 and the War in Ukraine*. Oxford: Oxford University Press.
Fabbrini, S. (2023). Going beyond the pandemic: Next Generation EU and the politics of sub-regional coalitions. *Comparative European Politics*21(1), 64–81.
Fabbrini, S., and Puetter, U. (2016). Integration without supranationalisation: The central role of the European Council in post-Lisbon EU politics. *Journal of European Integration* 38(5), 481–495.
Farrell, H., and Heritier, A. (2007). Contested competences in Europe: Incomplete contracts and interstitial institutional change. *West European Politics* 30(2), 227–243.
Ferrera, M., Mirò, J., and Ronchi, S. (2021). Walking the road together? EU polity maintenance during the COVID-19 crisis. *West European Politics* 44(5–6), 1329–1352.
Fleming, S. (2020). Is the Franco-German recovery plan a game-changer? *Financial Times*, 19 May.
Fossum, J. E. (2020). Politics versus law: The European Council and balancing European Union style. Unpublished EU-3D paper.
Genschel, P., and Jachtenfuchs, M. (eds.) (2014). *Beyond the Regulatory Polity: The European Integration of Core State Powers*. Oxford: Oxford University Press.
Hallerberg, M. (2014). Why is there fiscal capacity but little regulation in the US, but regulation and little fiscal capacity in Europe? The Global Financial Crisis as a test case. In P. Genschel and M. Jachtenfuchs (eds.), *Beyond the Regulatory Polity: The European Integration of Core State Powers*. Oxford: Oxford University Press, pp. 87–104.
Heldt, C. E., and Mueller, T. (2019). The (self-)empowerment of the European Central Bank during the sovereign debt crisis. *Journal of European Integration* 43(1), 83–98.
Heritier, A. (2007). *Explaining Institutional Change in Europe*. Oxford: Oxford University Press.
Howarth, D., and Quaglia, L. (2016). *The Political Economy of European Banking Union*. Oxford: Oxford University Press.
Howarth, D., and Spendzharova, A. (2019). Accountability in post-crisis eurozone governance: The tricky case of the European Stability Mechanism. *Journal of Common Market Studies* 57(4), 894–911.
Jacoby, W., and Hopkin, J. (2020). From lever to club? Conditionality in the European Union during the financial crisis. *Journal of European Public Policy* 27(8), 1157–1177.
Jones, E. (2020a). The politics of Economic and Monetary Union. In F. Amtenbrink and C. Hermann (eds.), *The EU Law of Economics and Monetary Union*. Oxford: Oxford University Press, pp. 523–596.
Jones, E. (2020b). COVID-19 and the EU economy: Try again, fail better. *Survival*, 62(4), 81-100.
Jones, E., Kelemen, R. D., and Meunier, S. (2016). Failing forward? The euro crisis and the incomplete nature of European integration. *Comparative Political Studies* 49(7), 1010–1034.

Ladi, S., and Tsarouhas, D. (2020). EU economic governance and Covid-19: Policy learning and windows of opportunity. *Journal of European Integration* 42(8), 1041–1056.

Letter of the nine (2020). Available at www.governo.it/sites/new.governo.it/files/letter_michel_20200325_eng.pdf

Matthijs, M. (2020). Lessons and learnings from a decade of EU crises. *Journal of European Public Policy* 27(8), 1127–1136.

Matthijs, M., and Blyth, M. (eds.) (2015). *The Future of the Euro*. Oxford: Oxford University Press.

Matthijs, M., Parsons, C., and Toenshoff, C. (2019). Ever tighter union? Brexit, Grexit, and frustrated differentiation in the single market and eurozone. *Comparative European Politics* 17(2), 209–230.

Morelli, P., and Seghezza, E. (2021). Why was the ECB's reaction to Covid-19 crisis faster than after the 2008 financial crash? *Journal of Policy Modeling* 43(1), 1–14.

Puetter, U. (2006). *The Eurogroup: How a Secretive Circle of Finance Ministers Shape European Economic Governance*. Manchester: Manchester University Press.

Puetter, U. (2014). *The European Council and the Council: New Intergovernmentalism and Institutional Change*. Oxford: Oxford University Press.

Quaglia, L., and Verdun, A. (2021). Explaining the response of the ECB to the Covid-19 related economic crisis: inter-crisis and intra-crisis learning. Paper delivered at the Conference on 'The Covid-19 Pandemic and the European Union', EUI, Florence, 9–10 December.

Richardson, J., and Mazey, S. (2015). *European Union: Power and Policy-Making*. London: Routledge.

RRF Regulation (2021). Available at https://data.consilium.europa.eu/doc/document/PE-75-2020-INIT/en/pdf

Schmidt, V. A. (2019). *Europe's Crisis of Legitimacy*. Oxford: Oxford University Press.

Truchlewski, Z., Schelkle, W., and Ganderson, J. (2021). Buying time for democracies? European Union emergency politics in the time of COVID-19. *West European Politics* 44(5–6), 1353–1375.

Tuori, K., and Tuori, K. (2014). *The Eurozone Crisis: A Constitutional Analysis*. Cambridge: Cambridge University Press.

Van Middelaar, L. (2019). *Alarums and Excursion: Improvising Politics on the European Stage*. English Translation. Newcastle upon Tyne: Agenda Publishing.

Verdun, A. (2015). A historical institutionalist explanation of the EU's responses to the euro area financial crisis. *Journal of European Public Policy* 22(2), 219–237.

Verdun, A. (2017). Political leadership of the European Central Bank. *Journal of European Integration* 39 (2), 207–221.

Verdun, A., and Zimmermann, H. (2006). *EMU Rules: The Political and Econimic Consequences of European Monetary Integration*. Baden-Baden: Nomos.

Wallace, H. (2000). The institutional setting: Five variations on a theme. In H. Wallace and W. Wallace (eds.), *Policy-Making in the European Union*. Oxford: Oxford University Press, pp. 3–37.

Wessels, W. (2016). *The European Council*. New York: Palgrave Macmillan.

21

Designing a Permanent EU-Wide Stabilization Facility

Roel Beetsma and George Kopits

21.1 INTRODUCTION

Since its creation, the European Union has faced two shocks that were extraordinary in scope, magnitude, and repercussions. The Global Financial Crisis (GFC) and the recent COVID-19 crisis (CC) imposed the most severe tests of the resilience of the EU. The Union coped with mixed results in both crises – albeit advancing on a learning curve by the second crisis – which exposed the weakest building blocks of the EU architecture, namely a limited capacity to deal in a timely manner with major exogenous shocks affecting multiple member countries, while relying excessively on a large, indefinite, and dysfunctional monetary expansion.

In general, federal and quasi-federal systems, consisting of partly or mostly decentralized fiscal policymaking under a unified monetary regime, need to contain the damage to subnational jurisdictions from major symmetric and asymmetric shocks using commensurate and timely resources. At the same time, it is necessary to design effective safeguards against moral hazard at subnational levels of government and thus avoid the proliferation of free-rider behaviour. To this end, EU law prescribes the subsidiarity (Article 5(3) TEU) and no-bailout principles (Article 125 TFEU), respectively. Yet institutional limitations and ad hoc application of these guiding principles reveal an apparent internal conflict between the two that undermines an effective mechanism to deal with unanticipated EU-wide exogenous shocks.

The purpose of this chapter is to learn from the EU experience with the GFC and the CC, with a view to outlining the design of an effective EU-wide central stabilization facility in line with the EU Treaties.[1] The remainder of this chapter is structured as follows. Section 21.2 reviews the relevant institutional context in the light of the subsidiarity and no-bailout principles. Against this background, Sections 21.3 and 21.4 highlight the fitful application of the principles before and during each crisis. Section 21.5 discusses possible lessons derived from the US experience relevant for the EU. Drawing from the EU and US track record, Section 21.6 explores ingredients for further institution-building to help contain major area-wide exogenous shocks and cyclical fluctuations and to complement a countercyclical discretionary policy

We are grateful for helpful comments received from participants in a preparatory workshop, and in particular to Dariusz Adamski and Jakob de Haan, on an earlier version of this chapter. The views expressed are those of the authors and do not necessarily coincide with the position of the institutions of their affiliation.

[1] Establishment of a central countercyclical facility, on the basis of the Treaty's subsidiarity principle, was proposed by Kopits (2017a). Similar proposals can be found in European Fiscal Board (2017, 2018), Arnold et al. (2018), Buti and Carnot (2018), and Beetsma et al. (2021). For further support for a permanent facility, see European Central Bank (2020).

stance – in addition to the effect of automatic stabilizers – at the national level. Section 21.7 describes a simple theoretical framework to evaluate the proposal and possible alternatives, against a stylized baseline for the euro area. The final section concludes the chapter.

21.2 PRINCIPLES AND INSTITUTIONS

According to the *principle of subsidiarity*, along with the companion *principle of proportionality*, enshrined in Article 5 TEU, each government function should be located at the lowest jurisdiction where it can be performed most efficiently, without externalities to other jurisdictions. Concomitantly, the Union assumes functions with cross-border repercussions, if such functions are exercised in proportion with their objectives.

Typically, municipal and local jurisdictions are in charge of police protection, sanitation, and primary education. Most other functions, such as higher education, health care, and social assistance, are shared between subnational and national governments. At higher levels, both national and supranational EU authorities (to the extent mandated by the EU Treaties) have a subsidiary role in designing and enforcing a range of regulatory responsibilities (environment, safety, banking, etc.) with significant externalities.

As regards macroeconomic policies, the EU institutions have had an evolving, yet uneven, set of functions. Notably, the Eurosystem is solely responsible for monetary policy within the euro area, which eventually all Member States (except Denmark under the opt-out) are expected to join. In fact, until the GFC, monetary policy had been the single instrument of macroeconomic stabilization to complement the conduct of national fiscal policy, constrained by the Stability and Growth Pact (SGP).[2] Since then, considerable progress has been made towards establishing a macro-prudential framework to ensure financial stability, under the authority of the European Central Bank (ECB), consisting of unified banking regulations (including countercyclical capital adequacy ratios), supervision (including periodic stress tests for large commercial banks operating across Member States), and resolution of banks facing insolvency.[3]

On the fiscal front, there have been relatively minor initiatives towards a common stabilization approach. Only the European Stability Mechanism (ESM), established in the wake of the GFC, can be regarded as a vehicle of stabilization for Member States facing a payments crisis.[4] The ESM is intended to provide funding subject to conditionality in the form of adjustment reform measures – modelled after standby arrangements with the International Monetary Fund (IMF).

Prominent in the Treaty of Maastricht (reaffirmed in the Treaty of Lisbon) is an explicitly stated *no-bailout clause*, which rules out any intra-EU financial rescue, or assumption of liabilities, of a Member State.[5] The motivation for this clause is to deter Member States from

[2] For a discussion of the SGP and the European Semester in which it is embedded, see De Haan and Gootjes, Chapter 18 in this volume, Eihmanis, Chapter 16 in this volume. On the legal aspects of its potential reform, see Dullien et al. (2021).

[3] During the transitional phase in which the Single Resolution Fund (SRF) is built up and the European Deposit Insurance Scheme (EDIS) formed (on which no concrete progress has been made to date), the development of a common backstop via the European Stability Mechanism (ESM) – besides its permanent remit as a facility to assist qualifying member countries in the context of a formal adjustment programme – would complete the Banking Union.

[4] The ECB's asset purchase programmes have similar effects (though absent conditionality) by compressing CDS spreads on sovereign debt. Since this can be regarded as an interest-free guarantee against CDS spreads, it is an infringement of the no-bailout clause; see Sinn (2018).

[5] Contrary to the journalistic misuse of the term – encompassing any form of financial rescue operation, including under IMF standby arrangements – a bailout consists only of an unconditional budgetary transfer, as for example in the case of central government transfers to insolvent local governments mandated by the German constitutional court.

financial indiscipline and dampen moral hazard, including that induced by the subsidiarity principle. In the strictest sense, the no-bailout clause can be defined as prohibition of any EU fiscal transfer (including direct support from any member government) to a member government in any circumstances. Under a realistic interpretation, the no-bailout clause permits financial assistance to a member government facing potential sovereign default, subject to conditionality under an adjustment programme, presumably qualifying for ESM lending.[6] Access to grants from the Structural Funds or Cohesion Funds requires a prescribed government contribution under the so-called additionality principle.

Further, the purpose of the SGP, created under the Treaty of Maastricht, is to promote fiscal discipline and avoid excessive indebtedness by member governments to the detriment of other Member States. The Pact's rules are supposed to play both preventive and dissuasive roles to obviate permanently a bailout from consideration. The preventive arm aims at monitoring budgetary positions over the medium term through the stability and convergence programmes submitted by Member States, with the support of national independent fiscal institutions and the European Fiscal Board (EFB). The dissuasive arm provides the Excess Deficit Procedure (EDP) for the correction of budget deficits incurred in excess over the statutory limit. Failure to comply with the EDP – without a waiver due to a contraction in activity – is subject to financial sanctions, which in fact were never imposed.[7] Whereas the Pact's rules were fairly well designed from an economic perspective, in practice they performed poorly in implementation, even after series of revisions.[8]

On the face of it, the subsidiarity and no-bailout principles may be incompatible as they are framed in the Treaty and embodied in a wide range of institutional arrangements. However, the former was designed as a constraint on the EU (together with the principle of conferral),[9] while the latter is meant to prevent any assistance that encourages free-rider behaviour as collateral damage. Without questioning the justification of each principle in the context of the theory of fiscal federalism, let us examine the practical application of each principle, as well as the adequacy of institutions, for the purpose of macroeconomic stabilization, as illustrated by the management of the GFC and CC, the most severe shocks suffered directly or indirectly by EU Member States so far.

21.3 COPING WITH THE GLOBAL FINANCIAL CRISIS[10]

From the very start of implementation, the EU macroeconomic policy framework revealed significant weaknesses, particularly in the euro area. The SGP suffered an erosion of credibility in several Member States due to insufficient ownership by political leaders; a pro-cyclical expansionary fiscal stance financed with windfall gains from the sharp interest rate decline

6 For an in-depth treatment from a legal point of view, see Ryvkin (2012).

7 Sinn (2018) documents 121 violations of the SGP deficit limit in member countries, unjustified by escape clauses.

8 The rules met rather well most criteria of design (definition, transparency, flexibility, adequacy, consistency, efficiency), but scored rather poorly on enforceability and simplicity; see Kopits (2018) and European Fiscal Board (2019). However, this does not exclude that they may have had some disciplining effect on fiscal policies, although such an effect is difficult to measure, because the counterfactual is not available.

9 If EU policymakers want to take a new initiative, they first need to verify whether there is a basis for action under the Treaty's principles of conferral and subsidiarity. They can proceed only if the initiative is consistent with both principles.

10 Actually, in Europe the GFC had manifested itself in closely interrelated crises undermining financial stability on the one hand and sovereign debt sustainability on the other. For presentational convenience and analytical simplicity, here the two crises are discussed under the same heading.

due to the vanishing currency risk; non-observance of stability or convergence programmes; and questionable effectiveness of the no-bailout clause.[11]

Indeed, widespread violation of the SGP, including by France and Germany, without the imposition of penalties by the European Council (rejecting the recommendation by the European Commission), contributed to moral hazard by member governments as well as in the financial markets. Moral hazard was exacerbated in a circular fashion by the ECB's open-market operations in rating uniformly all sovereign bonds issued within the euro area as riskless collateral,[12] echoing the favourable rating in the markets reflected in near-zero risk premia on such bonds, which in turn emulated the ECB's own rating – regardless of significant inter-country differences in public debt-to-GDP ratios. In addition, the ECB's Target settlement mechanism, permitting an indefinite accumulation of external imbalances by some member countries through the crisis, has been viewed as a channel for a back-door bailout.[13]

EU-wide application of the subsidiarity principle was absent not only in collective macro-fiscal stabilization, but also in a unified macroprudential regulation. In fact, uneven and lax banking regulation at the national level contributed to the onset of the financial crisis in peripheral Member States and to its propagation throughout the Union. This eventually aggravated public debt's sustainability risk within a doom loop between governments and banks.[14] Governments were called upon to bail out banks; banks in turn were encouraged to expand their holdings of national government paper in their balance sheets, already impaired due to sharp deleveraging and mounting default on liabilities by households and businesses in distress. The ECB was the only institution that assumed the role of a first responder by easing monetary policy within the euro area, though with limited effectiveness. Overall, during the GFC these conditions rendered the euro area Member States distinctly vulnerable to the exogenous shock emanating from the financial system under severe stress across the Atlantic.

Initially, each member government was left to its own devices to contain the crisis.[15] But unable to avoid a sudden loss of access to financial markets, Greece, Ireland, and Portugal sought assistance from the IMF, which paved the way to adjustment programmes[16] with the participation of the Commission and the ECB, which together exercised tutelage as the so-called Troika. The initial unwillingness to restructure Greece's public liabilities – especially to protect the exposure of French and German banks – and the onerous conditionality (including limits on the operation of automatic stabilizers) imposed by the Troika, while providing some financial assistance under the programmes, was a belated ad hoc application of both the no-bailout and subsidiarity principles. It was in partial recognition of the failure to implement an appropriate, timely, and orderly response to the crisis, and in an attempt to prevent future crises, that the ESM was established and initial steps were taken towards the formation of a banking union.

[11] See the evidence in Kopits (2017b). For recent confirmation of the procyclicality bias, see Gootjes and De Haan (2022).

[12] The risks of this approach were first observed by Buiter and Sibert (2005).

[13] Sinn (2014) examines this practice critically.

[14] Farhi and Tirole (2018) provide a detailed analysis of the mutually amplified lethal embrace between sovereigns and banks during the crisis.

[15] The European Economic Recovery Program of 2009 was an ad hoc common expansion in response to the GFC, which needs to be distinguished from our proposed stabilization capacity.

[16] For an assessment of the IMF's involvement in the design and implementation of these programmes, conducted by a team from the IMF Independent Evaluation Office, see Kopits (2016) on the fiscal policy aspects and Veron (2016) on the financial policy aspects.

As an upshot, in the wake of the crisis, the ECB launched massive unconventional quantitative easing to forestall the risk of deflation. The expansionary monetary stance prevailed well into the post-crisis period to restore financial intermediation and alleviate the hysteresis evidenced by lacklustre growth prospects. In broad terms, the interplay of macroeconomic policies shifted from monetary dominance in most member countries before the crisis – as their fiscal stance was supposed to be aligned with the ECB's implicit inflation-targeting regime – to some fiscal dominance at the start of the crisis,[17] but eventually to financial dominance as the monetary and fiscal authorities prioritized the recovery of the banking sector over their own conventional policy goals. With the COVID-19 crisis, the pendulum has swung back to fiscal dominance.

21.4 COPING WITH THE COVID-19 CRISIS

The GFC was a relatively straightforward occurrence that had begun in the international interconnected financial system, which, in combination with fiscal vulnerability, resulted in a contraction on the demand side of the economy. By comparison, the CC has been far more complex, rooted in a pandemic. This created and amplified shock waves through both demand and supply channels, depressing activity and income levels worldwide.[18] Apart from such differences between the crises, the initial reaction consisted in a familiar inward-looking policy response, securing the availability of medical services and equipment within each country's borders and erecting barriers to exporting to the rest of the Union – contrary to the most elementary interpretation of the subsidiarity principle.

Lacking a collective fiscal mechanism of protection, each member government faced an immediate revenue loss and a rise in spending needs, assisted by the effect of automatic stabilizers, which in some countries provided an insufficient fiscal backstop to the contraction in output. Unlike in the aftermath of the GFC, when their access to the capital markets came under pressure, highly indebted member governments were not prevented from adopting a countercyclical expansionary fiscal stance through discretionary spending measures – taking advantage of the SGP's general escape clause triggered by the extraordinary contraction.

At the Union level, however, monetary policy and recently adopted macroprudential tools were alone in alleviating the shock through stepped up and new asset purchase programmes and a temporary cut in the capital adequacy ratios for banks.[19] Yet excessive and indefinite reliance on quantitative easing in the form of massive purchases of sovereign bonds – depressing risk premia thereon – cannot be distinguished from outright monetization of government deficits, clearly a dysfunctional use of monetary policy, violating the spirit of the Treaty. Moreover, the apparent 'picking and choosing' winners and champions among sectors or corporations through dedicated bond purchases (for example, earmarked for mitigating climate change) by the ECB lies beyond the scope of central banking and can be questioned on allocative efficiency grounds.

In an improvised initiative, led by major member governments, a recovery plan was launched during the CC, following a protracted internal negotiation between governments that favour the subsidiarity principle and those that express concern about moral hazard. The plan represents an unprecedented step from a collection of uncoordinated national measures towards a unified response to the severe virus-induced contraction, consisting of a fiscal expansion financed with

[17] See estimates of the fiscal implications of the ECB's non-conventional monetary policy in Orphanides (2017).

[18] Fornaro and Wolf (2020) apply a simple new-Keynesian model to capture the macroeconomic effects of the virus. Additional studies can be found in Baldwin and Weder (2020).

[19] Purchases via the public sector purchase programme (PSPP) were in fact already restarted shortly before the CC. In addition, the ECB set up a new asset purchase programme, the Pandemic Emergency Purchase Programme (PEPP).

pooled resources from Member States through the issuance of EU debt. While welcome as a collective response to the depth of the crisis, and as a first clearance of the barrier to EU-level debt issuance, the final product, named Next Generation EU (essentially a fund the bulk of which is the Recovery and Resilience Facility, RRF), is a compromise of sorts as regards scale, timing, allocation, composition, conditionality, and financing.[20]

Yet the magnitude of the fund under the plan seems modest relative to the contraction in output. Extended well beyond 2022, the fund fails to provide timely financial assistance to the hardest-hit member countries. Allocation of assistance among member countries is calibrated according to lagged national indicators of need (population, unemployment, output loss, etc.)[21] instead of real-time high-frequency regional indicators. Disbursements from the RRF comprise a mix of grants, guarantees, and loans – the latter adding to the recipient country's indebtedness. The fund provides one-off assistance limited primarily to investment spending, disregarding other useful purposes such as manpower training. More importantly, it fails to meet the need for a permanent EU-wide fiscal stabilization scheme to be triggered in the event of future unanticipated exogenous shocks. Access to the fund is contingent on the recipient government's commitment to implementing growth-enhancing structural measures – and possibly to respecting the rule of law – albeit so far without a well-defined oversight procedure by the Council or the Commission (though subject to the Rule of Law Conditionality Regulation). The fund is financed with the issuance of special-purpose euro bonds, possibly supplemented with earmarked union-wide tax revenues from new resources (such as digital taxation and import carbon taxation) yet to be developed.

Apparently, the recovery plan is short of distinguishing innovations, which would set it apart from existing facilities and make it suitable as an EU-wide vehicle of stabilization. The fund lacks flexibility to be activated in the event of a sudden unanticipated shock. It resembles the Structural Funds or Cohesion Funds, failing to distinguish cyclical from structural indicators of unemployment, activity, and income levels of Member States. In addition, it seems to borrow features from the ESM in terms of lending being conditional on structural policy measures and from the European Investment Bank in terms of bond financing.

21.5 RELEVANT LESSONS FROM THE UNITED STATES

The policy trade-off in applying the subsidiarity principle and the no-bailout principle faced by the EU in tackling the economic consequences of the COVID-19 crisis arises to a greater or lesser extent in most federal or quasi-federal systems, including those with well-established practices. Nevertheless, the comparability of such a system in other countries with the EU is occasionally questioned because the EU's central budget is insignificant. For instance, in the United States, the share of the federal budget (including defence, infrastructure, public pensions, and other social entitlements) reaches nearly two-thirds of consolidated general government expenditures. However, given their earmarked nature, that share of the budget can only be utilized to a limited extent for discretionary countercyclical purposes – beyond the nationwide

[20] See the initial report on the formal proposal of a recovery fund in European Commission (2020), followed by the agreed version among member states in European Council (2020). For an assessment of its relationship with the EU Treaty, see Steinbach (2020). See also Wasserfallen, Chapter 19 in this volume.

[21] See the allocation criteria and country breakdown recommended by the Commission and approved by the Council in Darvas (2020).

effect of automatic stabilizers. Also, typically, federal fiscal transfers amount to less than one-tenth of the stabilization of output shocks in the United States.[22]

In any event, the resemblance of intergovernmental tensions in coping with the COVID-19 crisis and its aftermath within the EU and the United States is remarkable in several respects, and possibly of some relevance for the EU. The United States, comprising a mature federal structure, admittedly demonstrates a more advanced application of the subsidiarity principle, as evidenced by common monetary, defence, foreign, and environmental policies, as well as macroeconomic fiscal stabilization. Although a rational allocation of governmental functions and resources has evolved over more than 200 years, the state and local governments have been at loggerheads with the central government over the division of responsibilities in coping with the crisis.

Concern about moral hazard regarding US state governments dates to the early nineteenth century. Following the mutualization of debt overhang inherited by the states from the revolutionary war, state governments abused periodic federal bailouts for their fiscal profligacy. But by the 1840s, the US Congress refused any further bailouts – in what became a strictly observed implicit no-bailout clause, whereby nearly all states adopted a constitutional current budget balance rule (the so-called golden rule), to regain access to the international bond market.[23] Increasingly, over recent decades, some states have nominally complied with the rule by granting their employees future pension and healthcare benefits instead of wage increases, thereby raising their debt sustainability risk.

Against this backdrop, in 2020, a major partisan split emerged within Congress between those members who proposed a fiscal package that included a sizeable rescue for states and municipalities and those – including former President Trump – who resisted the proposal. The latter argued that states and municipalities currently facing severe fiscal stress should go bankrupt, on grounds that in the past they indulged in fiscal profligacy. However, the bankruptcy option is not available for the state governments by virtue of their constitutionally guaranteed status of fiscal sovereignty.[24] The counterargument, much as in the case of EU Member States, is that the crisis occurred beyond their control and calls for application of the subsidiarity principle. The latter view prevailed in the fiscal stimulus package enacted in 2021.

Since the central government has been fitful and slow in providing financial and medical assistance to the states from contingency reserves and procurement channels,[25] the Federal Reserve System (Fed) felt obliged to act in extending quantitative easing to purchases of state and municipal bonds, albeit through indirect channels, disregarding all precedent. A drawback of such a fiscal framework is that the golden rule allows states to borrow only to finance investment expenditures, excluding current spending. Furthermore, central bank support of state deficits can be questioned on grounds of monetizing state deficits and of allocative efficiency in earmarked lending: in effect, price signals coming from the financial markets can thereby become distorted.

[22] See the estimates in European Commission (2016).

[23] See Henning and Kessler (2012) for a historical summary of the US federal system.

[24] Under the Eleventh Amendment of the US Constitution, the states are immune from bankruptcy. Only local governments (municipalities and counties) have access to Chapter 9 of the Bankruptcy Code. As Puerto Rico is neither a state nor a municipality, Congress had to enact special legislation to manage its recent default.

[25] As interpreted in general, the no-bailout principle does not preclude immediate federal emergency assistance by the Federal Emergency Management Agency to a state or local government to relieve the impact of a natural disaster, such as floods, fire, hurricanes, or earthquakes – following an official declaration of emergency status.

Despite the highly politicized approach to dealing with the COVID-19 crisis in the United States, we can draw some lessons of potential relevance for the EU debacle. First and foremost, under the recent extraordinary shock, application of the subsidiarity principle to budgetary transfers, with appropriate safeguards, overrides the no-bailout clause. Second, the subsidiarity principle should elevate the Union-wide stabilization function to the highest level of government, given the size and the direct externalities of shocks (whether symmetric or asymmetric) or of cyclical swings at lower-level jurisdictions. Third, fiscal transfers should be targeted to lower-level governments preferably in the form of grants rather than loans, insofar as those governments are subject to rules-based constraints and are committed to reform their economies where necessary. And fourth, as noted, as a vehicle for macroeconomic stabilization, monetary policy through earmarked lending to lower-level governments is questionable on allocative efficiency grounds.

21.6 A PROPOSAL FOR A PERMANENT COMMON FISCAL STABILIZATION FACILITY

It is widely recognized that it is necessary to look ahead and complete the EU's institutional infrastructure and governance so that it can cope with new crises that will no doubt come at some point. In the past, crises were defining moments for the progress of European integration. The ESM and the initial steps toward a banking union resulted from the GFC – as indicated in Section 21.3. It is possible that the RRF will develop into a permanent EU budget with its own resources and transfer programmes, thereby enhancing the effect of national automatic stabilizers and contributing to the stabilization of the EU economy through discretionary countercyclical measures; thus also facilitating the stabilization of national economies relative to the aggregate. However, this development is uncertain and likely to be non-linear, and it may take a long time to reach a widely satisfactory end point. In particular, the required expansion of the EU's own resources would need to overcome substantial political resistance. In the meantime, there will be a need for an instrument that can provide immediate and adequate stabilization in the face of unanticipated shocks.[26]

The case for such an instrument rests on a number of factors (de Haan and Kosterink, 2018). Financial markets in the euro area provide only limited risk sharing, while, to a relatively large extent, firms are financed by non-state-contingent debt. Even if financial markets were complete, risk sharing via private channels would be inefficiently small-scale as private agents fail to internalize the beneficial externality of their own portfolio choice (Farhi and Werning, 2017). Further, it is suggested (Berger et al., 2019) that explicit risk sharing may be less prone to moral hazard than implicit bailout guarantees, as default becomes more acceptable, which in turn leads financial markets to impose more fiscal discipline. Another important factor is to what extent shocks are idiosyncratic and to what extent the ECB is able to stabilize common shocks. With monetary policy at the zero–lower bound, a potential case for the fiscal stabilization of common shocks emerges. A final factor concerns the relevance of the automatic stabilizers.

Considering most of the above considerations, we propose a *permanent* central fiscal stabilization facility (henceforth CFSF). How could it be designed? First, support should be

[26] Among alternative options, De Grauwe and Ji (2016) suggest simply utilizing the ESM as a stabilization fund. The ESM would issue ESM-bonds in the market to purchase sovereign bonds from crisis-hit member countries; these operations would be reversed during a boom, so that there would be no net accumulation of bonds over the business cycle.

concentrated where it is most needed. To this end, it is useful to distinguish regional shocks, country-specific shocks that affect all the regions in a country, and EU-wide shocks that affect all the member countries. In addition, a common shock may propagate in different ways through countries or regions, with a differential impact across countries. An example is the COVID-19 pandemic, which hit the Spanish economy relatively hard because of the size of the tourist industry with limited possibilities to work from home; similarly, certain manufacturing activities in Lombardy were hit harder than in the rest of Italy because of the large number of coronavirus cases detected there. Also, the diverse response of national and regional governments may have mitigated the crisis and its consequences in some countries, whereas in others it may have aggravated it.

Second, disbursement of support should be semi-automatically triggered (see later in this section) when certain threshold values for high-frequency real-time indicators are reached. These indicators should provide rapid information on an economy, enabling authorities to react quickly. Although the EU-level response to the COVID-19 pandemic was faster than the response to the GFC – with activation of the general escape clause of the SGP, Support to mitigate Unemployment Risks in an Emergency (SURE) intended to protect jobs during the COVID-19 pandemic, availability of ESM loans under light conditionality and the EU Recovery Fund – these response elements were the result of discretionary action and negotiations between the European Commission and the national governments. Discretion and negotiations during a crisis imply a loss of valuable time for action.

Examples of potentially useful real-time indicators are abrupt falls in energy use, a sudden steep increase in applications for unemployment benefits, steep drops in the number of financial transactions, and a sudden surge in medical emergencies and hospitalizations in the case of a pandemic. These indicators can be monitored continuously and provide information almost in real time. However, the use of real-time indicators is not without complications. For example, seasonal patterns may disturb the information from real-time indicators. However, the informational value of such indicators can be expected to increase with the increased availability of data (that can also be used for cross-checking)[27] and their intensified analysis.

Concomitantly, only large exogenous shocks, above threshold values of the specified indicators, should trigger support.[28] Smaller shocks, below those values, can in principle be dealt with at the national level. It is large shocks that may force governments to free up enough resources at the cost of forgoing regular spending or to secure additional funding in the financial markets. Moreover, while inaccuracies associated with real-time indicators are non-negligible, the size of the shock inferred from the indicators should be so large that, based on *ex post* data revisions, there can be no doubt that the timely support was justified.

Third, as regards the form the support from the CFSF should take, there are two extremes: grants or loans issued at concessionary rates. In the latter case, the net financial benefit would be the difference between projected interest payments at the market rate minus the concessionary rate. Hence, the net financial benefit to the Member State receiving support would be relatively small, while the loan itself adds to the existing debt burden. Still, loans allow a Member State to overcome an immediate liquidity need when private parties may be increasingly reluctant to lend, except at a widening risk premium. Grants have the advantage that they do not add to the debt burden of the receiver. However, they require the CFSF to secure financing either with

[27] Concretely, based on real-time indicators, a substantial drop in demand in Germany, say, can be inferred with more certainty if a similar development is observed for France.

[28] The losses resulting from moral hazard may only be justified in the case of large shocks; see Wyplosz (2020).

additional contributions from participating countries or with debt issuance in financial markets, or with revenue from EU-wide taxes. Both loans and grants may require conditionality based on reforms that enhance potential growth. This would raise the likelihood that a loan would be repaid or that the need for further future grants would be reduced.[29]

Fourth, the CFSF can be financed from different sources or some combination thereof. The required amount of financing might depend on whether support takes the form of grants or loans. In the case of loans, the required resources will depend on the estimated likelihood of repayment and the degree to which the interest rate charged is concessionary. For starters, it is necessary to construct some estimate of the size and frequency of exogenous shocks that form the basis for support. Financing of the support can be obtained through regular contributions by Member States.[30] As in the case of contributions to the Multiannual Financial Framework (MFF), these would typically be linked to national income: larger and richer countries would contribute more, while stabilizing their economy in response to a shock would generally also require more resources. A possibility is for countries that are less hurt by a shock, and that dispose of larger fiscal space, to contribute relatively more. A second source of funding could come from the EU's own resources with newly imposed taxes, beyond those needed to service the EU debt created in the context of the Next Generation EU scheme, such as further increases in the envisaged plastic waste tax, the carbon adjustment levy on imported energy, and a digital tax. The third source would be a CFSF bond issued to provide adequate stabilization in the event of a large shock or multiple shocks. The debt issued by the CFSF will then be serviced by future revenues from regular contributions and new taxes. The financing of the CFSF cannot be seen independently of its position relative to other EU arrangements. At some moment in the future, when all EU countries participate, it could become a demarcated part of the MFF, though, unlike the MFF, it must be sufficiently flexible for speedy authorization and disbursement.

Fifth, despite the semi-automatic character of disbursements, it is necessary to clearly define the authorization and disbursement process, as well as the authorities in charge of the CFSF. Following the logic under existing arrangements, the Economic and Financial Affairs Council (Ecofin) should be vested with the ultimate decision-making authority, supported by the opinion of the European Commission. Yet for the disbursements of funds to take place semi-automatically, it might be appropriate to appoint the EFB to make the technical case for disbursement on the basis of a significant fall in relevant real-time indicators below threshold values. Given the fast-track determination by the EFB and advice of the European Commission, the Ecofin decides on the proposal by qualified majority vote. Alternatively, a reverse-qualified majority voting procedure would ensure that the proposal is accepted, unless a qualified majority votes against. Thus, an observed drop in real-time indicators allows an independent estimate of the size (in terms of output loss) of the impact of an adverse shock on the EU economy, on national economies, and on regions. Given the likely disparity across regions, the focus of the

[29] The prospect of a better functioning economy would also lead private creditors to demand lower risk premia and speed up a return to the capital market.

[30] Consider a CFSF financed only with contributions from participating states. Suppose that countries contribute 0.25 per cent of GDP each year and that a major EU-wide crisis occurs every ten years. In that case 2.5 per cent of GDP would be available for a single support action for the entire EU economy within a ten-year period, assuming that the support would be fully spent on a discretionary stimulus. This number, which merely illustrates an order of magnitude, ignores potential interest earnings on accumulated assets and potential changes in GDP. A 2.5 per cent of GDP stimulus is already substantial, though unable to offset the output contraction due to the CC. If a severe shock is asymmetric across the EU, the support operation can be focused on those parts of the EU that are hit (hardest), and the degree of stabilization may be substantially larger.

impact assessment should possibly be undertaken according to the 'nomenclature of territorial units for statistics' (NUTS).[31]

Sixth, what form should the support take? There are several alternatives. One option is a general transfer to a country or region, as revealed by the real-time indicators. The advantage is that it offers freedom for the recipient jurisdiction to tailor spending as it deems fit. But the receiving government may prefer to spend the resources in a myopic way to maximize its popularity or to advance its own private interests. Hence, it may be more effective to earmark assistance spending for certain purposes, such as wage subsidies, for unemployment insurance or for retraining workers who have become unemployed by the shock.[32] A related question is through which level of government should the assistance be channelled. In principle, assistance should be concentrated towards areas hit hardest by the shock. This implies supporting local governments responsible for specific regions – identified under an appropriate NUTS level – rather than channelling resources to the central government of the recipient country. Supporting regions directly, of course, presupposes that the region has the capacity to allocate the transferred resources most efficiently.[33]

Seventh, to minimize moral hazard, support from the CFSF should be triggered only by exogenous shocks, whose nature, impact, and size are determined as discussed earlier. Examples are major natural disasters, accidents, epidemics, and turbulence in the financial sector, including those originating outside the EU. However, even when the original shock is exogenous, there may be a need for conditionality to be attached to support from the CFSF. More resilient economies featuring more flexible labour and product markets, or more ample fiscal space for discretionary action, are better placed to cope with exogenous shocks. Hence, conditionality reduces the need for further support. Conditionality may need to be country-specific and should be targeted at those obstacles that hamper the economy's ability to absorb such exogenous shocks. Importantly, conditionality is not necessarily aimed at improving fiscal discipline in the short run, although in some instances that may be necessary. A major question concerns practical implementation, namely whether it should involve a letter of intent that commits national authorities to undertake specific measures over a specified time period, subject to performance criteria that can be verified through objective indicators.

A priori it seems that a speedy disbursement of support in the case of a severe shock is difficult to reconcile with conditionality. However, annually, as part of the European Semester, countries submit their National Reform Programmes, the progress of which is monitored by the European Commission. Hence, the state of progress and the Commission's reform recommendations could form the basis for the conditionality attached to the support. While those recommendations normally have no legal bite and deviating from them is without sanctions, they could become legally binding when countries apply for and receive support from the CFSF. Hence, the appropriate conditionality could be designed with little time loss.

[31] The NUTS, established by Eurostat for data harmonization purposes, has been used since 1988 for allocating Structural Funds.

[32] The survey experiment conducted by Beetsma et al. (2022) suggests that respondents generally have a preference for earmarking assistance spending for certain specific causes, such as healthcare and education.

[33] On the one hand, paying transfers directly to the regions in line with the severity of the shocks hitting them may result in a more efficient and equitable spending allocation than transfers to the central governments when these do not come with certain qualification, because the lobbying power of the regions may be unevenly distributed and the central government may have its own spending priorities. On the other hand, it is not clear that hard-hit regions have the capacity for conducting effective stabilization programmes. In this regard, it may be noted that Structural Funds are not always fully used because of a lack of suitable projects. Moreover, the subsidiarity principle may actually call for national programmes with direct cross-regional externalities, such as investments in infrastructure.

The CFSF that we envisage is consistent with the Treaty's principle of subsidiarity, because, by definition, the insurance it provides can only be organized at a level above the unit that is to be insured, and the principle of proportionality, as the ensuing regional stabilization will not go beyond what is needed.

21.7 AN ILLUSTRATIVE MODEL

A simple model is presented in the Appendix to illustrate the operation and attributes of the proposed CFSF as applied to EU Member States, each consisting of several regions hit by shocks. These shocks can have a component common to all regions, which captures an EU-wide component, and/or a component common to all or some regions within a country. An example is the recent COVID-19 shock, which hit the entire EU, but worked out differently at the country level and, within each country, differently at the regional level. In any case, the shocks have negative potential externalities beyond the initially affected country or region.

In our model, we take the perspective of the entire EU, rather than merely the euro area. The monetary autonomy of the non-euro area members is effectively rather limited, while they are not immune to many of the shocks that also hit the euro area members. There are two periods, allowing the effects of shocks to be spread over time. In addition, economies feature distortions. Reducing these distortions is politically costly, which may lead to moral hazard in implementing structural reforms. The model also allows for hysteresis effects of shocks to output and of cross-regional externalities from economic stabilization.

For analytical convenience, the model abstracts from certain elements that may be relevant in practice. In particular, it is assumed that the CFSF only gives support in the form of grants financed by proportionate national contributions. Absent financial markets, the CFSF does not borrow for lending to regions in trouble. Admittedly, moral hazard leads to an inadequate reduction in structural distortions, insofar as the support transfers are spent on specific interests or grand projects intended to boost the recipient government's prestige. To prevent or minimize such behaviour, it is assumed that the Commission monitors to ensure that the grants are allocated to economic stabilization.

Economic activity in the second period is connected in two ways to the preceding period. First, we allow for hysteresis effects, which may arise either from a loss of skills during unemployment, or from an erosion of the capital stock, or from both, as a result of the shock. The other link between the two periods is the intertemporal budget constraint of the CFSF.

The European Commission operates the CFSF and establishes, through consultation with relevant EU institutions (Eurostat, EFB) and national institutions (national governments, independent fiscal institutions, statistical bureaus), the magnitude of the shocks hitting the regions. It then makes a proposal on the transfers to the individual regions, to be confirmed in a vote in the ECOFIN. The resulting set of transfers determines the contributions via the budget constraint of the CFSF. The proposed package is a set of transfers that minimizes the sum over the regions of the quadratic deviations of actual from 'non-distortionary' income in each of the two periods. Non-distortionary income is the exogenous level of income in the absence of any distortions, shocks, or policy actions. The other actors are the national governments, which choose the level of distortions trading off the beneficial effect of a reduction in distortions on income in both periods and the political cost associated with reducing distortions.

The model yields a number of useful insights. The first set of insights pertains to the authorities' response functions. First, the average transfer increases with the average level of distortions and the average shock, in both cases to make up for the income loss relative to non-distortionary income.

Second, the response of the average transfer increases with the intensity of externalities. The reason is that the benefit from transfers goes beyond the mere reduction of the shortfall of income from its non-distortionary level in each region, because a smaller shortfall in any given region also helps to reduce the shortfall in all other regions. The objective function of the CFSF internalizes this beneficial externality.

Third, the deviation of the region-specific from the average transfer increases proportionately with the region-specific component of the shock and the deviation of a country's distortions from the cross-country average level of distortions. Because the CFSF balances the quadratic deviations from its targets, and it has a sufficiently large set of instruments (one for each region), it eliminates the effect of the region-specific shock component with an equivalent deviation of the transfer from the average transfer. Likewise, it eliminates the cross-regional income differences resulting from differences in distortions.

Fourth, the choice of the level of distortions by governments can also be decomposed into a cross-country average, which responds to the average level of transfers and shocks, and a deviation from the average level of distortions. This deviation decreases with the average shock hitting a country's regions relative to the Union average shock and increases in the average transfer to a country's regions relative to the Union average.

The authorities' response functions are combined and solved for the eventual solutions as functions of the shocks. We find that the transfer settings are such that the effects of deviations of shocks from the Union average are completely eliminated, while distortions are equated across the countries. The common level of distortions falls with the Union average shock, while the average level of transfers increases with the Union average shock.

We also look at the outcomes in the absence of a CFSF and compare welfare with and without a CFSF. While an unambiguous welfare comparison is not feasible short of data-based quantitative simulations, it can be intuitively ascertained in the context of the model that an increase in the number of participating countries raises the relative attractiveness of installing a CFSF, because the impact and the alleviation of region-specific shocks, including externalities, can be shared over a broader group of regions.

21.8 CONCLUDING REMARKS

Establishment of the recovery fund, under the heading of Next Generation EU, represents an important step towards implementing the subsidiarity principle, against the background of two unprecedented macroeconomic crises that severely affected the majority of EU Member States. Commendable as it may be, the fund has some drawbacks: it is a one-off scheme, primarily focused on investment expenditures, with a considerable delay in disbursements, and allocated on the basis of lagged national indicators of need. The CFSF proposed here is an attempt to make up for those deficiencies by creating a permanent collective stabilization scheme in the presence of large common shocks, especially when the instruments of the ECB prove to be insufficient to contain the impact of such shocks, in particular in hard-hit member governments lacking fiscal space to adopt an effective countercyclical fiscal stance.

The proposed CFSF is designed to respond automatically to common exogenous shocks across regions in a timely fashion over an extended time period, if necessary. A major advantage of the proposed scheme is its reliance on real-time high-frequency indicators of economic activity at the regional level – a task that requires technical inputs and data from Eurostat, with support from national statistical agencies. As designed, the CFSF has several merits beyond stabilization during a crisis or a wide cyclical swing. First, the debt it issues would create a new safe asset with the future contributions of the participating countries as collateral.[34] It could be purchased by the ECB to provide liquidity or be held by commercial banks. Second, participating countries effectively commit to saving resources for a rainy day. If the contribution rate is linked to the business cycle, countries could contribute proportionally more during good times than during bad times. This would effectively amount to building up extra buffers in good times by accumulating assets via the CFSF. The well-documented expansionary pro-cyclicality of fiscal policy would thus be mitigated. Third, the concept of the appropriate euro area aggregate fiscal stance emphasizes that countries with fiscal space should use this space, which would create positive externalities vis-à-vis Member States without such space. However, Member States with fiscal space may be overheating at the same time. Fiscal expansion would contribute to further overheating. Disbursements from the CFSF can replace the deployment of the fiscal space by overheating economies. Fourth, as discussed, the disbursement of resources from the CFSF (or participation in the arrangement at all) could be made conditional on implementing reforms that enhance the resilience of the national economy. Participation in the CFSF may provide a sufficiently strong incentive for necessary reform that would otherwise not take place. Fifth, the CFSF could invest in pan-European infrastructure projects that would not be undertaken otherwise because their positive cross-border externalities would not be internalized at the national level.

A key caveat associated with any collective stabilization facility is the necessity to prevent moral hazard in Member States and financial markets. The CFSF should not give rise to complacency and a perception of a lax interpretation of the no-bailout clause enshrined in the Treaty. Hence, as mentioned, access to CFSF resources should be backed by adequate incentives and safeguards in the form of conditionality, to be monitored by the appropriate EU institutions. In light of the recent crises, governments of vulnerable member countries could be encouraged to strengthen automatic stabilizers (partly through raising the effective progressivity of tax systems), and, in addition, to generate sufficient fiscal space (through long-overdue structural reform) that will permit the conduct of discretionary expansion while possibly avoiding further build-up in government indebtedness. In all, recourse to the CFSF is to be treated as a complement to domestic countercyclical policies.

[34] As argued in Kopits (2017a), such a stabilization fund would operate symmetrically during the economic cycle, issuing bonds at a low interest rate in a recession and withdrawing them in an upswing as interest rates rise. Meanwhile, increased contributions would accumulate during a boom, to be made available for transfers during a recession.

Appendix: Designing a Permanent EU-Wide Stabilization Facility

This Appendix presents a simple model to illustrate the operation and attributes of the proposed CFSF as applied to EU member countries each consisting of several regions hit by shocks. These shocks can have an element common to all regions – which captures an EU-wide factor – and/or one common to all regions in a country. An example is the recent COVID-19 shock, which hit the entire EU, but worked out differently at the country level and, within each country, differently at the regional level. The shocks have negative potential externalities beyond the initially affected country or region. In our model, we take the perspective of the entire EU, rather than merely the euro area. The monetary autonomy of the non-euro area members is effectively rather limited, while they are not immune to many of the shocks that also hit the euro area members. There are two periods, allowing the effects of shocks to be spread over time. In addition, economies feature distortions. Reducing these distortions is politically costly, which may lead to moral hazard in implementing structural reforms. The model also allows for hysteresis effects of shocks to output and of cross-regional externalities from economic stabilization.[35]

For analytical convenience, the model abstracts from certain elements that may be relevant in practice. In particular, it is assumed that the CFSF only gives support in the form of grants financed by proportionate national contributions.[36] Absent financial markets, the CFSF does not borrow for lending to regions in trouble. To prevent the abuse of resources, it is assumed that the Commission monitors to ensure that the grants are allocated to economic stabilization.

Specifically, there are in total N countries, each consisting of R regions. Income in region j of country i in periods t and $t+1$ is:

$$y_{ijt} = y^*_{ij} - z_{it} - \tau - \varepsilon_{ijt} + g_{ijt} - \delta\left(\underline{y}^* - \underline{y}_t\right), \delta \geq 0, \tag{1}$$

$$y_{ij,t+1} = y^*_{ij} - \tau + \mu\left(y_{ijt} - y^*_{ij}\right), 0 \leq \mu \leq 1, \tag{2}$$

where y^*_{ij} is the exogenous level of income in the absence of any distortions, shocks and policy actions – we henceforth refer to it as 'non-distortionary income'; z_{it} are losses from inefficiencies

35 A detailed derivation of the model can be found in Beetsma and Kopits (2020).

36 Other financing arrangements can be thought of. For example, when a country's regions are on average hit by a more negative shock, the country may enjoy a lower contribution rate. The model would then imply that the average transfer to the country's regions responds less to this average shock than under the assumption of a constant contribution rate, implying an eventual allocation of resources that resembles the one derived below. Allowing for systematic differences in the contribution rate across countries (so independent of the shocks) would probably not be politically acceptable in the case of a permanent arrangement like the one envisaged here.

and market distortions, which are common for all regions in country i; τ is a contribution to the CFSF – we assume that the contributions are equal in both periods; $\varepsilon_{ijt} > 0$ is a shock leading to a fall in income; g_{ijt} is a transfer received from the CFSF; $\underline{y}_t$ is average income over all regions in all countries; and $\underline{y}^*$ is the average of y^*_{ij} over all regions in all countries.

The assumption behind a constant contribution over the two periods is made for tractability as well as realism – that is, it is not made conditional on the state of the aggregate economy. Alternatively, if the aggregate macroeconomic situation (i.e. the average across all regions over all countries) is unfavourable in period t, it would be optimal to reduce the contribution in period t and raise it in period $t + 1$. Parameter δ in (1) captures the intensity of cross-border externalities.[37] If average income falls short of y^*, this has a negative effect on all the regions. Such negative externality would primarily result from a reduction in trade and could be measured by estimating the sensitivity of intra-regional exports to a change in a region's income. Notably, by implication, if the value of δ collapses to zero, these externalities vanish.

No income shocks are assumed in period $t + 1$. Economic activity in this last period is connected to the preceding period in two ways. First, we allow for hysteresis effects, which may arise either from a loss of skills during unemployment, or from an erosion of the capital stock, or from both, as a result of the shock. These are present when $\mu > 0$. The other link between the two periods is the intertemporal budget constraint of the CFSF. To keep the algebra to a minimum we assume that the interest rate is zero and that all the regions are equally sized. [38] Hence, $\tau = \frac{g_t}{2}$.

The European Commission operates the CFSF and establishes, through consultation with relevant EU institutions (Eurostat, EFB) and national institutions (national governments, independent fiscal councils, statistical bureaus), the magnitude of the shocks hitting the regions. It then makes a proposal on the transfers to the individual regions, to be confirmed in a vote in the ECOFIN. The resulting set of transfers determines the contributions via the budget constraint of the CFSF. The proposed package is set so as to minimize over the set of g_{ijt} the sum over the regions of the quadratic deviations of actual from non-distortionary income in each of the two periods.

The other actors are the national governments, which choose the level of distortions trading off the beneficial effect of a reduction in distortions z_{it} on income in periods t and $t + 1$ and the political cost associated with reducing distortions γ. Hence, the government of country i sets z_{it} to minimize the sum of the quadratic deviations of actual from non-distortionary income in country i's regions and the quadratic deviation of distortions z_{it} from its minimum level of zero.

The described setting could give rise to moral hazard: if the Commission increases the level of transfers to the regions of a country, governments have less incentive to introduce politically costly reduction of distortions. A fear associated with EU-level transfers is that their design is suboptimal because the Commission is unable to disentangle to what extent a country's economic situation can be attributed to purely exogenous factors and to what extent to the quality of its policies. This would amount to the individual elements of the combination $z_{it} + \varepsilon_{ijt}$ not being directly observable to the Commission. However, interestingly, it is easy to ascertain that the instrument choices and hence all economic outcomes are independent of whether the Commission is able to observe z_{it} and ε_{ijt} separately, or only the sum $z_{it} + \varepsilon_{ijt}$. Obviously, in reality it will be difficult to disentangle

[37] For simplicity, the parameter is assumed to capture an equivalent negative externality of an adverse shock and positive externality of the offsetting transfer.

[38] In the presence of a positive interest rate, a negative average (across the regions) shock would produce an extra resource loss equal to interest paid on the debt incurred by the CFSF as a whole, implying an increase in the required contribution rate and a required reduction in the average distortion to compensate for the negative effect on output. Vice versa, for a positive average shock.

these two elements and what is opportune in terms of transfer policy is likely affected by the precision with which z_{it} can be assessed. In particular, public support for a transfer payment may be low if the size of the truly exogenous component ε_{ijt} cannot be ascertained.

In solving the model, we take account of externalities across regions. The solution for the transfers can be split into that for the average level of transfers and the deviation from the average. The former is given by:

$$\underline{g}_t = 2\frac{1+\beta\mu(\mu-1)}{\beta(1-\delta-\mu)(1-\delta)+1+\beta\mu(\mu-1)}\left(\underline{z}_t+\underline{\varepsilon}_t\right) \tag{3}$$

where β is the discount factor applied to next period's outcome. The average transfer is increasing in the average level of distortions and the average shock, in both cases to make up for the income loss relative to non-distortionary income. We observe that the response of the average transfer is increasing in the intensity of externalities. The reason is that the benefit from transfers goes beyond the mere reduction of the shortfall of income from its non-distortionary level in each region, because the reduction in any given region also helps to reduce the shortfall in all other regions. The objective function of the CFSF internalizes this beneficial externality.

The region-specific transfer is:

$$g_{ijt} = \underline{g}_t + \left(\varepsilon_{ijt} - \underline{\varepsilon}_t\right) + \left(z_{it} - \underline{z}_t\right). \tag{4}$$

In other words, the deviation of the region-specific from the average transfer is one-to-one increasing in the region-specific shock component, $\varepsilon_{ijt}-\underline{\varepsilon}_t$, and the deviation of country distortions from the cross-country average level of distortions, $z_{it}-\underline{z}_t$. Because the CFSF balances the quadratic deviations from its targets, and it has a sufficiently large set of instruments (one for each region), it eliminates the region-specific shock component with an equal deviation of the transfer beyond its average. Likewise, it eliminates the cross-regional income differences resulting from differences in distortions.

The solution for the choice of distortions can be split into an average and a deviation from this average. The average solution is:

$$\underline{z}_t = \left[1+\beta\mu^2+\widehat{\gamma}(1-\delta)\right]^{-1}\left[\left(1+\beta\mu^2\right)\left(\frac{1}{2}\underline{g}_t - \underline{\varepsilon}_t\right) - \frac{1}{2}\beta\mu(1-\delta)\underline{g}_t\right], \tag{5}$$

where

$$\widehat{\gamma} = \frac{\gamma}{R\left[1+\left(\frac{\delta}{1-\delta}\right)\frac{1}{N}\right]}.$$

Suppose that we hold $\underline{g}_t$ fixed. Then, a larger average adverse shock $\underline{\varepsilon}_t$ leads governments to produce smaller distortions $\underline{z}_t$ on average. Generally, there are two effects of $\underline{g}_t$ on distortions. On the one hand, supporting spending raises income, thereby weakening the incentive to reduce distortions. This is the moral hazard effect resulting from more external support. On the other hand, support spending needs to be financed by contributions paid out of the government's budget into the CFSF. As these lower income, they strengthen the incentive to reduce distortions. The term $\frac{1}{2}(1+\beta\mu^2)\underline{g}_t$ within square brackets reflects the net effect of the received transfer on income in period t and, via the hysteresis effect, in period $t+1$ and the contribution into the CFSF in period t. This net effect is positive and leads to higher distortions. The term $\frac{1}{2}\beta\mu(1-\delta)\underline{g}_t$ within brackets is the result of the contribution payment to the CFSF in period $t+1$ and leads to a reduction in distortions. Overall, a higher average transfer $\underline{g}_t$ produces an increase in average distortions $\underline{z}_t$. To obtain the summary solution for $\underline{g}_t$, it is necessary to substitute (3) into (5) and solve for $\underline{g}_t$ as a function of $\underline{\varepsilon}_t$ only.

The deviation of z_{it} from $\underline{z}_t$ is given by:

$$z_{it} = \underline{z}_t + \left[\frac{1+\beta\mu^2}{1+\beta\mu^2+\widehat{\gamma}}\right]\left[(\underline{\varepsilon}_t - \underline{\varepsilon}_{it}) + \left(\underline{g}_{it} - \underline{g}_t\right)\right] \tag{6}$$

where $\underline{\varepsilon}_{it}$ is the average shock hitting the regions of country i. If this average shock is larger than the average shock t across all the regions in the EU, then the government of country i reduces distortions more than does the average government, while a transfer g_{it} to country i higher than the average transfer g_t has the opposite effect on the amount of distortions. If $\gamma = 0$, i.e. the political cost of reducing distortions is zero, the difference between z_{it} and $\underline{z}_t$ exactly offsets the national deviations from the average shock and the average received transfer. The larger is γ, the more the response of the country-specific component $z_{it} - \underline{z}_t$ of distortions to the country-specific shock component $\underline{\varepsilon}_t - \underline{\varepsilon}_{it}$ and the country-specific spending component $\underline{g}_{it} - \underline{g}_t$ is dampened, while a stronger hysteresis effect μ, a higher discount factor β, larger externalities δ, and a smaller number of countries N, all lead to stronger responses of the deviation of distortions from the average.[39] Stronger hysteresis and a higher discount factor in effect both assign a larger weight to the effect of reducing distortions on future income. Larger externalities benefit income because the positive effect on other countries' income from reduced distortions in country i feeds back through second-round effects to country i. This feedback effect is proportional to $1/N$. If the number of countries N goes to infinity, the externality from country i on the union's average becomes negligible and so does the feedback effect.

Expressions (3) through (6) are response functions, but not the summary solutions solely expressed in terms of the exogenous shocks. Combining the 'average expressions' (3) and (5), one solves for $\underline{g}_t$ and $\underline{z}_t$ as linear functions of $\underline{\varepsilon}_t$ only:

$$\partial \underline{z}_t / \partial \underline{\varepsilon}_t < 0 \text{ and } \partial \underline{g}_t / \partial \underline{\varepsilon}_t > 0$$

Thus, a more adverse average shock leads countries to reduce distortions more on average, while it also implies higher transfers on average. Further, we find that:

$$z_{it} = \underline{z}_t \forall i \text{ and } \underline{g}_{it} - \underline{g}_t = \underline{\varepsilon}_{it} - \underline{\varepsilon}_t$$

That each country implements the same amount of reform may seem surprising but is easily explained. The difference between the transfer received by each country and the average transfer exactly offsets the effect of the difference in the shock hitting each country and the average shock, so that in equilibrium each country has the same incentive to reduce distortions – assuming a broadly equivalent political cost thereof.

The outcomes for a union with a transfer scheme and without a transfer scheme warrants comparison. In the absence of a transfer scheme, the average reduction in distortions is given by:

$$\underline{z}_t = -\left[\frac{1+\beta\mu^2}{1+\beta\mu^2+\widehat{\gamma}(1-\delta)}\right]\underline{\varepsilon}_t$$

Hence, the marginal effect of $\underline{\varepsilon}_t$ on $\underline{z}_t$ is identical without or with a CFSF, if in the latter case we hold $\underline{g}_t$ fixed, i.e. if we assume that transfers are not conditional on a reduction of distortions – see (5). Because $\underline{g}_t$ itself responds to both $\underline{z}_t$ and $\underline{\varepsilon}_t$, the overall response of $\underline{z}_t$ to $\underline{\varepsilon}_t$ will differ in the presence of a CFSF than without CFSF. In general, it is cumbersome to compare the responses

[39] Recall that a higher value of γ implies a higher value of $\widehat{\gamma}$ and that larger externalities δ and a smaller number of countries N imply a lower value of $\widehat{\gamma}$. Hence, a higher δ and a lower N cause an increase in the coefficients in front of $\underline{\varepsilon}_t - \underline{\varepsilon}_{it}$ and $\underline{g}_{it} - \underline{g}_t$ in (6).

of $\underline{z}_t$ to $\underline{\varepsilon}_t$ taking account of this effect. However, in the special case in which externalities are absent, $\delta = 0$,[40] and the hysteresis effect is at its maximum, $\mu = 1$, with and without CFSF we have, respectively,

$$\underline{z}_t = -\left[\frac{\beta}{\beta + \gamma/R}\right]\underline{\varepsilon}_t \text{ and } \underline{z}_t = -\left[\frac{1+\beta}{1+\beta+\gamma/R}\right]\underline{\varepsilon}_t.$$

Not surprisingly, without CFSF, distortions for $\underline{\varepsilon}_t > 0$ are smaller than with CFSF, because in the latter case, the compensation received from the CFSF disincentivizes the politically costly reduction in distortions. This disincentive would be weakened if the transfers were subject to structural conditionality. Turning to the solution in deviations, when a CFSF is absent we find:

$$z_{it} = \underline{z}_t + \left[\frac{1+\beta\mu^2}{1+\beta\mu^2+\widehat{\gamma}}\right](\underline{\varepsilon}_t - \underline{\varepsilon}_{it}),$$

which is the same direct response as in (6) under a CFSF. However, under a CFSF the country-specific transfer component eliminates cross-country differences in distortions.

With a CFSF, the regional component of a transfer, expression (4), offsets the country-specific component in distortion-reducing measures and the region-specific shock component. The average transfer, expression (3), in turn offsets the effect of the average shock and the average level of distortions on income, resulting in period t income equal to non-distortionary income and an elimination of the hysteresis effect in period $t + 1$.

While an unambiguous welfare comparison is not feasible short of data-based quantitative simulations, it can be intuitively ascertained in the context of the model that an increase in the number of participating countries N raises the relative attractiveness of installing a CFSF, because the impact and the alleviation of region-specific shocks, including externalities, can be shared over a broader group of regions.[41]

REFERENCES

Arnold, N., Barkbu, B., Ture, E., Wang, H., and J. Yao (2018). A central fiscal stabilization capacity for the euro area. IMF Staff Discussion Note No. 18/03.

Baldwin, R., and Weder di Mauro, B. (eds.) (2020). *Economics in the Time of COVID-19*. London: VoxEU eBook, CEPR Press.

Beetsma, R., Burgoon, B., Nicoli, F., de Ruijter, A., and Vandenbroucke, F. (2022). What kind of EU fiscal capacity? Evidence from a randomized survey experiment in five European countries in times of corona. *Economic Policy*, 37(111), 411–459.

Beetsma, R., Cima, S., and Cimadomo, J. (2021). Fiscal transfers without moral hazard? *International Journal of Central Banking* 17(3), 95–153.

Beetsma, R., and Kopits, G. (2020). Designing a permanent EU-wide stabilization facility. CESifo Working Paper No. 8735.

Berger, H., Dell'Ariccia, G., and Obstfeld, M. (2019). Revisiting the case for a fiscal union in the euro area. *IMF Economic Review* 67(3), 657–683.

Buiter, W. H., and Sibert, A. C. (2005). How the eurosystem's treatment of collateral in its open market operations weakens fiscal discipline in the eurozone. In *Fiscal Policy and the Road to the Euro*. Warsaw: National Bank of Poland.

40 Although analytically convenient, this case ignores an important rationale for establishing the CFSF, namely that alleviating the shock to one region benefits other regions by limiting negative spillovers.

41 Explicit expressions under a CFSF and without a CFSF for income in the two periods, as well as for the expected union welfare loss associated with income deviations from their non-distortionary levels, can be found in Beetsma and Kopits (2020).

Buti, M., and Carnot, N. (2018). The case for a central fiscal capacity in EMU. *VoxEU*, 7 December.
Darvas, Z. (2020). Having the cake, but slicing it differently: How is the grand EU recovery fund allocated? Bruegel, Brussels, 23 July.
De Grauwe, P., and Ji, Y. (2016). Flexibility versus stability: A difficult trade-off in the eurozone. CEPS Working Document No. 422.
de Haan, J., and Kosterink, P. (2018). The case for more fiscal risk sharing and coordination of fiscal and monetary policy. In N. F. Campos and J. E. Sturm (eds.), *Bretton Woods, Brussels, and Beyond Redesigning the Institutions of Europe*. London: A VoxEU.org Book, CEPR, Ch. 14, pp. 107–116.
Dullien, S., Paetz, C., Repasi, R., Watt, A., and Watzka, S. (2021). Between high ambition and pragmatism: Proposals for a reform of fiscal rules without treaty change, Study for the European Economic and Social Committee. www.eesc.europa.eu/sites/default/files/files/qe-01-21-510-en-n.pdf
European Central Bank (2020). The fiscal implications of the EU's recovery package. *ECB Economic Bulletin*, 6/2020, Frankfurt, 23 September.
European Commission (2016). Quarterly report on the euro area. Institutional Paper No. 30, Brussels, July.
European Commission (2020). The EU budget powering the recovery plan for Europe. Communication from the Commission to the European Parliament, the European Council, the Council, the European Economic and Social Committee and the Committee of the Regions, COM(2020) 442 final, Brussels, 27 May.
European Council (2020). Special meeting of the European Council (17, 18, 19, 20 and 21 July 2020) – Conclusions (CO EUR 8 CONCL 4). Brussels.
European Fiscal Board (2017). Annual report 2017. Brussels.
European Fiscal Board (2018). Assessment of the fiscal stance appropriate for the euro area in 2019. Brussels.
European Fiscal Board (2019). Assessment of EU fiscal rules – with a focus on the six and two-pack legislation. Brussels.
Farhi, E., and Tirole, J. (2018). Deadly embrace: Sovereign and financial balance sheets doom loops. *Review of Economic Studies* 85(3), 1781–1823.
Farhi, E., and Werning, I. (2017). Fiscal unions. *American Economic Review* 107(12), 3788–3834.
Fornaro, L., and Wolf, M. (2020). Coronavirus and macroeconomic policy. *VoxEU*, CEPR Portal, 10 March. https://cepr.org/voxeu/columns/coronavirus-and-macroeconomic-policy
Gootjes, B., and de Haan, J. (2022). Procyclicality of fiscal policy in the European Union. *Journal of International Money and Finance* 120, 102276.
Henning, C. R., and Kessler, M. (2012). *Fiscal Federalism: US History for Architects of Europe's Fiscal Union*. Brussels: Bruegel.
Kopits, G. (2016). The IMF and the euro area crisis: The fiscal dimension. IEO Background Paper No. BP/16-02/07, IMF Independent Evaluation Office, 8 July.
Kopits, G. (2017a). Toward a closer union in Europe: Elusive mirage or reality within grasp? In N. Costa Cabral et al. (eds), *The Euro and the Crisis: Future Perspectives for a Monetary and Budgetary Union*. Cham: Springer, 339–355.
Kopits, G. (2017b). Managing the euro debt crisis. In L. Odor (ed.), *Rethinking Fiscal Policy after the Crisis*. Cambridge: Cambridge University Press, 258–300.
Kopits, G. (2018). How could the Stability and Growth Pact be simplified? Economic and Monetary Committee, Brussels: European Parliament.
Orphanides, A. (2017). Fiscal implications of central balance sheet policies. In L. Odor (ed.), *Rethinking Fiscal Policy after the Crisis*. Cambridge: Cambridge University Press, pp. 71–100.
Ryvkin, B. (2012). Saving the euro: Tensions with European law to protect the common currency. *Cornell International Law Journal* 45(1), 227–255.
Sinn, H. W. (2014). *The Euro Trap: On Bursting Bubbles, Budgets, and Beliefs*. Oxford: Oxford University Press.
Sinn, H. W. (2018). The ECB's fiscal policy. NBER Working Paper No. 24613.
Steinbach, A. (2020). The Next Generation EU – Are we having a Hamiltonian moment? *EU Law Live*, No. 23, 27 June.
Veron, N. (2016). The IMF's role in the euro area crisis: Financial sector aspects. IEO Background Paper No. BP/16-02/10, IMF Independent Evaluation Office, 8 July.
Wyplosz, C. (2020). So far, so good: And now don't be afraid of moral hazard. *VoxEU*, 4 June. https://voxeu.org/article/so-far-so-good-and-now-don-t-be-afraid-moral-hazard

22

Enhancing Private and Public Risk Sharing

Lessons from the Literature and Reflections on the COVID-19 Crisis

Jacopo Cimadomo, Esther Gordo Mora, and Alessandra Anna Palazzo

22.1 INTRODUCTION

Since the Delors Report[1] conceived of the idea of a single currency, the resilience of the European Economic and Monetary Union (EMU) has been one of the main concerns of European policymakers. There are two fundamental nested dimensions of this debate. The first dimension concerns the mechanisms available at a *national level* to reduce the exposure to risks or to mitigate their effects (e.g. eliminating price and wage rigidities, building fiscal buffers). The second dimension concerns the notion of *international risk sharing*, which plays a central role in this debate, given that it focuses on the cross-border channels able to insure against idiosyncratic or country-specific output shocks (as opposed to shocks hitting the EMU as a whole). This chapter focuses on this latter dimension.

International risk sharing represents the capacity of a country to absorb shocks through *ex ante* insurance via cross-border investment on international capital markets or *ex post* compensation via cross-border credit or transfers. The issue of how countries and regions can better isolate themselves from idiosyncratic (country-specific) shocks by diversifying risks across borders has been extensively analysed in international finance (Obstfeld, 1994; Persson and Tabellini, 1996). When a country is hit by a negative shock there are different channels that may come into play to smooth out its impact on disposable income and consumption: the capital markets channel, the credit channel, and the fiscal channel. The first two channels are predominantly private channels while the latter is of a public nature. These channels could operate at the international level (across countries) or between states or regions in a federation, as in the United States.

First, the effects of the shock may be softened if the country's resident agents obtain income (whether financial or labour) from other countries (regions) not affected by the shock. The greater the cross-country financial integration or labour mobility, the greater the strength of this private channel. Financial and labour income from abroad are mainly generated by firms and households investing in foreign companies, or working in other countries. Nevertheless, this

We would like to thank Óscar Arce, Ettore Dorrucci, Alessandro Giovannini, Nadine Leiner-Killinger, and the members of the Eurosystem's Monetary Policy Committee and Working Group on Public Finances, and the staff of the ECB's Fiscal Policy Division, for their helpful suggestions and discussion. We are also grateful to the editors of this volume for their valuable comments. The opinions expressed herein are those of the authors and do not necessarily reflect those of the European Central Bank or the Eurosystem.

[1] See Committee for the Study of Economic and Monetary Union (1989): 'Report on Economic and Monetary Union in the European Community', European Council.

channel is generally referred to as the 'capital markets channel' due to the relatively lower importance of workers' remittances in comparison to cross-border capital flows.

Second, households and firms in the country hit by an adverse shock may protect their consumption by resorting to savings or to credit conceded by other countries, i.e. the 'credit channel'. This primarily includes credit from private financial (foreign) intermediaries but also foreign governments or international institutions (e.g. the International Monetary Fund), which provide official loans in the context of adjustment of other programmes.

Finally, in monetary unions or federal states, the effects of a shock may be smoothed through fiscal transfers drawn from the central or federal budget, which is typically referred to as the 'fiscal channel'.

Our review of the literature highlights the fact that the strength of the risk-sharing mechanisms in the euro area countries has remained rather limited compared with the United States. The lesser degree of risk sharing through European capital markets is the key difference as compared with the United States. In addition, the fiscal channel is virtually negligible in the euro area. Some studies document a significant decrease in risk sharing in euro area countries in periods of recession, precisely when it is most needed, owing to the fragmentation of financial markets. However, others highlight a progressive improvement of the shock-absorption capacity in the euro area in the aftermath of the European sovereign debt crisis of 2010–12, due to the activation of the European Financial Stability Facility (EFSF) and the European Stability Mechanism (ESM) channelling official loans to distressed eurozone economies (Cimadomo et al., 2020; Milano and Reichlin, 2017).

Our own empirical analysis is based on a sample from 1997 to 2022 for the eurozone, and on a sample from 1997 until 2020 for the United States, thus encompassing the peak of the COVID-19 crisis. Our findings show that risk sharing is more powerful across US states than across EMU countries. Furthermore, it can be seen that risk sharing has continued to improve in the United States since the Global Financial Crisis (GFC) of 2008–9, mainly owing to a stronger contribution by the credit channel.

As regards the euro area, our findings point to an improvement of risk sharing since the start of the COVID-19 pandemic, i.e. between 2020 and 2022, which is mainly explained by a stronger credit channel. In particular, on top of the significant fiscal support provided at the national level, which has contributed to prevent the fragmentation of capital markets and the decline in private risk-sharing channels, there have been significant advances in the provision of public support measures at the EU level. This includes the triple safety net that made €540 billion available in loans through the ESM to help to finance pandemic-related sovereign expenditures, on national short-time work schemes and in credit guarantees to firms provided through the European Investment Bank. While the temporary Support to mitigate Unemployment Risks in an Emergency (SURE) has been the only measure to be used to date, the announcement of these public support initiatives has undoubtedly contributed to boosting confidence and preventing sudden interruptions of cross-border financial flows.

The most significant step forward was the introduction of the EU's Recovery and Resilience Facility (RRF), the main component of the Next Generation EU (NGEU) package. The facility is a temporary instrument designed to bolster the recovery and structural transformation of EU economies through a combination of grants and loans to be financed by European debt issuance.[2]

[2] The RRF entered into force on 19 February 2021. It was launched to finance reforms and investments in EU Member States from the start of the coronavirus pandemic in February 2020 and is set to run until 31 December 2026. It has made a total of €723.8 billion available to EU countries – €385.8 billion in loans and €338 billion in grants. For an in-depth analysis of the impact of the RRF and NGEU on the euro area economy, see Bańkowski et al. (2022).

It amounts to €724 billion, and the expectation is that more than four-fifths will be taken up by euro area countries.

In addition, monetary policy measures of the ECB and particularly its Pandemic Emergency Purchase Programme (PEPP) may have prevented financial fragmentation during the COVID-19 crisis, thus indirectly contributing to enhance risk sharing through the credit and capital channels in this period.

The COVID-19 pandemic provides clear and tangible evidence of the benefits of having risk-sharing mechanisms to cope with such unexpected and unprecedented shocks with asymmetric effects. These effects have been shown to depend, among other things, on the stringency of the mitigation strategies applied to contain the crisis and on the productive structures that exist (Battistini and Stoevsky, 2021).

All in all, evaluating risk sharing is paramount for countries in a monetary union. Within monetary unions, countries face a loss of monetary policy independence and of exchange rate mechanisms for coping with idiosyncratic shocks (or with the divergent impact of common shocks). Building national fiscal buffers, eliminating structural rigidities and strengthening private and public risk-sharing channels are crucial to enhancing the capacity of the euro area to cope with future shocks. This is the principal rationale for most proposals to improve the institutional architecture of EMU, some of which are also reviewed here.[3]

This chapter is organized as follows. Section 22.2 reviews the risk-sharing literature, focusing on the impact of euro adoption, the differences between the EMU and the United States, the relationship between risk sharing and the economic cycle, and whether private and public channels can be thought of as complements or substitutes. Section 22.3 comments on our results and proposes some reflections on how risk sharing has operated during the COVID-19 crisis. Finally, Section 22.4 reviews some reform proposals aimed at enhancing risk sharing in the eurozone, and Section 22.5 concludes.

22.2 RESULTS FROM THE LITERATURE

The literature on international risk sharing has grown considerably over the past three decades, especially since the seminal paper on the United States by Asdrubali et al. (1996). That paper finds that 75 per cent of shocks to the per capita gross product of individual states between 1963 and 1990 were smoothed out, leaving a relatively small number of shocks that were not absorbed (25 per cent). Looking at the different channels, 39 per cent of income shocks were smoothed out by insurance or cross-ownership of assets and 23 per cent by borrowing or lending. Only 13 per cent of income shocks were absorbed by federal tax transfers and grant schemes, which is, however, significantly higher than has been estimated for the European Union or euro area (EA) in other studies. It should be noted in this regard that several US states have a balanced-budget rule in place, leaving limited scope for countercyclical fiscal policies at state level. Overall, the analysis in the aforementioned paper shows that state-specific shocks in the United States were, for the most part, smoothed out through private risk-sharing channels, i.e. market transactions, rather than through public channels.

22.2.1 *Impact on Risk Sharing of Euro Adoption and Financial Integration*

A number of studies published since Asdrubali et al. (1996) and other early literature on risk sharing have analysed whether the adoption of the single currency in Europe has strengthened

[3] See, for example, the Five Presidents' Report (Juncker et al., 2015) and other proposals summarized in Section 22.6.

risk sharing and consumption in the euro area. Building on the experience of the United States, where risk sharing was found to have increased over time following financial deregulation and integration (Athanasoulis and van Wincoop, 2001; Demyanyk et al., 2008), the general consensus was that creation of the EMU would have led to greater financial integration and thus more consumption smoothing (Jappelli and Pagano, 2008). Indeed, several studies identified a growing trend towards a smoothing out of consumption in the years running up to the Global Financial Crisis, primarily due to greater financial integration in the euro area.[4] However, Afonso and Furceri (2008) highlight a decline in risk sharing after the introduction of the euro. Ferrari and Rogantini-Picco (2016) suggest that this might be due to the credit market channel amplifying shocks in periphery countries rather than smoothing them out.

22.2.2 *Comparing the Euro Area with the United States and Other Countries*

Since the start of the EMU, a large part of the literature has focused on estimating the degree of shock absorption and risk sharing in the euro area, and in comparing it with the United States and other countries or federations. It is generally shown that the strength of the risk-sharing mechanisms in the euro area countries has remained rather limited compared with the United States. As shown in Table 22.1, on average, 60 per cent of an adverse shock in a euro area country translates into a decline in that country's consumption, compared with the 30 per cent estimated for the United States.

The degree to which risk is shared through capital markets is the key difference between the United States and Europe, with the capital market playing a much more important role in this regard in the United States, given that this market acts as a form of insurance (smoothing out close to 40 per cent of shocks to domestic income). In Europe, however, the role it plays is comparatively small, as shown in Table 22.1. This may be due to the more limited development of equity markets in Europe, the greater national bias seen in euro area countries in contrast to the United States, and the fact that cross-border investment is concentrated in just a few EU Member States (Goncalves-Raposo and Lehmann, 2019; Milano and Reichlin, 2017; Véron and Wolff, 2016).

The bulk of risk sharing in the euro area takes place through the credit channel, but it is not sufficient to compensate for the weakness of the other channels. Until the NGEU programme was launched, the fiscal channel was only marginally relevant in the euro area: EU structural funds, which are the main form of fiscal transfers from EU institutions to the Member States, are actually disbursed for convergence reasons and not for stabilization. In the United States, the fiscal channel is estimated to cushion between 10 and 20 per cent of adverse shocks owing to the sizeable US federal budget.

Other authors have focused on different groups of countries within the euro area and on subsamples, distinguishing in particular between the pre- and post-Global Financial Crisis periods. Kalemli-Ozcan et al. (2014) were among the first to estimate the degree of risk sharing focusing on the so-called periphery and core eurozone countries, and on the Great Recession between 2008 and 2010. Their findings suggest that during that crisis, international cross-border financial flows (i.e. the capital channel) did not provide any risk sharing for periphery countries. On the contrary, it may have acted procyclically as a shock amplifier due 'home bias' and 'flight-to-safety' during the crisis, as reflected in the fragmentation of European financial markets. More

[4] For instance, Balli et al. (2012) using data from 1992 to 2007 document an increase in risk sharing in EMU and other OECD countries through factor income and capital gains since 2000. See also Demyanyk et al. (2007) and Kalemli-Ozcan et al. (2008).

TABLE 22.1 *Summary of the findings of the literature*

			Capital markets	Public transfers	Credit channel	Unsmoothed
EU countries						
Asdrubali and Kim (2004)	1960–90		0.04	0.00	0.43	0.53
Poncela et al. (2016)	1960–2014		0.00	0.00	0.25	0.75
	1999–2014		0.01	0.00	0.13	0.86
		Total	–	0.07	0.42	0.55
Ferrari and Rogantini Pico (2016)	1990–2014	Core	–0.20	0.08	0.61	0.50
		Periphery	–	0.07	0.39	0.52
Furceri and Zdzienicka (2015)	1979–2010		0.08	0.04	0.31	0.66
Nikolov (2016) (2016)	2000–2015		0.06	0.00	0.18	0.76
Kalemli-Ozcan et al. (2014)	1990–2007	Total	0.05	0.00	0.49	0.46
		Periphery	0.12	0.00	0.31	0.57
	1970–2014		0.01	0.00	0.27	0.72
Milano (2017)	1999–2014		0.03	0.00	0.30	0.67
	2007–2014		0.02	0.00	0.39	0.59
Afonso and Furceri (2008)	1980–2005		0.01	0.02	0.39	0.58
	1998–2005		0.14	0.01	0.25	0.60
Hoffmann et al. (2018)	1998–2013		0.01	0.02	0.39	0.58
	1998–2005		0.14	0.01	0.25	0.60
Alcidi et al. (2017)	1998–2013		0.10	0.01	0.14	0.75
Cimadomo et al (2018)	1998–2016		0.20	0.05	–0.05	0.80
United States						
Asdrubali et al. (1996)	1963–90		0.39	0.13	0.23	0.25
Asdrubali and Kim (2004)	1960–90		0.34	0.07	0.21	0.38
Nikolov (2016)	1964–2013		0.45	0.08	0.27	0.18
Melitz and Zumer (1999)	1964–1990		0.24	0.13	0.24	0.39
Alcidi et al. (2017)	1998–2013		0.48	0.08	0.27	0.17
Cimadomo et al. (2018)	1998–2016		0.30	0.10	0.20	0.40
Other countries						
Hepp and Von Hagen (2013)	1970–94	Germany pre-unification	0.20	0.54	0.17	0.09
	1995–2006	Germany post-unification	0.50	0.11	0.18	0.22
Melitz and Zumer (1999)	1984–92	Italy	0.49	–0.01	–0.04	0.55
Dedola et al. (1999)	1983–92	Italy	0.67	0.18	0.15	0.00

(continued)

TABLE 22.1 (*cont.*)

			Capital markets	Public transfers	Credit channel	Unsmoothed
Fiorelli et al. (2020)	2000–2016	Italy	0.43	0.17	0.16	0.24
Alberola and Asdrubali (1997)	1973–93	Spain	0.25	0.03	0.23	0.49
Melitz and Zumer (1999)	1972–96	United Kingdom	0.34	0.00	0.05	0.61
Dedola et al. (1999)	1978–94	United Kingdom	0.40	0.00	0.27	0.33
Melitz and Zumer (1999)	1962–94	Canada	0.30	0.08	0.25	0.37

Note: The table shows the share of idiosyncratic output income shocks that were smoothed out through the capital, credit, and fiscal channels in the United States, the euro area, and other countries, together with the share of unsmoothed shocks as estimated in certain studies selected. The sum of the four columns is by construction equal to one (up to a decimal rounding). In Fiorelli et al. (2020), smoothing out through capital depreciation was allocated to the capital market channel.

recently, Cimadomo et al. (2020) looked at eleven euro area countries and at intra-euro area financial flows, finding that only about 40 per cent of shocks are absorbed in the early years of EMU, while in the aftermath of the 2010–12 sovereign debt crisis around 65 per cent of shocks are smoothed out. This could be in part attributed to the activation of office financial assistance for countries under stress, namely the Greek Loan Facility, the EFSF, the European Financial Stabilisation Mechanism (EFSM), and the ESM. Milano and Reichlin (2017) also found that there had been an increase in risk sharing in euro area countries since the sovereign debt crisis as a result of official financial assistance.

Table 22.1 also reports results for intra-regional risk sharing in other countries: Germany, Italy, Spain, Canada, and the United Kingdom. While these studies use different samples and methodologies, some interesting common insights can be drawn from them. In general, the literature suggests that the effectiveness of risk sharing at the inter-regional level tends to be higher than at the international level (Crucini, 1999; Dedola et al., 1999). In the case of Germany, Hepp and von Hagen (2013) found a very high level of risk sharing across German regions in the pre-unification period: 91 per cent of shocks to per capita state gross product were smoothed out. In the post-unification period, this level decreased somewhat but remained high (at about 80 per cent). A significant contribution came from the federal tax transfer and the grant system. For Italy, risk sharing appeared to be of a similar level (around 75 per cent of shocks smoothed out), whereas the level seems to have been lower, i.e. about 50 per cent, for Spanish regions (Alberola and Asdrubali, 1997).[5]

Figure 22.1 summarizes the results of the studies discussed by taking averages, for each country or federal state, for each risk-sharing channel. This sort of 'meta-analysis' again highlights the fact that the level of risk sharing across EMU (and EU) countries is significantly lower not only than for the United States, but also as compared with risk sharing between regions in Germany, Italy, and Spain. Canada and the United Kingdom exhibit slightly lower risk sharing compared to the United States. Overall, the experience of the United States and of some European countries points to the potential for greater risk sharing that has not so far been fully developed in the case of the euro area.

[5] To be best of our knowledge, there are no papers analysing the degree of risk sharing across French regions.

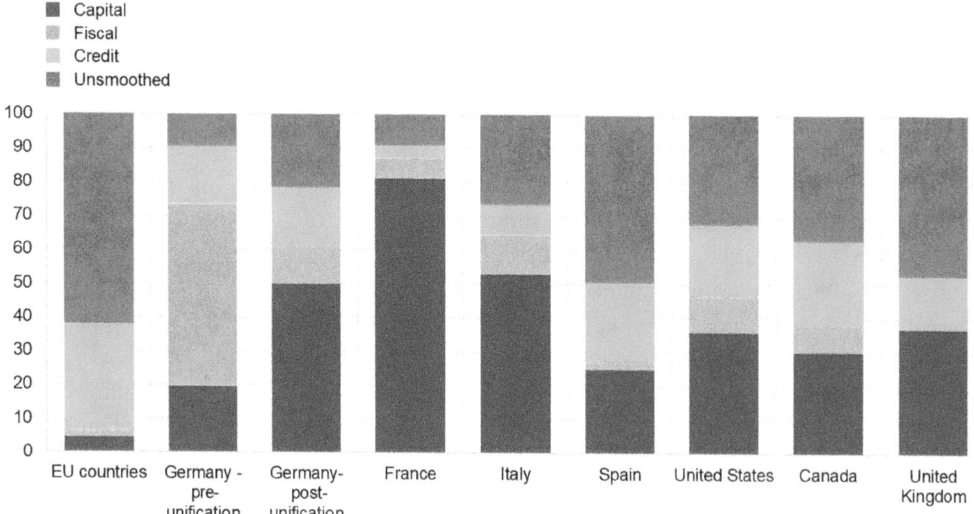

FIGURE 22.1. Strength of the risk-sharing channels in the various countries covered by the literature examined (x-axis: regions; y-axis: channel of smoothing).
Note: The table shows the average values for each country or federal state and for each channel referred to in Table 22.1.
Source: Authors' calculations.

22.2.3 *Relationship between Risk Sharing and the Economic Cycle*

Some of the literature has explored whether risk sharing has varied over the business cycle. In particular, consideration was given to whether it has been countercyclical, thus providing stronger absorption of local shocks when it was needed more (i.e. during economic downturns), or if it had instead been procyclical, thus amplifying the effects of shocks. Hoffmann and Shcherbakova-Stewen (2011) find that inter-state risk sharing in the United States varies over the business cycle, with risk sharing increasing in booms and decreasing during downturns. In the period 1963–2005, risk sharing during recessions was on average about 20 percentage points below its mean. This showed that income smoothing through capital income flows tended to be countercyclical, whereas the credit-saving channel was strongly procyclical, this latter effect turning out to dominate. In the case of the euro area, Furceri and Zdzienicka (2015) document a significant decrease of risk sharing in recessions among euro area countries, which becomes more intensive in severe downturns that are persistent and unanticipated. Moreover, several studies show that during the 2008–9 Global Financial Crisis and the subsequent 2010–12 euro area sovereign debt crisis there was a strong decrease in private risk sharing (Banco de Espana, 2016; Kalemli-Ozcan et al., 2014). The main driver was the behaviour of credit markets that typically collapse during financial crises. However, it should be borne in mind that in the euro area, in contrast to the United States, there was no other sizeable smoothing channel other than the ESM financial assistance and, more recently, the NGEU package.

22.2.4 *Private and Public Risk-Sharing Channels: Complements or Substitutes?*

Different views emerge on whether the main risk-sharing channels operate as complements, thus reinforcing each other, or as substitutes. With regard to the credit and capital market channels, Hoffmann et al. (2018) present empirical evidence – rationalized in a dynamic stochastic general equilibrium (DSGE)-model framework – that supports the complementarity of both channels. In their model, banking integration improves the access of bank-dependent firms to finance but at the cost of making those firms' profits more volatile and more procyclical. This, in turn, increases the benefits of international portfolio diversification and equity market integration. This finding is consistent with past literature which suggests that proper diversification of funding sources leads to more investment and to lower vulnerability to financial flows.

With regard to public versus private risk-sharing channels, the evidence is scarcer and tends to point to substitutability. Some authors consider that if risk sharing in the private sector was fostered through a fully fledged banking union and a capital markets union (CMU), the euro area could achieve significant capacity to absorb shocks that would be similar to that of other federal states. For example, Belke and Gros (2015) consider that financial institutions (e.g. through the Single Resolution Mechanism and the common deposit insurance scheme) are more important for restoring investor confidence than fiscal institutions. In contrast, others argue for fiscal insurance as a complement to private risk sharing. A central fiscal capacity might reduce the financial frictions associated with having foreign debt, serving as a backstop for cross-border private borrowing and lending (Beetsma et al., 2021a, 2021b; Giovannini et al., 2021b). For the United States, Schelkle (2017) argues that the Federal Deposit Insurance Corporation (FDIC) performs the role of fiscal backstop for state budgets in a systemic crisis. In addition, Farhi and Werning (2017) make a theoretical case for market-based insurance being suboptimal in currency unions given that private economic agents do not internalize the macroeconomic stabilization effects stemming from a higher diversification of asset portfolios. Others argue that a central fiscal stabilization capability could foster private risk sharing by reducing the possibility of a recession that could prompt procyclical credit flows. From a more practical perspective, some argue that the banking union currently in place falls short of realizing its potential for shock absorption and that it will take many years to develop a genuine banking and CMU. Fiscal union is a necessary complement to and not a substitute for a banking and capital markets union.

22.3 EMPIRICAL RESULTS

Tests of international risk sharing have typically been based on the relationship between total economy consumption growth and output growth, controlling for global economic shocks and other factors. A full risk-sharing scenario would be characterized by (local) consumption being uncorrelated with (local) output, indicating that idiosyncratic output shocks hitting a particular region in a federal state or a country in a monetary union would be smoothed out through financial market channels or inter-regional transfers. Empirically, initial descriptive evidence of the degree of risk sharing might be based on the approach proposed by Kalemli-Ozcan et al. (2014). They construct a measure of synchronization based on the negative absolute difference of GDP growth between country i and country j in year t. We have applied this measure to both GDP and consumption growth, and separately for the euro area and the United States. More specifically, we have calculated the measure of synchronization between all $n(n-1)/2$ country pairs, then computed the average of these pairs for each year t. The more negative is this measure, the less synchronized are the countries (states) in the two monetary unions analysed. A value of zero would indicate perfect synchronization.

Figure 22.2 shows, first, that consumption and output have a similar degree of dispersion across euro area countries while, for the United States, consumption is remarkably less dispersed

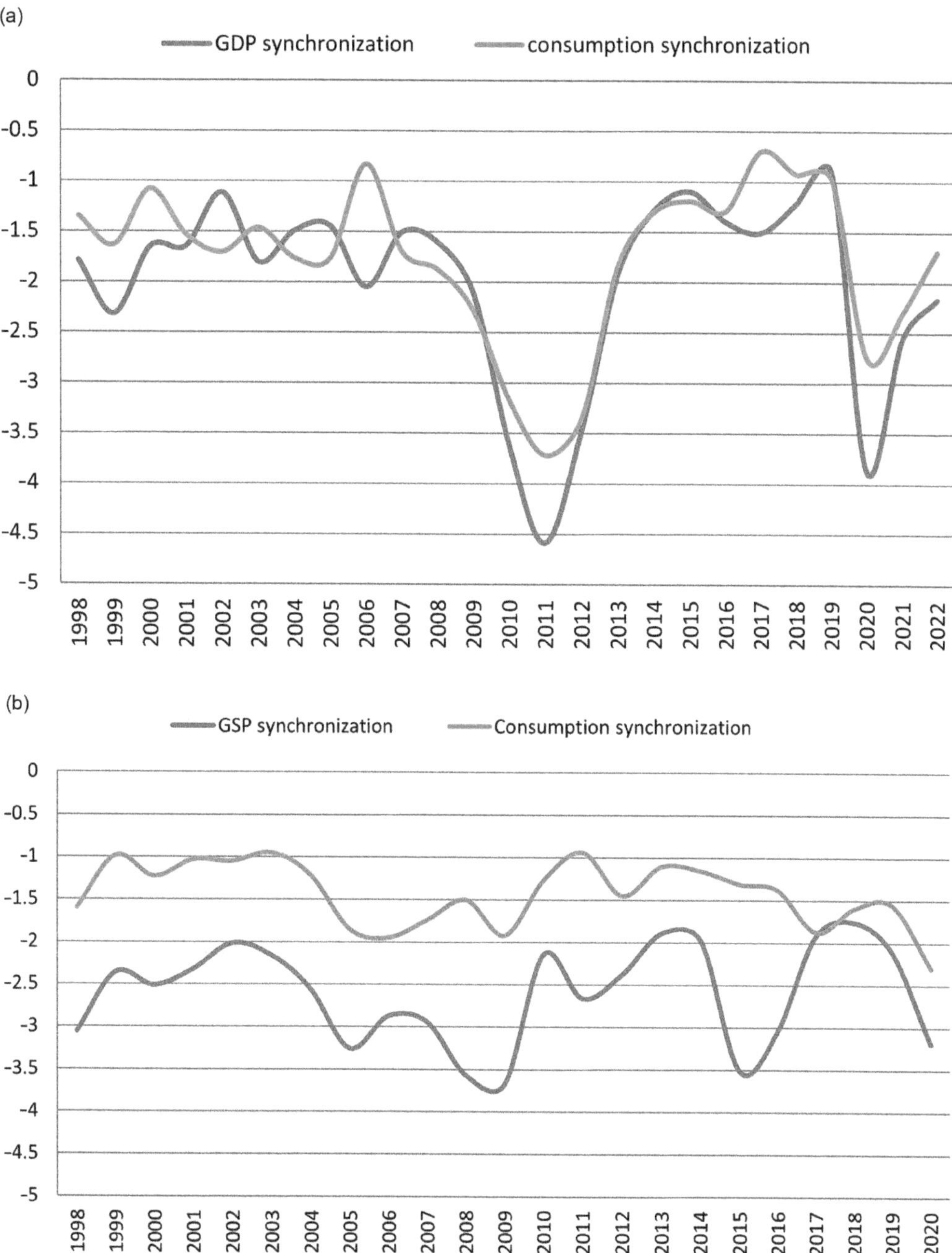

FIGURE 22.2. (a) Euro area: synchronization of Gross Domestic Product (GDP) and consumption across countries; (b) United States: synchronization of GSP (Gross State Product) and consumption across states (x-axis: years; y-axis: measure of synchronization).

Notes: The graphs show a measure of synchronization based on the negative absolute difference of GDP growth between country (state) *i* and country (state) *j* in year *t*. This measure is applied to both GDP and consumption growth, separately for the euro area and the United States. The measure of synchronization is calculated between all $n(n-1)/2$ country pairs, then averaged across all pairs for each year *t*. The more negative this measure is, the less synchronized the countries (states) will be within the two monetary unions considered. A value of zero would indicate perfect synchronization.

Source: Authors' calculations.

than output across states. This is already *prima facie* evidence of stronger risk sharing in the United States than in the euro area. Second, the United States experienced a sizeable increase in output dispersion during the Global Financial Crisis of 2008–9. However, this was accompanied by a smaller increase in dispersion for consumption. The euro area witnessed a bigger increase in dispersion, although this occurred at a later stage, namely during the 2010–12 European sovereign debt crisis. Dispersion also increased strongly in the euro area during the COVID-19 crisis, but then declined rapidly in 2021 and 2022 to pre-pandemic levels. Remarkably, consumption dispersion for the euro area was only slightly lower than output dispersion during both the European sovereign debt crisis and the COVID-19 crisis, signalling the limited role of risk sharing. Overall, this initial evidence suggests more powerful risk-sharing mechanisms in the United States than in the euro area, especially during severe recessions. Federal transfers, inter-state credit, and capital flows are likely to have contributed to smoothing out local output shocks, thus resulting in more synchronized consumption across states as compared with the situation in the euro area. However, preliminary evidence on the COVID-19 crisis indicates that *ex post* risk sharing through common instruments put in place in the EU seems to have limited income and consumption dispersion in the aftermath of the COVID-19 crisis.

Based on the empirical framework presented in the Appendix (which builds on Asdrubali and Kim, 2004) we estimate the overall degree of risk sharing and the contribution of the different risk-sharing channels in both the euro area and the United States. In contrast to previous studies, this approach allows us to evaluate not only the contemporaneous (i.e. within a year) effects of risk sharing, but also dynamic effects (i.e. shock absorption and the contribution of each channel) after some years.[6]

Figure 22.3 shows, for the euro area and the United States, the effect of the GDP shock on consumption growth at various horizons. In particular, the charts depict the contemporaneous response of each channel, and then the cumulative responses after one, two, three, and four years. The total impact is normalized at 100 at every horizon: for example, if a GDP shock occurs in year t, it may translate in a one-to-one change in consumption (i.e. no risk sharing). In this case, the 'unsmoothed' bar will take a value of 100, while the other bars will be at zero. In the opposite case of full risk sharing, the unsmoothed bar will be at zero, and the sum of the capital, fiscal, and credit channels will be 100. The advantage of the representation in Figure 22.3, which is novel, is that it allows for an evaluation not only of the contemporaneous effect of the output shock, but also of how it is dampened over time.

Figure 22.3 shows that, for both the euro area and the United States, risk sharing operated more effectively in the short to medium term, i.e. within one year after the realization of the shock (in t and $t + 1$), while the effectiveness of risk-sharing mechanisms weakens over time, as reflected in the 'unsmoothed' bars which increased over the four-year horizon. In the eurozone, the largest contribution was from the credit channel, which dampens about 30 per cent of the output shock within the first two years. In the United States, the contribution of the capital channel was high in the first year, before turning negative (the bars show the cumulated effect), while the contribution from the credit channel declines more slowly over the horizon. This is probably due to the fact that income from the equity and capital market is more volatile, while loans from financial intermediaries or governments have a longer duration and thus contribute to a steadier stabilization over time. The contribution of the fiscal channel was in the order

[6] See also European Central Bank (2016) and Cimadomo et al. (2018) for a related analysis.

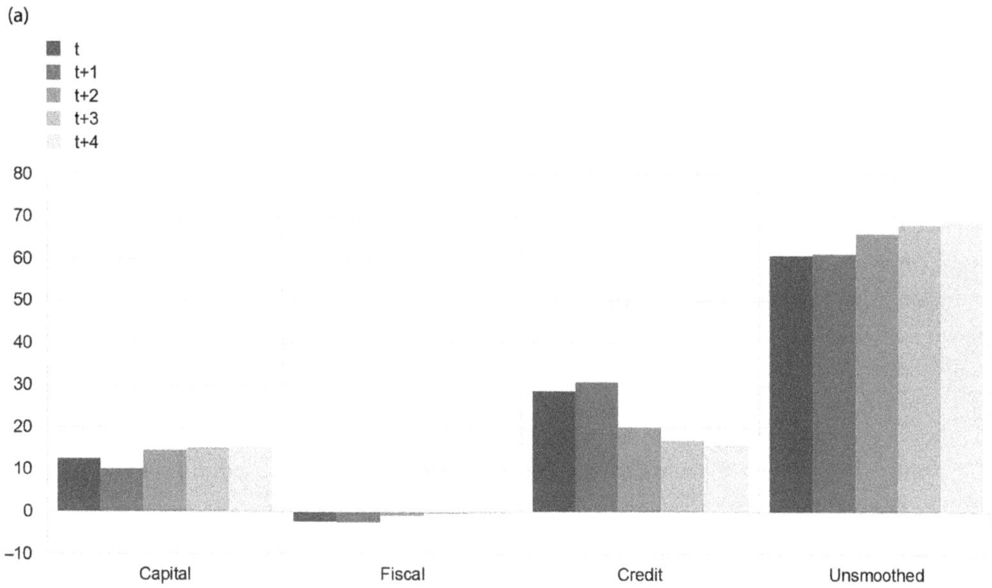

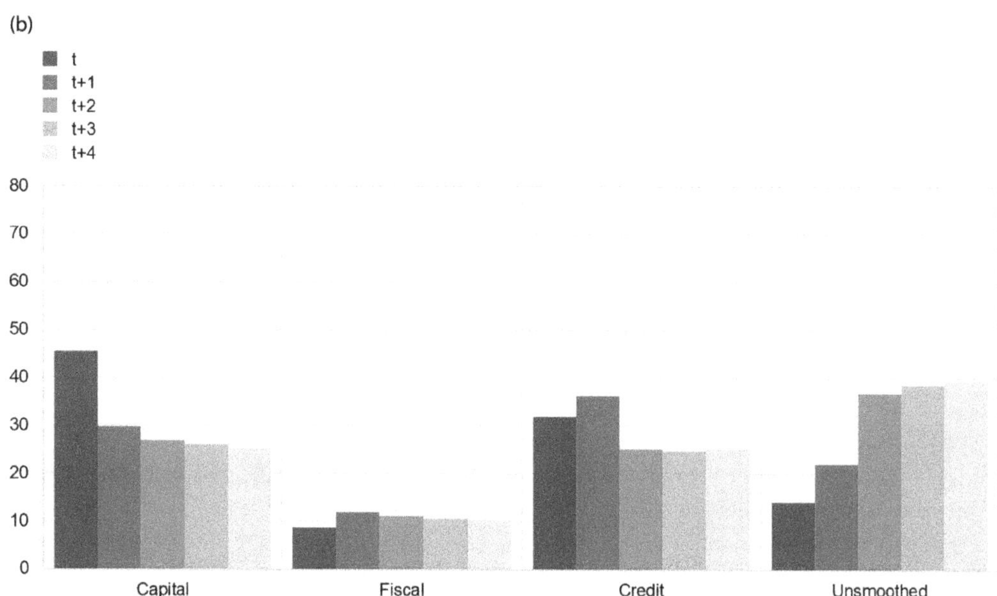

FIGURE 22.3. (a) Euro area: transmission of output shocks to consumption and the smoothing channels (y-axis: percentages).
Source: Authors' calculations. Sample: 1997–2022.
(b) United States: transmission of output shocks to consumption and the smoothing channels (y-axis: percentages).
Source: Authors' calculations.
Note: The charts depict the effect of a GDP shock on consumption growth at various horizons, based on impulse responses generated by the panel VAR model illustrated in the Appendix. The first bar represents the contemporaneous response of each channel, i.e. in the same year in which the output shock has occurred. Then, the cumulative responses after one, two, three, and four years is reported. The sum of all channels and the unsmoothed part is normalized at 100 at every horizon. Sample: 1997–2020.

of 10 per cent for all horizons in the United States, while it was close to zero in the euro area. The share of unsmoothed shocks increased over time for both the euro area (from around 55 to 70 per cent four years after the shock) and the United States (from around 15 to 40 per cent).

To evaluate how risk sharing has evolved over the last two decades, we estimated the effects of a GDP shock on consumption on the basis of twelve-year rolling windows. The results are reported in Figure 22.4. In these charts, each bar represents the contribution of the capital channel, fiscal channel, and credit channel respectively – together with the share of unsmoothed shocks – over the individual twelve-year windows, each of which end in the year reported on the x-axis. For example, the 2022 bar shows estimates for the sample 2010–22.[7] Year-on-year variation in the shares shown reflects changes in the re-estimated model parameters for each window. The remaining portion represents the share of the shock to country-specific real GDP growth that remains unsmoothed and is therefore fully reflected in country-specific consumption growth. The individual bars may fall below 0 per cent and rise above 100 per cent if one or more of the channels has a disruptive effect on the smoothing out of country-specific consumption growth. The sum of all channels equals 100 per cent.

Panel (a) of Figure 22.4 shows that the number of unsmoothed shocks increased across the euro area when the Global Financial Crisis of 2008–10 was included in the sample. Indeed, over that period, the role of the capital and credit markets became progressively less important, possibly reflecting financial market investor flight to safety and procyclical cross-border lending. However, the decline in risk sharing stops in 2012. This might be partially attributed to the activation of official assistance programmes in the eurozone, which are likely to have had a positive effect on risk sharing (see also Cimadomo et al., 2020). Moreover, ECB President Mario Draghi's 'whatever it takes' speech on 26 July 2012 and further ECB measures probably contributed to prevent financial fragmentation in EMU.

When the sample includes the COVID-19 pandemic, there was an improvement in risk sharing, mainly attributable to the credit channel. While an exact identification of the drivers of this channel is not possible in this framework, the evidence suggests that the provision of unprecedented policy support (including the activation of the EU's RRF which channels loans and grants to euro zone countries and the ECB's PEPP) probably prevented private risk-sharing channels from collapsing, reducing the risk of a sudden stop in cross-border financial flows. On the contrary, public risk sharing remained marginal. In addition to common initiatives at the EU level,[8] households may have resorted to their own savings to avoid large cuts in consumption during the pandemic, reflecting also significant support at the national level.[9]

Figure 22.4(b) shows that, for the United States, the Global Financial Crisis did not hamper risk sharing so severely, indicating that the credit and financial infrastructure in the United States operated effectively to dampen shocks and allow a relatively stable level of consumption

[7] The bars represent the cumulative responses two years after the shock has occurred. This is comparable to the bar $t+2$ in Figure 22.3, although the latter are estimated over the full sample.

[8] See also Bańkowski et al. (2022) for a related analysis of the importance of the confidence effects generated by the launch of the NGEU programme.

[9] Other studies point to the fact that risk sharing was relatively resilient during the COVID-19 crisis. For example, Giovannini et al. (2021a) suggest that lockdown measures taken to reduce the spread of COVID-19 prevented households from consuming a large share of their normal consumption basket. Consequently, for this period, it was recommended that analysis focus on income risk sharing, i.e. the ability to separate a country's change in GDP from changes in its output, rather than on consumption risk sharing. The findings of these authors suggest that income risk sharing was relatively stable during the crisis. Analysis of private intra-euro area cross-border flows confirms this, given that these flows exhibited a high degree of resilience during the COVID-19 crisis, in sharp contrast to the situation during the Global Financial Crisis (Gros and Alcidi, 2013).

(a)

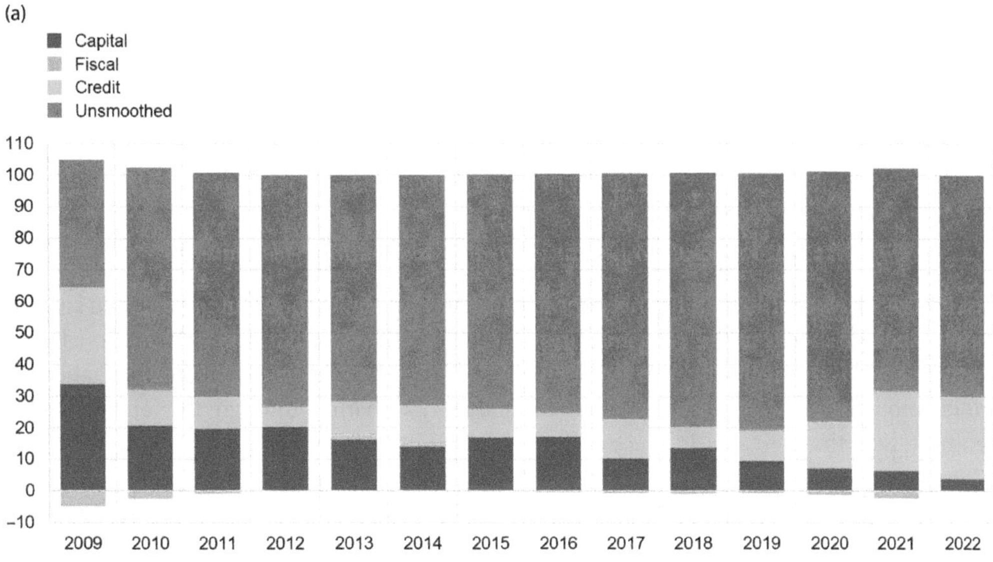

(b)

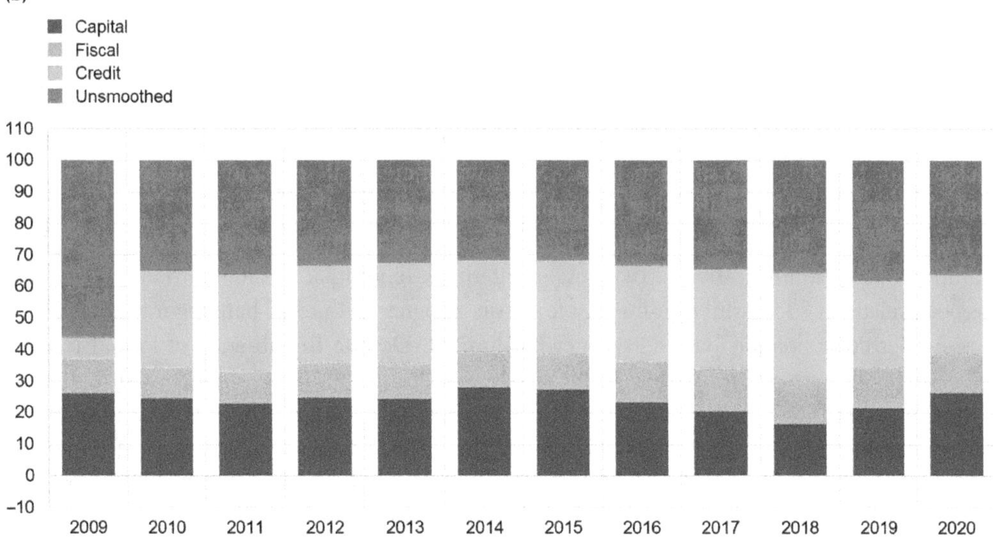

FIGURE 22.4. (a) Euro area: changes in consumption risk sharing and the smoothing channels (x-axis: end-year of the ten-year window; y-axis: percentages).
(b) United States: changes in consumption risk sharing and the smoothing channels (x-axis: end-year of the ten-year window; y-axis: percentages).
Notes: The charts show the percentage of consumption growth that is smoothed out through the capital, fiscal, and credit channels, as well as the unsmoothed component, following a shock to domestic GDP. These contributions are computed on the basis of the cumulative impact of the shock at the two-year horizon. The contributions of the channels are calculated using a panel Vector Autoregressive (VAR) model based on parameters estimated over a twelve-year rolling window of annual data. The x-axis reports the end-year for the twelve-year window. Panel a: the sample is for the period 1997–2022. Panel b: the sample covers the period 1997–2020.
Source: Authors' calculations.

across states. The contribution of the credit channel increased considerably after the Global Financial Crisis, possibly due to the emergence of new sources of consumer credit, such as non-bank financial institutions, and remained rather stable thereafter.

22.4 REFORM PROPOSALS

22.4.1 *Proposals to Enhance Private Risk-Sharing Mechanisms*

Past findings have highlighted the need for institutions that could contribute to insuring against country-specific shocks in the euro area. In particular, the finding that risk sharing through the credit channel is relatively effective in the euro area makes the process of banking integration of prime importance. Moreover, the observation that risk sharing through this channel falls significantly in the euro area in times of financial crisis or severe downturns points to the need for measures to avoid 'home bias' in credit flows in times of financial stress.

Substantial progress has been made to increase the soundness of the banking sector, which is a necessary prerequisite for increasing cross-border financial integration and enhancing risk sharing. The main catalyst for reform was the establishment of the Single Supervisory Mechanism (SSM). Currently, the ECB directly supervises all significant European credit institutions, which represent almost 82 per cent of total banking assets in the euro area.

Progress has also been made through the creation of the Single Resolution Mechanism that establishes homogeneous resolution criteria based on the principle of minimizing taxpayer cost. The agreement achieved at the euro summit in December 2018 to operationalize a common backstop for the Single Resolution Fund (SRF) will increase its capacity to deal with severe banking crises without destabilizing the public finances of countries affected.

There are still important challenges to achieving a truly integrated banking system. For example, while the integration of (wholesale) interbank lending across the euro area countries has been relatively successful over the past few years, progress with retail banking integration and cross-border consolidation has been somewhat limited. Despite the absence of formal restrictions, few banks have entered retail markets in other member countries and cross-border lending to the real sector has been less than adequate. As a result, the majority of firms and households in the euro area continue to be largely dependent on funding provided by their own domestic banking system, despite the clear benefits of having foreign banks operating in the domestic economy, as confirmed in the literature examined (see, for example, Albertazzi et al., 2021).[10]

Interbank flows have proved to be highly procyclical in the euro area, contributing to the deterioration in risk sharing after 2008. Among other factors, several authors have suggested that this might reflect significant differences in banking regulation across countries and the existence of national regulations that protect existing banks or regional banks, thereby reducing the incentive to expand their activities across borders (Angeloni, 2020; Restoy, 2015). Indeed, as shown in Hoffmann and Shcherbakova-Stewen (2011), state-level banking deregulation in the United States during the 1980s improved small firms' access to credit in recessions. These types of firms typically rely primarily on banking credit and, consequently, on the robustness of interstate risk sharing in economic downturns.

[10] Hoffmann et al. (2018) also suggest that what when banks direct cross-border lending direct to the real sector (i.e. through foreign intermediaries) this is associated with more risk sharing, while indirect integration through interbank flows is not.

In light of this, the euro area also needs to be equipped with a genuine banking union that would foster an increase in cross-border lending to the real economy. In this regard, the creation of a fully fledged European Deposit Insurance System (EDIS) might also facilitate cross-border banking operations and increase risk sharing. There have been some proposals along these lines. For instance, Gros (2015) suggests the introduction of an EDIS under which existing national deposit insurance schemes would retain their autonomous role based on a reinsurance system, at least in the initial stages (European Commission, 2017a). Other proposals include an EDIS funded by the countries concerned on the basis of their country-specific risks (Schnabel and Véron, 2018; Schoenmaker, 2018).

With regard to the capital market channel, a recent study by Goncalves-Raposo and Lehmann (2019) that was based on firm-level data showed that the use of equity financing is still rare in the euro area and has a strong home bias. This, combined with evidence that the more integrated financial markets in the United States contribute decisively to enhanced risk sharing, points clearly to the need for full completion of the Capital Markets Union (CMU) within the euro area. Unlike the banking union, the integration of capital markets in the euro area has received less institutional impetus recently. The European Commission launched the CMU project in 2015 to remove cross-border barriers and diversify the financing sources available to European firms and households. Greater diversification through capital markets can enhance cross-border risk sharing and alleviate the risks of financial fragmentation. Single or unified European supervision of capital markets and regulatory harmonization in areas such as insolvency law could contribute to achieving this goal. Full CMU could play a key role in funding recovery from crises such as that caused by COVID-19 and mitigate asymmetries across euro area countries (Friedrich and Thiemann, 2017; Sapir et al., 2018).

22.4.2 *Proposals to Enhance Public Risk-Sharing Mechanisms*

As mentioned, market-based risk-sharing mechanisms alone are not sufficient to withstand severe shocks (Farhi and Werning, 2017). Central fiscal capacity at euro area level might increase the capacity of budgetary policy to absorb common and idiosyncratic shocks, with the dual aim of softening the effects on individual countries and safeguarding stability in the euro area as a whole in the event of extreme shocks, such as those experienced in the past two decades (Juncker et al., 2015). The ESM could play a key role as a shock absorber (Cimadomo et al., 2020; Milano, 2017). However, the initial design of the ESM, which was conceived as an instrument of last resort, makes it ill-suited to prevent crises.[11]

Several proposals have been discussed for designing cross-country public insurance mechanisms within the euro area, all requiring very different degrees of political ambition (the surveys on which the proposals are based are given in Beetsma et al., 2021b; Burriel et al., 2020). The existing proposals mainly focus on a macroeconomic stabilization function (e.g. Balassone et al., 2018; Beetsma et al., 2021a, 2021b), a European investment protection scheme that would shield investment in the event of a downturn (Bara et al., 2017) or a European unemployment reinsurance scheme (Albrizio et al., 2017; Andor, 2016; Barkbu et al., 2018; Bénassy-Quéré et al., 2018; Dolls, 2020). Other proposals envisage a rainy-day fund with countries experiencing a boom being the net payers and countries in downturns

[11] Nevertheless, the recent reform of preventive credit lines strengthens the crisis-prevention capacity of the ESM.

being the net receivers. The most ambitious proposals include the creation of an economic government for the euro area, with its own budget for macroeconomic stabilization, that would have responsibility for a European debt agency entrusted with issuing joint debt instruments (see European Commission, 2017b). All these instruments would reallocate resources inter-temporally but also across participants in different positions along the economic cycle, thereby contributing to the synchronization of business cycles in the euro area. Some papers have simulated what would have happened had such mechanisms been in place since the creation of the euro area (see, for example, Banco de España, 2016; Furceri and Zdzienicka, 2015; Koester and Sondermann, 2018). Their findings suggest that a central fiscal capacity of a relatively moderate size would enable the euro area to achieve a stabilizing power close to that of federal budget transfers in the United States. Codogno and van den Noord (2019) applied a model-based framework to analyse how this type of instrument could improve the resilience of the euro area economy against shocks. They concluded that a central fiscal capacity combined with a safe asset would remove the doom loop between banks and sovereign states, reduce the loss in output for economies in the event of shocks, and improve the stabilization properties of fiscal policy for euro area countries; it would therefore be welfare enhancing.

A somewhat different perspective is offered by de Haan and Kosterink (2018). They argue that when governments have fiscal sustainability, they can use national fiscal policy to stabilize idiosyncratic shocks (see also Bayoumi and Masson, 1995; Dolls et al., 2012). At the same time, coordination of domestic monetary and fiscal policies with monetary policies adopted by the ECB to stabilize common shocks might make reinforcement of fiscal risk sharing unnecessary.

In general, a strong politico-economic argument against the establishment of central fiscal capacity is the increased risk of moral hazard and hence the need for the introduction of adequate safeguards in the form of strengthened surveillance and coordination mechanisms. In addition, there is little political appetite for sharing responsibilities on taxation at the EU level, which would be needed to underpin the funding side of the capacity.

The pandemic has further underlined the need for a common public risk-sharing mechanism in the euro area. In 2020 the EU rapidly set up what was called a triple safety net, amounting to €540 billion and providing loan-based support to governments through three schemes (of which only the first has been used so far): the SURE programme, the ESM's Pandemic Crisis Support credit line, and the European Investment Bank's pan-European guarantee fund to provide support to companies. By far the most sizeable EU public support programme is the NGEU economic recovery package aimed at supporting Member States hit by the COVID-19 pandemic with loans and grants worth up to €724 billion. These measures are an important milestone in public risk-sharing arrangements, even though they are temporary in nature. Codogno and van den Noord (2019), having applied a stylized macroeconomic model, argue that an alternative approach, with *ex ante* risk sharing through the creation of a Eurobond and permanent central fiscal capacity, would be at least as powerful, but more sustainable, automatic, and timely.

In general, while it is not contested that risk sharing increases the capacity to absorb shocks, some authors object to risk-sharing measures owing to the likely impact on the incentive structure in a currency union (e.g. Bargain et al., 2012). From a political perspective, the right balance must be found between additional central euro area stabilization and risk-sharing instruments on the one hand, and enforcement of fiscal rules and more market discipline on the other.

22.5 CONCLUSIONS

This chapter has presented a survey of the literature on consumption and income risk sharing, focusing on the euro area and the United States. It has also provided its own estimates of how risk sharing has evolved in both regions since the end of the 1990s. Overall, the literature finds a higher degree of risk sharing in the United States, rather than in the euro area. This is mainly due to the stronger role of private risk-sharing channels (the capital and credit channels) as compared with the fiscal channel, which has a relatively small part to play in the United States and is negligible in the euro area. Our own analysis confirms these findings and points to an improvement in risk sharing in the euro area during the COVID-19 crisis on the back of a stronger savings-credit channel. The Next Generation EU and its Recovery and Resilience Fund are likely to have contributed to consumption smoothing during the pandemic, both 'directly' (e.g. via loans and grants disbursed to Member States) and 'indirectly', through the confidence effects generated by the announcement of these initiatives. This added to the sizeable fiscal stimuli and the monetary policy measures implemented during the pandemic, which contributed to prevent financial market fragmentation. Overall, our findings point to the need to improve private and public risk-sharing mechanisms in the euro area, while at the same time weighing the trade-off between further common stabilization mechanisms and the risks of moral hazard.

Appendix: The Empirical Model

In their seminal paper on the United States, Asdrubali et al. (1996) propose a framework based on a cross-sectional variance decomposition of shocks to GDP to estimate risk-sharing channels. The approach has been extensively used in the literature as it has the merit of bringing together in an integrated framework the three smoothing channels previously mentioned. The approach is based on the following accounting identity:

$$GDP_{it} = \frac{GDP_{it}}{GNP_{it}} \frac{GNP_{it}}{GDI_{it}} \frac{GDI_{it}}{C_{it}} C_{it}$$

where GDP is gross domestic product, GNP is gross national product, GDI is gross disposable income, and C is total consumption.

With full risk sharing through capital markets ('capital' or 'income' channel), GDP and GNP should not co-move. Possible differences in GDP and GNP are explained by income from financial assets held abroad and labour income from employment abroad of citizens of the domestic country. The second channel depends on the difference between GNP and GDI, and it is defined as the 'fiscal channel'. This includes mainly cross-border transfers between governments (e.g. NGEU transfers or structural funds in the case of the EU) or, for the United States, federal transfers to states. The third channel is captured by the difference between GDI and C, and it is generally labelled as 'credit channel'. This includes, for example, borrowing abroad by individuals and governments, either in credit markets or through supranational insurance mechanisms such as the ESM. NGEU loans would also fall under this channel.

The first two channels capture *ex ante* risk sharing, as they refer to financial arrangements made before the GDP shock materializes. The last channel captures *ex post* risk sharing, as it reflects financial arrangements generally made after the GDP shock has taken place.

Empirically, Asdrubali et al. (1996) measure the strength of each channel using panel regressions of the following type:

$$\Delta GDP_{it} - \Delta GNP_{it} = \alpha_1 + \beta_1 \Delta GDP_{it} + \varepsilon_{1t}$$

$$\Delta GNP_{it} - \Delta GDI_{it} = \alpha_2 + \beta_2 \Delta GDP_{it} + \varepsilon_{2t}$$

$$\Delta GDI_{it} - \Delta C_{it} = \alpha_3 + \beta_3 \Delta GDP_{it} + \varepsilon_{3t}$$

$$\Delta C_{it} = \alpha_4 + \beta_4 \Delta GDP_{it} + \varepsilon_{4t}$$

The coefficients β_1, β_2, and β_3 approximate the percentage of risk shared through capital markets, fiscal transfers, and the credit markets, respectively. The coefficient β_4 measures the percentage of non-shared risk.

It is important to stress that the approach of Asdrubali et al. (1996) does not capture the dynamic behaviour of consumption smoothing. International consumption smoothing has not only a cross-border dimension but also a temporal one reflected in the behaviour of savings. As a result, there have been some proposals in the literature to address this issue. For instance, Del Negro (2002) measures risk sharing taking into account shocks to the overall level of wealth, and not only to income, in order to take better account of the intertemporal dimension of insurance.

We follow Asdrubali and Kim, 2004 (AK hereafter). These authors use a panel VAR model, where the four equations above are included in a single model featuring ΔGDP_{it}, $\Delta GDP_{it} - \Delta GNP_{it}$, $\Delta GNP_{it} - \Delta GDI_{it}$ and $\Delta GDI_{it} - \Delta C_{it}$ as endogenous variables. In our analysis, the panel VAR model has two lags and it also includes country fixed effects. It is estimated with the least squares dummy variable estimator (LSDV).

Previous studies, using a static system (as in Asdrubali et al., 1996), examined how ΔGDP_{it} is smoothed by different channels within the same year, and assumed ΔGDP_{it} as exogenous. AK, instead, studied how changes in GDP due to exogenous shocks are smoothed dynamically by different risk-sharing channels. This framework also allows us to assess smoothing properties over time, and not only contemporaneously. In order to derive the exogenous GDP shock, in their baseline formulation AK simply assume a recursive structure by ordering GDP first and applying a Cholesky identification scheme. Here we follow the same approach, which allows us not only to capture the dynamics of inter-regional risk sharing but also to endogenize the output process, i.e. taking into account potential feedback and interlinkages between output and the various smoothing channels. In practice, we estimate impulse responses of the capital channel ($\Delta GDP_{it} - \Delta GNP_{it}$,), the fiscal channel ($\Delta GNP_{it} - \Delta GDI_{it}$), and the credit channel ($\Delta GDI_{it} - \Delta C_{it}$) to an orthogonalized GDP shock. The response of GDP which is not absorbed by these three channels will be labelled as unsmoothed.

The sample used in the empirical analysis includes eleven euro area countries: Austria, Belgium, Germany, Spain, Finland, France, Greece, Italy, Luxemburg, the Netherlands, and Portugal. Ireland is excluded from the analysis due to unusually large revisions in main macroeconomic aggregates. The US dataset covers all fifty states. For the euro area, we include annual data spanning the period 1997–2022. Data are retrieved from the European Commission's spring 2022 AMECO dataset. We decided to include nowcasts for 2022. Although they are preliminary and likely to be somewhat revised in the future, they already help to provide a first insight on developments during the COVID-19 pandemic. For the United States, the dataset spans the period 1997–2020. We retrieve US data from various official sources, mainly the Bureau of Economic Analysis and Census. We proceed as follows. For the construction of the dataset, and in particular the definition of the key variables used in the empirical analysis, we closely follow the definitions reported in Asdrubali et al. (1996). First, we estimate the model on the full sample, then we estimate it on rolling windows of twelve years to explore how risk sharing has evolved over time.

REFERENCES

Afonso, A., and Furceri, D. (2008). EMU enlargement, stabilization costs and insurance mechanisms. *Journal of International Money and Finance* 27(2), 169–187.

Alberola, E., and Asdrubali, P. (1997). how do countries smooth regional disturbances? Risksharing in Spain: 1973–1993. Documento de Trabajo No. 9724, Madrid: Banco de España.

Albertazzi, U., Cimadomo, J., and Maffei-Faccioli, N. (2021). Foreign banks and the doom loop. ECB Working Paper No. 2540, Frankfurt: European Central Bank.

Albrizio, S., Berganza, J. C., and Kataryniuk, I. (2017). Federal unemployment insurance in the United States. *Economic Bulletin* No. 2, Madrid: Banco de España, 1–10.

Alcidi, C., D'Imperio, P., and Thirion, G. (2017). Risk-sharing and consumption-smoothing patterns in the US and the euro area: A comprehensive comparison. CEPS Working Document No. 2017/04, May 2017.

Andor, L. (2016). Towards shared unemployment insurance in the euro area. *IZA Journal of Labor Studies* 5, 1–15.

Angeloni, I. (2020). Time to address the shortcomings of the banking union. SAFE Policy Letter No. 77, Frankfurt: Leibniz Institute for Financial Research.

Asdrubali, P., and Kim, S. (2004). Dynamic risk-sharing in the United States and Europe. *Journal of Monetary Economics* 51(4), 809–836.

Asdrubali, P., Sørensen, B. E., and Yosha, O. (1996). Channels of interstate risk sharing: United States 1963–1990. *Quarterly Journal of Economics* 111(4), 1081–1110.

Athanasoulis, S. G., and van Wincoop, E. (2001). Risk-sharing within the United States: What do financial markets and fiscal federalism accomplish? *Review of Economics and Statistics* 83(4), 688–698.

Balassone, F., Momigliano, S., Romanelli, M., and Tommasino, P. (2018). Just around the corner? Pros, cons, and implementation issues of a fiscal union for the euro area. *Economia Pubblica*, Milan: Franco Angeli, 5–34.

Balli, F., Kalemli-Ozcan, S., and Sørensen, B. E. (2012). Risk-sharing through capital gains. *Canadian Journal of Economics/Revue canadienne d'economique* 45(2), 472–492.

Banco de España (2016). Fiscal policy in EMU. *Annual Report*, Madrid.

Bańkowski, K., Bouabdallah, O., Domingues Semeano, J., Dorrucci, E., Freier, M., Jacquinot, P., Modery, W., Rodríguez Vives, M., Valenta, V., and Zorell, N. (2022). The economic impact of Next Generation EU: A euro area perspective. ECB Occasional Paper, Frankfurt: European Central Bank, forthcoming.

Bara, Y.-E., Castets, L., Ernoult, T., and Zakhatchouk, A. (2017). A contribution to the work on the strengthening of the euro area. *Trésor-Economics*, No. 9, Ministère de l'Economie et des Finances et de la Relance, February.

Bargain, O., Dolls, M., Fuest, C., Neumann, D., Peichl, A., Pestel, N., and Siegloch, S. (2012). Fiscal Union in Europe? Redistributive and stabilising effects of an EU tax-benefit system. Discussion Paper Series, No. 6585, Institute of Labor Economics (IZA), May.

Barkbu, B., Wang, H., Ture, E., Yao, J., and Arnold, N. (2018). A central fiscal stabilization capacity for the euro area. IMF Staff Discussion Note, No. 2018/003, International Monetary Fund, Washington, March.

Battistini, N., and Stoevsky, G. (2021). The impact of containment measures across sectors and countries during the COVID-19 pandemic. *Economic Bulletin*, Issue 2, European Central Bank.

Bayoumi, T., and Masson, P. R. (1995). Fiscal flows in the United States and Canada: Lessons for monetary union in Europe. *European Economic Review* 39(2), 253–274.

Beetsma, R., Cima, S., and Cimadomo, J. (2021a). Fiscal transfers without moral hazard? *International Journal of Central Banking* 17, 95–153.

Beetsma, R., van Spronsen, J., and Cimadomo, J. (2021b). One scheme fits all: A central fiscal capacity for the EMU targeting euro area, national and regional shocks. CEPR Discussion Paper No. 16826, London: Centre for Economic Policy Research.

Belke, A., and Gros, D. (2015). Banking union as a shock absorber. Discussion paper series, No 15-02, Research on Money in the Economy research network, Rome network.

Bénassy-Quéré, A., Brunnermeier, M., Enderlein, H., Farhi, E., Fuest, C., Gourinchas, P.-O., Martin, P., Pisani-Ferry, J., Rey, H., and Schnabel, I. (2018). Reconciling risk-sharing with market discipline: A constructive approach to euro area reform. *CEPR Policy Insight* No. 91, Centre for Economic Policy Research, London.

Burriel, P., Chronis, P., Freier, M., Hauptmeier, S., Reiss, L., Stegarescu, D., and Van Parys, S. (2020). A fiscal capacity for the euro area: Lessons from existing fiscal-federal systems. *Occasional Paper Series* No. 239, European Central Bank, April.

Cimadomo, J., Ciminelli, G., Furtuna, O., and Giuliodori, M. (2020). Private and public risk-sharing in the euro area. *European Economic Review* 121, 103347.

Cimadomo, J., Hauptmeier, S., Palazzo, A. A., and Popov, A. (2018). Risk-sharing in the euro area. *Economic Bulletin* Issue 3, European Central Bank.

Codogno, L., and van den Noord, P. (2019). The rationale for a safe asset and fiscal capacity for the euro area. LSE 'Europe in Question' Discussion Paper Series, LEQS Paper No. 144, London School of Economics and Political Science, May.

Committee for the Study of Economic and Monetary Union (1989). Report on Economic and Monetary Union in the European Community. Technical report, European Council, Brussels.

Crucini, M. J. (1999). On international and national dimensions of risk sharing. *Review of Economics and Statistics* 81, 73–84.

De Haan, J., and Kosterink, P. (2018). The case for more fiscal risk-sharing and coordination of fiscal and monetary policy. In N. Campos and J.-E. Sturm (eds.), *Bretton Woods, Brussels and Beyond: Redesigning the Institutions of Europe*. London: Centre for Economic Policy Research, pp. 107–116.

Dedola, L., Usai, S., and Vannini, M. (1999). An assessment of regional risk-sharing in Italy and the United Kingdom. In J. Adams and F. Pigliaru (eds.), *Economic Growth and Change*. Cheltenham: Edward Elgar, Ch. 15.

Del Negro, M. (2002). Asymmetric shocks among US states. *Journal of International Economics*, 56(2), 273–297.

Demyanyk, Y., Ostergaard, C., and Sørensen, B. E. (2007). US banking deregulation, small businesses, and interstate insurance of personal income. *Journal of Finance* 62,2763–2801.

Demyanyk, Y., Ostergaard, C., and Sørensen, B. E. (2008). Risk-sharing and portfolio allocation in EMU. *European Economy – Economic Papers 2008–2015* 334, Directorate General Economic and Financial Affairs (DG ECFIN), European Commission, Brussels.

Dolls, M. (2020). An unemployment re-insurance scheme for the euro area? Stabilizing and redistributive effects. CESifo Working Paper Series, No. 8219, CESifo, Munich.

Dolls, M., Fuest, C., and Peichl, A. (2012). Automatic stabilizers and economic crisis: US vs. Europe. *Journal of Public Economics* 96(3–4), 279–294.

European Central Bank (2016). Financial integration in Europe. Technical Report, April.

European Commission (2017a). Communication to the European Parliament, the Council, the European Central Bank, the European Economic and Social Committee and the Committee of the Regions on completing the Banking Union. COM/2017/0592 final, 11 October.

European Commission (2017b). Roadmap for deepening Europe's Economic and Monetary Union. Technical report.

Farhi, E., and Werning, I. (2017). Fiscal unions. *American Economic Review* 107(12), 3788–3834.

Ferrari, A., and Rogantini-Picco, A. (2016), International risk-sharing in the EMU. ESM Working Paper No. 17, Luxembourg: European Stability Mechanism.

Fiorelli, C., Giannini, M., and Martini, B. (2020). Channels of interregional risk sharing in Italy. mimeo, University of Rome Tor Vergata.

Friedrich, J., and Thiemann, M. (2017). Capital markets union: The need for common laws and common supervision. *Vierteljahrshefte zur Wirtschaftsforschung* 86(2), 61–75.

Furceri, D., and Zdzienicka, A. (2015). The euro area crisis: Need for a supranational fiscal risk-sharing mechanism? *Open Economies Review* 26, 683–710.

Giovannini, A., Horn, C.-W., and Mongelli, F. P. (2021a). An early view on euro area risk-sharing during the COVID-19 crisis. Centre for Economic Policy Research, January.

Giovannini, A., Ioannou, D., and Stracca, S. (2021b). Public and private risk-sharing: Friends or foes? The interplay between different forms of risk sharing. Mimeo, European Central Bank.

Goncalves-Raposo, I., and Lehmann, A. (2019). Equity finance and capital market integration in Europe. Policy Contribution Issue No. 3, Bruegel.

Gros, D. (2015). Completing the banking union: Deposit insurance. CEPS Policy Brief No. 335, Centre for European Policy Studies.

Gros, D., and Alcidi, C. (2013). European economy – Country adjustment to a 'sudden stop': Does the euro make a difference? Economic Paper No. 492, Directorate General for Economic and Financial Affairs (DG ECFIN), European Commission, April.

Hepp, R., and von Hagen, J. (2013). Interstate risk-sharing in Germany: 1970–2006. *Oxford Economic Papers* 65, 1–24.

Hoffmann, M., Maslov, E., Sørensen, B. E., and Stewen, I. (2018). Are banking and capital markets union complements? Evidence from channels of risk-sharing in the euro area. CEPR Discussion Paper No. 13254, London: Centre for European Policy Research.

Hoffmann, M., and Shcherbakova-Stewen, I. (2011). Consumption risk-sharing over the business cycle: The role of small firms' access to credit markets. *Review of Economics and Statistics* 93(4), 1403–1416.

Jappelli, T., and Pagano, M. (2008). Financial market integration under EMU. CEPR Discussion Paper No. 7091, London: Centre for European Policy Research.

Juncker, J.-C., Tusk, D., Dijsselbloem, J., Draghi, M., and Schulz, M. (2015). Completing Europe's Economic and Monetary Union. mimeo, European Commission.

Kalemli-Ozcan, S., Luttini, E., and Sørensen, B. (2014). Debt crises and risk-sharing: The role of markets versus sovereigns. *Scandinavian Journal of Economics* 116(1), 253–276.

Kalemli-Ozcan, S., Manganelli, S., Papaioannou, E., and Peydró, J. L. (2008). Financial integration, macroeconomic volatility and risk-sharing – The role of monetary union. *Proceedings of the Fifth ECB Central Banking Conference. The Euro at Ten – Lessons and Challenges*. Frankfurt: European Central Bank, 116–155.

Koester, G., and Sondermann, D. (2018). A euro area macroeconomic stabilisation function: Assessing options in view of their redistribution and stabilisation properties. ECB Occasional Paper No. 216, Frankfurt: European Central Bank.

Melitz, J., and Zumer, F. (1999). Interregional and international risk-sharing and lessons for EMU. *Carnegie-Rochester Conference Series on Public Policy* 51(1), 149–188.

Milano, V. (2017). Risk-sharing in the euro zone: The role of European Institutions. CELEG Working Paper Series No. 01/17, Center for Labor and Economic Growth, Department of Economics and Finance, LUISS Guido Carli, March.

Milano, V., and Reichlin, P. (2017). Risk-sharing across the US and EMU: The role of public institutions. Policy Brief No. 9, LUISS School of European Political Economy, January.

Nikolov, P. (2016). Cross-border risk sharing after asymmetric shocks: evidence from the euro area and the United States. *Quarterly Report on the Euro Area (QREA), Directorate General Economic and Financial Affairs (DG ECFIN), European Commission* 15(2), 7–18.

Obstfeld, M. (1994). Risk-taking, global diversification, and growth. *American Economic Review* 84, 1310–1329.

Persson, T., and Tabellini, G. (1996). Federal fiscal constitutions: Risk-sharing and moral hazard. *Journal of Political Economy* 104, (5), 979–1009.

Poncela, P., Pericoli, F., Manca, A. R., and Nardo, M. (2016). Risk sharing in Europe. JRC Science for Policy Report, Joint Research Centre (Seville site).

Restoy, F. (2015). The banking union: Achievements and challenges. Speech by Mr Fernando Restoy, Deputy Governor of the Bank of Spain, at the closure of the presentation of the third report on the Banking Union 'La Uníon Bancaria: suma y sigue', organised by Centro de Sector Financiero PwC and IE Business School, Madrid, Bank for International Settlements, Basel, 2 December.

Sapir, A., Véron, N., and Wolff, G. B. (2018). Making a reality of Europe's capital markets union. Policy Contribution No. 7, Bruegel, April.

Schelkle, W. (2017). Hamilton's paradox revisited – Alternative lessons from US history. CEPS Working Document No. 2017/10, Brussels: Centre for European Policy Studies.

Schnabel, I., and Véron, N. (2018). Breaking the stalemate on European deposit insurance. Bruegel, blog post, March.

Schoenmaker, D. (2018). Building a stable European deposit insurance scheme. *Journal of Financial Regulation* 4(2), 314–320.

Véron, N., and Wolff, G. B. (2016). Capital markets union: A vision for the long term. *Journal of Financial Regulation* 2(1), 130–153.

PART IV

Financial Integration

23

Banking Regulation in Europe

From Reaction to Thinking Ahead

Katarzyna Parchimowicz

23.1 INTRODUCTION

Former chairman and CEO of General Electric, Jack Welch, used to say: 'Change before you have to.' Historically, banking regulators have tended to ignore this advice. Reforms of banking law in most cases occurred *after* financial and economic crises. Only when legal standards proved inadequate or insufficient did options to change them appear on the table. This was visible during banking panics in the Great Depression and the Global Financial Crisis (GFC) alike. The main aim of this chapter is to demonstrate that recently, this tendency has been changing. The COVID-19 pandemic, combined with the threat of climate change and digital challenges, seems to have altered the EU regulatory approach. Banking law in Europe may be entering a new phase.

The evolution of banking regulation in Europe has received plenty of scholarly attention (Armour et al., 2016, Chiu and Wilson, 2019; Gleeson, 2018). This chapter offers a slightly different angle – it does not go into the detail of what has changed in banking regulation, but constitutes a synopsis of this process, pointing out three main stages of banking law transformation in Europe, beginning with reforms triggered by bank runs during the Great Depression, through regulatory reaction to GFC materialization of systemic risk, up to the most recent shift that we have witnessed in relation to the COVID-19 pandemic, climate change, and digitalization, visible for instance in the increasing presence of cloud computing in the banking system.

Each of these stages has significantly shaped the regulatory landscape that banks are functioning in now. However, the first two waves of reforms constituted reactions to the issues exposed during respective crises, whereas the latest changes seem to be more future-oriented and attempt to address potential problems, mostly stemming from the real economy, that fortunately have not materialized yet.

Chronologically, in Section 23.2, attention will first be turned to bank runs and lack of capital – two issues that came to light during the Great Depression. Even though this crisis is often omitted in the European context, it had a vast impact on then-national banking regulations. It drew attention to the solution of deposit insurance and contributed to setting up the first, very

This chapter is a result of the research project No. 2020/37/N/HS5/00119 funded by the Polish National Science Centre. It came about within the framework of Academic Excellence Hub – Digital Justice Center carried out under Initiative of Excellence – Research University at the University of Wrocław.

modest, capital requirements, not to mention the liquidity reforms in the monetary policy context.

Further, the disruptive character of systemic risk revealed during the GFC and regulatory change brought about by this phenomenon will be analysed in Section 23.3. It constituted both a foundation for new, original reforms and a final impulse to shape the legal solutions already in place. As for the former, systemic risk forced regulators to draft provisions on global systemically important banks (G-SIBs) and on new macroprudential capital buffers. In terms of the latter, the strengthening of the banking system as a whole became the number one priority among the regulatory goals. Hence, we witnessed regulatory changes concerning leverage, liquidity, resolution, and supervision.[1] As in the case of the Great Depression, reforms during this period constituted a reaction to the downturn of 2008.

Section 23.4 explores the three areas reflecting the future-oriented shift in the regulatory approach. When the long underestimated exogenous risks[2] materialized in the form of the COVID-19 pandemic, the attention of regulators was drawn to the role that banks ought to play in aiding the real economy during such turmoil and in the context of a recovery from an economic shock. Their actions were forward-looking – aiming both to prevent a potential banking crisis and to stimulate the recovery. Similar to the case of the emerging provisions both on the climate risk in banking and on the use of cloud computing, regulators want to 'fix something before it breaks' (Bernanke et al., 2019, p. 25), and act even though no major banking crisis caused by these factors incentivized them to do so.

23.2 BANK RUNS

The Great Depression constitutes a milestone that taught the world how disruptive and consequential banking panics can be. It was an unprecedented financial and economic downturn, much more severe than the GFC of 2008 (Moessner and Allen, 2011). Banking failures undeniably played an important role during the Great Depression. Some consider them as an important reason for the Depression itself (Solimano, 2020), while for others they were a factor that simply contributed to the severity of the global crisis (Hetzel, 2012). Between 1930 and 1933, one-fifth of US banks failed. In Europe, failures were less numerous but equally significant. In Austria, both Bodencreditanstalt and Creditanstalt, the two most important banks, went under. One of the biggest German universal banks, Danatbank, followed suit. The behavioural phenomenon of banking panics (Dijk, 2017) attracted regulatory attention and forced lawmakers to find a remedy that would boost faith in banking institutions, even in troubled times.

23.2.1 *Deposit Insurance and Capital Requirements*

The mechanism of bank runs can be explained by the asymmetric information theory (Calomiris and Gorton, 1991). When financial stability is visibly in danger, depositors, due to lack of information, lose trust in credit institutions and start withdrawing their funds in order to protect them. It does not matter whether a particular bank is stable or not, usually the tendency to generalize takes over and all financial institutions are treated as unreliable (Brown et al.,

[1] In this chapter, a simple distinction between regulation and supervision recommended by the Federal Reserve Bank of San Francisco is used. Namely, regulation refers to setting rules and guidelines, whereas supervision encompasses examining and evaluating the functioning of supervised entities. See Federal Reserve Bank of San Francisco (2022).

[2] Understood as risks stemming from outside the financial sector, such as natural disasters, pandemics, industrial catastrophes (for instance, Majnoni and Powell, 2011).

2017). As a result of mass withdrawals, financial entities become illiquid, which in turn can (and often does) lead to bankruptcies. The way to avoid such herd behaviour is to guarantee depositors that they will not lose their money.

US regulators understood this lesson during the Great Depression and they immediately took regulatory action to remedy the situation and protect the US financial system from future mass bank failures. After re-establishing relative stability to the financial system disrupted by the wave of bankruptcies in 1932 and early 1933, President Roosevelt signed the Banking Act of 1933 (Glass–Steagall) into law. It established the Federal Deposit Insurance Corporation (FDIC) and introduced the first deposit insurance scheme protecting depositors' funds up to $2,500. As a result, 'bank failures dropped from over 4,000 in 1933 to only nine in 1934' (Barr et al., 2018, p. 249), which, in turn, started a worldwide wave of deposit insurance schemes (Demirgüç-Kunt et al., 2005).

Europe was also drawn in by this wave, but with quite some delay. As the scale of bank failures in Europe was smaller than in the United States, and the political concerns of the 1930s quickly overshadowed financial issues, the first deposit insurance system was introduced only years after World War II.[3] The first European schemes provided for voluntary membership (Fratianni, 1995), to some extent defeating the purpose of a guarantee applicable uniformly in the entire national banking system. In 1994, the level of insured deposits was harmonized in European Economic Area Member States.[4] This directive was a very concise piece of legislation and merely set a minimum amount of deposit guarantee at 20,000 ecu[5] per depositor per credit institution. It took a step in the right direction, but turned out to be insufficient. The run on Northern Rock and the GFC constituted a final push for the current system. The level of €20,000, or even the increased amount in the United Kingdom,[6] was insufficient to convince depositors that their money was safe. The wave of withdrawals from Northern Rock was triggered by the news that the bank had sought liquidity support from the Bank of England, resulting in a loss of confidence. Currently, Directive 2014/49/EU requires deposit protection to a maximum of €100,000 and participation in deposit insurance is compulsory for all credit institutions.

Deposit insurance undoubtedly increases trust in the banking system (Knell and Stix, 2015). Bank runs still sometimes occur, but often they are of wholesale nature when financial institutions decide to withdraw or withhold funding in the interbank market. However, there is another side to all the advantages of deposit insurance. Such a guarantee incentivizes reckless behaviour – in other words, deposit insurance contributes to moral hazard. Individual banks can look for more profitable, but riskier investments, as the potential losses will be divided between contributors to the deposit insurance fund. Similarly, depositors are not motivated to pay attention to their bank's financial condition, as they are certain no losses will be incurred on their part (Anginer and Demirgüç-Kunt, 2018).

For these reasons, deposit insurance cannot function in isolation. Bank runs during the Great Depression also revealed a dire need for recapitalization (Crafts and Fearon, 2010). Low levels of reserves contributed to the fragility of the banking sector (Calomiris and Mason, 2003). Stricter and more asset-dependent capital requirements balancing out the moral hazard potential of deposit insurance seemed essential for banks to remain stable. In the United States, the New Deal included capital adequacy in the conditions for deposit insurance eligibility. In

[3] In Germany in 1966.

[4] Directive 94/19/EC.

[5] European Currency Unit used between 1979 and 1999 before the introduction of the euro.

[6] £20,000 and 90 per cent of £33,000.

Germany, the Law of the German Reich on Banking was enacted and prescribed a possibility to implement capital restrictions, which were later formulated by the German central bank (Detzer, 2015).

These capital-oriented reforms were later continued after the Herstatt collapse and the creation of the Basel Committee on Banking Supervision (BCBS). The German bank went down because of over-trading on the foreign exchange markets. Its failure demonstrated the adverse consequences of internationalization of banking (Mourlon-Druol, 2015). This shock constituted a final impulse for bank regulators of G-10 to create the BCBS, an international body drafting non-binding standards that are supposed to be subsequently implemented nationally. Its initial set of standards published in 1988, Basel I, focused on two aspects – credit risk and risk-weighted assets (RWAs). Namely, it encompassed minimum capital adequacy ratio of 8 percent of RWAs and introduced categorization of various assets according to their riskiness. After the BCBS had adopted this first Capital Accord, capital adequacy based on the riskiness of assets became a basic standard in global banking regulation (Gleeson, 2018). In the EEA, Basel I was implemented by means of two directives adopted in 1989 – Own Funds Directive and Solvency Ratio Directive.[7] The system was further amended by the Capital Requirements Directive of 2006[8] introducing the Basel II Accord into EU law. The most relevant novelty was the reform of calculation of RWAs. In contrast to Basel I, Basel II[9] introduced two main methods of RWA calculation, standardized and internal ratings-based approaches. The latter effectively allowed banks to calculate risk using their own models. The next major overhaul of the capital adequacy system was triggered by the lessons learned about systemic risk in 2008.[10]

23.2.2 *Central Bank Liquidity*

Apart from the industry-centric measures, such as deposit insurance and capital requirements, the bank runs of the 1930s exposed the lack of an adequate governmental backstop that would constitute an ultimate guarantee for the depositors. Most central banks both in the USA and in Europe had no experience as lenders of last resort and were not ready to support struggling banking systems (Crafts and Fearon, 2010).[11] For instance, in Austria, instead of introducing central-bank-led refinancing options before liquidity issues turned into solvency drama, Creditanstalt was effectively taken over by the government in 1931. Also, the Reconstruction Finance Corporation (RFC), quickly established in 1932 in the USA to aid ailing financial entities, did not fulfil its function and has not stopped further bank bankruptcies.[12]

The failure to act as lender of last resort stemmed mostly from the gold standard preventing monetary authorities from attempting to proactively stabilize banking sectors. 'In moments of uncertainty that could undermine the exchange rate and the reserves of gold, the money supply

[7] Respectively Own Funds Directive 89/299/EC; Solvency Ratio Directive 89/647/EEC.

[8] Directive 2006/49/EC.

[9] Apart from novelties in the context of capital adequacy requirements, known as Pillar 1, Basel II also introduced a supervisory review process evaluating the capital and liquidity of a given entity (Pillar 2) and a disclosure framework aimed at imposing market discipline (Pillar 3).

[10] See Section 23.3.3.

[11] The Bank of England is an exception as a veteran of early forms of lender of last resort activity. Already in the nineteenth century it bought assets from discount houses in the face of market uncertainty (Anson et al., 2017). During the Great Depression it continued to discount frozen bills (Grossman, 1994).

[12] Some scholars claim that the RFC contributed to the scale of bank runs in the United States, as it revealed names of banks (Crafts and Fearon, 2010). Others identify different reasons for further aggravation of the banking system's condition in 1933 (Butkiewicz, 1999).

was tightened' (Solimano, 2020, p. 74). Providing liquidity to the market, in any form, seemed like disruption of this fragile balance worked out between currency, gold reserves, and fiscal policy. Hence, central banks were in practice deprived of the competence to provide targeted liquidity assistance. Lack of such an option effectively contributed to the scale of banking panics and the severity of the Great Depression as a whole (Friedman and Schwartz, 1971).

The abandonment of the gold standard during the Great Depression redefined opportunities for central banks – it allowed them to become a factual liquidity backstop for their banking systems. Since then, the Federal Reserve, as well as European national central banks and later the ECB, have been actively providing liquidity support to banks (and in the United States sometimes other financial institutions as well) in the face of any major crisis. Regulators have also tended to make refinancing aid subject to compliance with capital requirements or a bank's solvency, effectively completing the anti-bank run framework. First in 1951, the German central bank issued guidelines coupling liquidity assistance with compliance to capital requirements. The most recent formalized conditionality in this regard is embedded in the precautionary recapitalization clause of Article 32 (4) Bank Recovery and Resolution Directive (BRRD),[13] which, in compliance with Bagehot's rule,[14] prescribes a bank's solvency as a precondition of state support.

23.3 ADDRESSING SYSTEMIC RISK

After many reforms had been introduced to address the lessons taught by the Great Depression, the next wave of regulatory changes was triggered by the GFC. Even though throughout the years there were incidents pointing to the significant interdependencies between banking systems (e.g. the collapse of Herstatt) and financial globalization has constituted visible proof of the existence of such links, only the GFC of 2008 revealed the true relevance of the interconnectedness[15] between financial entities and drew attention to systemic risk stemming from it, defined as 'a risk of disruption to financial services that is (i) caused by an impairment of all or part of the financial system; and (ii) has the potential to have serious negative consequences for the real economy' (Staff of the IMF, BIS and FSB, 2009).[16] It showed that the entire financial system, and the broader economy with it, can collapse as a result of an individual failure of an important nexus in the financial network (Bernanke, 2009; Staff of the IMF, BIS and FSB, 2009).

Consequences of an individual collapse can reach far beyond the bank's direct counterparties (Freixas et al., 2015). Warren Buffett was thus right when he noted that financial institutions are all dominoes. The failure of Lehman Brothers and its externalities exposed regulatory aspects that had been neglected by the financial regulators: no consideration of differences between banks regarding systemicness, lack of adequate leverage and liquidity regulation, procyclical character of the capital framework, flawed (or non-existent) systems for resolution and supervision. These issues were addressed first by the international bodies, such as BCBS and the

[13] Directive 2014/59/EU.

[14] Walter Bagehot in his work *Lombard Street* outlined four conditions of central bank lending: they should lend without limit, to solvent entities, at high (some say penalty) rates, and against decent collateral. See Bagehot (1897).

[15] Interconnectedness between individual institutions is only one of the factors contributing to/exacerbating systemic risk. Common funding exposures, engagement in OTC derivatives market, or the custodian function of some banks could also be crucial in that regard.

[16] Many more attempts at defining this risk has been made, see Galati and Moessner (2013) for a literature review on systemic risk and macroprudential policy.

Financial Stability Board (FSB),[17] in their non-binding standards, and later implemented nationally, also in the EU. Importantly, regulators again acted reactively, only after it became clear during the GFC that the legal system was failing.

23.3.1 *Designation of Systemically Important Banks*

Even though the 1974 collapse of the Herstatt bank triggered an international discussion on the increasing globalization of banking services (Mourlon-Druol, 2015), no measure of interconnectedness or 'systemicness' was present in regulatory frameworks before the GFC. All banks were regulated similarly, with the exception of the activities-based differentiation.[18]

During the GFC the perception changed. Dominoes started falling. BNP's decision to stop withdrawals from its funds in 2007 adversely impacted repo markets and the entities funding themselves there, such as Countrywide, one of the largest mortgage issuers. The links of the small and seemingly insignificant German bank IKB were crucial in the context of its failure – it was investing in Goldman Sachs' synthetic collateralized debt obligations, and later received a loan from Commerzbank, Deutsche Bank, and KfW (Lybeck, 2016). The contagion reached a broader economy – for instance, General Motors had trouble financing its operations, as it mostly got its funding from commercial paper that was suddenly perceived unsafe (FCIC, 2011).

It became clear that banks should be diversified according to their potential systemic impact. The BCBS drafted a methodology aimed at the designation of systemically important banks (BCBS, 2011, 2013b, 2018). These are large, complex, interconnected financial institutions that may cause significant disruption to the wider financial system and economic activity if they fail. Therefore, these institutions are often considered *too big to fail* (TBTF). The BCBS methodology relies on five indicators: size, interconnectedness, substitutability, complexity, and cross-border activity. Every year the FSB publishes a list of G-SIBs based on this methodology. Soon after the first set of G-SIB-oriented designation standards was enacted, BCBS adopted an analogical framework for domestic systemically important banks (D-SIBs) (BCBS, 2012a). In their case, the designation relies on similar indicators, just without the cross-border element, as the main focus is on their influence on the local economy.

EU regulators implemented the international standards for G-SIBs in Article 131 of the Capital Requirements Directive (CRD).[19] In the EU legal system, G-SIBs function as global systemically important institutions (G-SIIs) and D-SIBs as other systemically important institutions (O-SIIs). Both types of entity are designated by national authorities. Importantly, in terms of indicators of systemic importance the EU approach to G-SIIs follows the BCBS's template. In contrast, when designating O-SIIs authorities are supposed to look at the importance for the EU economy or the economy of a given Member State, and at the significance of cross-border activities. This divergence in designation criteria shows that the O-SII framework is EU-made and not based on the D-SIB regime by BCBS. The EU decided to treat O-SIIs like 'little G-SIIs', also taking into account their international presence, whereas cross-border activities of D-SIBs are not included in their designation process.

[17] The Financial Stability Board is an international forum that allows financial regulators to agree on uniform regulatory standards aimed at maintaining financial stability. The results of its work are to be implemented nationally.

[18] For instance, in the United States we can historically distinguish three main types of bank charters – commercial bank (focused on short-term lending, corporate, mortgages, and consumer services), thrift (mostly accepting long-term funds), and credit union (an entity owned by participants, granting them personal and consumer loans). See more in Barr et al. (2018).

[19] Directive 2013/36/EU.

Designation of systemically relevant banks has profoundly transformed banking regulation in the EU. The goal of distinguishing between more and less systemically risky entities is to subject the systemically important institutions to stricter legal requirements. A gradation of the systemic relevance effectively introduces three levels of banking law – applicable to non-designated entities, O-SIIs, and G-SIIs, respectively. This differentiation is macroprudentially oriented, but could also be essential in the microprudential context, as the systemic risk levels interact with corporate governance or reputational issues (Addo et al., 2021; Iqbal et al., 2015). The designation process is far from perfect – for instance, G-SIBs have been rightly accused of window-dressing data that the designation process relies on (Behn et al., 2018; Berry et al., 2020). Regardless of such issues, the concept of distinguishing the systemically risky entities seems crucial for a smooth functioning of the financial system (FSB, 2021).

23.3.2 *Leverage*

Even in an interlinked system a failure of one financial entity would not be so threatening if it was not for the fragility of such a network. During the GFC, weaknesses of individual institutions stemmed from their leverage. Leverage – the measure of debt to equity – is vital for banking stability. As Admati and Hellwig (2014) explained vividly, an increase in leverage brutally exposes a given bank to market value fluctuations. Even a small drop in the value of some asset types can bring the said entity to the brink of failure, as substantial leverage means a modest equity buffer that such a drop could eat into. Risk-dependent capital requirements do not mitigate such danger entirely, as accurate calibration of risk weights is still highly problematic (King, 2017). Limits set on leverage are thus essential to create a backstop that would mitigate flaws of risk-weighted requirements.

Regulation of leverage constitutes an area of vast contrasts between the US and EU legal systems. In the United States, rules on leverage, even though excluding investment entities, were binding already before the GFC. In the EU, such provisions were adopted relatively long after this downturn and after the BCBS had issued its standards (BCBS, 2014a) in that regard.[20] Article 92 of the Capital Requirements Regulation (CRR)[21] introduces a leverage ratio at the level of 3 per cent as a binding minimum for all banks.[22] This measure does not differentiate between various types of exposure and treats all assets as equally risky. It mitigates systemic risk by addressing the debt-related fragility of the banking system.

In order to address the specific character of G-SIBs and the threat they can pose, the BCBS also adopted a G-SIB-oriented leverage ratio add-on (BCBS, 2017b). The level of the individual buffer depends on the higher loss absorbency requirement imposed proportionally to the 'systemicness' bucket that a given G-SIB is placed in during the designation process. Consequently, the leverage ratio increases with the systemic importance of a given financial institution. EU regulators included a G-SII-specific leverage buffer in the same regulation which also introduced the general ratio of 3 per cent.[23] It has been binding since 1 January 2023.[24]

Noticeably, O-SIIs are not subject to any stricter leverage requirements. The need to introduce such a standard is recognized by the EU regulators, though. In its recent report the

[20] A leverage ratio was introduced by Regulation (EU) 2019/876 amending Regulation (EU) 575/2013.

[21] Regulation (EU) 575/2013.

[22] This level is often perceived as far too low, given the impact leverage has on banks' stability (Admati and Hellwig, 2014).

[23] Regulation (EU) 2019/876.

[24] Its coming into force was postponed by one year due to the COVID pandemic. Art. 2(2) Regulation (EU) 2020/873.

Commission (EC, 2021b) indicated that this issue should be examined as part of a review of the macroprudential toolbox due by 30 June 2022.[25]

23.3.3 *New Capital Buffers*

Risk-dependent capital requirements were existent but highly flawed prior to the GFC (Tooze, 2018). The biggest banks at the end of 2007 followed the solvency ratio requirements (Lybeck, 2011). Considering the events of 2008 and thereafter, it is clear that capital-oriented provisions have been defective. The systemic failures which took place in this period revealed four main problems of the capital framework. First, banks simply did not hold enough capital to weather the storm. The required levels turned out to be too low. Second, the framework was vastly procyclical, not providing for requirements to accrue capital in good economic times. Further, it did not take into account the crucial aspect of interconnectedness. Capital requirements were supposed to ensure stability of the individual institutions. The crisis proved, though, that individual stability does not translate into robustness of the entire system. Even well-capitalized entities got into trouble in the face of write-downs and the funding freeze at the interbank market (e.g. Washington Mutual was one of the best capitalized banks in the United States in the second quarter of 2008, but due to a run on its deposits following Lehman's bankruptcy, it failed and was sold by the Federal Deposit Insurance Corporation). Lastly, calculations of risk-weighted assets did not reflect the true riskiness of the underlying instruments, which undermined the adequacy of the required levels of capital (Mariathasan and Merrouche, 2014).

Each of these aspects was addressed first by the BCBS and then by EU regulators. As for the capital minima, a general increase was not agreed upon but a framework of additional capital buffers was created. The first of them, the capital conservation buffer, implemented by Article 129 of CRD, effectively raises the required levels to 10.5 per cent of risk-weighted assets (RWAs), as it prescribes 2.5 per cent on top of the base 8 per cent (Gleeson, 2018). Further, a countercyclical buffer was introduced as an option for authorities to activate when credit growth indicates an increase in systemic risk (Article 136 CRD). It is supposed to incentivize capitalization during the so-called good times, in order to prepare financial institutions for possible losses in the future (Chiu and Wilson, 2019).

With regard to the systemicness, three new buffers are supposed to mitigate its potential impact on financial stability. The only one that was not prescribed by the Basel III Accord is the systemic risk buffer (Article 133 CRD). It can be set by national regulators depending on the long-term perspective of a given financial system. Also, regulators are not limited when it comes to selection of exposures subjected to this buffer. For instance, it can refer to domestic exposures, or the ones backed by residential property. Currently, thirteen EEA countries have introduced such a buffer.[26] In contrast, the G-SII buffer is imposed on each entity designated as a G-SII, according to its systemic status (Article 131 CRD). The O-SII buffer is even more targeted as it is imposed individually by the authorities. Consequently, EU law equips national authorities with significant powers over the capital framework. On the one hand, flexibility inherent in the system seems necessary to prevent and address crises, as it allows the framework to adjust quickly, should the financial situation deteriorate. On the other hand, it allows EU Member States to pursue different capital strategies and puts some financial institutions at a potential disadvantage

[25] The Commission is required by Art. 513 CRR to review macroprudential rules every five years.

[26] ESRB, Systemic risk buffer as of 24 June 2022.

depending on the country that they are based in, when one national regime requires compliance with higher buffers than the other.

The last change that addresses the systemic-risk-induced need to reshape the capital framework refers to the calculation of capital levels. In this context, a correct assessment of risk weights is crucial, as they build a foundation on which a final capital score is based. As many banks use internal models of calculations giving them an opportunity to adjust capital scores in a favourable way, the BCBS decided in 2017 to adopt a measure that would minimize the potential for gaming the final outcome. The output floor forces financial entities to compare scores received as a result of both standardized and internal RWA calculations. If the internal-based score is lower than 72.5 per cent of the standardized-based score, the entity applies the latter as its benchmark for capital calculation. 'This limits the benefit a bank can gain from using internal models to 27.5%' (BCBS, 2017a, p. 7). The EU is in the process of implementing this regulatory solution. The European Commission has proposed amendments to Article 92 CRR[27] in order to accurately transpose this output floor measure fixed at 72.5 per cent. If adopted, it should be gradually introduced starting on 1 January 2025.

23.3.4 *Liquidity*

After the hard lessons of the 1930s, banking panics and the subsequent regulatory adjustments, financial systems were relatively well prepared to prevent and tackle future bank runs. Retail depositors remain unpredictable, but with deposit insurance and capital requirements in place this threat was mitigated. However, regulators did not predict waves of bank runs in the interbank markets. During the GFC, banks started running on each other and so the systemic character of mutual exposures became visible. Collateral calls in the repo and swap transactions undermined the solvency of many institutions that were deemed stable, such as Bear Stearns or AIG. Refusals to roll over commercial paper and repos, that in normal circumstances would never occur, contributed to Lehman's and Bear Stearns' demise (FCIC, 2011). Central banks rushed to help the ailing institutions and flooded markets with liquidity of different sorts (Lybeck, 2011). Links between financial entities became even more visible and turned out to be more destabilizing than one would have predicted. Liquidity, always treated as an aspect less significant than solvency, was brought to the forefront of the regulatory agenda.

In 2013 and 2014, respectively, the BCBS introduced two main standards aimed at mitigating future liquidity problems of financial institutions: the Liquidity Coverage Ratio (LCR) and the Net Stable Funding Ratio (NSFR). The former is essentially a buffer of highly liquid assets equal to the thirty-day net outflow. It promotes short-term resilience (BCBS, 2013a). The latter complements the liquidity framework by adding a long-term (one-year) component. Namely, the NSFR limits the reliance on unstable and short-term wholesale funding by prescribing a ratio between the available and required stable funding, taking into account both on- and off-balance sheet exposures (BCBS, 2014b).

In the EU, the LCR and the NSFR have been implemented by Articles 412 and 413 CRR, respectively. Importantly, these ratios have been introduced into the banking legal system by means of a regulation – a legislative act binding directly. Just as in the case of the output floor and the leverage ratio, no room for manoeuvre was left to national regulators. Such a regulatory strategy underlines the relevance of these tools for all EU banks.

[27] Art. 1 (23) EC Proposal COM(2021) 664 final.

As the origins of liquidity regulation stem directly from systemically important links between financial institutions, it is surprising that the level of their systemic importance is not reflected in this legal framework. G-SIBs ought to fulfil the same requirements that are prescribed for all other banks. In the light of the G-SIB-specific capital buffer and the leverage add-on, the lack of a G-SIB-oriented liquidity requirement could be perceived as a dangerous omission, especially as it was suggested at the early stages of BCBS negotiations (Gleeson, 2018).

23.3.5 *Resolution*

Problems with liquidity of a bank often turn into problems with its solvency, and the GFC was no different in that regard. Contagious bank failures or almost-failures confirmed the inadequacy of the general insolvency law when it comes to banks. Bail-outs funded by taxpayers were used as an ad hoc solution but could not provide a universal remedy for the future problems of individual institutions. Specific bank-oriented international and then EU resolution regimes were needed, and establishing them constituted another outcome of the crisis-induced regulatory awakening.

Resolution is a process of restructuring of a bank conducted by the relevant authority supposed to assure continuity of the bank's functioning and to protect financial stability, without the use of taxpayers' money. In the case of resolution, it was the FSB that played the first fiddle in setting global standards. Its *Key Attributes of Effective Resolution Regimes for Financial Institutions* (FSB, 2014) and *Principles on Loss-Absorbing and Recapitalisation Capacity of G-SIBs in Resolution along with TLAC Term Sheet* (FSB, 2015) set the foundations for the EU resolution framework. The path of its development was two-pronged, though. Some reforms referred only to the European Banking Union (EBU) countries, namely eurozone countries and other participating Member States.[28] The experience during the GFC confirmed that harmonization of the cross-border euro area banking rules was needed, especially in the areas of resolution and supervision. The EBU is intended to constitute a remedy for the previous legal fragmentation and a tool for creating 'a more transparent, unified and safer market for banks' (ECB website). It is dubbed as a 'fundamental change ... for the pursuit of financial stability' (Lastra, 2015, p. 327).

As more broadly discussed elsewhere in this volume (see Ríos Camacho, Chapter 24 and Binder, Chapter 25 in this volume) the EBU has so far comprised the Single Supervisory Mechanism (SSM) and the Single Resolution Mechanism (SRM). Within the SRM, the Single Resolution Board (SRB) and national resolution authorities (NRAs) split responsibilities concerning resolution of banks subject to the consolidated supervision by the ECB.[29] Effectively, the SRM provides a centralized framework for regulatory actions that outside the EBU are conducted by the NRAs only.

This broader resolution regime, implemented in all EU countries, can be found in the BRRD. Apart from establishing resolution authorities, it also introduced requirements regarding recovery and resolution planning, resolvability assessment, and different legal options to be utilized in the case of serious problems with a given entity's solvency (resolution tools). These measures, even though applicable to all banks regardless of their systemic status, are aimed at mitigating systemic threats, maintaining stability, and tackling the potential funding advantage

[28] The ones that established close cooperation on the basis of Article 7 of the SSM Regulation and joined the Banking Union (since July 2020 Bulgaria and Croatia are members of the Banking Union after completing this procedure).

[29] See Section 23.3.6.

enjoyed by the banks expecting to be bailed out by the government due to their systemicness (Schillig, 2016).

Finally, EU regulators also addressed the issue of resolution-related loss absorbency by adopting minimum requirements for a bank's own funds and eligible liabilities (MREL) (see also Binder, Chapter 25 in this volume). In consequence, banks are to hold an amount of bail-in capital in order to make resolution feasible. A specific MREL level has also been set for G-SIIs, in an attempt to entangle this type of capital with the systemicness status. Hence, it should limit the externalities stemming from a disorderly failure of an ailing entity. Due to this resolution-linked role, the main perception is that MREL mitigates the risk of contagion *ex post*. However, even though no consensus can be found in this regard (Tröger, 2018), there are voices that it could also reinstate market discipline by forcing bail-inable creditors to consider their future losses (Zhou et al., 2012). Going one step further and bearing in mind the recent amendments introduced to the MREL regime,[30] it could be argued that MREL has preventive potential, at both micro- and macroprudential levels (Martino and Parchimowicz, 2021).

23.3.6 *Supervision*

The supervisory framework also changed after the GFC, in order to adjust it to the challenges of systemic risk and to avoid forcing them to 'fight the crisis with duct tape and baling wire' again (Bernanke et al., 2019, p. 54). The BCBS updated its *Core Principles for Effective Banking Supervision*, emphasizing three main aspects: the need for a particularly intense and effective supervision of the systemically important entities, the supervisory macro-focus allowing systemic risk to be identified and tackled, as well as crisis management and resolution tools necessary to mitigate potential externalities of a bank's collapse (BCBS, 2012b). The issue of systemic risk is also reflected in the FSB's *Intensity and Effectiveness of SIFI Supervision: Recommendations for Enhanced Supervision* (FSB, 2010). Even the concept of Pillar 2, a supervisory review process of capital and liquidity position, introduced by Basel II before the crisis (BCBS, 2006), gained momentum after this downturn and was implemented in different national forms.

Analogously to resolution, reforms of the supervisory structure took place at two levels: the establishment of the supervisory pillar of the EBU and EU-wide reforms. With regard to the former, another pillar of the EBU was established. The SSM added a supervisory role to the ECB's monetary policy function. In this system the ECB shares its SSM tasks with the national supervisory authorities. The centralization was necessary and constituted a natural remedy to the fragmentation and lack of cross-border coordination haunting the EU during the GFC (Ferran and Babis, 2013; Ríos Camacho, Chapter 24 in this volume). With the aim to gather significant entities under the ECB's supervision, a special designation framework was established. Significant institutions have been designated on the basis of size, importance to the EU or Member State's economy, and relevance of cross-border activities (Article 6 SSM Regulation).[31] Apart from being supervised directly by the ECB, they are also subject to specific methodology during their Supervisory Review and Evaluation Process (SREP). It takes into account 'the nature, scale and complexity of their activities and, where relevant, their situation within a group' (ECB, 2022d).

[30] The Banking Package of 2019 introduced BRRD II and CRR II – two legal acts reshaping the MREL framework.

[31] Council Regulation (EU) No. 1024/2013. Entities that received or requested public financial assistance from the EFSF or the ESM are automatically significant. The ECB also has some discretion to take over supervision in specific cases (Art. 6 SSM Regulation).

The focus on centralization and on tackling systemic risks was equally visible in supervisory reforms at the EU-wide level. The creation of the European Banking Authority (EBA) in 2011, tasked with issuing guidelines and technical standards, constituted a relevant step towards a uniform supervisory approach. Since the establishment of the EBU, the EBA's existence is also aimed at combating the persistent supervisory fragmentation between the EBU and non-EBU Member States. EBA conducts regular stress-testing exercises, pursuing an important goal of controlling banks' preparedness for different adverse scenarios. National supervisors are advised to utilize these results and formulate 'capital guidances' on its basis (EBA, 2016). The macro-prudential perspective is further strengthened by the European Systemic Risk Board (ESRB), a specialized body monitoring potential systemic risks in the EU's financial system. It does not have any directly binding tools at its disposal, but this feature should not be perceived as undermining its role in the EU banking system, as national authorities are required to 'act or explain' (Ferran and Alexander, 2011). On the contrary, the establishment of the ESRB in close proximity (both legal and actual) to the ECB started a trend of creating systemic-risk-oriented bodies within EU central banks' structures.[32]

23.4 THE PRESENT REGULATORY SHIFT

While after both the Great Depression and the GFC regulators focused on fixing revealed flaws and omissions, an equally crucial aspect requiring a forward-looking approach was omitted. The decades of banks' misconduct, supervisory mistakes and limitations to the central banks' mandate redirected attention from the centrepiece of global economic well-being – the real economy. It remained in the background – as an ultimate rationale for the standards enacted after each new downturn and an object of protection (Moloney, 2015). Regulators concentrated their efforts on reacting to financial crises and refrained from thinking ahead and answering the needs of the real economy. Everyone forgot that 'banks – and financial activity – follow where real activity goes' (Cetorelli, 2015, p. 819), so regulators should probably be one step ahead. The COVID-19 pandemic, the ongoing climate crisis, and the digitalization of our daily lives have constituted three important aspects that triggered the process of reshaping this regulatory strategy. In all of these instances, regulators started acting before a financial crisis materialized and forced them to act. They have attempted to create a legal environment ready for future challenges.

23.4.1 *Using Banks for Recovery*

The COVID-19 pandemic had its origins outside the financial system. Government-imposed restrictions on everyday lives to limit the spread of this disease had a major impact on economic activity. This adverse impact had two main causes (Ozili and Arun, 2020). First, people were required to stay at home; in almost all countries at some point businesses had to shut down or were allowed to operate only under strict health-related regulations. Second, the unprecedented situation of the pandemic produced uncertainty that lowered consumption and investments.

Even though the financial system seemed relatively stable nonetheless, regulators decided to take an unprecedented forward-looking, proactive approach, in order to minimize the threat of a

[32] For instance, the Financial Policy Committee within the Bank of England was established in 2013, the High Council for Financial Stability has existed in France since 2014, and the Financial Stability Committee was set up within the structures of the Polish National Central Bank in 2015.

banking crisis and to incentivize banks to contribute to the recovery. The key goal was to convince banks to lend out more, even though the worries of future non-performing loans (NPLs) or present loan losses persisted. The success of such a campaign was crucial, especially in the countries more affected by the pandemic, as the tendency to constrain bank lending was highly visible there (Çolak and Öztekin, 2021). On the other hand, regulators were faced with a tricky task, as they had to be careful not to incentivize poorly capitalized banks to lend excessively, because this could undermine financial stability (Özlem Dursun-de Neef and Schandlbauer, 2021).

In general, regulatory actions were aimed at freeing banks' capital without impairing their resilience. The ECB accepted the reduction of the market-risk-oriented capital requirements (ECB, 2020d) and let financial institutions use capital and liquidity surcharges (ECB, 2020c). Restrictions on the composition of the Pillar 2 requirements were loosened (ECB, 2020c). Namely, banks were allowed to use capital instruments not qualifying as Common Equity Tier 1 (e.g. Additional Tier 1) to fulfil Pillar 2 requirements. The ECB also announced its flexibility when it comes to NPLs, including preferential prudential treatment (ECB, 2020b). The guarantees and moratoriums granted by public authorities were taken into account in NPL assessment for loss absorbency calculations. The same guarantees could prevent the supervisor from granting 'unlikely to pay' status to some debtors. Further, banks did not have to take part in the stress-testing exercise, as the EBA decided to reschedule it for 2021 (EBA, 2020). Finally, in an attempt to keep the banking system stable, the ECB temporarily forbade banks from buying back their own shares and paying dividends (ECB, 2020a).

Reactions to this forward-looking and fast response offered by the ECB were mixed. Scholars analysed how 'usable' the capital gained by loosening the limits could be. Kleinnijenhuis et al. (2020) concluded that its usability was limited by both insufficient maximal buffer capacities and lack of usability of the capacity in place. Others highlighted threats to the recovery posed by the vast undercapitalization of EU banks (Schularick et al., 2020). In the end, however, it is crucial that these supervisory actions were taken quickly and decisively, regardless of the potential legal challenges they may still face, as the priority was to protect banking stability, ensure lending to the real economy, and start recovery as soon as possible (Ringe, 2020).

This experience has changed EU banking regulation in three main areas. First, it proved that regulators ought to act pre-emptively and follow a forward-looking approach. Second, it demonstrated that discretionary powers can (and should) be used, especially in such a dynamic environment as the banking system. Moreover, EU regulators proved that temporary measures really can be temporary, as they terminated capital relief in February 2022 (ECB, 2022c).

23.4.2 *Climate Change and Banking*

As the *Banking on Climate Chaos* report reveals, banks have not decreased fossil fuel financing since the Paris Agreement was signed (Rainforest Action Network, 2021). Quite to the contrary, EU banks have boosted funding of climate-harming projects. Even though banks' ability to contribute to the pursuit of environmental sustainability has been clear for a number of years (Bowman, 2010), regulators only recently realized that now is probably the last moment to act. Importantly, climate risks can be of a systemic nature and so are able to threaten the stability of the financial system by creating negative externalities (Alexander and Fisher, 2018). The main danger stems from transition risks and physical risks (Liu et al., 2021). The former can bring volatility to the markets as their severity depends on success of implementation of climate policies. The latter are generated by the rise in climate disasters, adversely impacting the economy and credit risk.

In the EU, environmental risks have been addressed by means of both supervisory measures and legislative action. Environmental risks have been taken up mainly by the ECB in its capacity of bank supervisor in the euro area (see also Schoenmaker and Stegeman, Chapter 12 in this volume). In November 2020, the ECB published its *Guide on Climate-Related and Environmental Risks*, which defines its supervisory expectations in that regard (ECB, 2020e). Institutions have since been expected to include climate-related risks at many stages of their operations, from formulating business strategy to defining risk appetite. A year later, the ECB reported on progress in that regard (ECB, 2021c) and as it was insufficient it decided to impose qualitative requirements on individual entities as part of the SREP (ECB, 2021a). It also announced the gradual integration of such risks into the SREP methodology (ECB, 2021a) and tackling them was named one of the supervisory priorities for 2022–24 (ECB, 2021b). As a next step, the ECB launched the first climate-oriented stress test (ECB, 2022b) and urged banks to improve disclosure of climate risks (Arnold, 2022; ECB, 2022a). The exercise showed that banks have made considerable progress with respect to their climate stress-testing capabilities. At the same time, the exercise also revealed many deficiencies, data gaps, and inconsistencies across institutions. Around 60 per cent of banks do not yet have a well-integrated climate risk stress-testing framework, and most of those banks envisage a medium to long-term time frame for incorporating physical and/or transition climate risk into their frameworks. The exercise also disclosed that many banks are still at an early stage in terms of factoring climate risk into their credit risk models. In many cases, credit risk parameters projected by banks were found to be fairly insensitive to the climate risk shocks depicted in the scenarios (ECB, 2022f).

On the legislative side, three important regulatory steps towards climate-friendly banking had been made earlier (de Arriba-Sellier, 2021). First, in 2019 climate change was recognized as a potential source of systemic risk for the financial system.[33] This created new supervisory possibilities to include environmental risks in the assessments made by the European Supervisory Authorities. Second, large banks are required from mid-2022 to disclose information on environmental, social, and corporate governance (ESG) risks.[34] Such public disclosures are crucial both for supervisory operations and as potential reputational threats. Lastly, the Taxonomy Regulation, as it is applicable to banks, too,[35] establishes a regime that allows them to identify environmentally sustainable activities.

Apart from the already adopted regulations, recent proposals of CRDVI[36]/CRRIII[37] reach even further and could impose more stringent requirements in the areas of governance and risk management of climate-oriented risks (de Arriba-Sellier, 2022). This draft Banking Package of 2021 would require 'banks to systematically identify, disclose and manage environmental, social and governance (ESG) risks as part of their risk management' (EC, 2021a). If adopted, banks would also be obliged to retain capital against climate-related risks for the first time.[38]

As in the case of the COVID-19 pandemic, reforms towards climate-oriented banking regulation do not constitute reactions to severe crises or bank collapses. They aim to ensure a better, more sustainable future and to align banks' operations with the transition to a sustainable

[33] Arts. 1(19), 2(20) and 3(20) of Regulation (EU) 2019/2175.
[34] Art. 1(119) Regulation 2019/876.
[35] Art. 1(2)(b) of Regulation 2020/852.
[36] Proposal COM/2021/663 final.
[37] Proposal COM/2021/664 final.
[38] Art. 1(12) CRDVI.

economy. In this vein, for the first time, banking regulation is to simultaneously serve a different, non-financial purpose. Naturally, as mentioned earlier, the climate crisis has economic consequences, so in the long term, banks have an interest in following a sustainable path. For now, however, regulators work on how to force them to do this, before it is too late.

23.4.3 *Digitalization of Banking Services: The Case of the Cloud*

Apart from other challenges, banking regulators face the dynamic progress especially visible in the technological context. Given the speed at which the financial environment is changing due to digital innovations, it is certain that banking regulation cannot just constitute an *ex post* solution when a specific problem materializes. In this respect, a forward-looking approach in the areas that are potentially problematic is needed and regulators seem to have noticed that.

One innovation has turned out to be especially crucial in recent years and has required regulatory attention. Cloud computing is rising in prominence among financial institutions (Lin et al., 2017). As one financial regulator said: 'Cloud will be a utility in 5 or 10 years, like electricity; that's where we're going in the end' (Hon and Millard, 2018, p. 605). Banks have already started turning to cloud computing. However, as banks constitute the most heavily regulated players in the financial system, the complexity and uncertainty of provisions applying to them in the context of cloud computing is additionally problematic.

Another reason for the cloud being particularly relevant for the banking system and its law is the fact that it constitutes common ground between Big Tech[39] and Big Banks. The two largest, most complex, and influential groups of entities are (often tightly) linked by cloud services. Importantly, over 60 per cent of the market for cloud providers is taken by the three biggest companies – Amazon Web Services, Microsoft, and Google (Cohen, 2021). Given this vast market concentration, systemic risks stemming from megabanks' presence in this network could be overwhelming for the financial system. Cooperation of these entities is likely to become more threatening to economic stability than potential competition between them.

No crisis linked to these cloud-oriented issues has materialized yet, but regulators decided to act pre-emptively and in September 2020 the EC tabled a ground-breaking proposal for a regulation on digital operational resilience for the financial sector (Digital Operational Resilience Act – DORA)[40] (see also Valiante et al., Chapter 28 and Lannoo, Chapter 29 in this volume). It requires financial entities to take adequate measures so that they can minimize the threat posed by problems related to information and communication technology (ICT). The list of financial institutions regulated by this legal act is very long, as it encompasses various entities, from credit institutions to institutions for occupational retirement pensions.[41]

Even though its scope is much broader, DORA also addresses the relation between banks and cloud providers. It tackles regulatory uncertainty accompanying the adoption and usage of cloud services. For instance, DORA sets requirements for potential future providers,[42] it defines critical

39 Big Tech could be defined as large technology conglomerates with extensive customer networks with core businesses in social media, telecommunications, internet search, and e-commerce (Adrian, 2021). Amazon, Google (Alphabet), Facebook (Meta), Microsoft, and Apple are usually identified as Big Tech companies.

40 Regulation (EU) 2022/2554. Digital finance-oriented regulation is covered in several different parts of this Handbook, so the focus of this contribution is placed on the forward-looking character of DORA in the banking context.

41 Art. 2(1) DORA.

42 Art. 28(4)(d) DORA; Art. 28(5) DORA.

or important functions[43] and requires banks to consider transferring them to cloud providers.[44] It also lists the obligatory contractual clauses.[45] This regulation, introduces clarity into the fragmented legal landscape binding before its adoption in the context of cloud services used by banks.[46]

In terms of the relation between Big Tech and Big Banks and the threat to financial stability that it could pose, DORA is moving operational stability to the forefront of legislative goals. Financial institutions should build their resilience in several areas: ICT Risk Management, ICT Incident Reporting, Digital Operational Resilience Testing, and ICT Third-Party Risk Management. In the context of cybersecurity, apart from incident reporting and information sharing, testing, especially the thread-led penetration variant of it,[47] is also crucial. Importantly, banks are not facing digital challenges on their own. DORA dares to introduce a long overdue measure – it places ICT third-party providers (including cloud service providers) that are considered critical under supervision of one of the ESAs.[48] Their oversight is not left toothless – the supervisor is able to impose fines of up to 1 per cent of daily worldwide turnover or to require termination of the contract in question.[49] This is the very first attempt to drag technological companies, including Big Tech, into regulatory parameters and it is highly promising for the future protection of financial stability.

Again, DORA shows a different face of EU financial policymakers – one that is willing to identify potential issues before they materialize in a way destructive to the financial system. The regulation addresses both the regulatory uncertainty haunting banks in the context of cloud services and the increase in systemic risk stemming from the strengthened cooperation between Big Tech and Big Banks. This act constitutes yet further proof that the regulators are attempting to act pre-emptively and follow a more forward-looking approach to banking regulation.

23.5 CONCLUSION

Until recently, banking regulation in the EU has been shaped by economic tragedies. Each crisis has had its main theme that defined the direction of legal reforms. Regulators acted *ex post*, correcting legal mistakes and filling regulatory gaps.

The Great Depression motivated them to create a framework preventing depositors from undermining the stability of the banking system. It is based on three pillars – straightforward guarantees (deposit insurance), safety nets minimizing moral hazard (capital requirements), and ultimate backstops (central bank liquidity). Today, all these elements constitute indispensable components of the regulatory framework for banking.

The GFC brought systemic risks to regulatory attention. This crisis had probably the most far-reaching consequences for the present shape of EU banking law. It resulted in a redefinition of the entire prudential framework, as it led to the division of legal standards into the rules

[43] Art. 3(22) DORA.
[44] Art. 28(4)(a) DORA.
[45] Art. 30 DORA.
[46] Before DORA's adoption the main legal source in this respect was the set of guidelines by EBA, treating cloud more as outsourcing than digital issue (EBA, 2019).
[47] Art. 26 DORA. Thread Led Penetration Testing constitutes a controlled attack at cybersecurity safeguards.
[48] Art. 31 DORA.
[49] Arts. 35 and 39 DORA.

applicable to all banks and those relevant for the systemically important entities. Additionally, it triggered reforms of capital requirements, leverage, liquidity, resolution, and supervision. Systemic risk changed EU banking law, materially and institutionally, as it motivated regulators to create an array of new supervisory bodies and instruments.

The most recent changes in the EU legal framework for banks differ from the previous regulatory shifts. They stem from dynamic needs of the real economy and point to forward-looking approaches of regulators. During the COVID-19 pandemic, regulators wanted to avoid banking crises and motivated banks to aid the real economy by loosening the supervisory grip over their balance sheets. This pre-emptive strategy has worked. It also showed how vital the flexibility of banking regulation really is. In line with this trend, supervisory tools and legislative acts incentivizing banks to contribute to the pursuit of climate sustainability prove that EU banking regulation can be future-oriented and its rationale reaches beyond the interests of the financial sector only. Lastly, policymakers have decided to address technological issues stemming from the increasing recourse to cloud services by banks. They have acknowledged the need to keep up with technological developments, to combat uncertainty and complexity in this area, as well as to create a prospective framework for the protection of financial stability.

REFERENCES

Addo, K. A., Hussain, N., and Iqbal, J. (2021). Corporate governance and banking systemic risk: A test of the bundling hypothesis. *Journal of International Money and Finance* 115, 102327.

Admati, A., and Hellwig, M. (2014). *The Bankers' New Clothes: What's Wrong with Banking and What to Do about It*. Princeton, NJ: Princeton University Press.

Adrian, T. (2021). BigTech in financial services. Speech for the European Parliament FinTech Working Group. www.imf.org/en/News/Articles/2021/06/16/sp061721-bigtech-in-financial-services

Alexander, K., and Fisher, P. (2018). *Banking Regulation and Sustainability*. http://dx.doi.org/10.2139/ssrn.3299351

Anginer, D. and Demirgüç-Kunt, A. (2018). Bank runs and moral hazard: A review of deposit insurance. World Bank Policy Research Working Paper No. 8589.

Anson, M., Bholat, D., Kang M., and Thomas, R. (2017). The Bank of England as lender of last resort: New historical evidence from daily transactional data. Bank of England Staff Working Paper No. 691.

Armour, J., Awrey, D., Davies, P., Enriques, L., Gordon, J., Mayer, C., and Payne, J. (2016). *The Principles of Financial Regulation*. Oxford: Oxford University Press.

Arnold, M. (2022). ECB accuses eurozone banks of 'white noise' on climate risks. *Financial Times*, 14 March.

Bagehot, W. ([1873] 1897). *Lombard Street: A Description of the Money Market*. New York: Charles Scribner's Sons.

Barr, M. S., Jackson, H. E., and Tahyar, M. E. (2018). *Financial Regulation: Law and Policy*. St. Paul: West Academic Foundation Press.

BCBS (2006). International convergence of capital measurement and capital standards. www.bis.org/publ/bcbs128.htm

BCBS (2011). Global Systemically Important Banks: Assessment methodology and the additional loss absorbency requirement. www.bis.org/publ/bcbs207.pdf

BCBS (2012a). A framework for dealing with domestic Systemically Important Banks. www.bis.org/publ/bcbs233.htm

BCBS (2012b). Core principles for effective banking supervision. www.bis.org/publ/bcbs230.htm

BCBS (2013a). Basel III: The liquidity coverage ratio and liquidity risk monitoring tools. www.bis.org/publ/bcbs238.pdf

BCBS (2013b). Global Systemically Important Banks: Updated assessment methodology and the higher loss absorbency requirement. www.bis.org/publ/bcbs255.htm

BCBS (2014a). Basel III: Leverage ratio framework and disclosure requirements. www.bis.org/publ/bcbs270.htm

BCBS (2014b). Basel III: The net stable funding ratio. www.bis.org/bcbs/publ/d295.pdf

BCBS (2017a). Finalising Basel III: In brief. www.bis.org/bcbs/publ/d424_inbrief.pdf

BCBS (2017b). Leverage ratio requirements for Global Systemically Important Banks. www.bis.org/basel_framework/chapter/LEV/40.htm?inforce=20220101&published=20191215

BCBS (2018). Global Systemically Important Banks: Revised assessment methodology and the higher loss absorbency requirement. www.bis.org/bcbs/publ/d445.htm

Behn, M., Mangiante, G., Parisi, L., and Wedow, M. (2018). Does the G-SIB framework incentivise window-dressing behaviour? Evidence of G-SIBs and reporting banks. *ECB Macroprudential Bulletin*, 2 October.

Bernanke, B. (2009). Financial reform to address systemic risk. Speech at the Council on Foreign Relations, Washington, DC.

Bernanke, B., Geithner, T., and Paulson, H. (2019). *Firefighting: The Financial Crisis and Its Lessons*. New York: Penguin Books.

Berry, J., Khan, A., and Rezende, M. (2020). How do US global systemically important banks lower their capital surcharges? *FEDS Notes*. Washington: Board of Governors of the Federal Reserve System, 31 January.

Bowman, M. (2010). The role of the banking industry in facilitating climate change mitigation and the transition to a low-carbon global economy. *Environment and Planning Law Journal* 27, 448–468.

Brown, M., Trautmann, S., and Vlahu, R. (2017). Understanding bank-run contagion. *Management Science* 63(7), 2272–2282.

Butkiewicz, J. L. (1999). The Reconstruction Finance Corporation, the gold standard, and the banking panic of 1933. *Southern Economic Journal* 66(2), 271–293.

Calomiris, C., and Gorton, G. (1991). The origins of banking panics: Models, facts, and bank regulation. In R. Glenn Hubbard (ed.), *Financial Markets and Financial Crises*. Chicago: University of Chicago Press.

Calomiris, C., and Mason, J. (2003). Fundamentals panics, and bank distress during the Depression, *American Economic Review* 93, 1615–1647.

Cetorelli, N. (2015). Banking and real economic activity. In N. Moloney, E. Ferran, and J. Payne (eds.), *The Oxford Handbook of Financial Regulation*. Oxford: Oxford University Press.

Chiu, I. H.-Y., and Wilson, J. (2019). *Banking Law and Regulation*. Oxford: Oxford University Press.

Cohen, J. (2021). 4 companies control 67% of the world's cloud infrastructure. *PCMag*. www.pcmag.com/news/four-companies-control-67-of-the-worlds-cloud-infrastructure

Council Directive 89/299/EEC of 17 April 1989 on the own funds of credit institutions, OJ L 124, 5.5.1989.

Council Directive 89/647/EEC of 18 December 1989 on a solvency ratio for credit institutions, OJ L 386, 30.12.1989.

Council Regulation (EU) No 1024/2013 of 15 October 2013 conferring specific tasks on the European Central Bank concerning policies relating to the prudential supervision of credit institutions, OJ L 287, 29.10.2013.

Crafts, N., and Fearon, P. (2010). Lessons from the 1930s Great Depression. *Oxford Review of Economic Policy* 26(3), 285–317.

Çolak, G., and Öztekin, Ö. (2021). The impact of COVID-19 pandemic on bank lending around the world. *Journal of Banking & Finance* 133, 106207.

De Arriba-Sellier, N. (2021). Turning gold into green: Green finance in the mandate of European financial supervision. *Common Market Law Review* 58, 1097–1140.

De Arriba-Sellier, N. (2022). Banking on green: Sustainability in the Commission's banking reform. *EU Law Live* 86, 22 January.

Demirgüç-Kunt, A., Karacaovali, B., and Laeven, L. (2005). Deposit insurance around the world: A comprehensive database. Policy Research Working Paper No. 3628. World Bank, Washington, DC.

Detzer, D. (2015). Financial market regulation in Germany – Capital requirements of financial institutions. *PSL Quarterly Review* 68(272), 57–87.

Dijk, O. (2017). Bank run psychology. *Journal of Economic Behavior & Organization* 144, 87–96.

Directive (EU) 2019/879 of the European Parliament and of the Council of 20 May 2019 amending Directive 2014/59/EU as regards the loss-absorbing and recapitalisation capacity of credit institutions and investment firms and Directive 98/26/EC.

Directive 2006/49/EC of the European Parliament and of the Council of 14 June 2006 on the capital adequacy of investment firms and credit institutions, OJ L 177, 30.6.2006.

Directive 2013/36/EU of the European Parliament and of the Council of 26 June 2013 on access to the activity of credit institutions and the prudential supervision of credit institutions and investment firms, amending Directive 2002/87/EC and repealing Directives 2006/48/EC and 2006/49/EC.

Directive 2014/49/EU of the European Parliament and of the Council of 16 April 2014 on deposit guarantee schemes, OJ L 173, 12.6.2014.

Directive 2014/59/EU of the European Parliament and of the Council of 15 May 2014 establishing a framework for the recovery and resolution of credit institutions and investment firms and amending Council Directive 82/891/EEC, and Directives 2001/24/EC, 2002/47/EC, 2004/25/EC, 2005/56/EC, 2007/36/EC, 2011/35/EU, 2012/30/EU and 2013/36/EU, and Regulations (EU) No 1093/2010 and (EU) No 648/2012, of the European Parliament and of the Council, OJ L 173/190, 12.6.2014.

Directive 94/19/EC of the European Parliament and of the Council of 30 May 1994 on deposit-guarantee schemes, OJ L 135, 31.5.1994.

EBA (2016). EBA clarifies use of 2016 EU-wide stress test results in the SREP process. Press Release, 1 July. https://eba.europa.eu/eba-clarifies-use-of-2016-eu-wide-stress-test-results-in-the-srep-process

EBA (2019). EBA Guidelines on outsourcing arrangements. 25 February. EBA/GL/2019/02.

EBA (2020). EBA statement on actions to mitigate the impact of COVID-19 on the EU banking sector. Press release, 12 March. www.eba.europa.eu/eba-statement-actions-mitigate-impact-covid-19-eu-banking-sector

EC (2021a). Banking Package 2021: new EU rules to strengthen banks' resilience and better prepare for the future. 27 October. https://ec.europa.eu/commission/presscorner/detail/en/IP_21_5401

EC (2021b). Report from the Commission to the European Parliament and the Council on a possible extension of the leverage ratio buffer framework to O-SIIs and on the definition and calculation of the total exposure measure, including the treatment of central bank reserves. COM(2021) 62 final, 16.2.2021.

ECB website. www.bankingsupervision.europa.eu/about/bankingunion/html/index.en.html

ECB (2020a). ECB asks banks not to pay dividends until at least October 2020. Press Release, 27 March. www.bankingsupervision.europa.eu/press/pr/date/2020/html/ssm.pr200327~d4d8f81a53.en.html

ECB (2020b). ECB banking supervision provides further flexibility to banks in reaction to coronavirus. 20 March.

ECB (2020c). ECB banking supervision provides temporary capital and operational relief in reaction to coronavirus. Press release, 12 March. www.bankingsupervision.europa.eu/press/pr/date/2020/html/ssm.pr200312~43351ac3ac.en.html

ECB (2020d). ECB banking supervision provides temporary relief for capital requirements for market risk. Press release, 16 April. www.bankingsupervision.europa.eu/press/pr/date/2020/html/ssm.pr200416~ecf270bca8.en.html

ECB (2020e). Guide on climate-related and environmental risks. Supervisory expectations relating to risk management and disclosure. November. www.bankingsupervision.europa.eu/legalframework/publiccons/pdf/climate-related_risks/ssm.202005_draft_guide_on_climate-related_and_environmental_risks.en.pdf

ECB (2021a). Banks must accelerate efforts to tackle climate risks, ECB supervisory assessment shows. Press release, 22 November. www.bankingsupervision.europa.eu/press/pr/date/2021/html/ssm.pr211122~6984deoae5.en.html

ECB (2021b). Supervisory priorities and risk assessment for 2022–2024. December. www.bankingsupervision.europa.eu/banking/priorities/html/ssm.supervisory_priorities2022~0f890c6b70.en.html

ECB (2021c). The state of climate and environmental risk management in the banking sector. Report on the supervisory review of banks' approaches to manage climate and environmental risks. November. www.bankingsupervision.europa.eu/ecb/pub/pdf/ssm.202111guideonclimate-relatedandenvironmentalrisks~4b25454055.en.pdf

ECB (2022a). Banks must get better at disclosing climate risks, ECB assessment shows. Press release, 14 March. www.bankingsupervision.europa.eu/press/pr/date/2022/html/ssm.pr220314~37303fd463.en.html

ECB (2022b). ECB banking supervision launches 2022 climate risk stress test. Press release, 27 January. www.bankingsupervision.europa.eu/press/pr/date/2022/html/ssm.pr220127~bd20df4d3a.en.html

ECB (2022c). ECB will not extend capital and leverage relief for banks. Press release, 10 February. www.bankingsupervision.europa.eu/press/pr/date/2022/html/ssm.pr220210_1~ea3ddocd51.en.html

ECB (2022d). SREP methodology. www.bankingsupervision.europa.eu/banking/srep/2022/html/ssm.srep202202_supervisorymethodology2022.en.html

ECB (2022f). 2022 climate risk stress test. July 2022. www.bankingsupervision.europa.eu/ecb/pub/pdf/ssm.climate_stress_test_report.20220708~2e3cc0999f.en.pdf

ESRB (2022). Systemic risk buffer as of 24th of June 2022. Retrieved from www.esrb.europa.eu/national_policy/systemic/html/index.en.html

Federal Reserve Bank of San Francisco. What is the Fed? www.frbsf.org/education/teacher-resources/what-is-the-fed/supervision-regulation/

Ferran, E. and Alexander, K. (2011). Can soft law bodies be effective? The special case of the European systemic risk board. *European Law Review* 37(6), 751–777.

Ferran, E. and Babis, V. (2013). The European Single Supervisory Mechanism. University of Cambridge Faculty of Law Research Paper, No. 10/2013.

Financial Crisis Inquiry Commission (FCIC) (2011). Final Report of the National Commission on the Causes of the Financial and Economic Crisis in the United States. January. www.govinfo.gov/app/details/GPO-FCIC

Fratianni, M. (1995). Bank deposit insurance in the European Union. In B. Eichengreen, J. Frieden, and J. von Hagen (eds.) *Politics and Institutions in an Integrated Europe*. Berlin: Springer, pp. 144–170.

Freixas, X., Laeven, L., and Peydró, J,-L. (2015). A primer on systemic risk. In X. Freixas, J.-L. Peydró, and L. Laeven (eds.), *Systemic Risk, Crises, and Macroprudential Regulation*. Cambridge, MA: MIT Press.

Friedman, M., and Schwartz, A. (1971). *A Monetary History of the United States, 1867–1960*. Princeton, NJ: Princeton University Press.

FSB (2010). Intensity and effectiveness of SIFI supervision: Recommendations for enhanced supervision. 2 November. www.imf.org/external/np/mcm/financialstability/papers/sifisup.pdf

FSB (2014). Key attributes of effective resolution regimes for financial institutions. www.fsb.org/wp-content/uploads/r_111104cc.pdf

FSB (2015). Principles on loss-absorbing and recapitalisation capacity of G-SIBs in resolution. Total Loss-Absorbing Capacity (TLAC) term sheet. www.fsb.org/2015/11/total-loss-absorbing-capacity-tlac-principles-and-term-sheet/

FSB (2021). Evaluation of the effects of too-big-to-fail reforms. Final Report, 31 March. www.fsb.org/2021/03/evaluation-of-the-effects-of-too-big-to-fail-reforms-final-report/

Galati, G., and Moessner, R. (2013). Macroprudential policy – A literature review. *Journal of Economic Surveys* 27, 846–878.

Gleeson, S. (2018). *Gleeson on the International Regulation of Banking*. Oxford: Oxford University Press.

Grossman, R. (1994). The shoe that didn't drop: Explaining banking stability during the Great Depression. *Journal of Economic History* 54(3), 654–682.

Hetzel, R. (2012). Monetary policy and bank runs in the Great Depression. In *The Great Recession: Market Failure or Policy Failure?* Studies in Macroeconomic History. Cambridge: Cambridge University Press, pp. 46–64.

Hon, W., and Millard, C. (2018). Banking in the cloud: Part 3 – contractual issues. *Computer Law and Security Review* 34, 595–614.

Iqbal, J., Strobl, S., and Vähämaa, S. (2015). Corporate governance and the systemic risk of financial institutions. *Journal of Economics and Business* 82, 42–61.

King, M. (2017). *The End of Alchemy: Money, Banking, and the Future of the Global Economy*. London: Abacus.

Kleinnijenhuis, A., Kodres, L., and Wetzer, T. (2020). Usable bank capital. *VoxEU*. 30 June.

Knell, M., and Stix, H. (2015). Trust in banks during normal and crisis times – Evidence from survey data. *Economica* 82, 995–1020.

Lastra, R. (2015). Systemic risk and macroprudential supervision. In N. Moloney, E. Ferran, and J. Payne (eds.), *The Oxford Handbook of Financial Regulation*. Oxford: Oxford University Press.

Lin, B., Wehkamp, R., and Kanniainen, J. (2017). Practitioner's guide on the use of cloud computing in finance. In M. A. H. Dempster, J, Kanniainen, J, Keane, and E. Vynckie (eds.), *High-Performance Computing in Finance: Problems, Methods, and Solutions*. New York: Chapman and Hall/CRC.

Liu, Z., Sun, H., and Tang, S. (2021). Assessing the impacts of climate change to financial stability: Evidence from China. *International Journal of Climate Change Strategies and Management* 13(3), 375–393.

Lybeck, J. (2011). *A Global History of the Financial Crash of 2007–2010*. Cambridge: Cambridge University Press.

Lybeck, J. (2016). *The Future of Financial Regulation: Who Should Pay for the Failure of American and European Banks?* Cambridge: Cambridge University Press.

Majnoni, G., and Powell, A. (2011). On endogenous risk, the amplification effects of financial systems and macro prudential policies. IDB Working Paper No. WP-276.

Mariathasan, M., and Merrouche, O. (2014). The manipulation of Basel risk-weights. *Journal of Financial Intermediation* 23(3), 300–321.

Martino, E., and Parchimowicz, K. (2021). Go preventive or go home – The double nature of MREL. *European Company and Financial Law Review* 18(4), 608–639.

Moessner, R., and Allen, W. (2011). Banking crises and the international monetary system in the Great Depression and now. *Financial History Review* 18(1), 1–20.

Moloney, N. (2015). Regulating the retail markets. In N. Moloney, E. Ferran, and J. Payne (eds.), *The Oxford Handbook of Financial Regulation*. Oxford: Oxford University Press.

Mourlon-Druol, E. (2015). Trust is good, control is better: The 1974 Herstatt Bank crisis and its implications for international regulatory reform. *Business History* 57(2), 311–334.

Ozili, P., and Arun, T. (2020). Spillover of COVID-19: Impact on the global economy. MPRA Paper No. 99850.

Özlem Dursun-de Neef, H., and Schandlbauer, A. (2021). COVID-19 and lending responses of European banks. *Journal of Banking & Finance* 133, 106236.

Proposal for a Directive of the European Parliament and of the Council amending Directive 2013/36/EU as regards supervisory powers, sanctions, third-country branches, and environmental, social and governance risks, and amending Directive 2014/59/EU, COM/2021/663 final.

Proposal for a Regulation of the European Parliament and of the Council amending Regulation (EU) No 575/2013 as regards requirements for credit risk, credit valuation adjustment risk, operational risk, market risk and the output floor COM/2021/664 final.

Rainforest Action Network. (2021). *Banking on Climate Chaos*. Fossil Fuel Finance Report 2021. www.ran.org/wp-content/uploads/2021/03/Banking-on-Climate-Chaos-2021.pdf

Regulation (EU) 2019/2088 of the European Parliament and of the Council of 27 November 2019 on sustainability-related disclosures in the financial services sector, OJ L 317, 9.12.2019.

Regulation (EU) 2019/2175 of the European Parliament and of the Council of 18 December 2019 amending Regulation (EU) No. 1093/2010 establishing a European Supervisory Authority (European Banking Authority), Regulation (EU) No. 1094/2010 establishing a European Supervisory Authority (European Insurance and Occupational Pensions Authority), Regulation (EU) No. 1095/2010 establishing a European Supervisory Authority (European Securities and Markets Authority), Regulation (EU) No. 600/2014 on markets in financial instruments, Regulation (EU) 2016/1011 on indices used as benchmarks in financial instruments and financial contracts or to measure the performance of investment funds, and Regulation (EU) 2015/847 on information accompanying transfers of funds, OJ L 334, 27.12.2019.

Regulation (EU) 2019/876 of the European Parliament and of the Council of 20 May 2019 amending Regulation (EU) No. 575/2013 as regards the leverage ratio, the net stable funding ratio, requirements for own funds and eligible liabilities, counterparty credit risk, market risk, exposures to central counterparties, exposures to collective investment undertakings, large exposures, reporting and disclosure requirements, and Regulation (EU) No. 648/2012, OJ L 150, 7.6.2019.

Regulation (EU) 2020/852 of the European Parliament and of the Council of 18 June 2020 on the establishment of a framework to facilitate sustainable investment, and amending Regulation (EU) 2019/2088, OJ L 198, 22.6.2020.

Regulation (EU) 2020/873 of the European Parliament and of the Council of 24 June 2020 amending Regulations (EU) No 575/2013 and (EU) 2019/876 as regards certain adjustments in response to the COVID-19 pandemic, OJ L 204/4, 26.6.2020.

Regulation (EU) 2022/2554 of the European Parliament and of the Council of 14 December 2022 on digital operational resilience for the financial sector and amending Regulations (EC) No 1060/2009,

(EU) No 648/2012, (EU) No 600/2014, (EU) No 909/2014 and (EU) 2016/1011, OJ L 333, 27.12.2022

Regulation (EU) No 575/2013 of the European Parliament and of the Council of 26 June 2013 on prudential requirements for credit institutions and amending Regulation (EU) No. 648/2012, OJ L 176, 27.6.2013.

Ringe, W.-G. (2020). COVID-19 and European banks: No time for lawyers. In C. Gorstos and W.-G. Ringe (eds.), Pandemic Crisis and Financial Stability. European Banking Institute Working Paper Series, 43–62. https://ebi-europa.eu/wp-content/uploads/2022/07/Gortsos-Ringe-eds-Pandemic-Crisis-and-Financial-Stability-2020-2.pdf

Schillig, M. (2016). *Resolution and Insolvency of Banks and Financial Institutions*. Oxford: Oxford University Press.

Schularick, M., Steffen, S., and Tröger, T. (2020). Bank capital and the European recovery from the COVID-19 crisis. SAFE White Paper, June, p. 69.

Solimano, A. (2020). *A History of Big Recessions in the Long Twentieth Century*. Cambridge: Cambridge University Press.

Staff of the International Monetary Fund and the Bank for International Settlements, and the Secretariat of the Financial Stability Board (2009). Report to G20 Finance Ministers and Governors, Guidance to Assess the Systemic Importance of Financial Institutions, Markets and Instruments: Initial Consideration, 28 October. www.bis.org/publ/othp07.pdf

Tooze, A. (2018). *Crashed: How a Decade of Financial Crises Changed the World*. New York: Viking.

Tröger, T. (2018). Too complex to work: A critical assessment of the bail-in tool under the European Bank Recovery and Resolution regime. *Journal of Financial Regulation* 4(1), 35–72.

Zhou, J., Rutledge, V., Bossu, W., Dobler, M., Jassaud, N., and Moore, M. (2012). From bail-out to bail-in: Mandatory debt restructuring of systemic financial institutions. IMF Staff Discussion Note 12/03, 24 April.

24

The Politics behind the Creation of the Banking Union

Elena Ríos Camacho

24.1 INTRODUCTION

The European banking sector is today far stronger and more resilient than before the sovereign debt crisis. During the COVID-19 pandemic, it has been able to maintain financing to the economy. This has been made possible partly due to the European Banking Union (EBU) created in a process which started in 2012 (Council of the EU, 2020a). Its aim was to restore confidence in the European banking systems and 'complete' the Economic and Monetary Union (EMU), thus saving the euro and protecting it better from future shocks (Van Rompuy, 2012).

The EBU represents the highest transfer of national sovereignty to the EU since the creation of the EMU. It is composed of three pillars: (1) the Single Supervisory Mechanism (SSM), which supervises the largest euro area banks; (2) the Single Resolution Mechanism (SRM) and the common backstop, in charge of banking resolution in the euro area, and the Single Resolution Fund (SRF); and (3) the European Deposit Insurance Scheme (EDIS) as an EU-wide deposit guarantee system, if ever agreed in the future (Howarth and Schild, 2020; Ríos Camacho, 2021).

This chapter analyses the politics behind the creation of the EBU. It aims to explain the agreement on the SSM and the SRM during the euro crisis, and the ongoing deadlock in the negotiations on the EDIS. In addition, it analyses the (partial) shift in national preferences towards a deposit reinsurance system. The negotiations on the banking union have mainly been characterized by Germany's moral hazard concerns and calls for mutualization of risks by the southern countries. In addition to these, in EDIS, national preferences are also characterized by interests of national deposit guarantee schemes (NDGSs) favouring a reinsurance system, rather than a system with full mutualization of funds. The SRF was also negotiated under an intergovernmental agreement and with numerous conditions attached to its financing structure and functioning, as mostly demanded by Germany.

By using two of the most common theories in European integration, namely liberal intergovernmentalism and historical institutionalism, I argue that the preferences and the bargaining power of the largest euro area countries, namely Germany, France, Italy, Spain, and the Netherlands, as well as unintended consequences from EMU and the EBU, can shed light on the establishment of an incomplete EBU without an EDIS.

This chapter is structured as follows. Section 24.2 conceptualizes the EBU as a case of European integration. Section 24.3 explains the creation of the SSM during the sovereign debt crisis. Section 24.4 analyses the establishment of the SRM taking into account the role played by the Netherlands in securing an agreement from Germany in a context where the SSM was already in place. Section 24.5 aims to explain the deadlock in the negotiations on the EDIS, by analysing national preferences and bargaining positions, as well as the status quo by looking at the influence of NDGSs on the positions of Germany, France, and Italy. The last section concludes.

24.2 THE ESTABLISHMENT OF THE EUROPEAN BANKING UNION: A CASE OF EUROPEAN INTEGRATION

Liberal intergovernmentalism is one of the key theories in the study of regional integration and draws on both liberal and institutionalist theories of international relations (Moravcsik, 1993, 1998; Moravcsik and Schimmelfennig, 2019). Liberal intergovernmentalism assumes Member States' national governments to be the most important political actors in European integration. In the first stage of the model, Member States' governments form their national preferences. The economic interests of powerful domestic groups determine Member States' preferences (Moravcsik, 1998, p. 18). Then, Member States take their preferences to the negotiating table in Brussels to obtain Pareto-improving solutions and solve distributional conflicts (Moravcsik and Schimmelfennig, 2019, p. 67). Their relative bargaining power is mainly based on power resources, threats of non-agreement, and the size and strength of their coalitions (Moravcsik and Schimmelfennig, 2019, p. 71). Member States that gain less from agreement enjoy more bargaining power than those that gain more from agreement (Moravcsik, 1993, pp. 499–500). Institutional design tends to reflect the preferences of the most powerful Member States (Moravcsik, 1998, p. 55).

Historical institutionalist scholars such as Paul Pierson admit that national governments play a key role in grand bargains, as liberal intergovernmentalism argues, but they assume that afterwards unanticipated consequences often develop. When the next bargain occurs, national governments play a central role again, but in a changed negotiation context where their decision-making power may be constrained (Pierson, 1996, p. 48). Therefore, it seems more appropriate to think about historical institutionalism as an extension of liberal intergovernmentalism rather than as an alternative to it (Ríos Camacho, 2021; Moravcsik, 2018; Schimmelfennig, 2014). In addition, external shocks can potentially be the trigger of the integration process (Niemann et al., 2019, p. 51; Niemann and Ioannou, 2015). When these external shocks have overwhelming negative effects, a so-called critical juncture would arise, allowing for institutional and policy changes, which may have been unthinkable in the past (Pollack, 2019, p. 111).

The EBU was established to tackle the sovereign–bank nexus[1] and the enforcement problems of national regulation in an integrated financial market. The euro area crisis showed that the banking systems of several Member States were weak and that the close relationships between

[1] This sovereign-bank nexus, also called 'vicious circle' is best understood as a combination of direct and indirect financial linkages (Schnabel and Véron, 2018a, pp. 2–3). Regarding direct linkages between sovereigns and their domestic banks, during the financial crisis, banks that were too systemic to fail ('too big to fail') and got into trouble turned to their national government for financial help. The stability of the banking sector could only be guaranteed to the detriment of the public finances of the governments concerned. When national governments provided financial assistance to banks, they increased their own debt, which decreased the value of sovereign bonds held by banks. When financial institutions were in trouble again and requested a bailout, they again triggered the 'vicious circle' (Schnabel and Véron, 2018a).

governments and their domestic institutions increased financial risks. Crises in domestic banking systems had contagious effects on other Member States across the euro area.

The SSM is responsible for directly supervising the largest and most significant banks in the euro area. The SSM supervises the smaller and less significant institutions indirectly in cooperation with the national competent authorities (NCAs) of the Member States. The SRM, which is governed by a Single Resolution Board (SRB), is responsible for limiting national discretion over how to restructure or resolve a failing bank. It is accompanied by the SRF, created by an intergovernmental agreement (IGA) outside the EU treaties. The SRF acts as a common backstop for the SRM and is principally funded by *ex ante* annual contributions raised at the national level by the National Resolution Authorities (NRAs) from the banking sector (Council of the EU and EP, 2014). Lastly, an EDIS would aim at creating an EU-wide deposit guarantee scheme and would include a Deposit Insurance Fund (DIF). The EBU, in line with liberal intergovernmentalism, can be seen as a grand bargain of European integration (Ríos Camacho, 2021). It was envisaged as a package following the publication of the Four Presidents' Report (Van Rompuy, 2012). However, it was not negotiated in one single bargain, but in closely interconnected bargaining sequences.

The outcome in the EBU is asymmetric and still incomplete. In contrast to the SSM, where Member States transferred to the European Central Bank (ECB) remarkable supervisory powers,[2] the SRM has a complex governance structure, allowing Member States to veto decisions they do not approve. Article 18 of the SRM Regulation establishes a complex procedure of power sharing with the SRB and the involvement of the European Commission and the Council of the EU (Council of the EU and EP, 2014). The large degree of discretion that Member States enjoy when applying the Bank Recovery and Resolution Directive (BRRD) can be seen in Italy's handling of its three troubled banks – the Monte dei Paschi, Veneto, and Vicenza banks – in 2016–17. Failing banks were bailed out despite having the SRM and the bail-in rule (Donnelly, 2018b; Donnelly and Asimakopoulos, 2020).

24.3 THE CREATION OF THE SINGLE SUPERVISORY MECHANISM: SPAIN'S SOVEREIGN DEBT CRISIS AND THE NEED TO BREAK THE VICIOUS CIRCLE

The SSM started operations in 2014 and established supranational banking supervision for the euro area Member States and those non-euro countries wishing to participate. The ECB within the SSM is responsible for the direct supervision of the 111 largest eurozone banks, referred to as Significant Institutions, and is in charge of the indirect supervision of the so-called Less Significant Institutions. Here, the ECB exercises some supervisory functions and the NCAs perform the rest of the supervisory tasks (Council of the European Union, 2013).

The preferences of the largest euro area countries, namely Germany, France, Spain, and Italy, and their bargaining power can explain the establishment of the SSM (Donnelly, 2013; Howarth and Quaglia, 2016; Ríos Camacho, 2021). In June 2012, when Spain was hit by the financial crisis, the country needed between €60 and €100 billion to recapitalize its cash-starved banks (Otero-Iglesias et al., 2016, p. 30). Spain found itself trapped in a 'doom loop' in which its banking and fiscal crises became intertwined (Otero-Iglesias et al., 2016; Schnabel and Véron,

[2] Although formally a coalition of national supervisors could outvote the ECB in the Single Supervisory Board (see Art. 26 Council Regulation (EU) No. 1024/2013 of 15 October 2013 conferring specific tasks on the European Central Bank concerning policies relating to the prudential supervision of credit institutions, OJ L 287, 29.10.2013, p. 63–89).

2018a). The financial and sovereign debt crises put the whole eurozone at risk (Otero-Iglesias et al., 2016). The Spanish government sought to make use of the European Stability Mechanism (ESM) for direct bank recapitalization rather than accepting a bail-out, which would have added more debt to the country's balance sheet (Schimmelfennig, 2014, p. 330). Spain, Italy, and France called for an EBU for the euro area (Ríos Camacho, 2021). Germany also called for an SSM, a European instrument for supervising the euro area banks, as a prerequisite for making ESM funds available to directly recapitalize Spanish banks (Emmanouilidis, 2012). Hence, Germany 'got the SSM rolling' and succeeded in imposing its preferences on the sequencing of the compromise to create the SSM (Ríos Camacho, 2021). At the June 2012 summit, euro area leaders agreed to break the 'vicious circle between banks and sovereigns' and to the establishment of a SSM involving the ECB (Euro area summit statement, 2012).

In line with liberal intergovernmentalism, national preferences reflected the interests of their domestic banking sectors (Epstein, 2014; Howarth and Quaglia, 2016). The two-level system whereby the ECB supervises the largest euro area banks directly, while day-to-day supervision for smaller banks is done by NCAs, was the preference of the largest euro area countries since they wanted their NCAs to be responsible for many of their banks (Ríos Camacho, 2021). Germany succeeded in limiting the scope of the SSM to the larger systemic banks in the euro area, thereby excluding its smaller banks and *Sparkassen* (Donnelly, 2013; Howarth and Quaglia, 2016; Ríos Camacho, 2021).

The SSM Regulation is based on Article 127(6) of the Treaty on the Functioning of the European Union (TFEU). This legal basis confers on the ECB specific tasks concerning policies relating to the prudential supervision of credit institutions, with the aim of contributing to their safety and the stability of the financial system within EMU (Council of the European Union, 2013). Article 127(6) TFEU has been interpreted as enabling Member States to establish the SSM upon an unanimous agreement in the Council and without a revision of the treaties (Ríos Camacho, 2021). Moreover, the ECB is a well-established and credible institution, given its solid reputation on monetary issues (Chang, 2015).

The SSM entered into force on 4 November 2014, after a transitional period necessary to perform a comprehensive assessment of credit institutions, as demanded by Germany and the Netherlands (Ríos Camacho, 2021). It included an Asset Quality Review (AQR) and rigorous stress tests, in order to tackle any possible legacy issues in the banking systems of the euro area countries before the SSM would become operational (Council of the European Union, 2013). The Commission's proposal for an SSM was significantly altered by the largest euro area Member States, in particular Germany, on the controversial issues of the scope of the mechanism by limiting it to the largest euro area banks and delaying its operational start by calling for a comprehensive assessment of euro area banks (Howarth and Quaglia, 2016). The Commission preferred to include all 6,000 euro area banks under the ECB's direct supervision instead of having a delegation system as was agreed in the end (Ríos Camacho, 2021). Moreover, the institution favoured a fast agreement on the SSM so that it would start operations as soon as possible given that it was set as a precondition to access the ESM's Direct Recapitalization Instrument (DRI) (Ríos Camacho, 2021). However, the operational start of the SSM was delayed due to the introduction of an AQR of the euro area banks.

In line with historical institutionalism, the euro area sovereign debt crisis brought to the fore some of EMU's shortcomings, which were not contemplated during its establishment in the Maastricht Treaty (1992) (Schimmelfennig, 2014). The EBU includes measures to decrease the functional dissonances originating from a European banking system that was working according to national policies (Niemann et al., 2019, pp. 55–56). The NCAs of the euro area countries were responsible for the financial institutions based within their national borders. Enforcement problems and lax supervision in Member States' national banking systems, due to cosy relationships between financial institutions and national supervisors, as well as different regulatory differences among Member States, contributed to the euro area crisis (Zeitlin, 2016, p. 9). Furthermore, Member States and NCAs were unable to manage risks to financial stability posed to Member States by cross-border financial markets operating beyond the scope of national jurisdictions (European Commission, 2017, p. 12).

In contrast to all euro area countries, which automatically participate in the SSM, non-euro area Member States have the choice whether to opt in or not. While the creation of the banking union heavily involved the governments of the 'old EU' belonging to the euro area, the central and eastern European countries played the role of bystanders. First, the so-called vicious circle between banks and sovereigns never developed there, largely due to the high level of internationalization of their banking sectors. Second, until very recently only the Baltic countries, Slovenia, and Slovakia adopted the euro. These two factors did not push them towards participating in the SSM (Mero and Piroska, 2016, p. 6). However, on 24 June 2020 the ECB Governing Council decided to establish close cooperation with the Bulgarian and Croatian central banks, as the two countries were aspiring to join the euro area. On 1 October 2020, when the close cooperation entered into force, the ECB started supervising the largest Bulgarian and Croatian banks after the completion of a significant assessment process (ECB, 2020).

24.4 SETTING UP THE SINGLE RESOLUTION MECHANISM: GERMANY, THE NETHERLANDS, AND THE SINGLE RESOLUTION FUND

The SRM negotiations resulted in the creation of a hybrid mechanism composed of two elements: the SRM Regulation based on Article 114 TFEU (the Treaty basis for the internal market harmonization), adopted via the ordinary legislative procedure, and an IGA for the transfer and mutualization of Member States' national contributions to the SRF. One of the main contested issues was the set-up of a SRF outside the EU treaties and the transfer and mutualization of funds in the SRF.

The Commission proposed a SRM including a SRF under Article 114 TFEU. This led to huge opposition by Germany, supported by the Netherlands and Finland, which argued that the EU could not levy contributions for the SRF. They conceived the SRF as a new EU budget item that would rely on bank levies or contributions, thereby mutualizing the risks of the banking sectors in the euro area (Ríos Camacho, 2021). Conversely, according to the legal services of the Commission, the Council, and the European Parliament (EP), setting up the SRF under the regulation was legally permitted, since the SRF would consist of levies integrated in a separate budget paid by the financial industry. Therefore, SRF contributions should not be considered direct taxes but insurance premiums (De Gregorio Merino, 2016). Nonetheless, Germany, the Netherlands and Finland were very sceptical about the mutualization of banking risks through a SRF because of moral hazard concerns and the desire of these countries to protect the credibility of their own banks (Howarth and Quaglia, 2016; Howarth and Schild, 2020; Ríos Camacho, 2021).

The German finance minister, Wolfgang Schäuble, argued that in order to create an EU-wide SRF it was first necessary to amend the EU treaties or alternatively there could be a system based on a network of national resolution funds backed up by bail-in rules (Schäuble, 2013, pp. 1–2). Schäuble's position reflected the preferences of the president of the Bundesbank, the conservative party CDU (Christian Democratic Union), the association of German Public Banks, and the association of German Cooperative and Savings Banks, which favoured the creation of a network of national resolution funds (Ríos Camacho, 2021; Schäfer, 2016). Banks with major international operations, like the Deutsche Bank, supported the establishment of the SRM and expressed their interest in centralized and simplified supervisory and regulatory power (Epstein, 2014, p. 7). In contrast, domestically oriented banks, like the German saving banks, are not in a position to enjoy the same cost savings from a single regulatory interface (Epstein, 2014, p. 6).

The preferences of the German government largely reflected the configuration of its national banking system with a high number of smaller public and savings banks, and moral hazard concerns related to the health of the banking sectors of the Member States (Howarth and Quaglia, 2016). In addition, Germany's bank resolution regime was able to provide the required resolution funds to its national banks, if necessary. In 2008, Germany established the Special Financial Market Stabilization Fund (*Sondervermögen Finanzmarktstabilisierungsfonds, SoFFin*), including tools such as recapitalization, risk transfers and bad bank schemes (Allen & Overy, 2012, p. 5). Furthermore, according to Germany, the key principle for the funding for the SRF was that the costs of resolution of troubled banks should be borne first by their shareholders and creditors (bail-in), and not by the taxpayers (Handelsblatt, 2012, pp. 2–3).

The German government was aware of the fact that if the EBU failed, i.e. if there was no agreement on the SRM, then EMU would be at risk because the EBU is connected to the euro, not to the internal market (Ríos Camacho, 2021). The set-up of the SRM with a SRF was considered necessary to place supervision and resolution at the same level and break the vicious circle between banks and sovereigns. The establishment of an SRM was the logical step after the SSM because Member States' national governments and resolution systems cannot be expected to pay for financial institutions, which are under the ECB's remit (Beck et al., 2013, p. 50). Germany's position based on the paradox between national constitutional and judicial concerns, on the one hand, and EU political needs, on the other, led the country to accept the SRF, albeit with a rather intergovernmental construction in the end (Ríos Camacho, 2021).

The German government was persuaded to accept the creation of a SRF by three concessions. First, the position of the German government was that in order to have a SRF, the provisions on the transfer and mutualization of contributions had to be carved out of the SRM Regulation and decided in an intergovernmental agreement (Ríos Camacho, 2021). Germany called for an IGA for the transfer and mutualization of contributions to the SRF because of the benefit of unanimity, which gave the country de facto veto power given its powerful economic position, thereby allowing it to set the conditions for designing the fund (Ríos Camacho, 2021). Second, the SRF was to be based on gradual mutualization of funds. During the negotiations, the Eurogroup president and Dutch finance minister, Jeroen Dijsselbloem, made a proposal for non-linear mutualization of contributions to the SRF, which was then agreed by all Member States including Germany (Ríos Camacho, 2021). The Eurogroup president played a key role in bringing Germany's position closer to that of the other Member States to find a compromise.

Furthermore, there were internal divisions in the German domestic politics arena hindering a strong common position against the SRF. There were important differences between the centre-right CDU, the free democrat party and Germany's social democratic party on the design of the fund. While the former favoured a network of national resolution funds, the latter supported a pan-European SRF (Ríos Camacho, 2021). Lastly, Germany moderated its position on creating a system of national resolution funds because of the Netherlands' proposal to structure the fund with national compartments and progressive mutualization (Ríos Camacho, 2021). During the transitional period of eight years, the resolution costs first had to be borne by national compartments. If a national compartment was not enough, recourse to all compartments ('mutualization') was possible. If the resolution costs were still not covered, there could be external borrowing and temporary transfers between national compartments. During the transitional period, banks paid their contributions to their national compartments. These compartments progressively merged and ceased to exist at the end of the transitional period (Council of the EU and EP, 2014, p. 5).

The Netherlands supported the SRM and the SRF because of the interests of its large international banks (Howarth and Quaglia, 2016). The Dutch government wanted to have the SRF in the regulation as the Commission proposed but based on gradual mutualization of contributions and subject to strict conditionality, that is, the bail-in rule. In case a troubled bank needed to be rescued, with 8 per cent bail-in as a first step, the potential use of the SRF would be reduced. The SRF intervenes only where, after having used the internal financial resources of the financial institution under resolution, namely the shareholders and the creditors – at least 8 per cent of total liabilities and own funds (bail-in) – resolution action could not be achieved without the SRF. In addition, for the Dutch government, an effective SSM had to be operational before establishing the SRM. Also, Member States' national resolution funds needed to be fully harmonized and the BRRD had to be adopted (Dutch government, 2012, p. 7). The main objective of this list of preconditions to set up the SRM with a SRF was first to improve the quality of supervision of euro area banks before any redistribution via the SRF could take place (Ríos Camacho, 2021). The Dutch finance minister, Jeroen Dijsselbloem, and the Dutch government called for a long progressive mutualization of contributions to the fund because the SSM was already operational and there would be less need to use the fund if supervision was effective (Dutch government, 2012, p. 3).

Spain, Italy, and France were the most vocal supporters of a SRM with a SRF (Ríos Camacho, 2021). They accepted the IGA as a part of the compromise but very reluctantly and as the price to pay for an SRF. Spain, Italy, and France pushed vehemently for the SRF no matter what it would look like whereas Germany had the last word on the sequence and conditions to access it (Ríos Camacho, 2021). Establishing the SRF by an IGA outside the EU treaties was strongly opposed by EU institutions and many euro area countries, among them France, Spain, and Italy.

Spain wanted to have a SRM with a SRF due to its inability and/or difficulties to resolve and pay for its banks in the short term (Donnelly, 2013). The Spanish government had called for the set-up of a DRI via the ESM and was under a financial assistance programme. A joint mission, including the Commission, ECB, EBA (European Banking Authority), EFSF (European Financial Stability Facility), and the International Monetary Fund (IMF) visited Madrid in June 2012 following the request by the Spanish government for external financial assistance under the terms of the Financial Assistance for the Recapitalisation of Financial Institutions by the EFSF (European Commission, 2012, p. 2). The agreement was a financial sector adjustment programme including a financing package of up to €100 billion for recapitalization and restructuring of the Spanish financial sector (European Commission, 2012, p. 2). In addition, Spanish banks were one of the main beneficiaries of the ECB long-term refinancing operations (LTROs) (European Commission, 2012, pp. 21–22). In addition, non-performing loans (NPLs) in Spain reached 9.9 per cent in July 2012 compared to only 0.9 per cent in December 2007 (European Commission, 2012, p. 22). Moreover, the Spanish bank resolution system did not have special resolution tools such as bail-in and the existing tools and resources were not sufficient (IMF, 2012, pp. 22–23).

Italy wanted to create common European mechanisms such as a SRF and maintain national state aid as a (traditional) alternative (Donnelly, 2018a, p. 216). During the crisis, the Italian deposit insurance system was primarily used to resolve and restructure troubled financial institutions. This allowed for the early and generous use of public funds for helping banks before they were wound down (Donnelly, 2018a, p. 216). Italy had one of the highest levels of NPLs in the eurozone (Donnelly, 2018a, p. 218). These factors lowered the bargaining power of these countries during the SRM and SRF negotiations.

France favoured the creation of an SRM and supported Italy and Spain because it wanted to avoid further strain on its economy given its exposure to these at-risk countries. At the end of 2012, the French banking system had one of the highest proportions (21.9 per cent, i.e. assets as a percentage of total bank assets) of exposure to at-risk countries such as Italy and Spain (Howarth and Quaglia, 2016, pp. 57–59). Although France was never at risk of losing access to financial markets, the public debt of this country was 90.2 per cent of GDP in 2012 (Eurostat, 2013).

In the conclusions of the European summit on 27–28 June 2013, EU leaders stated that in the short term, the main priority was to complete EBU and this required a SRM (European Council, 2014, pp. 11–12). In addition, participation in the SRM (and SRF) is mandatory for all Member States in the SSM, regardless of whether they have the euro or not. Thus, non-euro area countries must join the SRM if they have joined the SSM (Council of the EU and EP, 2014, p. 4). Bulgaria and Croatia were the first two non-euro countries that joined the SSM via close cooperation with the ECB (Darvas and Martins, 2022, p. 8). The Eurogroup stated that these countries would also participate in the SRM (including the SRF) from the date of entry into force of the ECB decision on close cooperation (Darvas and Martins, 2022, p. 9).

On 30 November 2020, nineteen euro area finance ministers committed to continue with the reform of the European Stability Mechanism (ESM),[3] which provided for establishing a common backstop to the SRF in the form of a credit line from the ESM to replace the DRI (Council of the European Union, 2020a, p. 1). The nineteen finance ministers committed to advancing the entry into force of the common backstop by the beginning of 2022, given the progress in risk reduction (Council of the European Union, 2020a, p. 1). The Commission, the ECB, and the SRB prepared a Risk Reduction Report, which showed a substantial reduction of NPLs in the banking system as well as continuous build-up of MREL (Minimum Requirement for own funds and Eligible Liabilities) capacity[4] (Council of the European Union, 2020a, p. 1). However, the Eurogroup stated that some vulnerabilities remained, as reflected in the levels of NPLs and MREL shortfalls regarding the agreed benchmarks. Moreover, the pandemic was likely to slow down the favourable trends observed in recent years (Council of the European Union, 2020a, p. 1).

On 27 January and 8 February 2021, ESM member countries signed the Agreement Amending the ESM Treaty. The reformed Treaty will come into force when ratified by the parliaments of all nineteen ESM members (ESM, 2021). The ESM common backstop will be

[3] The ESM was created in 2012 by an intergovernmental treaty among the euro area countries. The treaty established a permanent rescue fund headquartered in Luxembourg. The ESM's primary objective is to provide financial assistance in the form of loans to its members if necessary in order to maintain financial stability. Loans are subject to strict conditionality and are given to governments, not to private institutions such as banks. The ESM has provided financial assistance to Greece, Cyprus, and Spain (ESM, 2014).

[4] Minimum requirement for own funds and eligible liabilities (MREL) is set by the national resolution authorities to ensure that a bank maintains at all times sufficient quantity and quality of instruments capable of absorbing losses and recapitalizing a bank in resolution (SRB, 2021, p. 5).

used only as a last resort, where the SRF is depleted and the SRB is unable to raise sufficient contributions or borrow funds from other sources (ESM, 2021, p. 38). In this event, the ESM can act as a backstop and lend the necessary funds to the SRF to finance the resolution of a failing bank. The SRF will pay back the ESM loan with money from bank contributions within three years, although this period can be extended up to five years (ESM, 2021, p. 19).

Germany and the Netherlands had long pushed for a significant decrease in NPLs in the southern banking systems as a prerequisite for triggering the common backstop (Financial Times, 2020b). Italy opposed the part of the collective action clauses aimed at making it easier to force holdout investors to incur losses in a country's debt restructuring (Financial Times, 2020b). Its delegation feared that this would make debt restructuring not only more orderly in theoretical terms but more likely. The proposal to reform the ESM treaty became politically toxic in Italy as populist politicians equated any ESM assistance to national subjugation (Financial Times, 2020a, p. 2). Nevertheless, the COVID-19 pandemic and coordinated government action to alleviate the economic consequences altered the debate on the common backstop (Financial Times, 2020a).

In the context of the COVID-19 crisis, the common backstop will enhance the SRB's capacity should any issues arise. The common backstop is key to the SRF's credibility. It strengthens market participants' confidence by increasing the funds available to the SRB to manage a banking crisis (Reinder de Carpentier, 2020, p. 1). While the progress made in risk-reduction was the basis for finance ministers to decide its introduction, it should also decrease the possible need for the common backstop by ensuring that private sector funds are available to use before the SRF and the common backstop are tapped (Reinder de Carpentier, 2020, p. 3). However, activating the common backstop will be cumbersome since it will need unanimous support from the Member States, as it is an intergovernmental body where national vetoes rule.

24.5 DEADLOCK AND STATUS QUO ON THE EUROPEAN DEPOSIT INSURANCE SCHEME: TOWARDS A DEPOSIT REINSURANCE SYSTEM?

In 2015, the Commission published a proposal for a regulation establishing an EDIS (European Commission, 2015a). The EDIS proposal aimed at completing and strengthening the EBU by breaking the link between banks and sovereigns, thereby reducing the vulnerability of both to severe local shocks and reinforcing confidence across the EU (European Commission, 2015a, p. 6). In its communication 'Towards the Completion of the Banking Union', the Commission stated that negotiations on EDIS should proceed in parallel with negotiations on risk-reduction given the necessity to also decrease risks in Member States' banking sectors (European Commission, 2015b).

Germany rejected the Commission's proposal on EDIS contesting its timing and the creation of a Deposit Insurance Fund based on full mutualization of funds (Ríos Camacho, 2021). The German government feared that well-funded German deposit guarantee schemes (DGSs) would be responsible for insuring deposits of weaker foreign banks (Howarth and Quaglia, 2016). German commercial, savings, and cooperative banks, which have their own institutional protection schemes (IPSs), advocated for maintaining the system intact and attacked the EDIS as inferior (Donnelly, 2018a, p. 214; Howarth and Quaglia, 2016, p. 143).

The position of the German government on EDIS slightly changed in 2019 from 'we don't want EDIS' to 'Berlin should support a common deposit insurance scheme' in Europe. The shift in the position of the German government can be related to different factors. While pre-pandemic progress in risk reduction alleviated moral hazard concerns and commercial banks started supporting a reinsurance system, the German government's ideological shift from the conservative Wolfgang Schäuble to the pro-integration social democrat Olaf Scholz is another factor supporting the pro-integration position (Tümmler, 2022, p. 7).

Past efforts to reorient the debate on EDIS in Germany encountered opposition of conservatives in Merkel's CDU, as well as the IPS member institutions (Financial Times, 2019). However, advancing on EDIS meant that there had to be effective supervision and resolution in place based on harmonized bank insolvency rules and the further development of the European resolution regime (Scholz, 2019). Regarding limits on banks' sovereign debt exposures, the proposals included introduction of risk-based concentration charges, which would decrease home bias and contagion risks (Scholz, 2019). Furthermore, the proposals included, besides Member States' NDGSs, a DIF based on loans and negotiated via an IGA. A reinsurance model could be considered once all the elements were implemented (Scholz, 2019). However, the remarkable reduction of NPLs to around 3 per cent of the total volume, achieved before the COVID-19 pandemic, was not sufficient to persuade the German government to lift its veto on EDIS (Euractiv, 2020). Although the German government had become more pro-integration in the EBU, retaining NDGSs remained crucial (Tümmler, 2022, p. 8). To understand the position of the German government and this insistence, it is also important to consider the structural links between savings banks, on the one hand, and German elected politicians, who often hold the majority of board chairmanships, on the other (Markgraf and Véron, 2018).

The deadlock on EDIS is most commonly attributed to Germany's moral hazard concerns (Donnelly, 2018a; Howarth and Quaglia, 2016; Ríos Camacho, 2021). However, banking sector interests related to the institutional set-up and legal status of NDGS have also informed these concerns (Howarth and Quaglia, 2017; Tümmler, 2022). The German banking sector is composed of a few commercial banks with cross-border activities and a large number of domestic savings and cooperative banks. The position of savings and cooperative banks is determined by the IPSs they run, which are registered as a DGS. Deposit insurance only applies when a bank defaults despite the IPS, an event that is to be avoided at all costs (Tümmler, 2022, p. 6). A full-fledged EDIS replacing IPSs by moving DIFs to the supranational level is a primary concern for these banks since control over funds would be moved to the EU level, thereby potentially decreasing their ability to avoid defaults. In contrast, German commercial banks stand to benefit from a full-fledged EDIS, as it would reduce compliance costs, giving them competitive advantage towards domestic banks (Tümmler, 2022, p. 6). Moreover, developments on the institutional design of the EDIS reflected the preferences of the German government. The debate moved from establishing an EDIS based on full insurance and mutualization of funds to set up a reinsurance mechanism.

France, Italy, and Spain considered an EDIS as a priority and welcomed the Commission's proposal (Ríos Camacho, 2021). The Italian government argued that the SSM and the SRM should be complemented by an EU-wide DGS (Howarth and Quaglia, 2016, p. 147). In the case of Italy, given weaknesses of both state and bank finances, the goal would be to secure a mutually funded EDIS (Donnelly, 2018a, p. 216). However, Italy strongly opposed limits on its sovereign debt exposures (Donnelly, 2018a, p. 218). Setting limits on banks' sovereign debt exposures would penalize banks for holding sovereign debt of their countries, which has always been a non-starter for Italy and other southern European countries (The Economist, 2019). Italy firmly opposed any initiative that would discourage its banks from buying up Italian sovereign debt, since this could increase its borrowing costs, which is very dangerous for Italy given its public debt of over 155 per cent of economic output (Politico, 2021). Risk-weighting of national sovereigns (currently sovereign debt is risk-free) could lead to major adjustments in the banks' balance sheets and would affect the fragile sovereign markets of highly indebted Member States, for example, in case of large sales by banks (Micossi, 2017, p. 5).

The position of the Italian government is driven by the continuous fragility of its banking sector to the sovereign–bank nexus (Howarth and Quaglia, 2016; Ríos Camacho, 2021). However, the Italian position has developed in favour of a reinsurance system due to interests linked to its NDGSs. What differentiates Italian DGSs is their focus on alternative measures besides deposit insurance to recapitalize troubled banks (Tümmler, 2022, p. 10). Under a full-fledged EDIS, decisions on the use of DIFs would be taken at the supranational level, which would likely obstruct the use of alternative measures (Donnelly, 2018a). Italian banks consider it a negative outcome since possibilities for bank recapitalization would be reduced in accordance with the EBU framework (Tümmler, 2022, p. 10).

The Spanish government shared the position of the Italian government on limits on banks' sovereign debt exposures (Ríos Camacho, 2021). Furthermore, these countries would prefer an EDIS based on full insurance, which means full mutualization of funds (Ríos Camacho, 2021). However, Italy and Spain were willing to accept a less mutualized structure for the DIF, namely a reinsurance system rather than a full-fledged EDIS as originally proposed by the Commission (Ríos Camacho, 2021). In addition, there was some predisposition among the southern countries to set limits to banks' sovereign debt exposures, as Germany proposed, but with a red line: To leave out the risk-weighted assets, which would greatly reduce the capital ratios in the southern European banks (El Confidencial, 2019).

The position of the French government also started to favour a reinsurance system given its special benefits for a concentrated banking sector (Ríos Camacho, 2021; Tümmler, 2022). The French banking sector is characterized by a small number of large, cross-border banks. French banks developed a position in favour of a reinsurance system, as the 2014 Deposit Guarantee Scheme Directive (DGSD) grants a lower target level (percentage of eligible deposits)[5] for highly concentrated banking systems such as the French (Tümmler, 2022, p. 8). The French government pressed for a reinsurance system that retains NDGSs in order to keep the lower target level and the lower costs for the French banking sector (Tümmler, 2022, pp. 11–12).

The extreme positions of Germany and Italy on an EDIS have prevented an agreement. The main line of conflict was between those countries that feared that their banks would be net contributors (e.g. Germany, the Netherlands, and Finland) and those that were likely to benefit the most and use the EDIS because of their banking problems (e.g. Spain and Italy) (Howarth and Quaglia, 2016, p. 142). At the time, the levels of NPLs were highest in the Member States worst hit by the sovereign debt crisis, notably Spain and Italy. A German-led coalition of Member States whose banking sectors survived the euro crisis comparatively well considered that an EDIS creates moral hazard for Member States with weak banking sectors. The latter could benefit from EDIS in terms of financial stability without committing themselves to tackle the legacy issues in their domestic banking sectors (Howarth and Quaglia, 2017; Schnabel and Véron, 2018b).

Technical discussions have continued in the Ad Hoc Working Party on the Strengthening of the Banking Union, which the Council created in 2016 (Council of the European Union, 2016). In 2016, the EP rapporteur on EDIS published a new draft connecting progression from a reinsurance system to a loss-absorbing insurance system (Ríos Camacho, 2021). In case of a

[5] Instead of the 0.8 per cent of eligible deposits set as the regular target level in the DGSD, the target level can be decreased to 0.5 per cent after approval by the Commission. This target level has only been granted to the French DGS (Tümmler, 2022, p. 8).

payout, NDGSs would be depleted first, followed by the national compartments. This model aims to mitigate Germany's concerns over moral hazard and maintain NDGSs (Tümmler, 2022, p. 5). In 2017, the Commission proposed a two-tier scheme beginning with a reinsurance scheme, after which a co-insurance phase would be conditional upon risk reduction (Tümmler, 2022, p. 5). In this phase, losses would be gradually covered by the supranational fund up to full loss coverage (Tümmler, 2022, p. 5). In 2018, the Austrian Council presidency published a draft for a 'hybrid model', which maintained NDGSs, complementing them with a supranational reinsurance fund and mandatory lending among DGSs (High-Level Working Group on EDIS, 2019, p. 2; Council of the European Union, 2020b, p. 3). If the supranational reinsurance fund were depleted, it would be entitled to borrow from NDGSs (Council of the European Union, 2020b).

Negotiations centred around a watered down version of the EDIS with less mutualization of funds than originally envisioned by the Commission and the southern European countries (Ríos Camacho, 2021). National preferences became more aligned with a reinsurance system that maintained NDGSs (High-Level Working Group on EDIS, 2019). Discussions focused on how NGDSs were to be connected in a reinsurance system. Interests linked to the institutional structure of NDGSs influenced national preferences in favour of a reinsurance system after the initial Commission proposal on the EDIS failed (Tümmler, 2022, p. 2). A Commission survey of Member States' preferences on the different design choices was planned to serve as the basis for a new legislative proposal (High-Level Working Group on EDIS, 2019, p. 4). No proposal for a full-fledged EDIS has been tabled so far, though, and its publication in the foreseeable future is unlikely.

No shift in the position of the German ministry of finance in favour of further integration has prevailed over the insistence on maintaining NDGSs. The German savings and cooperative banks have remained highly critical since they fear that an agreement on a reinsurance system could be the first step towards a full-fledged EDIS (Tümmler, 2022, p. 6). Scholz's 2019 paper also conditioned agreement on a reinsurance system after a comprehensive list of risk-reduction measures, including the most controversial limits on banks' sovereign exposures (Tümmler, 2022, p. 7).

24.6 CONCLUSION

In the wake of the European financial and sovereign debt crises, the euro area embarked in 2012 on creating an EBU, starting with the first pillar, the SSM. A complete EBU, based on euro area leaders' commitments, should include three elements, namely the SSM, the SRM, and the EDIS, and equates it with breaking the bank–sovereign vicious circle. However, despite the establishment of the SSM and the SRM, Germany's and Italy's reticence, as well as Member States' national specificities, have remained the main obstacle to complete the EBU with a full-fledged EDIS.

In line with liberal intergovernmentalism, national preferences reflected the interests of euro area Member States' domestic banking sectors. In addition, in accordance with historical institutionalism, the euro crisis revealed the EMU's shortcomings and unintended consequences, setting the stage for the creation of the SSM. The sovereign debt crisis in Spain, however, represented a critical juncture that *triggered* integration. This crisis showed the vicious link between banks and sovereigns in southern Europe, which endangered the euro. The establishment of the SSM was led by the largest euro area countries and agreed as a result of intergovernmental bargaining.

The SRM was established following a compromise of Germany as one of its main initial opponents. An agreement from Germany was achieved in a context where the SSM had already been established and there was common agreement among the euro area countries (including Germany) that an SRM was necessary for it to function properly. However, the outcome, which was reached through the Netherlands acting as a broker, was a SRF negotiated under an IGA and with numerous conditions attached to its financing structure and functioning, as demanded mostly by Germany.

In a similar vein, negotiations on the EDIS have shifted to a reinsurance system retaining NDGSs and with less mutualization of funds than originally proposed by the Commission and favoured by the southern European countries. In line with liberal intergovernmentalism, the preferences of Germany based on moral hazard concerns can partly account for the deadlock in the EDIS. Furthermore, national specificities in deposit insurance in Germany, Italy, and France constitute other obstacles to a full-fledged EDIS, including full mutualization of insurance funds across the euro area. Nevertheless, although the positions of these countries became aligned in supporting a reinsurance system, no agreement has been reached yet. Any progress in the negotiations has heavily depended on the type and extent of risk reduction. The German government in particular has set a comprehensive list of risk-reduction measures, including the most controversial limits on banks' sovereign exposures, as preconditions for an agreement on the reinsurance system.

REFERENCES

Allen & Overy (2012). The German bank restructuring and bad bank regime: Its impact on investors. *German capital markets at a crossroads*. www.allenovery.com/

Beck, T., Gros, D., and Schoenmaker, D. (2013). On the design of a Single Resolution Mechanism. DG for Internal Policies, Policy department A: Economic and Scientific Policy, European Parliament. www.europarl.europa.eu/document/activities/cont/201302/20130214ATT61103/20130214ATT61103EN.pdf

Chang, M. (2015). The rising power of the ECB: The case of the Single Supervisory Mechanism. Paper presented at the European Union Studies Association, Boston.

Council of the European Union (2013). Council Regulation (EU) No 1024/2013 of 15 October 2013 conferring specific tasks on the European Central Bank concerning policies relating to the prudential supervision of credit institutions.

Council of the European Union (2016). Establishment of an ad hoc working party on the strengthening of the banking union. Interinstitutional File 2015/0270 (COD). https://data.consilium.europa.eu/doc/document/CM-1380-2016-INIT/en/pdf

Council of the European Union (2020a). Statement of the Eurogroup in inclusive format on the ESM reform and the early introduction of the backstop to the Single Resolution Fund. Press release. www.consilium.europa.eu/en/

Council of the European Union (2020b). Croatian Presidency progress report on the strengthening of the Banking Union. 29 May. https://data.consilium.europa.eu/doc/document/ST-8335-2020-ADD-1/en/pdf

Council of the European Union and the European Parliament (2014). Regulation of the European Parliament and of the Council establishing uniform rules and a uniform procedure for the resolution of credit institutions and certain investment firms in the framework of a Single Resolution Mechanism. http://eur-lex.europa.eu/legal-content/EN/TXT/PDF/?uri=CELEX:32014R0806&from=en

Darvas, Z., and Martins, C. (2022). Close cooperation for bank supervision: The cases of Bulgaria and Croatia. In-depth analysis requested by the ECON Committee, European Parliament. March 2022. www.europarl.europa.eu/RegData/etudes/IDAN/2022/699523/IPOL_IDA(2022)699523_EN.pdf

De Gregorio Merino, A. (2016). Institutional and constitutional aspects of banking union. In G. Bándi et al. (eds.), *European Banking Union. Congress Proceedings*, Vol. 1. *The XXVII FIDE (Fédération*

Internationale pour le Droit Européen) Congress in Budapest, 2016. Alphen aan der Rijn: Wolters Kluwer, 185–186.

Donnelly, S. (2013). Power politics and the undersupply of financial stability in Europe. *Review of International Political Economy* 21(4), 980–1005.

Donnelly, S. (2018a). Advocacy coalitions and the lack of deposit insurance in Banking Union. *Journal of Economic Policy Reform* 21(3), 210–223.

Donnelly, S. (2018b). Liberal economic nationalism, financial stability, and Commission leniency in Banking Union. *Journal of Economic Policy Reform* 21(2), 159–173.

Donnelly, S., and Asimakopoulos, I. G. (2020). Bending and breaking the Single Resolution Mechanism: The case of Italy. *Journal of Common Market Studies* 58(4), 856–871.

Dutch government (2012). Translation of parliamentary letter of 1 October 2012, 'Europees toezichtmechanisme voor banken en directe herkapitalisatie door het ESM', in which the Netherlands' position is outlined with regard to the European Commission's proposals for a single supervisory mechanism as well as with regard to direct recapitalization of banks by the ESM and possible further steps towards a full banking union. www.rijksoverheid.nl/

El Confidencial. (2019). Bruselas y la banca estudian concesiones a Alemania para culminar la unión bancaria. *El Confidencial*, 7 November.

Emmanouilidis, J. A. (2012). The prospects of ambitious muddling through – The results of an EU Summit in deep crisis mode. European Policy Centre. www.emmanouilidis.eu/download/Emmanouilidis_Prospects-of-ambitious-muddling-through-6-2012.pdf

Epstein, R. (2014). Choosing the lesser of two evils: Explaining multinational banking groups' push for supranational oversight in the EU. Cahiers Working Paper, European Union Series, Université de Montréal, 2.

Euractiv (2020). Commission eyes new proposal to unblock deposit insurance scheme. *Euractiv*, 7 December.

Euro area (2012). Euro area summit statement. 29 June.

European Central Bank (2020). ECB establishes close cooperation with Bulgaria's and Croatia's central banks. Press release. 10 July. www.bankingsupervision.europa.eu/press/pr/date/2020/html/ssm.pr200710~ae2abe1f23.en.html

European Commission (2012). The Financial Sector Adjustment Programme for Spain. Occasional Papers 118. https://ec.europa.eu/economy_finance/publications/occasional_paper/2012/pdf/ocp118_en.pdf

European Commission (2015a). Proposal for a Regulation of the European Parliament and of the Council amending Regulation (EU) 806/2014 in order to establish a European Deposit Insurance Scheme. https://eur-lex.europa.eu/legal-content/EN/TXT/PDF/?uri=CELEX:52015PC0586&from=EN

European Commission (2015b). Communication from the Commission. 'Towards the Completion of the Banking Union'. 24 November. https://eur-lex.europa.eu/legal-content/EN/TXT/PDF/?uri=CELEX:52015DC0587&from=en

European Commission (2017). Proposal for a Council regulation on the establishment of the European Monetary Fund. https://eur-lex.europa.eu/resource.html?uri=cellar:050797ec-db5b-11e7-a506-01aa75ed71a1.0002.02/DOC_1&format=PDF

European Council (2014). Banking union. Relevant European Council conclusions. www.consilium.europa.eu/

European Stability Mechanism (2021). ESM Treaty Amending Agreement. www.esm.europa.eu/about-esm/esm-reform-documents/esm-treaty-amending-agreement

European Stability Mechanism (2014). Press release. 8 December. www.esm.europa.eu/

Eurostat (2013). Maastricht debt as a percentage of GDP, 2011–2012. https://ec.europa.eu/eurostat/statistics-explained/index.php?title=File:Maastricht_debt_as_a_percentage_of_GDP,_2011%E2%80%932012.png

Financial Times (2019). Germany's Scholz gives ground on eurozone banking union plan. *Financial Times*, 6 November.

Financial Times (2020a). A chance to press on with EU banking union. *Financial Times*, 2 December.

Financial Times (2020b). Eurozone finance ministers strike deal over bailout fund reform. *Financial Times*, 30 November.

Handelsblatt (2012). *EU verschiebt Reformen. Handelsblatt*, 29 May.

High-Level Working Group on EDIS (2019). Letter by the High-Level Working Group on a EDIS Chair to the President of the Eurogroup: Further strengthening the Banking Union, including EDIS: A roadmap for political negotiations. www.consilium.europa.eu/media/41644/2019-12-03-letter-from-the-hlwg-chair-to-the-peg.pdf

Howarth, D., and Quaglia, L. (2016). *The Political Economy of European Banking Union*. Oxford: Oxford University Press.

Howarth, D., and Quaglia, L. (2017). The difficult construction of a European Deposit Insurance Scheme: A step too far in banking union? *Journal of Economic Policy Reform* 21(3), 1–20.

Howarth, D., and Schild, J. (2020). *The Difficult Construction of European Banking Union*. London: Routledge.

International Monetary Fund (2012). Financial Sector Assessment Program Update. Spain. Safety Net, Bank Resolution, and Crisis Management Framework. Technical Note. www.imf.org/external/pubs/ft/scr/2012/cr12145.pdf

Markgraf, J., and Véron, N. (2018). Germany's savings banks: Uniquely intertwined with local politics. Blog post. www.bruegel.org/2018/07/germanys-savings-banks-uniquely-intertwined-with-local-politics/

Mero, K., and Piroska, D. (2016). The persistence of national banking systems: Banking union and financial nationalism. *Policy and Society* 35(3), 215–226.

Micossi, S. (2017). A blueprint for completing the banking union. *CEPS Policy Insights*. www.ceps.eu/ceps-publications/blueprint-completing-banking-union/

Moravcsik, A. (1993). Preferences and power in the European Community: A liberal intergovernmentalist approach. *Journal of Common Market Studies* 31(4), 473–524.

Moravcsik, A. (1998). *The Choice for Europe. Social Purpose and State Power from Messina to Maastricht*. Ithaca, NY: Cornell University Press.

Moravcsik, A. (2018). Preferences, power and institutions in 21st-century Europe. *Journal of Common Market Studies* 56(7), 1648–1674.

Moravcsik, A., and Schimmelfennig, F. (2019). Liberal intergovernmentalism. In A. Wiener, T. A. Börzel, and T. Risse (eds.), *European Integration Theory*. Oxford: Oxford University Press, 64–84.

Niemann, A., and Ioannou, D. (2015). European economic integration in times of crisis: a case of neofunctionalism? *Journal of European Public Policy* 22(2), 196–218.

Niemann, A., Lefkofridi, Z., and Schmitter, P. C. (2019). Neofunctionalism. In A. Wiener, T. Börzel, and T. Risse (eds.), *European Integration Theory*. Oxford: Oxford University Press, pp. 43–64.

Otero-Iglesias, M., Royo, S., and Steinberg, F. (2016). The Spanish financial crisis: Lessons for the European Banking Union. Elcano Royal Institute. https://media.realinstitutoelcano.org/wp-content/uploads/2021/10/informe-elcano-20-spanish-financial-crisis-lessons-european-banking-union.pdf

Pierson, P. (1996). The path to European integration: A historical institutionalist analysis. *Comparative Political Studies* 29(2), 123–163.

Politico (2021). Germany says nein to eurozone banking safeguards. *Politico*, 15 June.

Pollack, M. (2019). Rational choice and historical institutionalism. In A. Wiener, T. Börzel, and T. Risse (eds.), *European Integration Theory*. Oxford: Oxford University Press, pp. 108–127.

Reinder de Carpentier, J. (2020). The common backstop – A welcome step forward. The SRB blog. www.srb.europa.eu/en/content/common-backstop-welcome-step-forward

Ríos Camacho, E. (2021). *The Choice for Banking Union: Power, Politics and the Trap of Credible Commitments*. New York: Routledge.

Schäfer, D. (2016). A banking union of ideas? The impact of ordoliberalism and the vicious circle on the EU banking union. *Journal of Common Market Studies* 54(4), 961–980.

Schäuble, W. (2013). Banking Union must be built on firm foundations. *Financial Times*, 12 May.

Schimmelfennig, F. (2014). European integration in the euro crisis: The limits of postfunctionalism. *Journal of European Integration* 36(3), 321–337.

Schnabel, I., and Véron, N. (2018a). Completing Europe's banking union means breaking the bank–sovereign vicious circle. *Bruegel*, 17 May. www.bruegel.org/2018/05/completing-europes-banking-union-means-breaking-the-bank-sovereign-vicious-circle/

Schnabel, I., and Véron, N. (2018b). Breaking the stalemate on European Deposit Insurance. Blog post. www.bruegel.org/2018/03/breaking-the-stalemate-on-european-deposit-insurance/

Scholz, O. (2019). Position paper on the goals of the banking union. BMF – non-paper. Bundesministerium der Finanzen, November. http://prod-upp-image-read.ft.com/b750c7e4-ffba-11e9-b7bc-f3fa4e77dd47

Single Resolution Board (2021). Minimum Requirement for Own Funds and Eligible Liabilities (MREL). SRB Policy under the Banking Package. May. www.srb.europa.eu/system/files/media/document/mrel_policy_may_2021_final_web_0.pdf

The Economist. (2019). What next for Europe's banking union? *The Economist*, 23 November.

Tümmler, M. (2022). Completing banking union? The role of national deposit guarantee schemes in shifting Member States' preferences on the European Deposit Insurance Scheme. *Journal of Common Market Studies* 60(6), 1556–1572.

Van Rompuy, H. (2012). Towards a genuine Economic and Monetary Union. Four Presidents' report. 5 December. www.consilium.europa.eu/media/23818/134069.pdf

Zeitlin, J. (2016). EU experimentalist governance in times of crisis. *West European Politics* 39(5), 1073–1094.

25

Failing Banks within the Banking Union at the Crossroads

A Great Step Forward, with Many Loose Ends

Jens-Hinrich Binder

25.1 INTRODUCTION

Among other things, the eurozone crisis since 2010 has exposed fundamental weaknesses in the regulation of banks in Member States participating in the common currency. While the substantive content of applicable regulations had, for a long time, been determined by European law (Parchimowicz, Chapter 23 in this volume), the ongoing supervision of credit institutions operating across the eurozone had remained solely within the responsibility of the respective home jurisdictions. Much the same applied, and even to a greater extent, in the area of bank crisis management, both with regard to individual bank failures and the management of systemic financial crises. In the eyes of policymakers and the general public, systemic financial distress in jurisdictions such as Cyprus, Greece, Italy, or Spain clearly illustrated the weaknesses of *national* crisis management in the light of financial problems that spread quickly beyond national borders, and whose containment exhausted public budgets in several states. As a corollary to centralized supervision, to be carried out by the European Central Bank (ECB) within the Single Supervisory Mechanism, a Single Resolution Mechanism was established as a framework for the prevention and the management of insolvencies of large ('significant') credit institutions within the eurozone.

In a variety of respects, the creation of that resolution framework, through Regulation (EU) No. 806/2014 (hereafter SRMR),[1] has changed dramatically the approach to dealing with failing banks within eurozone countries. First and foremost, the Single Resolution Mechanism, under the auspices of the Single Resolution Board (SRB), an EU agency in Brussels, has been created as an elaborate *institutional* framework distinct from, but interrelated with, existing national resolution authorities (see, in particular, Articles 5, 7, and 42 SRMR). Within this new framework, the SRB has since assumed and exercised core decision-making powers with regard to (a) the drafting of so-called resolution plans (i.e. preparatory plans for the treatment of failing banks by the SRB as resolution authority in an actual failure, see Article 8 SRMR), (b) the assessment of resolvability with corresponding powers to require credit institutions and financial groups to adopt changes with regard to, inter alia, funding arrangements, business activities, or even corporate structures (Article 10 SRMR), and (c) the initiation and calibration (i.e. the selection of resolution tools and definition of their specific use) in relation to actual resolution

[1] Regulation (EU) No. 806/2014 of the European Parliament and of the Council of 15 July 2014 establishing uniform rules and a uniform procedure for the resolution of credit institutions and certain investment firms in the framework of a Single Resolution Mechanism and a Single Resolution Fund, OJ L 225, p. 1.

cases (see, in particular, Article 23 SRMR, on the 'resolution scheme' to be adopted by the SRM).

Significantly, as part of its preventive powers, the SRB has also been responsible for the development of institution-specific minimum requirements on own funds and eligible liabilities (MREL) – a set of requirements designed so as to ensure that banks build up specific buffers of capital and debt instruments (to be held, ideally, by professional investors), which could be used, in the event of their failure, to absorb losses without affecting normal creditors.[2] These powers complement the resolution authority's powers, as part of its technical armoury for the management of bank failures, to restructure a failing bank's balance sheet by writing down the positions of shareholders (and other investors in capital instruments) and creditors, and by converting debt into equity instruments. Along with the application of such powers in actual resolution cases (Articles 21 and 27, on 'write-down and conversion powers' and the 'bail-in', respectively), the operationalization of MREL is supposed to provide a crucial precondition for resolution of financial institutions without recourse to public subsidies in future cases (Binder, 2019, pp. 313–314; Gardella, 2020; Lamandini and Ramos Muñoz, 2019; Santoro and Mecatti, 2019). As a fundamental characteristic, all relevant powers will be exercised within a wide margin of discretion granted to the SRB, with no creditor influence on the design and calibration of actions and with only very a limited degree of judicial review granted to them (see, generally, Binder, 2016c).

Moreover, a Single Resolution Fund (SRF) has been established under the auspices of the SRB, which is funded through mandatory contributions by credit institutions and designed to satisfy a broad range of funding needs in relation to resolution actions (Articles 67–77 SRMR; Gortsos, 2022a). Within this framework, for banks under the direct supervision of the ECB within the Single Supervisory Mechanism, National Resolution Authorities (NRAs) are largely left to the implementation of resolution schemes devised by the SRB, subject to the instructions laid down therein and to monitoring by the SRB (Articles 28 and 29 SRMR). All in all, these new arrangements have certainly created an impressive, highly ambitious new framework for the administration of the general European regime for the resolution of failing banking institutions. For the EU as a whole, a harmonized framework had been adopted with the Bank Recovery and Resolution Directive (BRRD) of 2014,[3] in response to (perceived) lessons learnt during the Global Financial Crisis. The legal framework for the SRM effectively replicates the BRRD's substantive and procedural provisions for application within the European Banking Union, but with centralized decision-making, leaving only very limited discretion for national authorities.

Against this (indisputably impressive) record, and considering that no institutional, procedural, and substantive arrangements for the resolution of large, systemically relevant banks had been in place before or during the Global Financial Crisis of 2007–9 or the subsequent eurozone crisis, a superficial observer could be forgiven for not noticing that the SRM's ability to effectively manage insolvencies in the financial sector of participating Member States is far from settled. To identify but three major areas of concern:

First, while the SRM, in tandem with the Single Supervisory Mechanism (SSM), certainly has gone a long way towards the creation of a reliable safety net for the preservation of systemic stability within the eurozone, effective bank crisis management, for decades now, has generally

[2] See, for details, Arts. 12–12j SRMR. While MREL requirements had been addressed by just one provision of the original version of the SRMR, the relevant regime has since been expanded substantially in the amended version of Art. 12 and the newly introduced provisions in Arts. 12a–j SRMR. See, generally, e.g. Haentjens (2022, paras. 1–4).

[3] Directive 2014/59/EU of the European Parliament and the Council of 15 May 2014 establishing a framework for the recovery and resolution of credit institutions and investment firms, OJ L 173, p. 190.

been believed to be incomplete without effective deposit guarantee schemes which, in the event of a bank failure, would offer protection to insured depositors. Deposit protection, in other words, has been considered part and parcel of the safety net for the financial sector, both as an instrument to ensure continuing access to indispensable liquid funds and as a safeguard against bank runs by depositors. Against this backdrop, it is certainly problematic that, to date, all attempts to complement the regime with a single European Deposit Insurance Scheme (EDIS),[4] as a 'third pillar' of the institutional architecture which would go beyond the existing minimum harmonization of deposit guarantees for the EU as a whole,[5] have remained unsuccessful.

Second, consider the issue of resolution funding, i.e. the provision of liquidity to entities in resolution, financial assistance in support of the implementation of resolution actions, or compensation to parties who have suffered a financial loss without legal basis as a result of resolution actions. Available resolution tools include: the sale of business tool (sale of the failing institution, or its assets and liabilities, to a competitor institution); the bridge institution tool (transfer to a bridge institution when a sale of business is not feasible); the asset separation tool (transfer of problem assets out of the failing bank's balance sheet to an asset management vehicle); and the bail-in tool (write-down of liabilities and their conversion into capital instruments).[6] Each of these tools can give rise to different funding needs.[7] Although the resolution toolbox established by the SRMR (in line with the BRRD) is designed to ultimately ensure full shareholder and creditor participation in the losses of an insolvent bank, it is nonetheless obvious from previous financial crises that the preservation of financial stability in the event of one or more insolvencies crucially depends on the availability of liquidity for other credit institutions (Gortsos, 2022a, paras. 1 and 2). While the SRF, within the EBU architecture, had been designed to provide just that (Article 76 SRMR), it was rather obvious that its target financial volume, in the event of a major crisis, would likely prove insufficient. By way of remedy, the financial resources of the SRF have been reinforced through the creation of an emergency lending facility from the European Stability Mechanism (ESM), undoubtedly yet another milestone enhancing greatly the framework's capability (Gortsos, 2022b, paras. 6–20; and see Aerz and Bizarro, 2020). While both the ESM and SRB have since gone a long way to establishing a predictable framework for cooperation in the event of a major crisis, in which ESM funding could be expected to be needed, the new arrangements remain untested. The availability of resolution funding is also crucial for the effective use of the bail-in tool (Article 27 SRMR), which, while expected to play an important role for incentive-compatible resolution actions, has never been used to date and remains fraught with considerable uncertainties (Binder, 2019, pp. 313–315).

And *third* but not least, while the SRM covers only large credit institutions which, by virtue of their size and relative market share, qualify as 'significant' and thus fall within the scope of direct supervision by the ECB within the SSM,[8] the legal and institutional frameworks for the management of insolvencies below that threshold remain largely unharmonized not just within

4 See European Commission (2015) and further Section 25.4.1.

5 Cf. Directive 2014/49/EU of the European Parliament and of the Council of 16 April 2014 on deposit guarantee schemes, OJ L 173, p. 149.

6 See Arts. 22(2), 24–27 SRMR, respectively, and, for further discussion, Binder (2016b, paras. 2.47–2.61, 2019, pp. 310–315).

7 While a detailed analysis of those differences would be outside the scope of the present chapter, consider the definition of the Fund's mandate in Art. 76(1) SRMR, which at least provides some guidance as to potential uses of Fund contributions in relation to the different resolution tools.

8 See, generally, Art. 7(2) and, in particular, 18(8) SRMR.

the EBU, but across the EU as a whole. The absence of harmonizing legislation in this regard has been decried mainly for two reasons. On the one hand, the divergence of national bank insolvency regimes for banks falling outside the scope of single supervision and resolution, in terms of substantive rules and both procedural and institutional frameworks, is very likely to leave creditors and other market participants not just with substantially different economic outcomes, but also with a considerable degree of legal uncertainty, especially in cross-border settings (Binder, 2021, pp. 565–573; Binder et al., 2019, pp. 200–201). On the other hand, it is important to understand that the SRB's powers are restricted even in the case of 'significant' banks within the meaning defined above. In order for a bank to be resolved under the auspices of the SRB, it must pass what has become known as the 'Public Interest Assessment', whereby the public interest to avoid outright liquidation, in the circumstances, must be deemed to outweigh the disadvantages that resolution might have in terms of shareholder and creditor rights.[9] *If* resolution is denied on these grounds, the relevant bank will then be submitted to liquidation under national insolvency rules. Thus, residual divergences of national insolvency regimes translate into difficulties also with regard to the operational treatment of failing banks in such cases, leaving a high degree of uncertainty as to the economic outcome of liquidation (Binder, 2021, pp. 560–565).

Against that backdrop, this chapter seeks to take stock of the ever-growing policy discussion and recent policy initiatives aiming at the further reform of the EBU. With the fate of the EDIS proposal still uncertain,[10] it cannot be expected to discuss ultimate outcomes. Nonetheless, it is obvious that, with both proposals, the Monetary Union will have reached yet another critical junction; only if and when the residual structural and procedural shortcomings have been addressed, will the management of bank failures and sector-wide crises stand a chance of being carried out anywhere near as effectively as the supervision of systemically relevant banking institutions within the eurozone.

Exploring this agenda, the remainder of the chapter will be organized in three sections. Section 25.2 briefly recalls the policy rationale of the EBU as a whole and the SRM in particular. Taking into account both the evidence from the available cases and the relevant academic literature, Section 25.3 then moves on to analysing the identified shortcomings in more detail. Finally, Section 25.4 presents a preliminary assessment of the two major policy initiatives outstanding, i.e. the EDIS proposal and the incoming BRRD/SRMR review package. Section 25.5 concludes.

25.2 THE SRM IN LIGHT OF THE FUNDAMENTAL POLICY OBJECTIVES OF THE EBU

Looking back at the legal history of the EBU (see e.g. Binder, 2015a; Teixeira, 2020), the creation of the institutional framework of the SRM and the centralization of decision-making powers also in the realm of bank insolvency management clearly has featured as a central objective from the very beginning. As early as 2010, a paper by IMF economists on crisis management and resolution arrangements in Europe anticipated both a single European

9 See Art. 18(1)(c), (5) SRMR. Pursuant to Art. 18(5) SRMR, 'a resolution action shall be treated as in the public interest if it is necessary for the achievement of, and is proportionate to one or more of the resolution objectives referred to in Article 14 and winding up of the entity under normal insolvency proceedings would not meet those resolution objectives to the same extent'.

10 The European Commission published its proposals only in April 2023, following the completion of the present chapter: see https://finance.ec.europa.eu/publications/reform-bank-crisis-management-and-deposit-insurance-framework_en.

resolution authority and a unified European deposit insurance system (Fonteyne at al., 2010, pp. 52–54). This is by no means the first time that the case for such centralization had been advanced with respect to some parts of the financial safety net, however. Proposals for centralization of deposit insurance and other relevant functions had been made much earlier – and well ahead of the eurozone crisis, reflecting fundamental concerns about a financial landscape with an integrated framework in terms of monetary policy but without centralized regulatory and supervisory functions, far beyond the debate on responses to the immediate systemic problems in some national banking systems as of 2012 onwards (see, for a review, Binder, 2015a, pp. 2–3). To be sure, similar problems could have arisen, to some extent, also in the EU as a whole, under conditions of full mobility of capital. In other words, systemic financial problems within one EU Member State could also cause destabilization in other Member States, such as through a flight into another currency and the transfer of deposits into other markets perceived as safer. Within the eurozone, however, that potential is aggravated, first, by the existence of the common currency, which certainly facilitates the transfer of funds: As no conversion into other currency is required to shift funds into a safer environment, transaction costs are reduced, while the funds remain easily accessible for payments in the depositors' home market. Moreover, the relevance of banking systems for the effective transmission of monetary policy also means that systemic problems within a Member State participating in the eurozone can hamper the monetary transmission mechanism.

In the light of this set-up, it is obvious that the introduction of centralized resolution (and supervision) within the eurozone essentially responded to fundamental structural deficiencies in the institutional design of the monetary union which, even without the financial and political disruptions caused by the sovereign debt crisis in a number of eurozone countries, would have become obvious and required solutions at some later point anyhow. These deficiencies have been discussed at length both in academic contributions and in the policy debate preceding the creation of the EBU. Key aspects include:

- the vulnerability of national financial markets to broader economic shocks, enhanced by the desperate state of public finances in a number of south European jurisdictions, which ultimately affected credit institutions and, jointly with the economic crisis in the relevant countries, caused widespread systemic distress;
- the inadequacy of decentralized supervision and bank insolvency management by national authorities in terms of both crisis prevention and crisis management, due not just to deficient institutional arrangements but also adverse incentive structures and national biases;
- the absence of reliable transnational safety nets in the form of robust deposit guarantee schemes and reliable sources of funding for the management of bank failures, in particular in scenarios of sector-wide distress;
- the resulting lack of trust among depositors in problem economies, causing flights into currency and the massive transfer of funds into more stable markets, which enhanced the systemic crisis yet further;
- and the residual incentives for Member States to provide public financial support to failing banks rather than resort to formal resolution measures which could and should have prevented a further deterioration in their public budgets (see e.g., for a detailed discussion and a review of the relevant literature, Binder, 2015a, pp. 3–16).

The creation of the EBU has sought to address these concerns not just by way of a new procedural framework, but also by the addition of a new European governance level to the existing institutional landscape that, hitherto, was confined exclusively to national authorities (including, where applicable, insolvency courts). In terms of the technical content of the resolution toolbox, the creation of the SRM, as mentioned before, has effectively replicated the framework adopted for the EU as a whole, with the adoption of the BRRD in 2014, which in turn reflects a broader international convergence of approaches for the management of failures of systemically important institutions.[11]

Even if, following the full implementation of the BRRD across the EU as a whole, the technical toolbox – both preventive and reactive – is identical for the eurozone and the remainder of the EU, it is particularly the creation of the *institutional* framework in the EBU that has opened new horizons in terms of effectiveness. In comparison to the situation in EU Member States not participating in the eurozone, where the application of the harmonized framework continues to be contingent on the capability of national authorities, the centralization of the decision-making process for both preventive measures in the area of crisis management – i.e. recovery and resolution planning and the 'assessment of resolvability' with corresponding powers to require institutions to adopt changes to business models, funding, and legal arrangements – *and* the initiation and calibration of resolution measures has gone a substantial step further. This should ensure not just a higher degree of consistency in terms of both resolution strategies and the interpretation of the relevant provisions,[12] thereby facilitating also a higher degree of legal certainty in terms of the operationalization of the complex resolution toolbox. Entirely consistent with one of the core objectives of the EBU, the transfer of decision-making powers from the national levels to a European agency is also expected to reduce the potential for discretionary exemptions from the general rule that insolvencies in the financial sector should be dealt with in a manner that avoids the use of public funds.[13] The recent allocation of the new backstop powers to the ESM, whereby the ESM will eventually provide additional sources of funding to resolution actions in cases where the Single Resolution Fund has been exhausted, has undoubtedly reinforced the institutional capabilities of the SRM yet further. Notwithstanding these impressive successes, it remains entirely obvious that the rather high-flying policy objectives summarized above remain almost stunningly ambitious in the light of the economic divergences between the financial systems of the EBU Member States.

25.3 TAKING STOCK: WHAT HAS BEEN ACCOMPLISHED SO FAR?

If one accepts the policy objectives discussed previously as a benchmark against which all implementation efforts have to be evaluated, the picture, to date, is mixed. Moreover, any stock-taking exercise remains inevitably difficult for a number of reasons. The situation is particularly difficult to assess with regard to the current state of affairs in the area of preventive measures (Section 25.3.1). While the picture is clearer by comparison with actual resolution decisions adopted under the auspices of the SRM (Section 25.3.2), it is still difficult to reach an ultimate judgement in this respect. Some of the reasons are to be found in the problem of large

[11] Cf. Financial Stability Board (FSB) (2011/2014); BCBS (2010); and see, for further discussion of the international background, e.g. Binder (2016b, paras. 2.05–2.19); Schillig (2016, paras. 1.05–1.08).

[12] It should be noted, in this context, that the implementation of resolution schemes, as a rule, is subject to the national laws transposing the BRRD (Art. 29 SRMR), while the SRB retains certain rights of control and, if necessary, interference (Art. 28 SRMR). However, pursuant to Art. 7(3), sub-para. (3) SRMR, important aspects are governed by direct application of the relevant provisions of the SRMR, in this respect substituting the national laws transposing the BRRD.

[13] A representative statement to that effect has been formulated in Recitals 8–10 and 12 SRMR.

volumes of non-performing loans, which continues to burden the banking sectors in a number of participating Member States (Section 25.3.3).

25.3.1 *The Invisible: Why the SRB's Preventive Work Is Impossible to Assess*

To start with, a substantial part of the SRB's work, including, in particular, its efforts on the *preventive* side of bank resolution, to date remains broadly inaccessible for outside observers. To be sure, the SRB's general strategy regarding resolution planning has been summarized in – rather high-level and abstract – documents published on the SRB's website (SRB, 2016, 2021a). Additional details have been published in the annual reports (e.g. SRB, 2021b, pp. 26–27). Much more granular information has been made available regarding the development of MREL requirements.[14] However, institution-specific information is *not* available, keeping both the fundamental policies and technical details with regard to individual resolution plans out of scrutiny by interested researchers.[15] Likewise, individual remedial actions taken in order to enhance the resolvability of institutions and groups (Article 10(10)–(13) SRMR) are not reported in public.

While perfectly understandable in view of the highly sensitive nature of such information, confidentiality in this respect inevitably precludes reliable assessments by observers other than EU insiders. It is worth noting, in this regard, that rigorous evaluations of the SRB's work, including in the area of preventive activities, have been published by the European Court of Auditors (ECA), which is under an on-going obligation to assess the SRB's activities and financing practices. Presenting, in part, a rather critical analysis of the status quo, the relevant reports, to the extent that they have been published (e.g. ECA, 2017, 2021), represent a very useful source of information which complements the reporting by SRB.

All the same, it remains entirely impossible, based on publicly available data, to fully assess the practical dimension of relevant activities, let alone their impact on institutions' business models and corporate structures. Given the potential of relevant powers to trigger far-reaching changes in this regard which, if used expansively, could fundamentally change market structures across the eurozone and the EU as a whole (see, for further discussion, Binder, 2015b, 2016a), the significance of preventive measures adopted by the SRB can hardly be underestimated, which renders the absence of reliable information all the more deplorable. It should be noted that none of the foregoing should be misread as belittling the SRB's efforts in the area. In all likelihood, the identification of potential strategies for future resolution cases and the removal of foreseeable impediments in this regard in cooperation between the SRB and the relevant credit institution, as well as the gradual build-up of MREL buffers, i.e. the creation of financial buffers by banks designated to be used in future bail-ins, across the EBU can be expected to have made an important contribution to enhancing the resilience of the relevant banking systems and thus the preservation of financial stability within the eurozone.

25.3.2 *The (Un)Happy Few: What Can Be Learnt from the First Resolution Decisions?*

If then, with regard to the preventive stage, it remains impossible to formulate a meaningful analysis of what has and has not been achieved over the first five years of the SRB's existence, the

[14] See www.srb.europa.eu/en/content/mrel.

[15] It should be noted that an edited version of the group resolution plan has been published in relation to Banco Popular Español SA, which went into resolution in 2017 (see SRB, 2016).

situation with regard to the *reactive* stage – i.e. resolution actions proper – is hardly more certain. While a number of decisions on the initiation of resolution actions have been taken with regard to individual banks under the supervision of the SSM, in only two cases so far, involving Banco Popular Español SA (in 2017, SRB, 2017a) as well as Sberbank d.d. and Sberbank banka d.d. (in 2022, SRB, 2022a, 2022b), the SRB actually adopted resolution schemes pursuant to Article 23 SRMR and thus initiated a regular resolution procedure as prescribed by the SRM Regulation. By contrast, in two cases originating from Italy, involving Banca Popolare di Vicenza S.p.A. and Veneto Banca S.p.A., the SRB decided *not* to take resolution on the grounds that neither institution provided critical functions, their failure was unlikely to result in significant adverse effects on financial stability, and that, consequently, the 'Public Interest' test required by Article 18(1)(c), (5) SRMR was not fulfilled (SRB, 2017b, 2017c). Both institutions were then liquidated in insolvency proceedings pursuant to Italian law, to which the Italian state contributed extraordinary financial support of €17 billion to facilitate the process and fund special protection for senior creditors who had invested in debt securities issued by the two institutions (see di Goia-Callabrese, 2021; Donnelly and Asimakopoulos, 2019; European Commission, 2017; Ferrarini and Piantelli, 2020, paras. 12.40–12.63; Miglionico, 2018; Stanghellini, 2016). Similarly, in February 2018, the SRB decided not to take resolution action against ABLV Bank A.S., of Latvia, and its subsidiary ABLV Bank Luxembourg S.A., again on the grounds that the public interest was not met, given the institutions' limited role in the markets (SRB, 2018a, 2018b). Likewise, the 'public interest' assessment ended the 2019 case of AS PNB Banka, in August 2019 (SRB, 2019). In yet another controversial case, involving the Italian bank Monte dei Paschi di Siena, resolution was avoided altogether by way of a precautionary recapitalization pursuant to Article 18(4)(d)(iii) SRMR (see e.g. di Goia-Callabrese, 2021, pp. 100–102; Ferrarini and Piantelli, 2020, paras. 12.36–12.39; Hadjiemmanuil, 2017; Miglionico, 2018).

25.3.2.1 Substantive and Procedural Aspects

In substantive and procedural terms, although certainly limited in number and scope, these first cases have revealed important insights into both the strengths and, in particular, the weaknesses of the resolution framework in general and the use of the resolution toolbox in particular (see generally, e.g., Binder, 2019; Morais, 2019). In particular, the following aspects are worth highlighting.

First, at a very fundamental level, it has become obvious that the classification of a credit institution as 'significant' within the meaning of Article 6 SSMR, and thus as potentially falling within the direct responsibility of the SRB pursuant to Article 7(2) SRMR, should not, for the time being, be interpreted as a guarantee that the insolvency of that institution would automatically result in the application of the new resolution framework under the auspices of the SRM. Instead, as demonstrated by the SRB's decision in the *Banca Popolare di Vicenza*, *Veneto Banca*, *ABLV*, and *PNB* cases mentioned, the Board has chosen to apply the Public Interest Assessment (PIA) – the fundamental test of whether a failing institution can be liquidated under national insolvency law without systemic repercussions – on a case-by-case basis and to engage in a detailed assessment of the likely impact of its liquidation on the 'resolution objectives' (Article 18 (5) in conjunction with Article 14(2) SRMR), including, most notably, the preservation of 'critical functions' of credit institutions and the preservation of systemic stability. This approach may have come as a surprise to observers, who may have assumed that the classification of an institution as 'significant' would per se justify the application of the new resolution framework, thus allocating the full responsibility for crisis management to the European level and facilitating the use of the SRF as a source of funding for the resolution costs. A restrictive interpretation of the PIA is nonetheless perfectly justifiable in light of the underlying policy rationale. Along with other conditions for resolution, the PIA has been designed so as to ensure proportionality of resolution actions. As the new resolution toolbox, in comparison with more traditional instruments for the management of insolvencies of financial institutions, comes with a rather wide range of powers for the resolution authority on the one hand and very limited creditor participation on the other, its application should be restricted to cases where the public interest in the preservation of financial stability outweighs the rights of individual stakeholders, which is precisely what the PIA is intended to ensure (see, for further discussion, Binder, 2019, pp. 306–308, 2020, pp. 459–472, 2021, pp. 558–560). If, consequently, smaller institutions under the direct supervision of the ECB have been, and likely will be, resolved outside the framework established by the SRMR, under *national* laws and under the auspices of *national* authorities and courts, this result is difficult to reconcile with the overarching policy objective to *centralize* decision-making powers at least in relation to the most significant banks within the eurozone. This is unsatisfactory in view of the existing differences between national insolvency laws and resolution strategies for banks not falling within the direct responsibility of the SRB. While it remains to be seen whether, and how, the SRB will, over time, adjust its interpretation of the PIA,[16] the resulting gap between centralized resolution under the auspices of the SRM on the one hand and national insolvency liquidation on the other may eventually be closed by a comprehensive reform of national bank insolvency frameworks within the EU with or without a further centralization of decision-making powers within the eurozone.

Second, the *Banco Popular* case, as one of two resolution actions implemented so far, offers only limited information as to the relevance of the individual resolution tools in future cases (Binder, 2019). Following a drastic write-down of equity and capital instruments, the institution was sold under the 'sale of business tool' (Articles 22(2)(a), 24 SRMR) to Banco Santander S.A., a competitor operating in the same market. The use of the write-down powers, in this case, clearly demonstrated their effectiveness as a means of allocating losses to shareholders and investors in capital instruments. Their quantitative calibration, however, on the basis of a valuation report that put the equity of the institution 'in a range between € 1.3 bn and € –8.2 with our best estimate within that range being € –2.0 bn' (Deloitte, 2017, p. 4), also illustrated the immense difficulties involved in value verification of a failing institution within a short timeframe, which proved highly controversial and resulted in a host of litigation, inter alia, before the European Court of Justice.[17] Even more significant is the fact that the resolution scheme ultimately adopted in this case deviated from the strategy originally identified in the group resolution plan adopted pursuant to Article 8 SRMR, which had anticipated the implementation of a bail-in (SRB, 2016, pp. 24–25, noting that '[v]ariant strategies based on other tool [sic!] than the bail-in tool had not been considered'). Thus, while the sale of Banco Popular to Santander clearly proved to be an effective instrument to facilitate an orderly resolution without disruptions in the failing bank's relationships with clients, professional counterparties, and financial market infrastructures, the practicability of the bail-in tool – designed specifically for cases where neither a sale of business nor the application of the bridge institution – continues to be untested, which is particularly problematic because neither a sale of business transaction nor the transfer to a bridge institution might work in the case of a very large, systemically relevant institution that

[16] Some aspects of the PIA have been under revision of late, see Laviola (2021, 2022).

[17] See, for a useful overview of pending litigation, https://ebi-europa.eu/publications/eu-cases-or-jurisprudence.

operates across a number of jurisdictions (see, for further discussion, Binder, 2019, pp. 312–316).

25.3.2.2 Institutional Aspects

In institutional terms, progress has been remarkable. Having started, literally, from scratch following the adoption of the legal foundation back in 2014, the SRB, having become operational from 2015 and fully assuming its powers from 2016, with a workforce of close to 400 permanent and temporary professionals (see SRB, 2021b, pp. 48–49), clearly has turned into a highly capable and effective supranational actor, which has by now successfully overseen two resolution cases and taken a wide range of decisions with regard to preventive measures. Moreover, the institutional build-up of the SRB (and the SRF) has obviously been matched by the establishment of effective procedures which, in principle, should facilitate a smooth and swift inter-agency cooperation with all other relevant players, as evidenced not least by the adoption of resolution actions within a matter of a few days. This is particularly noteworthy because both effective preventive measures and the swift and effective implementation of resolution measures, within the framework established by the SRMR, depend on cooperation with (a) the ECB and the SRM,[18] (b) the Commission, including in its capacity as authority responsible for monitoring compliance with the EU State Aid regime,[19] and the Council, in the process leading to the adoption of resolution schemes pursuant to Article 18(7) SRMR, (c) national resolution authorities,[20] and, ultimately, (d) the ESM under the backstop arrangement.[21]

To date, all actors appear to have exercised their powers within this framework in a sufficiently flexible way, and to have cooperated without disruptions. Illustrative was the *Banco Popular* case, where the ECB's determination that the institution was 'failing or likely to fail' for the purposes of Article 18(1) SRMR was immediately followed by the adoption of the resolution scheme, and its implementation on the following day[22] – clearly an impressive course of events which demonstrates the institutional capacity to act without undue delay in the face of a dramatic deterioration of the relevant institution's finances.

Even *if* institutions and procedures proved sufficiently reliable in a case where all relevant actors appear to have been in broad agreement not just regarding the *need* to act, but also regarding the appropriate response, it would nevertheless be premature to conclude that a similar outcome can always be taken for granted. Especially in cases where political interests are at stake, e.g. in the insolvency of a very large banking institution with a sizeable share in a Member State's domestic market, it is at least conceivable that political disagreement between that state's government and the SRB could translate into disagreement with potentially obstructive implications, in both the preparation and implementation of resolution schemes. As has

18 See, in particular, Arts. 8(2) and (13) (consultation with regard to resolution plans), 10(1), (2), (7) (consultation with regard to the assessment of resolvability), 10a(2) and (3) (consultation before restrictions on payments to shareholders), 12(1) and (6), 12c(9), 12d(1) and (3), 12g(1) (consultation prior to the setting of MREL), 13 (collaboration with regard to the exercise of early intervention powers), 18(1) (division of powers with regard to the determination that an institution is 'failing or likely to fail' as the fundamental precondition to the initiation of resolution actions), 21(1) and (2) (division of powers with regard to the write-down and conversion of capital instruments) and 30 (general rules of cooperation) SRMR.

19 See Art. 19(3) SRMR.

20 See, generally, Art. 31 SRMR.

21 See, generally, e.g. Busch (2020, paras. 9.97–9.120); Tröger and Kotovskaia (2022).

22 See www.srb.europa.eu/en/node/315.

been pointed out in a recent paper, neither the voting rules prescribed by the SRMR nor the existence of the SRF as a supranational source of funding should be relied upon as precluding such effects in all conceivable scenarios (Tröger and Kotovskaia, 2022). With national incentives – e.g. favouring the protection of national 'champions' against interference by European authorities or the protection of specific (groups of) national stakeholders against the economic outcomes of resolution actions – still alive, it certainly remains to be seen whether national players (governments or national resolution authorities) will in all cases be prepared to fully accept SRB's decisions, and to implement them against the resistance of national constituents. Although practical experience with the institutional and procedural framework has to date been rather positive, the real test for its reliability could yet occur. It remains to be seen, in other words, if the institutional and procedural framework will ultimately prove sufficiently resilient also in the face of potential impediments to the use of the resolution toolbox in cases where potentially overwhelming political economy pressures might stand in the way of its application that may come with substantial costs to vested interests in the respective Member States.

25.3.3 *The Looming Ghost of the (Not So Distant) Past: Legacy Problems in the Context of the SRM*

The concerns discussed are all the more pressing in light of residual problems associated with the massive accumulation of non-performing loans (NPLs) in the banking system of certain Member States that have both motivated and burdened the development of the EBU ever since its conception during, and in the immediate aftermath of, the eurozone crisis.[23] Already during the political negotiations leading up to the adoption of the legal framework, concerns had been voiced that its creation without a prior restructuring of the legacy problems affecting some banking systems in the European south could damage the capacity of the new framework to operate effectively (see, for an early assessment, Buch and Weigert, 2012).

As discussed elsewhere, there are reasons to assume that the functional limits of the new resolution toolbox will be particularly strong in the context of system-wide distress, where the financial sector as a whole is adversely affected by more general macroeconomic problems (see, for a more detailed analysis, Binder, 2019; see also Lamandini et al., 2018, pp. 239–256). In a setting where an entire financial system suffers, applying the sale of business tool according to the book to any one failing institution will likely be difficult, as competitor institutions both willing to assume the additional business, and financially sound enough to actually be capable of doing so, will be rare in distressed markets. While the application of the bridge institution tool could help to overcome this problem, the simultaneous creation and operation of a number of bridge institutions in relation to a number of failing institutions in distressed markets may well prove impossible to orchestrate and finance in such circumstances. Whether the bail-in tool could be used as an alternative in relevant cases also remains an open question. Its potential weaknesses discussed before may be particularly problematic in distressed markets, where both public and wholesale investor confidence is wanting, and where the broader economic implications of burden-sharing by stakeholders may be difficult to control.

In principle, the use of asset management vehicles set up by public authorities, the core element of the asset separation tool (Article 26 SRMR), would commend itself precisely in such scenarios. In fact, the transfer of entire portfolios of problem assets out of banks' balance sheets to

[23] For a recent survey of the dimension of structural NPL problems within the EU, see Lamandini et al. (2018, pp. 236–239).

designated asset management vehicles, set up for the purposes of managing, and gradually winding down, the relevant assets without disruption to the provision of critical banking services on the one hand and to the broader economy as a whole has been used widely in systemic banking crises across a wide range of jurisdictions for some time (for a detailed review of past experience, see Binder, 2016b, para. 2.5.2; Brescia Morra et al., 2021; Grünewald and Louisse, 2022).

These considerations are also consistent with the recent initiative for the adoption of comprehensive strategies addressing systemic non-performing loans in the Member States by the European Commission, which include recommendations for the use of asset management vehicles (European Commission, 2018a, 2018b; Lamandini et al., 2018, pp. 257–262). However, as discussed elsewhere (Binder, 2019, pp. 312–313, 2022, paras. 4–6), given that the use of asset management vehicles to remedy structural problems in national banking systems will inevitably have to be orchestrated, and funded, with substantial involvement of national governments and authorities, it is hardly conceivable that the implementation of resolution actions involving the use of the asset separation tool could ever be initiated under the auspices of the SRM in the same way as the use of other resolution instruments. In sum, although the resolution toolbox established by the SRMR (and the BRRD) *would* provide an effective remedy for structural problems with NPL, facilitating their effective removal from banks' balance sheets, and thus the recovery of banks' lending capacity, the de facto conditions render its comprehensive use almost impossible within the given procedural framework. Despite the (theoretical) availability of the tool it would follow that comprehensive solutions to the problem *within* the institutional setting established by the SRM, in compliance with the procedural requirements for resolution actions under its auspices, are hardly conceivable. If and to the extent that the existence of structural NPL problems, as discussed before, stand in the way of the full use of the resolution toolbox for the management of individual bank failures in the respective jurisdictions, this result clearly comes with substantial repercussions on the viability of the SRM as a whole. In those jurisdictions whose banking systems continue to be burdened by unsustainable levels of non-performing loans, resorting to the formal resolution tools (other than the use of asset management tools), given their focus on idiosyncratic failures, may prove infeasible and potentially outright counterproductive, as no remedy could work without addressing the fundamental problem in the first place.

25.4 THE CURRENT REFORM AGENDA: EDIS AND THE FURTHER HARMONIZATION OF BANK INSOLVENCY LAWS

In the light of the considerations developed earlier, it is hardly surprising that additional steps towards further harmonization of the institutional and procedural framework for the management of bank failures within the eurozone have been discussed for some time. While a detailed analysis of these proposals would be outside the scope of this chapter, some aspects are nonetheless worth noting. Against this backdrop, the following subsections briefly address, in turn, the on-going discussion of proposals for the creation of a European Deposit Insurance Scheme as a 'third pillar' of the EBU (Section 25.4.1), and the more recent policy discussion promoting the integration of resolution frameworks also for less significant institutions (Section 25.4.2).

25.4.1 *EDIS*

Deposit guarantee schemes have been a core element of national approaches to addressing the systemic implications of banking business (collectively referred to as 'safety nets' for the banking sector) across most jurisdictions worldwide for decades (for a representative survey, see Demirgüç-Kunt and Detragiache, 2002; for a concise summary of the functions, see Colaert and Bens, 2020, para. 14.04; Kleftouri, 2015, ch. 1). The introduction of mandatory deposit guarantee schemes had already been prescribed, for the EU as a whole, by Directive 94/19/EC,[24] later superseded by Directive 2014/49/EU.[25] While both instruments provided for the mandatory protection of depositors in the case of an insolvency of their bank, the 2014 reform reinforced that further, including by more restrictive provisions on banks' contributions to the respective scheme (see, for further discussion, Kleftouri, 2015, paras. 3.28–3.41). Nonetheless, in light of substantial structural differences between the existing national schemes, including, in particular, the number and size of participating banks and the size of the available financial resources, it is widely agreed that the effective level of protection afforded to depositors, and the sustainability of the respective schemes, particularly in the context of a multitude of failures within a short period of time, continue to differ widely across Member States, weakening not just the position of depositors in comparison with their peers in other jurisdictions with stronger systems, but also the competitiveness of individual banking sectors within the eurozone (Colaert and Bens, 2020, paras. 14.15 and 14.16).[26]

Against this backdrop, it should not come as a surprise that the creation of an integrated deposit guarantee framework as a corollary to the SSM and the SRM has been promoted from the outset (Fonteyne et al., 2010, pp. 52–53; see also Binder, 2015a, pp. 2–4; Colaert and Bens, 2020, paras. 14.02, 14.20–14.32). A Commission proposal for the creation of a European Deposit Insurance Scheme was published in November 2015, aiming at the gradual development of common deposit insurance, which would initially create a reinsurance scheme, followed by transfer into a co-insurance scheme and, finally, a full insurance scheme (European Commission, 2015, p. 8; for a detailed assessment, see Brescia-Morra, 2019, pp. 396–397 and 405–407; Colaert and Bens, 2020, paras. 14.22–14.26, 14.33–14.68). For a number of reasons, however, the political process since then has been burdensome, and failed to produce agreement as yet (Colaert and Bens, 2020, paras. 14.30–14.30, Ríos Camacho, Chapter 24 in this volume).[27] Resistance to the mutualization of deposit guarantee schemes has been particularly strong in northern euro area Member States. Not least because of residual NPL problems in several Member States, the opposition has expressed concerns that this might lead to cross-subsidiarization of weaker by stronger banking systems, despite all the subsequent proposals to mitigate such problems (Colaert and Bens, 2020, paras. 14.30–14.32). Independently from these considerations, it has also been debated whether Article 114 TFEU, which had also been used as the legal basis for the creation of the SRB, would provide a

[24] Directive 94/19/EC of the European Parliament and of the Council of 30 May 1994 on deposit-guarantee schemes, OJ L 135, p. 5.

[25] Directive 2014/49/EU of the European Parliament and of the Council of 16 April 2014 on deposit guarantee schemes, OJ L 173, p. 149.

[26] See also European Commission (2015, p. 6): 'In the Banking Union, deposit insurance remains purely national, which leaves national DGSs vulnerable to large local shocks and Member States' budgets continue to be exposed to risks in their banking sectors. This prevents the realisation of the full benefits of the internal market and of the Banking Union and potentially negatively affects depositor confidence and the rights of establishment of credit institutions and depositors. DGSs are in place in all Member States, as required by the DGS Directive. Although they already share some common aspects regarding their main features and their functioning, important aspects are still left at the discretion of Member States. Member States can also authorise, upon approval by the European Commission, reduced target levels for available financial means. The differences in funding levels and size of the existing 38 DGSs in the EU may negatively affect depositors' confidence and could impair the functioning of the internal market.'

[27] For an account of the most recent developments, see Council of the European Union, Information Note regarding 2015/0270(COD) (EF 36 ECOFIN 93 CODEC 122) (3 February 2022).

sufficient legal basis for the adoption of the EDIS regulation (Brescia-Morra, 2019, pp. 401–405).

In light of these lengthy debates it seems inconceivable that the proposals will move forward in the absence of a comprehensive solution for the on-going problem of specific national banking systems suffering from structural non-performing loans discussed before. The controversial issue of mutualization of resources, in this context, clearly reflects broader concerns about the implications of further integration in highly heterogenous banking systems, but also about the systemic soundness of several banking systems. Even if and to the extent that progress has been made towards reduction of systemic NPL levels in recent years (Brescia-Morra, 2019, pp. 398–400), such concerns are probably unlikely to fade away soon, and the political case for integration is likely to remain controversial irrespective of the underlying economic rationale in general and the merits of having a coinsurance scheme with the broadest possible funding base in particular. Moreover, unresolved problems pertaining to residual differences between the insolvency laws of participating Member States, which also have a bearing on the economic outcomes of liquidation procedures for banks that are not resolved under the auspices of the SRM, stand in the way of political agreement in this regard (Binder et al., 2019, pp. 194–198; Brescia-Morra, 2019, p. 399). Given these differences, it may be premature to expect a reliable commitment to the integration of DGS arrangements on the part of all participating Member States anytime soon.[28]

25.4.2 *Further Harmonization of Bank Insolvency Laws*

Much the same assessment is probably warranted regarding recent proposals for an even more comprehensive institutional, substantive, and procedural reform aiming at the further harmonization of bank insolvency procedures for *all* banks operating within the eurozone, i.e. irrespective of the current delineation of powers between the SRB and national authorities, and irrespective also of the PIA as it currently stands. Some authors have promoted targeted reforms of the status quo – including by removing the PIA requirement so as to broaden the scope of the SRM (see, in particular, Schillig, 2020; see also Restoy et al., 2020; VVA et al., 2019). Other proposals have been considerably more ambitious, promoting a fully fledged harmonization of national insolvency regimes that would be coupled with the further centralization of decision-making powers, allocated either to the SRB (Sciascia, 2020), or to a new institution, modelled to some extent after the US Federal Deposit Insurance Corporation (FDIC), that would combine the functions of a DGS and a resolution authority (Gelpern and Véron, 2019; see also De Aldisio et al., 2019; European Parliament, 2019; Huertas, 2021; Restoy et al., 2020, pp. 20–21; VVA et al., 2019, pp. 56–60). The European Commission carried out a comprehensive public consultation addressing both procedural and institutional aspects in 2020,[29] but has not published any legislative proposals in the field so far.

To be sure, the concept of further institutional convergence between providers of deposit guarantees and resolution functions is not new (see, for an early proposal, Gros and Schoenmaker, 2014). All the same, given the need to reconcile liquidation regimes with national substantive law regimes (e.g. in the areas of property and company law) and insolvency

[28] See, for a rather bleak assessment from an insider's perspective, also *Börsen-Zeitung*, Interview with Elke König, Chair of the SRB (17 November 2021).

[29] See https://ec.europa.eu/info/law/better-regulation/have-your-say/initiatives/12737-Banking-Union-Review-of-the-bank-crisis-management-and-deposit-insuranceframework-DGSD-review-/public-consultation.

frameworks, already the creation of a fully integrated insolvency regime for *all* banks, irrespective of their size and market share, applicable across the eurozone or the EU, could well prove even more ambitious than the creation of the SRM as a whole, whose focus on 'significant' institutions facilitates concentration on relatively large banks with similar corporate structures or more homogenous business models. While international standards in this regard are currently being developed under the auspices of UNIDROIT,[30] it is worth noting that consensus about both fundamental features of such regimes and technical details hardly exists. In view of highly diverse market structures such consensus could arguably develop only gradually and on the basis of comprehensive comparative analyses of the existing frameworks (see, for further discussion, Binder, 2021, pp. 563–565, 578–581). It should be borne in mind that the question how the institutional and legal foundations of the SRM could, and should, develop further over the years to come is *not* confined to the division of powers between the European and the national levels, but is deeply intertwined and charged with problems of a more fundamental nature: Which are the functional requirements bank insolvency regimes should be designed to meet? In view of highly divergent approaches and policies observable across the EU, what should be the institutional and procedural relationship of such regimes with the general legal and institutional framework for corporate insolvency? Specifically, should the management of insolvencies in the financial sector be entrusted to administrative agencies or to the general insolvency courts, with or without the involvement of private sector insolvency officials?

While it should be possible to reach broad consensus that the 'single' mechanisms for preventing and managing systemic risks in the banking sector created with the EBU are far from being uniform and, hence, give rise to substantial problems for the treatment of both 'significant' and 'less significant' failing institutions, the adoption and implementation of an altogether new framework would clearly be a particularly daunting task. In theory, a comprehensive reform, including both centralization of powers *and* a common liquidation and resolution toolbox, would commend itself as an effective remedy to the shortcomings identified in relation to the present arrangements. However, in order to be acceptable to Member States, any legislative proposal would have to balance carefully the existing controversies among the Member States over the appropriate level of centralization of powers, as well as technical difficulties to be overcome in view of the interplay between the existing national institutional, procedural, and substantive approaches, developed path-dependently over decades (Binder, 2021, p. 587). The fact that political progress in relation to the EDIS proposals, with which a broader institutional and procedural overhaul would have to be realigned, has stalled for some time now, certainly does not inspire much optimism in this respect.

25.5 CONCLUSIONS

It should be stressed that none of the considerations developed here should be (mis)interpreted as an attempt to belittle the progress made in the creation of the SRM since 2014. While a host of unresolved problems and loose ends in terms of its interplay with national laws and institutions can be identified with regard to the preventive stage, but also, and particularly with regard to the SRM as a whole, the case for the centralization of powers remains strong at least for those banks whose failure – owing to their size, market share and business activities – would present substantial problems to public budgets within their own Member State and for the preservation of financial stability within and beyond that jurisdiction. Moreover, it is certainly

[30] See www.unidroit.org/work-in-progress/bank-insolvency/.

plausible to assume that the exercise of the SRB's powers to address impediments to swift and effective resolution in institutions within its remit will, in all likelihood, trigger a welcome trend to enhance the resolvability of banks and thus, ultimately, the chance that they can be resolved without major exposures to public budgets in the future.

Still, both the limited use of the resolution toolbox and the residual deficiencies and limitations discussed may provoke the fundamental question whether the success achieved justifies the costs incurred so far. To be sure, the costs incurred as a result of both the creation and the on-going operation of the institutional and procedural framework for Member States and market participants are, in all likelihood, impossible to quantify with a reasonable degree of precision. At the same time, the framework's capacity to prevent any further large-scale exposure to public budgets in the event of large failures and, in particular, system-wide financial crisis is difficult to predict with certainty. Thus, even though the social costs triggered by the extraordinary burden on national economies and public budgets were measurable, the question whether benefits outweigh the financial efforts incurred in the course of the creation of the SRM and the relevant institutions, as well as in the on-going operation on market participants and public budgets remains open. Highly speculative though it certainly is, the question might still remain worth asking, in particular in view of the even more ambitious reforms discussed in Section 25.4. Be that as it may, the EBU, in all likelihood, will remain a moving target. It is currently at a crossroads and, even if only part of the reform agenda should ultimately succeed, is likely to change dramatically in years to come.

REFERENCES

Aerz, J., and Bizarro, P. (2020). The reform of the European Stability Mechanism. *Capital Markets Law Journal* 15, 159–174.

BCBS (Basel Committee on Banking Supervision) (2010). Report and Recommendations of the Cross-border Bank Resolution Group. March 2010. www.bis.org/publ/bcbs169.pdf

Binder, J.-H. (2015a). The European Banking Union – Rationale and key policy issues. In J.-H. Binder and C. Gortsos (eds.), *Banking Union: A Compendium*. Baden-Baden: Nomos, pp. 1–16.

Binder, J.-H. (2015b). The Banking Union and the governance of credit institutions. *European Business Organization Law Review* 16, 469–490.

Binder, J.-H. (2016a). Resolution planning and structural bank reform within the Banking Union. In J. E. Castañeda, D. G. Mayes, and G. Wood (eds.), *European Banking Union: Prospects and Challenges*. London: Routledge, pp. 129–155.

Binder, J.-H. (2016b). Resolution: Concepts, requirements, and tools. In J.-H. Binder and D. Singh (eds.), *Bank Resolution: The European Regime*. Oxford: Oxford University Press, pp. 25–59.

Binder, J.-H. (2016c). The position of creditors under the BRRD. In Bank of Greece (ed.), *Commemorative Volume for Leonidas Georgakopoulos*, Vol. 1. Athens: Bank of Greece, pp. 37–61.

Binder, J.-H. (2019). The relevance of the resolution tools within the single resolution mechanism. In M. P. Chiti and V. Santoro (eds.), *The Palgrave Handbook of European Banking Union Law*. Cham: Palgrave Macmillan, pp. 299–320.

Binder, J.-H. (2020). Proportionality at the resolution stage: Calibration of resolution measures and the public interest test. *European Business Organization Law Review* 21, 453–474.

Binder, J.-H. (2021). Towards harmonised frameworks for the liquidation of non-systemically relevant credit institutions in the EU? A discussion of policy choices and potential impediments. *European Company and Financial Law Review* 18, 555–587.

Binder, J.-H. (2022). Art. 26 SRMR. In J. H. Binder, C. Gortsos, K. Lackhoff, and C. Ohler (eds.), *Brussels Commentary European Banking Union*. Baden-Baden: Nomos, pp. 759–762.

Binder, J.-H., Krimminger, M., Nieto, M., and Singh, D. (2019). The choice between judicial and administrative sanctioned procedures to manage liquidation of banks: a transatlantic perspective. *Capital Markets Law Journal* 14, 178–216.

Brescia Morra, C. (2019). The third pillar of the banking union and its troubled implementation. In M. P. Chiti and V. Santoro (eds.), *The Palgrave Handbook of European Banking Union Law*. Cham: Palgrave Macmillan, pp. 393–407.

Brescia Morra, C., et al. (2021). Non-performing loans – New risks and policies? What factors drive the performance of national asset management companies? Study requested by the ECON Committee of the European Parliament. www.europarl.europa.eu/RegData/etudes/STUD/2021/651390/IPOL_STU(2021)651390_EN.pdf

Buch, C. and Weigert, B. (2012). Legacy problems in transition to a banking union. In T. Beck (ed.), *Banking Union for Europe: Risks and Challenges*. Brussels: Centre for Economic Policy Research, pp. 25–35.

Busch, D. (2020). Governance of the single resolution scheme. In D. Busch and G. Ferrarini (eds.), *European Banking Union*, 2nd ed. Oxford: Oxford University Press, pp. 343–401.

Colaert, V. and Bens, G. (2020). European Deposit Insurance System (EDIS) – Cornerstone of the banking union or dead end? In D. Busch and G. Ferrarini (eds.), *European Banking Union*, 2nd ed. Oxford: Oxford University Press, pp. 541–575.

De Aldisio, A., et al. (2019). Towards a framework for orderly liquidation of banks in the EU. *Banca d'Italia Notes on Financial Stability and Supervision* No. 15. www.bancaditalia.it/pubblicazioni/note-stabilita/2019-0015/Note-stabilita-finanziaria-n15.pdf?language_id=1

Di Goia-Callabrese, P. (2021). Bail-in: Do Italians do it better (or worse, or not at all)? *European Business Law Review* 32, 93–116.

Deloitte (2017). Hippocrates Provisional Report (Sale of Business Scenario). [i.e. provisional valuation report in relation to Banco Popular], 6 June . www.srb.europa.eu/system/files/media/document/Valuation%202%20report%20-%20Hippocrates%20Provisional%20Valuation%20Report.pdf

Demirgüç-Kunt, A., and Detragiache, E. (2002). Does deposit insurance increase banking system stability? An empirical investigation. *Journal of Monetary Economics* 49, 1373–1406.

Donnelly, S., and Asimakopoulos, I. G. (2019). Bending and breaking the single resolution mechanism: The case of Italy. *Journal of Common Market Studies* 57 1–16.

ECA (European Court of Auditors) (2017). Special Report – Single Resolution Board: Work on a challenging Banking Union task started, but still a long way to go. www.eca.europa.eu/lists/ecadocuments/sr17_23/sr_srb-bu_en.pdf

ECA (2021). Special Report – Resolution planning in the Single Resolution Mechanism. www.eca.europa.eu/lists/ecadocuments/sr21_01/sr_single_resolution_mechanism_en.pdf

European Commission (2015). Proposal for a Regulation of the European Parliament and of the Council amending Regulation (EU) 806/2014 in order to establish a European Deposit Insurance Scheme, COM(2015) 586 final, 24 November.

European Commission (2017). European Commission, Decision: State Aid SA. 45664 (2017/N) – Italy – Orderly liquidation of Banca Popolare di Vicenza and Veneto Banca – Liquidation aid (25 June 2017), C(2017) 4501 final.

European Commission (2018a). Proposal for a Directive of the European Parliament and of the Council on credit servicers, credit purchasers and the recovery of collateral, COM(2018) 135 final.

European Commission (2018b). Commission Staff Working Document: 'AMC Blueprint' of 14 March 2018 (SWD(2018) 72 final.

European Parliament (2019). In-depth analysis: Liquidation of banks: Towards an 'FDIC' for the Banking Union? February. www.europarl.europa.eu/RegData/etudes/IDAN/2019/634385/IPOL_IDA(2019)634385_EN.pdf

Ferrarini, G., and Piantelli, A. M. (2020). Bank resolution in practice – Analysis of early European cases. In D. Busch and G. Ferrarini (eds.), *European Banking Union*, 2nd ed. Oxford: Oxford University Press, pp. 475–511.

Fonteyne, W., et al. (2010). Crisis management and resolution for a European banking system. IMF Working Paper WP/10/70. www.imf.org/external/pubs/ft/wp/2010/wp1070.pdf

FSB (Financial Stability Board) (2011/2014). Key attributes of effective resolution regimes for financial institutions. October. www.financialstabilityboard.org/publications/r_111104cc.pdf; updated October 2014 www.financialstabilityboard.org/wp-content/uploads/r_141015.pdf

Gardella, A. (2020). Bail-in: Preparedness and execution. In D. Busch and G. Ferrarini (eds.), *European Banking Union*, 2nd ed. Oxford: Oxford University Press, pp. 451–474.

Gelpern, A., and Véron, N. (2019). An effective regime for non-viable banks: US experience and considerations for EU reform – Banking union scrutiny. Study requested by the ECON Committee of the European Parliament. www.europarl.europa.eu/RegData/etudes/STUD/2019/624432/IPOL_STU(2019)624432_EN.pdf

Gortsos, C. (2022a). Introduction to Arts. 67–74 SRMR. In J. H. Binder, C. Gortsos, K. Lackhoff, and C. Ohler (eds.), *Brussels Commentary European Banking Union*. Baden-Baden: Nomos, pp. 1075–1084.

Gortsos, C. (2022b). Art. 74 SRMR. In J. H. Binder, C. Gortsos, K. Lackhoff, and C. Ohler (eds.), *Brussels Commentary European Banking Union*. Baden-Baden: Nomos, pp. 1112–1119.

Gros, D., and Schoenmaker, D. (2014). European deposit insurance and resolution in the banking union. *Journal of Common Market Studies* 52, 529–546.

Grünewald, S., and Louisse, M. (2022). How asset management companies can help tackle the NPL crisis – A state aid perspective within the resolution framework. EBI Working Paper No. 109. https://ssrn.com/abstract=3999059

Hadjiemmanuil, C. (2017). Limits on state-funded bailouts in the EU bank resolution regime (2017). European Banking Institute Working Paper Series 2017 No. 2. https://ssrn.com/abstract=2912165

Haentjens, M. (2022). Arts. 12–12k SRMR. In J. H. Binder, C. Gortsos, K. Lackhoff, and C. Ohler (eds.), *Brussels Commentary European Banking Union*. Baden-Baden: Nomos, pp. 570–604.

Huertas, T. (2021). Reset required: The euro area crisis management and deposit insurance framework. SAFE White Paper No. 85. https://safe-frankfurt.de/fileadmin/user_upload/editor_common/Policy_Center/SAFE_White_Paper_85.pdf

Kleftouri, N. (2015). *Deposit Protection and Bank Resolution*. Oxford: Oxford University Press.

Lamandini, M., and Ramos Muñoz, D. (2019). Minimum requirement for own capital and eligible liabilities. In M. P. Chiti and V. Santoro (eds.), *The Palgrave Handbook of European Banking Union Law*. Cham: Palgrave Macmillan, pp. 321–348.

Lamandini, M., Lusignani, G., and Muñoz, D. R. (2018). Does Europe have what it takes to finish the banking union? *Columbia Journal of European Law* 24, 233–289.

Laviola, S. (2021). System-wide events in the Public Interest Assessment. The SRB blog, 31 May. www.srb.europa.eu/en/content/system-wide-events-public-interest-assessment

Laviola, S. (2022). The public interest assessment and bank-insurance contagion. The SRB blog, 26 January. www.srb.europa.eu/en/content/public-interest-assessment-and-bank-insurance-contagion

Miglionico, A. (2018). Rescuing failing banks for financial stability: The unintended outcomes of bail-in rules. *International Company and Commercial Law Review* 29(10), 608–617.

Morais, L. S. (2019). Lessons from the first resolution experiences in the context of banking recovery and resolution directive. In M. P. Chiti and V. Santoro (eds.), *The Palgrave Handbook of European Banking Union Law*. Cham: Palgrave Macmillan, pp. 371–391.

Restoy, F., Vrbaski, R., and Walters, R. (2020). Bank failure management in the European banking union: What's wrong and how to fix it. Financial Stability Institute Occasional Paper No. 15. www.bis.org/fsi/publ/insights10.pdf

Santoro, V., and Mecatti, I. (2019). Write-down and conversion of capital instruments. In M. P. Chiti and V. Santoro (eds.), *The Palgrave Handbook of European Banking Union Law*. Cham: Palgrave Macmillan, pp. 349–370.

Schillig, M. (2016). *Resolution and Insolvency of Banks and Financial Institutions*. Oxford: Oxford University Press.

Schillig, M. (2020). EU bank insolvency law harmonisation: What next? *International Insolvency Review* 30(2), 1–28.

Sciascia, G. (2020). Expanding the scope of the EU BRR framework: An administrative receivership for the banking union. https://ssrn.com/abstract=3748525

SRB (2016). The single resolution mechanism: Introduction to resolution planning. September. www.srb.europa.eu/system/files/media/document/intro_resplanning.pdf.pdf

SRB (2017a). Single Resolution Board, Decision of the Single Resolution Board in its executive session of 7 June 2017 concerning the adoption of a resolution scheme in respect of Banco Popular Español, S.A., … Addressed to FROB (SRB/EES/2017/08) (non-confidential version). https://srb.europa.eu/sites/srbsite/files/resolution_decision.pdf

SRB (2017b). Decision of the Single Resolution Board in its executive session of 23 June 2017 concerning the assessment of the conditions for resolution in respect of Veneto Banca S.p.A. … addressed to

Banca d'Italia in its capacity as National Resolution Authority (SRB/EES/2017/11) (non-confidential version). https://srb.europa.eu/sites/srbsite/files/srb-ees-2017-11_non-confidential.pdf

SRB (2017c). Decision of the Single Resolution Board in its executive session of 23 June 2017 concerning the assessment of the conditions for resolution in respect of Banca Popolare di Vicenza S.p.A. … addressed to Banca d'Italia in its capacity as National Resolution Authority (SRB/EES/2017/12) (non-confidential version). https://srb.europa.eu/sites/srbsite/files/srb-ees-2017-12_non-confidential.pdf

SRB (2018a). Single Resolution Board, Notice summarising the decision taken in respect of ABLV Bank, AS. https://srb.europa.eu/sites/srbsite/files/20180223-summary_decision_-_latvia.pdf

SRB (2018b). Single Resolution Board, Notice summarising the decision taken in respect of ABLV Bank Luxembourg S.A. https://srb.europa.eu/sites/srbsite/files/20180223_summary-decision_-_luxembourg.pdf

SRB (2019). Decision of the Single Resolution Board of 15 August 2019 concerning the assessment of the conditions for resolution in respect of AS PNB (SRB/EES/2019/131). www.srb.europa.eu/system/files/media/document/non-confidential_version_of_the_resolution_decision_in_relation_to_as_pnb_banka.pdf

SRB (2021a). 2021 resolution planning cycle (RPC) booklet. www.srb.europa.eu/system/files/media/document/srb_rpc_booklet_2021.pdf

SRB (2021b). Annual report 2020. www.srb.europa.eu/system/files/media/document/Annual%20Report%202020_Final_web.pdf

SRB (2022a). Notice summarising the decision taken in respect of Sberbank banka d.d. www.srb.europa.eu/system/files/media/document/20220103%20SRB%20Notice%20summarising%20the%20decision%20taken%20in%20respect%20of%20Sberbank%20banka%20d.d..pdf

SRB (2022b). Notice summarising the decision taken in respect of Sberbank d.d. www.srb.europa.eu/system/files/media/document/20220103%20SRB%20Notice%20summarising%20the%20decision%20taken%20in%20respect%20of%20Sberbank%20d.d._0.pdf

Stanghellini, L. (2016). The implementation of the BRRD in Italy and its first test: Policy implications. *Journal of Financial Regulation* 2, 154–161.

Teixeira, P. G. (2020). *The Legal History of the European Banking Union.* Oxford: Hart Publishing.

Tröger, T., and Kotovskaia, A. (2022): National interests and supranational resolution in the European Banking Union. SAFE Working Paper No. 340 / EBI Working Paper No. 114. https://ssrn.com/abstract=4024343

VVA, Grimaldi and Bruegel (2019). Study on the differences between bank insolvency laws and on their potential harmonisation – Final report (commissioned by the European Commission). https://finance.ec.europa.eu/document/download/dd2e21c2-f56a-4126-8b4f-4aa8f1fe5e9a_en?filename=191106-study-bank-insolvency_en.pdf

26

The Banking Union

Supervision and Crisis Management

Willem Pieter de Groen

26.1 INTRODUCTION

The global financial and economic crises of 2008–12 put the financial stability of the European banking sector at risk. To stabilize the banking sector, monetary authorities and national governments intervened by providing significant liquidity and capital support (De Groen and Gros, 2015). In response, EU policymakers set up the European Banking Union (EBU) to tackle potential negative cross-border spill-over effects and avoid the situation in which governments of the euro area would again need bailouts in the banking sector (European Commission, 2012).

A fully fledged EBU ought to consist of three pillars: (i) Single Supervisory Mechanism (SSM);[1] (ii) Single Resolution Mechanism (SRM);[2] and (iii) European Deposit Insurance Scheme (EDIS). The three pillars of the EBU are underpinned by the Single Rulebook, which is the single set of harmonized prudential rules applicable to EU institutions (Lannoo, 2019).

The SSM was established to enhance the coordination between supervisors and consistent application of prudential rules (European Commission, 2012; Van Rompuy, 2012). As part of the SSM, the European Central Bank (ECB) is since November 2014 responsible for the direct supervision of significant banking groups (111 banking groups in June 2022[3] representing the large majority of banking assets) and indirect supervision of the less significant banks (more than 2,000 institutions) in the EBU.

The SRM has been set up to avoid negative spill-over effects of financial crises to depositors and taxpayers (European Commission, 2012). Failures of large banks under standard liquidation regimes are likely to disrupt the real economy, with – among others – restricted access to payment systems and bank credit. To avoid this, governments traditionally bail out large failing banks, which gives these 'too big to fail' banks an implicit government guarantee.

As a part of the SRM, the Single Resolution Board (SRB) and Single Resolution Fund (SRF) are responsible for the resolution planning and execution of the resolution of banks in the EBU since 1 January 2016. The SRB has all significant banking groups directly supervised by the ECB under its remit, as well as other less significant cross-border banking groups (five banking

[1] Council Regulation (EU) No. 1024/2013 of 15 October 2013 conferring specific tasks on the European Central Bank concerning policies relating to the prudential supervision of credit institutions, OJ L 287, 29.10.2013, pp. 63–89.

[2] Regulation (EU) No. 806/2014 of the European Parliament and of the Council of 15 July 2014 establishing uniform rules and a uniform procedure for the resolution of credit institutions and certain investment firms in the framework of a Single Resolution Mechanism and a Single Resolution Fund and amending Regulation (EU) No. 1093/2010, OJ L 225, 30.7.2014, pp. 1–90 (hereinafter SRM Regulation).

[3] See ECB (2022) for the list of supervised institutions.

groups in June 2022).[4] Additionally, other less significant banks come under the remit of the SRB when they require funds from the SRF.[5] Besides resolution, the SRB also prepares plans for potential resolutions (De Groen and Gros, 2015). Additionally, the SRB is responsible for managing the SRF, which provides funds for resolution actions and compensates those creditors worse off in resolution than under a regular insolvency. The resources of the SRF are collected through contributions from all credit institutions in the EBU. The fund should reach the target level of 1.0 per cent of covered deposits by 2024.

The rules for deposit guarantee schemes (DGS) have been harmonized across EU Member States with the adoption of the DGS Directive in 2014,[6] but there is still no single EBU-wide DGS. The European Commission (2015a) launched a proposal for an EBU-wide DGS in 2015, on which no political agreement has been reached so far.

The EBU applies to all euro area countries, but also non-euro area countries have the possibility to join or participate. In October 2020, both Bulgaria and Croatia entered into a close cooperation with the ECB on bank supervision (ECB, 2014b).

The EBU has undoubtedly contributed to the strengthening of the supervisory framework. However, there remain important legal, economic, political, and operational challenges. This chapter discusses the main remaining challenges and potential feasible strategies to address these challenges.

26.2 THE MAIN REMAINING CHALLENGES FOR THE EBU

More than five years into operation, several important flaws in the design of the EBU have come to light. Most of the critical information about the functioning of the SSM and SRM is confidential. Therefore, the examinations by the European Court of Auditors (ECA), which has access to most of the information, form an important source of information. The ECA has in past years conducted various examinations of the Banking Union, covering the SSM, SRB, and the SRM.

The ECA found in its 2016 examination that the SSM was set up by the ECB as scheduled and faces practical and institutional design challenges, including complex procedures, the necessity of separating between the monetary policy and supervisory mandates of the ECB, sufficient human resources for on-site supervision, qualified human resources at national level, and adequate IT systems (ECA, 2016). Many of these issues have in the meantime been addressed and no longer hamper the effective functioning of the SSM.

Turning to the SRM, in its 2017 examination the ECA concluded that the mechanism was still in a start-up phase. As at this stage, no actual resolutions had been effectuated, and the examination primarily focused on the preparation for resolution processes. According to the ECA, in 2017 the SRB still had not managed to prepare the resolution plans for all institutions under its remit. This was partially due to its inability to find sufficient skilled staff. Moreover, there was unclarity in the division of tasks between the SRB and the national resolution authorities (ECA, 2017).

The second examination of the resolution mechanism by the ECA (in 2021) showed that the SRB was making important progress, but that operational challenges still persisted. Moreover, the broadening of the scope to the SRM also led to additional legislative recommendations.

[4] See SRB (2022) for the list of banks under remit.

[5] Article 7 SRM Regulation.

[6] Directive 2014/49/EU of the European Parliament and of the Council of 16 April 2014 on deposit guarantee schemes (recast), OJ L 173, 12.6.2014, pp. 149–178 (hereinafter DGS Directive).

The ECA concluded that key elements in resolution planning are missing (e.g. identification of significant impediments, no resolution plans for some banks, many plans were not fully compliant with the EU rules, and there were deviations across countries) and that the first guidance documents were only issued in late 2020 to NRAs for banks under its remit. In the meantime, the SRB has been able to attract more staff, while NRAs reduced their staff contribution.

The ECA noted two important shortcomings in the legislation: insufficient funding for resolutions and differences in national insolvency proceedings. The lack of resolution funding forms a barrier to executing the preferred strategy in resolution, while the differences in the insolvency regimes hinder the preparation and execution of resolutions. For example, the impact of a failure on the value of assets as well as procedures for treatment of failed banks differ. In addition, ECA also pointed to the difference in burden sharing required for banks under resolution and banks receiving state aid (i.e. difference in bailed-in liabilities),[7] as well as missing objectives and quantitative criteria for early intervention measures by the ECB (ECA, 2021).

To conclude, based on ECA's examination, there is still one important policy challenge remaining for the completion of an effectively functioning EBU: the use and financing of the resolution fund and tools (i.e. sale of business, bridge institution, and asset separation). This comes in addition to the completion of the EBU with an agreement on the EDIS. The following sections assess these challenges.

26.2.1 *Challenge 1: Use and Funding of the Resolution Fund and Tools*

The first challenge is ensuring sufficient funding for resolution. The SRF has been established to gather the funds required to finance bank resolutions, in order to avoid bail-outs with taxpayers' money, as was common during the financial and economic crises of 2008–12.

During and after the crises, banks and other financial institutions received cumulatively about €4.8 trillion in state aid. Most aid consisted of liquidity measures (87 per cent), which comprised both guarantees (€3.8 trillion or 79 per cent of state aid) and other liquidity measures (€0.3 trillion or 7 per cent of state aid) such as loans. The remaining support consisted of capital support (€0.5 trillion or 10 per cent of state aid) and impaired asset measures (€0.2 trillion or 4 per cent of state aid) (DG Competition, 2016). Additionally, banks benefited from funds from monetary authorities. For instance, at one point in time the ECB provided up to €1.4 trillion in loans to euro area banks. These monetary means also included emergency liquidity assistance (ELA). The liquidity support for individual banks was in some instances significant. For example, Belgian Dexia and German Hypo Real Estate received about €100 billion in guarantees each and Greek banks received up to €135 billion ELA (De Groen and Gros, 2015).

In a future crisis, the liquidity needs in resolution are expected to be lower than during the financial and economic crises of 2008–12 due to some measures introduced to strengthen the financial position of the banking sector. First, the liquidity coverage ratio (LCR) and the net stable funding ratio (NSFR) that have been added to the rulebook after the Global Financial Crisis (GFC) limit the maximum short-term liquidity mismatch between assets with long maturities (such as mortgages) and liabilities with short maturities (such as deposits) (BCBS,

[7] Communication from the Commission on the application, from 1 August 2013, of state aid rules to support measures in favour of banks in the context of the financial crisis (hereinafter Banking Communication), OJ C216 of 30.7.2013, p. 1.

2013, 2014). The LCR gauges the ability of banks to cover the thirty-day liquidity needs by highly liquid assets, while the NSFR determines the extent to which the available resources are sufficient to cover the required stable funding for a one-year period. Second, the introduction of the crisis management framework should allow for earlier interventions, limiting liquidity outflows before bank failures (De Groen and Gros, 2015). However, if the crisis is persistent and severe, and there are uncertainties about the viability of the bank under resolution, there will be additional losses and liquidity outflows, leading to substantial liquidity needs.

The liquidity and funding needs are unlikely to disappear as they are inherent to the banks. There might be significant liquidity and funding shortfalls due to the inherent maturity mismatch, i.e. assets have longer maturities than liabilities. Indeed, the maturity mismatch might lead to financial difficulties when a bank does not have access to sufficient funds (or only against high costs) to finance new assets or replace existing funding (De Haan and Van den End, 2013).

The funding available to the SRF will be significantly lower than the financial resources used during the financial and economic crises of 2008–12. The SRF has a target size of 1 per cent of covered deposits, equivalent to about €70 to €75 billion (SRB, 2021).

These funds, which are *ex ante* collected, can be increased in case of a potential resolution with additional funds:

- ***Ex post* contributions** equivalent to up to three times the annual contributions (37.5 per cent of the target level = 0.375 per cent of covered deposits).
- Additional funds can be **borrowed** from third parties when the funds collected *ex ante* and *ex post* are not immediately available or sufficient.[8] The exact amount of additional funds this option could deliver is uncertain. I assume that it is at least possible to borrow an amount equivalent to the *ex post* contributions which the SRF could levy on banks (37.5 per cent of the target level = 0.375 per cent of covered deposits).
- **Funds obtained from the sale of the shares** the SRF holds from banks that have previously undergone resolution.[9] The amounts that can be obtained through this means are highly dependent on the financial position of those banks and market conditions. In general, the sale of the shares is unattractive shortly after the intervention when the banks are recovering and the economy distressed.
- **Common backstop** facility provided by the ESM is also available to address capital needs. The common backstop amounts to a maximum €68 billion and takes the form of a revolving credit line.
- Resources can be **borrowed from resolution funds** in non-EBU Member States.[10] Besides that, it is questionable whether the other resolution funds are willing and able to lend funds to the SRF; the available *ex ante* funds they are collecting are relatively limited after Brexit. Hence, the funds of the non-EBU Member States are likely to be only about one-tenth of the SRF.
- Contributions from national **Deposit Guarantee Schemes** (DGSs) if certain conditions are fulfilled. A DGS aims to protect customer deposits, in order to limit the possibility for bank runs, and to avoid or address bank failures. The contribution from DGSs shall (i) not be greater than the size of the losses attributed to the DGS if the bank had been liquidated, and (ii) maximum 0.4 per cent of covered deposits of the DGS per resolution. The DGS

[8] Article 73 SRM Regulation.
[9] Article 24 SRM Regulation.
[10] Article 72 SRM Regulation.

TABLE 26.1 *Estimated maximum funds available for resolution (€ billion)*

Measures	Potentially available funds
Ex ante contributions	70–75
Ex post contributions	26–28
Total SRF funds	**96–103**
Borrowing from third parties	26–28
Sales of shares	n/a
Common backstop from ESM	68
Borrowing from other resolution schemes	8
Deposit Guarantee Schemes (50%)	28–30
Total alternative funds	**130–134**
Total funds potentially available	**226–237**

Note: For the DGS contribution it is assumed that all DGSs have funds equal to the target size of 0.8 per cent and only these funds are used. See text for additional assumptions as well as conditions to obtain the funds.
Source: Author's own calculations based on De Groen and Gros (2015), EBA (2022). See EBA (2022) for the data on EU deposit guarantee schemes.

funds are fragmented across the Member States, which significantly limits the amounts that can be contributed to a single resolution. Furthermore, only DGS funds that insure deposits of the failing banks can contribute. The funds the DGSs can contribute in a range between about €37 million in Latvia and €5 billion in France (40 per cent of the target level = 0.4 per cent of covered deposits).[11]

In total, this means that the SRF could have between €226 and €237 billion available for resolution (see Table 26.1), which seems largely insufficient for a systemic crisis based on the funds used during the financial and economic crises of 2008–12.

Although various policymakers such as the Eurogroup (2018), SRB (König, 2018), and IMF (2018) are aware that the liquidity needs are insufficiently addressed, there are still no concrete measures agreed to remedy this shortcoming.

26.2.2 *Challenge 2: Establishment of a Common Deposit Insurance*

The second challenge is the completion of the third pillar of the EBU: establishing a common deposit insurance mechanism (Figure 26.1). The DGSs in the EU are for the most part *ex ante* funded. Nevertheless, governments can be exposed when the DGSs do not have or are unable to raise the necessary funds.

A common deposit insurance mechanism, or a European Deposit Insurance Scheme as it was labelled by the European Commission, aims to avoid the national DGSs destabilizing government finances of individual euro area countries. This detrimental effect would happen if the funds of the (national) DGS are insufficient to pay out the covered deposits in case of the failure of one or more banks and the national government does not have the ability to raise the necessary funds or can do so only at a high cost. As a consequence, countries with weak government finances would encounter a higher risk of bank runs.

The EDIS proposal envisaged a gradual transition from the national DGSs to a supranational insurance scheme. The deposit guarantee fund would have to cover the pay-outs of all member

[11] The funds are estimated based on the relative size of covered deposits at the end of 2012 and the relative size of the DGS (0.8 per cent covered deposits) compared to the SRF (1.0 per cent covered deposits).

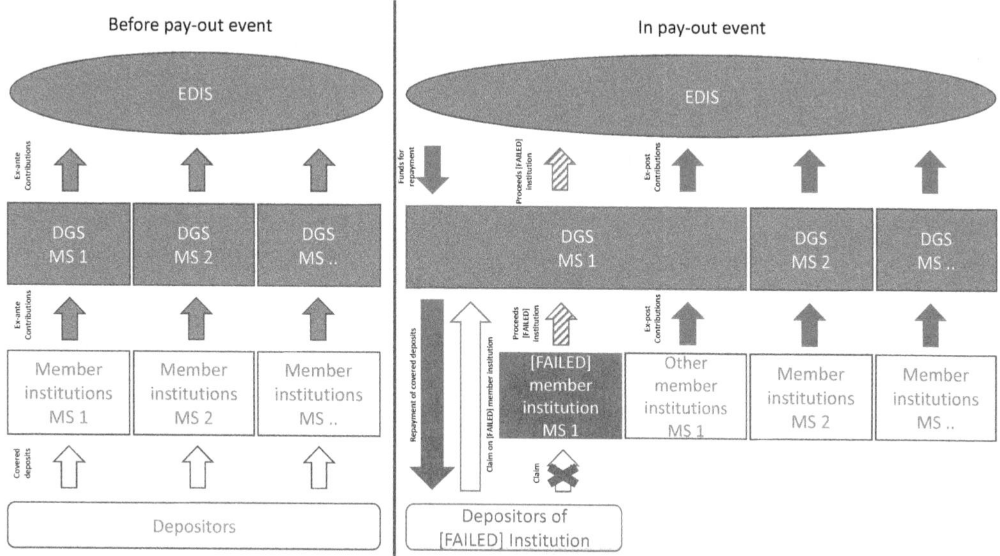

FIGURE 26.1. Graphic illustration of full insurance scheme

Note: The figure shows the (simplified) financial relations of EDIS and the national DGSs under a full insurance scheme. The panel on the left-hand side illustrates the relations during normal times, i.e. before a pay-out event, while the panel on the right-hand side illustrates the situation in a regular - pay-out event, i.e. no preventive or alternative measures. In this exemplary case, a member institution in country A failed. Only the actors financially involved have been included in the graphic.

institutions or contributions to resolutions after the national DGSs funds was consolidated into a common fund. The national DGSs would continue to exist and remain responsible for the collection of the funds and execution of the pay-outs, while the common fund would ensure uniform policies. The contributions would be calculated at the national rather than the EBU level.

Despite the common understanding of the potential financial stability risks related to the lack of the deposit guarantee scheme, there is no agreement on EDIS yet. The Commission's proposal of November 2015 for a deposit insurance for the EBU (see European Commission, 2017) did not get the necessary support from the Council and European Parliament to be adopted. In fact, it got stuck at the technical level, indicating a large division in views on when and how a common deposit insurance mechanism could be implemented (De Groen and Alcidi, 2019).

The key challenges in finding an agreement on a common deposit insurance mechanism were twofold. On the one hand, there was a question about the solidity of the banking sectors in different EBU countries, i.e. countries with a robust banking sector feared they would have to contribute to pay-outs to depositors in the countries with weaker banks. On the other hand, a common deposit insurance mechanism would reduce national discretion.

Without an agreement on EDIS, the deposit insurance is still legislated by the DGS Directive, which exhibits a minimum degree of harmonization. Under the directive, each Member State is required to (i) ensure that one or more DGSs are set up, (ii) collect *ex ante* funds of at least 0.8 per cent of covered deposits by 2024, (iii) harmonize the protection of depositors, covering €100,000 per depositor per bank of both individuals and businesses, and (iv) pay-out in a maximum of seven working days by 2024.

Although the DGS Directive limits potential differences between EU Member States, it still contains several tens of national options and discretions (NODs). Most of the NODs related to coverage, pay-out, and transitional provisions are either not used much or harmonization will have limited impact. However, there are also NODs deemed important by the Member States, which are more difficult to harmonize, as they allow for a different use of the DGS.

The failure *prevention measure* provision (Article 11(3) DGS Directive) has been transposed in nine Member States, including countries with institutional protection schemes (IPSs), such as Germany and Italy. The IPSs provide protection to the members of cooperative and saving banks networks. It is unclear whether the provision has been used since the adoption of the DGS Directive, as not all DGSs disclose information on preventive measures. Nevertheless, for the DGSs which are also an IPS it is important to be able to use the collected funds of the DGSs for preventing failures of their member institutions. Although the DGS Directive includes several provisions for the use of the preventive measures, it leaves considerable room for interpretation to Member States, especially the selection of the measures, appropriateness of the systems, and procedures in place for using them and determining whether the costs for the DGS do not exceed those of the conventional pay-out (De Groen and Alcidi, 2019).

The **alternative measure** provision to finance measures to preserve the access to covered deposits (Article 11(6) DGS Directive) has been transposed in ten Member States, including Italy and Poland. It allows for funding the transfer of all or a part of the assets and liabilities of a failing bank to another bank. It has the potential for reducing the pay-out costs and disturbances that a failing bank may cause. For the use of the alternative measures to a pay-out, the costs borne by the DGS may not exceed those that would have been necessary to compensate depositors of the failing member institution (De Groen and Alcidi, 2019).

The EDIS proposal did not include provisions for preventive and alternative measures financed with deposit funds, which raised objections among Member States using such provisions. In turn, the other Member States were hesitant to accept their inclusion, as they might imply transfers between countries.

26.3 REFORM PROPOSALS TO ADDRESS ECONOMIC CHALLENGES FOR THE EBU

Giving the resolution mechanism access to additional funding and establishing a common deposit insurance mechanism have been recognized by the European Commission as necessary, with several legislative proposals dealing with them tabled. However, it is difficult to find a political agreement, as not all euro area Member States deem the proposed solutions mutually beneficial. This section aims to come up with some pragmatic solutions to address the challenges identified. Solutions that increase the mutualization of losses and significantly restrict national discretion have been disregarded as they do not seem politically feasible. For example, the creation of an equivalent of the FDIC in Europe might be a sensible solution to create a single DGS and increase the available funding for resolution, but would be unlikely to receive the required political support (Restoy, 2019).

26.3.1 *Proposal 1: A Backstop and Liquidity Facility in Resolution*

The resolution tools included in the crisis management framework need to ensure an orderly resolution of failing or likely to fail (FOLTF) banks, which contributes to financial stability. The resolution tools allow the costs of resolution to be reduced and the burden sharing to be

TABLE 26.2 *Potential needs from the SRF of resolution tools*

Resolution tool	Sale of business	Bridge institution	Asset separation	Bail-in
Description	Bank assets are sold to another bank or investor	Selected assets and liabilities are transferred to new bank	Legacy assets are transferred to asset management company (AMC)	Writing down or conversion of equity/ debt
Type of institution	Bank	Bank	Non-bank	Bank
Access to central bank facilities	Through acquiring bank	If ECB grants a licence to new/rescued institution	No	N/A
Access to SRF	Potentially	Potentially	Potentially	N/A
Liquidity	Liquidity is in principle the responsibility of the acquirer, but SRF can deliver contribution	Liquidity can be arranged as for other banking institutions and SRF can deliver a contribution	Liquidity can be arranged by AMC itself as well as provided by the SRF	Reducing liquidity needs
Capital	Capitalization is in principle the responsibility of the acquirer, but SRF can deliver contribution	Capital required to meet capital requirements plus potential buffer, which can be financed through bail-in, rescued institution and SRF	Limited to no capital required from SRF	Reducing capital needs

Note: The information in the table is based on experiences in past state aid cases.

enhanced. However, a failing institution in resolution as well as resolution tools might need funds for liquidity and capitalization.

Looking at the four different tools (see Table 26.2), the **bail-in tool** reduces the need for liquidity and capital from the SRF. The **sale of business tool** also in principle does not require funds from the SRF, as the acquiring institution has to provide the liquidity and capital needed. The SRF is primarily needed to provide liquidity and/or capital to the **bridge institution tool** and only liquidity to the **asset separation tool** as well as the **failing institution in resolution**. Both the bridge bank and the failing institution could potentially use monetary financing from the ECB, when they meet the conditions for emergency liquidity assistance (i.e. being a solvent credit institution with sufficient collateral) after the resolution action by the SRB.

The SRF was created to effectively apply the resolution tools (sale of business, asset management company (AMC), bridge bank, and bail-in). According to Article 76 SRM Regulation SRF can be used for capital, liquidity, and compensation purposes. Specific measures include:

- **Guarantees on assets and liabilities** of the institution, bridge bank or AMC;
- **Loans** to the institution, bridge bank, or AMC;
- **Purchase assets** of the institution;
- **Contributions** to the bridge bank or AMC;
- **Compensation** for creditors which are worse off than if the institution had been liquidated;
- **Contribution** to the institution to compensate for certain liabilities excluded from bail-in.

The SRF is not supposed to absorb losses of the rescued entity or recapitalization by law,[12] however it cannot be ruled out that this will nevertheless occur. The losses are uncertain, as they are based on the asset values at the time of resolution, while the situation can deteriorate afterwards. Moreover, when the SRF is used for providing capital support, first at least 8 per cent of total liabilities including own funds (TLOF) needs to be bailed in before a maximum contribution of 5 per cent of TLOF can be provided (Article 27(6) SRM Regulation).

At the time that the target level of 1 per cent of covered deposits is reached for the first time by the end of 2023, the SRF is likely to be able to provide sufficient capital support, but this does not hold for liquidity support. For the latter purpose, monetary funding from the Eurosystem may be required, which is able to provide large amounts of liquidity immediately. To obtain the liquidity, the rescued institution/bridge institution needs to meet the corresponding conditions (i.e. being a solvent credit institution with sufficient collateral).

26.3.1.1 Capital Support[13]

The funds required for capital support from the SRF are substantially less than the capital support provided by governments to support banks during the financial and economic crises of 2008–12. This is primarily because of the bail-in requirement of at least 8 per cent of total liabilities including own funds and a maximum contribution of the SRF of 5 per cent of TLOF. The potential needs from the SRF were estimated based on the losses incurred by the seventy-two banking groups in the euro area country that received capital support in the period 2008–14. These banks had total assets of around €14.2 trillion at the end of the book year preceding the interventions, which is equivalent to approximately 45 per cent of the total euro area banking assets.[14] Two-thirds of these banks could be classified as significant according to the definition applied by the SSM.[15] The significant banks held 98 per cent of the total assets of the banks that received support.

The losses are calculated using the profit before tax minus the tax paid and the write-downs of goodwill after the initial bail-out. The maximum cumulative loss is €313 billion, or 2.2 per cent of total liabilities (including own funds), €304 billion excluding tax and goodwill.[16] The losses before tax are primarily due to high loan loss provisions and to a lesser extent due to losses on other financial assets (i.e. trading losses) and discontinued operations. The total estimated losses plus capital shortfalls are around €32 billion below the €335 billion total capital aid provided to euro area financial institutions during the financial and economic crises of 2008–12 (European Commission, 2015b). The difference can be partially explained through the banks for which no performance data was available, the non-bank institutions that also received state aid, as well as the part of the capital support used to increase the buffers of the banks.

The cumulative losses are unequally divided across the banks that received aid. About 10 per cent of the banks did not report any losses and about another 40 per cent of the banks reported peak cumulative losses of up to 4 per cent of total liabilities, including own funds. These banks

[12] Article 76(3) SRM Regulation.

[13] This section is based on De Groen and Gros (2015).

[14] The total banking assets (i.e. MFIs excl. euro area central banks) were on average €31.5 trillion (varying between €26.4 and €34.9 trillion) during the period from January 2007 to December 2014, see ECB (2015).

[15] Banks are considered significant in case the assets are over €30 billion or over €5 billion and 20 per cent of GDP or if the bank is one of the three largest banks in a country or has significant cross-border activities (ECB, 2014a).

[16] Since the exact losses and financial accounts at the moment of the intervention are not disclosed, the amounts at the end of the last book year before the intervention in the aftermath of the financial and economic crises of 2008–12 are used to determine the own funds requirement, the maximum bail-in, and the contribution from the SRF.

are less likely to need any recapitalization with SRF funds. Indeed, with a minimum bail-in of 8 per cent of total liabilities, minimum capital requirements excluding buffers of 8 per cent of risk-weighted assets, and the risk-weighted assets to total liabilities of around 50 per cent on average, the average maximum capital contribution of excess own funds and bail-in is expected to be around 4 per cent. About a fifth of the banks reported peak losses of between 4 and 9 per cent, the likely range in which the SRF will be most effective. The remaining quarter noted peak losses of 9 per cent or more, with a maximum of 34.5 per cent, for which minimum bail-in and maximum contribution from the SRF are likely to be insufficient to cover the losses. The losses could not be calculated for ten banks because of a lack of data on their profitability. These banks are primarily less significant and were absorbed or liquidated in the past few years. The maximum amount required for these banks would probably not be more than €2.7 billion.

The distribution across resolution tools largely confirms the intuition about the number of banks that would have required funds from the SRF. The banks of which the losses and recapitalization requirement exceeded 8 per cent of TLOF could have demanded support for up to €72 billion from the SRF. Thirteen banks with an aggregated loss of around €32 billion would have needed around €10 billion from the Fund in combination with €13 billion own funds and €9 billion through bail-in of creditors. The remaining eighteen banks had to recoup €182 billion, of which only €33 billion could have been absorbed through own funds and bail-in. On top of the minimum bail-in amount the banks would have required another €149 billion. The SRF might have contributed up to €62 billion, while the remaining €87 billion would need to be absorbed by other creditors and/or the deposit guarantee scheme.

The total assets of the banks that might have received support from the SRF account for around 6 per cent of total euro area banking assets, just a fraction of the 45 per cent of the entire sample of aided banks. Besides Irish AIB, Spanish BFA/Bankia, and Italian Monte dei Paschi di Siena, the list only contains small and medium-sized banks (i.e. banks with less than €150 billion in total assets). Interestingly, two large Belgium banks (Fortis and Dexia) were responsible for more than one-sixth of the losses. These banks could have been recapitalized through a bail-in of €37 billion. The bail-in capacity of these and other large banks is particularly high due to the size of the banks as well as the relatively low capital as share of the 8 per cent bail-in threshold.

Notwithstanding that the losses during the sample period were extreme due to the largest financial and economic crises in seventy years, the high costs if a second resolution had to be undertaken might spur the ECB to build in some safety margins in the form of additional capital buffers. For example, 4 per cent extra capital would have resulted in €17 billion or about a quarter of extra contributions from the SRF. The limited increase is partially due to the cap of 5 per cent of total liabilities on the SRF contributions. In turn, the use of resolution tools could reduce the funds required from the SRF. Several forms of capital relief measures were used for the resolution of banks during the sample period. Assuming that these measures will be used similarly as during the global financial and economic crises and will not require any funds from the SRF, the risk-weighted assets and the amounts necessary for recapitalization will decrease.

Combining both the estimations of the funds required and the availability of the funds, this section will further discuss the need for additional financing for the SRF funding under various scenarios:

(i) failure of a single bank (requiring up to €16 billion from SRF);
(ii) a small group of banks, like the ones requiring funds during the period from 2011 to 2014 (requiring €4 billion); and

(iii) a large number of failing banks, as during the last financial and economic crises of 2008–12 (requiring €58 billion).

Overall, the SRF would be sufficient to cover the demands during a significant banking crisis as in 2009 and 2010, even if higher capital buffers were assumed. The SRF will thus most likely be able to withstand the crisis, provided its full financing capacity is available, which will be an estimated €96 billion (excluding the common backstop of €68 billion).

26.3.1.2 Liquidity Support[17]

The target size of the SRF is expected to be insufficient to address the liquidity needs in a systemic crisis when governments do not intervene in the economy at a large scale (as was the case during the COVID-19 pandemic) by providing for the cash needs of the banks and the resolution tools. The proposal envisages leveraging the SRF, which can bring its effective size to the same magnitude as the liquidity support during the financial and economic crises of 2008–12 (€4.1 trillion).

26.3.1.3 Difficulties in Determining Liquidity Needs

Liquidity shortages generally arise in the run-up to the failure of the bank, but might worsen when a resolution scheme is implemented. Market analysts, creditors, and shareholders are likely to need some time to assess the viability of the banks after the resolution is implemented. Investors might be hesitant to entrust funds to the banks before they have certainty about their viability, creating a liquidity shortfall that needs to be addressed in a resolution.

The SRB is expected to describe liquidity needs in its resolution plans. However, their size is difficult to determine in advance for the supervisors and the resolution funds involved. Liquidity needs are strongly contingent on the moment of the intervention and the market conditions around that time, as well as on the resolution strategy and tools. Moreover, the SRB would also need to identify the collateral available, as a large share might already be encumbered for liquidity purposes before the resolution. Additionally, collateral requirements are likely to become more stringent with more extreme haircuts during periods of severe stress. Liquidity needs anticipated in the resolution plans will take central bank financing into consideration, but not the liquidity that could potentially be obtained under the ELA.

Ideally, the crisis management framework should also be able to address liquidity needs in these extreme events. The current SRF, with maximum firepower of about €70 to €75 billion immediately available (plus €68 billion of the ESM common backstop), seems insufficient for such extreme conditions.

26.3.1.4 Proposal for a Transitional Liquidity Assistance

The SRB has to be able to ensure liquidity for the banks and resolution tools. However, the SRF does not have similar means available to the monetary authorities. The most straightforward solution to this limitation would be to give a government guarantee to cover the default risks to the Eurosystem, allowing it to provide the necessary liquidity in resolution. Another solution would be to provide ESM claims on governments as collateral to the Eurosystem in addition to

[17] This section is based on De Groen (2018).

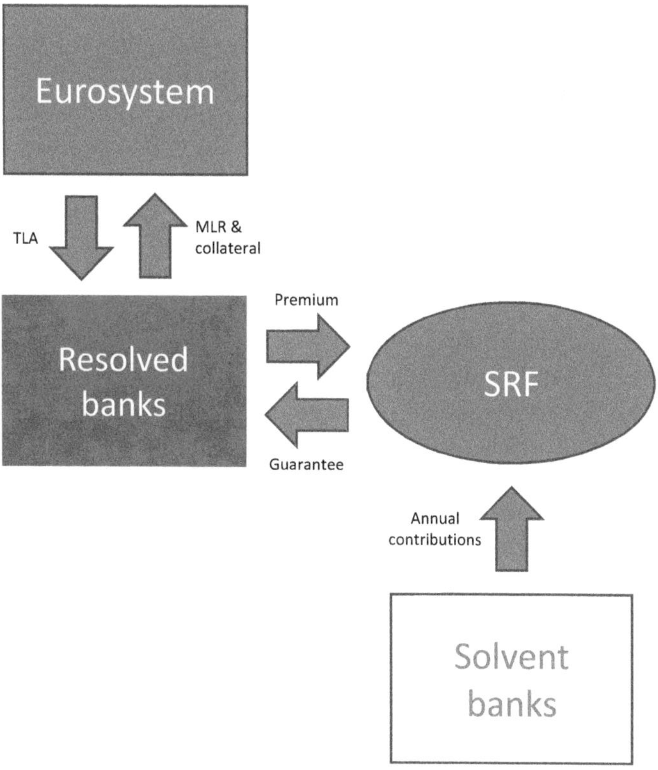

FIGURE 26.2. Graphic description of transitional liquidity assistance for rescued banks
Note: **MLR**: Marginal Lending Rate; **SRF**: Single Resolution Fund; **TLA**: Transitional Liquidity Assistance.

the common backstop, or to increase the size of the revolving credit line from the ESM to the SRF, to specifically address liquidity needs during resolution. However, even though liquidity support might not in principle be costly, these solutions would also go against the objectives of the resolution mechanism and the EBU to minimize the costs of resolution for taxpayers and break the 'doom loop' between banks and their sovereigns. Moreover, these solutions do not appear politically feasible, given the resistance against potential mutualization of losses (Löyttyniemi, 2018), as also illustrated by the discussion on EDIS.

Alternatively, the SRF could provide a **substantial guarantee to rescued banks**, which in turn could obtain the required liquidity immediately from the Eurosystem (see Figure 26.2). The SRF would be able to give a credible guarantee as long as it has the possibility to raise additional *ex post* contributions from banks in the unlikely event that the guarantees are called.[18] In the proposal this would be an additional annual contribution equal to the current annual contribution (i.e. 0.125 per cent of covered deposits). The liquidity could be provided under a new facility, named *Transitional Liquidity Assistance* (TLA) in this proposal. The bank receiving liquidity support under the TLA (or revised ELA) should pay interest similar to that of the marginal lending facility of the Eurosystem. In addition, the beneficiary banks should pay a

[18] Since the guarantee is for liquidity and not capital support, it should in principle not lead to any costs to the SRF. However, in order for the SRF to credibly grant a guarantee, there would be a need to raise the guaranteed amounts.

premium for the guarantee. Based on the current ELA framework and the previous state aid decisions this should be at least 100 basis points, or 1 per cent of the guarantee.

The liquidity facility would have to be **provided by the Eurosystem** instead of individual national central banks (currently responsible for ELA), and under predetermined conditions, making the availability of the facility predictable and reliable to the SRB. The main conditions could be agreed between the Eurosystem/ECB and the SRB/SRF in a Memorandum of Understanding (MoU). This should at least include the following **conditions** for the liquidity support:

- TLA is available to banks with a guarantee from the SRF;
- Minimum total amount of liquidity that can be provided under TLA;
- TLA can only be used when the other central bank facilities have been exhausted;
- The use of TLA should be collateralized as much as possible to reduce the likelihood that the guarantee from the SRF needs to be used and is called;
- TLA is only a temporary facility, limiting the amount allotted;
- The use of TLA is accompanied by a plan for regaining the viability of the bank and phasing out the liquidity support;
- A summary of the viability plan should be published to regain the confidence of market participants.

The TLA would, according to the Banking Communication, be **subject to state aid rules**. Standard monetary policy facilities are excluded from state aid rules and the current ELA is also exempted under specific conditions. However, the TLA would not be provided at the initiative of a central bank. Furthermore, it would be fully secured by collateral and would potentially be a part of a broader package, which are all requirements for state aid rules exemptions. Ideally, in order to avoid uncertainties produced by *ex post* approvals of liquidity support, which is by definition time-sensitive in a resolution, the DG Competition should include a special section for the TLA in the revised 2013 Banking Communication.

Although the facility causes fewer moral hazard issues than most other solutions (such as a credit line from governments) the guarantee from the SRF to the Eurosystem might also have some **unintended consequences**. The guarantee might potentially reduce the urgency for the SRB to act, since the banks concerned would know sufficient liquidity is available for resolution. However, a reduction of the firepower of the fund due to an increase in the guarantees might mitigate this potential unintended consequence. In addition, the ECB and national central banks (NCBs) might be less tempted to provide ELA when the alternative of TLA is available, with no or less credit risk. Lower compensation for the ECB and NCBs under the TLA than ELA should account for this. The rescued banks might also prefer to use the TLA, which requires no or less collateral. To avoid this, the TLA might be granted super senior creditor status. Although the super senior status might delay access to market funding for the bank, it lowers the risk that the guarantees are called. The latter could happen when losses are underestimated and capital buffers of the bank are insufficient.

26.3.1.5 Potential Size of the TLA

Size remains critical for the credibility of the liquidity facility. Using the financial and economic crises of 2008–12 as a benchmark, about €4.1 trillion would be sufficient in a severe financial and economic crises. Looking at the experiences of the previous decade, the costs of guarantees are only a fraction of the total amount guaranteed. Indeed, a total of around €7.1 billion of

TABLE 26.3 *Estimation of available funds for Transitional Liquidity Assistance (€ million)*

Marginal lending rate	SRF guarantee	Rescued bank collateral	TLA
0.00%	Unlimited	Unlimited	Unlimited
0.25%	3,596,250	3,596,250	7,192,500
0.50%	1,846,250	1,846,250	3,692,500
0.75% (current)	1,262,917	1,262,917	2,525,833
1.00% (financial crisis)	971,250	971,250	1,942,500
1.25%	796,250	796,250	1,592,500
1.50%	679,583	679,583	1,359,167
1.75%	596,250	596,250	1,192,500
2.00%	533,750	533,750	1,067,500
2.25%	485,139	485,139	970,278
2.50% (50% collateral)	446,250	446,250	892,500
3.00%	387,917	387,917	775,833
4.00%	315,000	315,000	630,000
5.00%	271,250	271,250	542,500
6.00%	242,083	242,083	484,167

Note: The estimation of the amounts of the SRF guarantee are equal to the *ex ante* and *ex post* funding for the SRF (€96.25 billion) and cash-flow from a potential annual contribution (€8.8 billion) that should at least cover interest payments. The calculation is expressed by the following formula. SRF Guarantee = Annual contribution SRF Marginal Lending Rate + SRF + ESM backstop.

guarantees was called in the euro area between 2007 and 2017 (0.21 per cent of the guaranteed amount per annum). This is substantially less than the approximately 0.86 per cent per annum that the guarantors received for providing the guarantees. Provided that the guarantee should indeed generate profits for the SRF on average, no additional contributions from other banks in the EBU or ESM will be necessary.

Nevertheless, in order for the Eurosystem to accept the guarantee as collateral, it must be certain that the SRF can provide the funds if the guarantees are called. This limits the guarantee to the potential cash flows of the SRF. The guarantee could be based on the target size of the SRF (*ex ante* plus *ex post*), the potential backstop, and the additional annual contributions. The proposed solution assumes that if the SRF cannot pay the entire guarantee at once, it should at least be able to pay the interest. This means that, based on the current MLR of 0.75 per cent, for each euro of annual contribution more than €130 can be guaranteed. However, the policy rates of the Eurosystem change over time, which requires introducing a margin to cover interest payments if the ECB increases the MLR. The additional collateral could substantially increase the liquidity available. For example, in Table 26.3 it is assumed that the banks can obtain a similar amount to the guarantee with unencumbered assets.

Overall, the proposed solution seems to be able to mobilize more than enough of the funds to guarantee substantial liquidity provisioning. Based on the current policy rates, the SRF could potentially guarantee more than €1,263 billion. The amounts the SRF could potentially guarantee are substantial, but highly dependent on the level of the MLR. The MLR is still at historically low levels and is expected to increase further in the near future. The MLR is likely not to decrease in periods of stress and increase in periods of economic recovery and prosperity. For example, the Eurosystem decreased the MLR during the past crises from 5.25 per cent in

July 2008 to 0.25 per cent in March 2016. The MLR had been kept at the same level for quite some time, increased in July 2022 (last update April 2022).

Except for situations with high monetary interest rates, this proposal would ensure that there is sufficient and readily available liquidity support to allow the SRB to be able to execute the resolution strategy that best meets the objectives of the resolution mechanism.

26.3.2 *Proposal 2: Common Deposit Insurance Scheme*

The proposal for a common deposit insurance scheme concerns a revision of the latest EDIS proposal, in the sense that it will allow some important national specificities to persist (see De Groen and Alcidi, 2019) and limit the transfer of funds to a temporary transfer between the national DGSs.

26.3.2.1 National Specificities

There are several Member States with decentralized cooperative and savings bank networks with the IPSs, for which it is particularly important that the liquidation of members is avoided. On the one hand, these bank networks are often more financially interconnected than other banks. On the other hand, a failure of a single cooperative or savings bank can have ramifications for the perceived risk of the entire network by customers and counterparts.

There are basically two broad options to include the preventive and alternative measures under a common deposit insurance scheme: First, add private IPS to the DGS/EDIS framework. The preventive measures could be arranged through private IPSs, which are added on top of the DGS or EDIS frameworks. This means that the IPSs would have to collect contributions in addition to those already collected by the DGS/EDIS. Although this would give the IPS more liberty in preventing a potential failure or limiting the impact of a potential failure. However, it might be difficult to agree upon with the Member States involved. The costs for the members of the IPS would be higher, as they have to contribute to both the IPS and DGS/EDIS. This could be solved by giving the members of a private IPS a discount on their contribution to the DGS/EDIS as they are less likely to need funds from the DGS/EDIS to pay out covered deposits. Lower contributions by IPS members are unlikely to be accepted by Member States without an IPS, however, as they would imply higher contributions from banks in the countries without an IPS. Indeed, the total contributions to the DGS is a fixed share of total covered deposits (0.8 per cent of covered deposits), so if some banks receive a discount, this needs to be compensated by higher contributions from other banks.

Second, integrate private measures within the EDIS framework. The preventive and alternative measures could be fully integrated within the EDIS framework, notwithstanding whether there are IPSs in a Member State or not. This would require: (i) that the Member States demanding preventive and alternative measures can count on them when necessary; (ii) the preventive and alternative measures would not lead to higher contributions for the other Member States; and (iii) the preventive and alternative measures fit well within the EU bank crisis management framework. The full integration of the preventive and alternative measures in EDIS would limit the need for maintaining standalone IPSs. The use of both preventive and alternative measures effectively requires an organizational capacity to assess, implement, and monitor the concomitant risks, which an EBU-wide DGS is unlikely to possess. Therefore, a national DGS would in general be best placed to execute the preventive and alternative measures. The critical aspect in this remains the financial contributions and thus potential mutualization. Indeed, the costs of the measures should not exceed the costs of the contractual/ statutory mandate of the DGS.

This latter option to integrate the preventive and alternative measures in EDIS seems preferred if national DGSs remain responsible for the organization of pay-outs, as they are more likely to have the necessary expertise. Moreover, to ensure that the net costs are not higher to the DGS, harmonization of the least cost test is required.

26.3.2.2 The Least-Cost Test

The current DGS Directive does not specify how it should be determined whether the (net) costs for the DGS do not exceed the costs of a regular pay-out. Hence, for the preventive measures the costs should not exceed 'the costs of fulfilling the statutory or contractual mandate of the DGS' as specified in Article 11(3) DGS Directive and alternative measures only the 'net amount of compensating covered depositors' as specified in Article 11(6) DGS Directive. In order to limit the chances that in practice the costs for the DGS exceed those of a regular pay-out and the alternative and preventive measures are applied similarly across the EBU countries, the so-called least-cost test would have to be defined in detail, for instance through technical standards to be drafted by the European Banking Authority.

The least-cost test could also benefit from the logic used by the FDIC in the United States. The FDIC is obliged to choose the least-cost option (FDIC, 2019). Searching for the least-cost option is also appropriate for interventions of DGSs in the EBU, as the failing banks which put the financial stability at risk are in principle subject to a resolution instead of a DGS pay-out.

To contribute to a level playing field, a few additional requirements should be included for alternative measures to open the search to find a potential acquirer for all banks in the EBU, stakeholder bank networks should have the possibility to match the best offer to limit the demutualization, and the acquisition should not put the acquirer at risk.

26.3.2.3 Roles within the Crisis Management Framework

The use of preventive and alternative measures would also have to fit into the bank crisis management framework and state aid rules. The state aid rules form the main obstacle to a use of preventive measures, as some private IPSs seem to be allowed to use their funds for preventive measures, while public DGSs are not. Alternative measures could have a clear contribution to the reduction of costs for the DGSs as well as preservation of the economic value by avoiding insolvency. Moreover, the alternative measures could form an option for the failing banks not subject to resolution (Figure 26.3).

26.3.2.4 Limit the Potential Mutualization

The main obstacle to finding a political consensus on a common deposit insurance is the lack of support for risk sharing between Member States, especially if the risks in the banking system are not reduced. Looking at the deposit insurance, sovereigns are exposed to failing institutions as implicit or explicit ultimate guarantors of the national DGSs. Although some have questioned the extent to which systematic cross-subsidization would be necessary (Carmassi et al., 2018), there are varying risks of bank failures across countries due to bank-specific factors (concentration, presence of stakeholder banks, branches, and foreign banks), but also differences in insolvency frameworks, and legal and tax systems (see e.g. De Aldisio et al., 2019).

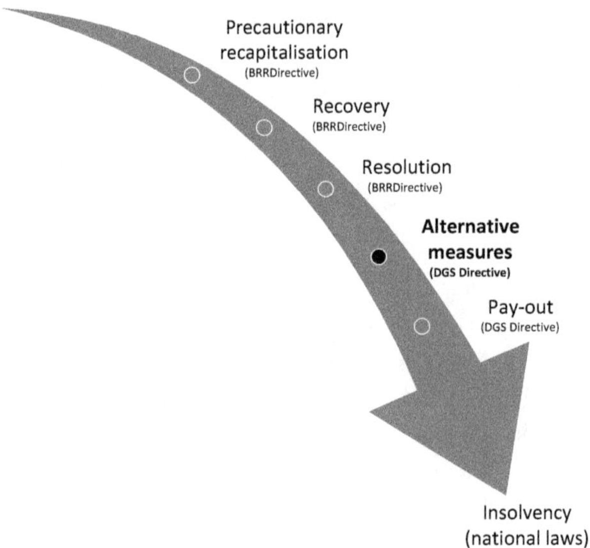

FIGURE 26.3. Role of alternative measures in crisis management framework
Note: The figure shows the order of the various crisis management measures as envisaged under the proposed option. The figure is a simplification as some of the measures can be taken in parallel or connected. For example, the precautionary recapitalization and preventive measures can be taken at the same time and DGS can contribute to resolution.

There are broadly four different possible forms of a common deposit insurance scheme. First, a full insurance scheme, which requires a EBU-wide DGS that covers all the liquidity needs and losses related to the pay-out events or contributions to resolutions in the EBU. The full insurance scheme would imply that all the funds and thus risks of the national DGSs in the EBU countries are merged into a single fund. The national DGSs could still collect the funds and execute the pay-out procedures or alternative measures.

Second, a co-insurance scheme shares liquidity needs and losses related to deposit pay-outs from the 'first euro' between national DGSs and a EBU-wide DGS. The collected funds would be distributed among national DGSs and EBU-wide DGS. The larger the share covered by the common DGS, the less the risk for the sovereign and the higher the risk-sharing.

Third, a reinsurance scheme would meet liquidity needs and losses until the funds of the national DGSs are depleted (Figure 26.4). Afterwards the common DGS would cover the remainder. The contributions would have to be split between national DGSs and the EBU-wide DGS. The contribution to the EBU-wide DGS would have to be calculated based on the risks the national DGSs pose to the EBU-wide DGS.

The fourth is **a mandatory lending scheme** between the national DGSs to cover the liquidity needs in excess of the liquidity available to national DGS that is confronted with a pay-out event. The loans would have to be repaid within a given maturity and require an interest payment. The mandatory lending scheme would imply no risk sharing, as all the losses would be carried by the national DGS confronted with a pay-out event. The loans could be provided by the national DGSs pro rata the share in the covered deposits. These forms can be applied as standalones or in combination. For example, the EDIS, as proposed by the Commission, could initially take the form of a reinsurance, followed by co-insurance, and full insurance.[19]

[19] See European Commission (2015a) for the EDIS proposal.

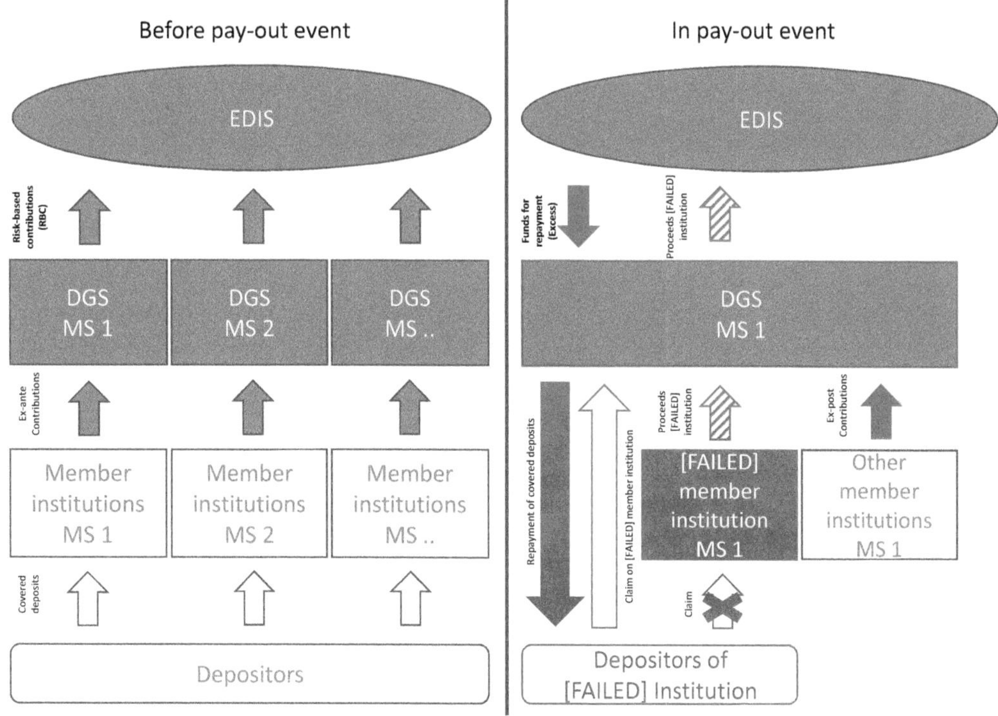

FIGURE 26.4. A reinsurance scheme

Considering the opposition of the Member States against cross-subsidization of losses and the need of measures to fully align the risks of the banks across countries, in principle only reinsurance with a risk-based contribution and mandatory lending would remain a feasible option. The reinsurance scheme would be preferred to ensure that the national DGSs do not become dysfunctional after multiple pay-outs.

26.4 CONCLUSIONS

The EBU has been a major step towards breaking the 'doom loop' between banks and their sovereigns. Of the three pillars of the EBU, the SSM and SRM have already been established, while the EDIS still needs to be established as a third pillar. Besides the creation of the deposit insurance, the liquidity in resolution is still a major challenge that needs to be addressed.

This chapter presented two pragmatic proposals to solve these two key challenges for the EBU.

The first proposal is a transitional liquidity assistance tool to provide the necessary liquidity in a resolution. The proposal anticipates that the SRF guarantees the funds provided by the ECB to the banks under resolution. The TLA needs to provide the SRB the predictability needed when resolving a bank, while taking away credit risks for the ECB.

The second proposal is to create an EDIS that takes the form of a reinsurance scheme to overcome objections against mutualization. The reinsurance scheme would also include some national features for the inclusion of preventive and alternative measures if the methodology for the least-cost test could be worked out, to ensure that there is no negative outcome for the deposit insurance scheme and the EDIS in particular.

REFERENCES

BCBS (2013). Basel III: The liquidity coverage ratio and liquidity risk monitoring tools (January). www.bis.org/publ/bcbs238.htm

BCBS (2014). Basel III: the net stable funding ratio. Bank for International Settlements, Basel (October). www.bis.org/bcbs/publ/d295.htm.

Carmassi, J., Dobkowitz, S., Evrard, J., Parisi, L., and Silva, A. (2018). Completing the Banking Union with a European Deposit Insurance Scheme: who is afraid of cross-subsidisation? Occasional Paper Series, 208.

De Aldisio, A., Aloia, G., Bentivegna, A., Gagliano, A., Giorgiantonio, E., Lanfranchi, C., and Maltese, M. (2019). Notes on financial stability and supervision. *Notes on Financial Stability and Supervision*, 15, 1–6. www.bancaditalia.it/pubblicazioni/note-stabilita/2019-0015/index.html?com.dotmarketing.htmlpage.language=1

De Groen, W. P. (2018). Financing bank resolution: An alternative solution for arranging the liquidity required (November). www.europarl.europa.eu/RegData/etudes/IDAN/2018/624423/IPOL_IDA(2018)624423_EN.pdf

De Groen, W. P., and Alcidi, C. (2019). Options and national discretions under the Deposit Guarantee Scheme Directive and their treatment in the context of a European Deposit Insurance Scheme (November). European Commission. https://doi.org/10.2874/648805

De Groen, W. P., and Gros, D. (2015). Estimating the bridge financing needs of the Single Resolution Fund: How expensive is it to resolve a bank? www.ceps.eu/ceps-publications/estimating-bridge-financing-needs-single-resolution-fund-how-expensive-it-resolve-bank/

DG Competition (2016). State aid used. European Commission.

De Haan, L., and van den End, J. W. (2013). Bank liquidity, the maturity ladder, and regulation. *Journal of Banking and Finance* 37(10), 3930–3950.

EBA (2022). Deposit guarantee schemes data. www.eba.europa.eu/regulation-and-policy/recovery-and-resolution/deposit-guarantee-schemes-data

ECA (2016). Single Supervisory Mechanism – Good start but further improvements needed (Issue 29). https://doi.org/10.2865/233213

ECA (2017). Single Resolution Board: Work on a challenging Banking Union task started, but still a long way to go. Special Report (Vol. 287, No. 23). www.eca.europa.eu/Lists/ECADocuments/SR17_23/SR_SRB-BU_EN.pdf

ECA (2021). Resolution planning in the Single Resolution Mechanism. Special Report. www.eca.europa.eu/Lists/ECADocuments/SR21_01/SR_Single_resolution_mechanism_EN.pdf

ECB (2014a). Guide to banking supervision. European Central Bank (November). www.bankingsupervision.europa.eu/ecb/pub/pdf/ssmguidebankingsupervision201411.en.pdf?404fd6cb61dbde0095c8722d5aff29cd

ECB (2014b). Decision of the European Central Bank of 31 January 2014 on the close cooperation with the national competent authorities of participating Member States whose currency is not the euro (ECB/2014/5). www.ecb.europa.eu/pub/pdf/other/en_dec_2014_05_fen.pdf?5105e4c768e886be0f5844b03a868418

ECB (2015). Statistical Data Warehouse: Total assets/liabilities reported by MFI excluding ESCB in the euro area (stock). https://sdw.ecb.europa.eu/quickview.do?SERIES_KEY=117.BSI.M.U2.N.A.T00.A.1.Z5.0000.Z01.E

ECB (2022). List of supervised banks. www.bankingsupervision.europa.eu/banking/list/html/index.en.html

Eurogroup (2018). Letter President Centeno to President Tusk. 25 June. www.consilium.europa.eu/media/35798/2018-06-25-letter-president-centeno-to-president-tusk.pdf

European Commission (2012). A roadmap towards a banking union. In *Communication from the Commission to the European Parliament and the Council*. https://eur-lex.europa.eu/legal-content/EN/TXT/PDF/?uri=CELEX:52012DC0510&from=EN

European Commission (2015a). Proposal for a Regulation of the European parliament and of the Council amending Regulation (EU) 806/2014 in order to establish a European Deposit Insurance Scheme. https://eur-lex.europa.eu/legal-content/EN/TXT/PDF/?uri=CELEX:52015PC0586&from=EN

European Commission (2015b). State Aid Scoreboard 2014: Aid in the context of the financial and economic crisis. https://ec.europa.eu/competition-policy/state-aid/scoreboard_en

European Commission (2017). Communication on completing the Banking Union. https://ec.europa.eu/commission/state-union-2017_en

FDIC (2019). Resolutions Handbook. https://ypfsresourcelibrary.blob.core.windows.net/fcic/YPFS/resolutions-handbook.pdf

IMF (2018). Euro area policies: Financial sector assessment program–technical note–bank resolution and crisis management. *IMF Staff Country Reports*, 18(232), 1. https://doi.org/10.5089/9781484369661.002

König, E. (2018). Gaps in the Banking Union regarding funding in resolution and how to close them. *Eurofi Magazine* (September). https://srb.europa.eu/en/content/eurofi-article-elke-konig-gaps-banking-union-regarding-funding-resolution-and-how-close

Lannoo, K. (2019). Stock take of the SRB's activities over the past years: What to improve and focus on? (March). www.europarl.europa.eu/RegData/etudes/IDAN/2019/634394/IPOL_IDA(2019)634394_EN.pdf

Löyttyniemi, T. (2018). The common backstop: How it will strengthen the Single Resolution Fund. *SRB Article* (October). https://srb.europa.eu/en/node/664

Restoy, F. (2019). How to improve crisis management in the banking union: A European FDIC? CIRSF Annual International Conference 2019 on 'Financial Supervision and Financial Stability 10 Years after the Crisis: Achievements and next steps' (July), 1–8. www.bis.org/speeches/sp190715.pdf

SRB (2021). Single Resolution Fund (SRF) – Fact Sheet 2021. 1(806), 2020–2021. www.srb.europa.eu/en/content/single-resolution-fund

SRB (2022). Banks under the SRB's remit. www.srb.europa.eu/en/content/banks-under-srbs-remit

Van Rompuy, H. (2012). Towards a genuine economic and monetary union. Report by President of the European Council. https://doi.org/10.1007/978-3-319-30707-7_6

27

The Re-emergence of Market-Based Finance?

The Politics of the Capital Markets Union

Giuseppe Montalbano and Markus Haverland

27.1 INTRODUCTION

This chapter focuses on the Capital Markets Union (CMU) approached from a political science viewpoint. While taking different theoretical perspectives, political scientists so far have looked at explaining the main motives and driving forces behind the CMU, at the same time focusing less on its actual policy outcomes. Also, most of the attention has been directed to the reform of the regulatory framework for securitization, whereas the other priorities and measures of the CMU agenda have received little scrutiny. However, a comprehensive assessment of the rationale, goals, and policy outcomes is necessary to grasp the CMU's significance.

To explain the initiation and content of the CMU agenda, its fluctuating fortunes and prospects, we focus on intergovernmentalist, supranationalist, and transnationalist approaches in international political economy (IPE), assessing their explanatory potentials and flaws. The three theoretical streams point to different actors and dynamics, which can complement each other and be integrated according to a more holistic approach in IPE, looking at disentangling the multiple processes within the complex policy initiative. While intergovernmentalism concerns Member State preferences, electoral incentives, and bargaining power, supranationalism focuses on functional spill-overs and the role of supranational actors such as the European Commission and the European Central Bank (ECB). At the intersection between national and supranational dimensions, transnationalist frameworks put at the centre the role of cross-border socioeconomic interests in shaping dominant discourses and political orientations.

By relying on these main political science perspectives towards European financial integration, this chapter addresses some critical puzzles: Why did the CMU emerge as a market-based solution in the wake of the European economic crisis? After being seen as part of the problem in the context of the Global Financial Crisis (GFC), how did financial markets integration and expansion again become a tool for public policy goals? Did the CMU represent an actual historical turn in the EU financial markets integration process? As we will argue, the CMU represented a significant shift in the EU approach towards financial market regulation compared to the post-crisis reform wave. Yet, far from being a fully coherent and successful initiative, in its policy outcomes the CMU revealed the fragmentation, diverging political logics, and multiple conflicts beneath its surface. It has become a relatively narrow and technocratic battlefield among competing coalitions of corporate and policymakers' interests for the future of financial integration in the EU.

The chapter starts by describing the initiation of the CMU through the 2015 Action Plan, focusing first on its rationales and assumptions and then its various actions, also considering the redefinition of the CMU strategic priorities in the 2017 mid-term review (and in the face of Brexit). The achievements and non-achievements are then described using the theoretical framework's explanatory elements. Finally, the political feasibility of the new 2020 Action Plan is discussed.

27.2 MAIN FEATURES OF THE CAPITAL MARKETS UNION

27.2.1 *Rationale and Assumptions*

The CMU was initially launched as a flagship initiative of the incoming Juncker Commission in 2015 to respond to a set of fundamental challenges for the EU struggling with a prolonged economic crisis. Resuming the longstanding project of European capital markets integration was framed as an essential priority to address both the immediate challenges for the EU's economic recovery and financial stability and the long-term viability of the EMU and European integration at large. In his speech as the leading candidate for the Presidency of the European Commission in July 2014, Juncker firstly presented the need to 'further develop and integrate capital markets' as a grounding condition to boost economic growth by cutting the costs of financing 'particularly for small and medium-size enterprises [SMEs]' (Juncker, 2014; building on European Commission 2014). A few months later, the Commission's green paper *Building a Capital Markets Union* set the ambitious target of creating an effective single European market for capital across all then twenty-eight EU Member States by 2019 (European Commission, 2015a, p. 4).

The general CMU rationale was linked to the new Commission's priority to foster growth and employment in Europe through long-term investments in the context of a €315 billion *Investment Plan for Europe*. Integrated capital markets were intended to provide the needed financial leverage for Juncker's investment package by diversifying and broadening funding sources for entrepreneurs (emphasizing SMEs and infrastructural projects), thus reducing the overreliance on banks. The growth argument was intertwined with the enduring concern for ensuring financial stability. From this angle, market-based finance in the European bank-based financial systems was presented as an essential step in improving market-based risk-sharing mechanisms (European Commission, 2015a, pp. 2–3, 9). In this way, the CMU emerged as the third 'Union' to build up alongside the (partly achieved) Banking Union and the (still distant) Fiscal Union, to secure the stabilization of the EMU and the whole EU project (Juncker et al., 2015). The growth and stability goals of the CMU were then articulated in a set of core economic and political assumptions and objectives.

The CMU policy narrative framed the problem of the sluggish and asymmetric economic recovery in the EU in terms of a supply shortage of credit availability for the business sectors (Braun and Hübner, 2018; Finance Watch, 2015). Therefore, a supply-side-oriented approach targeted the regulatory burdens and barriers to improving cross-border capital flow in Europe and lowering the cost of credit, particularly for SMEs. The latter was presented as the primary intended beneficiaries of diversification of the EU's financial system, making it less reliant on banking lending. In the distressed eurozone countries, SMEs experienced a prolonged shrinkage in the traditional bank funding channels, on which they are most dependent, due to the fragmentation of interbank markets, the high level of non-performing loans, and the stricter capital adequacy requirements introduced in the EU post-regulation, resulting in an overall pressure to deleverage. The Commission stressed the benefits for SMEs resulting from the Action Plan as a fundamental discursive strategy to frame the CMU project as a win–win game for non-financial firms and capital markets incumbents, and to build up a broad consensus around it, as plainly admitted by Commissioner Hill (2015; see also Quaglia and Howarth, 2018).

Hence, the CMU's second critical assumption targeted European firms' overreliance on banks and their limited funding opportunities, exposing the EU's economies to the tightening of bank lending conditions. Retrieving a recurrent argument used since the first plans for an integrated EU financial services markets emerged at the end of the 1990s (European Commission, 1998), the US capital market-based system was taken as a paradigmatic model as regards the untapped potential for European SME funding and economic growth, attributed to the overreliance on traditional bank credit (European Commission, 2015a, pp. 3–4; for a critical discussion of the assumed superiority of capital market-based system against bank-based ones, see Aldasoro and Unger, 2017; Sahay et al., 2015). Such diversification efforts entailed the promotion of non-bank intermediaries and equity markets, together with market-based banking. The latter refers to the increasing exposure to global financial markets and complex financial products by the whole banking sector, including small and alternative banks (Hardie and Howarth, 2013; Pesendorfer, 2020, pp. 265–266). Some key CMU 2015 priorities aimed first at improving the conditions for investment banking activities (see Section 27.2.2), giving them some relief in the ongoing tightening of prudential requirements and generally restoring the profitability of the European banking sector. Revitalization of market-based banking and the banks mainly engaged with it stands at the core of the CMU project, against those banking sectors less involved in financial markets activities (such as the small alternative banks).

The third main CMU rationale addressed the importance of restoring key market-based banking activities to ensure the efficient transmission of the ECB monetary policy in open market operations in the context of the European sovereign debt crisis. From the very outset, the ECB looked favourably at the proposals to relaunch those market segments on which the transmission of its extraordinary stimulus policies relied, like securitization, thus sustaining the recovery of the EU banking sector and its lending capacity to the real economy. For example, most of the securitization business is based on residential and commercial mortgage loans, which represent a key item in the banks' balance sheets. At the same time, the ECB purchased large amounts of asset-backed securities and other securitized products in its asset purchase programmes (Adamski, Chapter 9 in this volume), thus having an interest in maintaining the liquidity of these markets (Braun et al. 2018, pp. 104–105; Gonzalez, 2014, p. 32).

Alongside the ECB's expansionary monetary policy, as the fourth main rationale, the CMU became the market-led complementary tool to stimulate growth in substitution for the restrained fiscal leeway left to the eurozone countries under the EU's austerity response to the crisis. Strengthening of the debt and deficit rules (Markakis, Chapter 17 in this volume), together with the European Semester as a significant innovation in the macroeconomic coordination of the EU countries (Eihmanis, Chapter 16 this volume), severely repressed spending capacity in the distressed Member States, together with their ability to finance public investments (Amtenbrink, 2015; Fitoussi and Saraceno, 2013; Laffan and Schlosser, 2016; Oberndorfer, 2015). Again, the financial markets would step in to provide budget-neutral cross-border investment opportunities, private welfare provisions (such as personal and occupational pensions), and cheap funding for firms while the distressed states repaired their budgets. In this way, capital markets were intended to give a financial market 'fix' to the lacking distributional mechanisms in the EMU and the caps put on the eurozone governments' expenditures (Braun and Hübner, 2018, p. 7; Hübner, 2019).

In addition, more integrated and liquid markets for financial instruments were a condition for the Juncker Commission's Investment Plan for Europe, the short-term public stimulus programme relying on a substantial leveraging of private financing (ratio of 1:15) through the European Fund of Strategic Investments (EFSI) managed by the European Investment Bank (EIB). A public guarantee of €21 billion allowed the EFSI to issue bonds amounting to around three times as much and then use the raised funds to finance further investments, providing substantive guarantees to private investors by committing to absorb potential losses on junior investment tranches (European Commission, 2015c). The EFSI was then given the flexibility to manage 'a wide range of different financial instruments', such as debt financing, guarantees, equity, private equity, and venture capital, with the aim to 'crowd-in private investors' (Katainen, 2015), thus incentivizing the participation of financial market investors in riskier long-term investments. In this context, the CMU would provide a critical market infrastructure for the functioning of the Investment Plan.

As the fifth core assumption, the Commission and the ECB presented the CMU as the necessary premise to put in place adequate capital market-based shock-absorption mechanism. The latter was meant to enhance the stability and resilience of the European economies. The sovereign debt crisis brought to the fore the vulnerability of the Monetary Union in face of asymmetric economic shocks and the essential need for public risk-sharing arrangements, while fully exposing at the same time the formidable political obstacles to achieving it.

Most of the hardest political conflicts dividing the eurozone countries in response to the crisis revolved around the introduction of cross-border burden sharing and (indirect) fiscal transfer mechanisms. A significant cleavage between creditor and crisis-prone states emerged. The former feared worsening their conditions as they were increasingly becoming net contributors at the expense of their domestic taxpayers' and policymakers' electoral consensus. In the end, the European Stability Mechanism (ESM) and the Single Resolution Fund (SRF) for the distressed eurozone banks provide for cross-border risk sharing, although the conditionalities and attached requirements called into question their actual effectiveness (Camacho, 2021; Montalbano, 2021). Similarly, the setting up of a Europeanized bank deposit insurance scheme, proposed by the Commission at the end of 2015 as the third pillar of the Banking Union, would have remained in a deadlock due to the resolute opposition of the creditor countries (Donnelly, 2018, Ríos Camacho, Chapter 24 in this volume; Binder, Chapter25 in this volume). On the contrary, private cross-border risk sharing, such as that offered by capital markets integration, represented a far less politically controversial solution, meeting concerns of the creditor countries (Epstein and Rhodes, 2018, p. 219). According to the argument defended by its supporters, the CMU could improve cross-border and cross-sectional market risk sharing through geographical and product diversification of investment portfolios, preventing the concentration of losses to domestic investors in case of an economic shock (Cimadomo et al., 2018; ECB, 2016; Lannoo and Thomadakis, 2019, p. 29; Schelkle, 2017; Valiante, 2016, p. 58).

While the CMU Action Plan fully assumed the economic theory beyond capital market risk absorption efficacy (Juncker et al., 2015, p. 4), the risks stemming from the impact of significant economic shocks on integrated financial markets, like the spread of crisis contagion into systemic events, were put aside (Lannoo and Thomadakis, 2019, p. 5; Valiante, 2016, pp. 46–47). Just three years before, the Four Presidents' Report put on paper the then prevailing scepticism about the efficacy of private risk sharing as a tool to deal with the European crisis, pointing at its implicit risks for financial stability (Van Rompuy, 2012, p. 10). Since then, key experts and officials in the Commission and the ECB have led the conversion of the EU policymakers towards private risk-sharing solutions, faced with the enduring impasse among

Member States' governments around public-based risk sharing (Braun and Hübner, 2018, pp. 12–13). However, the actual ability of cross-border capital market integration to bring the intended benefits of private risk sharing without a full-fledged Banking Union and a functioning Fiscal Union has been questioned in the literature, stressing the complementarity of the 'three Unions' (Acharya and Steffen, 2016; Farhi and Werning, 2017; Iannou and Schäfer, 2017).

Lastly, as a final remark, the CMU Plan represented a relevant turn in the post-crisis regulatory approach towards the financial industry. If the latter was at the centre of the public bias and policy reforms to plug the pre-crisis regulatory loopholes, the CMU opened a new season of dialogue and cooperation between EU authorities and the financial sector. Market-based finance and its actors switched from the problem to a solution to the EU's new pressing urgency of growth. A more inclusive approach toward financial interests and expertise in the agenda-setting and policy-making process underlies the CMU, ushering in new forms of public–private regulatory partnerships (Dorn, 2016) and a more proactive stance from financial lobbying (Engelen and Glasmacher, 2016, 2018; Montalbano, 2020) compared to the years immediately after the GFC. As Commissioner Hill put it, shortly after taking charge of the new Directorate General on Financial Stability, Financial Services, and Capital Markets Union, 'we do not make our economy stronger by making our financial services weaker', so that financial regulation had to be addressed 'through the prism of jobs and growth' (Hill, 2014).

The designation of Lord Jonathan Hill, a leading figure of the British Conservative Party with a professional background in the City of London, to the Commission's financial services directorate, was part of Juncker's strategy to involve the United Kingdom in the renewed EU financial integration efforts. As the most important financial centre and global financial hub in Europe, the United Kingdom was meant to play a vital role in the EU-wide CMU project, thus emerging from its isolation in the wake of the eurozone-centred Banking Union and the German–French leading role in the management of the European financial and sovereign debt crisis. Moreover, a closer engagement of the United Kingdom with the CMU soon acquired a political meaning for the Commission, in face of the threat of an anti-EU referendum, promised by David Cameron if the Conservatives won the 2015 general elections (Cameron, 2013; Guardian, 2014; Ringe, 2015, p. 3).

27.2.2 *The Initial CMU Agenda and Policy Initiatives*

The CMU Action Plan, issued in September 2015, contained thirty-three actions across six areas of intervention, corresponding to the vital political objectives entailed in deepening capital markets integration. A broad array of policy tools and types of intervention was announced, combining regulatory initiatives with public consultations, impact assessments, and white papers. Moreover, the plan called for proactive participation of financial actors and the strategic use of industry self-regulation and market-led initiatives, limiting public regulation only where strictly necessary (European Commission, 2015b, p. 28). Such an approach was coherent with the general aim of relieving the financial industry's regulatory pressure and grounding the CMU project in a public–private policy partnership (Dorn, 2016; Montalbano, 2020, 2022). Lastly, non-legislative measures were foreseen to foster convergence among the Member States and remove barriers to highly sensitive policy issues.

The first two priority areas referred to the expansion of financing options for firms, emphasizing SMEs' access to public and private equity markets. Relevant initiatives under this policy area included notably the streamlining of the Prospectus Directive to 'make it less costly for businesses', and foremost SMEs, 'to raise funds publicly' (European Commission, 2015b,

p. 4), together with a package to foster venture capital markets in Europe, containing both a review of the 2013 Regulation on the EU passport for venture capital fund managers and the launch of a public fund-of-funds to kick-start such investments (European Commission, 2015b, pp. 7–9).

Promoting long-term, sustainable infrastructure-related investments constituted the third main line of action. The advanced measures pointed at revising the capital adequacy requirements for banks and insurance firms investing in infrastructure projects, thus amending the post-crisis legislation on prudential standards (the Solvency II and the Capital Requirements Regulation and Directive, see also Parchimowicz, Chapter 23 in this volume). Moreover, as part of the Better Regulation initiative, the Commission committed to starting an overall cumulative impact assessment of all the post-crisis financial regulations implemented until then.

The fourth policy area aimed to incentivize the inclusion of small savers into the capital markets. In this way, the CMU aimed to promote further financialization, hoping to channel households' savings into the markets and induce less risk-averse saving habits, moving them from home equities and bank deposits (European Commission, 2015b, pp. 18–19). At the same time, the Action Plan drafted a future policy initiative to build up an EU market for personal private pensions to complement public pension schemes. A European private pension product was thus proposed to support households in making efficient provisions for their retirement given the challenges faced by public welfare systems due to increased life expectancy and fiscal pressures (European Commission, 2015b, p. 19). Therefore, a key CMU goal was to strengthen privatized and asset-based welfare mechanisms.

A specific chapter was dedicated to the measures needed to enhance lending capacities of EU banks. At the centre of these priority areas, the Commission included what has been considered by many scholars as the most representative and influential initiative in the CMU: the launch of 'simple, transparent and standardized' (STS) securitization (European Commission, 2015b, pp. 21–22). The latter was presented as a fundamental move to restore the important market for bank lending and risk management 'in a safe way', heeding the lessons of the Global Financial Crisis. In addition, the Action Plan addressed the problem raised by the exemption of credit unions in some Member States from the Capital Requirements Directive (CRD IV), justifying it by their low level of risks and the unfair treatment received by the one-size-fits-all approach of the new prudential standards in the EU.

Lastly, as the sixth line of action, the Commission planned to break down 'the most important barriers to the free flow of capital' concerning domestic business insolvency, taxation, and securities legislation, aiming at a legal convergence in the EU (European Commission, 2015b, pp. 24–25). Direct taxation requires unanimous voting in the Council according to the special legislative procedure established by Article 115 of the Treaty on the Functioning of the European Union (TFEU). For this reason, the Commission advanced targeted proposals for a code of conduct and voluntary cooperation in the tax treatment of cross-border investments and mechanisms of withholding tax reliefs. Yet a significant effort was envisaged in the Action Plan to address the generalized preferential tax treatment of debt over equity instruments in the EU, a fundamental bias in developing cross-border equity markets integration.

Most importantly, the Action Plan foresaw the gradual empowerment of the EU oversight on securities markets to foster supranationalization of supervision and building up of a single rule book for the EU capital markets (European Commission, 2015a, p. 26). However, whereas the Five Presidents' Report put the construction of a single capital markets authority as the ultimate goal of the CMU (Juncker et al., 2015, p. 12), no mention of the latter appeared in the final 2015 Action Plan. As is evident, a unique EU supervisor for, at that time, twenty-eight different capital markets and their regulatory settings would have been a far more contentious institutional development than the single supervisory mechanism under the eurozone-centred Banking Union (Epstein and Rhodes, 2018). Any plan for a centralized supranational oversight was suddenly opposed by the British government, in line with its growing aversion to the influence of the ECB and the eurozone core economies over the EU financial markets, reflected in the EU–UK agreement in February 2016 (Howarth and Quaglia, 2017, pp. 153–157).

27.2.3 *Recasting the CMU in Light of Brexit, the Digital Revolution and Ecological Transition*

The CMU mid-term review, issued in June 2017, took stock of the achieved and ongoing initiatives, reporting twenty delivered measures out of the thirty-three envisaged in the original Action Plan (European Commission, 2017a, p. 4). The remaining reform projects were reoriented and integrated according to the general redefinition of the CMU's strategic goals in a profoundly different political context compared to that in 2015.

The perspective of a British exit from the EU induced a reorientation of the CMU's overall political rationale. If the United Kingdom was the main character on the CMU stage, the Brexit victory cast a shadow over the future of European financial markets integration (Howarth and Quaglia, 2017; Ständer, 2016). The City of London represented the largest financial hub in Europe and the main access point to global capital markets for the EU's large firms. Moreover, the United Kingdom was the primary market in euro-denominated derivatives clearing (James and Quaglia, 2020, 2022). On the one hand, therefore, the EU and UK financial regulators had an interest in preventing the disruption of the regulatory framework upholding the European financial markets (Ringe, 2015). On the other hand, the EU's core financial powers soon found themselves competing 'to lure financial business away from the UK' (Howarth and Quaglia, 2018, p. 1119). For its part, the United Kingdom ran the long-term risk of becoming a rule-taker of financial regulation from the EU, being threatened in its capacity to influence the international regulatory agenda (James and Quaglia, 2020, p. 150).

In the end, the Commission framed Brexit as an event requiring a speeding up in the finalization of the key legislative initiatives envisaged in the original Action Plan and the definition of new strategic priorities (European Commission, 2017a, p. 8).

The first new priority set in the 2017 Communication thus pointed to strengthening the supervisory powers of the European Securities and Markets Authority (ESMA), including its 'ability to identify and tackle weaknesses in national supervision', with the possibility to grant to it, 'where warranted', the 'direct supervision to support a functioning CMU' (European Commission, 2017a, pp. 10–11). The UK withdrawal opened an unexpected window of opportunity for the Commission to bring the centralization of capital markets supervision to the fore, winning against the resistance of the remaining EU governments.

Supervisory and regulatory convergence was also related to the second main initiative prompted by the Commission on the development of innovative financial business, based on digitalization and data-driven tools, labelled under the 'FinTech' acronym (Demertzis et al., 2017; Navaretti et al., 2018). Again, the FinTech narrative revolved around the expanded opportunities and cheaper funding for consumers and SMEs, brought by the competition among financial actors, and the digitalization of finance as a tool to enhance financial inclusion (European Commission, 2017a, p. 7).

A third new priority field highlighted in the CMU mid-term review was sustainable finance. Responding to commitments made at the UN Conference in Paris on Climate (COP21) to set a pathway for financing the transition to a climate-resilient economy, the Commission established a high-level expert group in December 2016 to advise on how to increase public and private capital flows towards environmentally sustainable investments and to integrate environmental, social, and governance factors (ESG) to financial stability risk assessment (European Commission, 2017a, pp. 14–15). Sustainable finance thus emerged as an occasion for the Commission to rebuild consensus from civil society around the CMU agenda (Ahlström and Monciardini, 2022), loudly denounced on various occasions by public interest groups as a return to a pre-crisis-like path to financialization. At the same time, an environmentally oriented CMU responded to the broadly shared goal to strengthen the EU leadership on green finance as a key strength for its global competitiveness.

27.3 EXPLAINING CMU'S SUCCESS AND FAILURES

27.3.1 *Overview of the Main Theories*

To assess and explain both the achievements and failures of the CMU agendas, we build on the main theoretical approaches in the European financial market integration and political economy that have been used in the growing literature on the CMU. In particular, this section looks at the intergovernmentalist, supranationalist, and transnationalist strands to derive a set of competing hypotheses for testing in our analysis of the policy outcomes.

The domestic-centred focus adopted in the first analyses of the CMU agenda showed how the core EU financial centres, hosting the large cross-border banks and most developed capital markets, have been the core constituency of the CMU (Quaglia et al., 2016; Pesendorfer, 2015). As the leading European financial hub, the United Kingdom emerged as the main potential beneficiary, and its involvement in this new chapter of the EU integration process has been considered a crucial political objective of the CMU (Ringe, 2015). From an intergovernmentalist perspective in the European political economy (for example, Howarth and Quaglia, 2016; Moravcsik, 1998), we would expect the CMU achievements and the extent of the cross-border capital market integration to depend on the interests of EU's core financial powers.

Most of the literature on the CMU so far, however, mainly relied on supranationalist and neofunctionalist accounts (see, for example, Jabko, 2006; Posner, 2009; Stone Sweet and Sandholtz, 1998), pointing to the role of functional pressures unleashed by the structural interdependence of the ECB's monetary policy and the Commission's growth objectives on the liquidity, depth, and integration of the EU financial markets (see earlier). Such a mode of 'governing-through-the-markets' (Braun, 2020; Braun and Hübner, 2018; Braun et al., 2018) in the wake of the prolonged European crisis allowed the Commission and the ECB to play a significant role in defining and pushing forward the CMU's goals (Epstein and Rhodes, 2018, pp. 209, 213–214). Along the supranationalist strand, from a constructivist-like viewpoint, Howarth and Quaglia (2018) examined the rhetorical strategy of the Juncker Commission in framing the CMU as a win–win game for the financial industry, governments, and consumer interests. According to this supranational framework, we would expect that functionalist pressures and entrepreneurship of the supranational policymakers will explain CMU's outcomes.

Lastly, other transnationalist and critical political economy approaches considered the role of European and domestic lobbying and narratives (Engelen and Glasmacher, 2016, 2018; Fernandez and Aalbers, 2017), as well as the interplay between corporate power and public salience of financial regulation after the crisis in shaping the policy entrepreneurship of the financial industry (Montalbano, 2020). From this point of view, the underlying factors of the CMU's success must be found in the lobbying power of the financial industry and its coalition-making capacity in the context of different levels of salience for the policy at stake. The less the interest groups' variety and fragmentation, combined with a context of low policy salience, the more the public–private interest coalition pushed for deepening capital markets integration (Montalbano, 2021). However, both supranationalist and transnationalist accounts variously stressed the importance of the GFC as a critical juncture and the efforts of policymakers and interest groups to frame the CMU accordingly. If the CMU represented a turn concerning the post-crisis priority for financial (re)regulation, the former could not be regarded as a simple return to a pre-crisis 'business as usual'. While the overall goal of 'financial stability' had to fit with the growth objective, the EU policymakers' discourses retained the appeal for a 'safe finance', mindful of the past mistakes, as the veritable leitmotiv of the CMU (Montalbano, 2020).

Based on these competing explanations, the following sections will analyse the main CMU policy initiatives and assess the factors enabling or impeding them.

27.3.2 *Venture Capital*

Concerning the promotion of risk capital, the review of the Regulation establishing an EU passport for venture capital funds (EuVECA) and the European Social Entrepreneurship Funds (EuSEF) was agreed by the Council and the Parliament in May 2017, allowing these funds to invest in larger SMEs and expanding the EU label to private equity funds managing venture capital under the Alternative Investment Fund Managers Directive (AIFMD) (EU, 2017a). EU institutions invested €410 million to establish six public–private VentureEU funds to bring private investors into venture capital funds, with an estimated €6.5 billion of new investment in innovative start-ups and SMEs across Europe (European Commission, 2018). Moreover, the Commission published a study on good practices in tax incentives for venture capital and business angels, providing guidance for Member States' tax policies through the European Semester. The achievements in the area of venture capital can be linked to a broad consensus built in the run-up to the Action Plan between the private equity industry and the Commission, combined with the low political salience of the issue and the perceived small risks for financial stability entailed in these investments in relation to the expected benefits. The plan for a comprehensive package to boost venture capital funds already emerged in the wake of the introduction of the AIFM Directive, depicted by the EU and national venture capital associations as excessively penalizing and stifling this type of investment, aimed at funding innovative and high-growth potential SMEs, on the model of the US Silicon Valley. The Commission sided with the venture capital industry, framing the promotion of such investments as an essential step to unlock funding for innovation in the EU and creating a more US-like equity financing ecosystem. The reduced size of such investment funds in Europe and the related low risks, together with their irrelevance to the underlying causes of the financial crisis, contributed to making venture capital perceived as a rather niche policy issue and as a focused tool to expand funding opportunities for innovative SMEs (the stakeholder consultation showed little participation by non-corporate and other business groups: see EU, 2015). From a functionalist perspective, creating a vibrant cross-border venture capital market would respond to Europe's post-crisis growth and competitive concerns by expanding long-term investment in crucial innovation areas with reduced use of the EU budget. On the other side, the venture capital plan received the staunch support of the United Kingdom, as the leading EU hub of private equity funds, while not being opposed by Germany and France (as the largest venture capital markets on the continent, although at a lower scale than the United Kingdom), which, however, stood with the Commission in preventing the excessive lightening of the EuVECA Regulation, as demanded by the venture capital industry (see EU, 2015).

27.3.3 *Revision of Prospectus Regulation*

As regards the simplification of firms' access to stock markets, the new Regulation on the Prospectus (Regulation (EU) 2017/1129) was published one week after the Communication on the mid-term review, streamlining the requirements related to the companies' information to investors and regulatory authorities when its securities are offered in public and regulated markets. In particular, the Regulation introduced a tailored 'EU Growth Prospectus' for SMEs, designed to simplify their access to the capital markets (EU, 2017b, p. 44). Moreover, the issuance threshold for the obligatory Prospectus was raised from €5 million to €8 million, below which Member States could fix their national thresholds, while for issuance less than €1 million there would be no requirement for a prospectus at all.

Here again, the alliance between the Commission and corporate interests proved crucial in shaping the revision of the Prospectus requirements as a critical theme for expanding European firms' financing opportunities by favouring their access to securities markets. In this way, streamlining such disclosure requirements responded to the primary CMU goal of promoting capital market financing channels for companies, emphasizing SMEs, loosening the dependence on traditional bank lending, and thus improving the EU's recovery and private risk-sharing capacity. Yet, as this measure entailed investor protection and transparency concerns that gained salience in the post-crisis scenario (Kastner, 2017), it drew some attention from the Member States and the European Parliament, under the pressure of consumers' and investors' associations. In the end, Member States obtained more discretion in defining Prospectus exemption thresholds, while the Parliament's amendments favoured SMEs' simplified obligations over those of larger firms. However, the broad consensus around the need for a tailored Prospectus for SMEs signalled a substantive alignment between core governments and EU policymakers on the overall rationale of the policy initiative, against the concerns expressed by European consumers and investors' organizations.

27.3.4 *Securitization*

The most significant result of the first CMU reform period can be identified in the EU legislators' agreement on a regulatory framework for defining 'safe' securitization (Regulation (EU) 2017/2402). The Regulation established a set of product requirements, as well as disclosure and risk retention obligations to issue simple, transparent, and standardized securities, under which banks could benefit from reduced capital requirements. This reform represented a notable case of rehabilitation of a financial instrument that was the first cause of the GFC, drawing the attention of financial regulators and governments on the international regulatory agenda (Bavoso, 2017). This outcome can be explained by considering both the policy entrepreneurship of the financial industry, sponsorship from key EU regulators, and the building up of a supportive transnational business coalition. The launch of a market-led quality label for securitization in the aftermath of the crisis (the Prime Collateralized Securities initiative), under the leadership of the European Roundtable of Financial Services (EFR) and the Association for Financial Markets in Europe

(AFME) triggered a consensus-building process on the benefits of promoting a market for safe asset-backed securities (Montalbano, 2020). The initiative was soon supported by the ECB and the Bank of England. They targeted securitization as a fundamental market segment to be restored in Europe, to secure the sound transmission of their unconventional monetary policies (Braun, 2020). The strategic framing of a safe revival of securitization, in a break with the pre-crisis practices (Engelen and Glasmacher, 2018), as well as the construction of a powerful alliance with fundamental business interests in core EU countries (such as the German automotive sector), allowed a supranational coalition to win the consensus from the governments and the Commission, defeating the opposition of public interest groups (Montalbano, 2020). Again, the United Kingdom emerged as the primary sponsor of the demands raised by the financial industry. At the same time, Germany and France aligned with the Commission in defending a more rigid regulatory framework, mostly related to the penalty regime, the partial ban on re-securitization, and the definition of stricter criteria for asset-backed commercial papers.

27.3.5 *Covered Bonds*

The EU covered bond framework was agreed upon by the co-legislators in April 2019, and an EU covered bond label was set up, entailing regulatory requirements and supervisory responsibilities (Directive 2019/2162), together with tailored (and softened) prudential requirements for the latter (Regulation 2019/2160). As in the case of STS securitization, the covered bond reform initiative was born out of a market-led standard-setting initiative supported by the ECB and the Commission. In the aftermath of the crisis, the European Covered Bond Council (the pan-European organization representing the covered bonds market participants and stakeholders) worked on a high-quality industry-led label aiming at restoring investors' confidence and revitalizing the covered bond markets. The ECB warmly supported the recovery of covered bonds, as they provided long-term funding and maturity management instruments for distressed European banks. From July 2009 to the end of June 2010, the ECB launched two covered bond purchase programmes, spurring fast recovery of the covered bond markets (Kemmish et al., 2017, p. 19). Exposure to covered bonds led the ECB to develop an interest in ensuring lasting liquidity in the covered bonds market, in an interdependence dynamic similar to that observed in the case of securitization. The Commission would soon meet the demands of such a transnational coalition, putting the relaunch of 'high-quality' covered bond markets as the main CMU goal to boost banks' profits, building on industry-led standards (Montalbano, 2022). The limited participation of non-financial and non-corporate interests in the dedicated stakeholder consultation and the minimum debate in the negotiations between the Council and Parliament testified to the low political salience of the issue. The core eurozone powers, notably Germany, hosted the largest markets in covered bonds and were eager to develop them further cross-border, provided that no significant changes to the entrenched regulatory and supervisory practices were introduced. At the same time, covered bonds remained substantially unrelated to the causes of the financial crisis. They were strategically framed by the ECB and the Commission as low-risk structured products, not comparable to securitization. In this way, a transnational public–private coalition of EU policy-makers and financial industry interests managed to build covered bonds integration in the EU.

27.3.6 *The Pan-European Personal Pension Product*

Another key achievement was a Pan-European Personal Pension Product (Regulation (EU) 2019/1238). The initial push for an EU initiative to create a European market for private pensions was spurred by the European Roundtable of Financial Services (EFR), a forum of CEOs from cross-border banks and insurance firms. The EFR advanced a proposal for an EU pension product as the best viable way to overcome governments' resistance to harmonizing profoundly different national systems (Schelkle, 2019). Such a solution was substantively mirrored in the European Insurance and Occupational Pensions Authority (EIOPA) preliminary report to the Commission and then supported by the European equity investment industry as a crucial element in the CMU plan (EIOPA, 2014; IPO Task Force, 2015). An EU private pension scheme was presented in the final Commission proposal as an additional, and not substitutive, tool to allow for better pensions, contributing to unloading the public pension systems under pressure in various Member States while fostering the access of small savers and households to cross-border capital markets. However, the competitive concerns and contrasts between the occupational and private pension fund industry representatives was coupled with the commitment of Member States to retain control over the PEPP authorization. Moreover, many amendments from the European Parliament pointed at strengthening consumer protection for PEPP users, thus increasing regulatory burdens for potential providers. The significant stakes for both governments and Members of the European Parliament over pension policies thus resulted in a contested policy process, leading to final legislation differing substantially from the original proposal (Lannoo, 2019).

27.3.7 *Small Investment Firms and SMEs*

Low politicization and broad support from a niche policy community composed of the transnational financial industry and supranational policymakers underlay other successful outcomes of the CMU by 2019. They included streamlining and harmonization of national rules on cross-border distribution of collective investment undertakings (enacted in June 2019); the Investment Firms Review (IFR), introducing a tailored prudential requirement framework for small and medium-sized investment companies (while systemically relevant firms will remain under the Capital Requirements Regulation/Capital Requirements Directive framework); the reduction of administrative burdens for SMEs listing under the SME growth market.

27.3.8 *Insolvency Procedures*

Divergence in business insolvency procedures figured among the longstanding obstacles to cross-border market integration entrenched in national laws. Different definitions of property rights and their treatment in business failure were considered a significant source of uncertainty and administrative burden for multinational companies. Since the start of EU financial market integration, poor progress in this field was rooted in the technical complexity of harmonizing the domestic legal frameworks underpinning insolvency rules and the political significance of such a move towards supranationalization. Restructuring and liquidation rules directly impact on the treatment of bank loans, investors' claims and occupational interests, making business insolvency issues a salient policy area for economic and financial stability.

On the eve of the CMU Action Plan the Commission attempted a cautious move towards harmonizing insolvency rules. In 2014 a Recommendation was published to encourage adoption by the Member States of shared principles on early restructuring procedures, aiming at reducing their costs and duration while allowing entrepreneurs to have a 'second chance' before closing their business. Yet the 2015 Action Plan soon certified the substantive failure of this voluntary approach, taking it as a significant reason to advance a targeted legislative initiative, building on the content of the Recommendation (European Commission, 2015b, p. 25). In November 2016, a Commission proposal for a Directive on preventive restructuring was presented, introducing standard procedures to prevent early liquidation of firms in trouble and to streamline insolvency procedures. The legislative journey of such a piece of reform proved particularly hard, due to the reluctance of EU governments to give away their national laws, underpinned by the opposition of core domestic-oriented business and financial interests, fearing the loss of their competitive positions. In the end, in June 2019, Directive 2019/1023 on restructuring and insolvency was adopted, representing a milestone in the harmonization of European insolvency law. Yet, as the IMF analysts have noted, its initial ambitions have been watered down, leading to a low level of harmonization and the persistence of substantive differences and regulatory competition among the Member States (Garrido et al., 2021). Thus, in this case, intergovernmental conflicts and domestic-centred interests proved to be dominant, under the high salience of the issue at stake, in determining the partial achievements of the CMU agenda in insolvency harmonization.

27.3.9 *Taxation*

The variety of national taxation regimes for cross-border investments and business operations was identified as a formidable barrier to overcome given high Member State stakes and the unanimity in the Council required in matters of direct taxation. The coordination of tax matters has direct fiscal and redistributive implications for the EU Member States, which retain sovereign prerogatives in this policy area as recognized in Article 115 TFEU. Most of the CMU's original proposals were thus limited to improving voluntary cooperation and convergence in the tax treatment of private equity, venture capital, investment funds, and withholding tax relief systems. As non-binding measures constructed through a lengthy consultation process with governments, introducing a code of conduct on withholding tax treatment (European Commission, 2017a) and specific guidelines on cross-border investment taxation were not particularly controversial.

However, the ambitious plan for a common consolidated corporate tax base, addressing (among other issues) the debt-equity bias, was a somewhat different story. The new Commission proposal was issued in October 2016. It was designed to meet a key concern raised by the Member States (and echoed by EU multinational companies) on the *consolidated* treatment of cross-border taxable activities. The proposal thus focused on defining a joint tax computation *base* under an allocation key targeting the sources of profit along the business activities allocated in the different countries. The consolidation requirement was then postponed to a future step. Yet the proposal included some anti-avoidance rules, such as the permanent establishment requirement (ensuring that companies have a taxable presence in a Member State where they conduct economic activities).

Moreover, while an earlier proposal foresaw the *voluntary* subjection of multinational firms to the EU corporate tax base, the Commission now advanced the *mandatory* nature of the proposed regime. While postponing the consolidation rule, the new text was in many respects more burdensome and more intrusive than the first version, making it a highly salient political issue for a powerful minority of EU tax havens (such as Luxembourg, Malta, Ireland, and the Netherlands) which would have been penalized mainly by the Common Consolidated Corporate Tax Base (CCCBT) (Hentze, 2019, p. 12). At the same time, EU cross-border corporate interests soon coalesced in their opposition against the Commission's plan, siding with the reluctant EU governments. Little surprise that the new proposal rapidly ran aground, with no recorded progress since then.

27.3.10 *Supervision*

Since its creation, the ESMA has gradually expanded its powers, thanks to the entrepreneurship of the Commission and an emerging favourable European jurisprudence. Since 2011, it has been entrusted with direct supervision of specific entities with a relevant EU cross-border scope, such as the EU-based credit rating agencies and trade repositories under the European Market Infrastructure Regulation (EMIR), together with the recognition of such third-country institutions. In a landmark decision issued in 2014, the Court of Justice of the EU recognized that ESMA was authorized to issue legally binding decisions directed at individual entities in case of inaction by the competent national authorities (Avgouleas and Ferrarini, 2018). As already noted, the prospect of the British withdrawal from the EU gave the Commission a unique opportunity to push towards a complete centralization of EU capital markets supervision under the ESMA. Freed from the opposition of the United Kingdom and given the subjection of the EU's remaining core financial centres under the ECB-led single banking supervision, both the functional pressures and political conditions seemed favourable to overcome the longstanding reluctance of the Member States (see Montalbano, 2021) to establish an EU capital markets supervisory authority. Yet the Commission's efforts encountered the enduring concerns of both the largest eurozone and non-euro area countries for a significant transfer of supervisory powers to the supranational level, echoing the opposition from critical domestic industry interests. While non-euro area countries, particularly the central and eastern EU countries, were reluctant to cede control of their poorly developed financial markets to an authority potentially dominated by the eurozone states, the latter – notably Germany and the northern countries – reiterated the question of the sensitive implications for financial, stability, national competitiveness, and fiscal responsibilities of supranational oversight of key financial activities. A powerful coalition of Member States, supported by core domestic financial incumbents (Lagaria, 2018) managed to water down the initial Commission proposals, while showing willingness to engage in discussion for a more targeted approach. The EU authority could have expanded its powers in selected financial market segments, responding to the most pressing coordination problems raised by the cross-border financial operations in the wake of Brexit. A significant area for ESMA's expansion of competencies was then represented by the supervision of central clearing counterparties (CCPs) after the withdrawal from the Single Market of the City of London, which hosted the main volume of clearing and settlements in the EU. The review of the EMIR Regulation thus conferred new powers on the European CCPs and in the relationship with third-country clearing and settlements. Following such a targeted approach, the finalization of the overall review of the European Supervisory Authorities in 2019 resulted in a selective expansion of ESMA's supervisory powers on some cross-border entities (such as venture capital and the European Long-Term Investment funds) and activities (overseeing measures to prevent market abuse and in monitoring critical benchmarks). Far from realizing a single supervisor for capital markets, the new ESMA powers had an 'incremental quality' and were 'limited to a small population of regulated actors/activities with distinct cross-border settings' (Moloney, 2018, p. 306).

27.4 THE CMU 2020 AGENDA

The outbreak of the COVID-19 pandemic and the ensuing economic crisis in 2020 set a new window of opportunity for relaunching the CMU project. The original Action Plan set out 2019 as a deadline for full-fledged CMU. Yet on reaching the deadline, EU capital markets integration still had a long way to go (European Commission, 2019). Before the end of its mandate, the outgoing Juncker Commission locked in the agenda for cross-border capital market integration by establishing a High-Level Forum (HLF) on a new CMU agenda. Starting its work in November 2019, the meetings and discussions of the HLF were soon shaped by the outbreak of the COVID-19 pandemic and its economic consequences in Europe. In this context, the CMU acquired a new justification and rationale. The HLF final report in June 2020 presented the relaunch of the CMU project as a fundamental pillar to 'rebuild the European economy' and recover from 'the biggest economic crisis in peacetime in 90 years' (HLF, 2020, p. 4). Three months later, the CMU's 'new Action Plan' linked the old and unsolved challenges in the development and integration of EU capital markets to the pressing urgency of the European recovery from the economic crisis brought about by COVID-19. According to the von der Leyen Commission, although necessary to get Europe out of the crisis, the unprecedented Next Generation EU stimulus package would not have been 'sufficient given the magnitude and expected duration of financing needs' (European Commission, 2020, p. 3).

For this reason, in addition to public funding, as the new Action Plan put it, 'market financing will be the lifeblood that sustains the recovery and future growth over the long-term' (European Commission, 2020, p. 3). Furthermore, the push for more integrated and liquid capital markets was presented as a renewed priority to allow the Commission to raise the required funding from international investors through bond issuance. As in 2015, capital markets appeared as crucial private infrastructure to provide for the public good of the post-crisis economic recovery. As already noted in previous studies (Quaglia and Howarth, 2018), the Commission narrative strategy again presented the CMU as a core part of an EU response to an economic crisis.

Under such a new general orientation, the 2020 Action Plan relaunched the central CMU initiatives. A particular emphasis was put on developing the sustainable finance plan under the new European Green Deal, the flagship initiative of the von der Leyen Commission aiming to make Europe climate neutral by 2050. Here again, market-based financing was assumed to provide the primary source of investments for the ecological transition, given that public funding 'will not be sufficient' for the increasing green conversion of the financial industry. Next to the EU climate goals, the CMU would have prompted Europe's digital competitiveness, starting from the role of the FinTech industry and its strategic importance in the confrontation with the non-EU City of London. The FinTech plan launched in March 2018 was then incorporated into the more comprehensive EU Digital Finance Strategy, issued in September 2020 together with the new CMU Action Plan.

Moreover, the new plan represented an occasion for the Commission to return to the most contentious policy dossiers of the original Action Plan, such as those on taxation, insolvency, and supervision, to advance ambitious objectives. Having noted the poor success of the existing code of conduct, the Commission announced a legislative proposal for a harmonized system for withholding tax relief at source (European Commission, 2020, p. 12). A new central intervention was also planned on the insolvency rules to foster minimum harmonization in targeted insolvency procedures (European Commission, 2020, p. 13). Even on financial markets supervision, the Action Plan introduced supervisory convergence as an explicit goal, with the possible presence of specific measures 'for stronger supervisory coordination or direct supervision by the European Supervisory Authorities' (European Commission, 2020, p. 14). The Commission appealed again for a single rulebook and a unique oversight authority for a 'post-Brexit' European financial system to help it remain globally competitive. However, looking at the continuing resistance of Member States on the most politically sensitive issues and competitive pressures among the continental financial centres to become the new EU core financial hub, it is doubtful that the post-Brexit world would offer better political conditions for a further step in supervisory supranationalization.

Yet, on the other side, the economic disruption brought by the pandemic crisis offered a unique window of opportunity to bring forward and accelerate those policy initiatives mostly related to softening the regulatory pressures on banks and unlocking their funding capacity. Resulting from an assessment process by the EBA, a package of amendments to the Securitization Regulation was published in April 2021, introducing the STS framework on balance sheet synthetic securitizations (while previously only 'true sale' securitization was admitted) and removing existing regulatory constraints to securitizing non-performing exposures. At the same time, as part of the same 'Capital Markets Recovery Package', the disclosure requirements under the Market in Financial Instruments Directive (MiFID) II and Prospectus Regulation have been simplified to speed up access to funding for companies. In this case, the COVID-19 crisis triggered a rapid and targeted regulatory simplification on some critical policy issues, such as securitization and disclosure requirements, allowing the Commission to add other pieces to the CMU mosaic.

27.5 CONCLUSIONS

The CMU represented a significant reorientation in the EU's post-GFC attitude, discourse, and approach towards the role of financial markets. From being a source of financial instability to being regulated against their participants' reckless behaviour, financial markets again become part of the solution for the EU's sluggish economic recovery and inadequate cross-border risk sharing. If the regulatory reforms in the aftermath of the GFC aimed at reining in the financial industry, the CMU reoriented regulation as an *enabling* condition for the financial markets to unleash their untapped potential and deliver those collective goods of growth and stability in the EU that the Member States' governments could not reach on their own. The CMU thus emerged as the 'logical' market supply-side complement to the shrinking of aggregate demand and the enhanced budgetary discipline of post-crisis EU economic governance. The reconstruction of more open dialogue and regulatory cooperation between EU policymakers and the financial industry appeared as a consequence of such a new orientation that emerged within the EU institutions, starting from the Commission.

However, the CMU agenda and outcomes were the terrain of differing degrees of political salience and industry influence. While the interdependence and functional pressures raised by the EU's austerity-led crisis response, the ECB's extraordinary policies, and the Banking Union constituted some fundamental determinants of the CMU, this chapter integrated them with the enabling and impeding political factors leading to the achievements and failures of the CMU agenda. To summarize the main findings of our analysis, the CMU achievements can be linked to the presence of functional pressures when combined with the low political salience of the policy initiatives at stake for the Member States' governments and the proactive support from the financial industry. Examples of such a dynamic were the reforms relating to venture capital, covered bonds, pan-European private pension products, and measures to improve SMEs' access to capital markets. Yet, on the contrary, the limited achievements and failures of the CMU plan have been assessed concerning the most politicized issues, mostly impinging on the state's fiscal responsibilities and impacting on core domestic constituencies, such as the supranationalization of supervision and the harmonization of taxation and insolvency rules. When the CMU policy reforms touched on the most sensitive political areas, an intergovernmental and domestic-centred logic of power emerged. Even the withdrawal of the United Kingdom did not open the doors for a full-fledged supranationalization of capital market governance in the EU.

A crucial case in the CMU plan was that of securitization. Although a salient and contested issue in the post-crisis debate, securitization has been rehabilitated thanks to the joint efforts of key market policy entrepreneurs and supranational actors (foremost the ECB and the Bank of England) and the affirmation of a new framing about safe securitization. This transnational coalition proved successful thanks to the reframing strategy adopted, responding to the political need to justify the revival of securitization in terms of a 'safe' financial product, making it acceptable for both Member States and the European Parliament.

The redefinition of the CMU strategic priorities in the 2017 mid-term review and the new 2020 Action Plan shows the adaptability of the imperatives of capital market integration as a crucial governance tool for the EU to attain its key political goals, together with the continuing need to build up political consensus around the CMU. The sustainable and digital finance agendas were thus crucial to steer capital markets integration in response to general goals strongly supported by both public interest groups and social movements (such as climate issues), core industry concerns in the wake of Brexit, and the increasing technological competition with the United States and China (for example in the digital economy). Constructing political consensus on the primary role of capital markets in delivering such new public objectives as the ecological transition and digital development is at the same time functional to the attempt to increasingly depoliticize the latter by progressively shifting away from the centrality of state-led and public investments, or at least making the latter dependent on the capacity to raise the former.

In this respect, the COVID-19 crisis has been presented by the Commission as a window for a new round of capital markets integration. The CMU's new Action Plan again framed market-based finance in terms of a vital source of funding and risk-sharing mechanism in the post-pandemic recovery, linked to the enhanced EU plan on sustainable finance and FinTech. Indeed, the pandemic-driven economic disruption already offered an opportunity to soften the regulatory burdens on banks' prudential requirements for complex securitization and on firms' access to capital markets. However, as we showed in our analysis, the enduring competing national interests, together with the differing levels of political salience and the entrenched Member State opposition to full-fledged public risk-sharing arrangements, can be expected to represent an enduring source of resistance to any future efforts towards a fully integrated EU capital market under a centralized supervisory authority.

REFERENCES

Acharya, V. V., and Steffen, S. (2016). Capital markets union in Europe: Why other unions must lead the way. *Swiss Journal of Economics and Statistics* 152(4), 319–329.

Ahlström, H., and Monciardini, D. (2022). The regulatory dynamics of sustainable finance: Paradoxical success and limitations of EU reforms. *Journal of Business Ethics* 177(1), 193–201.

Aldasoro, I., and Unger, R. (2017). External financing and economic activity in the euro area: Why are bank loans special? BIS Working Papers No. 622. www.bis.org/publ/work622.pdf

Amtenbrink, F. (2015). The metamorphosis of European economic and monetary union. In D. Chalmers and A. Arnull (eds.), *The Oxford Handbook of European Union Law*. Oxford: Oxford University Press, pp. 719–756.

Avgouleas, A., and Ferrarini, G. (2018). The future of ESMA and a single listing authority and securities regulator for the CMU: Costs, benefits and legal impediments. In A. Avgouleas (ed.), *Capital Markets Union in Europe*. Oxford: Oxford University Press, pp. 55–77.

Bavoso, V. (2017). High quality securitisation and EU capital markets union – Is it possible? *Accounting, Economics and Law: A Convivium* 7(3), 1–29.

Braun, B. (2020). Central banking and the infrastructural power of finance: The case of ECB support for repo and securitization markets. *Socio-Economic Review* 18(2), 395–418.
Braun, B., and Hübner, M. (2018). Fiscal fault, financial fix? Capital Markets Union and the quest for macroeconomic stabilization in the euro area. *Competition & Change* 22(2), 117-138.
Braun, B., Gabor, D., and Hübner, M. (2018). Governing through financial markets: Towards a critical political economy of Capital Markets Union. *Competition and Change* 22(2), 101–116.
Camacho, E. R. (2021). *The Choice for Banking Union: Power, Politics and the Trap of Credible Commitments.* London: Routledge.
Cameron, D. (2013). David Cameron's EU speech – full text. *The Guardian*, 23 January. www.theguardian.com/politics/2013/jan/23/david-cameron-eu-speech-referendum
Cimadomo, J., Furtuna, O., and Giuliodori, M. (2018). Private and public risk sharing in the euro area. ECB Working Paper Series. www.ecb.europa.eu/pub/pdf/scpwps/ecb.wp2148.en.pdf?7eb7d8a2582e8da2d6d4f25d8ac0c582
Demertzis, M., Merler, S., and Wolff, G. B. (2017). Capital Markets Union and the Fintech opportunity. Bruegel Policy Contribution, No. 22, Brussels. www.bruegel.org/policy-brief/capital-markets-union-and-fintech-opportunity
Donnelly, S. (2018). *Power Politics, Banking Union and EMU: Adjusting Europe to Germany.* New York: Routledge.
Dorn, N. (2016). Capital cohabitation: EU Capital Markets Union as public and private co-regulation. *Capital Markets Law Journal* 11(1), 84–102.
ECB (2016). Capital Markets Union and the European monetary and financial framework. Keynote speech by Vítor Constâncio, Vice-President of the ECB, at Chatham House, London, 21 March. www.ecb.europa.eu/press/key/date/2016/html/sp160321_1.en.html
EIOPA (2014). Towards an EU single market for personal pensions. An EIOPA Preliminary Report to COM, EIOPA-BoS/14/029. www.eiopa.europa.eu/system/files/2020-02/eiopa-bos-14-029_towards_an_eu_single_market_for_personal_pensions-_an_eiopa_preliminary_report_to_com_1.pdf
Engelen, E., and Glasmacher, A. (2016). The Trojan Horse of Europe's Capital Markets Union. Part III. Follow the money. www.ftm.nl/artikelen/the-trojan-horse-of-europes-capital-markets-union-part-iii
Engelen, E., and Glasmacher, A. (2018). The waiting game: How securitization became the solution for the growth problem of the eurozone. *Competition & Change* 22(2), 165–183.
Epstein, R., and Rhodes, M. (2018). From governance to government: Banking union, capital markets union and the new EU. *Competition & Change* 22(2), 205–224.
EU (2015). Public consultation on the review of the European Venture Capital Funds (EuVECA) and European Social Entrepreneurship Funds (EuSEF) regulations. https://ec.europa.eu/eusurvey/publication/venture-capital-funds-2015?language=en
EU (2017a). Capital Markets Union: EU agrees to more support for venture capital and social enterprises. Brussels. https://ec.europa.eu/commission/presscorner/detail/en/IP_17_1477
EU (2017b). Regulation (EU) 2017/1129 of the European Parliament and of the Council of 14 June 2017 on the Prospectus to be published when securities are offered to the public or admitted to trading on a regulated market, and repealing Directive 2003/71/EC. Brussels. https://eur-lex.europa.eu/legal-content/EN/TXT/?uri=celex:32017R1129
European Commission (1998). Communication from the European Commission. Risk capital: A key to job creation in the European Union. SEC(1998)552 final. Brussels. http://aei.pitt.edu/6987/1/003657_1.pdf
European Commission. (2014). Communication from the Commission to the European Parliament and the Council on Long-Term Financing of the European Economy. COM(2014) 168 final, Brussels, 27.3. https://eur-lex.europa.eu/LexUriServ/LexUriServ.do?uri=COM:2014:0168:FIN:EN:PDF
European Commission (2015a). Building a capital markets union. Green paper. COM(2015) 63 final. Brussels. https://eur-lex.europa.eu/legal-content/EN/TXT/PDF/?uri=CELEX:52015DC0063&from=EN
European Commission (2015b). Action Plan on building a Capital Markets Union. COM(2015) 468 final. Brussels. https://eur-lex.europa.eu/legal-content/EN/TXT/PDF/?uri=CELEX:52015DC0468&from=HU
European Commission (2015c). The investment plan for Europe: Questions and answers. Brussels. https://ec.europa.eu/commission/presscorner/detail/en/MEMO_15_5419

European Commission (2016). Commission delegated Regulation (EU) 2016/467 of 30 September 2015 amending Commission Delegated Regulation (EU) 2015/35 [...]. Brussels. https://eur-lex.europa.eu/legal-content/EN/TXT/PDF/?uri=CELEX:32016R0467&from=DA

European Commission (2017a). Communication from the Commission [...] on the Mid-Term Review of the Capital Markets Union Action Plan. COM(2017) 292 final. https://eur-lex.europa.eu/legal-content/EN/TXT/?uri=CELEX%3A52017DC0292

European Commission (2017b). Consultation document. FinTech: A more competitive and Innovative European Financial Sector. https://ec.europa.eu/info/sites/default/files/2017-fintech-consultation-document_en_0.pdf

European Commission (2018). VentureEU: €2.1 billion to boost venture capital investment in Europe's innovative start-ups. Press Release, 10 April, Brussels. https://ec.europa.eu/commission/presscorner/detail/en/IP_18_2763

European Commission, E. (2019). Delivering on the Capital Markets Union. Progress Report. Brussels. https://ec.europa.eu/finance/docs/policy/190315-cmu-factsheet_en.pdf

European Commission (2020). A Capital Markets Union for people and businesses – New action plan. COM(2020) 590 final. https://ec.europa.eu/info/business-economy-euro/growth-and-investment/capital-markets-union/capital-markets-union-2020-action-plan_en

Farhi, E., and Werning, I. (2017). Fiscal unions. *American Economic Review* 107(12), 3788–3834.

Fernandez, R., and Aalbers, M. B. (2017). Capital Markets Union and residential capitalism in Europe: Rescaling the housing-centred model of financialization. *Finance and Society* 3(1), 32–50.

Finance Watch (2015). Who will benefit from the Capital Markets Union? Brussels. www.finance-watch.org/who-will-benefit-from-the-capital-markets-union/

Fitoussi, J. P., and Saraceno, F. (2013). European economic governance: the Berlin–Washington consensus. *Cambridge Journal of Economics* 37(3), 479–496.

Garrido, J., DeLong, C., Rasekh, A., and Rosha, A. (2021). Restructuring and insolvency in Europe: Policy options in the implementation of the EU Directive. IMF Working Paper. www.imf.org/en/Publications/WP/Issues/2021/05/27/Restructuring-and-Insolvency-in-Europe-Policy-Options-in-the-Implementation-of-the-EU-50235

Gonzalez, F. (2014). Transparency in the European loan markets: From words to facts. *Zeitschrift Fur Das Gesamte Kreditwesen* 19, 32–34.

Guardian (2014). David Cameron: In–out referendum on EU by 2017 is cast-iron pledge. 11 May. www.theguardian.com/world/2014/may/11/david-cameron-european-union-referendum-pledge

Hardie, I., and Howarth, D. (2013). Framing market-based banking and the financial crisis. In I. Hardie and D. Howarth (eds.), *Market-Based Banking and the International Financial Crisis*. Oxford: Oxford University Press, pp. 22–55.

Hentze, T. (2019). The challenge of moving to a Common Consolidated Corporate Tax Base in the EU. IW-Report, No. 2, Köln. www.iwkoeln.de/en/studies/tobias-hentze-the-challenge-of-moving-to-a-common-consolidated-corporate-tax-base-in-the-eu.html

High Level Forum (2020). A new vision for Europe's capital markets. Final Report of the High-Level Forum on the Capital Markets Union. Brussels, June. https://finance.ec.europa.eu/system/files/2020-06/200610-cmu-high-level-forum-final-report_en.pdf

Hill, J. (2014). Commissioner Hill on Capital Markets Union: Finance serving the economy. Brussels. https://ec.europa.eu/commission/presscorner/detail/en/AC_16_1535

Hill, J. (2015). Q&A session. European Financial Regulation and Transatlantic Collaboration. Brookings Institution, Washington, DC. www.brookings.edu/events/european-financial-regulation-and-transatlantic-collaboration/

Howarth, D., and Quaglia, L. (2016). *The Political Economy of European Banking Union*. Oxford: Oxford University Press.

Howarth, D., and Quaglia, L. (2017). Brexit and the single European financial market. *Journal of Common Market Studies* 55(149), 149–164.

Howarth, D., and Quaglia, L. (2018). Brexit and the battle for financial services. *Journal of European Public Policy* 25(8), 1118–1136.

Hübner, M. (2019). *Wenn der Markt regiert: die politische Ökonomie der Europäischen Kapitalmarktunion*, Vol. 92. Frankfurt: Campus Verlag.

Ioannou, D., and Schäfer, D. (2017). Risk sharing in EMU: Key insights from a literature review. SUERF Policy Note Issue, No. 21, November: www.suerf.org/policynotes/1771/risk-sharing-in-emu-key-insights-from-a-literature-review

IPO Task Force (2015). EU IPO Report: Rebuilding IPOs in Europe; Creating jobs and growth in European capital markets. www.fese.eu/blog/eu-ipo-report-rebuilding-ipos-in-europe-creating-jobs-and-growth-in-european-capital-markets/

Jabko, N. (2006). *Playing the Market: A Political Strategy for Uniting Europe, 1985–2005*. Ithaca, NY: Cornell University Press.

James, S., and Quaglia, L. (2020). *The UK and Multi-Level Financial Regulation: From Post-Crisis Reform to Brexit*. Oxford: Oxford University Press.

James, S. and Quaglia, L. (2022). Rule maker or rule taker? Brexit, finance and UK regulatory autonomy. *International Political Science Review* 43(3), 390–403.

Juncker, J.-C. (2014). A new start for Europe. Opening statement in the European Parliament plenary session. Strasbourg, 15 July 2014. https://ec.europa.eu/commission/presscorner/detail/en/SPEECH_14_567

Juncker, J.-C., Tusk, D., Dijsselbloem, J., Draghi, M., and Schulz, M. (2015). The Five Presidents' Report: Completing Europe's Economic and Monetary Union. Brussels, 22 June. https://ec.europa.eu/commission/sites/beta-political/files/5-presidents-report_en.pdf

Kastner, L. (2017). *Civil Society and Financial Regulation: Consumer Finance Protection and Taxation after the Financial Crisis*. London: Routledge.

Katainen, J. (2015). An investment plan for Europe. The speech by Jyrki Katainen's, Vice President of the Commission, at the Bruegel event 'An investment plan for Europe'. Bruegel, 14 January. www.bruegel.org/2015/01/an-investment-plan-for-europe/

Kemmish, R., Wilkinson, C., and Andruszkiewicz, O. (2017). Covered bonds in the European Union: Harmonisation of legal frameworks and market behaviours. Final Report. Brussels: European Commission. https://publications.europa.eu/resource/cellar/8df6d9cd-8c65-11e7-b5c6-01aa75ed71a1.0001.01/DOC_1

Laffan, B., and Schlosser, P. (2016). Public finances in Europe: Fortifying EU economic governance in the shadow of the crisis. *Journal of European Integration* 38(3), 237–249.

Lagaria, K. (2018). Towards a single capital markets supervisor in the EU: The proposed extension of ESMA's supervisory powers. *Competition and Regulation Journal* 33–34, 39–62.

Lannoo, K. (2019). The Final PEPP or how to kill an important EU Commission proposal. In N. Costa Cabral and N. Cunha Rodrigues (eds.), *The Future of Pension Plans in the EU Internal Market*. Cham: Springer, pp. 193–197.

Lannoo, K., and Thomadakis, A. (2019). Rebranding Capital Markets Union: A market finance action plan. Brussels: CEPS-ECMI Task Force. www.ecmi.eu/publications/books/rebranding-capital-markets-union-market-finance-action-plan

Moloney, N. (2018). *The Age of ESMA: Governing EU Financial Markets*. Oxford: Hart Publishing.

Montalbano, G. (2020). Policy entrepreneurship and the influence of the transnational financial industry in the EU reform of securitization. *Business and Politics* 22(1), 85–112.

Montalbano, G. (2021). *Competing Interest Groups and Lobbying in the Construction of the European Banking Union*. Houndmills: Palgrave Macmillan.

Montalbano, G. (2022). Public–private co-regulation in the making of the capital markets union. *Journal of Economic Policy Reform* 1, 1–17.

Moravcsik, A. (1998). *The Choice for Europe: Social Purpose and State Power from Messina to Maastricht*. Ithaca, NY: Cornell University Press.

Navaretti, G. B., Calzolari, G., Mansilla-Fernandez, J. M., and Pozzolo, A. F. (2018). Fintech and banking. Friends or foes? *European Economy – Banks, Regulation, and the Real Sector* 2, 9–30.

Oberndorfer, L. (2015). From new constitutionalism to authoritarian constitutionalism: New economic governance and the state of European democracy. In J. Jäger and E. Springler (eds.), *Asymmetric Crisis in Europe and Possible Futures: Critical Political Economy and Post-Keynesian Perspectives*. London: Routledge, pp. 206–227.

Pesendorfer, D. (2015). Capital Markets Union and ending short-termism: Lessons from the European Commission's public consultation. *Law and Financial Markets Review* 9(3), 202–209.

Pesendorfer, D. (2020). *Financial Markets (Dis)Integration in a Post-Brexit EU: Towards a More Resilient Financial System in Europe*. Cham: Palgrave.

Posner, E. (2009). *The Origins of Europe's New Stock Markets*. Cambridge, MA: Harvard University Press.

Quaglia, L., and Howarth, D. (2018). The policy narratives of European capital markets union. *Journal of European Public Policy* 25(7), 990–1009.

Quaglia, L., Howarth, D., and Liebe, M.(2016). The political economy of European capital markets union. *Journal of Common Market Studies* 54, 185–203.

Ringe, W.-G. (2015). Capital Markets Union for Europe: A commitment to the Single Market of 28. *Law and Financial Markets Review* 9(1), 5–7.

Sahay, R., Čihák, M., N'diaye, P., Barajas, A., Bi, R., Ayala, D., Gao, Y., Kyobe, A., Nguyen, L., Saborowski, C., and Svirydzenka, K. (2015). Rethinking financial deepening: Stability and growth in emerging markets IMF Staff Discussion Note 15(8). Washington: IMF. www.imf.org/external/pubs/ft/sdn/2015/sdn1508.pdf

Schelkle, W. (2017). *The Political Economy of Monetary Solidarity: Understanding the Euro Experiment*. Cambridge: Cambridge University Press.

Schelkle, W. (2019). EU Pension policy and financialisation: Purpose without power? *Journal of European Public Policy* 26(4), 599–616.

Ständer, P. (2016). *What Will Happen with the Capital Markets Union after Brexit?* Brussels: Jacques Delors Institut.

Stone Sweet, A., and Sandholtz, A. (1998). Integration, supranational governance, and the institutionalization of the European polity. In W. Sandholtz and A. Stone Sweet (eds.), *European Integration and Supranational Governance*. Oxford: Oxford University Press, pp. 1–26.

Valiante, D. (2016). *Europe's Untapped Capital Market: Rethinking Integration after the Great Financial Crisis*. London: Rowman & Littlefield International.

Van Rompuy, H. (2012b). Towards a genuine Economic and Monetary Union. Report by President of the European Council Herman Van Rompuy. EUCO 120/12. Brussels: European Council. www.consilium.europa.eu/media/33785/131201.pdf

28

The European Strategy on Digital Finance and Its Interplay with Capital Markets Integration in the EU

Diego Valiante, Marco Lamandini, and David Ramos Muñoz

28.1 INTRODUCTION

The digitalization of finance is changing the financial system and its interaction with the rest of the economy. This process, which affects financial and non-financial entities, raises key policy, legal, and economic questions vis-à-vis the integrity and the development of the European Single Market for capital. In recent years, European policies have embraced the digitalization process with an ad hoc Digital Finance Strategy (DFS). This chapter reviews the defining elements of the DFS that can have a lasting impact on capital markets integration and explores the links with the Capital Markets Union project. In particular, it focuses on the impact of two important legislative measures on capital market integration under the DFS, i.e. the Market in Crypto-Assets Regulation (MiCAR)[1] and the Distributed Ledger Technology Pilot Project Regulation (DLTR) (see also Lannoo, Chapter 29 in this volume).[2] It concludes by providing a forward-looking view of the impact of the DFS and about the prospects of 'digital security' on capital markets integration in the EU.

28.2 A BRIEF HISTORICAL PERSPECTIVE SINCE THE GLOBAL FINANCIAL CRISIS

The Global Financial Crisis (GFC), technological developments in the financial market infrastructure, and the COVID-19 pandemic have made the digitalization of finance ever more relevant. While these events or trends have different root causes, they have all led to policy goals that are fully aligned with the digitalization of finance. In particular, the call for more transparency and accountability post-GFC (Group of Thirty, 2009, p. 21), massive infrastructure investments (and entries of new players) in the securities exchange and payments industries to improve quality and speed of execution and, finally, the post-COVID-19 shift away from in-person service provision, are developments strategically aligned with the opportunities and development of digitalization in finance. The GFC was also a symbolic catalyst of technological

[1] See Regulation 2023/1114 of 31 May 2023 on markets in crypto-assets, and amending Regulations (EU) No 1093/2010 and (EU) No 1095/2010 and Directives 2013/36/EU and (EU) 2019/1937. https://eur-lex.europa.eu/legal-content/EN/TXT/PDF/? The proposal was approved when the book was on print, on 16 May 2023, and the Regulation published on the OJ on 9 June 2023 to enter into force on 29 June 2023 (though most provisions apply after 12 to 18 months).

[2] Regulation 2022/858 of 30 May 2022, on a pilot regime for market infrastructures based on distributed ledger technology, and amending Regulations (EU) No 600/2014 and (EU) No 909/2014 and Directive 2014/65/EU. https://eur-lex.europa.eu/legal-content/EN/TXT/PDF/?uri=CELEX:32022R0858

change. The reputational failure of the banking system stimulated initiatives towards a system that does not rely on trust among financial institutions and towards a more cost-effective financial (payment) system. As a result, at the end of October 2008, a group of individuals (most likely) under the name of 'Satoshi Nakamoto', published a paper describing the first peer-to-peer electronic cash based on distributed ledgers and cryptography, creating de facto a new source of digital disruption in the financial system (Nakamoto, 2008).

The introduction of new technologies and new tools, such as mobile apps (with internet application programming interfaces, or APIs), machine learning and algorithmic trading based on big data analytics, as well as a combination of decentralized architecture and cryptography into the distributed-ledger technology (DLT), have largely improved transparency, competition, and accessibility to financial services (see, for instance, a recap by Beck, 2020 and 2021). Against this backdrop, in recent years, European policies have embraced the digitalization process with an ad hoc Digital Finance Strategy (European Commission, 2020a). This chapter does not discuss the second element of the Digital Finance Strategy, which concerns retail payments (see, for instance, European Commission, 2020b).

At the outset, the European Commission embraced digital transformation and put it at the centre of a dedicated Digital Single Market Strategy in 2015, which promoted three policy objectives: (1) supporting digital infrastructure development; (2) improving access to digital goods and services; and (3) designing rules that foster technological development (European Commission, 2015). A bolder approach to foster digitalization specifically for financial services came only in 2017, with a public consultation on the topic (European Commission, 2017). The consultation paper affirmed for the first time three principles for future policy action:

(a) Technological neutrality (i.e. the same activity should be subject to the same regulation irrespective of the way in which the service is delivered);
(b) Proportionality (i.e. any intervention should take into account the size and significance of the business model, as well as its complexity);
(c) Integrity (i.e. application of new technologies to financial service should promote market transparency without creating unnecessary risks potentially stemming from cyber security, market abuse, and mis-selling practices).

The Commission reaffirmed its 'technology neutral' approach when assessing policy intervention in 2018, with a dedicated Fintech Action Plan (European Commission, 2018). It included one regulatory action for crowdfunding service providers (the European Crowdfunding Service Providers Regulation, ECSPR), which resulted in an EU-wide framework. This new framework[3] regulates for the first time 'internet-based' platforms that provide financial services, such as investment services or credit intermediation, exclusively in a digital form.

The EU Regulation builds upon the already existing framework for investment services (Markets in Financial Instrument Directive 2, MiFID 2),[4] but it expands it to credit intermediation for the first time at the European level (Valiante, 2022). The crowdfunding regime also tests new boundaries in investor protection with the introduction of a system of warnings and targeted transparency (nudges) to ensure that the platform acts as a risk-neutral gatekeeper. As a

[3] Regulation (EU) 2020/1503 of the European Parliament and of the Council of 7 October 2020 on European crowdfunding service providers for business amending Regulation (EU) 2017/1129 and Directive (EU) 2019/1937, OJ L 347.

[4] Markets in Financial Instruments Directive (MiFID), Directive 2014/65/EU of the European Parliament and of the Council of 15 May 2014 on markets in financial instruments and amending Directive 2002/92/EC and Directive 2011/61/EU, OJ L 173.

result, while the fundamental objectives remain the same, there is an implicit recognition that investor protection mechanisms and other integrity-enhancing measures need a different design when financial services are fully provided in a digital form.

The second key element reflected in the 2018 Action Plan was the need to better understand the obstacles to cross-border provision of digital financial services, especially payment and investment services. In particular, the European Banking Authority (EBA) highlighted the importance of harmonized rules for identifying when an activity offered via digital means is considered 'cross-border' (to establish if it is provided under the internal market 'right of establishment' or the 'freedom to provide services'). Here again, the new ECSPR regime resolves this issue by de facto opting for 'freedom to provide services', as in this case the provider will remain exclusively under the supervision of its home competent authority – where the provider is established. Licensing (versus the use of sandboxes in some countries), business conduct, consumer protection, anti-money laundering, and countering the financing of terrorism were other regulatory areas of significant cross-country divergences, which create obstacles to the cross-border provision of financial services (EBA, 2019a).

As a follow-up to the 2018 Action Plan, the Commission also launched an expert group to look into 'regulatory obstacles to financial innovation in the financial services regulatory framework', also called the Expert Group on Regulatory Obstacles to Financial Innovation (ROFIEG). The Expert Group issued thirty recommendations (ROFIEG, 2019), warning about the risks when new players and new technologies enter the market for financial services, such as regulatory fragmentation (imposed over an underlying technology that is the same everywhere), unfair commercial practices of vertically integrated incumbent digital infrastructures (and the need for an open data architecture), and the lack of cooperation among supervisors, at both international and sectoral levels (i.e. competition authorities, financial markets authorities, and central banks). Moreover, the ROFIEG highlighted the lack of regulatory attention to how to fit financial networks built on distributed ledger technology under the existing regulatory framework.

After the 2018 Action Plan and the ROFIEG report, the scaling up problem for the FinTech companies advanced on the European agenda. In 2019, the European Supervisory Authorities (ESAs) first published a joint report on regulatory sandboxes and innovation hubs (ESMA et al., 2018), in which they highlighted existing best practices. Later on, EBA identified a list of 'conditions, limitations and restrictions' to authorization procedures in the context of banking and payment legislation, which may impede a 'fully level playing field in this area' (EBA, 2019b, p. 5). Most recently, the EBA highlighted the growing importance of digital platforms to 'bridge' customers and financial institutions as they create 'new forms of financial, operational and reputational interdependencies', which call for a strengthening of the 'supervisory capacity' to deal properly with this market trend (EBA, 2021). Nonetheless, no evidence has emerged about a bias or favourable treatment towards new innovative business models.

Meanwhile, the European Securities and Markets Authority (ESMA) published its advice on crypto-assets regulation in January 2019 (ESMA, 2019a). The advice concluded that, despite not being (yet) a financial stability concern, crypto-assets are a source of risks for market integrity and investor protection and financial services relating to crypto-assets currently fall outside the scope of EU regulation.

On top of these actions, the European Parliament called for even more ambition, with a 'transition from open banking (in the payment space) to open finance (for all financial services)', 'to improve efficiency, reduce concentration risk and enhance financial inclusion' (European Parliament, 2020, p. 18).

Finally, international organizations, such as the Bank for International Settlements (BIS), the Financial Stability Board (FSB), and the International Organization of Securities Commissions (IOSCO), have been researching in different areas of digitalization of financial services, with greater focus on the policy implications of cryptocurrencies as a means of payment, such as the use of stablecoins and central bank digital currencies (Auer et al., 2020; IOSCO, 2020a), cybersecurity (IOSCO, 2019a; FSB, 2020b) and the market infrastructure developments (including on access and use of data; IOSCO, 2020b; Linnemann et al., 2020).

28.3 A DIGITAL FINANCE STRATEGY FOR THE EU

In this context, the European Commission renewed its strategy on digitalization of financial services with the new Digital Finance Strategy in September 2020 (European Commission, 2020a). The DFS looks at four priority areas:

1. Removing obstacles to the Single Market in areas like the use of digital identities for onboarding clients, cloud computing, and gold-plating practices when it comes to passporting digital financial services (the latter is in line with the work of the ESAs on regulatory sandboxes and innovation hubs);
2. Adapting the EU regulatory framework to digital innovation, by clarifying (among others) the legal status of crypto-assets (e.g. stablecoins) and tokenized financial instruments;
3. Promoting data-driven innovation in finance, focused on improving standardization of supervisory data and open data architecture (also called open finance);[5]
4. Addressing risks and vulnerabilities of the digital transition, with a special focus on resilience to cybersecurity risks.

For the purpose of this chapter, the next sections will focus on two key measures of the DFS for capital market development in the EU: (a) the crypto-assets legislation; and (b) the DLT pilot regime (see also Lannoo, Chapter 29 in this volume). The cyber resilience legislative proposal and the 'open finance' framework (learning from other experiences, since there is no EU proposal yet) will also be briefly discussed.

28.4 THE NEW EU FRAMEWORK FOR (GLOBAL) STABLECOINS AND DEFI: THE MICAR PROPOSAL

The most important piece of the digital finance strategy is a Regulation on the Markets for Crypto-Assets,[6] mainly for its overarching objective to bring crypto-assets (including stablecoins and Decentralized Finance – DeFi – tokens) under regulatory scrutiny. The boom and bust of markets for stablecoins and DeFi tokens (for a recap see IMF, 2021, chapter 2), as well as the failed attempt to introduce Facebook-sponsored stablecoins (under the Diem brand, formerly

[5] 'Open finance' arguably refers to all the policies to make data about financial services/products users sufficiently standardized and accessible to all service providers, to enable interoperability and competition (by minimizing switching and access costs to financial services and products).

[6] Regulation 2023/1114 of 31 May 2023 on markets in crypto-assets, and amending Regulations (EU) No 1093/2010 and (EU) No 1095/2010 and Directives 2013/36/EU and (EU) 2019/1937. https://eur-lex.europa.eu/legal-content/EN/TXT/PDF/?

Libra), have been a significant catalyst for action on both sides of the Atlantic. The prospects of suddenly introducing a new means of payment adopted by billions of users without common standards and legal clarity about rights and obligations surrounding the issuance of such tokens have led regulators across the world to speed up discussions on the new framework. This section will focus on the key defining elements of MiCAR: the scope, the key instruments, the key requirements for stablecoins, and the supervisory framework.

28.4.1 *Scope*

The scope of the Regulation is to establish minimum standards for issuers of crypto-assets, whereby a 'crypto-asset' is 'a digital representation of value or rights which may be transferred and stored electronically, using distributed ledger technology or similar technology'.[7] This definition includes all kinds of DLT tokens,[8] including virtual currencies. Central Bank Digital Currencies (CBDCs) are, nonetheless, partially excluded, insofar as it concerns the requirements applicable to the issuers such as the ECB, national central banks, and other public authorities. There is no further definition of what a 'public authority' is and whether this exemption applies also to non-EU public authorities. As the exemption applies at issuer level, intermediaries providing services in relation to CBDCs will remain in the scope of the legislation.

As MiCAR introduces requirements applicable to issuers of such instruments, there are essentially no requirements that are applicable to well-known existing virtual currencies, such as Bitcoin and Ethereum, as the issuer (or, more precisely, the legal person who made an offer to the public) is no longer identifiable. The existence of a claim on the issuer that is dependent on the future value of an underlying asset is de facto what makes financial assets different from intangibles or real assets.

Virtual currencies on decentralized blockchains (with no identifiable issuer) are closer to intangibles (as a form of digital asset) than financial assets, as their value is not derived from a contractual claim or similar, but rather from the scarcity of that asset. While the outcome is largely aligned with the Commodity Futures Trading Commission's (CFTC) decision to classify major virtual currencies (e.g. Bitcoin) as commodities and to exclude them from the regulatory framework for securities, the MiCAR does include such digital assets in its scope. In effect, the measure may cover issuance of virtual currencies even on decentralized infrastructures, if there is the possibility to link the issuance back to a legal person. Natural persons cannot offer to the public crypto-assets authorized under the Regulation, or provide crypto-assets services (unless under strict conditions), but they can distribute e-money tokens if they are authorized under the Directive 2009/110/EC on E-money.

The clear reference in the rules to 'offers of crypto-assets to the public' or 'admission to trading on a trading platform for crypto-assets' restricts the application of the legislation only to crypto-assets actively traded and marketed in the EU, perhaps via Initial Coin Offerings (ICOs) or an Initial Exchange Offering (IEO) directly on a trading platform. Moreover, no tokens can be offered to the public in the Union or admitted to trading on a trading platform for crypto-assets if

7 Article 3(1)(5) MiCAR.

8 Article 3(1)(1) MiCAR refers to DLT as 'a technology that enables the operation and use of distributed ledgers', while a 'distributed ledger' is 'an information repository that keeps records of transactions and that is shared across, and synchronised between, a set of DLT network nodes using a consensus mechanism'.

the issuer is not authorized in the EU and does not publish a crypto-asset white paper[9] approved by its competent authority. Nonetheless, in the crypto world, it is not always straightforward to establish whether an offer is being made to the public in the EU by a non-EU-established venue or a website not registered in the EU. Things may potentially be easier for well-known US-based stablecoin providers, which may be interested in reaching out to investors across Europe by establishing a branch in the EU and requesting an admission to trading on EU crypto exchanges.

The scope of the rules, moreover, excludes, among others, security tokens or tokenized securities classified as 'financial instruments', funds, deposits, structured deposits, securitization, which are covered under their respective legal frameworks. This classification is typically done by national competent authorities (NCAs), which often apply the EU legal framework differently. For instance, crypto-assets (tokens) that are not means of payment (e-money) often have to undergo an assessment of whether they are 'transferable securities'. Despite the cross-border nature of crypto-assets, MiCAR does not determine the crypto-assets to be classified as financial instruments or transferable securities, leaving this up to MiFID 2. The MiFID 2 definition of 'transferable security' in turn leaves some of the key notions, such as the 'transferability' properties (including when it is 'negotiable on capital markets'), to national laws (ESMA, 2019b, p. 5). The transferability constraints typically come from statutory or technical restrictions, which can vary across Member States according to legal customs or market developments. Moreover, the definition of 'capital markets' typically refers to Regulated Markets and Multilateral Trading Facilities (defined under MiFID 2), which currently exclude crypto exchanges in most Member States. In order to deal with the potential risk of some crypto-assets being captured under the 'transferable security' definition in some countries, but not in others, with potential risks of conflicts of laws, some have called for an *ex ante* review by NCAs (coordinated by ESMA): a non-binding legal opinion supporting the final supervisory decision (Zetzsche et al., 2021, p. 24).

28.4.2 *Key Instruments*

MiCAR identifies three key instruments subject to specific requirements: (1) E-Money Tokens (EMTs); (2) Asset-Referenced Tokens (ARTs); and (3) other tokens that are neither ARTs nor EMTs, including Utility Tokens (UTs). This classification attempts de facto to capture all assets currently available in the crypto ecosystem.

More specifically, EMTs are tokens whose objective is to maintain stable value 'by referring to the value' of a legal tender, typically an official currency. This is by far the most diffused category of stablecoins, which includes Tether, Binance USD, and USD Coin. EMTs aim at being as close to parity as possible, but there is no guaranteed parity among the major stablecoins currently available (for instance, through the use of sponsoring entities or through a direct legal claim that can be redeemed at par). As the objective of EMTs is parity against a single currency, money that is being collected should be invested in multiple (but highly liquid and low-risk, such as government bonds) assets that are denominated in the same currency.

These two characteristics – being low risk (in the meaning of Directive 2009/110/EC) and denominated in the same currency – make most of the current stablecoins non-compliant with MiCAR and therefore they would not be marketable and tradable in the EU. In particular,

[9] A white paper is a short document containing, among others, information on the issuer, the offer, the crypto-asset, and the underlying project being funded.

stablecoins invested in commercial papers, such as Tether, or other crypto-asset tokens, such as DIA, would need to adjust their underlying basket of investments in order to actively solicit an offer of their tokens or admit the token to trade on a crypto-asset trading venue or provide a crypto-asset service in the EU under MiCAR. An EMT may show similarities with e-money, governed by Directive 2009/110/EC, but there are two main differences that still set them apart: (1) some crypto-assets do not explicitly provide a claim on the issuer, and (2) the claim (if it exists) is typically for redemption not at par (Gortsos, 2020).

The second group of crypto-assets classified under MiCAR are ARTs. These are tokens whose objective is to maintain a stable value by referring to the value of a basket of official currencies (legal tenders), or any other value (such as one or several commodities or one or several crypto-assets), or a combination of all of them. This definition captures more complex stablecoins, like the model designed by Diem. A token that keeps its value stable in relation to a basket of fiat currencies potentially offers a tool to protect from excessive currency risk, especially in emerging economies.

While EMTs and ARTs would capture most of the stablecoins, there are also stablecoins that are algorithmic-based, i.e. they keep a stable value by adjusting the supply of tokens in the system and through the use of smart contracts. Their future has been challenged by some (Bullman et al., 2019). and they represent today around 1 per cent of total market capitalization of stablecoins (Xiao, 2021). As a result, they are captured by a residual category under MiCAR, which includes UTs and crypto-assets that are not UTs, EMTs, or ARTs and will be required to issue a white paper (not pre-approved by the NCA). The residual category includes algorithmic stablecoins, native cryptocurrencies (e.g. Bitcoin or Ethereum), and so on. The regulatory treatment of algorithm-based stablecoins, under Title II of MiCAR, requires the existence of an identifiable issuer (a legal person) that has to prepare and publish a white paper. As the requirements are addressed to the issuer, they will not apply when there is no identifiable issuer. Moreover, no white paper is required for a restricted offer (to fewer than 150 natural or legal persons or only to qualified investors with no possibility to be held by non-qualified investors), or small offers (below €1 million over twelve months). Title II of MiCAR does not apply to specific one-time events, such as airdrops, mining rewards, or utility tokens for goods or services in operation, while the whole Regulation does not apply to non-fungible tokens (NFTs).

28.4.3 *Crypto-Assets Service Providers*

Besides the issuers, there is an additional category of entities that would fall under the MiCAR. Those are Crypto-Asset Service Providers (CASPs) – legal persons that offer services in relation to the crypto-assets under MiCAR's scope. The explanatory memorandum clarifies that CASPs are currently unable to provide cross-border services due to diverging bespoke national regimes or a lack of regulation,[10] which adds to the legal uncertainty and lack of protection, especially for investors that need to use services provided by CASPs. This creates two problems. First, an uneven playing field among firms located sparsely across the EU, coupled with inadequate or no regulation in some EU countries, increases the risks of a large loss of confidence in those jurisdictions, with potential rippling effects across the EU. Second, there are increasing concerns that uncoordinated national interventions are ineffective when dealing with internet-based services and financial product offerings. An EU-level intervention might be the bare minimum,

[10] See European Commission, MiCAR Proposal, p. 4.

TABLE 28.1 *Crypto-asset vs (core) investment services*

	MiCAR	MiFID 2/R
1	Operation of a trading platform for crypto-assets	Operation of a multilateral trading facility/ organized trading facility
2	Exchange of crypto-assets for other crypto-assets or fiat	Dealing on own account
3	Execution of crypto orders on behalf of third parties	Execution of orders on behalf
4	Placing of crypto-assets	Placement with or without firm commitment
5	Reception and transmission of crypto orders	Reception and transmission of orders
6	Advice on crypto-assets	Investment advice
7	The custody and administration of crypto-assets on behalf of third parties	
8	Portfolio management in crypto-assets	Individual portfolio management

while coordination with other major jurisdictions (such as G-20 countries) would be the optimal solution.

Beyond broader considerations, the measure introduces a unified regime for CASPs (Title V, MiCAR), which requires them to seek authorization from the competent authority of the Member State in which they have their registered office. In line with the recent Regulation (EU) 2020/1503 on crowdfunding service providers for business, MiCAR introduces an agile passporting framework if the CASP intends to provide services cross-border. In consequence, the authorities of the home Member State for the CASP are to inform the single point of contact of the competent authorities of the host Member States about the CASP providing services in their jurisdiction. Moreover, CASPs will be included in a register managed by ESMA that will provide an overall picture of their operations across the EU.

MiCAR also establishes a list of services that CASPs can provide and those that investment firms authorized under MiFID 2 already provide and that are considered 'equivalent' to crypto-asset services, which in turn reduces the regulatory burden for MiFID firms under MiCAR (see Table 28.1).

Other financial institutions, such as credit institutions, market operators (such as trading platforms), e-money institutions, Undertakings for Collective Investments in Transferable Securities (UCITS) management companies and alternative investment fund managers will be able to provide equivalent services they offer in respect to crypto-assets, under the provision of specific information to check the risks of non-compliance with MiCAR requirements. In effect, MiCAR is the first attempt to regulate platforms, asset managers, and financial institutions that are exclusively dealing with crypto-assets.

Notably, for trading platforms in crypto-assets, there are two sets of requirements. The first is for the operations of trading platforms, i.e. the matching of multiple buying and selling interests for crypto-assets to be exchanged for other crypto-assets or fiat currency. A set of 'operating rules' – for example, the due diligence of crypto-assets admitted to trading and exclusion categories also requires the platform operator to ensure orderly trading, to create a reporting system, and set 'objective and proportionate' criteria for participation in the platform. These requirements create an important distinction (existing also for MiFID trading platforms) between multilateral trading platforms, i.e. where operators act as riskless counterparts, and bilateral trading platforms (exchange of crypto-assets), i.e. largely those involving the proprietary capital of the operator. As a result, the second set of requirements for 'crypto-assets exchanges' is focused on ensuring that the operator does not commercially discriminate against clients and, more generally, acts in a transparent and fair way.

All CASPs need to comply with a list of organizational and prudential requirements, including complaint handling, conflicts of interest management, own funds, and safekeeping of crypto-assets and funds. Moreover, MiCAR introduces requirements specifically for services 3 to 6 (see Table 28.1) to ensure that CASPs operate in the best interest of the client, for instance by managing conflicts of interest, disclosing relevant information (such as third parties' remuneration), and understanding clients' needs. This is very much along the lines of the requirements imposed on MiFID investment firms for equivalent services.

Finally, MiCAR provides a framework for providers of custodial and administration of crypto-assets on behalf of third parties. In line with the inclusion of custodian wallet providers and crypto exchanges under the money-laundering legislation,[11] MiCAR determines the information to be collected and the information to be disclosed by a CASP. Notably, a CASP that provides custody and administration of crypto-assets will be liable for a loss. The original Commission proposal also included a loss 'from a malfunction or hacks up to the market value of the crypto-assets lost',[12] but the Council amended it by only referring to a loss where the CASP cannot demonstrate that it occurred independently of its operations. This could be the case of a problem 'inherent in the operation of the distributed ledger'[13] that is beyond the control of the CASP.

28.4.4 *Key Requirements for (Global) Stablecoins*

According to the explanatory memorandum of the original Commission proposal, 'the proposal imposes more stringent requirements on "stablecoins", which are more likely to grow quickly in scale and possibly result in higher levels of risk to investors, counterparties and the financial system'.[14] As native financial instruments and tokenized securities will remain subject to the existing EU financial legislation, stablecoins are thus directly addressed by MiCAR. Their importance is also emphasized by their 'clear monetary substitution dimension', which can mainly affect the conduct of monetary policies and the smooth operation of payment systems (ECB, 2021, pp. 1–9).

Issuers of ARTs would need to seek authorization, unless tokens are only offered or held by qualified investors or the average outstanding amount does not exceed €5 million over twelve months or they are credit institutions. Whether below or above the threshold, the preparation and publication of a white paper is mandatory. It needs to be pre-approved by the NCA within the authorization procedure (and outside of it for credit institutions) for ARTs. No pre-approval is required for white papers issued in relation to EMTs and tokens that are neither ARTs nor EMTs. For ARTs, their content (for which the issuer is liable) includes a description of the issuer's governance arrangements, reserve assets composition, rights on referenced assets, or alternative arrangements with CASPs, and a legal opinion that the ART is not a financial instrument, electronic money, or (structured) deposit. Similar information is included in the EMT white paper, although obviously there is no focus on reserve assets in this case, but rather on rights and obligations attached to the token and in particular a statement on the holders benefiting from redemption rights 'at any moment and at par value' and related conditions.

[11] Directive (EU) 2015/849 of the European Parliament and of the Council of 20 May 2015 on the prevention of the use of the financial system for the purposes of money laundering or terrorist financing, OJ L 141 5.6.2015, p. 73, as subsequently amended.

[12] Article 67(8) MiCAR COM Proposal.

[13] Article 67(8) MiCAR Council Proposal, now Article 75(8) para. 2nd MiCAR.

[14] European Commission, MiCAR Proposal, p. 5.

Moreover, an e-money token pegging one of the European Union's official currencies will be 'deemed to be offered to the public in the Union'.

In line with the regulatory treatment of e-money in Article 12 Directive 2009/110/EC, MiCAR prohibits the granting of interest for both EMTs and ARTs, also to limit the possibility of being considered as a deposit-taking activity and creating a de facto shadow bank.

Due to the complexity of asset-referenced tokens, ARTs issuers are subject to additional organizational and prudential requirements compared to EMT issuers (which can only be credit institutions or electronic money institutions), in relation to the rights granted to holders, reserve assets, conflicts of interests, complaint handling, and own funds. In particular, MiCAR prescribes the creation of reserve assets for each category of an ART and a specific policy for the management of the reserve assets backing ARTs. Their value and composition should be publicly disclosed and subject to an independent audit every six months. Assets need to be entrusted to credit institutions or CASPs and not encumbered or pledged as collateral. Reserve assets shall be invested in 'highly liquid financial instruments with minimal market and credit risk'[15]. Finally, MiCAR requires ARTs to have disclosed policies setting out conditions and procedures in relation to the rights of the token holder on the issuer or on the reserve assets.

MiCAR also introduces requirements for the prevention of market abuse involving crypto-assets admitted on a trading platform. The requirements mirror to a large extent existing market abuse legislation in relation to insider trading and market manipulation. Nonetheless, they introduce new elements, such as market manipulation, by 'securing a dominant position over the supply of or demand for a crypto asset' with impact on prices and trading conditions, [16] which potentially applies to all crypto-assets transactions and not just to specific cornering actions in the cash forward or Emission Trading Scheme markets (as per Market Abuse Regulation (EU) 596/2014, Article 12(2)).

28.4.5 *The Supervisory Framework and 'Significant Tokens'*

In line with the recommendations of international policy fora, such as the Financial Stability Board (2020a), MiCAR recognizes that there are heightened financial stability risks when a stablecoin reaches a significant scale. As a result, MiCAR classifies ARTs and EMTs as 'significant' tokens when they reach a specific size and interconnection with the financial system. Moreover, the issuer can ask for its token(s) to be classified by the competent authority as 'significant' if it can demonstrate that it is likely to meet at least three of the criteria to be classified as 'significant'.

On top of additional organizational and own funds requirements, such as additional own funds or custody arrangements, the key feature of this targeted regime is the supervisory framework. In particular, EBA will be in charge of classifying tokens as 'significant'. Once this has been determined, EBA becomes the sole supervisor of the issuer in relation to the issuance of Significant ARTs (SARTs) or Significant EMTs (SEMTs) and, for SEMTs, EBA will only supervise the application of specific requirements. The EBA should also establish a college of supervisors (including ECB and ESMA) for each issuer. The colleges will address EBA and national competent authorities with non-binding opinions.

When it comes to regulation and supervision of third-country issuers, the FSB called for 'cooperation' both domestically and internationally, as one of the key factors for effective

[15] This also includes UCITS investing in low-risk assets; see Article 34(4) MiCAR, Council Proposal.
[16] See Article 91(3)(a) MiCAR.

supervision of global stablecoins (FSB, 2020a, p. 21). MiCAR does not include any framework to recognize third-country regimes, whose existence would often imply some level of coordination with major non-EU jurisdictions. Non-EU issuers offering stablecoins in the EU would need to be established in the EU, forcing current global players to create a European legal entity to fulfil legal requirements of the MiCAR. Nonetheless, the EBA would be empowered to seek agreements on exchanges of information with competent authorities in third countries to best perform its own tasks.

28.5 DLT-BASED MARKET INFRASTRUCTURE: A REGULATORY SANDBOX

Another important piece of the DFS is the so-called DLT Pilot regime, i.e. Regulation 2022/858 on a pilot regime for market infrastructures based on distributed ledger technology. In line with the well-established preference by European institutions (including national competent authorities) and the international community more broadly (FSB, 2017, p. 31; IOSCO, 2019b, p. 3) to test new technological solutions for the financial system, DLTR creates a 'statutory' (regulatory) sandbox for market infrastructures that want to transfer the traditional securities trading 'on chain'. The regulation is addressed to 'multilateral trading facilities' authorized under MiFID 2 and 'securities settlement systems' (central securities depositories, as defined by Regulation 909/2014, also called Central Securities Depositories Regulation, CSDR) using DLT technology – broadly defined as 'a technology that enables the operation and use of distributed ledgers'.[17] An authorization to operate a DLT infrastructure under DLTR (and its ongoing supervision) is provided by the national competent authority, which authorizes multilateral trading facilities and central securities depositories, respectively under MiFID 2 and CSDR. National authorities should consult ESMA on this authorization decision and receive a non-binding opinion, as well as recommendations on the application or the exemptions requested.

An agile sandbox approach was necessary, as many Member States shy away from standard regulatory sandboxes, which could have implied only temporary disapplication of EU financial law (up to twenty-four months in most cases; Zetzsche and Woxholth, 2021). In particular, DLTR offers a more long-term and size-based sandbox, which will be currently in place for six years. As a result, DLTR aims to create a new viable and live DLT-based market infrastructure that would potentially compete with current market infrastructure, insofar as it can prove that it is more effective and cost-efficient than current centralized bookkeeping infrastructures.

The scope of DLTR covers DLT financial instruments, including DLT transferable securities, such as shares and bonds either tokenized or issued natively on DLT with a maximum market capitalization of €500 million for shares and UCITS (assets under management), and €1 billion for bonds. The DLT market infrastructure cannot admit to trading DLT financial instruments with initial market value above €6 billion and the infrastructure can continue to operate until the market value of the registered DLT financial instruments, traded on the DLT multilateral trading facilities and settled with central securities depositories in the DLT securities settlement system reaches €9 billion. While there is no official explanation of why these specific amounts have been chosen, these thresholds are largely linked to discussions in other pieces of EU legislation (also with limited cross-border impact).

As these DLT markets may grow in size and go well above the thresholds set in DLTR, a transition strategy is imposed by DLTR to transfer activities 'off chain', so in traditional marketplaces, starting from a market value of DLT instruments admitted to trading of €9 billion.

[17] Article 2(1) DLTR.

Another interesting feature of DLTR includes the possibility for investment firms that are DLT MTFs to also run the 'security settlement system', and so a DLT trading and settlement system (DLT TSS), and for central securities depositories to run DLT MTFs, as long as they both comply with MiFID 2 and CSDR requirements (and the conditions for targeted exemptions from the legislation under DLTR). This is an interesting development since it shows the great potential of DLT systems to integrate the securities value chain into a single market infrastructure, with potential operational synergies and cost reductions. Moreover, the DLT financial instruments that can be admitted to trading on such DLTR-compliant infrastructure could potentially include (for the first time) all DeFi tokens that are natively on chain and meet the characteristics of a transferable security, provided that the issuance is not large in size.

The central securities depositories operating the DLT securities settlement system or the DLT TSS may be exempted from targeted requirements under CSDR for account-based settlement of book entry securities that may be incompatible with DLT infrastructures, such as the requirement to be in dematerialized (book entry) form (Article 2(4) and 3 CSDR), the transfer of orders (Article 2(9), CSDR), and the use of securities accounts (Article 2(28), CSDR). There are no exemptions for the application of market abuse rules under Regulation (EU) 596/2014.

Overall, this framework creates a 'safe space' for trading and settlement of DLT transferable securities both in respect to tokenized existing transferable securities and native tokens issued 'on chain'. However, critical questions remain regarding its applicability on the ground. In particular, there are profound legal questions about the fitness of the current regulatory framework applicable to traditional securities infrastructure in relation to DLT systems. For instance, implementing delivery-versus-payment (DvP) in the context of DLT systems under the current Settlement Finality Directive 98/26/EC, which is at the heart of securities settlement, is difficult. The Directive constructs settlement finality around market infrastructure with bookkeeping entries, where 'the moment of entry and of irrevocability of transfer orders' is clearly identifiable. This is not straightforward in a DLT environment. For now, DLTR tries to escape this issue by offering the DLT settlement system the possibility to avoid the settlement finality requirement if it puts in place 'robust procedures and arrangements' to, among other, mitigate any risk arising from the non-designation of the DLT securities system as a system for the purposes of Directive 98/26/EC, in particular with regard to insolvency proceedings. This implies that the DLT system may be incompatible with the transfer of ownership of securities (and overall DvP process) under the national laws of Member States where the transaction needs to be considered effected. The DLT securities settlement system may also not qualify as a 'system' under the Settlement Finality Directive and therefore lose the protection from insolvency proceedings that is essential for settlement finality. As a result, while the conditional disapplication of specific EU laws is indeed possible under DLTR, it may be hard to circumvent application of national private law on ownership transfer. It needs to be seen whether this level of legal uncertainty will discourage market operators from taking on this challenge.

28.6 MEASURES TO ENHANCE CYBER RESILIENCE AND TO FOSTER COMPETITION

The DFS also includes another important legislative initiative, i.e. Regulation on Digital Operational Resilience for the financial sector (DORA),[18] and a commitment for further action under the

[18] Regulation (EU) 2022/2554 of the European Parliament and of the Council of 14 December 2022 on digital operational resilience for the financial sector and amending Regulations (EC) No. 1060/2009, (EU) No. 648/2012, (EU) No. 600/2014, (EU) No. 909/2014 and (EU) 2016/101, OJ L 333, 27.12.2022, pp. 1–79.

so-called open finance framework, which promises to open access to data held by financial institutions and big tech involved in financial services for the benefit of retail investors and consumers.

The measure recognizes that the principle of technological neutrality can apply to the objectives (outcome) of financial regulation, but organizational requirements need to be calibrated depending on how the service is delivered to users. MiFD 2 and the Markets in Financial Instruments Regulation did that when they introduced additional requirements targeted to algorithmic trading, as that technology became dominant in financial markets. In the same way, DORA aims to factor in 'new risks' brought about by new technological uses. In particular, DORA aims 'to build, assure and review [...] operational integrity'.[19] It creates a framework to report, test, and manage ICT risks for all the entities in the financial sector, where 'ICT risk' means 'any reasonably identifiable circumstance or event having a potential adverse effect on the network and information systems – including any malfunction, capacity overrun, failure, disruption, impairment, misuse, loss or other type of malicious or non-malicious event – which, if materialised, may compromise the security of the network and information systems'.[20] This is a long overdue action in a sector where cyber resilience has become a key priority for an ever more digital and internet-based business.

The DFS also pledges to reinforce its 'open finance' strategy launched with the Payment Service Directive 2,[21] which required credit institutions to give payment providers access to accounts for the purpose of allowing an 'unhindered and efficient' provision of payment services. This required banks to open up data on clients' accounts to new payment service providers that have over the years increasingly gained market share and eroded profits of major banks, while revolutionizing accessibility to payments via new apps and interfaces. The follow-up step, according to the DFS, is to move from 'open banking' to 'open finance', i.e. to expand the access to 'more customer data' (this potentially includes securities accounts, suitability and appropriateness assessments, etc.), in order to provide better and more targeted financial advice, while ensuring appropriate data protection.

28.7 LOOKING FORWARD: IS DIGITAL SECURITY THE 'PROMISED LAND' OF CAPITAL MARKETS INTEGRATION?

All the initiatives described pose a wide array of legal questions, including some on the adaptations needed for company law and capital markets law to the new digital context. Among others, a remarkable example is 'tokenization', or digitalization of securities. The DFS inevitably brings to the forefront new and underexplored questions about the need to identify what digital security is, what the market infrastructure of a digital security looks like, and what is the added value of such instruments, for instance, in corporate governance.

28.7.1 *What Is Digital Security', When Is It a 'Financial Instrument' and Why Is This Question Relevant?*

From a legal perspective, it is hard to capture crypto-assets under a simple taxonomy and to define an appropriate regulatory and supervisory regime for them. Some of the digital assets

[19] Article 3(1) DORA.

[20] Article 3(5) DORA.

[21] Directive (EU) 2015/2366 on payment services in the internal market, amending Directives 2002/65/EC, 2009/110/EC and 2013/36/EU and Regulation (EU) No 1093/2010, and repealing Directive 2007/64/EC, OJ L 337 23.12.2015, p. 35, https://eur-lex.europa.eu/legal-content/EN/TXT/HTML/?uri=CELEX:02015L2366-20151223&from=EN.

using DLT may result in rights or endowments, which do not fit well into the traditional understanding of rights of a shareholder or a bondholder, or, more generally, of the holder of a 'financial instrument' as an investment characterized by rights to a financial return.

Regulatory agencies such as ESMA and EBA have conducted surveys and made studies using a tripartite classification of crypto-assets as 'investment type' (rights to financial returns), 'payment type' (services of exchange), and 'utility type' (access to a good or service; EBA, 2019c). Some jurisdictions follow this tripartite classification to regulate the first type of the three as 'financial products', the second type as payment systems, and leaving the third type outside the reach of securities laws. Yet things are seldom that simple. An ESMA survey of national supervisors showed that, whereas a 'pure utility type' crypto-asset[22] was considered outside the scope of securities regulation, 'hybrid' types, which include features of 'investment', 'payment/ exchange', and utility, could be classified differently. For example, crypto-assets that offered the right to participate in a firm's profits were classified as a 'security', but national approaches differ when crypto-assets offer a mixture of investment and payment characteristics. In the United States, the Securities and Exchange Commission introduced a concept of 'security' encompassing a large part of crypto-assets on the basis of the so-called Howey test devised by the courts.[23] So far, the European strategy is two-pronged, and consists of combining a bespoke regulation for utility assets and stable coins, including payments tokens, while using the existing capital markets regulatory framework (with minimal changes, if needed) for investment assets.

Yet the question of whether a crypto-asset is a 'security' (or a 'payment service' or 'money') actually masks a series of different issues. The emergence of digital assets carrying the rights of shares or bonds (albeit adapted to the reality of the digital 'metaverse'), as 'equity tokens' or 'debt tokens', impacts not only on capital markets regulation but also on corporate law. Indeed, depending on their specific technological features, they may pose specific corporate law issues in their own right. Anonymity of shares could be an example. Indeed, in a corporate law context shareholders' anonymity is often not allowed. However, in many DLT settings, identification of shareholders for equity token holders may be impossible beyond the use of a pseudonym for allocation of a wallet, unless investor whitelisting and other validation processes are put in place and the applicable technological ecosystem is a so-called permissioned DLT (notably a private and restricted blockchain network offered for service by approved market players), whose service provider can precisely identify the holders of such equity tokens (also for anti-money-laundering and know-your-customer purposes) (Blemus and Guegan, 2019, p. 19).

28.7.2 *The Market Dimension of a Permissioned DLT Digital Security: Central Depositories, Clearing and Settlement*

Leaving aside the new 'bundles of rights' packaged as crypto-assets, and focusing merely on the technological side, the use of DLT in this context appears to be less controversial. From a market perspective, a permissioned DLT may be useful for the issuance, holding, and transfer of securities. There are pilot tests ongoing for shares, bonds, and units of mutual funds in blockchain technology (ESMA, 2021, p. 13). In France, for instance, non-listed shares and

[22] ESMA (2019b, p. 24) considers a pure utility type Filecoin, a decentralized storage network that turns cloud storage into an algorithmic market, where Filecoins can be spent to get access to unused storage capacity on computers worldwide, and providers of said unused storage capacity can earn filecoins, which then can be sold for cryptocurrencies or fiat money.

[23] *SEC* v. *Howey Co.*, 328 U.S. 293 (1946). See also SEC Framework for 'Investment Contract' Analysis of Digital Assets, www.sec.gov/corpfin/framework-investment-contract-analysis-digital-assets.

debt instruments can be registered and transferred on a distributed ledger since 2016. There is a wide consensus that DLT may progressively compete and even replace in the long term the centrally maintained securities depositor's services. For the time being, several existing pilot initiatives seem to deliver on their promises. This justifies a pause for thought to discuss how central depository and securities settlement services may be organized and operated in a DLT environment.

As shown by the DLT Pilot Regulation 2022/858, in such a new technological context, central securities depositories (CSDs) may rely on a permissioned DLT where listed securities are no longer centrally deposited with the CSD but rather deposited in several nodes of the network, whose integrity is ensured by the CSD, but participants to the network are enabled to run parts of the operations themselves and to act autonomously or bilaterally with each other under predefined legal and technological rulebooks. This, in principle, may allow market efficiency to increase among a larger number of clients, standardize pre-issuance and issuance processes through smart contracts, and enhance asset servicing. It may also have visible implications not only for the existing securities settlement environment but also for its European regulatory environment and for market integration.

Both Regulation (EU) No. 909/2014 on central securities depositories (together with its Delegated Regulations 2017/392 and 2018/1229) and the Settlement Finality Directive 98/26/EC (SFD) are, in principle, technologically neutral and thus should also accommodate the use of new DLT technology by CSD, provided that the adopted technology is not based on a purely decentralized and public network, but rather on a permissioned DLT platform with a validation model allowing for the needed centralized controls. The DLT Pilot regime brought about by Regulation 2022/858 facilitates this, by removing impediments, but also specifies in recital (7) of its preamble that

> the status as DLT market infrastructure should be optional and should not prevent financial market infrastructures, such as trading venues, central securities depositories (CSDs) and central counterparties (CCPs), from developing trading and post-trading services and activities for crypto-assets that qualify as financial instruments, or are based on distributed ledger technology, under existing Union financial services legislation.[24]

Anecdotal evidence, however, shows that existing examples of central securities depositories already using DLT technology are confined to notary and central maintenance services to keep records of every change resulting from transactions settled through the established Target 2 Securities (the CSD does not, therefore, use DLT as a security settlement system; ESMA, 2021, p.17). Moreover, while the transfer of securities may, in principle, be settled in the DLT context (e.g. when a transaction is 'validated' on a DLT platform, data is recorded to the transferor's and the transferee's DLT addresses, which results in a 'transfer' of the token), payment in cryptocurrency appears to be currently not possible on a DLT platform (Article 40 CSDR still prevents this). As long as this regulatory bottleneck is not removed (by allowing cryptocurrencies or by making available central bank money on a DLT platform, notably a digital euro, or by developing new technologies offering interfaced settlement off-ledger), the complete tokenization of the settlement and delivery of security tokens is impossible. The CSD has to settle the cash leg of the transaction through movements in its cash accounts at the same time as the securities leg of the transaction takes place on the DLT platform.

[24] https://eur-lex.europa.eu/eli/reg/2022/858/oj

28.7.3 *Towards a DLT-Based Platform Corporate Governance?*

DLT-based technologies appear to also have potential to reframe several important aspects of the 'legacy' corporate law. In the corporate setting, technology may help curb collective action problems. This may fundamentally modify the principal/agent relationship, questioning the traditional agency model applied to the shareholders/managers relation in offline, 'legacy' companies, which deeply inspired existing company laws.

This situation may have corporate governance implications (Abriani and Schneider, 2021). Thus, from a regulatory perspective, the advent of new technologies may call for company law adjustments. Some argue that in a technology-driven, digital world, 'platform companies' are already disrupting many industries and offer a new model of 'platform governance', where digital technologies are leveraged to create less hierarchical, more 'community-driven' forms of corporate organizations (Fenwick et al., 2018a, 2018b).

Others note that DLT and smart contracts have the potential 'greatly to reduce the costs of organising business activities by contract, as opposed to using firms' and this will 'likely reduce the scope of business activities for which the corporate form is used as an organising device and therefore the scope of activity governed by corporate law' (Armour et al., 2019, p. 8). In a seminal study, Lafarre and Van der Elst (2018, p. 1) argue that 'blockchain is a technology that can offer smart solutions for classical corporate governance inefficiencies, especially in the relationship between shareholders and the company'; because 'blockchain technology can lower shareholder voting costs and the organization costs for companies substantially', it can 'increase the speed of decision making, facilitate fast and efficient involvement of the shareholders'. In short, blockchain technology may prove a promising tool for better shareholder engagement.

This has interesting implications from the perspective of company law. A first example is shareholder identification. The Shareholders Right Directive (SRD II)[25] allows companies to make use of electronic means in their corporate governance provided that the proper identification of shareholders (including the name of the shareholder, contact details, and, if applicable, information such as the Legal Entity Identifier Code) is ensured. In practice, in many jurisdictions, companies identify shareholders via individual access codes ('access cards') sent to shareholders, often via specialized service providers. Currently, the SRD II defines a 'shareholder' as a natural or a legal person recognized as a shareholder under the national law. The Capital Market Union Action Plan[26] envisaged identifying shareholders by the issuer. In the context of a permissioned DLT, the proper identification of the shareholder would need something more than a digital identity of the shareholder's wallet. It would also require proof of authentication outside the blockchain with the holder's real identity, which could also be stored in the blockchain (Lafarre and Van der Elst, 2018, p. 16). In turn, however, a permissioned DLT may eliminate many of the practical impediments that shareholders of listed companies currently face in getting their access cards for the shareholders' meetings on time due to the complex (and often inefficient) chain of intermediaries participating in the central depository system.

A second example of company law implications of digitalization is the exercise of voting rights electronically. Here again, the Capital Market Union Action Plan envisaged an assessment of

[25] Directive (EU) 2017/828 of the European Parliament and of the Council of 17 May 2017 amending Directive 2007/36/EC as regards the encouragement of long-term shareholder engagement, OJ L 132, 20.5.2017, pp. 1–25.

[26] European Commission, Communication on A Capital Markets Union for people and businesses. New action plan, COM(2020) 590 final, September 2020.

whether and how the 'rules governing the interaction between investors, intermediaries and issuers' as regards the exercise of voting rights and corporate action processing can be further clarified and harmonized, also looking at new digital technologies.[27] The Action Plan is based on the Final Report of the High-Level Forum for Europe's Capital Markets, 'A New Vision for Europe's Capital Markets', of June 2020, which contains a recommendation on shareholders' exercise of voting rights and corporate actions. This encompasses attendance in purely digital or hybrid (both in person and digital) meetings, where all shareholders must be able to exercise the same rights as in physical meetings, i.e. viewing, hearing, speaking, proposing, and voting. In contrast to some US state laws, so far, law in many European countries does not allow for virtual shareholders' meetings only, except for the exceptional circumstances of the COVID-19 pandemic. However, digital means, including blockchain technology, may facilitate dialogue between shareholders and board members. Although this may deprive shareholders of the opportunity of face-to-face in-person discussions, the benefits may outweigh the costs.

A third example is the transmission of information across the investment chain. Again, blockchain technology seems capable of remedying the fact that currently the chain of intermediaries maintaining securities accounts on behalf of shareholders often fails in its duties towards shareholders and issuers and, as witnessed by recital (8) of the preamble to the SRD II, in practice 'information is not always passed from the company to its shareholders and shareholders votes are not always correctly transmitted to the company' (see also Laster, 2017). In a 'permission-based' system, instead, information can be transmitted automatically to the parties formally authorized to be in the DLT system.

These and many other advantages are the promises of the transition of company law from the offline to the online world and the use of DLT for enhanced corporate governance. Only time will tell what promises are kept, and what unanticipated challenges will need to be addressed to bridge past and future of company and capital markets law.

28.8 WHAT DOES THE DIGITAL FINANCE STRATEGY IMPLY FOR CAPITAL MARKET INTEGRATION IN THE EU?

Capital markets are one of the sectors where digitalization is changing old paradigms as to how services are provided and how providers approach their clients. Capital markets, as a funding tool, also tend to be more open to innovation, as by definition they require a dialogue with multiple parties, whether issuers or investors. As a result, any technology that helps to better connect investors with issuers will be easily taken up. Moreover, the DFS also has a formal link with capital market policies, via the CMU project, which was the main catalyst for action in the FinTech space with the launch of the FinTech Action Plan in March 2018. As a continuation of the original plan, while the DFS expands into other areas of finance, the most significant impact can be expected in the area of capital market integration. This contribution to integration takes different forms, such as the need for greater supervisory and regulatory coordination or the synergies and vertical integration that some technologies could bring for the traditional market infrastructure and securities value chain.

MiCAR (together with the 5th Anti-Money Laundering Directive)[28] in particular will increase the need for coordination on the classification of transferable securities by increasing

[27] Ibid., p. 13.

[28] Directive (EU) 2018/843 of the European Parliament and of the Council of 30 May 2018 amending Directive (EU) 2015/849 on the prevention of the use of the financial system for the purposes of money laundering or terrorist financing, and amending Directives 2009/138/EC and 2013/36/EU, OJ L 156, 19.6.2018, pp. 43–74.

tensions between national interpretations of concepts like transferability and negotiability (for the definition of transferable securities discussed earlier), and the new European framework for (global) stablecoins, utility, and other coins, which needs to be able to identify in a more homogenous way tokens that are securities from those that are not. For instance, some utility coins (especially those for which the service or good is still in the development phase) are instruments that lie on the border between utility tokens and transferable securities, due to the nature of claims over products that might or might not ever be produced. Moreover, the measure clearly spells out that DLT-based MiFID financial instruments should always be in the MiFID 2 scope, which was not something to be taken for granted. Whether or not a more detailed definition of transferable security will be included in a legal text anytime soon, market developments and the pressure coming from this legislative action may increasingly force Member States to coordinate their approach, to avoid unpredictable spill-over effects and legal uncertainty due to different national classifications of large phenomena, such as widespread adoption of stablecoins by the EU public.

A euro-based stablecoin or a European Central Bank Digital Currency can be a key driver to lower cross-border friction for investments in terms of a cost reduction and a market infrastructure integration. This could also be the case for non-legal barriers, such as withholding tax procedures, which can then be programmed to retain or release funds at source via smart contracts. Moreover, a token that can keep a stable value against a basket of fiat currencies offers a good hedging tool for international investors and companies that want to raise money or invest in multiple countries and be protected from currency risks with cost-saving alternatives.

The introduction of harmonized requirements on cyber resilience (DORA) increases trust and stimulates the take-up of new technological solutions by issuers and investors, which can further reduce friction to cross-border capital market integration.

A gradual take-up of DLT technologies for the issuance in the traditional securities trading sector can produce positive spill-over effects for coordination of supervision among national supervisors, which is the core of the European Single Rulebook. In particular, some aspects of supervision can even be embedded into smart contracts (Auer, 2019), such as automatic application of a supervisory order when specific circumstances are met. This possibility makes the *ex ante* examination related to the approval and monitoring of smart contract codes easier than other situations, in which the supervisory check comes *ex post* (i.e. when the conduct has materialized and the smart contract triggered with no possibility to revert the action using 'specific performance' measures).

REFERENCES

Abriani, N., and Schneider, G. (2021). *Diritto delle imprese e intelligenza artificiale*. Bologna: Il Mulino, pp. 191–225.

Armour, J., Enriques, L., Ezrachi, A., and Vella, J. (2019). Putting technology to good use for society: The role of corporate, competition and tax law. ECGI Law Working Paper, No. 427/2018.

Auer, R. (2019). Embedded supervision: How to build regulation into blockchain finance. BIS Working Paper, No. 811, 16 September. www.bis.org/publ/work811.htm

Auer, R., Cornelli, G., and Frost, J. (2020). Rise of the central bank digital currencies: Drivers, approaches and technologies. BIS Working Paper, No. 880, 24 August.

Beck, T. (2020). FinTech and financial inclusion: Opportunities and pitfalls. ADBI Working Paper Series, No. 1165, July. www.adb.org/sites/default/files/publication/623276/adbi-wp1165.pdf

Beck, T. (2021). Digital technology and financial innovation: A literature survey. In T. Beck and Y. C. Park (eds.), *Fostering FinTech for Financial Transformation: The Case of South Korea*.London: CEPR Press, 143–188. https://voxeu.org/content/fostering-fintech-financial-transformation-case-south-korea.

Blemus, S., and Guegan, D. (2019). Initial crypto-assets offerings (ICOs), tokenisation and corporate governance. CES Working Papers, No. 2019.04, pp. 1–31.

Bullmann, D., Klemm, J., and Pinna, A. (2019). In search for stability in crypto-assets: Are stablecoins the solutions? ECB Occasional Paper Series, No. 230, August.

European Banking Authority (2019a). Report on potential impediments to the cross-border provision of banking and payment services. EBA Report, 29 October. www.eba.europa.eu/eba-calls-european-commission-take-action-facilitate-scaling-cross-border-activity

European Banking Authority (2019b). Regulatory perimeter, regulatory status and authorisation approaches in relation to FinTech activities. Final Report. www.eba.europa.eu/eba-publishes-report-on-regulatory-perimeter-regulatory-status-and-authorisation-approaches-in-relation-to-fintech-activities

European Banking Authority (2019c). Report with advice for the European Commission on Crypto Assets. 9 January. www.eba.europa.eu/eba-reports-on-crypto-assets

European Banking Authority (2021). Report on the use of digital platforms in the EU banking and payment sector. EBA/REP/2021/26, September. www.eba.europa.eu/eba-sees-rapid-growth-use-digital-platforms-eu%E2%80%99s-banking-and-payments-sector-and-identifies-steps

European Central Bank (2021). Opinion on a proposal for regulation on Markets in Crypto-assets, and amending Directive (EU) 2019/1937, CON/2021/4, OJ C 152. 29 April. https://eur-lex.europa.eu/legal-content/EN/TXT/?uri=CELEX%3A52021AB0004

European Commission (2015). A digital single market strategy for Europe. Communication from the Commission to the European Parliament, the Council, the European Economic and Social Committee and the Committee of the Regions, COM(2015) 192 final. https://eur-lex.europa.eu/legal-content/EN/TXT/HTML/?uri=CELEX:52015DC0192&from=EN

European Commission (2017). FinTech: A more competitive and innovative European financial sector. Consultation Document. https://ec.europa.eu/info/sites/default/files/2017-fintech-consultation-document_en_0.pdf

European Commission (2018). FinTech action plan: For a more competitive and innovative European financial sector. Communication from the Commission, COM(2018) 109 final, 8 March. https://eur-lex.europa.eu/legal-content/EN/TXT/HTML/?uri=CELEX:52018DC0109&from=EN

European Commission (2020a). Digital finance package. Commission Communication, COM/2020/591 final, 24 September. https://ec.europa.eu/info/publications/200924-digital-finance-proposals_en

European Commission (2020b). Retail payments strategy for the EU. Communication from the Commission to the European Parliament, the Council, the European Economic and Social Committee and the Committee of the Regions. COM(2020) 591 final, 24 September. https://eur-lex.europa.eu/legal-content/EN/TXT/HTML/?uri=CELEX:52020DC0591&from=EN

European Parliament (2020). Digital finance: Emerging risks in crypto-assets – regulatory and supervisory challenges in the area of financial services, institutions and markets. European Parliament Regulation of 8 October 2020, P9_TA(2020)0265. www.europarl.europa.eu/doceo/document/TA-9-2020-0265_EN.html

European Securities and Markets Authority (ESMA) (2019a). Initial coin offerings and crypto-assets. Advice to the European Commission, ESMA50-157-1391, 9 January. www.esma.europa.eu/sites/default/files/library/esma50-157-1391_crypto_advice.pdf

European Securities and Markets Authority (ESMA) (2019b). Legal qualification of crypto-assets – Survey to NCAs. Annex to ESMA50-157-1391, 9 January). www.esma.europa.eu/sites/default/files/library/esma50-157-1384_annex.pdf

European Securities and Markets Authority (ESMA) (2021). Use of FinTech by CSDs, Report to the European Commission. ESMA70-156-4576, 2 August.

European Securities and Markets Authority, European Banking Authority and European Insurance and Occupational Pensions Authority (ESMA, EBA, and EIOPA) (2018). FinTech: Regulatory sandboxes and innovation hubs. Report, JC 2018/74. www.esma.europa.eu/sites/default/files/library/jc_2018_74_joint_report_on_regulatory_sandboxes_and_innovation_hubs.pdf

Fenwick, M., Kaal, W. A., and Vermeulen, E. P. M. (2018a). Why blockchain will disrupt corporate organizations. TILEC Discussion Paper and ECGI Law Working Paper No. 419/2018, October.

Fenwick, M., McCahery, J. A., and Vermeulen, E. P. M. (2018b). The end of 'corporate' governance (hello 'platform' governance). ECGI Law Working Paper, No. 430/2018, December.

Feyen, E., Frost, J., Gambacorta, L., Natarajan, H., and Saal, M. (2021). Fintech and the digital transformation of financial services: Implications for market structure and public policy. BIS Papers, No. 117.

Financial Stability Board (2017). Financial stability implications from FinTech: Supervisory and regulatory issues that merit authorities' attention. www.fsb.org/wp-content/uploads/R270617.pdf

Financial Stability Board (2020a). Regulation, supervision and oversight of 'global stablecoin' arrangements. Final report and high-level recommendations, October. www.fsb.org/wp-content/uploads/P131020-3.pdf

Financial Stability Board (2020b). Effective practices for cyber incident response and recovery: Final Report. Final Report of Public Consultation. www.fsb.org/2020/10/effective-practices-for-cyber-incident-response-and-recovery-final-report/

Gortsos, C. V. (2020). The Commission's 2020 proposal for a markets in crypto-assets regulation ('MiCAR'): A brief introductory overview. Notes for students. https://papers.ssrn.com/sol3/papers.cfm?abstract_id=3842824

Group of Thirty (2009). Financial reform: A framework for financial stability. Report of Working Group on Financial Reform. https://group30.org/publications/detail/146

International Monetary Fund (2021). COVID-19, crypto, and climate: Navigating challenging transitions. Global Financial Stability Report, October.

International Organization of Securities Commissions (2019a). Board priorities – IOSCO work program for 2019. www.iosco.org/library/pubdocs/pdf/IOSCOPD625.pdf

International Organization of Securities Commissions (2019b). Cyber Task Force: Final Report. FR09/2019, June. www.iosco.org/library/pubdocs/pdf/IOSCOPD633.pdf

International Organization of Securities Commissions (2020a). Global Stablecoin Initiative. Public Report, OR01/2020, March.

International Organization of Securities Commissions (2020b). Issues, risks and regulatory considerations relating to crypto-asset trading platforms. Final Report, FR02/2020, February. www.iosco.org/library/pubdocs/pdf/IOSCOPD649.pdf

Lafarre, A., and Van der Elst, C. (2018). Blockchain technology for corporate governance and shareholder activism. Tilburg Law School Legal Studies Research Paper Series, No. 7/2018.

Laster, T. J. (2017). The block chain plunger: Using technology to clean up proxy plumbing and take back the vote available. Keynote Speech at the Council of Institutional Investors, Chicago, 29 September.

Linnemann Bech, M., Hancock, J., Rice, T., and Wadsworth, A. (2020). On the future of securities settlement. *BIS Quarterly Review* March. www.bis.org/publ/qtrpdf/r_qt2003i.htm

Nakamoto, S. (2008). Bitcoin: A peer-to-peer electronic cash system. https://bitcoin.org/bitcoin.pdf

ROFIEG (Expert Group on Regulatory Obstacles to Financial Innovation) (2019). Thirty recommendations on regulation, innovation and finance. Final Report to the European Commission, December. https://ec.europa.eu/info/files/191113-report-expert-group-regulatory-obstacles-financial-innovation_en

Valiante, D. (2022). Regulating digital platforms: The European experience with financial return crowdfunding. *European Company and Financial Law Review* 19(5), n.p.

Xiao, R. (2021). Decentralized central bank's currency experiment. Medium blog post, 30 August. https://medium.com/iosg-ventures/decentralized-central-banks-currency-experiment-6e3120438a94

Zetzsche, D. A., and Woxholth, J. (2021). The DLT sandbox under the pilot regulation. Law Working Paper Series, No. 2021-001, University of Luxembourg. https://papers.ssrn.com/sol3/papers.cfm?abstract_id=3833766

Zetzsche, D. A., Annunziata, F., Arner, D., and Buckley, R. P. (2021). The markets in crypto-assets regulation (MiCA) and the EU digital finance strategy. *Capital Markets Law Journal* 16(2), 203–225.

29

Regulating Crypto and Cyberware in the EU

Karel Lannoo

29.1 INTRODUCTION

The biggest opportunities and threats in finance these days come from the digital sphere. Fintech firms have made big inroads into financial intermediation, and several relatively new companies have a higher stock value than large banks. Blockchain and Artificial Intelligence (AI) have the potential to revolutionize the ways finance firms interact with their clients and structure their operations internally. The growing use of digital currencies in its different forms has created a large controversy among regulators and central bankers about the creation of a new asset outside the classic institutions. It has led several central banks to announce the creation of a central bank digital currency (CBDC).

Innovation in the financial sector should be welcomed, but the policy response is not uniform, at the global or the European level. Innovation brings more competition and lowers costs for users; it creates new funding channels for enterprises, and more integration of payment systems. But unlike a decade ago with the response to the challenges posed by the Global Financial Crisis, views differ on how to deal with this development. Bitcoins are an opportunity for small or rogue states to escape from the dominance of the big reserve currencies. Crypto-asset offerings carry huge financial and investor protection risks, and while some countries have adopted rules to facilitate token or Initial Currency Offerings (ICOs), and have important volumes of issuance, others are resisting. Approaches also differ for regulating FinTech and decentralized finance: some are registered as banks or trading platforms, others are under a much lighter scheme, or follow the regulatory sandbox approach.

An important element explaining the confusion is related to the definition of cryptofinance: Is it related to payments, to intangible assets or simply to tradable tokens or virtual gadgets? How are crypto 'transactions' regulated and supervised? What are the implications for financial institutions and central banks? What is the impact on financial inclusion and financial literacy?

After a period of long hesitation – and then consultation – the European Commission in September 2020 proposed to regulate cryptocurrencies under the Markets in Crypto-Assets (MiCA) proposal (EC, 2020). This complex piece of regulation covers three different forms of crypto-assets that are based on distributed ledger technology (DLT): non-fungible and utility tokens, asset-referenced tokens, and e-money tokens. Another proposed regulation, the Digital Operational Resilience Act (DORA), sets general rules for managing ICT and cybersecurity risks in the financial sector, including oversight of third-party providers, to strengthen business continuity (EC, 2020b). Both pieces of legislation give important new tasks for the European

Supervisory Authorities (ESAs) and national authorities in supervising technology and its providers in the financial sector. The drafts have in the meantime been adopted by the EU institutions and are being implemented with secondary legislation.

This chapter discusses the EU's digital finance acts in the context of the broader regulatory and supervisory structure at the EU level. MiCA and DORA have not received the attention they deserve. With MiCA, the EU is the first international jurisdiction to come up with a distinct regulatory approach for crypto-assets, but it renders the framework rather complex, with an unclear supervisory set-up. As for DORA, the EU introduces a common regulatory approach in tackling digital dependence in the financial sector. The question remains whether European supervisors will have sufficient expertise to take on their new tasks. More broadly, these rules also interact with other horizontal rules, related to digital identity and privacy, e-commerce and digital markets and services, or specific rules on anti-money laundering (AML) and crowdfunding. First, we start with some broader conceptual and policy considerations raised by these technological developments, and then we go on to discuss the proposals and their implications in more detail, while also indicating where the central bank digital currency fits into these discussions. We conclude with some specific recommendations for EU policy-making in this domain.

29.2 DLT AND FINANCE

Crypto-assets are any digital representation of value that utilizes some kind of DLT or blockchain technology. DLT is a shared and synchronized digital database that is maintained by a consensus algorithm, the procedure through which all peers of the blockchain network reach a common agreement about the present state of the distributed ledger, and stored on multiple nodes (i.e. computers that store a local version of the database). It is decentralized in distributed ledgers, or databases, shared across public or private computing networks, meaning that there are often many parties involved in the maintenance of these databases. Every piece of information is validated and stored as a new 'block' in the chain of historical records. The encrypted data reveals a user and transaction nexus that allows for transactions to be traced back to users (Reid and Harrigan, 2011). This decentralized structure brings efficiencies (BIS-SIX-SNB, 2020; Nascimento and Pólvora, 2019),[1] promotes competition (Lianos, 2019; Pike and Capobianco, 2020), but also entails inefficiencies (Atzori, 2021; Casey et al., 2018). The 'tokenization' of assets facilitates the processing of securities trades, in further automating and integrating the different steps post-trade. But it raises control and authorization issues of these networks, which can be public permissionless and private permissioned blockchains.[2] DLT includes different technologies, which are in full evolution, hence any clear description or definition remains difficult to formulate.

Definitional problems are key, given that crypto-assets can cover many different realities. Is it a security, a commodity, a currency, a means of payment, or simply a token? The definition

[1] An area, for example, in which such efficiencies might occur is post-trading. DLT offers the potential of merging/ rendering obsolete back-office functions that are currently distributed to clear intermediaries along the value chain (e.g. trading, clearing, settlement).

[2] A permissionless blockchain is a type of blockchain network that allows anyone (i.e. open to the public) to become part of the network and contribute towards its upkeep. For example, cryptocurrencies like Bitcoin are powered by permissionless blockchain networks. The main characteristics of such a network are transparency, anonymity, and full decentralization. On the other hand, in a permissioned blockchain one needs, as the name implies, permission to become part of the network. The owner of the network dictates who can or cannot join it. As a result, such a network has a defined governance structure, a varying degree of decentralization, but does not provide transparency.

provided in the EU's MiCA proposal – 'a digital representation of value or rights this is able to be transferred and stored electronically, using distributed ledger or similar technology' (REGULATION (EU) 2023/1114 Art. 3.1(5)) – is rather vague and broad. It certainly requires further clarification, as was highlighted by the European Central Bank (ECB, 2021). But the question is: can a clear definition be made with a still evolving technology? And would a clear definition stifle innovation?

Blockchain has been around for some time, and although it has advanced, it is still nascent. The big breakthrough and broad adoption have been announced several times ('three to five years away from feasibility', according to McKinsey, 2018) but have always been delayed. Some have compared it to the emergence of the World Wide Web in the early 1990s (Iansiti and Lakhani, 2017), which also required fundamental governance issues to be resolved before it could really take off. Apart from that, there is the issue of blockchains' huge energy consumption, which in a world of high energy prices and decarbonization is a no-go.[3]

Blockchain has clearly advanced as the basic technology for 'cryptocurrencies'. New types of cryptocurrencies have emerged, and its formal adoption in several jurisdictions has increased. Over the year 2021 and early 2022, the total value of outstanding crypto tokens fluctuated around $2 trillion, which is roughly the same value as all US dollars in circulation, or double all euro banknotes in circulation, but it plunged to just below $1 trillion by mid-2022 and has fluctuated around that level since.[4] This rapid emergence has impacted central banks' views on digital currencies. Until about the middle of 2018, central banks were clearly against the very notion of digital currency, as it was seen as a threat to their core task. Today, central banks have accepted that important inefficiencies exist in cross-border and international payments, and that digital currencies can revolutionize the way money is provided and enhance the transmission of monetary policy.

The same applies for decentralized finance (DeFi), where DLT is a response to the inefficiencies in financial infrastructures and back-offices, certainly for more complex products such as derivatives or collateralized debt positions. It eliminates intermediaries by allowing people, merchants, and businesses to conduct transactions through DLT technology, that is easily accessible. DeFi refers to financial services using smart contracts, which are automated enforceable agreements that operate entirely on blockchain networks, with tight security protocols and open connectivity, rather than through intermediaries like brokers or custodians. DeFi is seen to be more accessible, efficient, and transparent, a new way to disintermediate finance and to democratize the creation of markets and consumption. It is called the 'money-lego' concept, due to the simplicity of the building blocks.

Both public and private blockchains trigger specific security issues related to scalability and network congestion, as well as concentration of risk and interdependence. Moreover, the use of blockchain technology raises concerns about governance (who controls the protocol and where is it based?), about market abuse, inside information, and money laundering. DORA attempts to address some of the cyber-operational matters, but the question remains whether the European

[3] According to the Cambridge Bitcoin Electricity Index (https://ccaf.io/cbeci/index), Bitcoin's current yearly electricity consumption is at around 96 terawatt-hours (TWh) or at around 0.5 per cent of global electricity consumption. In fact, the bitcoin economy has more CO_2 emissions than countries such as Belgium or Finland, and just a bit less than the Netherlands. However, there are differences between different types of blockchains depending on the approach followed to validate new blocks of information. Bitcoin is particularly demanding in energy due to the 'proof of work' approach, which requires huge computing power to validate new blocks. However, other methods might consume much less energy, such as the 'proof of stake', which only validates block transactions based on the amount of coins a miner holds (Gallersdörfer et al., 2020; Martin and Nauman, 2021).

[4] See Coinmarketcap, https://coinmarketcap.com/charts/.

Commission has taken consumer protection issues sufficiently into consideration, which is discussed in the next section.

29.3 REGULATORY APPROACHES TO DLT

Definitional problems of DLT have prevented a consistent regulatory approach. In addressing DLT, the EU and regulators around the world have followed different approaches. This problem predates DLT, however, as payment systems – the most disruptive part in FinTech – have been undergoing deep change for the last two decades, following the emergence of e-commerce. This relates to the level-playing-field discussions and same risks/same rules debates, which are not easy to conclude. Payments traditionally formed part of the banking functions, but have moved out as a result of market developments.

Regulation has followed these developments, but not uncontested by the incumbents. The EU's first E-Money Directive (Directive 2000/46/EC) was adopted in 2000 and the first Payments Services Directive (PSD) in 2007 (Directive 2007/64/EC). Cross-border payments in the EU have been regulated since 2001 after long and protracted discussions with the banking sector on their costs (Regulation (EC) 2560/2001). For a long time, high credit card sector interchange fees have been a stumbling block for the EU's competition policy authorities. Fees were capped at 0.2 per cent of the value of a transaction for debit cards and 0.3 per cent for credit cards in a 2015 regulation (Regulation (EU) 2015/751). But this remains contested, as some have argued that it maintains the credit card duopoly of Visa and Mastercard (Dolmans et al., 2019).

Payment transmitters can operate under several regulatory regimes, at the EU or global level. Regarding cryptocurrency schemes, they have worked under regulatory sandboxes at the local level, or were seen to be illegal, provided they did not qualify as a financial instrument under the Markets in Financial Instruments Directive (MiFID), the EU regulation concerning investment services providers. With MiCA, the European Commission wants to fill the void and set a common approach in the EU for DLT-based operators, ensuring consumer and investor protection, and market integrity. However, the question emerges why the EU has not tried to cover crypto-assets and cryptocurrencies under existing rules, as is the approach taken in the United States and Hong Kong, rather than creating another new regime for a still emerging and fast-changing technology.[5] Moreover, the EU has brought three distinct forms of crypto-based services under one regulation, instead of having it under separate rules. In doing so, the EU may contribute to regulatory complexity, rather than reducing it.

It could be argued that the EU's approach is correct, given that the main difficulty in regulating crypto-assets is that they bring new risks related to new 'functions', hence they require specific regulation. For example, contracts that automate contingent transfers depending on the success of delivering goods or services can pose new risks of collusion (Cong and He, 2019). Through the decentralized consensus, sellers will have greater knowledge of aggregate business conditions on the blockchain, which can lead to tacit collusion among sellers. Another new

[5] See the speeches by Gary Gensler of the SEC on the US approach, asserting crypto-assets should be regulated the same way as existing securities under the existing securities laws, whereas the industry argues for a new approach (i.e. speech of 4 April 2022, available at www.sec.gov/). See also the First Fraud Case against a Defi Network on 6 August 2021 (Press release, www.sec.gov/). For the Hong Kong Securities and Futures Commission (SFC), ICO tokens are regulated as securities under Hong Kong's Securities and Futures rules and must be licensed and authorized by the SFC.

functionality made possible through blockchain is the 'fork' – an either accidental or intentional change in protocol – that can make the ledger less stable, reliable, and useful (Biais et al., 2021). In an ideal blockchain, there is a single sequence of blocks, with each of them offering an updated version of the ledger (taking into account the most recent transactions), on which all participants agree. However, if there are forks in the blockchain, it means that there are competing branches, with each of them trying to register a potentially different version of the ledger. Lastly, a new functionality also arises from decentralization, which allows greater ease in benefiting from regulatory arbitrage (Amstad, 2019; Nabilou, 2019).

29.4 EU CRYPTO REGULATION UNDER MICA

MiCA provides for a broad definition of crypto-assets and stablecoins, sets rules on their providers, including the trading platforms, and defines the role of the supervisors. Crypto-assets include three groups: (1) utility tokens, (2) asset-referenced tokens, and (3) e-money tokens, with the lightest rules for the first group. Utility tokens are intended to provide digital access to a specific good or service, they are non-fungible tokens (NFT). Under DLT, NFTs are uniquely identifiable representations of information, art, music, etc., providing strong intellectual property protection. Asset-referenced tokens are the so-called 'stablecoins', coins that reference baskets of currencies or commodities. An e-money token is also a stablecoin, but they are like traditional e-money, meaning they should have a fixed value to a hard currency. The rules will not apply to security tokens that are already subject to an existing EU regulatory regime, or to central bank digital currencies, as discussed below.

Specific stipulations of MiCA include:

- Providers of crypto-assets and **utility or non-fungible tokens**, or virtual gadgets, shall draw up a 'crypto-asset white paper' for notification to the authorities before issuing and commercializing this product. The white paper will contain disclosure, conduct, and liability rules that are in principle prospectus requirements to address the inadequate disclosures, misrepresentations, and fraud currently often observed in certain initial coin offerings. White paper issuers will be allowed to benefit from a European passport. There is no formal *ex ante* approval requirement (Article 8(3): 'Competent authorities shall not require prior approval of crypto-asset white papers, nor of any marketing communications relating thereto, before their respective publication'), which is justified by the goal of not placing excessive burdens on supervisors (Recital 6).
- Issuers of **asset-referenced tokens** or stablecoins must be formally authorized. They shall respect a minimum capital of €350,000 and an ongoing capital requirement of 2 per cent of the average amount of the reserve assets in the last six months in Tier 1 capital. Reserves must be kept in triple A securities and be prudently managed. The rules also contain a value stabilization mechanism, or the investment policy (Article 36.8d), including among others 'the procedure by which the asset-referenced tokens are issued and redeemed, and the procedure by which such issuance or redemption will result in the increase and decrease in the reserve of assets'. This also raises issues of custody of these assets, which is detailed in Article 36. Furthermore, issuers need to meet governance and conduct rules – minimum operational requirements for the managers of a crypto platform (Article 76).
- **E-money tokens** can only be offered to the public by an issuer authorized as a credit institution or as an 'electronic money institution' within the meaning of the E-Money Directive (2009/110/EC). E-money tokens shall be issued at par value and on the receipt of

funds, and upon request by the holder of e-money tokens, the issuers must redeem them at any moment and at par value.

The supervisory regime for MiCA is a mix: national authorities are in charge, but for significant issuers of asset-referenced and e-money tokens, the European Banking Authority (EBA) is responsible, based on minimum criteria. The EBA chairs the supervisory colleges for these crypto-assets (with national competent authorities (NCAs), the European Securities and Markets Authority (ESMA), and the ECB), with the frequency of meetings to be determined. EBA will have general investigative powers, can make on-site inspections, and request information from NCAs, also in third countries. ESMA, on the other hand, has implementing powers for crypto-asset providers, of which it needs to establish a register. The complexity of this set-up led the European Parliament in its reading to ask for a clearer, better-defined role for the European Supervisory Authorities.

The regime for third-country issuers is highly rudimentary, considering that crypto-assets are global and most activity is outside the EU. NCAs shall conclude cooperation agreements with these countries. Whenever there is an issuance of a global stablecoin in the EU, the EBA should be leading the supervisory college, with no voting rights for third countries. Third-country providers will thus need to fully conform to EU rules in case they want to sell cryptocurrencies in the EU. There is no reference to equivalence agreements with third-country regimes, only a request to examine the need for equivalence agreements three years after adoption of the measure. This is particularly problematic as MiFID II establishes a full framework for the operation of third-country firms (via Article 39 and following), while this is not the case at all under the MiCA Regulation.

Rules on the prohibition of market abuse, insider trading, and market manipulation will apply (Title VI), but they are much lighter than the existing rules applicable to securities markets operators (Regulation 596/2014). According to Recital 95, 'Issuers of crypto-assets and crypto-asset service providers are very often SMEs, it would be disproportionate to apply all of the provisions of Regulation (EU) No 596/2014'. Hence a crypto trading platform that clears crypto-asset transactions can be created very easily without a high regulatory burden. The question remains whether this is justified.

Overall, the problem with MiCA is that it brings together three distinct forms of crypto-assets under one regulation, but it does not clarify when the second group (i.e. asset-referenced tokens) falls within or outside the framework of existing EU securities markets law, in particular the prospectus rules and MiFID. In practice, MiCA will apply, unless it is within the scope of MiFID, which creates ample scope for arbitrage. The same lack of clarity exists for crypto trading platforms, where the question will emerge whether a MiFID licensed trading platform can trade crypto, or whether it should be authorized separately under MiCA. Because of this complexity, some have called MiCA 'a job-creation programme for lawyers' (Godschalk, 2021). In fact, it has been argued that even if it harmonizes EU law for crypto instruments, it renders the overall application of financial law more difficult (Zetzsche et al., 2021). Compared to this, the approach of the US Securities and Exchange Commission (SEC) is more straightforward. It checks whether the basic objectives of the 1933 and 1934 securities acts are respected, the protection of investors and the orderly functioning of markets, irrespective of new market functionalities.

The EU would have been better off to consider crypto under existing laws, rather than creating a new regulatory framework. This means applying prospectus rules for issuers and MiFID for crypto-assets service providers (considering these as financial instruments, not as a separate class of assets); and applying e-money, FinTech, or banking rules for digital money. NFTs do not require sperate rules, but can be covered under existing consumer or intellectual property legislation. This would be much easier for consumers as well as regulators. Market and conduct of business rules should apply regardless of the 'packaging'.[6]

Instead, it will take another 18 months, until end 2024, until the new rules will apply. After the publication of the new MiCA rules in the EU Official Journal on 9 June, some 18 different pieces of level 2 legislation or guidelines will have to be adopted by EBA and the European Commission. In the meantime, markets have moved on, and many citizens have been defrauded by crypto scams, with unclear redress procedures.

29.5 WHERE DOES THE CBDC FIT INTO THE PICTURE?

Central bank digital currency has added to the confusion about cryptocurrency. In the case of the large, well-established central banks, CBDC will be nothing else than digital money but now directly issued by the central bank as legal tender, with the modalities still to be decided upon. In some developing countries, on the contrary, a CBDC resembles a stablecoin, where the composing parts and reserves will need to be controlled. It could be an 'illegal' tender, if the rules or governance cannot guarantee stability of the tender. But whether or not these CBDCs will be based upon DLT remains to be seen. In principle, they are at opposed ends of the spectrum, as a DLT-based system is decentralized by definition, whereas a CBDC is not.

After a lengthy consultation phase, the ECB's Governing Council decided on 14 July 2021 to launch an investigation phase of a digital euro project that will last two years. The project also considers changes to the EU's legislative framework that might be needed. The key issue is the modalities for the circulation of the digital euro, which will be closely watched by the European banking sector. If citizens store their digital currency with the central bank, it will be a further threat to the traditional retail banks for which payments in all their forms are a core part of their business, contributing to around one-quarter of their revenues. The Federal Reserve and the People's Bank of China (PBoC) are also examining digital currencies. The PBoC already has pilot schemes of e-RMB running, involving private citizens, as a reaction against the blockchain-based currencies that are decentralized by definition. In the United States, a 9 March 2022 executive order of President Biden supports the potential of CBDC and asked for a report on the possible design options, while insisting upon the benefits for efficiency of payments systems and protection of consumers (The White House, 2022).

The digital euro impacts core and critical bank regulatory matters. It could facilitate financial inclusion, although financial literacy will remain an issue, as the onus will be on central banks to explain the functioning of CBDCs. Access to and the cost of bank accounts for European citizens has long been a matter of concern for consumer lobbies, as it determines overall societal participation in the financial system. But direct 'accounts' at the central bank could threaten the stability of the financial system, as only central bank accounts may be seen to be safe. A 'bank run' in a system with a CBDC may thus provoke even more volatility, and could lead to a total gridlock in the financial system. It would profoundly alter the liquidity transformation function of commercial banks, as banks would no longer be the main storage point for money, which could lead to liquidity shortages in times of stress. Creating a CBDC could mean the end of commercial banking as we know it, as the central bank would become the focal point of retail

[6] As we argued in the Financial Times (2022), EU's proposed crypto regulations are flawed, 16 May.

accounts, by which the source for the loan function of banks will disappear. This would profoundly change the role of markets in a financial system.

The ECB may be attracted by the perspective of a bigger role in the payment system, which it has been trying to do since the launch of the TARGET (Trans-European Automated Real-Time Gross Settlement Express Transfer) system in 1999, and also recently through its involvement in the European Payments Initiative (EPI). But this stands in contrast with its statute and origin as a 'narrow' central bank, focusing on monetary policy and price stability. Payments systems raise a host of microeconomic and allocative efficiency issues – how to get cash, in which form, and where – beyond merely the payment assets, which are not core to the ECB's mandate, and which globally active providers can do better (Bofinger and Haas, 2021). The ECB is a supervisor of payment systems, not an operator, which is the task of private agents. Central banks should monitor these markets based on their financial stability mandate.

Data protection and privacy matters will also be affected by a CBDC. Control on illicit activities and money laundering are raised as a big advantage of the digital euro, because of the technology used – DLT – which allows transactions to be traced back to users through the digital identities (e-ID) and digital signature components. However, this brings the 'Big Brother' state much closer to reality.[7] Moreover, it is by no means certain that the ECB, let alone the EU-27, will manage to get all its members aligned on these matters. Some Member States may wish the digital euro to be a substitute for cash, with less traceability than DLT allows. The discussions on the latest AML package of the EU Commission demonstrates that more restrictions on cash payments remains very sensitive, not the least in Germany.

29.6 CYBER RESILIENCE RULES IN DORA

Cybersecurity has been on the minds of many finance professionals and policymakers as a major concern and priority. DORA aims to meet the need for a more EU-wide standardized approach for cyber risks and disclosure by the financial sector of cyber-attacks. It clearly defines the applicable entities and requires them to have the necessary governance framework in place. It also gives a huge (but difficult) additional role to the ESAs to monitor digital resilience. A key novelty of DORA is that it brings third-party ICT providers into the financial supervisory domain. The challenge here is to find the right balance in financial supervision in an ecosystem where tech companies are increasingly important actors for the effective provision of financial services, and to maintain a clear separation between both.[8]

DORA's principle-based approach aims to streamline the provisions of financial legislation to create a minimum baseline for the digital operational resilience of the financial sector, and hence financial stability. It completes the existing but generic Network of Information Systems Directive (NISD),[9] with much more detailed provisions and oversight. Furthermore, it aims to cover almost the entire financial sector, including crypto-asset providers, and address five main areas that are relevant from a digital operational resilience perspective: (1) ICT risk management; (2) incident reporting; (3) testing; (4) third-party risk; and (5) information sharing. Importantly, the proportionality of application is embedded in the rules and addressed by

[7] See the blog post by Fabio Panetta, member of the Executive Board of the ECB on 'Preparing for the euro's digital finance', 14 July 2021 (www.ecb.europa.eu).

[8] See Deloitte (2022) for an assessment of the agreement and the implications for firms.

[9] Directive (EU) 2016/1148 sets overall standards for cybersecurity in society and the economy, with a central role for ENIAS, the EU cyber agency.

specific exemptions.[10] As for the supervision of DORA's application, this is up to the competent responsible authorities as defined in the respective EU legislation, which may be the ECB, or specialized or generic financial supervisory authorities.

The key components of DORA can be summarized as follows:

- A clear taxonomy – what is cybersecurity and what is not? The draft defines 'digital operational resilience', 'ICT risk', 'cyber threat', 'cyber-attack', 'vulnerability', 'threat-led penetration testing' ('a framework that mimics the tactics, techniques and procedures of real-life threat'), 'ICT concentration risk', etc., all elements that had not previously been clearly defined for the financial sector, and which will allow a better framing of the risk.
- A clear ICT management framework. Every financial entity shall have a management body in charge of the implementation of all arrangements related to ICT risk, including the obligation to have a business continuity plan. Firms are required to set risk tolerance for ICT disruptions, they must identify their 'critical or important functions' (CIFs), and map their assets and dependencies.
- Procedures for stress testing of cyber resilience, vulnerability disclosure, and incident reporting, including cyber-attacks. These are based on common templates, building upon the work already undertaken by the ECB (in its so-called TIBER-EU programme). Firms will need to assess the quantitative impact of incidents and analyse their root cause. Reporting deadlines to NCAs will be specified in technical standards.
- Procedures for ICT third-party service providers (ITPP) that are critical for financial entities, with a clear division of responsibilities, and reporting to authorities of contractual arrangements, with a definition of the required provisions (Article 28).
- The ESAs – based upon systemic stability criteria – will designate the ITPP that are critical for financial entities. EBA, ESMA, or the European Insurance and Occupational Pensions Authority (EIOPA) will be appointed as their Lead Overseers, with on-site inspections (Article 36), covered by fees charged to the ICT providers.
- A central role for the ESAs Joint Committee, which together with the European Union Agency for Cybersecurity (ENISA) will aim to reinforce cross-border cooperation and improve the process of attribution and eventually criminalization of cybersecurity risks. A Joint Oversight Forum as a specialized ICT subcommittee will support the work of the Joint Committee.

When implemented, DORA should be a big step forward in improving digital resilience at EU level and creating a common approach for the disclosure of software vulnerability, although the definitions and risks will need to be clarified in delegated acts. Only clearly identifiable incidents should be reported. DORA refrains from proposing an EU-wide cyber hub, but central incident reporting for major incidents will be explored (see Recital 53 and Article 19). Another element that is missing is the link with the fight against money laundering, which digitization is facilitating. A new Anti-Money Laundering (AML) agency, as the European Commission has proposed (EC, 2021), will require close cooperation with the Joint Committee to facilitate action in this domain.

A third critical element for DORA is data localization. The act prohibits using critical ITPP only based in a third country (Article 31.12) or subcontracting (Recital 67) to a third country. As

[10] For example, certain provisions do not apply to micro-enterprises, while some rules are only applicable to significant institutions (e.g. the threat-led penetration testing and the reporting of incidents are only for major ICT-related incidents).

TABLE 29.1 *Supervisory responsibilities under MiCA and DORA*

		NCAs	ESAs
MiCA	Tokens	White Paper notification	
	Stablecoins	White Paper authorization	Significant issuers supervised by EBA, and registered by ESMA
	E-money	Issuers	Significant issuers supervised by EBA
DORA	Cyber-attacks	Incident reporting	ESAs as Lead Overseers for critical third-party ICT providers
	Third-party service providers (TPP)	Reporting of ICT contractual engagements	ESAs Joint Committee for cross-border cooperation; ESAs as Lead Overseers

for the United Kingdom, as part of the Trade and Cooperation Agreement (TCA), it can, as a major financial centre, be part of the European data sphere, and decide whether to be a member of ENISA, thus allowing its involvement to some degree in such a scheme. But this will need to be formally agreed, and will have drawbacks due to the United Kingdom's status as a non-Member State.

DORA goes a long way to bringing a harmonized approach to tackling cyber problems in the financial sector. It was formally adopted in October 2022, but it will take another two years before the provisions will apply in full, as twelve different Level 2 mandates will need to be substantiated in technical standards and delegated acts in the eighteen months following adoption.

Table 29.1 gives an overview of the new digital supervisory responsibilities under both acts.

29.7 A DEFI REGULATORY SANDBOX

As part of the digital finance package, the European Commission also proposed the DLT infrastructures pilot regime regulation, or an EU-wide regulatory sandbox, for market infrastructures (or DeFi) based on DLT.[11] It can be used by a DLT multilateral trading facility, a DLT securities settlement system, a DLT market infrastructure for DLT transferable securities, market facilities as defined in EU law. It has several exemptions from the existing rules (such as the Central Securities Depositories Regulation), but with thresholds over which the structures cannot be used, and to be reviewed in five years. For DLT transferable securities, for example, the limit is €200 million, for a DLT market infrastructure, €2.5 billion. The pilot regime sets the operational requirements for these entities, the supervisory regime applicable, and the cooperation amongst authorities in the EU. This is the first time the Commission is using such a regime, to our knowledge, but it has been used in Member States for some time, with varying degrees of success. It facilitated innovation in some, such as the United Kingdom, but much less in other states, such as France.

29.8 CONCLUSIONS

With its digital finance strategy, the European Commission is embracing innovation in finance, aligning it with the single market and further facilitating access to finance. Enhancing competition and market access in the retail and small business segments of EU financial markets is a

[11] Regulation (EU) 2022/858 was adopted in June 2022.

priority for the EU, and the ambition to facilitate payments and digital innovation in finance should be welcomed. Crypto and cyberware have made big inroads in finance and will continue to shake up the supply and operation of financial services, and payments in particular. Consumer and investor protection should be guaranteed, or they should at least be well informed, as many Europeans are involved as providers or customers.

The question remains, however, whether a specific regulatory response and new rules are needed for crypto-assets and cryptocurrencies for still very rapidly evolving blockchain or distributed ledger technologies. For the EU Commission, most crypto-assets fall outside the scope of EU financial services legislation and are therefore not subject to the existing provisions on consumer and investor protection and market integrity, among others, although they give rise to risks. And in regulating DLT-based providers, the Commission wants to place the EU at the forefront of change, as it is the first international jurisdiction to propose rules on the matter. Other regulators around the globe are following different approaches, however, and prefer to stand on the side-lines or prohibit cryptocurrencies.

The classification of the different tokens as proposed in MiCA is very confusing for citizens, and a huge new task for supervisors. The value of a token or a crypto-asset is difficult to know for a citizen: How are they valued and what accounting or tax rules apply? What are the reliable sources of price information about crypto-assets? What is a stablecoin, what is e-money, and what is a CBDC? Keeping e-money out of the MiCA regulation could have facilitated the understanding that crypto is about a highly speculative and volatile asset, not money.

For supervisors, the new tasks to monitor the different regimes, with different degrees of involvement, is also an enormous challenge. They will need to understand the motives of investors and judge the intentions of the crypto providers (see e.g. BIS, 2021a). They should assess whether consumer protection and financial stability will be affected, but will be unsure how to react in case of trouble, as they may not have all the information. In the latter case, a clearer division of labour between (and among) the ESAs and the national authorities is required, which is not the case in the proposal. The same applies to DORA: monitoring the cyber resilience of financial services firms and their third-party ICT providers is a substantial new task, for the ESAs, as well as for the NCAs, let alone central banks. More centralization of tasks would be better, given the competences needed.

Rather than amplifying and fragmenting the regulatory schemes, it would have been preferable to bring crypto-assets as much as possible under the existing rules, with possible derogations. How will the different regulatory regimes apply with the new MiCA rules on the one hand, and the existing EU's prospectus rules for issuers and the MiFID rules for investment service providers and trading platforms on the other. Is it appropriate to have a much lighter regime for crypto-asset trading platforms, or for market abuse and insider trading in crypto-assets? Are stablecoins not like money market funds? In the MiCA regulation, the reference to existing law is only made for e-money tokens, by limiting the issuance to those subject to the banking and e-money directives.

The danger with a distinct regulatory set-up is the possibility for arbitrage, with clearly much lighter rules for crypto-asset providers and their platforms than for providers of traditional financial instruments and their platforms. It gives the impression that these are different financial products to which lighter forms of investor protection can apply, rather than those that already exist. And will investors notice the difference between EU and non-EU crypto-assets and offerings, or are the products potentially forbidden in the EU? For Europe to stimulate innovation in digital finance, investors need the same level of protection. The EU will definitely need to follow up – and quickly – with its international counterparts and ensure both international consistency and cooperation.

REFERENCES

Amstad, M. (2019). Regulating FinTech: Objectives, principles, and practices. Working Paper, No. 1016, October, Asian Development Bank.

Atzori, M. (2021). Blockchain technology and decentralised governance: Is the state still necessary? *Journal of Governance and Regulation* 6(1), 45–62.

Biais, B., Bisière, C., Bouvard, M., and Casamatta, C. (2021). The blockchain folk theorem. *Review of Financial Studies* 32(5), 1662–1715.

BIS (2021a). Distrust or speculation? The socioeconomic drivers of US cryptocurrency investments by Raphael Auer and David Tercero-Lucas.

BIS Working Papers No. 951. www.bis.org/publ/work951.pdf

BIS (2021b). Central bank digital currencies for cross-border payments. Report to the G-20, July. www.bis.org/publ/othp38.pdf

BIS-SIX-SNB (2020). Project Helvetia: Settling tokenised assets in central bank money. Bank for International Settlements, SIX Group AG, and Swiss National Bank, December.

Bofinger, P., and Haas, T. (2021). Central bank digital currencies: Can central banks succeed in the marketplace for digital monies? ECMI Working Paper, December.

Bouyon, S., and Krause, S. (2018). Cybersecurity in finance: Getting the policy mix right. Report of a CEPS-ECRI Task Force, June, Centre for European Policy Studies and European Credit Research Institute.

Casey, M., Crane, J., Gensler, G., Johnson, S., and Narula, N. (2018). The impact of blockchain technology on finance: A catalyst for change. Geneva Reports on the World Economy No. 21.

Cong, L., and He, Z. (2019). Blockchain disruption and smart contracts. *Review of Financial Studies* 32(5), 1754–1797.

Deloitte (2022). The EU's Digital Operational Resilience Act has been agreed: implications for the financial services sector for an assessment of the agreement and the implications for firms. July. www2.deloitte.com/lu/en/pages/risk/articles/eu-dora-agreed-implications-financial-services-sector.html?icid=wn_eu-dora-agreed-implications-financial-services-sector

Dolmans, M., Gilbert, P., Messent, J., Siragusa, M., and Subiotto, R. (2019). Payment services in the EU: Price regulation to protect a duopoly. *Competition Law Journal* 18(4), 175–189.

European Commission (2020a). Proposal for a Regulation of the European Parliament and of the Council on Markets in Crypto-Assets, and Amending Directive (EU) 2019/1937, (MiCA), COM(2020) 593 final, 24 September.

European Commission (2020b). Proposal for a Regulation of the European Parliament and of the Council on digital operational resilience for the financial sector and amending Regulations (EC) No. 1060/2009, (EU) No. 648/2012, (EU) No. 600/2014 and (EU) No. 909/2014 (DORA), COM(2020) 595 final, 24 September.

European Commission (2021). Proposal for a Regulation of the European Parliament and of the Council Establishing the Authority for Anti-Money Laundering and Countering the Financing of Terrorism and Amending Regulations (EU) No. 1093/2010, (EU) 1094/2010, (EU) 1095/2010, COM(2021) 421 final, 20 June.

European Union (2022), Regulation (EU) 2022/2554 of the European Parliament and of the Council of 14 December 2022 on digital operational resilience for the financial sector (DORA), and amending Regulations (EC) No 1060/2009, (EU) No 648/2012, (EU) No 600/2014, (EU) No 909/2014 and (EU) 2016/1011

European Union (2023), Regulation (EU) 2023/1114 of the European Parliament and of the Council of 31 May 2023 on markets in crypto-assets (MiCA), and amending Regulations (EU) No 1093/2010 and (EU) No 1095/2010 and Directives 2013/36/EU and (EU) 2019/1937. Official Journal, 9 June 2023.

ECB (2021). Opinion of the European Central Bank of 19 February 2021 on a proposal for a regulation on Markets in Crypto-assets, and amending Directive (EU) 2019/1937. https://eur-lex.europa.eu/legal-content/EN/TXT/?uri=CELEX%3A52021AB0004

EPRS (2021). Updating the Crypto Assets Regulation and establishing a pilot regime for distributed ledger technology, PE 612.617 – March.

Gallersdörfer, U., KlaaÔen, L., and Stoll, C. (2020). Energy consumption of cryptocurrencies beyond bitcoin. *Joule* 4(9), 1843–1846.

Godschalk, H. (2021). Crypto-assets, fiat currency and Aa: Some notes on the MiCAR. 16 March. https://paytechlaw.com/en/crypto-assets-fiat-currency-micar/

Iansiti, M., and Lakhani, K. (2017). The truth about blockchain: It will take years to transform business, but the journey begins now. *Harvard Business Review*, January–February. https://hbr.org/2017/01/the-truth-about-blockchain

Lannoo, K. (2021). Cyberfinance challenges require a common response. CEPS Policy Insight, No. 2018/12, October. www.ceps.eu/ceps-publications/cyber-finance-challenges-demand-unified-response/

Lannoo, K. (2022). The EU's proposed crypto regulations are flawed. 16 May. www.ft.com/content/83ddff31-fb9a-4765-becf-82a52cc7291d

Lastra, R., and Allen, J. G. (2019). Towards a European governance framework for cryptoassets. SUERF Policy Note 110, November.

Lianos, I. (2019). Blockchain competition – gaining competitive advantage in the digital economy: Competition law implications. In P. Hacker, I. Lianos, G. Dimitropoulos, and S. Eich (eds.), *Regulating Blockchain: Techno-Social and Legal Challenges*. Oxford: Oxford University Press, p. 329.

Martin, K., and Nauman, B. (2021). Bitcoin's growing energy problem: 'It's a dirty currency'. *Financial Times*, 20 May. www.ft.com/content/1aecb2db-8f61-427c-a413-3b929291c8ac

McKinsey (2018). Blockchain beyond the hype: What is the strategic business value? www.mckinsey.com/capabilities/mckinsey-digital/our-insights/blockchain-beyond-the-hype-what-is-the-strategic-business-value

Nabilou, H. (2019). How to regulate bitcoin? Decentralized regulation for a decentralized cryptocurrency. *International Journal of Law and Information Technology* 27(3), 266–291.

Nascimento, S., and Pólvora, A. (2019). Blockchain now and tomorrow: Assessing multidimensional impacts of distributed ledger technologies. Joint Research Centre, European Commission.

Pike, C., and Capobianco, A. (2020). Antitrust and the trust machine. OECD Blockchain Policy Series, Organisation for Economic Co-operation and Development, 4 November.

Pupillo, L., Ferreira, A., and Varisco, G. (2018). Software vulnerability disclosure in Europe: Technology, policies and legal challenges. Report of a CEPS Task Force, June, Centre for European Policy Studies.

Reid, F., and Harrigan, M. (2011). An analysis of anonymity in the bitcoin system. IIEEE International Conference on Privacy, Security, Risk, and Trust, Boston, 9–11 October.

Thomadakis, A. (2021). How crisis-proof are financial market infrastructures? ECMI event report. www.ecmi.eu/sites/default/files/event_report_operational_resilience.docx.pdf

Villeroy de Galhau, F. (2021). Roads towards the future for CBDC and innovative payments. SUERF Policy Notes. www.suerf.org/policynotes/29965/roads-for-the-future-central-bank-digital-currency-cbdc-and-innovative-payments

The White House (2022). Executive Order on Ensuring Responsible Development of Digital Assets. Presidential actions. 9 March.

Zetzsche, D., Annunziata, F., Arner, D., and Buckley, R. (2021). The Markets in Crypto-Assets Regulation (MiCA) and the EU digital finance strategy. *Capital Markets Law Journal* 16(2), 203–225.

Index

Numbers: **bold**=table, *italics*=figure

Printed in the USA
CPSIA information can be obtained
at www.ICGtesting.com
LVHW070755211123
764314LV00023B/111